The Wordsworth

Encyclopedia

D0244928

The Wordsworth
Encyclopedia

Volume 1

A – chub

Wordsworth Reference

This edition published 1995 by Wordsworth Editions Ltd,
Cumberland House, Crib Street, Ware, Hertfordshire SG12 9ET
and produced for Wordsworth Editions by Helicon Publishing Ltd.

Copyright © Helicon Publishing Ltd 1995

ISBN 1–85326–860–7

Printed and bound in Denmark by Nørhaven

The paper in this book is produced from pure wood pulp,
without the use of chlorine or any other substance
harmful to the environment. The energy used in its
production consists almost entirely of hydroelectricity
and heat generated from waste materials, thereby
conserving fossil fuels and contributing little to
the greenhouse effect.

Introduction

The Wordsworth Encyclopedia is a five-volume companion to world events, history, arts, and sciences, for home, school, college, or library use. The aim throughout has been to provide up-to-date, readable entries, using clear and non-technical language, with an inclusion policy based on what is most relevant for the modern world. It is hoped that the encyclopedia will also be useful in providing, wherever possible, background details for particular subject areas such as current affairs and major historical events, in addition to basic facts and dates.

Arrangement of entries

Entries are ordered alphabetically, as if there were no spaces between words. Thus, entries for words beginning 'federal' follow the order:

> Federal Bureau of Investigation
> federalism
> Federalist
> Federalist Papers, the

However, we have avoided a purely mechanical alphabetization in cases where a different order corresponds more with human logic. For example, sovereigns with the same name are grouped according to country before number, so that King George II of England is placed before George III of England, and not next to King George II of Greece. Words beginning 'Mc' and 'Mac' are treated as if they begin 'Mac' and 'St' and 'Saint' are both treated as if they were spelt 'Saint'.

Foreign names and titles

Names of foreign sovereigns and places are usually shown in their English form, except where the foreign name is more familiar; thus, there are entries for Charles V of Spain, but Juan Carlos (not John Charles), and for Florence, not Firenze. Entries for titled people are under the name by which they are best known to the general reader: thus, Anthony Eden, not Lord Avon. Cross-references are provided in cases where confusion is possible.

Cross-references

Cross-references are shown by ◊ immediately preceding the reference. Cross-referencing is selective; a cross-reference is shown when another entry contains material directly relevant to the subject matter of an entry, in cases where the reader may not otherwise think of looking. Common alternative spellings, where there is no agreed consistent form, are also shown; thus there is a cross-reference to Muhammad at Mohammed.

Units

SI (metric) units are used throughout for scientific entries. Commonly used measurements of distances, temperatures, sizes, and so on include an approximate imperial equivalent.

Science and technology

Scientific and technical terms are usually placed under the better-known name rather than the technical name (thus, chloroform is placed under C and not under its technically correct name trichloromethane), but the technical term is also given. To aid comprehension for the non-specialist, technical terms are frequently explained when used within the text of an entry, even though they may have their own entry elsewhere.

World Changes

Entries and maps have been included for the independent countries that have emerged from the secession of Croatia, Slovenia, Bosnia-Herzegovina from Yugoslavia 1992 and the peaceful split of Czechoslovakia into the Czech Republic and the Slovak Republic 1993.

Chinese names

Pinyin, the preferred system for transcribing Chinese names of people and places, is generally used: thus, there is an entry at Mao Zedong, not Mao Tse-tung; an exception is made for a few names which are more familiar in their former (Wade-Giles) form, such as Sun Yat-sen and Chiang Kai-shek. Where confusion is likely, Wade-Giles forms are given as cross-references.

Pronunciations

Pronunciations are given for the names of people and places, using a transcription which conforms to the International Phonetic Alphabet (IPA). If the name is from a foreign language, the pronunciation given is the nearest English equivalent; this provides the English speaker with an intelligible pronunciation of the name. A key to the pronunciation symbols is shown on p. viii of Volume 1 and p. ii of Volumes 2-5.

Contributors

Owen Adikibi PhD
Lesley and Roy Adkins
Christine Avery PhD
John Ayto MA
Paul Bahn
Bernard Balleine
Tia Cockerell LLB
Sue Cusworth
Nigel Davis MSc
Ian D Derbyshire PhD
J Denis Derbyshire PhD, FBIM
Col Michael Dewar
Dougal Dixon BSc, MSc
Nigel Dudley
George du Boulay FRCR, FRCP, Hon FACR
Ingrid von Essen
Eric Farge
Anna Farkas
Peter Fleming PhD
Kent Fedorowich BA, MA, PhD
Derek Gjertsen BA
Lawrence Garner BA
Wendy Grossman
Joseph Harrison BA, PhD
Michael Hitchcock PhD
Stuart Holroyd
Gerald M D Howat MA, MLitt, PhD, FRHist C
H G Jerrard PhD
Robin Kerrod FRAS
Charles Kidd
Stephen Kite B Arch, RIBA
Peter Lafferty MSc
Mike Lewis MBCS
Graham Ley MPhil
Carol Lister PhD, FSS
Graham Littler BSc, MSc, FSS
Robin Maconie MA
Morven MacKillop
Tom McArthur PhD
Isabel Miller BA PhD
Karin Mogg MSc PhD
Bob Moore PhD
David Munro PhD
Joanne O'Brien
Maureen O'Connor

Roger Owen MA, DPhil
Robert Paisley PhD
Martin Palmer
David Penfold PhD, MBCS
Paulette Pratt
Michael Pudlo MSc, PhD
Tim Pulleine
Chris Rhys
Ian Ridpath FRAS
Adrian Room MA
Simon Ross
Julian Rowe PhD
Paul Rowntree MA
Jack Schofield BA, MA
Emma Shackleton
Mark Slade MA
Steve Smyth
Jennifer Speake MPhil
Joe Staines
Glyn Stone
Calum Storrie
Michael Thum
Norman Vance, PhD, Professor of English, Univ. of Sussex
Stephen Webster BSc, MPhil
Liz Whitelegg BSc

Editors

Managing Editor
Hilary McGlynn

Text Editor
Avril Cridlan

Artwork Editor
Terence Caven

Production
Tony Ballsdon

Typesetting
Pure Tech

Pronunciation key

Pronunciations are transcribed using the International Phonetic Alphabet (IPA). In general, only one pronunciation is given for each word. The pronunciation given for foreign names is the generally agreed English form, if there is one; otherwise an approximation using English sounds is given.

ɑː	father /ˈfɑːðə/, start /stɑːt/	ɬ	Llanelli /ɬæˈneɬɪ
aɪ	price /praɪs/, high /haɪ/	m	minimum /ˈmɪnɪməm/
aʊ	mouth /maʊθ/, how /haʊ/	n	nine /naɪn/
æ	trap /træp/, man /mæn/	ŋ	sing /sɪŋ/, uncle /ˈʌŋkl/
b	baby /ˈbeɪbɪ/	ɒ	lot / lɒt/, watch /wɒtʃ/
d	dead / ded/	ɔː	thought /θɔːt/, north /nɔːθ/
dʒ	judge /dʒʌdʒ/	ɔɪ	choice /tʃɔɪs/, boy /bɔɪ/
ð	this /ðɪs/, other /ˈʌðə/	p	paper /ˈpeɪpə/
e	dress /dres/, men /men/	r	red /red/, carry /ˈkærɪ/
eɪ	face /feɪs/, wait /weɪt/	s	space /speɪs/
eə	square /skweə/, fair /feə/	ʃ	ship /ʃɪp/, motion /ˈməʊʃən/
ɜː	nurse /nɜːs/, pearl /pɜːl/	t	totter /ˈtɒtə/
ə	another /əˈnʌðə/	tʃ	church /tʃɜːtʃ/
əʊ	goat /gəʊt/, snow /snəʊ/	θ	thick /θɪk/, author /ˈɔːθə/
f	fifty /ˈfɪftɪ/	uː	goose /ˈguːs/, soup /suːp/
g	giggle /ˈgɪgl/	u	influence /ˈɪnfluəns/
h	hot /hɒt/	ʊ	foot /fʊt/, push /pʊʃ/
iː	fleece /fliːs/, sea /siː/	ʊə	poor /pʊə/, cure /kjʊə/
i	happy /ˈhæpi/, glorious /ˈglɔːriəs/	v	vivid /ˈvɪvɪd/
ɪ	kit /kɪt/, tin /tɪn/	ʌ	strut /strʌt/, love /lʌv/
ɪə	near /nɪə/, idea /aɪˈdɪə/	w	west /west/
j	yellow /ˈjeləʊ/, few /fjuː/	x	loch /lɒx/
k	kick /kɪk/	z	zones /zəʊnz/
l	little /ˈlɪtl/	ʒ	pleasure [ˈpleʒə]

Consonants

p b t d k g tʃ dʒ f h v θ ð s z ʃ ʒ m n ŋ r l w j ɬ x

Vowels and Diphthongs

iː ɪ e æ ɑː ɒ ɔː u ʊ uː ʌ ɜː ə eɪ əʊ aɪ aʊ ɔɪ ɪə eə ʊə

Stress marks

ˈ (primary word stress) ˌ (secondary word stress)

A

A in physics, symbol for ◊ampere, a unit of electrical current.

AA abbreviation for ◊Alcoholics Anonymous; the British *Automobile Association*.

AAA abbreviation for *Amateur Athletics Association* the UK governing body for men's athletics, founded 1880.

Aachen /ˈɑːxən/ (French *Aix-la-Chapelle*) German cathedral city and spa in the *Land* of North Rhine–Westphalia, 72 km/45 mi SW of Cologne; population (1988) 239,000. It has thriving electronic, glass, and rubber industries, and is one of Germany's principal railway junctions.

Aachen was the Roman Aquisgranum, and from the time of Charlemagne until 1531 the German emperors were crowned there. Charlemagne was born and buried in Aachen, and founded the cathedral 796. The 14th century town hall, containing the hall of the emperors, is built on the site of Charlemagne's palace.

Aalborg /ˈɔːlbɔːg/ (Danish *Ålborg*) port in Denmark 32 km/20 mi inland from the Kattegat, on the south shore of the Limfjord; population (1988) 155,000. One of Denmark's oldest towns, it has a castle and the fine Budolfi church. It is the capital of Nordjylland county in Jylland (Jutland); the port is linked to Nørresundby on the north side of the fjord by a tunnel built 1969.

Aalst /ɑːlst/ (French *Alost*) industrial town (brewing, textiles) in East Flanders, Belgium, on the river Dender 24 km/15 mi NW of Brussels; population (1982) 78,700.

Aalto /ˈɑːltəʊ/ Alvar 1898–1976. Finnish architect and designer. One of Finland's first Modernists, his architectural style was unique, characterized by asymmetry, curved walls, and contrast of natural materials. His

buildings include the Hall of Residence at the Massachusetts Institute of Technology, Cambridge, Massachusetts 1947–49; Technical High School, Otaniemi 1962–65; and Finlandia Hall, Helsinki 1972. He invented a new form of laminated bent plywood furniture in 1932 and won many design awards for household and industrial items.

Aaltonen /ˈɑːltənen/ Wäinö 1894–1966. Finnish sculptor best known for his monumental figures and busts portraying citizens of Finland, following the country's independence in 1917. He was one of the early 20th-century pioneers of direct carving and favoured granite as his medium.

aardvark (Afrikaans 'earth-pig') nocturnal mammal *Orycteropus afer*, order Tubulidentata, found in central and southern Africa. A timid, defenceless animal about the size of a pig, it has a long head, piglike snout, and large asinine ears. It feeds on termites, which it licks up with its long sticky tongue.

aardwolf nocturnal mammal *Proteles cristatus* of the ◊hyena family, Hyaenidae. It is found in E and southern Africa, usually in the burrows of the aardvark, and feeds on termites.

Aarhus /ˈɔːhuːs/ (Danish *Århus*) second-largest city of Denmark, on the E coast overlooking the Kattegat; population (1988) 258,000. It is the capital of Aarhus county in Jylland (Jutland) and a shipping and commercial centre.

Aaron /ˈeərən/ *c.* 13th century BC. In the Old Testament, the elder brother of Moses and co-leader of the ◊Hebrews in their march from Egypt to the Promised Land of Canaan. He made the Golden Calf for the Hebrews to worship when they despaired of Moses' return from Mount Sinai, but he was allowed to continue as high priest. All his descendants are hereditary high priests, called the *cohanim*, or cohens, and maintain a special place in worship and ceremony in the synagogue. See also ◊Levite.

Aaron /ˈeərən/ Hank (Henry Louis) 1934– . US baseball player. He played for 23 years with the Milwaukee (later Atlanta) Braves (1954–74) and the Milwaukee Brewers (1975–76), hitting a major-league record of 755 home runs and 2,297 runs batted in. He was elected to the Baseball Hall of Fame 1982.

abacus method of calculating with a handful of stones on 'a flat surface' (Latin *abacus*), familiar to the Greeks and Romans, and used by earlier peoples, possibly even in ancient Babylon; it still survives in the more sophisticated bead-frame form of the Russian *schoty* and the Japanese *soroban*. The abacus has been superseded by the electronic calculator.

Abadan /ˌæbəˈdɑːn/ Iranian oil port on the E side of the Shatt-al-Arab; population (1986) 294,000. Abadan is the chief refinery and shipping centre for Iran's oil industry, nationalized 1951. This measure was the beginning of the worldwide movement by oil-producing countries to assume control of profits from their own resources.

Abakan /ˌæbəˈkæn/ coal-mining city and capital of Khakass Autonomous Region, Krasnoyarsk Territory, in S Russia, population (1987) 181,000.

abalone edible marine snail of the worldwide genus *Haliotis*, family Haliotidae. They have flattened, oval, spiralled shells, which have holes around the outer edge and a bluish mother-of-pearl lining. This lining is used in ornamental work.

Abbadid dynasty /ˈæbədɪd/ 11th century. Muslim dynasty based in Seville, Spain, which lasted from 1023 until 1091. The dynasty was founded by Abu-el-Kasim Muhammad Ibn Abbad, who led the townspeople against the Berbers when the Spanish caliphate fell. The dynasty continued under Motadid (1042–1069) and Motamid (1069–1091) when the city was taken by the ◊Almoravids.

Abbas I /ˈæbəs/ *the Great* · *c.* 1557–1629. Shah of Persia from 1588. He expanded Persian territory by conquest, defeating the Uzbeks near Herat in 1597 and also the Turks. The port of Bandar-Abbas is named after him. At his death his empire reached from the river Tigris to the Indus. He was a patron of the arts.

Abbas II /ˈæbəs/ Hilmi 1874–1944. Last ◊khedive (viceroy) of Egypt, 1892–1914. On the outbreak of war between Britain and Turkey in 1914, he sided with Turkey and was deposed following the establishment of a British protectorate over Egypt.

Abbasid dynasty /ˈæbəsɪd/ dynasty of the Islamic empire, whose ◊caliphs reigned in Baghdad 750–1258. They were descended from Abbas, the prophet Muhammad's uncle, and some of them, such as Harun al-Rashid and Mamun (reigned 813–33), were outstanding patrons of cultural development. Later their power dwindled, and in 1258 Baghdad was burned by the Tatars. From then until 1517 the Abbasids retained limited power as caliphs of Egypt.

abbey in the Christian church, a monastery (of monks) or a nunnery or convent (of nuns), all dedicated to a life of celibacy and religious seclusion, governed by an abbot or abbess respectively. The word is also applied to a building that was once the church of an abbey, for example, Westminster Abbey, London.

Abbey Theatre playhouse in Dublin associated with the Irish literary revival of the early 1900s. The theatre, opened in 1904, staged the works of a number of Irish dramatists, including Lady Gregory, W B Yeats, J M Synge, and Sean O'Casey. Burned down in 1951, the Abbey Theatre was rebuilt 1966.

Abbott and Costello /ˈæbət, kɒˈsteləʊ/ stage names of William Abbott (1895–1974) and Louis Cristillo (1906–1959) US comedy duo. They moved to the cinema from vaudeville, and their films, including *Buck Privates* 1941 and *Lost in a Harem* 1944, were showcases for their routines.

Abd Allah Sudanese dervish leader *Abdullah el Taaisha* 1846–1899. Successor to the Mahdi as Sudanese ruler from 1885, he was defeated by British forces under General ◊Kitchener at Omdurman 1898 and later killed in Kordofan.

Abd al-Malik /ˈæbd ælˈmɑːlɪk/ Ibn Marwan AD 647– . Caliph who reigned 685–705. Based in Damascus, he waged military campaigns to unite Muslim groups and battled against the Greeks. He instituted a purely Arab coinage and replaced Syriac, Coptic, and Greek with Arabic as the language for his lands. His reign was turbulent but succeeded in extending and strengthening ◊Omayed power. He was also a patron of the arts.

Abd el-Kader /ˈæbd el ˈkɑːdə/ *c.* 1807–1873. Algerian nationalist. Emir (Islamic chieftain) of Mascara from 1832, he led a struggle against the French until his surrender in 1847.

Abd el-Krim /ˈæbd el ˈkrɪm/ el-Khettabi 1881–1963. Moroccan chief known as the 'Wolf of the ◊Riff'. With his brother Muhammad, he led the *Riff revolt* against the French and Spanish invaders, inflicting disastrous defeat on the Spanish at Anual in 1921, but surrendered to a large French army under Pétain in 1926. Banished to the island of Réunion, he was released in 1947 and died in voluntary exile in Cairo.

abdication crisis in British history, the constitutional upheaval of the period 16 Nov 1936 to 10 Dec 1936, brought about by the English king Edward VIII's decision to marry Wallis Simpson, an American divorcee. The marriage of the 'Supreme Governor' of the Church of England to a divorced person was considered unsuitable and the king was finally forced to abdicate on 10 Dec and left for voluntary exile in France. He was created Duke of Windsor and married Mrs Simpson on 3 June 1937.

abdomen in invertebrates, the part of the body below the ◊thorax, containing the digestive organs; in insects and other arthropods, it is the hind part of the body. In mammals, the abdomen is separated from the thorax by the diaphragm, a sheet of muscular tissue; in arthropods, commonly by a narrow constriction. In insects and spiders, the abdomen is characterized by the absence of limbs.

Abdul-Hamid II /ˈæbdʊl ˈhæmɪd/ 1842–1918. Last sultan of Turkey 1876–1909. In 1908 the ◊Young Turks under Enver Pasha forced Abdul-Hamid to restore the constitution of 1876 and in 1909 insisted on his deposition. He died in confinement. For his part in the ◊Armenian massacres suppressing the revolt of 1894–96 he was known as 'the Great Assassin'; his actions still motivate Armenian violence against the Turks.

Abdullah /æbˈdʌlə/ ibn Hussein 1882–1951. King of Jordan from 1946. He worked with the British guerrilla leader T E ◊Lawrence in the Arab revolt of World War I. Abdullah became king of Trans-Jordan 1946; on the incorporation of Arab Palestine (after the 1948–49 Arab–Israeli War) he renamed the country the Hashemite Kingdom of Jordan. He was assassinated.

Abdullah /æbˈdʌlə/ Sheik Muhammad 1905–1982. Indian politician, known as the 'Lion of Kashmir'. He headed the struggle for constitutional government against the Maharajah of Kashmir, and in 1948, following a coup, became prime minister. He agreed to the accession of the state to India, but was dismissed and imprisoned from 1953 (with brief intervals) until 1966, when he called for Kashmiri self-determination. He became chief minister of Jammu and Kashmir 1975, accepting the sovereignty of India.

Abel /ˈeɪbəl/ in the Old Testament, the second son of Adam and Eve; as a shepherd, he made burnt offerings of meat to God which were more acceptable than the fruits offered by his brother Cain; he was killed by the jealous Cain.

Abel /ˈeɪbəl/ Frederick Augustus 1827–1902. British scientist and inventor who developed explosives. As a chemist to the War Department, he introduced a method of making gun-cotton and was joint inventor with James ◊Dewar of cordite. He also invented the Abel close-test instrument for determining the ◊flash point (ignition temperature) of petroleum.

Abel /ˈeɪbəl/ John Jacob 1857–1938. US biochemist, discoverer of ◊adrenaline. He studied the chemical composition of body tissues, and this led, in 1898, to the discovery of adrenaline, the first hormone to be identified, which Abel called epinephrine. He later became the first to isolate ◊amino acids from blood.

Abelard /ˈæbəlɑːd/ Peter 1079–1142. French scholastic philosopher, who worked on logic and theology. His romantic liaison with his pupil, ◊Héloïse, caused a medieval scandal. Details of his controversial life are contained in the autobiographical *Historia Calamitatum Mearum/The History of My Misfortunes.*

Abelard, born near Nantes, became canon of Notre Dame in Paris and master of the cathedral school 1115. When his seduction of, and secret marriage to, Héloïse became known, she entered a convent and he was castrated at the instigation of her uncle, Canon Fulbert, and became a monk. Resuming teaching a year later, he was cited for heresy and became a hermit at Nogent, where he built the oratory of the Paraclete, and later abbot of a monastery in Brittany. He died at Châlon-sur-Saône on his way to defend himself against a new charge of heresy. Héloïse was buried beside him at the Paraclete 1164; their remains were taken to Père Lachaise cemetery, Paris, 1817.

Abeokuta /ˌæbiəʊˈkuːtə/ agricultural trade centre in Nigeria, W Africa, on the Ogun River, 103 km/64 mi N of Lagos; population (1983) 309,000.

Aberbrothock another name for ◊Arbroath, town in Scotland.

Abercrombie /ˈebəkrʌmbi/ Leslie Patrick 1879–1957. Pioneer of British town planning. He is known for his work replanning British cities after damage in World War II (such as the Greater London Plan, 1944) and for the ◊new town policy. See also ◊garden city.

Abercromby /ˈæbəkrʌmbi/ Ralph 1734–1801. Scots soldier who in 1801 commanded an expedition to the Mediterranean, charged with the liquidation of the French forces left behind by Napoleon in Egypt. He fought a brilliant action against the French at Aboukir Bay in 1801, but was mortally wounded at the battle of Alexandria a few days later.

Aberdeen /ˌæbəˈdiːn/ city and seaport on the E coast of Scotland, administrative headquarters of Grampian region; population (1986) 214,082. It has shore-based maintenance and service depots for the North Sea oil rigs. It is Scotland's third largest city.

It is rich in historical interest and fine buildings, including the Municipal Buildings (1867); King's College (1494) and Marischal College (founded 1593, and housed in one of the largest granite buildings in the world 1836), which together form Aberdeen University; St Machar Cathedral (1378); and the Auld Brig o'Balgownie (1320). Industries include agricultural machinery, paper, and textiles; fishing; ship-building; granite-quarrying; and engineering. Oil discoveries in the North Sea in the 1960s–70s transformed Aberdeen into the European 'offshore capital', with an airport and heliport linking the mainland to the rigs.

Aberdeen /ˌæbəˈdiːn/ George Hamilton Gordon, 4th Earl of Aberdeen 1784–1860. British Tory politician, prime minister 1852–55 when he resigned because of the Crimean War losses.

Aberdeen began his career as a diplomat. In 1828 and again in 1841 he was foreign secretary under Wellington. In 1852 he became prime minister in a government of Peelites and Whigs (Liberals), but resigned in 1855 because of the criticism aroused by the miseries and mismanagement of the Crimean War. Although a Tory, he supported Catholic emancipation and followed Robert Peel in his conversion to free trade.

Aberdeenshire /ˌæbəˈdiːnʃə/ former county in E Scotland, merged in 1975 into Grampian Region.

Aberfan /ˌæbəˈvæn/ mining village in Mid Glamorgan, Wales. Coal waste overwhelmed a school and houses in 1966; of 144 dead, 116 were children.

aberration of starlight the apparent displacement of a star from its true position, due to the combined effects of the speed of light and the speed of the Earth in orbit around the Sun (about 30 km per second/18.5 mi per second).

Aberration, discovered in 1728 by James ◊Bradley, was the first observational proof that the Earth orbits the Sun.

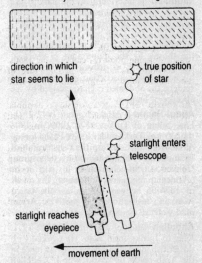

Aberration of starlight The aberration of starlight is an optical illusion caused by the motion of the Earth.

aberration, optical any of a number of defects that impair the image in an optical instrument. Aberration occurs because of minute variations in lenses and mirrors, and because different parts of the light ◊spectrum are reflected or refracted by varying amounts. In *chromatic aberration* the image is surrounded by coloured fringes, because light of different colours is brought to different focal points by a lens. In *spherical aberration* the image is blurred because different parts of a spherical lens or mirror have different focal lengths. In *astigmatism* the image appears elliptical or cross-shaped because of an irregularity in the curvature of the lens. In *coma* the images appear progressively elongated towards the edge of the field of view.

Aberystwyth /ˌæbəˈrɪstwɪθ/ resort town in Wales; population (1981) 8,500. It is the unofficial capital of the Welsh-speaking area of Wales. The University College of Wales 1872, Welsh Plant Breeding Station, and National Library of Wales are here.

Abidja'n /ˌæbiːˈdʒɑːn/ port and former capital (to 1983) of the Republic of Ivory Coast, W Africa; population (1982) 1,850,000. Products include coffee, palm oil, cocoa, and timber (mahogany). It was replaced as capital by Yamoussoukro.

Abilene /ˈæbəliːn/ town in Kansas, USA, on the Smoky Hill River; population (1980) 98,500. A western railway terminus, Abilene was a shipping point for cattle in the 1860s. Its economy includes the manufacture of aircraft and missile components and oil-field equipment.

Abkhazia /æbˈkɑːziə/ autonomous republic within Georgia, situated on the Black Sea; area 8,600 sq km/3,320 sq mi; population (1989) 526,000. Abkhazia, a Georgian kingdom from the 4th century, was inhabited traditionally by Abkhazis, an ethnic group converted from Christianity to Islam in the 17th century. By the 1980s some 17% of the population were Muslims and two-thirds were of Georgian origin. In March-April and July 1989, Abkhazis demanded secession from Georgia and reinstatement as a full Union republic; violent interethnic clashes erupted in which at least 20 people died. Georgian nationalists, however, wanted the republic to be incorporated as part of Georgia. The dispute triggered nationalist demonstrations throughout Georgia.

ablution washing for a religious purpose, to purify the soul. Hindus, for example, believe that bathing in the river Ganges will purify them. Similar beliefs are found in Christianity and Shinto (for example, the mythical Izanagi purifies himself by diving to the bottom of the sea and washing himself).

ABM abbreviation for *anti-ballistic missile*; see ◊nuclear warfare.

Åbo /ˈɔːbuː/ Swedish name for ◊Turku in Finland.

abolitionism in UK and US history, a movement culminating in the late 18th and early 19th centuries, which aimed first to end the slave trade, and then to abolish the institution of ◊slavery and emancipate slaves. In the USA, Benjamin ◊Franklin had argued against slavery as early as 1775. It was officially abolished by the Emancipation Proclamation 1863 of President Abraham ◊Lincoln, but it could not be enforced until 1865 after the Union victory in the civil war. The question of whether newly admitted states would allow slavery was a major issue in the break up of the Union.

In the UK, the leading abolitionist was William ◊Wilberforce, who secured passage of a bill abolishing the slave trade in 1807.

Abomey /əˈbəʊmi/ town and port of ◊Benin, W Africa; population (1982) 54,500. It was once the capital of the kingdom of Dahomey, which flourished in the 17th–19th centuries, and had a mud-built defence wall 10 km/6 mi in circumference.

Aboriginal art art of the Australian Aborigines. Traditionally this was in the main religious and directed towards portraying the stories of the ◊Dreamtime. Perishable materials were used, such as in ◊bark painting and carved trees and logs, and apart from some sheltered cave paintings and rock engravings few early works survive. Abstract patterns and stylized figures predominate.

Rock engravings are found throughout the continent. The earliest, such as those found in Koon-alda Cave beneath the Nullarbor Plain and at the Early Man site on Cape York Peninsula, are characterized by stylized designs of circles, animal tracks and meandering patterns, and are between 15,000 and 20,000 years old. In the Hawkesbury River region of New South Wales large figures of animals, birds, fish, and spirit beings have been engraved into the sandstone. Cave walls were painted using natural ochres of red and yellow, white pipeclay, and charcoal. Such paintings are the most common form of Aboriginal fixed art, and include the vast galleries in the Laura district of Cape York, which feature the sticklike Quinkan spirit figures, and in the Kimberleys the Wandjina figures, towering red and white creatures with halolike headdresses. Stencils, frequently of hands, are found in all rock-painting areas and were produced by placing an object against the rock wall and then blowing a mouthful of paint over it. Trees and logs carved for ceremonial purposes include the burial poles made by the Tiwi people of Bathurst and Melville

Islands, which are painted in complex designs using black, white, red, and yellow, and the carved trees (*dendroglyphs*) of the Darling Basin region of New South Wales, which were associated with initiation ceremonies and burial rites.

aborigine (Latin *ab origine* 'from the beginning') any indigenous inhabitant of a region or country. The word often refers to the original peoples of areas colonized by Europeans, and especially to ⟡Australian Aborigines.

abortion the ending of a pregnancy before the fetus is developed sufficiently to survive outside the uterus. Loss of a fetus at a later gestational age is termed premature stillbirth. Abortion may be accidental (miscarriage) or deliberate (termination of pregnancy).

Methods of deliberate abortion vary according to the gestational age of the fetus. Up to 12 weeks, the cervix is dilated and a suction curette passed into the uterus to remove its contents (*D and C*). Over 12 weeks, a prostaglandin pessary is introduced into the vagina, which induces labour, producing a miscarriage.

In 1989 an anti-progesterone pill was introduced in France, under the name RU 486; in 1991 it was licensed in the UK, known as ⟡mefipristone. Within 24 hours of ingestion, it leads to the expulsion of the fetus from the uterus, and can be used at an earlier stage in pregnancy. The pill is also an effective contraceptive when taken up to 72 hours after intercourse.

Abortion as a means of birth control has long been the subject of controversy. The argument centres largely upon whether a woman should legally be permitted to have an abortion and, that being so, under what circumstances. Another aspect is whether, and to what extent, the law should protect the fetus. Those who oppose abortion generally believe that human life begins at the moment of conception, when a sperm fertilizes an egg. This is the view held, for example, by the Roman Catholic Church. Those who support unrestricted legal abortion may believe in a woman's right to choose whether she wants a child, and may take into account the large numbers of deaths and injuries from back-street abortions that are thus avoided. Others approve abortion for specific reasons. For example, if a woman's life or health is jeopardized, abortion may be recommended; and if there

is a strong likelihood that the child will be born with severe mental or physical handicap. Other grounds for abortion include pregnancy resulting from sexual assault such as rape or incest.

In the USA in 1989, a Supreme Court decision gave state legislatures the right to introduce some restrictions on the unconditional right, established by the Supreme Court in an earlier decision (Roe v. Wade), for any woman to decide to have an abortion.

In the UK an abortion must be carried out under the terms of the 1967 Abortion Act, which states that two doctors must agree that termination of the pregnancy is necessary, and the operation must be performed on approved premises.

The legal cut-off point for therapeutic abortion — in Britain 24 weeks — is largely arbitrary. Techniques have been developed to sustain babies delivered at an earlier stage of gestation (some as young as 23 weeks). In 1988, there were 183,978 abortions performed in England and Wales, an increase of 5.5% on 1987 figures. In the UK, 20% of conceptions in 1988 were terminated by abortion, mostly in the 16–24 age group.

Aboukir Bay, Battle of /ˌæbuːˈkɪə/ also known as the *Battle of the Nile*; naval battle between Great Britain and France, in which Admiral Nelson defeated Napoleon's fleet at the Egyptian seaport of Aboukir on 1 Aug 1798.

abracadabra magic word first recorded in a Latin poem of the 2nd century AD by the Gnostic poet Serenus Sammonicus. When written in the form of an inverted pyramid, so as to be read across the top and up the right side, it was worn as a health amulet, to ward off illnesses.

Abraham /ˈeɪbrəhæm/ *c.* 2300 BC. in the Old Testament, founder of the Jewish nation. In his early life he was called Abram. God promised him heirs and land for his people in Canaan, (Israel), renamed him Abraham ('father of many nations') and tested his faith by a command (later retracted) to sacrifice his son Isaac.

Abraham was born in Ur, in ⟡Sumeria, the son of Terah. With his father, wife Sarah, and nephew Lot, he migrated to Haran, N Mesopotamia, then to Canaan where he received God's promise of land. After visiting Egypt he separated from Lot at Bethel and settled in Hebron (now in Israel). He was still childless at the age of 76, subsequently had a son (Ishmael) with his wife's maidservant Hagar, and then, at the age of 100, a son Isaac with his wife Sarah. God's promise to Abraham that his descendants would be a nation and Canaan their land was fulfilled when the descendants of Abraham's grandson, Jacob, were led out of Egypt by Moses. Abraham was buried in Machpelah Cave, Hebron.

Abraham /ˈeɪbrəhæm/ Edward Penley 1913– . British biochemist who isolated the antibiotic *cephalosporin*, capable of destroying penicillin-resistant bacteria.

Abraham, Plains of /ˈeɪbrəhæm/ plateau near Québec, Canada, where the British commander ◊Wolfe defeated the French under ◊Montcalm, 13 Sept 1759, during the French and Indian War (1754–63).

abrasive substance used for cutting and polishing or for removing small amounts of the surface of hard materials. There are two types: natural and artificial abrasives, and their hardness is measured using the ◊Mohs' scale. Natural abrasives include quartz, sandstone, pumice, diamond, and corundum; artificial abrasives include rouge, whiting, and carborundum.

abraxas mystical word found engraved on ancient stones, used as a superstitious charm. The Greek letters of the word, when interpreted as numbers, are equivalent to 365. The title was used by Egyptian Gnostics to describe the supreme being.

Abruzzi /əˈbrutsi/ mountainous region of S central Italy, comprising the provinces of L'Aquila, Chieti, Pescara, and Teramo; area 10,800 sq km/4,169 sq mi; population (1988) 1,258,000; capital L'Aquila. Gran Sasso d'Italia, 2,914 m/9,564 ft, is the highest point of the ◊Apennines.

Absalom /ˈæbsələm/ in the Old Testament, the favourite son of King David; when defeated in a revolt against his father he fled on a mule, but caught his hair in a tree branch and was killed by Joab, one of David's officers.

abscess collection of ◊pus in the tissues forming in response to infection. Its presence is signalled by pain and inflammation.

abscissa in coordinate geometry, the horizontal or *x*-coordinate—that is, the distance of a point from the vertical or *y*-axis. For example, a point with the coordinates (3,4) has an abscissa of 3.

abscissin or *abscissic acid* plant hormone found in all higher plants. It is involved in the process of abscission and also inhibits stem elongation, germination of seeds, and the sprouting of buds.

abscission in botany, the controlled separation of part of a plant from the main plant body—most commonly, the falling of leaves or the dropping of fruit. In ◊deciduous plants the leaves are shed before the winter or dry season, whereas ◊evergreen plants drop their leaves continually throughout the year. Fruit drop, the abscission of fruit while still immature, is a naturally occurring process.

Abscission occurs after the formation of an abscission zone at the point of separation. Within this, a thin layer of cells, the abscission layer, becomes weakened and breaks down through the conversion of pectic acid to pectin. Consequently the leaf, fruit, or other part can easily be dislodged by wind or rain. The process is thought to be controlled by the amount of ◊auxin present. Fruit-drop is particularly common in fruit trees such as apples, and orchards are often sprayed with artificial auxin as a preventive measure.

absinthe green liqueur containing 60–80% alcohol and made with anise. It was originally flavoured with oil of wormwood, which, because it attacks the nervous system, is widely banned, so substitutes are now used.

Absinthe was made in Switzerland in the 18th century, and in 1805 the Pernod family in France set up in business on the strength of this drink. By 1910, 20 million litres of absinthe was consumed annually, and many crimes were attributed to its effects; it was banned in Switzerland in 1907, in the USA 1912, and in France after 1918.

absolute value or *modulus* in mathematics, the value, or magnitude, of a number irrespective of its sign (denoted $|n|$), and defined as the positive square root of n^2.

For example, 5 and –5 have the same absolute value: $|5| = |-5| = 5$. For a ◊complex number, the absolute value is its distance to the origin when it is plotted on an Argand diagram, and can be calculated (without plotting) by applying the ◊Pythagorean theorem. By definition, the absolute value of any complex number $a + bi$ is given by the expression $|a + bi| = (\sqrt{a^2 + b^2})$.

absolute zero lowest temperature theoretically possible, zero kelvin, equivalent to $-273.16°C/-459.67°F$, at which molecules are motionless. Although the third law of ◊thermodynamics indicates the impossibility of reaching absolute zero exactly, a temperature within 3×10^{-8} kelvin of it was produced in 1984 by Finnish scientists. Near absolute zero, the physical properties of some materials change substantially; for example, some metals lose their electrical resistance and become superconductive. See ◊ cryogenics.

absolutism or *absolute monarchy* system of government in which the ruler or rulers have unlimited power. The principle of an absolute monarch, given a right to rule by God (see ◊ divine right of kings), was extensively used in Europe during the 17th and 18th centuries. Absolute monarchy is contrasted with limited or constitutional monarchy, in which the sovereign's powers are defined or limited.

absorption in science, the taking up of one substance by another, such as a liquid by a solid (ink by blotting paper) or a gas by a liquid (ammonia by water). In biology, absorption describes the passing of nutrients or medication into and through tissues such as intestinal walls and blood vessels. In physics, absorption is the phenomenon by which a substance retains radiation of particular wavelengths; for example, a piece of blue glass absorbs all visible light except the wavelengths in the blue part of the spectrum; it also refers to the partial loss of energy resulting from light and other electromagnetic waves passing through a medium. In nuclear physics, absorption is the capture by elements, such as boron, of neutrons produced by fission in a reactor.

absorption spectroscopy or *absorptiometry* in analytical chemistry, a technique for determining the identity or amount present of a chemical substance by measuring the amount of electromagnetic radiation the substance absorbs at specific wavelengths; see ◊ spectroscopy.

abstract art nonrepresentational art. Ornamental art without figurative representation occurs in most cultures. The modern abstract movement in sculpture and painting emerged in Europe and North America between 1910 and 1920. Two approaches produce different abstract styles: images that have been 'abstracted' from nature to the point where they no longer reflect a conventional reality and nonobjective, or 'pure', art forms, supposedly without reference to reality.

Abstract art began in the avant-garde movements of the late 19th century, in Impressionism, Neo-Impressionism, and Post-Impressionism. These styles of painting reduced the importance of the original subject matter and emphasized the creative process of painting itself. In the first decade of the 20th century, some painters in Western Europe began to abandon the established Western convention of imitating nature and storytelling in pictures and developed a new artistic form and expression. Kandinsky is generally regarded as the first abstract artist. His highly coloured canvases influenced many younger European artists. In France, the Cubists Picasso and Braque also developed, around 1907, an abstract style; their pictures, some partly collage, were composed mainly of fragmented natural images.

Many variations of abstract art developed in Europe, as shown in the work of Mondrian, Malevich, the Futurists, the Vorticists, and the Dadaists.

Sculptors, including Brancusi and Epstein, were inspired by the new freedom in form and content, and Brancusi's *The Kiss* 1910 is one of the earliest abstract sculptures.

Two exhibitions of European art, one in New York in 1913 (the Armory Show), the other in San Francisco in 1917, opened the way for abstraction in US art. Many painters, including the young Georgia O'Keeffe, experimented with new styles. Morgan Russell (1886–1953) and Stanton Mac-donald-Wright (1890–1973) invented their own school, Synchronism, a rival to Orphism, a similar style developed in France by Robert Delaunay.

Abstract art has dominated Western art from 1920 and has continued to produce many variations. In the 1940s it gained renewed vigour in the works of the Abstract Expressionists. From the 1950s Minimal art provoked more outraged reactions from critics and the general public alike.

Abstract Expressionism US movement in abstract art that emphasized the act of painting, the expression inherent in paint itself, and the interaction of artist, paint, and canvas. Abstract Expressionism emerged in New York in the early 1940s. Arshile Gorky, Franz Kline, Jackson Pollock, and Mark Rothko are associated with the movement.

Abstract Expressionism may have been inspired by Hans Hofmann and Gorky, who were both working in the USA in the 1940s. Hofmann, who emigrated from Germany in the 1930s, had started to use dribbles and blobs of paint to create expressive abstract patterns, while Gorky, a Turkish Armenian refugee, was developing his highly coloured abstracts with wild organic forms. Abstract Expressionism was not a distinct school but rather a convergence of artistic personalities, each revolting against restricting conventions in US art. The styles of the movement's exponents varied widely: Pollock's huge dripped and splashed work, Willem de Kooning's grotesque figures, Kline's strong calligraphic style, and Robert Motherwell's and Rothko's calmer large abstract canvases. The movement made a strong impression on European painting in the late 1950s.

Absurd, Theatre of the avant-garde drama originating with a group of playwrights in the 1950s, including Beckett, Ionesco, Genet, and Pinter. Their work expressed the belief that in a godless universe human existence has no meaning or purpose and therefore all communication breaks down. Logical construction and argument gives way to irrational and illogical speech and to its ultimate conclusion, silence, as in Beckett's play *Breath* 1970.

Abu Bakr /ˌæbuːˈbækə/ or *Abu-Bekr* 573–634. 'Father of the virgin', name used by Abd-el-Ka'aba from about 618 when the prophet Muhammad married his daughter Ayesha. He was a close adviser to Muhammad in the period 622–32. On the prophet's death, he became the first ◊caliph, adding Mesopotamia to the Muslim world and instigating expansion into Iraq and Syria.

Traditionally he is supposed to have encouraged some of those who had known Muhammad to memorize his teachings; these words were later written down to form the Koran.

Abu Dhabi /ˌæbuːˈdɑːbi/ sheikdom in SW Asia, on the Arabian Gulf, capital of the ◊United Arab Emirates. Formerly under British protection, it has been ruled since 1971 by Sheik Sultan Zayed bin al-Nahayan, who is also president of the Supreme Council of Rulers of the United Arab Emirates.

Abuja /əˈbuːdʒə/ city in Nigeria that began construction in 1976 as a replacement for Lagos. Shaped like a crescent, it was designed by the Japanese architect Kenzo Tange.

Abu Musa /ˈaebuː ˈmuːsɑː/ small island in the Persian Gulf. Formerly owned by the ruler of Sharjah, it was forcibly occupied by Iran in 1971.

Abú Nuwás /ˈæbuː ˈnuːwæs/ Hasan ibn Háni 762–*c*. 815. Arab poet celebrated for the freedom, eroticism and ironic lightness of touch he brought to traditional forms.

Abu Simbel /ˌæbuː ˈsɪmbəl/ former site of two ancient temples cut into the rock on the banks of the Nile in S Egypt during the reign of Ramses II, commemorating him and his wife Nefertari. The temples were moved, in sections, 1966–67 before the site was flooded by the Aswan High Dam.

Abydos /əˈbaɪdɒs/ ancient city in Upper Egypt; the Great Temple of Seti I dates from about 1300 BC.

abyssal zone dark ocean area 2,000–6,000 m/6,500–19,500 ft deep; temperature 4°C/39°F. Three-quarters of the area of the deep ocean floor lies in the abyssal zone, which is too far from the surface for photosynthesis to take place. Some fish and crustaceans living there are blind or have their own light sources. The region above is the bathyal zone; the region below, the hadal zone.

Abyssinia /ˌæbɪˈsɪniə/ former name of ◊Ethiopia.

AC in physics, abbreviation for ◊alternating current.

acacia any of a large group of shrubs and trees of the genus *Acacia*, family Leguminosae, found in warm regions of the world, notably Australia. Acacias include the thorn trees of the African savanna, the gum arabic tree *A. senegal* of N Africa which is used in manufacturing jellies and sweets, and several species of the SW USA and Mexico.

Academy originally, the school of philosophy founded by ◊Plato in the gardens of Academe, NW of Athens; it was closed by the Byzantine Emperor ◊Justinian I, with the other pagan schools, in AD 529. The first academy (in the present-day sense of a recognized society established for the promotion of one or more of the arts and sciences) was the Museum of Alexandria, founded by Ptolemy Soter in the 3rd century BC.

Academy Award annual cinema award in many categories, given since 1927 by the American Academy of Motion Picture Arts and Sciences (founded by Louis B Mayer of Metro-Goldwyn-Mayer 1927). The award is cinema's most prestigious accolade, taking the form of a gold-plated statuette, nicknamed *Oscar* since 1931.

Academy Awards: recent winners

1984	Best Picture: *Amadeus*; Best Director: Milos Forman *Amadeus*; Best Actor: F Murray Abraham *Amadeus*; Best Actress: Sally Field *Places in the Heart*
1985	Best Picture: *Out of Africa*; Best Director: Sidney Pollack *Out of Africa*; Best Actor: William Hurt *Kiss of the Spiderwoman*; Best Actress: Geraldine Page *The Trip to Bountiful*
1986	Best Picture: *Platoon*; Best Director: Oliver Stone *Platoon*; Best Actor: Paul Newman *The Color of Money*; Best Actress: Marlee Matlin *Children of a Lesser God*
1987	Best Picture: *The Last Emperor*; Best Director: Bernardo Bertolucci *The Last Emperor*; Best Actor: Michael Douglas *Wall Street*; Best Actress: Cher *Moonstruck*
1988	Best Picture: *Rain Man*; Best Director: Barry Levinson *Rain Man*; Best Actor: Dustin Hoffman *Rain Man*; Best Actress: Jodie Foster *The Accused*
1989	Best Picture: *My Left Foot*; Best Director: Oliver Stone *Born on the 4th of July*; Best Actor: Daniel Day-Lewis *My Left Foot*; Best Actress: Jessica Tandy *Driving Miss Daisy*
1990	Best Picture: *Dances with Wolves*; Best Director: Kevin Costner *Dances with Wolves*; Best Actor: Jeremy Irons *Reversal of Fortune*; Best Actress: Kathy Bates *Misery*
1991	Best Picture: *The Silence of the Lambs*; Best Director: Jonathan Demme *The Silence of the Lambs*; Best Actor: Anthony Hopkins *The Silence of the Lambs*; Best Actress: Jodie Foster *The Silence of the Lambs*
1992	Best Picture: *Unforgiven*; Best Director: Clint Eastwood *Unforgiven*; Best Actor: Al Pacino *Scent of a Woman*; Best Actress: Emma Thompson *Howards End*
1993	Best Picture: *Schindler's List*; Best Director: Steven Spielberg *Schindler's List*; Best Actor: Tom Hanks *Philadelphia*; Best Actress: Holly Hunter *The Piano*

Academy, French or *Académie Française* literary society concerned with maintaining the purity of the French language, founded by ◊Richelieu 1635. Membership is limited to 40 'Immortals' at a time.

Acadia /əˈkeɪdɪə/ (French *Acadie*) name given to ◊Nova Scotia by French settlers 1604, from which the term ◊Cajun derives.

acanthus any herbaceous plant of the genus *Acanthus* with handsome lobed leaves. Twenty species are found in the Mediterranean region and Old World tropics, including bear's breech *A. mollis*, whose leaves were used as a motif in classical architecture, for example, on Corinthian columns.

a cappella (Italian 'in the style of the chapel') choral music sung without instrumental accompaniment. It is characteristic of ◊gospel music, ◊doo-wop, and the evangelical Christian church movement.

Acapulco /ˌækəˈpʊlkəʊ/ or *Acapulco de Juarez* port and holiday resort in Mexico; population (1990) 592,187.

ACAS acronym for ◊*Advisory, Conciliation and Arbitration Service*.

Accad /ˈækæd/ alternative form of ◊Akkad, ancient city of Mesopotamia.

accelerated freeze drying (AFD) common method of food preservation. See ◊food technology.

acceleration the rate of change of the velocity of a moving body. Acceleration due to gravity is the acceleration of a body falling freely under the influence of gravity; it varies slightly at different latitudes and altitudes. Retardation (deceleration) is negative acceleration; for example, as a rising rocket slows down, it is being negatively accelerated towards the centre of the Earth. Acceleration is expressed in metres per second per second (m s^{-2}) or feet per second per second (ft s^{-2}).

The value adopted internationally for gravitational acceleration on Earth is 9.806 m s^{-2}/32.174 ft s^{-2}.

acceleration, secular in astronomy, the continuous and nonperiodic change in orbital velocity of one body around another, or the axial rotation period of a body.

An example is the axial rotation of the Earth. This is gradually slowing down owing to the gravitational effects of the Moon and the resulting production of tides, which have a frictional effect on the Earth. However, the angular ◊momentum of the Earth–Moon system is maintained, because the momentum lost by the Earth is passed to the Moon. This results in an increase in the Moon's orbital period and a consequential moving away from the Earth. The overall effect is that the Earth's axial rotation period is increasing by about 15-millionths of a second a year, and the Moon is receding from the Earth at about 4 cm/1.5 in a year.

accelerator in physics, a device to bring charged particles (such as ◊protons) up to high speeds and energies, at which they can be of use in industry, medicine, and pure physics: when high energy particles collide with other particles, the fragments formed reveal the nature of the fundamental forces of nature. For particles to achieve the energies required, successive applications of a high voltage are given to electrodes placed in the path of the particles. During acceleration, the particles are confined within a circular or linear track using a magnetic field.

The first circular accelerator, the *cyclotron*, was built in the early 1930s. The early cyclotrons had circumferences of about 10 cm/4 in, whereas the ◊Large Electron–Positron Collider (LEP) at ◊CERN near Geneva, which came into operation 1989, has a circumference of 27 km/16.8 mi, around which ◊electrons and ◊positrons are accelerated before being allowed to collide. In 1988, the USA announced plans to build the Superconducting Super Collider (to be completed 1996), in Waxahachie, Texas, with a circumference of 85 km/53 mi.

The world's largest *linear accelerator* is the Stanford Linear Collider, in which electrons and positrons are accelerated along a straight track, 3.2 km/2 mi long, and then steered into a head-on collision.

accelerometer apparatus, either mechanical or electromechanical, for measuring ◊acceleration or deceleration—that is, the rate of increase or decrease in the ◊velocity of a moving object.

Accelerometers are used to measure the efficiency of the braking systems on road and rail vehicles; those used in aircraft and spacecraft can determine accelerations in several directions simultaneously. There are also accelerometers for detecting vibrations in machinery.

accent way of speaking that identifies a person with a particular country, region, language, social class, linguistic style, or some mixture of these.

People often describe only those who belong to groups other than their own as having accents and may give them special names, for example, an Irish brogue or a Northumbrian burr.

accessory in law, a party to a crime that is actually committed by someone else. An accessory either incites someone to commit a crime or assists and abets them.

access time in computing, the time taken by a computer after an instruction has being given before it reads from, or writes to, ◊memory; otherwise known as the 'reaction time'.

acclimation or *acclimatization* the physiological changes induced in an organism by exposure to new environmental conditions. When humans move to higher altitudes, for example, the number of red blood cells rises to increase the oxygen-carrying capacity of the blood in order to compensate for the lower levels of oxygen in the air.

accommodation in biology, the ability of the vertebrate ◊eye to focus on near or far objects by changing the shape of the lens.

For something to be viewed clearly the image must be precisely focused on the retina, the light-sensitive sheet of cells at the rear of the eye. Close objects can be seen when the lens takes up a more spherical shape, far objects when the lens is stretched and made thinner. These changes in shape are directed by the brain and by a ring of ciliary muscles lying beneath the iris.

From about the age of 40, the lens in the human eye becomes less flexible, causing the defect of vision known as *presbyopia* or lack of accommodation. People with this defect need different spectacles for reading and distance vision.

accomplice in law, a person who acts with another in the commission or attempted commission of a crime, either as a principal or as an ◊accessory.

accordion musical instrument of the reed organ type comprising left and right wind chests connected by flexible bellows. The right hand plays melody on a piano-style keyboard while the left hand has a system of push buttons for selecting single notes or chord harmonies.

Invented by Cyrill Damien (1772–1847) in Vienna 1829, the accordion came into use throughout the world and can be heard in the popular music of France, China, Russia, and the southern USA.

accountancy financial management of businesses and other organizations, from balance sheets to policy decisions.

Forms of ◊inflation accounting, such as CCA (current cost accounting) and CPP (current purchasing power), are aimed at providing valid financial comparisons over a period in which money values change.

Accra /ˈækrɑː/ capital and port of Ghana; population of greater Accra region (1984) 1,420,000. The port trades in cacao, gold, and timber. Industries include engineering, brewing, and food processing. Osu (Christiansborg) Castle is the presidential residence.

accumulator in electricity, a storage ◊battery—that is, a group of rechargeable secondary cells.

An ordinary 12-volt car battery is an accumulator consisting of six lead–acid cells which are continually recharged by the car's alternator or dynamo. It has electrodes of lead and lead oxide in an electrolyte of sulphuric acid. Another common type of accumulator is the 'nife' or Ni Fe cell, which has electrodes of nickel and iron in a potas-sium hydroxide electrolyte.

acetaldehyde common name for ◊ethanal.

acetate common name for ◊ethanoate.

acetic acid common name for ◊ethanoic acid.

acetone common name for ◊propanone.

acetylene common name for ◊ethyne.

acetylsalicylic acid chemical name for the painkilling drug ◊aspirin.

Achaea /əˈkiːə/ in ancient Greece, and also today, an area of the N Peloponnese. The *Achaeans* were the predominant society during the Mycenaean period and are said by Homer to have taken part in the siege of Troy.

Achaean League /əˈkiːən/ union in 275 BC of most of the cities of the N Peloponnese, which managed to defeat ◊Sparta, but was itself defeated by the Romans 146 BC.

Achaemenid dynasty /əˈkiːmənɪd/ family ruling the Persian Empire 550–330 BC, and named after Achaemenes, ancestor of Cyrus the Great, founder of the empire. His successors included Cambyses, Darius I, Xerxes, and Darius III, who, as the last Achaemenid ruler, was killed after defeat in battle against Alexander the Great 330 BC.

Achard /ˈæxɑːt/ Franz Karl 1753–1821. German chemist who was largely responsible for developing the industrial process by which table sugar (sucrose) is extracted from beet. He improved the quality of available beet and erected the first factory for the extraction of sugar in Silesia (now in Poland) 1802.

Achebe /əˈtʃeɪbi/ Chinua 1930– . Nigerian novelist, whose themes include the social and political impact of European colonialism on African people, and the problems of newly independent African nations. His novels include the widely acclaimed *Things Fall Apart* 1958 and *Anthills of the Savannah* 1987.

achene dry, one-seeded ◊fruit that develops from a single ◊ovary and does not split open to disperse the seed. Achenes commonly occur in groups, for example, the fruiting heads of buttercup *Ranunculus* and clematis. The outer surface may be smooth, spiny, ribbed, or tuberculate, depending on the species.

An achene with part of the fruit wall extended to form a membranous wing is called a *samara*; an example is the pendulous fruit of the ash *Fraxinus*. A ◊*caryopsis*, another type of achene, is formed when the ◊carpel wall becomes fused to the seed coat and is typical of grasses and cereals. A *cypsela* is derived from an inferior ovary and is characteristic of the daisy family (Compositae). It often has a ◊pappus of hairs attached, which aids its dispersal by the wind, as in the dandelion.

Acheron /ˈækərən/ in Greek mythology, one of the rivers of the lower world. The name was taken from a river in S Epirus that flowed through a deep gorge into the Ionian Sea.

Acheson /ˈætʃɪsən/ Dean (Gooderham) 1893–1971. US politician. As undersecretary of state 1945–47 in Truman's Democratic administration, he was associated with George C Marshall in preparing the ◊Marshall Plan, and succeeded him as secretary of state 1949–53.

Achilles /əˈkɪliːz/ Greek hero of Homer's ◊Iliad. He was the son of Peleus, king of the Myrmidons in Thessaly, and the sea nymph Thetis, who rendered him invulnerable, except for the heel by which she held him when dipping him in the river Styx. Achilles killed Hector in the Trojan War and was himself killed by Paris who shot a poisoned arrow into his vulnerable heel.

Achilles tendon tendon pinning the calf muscle to the heel bone. It is one of the largest in the human body.

achromatic lens combination of lenses made from materials of different refractive indexes, constructed in such a way as to minimize chromatic aberration (which in a single lens causes coloured fringes around images because the lens diffracts the different wavelengths in white light to slightly different extents).

acid compound that, in solution in an ionizing solvent (usually water), gives rise to hydrogen ions (H^+ or protons). In modern chemistry, acids are defined as substances that are proton donors and accept electrons to form ◊ionic bonds. Acids react with ◊bases to form salts, and they act as solvents. Strong acids are corrosive; dilute acids have a sour or sharp taste, although in some organic acids this may be partially masked by other flavour characteristics. Acids are classified as monobasic, dibasic, tribasic, and so forth, according to the number of replaceable hydrogen atoms in a molecule.

Acids can be detected by using coloured indicators such as ◊litmus and methyl orange. The strength of an acid is measured by its hydrogen-ion concentration, indicated by the ◊pH value. The first known acid was vinegar (ethanoic or acetic acid). Inorganic acids include boric, carbonic, hydrochloric, hydrofluoric, nitric, phosphoric, and sulphuric. Organic acids include acetic, benzoic, citric, formic, lactic, oxalic, and salicylic, as well as complex substances such as ◊nucleic acids and ◊amino acids.

acid house type of ◊house music. The derivation of the term is disputed but may be from 'acid burning', Chicago slang for 'sampling', a recording technique much featured in acid house (see ◊digital sampling).

acid rain acidic rainfall, thought to be caused principally by the release into the atmosphere of sulphur dioxide (SO_2) and oxides of nitrogen. Sulphur dioxide is formed from the burning of fossil fuels, such as coal, that contain high quantities of sulphur; nitrogen oxides are contributed from various industrial activities and from car exhaust fumes.

Acid rain is linked with damage to and death of forests and lake organisms in Scandinavia, Europe, and eastern North America. It also results in damage to buildings and statues. US and European power stations burning fossil fuel release some 8 grams of sulphur dioxides and 3 grams of nitrogen oxides per kilowatt-hour. According to UK Department of Environment figures emissions of sulphur dioxide from power stations would have to be decreased by 81% in order to arrest such damage.

acid salt chemical compound formed by the partial neutralization of a dibasic or tribasic ◊acid (one that contains two or three hydrogen atoms). Although a salt, it contains replaceable hydrogen, so it may undergo the typical reactions of an acid. Examples are sodium hydrogen sulphate ($NaHSO_4$) and acid phosphates.

aclinic line the magnetic equator, an imaginary line near the equator, where the compass needle balances horizontally, the attraction of the north and south magnetic poles being equal.

acne skin eruption, mainly occurring among adolescents and young adults, caused by inflammation of the sebaceous glands which secrete an oily substance (sebum), the natural lubricant of the skin. Sometimes the glands' openings become blocked and they swell; the contents decompose and pimples form on the face, back, and chest.

Aconcagua /ˌækənˈkægwə/ extinct volcano in the Argentine Andes, the highest peak in the Americas; 6,960 m/22,834 ft. It was first climbed by Vines and Zeebruggen 1897.

aconite or **monkshood** herbaceous Eurasian plant *Aconitum napellus* of the buttercup family Ranunculaceae, with hooded blue-mauve flowers. It produces aconitine, a powerful alkaloid with narcotic and analgesic properties.

acorn fruit of the oak tree, a ◊nut growing in a shallow cup.

acoustic ohm c.g.s. unit of acoustic impedance (the ratio of the sound pressure on a surface to the sound flux through the surface). It is analogous to the ohm as the unit of electrical ◊impedance.

acoustics in general, the experimental and theoretical science of sound and its transmission; in particular, that branch of the science that has to do with the phenomena of sound in a particular space such as a room or theatre.

Acoustical engineering is concerned with the technical control of sound, and involves architecture and construction, studying control of vibration, soundproofing, and the elimination of noise. It also includes all forms of sound recording and reinforcement, the hearing and perception of sounds, and hearing aids.

acquired character feature of the body that develops during the lifetime of an individual, usually as a result of repeated use or disuse, such as the enlarged muscles of a weightlifter.

◊Lamarck's theory of evolution assumed that acquired characters were passed from parent to offspring. Modern evolutionary theory does not recognize the inheritance of acquired characters because there is no reliable scientific evidence that it occurs, and because no mechanism is known whereby bodily changes can influence the genetic material. See also ◊central dogma.

acquired immune deficiency syndrome full name for the disease ◊AIDS.

acquittal in law, the setting free of someone charged with a crime after a trial.

In English courts it follows a verdict of 'not guilty', but in Scotland the verdict may be either 'not guilty' or 'not proven'. Acquittal by the jury must be confirmed by the judge.

acre /eɪkə/ traditional English land measure equal to 4,840 square yards (4,047 sq m/ 0.405 ha). Originally meaning a field, it was the size that a yoke of oxen could plough in a day. It may be subdivided into 160 square rods (one square rod equalling 25.29 sq m/ 30.25 sq yd).

Acre /eɪkə/ or *Akko* seaport in Israel; population (1983) 37,000. Taken by the Crusaders 1104, it was captured by Saladin 1187 and retaken by Richard I (the Lionheart) 1191. Napoleon failed in a siege 1799. British field marshal Allenby captured the port 1918. From being part of British mandated Palestine, it became part of Israel 1948.

acridine $C_{13}H_9N$ organic compound that occurs in coal tar. It is extracted by dilute acids but can also be obtained synthetically. It is used to make dyes and drugs.

acromegaly rare condition in which enlargement of prominent parts of the body, for example hands, feet, heart, and, conspicuously, the eyebrow ridges and lower jaw, is caused by excessive output of growth hormone in adult life by a nonmalignant tumour of the ◊pituitary gland.

acronym word formed from the initial letters and/or syllables of other words, intended as a pronounceable abbreviation, for example NATO (*N*orth *A*tlantic *T*reaty *Or*ganization), radar (*ra*dio *d*etecting *a*nd *rang*ing), and sitrep (*sit*uation *rep*ort).

acrophobia ◊phobia involving fear of heights.

acropolis (Greek 'high city') citadel of an ancient Greek town. The Acropolis and surrounding complexes at Athens contain the ruins of the Parthenon, built there during the days of the Athenian empire. The term is also used for analogous structures, as in the massive granite-built ruins of Great ◊Zimbabwe.

acrostic (Greek 'at the extremity of a line or row') a number of lines of writing, usually verse, whose initial letters (read downwards) form a word, phrase, or sentence. A *single acrostic* is formed by the initial letters of lines only, while a *double acrostic* is formed by both initial and final letters.

acrylic acid common name for ◊propenoic acid.

acrylic fibre synthetic fibre often used as a substitute for wool. It was first developed 1947 but not produced in great volumes until the 1950s. Strong and warm, acrylic fibre is often used for sweaters and tracksuits, and as linings for boots and gloves.

ACT abbreviation for ◊*Australian Capital Territory*.

Actaeon /ækˈtiː ən/ in Greek mythology, a hunter, son of Aristaeus and Autonöe. He surprised ◊Artemis bathing; she changed him into a stag and he was torn to pieces by his own hounds.

ACTH abbreviation for *adrenocorticotropic hormone*.

actinide any of a series of 15 radioactive metallic chemical elements with atomic numbers 89 (actinium) to 103 (lawrencium). Elements 89 to 95 occur in nature; the rest of the series are synthetic elements only. Actinides are grouped together because of their chemical similarities (for example, they are all bivalent), the properties differing only slightly with atomic number. The series is set out in a band in the ◊periodic table of the elements, as are the ◊lanthanides.

actinium (Greek *aktis* 'ray') white, radioactive, metallic element, the first of the actinide series, symbol Ac, atomic number 89, relative atomic mass 227; it is a weak emitter of high-energy alpha particles. Actinium occurs with uranium and radium in ◊pitchblende and other ores, and can be synthesized by bombarding radium with neutrons. The longest-lived isotope, Ac-227, has a half-life of 21.8 years (all the other isotopes have very short half-lives). Actinium was discovered in 1899 by the French chemist André Debierne.

action in law, one of the proceedings whereby a person or agency seeks to enforce rights in a civil court.

In the UK, civil actions (for example, the enforcement of a debt) are distinguished from criminal proceedings (where the Crown prosecutes a defendant accused of an offence).

action and reaction in physical mechanics, equal and opposite effects produced by a force acting on an object. For example, the pressure of expanding gases from the burning of fuel in a rocket engine (a force) produces an equal and opposite reaction, which causes the rocket to move.

Action Française French extreme nationalist political movement founded 1899, first led by Charles Maurras (1868–1952). It stressed the essential unity of all French people in contrast to the socialist doctrines of class warfare. Its influence peaked in the 1920s.

action painting or *gesture painting* in US art, a dynamic school of Abstract Expressionism. It emphasized the importance of the physical act of painting, sometimes expressed with both inventiveness and aggression, and on occasion performed for the camera. Jackson ◊Pollock was the leading exponent. The term 'action painting' was coined by the US art critic Harold Rosenberg 1952.

action potential in biology, a change in the potential difference (voltage) across the membrane of a nerve cell when an impulse passes along it. A change in potential (from about –60 to +45 millivolts) accompanies the passage of sodium and potassium ions across the membrane.

Actium, Battle of /ˈæktiəm/ naval battle in which ◊Augustus defeated the combined fleets of ◊Mark Antony and ◊Cleopatra in 31 BC. The site is at Akri, a promontory in W Greece.

activation energy in chemistry, the energy required in order to start a chemical reaction. Some elements and compounds will react together merely by bringing them into contact (spontaneous reaction). For others it is necessary to supply energy in order to start the reaction, even if there is ultimately a net output of energy. This initial energy is the activation energy.

active transport in cells, the use of energy to move substances, usually molecules or ions, across a membrane.

Energy is needed because movement occurs against a concentration gradient, with substances being passed into a region where they are already present in significant quantities. Active transport thus differs from diffusion, the process by which substances move towards a region where they are in lower concentration, as when oxygen passes into the blood vessels of the lungs. Diffusion requires no input of energy.

act of Congress in the USA, a bill or resolution passed by both houses of Congress, the Senate and the House of Representatives, which becomes law with the signature of the president. If vetoed by the president, it may still become law if it returns to Congress again and is passed by a majority of two-thirds in each house.

act of God legal term meaning some sudden and irresistible act of nature that could not reasonably have been foreseen or prevented, such as floods, storms, earthquakes, or sudden death.

act of indemnity in Britain, an act of Parliament relieving someone from the consequences of some action or omission that, at the time it took place, was illegal or of doubtful legality.

act of Parliament in Britain, a change in the law originating in Parliament and called a statute. Before an act receives the royal assent and becomes law it is a *bill*. The US equivalent is an ◊act of Congress.

An act of Parliament may be either public (of general effect), local, or private. The body of English statute law comprises all the acts passed by Parliament: the existing list opens with the Statute of Merton, passed in 1235. An act (unless it is stated to be for a definite period and then to come to an end) remains on the statute book until it is repealed.

How an act of Parliament becomes law:
1 first reading of the bill The title is read out in the House of Commons (H of C) and a minister names a day for the second reading.
2 The bill is officially printed.
3 second reading A debate on the whole bill in the H of C followed by a vote on whether or not the bill should go on to the next stage.
4 committee stage A committee of MPs considers the bill in detail and makes amendments.
5 report stage The bill is referred back to the H of C which may make further amendments.
6 third reading The H of C votes whether the bill should be sent on to the House of Lords.

7 House of Lords The bill passes through much the same stages in the Lords as in the H of C. (Bills may be introduced in the Lords, in which case the H of C considers them at this stage.)

8 last amendments The H of C considers any Lords' amendments, and may make further amendments which must usually be agreed by the Lords.

9 royal assent The Queen gives her formal assent.

10 The bill becomes an act of Parliament at royal assent, although it may not come into force until a day appointed in the act.

Acton /ˈæktən/ Eliza 1799–1859. English cookery writer and poet, whose *Modern Cookery for Private Families* 1845 influenced ◊Mrs Beeton.

Actors Studio theatre workshop in New York City, established 1947 by Cheryl Crawford and Elia Kazan. Under Lee Strasberg, who became artistic director 1948, it became known for the study of Stanislavsky's ◊Method acting.

Acts of the Apostles book of the New Testament, attributed to ◊Luke, which describes the history of the early Christian church.

actuary mathematician who makes statistical calculations concerning human life expectancy and other risks, on which insurance premiums are based.

Professional bodies are the Institute of Actuaries (England, 1848), Faculty of Actuaries (Scotland, 1856; Australia, 1977, incorporating earlier bodies), and Society of Actuaries (USA, 1949, by a merger of two earlier bodies).

acupuncture system of inserting long, thin metal needles into the body at predetermined points to relieve pain, as an anaesthetic in surgery, and to assist healing. The needles are rotated manually or electrically. The method, developed in ancient China and increasingly popular in the West, is thought to work by somehow stimulating the brain's own painkillers, the ◊endorphins.

acute in medicine, pertaining to a condition that develops and resolves quickly; for example, the common cold and meningitis. In contrast, a *chronic* condition develops and remains over a long period.

ACV abbreviation for *air-cushion vehicle*; see ◊hovercraft.

AD in the Christian calendar, abbreviation for *Anno Domini* (Latin 'in the year of the Lord'); used with dates.

ADA computer-programming language, developed and owned by the US Department of Defense, designed for use in situations in which a computer directly controls a process or machine, such as a military aircraft. The language took more than five years to specify, and became commercially available only in the late 1980s. It is named after Ada Augusta ◊Byron, regarded as the world's first computer programmer.

Adam /ˈædəm/ family of Scottish architects and designers. *William Adam* (1689–1748) was the leading Scottish architect of his day, and his son *Robert Adam* (1728–1792) is considered one of the greatest British architects of the late 18th century, who transformed the prevailing Palladian fashion in architecture to a Neo-Classical style. He designed interiors for many great country houses and earned a considerable reputation as a furniture designer. With his brother *James Adam* (1732–1794), also an architect, he speculatively developed the Adelphi near Charing Cross, London, largely rebuilt 1936.

Adam /ˈædəm/ (Hebrew *adham* 'man') in the Old Testament, founder of the human race. Formed by God from dust and given the breath of life, Adam was placed in the Garden of Eden, where ◊Eve was created from his rib and given to him as a companion. Because she tempted him, he tasted the forbidden fruit of the Tree of Knowledge of Good and Evil, for which trespass they were expelled from the Garden.

Adam /æˈdɒm/ Adolphe Charles 1803–1856. French composer of light operas. Some 50 of his works were staged, including the classic ballet *Giselle*.

Adams /ˈædəmz/ Ansel 1902–1984. US photographer known for his printed images of dramatic landscapes and organic forms of the American West. He was associated with the ◊zone system of exposure estimation.

Adams /ˈædəmz/ Gerry (Gerard) 1948– . Northern Ireland politician, president of Provisional Sinn Féin from 1978 (the political wing of the IRA). He was elected member of Parliament for Belfast West 1983 but declined to take up his Westminster seat, stating that he did not believe in the British government. In Aug 1994 he announced a 'complete cessation of military operations'. The British government subsequently removed all restrictions on his public appearances and freedom to travel in the UK.

Adams /ˈædəmz/ Henry Brooks 1838–1918. US historian and novelist, a grandson of President John Quincy Adams. He published the acclaimed nine-volume *A History of the United States During the Administrations of Jefferson and Madison* 1889–91, a study of the evolution of democracy in the USA.

His other works include *Mont-Saint-Michel and Chartres* 1904, and a classic autobiography *The Education of Henry Adams* 1907.

Adams /ˈædəmz/ John 1735–1826. 2nd president of the USA 1797–1801, and vice president 1789–97. He was a member of the Continental Congress 1774–78 and signed the Declaration of Independence. In 1779 he went to France and negotiated the treaties that ended the American Revolution. He was suspicious of the French Revolution, but resisted calls for war with France. He became the first US ambassador in London 1785.

Adams /ˈædəmz/ John Coolidge 1947– . US composer and conductor, director of the New Music Ensemble 1972–81, and artistic adviser to the San Francisco Symphony Orchestra from 1978. His works include *Electric Wake* 1968, *Heavy Metal* 1971, *Bridge of Dreams* 1982, and the operas *Nixon in China* 1988 and *The Death of Klinghoffer* 1990.

Adams /ˈædəmz/ John Couch 1819–1892. English astronomer who mathematically deduced the existence of the planet Neptune 1845 from the effects of its gravitational pull on the motion of Uranus, although it was not found until 1846 by J G ◊Galle. Adams also studied the Moon's motion, the Leonid meteors, and terrestrial magnetism.

Adams /ˈædəmz/ John Quincy 1767–1848. 6th president of the USA 1825–29. Eldest son of President John Adams, he was born at Quincy, Massachusetts, and became US minister in The Hague, Berlin, St Petersburg, and London. He negotiated the Treaty of Ghent to end the ◊War of 1812 (between Britain and the USA) on generous terms for the USA. In 1817 he became ◊Monroe's secretary of state, formulated the ◊Monroe Doctrine 1823, and was elected president by the House of Representatives, despite receiving fewer votes than his main rival, Andrew ◊Jackson. As president, Adams was an advocate of strong federal government.

Adams /ˈædəmz/ Neil 1958– . English judo champion. He won two junior and five senior European titles 1974–85, eight senior national titles, and two Olympic silver medals 1980, 1984. In 1981 he was world champion in the 78 kg class.

Adams /ˈædəmz/ Richard 1920– . English novelist. A civil servant 1948–72, he wrote *Watership Down* 1972, a tale of a rabbit community, which is read by adults and children. Later novels include *Shardik* 1974, *The Plague Dogs* 1977, and *Girl on a Swing* 1980.

Adams /ˈædəmz/ Samuel 1722–1803. US politician, second cousin of President John Adams. He was the chief instigator of the Boston Tea Party (see ◊American Revolution). He was also a signatory to the Declaration of Independence, served in the ◊Continental Congress, and anticipated the French emperor Napoleon in calling the British a 'nation of shopkeepers'.

Adams /ˈædəmz/ William 1564–1620. English sailor and shipbuilder, the only foreigner ever to become a samurai. He piloted a Dutch vessel that reached Japan in 1600, and became adviser to the first ◊Tokugawa shogun, for whom he built two warships, the first Western-style ships in Japan. He is regarded by the Japanese as the symbolic founder of the Japanese navy.

Adamson /ˈædəmsən/ Joy 1910–1985. German-born naturalist whose work with wildlife in Kenya, including the lioness Elsa, is described in *Born Free* 1960 which was adapted for the cinema in 1975. She was murdered at her home in Kenya. She worked with her third husband, British game warden *George Adamson* (1906–1989), who was murdered by bandits.

Adamson /ˈædəmsən/ Robert R 1821–1848. Scottish photographer who, with David Octavius Hill, produced 2,500 ◊calotypes (mostly portraits) in five years from 1843.

Adana /ˈædənə/ capital of Adana (Seyhan) province, S Turkey; population (1985) 776,000. It is a major cotton-growing centre and Turkey's fourth largest city.

adaptation in biology, any change in the structure or function of an organism that allows it to survive and reproduce more effectively in its environment. In ◊evolution, adaptation is thought to occur as a result of random variation in the genetic make-up of organisms (produced by ◊mutation and

◊recombination) coupled with ◊natural selection.

adaptive radiation in evolution, the formation of several species, with ◊adaptations to different ways of life, from a single ancestral type. Adaptive radiation is likely to occur whenever members of a species migrate to a new habitat with unoccupied ecological niches. It is thought that the lack of competition in such niches allows sections of the migrant population to develop new adaptations, and eventually to become new species.

The colonisation of newly formed volcanic islands has led to the development of many unique species. The 13 species of Darwin's finch on the Galápagos Islands, for example, are probably descended from a single species from the South American mainland. The parent stock evolved into different species that now occupy a range of diverse niches.

ADB abbreviation for ◊*Asian Development Bank*.

Addams /ˈædəmz/ Charles 1912–1988. US cartoonist, creator of the ghoulish family featured in the *New Yorker* magazine. A successful television comedy series was based on the cartoon in the 1960s.

Addams /ˈædəmz/ Jane 1860–1935. US sociologist and campaigner for women's rights. In 1889 she founded and led the social settlement of Hull House, Chicago, one of the earliest community centres. She was vice president of the National American Women Suffrage Alliance 1911–14, and in 1915 led the Women's Peace Party and the first Women's Peace Congress. She shared the Nobel Peace Prize 1931.

addax light-coloured ◊antelope *Addax nasomaculatus* of the family Bovidae. It lives in the Sahara desert where it exists on scanty vegetation without drinking. It is about 1.1 m/3.5 ft at the shoulder, and both sexes have spirally twisted horns.

added value in economics, the difference between the cost of producing something and the price at which it is sold. Added value is the basis of VAT or ◊value-added tax, a tax on the value added at each stage of the production process of a commodity.

adder European venomous snake, the common ◊viper, *Vipera berus*. Growing to about 60 cm/24 in in length, it has a thick body, triangular head, a characteristic V-shaped mark on its head and, often, zig-zag markings along the back. A shy animal, it feeds on small mammals and lizards. The *puff adder, Bitis arietans*, is a large, yellowish, thick-bodied viper up to 1.6 m/5 ft long, living in Africa and Arabia.

Adder The puff adder, from Africa and western Arabia, grows up to 1.6 m/5 ft long.

addiction state of dependence on drugs, alcohol, or other substances. Symptoms include uncontrolled craving, tolerance, and symptoms of withdrawal when access is denied. Habitual use produces changes in chemical processes in the brain; when the substance is withheld, severe neurological manifestations, even death, may follow. These are reversed by the administration of the addictive substance, and mitigated by a gradual reduction in dosage.

Initially, only opium and its derivatives (morphine, heroin, codeine) were recognized as addictive, but many other drugs, whether therapeutic (for example, tranquillizers or ergotamine) or recreational (such as cocaine and alcohol), are now known to be addictive.

Addington /ˈædɪŋtən/ Henry 1757–1844. British Tory politician and prime minister 1801–04, he was created Viscount Sidmouth 1805. As home secretary 1812–1822, he was responsible for much reprieve legislation, including the notorious ◊Six Acts.

Addis Ababa /ˈædɪs ˈæbəbə/ or *Adis Abeba* capital of Ethiopia; population (1984) 1,413,000. It was founded 1887 by Menelik, chief of Shoa, who ascended the throne of Ethiopia 1889. His former residence, Menelik Palace, is now occupied by the government. The city is the headquarters of the ◊Organization of African Unity.

Addison /ˈædɪsən/ Joseph 1672–1719. English writer. In 1704 he celebrated ◊Marlborough's victory at Blenheim in a poem, 'The Campaign', and subsequently held political appointments, including undersecretary of state and secretary to the Lord-Lieutenant of Ireland 1708. In 1709 he contributed to the *Tatler*, begun by Richard ◊Steele, with whom he was cofounder in 1711 of the *Spectator*.

Addison's disease rare deficiency or failure of the ◊adrenal glands to produce corticosteroid hormones; it is treated with hormones. The condition, formerly fatal, is characterized by anaemia, weakness, low blood pressure, and brownish pigmentation of the skin.

addition reaction chemical reaction in which the atoms of an element or compound react with a double bond or triple bond in an organic compound by opening up one of the bonds and becoming attached to it — for example,
$$CH_2 = CH_2 + HCl \rightarrow CH_3CH_2Cl.$$
An example is the addition of hydrogen atoms to ◊unsaturated compounds in vegetable oils to produce margarine.

additive in food, any natural or artificial chemical added to prolong the shelf life of processed foods (salt or nitrates), alter the colour or flavour of food, or improve its food value (vitamins or minerals). Many chemical additives are used and they are subject to regulation, since individuals may be affected by constant exposure even to traces of certain additives and may suffer side effects ranging from headaches and hyperactivity to cancer. Within the European Community, approved additives are given an official ◊E number.

flavours are said to increase the appeal of the food. They may be natural or artificial, and include artificial ◊sweeteners and monosodium glutamate (m.s.g.).

colourings are used to enhance the visual appeal of certain foods.

enhancers are used to increase or reduce the taste and smell of a food without imparting a flavour of its own.

nutrients replace or enhance food value. Minerals and vitamins are added if the diet might otherwise be deficient, to prevent diseases such as beriberi and pellagra.

preservatives are antioxidants and antimicrobials that control natural oxidation and the action of microorganisms. See ◊food technology.

emulsifiers and *surfactants* regulate the consistency of fats in the food and on the surface of the food in contact with the air.

thickeners, primarily vegetable gums, regulate the consistency of food. Pectin acts in this way on fruit products.

leavening agents lighten the texture of baked goods without the use of yeasts. Sodium bicarbonate is an example.

acidulants sharpen the taste of foods but may also perform a buffering function in the control of acidity.

bleaching agents assist in the ageing of flours.

anti-caking agents prevent powdered products coagulating into solid lumps.

humectants control the humidity of the product by absorbing and retaining moisture.

clarifying agents are used in fruit juices, vinegars, and other fermented liquids. Gelatin is the most common.

firming agents restore the texture of vegetables that may be damaged during processing.

foam regulators are used in beer to provide a controlled 'head' on top of the poured product.

Addled Parliament the English Parliament that met for two months in 1614 but failed to pass a single bill before being dissolved by James I.

address in a computer memory, a number indicating a specific location. At each address, a single piece of data can be stored. For microcomputers, this normally amounts to 1 ◊byte (enough to represent a single character such as a letter or number).

The maximum capacity of a computer memory depends on how many memory addresses it can have. This is normally measured in units of 1,024 bytes (known as ◊kilobytes, or KB).

Adelaide /ˈædɪleɪd/ capital and industrial city of South Australia; population (1986) 993,100. Industries include oil refining, shipbuilding, and the manufacture of electrical goods and cars. Grain, wool, fruit, and wine are exported. Founded in 1836, Adelaide was named after William IV's queen.

It is a fine example of town planning, with residential districts separated from the commercial area by the river Torrens, dammed to form a lake. Impressive streets include King William Street and North Terrace, and fine buildings include Parliament House, Government House, the Anglican cathedral of St Peter, the Roman Catholic cathedral, two universities, the state observatory, and the museum and art gallery.

Adélie Land /əˈdeɪli/ (French *Terre Adélie*) region of Antarctica which is about 140 km/87 mi long, mountainous, covered in snow and ice, and inhabited only by a research team. It was claimed for France 1840.

Aden /ˈeɪdn/ (Arabic *'Adan*) main port and commercial centre of Yemen, on a rocky peninsula at the SW corner of Arabia, commanding the entrance to the Red Sea; population (1984) 318,000. It was the capital of South Yemen until 1990. It comprises the new administrative centre Madinet al-Sha'ab; the commercial and business quarters of Crater and Tawahi, and the harbour area of Ma'alla. The city's economy is based on oil refining, fishing, and shipping. A British territory from 1839, Aden became part of independent South Yemen 1967.

history After annexation by Britain, Aden and its immediately surrounding area (121 sq km/47 sq mi) were developed as a ship-refuelling station following the opening of the Suez Canal 1869.

It was a colony 1937–63 and then, after a period of transitional violence among rival nationalist groups and British forces, was combined with the former Aden protectorate (290,000 sq km/ 112,000 sq mi) to create the Southern Yemen People's Republic 1967, later renamed the People's Democratic Republic of Yemen.

Adenauer /ˈædənaʊə/ Konrad 1876–1967. German Christian Democrat politician, chancellor of West Germany 1949–63. With the French president de Gaulle he achieved the postwar reconciliation of France and Germany and strongly supported all measures designed to strengthen the Western bloc in Europe.

Adenauer was mayor of his native city of Cologne from 1917 until his imprisonment by Hitler in 1933 for opposition to the Nazi regime. After the war he headed the Christian Democratic Union and became chancellor.

adenoids masses of lymphoid tissue, similar to ◊tonsils, located in the upper part of the throat, behind the nose. They are part of a child's natural defences against the entry of germs but usually shrink and disappear by the age of ten.

Adenoids may swell and grow, particularly if infected, and block the breathing passages. If they become repeatedly infected, they may be removed surgically (*adenoidectomy*).

Ader /æˈdeə/ Clément 1841–1925. French aviation pioneer and inventor. He demonstrated stereo-phonic sound transmission by telephone at the 1881 Paris Exhibition of Electricity. His steam-driven aeroplane, the *Eole*, made the first powered takeoff in history 1890, but it could not fly. In 1897, with his *Avion III*, he failed completely, despite false claims made later.

ADH in biology, abbreviation for *antidiuretic hormone*, part of the system maintaining a correct salt/water balance in vertebrates.

Its release is stimulated by the hypothalamus in the brain, which constantly receives information about salt concentration from receptors situated in the neck. In conditions of water shortage increased ADH secretion from the brain will cause more efficient conservation of water in the kidney, so that water is retained by the body. When an animal is able to take in plenty of water, decreased ADH secretion will cause the urine to become dilute so that more water leaves the body. The system allows the body to compensate for a varying water intake and maintains a correct blood concentration.

adhesion in medicine, the abnormal binding of two tissues as a result of inflammation. The moving surfaces of joints or internal organs may merge together if they have been inflamed.

adhesive substance that sticks two surfaces together. Natural adhesives (glues) include gelatin in its crude industrial form (made from bones, hide fragments, and fish offal) and vegetable gums. Synthetic adhesives include thermoplastic and thermosetting resins, which are often stronger than the substances they join; mixtures of epoxy resin and hardener that set by chemical reaction; and elastomeric (stretching) adhesives for flexible joints. Superglues are fast-setting adhesives used in very small quantities.

adiabatic in physics, a process occuring without loss or gain of heat, especially the expansion or contraction of a gas in which a change takes place in the pressure or volume, although no heat is allowed to enter or leave.

Adige /ˈɑːdɪdʒeɪ/ second-longest river (after the Po) in Italy, 410 km/255 mi in length. It crosses the Lombardy Plain and enters the Adriatic just N of the Po delta.

Adi Granth /ˈɑːdi ˈgrɑːnθ/ or *Guru Granth Sahib* the holy book of Sikhism.

adipose tissue type of ◊connective tissue of vertebrates that serves as an energy reserve, and also pads some organs. It is commonly called fat tissue, and consists of large spherical cells filled with fat. In mammals, major layers are in the inner layer of skin and around the kidneys and heart.

Adirondacks /ˌædəˈrɒndæks/ mountainous area in NE New York State, USA; rising to 1,629 m/ 5,344 ft at Mount Marcy; the source of the Hudson and Ausable rivers; named after a native American people. It is known for its scenery and sports facilities.

adit in mining, a horizontal shaft from the surface to reach the mineral seam. It was a common method of mining in hilly districts, and was also used to drain water.

adjective grammatical ◊part of speech for words that describe nouns (for example, *new* and *beautiful*, as in 'a new hat' and 'a beautiful day'). Adjectives generally have three degrees (grades or levels for the description of relationships): the positive degree (*new*, *beautiful*), the comparative degree (*newer*, *more beautiful*), and the superlative degree (*newest*, *most beautiful*).

Some adjectives do not normally need comparative and superlative forms; one person cannot be 'more asleep' than someone else, a lone action is unlikely to be 'the most single-handed action ever seen', and many people dislike the expression 'most unique' or 'almost unique', because something unique is supposed to be the only one that exists. For purposes of emphasis or style these conventions may be set aside ('I don't know who is more unique; they are both remarkable people'). Double comparatives such as 'more bigger' are not grammatical in Standard English, but Shakespeare used a double superlative ('the most unkindest cut of all'). Some adjectives may have both the comparative and superlative forms (*commoner* and *more common*; *commonest* and *most common*), usually shorter words take on the suffixes *-er/-est* but occasionally they may be given the *more/most* forms for emphasis or other reasons ('Which of them is the *most clear*?').

When an adjective comes before a noun it is attributive; when it comes after noun and verb (for example, 'It looks *good*') it is predicative. Some adjectives can only be used predicatively ('The child was asleep', but not 'the asleep child'). The participles of verbs are regularly used adjectivally ('a *sleeping* child', '*boiled* milk'), often in compound forms ('a *quick-acting* medicine', 'a *glass-making* factory'; 'a *hard-boiled* egg', '*well-trained* teachers'). Adjectives are often formed by adding suffixes to nouns (sand: sand*y*; nation: nation*al*).

adjutant in military usage, the commanding officer's personal staff officer. The adjutant is responsible for discipline in a military unit.

Adler /ˈɑːdlə/ Alfred 1870–1937. Austrian psychologist. Adler saw the 'will to power' as more influential in accounting for human behaviour than the sexual drive theory. A dispute over this theory led to the dissolution of his ten-year collaboration with ◊Freud.

Born in Vienna, he was a general practitioner and nerve specialist there 1897–1927, serving as an army doctor in World War I. He joined the circle of Freudian doctors in Vienna about 1900. The concepts of inferiority complex and overcompensation originated with Adler, for example in his books *Organic Inferiority and Psychic Compensation* 1907 and *Understanding Human Nature* 1927.

ad lib(itum) (Latin) 'freely' interpreted.

administrative law law concerning the powers and control of government agencies or those agencies granted statutory powers of administration.

These powers include those necessary to operate the agency or to implement its purposes, and making quasi-judicial decisions (such as determining tax liability, granting licenses or permits, or hearing complaints against the agency or its officers). The vast increase in these powers in the 20th century in many countries has been widely criticized.

In the UK, powers delegated to ministers of the Crown are so wide that they sometimes enable ministers to make regulations that amend or override acts of Parliament. The courts can exercise some control over administrative action through ◊judicial review, for example a declaration that certain regulations are void because they exceed their authority (◊ultra vires). In the USA the Administrative Procedure Act 1946 was an attempt to cope with the problem.

admiral highest-ranking naval officer. In the UK Royal Navy and the US Navy, in descending order, the ranks of admiral are: admiral of the fleet (fleet admiral in the USA), admiral, vice admiral, and rear admiral.

admiral any of several species of butterfly in the same family (Nymphalidae) as the ◊tortoiseshells. The red admiral *Vanessa atalanta*, wingspan 6 cm/2.5 in, is found worldwide in the N hemisphere. It migrates S each year from N areas to subtropical zones.

Admiral's Cup sailing series first held in 1957 and held biennially. National teams consisting of three boats compete over three inshore courses (in the Solent) and two off-shore courses (378 km/ 235 mi across the Channel from Cherbourg to the Isle of Wight and 1,045 km/650 mi from Plymouth to Fastnet lighthouse off Ireland, and back). The highlight is the Fastnet race.

Admiralty, Board of the in Britain, the controlling department of state for the Royal Navy from the reign of Henry VIII until 1964, when most of its functions—apart from that of management—passed to the Ministry of Defence. The 600-year-old office of Lord High Admiral reverted to the sovereign.

Admiralty Islands a group of small islands in the SW Pacific, part of Papua New Guinea; population (1980) 25,000. The main island is Manus. The islands became a German protectorate 1884 and an Australian mandate 1920.

adobe in architecture, building with earth bricks. The formation of earth bricks ('adobe') and the construction of walls by enclosing earth within moulds (*pisé de terre*) are the two principal methods of earth build-ing. The techniques are commonly found in Spain, Latin America, and New Mexico.

Jericho is the site of the earliest evidence of building in sun-dried mud bricks, dating to the 8th millennium BC. Firing bricks did not come into practice until the 3rd millen-nium BC, and then only rarely because it was costly in terms of fuel.

The Great Wall of China is largely con-structed of earth; whole cities of mud con-struction exist throughout the Middle East and North Africa, for example ◊San'a in Yemen and ◊Yazd in Iran. It remains a vigorous vernacular tradition in these areas. A variation of it is found as cob (a mixture of clay and chopped straw) in Devon, Eng-land and in the pueblos of North America.

The most influential contemporary advo-cate of raw-earth building was Hassan Fathy (1900–1989). In 1945–47 he built the new village of Gourna for 7,000 inhabitants in Egypt, and demonstrated the value of adobe material in helping to solve the housing problems of the Third World.

Recent years have seen a revival of interest in the technique and a number of schemes have been built. Examples are La Luz new

town, USA by architect Antoine Predock (1967–73); Great Mosque of Niono, Mali 1955–72 by architect Mason-Lassiné Minta; Wissa Wassef Arts Centre, Harrania, Egypt 1952 by architect Ramses Wissa Wassef (1911-74).

Adonis /əˈdəʊnɪs/ in Greek mythology, a beautiful youth beloved by the goddess ◊Aph-rodite. He was killed while boar-hunting but was allowed to return from the lower world for six months every year to rejoin her. The anemone sprang from his blood.

Worshipped as a god of vegetation, he was known as *Tammuz* in Babylonia, Assyria, and Phoenicia (where it was his sister, ◊Ish-tar, who brought him from the lower world). He seems also to have been identified with ◊Osiris, the Egyptian god of the underworld.

adoption permanent legal transfer of paren-tal rights and duties in respect of a child from one person to another.

In the UK adoption can take place only by means of an order of the court, either with or without the natural parent's consent. It was first legalized in England in 1926; in 1958 an adopted child was enabled to inherit on parental intestacy. The Children's Act 1975 enables an adopted child at the age of 18 to know its original name. See also ◊cus-tody of children.

The adoption by wealthy Western families of children from poor countries, sometimes for payment, became a contentious issue in the 1980s, with cases of babies in, for example, Brazil being kidnapped and then sold to adoptive parents abroad. About 50 couples a year apply to the Home Office for permission to bring in a child, but many others avoid official procedures. According to the Adoption Act 1976, home-study re-ports on prospective parents must be made by approved agencies before permission to adopt from other countries can be granted.

Adowa /ˈædəwɑː/ alternative form of ◊Adu-wa, former capital of Ethiopia.

ADP in biology, abbreviation for *adenosine diphosphate*, a raw material in the manufac-ture of ◊ATP, the molecule used by all cells to drive their chemical reactions.

adrenal gland or *suprarenal gland* gland situated on top of the kidney. The adrenals are soft and yellow, and consist of two parts: the cortex and medulla. The *cortex* (outer part) secretes various steroid hormones, con-trols salt and water metabolism, and regu-lates the use of carbohydrates, proteins, and fats. The *medulla* (inner part) secretes the hormones adrenaline and noradrenaline which constrict the blood vessels of the belly and skin so that more blood is available for the heart, lungs, and voluntary muscles, an emergency preparation for the stress reaction 'fight or flight'.

adrenaline or *epinephrine* hormone secreted by the medulla of the adrenal glands.

adrenocorticotropic hormone (ACTH) a hormone, secreted by the anterior lobe of the ◊pituitary gland, that controls the production of corticosteroid hormones by the ◊adrenal gland. It is commonly produced as a response to stress.

Adrian /ˈeɪdriən/ Edgar, 1st Baron Adrian 1889–1977. British physiologist who received the Nobel Prize for Medicine in 1932 for his work with Charles Sherrington in the field of nerve impulses and the function of the nerve cell.

Adrian IV /ˈeɪdriən/ (Nicholas Breakspear) *c.* 1100–1159. Pope 1154–59, the only British pope. He secured the execution of Arnold of Brescia; crowned Frederick I Barbarossa as German emperor; refused Henry II's request that Ireland should be granted to the English crown in absolute ownership; and was at the height of a quarrel with the emperor when he died.

Adrianople /ˌeɪdriənˈəʊpəl/ older name of the Turkish town ◊Edirne, after the Emperor Hadrian, who rebuilt it about AD 125.

Adriatic Sea /ˌeɪdriˈætɪk/ large arm of the Mediterranean Sea, lying NW to SE between the Italian and the Balkan peninsulas. The sea is about 805 km/500 mi long, and its area is 135,250 sq km/52,220 sq mi.

adsorption the taking up of a gas or liquid at the surface of another substance, usually a solid (for example, activated charcoal adsorbs gases). It involves molecular attraction at the surface, and should be distinguished from ◊absorption (in which a uniform solution results from a gas or liquid being incorporated into the bulk structure of a liquid or solid).

adult education in the UK, voluntary classes and courses for adults provided mainly in further-education colleges, adult-education institutes, and school premises. Adult education covers a range of subjects from flower arranging to electronics and can lead to examinations and qualifications. Small fees are usually charged. The ◊Open College, ◊Open University, and ◊Workers'

Educational Association are adult-education bodies.

Most adult education is provided by local education authorities and fees for classes are subsidized. In 1991 the government proposed restricting subsidy to work-related courses, a proposal which met with strong opposition from bodies as diverse as the LEAs and the Women's Institute. Adult students are also provided for by extra-mural departments of universities and by a small number of residential colleges such as Ruskin College, Oxford and Fircroft, Birmingham.

adultery voluntary sexual intercourse between a married person and someone other than his or her legal partner.

It is one factor that may prove 'irretrievable breakdown' of marriage in actions for judicial separation or ◊divorce in Britain.

Aduwa /ˈædəwɑː/ or *Adwa*, *Adowa* former capital of Ethiopia, about 180 km/110 mi SW of Massawa at an altitude of 1,910 m/6,270 ft; population (1982) 27,000.

Aduwa, Battle of /ˈæduɑː/ defeat of the Italians by the Ethiopians at Aduwa in 1896 under Emperor ◊Menelik II. It marked the end of Italian ambitions in this part of Africa until Mussolini's reconquest in 1935.

advanced gas-cooled reactor (AGR) type of ◊nuclear reactor widely used in W Europe. The AGR uses a fuel of enriched uranium dioxide in stainless-steel cladding and a moderator of graphite. Carbon dioxide gas is pumped through the reactor core to extract the heat produced by the ◊fission of the uranium. The heat is transferred to water in a steam generator, and the steam drives a turbogenerator to produce electricity.

Advent in the Christian calendar, the preparatory season for Christmas, including the four Sundays preceding it, beginning with the Sunday that falls nearest (before or after) St Andrew's Day (30 Nov).

Adventist person who believes that Jesus will return to make a second appearance on Earth. Expectation of the Second Coming of Christ is found in New Testament writings generally. Adventist views are held by the Seventh-Day Adventists, Christadelphians, Jehovah's Witnesses, and the Four Square Gospel Alliance.

adventitious root in plants, a root developing in an unusual position, as in the ivy, where roots grow sideways out of the stem and cling to trees or walls.

adverb grammatical ◊part of speech for words that modify or describe verbs ('She ran *quickly*'), adjectives ('a *beautifully* clear day'), and adverbs ('They did it *really* well'). Most adverbs are formed from adjectives or past participles by adding -*ly* (*quick: quickly*) or -*ally* (*automatic: automatically*).

Sometimes adverbs are formed by adding-*wise* (*likewise* and *clockwise*, as in 'moving *clockwise*'; in 'a *clockwise* direction', *clockwise* is an adjective). Some adverbs have a distinct form from their partnering adjective; for example, *good/well* ('It was *good* work; they did it *well* '). Others do not derive from adjectives (*very*, in '*very* nice'; *tomorrow*, in 'I'll do it *tomorrow*'); and some are unadapted adjectives (*pretty*, as in 'It's *pretty* good'). Sentence adverbs modify whole sentences or phrases: '*Generally*, it rains a lot here'; '*Usually*, the town is busy at this time of year.' Sometimes there is controversy in such matters. *Hopefully* is universally accepted in sentences like 'He looked at them *hopefully*' (= in a hopeful way), but some people dislike it in '*Hopefully*, we'll see you again next year' (= We hope that we'll see you again next year).

advertising any of various methods used by a company to increase the sales of its products or to promote a brand name. Advertising can be seen by economists as either beneficial (since it conveys information about a product and so brings the market closer to a state of ◊perfect competition) or as a hindrance to perfect competition, since it attempts to make illusory distinctions (such as greater sex appeal) between essentially similar products.

The UK's national advertising budget was £6 billion in 1988 (newspapers 40%; television 33%, magazines 20%; posters and radio taking the rest). The UK government spent over £120 million in 1988 on advertising.

Advertising Standards Authority (ASA) org-anization founded by the UK advertising industry 1962 to promote higher standards of advertising in the media (excluding television and radio, which have their own authority). It is financed by the advertisers, who pay 0.1% supplement on the cost of advertisements. It recommends to the media that advertisements which might breach the British Code of Advertising Practice are not published, but has no statutory power.

Advisory, Conciliation, and Arbitration Service (ACAS) in the UK, the independent body set up under the Employment Protection Act 1975 to improve industrial relations. Specifically, ACAS aims to encourage the extension of collective bargaining and, wherever possible, the reform of collective-bargaining machinery.

Its chair is appointed by the secretary of state for employment and a third of its nine-member council is nominated by the TUC, a third by the CBI, and a third are independents.

advocate (Latin *advocatus*, one summoned to one's aid, especially in a lawcourt) pleader in a court of justice. A more common term for a professional advocate is ◊barrister or counsel. In many tribunals lay persons may appear as advocates.

Advocate Judge manager of the prosecution in British courts martial.

Advocates, Faculty of professional organization for Scottish advocates, the equivalent of English ◊barristers. It was incorporated 1532 under James V.

advowson the right of selecting a person to a church living or benefice; a form of ◊patronage.

Aegean civilization the cultures of Bronze Age Greece, including the ◊*Minoan civilization* of Crete and the ◊*Mycenaean civilization* of the E Peloponnese.

Aegean Islands /i:ˈdziːən/ islands of the Aegean Sea, but more specifically a region of Greece comprising the Dodecanese islands, the Cyclades islands, Lesvos, Samos, and Chios; population (1981) 428,500; area 9,122 sq km/3,523 sq mi.

Aegean Sea /i:ˈdʒiːən/ branch of the Mediterranean between Greece and Turkey; the Dardan-elles connect it with the Sea of Marmara. The numerous islands in the Aegean Sea include Crete, the Cyclades, the Sporades, and the Dodecanese. There is political tension between Greece and Turkey over sea limits claimed by Greece around such islands as Lesvos, Chios, Samos, and Kos.

The Aegean Sea is named after the legendary Aegeus, who drowned himself in the belief that Theseus, his son, had been killed.

Aegeus in Greek mythology, king of Athens, and father of ◊Theseus. On his return from Crete, Theseus forgot to substitute white sails for black to indicate his success in killing the ◊Minotaur. Believing his son dead, Aegeus leapt into the Aegean Sea.

Aegina /iːdʒaɪnə/ (Greek *Aíyna* or *Aíyina*) Greek island in the Gulf of Aegina about 32 km/20 mi SW of Piraeus; area 83 sq km/32 sq mi; population (1981) 11,100. In 1811 remarkable sculptures were recovered from a Doric temple in the northeast, restored by Thorwaldsen, and taken to Munich.

Aegir /ægə/ in Scandinavian mythology, the god of the sea.

Aegis in Greek mythology, the shield of Zeus, symbolic of the storm cloud associated with him. In representations of deities it is commonly shown as a protective animal skin.

Aelfric /ælfrɪk/ *c.* 955–1020. Anglo-Saxon writer and abbot, author of two collections of *Catholic Homilies* 990–92, sermons, and the *Lives of the Saints* 996–97, written in vernacular Old English prose.

Aeneas /iːnˈiːəs/ in Classical legend, a Trojan prince who became the ancestral hero of the Romans. According to Homer, he was the son of Anchises and the goddess Aphrodite. During the Trojan War he owed his life to the frequent intervention of the gods. The legend on which Virgil's epic poem the ◊*Aeneid* is based describes his escape from Troy and his eventual settlement in Latium, on the Italian peninsula.

Aeneid /iːnɪɪd/ epic poem by Virgil, written in Latin in 12 books of hexameters and composed during the last 11 years of his life (30–19 BC). It celebrates the founding of Rome through the legend of Aeneas. After the fall of Troy, Aeneas wanders the Mediterranean for seven years and becomes shipwrecked off North Africa. He is received by Dido, Queen of Carthage, and they fall in love. Aeneas, however, renounces their love and sails on to Italy where he settles as the founder of Latium and the Roman state.

Aeolian harp wind-blown instrument consisting of a shallow soundbox supporting gut strings at low tension and tuned to the same pitch. It produces an eerie harmony that rises and falls with the changing pressure of the wind. It was common in parts of central Europe during the 19th century.

Aeolian Islands /iːˈəʊlɪən/ another name for the ◊Lipari Islands.

Aeolus /iːələs/ in Greek mythology, the god of the winds, who kept them imprisoned in a cave on the ◊Lipari Islands.

Aequi /iːkwiː/ Italian people, originating around the river Velino, who were turned back from their advance on Rome 431 BC and were conquered 304 BC, during the Samnite Wars. Like many other peoples conquered by the Romans, they adopted Roman customs and culture.

aerated water water that has had air (oxygen) blown through it. Such water supports aquatic life and prevents the growth of putrefying bacteria.

aerenchyma plant tissue with numerous air-filled spaces between the cells. It occurs in the stems and roots of many aquatic plants where it aids buoyancy and facilitates transport of oxygen around the plant.

aerial or *antenna* in radio and television broadcasting, a conducting device that radiates or receives electromagnetic waves. The design of an aerial depends principally on the wavelength of the signal. Long waves (hundreds of metres in wavelength) may employ long wire aerials; short waves (several centimetres in wavelength) may employ rods and dipoles; microwaves may also use dipoles—often with reflectors arranged like a toast rack—or highly directional parabolic dish aerials. Because microwaves travel in straight lines, giving line-of-sight communication, microwave aerials are usually located at the tops of tall masts or towers.

aerobic in biology, a description of those living organisms that require oxygen (usually dissolved in water) for the efficient release of energy contained in food molecules, such as glucose. Almost all living organisms (plants as well as animals) are aerobes.

Aerobic reactions occur inside every cell and lead to the formation of energy-rich ◊ATP, subsequently used by the cell for driving its metabolic processes. Water and carbon dioxide are also formed.

Most aerobic organisms die in the absence of oxygen, but certain organisms and cells, such as those found in muscle tissue, are able to function for short periods anaerobically (without oxygen). Other ◊anaerobic organisms can survive without oxygen.

aerobics (Greek 'air' and 'life') strenuous combination of dance, stretch exercises, and running, which aims to improve the performance of the heart and lungs system, and became a health and fitness fashion in the 1980s.

aerodynamics branch of fluid physics that studies the forces exerted by air or other gases in motion—for example, the airflow around bodies (such as land vehicles, bullets, rockets, and aircraft) moving at speed through the atmosphere. For maximum efficiency, the aim is usually to design the shape of an object to produce a streamlined flow, with a minimum of turbulence in the moving air.

aeronautics science of travel through the Earth's atmosphere, including ◊aerodynamics, aircraft structures, jet and rocket propulsion, and aerial navigation.

In *subsonic aeronautics* (below the speed of sound), aerodynamic forces increase as the rate of the square of the speed. *Transsonic aeronautics* covers the speed range from just below to just above the speed of sound and is crucial to aircraft design. Ordinary sound waves move at about 1,225 kph/760 mph at sea level, and air in front of an aircraft moving slower than this is 'warned' by the waves so that it can move aside. However, as the flying speed approaches that of the sound waves, the warning is too late for the air to escape, and the aircraft pushes the air aside, creating shock waves, which absorb much power and create design problems. On the ground the shock waves give rise to a ◊sonic boom. It was once thought that the speed of sound was a speed limit to aircraft, and the term ◊sound barrier came into use. *Supersonic aeronautics* concerns speeds above that of sound and in one sense may be considered a much older study than aeronautics itself, since the study of the flight of bullets, known as ◊ballistics, was undertaken soon after the introduction of firearms. *Hypersonics* is the study of airflows and forces at speeds above five times that of sound (Mach 5); for example, for guided missiles, space rockets, and advanced concepts such as ◊HOTOL (horizontal takeoff and landing). For all flight speeds streamlining is necessary to reduce the effects of air resistance.

Aeronautics is distinguished from astronautics, which is the science of travel through space. Astronavigation (navigation by reference to the stars) is used in aircraft as well as in ships and is a part of aeronautics.

aeroplane (North American *airplane*) powered heavier-than-air craft supported in flight by fixed wings. Aeroplanes are propelled by the thrust of a jet engine or airscrew (propeller). They must be designed aerodynamically, since streamlining ensures maximum flight efficiency. The shape of a plane depends on its use and operating speed—aircraft operating at well below the speed of sound need not be as streamlined as supersonic aircraft. The Wright brothers flew the first powered plane (a biplane) in Kitty Hawk, North Carolina, USA, 1903. For the history of aircraft and aviation, see ◊flight.

design Efficient streamlining prevents the formation of shock waves over the body surface and wings, which would cause instability and power loss. The wing of an aeroplane has the cross-sectional shape of an aerofoil, being broad and curved at the front, flat underneath, curved on top, and tapered to a sharp point at the rear. It is so shaped that air passing above it is speeded up, reducing pressure below atmospheric pressure. This follows from ◊Bernoulli's principle and results in a force acting vertically upwards, called lift, which counters the plane's weight. In level flight lift equals weight. The wings develop sufficient lift to support the plane when they move quickly through the air. The thrust that causes propulsion comes from the reaction to the air stream accelerated backwards by the propeller or the gases shooting backwards from the jet exhaust. In flight the engine thrust must overcome the air resistance, or ◊drag. Drag depends on frontal area (for example, large, airliner; small, fighter plane) and shape (drag coefficient); in level flight, drag equals thrust. The drag is reduced by streamlining the plane, resulting in higher speed and reduced fuel consumption for a given power. Less fuel need be carried for a given distance of travel, so a larger payload (cargo or passengers) can be carried.

The shape of a plane is dictated principally by the speed at which it will operate (see ◊aeronautics). A low-speed plane operating at well below the speed of sound (about 965 kph/600 mph) need not be particularly well streamlined, and it can have its wings broad and projecting at right angles from the fuselage. An aircraft operating close to the speed of sound must be well streamlined and have swept-back wings. This prevents the formation of shock waves over the body surface and wings, which would result in instability and high power loss. Supersonic planes (faster than sound) need to be severely streamlined, and require a needle nose, extremely swept-back wings, and what is often termed a 'Coke-bottle' (narrow-waisted) fuselage, in order to pass through the sound barrier without suffering undue disturbance. To give great flexibility of operation at low as well as high speeds, some supersonic planes are designed with variable geometry, or ◊swing wings. For low-speed flight the wings are outstretched; for high-speed flight they are swung close to the fuselage to form an efficient ◊delta wing configuration.

Aircraft designers experiment with different designs in ◊wind tunnel tests, which indicate how their designs will behave in practice. Fighter jets in the 1990s are being deliberately designed to be aerodynamically unstable, to ensure greater agility; an example is the European Fighter Aircraft under development by the UK, Germany, Italy, and Spain. This is achieved by a main wing of continuously modifiable shape, the airflow over which is controlled by a smaller tilting foreplane. New aircraft are being made lighter and faster (to Mach 3) by the use of heat-resistant materials, some of which are also radar-absorbing, making the aircraft 'invisible' to enemy defences.

construction Planes are constructed using light but strong aluminium alloys such as duralumin (with copper, magnesium, and so on). For supersonic planes special stainless steel and titanium may be used in areas subjected to high heat loads. The structure of the plane, or the airframe (wings, fuselage, and so on) consists of a surface skin of alloy sheets supported at intervals by struts known as ribs and stringers. The structure is bonded together by riveting or by powerful adhesives such as ◊epoxy resins. In certain critical areas, which have to withstand very high stresses (such as the wing roots), body panels are machined from solid metal for extra strength.

On the ground a plane rests on wheels, usually in a tricycle arrangement, with a nose wheel and two wheels behind, one under each wing. For all except some light planes the landing gear, or undercarriage, is retracted in flight to reduce drag. Seaplanes, which take off and land on water, are fitted with nonretractable hydrofoils.

flight control Wings by themselves are unstable in flight, and a plane requires a tail to provide stability. The tail comprises a horizontal tailplane and vertical tailfin, called the horizontal and vertical stabilizer respectively. The tailplane has hinged flaps at the rear called elevators to control pitch (attitude). Raising the elevators depresses the tail and inclines the wings upwards (increases the angle of attack). This speeds the airflow above the wings until lift exceeds weight and

the plane climbs. However, the steeper attitude increases drag, so more power is needed to maintain speed and the engine throttle must be opened up. Moving the elevators in the opposite direction produces the reverse effect. The angle of attack is reduced, and the plane descends. Speed builds up rapidly if the engine is not throttled back. Turning (changing direction) is effected by moving the rudder hinged to the rear of the tailfin, and by backing (rolling) the plane. It is banked by moving the ailerons, interconnected flaps at the rear of the wings which move in opposite directions, one up, the other down. In planes with a delta wing, such as ◊Concorde, the ailerons and elevators are combined. Other movable control surfaces, called flaps, are fitted at the rear of the wings closer to the fuselage. They are extended to increase the width and camber (curve) of the wings during takeoff and landing, thereby creating extra lift, while movable sections at the front, or leading edges, of the wing, called slats, are also extended at these times to improve the airflow. To land, the nose of the plane is brought up so that the angle of attack of the wings exceeds a critical point and the airflow around them breaks down; lift is lost (a condition known as stalling), and the plane drops to the runway. A few planes, (for example, the Harrier) have a novel method of takeoff and landing, rising and dropping vertically by swivelling nozzles to direct the exhaust of their jet engines downwards. The ◊helicopter and ◊convertiplane use rotating propellers (rotors) to obtain lift to take off vertically.

operation The control surfaces of a plane are operated by the pilot on the flight deck, by means of a control stick, or wheel, and by foot pedals (for the rudder). The controls are brought into action by hydraulic power systems. Advanced experimental high-speed craft known as control-configured vehicles use a sophisticated computer-controlled system. The pilot instructs the computer which manoeuvre the plane must perform, and the computer, informed by a series of sensors around the craft about the altitude, speed, and turning rate of the plane, sends signals to the control surface and throttle to enable the manoeuvre to be executed.

aerosol particles of liquid or solid suspended in a gas. Fog is a common natural example. Aerosol cans, which contain pressurized gas mixed with a propellant, are used to spray liquid in the form of tiny drops of

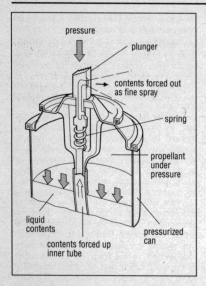

pressure

plunger

contents forced out
as fine spray

spring

propellant
under
pressure

liquid
contents

pressurized
can

contents forced up
inner tube

Aerosol The aerosol can produces a fine spray
of liquid particles, called an aerosol.

such products as scents and cleaners. Until
recently, most aerosols used chlorofluorocarbons (CFCs) as propellants. However,
these were found to cause destruction of the
◊ozone layer in the stratosphere, and the
international community has agreed to
phase out their use. Most so-called 'ozone-
friendly' aerosols also use ozone-depleting
chemicals, although they are not as destructive as CFCs. Some of the products sprayed,
such as pesticides, can be directly toxic to
humans.

Aeschylus /ˈiːskələs/ *c.* 525–*c.* 456 BC. Greek
dramatist, widely regarded as the founder of
Greek tragedy (see ◊Euripides; ◊Sophocles).
By the introduction of a second actor he
made true dialogue and dramatic action
possible. Aeschylus wrote some 90 plays between 499 and 458 BC, of which seven survive. These are *The Suppliant Women*
performed about 490 BC, *The Persians* 472 BC,
Seven against Thebes 467 BC, *Prometheus
Bound c.* 460 BC, and the ◊*Oresteia* trilogy
458 BC.

Aeschylus was born at Eleusis, near Athens, of a noble family. He took part in the
Persian Wars and fought at Marathon 490
BC. He twice visited the court of Hieron I,
king of Syracuse, and died at Gela in Sicily.

Aesculapius /ˌiːskjʊˈleɪpiəs/ in Greek and
Roman mythology, the god of medicine; his
emblem was a staff with a snake coiled
around it, since snakes seemed to renew life
by shedding their skin.

Aesir /ˈiːsə(r)/ principal gods of Norse mythology—Odin, Thor, Balder, Loki, Freya, and
Tyr—whose dwelling place was Asgard.

Aesop /ˈiːsɒp/ traditional writer of Greek
fables. According to Herodotus he lived in
the reign of Amasis of Egypt (mid-6th century BC) and was a slave of Iadmon, a Thra-
cian. The fables, for which no evidence of his
authorship exists, are anecdotal stories using
animal characters to illustrate moral or satirical points.

Aesthetic movement English artistic
movement of the late 19th century, dedicated to the doctrine 'art for art's sake'—
that is, art as self-sufficient, not needing to
justify its existence by serving any particular
use. Artists associated with the movement
include Beardsley and Whistler. The writer
Oscar Wilde was, in his twenties, an exemplary aesthete.

aesthetics branch of philosophy that deals
with the nature of beauty, especially in art.
It emerged as a distinct branch of enquiry in
the mid-18th century.

The subject of aesthetics was introduced
by Plato and enlarged upon by Aristotle, but
the term was first used by the German philosopher Baumgarten (1714–1762). Other
philosophers interested in this area were Im-
manuel Kant, David Hume, Benedetto
Croce, John Dewey, and George Santayana.

aestivation in zoology, a state of inactivity
and reduced metabolic activity, similar to
◊hibernation, that occurs during the dry season in species such as lungfish and snails. In
botany, the term is used to describe the way
in which flower petals and sepals are folded
in the buds. It is an important feature in
◊plant classification.

Aetolia /iːˈtəʊliə/ district of ancient Greece
on the NW of the gulf of Corinth. The
Aetolian League was a confederation of the
cities of Aetolia which, following the death
of Alexander the Great, became the chief
rival of Macedonian power and the Achaean
League.

AEW abbreviation for *airborne early warning*, a military surveillance system; see
◊AWACS and ◊early warning.

Afars and the Issas, French Territory of the/'æfɑːz, 'ısəz/ former French territory that became the Republic of ◊Djibouti 1977.

AFD abbreviation for *accelerated freeze drying*, a common method of food preservation. See ◊food technology.

affidavit legal document, used in court applications and proceedings, in which a person swears that certain facts are true.

In England, an affidavit is usually sworn before a solicitor or commissioner for oaths.

affiliation order in English law, formerly a court order for maintenance against the alleged father of an illegitimate child. Under the Family Law Reform Act 1987, either parent can apply for a court order for maintenance of children, no distinction being made between legitimate and illegitimate children.

In 1969 blood tests were first used to prove 'nonpaternity'; they are not equally conclusive of paternity. Genetic fingerprinting was first used 1988 in Britain to prove paternity and thereby allow immigration to the UK.

affinity in law, relationship by marriage not blood (for example, between a husband and his wife's blood relatives, between a wife and her husband's blood relatives, or step-parent and stepchild), which may legally preclude their marriage. It is distinguished from consanguinity or blood relationship. In Britain, the right to marry was extended to many relationships formerly prohibited by the Marriage (Prohibited Degrees of Relationship) Act 1986.

affinity in chemistry, the force of attraction (see ◊bond) between atoms that helps to keep them in combination in a molecule. The term is also applied to attraction between molecules, such as those of biochemical significance (for example, between ◊enzymes and substrate molecules). This is the basis for affinity ◊chromatography, by which biologically important compounds are separated.

The atoms of a given element may have a greater affinity for the atoms of one element than for another (for example, hydrogen has a great affinity for chlorine, with which it easily and rapidly combines to form hydrochloric acid, but has little or no affinity for argon).

affirmation solemn declaration made instead of taking the oath by a person who has no religious belief or objects to taking an oath on religious grounds.

affirmative action in the USA and Australia, a government policy of positive discrimination that favours members of minority ethnic groups and women in such areas as employment and education, designed to counter the effects of long-term discrimination against them.

In the USA, the Equal Opportunities Act 1972 set up a commission to enforce the policy in organizations receiving public funds, so many private institutions and employers adopted voluntary affirmative action programmes at the same time. In the 1980s the policy was sometimes not rig-orously enforced.

affluent society society in which most people have money left over after satisfying their basic needs such as food and shelter. They are then able to decide how to spend their excess ('disposable') income, and become 'consumers'. The term was popularized by the US economist John Kenneth ◊Galbraith.

Afghan /'æfgæn/ native to or an inhabitant of Afghanistan. The dominant group, particularly in Kabul, are the Pathans. The Tajiks, a smaller ethnic group, are predominantly traders and farmers in the province of Herat and around Kabul. The Hazaras, another farming group, are found in the southern mountain ranges of the Hindu Kush. The Uzbeks and Turkomen are farmers and speak Altaic-family languages. The smallest Altaic minority are the Kirghiz, who live in the Pamir. Baluchi nomads live in the south, and Nuristani farmers live in the mountains of the northeast.

The Pathans, Tajiks, and Hazaras are traditionally nomadic horse breeders and speak languages belonging to the Iranian branch of the Indo-European family. The majority of the population are Sunni Muslims, the most recent converts being the Nuristanis.

Afghan hound breed of fast hunting dog resembling the ◊saluki, though more thickly coated, first introduced to the W by British army officers serving on India's North-West Frontier along the Afghanistan border in the late 19th century. The Afghan hound is about 70 cm/28 in tall and has a long, silky coat.

In 1989, it was still being raced at five greyhound tracks in the UK, though no betting was allowed. It can reach a speed of 56 kph/35 mph.

Afghanistan /æfgænɪstɑːn/ mountainous, landlocked country in S central Asia, bounded N by Tajikistan, Turkmenistan and Uzbekistan, W by Iran, and S and E by Pakistan and China.

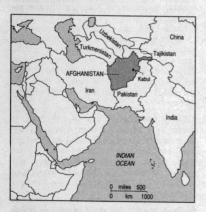

government In Nov 1987 a grand national assembly (Loya Jirgah) of indirectly elected elders from various ethnic groups approved a new permanent constitution, establishing Islam as the state religion and creating a multiparty, presidential system of government. Under the terms of this constitution, the president, who is elected for a seven-year term by the Loya Jirgah, appoints the prime minister and is empowered to approve the laws and resolutions of the elected two-chamber national assembly (Meli Shura). The constitution was suspended following the withdrawal of Soviet troops Feb 1989 and an emergency military–PDPA regime was established.

history Part of the ancient Persian Empire, the region was used by Darius I and Alexander the Great as a path to India; Islamic conquerors arrived in the 7th century, then Genghis Khan and Tamerlane in the 13th and 14th respectively. Afghanistan first became an independent emirate 1747. During the 19th century two ◊Afghan Wars were fought in which imperial Britain checked Russian influence extending towards India. The Anglo-Russian treaty 1907 gave autonomy to Afghanistan, with independence achieved by the Treaty of Rawalpindi 1919 following the third Afghan War. The kingdom was founded 1926 by Emir Amanullah.

During the 1950s, Lt-Gen Sardar Mohammad Daud Khan, cousin of King Mohammad Zahir Shah (ruled 1933–73), governed as prime minister and introduced a programme of social and economic modernization with Soviet aid. Opposition to his authoritarian rule forced Daud's resignation 1963; the king was made a constitutional monarch, but political parties were outlawed.

republic After a famine 1972, General Daud Khan overthrew the monarchy in a Soviet-backed military coup 1973. The King fled to exile, and a republic was declared. President Daud was assassinated 1978 in a military coup, and Nur Mohammad Taraki, the imprisoned leader of the radical Khalq (masses) faction of the banned communist People's Democratic Party of Afghanistan (PDPA), took charge as president of a revolutionary council. A one-party constitution was adopted, a Treaty of Friendship and Mutual Defence signed with the USSR, and major reforms introduced. Conservative Muslims opposed these initiatives, and thousands of refugees fled to Iran and Pakistan. Taraki was replaced 1979 by foreign minister Hafizullah Amin.

Soviet invasion Internal unrest continued, and the USSR organized a further coup Dec 1979. Amin was executed and Babrak Karmal (1929–), the exiled leader of the gradualist Parcham (banner) faction of the PDPA, was installed as leader. The numbers of Soviet forces in Afghanistan grew to over 120,000 by 1985 as Muslim guerrilla resistance by the 'mujaheddin' ('holy warriors') continued.

Soviet withdrawal Faced with high troop casualties and a drain of economic resources, the new Soviet administration of ◊Gorbachev moved towards a compromise settlement 1986. Karmal was replaced as PDPA leader May 1986 by the Pathan former secret police chief Dr Najibullah Ahmadzai (1947–), and several non-communist politicians joined the new government. In Oct 1986, 8,000 Soviet troops were withdrawn as a goodwill gesture, and the Afghan government announced a six-month unilateral cease-fire Jan 1987. The mujaheddin rejected this initiative, however, insisting on a full Soviet withdrawal and replacement of the communist government. The Najibullah government extended the cease-fire, and a new multiparty Islamic constitution was ratified Nov 1987 in an attempt to promote 'national reconciliation'. On the completion of Soviet troop withdrawal Feb 1989 the constitution was suspended and a 'state of emergency' was imposed by the Najibullah government, which was faced with a mounting military onslaught by the mujaheddin. The guerrillas continued to resist the PDPA regime's 'power-sharing' entreaties, demanding that Najibullah should first resign.

government in exile formed The mujaheddin met in Peshawar (Pakistan) Feb 1989 and elected Prof Sibghatullah Mojadidi (head of the Afghan National Liberation Front), as president, and the fundamentalist Prof Abdur-Rabbur Rasul Sayaf as prime minister of the Afghan Interim Government (AIG). AIG was not accorded international recognition.

areas of respective control The ruling PDPA was renamed the Homeland Party (Hezb-i-Watan) June 1990, with President Najibullah being elected its chair. The small garrison of Khost, near the Pakistan border, fell to the mujaheddin March 1991. It was a significant victory for the guerrillas, who had reportedly received logistical support from the CIA and Pakistan's Inter Services Intelligence directorate. The mujaheddin, now in receipt of diminishing amounts of aid from the USA, Saudi Arabia, and Pakistan, also controlled 90% of the mountainous Afghan countryside.

UN peace plan The Najibullah government accepted a UN peace plan for Afghanistan May 1991 but the Hezb-i-Islami mujaheddin leader, Gulbuddin Hekmatyar, and the prime minister of the AIG, Abdur-Rabbur Rasul Sayaf, both rejected the plan, refusing to accept any settlement under the Najibullah regime.

Mujaheddin seize power The Najibullah regime collapsed April 1992 when government troops defected to the mujaheddin forces led by Ahmad Shah Massoud, and Kabul was captured. Najibullah fled and was placed under UN protection. An attempt by the Islamic fundamentalist Gulbuddin Hekmatyar to seize power was thwarted and an interim government April–June under the moderate Sibghatullah Mojadidi failed to restore order to Kabul. Power was transferred to guerrilla leader Burhanuddin Rabbani with Hezb-i-Islami representative Abdul Sabur Farid as prime minister. Rabbani pledged to seek unity between the country's warring guerrillas and abolished all laws contrary to *Sharia* (Islamic law). However, tensions between the government and the Hekmatyar faction culminated Aug 1992 in indiscriminate and heavy bombardment of the city by the rebels' forces. Rabbani removed Farid from the premiership and banned Hezb-i-Islami from all government activity. In Jan 1993 Kabul suffered renewed bombardment by Hezb-i-Islami and other rebel forces.   In March 1993 a peace agreement between Rabbani and Hekmatyar followed intense fighting around Kabul during which 1,000 lives were lost. Hekmatyar became prime minister, but was dismissed Jan 1994 after he formed an alliance with ex-communist mujaheddin leader, Rashid Dostam.

Afghan Wars three wars waged between Britain and Afghanistan to counter the threat to British India from expanding Russian influence in Afghanistan.
First Afghan War 1838–42, when the British garrison at Kabul was wiped out.
Second Afghan War 1878–80, when General ◊Roberts captured Kabul and relieved Kandahar.
Third Afghan War 1919, when peace followed the dispatch by the UK of the first aeroplane ever seen in Kabul.

AFL-CIO abbreviation for ◊*American Federation of Labor and Congress of Industrial Organizations*.

Afonso /æ'fɒnseʊ/ six kings of Portugal, including:

Afonso I 1094–1185. King of Portugal from 1112. He made Portugal independent from León.

Africa /'æfrɪkə/ second largest of the continents, three times the area of Europe
area 30,097,000 sq km/11,620,451 sq mi
largest cities (population over 1 million) Cairo, Algiers, Lagos, Kinshasa, Abidjan, Cape Town, Nairobi, Casablanca, El Gîza, Addis Ababa, Luanda, Dar-es Salaam, Ibadan, Douala, Mogadishu.
physical dominated by a uniform central plateau comprising a southern tableland with a mean altitude of 1,070 m/3,000 ft that falls northwards to a lower elevated plain with a mean altitude of 400 m/1,300 ft. Although there are no great alpine regions or extensive coastal plains, Africa has a mean altitude of 610 m/2,000 ft, two times greater than Europe. The highest points are Mount Kilimanjaro 5,900 m/19,364 ft, and Mount Kenya 5,200 m/17,058 ft; the lowest point is Lac Assal in Djibouti –144 m/–471 ft. Compared with other continents, Africa has few broad estuaries or inlets and therefore has proportionately the shortest coastline

(24,000 km/15,000 mi). The geographical extremities of the continental mainland are Cape Hafun in the E, Cape Almadies in the W, Ras Ben Sekka in the N, and Cape Agulhas in the S. The Sahel is a narrow belt of savanna and scrub forest which covers 700 million hectares of west and central Africa; 75% of the continents lies within the tropics

features Great Rift Valley, containing most of the great lakes of E Africa (except Lake Victoria); Atlas Mountains in NW; Drakensberg mountain range in SE; Sahara Desert (world's largest desert) in N; Namib, Kalahari, and Great Karoo deserts in S; Nile, Zaïre, Niger, Zambezi, Limpopo, Volta, and Orange rivers

products has 30% of the world's minerals including diamonds (51%) and gold (47%); produces 11% of world's crude petroleum, 58% of world's cocoa (Ivory Coast, Ghana, Cameroon, Nigeria) 23% of world's coffee (Uganda, Ivory Coast, Zaïre, Ethiopia, Cameroon, Kenya), 20% of the world's groundnuts (Senegal, Nigeria, Sudan, Zaïre), and 21% of the world's hardwood timber (Nigeria, Zaire, Tanzania, Kenya)

population (1988) 610 million; more than double the 1960 population of 278 million, and rising to an estimated 900 million by 2000; annual growth rate 3% (10 times greater than Europe); 27% of the world's undernourished people live in sub-Saharan Africa where an estimated 25 million are facing famine

language over 1,000 languages spoken in Africa; Niger-Kordofanian languages including Mandinke, Kwa, Lingala, Bemba, and Bantu (Zulu, Swahili, Kikuyu), spoken over half of Africa from Mauritania in the W to South Africa; Nilo-Saharan languages, including Dinka, Shilluk, Nuer, and Masai, spoken in Central Africa from the bend of the Niger river to the foothills of Ethiopia; Afro-Asiatic (Hamito-Semitic) languages, including Arabic, Berber, Ethiopian, and Amharic, N of Equator; Khoisan languages with 'click' consonants spoken in SW by Bushmen, Hottentots, and Nama people of Namibia

religion Islam in the N and on the E coast as far S as N Mozambique; animism below the Sahara, which survives alongside Christianity (both Catholic and Protestant) in many central and S areas

Africa, Horn of /ˈæfrɪkə/ projection constituted by Somalia and adjacent territories.

African art art of sub-Saharan Africa, from prehistory onwards, ranging from the art of ancient civilizations to the new styles of post-imperialist African nations. Examples of historic African art are bronze figures from Benin and Ife (in Nigeria) dating from about 1500 and, also on the west coast, in the same period, bronze or brass figures for weighing gold, made by the Ashanti.

prehistoric art Rock paintings are found in various regions, notably in the western Sahara, Zimbabwe, South Africa, and, from the end of the period, East Africa. Some of the earliest pictures are of elephants. The images tend to be linear and heavily stylized and sometimes show a geometric style. Terracotta figures from Nigeria, dating from several centuries BC, have stylized features similar to Oceanic art forms and some early South American styles.

Zimbabwe Ruins of ancient stone buildings from before 300 AD suggest a time of outstanding craft skill in the country's history; sculptures have also been found in the ruins.

Benin and Ife The bronze sculptures from the 13th to 16th-century realms of Benin and Ife on the west coast of Africa (examples in the British Museum, London) are distinctive in style and demonstrate technical refinement in casting by the lost-wax method (see ◊sculpture). The Ife heads are naturalistic, while those of Benin are more stylized. The art of Benin includes high-relief bronze plaques with figurative scenes, and ivory carvings. Some of these appear to have been designed for the Portuguese trade.

Ashanti Metalworkers of the Ashanti people (in present-day Ghana) made weights, highly inventive forms with comically exaggerated figures.

general Over the centuries, much artistic effort was invested in religious objects and masks, with wooden sculpture playing a large role. Many everyday items, such as bowls, stools, drums, and combs, also display fine craft and a vitality of artistic invention.

Since much of Africa's history up to the late 19th century has not been researched, African art has occupied a meagre place in Western art-history studies. In the early 20th century West African art had a profound influence on the work of many European painters and sculptors.

African National Congress (ANC) multiracial nationalist organization formed in South Africa 1912 to extend the franchise to the whole population and end all racial discrimination there. Its president is Nelson ◊Mandela. Although originally nonviolent, the ANC was banned by the government from 1960 to Jan 1990, and in exile in Mozambique developed a military wing, *Umkhonto we Sizwe*, which engaged in sabotage and guerrilla training. The armed struggle was suspended August 1990 after Mandela's release from prison and the organization's headquarters were moved from Zambia to Johannesburg.

Talks between the ANC and the South African government began Dec 1991, culminating in the adoption of a nonracial constitution 1993. In April 1994 the ANC won the majority of seats in the country's first free nonracial elections. Nelson Mandela became president of the new government May 1994.

African nationalism political movement for the unification of Africa. African nationalism has its roots among the educated elite (mainly 'returned' Americans of African descent and freed slaves or their descendents) in W Africa in the 19th century. Christian mission-educated, many challenged overseas mission control and founded independent churches. These were often involved in anticolonial rebellions, for example in Natal 1906 and Nyasaland 1915. The Kitwala (Watchtower Movement) and Kimbanguist churches provided strong support for the nationalist cause in the 1950s. Early African political organizations included the Aborigines Rights Protection Society in the Gold Coast 1897, the African National Congress in South Africa 1912, and the National Congress of West Africa 1920.

After World War I nationalists fostered moves for self-determination. The ◊Fourteen Points encouraged such demands in Tunisia, and delegates to London 1919 from the Native National Congress in South Africa stressed the contribution to the war effort by the South African Native Labour Corps. Most nationalist groups functioned within the territorial boundaries of single colonies, for example the Tanganyika African Association and the Rhodesian Bantu Voters Association. One or two groups, including the National Congress of British West Africa, had wider pan-African visions. The first pan-African Congress was held in London 1900 and others followed after 1919.

Pan-African sentiment in Africa and the Americas was intensified with the Italian invasion of ◊Ethiopia in 1935. By 1939 African nationalist groups existed in nearly every territory of the continent. Africa's direct involvement in World War II, the weakening of the principal colonial powers, increasing anticolonialism from America (the ◊Atlantic Charter 1941 encouraged self-government), and Soviet criticism of imperialism inspired African nationalists.

Since 1958 pan-Africanism has become partially absorbed into wider Third World movements. In May 1963 it was decided to establish the ◊Organization of African Unity (OAU).

African violet herbaceous plant *Saintpaulia ionantha* from tropical central and E Africa, with velvety green leaves and scentless purple flowers. Different colours and double varieties have been bred.

Afrikaans language an official language (with English) of the Republic of South Africa and Namibia. Spoken mainly by the Afrikaners—descendants of Dutch and other 17th-century colonists—it is a variety of the Dutch language, modified by circumstance and the influence of German, French, and other immigrant as well as local languages. It became a standardized written language about 1875.

Afrika Korps German army in N Africa 1941–43 during World War II, commanded by Field Marshal Rommel. They were driven out of N Africa by May 1943.

Afrikaner (formerly known as *Boer*) inhabitant of South Africa descended from the original Dutch, Flemish, and ◊Huguenot settlers of the 17th century. Comprising approximately 60% of the white population in South Africa, they were originally farmers but have now become mainly urbanized. Their language is Afrikaans.

Afro-Caribbean West Indian person of African descent. Afro-Caribbeans are the descendants of W Africans captured or obtained in trade from African procurers. European slave traders then shipped them to the West Indies to English, French, Dutch, Spanish, and Portugese colonies founded from the 16th century. Since World War II many Afro-Caribbeans have migrated to North America and to Europe, especially to the USA, the UK, and the Netherlands.

afterbirth in mammals, the placenta and other material, including blood and membranes, expelled from the uterus soon after birth. In the natural world it is often eaten.

afterburning method of increasing the thrust of a gas turbine (jet) aeroplane engine by spraying additional fuel into the hot exhaust duct between the turbojet and the the tailpipe where it ignites. Used for short-term increase of power during take-off, or during combat in military aircraft.

afterimage persistence of an image on the retina of the eye after the object producing it has been removed. This leads to persistence of vision, a necessary phenomenon for the illusion of continuous movement in films and television. The term is also used for the persistence of sensations other than vision.

after-ripening process undergone by the seeds of some plants before germination can occur. The length of the after-ripening period in different species may vary from a few weeks to many months. It helps seeds to germinate at a time when conditions are most favourable for growth. In some cases the embryo is not fully mature at the time of dispersal and must develop further before germination can take place. Other seeds do not germinate even when the embryo is mature, probably owing to growth inhibitors within the seed that must be leached out or broken down before germination can begin.

AG abbreviation for *Aktiengesellschaft* (German 'limited company').

aga (Turkish 'lord') title of nobility, applied by the Turks to military commanders and, in general, to men of high station in some Muslim countries.

Agadir Incident or the *Second Moroccan Crisis* international crisis provoked by Kaiser Wilhelm II of Germany, July–Nov 1911. By sending the gunboat *Panther* to demand territorial concessions from the French, he hoped to drive a wedge into the Anglo-French entente. In fact, German aggression during the second Moroccan crisis merely served to reinforce Anglo-French fears of Germany's intentions. The crisis gave rise to the term 'gunboat diplomacy'.

Aga Khan IV /ˈɑːgə ˈkɑːn/ 1936– . Spiritual head (*imam*) of the *Ismaili* Muslim sect (see ◊Islam). He succeeded his grandfather 1957.

Agamemnon /ˌægəˈmemnən/ in Greek mythology, a Greek hero, son of Atreus, king of Mycenae. He married Clytemnestra, and their children included ◊Electra, ◊Iphigenia, and ◊Orestes. He led the capture of Troy, received Priam's daughter Cassandra as a prize, and was murdered by Clytemnestra and her lover, Aegisthus, on his return home. His children Orestes and Electra later killed the guilty couple.

Agaña /əˈgɑːnjə/ capital of Guam, in the W Pacific; population (1981) 110,000. It is a US naval base.

agar jellylike carbohydrate, obtained from seaweeds. It is used mainly in microbiological experiments as a culture medium for growing bacteria and other microorganisms. The agar is resistant to breakdown by microorganisms, remaining a solid jelly throughout the course of the experiment. It is also used in the food industry as a thickening agent in ice cream and other desserts, and in the canning of meat and fish.

agaric fungus of typical mushroom shape. Agarics include the field mushroom *Agaricus campestris* and the cultivated edible mushroom *A. brunnesiens*. Closely related is the ◊*Amanita* genus, including the fly agaric *Amanita muscaria*.

Agassiz /ˈægəsi/ Jean Louis Rodolphe 1807–1873. Swiss-born US palaeontologist and geologist, one of the foremost scientists of the 19th century. He established his name through his work on the classification of the fossil fishes. Unlike Darwin, he did not believe that individual species themselves changed, but that new species were created from time to time.

Agassiz was the first to realize that an ice age had taken place in the northern hemisphere, when, in 1840, he observed ice scratches on rocks in Edinburgh. He is now criticized for holding racist views concerning the position of blacks in American society.

agate banded or cloudy type of ◊chalcedony, a silica, SiO_2, that forms in rock cavities. Agates are used as ornamental stones and for art objects.

Agate stones, being hard, are also used to burnish and polish gold applied to glass and ceramics.

agave any of several related plants with stiff sword-shaped spiny leaves arranged in a rosette. All species of the genus *Agave* come from the warmer parts of the New World. They include *A. sisalina*, whose fibres are used for rope making, and the Mexican century plant *A. americana*. Alcoholic drinks such as ◊tequila and pulque are made from the sap of agave plants.

Agee /ˈeɪdʒiː/ James 1909–1955. US journalist, screenwriter, and author. He rose to national prominence as a result of his investigation of the plight of Alabama sharecroppers during the Depression. In collaboration with photographer Walker Evans, he published the photo and text essay *Let Us Now Praise Famous Men* 1941. Agee's screenwriting credits include *The African Queen* 1951 and *The Night of the Hunter* 1955. His novel *A Death in the Family* won a Pulitzer Prize 1958.

ageing in common usage, the period of deterioration of the physical condition of a living organism that leads to death; in biological terms, the entire life process.

Three current theories attempt to account for ageing. The first suggests that the process is genetically determined, to remove individuals that can no longer reproduce. The second suggests that it is due to the accumulation of mistakes during the replication of ◊DNA at cell division. The third suggests that it is actively induced by pieces of DNA that move between cells, or by cancer-causing viruses; these may become abundant in old cells and induce them to produce unwanted ◊proteins or interfere with the control functions of their DNA.

ageism discrimination against older people in employment, pensions, housing, and health care. To combat it the American Association of Retired Persons (AARP) has 30 million members, and in 1988 a similar organization was founded in the UK. In the USA the association has been responsible for legislation forbidding employers to discriminate; for example, making it illegal to fail to employ people aged 40–69, to dismiss them or to reduce their working conditions or wages.

Agent Orange selective ◊weedkiller, notorious for its use in the 1960s during the Vietnam War by US forces to eliminate ground cover which could protect communists; it was subsequently discovered to contain highly poisonous ◊dioxin. Thousands of US troops who had handled it later developed cancer or fathered deformed babies.

Agent Orange, named after the distinctive orange stripe on its packaging, combines equal parts of 2,4-D (2,4-trichlorophenoxyacetic acid) and 2,4,5-T (2,4,5-trichlorophenoxyacetic acid), both now banned in the USA. Companies that had manufactured the chemicals faced an increasing number of lawsuits in the 1970s. All the suits were settled out of court in a single ◊class action, resulting in the largest ever payment of its kind ($180 million) to claimants.

agglutination in medicine, the clumping together of ◊antigens, such as blood cells or bacteria, to form larger, visible masses, under the influence of ◊antibodies. As each antigen clumps only in response to its particular antibody, agglutination provides a way of determining ◊blood groups and the identity of unknown bacteria.

aggression in biology, behaviour used to intimidate or injure another organism (of the same or of a different species), usually for the purposes of gaining a territory, a mate, or food. Aggression often involves an escalating series of threats aimed at intimidating an opponent without having to engage in potentially dangerous physical contact. Aggressive signals include roaring by red deer, snarling by dogs, the fluffing up of feathers by birds, and the raising of fins by some species of fish.

Agincourt, Battle of /ˈædʒɪnkɔː/ battle of the Hundred Years' War in which Henry V of England defeated the French on 25 Oct 1415, mainly through the overwhelming superiority of the English longbow. The French lost more than 6,000 men to about 1,600 English casualties. As a result of the battle, Henry gained France and the French princess, Catherine of Valois, as his wife. The village of Agincourt (modern *Azincourt*) is south of Calais, in N France.

Agnew /ˈæɡnjuː/ Spiro 1918– . US vice president 1969–1973. A Republican, he was governor of Maryland 1966–69, and vice president under ◊Nixon. He took the lead in a campaign against the press and opponents of the ◊Vietnam War. Although he was one of the few administration officials not to be implicated in the ◊Watergate affair, he resigned 1973, shortly before pleading 'no contest' to a charge of income-tax evasion.

Agni /ˈʌɡni/ in Hindu mythology, the god of fire, the guardian of homes, and the protector of humans against the powers of darkness.

Agnon /ˈæɡnɒn/ Shmuel Yosef 1888–1970. Israeli novelist. Born in Buczacz, Galicia (now in the Ukraine), he made it the setting of his most celebrated work, *A Guest for the Night* 1945. He shared a Nobel prize 1966.

agnosticism belief that the existence of God cannot be proven; that in the nature of things the individual cannot know anything of what lies behind or beyond the world of natural phenomena. The term was coined 1869 by T H ◊Huxley.

Whereas an atheist (see ◊atheism) denies the existence of God or gods, an agnostic asserts that God or a First Cause is one of those concepts—others include the Absolute, infinity, eternity, and immortality—that lie beyond the reach of human intelligence, and therefore can be neither confirmed nor denied.

Agostini /ˌægɒˈstiːni/ Giacomo 1943– . Italian motorcyclist. He won a record 122 grand prix and 15 world titles. His world titles were at 350cc and 500cc and he was five times a dual champion.

In addition he was ten times winner of the Isle of Man TT races; a figure bettered only by Mike ◊Hailwood and Joey Dunlop.

AGR abbreviation for ◊*advanced gas-cooled reactor*, a type of nuclear reactor.

Agra /ˈɑːgrə/ city of Uttar Pradesh, India, on the river Jumna, 160 km/100 mi SE of Delhi; population (1981) 747,318. A commercial and university centre, it was the capital of the Mogul empire 1527–1628, from which period the Taj Mahal dates.

history ◊Zahir ud-din Muhammad (known as 'Babur'), the first great Mogul ruler, made Agra his capital 1527. His grandson Akbar rebuilt the Red Fort of Salim Shah 1566, and is buried outside the city in the tomb at Sikandra. In the 17th century the buildings of ◊Shah Jahan made Agra one of the most beautiful cities in the world. The Taj Mahal, erected as a tomb for the emperor's wife Mumtaz Mahal, was completed 1650. Agra's political importance dwindled from 1658, when Aurangzeb moved the capital back to Delhi. It was taken from the Marathas by Lord Lake 1803.

Agricola /əˈgrɪkələ/ Gnaeus Julius AD 37–93. Roman general and politician. Born in Provence, he became Consul of the Roman Republic AD 77, and then governor of Britain AD 78–85. He extended Roman rule to the Firth of Forth in Scotland and won the battle of Mons Graupius. His fleet sailed round the north of Scotland and proved Britain an island.

agricultural revolution sweeping changes that took place in British agriculture over the period 1750–1850 in response to the increased demand for food from a rapidly expanding population. Recent research has shown these changes to be only part of a much larger, ongoing process of development.

Changes of the latter half of the 18th century included the enclosure of open fields, the introduction of four-course rotation together with new fodder crops such as turnip, and the development of improved breeds of livestock. Pioneers of the new farming were Viscount ◊Townshend (known as 'Turnip' Townshend), Jethro ◊Tull, Robert ◊Bakewell, and enlightened landowners such as Thomas Coke of Norfolk (1752–1842).

agriculture the practice of farming, including the cultivation of the soil (for raising crops) and the raising of domesticated animals. Crops are for human nourishment, animal fodder, or commodities such as cotton and sisal. Animals are raised for wool, milk, leather, dung (as fuel), or meat. The units for managing agricultural production vary from small holdings and individually owned farms to corporate-run farms and collective farms run by entire communities. Agriculture developed in Egypt and the near East at least 7,000 years ago. Soon, farming communities became the base for society in China, India, Europe, Mexico, and Peru, then spread throughout the world. Reorganization along more scientific and productive lines took place in Europe in the 18th century in response to dramatic population growth. Mechanization made considerable progress in the USA and Europe during the 19th century. After World War II, there was an explosive growth in the use of agricultural chemicals: herbicides, insecticides, fungicides, and fertilizers. In the 1960s there was development of high-yielding species in the ◊*green revolution* of the Third World, and the industrialized countries began intensive farming of cattle, poultry, and pigs. In the 1980s, hybridization by genetic engineering methods and pest control by the use of chemicals plus ◊pheromones were developed. However, there was also a reaction against some forms of intensive agriculture because of the pollution and habitat destruction caused. One result of this was a growth of alternative methods, including organic agriculture.

plants For plant products, the land must be prepared (ploughing, cultivating, harrowing, and rolling). Seed must be planted and the growing plant nurtured. This may involve fertilizers, irrigation, pest control by chemicals, and monitoring of acidity or nutrients. When the crop has grown, it must be harvested and, depending on the crop, processed in a variety of ways before it is stored or sold.

Greenhouses allow cultivation of plants that would otherwise find the climate too harsh. ◊Hydroponics allows commercial cultivation of crops using nutrient-enriched sol-utions instead of soil. Special methods, such as terracing, may be adopted to allow culti-vation in hostile terrain and to retain topsoil in mountainous areas with heavy rainfall.

livestock Animals may be semi-domest-icated, such as reindeer, or fully domesticated but nomadic (where naturally growing or cultivated food supplies are sparse), or kept in one location. Animal farming involves accommodation (buildings, fencing, or pas-ture), feeding, breeding, gathering the pro-duce (eggs, milk, or wool), slaughtering, and further processing (such as butchery or tanning).

organic farming From the 1970s there has been a movement towards more sophisti-cated natural methods without chemical sprays and fertilizers. Nitrates have been seeping into the ground water, insecticides are found in lethal concentrations at the top of the ◊food chain, some herbicides are asso-ciated with human birth defects, and hor-mones fed to animals to promote fast growth have damaging effects on humans.

overproduction The greater efficiency in agri-culture achieved since the 19th century, coupled with post-World War II govern-ment subsidies for domestic production in the USA and the European Community (EC), have led to the development of high stocks, nicknamed 'lakes' (wine, milk) and 'mountains' (butter, beef, grain). There is no simple solution to this problem, as any large-scale dumping onto the market dis-places regular merchandise. Increasing con-cern about the starving and the cost of storage has led the USA and the EC to develop measures for limiting production, such as letting arable land lie fallow to re-duce grain crops. The USA has had some success at selling surplus wheat to the USSR when the Soviet crop is poor, but the overall cost of bulk transport and the potential destabilization of other economies acts against the high producers exporting their excess on a regular basis to needy countries. Intensive farming methods also contribute to soil ◊erosion and water pollution.

In the EC, a quota system for milk pro-duction coupled with price controls has re-duced liquid milk and butter surpluses to manageable levels but has also driven out many small uneconomic producers who, by switching to other enterprises, risk upsetting the balance elsewhere. A voluntary 'set aside' scheme of this sort was proposed in the UK 1988.

Agrigento /ˌægrɪˈdʒentəʊ/ town in Sicily, known for Greek temples; population (1981) 51,300. The Roman *Agrigentum*, it was long called *Girgenti* until renamed Agrigento 1927 under the Fascist regime.

agrimony herbaceous plant *Agrimonia eu-patoria* of the rose family Rosaceae, with small yellow flowers on a slender spike. It grows along hedges and in fields.

Agrippa /əˈgrɪpə/ Marcus Vipsanius 63–12 BC. Roman general. He commanded the vic-torious fleet at the battle of Actium and married Julia, daughter of the emperor ◊Augustus.

agrochemicals artificially produced chem-icals used in modern, intensive agricultural systems, including nitrate and phosphate fer-tilizers, pesticides, some animal-feed addi-tives, and pharmaceuticals. Many are responsible for pollution and almost all are avoided by organic farmers.

agronomy study of crops and soils, a branch of agricultural science. Agronomy includes such topics as selective breeding (of plants and animals), irrigation, pest control, and soil analysis and modification.

Aguascalientes /ˌægwəskæliˈenteɪs/ city in central Mexico, and capital of a state of the same name; population (1990) 506,384. It has hot mineral springs.

Agulhas /əˈgʌləs/ southernmost cape in Af-rica. In 1852 the British troopship *Birken-head* sank off the cape with the loss of over 400 lives.

AH with reference to the Muslim calendar, abbreviation for *anno hegirae* (Latin 'year of the flight'—of ◊Muhammad, from Mecca to Medina).

Ahab /ˈeɪhæb/ *c.* 875–854 BC. King of Israel. His empire included the suzerainty of Moab, and Judah was his subordinate ally, but his kingdom was weakened by constant wars with Syria. By his marriage with Jezebel, princess of Sidon, Ahab introduced into Is-rael the worship of the Phoenician god Baal, thus provoking the hostility of Elijah and other prophets. Ahab died in battle against the Syrians at Ramoth Gilead.

Ahaggar /əˈhægə/ or *Hoggar* mountainous plateau of the central Sahara, Algeria, whose highest point, Tahat, at 2,918 m/9,576 ft, lies between Algiers and the mouth of the Niger. It is the home of the formerly nomadic Tuaregs.

Ahasuerus /əˌhæzjuˈɪərəs/ (Latinized Hebrew form of the Persian *Khshayarsha*, Greek *Xerxes*) name of several Persian kings in the Bible, notably the husband of ◊Esther. Traditionally it was also the name of the ◊Wandering Jew.

ahimsa in Hinduism, Buddhism, and Jainism, the doctrine of respect for all life (including the lowest forms and even the elements themselves) and consequently an extreme form of nonviolence. It arises in part from the concept of *karma*, which holds that a person's actions (and thus any injury caused to any form of life) are carried forward from one life to the next, determining each stage of reincarnation.

Ahmadiyya /ˌɑːməˈdiːə/ Islamic religious movement founded by Mirza Ghulam Ahmad (1839–1908). His followers reject the doctrine that Muhammad was the last of the prophets and accept Ahmad's claim to be the Mahdi and Promised Messiah. In 1974 the Ahmadis were denounced as non-Muslims by other Muslims.

Ahmadnagar /ˌɑːmədˈnʌgə/ city in Maharashtra, India, 195 km/120 mi E of Bombay, on the left bank of the river Sina; population (1981) 181,000. It is a centre of cotton trade and manufacture.

Ahmad Shah Durrani /ˈɑːmæd ˈʃɑː/ 1724–1773. Founder and first ruler of Afghanistan. Elected shah in 1747, he had conquered the Punjab by 1751.

Ahmedabad /ˈɑːmədəbɑːd/ or *Ahmadabad* capital of Gujarat, India; population (1981) 2,515,195. It is a cotton-manufacturing centre, and has many sacred buildings of the Hindu, Muslim, and Jain faiths.

Ahmedabad was founded in the reign of Ahmad Shah 1412, and came under the control of the East India Company 1818. In 1930 ◊Gandhi marched to the sea from here to protest against the government salt monopoly.

Ahriman /ˈɑːrɪmən/ in Zoroastrianism, the supreme evil spirit, lord of the darkness and death, waging war with his counterpart Ahura Mazda (Ormuzd) until a time when human beings choose to lead good lives and Ahriman is finally destroyed.

Ahura Mazda /əˈhuərə ˈmæzdə/ or *Ormuzd* in Zoroastrianism, the spirit of supreme good. As god of life and light he will finally prevail over his enemy, Ahriman.

Ahváz /ɑːˈvɑːz/ industrial capital of the province of Khuzestan, W Iran; population (1986) 590,000.

AI(D) abbreviation for ◊*artificial insemination (by donor)*. AIH is *artificial insemination by husband*.

Aidan, St /ˈeɪdn/ *c.* 600–651. Irish monk who converted Northumbria to Christianity and founded Lindisfarne monastery on Holy Island off the NE coast of England. His feast day is 31 Aug.

aid, development money given or lent on concessional terms to developing countries or spent on maintaining agencies for this purpose. In the late 1980s official aid from governments of richer nations amounted to $45–60 billion annually whereas voluntary organizations in the West received about $2.4 billion a year for the Third World. The ◊World Bank is the largest dispenser of aid. All industrialized United Nations (UN) member countries devote a proportion of their gross national product to aid, ranging from 0.20% of GNP (Ireland) to 1.10% (Norway) (1988 figures). Each country spends more than half this contribution on direct bilateral assistance to countries with which they have historical or military links or hope to encourage trade. The rest goes to international organizations such as UN and World Bank agencies, which distribute aid multilaterally.

The UK development-aid budget in 1988 was 0.32% of GNP, with India and Kenya among the principal beneficiaries. The European Development Fund (an arm of the European Community) and the ◊International Development Association (an arm of the World Bank) receive approximately 5% and 8% respectively of the UK development-aid budget.

In 1988, the US development-aid budget was 0.21% of GNP, with Israel and Egypt among the principal beneficiaries; Turkey, Pakistan, and the Philippines are also major beneficiaries. The United States Agency for International Development (USAID) is the State Department body responsible for bilateral aid. The USA is the largest contributor to, and thus the most powerful member of, the International Development Association.

In the UK, the Overseas Development Administration is the department of the Foreign Office that handles bilateral aid. The combined overseas development aid of all EC member countries is less than the sum ($20 billion) the EC spends every year on storing surplus food produced by European farmers.

aid, foreign another name for *development aid* (see ◊aid, development).

AIDS (acronym for *a*cquired *i*mmune *d*eficiency *s*yndrome) the newest and gravest of the sexually transmitted diseases, or ◊STDs. It is caused by the human immunodeficiency virus (HIV), now known to be a ◊retrovirus, an organism first identified 1983. HIV is transmitted in body fluids, mainly blood and sexual secretions.

Sexual transmission of the AIDS virus endangers heterosexual men and women as well as high-risk groups, such as homosexual and bisexual men, prostitutes, intravenous drug-users sharing needles, and haemophiliacs and surgical patients treated with contaminated blood products. The virus itself is not selective, and infection is spreading to the population at large. The virus has a short life outside the body, which makes transmission of the infection by methods other than sexual contact, blood transfusion, and shared syringes extremely unlikely.

Infection with HIV is not synonymous with having AIDS; many people who have the virus in their blood are not ill, and only about half of those infected will develop AIDS within ten years. Some suffer AIDS-related illnesses but not the full-blown disease. However, there is no firm evidence to suggest that the proportion of those developing AIDS from being HIV-positive is less than 100%. The effect of the virus in those who become ill is the devastation of the immune system, leaving the victim susceptible to diseases that would not otherwise develop. In fact, diagnosis of AIDS is based on the appearance of rare tumours or opportunistic infections in unexpected candidates. Pneumocystis pneumonia, for instance, normally seen only in the malnourished or those whose immune systems have been deliberately suppressed, is common among AIDS victims and, for them, a leading cause of death.

The estimated incubation period is 9.8 years. Some AIDS victims die within a few months of the outbreak of symptoms, some survive for several years; roughly 50% are dead within three years. There is no cure for the disease, although the new drug ◊zidovudine is claimed to delay the onset of AIDS and diminish its effects. The search continues for an effective vaccine.

In the USA, attempts to carry out clinical trials of HIV vaccines on HIV-positive pregnant women were started 1991 in the hope that they might prevent the transmission of the virus to the fetus.

In the UK, 2,256 people had died of AIDS by Dec 1990, and between 30,000 and 50,000 people were thought to be carriers of the disease. Altogether 1,276 new cases of AIDS were reported in the UK in 1990, a 51% increase over the 1988 figure. The rise was 44% among homosexual men, 78% among heterosexuals, and 102% among those who inject drugs. In the USA, there were 100,777 deaths from AIDS by Dec 1990, and 161,075 persons with the disease. One million Americans are thought to be infected with the virus.

The HIV virus originated in Africa, where the total number of cases up to Oct 1988 was 19,141. In Africa, the prevalence of AIDS among high-risk groups such as prostitutes may approach 30%. Previous reports of up to 80% of certain populations being affected are thought to have been grossly exaggerated by inaccurate testing methods. By Feb 1991, 323,378 AIDS cases in 159 countries had been reported to the World Health Organization (WHO), which estimated that over 1.3 million cases might have occurred worldwide, of which about 400,000 were a result of transmission before, during, or shortly after birth.

WHO also estimated that at least 8–10 million individuals had been infected with HIV, and about half of these would develop AIDS within ten years of infection. By the year 2000 WHO expects that 15–20 million adults and 10 million children will have been infected with HIV.

Aiken /ˈeɪkən/ Conrad (Potter) 1899–1973. US poet, novelist, and short-story writer whose *Selected Poems* 1929 won the Pulitzer prize. His works were influenced by early psychoanalytic theory and the use of the stream-of-consciousness technique.

Aiken /ˈeɪkən/ Howard 1900– . US mathematician. In 1939, in conjunction with engineers from ◊IBM, he started work on the design of an automatic calculator using standard business machine components. In 1944 the team completed one of the first computers, the Automatic Sequence Controlled Calculator (known as the Mark 1), a programmable computer controlled by punched paper tape and using ◊punched cards.

aikido Japanese art of self-defence; one of the ◊martial arts. Two main systems of aikido are tomiki and uyeshiba.

Ailey /ˈeɪli/ Alvin 1931–1989. US dancer, choreographer, and director whose Alvin Ailey City Center Dance Theater, formed 1958, was the first truly interracial dance company and opened dance to a wider audience. Ailey studied modern, ethnic, jazz, and academic dance, and his highly individual work celebrates rural and urban black America in pieces like *Blues Suite* 1958 and the company signature piece *Revelations* 1960.

Aintab /aɪnˈtɑːb/ Syrian name of ◊Gaziantep, city in Turkey.

Aintree racecourse situated on outskirts of Liverpool, Merseyside, NE England. The ◊Grand National steeplechase (established 1839) is held every spring.

Ainu aboriginal people of Japan, driven north in the 4th century AD by ancestors of the Japanese. They now number about 25,000, inhabiting Japanese and Soviet territory on Sakhalin, Hokkaido, and the Kuril Islands. Their language has no written form, and is unrelated to any other.

air see ◊atmosphere.

air conditioning system that controls the state of the air inside a building or vehicle. A complete air-conditioning unit controls the temperature and humidity of the air, removes dust and odours from it, and circulates it by means of a fan. US inventor W H Carrier developed the first effective air-conditioning unit 1902 for a New York printing plant.

The air in an air conditioner is cooled by a type of ◊refrigeration unit comprising a compressor and a condenser. The air is cleaned by means of filters and activated charcoal. Moisture is extracted by condensation on cool metal plates. The air can also be heated by electrical wires or, in large systems, pipes carrying hot water or steam; and cool, dry air may be humidified by circulating it over pans of water or through a water spray.

A specialized air-conditioning system is installed in spacecraft as part of the life-support system. This includes the provision of oxygen to breathe and the removal of exhaled carbon dioxide.

aircraft any aeronautical vehicle, which may be lighter than air (supported by buoyancy) or heavier than air (supported by the dy-namic action of air on its surfaces). ◊Balloons and ◊airships are lighter-than-air craft. Heavier-than-air craft include the ◊aeroplane, glider, autogyro, and helicopter.

aircraft carrier sea-going base for military aircraft. The first purpose-designed aircraft carrier was the British HMS *Hermes*, completed 1913. Carriers such as HMS *Ark Royal*, completed 1938, played a major role in World War II, but in postwar years the cost and vulnerability of such large vessels were thought to have outweighed their advantages.

However, by 1980 the desire to have a means of destroying enemy aircraft beyond the range of a ship's own weapons—for instance, when on convoy duty—led to a widespread revival of aircraft carriers of 20,000–30,000 tonnes.

Despite the cost, aircraft carriers have always remained popular with the USSR and the USA. Examples include the USSR's *Komsomolec* 1979 (40,000 tonnes, 15 fixed-wing aircraft, 20 helicopters), the USA's *Eisenhower* 1979 (81,600 tonnes, 95 aircraft), and the British *Invincible* 1980 (19,500 tonnes). Aircraft carriers are equipped with combinations of fixed-wing aircraft, helicopters, missile launchers, and anti-aircraft guns.

air-cushion vehicle (ACV) craft that is supported by a layer, or cushion, of high-pressure air. The ◊hovercraft is one form of ACV.

Airedale terrier /ˈeədeɪl/ breed of large ◊terrier dog, about 60 cm/2 ft tall, with a rough red-brown coat. It originated about 1850 in England, as a cross of the otter hound and Irish and Welsh terriers.

air force a nation's fighting aircraft and the organization that maintains them.

history The emergence of the aeroplane at first brought only limited recognition of its potential value as a means of waging war. Like the balloon, used since the American Civil War, it was considered a way of extending the vision of ground forces. A unified air force was established in the UK 1918, Italy 1923, France 1928, Germany 1935 (after repudiating the arms limitations of the Versailles treaty), and the USA 1947 (it began as the Aeronautical Division of the Army Signal Corps in 1907, and evolved into the Army's Air Service Division by 1918; by 1926 it was the Air Corps and in World War II the Army Air Force). The main specialized groupings formed during

World War I—such as *combat*, *bombing* (see ◊bomb), *reconnaissance*, and *transport*—were adapted and modified in World War II; activity was extended, with self-contained tactical air forces to meet the needs of ground commanders in the main theatres of land operations and for the attack on and defence of shipping over narrow seas.

During the period 1945–60 the piston engine was superseded by the jet engine, which propelled aircraft at supersonic speeds; extremely precise electronic guidance systems made both missiles and aircraft equally reliable delivery systems; and flights of much longer duration became possible with air-to-air refuelling. The US Strategic Air Command's bombers can patrol 24 hours a day armed with thermonuclear weapons. It was briefly anticipated that the pilot might become redundant, but the continuation of conventional warfare and the evolution of tactical nuclear weapons led in the 1970s and 1980s to the development of advanced combat aircraft able to fly supersonically beneath an enemy's radar on strike and reconnaissance missions, as well as so-called stealth aircraft that cannot be detected by radar.

airglow faint and variable light in the Earth's atmosphere produced by chemical reactions in the ionosphere.

airlock airtight chamber that allows people to pass between areas of different pressure; also an air bubble in a pipe that impedes fluid flow. An airlock may connect an environment at ordinary pressure and an environment that has high air pressure (such as a submerged caisson used for tunnelling or building dams or bridge foundations).

air pollution contamination of the atmosphere caused by the discharge, accidental or deliberate, of a wide range of toxic substances. Often the amount of the released substance is relatively high in a certain locality, so the harmful effects are more noticeable. The cost of preventing any discharge of pollutants into the air is prohibitive, so attempts are more usually made to reduce gradually the amount of discharge and o disperse this as quickly as possible by using a very tall chimney, or by intermittent release.

air raid aerial attack, usually on a civilian population. In World War II (1939–45), raids were usually made by bomber aircraft, but many thousands were killed in London 1944 by German V1 and V2 rockets. The air raids on Britain 1940–41 became known as *the Blitz*. The Allies carried out a bombing campaign over Germany 1942–45.

air sac in birds, a thin-walled extension of the lungs. There are nine of these and they extend into the abdomen and bones, effectively increasing lung capacity. In mammals, it is another name for the alveoli in the lungs, and in some insects, for widenings of the trachea.

airship power-driven balloon. All airships have streamlined envelopes or hulls, which contain the inflation gas (originally hydrogen, now helium) and are nonrigid, semirigid, or rigid.

Count Ferdinand von Zeppelin pioneered the rigid airship, used for bombing raids on Britain in World War I. The destruction by fire of the British R101 in 1930 halted airship building in Britain, but the Germans continued and built the 248 m/812 ft long *Hindenburg*, which exploded at Lakehurst, New Jersey, USA, 1937, marking the effective end of airship travel.

Early airships were vulnerable because they used highly flammable hydrogen for inflation. After World War II, interest grew in airships using the nonflammable gas helium. They cause minimum noise, can lift enormous loads, and are economical on fuel. Britain's Airship Industries received large orders 1987 from the US Navy for airships to be used for coastguard patrols, and the Advanced Airship Corporation on the Isle of Man was reported in 1989 to be constructing the fastest passenger airship ever built, capable of travelling at 80 knots (148 kph/92 mph), powered by twin-propeller turbine engines.

air transport means of conveying goods or passengers by air from one place to another. See ◊flight.

Airy /ˈeəri/ George Biddell 1801–1892. English astronomer. He installed a transit telescope at the Royal Observatory at Greenwich, England, and accurately measured ◊Greenwich Mean Time by the stars as they crossed the meridian.

Aisne /eɪn/ river of N France, giving its name to a *département* (administrative region); length 282 km/175 mi.

Aix-en-Provence /ˈeɪks ɒm prəˈvɒns/ town in the *département* of Bouches-du-Rhône, France, 29 km/18 mi N of Marseille; population (1982) 127,000. It is the capital of Provence and dates from Roman times.

Aix-la-Chapelle /ˈeɪks læ ʃæˈpel/ French name of ◊Aachen, ancient city in Germany.

Aix-les-Bains /ˈeɪks leɪ ˈbæn/ spa with hot springs in the *département* of Savoie, France, near Lake Bourget, 13 km/8 mi N of Chambéry; population (1982) 22,534.

Ajaccio /æˈʒæksiəʊ/ capital and second-largest port of Corsica; population (1982) 55,279. Founded by the Genoese 1492, it was the birthplace of Napoleon; it has been French since 1768.

Ajax /ˈeɪdʒæks/ Greek hero in Homer's ◊*Iliad*. Son of Telamon, king of Salamis, he was second only to Achilles among the Greek heroes in the Trojan War. When ◊Agamemnon awarded the armour of the dead Achilles to ◊Odysseus, Ajax is said to have gone mad with jealousy, and then committed suicide in shame.

Ajman /ˈædʒmɑːn/ smallest of the seven states that make up the ◊United Arab Emirates; area 250 sq km/96 sq mi; population (1985) 64,318.

Ajmer /ɑːdʒˈmɪə/ town in Rajasthan, India; population (1981) 376,000. Situated in a deep valley in the Aravalli mountains, it is a commercial and industrial centre, notably of cotton manufacture. It has many ancient remains, including a Jain temple.

It was formerly the capital of the small state of Ajmer, which was merged with Rajasthan 1956.

ajolote Mexican reptile of the genus *Bipes*. It and several other tropical burrowing species are placed in the Amphisbaenia, a group separate from lizards and snakes among the Squamata. Unlike the others, however, which have no legs, it has a pair of short but well-developed front legs. In line with its burrowing habits, the skull is very solid, the eyes small, and external ears absent. The scales are arranged in rings, giving the body a wormlike appearance.

AK abbreviation for ◊*Alaska*.

Akaba /ˈækəbə/ alternative transliteration of ◊Aqaba, gulf of the Red Sea.

Akbar /ˈækbɑː/ Jalal ud-Din Muhammad 1542–1605. Mogul emperor of N India from 1556, when he succeeded his father. He gradually established his rule throughout N India. He is considered the greatest of the Mogul emperors, and the firmness and wisdom of his rule won him the title 'Guardian of Mankind'; he was a patron of the arts.

à Kempis Thomas see ◊Thomas à Kempis, religious writer.

Akhenaton /ˌækəˈnɑːtɒn/ another name for ◊Ikhnaton, pharaoh of Egypt.

Akhetaton /ˌækɪˈtɑːtɒn/ capital of ancient Egypt established by the monotheistic pharaoh ◊Ikhnaton as the centre for his cult of the Aton, the sun's disc; it is the modern Tell el Amarna 300 km/ 190 mi S of Cairo. Ikhnaton's palace had formal enclosed gardens. After his death it was abandoned, and the ◊*Amarna tablets*, found in the ruins, were probably discarded by his officials.

Akhmatova /ækˈmætəvə/ Anna. Pen name of Anna Andreevna Gorenko 1889–1966. Russian poet. Among her works are the cycle *Requiem* 1963 (written in the 1930s), which deals with the Stalinist terror, and *Poem Without a Hero* 1962 (begun 1940).

Akihito /ˌækɪˈhiːtəʊ/ 1933– . Emperor of Japan from 1989, succeeding his father Hirohito (Showa). His reign is called the Heisei ('achievement of universal peace') era.

Unlike previous crown princes, Akihito was educated alongside commoners at the elite Gakushuin school and in 1959 he married Michiko Shoda (1934–), the daughter of a flour-company president. Their three children, the Oxford university-educated Crown Prince Hiro, Prince Aya, and Princess Nori, were raised at Akihito's home instead of being reared by tutors and chamberlains in a separate imperial dormitory.

Akkad /ˈækæd/ northern Semitic people who conquered the Sumerians in 2350 BC and ruled Mesopotamia. The ancient city of Akkad in central Mesopotamia, founded by ◊Sargon I, was an imperial centre in the 3rd millennium BC; the site is unidentified, but it was on the Euphrates.

Akkaia alternative form of ◊Achaea.

'Akko /ˈækəʊ/ Israeli name for the port of ◊Acre.

Akola /əˈkəʊlə/ town in Maharashtra, India, near the Purnar; population (1981) 176,000. It is a major cotton and grain centre.

Akron /ˈækrən/ (Greek 'summit') city in Ohio, USA, on the Cuyahoga River, 56 km/35 mi SE of Cleveland; population (1980) 660,000. Almost half the world supply of rubber is processed here.

history Akron was first settled 1807. B F Goodrich established a rubber factory 1870, and the industry grew immensely with the rising demand for car tyres from about 1910.

Aksai Chin /ˌæksaɪ/ part of Himalayan Kashmir lying to the east of the Karakoram range. It is occupied by China but claimed by India.

Aksum /ˈɑːksʊm/ ancient Greek-influenced Semitic kingdom that flourished 1st–6th centuries AD and covered a large part of modern Ethiopia as well as the Sudan. The ruins of its capital, also called Aksum, lie NW of Aduwa, but the site has been developed as a modern city.

Aktyubinsk /ækˈtjuːbɪnsk/ industrial city in the republic of Kazakhstan; population (1987) 248,000. Established 1869, it expanded after the opening of the Trans-Caspian railway 1905.

al- for Arabic names beginning *al-*, see rest of name; for example, for 'al-Fatah', see ◊Fatah, al-.

AL abbreviation for ◊*Alabama*.

Alabama /ˌæləˈbæmə/ state of southern USA; nickname Heart of Dixie/Camellia State
area 134,700 sq km/51,994 sq mi
capital Montgomery
towns Birmingham, Mobile, Huntsville, Tuscaloosa
physical the state comprises the Cumberland Plateau in the north; the Black Belt, or Canebrake, which is excellent cotton-growing country, in the centre; and south of this, the coastal plain of Piny Woods
features Alabama and Tennessee rivers; Appalachian mountains; George Washington Carver Museum at the Tuskegee Institute (a college founded for blacks by Booker T Washington) and Helen Keller's birthplace at Tuscumbia
products cotton still important though no longer prime crop; soya beans, peanuts, wood products, coal, iron, chemicals, textiles, paper
population (1987) 4,149,000
famous people Nat King Cole, Helen Keller, Joe Louis, Jesse Owens, Booker T Washington
history first settled by the French in the early 18th century, it was ceded to Britain 1763, passed to the USA 1783, and became a state 1819. It was one of the ◊Confederate States in the American Civil War.

Alabama /ˌæləˈbæmə/ Confederate cruiser (1,040 tonnes) in the ◊American Civil War. Built in Great Britain, it was allowed to leave port by the British, and sank 68 Union merchant ships before it was itself sunk by a Union warship off the coast of France in 1864. In 1871 the international court awarded damages of $15.5 million to the USA, a legal precedent.

alabaster naturally occurring fine-grained white or light-coloured translucent form of ◊gypsum, often streaked or mottled. It is a soft material, used for carvings, and ranks second on the ◊Mohs' scale of hardness.

Aladdin /əˈlædɪn/ in the ◊*Arabian Nights*, a poor boy who obtains a magic lamp: when the lamp is rubbed, a jinn (genie, or spirit) appears and fulfils its owner's wishes.

ALADI abbreviation for *Asociacion Latino-Americana de Integration* or ◊Latin American Integration Association, organization promoting trade in the region.

Alain-Fournier /æˈlæ̃ ˈfʊəniei/ Pen name of Henri-Alban Fournier 1886–1914. French novelist. His haunting semi-autobiographical fantasy *Le Grand Meaulnes/The Lost Domain* 1913 was a cult novel of the 1920s and 1930s. His life is intimately recorded in his correspondence with his brother-in-law Jacques Rivière.

Alamein, El, Battles of /ˈæləmeɪn/ in World War II, two decisive battles in the western desert, N Egypt. In the *First Battle of El Alamein* 1–27 July 1942 the British 8th Army under Auchinleck held the German and Italian forces under Rommel. In the *Second Battle of El Alamein* 23 Oct–4 Nov 1942 ◊Montgomery defeated Rommel.

Alamo, the /ˈæləməʊ/ mission fortress in San Antonio, Texas, USA. It was besieged 23 Feb–6 March 1836 by ◊Santa Anna and 4,000 Mexicans; they killed the garrison of about 180, including frontiersmen Davy ◊Crockett and Jim Bowie (1796–1836).

Alamogordo /ˌæləməˈɡɔːdəʊ/ town in New Mexico, USA, associated with nuclear testing. The first atom bomb was exploded nearby at Trinity Site 16 July 1945. It is now a test site for guided missiles.

Alanbrooke /ˈælənbrʊk/ Alan Francis Brooke, 1st Viscount Alanbrooke 1883–1963. British army officer, chief of staff in World War II and largely responsible for the strategy that led to the German defeat.

Åland Islands /ˈɔːlənd/ (Finnish *Ahvenanmaa* 'land of waters') group of some 6,000 islands in the Baltic Sea, at the southern extremity of the Gulf of Bothnia; area 1,481 sq km/572 sq mi; population (1988) 23,900. Only 80 are inhabited; the largest island has a small town, Mariehamn. The main sectors of the island economy are tourism, agriculture, and shipping.

history The islands were Swedish until 1809, when they came, (with Finland), under Russian control. The Swedes tried, unsuccessfully, to recover the islands at the time of the Russian Revolution 1917. In 1921 the League of Nations ruled that the islands remain under Finnish sovereignty, be demilitarized, and granted autonomous status. Although the islands' assembly voted for union with Sweden 1945, the 1921 declaration remains valid.

Alarcón /ˌæloˈkɒn/ Pedro Antonio de 1833–1891. Spanish journalist and writer. The acclaimed *Diario/Diary* was based upon his experiences as a soldier in Morocco. His *El Sombrero de tres picos/The Three-Cornered Hat* 1874 was the basis of Manuel de Falla's ballet.

Alaric /ˈælərɪk/ *c.* 370–410. King of the Visigoths. In 396 he invaded Greece and retired with much booty to Illyria. In 400 and 408 he invaded Italy, and in 410 captured and sacked Rome, but he died the same year on his way to invade Sicily.

Alaska /əˈlæskə/ largest state of the USA, on the NW extremity of North America, separated from the lower 48 states by British Columbia; nickname Last Frontier

total area 1,530,700 sq km/591,004 sq mi
land area 1,478,457 sq km/570,833 sq mi
capital Juneau

towns Anchorage, Fairbanks, Fort Yukon, Holy Cross, Nome

physical much of Alaska is mountainous and includes Mount McKinley (Denali), 6,194 m/20,322 ft, the highest peak in North America, surrounded by Denali National Park. Caribou thrive in the Arctic tundra, and elsewhere there are extensive forests

features Yukon river; Rocky Mountains, including Mount McKinley and Mount Katmai, a volcano that erupted 1912 and formed the Valley of Ten Thousand Smokes (from which smoke and steam still escape and which is now a national monument); Arctic Wild Life Range, with the only large herd of North American caribou; Little Diomede Island, which is only 4 km/2.5 mi from Big Diomede/Ratmanov Island in the USSR; caribou herds on the tundra. A Congressional act 1980 gave environmental protection to 104 million acres/42 million ha. The chief railway line runs from Seward to Fairbanks, which is linked by highway (via

Canada) with Seattle. Near Fairbanks is the University of Alaska

products oil, natural gas, coal, copper, iron, gold, tin, fur, salmon fisheries and canneries, lumber

population (1987) 538,000; including 9% American Indians, Aleuts, and Inuits

history Various groups of Indians crossed the Bering land bridge 60,000–15,000 years ago; the Eskimo began to settle the Arctic coast from Siberia about 2000 BC; the Aleuts settled the Aleutian archipelago about 1000 BC. The first European to visit Alaska was Vitus Bering 1741. Alaska was a Russian colony from 1744 until purchased by the USA 1867 for $7,200,000; gold was discovered five years later. It became a state 1959. Exploited from 1968, especially in the Prudhoe Bay area to the SE of Point Barrow, are the most valuable mineral resources. An oil pipeline (1977) runs from Prudhoe Bay to the port of Valdez. Oilspill from a tanker in Prince William Sound caused great environmental damage in 1989. Under construction is an underground natural-gas pipeline to Chicago and San Francisco.

Alaska Highway road that runs from Fort St John, British Columbia, to Fairbanks, Alaska (2,450 km/1,522 mi). It was built 1942 as a supply route for US forces in Alaska.

Alba /ˈælbə/ Celtic name for Scotland; also an alternate spelling for ◊Alva, Ferdinand Alvarez de Toledo, duke of Alva, Spanish politician and general.

albacore name loosely applied to several species of fishes found in warm regions of the Atlantic and Pacific oceans, in particular to a large tuna, *Thunnus alalunga*, and to several other species of the mackerel family.

Albania /ælˈbeɪnɪə/ country in SE Europe, bounded W and SW by the Adriatic Sea, N by Yugoslavia, E by Macedonia, and SE by Greece.

government Under the 1991 interim constitution, Albania has a single-chamber legislature, the 140-member People's Assembly. It is elected every four years by universal suffrage by means of the two-ballet majority vote system. An executive president, who is also commander in chief of the armed forces and who is debarred from concurrently holding party office, is elected by People's Assembly. A prime minister and council of ministers (cabinet), drawn from the majority grouping within the assembly, have day-to-day charge of government. Private property, freedom of worship and expression, and po-

litical pluralism are endorsed by the interim constitution.

history In the ancient world the area was occupied by the Illyrians, later becoming a Roman province until the end of the 4th century AD. Albania then came under Byzantine rule, which lasted until 1347. There followed about 100 years of invasions by Bulgarians, Serbs, Venetians, and finally Turks, who arrived 1385 and, after the death of the nationalist leader Skanderbeg (George Castriota) (1403–1468), eventually made Albania part of the ◊Ottoman empire *c.* 1468.

Albania became independent 1912 and a republic 1925. In 1928 President Ahmed Beg Zogu was proclaimed King Zog. Overrun by Italy and Germany 1939–44, Albania became a republic with a communist government 1946 after a guerrilla struggle led by Enver ◊Hoxha (1908–1985).

the 'Hoxha experiment' At first closely allied with Yugoslavia, Albania backed ◊Stalin in his 1948 dispute with ◊Tito and developed close links with the USSR 1949–55, entering ◊Comecon 1949. Hoxha imposed a Stalinist system with rural collectivization, industrial nationalization, central planning, and one-party control. Mosques and churches were closed in an effort to create the 'first atheist state'. Hoxha remained a committed Stalinist and, rejecting ◊Khrushchev's denunciations of the Stalin era, broke off diplomatic relations with the USSR 1961 and withdrew from Comecon. Albania also severed diplomatic relations with China 1978, after the post-Mao accommodation with the USA, choosing isolation and neutrality. The

'Hoxha experiment', however, left Albania with the lowest income per head of population in Europe. After Hoxha's death 1985, there was a widening of external economic contacts and the number of countries with which Albania had formal diplomatic relations increased from 74 in 1978 to 111 in 1988.

open dissent Opposition to the regime began to mount during 1990 around the NW border town of Shkodër. In early July unprecedented anti-government street demonstrations erupted in Tiranë. Faced with a government crackdown, 5,000 demonstrators sought refuge in foreign embassies and were later allowed to leave the country. Later the same month diplomatic relations with the USSR were restored and embassies re-established.

end of one-party system In Dec 1990, amid continuing protests in Tiranë and economic collapse, the Communist Party leadership announced that the existence of opposition parties had finally been authorized and the ban on religion lifted. An opposition party was immediately formed by the Tiranë intelligentsia: the Democratic Party (DP), led by Sali Berisha. Elections (secret ballot) to the People's Assembly due to be held Feb 1991 were postponed to give the new party some time to organize, and in return the opposition agreed to a temporary wage freeze and ban on strikes.

civil unrest A huge bronze statue of Hoxha in Tiranë was toppled by demonstrators Feb 1991, and there were riots in several other towns. President Alia replaced the unpopular premier Adil Çarçani with Fatos Nano (1951–), a reform economist. Alia also declared the imposition of presidential rule and tanks were moved into the streets of Tiranë. Fears of a right-wing coup prompted a flight of thousands of Albanians to Greece, Yugoslavia, and Italy; the port of Brindisi alone had received more than 20,000 refugees by mid-March 1991. 'Non-political' refugees were sent back to Albania.

first multiparty elections Diplomatic relations with the USA and the UK, suspended since 1946, were restored March and May 1991 respectively. In Albania's first free multiparty elections, held March–April 1991, the ruling Party of Labour of Albania (PLA) captured 169 of the 250 seats in the new People's Assembly. It secured sufficient seats for the necessary two-thirds majority to make constitutional changes. PLA support came predominantly from rural areas.

In the major towns the DP, which captured 75 seats, polled strongly, convincingly defeating President Alia in the first round in a Tiranë constituency. The frustration of the opposition's supporters was ventilated in anti-communist rioting in Shkodë April 1991, with four persons being shot dead by the police, including the local DP leader. The report of a commission subsequently blamed the security forces for these deaths and the Siqurimi (secret police) were replaced May 1991 by a new national Security Council.

economic problems A new interim constitution was adopted April 1991, with the country being renamed the Republic of Albania, the PLA's leading role being abandoned, and private property being endorsed. The new People's Assembly elected Ramiz Alia as both the new executive president of the republic, replacing the presidium, and commander-in-chief of the armed forces. Alia, conforming with the provisions of the new interim constitution, which debarred the republic's president from holding party office, resigned as PLA first secretary and from its politburo and central committee May 1991. Fatos Nano was reappointed prime minister the same month. However, faced with a rapidly deteriorating economy—agricultural, industrial products, and exports declining and unemployment standing at almost 40%-exacerbated by the exodus of thousands of Albanians to Italy and the opposition's calling of a three-week-long strike, Nano resigned June 1991. He was replaced by Ylli Bufi, the former food minister. Bufi headed a new, interim 'government of national stability' with some members from the opposition parties. In July 1991 a land-privatization bill was passed to restore land to peasants dispossessed under communist rule. In Jan 1992, 20 former Albanian communist officials were arrested on corruption charges. The DP won 62% of the national vote in March 1992 elections. The new parliament elected Dr Sali Berisha, founder and leader of the DP, as the country's president. In Sept former president, Ramos Alia, was charged with abuse of power and misuse of state funds. In Jan 1993 Nexhmije Hoxha, widow of Enver Hoxha, was sentenced to nine years' imprisonment for misuse of government funds.

Albanian person of Albanian culture from Albania and the surrounding area. The Al-banian language belongs to a separate group within the Indo-European family and has 3–4½ million speakers. There are both Christian and Muslim Albanians, the latter having been converted by the Ottoman Turks. Albanians comprise the majority of Kosovo in Yugoslavia and are in conflict with the Serbs, for whom the province is historically and culturally significant.

Alban, St /ˈɔːlbən/ died AD 303. First Christian martyr in England. In 793 King Offa founded a monastery on the site of Alban's martyrdom, around which the city of St Albans grew up.

According to tradition, he was born at Verulamium, served in the Roman army, became a convert to Christianity after giving shelter to a priest, and, on openly professing his belief, was beheaded.

Albany /ˈɔːlbəni/ capital of New York state, USA, situated on the W bank of the Hudson River, about 225 km/140 mi N of New York City; population (1980) 101,727. With Schenectady and Troy it forms a metropolitan area, population (1980) 794,298.

Albany /ˈɔːlbəni/ port in Western Australia, population (1986) 14,100. It suffered from the initial development of ◊Fremantle, but has grown with the greater exploitation of the surrounding area.

albatross large seabird, genus *Diomedea*, with long narrow wings adapted for gliding and a wingspan of up to 3 m/10 ft, mainly found in the southern hemisphere. It belongs to the order Procellariiformes, the same group as petrels and shearwaters.

Albatrosses cover enormous distances, flying as far as 10,000 miles in 33 days, or up to 600 miles in one day. They continue flying even after dark, at speeds of up to 50 mph, though they may stop for an hour's rest and to feed during the night. They are sometimes called 'gooney birds', probably because of their clumsy way of landing. Albatrosses are becoming increasingly rare, and are in danger of extinction.

albedo the fraction of the incoming light reflected by a body such as a planet. A body with a high albedo, near 1, is very bright, while a body with a low albedo, near 0, is dark. The Moon has an average albedo of 0.12, Venus 0.65, Earth 0.37.

Albee /ˈælbiː/ Edward 1928– . US playwright. His internationally performed plays are associated with the Theatre of the ◊Absurd and include *The Zoo Story* 1960,

The American Dream 1961, *Who's Afraid of Virginia Woolf?* 1962 (his most successful play; also filmed with Elizabeth Taylor and Richard Burton as the quarrelling, alcoholic, academic couple in 1966), and *Tiny Alice* 1965. *A Delicate Balance* 1966 and *Seascape* 1975 both won Pulitzer prizes.

Albéniz /æl'beɪnɪθ/ Isaac 1860–1909. Spanish composer and pianist, born in Catalonia. He composed the suite *Iberia* and other piano pieces, making use of traditional Spanish melodies.

Albert /ˈælbət/ Prince Consort 1819–1861. Husband of British Queen ◊Victoria from 1840; a patron of the arts, science, and industry. Albert was the second son of the Duke of Saxe-Coburg-Gotha and first cousin to Queen Victoria, whose chief adviser he became. He planned the Great Exhibition of 1851; the profit was used to buy the sites in London of all the South Kensington museums and colleges and the Royal Albert Hall, built 1871. He died of typhoid.

The *Albert Memorial* 1872, designed by Sir Gilbert Scott, in Kensington Gardens, London, typifies Victorian decorative art.

Albert I /ˈælbət/ 1875–1934. King of the Belgians from 1909, the younger son of Philip, Count of Flanders, and the nephew of Leopold II. In 1900 he married Duchess Elisabeth of Bavaria. In World War I he commanded the Allied army that retook the Belgian coast in 1918.

Alberta /æl'bɜːtə/ province of W Canada
area 661,200 sq km/255,223 sq mi
capital Edmonton
towns Calgary, Lethbridge, Medicine Hat, Red Deer
physical the Rocky Mountains; dry, treeless prairie in the centre and south; towards the north this merges into a zone of poplar, then mixed forest. The valley of the Peace River is the most northerly farming land in Canada (except for Inuit pastures), and there are good grazing lands in the foothills of the Rockies
features Banff, Jasper, and Waterton Lake national parks; annual Calgary stampede; extensive dinosaur finds near Drumheller
products coal; wheat, barley, oats, sugar beet in the south; more than a million head of cattle; oil and natural gas.
population (1986) 2,375,000
history in the 17th century much of its area was part of a grant to the ◊Hudson's Bay Company for the fur trade. It became a province in 1905.

Albert Canal /ˈælbət/ canal designed as part of Belgium's frontier defences; it also links the industrial basin of Liège with the port of Antwerp.. It was built 1930–39 and named after King Albert I.

Alberti /æl'beəti/ Leon Battista 1404–1472. Italian ◊Renaissance architect and theorist who recognized the principles of Classical architecture and their modification for Renaissance practice in *On Architecture* 1452.

Albert, Lake /ˈælbət/ former name of Lake ◊Mobutu in central Africa.

Albertus Magnus, St /æl'bɜːtəs 'mægnəs/ 1206–1280. German scholar of Christian theology, philosophy (especially Aristotle), natural science, chemistry, and physics. He was known as 'doctor universalis' because of the breadth of his knowledge. Feast day 15 Nov.

Albi /æl'biː/ chief town in Tarn *département*, Midi-Pyrénées, SW France, on the river Tarn, 72 km/45 mi NE of Toulouse; population (1983) 45,000. It was the centre of the Albigensian heresy (see ◊Albigenses) and the birthplace of the artist Toulouse-Lautrec. It has a 13th-century cathedral.

Albigenses /ˌælbɪ'dʒensiːz/ heretical sect of Christians (associated with the ◊Cathars) who flourished in S France near Albi and Toulouse during the 11th–13th centuries. They adopted the Manichean belief in the duality of good and evil and pictured Jesus as being a rebel against the cruelty of an omnipotent God.

The Albigensians showed a consistently anti-Catholic attitude with distinctive sacraments, especially the *consolamentum*, or baptism of the spirit. An inquisition was initiated against the Albigensians in 1184 by Pope Lucius III (although the ◊Inquisition as we know it was not established until 1233); it was, however, ineffective, and in 1208 a crusade (1208–29) was launched against them under the elder Simon de Montfort. Thousands were killed before the movement was crushed in 1244.

albinism rare hereditary condition in which the body has no tyrosinase, one of the enzymes that form the pigment melanin, normally found in the skin, hair, and eyes. As a result, the hair is white and the skin and eyes are pink. The skin and eyes are abnormally sensitive to light, and vision is often impaired. The condition occurs among all human and animal groups.

Albinoni /ælbɪˈnəʊni/ Tomaso 1671–1751. Italian Baroque composer and violinist, whose work was studied and adapted by ◊Bach. He composed over 40 operas.

The popular *Adagio* often described as being by Albinoni was actually composed by his biographer Remo Giazotto (1910–).

Albion /ˈælbiən/ ancient name for Britain used by the Greeks and Romans. It was mentioned by Pytheas of Massilia (4th century BC), and is probably of Celtic origin, but the Romans, having in mind the white cliffs of Dover, assumed it to be derived from *albus* (white).

Alboin /ˈælbɔɪn/ 6th century. King of the ◊Lombards about 561–573. At that time the Lombards were settled north of the Alps. Early in his reign he attacked the Gepidae, a Germanic tribe occupying present-day Romania, killing their king and taking his daughter Rosamund to be his wife. About 568 he crossed the Alps to invade Italy, conquering the country as far S as Rome. He was murdered at the instigation of his wife, after he forced her to drink wine from a cup made from her father's skull.

Ålborg alternative form of ◊Aalborg, Denmark.

albumin or *albumen* any of a group of sulphur-containing ◊proteins. The best known is in the form of egg white; others occur in milk, and as a major component of serum. They are soluble in water and dilute salt solutions, and are coagulated by heat.

Albuquerque /ˈælbəkɜːki/ largest city of New Mexico, USA, situated east of the Rio Grande, in the Pueblo district; population (1982) 342,000. Founded 1706, it was named after Alfonso de Albuquerque. It is a resort and industrial centre, specializing in electronics.

Albury-Wodonga /ˈɔːbəri wəˈdɒŋgə/ twin town on the New South Wales/Victoria border, Australia; population (1981) 54,214. It was planned to relieve overspill from Melbourne and Sydney, and produces car components.

Alcatraz /ˈælkətræz/ small island in San Francisco Bay, California, USA. Its fortress was a military prison 1886–1934 and then a federal penitentiary until closed 1963. The dangerous tides allowed few successful escapes. Inmates included the gangster Al Capone and the 'Birdman of Alcatraz', a prisoner who used his time in solitary confinement to become an authority on caged birds. American Indian 'nationalists' briefly took over the island 1970 as a symbol of their lost heritage.

alcázar /ælˈkæθɑː/ (Arabic 'fortress') Moorish palace in Spain; one of five in Toledo defended by the Nationalists against the Republicans for 71 days in 1936 during the Spanish ◊Civil War.

Alcazarquivir, Battle of /ˈælkæθəˈkɪvɪə/ battle on 4 Aug 1578 between the forces of Sebastian, king of Portugal (1554–1578), and those of the Berber kingdom of Fez. Sebastian's death on the field of battle paved the way for the incorporation of Portugal into the Spanish kingdom of Philip II.

Alcestis in Greek mythology, wife of Admetus, king of Thessaly. At their wedding, the god Apollo secured a promise from the ◊Fates that Admetus might postpone his death if he could persuade someone else to die for him. Only his wife proved willing, but she was restored to life by ◊Heracles.

alchemy (Arabic *al-Kimya*) the supposed technique of transmuting base metals, such as lead and mercury, into silver and gold by the philosopher's stone, a hypothetical substance, to which was also attributed the power to give eternal life.

This aspect of alchemy constituted much of the chemistry of the Middle Ages. More broadly, however, alchemy was a system of philosophy that dealt both with the mystery of life and the formation of inanimate substances. Alchemy was a complex and indefinite conglomeration of chemistry, astrology, occultism, and magic, blended with obscure and abstruse ideas derived from various religious systems and other sources. It was practised in Europe from ancient times to the Middle Ages but later fell into disrepute.

Alcibiades /ˈælsɪbaɪədiːz/ 450–404 BC. Athenian general. Handsome and dissolute, he became the archetype of capricious treachery for his military intrigues against his native state with Sparta and Persia; the Persians eventually had him assassinated. He was brought up by ◊Pericles and was a friend of ◊Socrates, whose reputation as a teacher suffered from the association.

Alcmene /ælkˈmiːni/ in Greek mythology, the wife of Amphitryon, and mother of Heracles (the father was Zeus, king of the gods, who visited Alcmene in the form of her husband).

Alcock /ˈælkɒk/ John William 1892–1919. British aviator. On 14 June 1919, he and

Arthur Whitten Brown (1886–1948) made the first nonstop transAtlantic flight, from Newfoundland to Ireland.

alcohol any member of a group of organic chemical compounds characterized by the presence of one or more aliphatic OH (hydroxyl) groups in the molecule, and which form ◊esters with acids. The main uses of alcohols are as solvents for gums, resins, lacquers, and varnishes; in the making of dyes; for essential oils in perfumery; and for medical substances in pharmacy. Alcohol (ethanol) is produced naturally in the ◊fermentation process and is consumed as part of alcoholic beverages.

Alcohols may be liquids or solids, according to the size and complexity of the molecule. The five simplest alcohols form a series in which the number of carbon and hydrogen atoms increases progressively, each one having an extra CH_2 (methylene) group in the molecule: methanol or wood spirit (methyl alcohol, CH_3OH); ethanol (ethyl alcohol, C_2H_5OH); propanol (propyl alcohol, C_3H_7OH); butanol (butyl alcohol, C_4H_9OH); and pentanol (amyl alcohol, $C_5H_{11}OH$). The lower alcohols are liquids that mix with water; the higher alcohols, such as pentanol, are oily liquids immiscible with water and the highest are waxy solids;—for example, hexadecanol (cetyl alcohol, $C_{16}H_{33}OH$) and melissyl alcohol ($C_{30}H_{61}OH$) which occur in sperm-whale oil and beeswax respectively. Alcohols containing the CH_2OH group are primary; those containing CHOH are secondary; while those containing COH are tertiary.

alcoholic liquor intoxicating drink. ◊Ethanol (ethyl alcohol), a colourless liquid C_2H_5OH, is the basis of all common intoxicants: *wines, ciders, and sherry* contain alcohol produced by direct fermentation with yeasts of the sugar in the fruit forming the basis of the drink; *malt liquors* are beers and stouts, in which the starch of a grain is converted to sugar by malting, and the sugar then fermented into alcohol by yeasts (fermented drinks contain less than 20% alcohol); *spirits* are distilled from malted liquors or wines, and can contain up to 55% alcohol. When consumed, alcohol is rapidly absorbed from the stomach and upper intestine and affects nearly every tissue, particularly the central nervous system. Tests have shown that the feeling of elation usually associated with drinking alcoholic liquors is caused by the loss of inhibitions through

removal of the restraining influences of the higher cerebral centres. It also results in dilatation of the blood vessels, including those of the skin. The resulting loss of heat from the skin causes the body to cool, although the drinker feels warm. A concentration of 0.15% alcohol in the blood causes mild intoxication; 0.3% definite drunkenness and partial loss of consciousness; 0.6% endangers life. In 1990 it was found that women produce a lower level than men of the enzyme in the stomach that breaks down alcohol. Alcohol is more rapidly absorbed at higher altitudes, as in, for example, the slightly reduced pressure of an aircraft cabin.

Alcohol consumption in the UK has been declining for more than two centuries.

Alcoholics Anonymous (AA) voluntary self-help organization established 1934 in the USA to combat alcoholism; branches now exist in many other countries.

alcoholism dependence on alcoholic liquor. It is characterized as an illness when consumption of alcohol interferes with normal physical or emotional health. Excessive alcohol consumption may produce physical and psychological addiction and lead to nutritional and emotional disorders. The direct effect is cirrhosis of the liver, nerve damage, and heart disease, and the condition is now showing genetic predisposition.

In Britain, the cost of treating alcohol-related diseases in 1985 was estimated as at least £100 million. Alcohol consumption is measured in standard units. One unit is approximately equal to a single glass of wine or measure of spirits, or half a pint of normal-strength beer. The recommended maximum weekly intake is 21 units for men and 14 units for women.

alcohol strength measure of the amount of alcohol in a drink. Wine is measured as the percentage volume of alcohol at 20°C; spirits in litres of alcohol at 20°C, although the percentage volume measure is also commonly used. A 75 cl bottle at 40% volume is equivalent to 0.3 litres of alcohol. See also ◊proof spirit.

Alcott /ˈɔːlkət/ Louisa M(ay) 1832–1888. US author of the children's classic *Little Women* 1869, which drew on her own home circumstances, the heroine Jo being a partial self-portrait. *Good Wives* 1869 was among its sequels.

Alcuin /ˈælkwɪn/ 735–804. English scholar. Born in York, he went to Rome in 780, and in 782 took up residence at Charlemagne's court in Aachen. From 796 he was abbot of Tours. He disseminated Anglo-Saxon scholarship, organized education and learning in the Frankish empire, gave a strong impulse to the Carolingian Renaissance, and was a prominent member of Charlemagne's academy.

Aldebaran /ælˈdebərən/ or *Alpha Tauri* brightest star in the constellation Taurus and the 14th brightest star in the sky; it marks the eye of the 'bull'. Aldebaran is a red giant 60 light years away, shining with a true luminosity of about 100 times that of the Sun.

Aldeburgh /ˈɔːldbərə/ small town and coastal resort in Suffolk, England; site of an annual music festival founded by Benjamin ◊Britten. It is also the home of the Britten–Pears School for Advanced Musical Studies.

aldehyde any of a group of organic chemical compounds prepared by oxidation of primary alcohols, so that the OH (hydroxyl) group loses its hydrogen to give an oxygen joined by a double bond to a carbon atom (the aldehyde group, with the formula CHO).

The name is made up from *alcohol dehydrogenation*—that is, alcohol from which hydrogen has been removed. Aldehydes are usually liquids and include methanal (formaldehyde), ethanal (acetaldehyde), and benzaldehyde.

alder any tree or shrub of the genus *Alnus*, in the birch family Betulaceae, found mainly in cooler parts of the northern hemisphere and characterized by toothed leaves and catkins.

alderman (Old English *ealdor mann* 'older man') Anglo-Saxon term for the noble governor of a shire; after the Norman Conquest the office was replaced with that of sheriff. From the 19th century aldermen were the senior members of the borough or county councils in England and Wales, elected by the other councillors, until the abolition of the office in 1974; the title is still used in the City of London, and for members of a municipal corporation in certain towns in the USA.

Aldermaston /ˈɔːldəmɑːstən/ village in Berkshire, England; site of an atomic and biological weapons research establishment, which employs some 7,000 people to work on the production of nuclear warheads. During 1958–63 the Campaign for Nuclear Disarmament (CND) made it the focus of an annual Easter protest march.

Alderney /ˈɔːldəni/ third largest of the ◊Channel Islands, with its capital at St Anne's; area 8 sq km/3 sq mi; population (1980) 2,000. It gives its name to a breed of cattle, better known as the Guernsey.

Aldershot /ˈɔːldəʃɒt/ town in Hampshire, England, SW of London; population (1981) 32,500. It has a military camp and barracks dating from 1854.

Aldhelm, St /ˈɔːldhelm/ c. 640–709. English prelate and scholar. He was abbot of Malmesbury from 673 and bishop of Sherborne from 705. Of his poems and treatises in Latin, some survive, notably his *Riddles* in hexameters, but his English verse has been lost. He was also known as a skilled architect.

Aldiss /ˈɔːldɪs/ Brian 1925– . English science-fiction writer, anthologist, and critic. His novels include *Non-Stop* 1958, *The Malacia Tapestry* 1976, and the 'Helliconia' trilogy. *Trillion Year Spree* 1986 is a history of science fiction.

Aldrin /ˈɔːldrɪn/ Edwin (Eugene 'Buzz') 1930– . US astronaut who landed on the Moon with Neil ◊Armstrong during the *Apollo 11* mission in July 1969, becoming the second person to set foot on the Moon.

aleatory music (Latin *alea* 'dice') method of composition (pioneered by John ◊Cage) dating from about 1945 in which the elements are assembled by chance by using, for example, dice or computer.

Aleksandrovsk /ˌælɪkˈsɑːndrɒfsk/ former name (until 1921) of ◊Zaporozhye, city in the Ukraine.

Alembert /ˌælɒmˈbeə/ Jean le Rond d' 1717–1783. French mathematician and encyclopedist. He was associated with ◊Diderot in planning the great ◊Encyclopédie.

Alençon /ˌælɒnˈsɒn/ capital of the Orne *département* of France, situated in a rich agricultural plain to the SE of Caen; population (1983) 33,000. Lace, now a declining industry, was once a major product.

Alençon /ˌælɒnˈsɒn/ François, duke of, later duke of Anjou 1554–1584. Fourth son of Henry II of France and Catherine de' Medici. At one time he was considered as a suitor to Elizabeth I of England.

Aleppo /əˈlepəʊ/ (Syrian *Halab*) ancient city in NW Syria; population (1981) 977,000. There has been a settlement on the site for at least 4,000 years.

Alessandria /ˌælɪˈsændriə/ town in N Italy on the river Tanaro; population (1981) 100,500. It was founded 1168 by Pope Alexander III as a defence against Frederick I Barbarossa.

Aletsch /ˈɑːletʃ/ most extensive glacier in Europe, 23.6 km/14.7 mi long, beginning on the southern slopes of the Jungfrau in the Bernese Alps, Switzerland.

Aleut member of a people indigenous to the Aleutian Islands; a few thousand remain worldwide, most in the Aleuts and Alaska. They were exploited by Russian fur traders in the 18th and 19th centuries, and their forced evacuation 1942–45 earned the USA a United Nations reprimand 1959; compensation was paid 1990. From the 1980s, concern for wildlife and diminishing demand for furs threatened their traditional livelihood of seal trapping.

Aleutian Islands /əˈluːʃən/ volcanic island chain in the N Pacific, stretching 1,900 km/1,200 mi SW of Alaska, of which it forms part; population 5,000 Inuit (most of whom belong to the Greek Orthodox Church), 1,600 Aleuts, plus a large US military establishment. There are 14 large and over 100 small islands, running along the Aleutian Trench.

A level or *Advanced level* in the UK, examinations taken by some students in no more than four subjects at one time, usually at the age of 18 after two years' study. Two A-level passes are normally required for entry to a university degree course.

alewife fish *Alosa pseudoharengus* of the ◊herring group, up to 30 cm/1 ft long, found in the NW Atlantic and in the Great Lakes of North America.

Alexander /ˌælɪgˈzɑːndə/ Harold Rupert Leofric George, 1st Earl Alexander of Tunis 1891–1969. British field marshal, a commander in World War II in Burma (now Myanmar), N Africa, and the Mediterranean. He was governor general of Canada 1946–52 and UK minister of defence 1952–54.

Alexander /ˌælɪgˈzɑːndə/ eight popes, including:

Alexander III (Orlando Barninelli) Pope 1159–81. His authority was opposed by Frederick I Barbarossa, but Alexander

eventually compelled him to render homage 1178. He supported Henry II of England in his invasion of Ireland, but imposed penance on him after the murder of Thomas à ◊Becket.

Alexander VI (Rodrigo Borgia) 1431–1503. Pope 1492–1503. Of Spanish origin, he bribed his way to the papacy, where he furthered the advancement of his illegitimate children, who included Cesare and Lucrezia ◊Borgia. When ◊Savonarola preached against his corrupt practices Alexander had him executed.

Alexander was a great patron of the arts in Italy, as were his children. He is said to have died of a poison he had prepared for his cardinals.

Alexander /ˌælɪgˈzɑːndə/ three tsars of Russia:

Alexander I 1777–1825. Tsar from 1801. Defeated by Napoleon at Austerlitz 1805, he made peace at Tilsit 1807, but economic crisis led to a break with Napoleon's ◊continental system and the opening of Russian ports o British trade; this led to Napoleon's ill-fated invasion of Russia 1812. After the Congress of Vienna 1815, Alexander hoped through the Holy Alliance with Austria and Prussia to establish a new Christian order in Europe.

He gave a new constitution to Poland, presented to him at the Congress of Vienna.

Alexander II 1818–1881. Tsar from 1855. He embarked on reforms of the army, the government, and education, and is remembered as 'the Liberator' for his emancipation of the serfs 1861. However, the revolutionary element remained unsatisfied, and Alexander became increasingly autocratic and reactionary. He was assassinated by an anarchistic terrorist group, the ◊Nihilists.

Alexander III 1845–1894. Tsar from 1881, when he succeeded his father, Alexander II. He pursued a reactionary policy, promoting Russification and persecuting the Jews. He married Dagmar (1847–1928), daughter of Christian IX of Denmark and sister of Queen Alexandra of Britain, 1866.

Alexander /ˌælɪgˈzɑːndə/ three kings of Scotland:

Alexander I *c.* 1078–1124. King of Scotland from 1107, known as *the Fierce*. He was succeeded by his brother David I.

Alexander II 1198–1249. King of Scotland from 1214, when he succeeded his father William the Lion. Alexander supported the

English barons in their struggle with King John after the ◊Magna Carta.

Alexander III 1241–1285. King of Scotland from 1249, son of Alexander II. In 1263, by military defeat of Norwegian forces, he extended his authority over the Western Isles, which had been dependent on Norway. He strengthened the power of the central Scottish government.

He died as the result of a fall from his horse, leaving his granddaughter Margaret, the Maid of Norway, to become queen of Scotland.

Alexander I /ˌælɪgˈzɑːndə/ Karageorgevich 1888–1934. Regent of Serbia 1912–21 and king of Yugoslavia 1921–34 (dictator from 1929). He was assassinated, possibly by Italian Fascists.

Second son of ◊Peter I, king of Serbia, he was declared regent for his father 1912 and on his father's death became king of the state of South Slavs—Yugoslavia—that had come into being 1918. Rivalries both with neighbouring powers and among the Croats, Serbs, and Slovenes within his country led Alexander to establish a dictatorship. He was assassinated on a state visit to France, and Mussolini's government was later declared to have instigated the crime.

Alexander Nevski, St /nevski/ 1220–1263. Russian military leader, son of the grand duke of Novgorod. In 1240 he defeated the Swedes on the banks of the Neva (hence Nevski), and 1242 defeated the Teutonic Knights on the frozen Lake Peipus.

Alexander Obrenovich /oˈbrenevits/ 1876–1903. King of Serbia from 1889 while still a minor, on the abdication of his father, King Milan. He took power into his own hands 1893 and in 1900 married a widow, Draga Mashin. In 1903 Alexander and his queen were murdered, and ◊Peter I Karageorgevich was placed on the throne.

Alexander technique method of correcting established bad habits of posture, breathing, and muscular tension which Australian therapist F M Alexander (1869-1955) maintained cause many ailments. Back troubles, migraine, asthma, hypertension, and some gastric and gynaecological disorders are among the conditions said to be alleviated by the technique, which is also effective in the prevention of disorders, particularly those of later life. The technique also acts as a general health promoter, promoting relaxation and enhancing vitality.

Alexander the Great /ˌælɪgˈzɑːndə/ 356–323 BC. King of Macedonia and conqueror of the large Persian empire. As commander of the vast Macedonian army he conquered Greece 336. He defeated the Persian king Darius in Asia Minor 333, then moved on to Egypt, where he founded Alexandria. He defeated the Persians again in Assyria 331, then advanced further east to reach the Indus. He conquered the Punjab before diminished troops forced his retreat.

The son of King Philip of Macedonia and Queen Olympias, Alexander was educated by the philosopher Aristotle. He first saw fighting in 340, and at the battle of Chaeronea 338 contributed to the victory by a cavalry charge. At the age of 20, when his father was murdered, he assumed command of the throne and the army. He secured his northern frontier, suppressed an attempted rising in Greece by his capture of Thebes, and in 334 crossed the Dardanelles for the campaign against the vast Persian empire; at the river Granicus near the Dardanelles he won his first victory. In 333 he routed the Darius at Issus, and then set out for Egypt, where he was greeted as Pharaoh. Meanwhile, Darius assembled half a million men for a final battle but at Arbela on the Tigris in 331 Alexander, with 47,000 men, drove the Persians into retreat. After the victory he stayed a month in Babylon, then marched to Susa and Persepolis and in 330 to Ecbatana (now Hamadán, Iran). Soon after, he learned that Darius was dead. In Afghanistan he founded colonies at Herat and Kandahar, and in 328 reached the plains of Sogdiana, where he married Roxana, daughter of King Òxyartes. India now lay before him, and he pressed on to the Indus. Near the river Hydaspes (now Jhelum) he fought one of his fiercest battles against the rajah Porus. At the river Hyphasis (now Beas) his men refused to go farther, and reluctantly he turned back down the Indus and along the coast. They reached Susa 324, where Alexander made Darius's daughter his second wife. He died in Babylon of a malarial fever.

Alexandra /ˌælɪgˈzɑːndrə/ 1936– . Princess of the UK. Daughter of the Duke of Kent and Princess Marina, she married Angus Ogilvy (1928–), younger son of the earl of Airlie. They have two children, James (1964–) and Marina (1966–).

Alexandra /ˌælɪgˈzɑːndrə/ 1844–1925. Queen consort of ◊Edward VII of the UK, whom she married 1863. She was the daughter of Christian IX of Denmark. An annual Alexandra Rose Day in aid of hospitals commemorates her charitable work.

Alexandra /ˌælɪgˈzɑːndrə/ 1872–1918. Last tsarina of Russia 1894–1917. She was the former Princess Alix of Hessen and granddaughter of Britain's Queen Victoria. She married ◊Nicholas II and, from 1907, fell under the spell of ◊Rasputin, a 'holy man' brought to the palace to try to cure her son of haemophilia. She was shot with the rest of her family by the Bolsheviks in the Russian Revolution.

Alexandretta /ˌælɪgzɑːnˈdretə/ former name of ◊Iskenderun, port in S Turkey.

Alexandria /ˌælɪgˈzɑːndriə/ or *El Iskandariya* city, chief port, and second largest city of Egypt, situated between the Mediterranean and Lake Maryut; population (1986) 5,000,000. It is linked by canal with the Nile and is an industrial city (oil refining, gas processing, and cotton and grain trading). Founded 331 BC by Alexander the Great, Alexandria was for over 1,000 years the capital of Egypt.

history The principal centre of Hellenistic culture, Alexandria has since the 4th century AD been the seat of a Christian patriarch. In 641 it was captured by the Muslim Arabs, and after the opening of the Cape route its trade rapidly declined. Early in the 19th century it began to recover its prosperity, and its growth was encouraged by its use as the main British naval base in the Mediterranean during both world wars. Of the large European community, most were expelled after the Suez Crisis 1956 and their property confiscated.

Few relics of antiquity remain. The Pharos, the first lighthouse and one of the seven wonders of the ancient world, has long since disappeared. The library, said to have contained 700,000 volumes, was destroyed by the caliph ◊Omar 640. Pompey's Pillar is a column erected, as a landmark from the sea, by the emperor Diocletian. Two obelisks that once stood before the Caesarum temple are now in London (Cleopatra's Needle) and New York respectively.

Alexandria, school of /ˌælɪgˈzɑːndriə/ the writers and scholars of Alexandria who made the city the chief centre of culture in the Western world from about 331 BC to AD 642. They include the poets Callimachus, Apollonius Rhodius, and Theocritus; Euclid, pioneer of geometry; Eratosthenes, the

geographer; Hipparchus, who developed a system of trigonometry; the astronomer Ptolemy, who gave his name to the Ptolemaic system of astronomy that endured for over 1,000 years; and the Jewish philosopher Philo. The Gnostics and neo-Platonists also flourished in Alexandria.

alexandrite rare gemstone variety of the mineral chrysoberyl (beryllium aluminium oxide $BeAl_2O_4$), which is green in daylight but appears red in artificial light.

Alexandros in Greek mythology, an alternative name for ◊Paris.

Alexeev /æˈleksief/ Vasiliy 1942– . Soviet weightlifter who broke 80 world records 1970–77, a record for any sport.

He was Olympic super-heavyweight champion twice, world champion seven times, and European champion on eight occasions. At one time the most decorated man in the USSR, he was regarded as the strongest man in the world. He carried the Soviet flag at the 1980 Moscow Olympics opening ceremony, but retired shortly afterwards.

Alexius /əˈleksies/ five emperors of Byzantium, including:

Alexius I /əˈleksies kɒmˈniːnəs/ (Comnenus) 1048–1118. Byzantine emperor 1081–1118. The Latin (W European) Crusaders helped him repel Norman and Turkish invasions, and he devoted great skill to buttressing the threatened empire. His daughter ◊Anna Comnena chronicled his reign.

Alexius IV (Angelos) 1182–1204. Byzantine emperor from 1203, when, with the aid of the army of the Fourth Crusade, he deposed his uncle Alexius III. He soon lost the support of the Crusaders (by that time occupying Constantinople), and was overthrown and murdered by another Alexius, Alexius Mourtzouphlus (son-in-law of Alexius III) 1204, an act which the Crusaders used as a pretext to sack the city the same year.

alfalfa or *lucerne* perennial tall herbaceous plant *Medicago sativa* of the pea family (Leguminosae). It is native to Eurasia and bears spikes of small purple flowers in late summer. It is now a major fodder crop, generally processed into hay, meal, or silage.

Alfa Romeo /ˈælfə rəʊˈmeɪəʊ/ Italian car-manufacturing company, known for its racing cars. In 1985 the company was bought by Fiat.

The Alfa Romeo racing car made its debut 1919. In the 1930s it was dominant in the great long-distance races such as the *Targo*

Florio and *Mille Miglia.* An Italian, Giuseppe Farina, drove the Alfa Romeo 158 to win the 1950 British Grand Prix, the first world championship race; he also won the world title that year. Alfa left Grand Prix racing 1951 only to return for a brief spell 1978.

Alfonsín Foulkes /ælfɒnˈsiːn ˈfuːks/ Raúl Ricardo 1927– . Argentinian politician, president 1983–89, leader of the moderate Radical Union Party (UCR). As president from the country's return to civilian government, he set up an investigation of the army's human-rights violations. Economic problems forced him to seek help from the International Monetary Fund and introduce austerity measures.

Alfonso kings of Portugal; see ◊Afonso.

Alfonso /ælˈfonseʊ/ thirteen kings of León, Castile, and Spain, including:

Alfonso VII *c.* 1107–1157. King of León and Castile from 1126, who attempted to unite Spain. Although he protected the Moors, he was killed trying to check a Moorish rising.

Alfonso X *el Sabio* ('the Wise') 1221–1284. King of Castile from 1252. His reign was politically unsuccessful but he contributed to learning: he made Castilian the official language of the country and commissioned a history of Spain and an encyclopedia, as well as several translations from Arabic concerning, among other subjects, astronomy and games.

Alfonso XI *the Avenger* 1311–1350. King of Castile from 1312. He ruled cruelly, repressed a rebellion by his nobles, and defeated the last Moorish invasion 1340.

Alfonso XII 1857–1885. King of Spain from 1875, son of ◊Isabella II. He assumed the throne after a period of republican government following his mother's flight and effective abdication 1868.

Alfonso XIII /ælˈfonsəʊ/ 1886–1941. King of Spain 1886–1931. He assumed power 1906 and married Princess Ena, granddaughter of Queen Victoria of the United Kingdom, in the same year. He abdicated 1931 soon after the fall of the Primo de Rivera dictatorship 1923–30 (which he supported), and Spain became a republic. His assassination was attempted several times.

Alfred /ˈælfrɪd/ *the Great* *c.* 848–*c.* 900. King of Wessex from 871. He defended England against Danish invasion, founded the first English navy, and put into operation a legal code.

He encouraged the translation of works from Latin (some of which he translated himself), and promoted the development of the ◊Anglo-Saxon Chronicle.

Alfred was born at Wantage, Berkshire, the youngest son of Ethelwulf (died 858), king of the West Saxons. In 870 Alfred and his brother Ethelred fought many battles against the Danes. He gained a victory over the Danes at Ashdown 871, and succeeded Ethelred as king April 871 after a series of defeats. Five years of uneasy peace followed while the Danes were occupied in other parts of England. In 876 the Danes attacked again, and in 878 Alfred was forced to retire to the stronghold of ◊Athelney, from where he finally emerged to win the victory of Edington, Wiltshire. By the Peace of Wedmore 878 the Danish leader Guthrum (died 890) agreed to withdraw from Wessex and from Mercia west of Watling Street. A new landing in Kent encouraged a revolt of the East Anglian Danes, which was suppressed 884–86, and after the final foreign invasion was defeated 892–96, Alfred strengthened the navy to prevent fresh incursions.

algae (singular *alga*) diverse group of plants (including those commonly called seaweeds) that shows great variety of form, ranging from single-celled forms to multicellular seaweeds of considerable size and complexity.

Algae were formerly included within the division Thallophyta, together with fungi and bacteria. Their classification changed with increased awareness of the important differences existing between the algae and Thallophyta, and also between the groups of algae themselves; many botanists now place each algal group in a separate class or division of its own.

They can be classified into 12 divisions, largely to be distinguished by their pigmentation, including the *green algae* Chlorophyta, freshwater or terrestrial; *stoneworts* Charophyta; *golden-brown algae* Chrysophyta; *brown algae* Phaeophyta, mainly marine and including the *kelps Laminaria* and allies, the largest of all algae; *red algae* Rhodophyta, mainly marine and often living parasitically or as epiphytes on other algae; *diatoms* Bacillariophyta; *yellow-green algae* Xanthophyta, mostly freshwater and terrestrial; and *blue-green algae* Cyanophyta, of simple cell structure and without sexual reproduction, mostly freshwater or terrestrial.

Algardi /æl'gɑːdi/ Alessandro *c.* 1595–1654. Italian Baroque sculptor, active in Rome and at the papal court. His major work, on which he was intermittently occupied from 1634 to 1652, is the tomb of Pope Leo XI (Medici) in St Peter's, Rome.

Algarve /æl'gɑːv/ (Arabic *al-gharb* 'the west') ancient kingdom in S Portugal, the modern district of Faro, a popular holiday resort; population (1981) 323,500.

The Algarve began to be wrested from the ◊Moors in the 12th century and was united with Portugal as a kingdom 1253. It includes the SW extremity of Europe, Cape St Vincent, where the British fleet defeated the Spanish 1797.

algebra system of arithmetic applying to any set of nonnumerical symbols, and the axioms and rules by which they are combined or operated upon; sometimes known as *generalized arithmetic*.

The basics of algebra were familiar in Babylon 2000 BC, and were practised by the Arabs in the Middle Ages. In the 9th century, the Arab mathematician Muhammad ibn-Musa al-◊Khwarizmi first used the words *hisäb al-jabr* ('calculus of reduction') as part of the title of a treatise. Algebra is used in many branches of mathematics, for example, matrix algebra and Boolean algebra (the latter method was first devised in the 19th century by the British mathematician George Boole and used in working out the logic for computers).

Algeciras /ˌældʒɪˈsɪərəs/ port in S Spain, to the W of Gibraltar across the Bay of Algeciras; population (1986) 97,000. Founded by the ◊Moors 713, it was taken from them by Alfonso XI of Castile 1344. Following a conference of European Powers held here 1906, France and Spain were given control of Morocco.

Algeciras Conference international conference held Jan–April 1906 when France, Germany, Britain, Russia, and Austria-Hungary, together with the USA, Spain, the Low Countries, Portugal, and Sweden, met to settle the question of Morocco. The conference was prompted by increased German demands in what had traditionally been seen as a French area of influence, but it resulted in a reassertion of Anglo-French friendship and the increased isolation of Germany. France and Spain gained control of Morocco.

Alger /ˈældʒə/ Horatio 1834–1899. US writer of children's books. He wrote over 100 didactic moral tales in which the heroes rise from poverty to riches through hard work, luck, and good deeds, including the series 'Ragged Dick' from 1867 and 'Tattered Tom' from 1871.

It is estimated that his books sold more than 20 million copies. In US usage a 'Horatio Alger tale' has now come to mean any rags-to-riches story, often an implausible one.

Algeria /ælˈdʒɪəriə/ country in N Africa, bounded E by Tunisia and Libya, SE by Niger, SW by Mali and Mauritania, NW by Morocco, and N by the Mediterranean Sea.

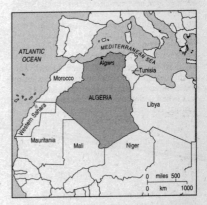

government The constitution dates from 1989. Algeria is a multiparty state, There is a president and a single-chamber national people's assembly of 295 deputies, elected for a five-year term. Islam is the state religion.

history From the 9th century BC the area now known as Algeria was ruled by ◊Carthage, and subsequently by Rome 2nd century BC–AD 5th century. In the early Christian era, St ◊Augustine was bishop of Hippo (now called Annaba) 396–430. The area was invaded by the ◊Vandals after the decline of Roman rule and was ruled by ◊Byzantium from the 6th–8th centuries, after which the ◊Arabs invaded the region, introducing ◊Islam and ◊Arabic. Islamic influence continued to dominate, despite Spain's attempts to take control in the 15th–16th centuries. From the 16th century Algeria was under ◊Ottoman rule and flourished as a centre for the slave trade. However, the Sultan's rule was often nominal, and in the 18th century Algeria became a pirate state, preying on Mediterranean shipping. European intervention became inevitable, and an Anglo–Dutch force bombarded Algiers 1816.

French colonization A French army landed 1830 and seized Algiers. By 1847 the north had been brought under French control, and was formed 1848 into the *départements* of Algiers, Oran, and Constantine. Many French colonists settled in these *départements*, which were made part of metropolitan France 1881. The mountainous region inland, inhabited by the Kabyles, was occupied 1850–70, and the Sahara region, subdued 1900–09, remained under military rule.

Struggle for independence After the defeat of France 1940, Algeria came under the control of the ◊Vichy government until the Allies landed in North Africa 1942. Postwar hopes of integrating Algeria more closely with France were frustrated by opposition in Algeria from those of both non-French and French origin. An embittered struggle for independence from France continued 1954–62, when referenda in both Algeria and France resulted 1962 in the recognition of Algeria as an independent one-party republic with ◊Ben Bella as prime minister 1962 and the country's first president 1963. Colonel Houari ◊Boumédienne deposed Ben Bella in a military coup 1965, suspended the constitution, and ruled through a revolutionary council.

Chadli's presidency A new constitution confirmed Algeria as an Islamic, socialist, one-party state 1976. Boumédienne died 1978, and power was transferred to Benjedid ◊Chadli, secretary general of the FLN. During Chadli's presidency, relations with France and the USA improved, and there was some progress in achieving greater cooperation with neighbouring states, such as Tunisia. Algeria acted as an intermediary in securing the release of the US hostages in ◊Iran 1981. A proposal by Colonel ◊Khaddhafi for political union with Libya received a cool response 1987. Following public unrest 1988, Chadli promised to make the government more responsive to public opinion. A referendum approved a new constitution Feb 1989, deleting any reference to socialism, and opened the way for a multiparty system. Islam remained the state religion, and the political reforms were designed, at least in part, to stem the growing fundamentalist movement. Ben Bella returned Sept 1990 after nine years in exile. Chadli promised multiparty elections 1991 but declared a state of emergency following clashes between the fundamentalist Islamic Salvation Front (FIS) and government forces.

military rule In the first round of assembly elections in Dec 1991, the Islamic Salvation Front (FIS) won 188 of the 231 seats contested. Chadli resigned in Jan 1992. The army stepped in and cancelled the second round of the elections. It formed a junta headed by a former opponent of the president, Mohamed Boudiaf. The army banned political activity in mosques and detained FIS leaders in an attempt to halt the rise of Islamic fundamentalism. A state of emergency was declared Feb 1992 and in March the FIS was ordered to disband. Disquiet and potential violence persisted; Boudiaf was assassinated in June and replaced by Ali Kafi. Belnid Absessalem was appointed prime minister. In Jan 1994 Kafi was replaced as president by General Lamine Zeroual.

Algiers /æl'dʒɪəz/ (Arabic *al-Jazair*; French *Alger*) capital of Algeria, situated on the narrow coastal plain between the Atlas mountains and the Mediterranean; population (1984) 2,442,300.

Founded by the Arabs AD 935, Algiers was taken by the Turks 1518 and by the French 1830. The old town is dominated by the Kasbah, the palace and prison of the Turkish rulers. The new town, constructed under French rule, is in European style.

Algiers, Battle of /æl'dʒɪəz/ bitter conflict in Algiers 1954–62 between the Algerian nationalist population and the French colonial army and French settlers. The conflict ended with Algerian independence 1962.

Algoa Bay /æl'ɡəʊə/ broad and shallow inlet in Cape Province, South Africa, where Diaz landed after rounding the Cape 1488.

ALGOL /'ælɡɒl/ (acronym from *algo*rithmic *l*anguage) in computing, an early high-level programming language, developed in the 1950s and 1960s for scientific applications. A general-purpose language, ALGOL is best suited to mathematical work and has an algebraic style. Although no longer in common use, it has greatly influenced more recent languages, such as ADA and PASCAL.

Algol or *Beta Persei* ◊eclipsing binary, a pair of rotating stars in the constellation Perseus, one of which eclipses the other every 69 hours, causing its brightness to drop by two-thirds.

The brightness changes were first explained 1782 by English amateur astronomer John Goodricke (1764–1786).

Algonquin /æl'gɒŋkwɪn/ member of the Algonquian-speaking hunting and fishing people formerly living around the Ottawa River in E Canada. Many now live on reservations in NE USA, E Ontario, and W Québec; others have chosen to live among the general populations of Canada and the USA.

algorithm procedure or series of steps that can be used to solve a problem. The word derives from the name of the 9th-century Arab mathematician, ibn-Masa al-◊Khwarizmi. In computer science, where the term is most often used, algorithm describes the logical sequence of operations to be performed by a program. A ◊flow chart is a visual representation of an algorithm.

Alhambra /æl'hæmbrə/ fortified palace in Granada, Spain, built by Moorish kings mainly between 1248 and 1354. The finest example of Moorish architecture, it stands on a rocky hill.

Alhazen /æl'hɑːzən/ Ibn al Haytham *c.* 965–1038. Arabian scientist, author of the *Kitab al Manazir/Book of Optics*, translated into Latin as *Perspectiva*. For centuries it remained the most comprehensive and authoritative treatment of optics in both East and West.

Ali /'ɑːli/ *c.* 598–660. 4th caliph of Islam. He was born in Mecca, the son of Abu Talib, uncle to the prophet Muhammad, who gave him his daughter Fatima in marriage. On Muhammad's death 632, Ali had a claim to succeed him, but this was not conceded until 656. After a stormy reign, he was assassinated. Around Ali's name the controversy has raged between the Sunni and the Shi'ites (see ◊Islam), the former denying his right to the caliphate and the latter supporting it.

Ali /'ɑːli/ (Ali Pasha) 1741–1822. Turkish politician, known as *Arslan* ('the Lion'). An Albanian, he was appointed pasha (governor) of the Janina region 1788 (now Ioánnina, Greece). His court was visited by the British poet Byron. He was assassinated.

Ali /ɑːˈliː/ Muhammad. Born Cassius Marcellus Clay, Jr. 1942– . US boxer. Olympic light-heavyweight champion 1960, he went on to become world professional heavyweight champion 1964, and was the only

man to regain the title twice. He was known for his fast footwork and extrovert nature.

He had his title stripped from him 1967 for refusing to be drafted into the US Army. He regained his title 1974, lost it Feb 1978, and regained it seven months later.

Âli /'ɑːli/ Mustafa 1541–1600. historian and writer of the Ottoman Empire. Âli was responsible for much of the myth of the preceding reign of Suleyman (1520–1566) as a golden age.

Alia /'æliə/ Ramiz 1925– . Albanian communist politician, head of state 1982–92. He gradually relaxed the isolationist policies of his predecessor Hoxha and following public unrest introduced political and economic reforms, including free elections 1991, when he was elected executive president.

Born in Shkodër in NW Albania, the son of poor Muslim peasants, Alia joined the National Liberation Army 1944, actively opposing Nazi control. After a period in charge of agitation and propaganda, Alia was inducted into the secretariat and politburo of the ruling Party of Labour of Albania (PLA) 1960–61. On the death of Enver Hoxha he became party leader, soon earning the description of the Albanian Gorbachev. In April 1991, he was elected executive president of the Republic of Albania, following the PLA's victory in multiparty elections. A month later, in conformity with the provisions of the new interim constitution, which debarred the Republic's president from holding party office, he resigned as PLA first secretary and from its politburo and central committee.

alibi (Latin 'elsewhere') in law, a provable assertion that the accused was at some other place when a crime was committed.

In Britain it can usually only be used as a defence in a ◊crown court trial if the prosecution is supplied with details before the trial.

Alice's Adventures in Wonderland children's story by Lewis Carroll, published 1865. Alice dreams she follows the White Rabbit down a rabbit hole and meets fantastic characters such as the Cheshire Cat, the Mad Hatter, and the King and Queen of Hearts.

An Alice-in-Wonderland situation has come to mean an absurd or irrational situation, because of the dreamlike logic of Alice's adventures in the book. With its companion volume *Through the Looking-*

Glass 1872, it is one of the most quoted works in the English language.

alien in law, a person who is not a citizen of a particular state. In the UK, under the British Nationality Act 1981, an alien is anyone who is neither a British Overseas citizen (for example Commonwealth) nor a member of certain other categories; citizens of the Republic of Ireland are not regarded as aliens. Aliens may not vote or hold public office in the UK.

alienation sense of isolation, powerlessness, and therefore frustration; a feeling of loss of control over one's life; a sense of estrangement from society or even from oneself. As a concept it was developed by the German philosophers Hegel and Marx; the latter used it as a description and criticism of the condition that developed among workers in capitalist society.

The term has also been used by non-Marxist writers and sociologists (in particular Durkheim in his work *Suicide* 1897) to explain unrest in factories and to describe the sense of powerlessness felt by groups such as young people, black people, and women in Western industrial society.

alimentary canal in animals, the tube through which food passes; it extends from the mouth to the anus. It is a complex organ, adapted for ◊digestion. In human adults, it is about 9 m/30 ft long, consisting of the mouth cavity, pharynx, oesophagus, stomach, and the small and large intestines.

A constant stream of enzymes from the canal wall and from the pancreas assists the breakdown of food molecules into smaller, soluble nutrient molecules, which are absorbed through the canal wall into the bloodstream and carried to individual cells. The muscles of the alimentary canal keep the incoming food moving, mix it with the enzymes and other juices, and slowly push it in the direction of the anus, a process known as ◊peristalsis. The wall of the canal receives an excellent supply of blood and is folded so as to increase its surface area. These two adaptations ensure efficient absorption of nutrient molecules.

alimony in the USA, money allowance given by court order to a former spouse after separation or ◊divorce. The right has been extended to relationships outside marriage and is colloquially termed ◊palimony.

In the UK the legal term is ◊maintenance.

Ali Pasha /ɑːliˈpɑːʃə/ Mehmed Emin 1815–1871. Grand vizier (chief minister) of the Ottoman empire 1855–56, 1858–59, 1861, and 1867–71, noted for his attempts to westernize the Ottoman Empire.

After a career as ambassador to the UK, minister of foreign affairs 1846, delegate to the Congress of ◊Vienna 1855 and of Paris 1856, he was grand vizier a total of five times. While promoting friendship with Britain and France, he defended the vizier's powers against those of the sultan.

aliphatic compound organic chemical compound in which the bonding electrons are localized within the vicinity of the bonded atoms. Its carbon atoms are joined in straight chains, as in hexane (C_6H_{14}), or in branched chains, as in 2-methylpentane ($CH_3CH(CH_3)CH_2CH_2CH_3$). ◊Cyclic compounds that do not have delocalized electrons are also aliphatic, as in the alicyclic compound cyclohexane (C_6H_{12}) or the heterocyclic piperidine ($C_5H_{11}N$). Compare ◊aromatic compound.

alkali (Arabic *al-quaḥy* 'ashes') in chemistry, a compound classed as a ◊base that is soluble in water. Alkalis neutralize acids and are soapy to the touch. The hydroxides of metals are alkalis; those of sodium (sodium hydroxide, NaOH) and of potassium (potassium hydroxide, KOH) are chemically powerful and were formerly derived from the ashes of plants.

alkali metal any of a group of six metallic elements with similar chemical bonding properties: lithium, sodium, potassium, rubidium, caesium, and francium. They form a linked group in the ◊periodic table of the elements. They are univalent (have a valency of one) and of very low density (lithium, sodium, and potassium float on water); in general they are reactive, soft, low-melting-point metals. Because of their reactivity they are only found as compounds in nature, and are used as chemical reactants rather than as structural metals.

alkaline-earth metal any of a group of six metallic elements with similar bonding properties: beryllium, magnesium, calcium, strontium, barium, and radium. They form a linked group in the ◊periodic table of the elements. They are strongly basic, bivalent (have a valency of two), and occur in nature only in compounds. They and their compounds are used to make alloys, oxidizers, and drying agents.

alkaloid any of a number of physiologically active and frequently poisonous substances contained in some plants. They are usually organic bases and contain nitrogen. They form salts with acids and, when soluble, give alkaline solutions.

Substances in this group are included by custom rather than by scientific rules. Examples include morphine, cocaine, quinine, caffeine, strychnine, nicotine, and atropine.

alkane member of a group of ◊hydrocarbons having the general formula C_nH_{2n+2}, commonly known as *paraffins*. Lighter alkanes, such as methane, ethane, propane, and butane, are colourless gases; heavier ones are liquids or solids. In nature they are found in natural gas and petroleum. As alkanes contain only single ◊covalent bonds, they are said to be saturated.

alkene member of the group of ◊hydrocarbons having the general formula C_nH_{2n}, formerly known as *olefins*. Lighter alkenes, such as ethene and propene, are gases, obtained from the ◊cracking of oil fractions. Alkenes are unsaturated compounds, characterized by one or more double bonds between adjacent carbon atoms. They react by addition, and many useful compounds, such as poly(ethene), are made from them.

al-Khalil Arabic name for ◊Hebron in the Israeli-occupied West Bank.

al Kut /ælˈkuːt/ alternative term for ◊Kūt-al-Imāra, a city in Iraq.

alkyne member of the group of ◊hydrocarbons with the general formula C_nH_{2n-2}, formerly known as the *acetylenes*. They are unsaturated compounds, characterized by one or more triple bonds between adjacent carbon atoms. Lighter alkynes, such as ethyne, are gases; heavier ones are liquids or solids.

Allah /ˈælə/ (Arabic *al-Ilah* 'the God') Islamic name for God.

Allahabad /ˌæləhəˈbɑːd/ ('city of god') historic city in Uttar Pradesh state, NE India, 580 km/360 mi SE of Delhi, on the Yamuna River where it meets the Ganges and the mythical Seraswati River; population (1981) 642,000. A Hindu religious festival is held here every 12 years with the participants washing away sin and sickness by bathing in the rivers.

Fifteen million people attended the festival of the jar of nectar of immortality (Khumbha-mela) Jan–March 1989.

Allan /ˈælən/ William 1782–1850. Scottish historical painter, born in Edinburgh, who spent several years in Russia and neighbouring countries, and returned to Edinburgh 1814. He was elected president of the Royal Scottish Academy 1838. His paintings include scenes from Walter Scott's Waverley novels.

Allegheny Mountains /ˌælɪˈɡeɪnɪ/ range over 800 km/500 mi long extending from Pennsylvania to Virginia, USA, rising to more than 1,500 m/4,900 ft and averaging 750 m/2,500 ft. The mountains are a major source of timber, coal, iron, and limestone. They initially hindered western migration, the first settlement to the west being Marietta 1788.

allegory in literature, the description or illustration of one thing in terms of another; a work of poetry or prose in the form of an extended metaphor or parable that makes use of symbolic fictional characters.

An example of the use of symbolic fictional character in allegory is the romantic epic *The Faerie Queene* 1590–96 by Edmund Spenser in homage to Queen Elizabeth I. Allegory is often used for moral purposes, as in John Bunyan's *Pilgrim's Progress* 1678. Medieval allegory often used animals as characters; this tradition survives in such works as *Animal Farm* 1945 by George Orwell.

Allegri /əˈleɪɡriː/ Gregorio 1582–1652. Italian Baroque composer, born in Rome, who became a priest and entered the Sistine chapel choir 1629. His *Miserere* for nine voices was reserved for performance by the chapel choir until Mozart, at the age of 14, wrote out the music from memory.

allegro (Italian 'merry, lively') in music, a lively or quick passage, movement, or composition.

allele one of two or more alternative forms of a ◊gene at a given position (locus) on a chromosome, caused by a difference in the ◊DNA. Blue and brown eyes in humans are determined by different alleles of the gene for eye colour.

Organisms with two sets of chromosomes (diploids) will have two copies of each gene. If the two alleles are identical the individual is said to be ◊homozygous at that locus; if different, the individual is ◊heterozygous at that locus. Some alleles show ◊dominance over others.

Allen /'ælən/ Woody. Adopted name of Allen Stewart Konigsberg 1935– . US film director and actor, known for his self-deprecating parody and offbeat humour. His films include *Sleeper* 1973, *Annie Hall* 1977 (for which he won three Academy Awards), *Manhattan* 1979, and *Hannah and Her Sisters* 1986, all of which he directed, wrote, and appeared in. From the late 1970s, Allen has mixed his output of comedies with straight dramas, such as *Interiors* 1978 and *Another Woman* 1988, but *Crimes and Misdemeanors* 1990 broke with tradition by combining humour and straight drama.

Allen, Bog of /'ælən/ wetland E of the river Shannon in the Republic of Ireland, comprising some 96,000 ha/240,000 acres of the counties of Offaly, Leix, and Kildare; the country's main source of peat fuel.

Allenby /'ælənbi/ Henry Hynman, 1st Viscount Allenby 1861–1936. English field marshal. In World War I he served in France before taking command 1917–19 of the British forces in the Middle East. His defeat of the Turkish forces at Megiddo in Palestine in Sept 1918 was followed almost at once by the capitulation of Turkey. He was high commissioner in Egypt 1919—35.

Allende (Gossens) /ar'endi/ Salvador 1908–1973. Chilean left-wing politician. Elected president 1970 as the candidate of the Popular Front alliance, Allende never succeeded in keeping the electoral alliance together in government. His failure to solve the country's economic problems or to deal with political subversion allowed the army, backed by the CIA, to stage the 1973 coup which brought about the death of Allende and many of his supporters.

Allende became a Marxist activist in the 1930s and rose to prominence as a presidential candidate in 1952, 1958, and 1964. In each election he had the support of the socialist and communist movements but was defeated by the Christian Democrats and Nationalists. As president, his socialism and nationalization of US-owned copper mines led the CIA to regard him as a communist and to their involvement in the coup that replaced him by General Pinochet.

Allen, Lough /'ælən/ lake in County Leitrim, Republic of Ireland, on the upper course of the river Shannon. It is 11 km/7 mi long and 5 km/3 mi broad.

allergy special sensitivity of the body that makes it react, with an exaggerated response of the natural immune defence mechanism, to the introduction of an otherwise harmless foreign substance (*allergen*).

The person subject to hay fever in summer is allergic to one or more kinds of pollen. Many asthmatics are allergic to certain kinds of dust or to microorganisms in animal fur or feathers. Others come out in nettle rash or are violently sick if they eat shellfish or eggs. Drugs such as antihistamines and corticosteroids are used.

All Fools' Day another name for ◊April Fools' Day.

alliance agreement between two or more states to come to each other's assistance in the event of war. Alliances were criticized after World War I as having contributed to the outbreak of war but NATO and, until 1991, the Warsaw Pact have been major parts of the post-1945 structure of international relations.

Alliance, the in UK politics, a loose union 1981–87 formed by the ◊Liberal Party and ◊Social Democratic Party (SDP) for electoral purposes.

The Alliance was set up soon after the formation of the SDP, and involved a joint manifesto at national elections and the apportionment of constituencies in equal numbers to Liberal and SDP candidates. The difficulties of presenting two separate parties to the electorate as if they were one proved insurmountable, and after the Alliance's poor showing in the 1987 general election the majority of the SDP voted to merge with the Liberals to form the Social and Liberal Democrats.

Allied Coordination Committee or *Operation Stay Behind* or *Gladio* secret right-wing paramilitary network in W Europe set up in the 1950s to arm guerrillas chosen from the civilian population in the event of Soviet invasion or communist takeover. Initiated and partly funded by the CIA, it is linked to NATO. Its past or present existence was officially acknowledged 1990 by Belgium, France, (West) Germany, Greece, Italy, the Netherlands, Norway, and Portugal; in the UK the matter is covered by the Official Secrets Act. In 1990 those governments that confirmed their countries' participation said that the branches had been or would be closed down; the European Parliament set up a commission of inquiry.

The network was operated by the secret services and armed forces of member countries, and was reported to have links with right-wing extremist groups—at least in Belgium and Italy. Switzerland officially stated 1990 that its secret resistance army, P-26, had no links with the NATO network, although it had cooperated with British secret services.

Allied Mobile Force (AMF) permanent multinational military force established 1960 to move immediately to any NATO country under threat of attack. Its headquarters are in Heidelberg, Germany.

Allies, the in World War I, the 23 countries allied against the Central Powers (Germany, Austria–Hungary, Turkey, and Bulgaria), including France, Italy, Russia, the UK, Australia and other Commonwealth nations, and, in the latter part of the war, the USA; and in World War II, the 49 countries allied against the ◊Axis powers (Germany, Italy, and Japan), including France, the UK, Australia and other Commonwealth nations, the USA, and the USSR. In the 1991 Gulf War, there were 28 countries in the Allied coalition.

alligator reptile of the genus *Alligator*, related to the crocodile. There are two species: *A. mississipiensis*, the Mississippi alligator of the southern states of the USA, and *A. sinensis* from the swamps of the lower Chang Jiang river in China. The former grows to about 4 m/12 ft, but the latter only to 1.5 m/5 ft. Alligators swim well with lashing movements of the tail; they feed on fish and mammals but seldom attack people.

The skin is of value for fancy leather, and alligator farms have been established in the USA. Closely related are the caymans of South America; these belong to the genus *Caiman*.

Allingham /ˈælɪŋəm/ Margery (Louise) 1904–1966. English detective novelist, creator of detective Albert Campion, as in *More Work for the Undertaker* 1949.

alliteration in poetry and prose, the use, within a line or phrase, of words beginning with the same sound, as in 'Two tired toads trotting to Tewkesbury'. It was a common device in Old English poetry, and its use survives in many traditional English phrases, such as *kith and kin, hearth and home*.

allometry in biology, a regular relationship between a given feature (for example, the size of an organ) and the size of the body as a whole, when this relationship is not a simple proportion of body size. Thus, an organ may increase in size proportionally faster, or slower, than body size does. For example, a human baby's head is much larger in relation to its body than is an adult's.

allopathy the usual contemporary method of treating disease, using therapies designed to counteract the manifestations of the disease. In strict usage, allopathy is the opposite of ◊homeopathy.

allopurinol drug prescribed for the treatment of ◊gout; it is an isomer of hypexanthine $C_5H_4N_4O$, and acts by reducing levels of ◊uric acid in the blood.

allotment small plot of rented land used for growing vegetables and flowers. Allotments originated in the UK during the 18th and 19th centuries, when much of the common land was enclosed (see ◊enclosure) and efforts were made to provide plots for poor people to cultivate.

Later, acts of Parliament made this provision obligatory for local councils. In 1978 there were about 480,000 allotment plots in the UK, covering 49,105 acres.

allotropy property whereby an element can exist in two or more forms (allotropes), each possessing different physical properties but the same state of matter (gas, liquid, or solid). The allotropes of carbon are diamond and graphite. Sulphur has several different forms (flowers of sulphur, plastic, rhombic, and monoclinic). These solids have different crystal structures, as do the the white and grey forms of tin and the black, red, and white forms of phosphorus.

Oxygen exists as two gaseous allotropes, 'normal' oxygen (O_2) and ozone (O_3), which differ in their molecular configurations.

alloy metal blended with some other metallic or nonmetallic substance to give it special qualities, such as resistance to corrosion, greater hardness, or tensile strength. Useful alloys include bronze, brass, cupronickel, duralumin, German silver, gunmetal, pewter, solder, steel, and stainless steel. The most recent alloys include the superplastics: alloys that can stretch to double their length at specific temperatures, permitting, for example, their injection into moulds as easily as plastic.

Among the oldest alloys is bronze, whose widespread use ushered in the Bronze Age. Complex alloys are now widespread—for example, in dentistry, where a cheaper alternative to gold is made of chromium, cobalt, molybdenum, and titanium.

All Saints' Day or *All-Hallows* or *Hallowmas* festival on 1 Nov for all Christian saints and martyrs who have no special day of their own.

All Souls' Day festival in the Roman Catholic church, held on 2 Nov (following All Saints' Day) in the conviction that through prayer and self-denial the faithful can hasten the deliverance of souls expiating their sins in purgatory.

allspice spice prepared from the dried berries of the evergreen pimento tree or West Indian pepper tree *Pimenta dioica* of the myrtle family, cultivated chiefly in Jamaica. It has an aroma similar to that of a mixture of cinnamon, cloves, and nutmeg.

Allston /ˈɔːlstən/ Washington 1779–1843. US painter of sea- and landscapes, a pioneer of the Romantic movement in the USA. His handling of light and colour earned him the title 'the American Titian'. He also painted classical, religious, and historical subjects.

alluvial deposit layer of broken rocky matter, or sediment, formed from material that has been carried in suspension by a river or stream and dropped as the velocity of the current changes. River plains and deltas are made entirely of alluvial deposits, but smaller pockets can be found in the beds of upland torrents.

Alluvial deposits can consist of a whole range of particle sizes, from boulders down through cobbles, pebbles, gravel, sand, silt, and clay. The raw materials are the rocks and soils of upland areas that are loosened by erosion and washed away by mountain streams. Much of the world's richest farmland lies on alluvial deposits. These deposits can also provide an economic source of minerals. River currents produce a sorting action, with particles of heavy material deposited first while lighter materials are washed downstream. Hence heavy minerals such as gold and tin, present in the original rocks in small amounts, can be concentrated and deposited on stream beds in commercial quantities. Such deposits are called 'placer ores'.

alluvial fan a roughly triangular sedimentary formation found at the base of slopes. An alluvial fan results when a sediment-laden stream or river rapidly deposits its load of gravel and silt as its speed is reduced on entering a plain.

The surface of such a fan slopes outward in a wide arc from an apex at the mouth of the steep valley. A small stream carrying a load of coarse particles builds a shorter, steeper fan than a large stream carrying a load of fine particles. Over time, the fan tends to become destroyed piecemeal by the continuing headward and downward erosion leveling the slope.

Alma-Ata /ˈælmɑː əˈtɑː/ formerly (to 1921) *Vernyi* capital of Kazakhstan; population (1987) 1,108,000. Industries include engineering, printing, tobacco processing, textile manufacturing, and leather products.

Established 1854 as a military fortress and trading centre, the town was destroyed by an earthquake 1887.

Alma, Battle of the in the Crimean War, battle 20 Sept 1854 in which British, French, and Turkish forces defeated Russian troops, with a loss of about 9,000 men, 6,000 being Russian.

Almagest (Arabic *al* 'the' and Greek *majisti* 'greatest') book compiled by the Greek astronomer ◊Ptolemy during the 2nd century AD, which included the idea of an Earth-centred universe. It survived in an Arabic translation. Some medieval books on astronomy, astrology, and alchemy were given the same title.

Each section of the book deals with a different branch of astronomy. The introduction describes the universe as spherical and contains arguments for the Earth being stationary at the centre. From this mistaken assumption, it goes on to describe the motions of the Sun, Moon, and planets; eclipses; and the positions, brightness, and precession of the 'fixed stars'. The book drew on the work of earlier astronomers such as ◊Hipparchus.

alma mater (Latin 'bounteous mother') term applied to universities and schools, as though they are the foster mothers of their students. Also, the official school song. It was the title given by the Romans to Ceres, the goddess of agriculture.

Almansa, Battle of /ælˈmænsə/ in the War of the Spanish Succession, battle 25 April 1707 in which British, Portuguese and Spanish forces were defeated by the French under the Duke of Berwick at a Spanish town in Albacete, about 80 km/50 mi NW of Alicante.

Alma-Tadema /ˈælmə ˈtædɪmə/ Laurence 1836–1912. Dutch painter who settled in the

UK 1870. He painted romantic, idealized scenes from Greek, Roman, and Egyptian life in a distinctive, detailed style.

Almeida /æl'meɪdə/ Francisco de *c.* 1450–1510. First viceroy of Portuguese India 1505–08. He was killed in a skirmish with the Hottentots at Table Bay, S Africa.

Almohad /'ælməhæd/ Berber dynasty 1130–1269 founded by the Berber prophet Muhammad ibn Tumart (*c.* 1080–1130). The Almohads ruled much of Morocco and Spain, which they took by defeating the ◊Almoravids; they later took the area that today forms Algeria and Tunis. Their policy of religious 'purity' involved the forced conversion and massacre of the Jewish population of Spain. They were themselves defeated by the Christian kings of Spain in 1212, and in Morocco in 1269.

almond tree *Prunus amygdalus*, family Rosaceae, related to the peach and apricot. Dessert almonds are the kernels of the fruit of the sweet variety *P. amygdalus dulcis*, which is also the source of a low-cholesterol culinary oil. Oil of bitter almonds, from the variety *P. amygdalus amara*, is used in flavouring. Almond oil is also used for cosmetics, perfumes, and fine lubricants.

Almoravid /æl'mɔːrəvɪd/ Berber dynasty 1056–1147 founded by the prophet Abdullah ibn Tashfin, ruling much of Morocco and Spain in the 11th–12th centuries. The Almoravids came from the Sahara and in the 11th century began laying the foundations of an empire covering the whole of Morocco and parts of Algeria; their capital was the newly founded Marrakesh. In 1086 they defeated Alfonso VI of Castile to gain much of Spain. They were later overthrown by the ◊Almohads.

aloe plant of the genus *Aloe* of African plants, family Liliaceae, distinguished by its long, fleshy, spiny-edged leaves. The drug usually referred to as 'bitter aloes' is a powerful cathartic prepared from the juice of the leaves of several of the species.

Alost /ɑːˈlɒst/ French name for the Belgian town of ◊Aalst.

alpaca domesticated South American hoofed mammal, *Lama pacos*, of the camel family, found in Chile, Peru, and Bolivia, and herded at high elevations in the Andes. About 1 m/3 ft tall at the shoulder with neck and head another 60 cm/2 ft, it is bred mainly for its long, fine, silky wool and used for food at the end of its fleece-producing years.

Alpaca The alpaca is related to the llama, and has been known since 200 BC.

Like the ◊llama it was probably bred from the wild ◊guanaco and is a close relative of the ◊vicuna.

alpha and omega first (α) and last (ω) letters of the Greek alphabet, a phrase hence meaning the beginning and end, or sum total, of anything.

alphabet set of conventional symbols used for writing, based on a correlation between individual symbols and spoken sounds, so called from *alpha* (α) and *beta* (β), the names of the first two letters of the classical Greek alphabet.

The earliest known alphabet is from Palestine, about 1700 BC. Alphabetic writing now takes many forms, for example the Hebrew *aleph-beth* and the Arabic script, both written from right to left; the Devanagari script of the Hindus, in which the symbols 'hang' from a line common to all the symbols; and the Greek alphabet, with the first clearly delineated vowel symbols. Each letter of the alphabets descended from Greek represents a particular sound or sounds, usually grouped into *vowels* (*a, e, i, o, u,* in the English version of the Roman alphabet), *consonants* (*b, p, d, t,* and so on) and *semivowels* (*w, y*). Letters may be combined to produce distinct sounds (for example *a* and *e* in words like *tale* and *take*, or *o* and *i* together to produce a 'wa' sound in the French *loi*), or may have no sound whatsoever (for example the silent letters *gh* in *high* and *through*).

Alpha Centauri /ˈælfə senˈtɔːraɪ/ or *Rigil Kent* the brightest star in the constellation Centaurus and the third brightest star in the sky. It is actually a triple star (see ◊binary star); the two brighter stars orbit each other every 80 years, and the third, Proxima Centauri is the closest star to the Sun, 4.2 light years away, 0.1 light years closer than the other two.

alpha decay the disintegration of the nucleus of an atom to produce an ◊alpha particle. See also ◊radioactivity.

alpha particle positively charged particle emitted from the nucleus of a radioactive ◊atom. It is one of the products of the spontaneous disintegration of radioactive elements such as radium and thorium, and is identical with the nucleus of a helium atom —that is, it consists of two protons and two neutrons. The process of emission, alpha decay, transforms one element into another, decreasing the atomic number by two, and the atomic mass by four. See ◊radioactivity.

Because of their large mass alpha particles have a short range of only a few centimetres in air, and can be stopped by a sheet of paper. They have a strongly ionizing effect (see ◊ionizing radiation) on the molecules that they strike, and are therefore capable of damaging living cells. Alpha particles travelling in a vacuum are deflected slightly by magnetic and electric fields.

Alphege, St /ˈælfɪdʒ/ 954–1012. Anglo-Saxon priest, bishop of Winchester from 984, archbishop of Canterbury from 1006. When the Danes attacked Canterbury he tried to protect the city, was thrown into prison, and, refusing to deliver the treasures of his cathedral, was stoned and beheaded at Greenwich on 19 April, his feast day.

alphorn wind instrument consisting of a straight wooden tube terminating in a conical endpiece with upturned bell, sometimes up to 4 m/12 ft in length. It sounds a harmonic series and is used to summon cattle and serenade tourists in the highlands of central Europe.

Alps /ælps/ mountain chain, the barrier between N Italy and France, Germany and Austria.
Famous peaks include *Mont Blanc*, the highest at 4,809 m/15,777 ft, first climbed by Jacques Balmat and Michel Paccard 1786; *Matterhorn* in the Pennine Alps, 4,479 m/14,694 ft, first climbed by Edward Whymper 1865 (four of the party of seven were

killed when the rope broke during their descent); *Eiger* in the Bernese Alps/Oberland, 3,970 m/13,030 ft, with a near-vertical rock wall on the N face, first climbed 1858; *Jungfrau*, 4,166 m/13,673 ft; and *Finsteraarhorn* 4,275 m/14,027 ft. *Famous passes* include *Brenner*, the lowest, Austria/Italy; *Great St Bernard*, one of the highest, 2,472 m/8,113 ft, Italy/Switzerland (by which Napoleon marched into Italy 1800); *Little St Bernard*, Italy/France (which Hannibal is thought to have used); and *St Gotthard*, S Switzerland, which Suvorov used when ordered by the tsar to withdraw his troops from Italy. All have been superseded by all-weather road/rail tunnels. The Alps extend into Slovenia, Croatia, Bosnia-Herzegovina, Yugoslavia, and N Albania with the Julian and Dinaric Alps.

Alps, Australian /ælps/ highest area of the E Highlands in Victoria/New South Wales, Australia, noted for winter sports. They include the *Snowy mountains* and *Mount Kosciusko*, Australia's highest mountain, 2,229 m/7,316 ft, first noted by Polish-born Paul Strzelecki 1829 and named after a Polish hero.

Alps, Southern /ælps/ range of mountains running the entire length of South Island, New Zealand. They are forested to the west, with scanty scrub to the east. The highest point is Mt Cook, 3,764 m/12,349 ft. Scenic features include gorges, glaciers, lakes, and waterfalls. Among its lakes are those at the southern end of the range: Manapouri, Te Anau, and the largest, Wakatipu, 83 km/52 mi long, which lies about 300 m/1,000 ft above sea level and has a depth of 378 m/1,242 ft.

Alsace /ælˈsæs/ region of France; area 8,300 sq km/3,204 sq mi; population (1986) 1,600,000. It consists of the *départements* of Bas-Rhin and Haut-Rhin, and its capital is Strasbourg.

Alsace-Lorraine /ælˈsæs lɒˈreɪn/ area of NE France, lying west of the river Rhine. It forms the French regions of ◊Alsace and ◊Lorraine. The former iron and steel industries are being replaced by electronics, chemicals, and precision engineering. The German dialect spoken does not have equal rights with French, and there is autonomist sentiment. Alsace-Lorraine formed part of Celtic Gaul in Caesar's time, was invaded by the Alemanni and other Germanic tribes in the 4th century, and remained part of the German Empire until the 17th century. In 1648 part of the territory was ceded to France; in 1681 Louis XIV seized Strasbourg. The few remaining districts were seized by France after the French Revolution. Conquered by Germany 1870–71 (chiefly for its iron ores), it was regained by France 1919, then again annexed by Germany 1940–44, when it was liberated by the Allies.

Alsatian breed of dog known officially from 1977 as the German shepherd. It is about 63 cm/26 in tall, and has a wolflike appearance, a thick coat with many varieties of colouring, and a distinctive gait. Alsatians are used as police dogs because of their high intelligence. Alsatians were introduced from Germany into Britain and the USA after World War I.

Altai /ɑːlˈtaɪ/ territory of Russian Federation in SW Siberia; area 261,700 sq km/101,043 sq mi; population (1985) 2,744,000. The capital is Barnaul.

Altai Mountains /ælˈtaɪ/ mountain system of Kazakhstan, W Siberia, Mongolia and N China. It is divided into two parts, the Russian Altai, which includes the highest peak, Mount Belukha, 4,506 m/14,783 ft, and the Mongolian or Great Altai.

Altamira /ˌæltəˈmɪərə/ Amazonian town in the state of Pará, NE Brazil, situated at the junction of the Trans-Amazonian Highway with the Xingu river, 700 km/400 mi SW of Belem. In 1989 a protest by Brazilian Indians and environmentalists against the building of six dams, focused world attention on the devastation of the Amazon rainforest.

Altamira caves decorated with Palaeolithic wall paintings, the first discovered in 1879. The paintings are realistic depictions of bison, deer and horses in several colours. The caves are near the village of Santillana del Mar in Santander province, north Spain; other well-known Palaeolithic cave paintings are in ◊Lescaux.

Altdorfer /ˈæltdɔːfə/ Albrecht c. 1480–1538. German painter and printmaker, active in Regensburg, Bavaria. Altdorfer's work, inspired by the linear, Classical style of the Italian Renaissance, often depicts dramatic landscapes that are out of scale with the figures in the paintings. His use of light creates tension and effects of movement. Many of his works are of religious subjects.

alternate angle in geometry, one of a pair of angles that lie on opposite sides of a transversal (a line that intersects two or more lines in the same plane). The alternate angles formed by a transversal of two parallel lines are equal.

alternating current (AC) electric current that flows for an interval of time in one direction and then in the opposite direction, that is, a current that flows in alternately reversed directions through or around a circuit. Electric energy is usually generated as alternating current in a power station, and alternating currents may be used for both power and lighting.

The advantage of alternating current over direct current (DC), as from a battery, is that its voltage can be raised or lowered economically by a transformer: high voltage for generation and transmission, and low voltage for safe utilization. Railways, factories, and domestic appliances, for example, use alternating current.

alternation of generations typical life cycle of terrestrial plants and some seaweeds, in which there are two distinct forms occurring alternately: *diploid* (having two sets of chromosomes) and *haploid* (one set of chromosomes). The diploid generation produces haploid spores by ◊meiosis, and is called the sporophyte, while the haploid generation produces gametes (sex cells), and is called the gametophyte. The gametes fuse to form a diploid ◊zygote which develops into a new sporophyte; thus the sporophyte and gametophyte alternate.

alternative energy energy from sources that are renewable and ecologically safe, as opposed to sources that are nonrenewable with toxic by-products, such as coal, oil, or gas (fossil fuels), and uranium (for nuclear power). The most important alternative energy source is flowing water, harnessed as ◊hydroelectric power. Other sources include the ocean's tides and waves (see ◊tidal power station and ◊wave power), wind (harnessed by windmills and wind turbines), the Sun (◊solar energy), and the heat trapped in the Earth's crust (◊geothermal energy).

The Centre for Alternative Technology, near Machynlleth in mid-Wales, was established 1975 to research and demonstrate methods of harnessing wind, water, and solar energy.

alternative medicine see ◊medicine, alternative.

alternator electricity ◊generator that produces an alternating current.

Althing /ˈælθɪŋ/ parliament of Iceland, established about 930, the oldest in the world.

Althusser /ˌæltʊˈseə/ Louis 1918–1990. French philosopher and Marxist, born in Algeria, who argued that the idea that economic systems determine family and political systems is too simple. He attempted to show how the ruling class ideology of a particular era is a crucial form of class control.

Althusser divides each mode of production into four key elements—the economic, political, ideological, and theoretical—all of which interact. His structuralist analysis of capitalism sees individuals and groups as agents or bearers of the structures of social relations, rather than as independent influences on history. His works include *For Marx* 1965, *Lenin and Philosophy* 1969, and *Essays in Self-Criticism* 1976.

altimeter instrument used in aircraft that measures altitude, or height above sea level. The common type is a form of aneroid ◊barometer, which works by sensing the differences in air pressure at different altitudes. This must continually be recalibrated because of the change in air pressure with changing weather conditions. The ◊radar altimeter measures the height of the aircraft above the ground, measuring the time it takes for radio pulses emitted by the aircraft to be reflected. Radar altimeters are essential features of automatic and blind-landing systems.

Altiplano /ˌæltʊˈplɑːnəʊ/ densely populated upland plateau of the Andes of South America, stretching from S Peru to NW Argentina. Height 3,000–4,000 m/10,000–13,000 ft.

altitude in geometry, the perpendicular distance from a ◊vertex (corner) of a figure (such as a triangle) to the base (the side opposite the vertex); also the perpendicular line that goes through the vertex to the base.

Altman /ˈæltmən/ Robert 1925– . US maverick film director. His antiwar comedy *M.A.S.H.* 1970 was a critical and commercial success; subsequent films include *McCabe and Mrs Miller* 1971, *The Long Goodbye* 1973, *Nashville* 1975, and *Popeye* 1980.

alto (Italian 'high') (1) low-register female voice, also called *contralto*; (2) high adult male voice, also known as counter tenor; (3) (French) viola.

altruism in biology, helping another individual of the same species to reproduce more effectively, as a direct result of which the altruist may leave fewer offspring itself. Female honey bees (workers) behave altruistic-

ally by rearing sisters in order to help their mother, the queen bee, reproduce, and forego any possibility of reproducing themselves.

ALU abbreviation for *arithmetic and logic unit* in a computer, the part of the ◊central processing unit (CPU) that performs the basic arithmetic and logic operations on data.

alum any double sulphate of a monovalent metal or radical (such as sodium, potassium, or ammonium) and a trivalent metal (such as aluminium or iron). The commonest alum is the double sulphate of potassium and aluminium, $K_2Al_2(SO_4)_4.24H_2O$, a white crystalline powder that is readily soluble in water. It is used in curing animal skins. Other alums are used in papermaking and to fix dye in the textile industry.

alumina or *corundum* Al_2O_3 oxide of aluminium, widely distributed in clays, slates, and shales. It is formed by the decomposition of the feldspars in granite and used as an abrasive. Typically it is a white powder, soluble in most strong acids or caustic alkalis but not in water. Impure alumina is called 'emery'. Rubies and sapphires are corundum gemstones.

aluminium lightweight, silver-white, ductile and malleable, metallic element, symbol Al, atomic number 13, relative atomic mass 26.9815. It is the third most abundant element (and the most abundant metal) in the Earth's crust, of which it makes up about 8.1% by mass. It is an excellent conductor of electricity and oxidizes easily, the layer of oxide on its surface making it highly resistant to tarnish. Because of its rapid oxidation a great deal of energy is needed in order to separate aluminium from its ores, and the pure metal was not readily obtainable until the middle of the 19th century. Commercially, it is prepared by the electrolysis of ◊bauxite. In its pure state aluminium is a weak metal, but when combined with elements such as copper, silicon, or magnesium it forms alloys of great strength.

Because of its light weight (specific gravity 2.70), aluminium is widely used in the shipbuilding and aircraft industries. It is also used in making cooking utensils, cans for beer and soft drinks, and foil. It is much used in steel-cored overhead cables and for canning uranium slugs for nuclear reactors. Aluminium is an essential constituent in some magnetic materials; and, as a good conductor of electricity, is used as foil in electrical capacitors. A plastic form of aluminium, developed 1976, which moulds to any shape and extends to several times its original length, has uses in electronics, cars, building construction, and so on.

Aluminium sulphate is the most widely used chemical in water treatment worldwide, but accidental excess (as at Camelford, N Cornwall, England, July 1989) makes drinking water highly toxic, and discharge into rivers kills all fish.

In the USA the original name suggested by the scientist Humphry Davy, 'aluminum', is retained.

aluminium ore raw material from which aluminium is extracted. The main ore is bauxite, a mixture of minerals, found in economic quantities in Australia, Guinea, West Indies, and several other countries.

Alva /ˈælvə/ or **Alba** Ferdinand Alvarez de Toledo, duke of 1508–1582. Spanish politician and general. He successfully commanded the Spanish armies of the Holy Roman emperor Charles V and his son Philip II of Spain. In 1567 he was appointed governor of the Netherlands, where he set up a reign of terror to suppress Protestantism and the revolt of the Netherlands. In 1573 he was recalled by his own wish. He later led a successful expedition against Portugal 1580–81.

Alvarado /ˌælvəˈrɑːdəʊ/ Pedro de c. 1485–1541. Spanish conquistador. In 1519 he accompanied Hernándo Cortés in the conquest of Mexico. In 1523–24 he conquered Guatemala.

Alvarez /ˈælvarez/ Luis Walter 1911–1988. US physicist who led the research team that discovered the Xi-zero atomic particle 1959. He had worked on the US atom bomb project for two years, at Chicago and Los Alamos, New Mexico, during World War II. He was awarded a Nobel prize 1968.

Alvarez was professor of physics at the University of California from 1945 and an associate director of the Lawrence Livermore Radiation Laboratory 1954–59. In 1980 he was responsible for the theory that dinosaurs disappeared because a meteorite crashed into Earth 70 million years ago, producing a dust cloud that blocked out the Sun for several years, and causing dinosaurs and plants to die.

Alvarez Quintero /kɪnˈteərəʊ/ Serafin 1871–1938 and Joàquin 1873–1945. Spanish dramatists. The brothers, born near Seville, always worked together and from 1897 pro-duced some 200 plays, principally dealing with Andalusia. Among them are *Papá Juan: Centenario* 1909 and *Los Mosquitos* 1928.

alveolus (plural *alveoli*) one of the many thousands of tiny air sacs in the ◊lungs in which exchange of oxygen and carbon dioxide takes place between air and the bloodstream.

Alwar /ˈʌlwɑː/ city in Rajasthan, India, chief town of the district (formerly princely state) of the same name; population (1981) 146,000. It has fine palaces, temples, and tombs. Flour milling and trade in cotton goods and millet are major occupations.

Alzheimer's disease /ˈæltshaɪməz/ common cause of ◊dementia, thought to afflict one in 20 people over 65. Attacking the brain's 'grey matter', it is a disease of mental processes rather than physical function, characterized by memory loss and progressive intellectual impairment.

It was first described by Alois Alzheimer 1906. The cause is unknown, although a link with high levels of aluminium in drinking water was discovered 1989. It has also been suggested that the disease may result from a defective protein circulating in the blood. Under the electron microscope, small plaques of abnormal protein can be seen within the brain, and tiny fibres, called neurofibrils, which are normally aligned with the nerve cells, are seen to form 'tangles'. There is no treatment, but recent insights into the molecular basis of the disease may aid the search for a drug to counter its effects. For example, one type of early-onset Alzheimer's disease has been shown to be related to a defective gene on chromosome 21.

AM in physics, abbreviation for ◊amplitude modulation.

a.m. or *A.M.* abbreviation for *ante meridiem* (Latin 'before noon').

Amagasaki /ˌæməɡəˈsɑːki/ industrial city on the NW outskirts of Osaka, Honshu island, Japan; population (1987) 500,000.

Amal /ˈæmæl/ radical Lebanese ◊Shi'ite military force, established by Musa Sadr in the 1970s; its headquarters are at Borj al-Barajneh. The movement split into extremist and moderate groups 1982, but both sides agreed on the aim of increasing Shi'ite political representation in Lebanon. The Amal militia under Nabi Berri fought several bloody battles against the Hezbollah (Party of God) in 1988. Amal guerrillas were responsible for many of the attacks and kidnappings in Lebanon during the 1980s, although subsequently the group came to be considered one of the more mainstream elements on the Lebanese political scene.

Amalekite /əˈmæləkaɪt/ in the Old Testament, a member of an ancient Semitic people of SW Palestine and the Sinai peninsula. According to Exodus 17 they harried the rear of the Israelites after their crossing of the Red Sea, were defeated by Saul and David, and were destroyed in the reign of Hezekiah.

Amalfi /əˈmælfi/ port 39 km/24 mi SE of Naples, Italy, situated at the foot of Monte Cerrato, on the Gulf of Salerno; population 7,000. For 700 years it was an independent republic. It is an ancient archiepiscopal see (seat of an archbishop) and has a Romanesque cathedral.

amalgam any alloy of mercury with other metals. Most metals will form amalgams, except iron and platinum. Amalgam is used in dentistry for filling teeth, and usually contains copper, silver, and zinc as the main alloying ingredients. This amalgam is pliable when first mixed and then sets hard, but the mercury leaches out and may cause a type of heavy-metal poisoning.

Amalgamation, the process of forming an amalgam, is a technique sometimes used to extract gold and silver from their ores.

Amalia /əˈmɑːliə/ Anna 1739–1807. Duchess of Saxe-Weimar-Eisenach. As widow of Duke Ernest, she reigned 1758–75, when her son Karl August succeeded her with prudence and skill, making the court of Weimar a literary centre of Germany. She was a friend of the writers Wieland, Goethe, and Herder.

Amanita /ˌæməˈnaɪtə/ genus of fungi (see ◊fungus), distinguished by a ring, or *volva*, round the stem, warty patches on the cap, and a clear white colour of the gills. Many of the species are brightly coloured and highly poisonous.

The fly agaric *A. muscaria*, a poisonous toadstool with a white-spotted red cap, which grows under birch or pine, and the deadly buff- coloured ◊death cap *A. phalloides* are both found in Britain.

Amar Das /əˈmɑːdəs/ 1495–1574. Indian religious leader, third guru (teacher) of Sikhism 1552–74. He laid emphasis on equality and opposed the caste system. He initiated the custom of the *langar* (communal meal).

Amarna tablets /əˈmɑːnə/ collection of Egyptian clay tablets with cuneiform inscriptions, found in the ruins of the ancient city of ◊Akhetaton on the east bank of the Nile. The majority of the tablets, which comprise royal archives and letters of 1411–1375 BC, are in the British Museum.

Amaterasu /əˌmɑːtəˈrɑːsuː/ in Japanese mythology, the sun-goddess, grandmother of Jimmu Tenno, first ruler of Japan, from whom the emperors claimed to be descended.

Amati /əˈmɑːti/ Italian family of violinmakers, who worked in Cremona, about 1550–1700. *Nicolo Amati* (1596–1684) taught Andrea ◊Guarneri and Antonio ◊Stradivari.

Amazon /ˈæməzən/ (Indian *Amossona* 'destroyer of boats') South American river, the world's second longest, 6,570 km/4,080 mi, and the largest in volume of water. Its main headstreams, the Marañón and the Ucayali, rise in central Peru and unite to flow E across Brazil for about 4,000 km/2,500 mi. It has 48,280 km/30,000 mi of navigable waterways, draining 7,000,000 sq km/2,750,000 sq mi, nearly half the South American land mass. It reaches the Atlantic on the equator, its estuary 80 km/50 mi wide, discharging a volume of water so immense that 64 km/40 mi out to sea, fresh water remains at the surface. The Amazon basin covers 7.5 million sq km/3 million sq mi, of which 5 million sq km/2 million sq mi is tropical forest containing 30% of all known plant and animal species (80,000 known species of trees, 3,000 known species of land vertebrates, 2,000 fresh-water fish). It is the wettest region on Earth; average rainfall 2.54 m/8.3 ft a year. Independent estimates and Landsat surveys indicated a deforestation of 12% by 1985 (up from 0.6% in 1975).

The opening up of the Amazon river basin to settlers from the overpopulated east coast has resulted in a massive burning of tropical forest to create both arable and pasture land. Brazil, with one third of the world's remaining tropical rainforest, has 55,000 species of flowering plant; half of which are only found in Brazilian Amazonia. The problems of soil erosion, the disappearance of potentially useful plant and animal species, and the possible impact of large-scale forest clearance on global warming of the atmosphere have become environmental issues of international concern.

Amazon /ˈæməzən/ in Greek mythology, a member of a group of legendary female warriors living near the Black Sea, who cut off their right breasts to use the bow more easily. Their queen, Penthesilea, was killed by Achilles at the siege of Troy. The Amazons attacked Theseus and besieged him at Athens, but were defeated, and Theseus took the Amazon Hippolyta captive; she later gave birth to ◊Hippolytus. The term Amazon has come to mean a large, strong woman.

Amazonian Indian indigenous inhabitant of the Amazon River Basin in South America. The majority of the societies are kin-based; traditional livelihood includes hunting and gathering, fishing, and shifting cultivation. A wide range of indigenous languages are spoken. Numbering perhaps 2.5 million in the 16th century, they had been reduced to perhaps one-tenth of that number by the 1820s. Their rainforests are being destroyed for mining and ranching, and Indians are being killed, transported, or assimilated.

Amazon Pact treaty signed in 1978 by Bolivia, Brazil, Colombia, Ecuador, Guyana, Peru, Surinam, and Venezuela to protect and control the industrial or commercial development of the Amazon River.

amber fossilized resin from coniferous trees of the Middle Tertiary period. It is often washed ashore on the Baltic coast with plant and animal specimens preserved in it; many extinct species have been found preserved in this way. It ranges in colour from red to yellow, and is used to make jewellery.

ambergris fatty substance, resembling wax, found in the stomach and intestines of the sperm ◊whale. It is found floating in warm seas, and was used in perfumery as a fixative.

Basically intestinal matter, ambergris is not the result of disease, but the product of an otherwise normal intestine. The name derives from the French *ambre gris* (grey amber).

Ambler /ˈæmblə/ Eric 1909–1986. English novelist. He used Balkan/Levant settings in the thrillers *The Mask of Dimitrios* 1939 and *Journey into Fear* 1940.

Amboina /æmˈbɔɪnə/ or ***Ambon*** small island in the Moluccas, republic of Indonesia; population (1980) 209,000. The town of Amboina, formerly an historic centre of Dutch influence, has shipyards.

Amboise /dæmˈbɔɪz/ Jacques d' 1934– . US dancer who created roles in many of George ◊Balanchine's greatest works as a principal dancer with New York City Ballet. He also appeared in films and TV productions, including *Seven Brides for Seven Brothers* 1954.

Ambrose, St /ˈæmbrəʊz/ *c.* 340–397. One of the early Christian leaders and theologians known as the Fathers of the Church. Feast day 7 Dec.

Born at Trèves, in S Gaul, the son of a Roman prefect, Ambrose became governor of N Italy. In 374 he was chosen bishop of Milan, although he was not yet a member of the church. He was then baptized and consecrated. He wrote many hymns, and devised the regulation of church music known as the *Ambrosian Chant*, which is still used in Milan.

ambrosia (Greek 'immortal') the food of the gods, which was supposed to confer eternal life upon all who ate it.

amen Hebrew word signifying affirmation ('so be it'), commonly used at the close of a Jewish or Christian prayer or hymn. As used by Jesus in the New Testament it was traditionally translated 'verily'.

Amenhotep /ˌɑːmənˈhəʊtep/ four Egyptian pharaohs, including:

Amenhotep III King of Egypt (*c.* 1400 BC) who built great monuments at Thebes, including the temples at Luxor. Two portrait statues at his tomb were known to the Greeks as the colossi of Memnon; one was cracked, and when the temperature changed at dawn it gave out an eerie sound, then thought supernatural. His son *Amenhotep IV* changed his name to ◊Ikhnaton.

America /əˈmerɪkə/ western hemisphere of the Earth, containing the continents of North America and South America, with Central America in between. This great land mass extends from the Arctic to the Antarctic, from beyond 75° N to past 55° S. The area is about 42,000,000 sq km/16,000,000 sq mi, and the estimated population is over 500,000,000.

The name America is derived from Amerigo Vespucci, the Florentine navigator who was falsely supposed to have been the first European to reach the American mainland 1497. The name is also popularly used to refer to the United States of America, a usage which many Canadians, South Americans, and other non-US Americans dislike.

American Revolution: chronology

1773	A government tax on tea led Massachusetts citizens disguised as North American Indians to board British ships carrying tea and throw it into Boston harbour, the Boston Tea Party.
1774–75	The First Continental Congress was held in Philadelphia to call for civil disobedience in reply to British measures such as the Intolerable Acts, which closed the port of Boston and quartered British troops in private homes.
1775 19 April	Hostilities began at Lexington and Concord, Massachusetts. The first shots were fired when British troops, sent to seize illegal military stores and arrest rebel leaders John Hancock and Samuel Adams, were attacked by the local militia (minutemen).
10 May	Fort Ticonderoga, New York, was captured from the British.
17 June	The colonialists were defeated in the first battle of the Revolution, the Battle of Breed's Hill, Massachusetts; George Washington was appointed colonial commander soon afterwards.
1776 4 July	The Second Continental Congress issued the Declaration of Independence, which specified some of the colonists' grievances and called for a new form of government.
27 Aug	Washington was defeated at Long Island and was forced to evacuate New York and retire to Pennsylvania.
26 Dec	Washington recrossed the Delaware River and defeated the British at Trenton, New Jersey.
1777 3 Jan	Washington defeated the British at Princeton, New Jersey.
11 Sept–4 Oct	British general William Howe defeated Washington at Brandywine and Germantown, and occupied Philadelphia.
17 Oct	British general John Burgoyne surrendered at Saratoga, New York State, and was therefore unable to link up with Howe.
1778–78	Washington wintered at Valley Forge, Pennsylvania, enduring harsh conditions and seeing many of his troops leave to return to their families.
1778	France, with the support of its ally Spain, entered the war on the US side (John Paul Jones led a French-sponsored naval unit).
1780 12 May	The British captured Charleston, South Carolina, one of a series of British victories in the South, but alienated support by enforcing conscription.
1781 19 Oct	British general Charles Cornwallis, besieged in Yorktown, Virginia by Washington and the French fleet, surrendered.
1782	Peace negotiations opened.
1783 3 Sept	The Treaty of Paris recognized American independence.

American Ballet Theater (ABT) US company founded 1939 (as Ballet Theater), aiming to present both classical and contemporary American ballet. ABT has a repertoire of exemplary range and quality with celebrity guest appearances. Based in New York, the company tours annually, and is considered one of the top six ballet companies in the world.

American Civil War 1861–65; see ◊Civil War, American.

American Federation of Labor and Congress of Industrial Organizations (AFL–CIO) federation of North American trade unions. The AFL was founded 1886, superseding the Federation of Organized Trades and Labor Unions of the USA and Canada, and was initially a union of skilled craftworkers. The CIO was known in 1935 as the Committee on Industrial Organiza-

tion (it adopted its present title 1937 after expulsion from the AFL for its opposition to the AFL policy of including only skilled workers). A merger reunited them 1955, bringing most unions into the national federation, currently representing about 17% of the workforce in North America.

American Independence, War of alternative name of the ◊American Revolution, the revolt 1775–83 of the British North American colonies that resulted in the establishment of the United States of America.

American Indian one of the aboriginal peoples of the Americas. Columbus named them Indians in 1492 because he believed he had found not the New World, but a new route to India. The Asian ancestors of the Indians are thought to have entered North America on the land bridge, Beringia, exposed by the lowered sea level between

Siberia and Alaska during the last ice age, 60,000–35,000 BC.

Hunting, fishing, and moving camp throughout the Americas, the migrants inhabited both continents and their nearby islands, and settled all the ecological zones, from the most tropical to the most frozen, including the woodlands, deserts, plains, mountains, and river valleys. As they specialized, many kinds of societies evolved, speaking many languages. Some became farmers, the first cultivators of maize, potatoes, sweet potatoes, manioc, peanuts, peppers, tomatoes, pumpkins, cacao, and chicle. They also grew tobacco, coca, peyote, and cinchona (the last three are sources of cocaine, mescalin, and quinine respectively.) *distribution*: *Canada* 300,000, including the Inuit; the largest group is he Six Nations (Iroquois), with a reserve near Brantford, Ontario, for 7,000. They are organized in the National Indian Brotherhood of Canada. *United States* 1.6 million, almost 900,000 (including Inuit and Aleuts) living on or near reservations, mainly in Arizona, New Mexico, Utah (where the Navajo have the largest of all reservations), Oklahoma, Texas, Montana, Washington, and North and South Dakota. The population level is thought to be about the same as at the time of Columbus, but now includes many people who are of mixed ancestry. Indians were made citizens of the US in 1924. There is an organized American Indian Movement (AIM). *Latin America* many mestizo (mixed Indian-Spanish descent), among them half the 12 million in Bolivia and Peru. Since the 1960s hey have increasingly stressed their Indian inheritance in terms of language and culture. The few Indians formerly beyond white contact are having their environment destroyed by the clearing and industrialization of the Amazon Basin.

American literature see ◊United States literature.

American Revolution revolt 1775–83 of the British North American colonies that resulted in the establishment of the United States of America. It was caused by colonial resentment at the contemporary attitude that commercial or industrial interests of any colony should be subordinate to those of the mother country; and by the unwillingness of the colonists to pay for a standing army. It was also fuelled by the colonists' anti-monarchist sentiment and a desire to participate in the policies affecting them.

American Samoa see ◊Samoa, American.

America's Cup international yacht-racing tro-phy named after the US schooner *America*, owned by J L Stevens, who won a race around the Isle of Wight 1851.

Offered for a challenge in 1870, it is now contested every three or four years, and is a seven-race series. The USA have dominated the race, only twice losing possession, in 1983 to Australia and in 1989 to New Zealand, then regaining it after a court battle. All races were held at Newport, Rhode Island, until 1987 when the Perth Yacht Club, Australia, hosted the series. Yachts are very expensive to produce and only syndicates can afford to provide a yacht capable of winning the trophy.

americium radioactive metallic element of the actinide series, symbol Am, atomic number 95, relative atomic mass 243.13; it was first synthesized in 1944. It occurs in nature in minute quantities in ◊pitchblende and other uranium ores, where it is produced from the decay of neutron-bombarded plutonium, and is the element with the highest atomic number that occurs in nature. It is synthesized in quantity only in nuclear reactors by the bombardment of plutonium with neutrons. Its longest-lived isotope is Am-243, with a half-life of 7,650 years.

The element was named by Glenn Seaborg, one of the team who first synthesized it, after the United States of America, where transuranics (elements with an atomic number greater than 92) were first produced.

Amerindian contraction of ◊American Indian.

Ames Research Center US space-research (NASA) installation at Mountain View, California, for the study of aeronautics and life sciences. It has managed the Pioneer series of planetary probes and is involved in the search for extraterrestial life.

amethyst variety of ◊quartz, SiO$_2$, coloured violet by the presence of small quantities of manganese; used as a semiprecious stone. Amethysts are found chiefly in the USSR, India, the USA, Uruguay, and Brazil.

AMF abbreviation of ◊*Arab Monetary Fund*.

Amhara /æmˈhɑːrə/ member of an ethnic group comprising approximately 25% of the population of Ethiopia; 13,000,000 (1987). The Amhara are traditionally farmers. They speak Amharic, a language of the Semitic branch of the Afro-Asiatic family. Most are members of the Ethiopian Christian Church.

amicus curiae (Latin 'friend of the court') in law, a barrister advising the court in a legal case as a neutral person, not representing either side.

In England and Wales, for example, where the public interest is concerned, the Attorney General (or his or her representative) may be asked to express an opinion. Professional bodies such as the Law Society may be represented in order to give an opinion on matters affecting their members. In the USA, a person with a strong interest in or views on the subject matter of an action, but who is not a party to it, may be given the court's permission to act as amicus curiae, usually only in matters of broad public interest.

Amida Buddha /ˈɑːmɪdə/ the 'Buddha of immeasurable light'. Japanese name for *Amitābha*, the Buddha venerated in Pure Land Buddhism. He presides over the Western Paradise (the Buddha-land of his own creation), and through his unlimited compassion and power to save, true believers can achieve enlightenment and be reborn.

amide any organic chemical derived from a fatty acid by the replacement of the hydroxyl group (–OH) by an amino group (–NH₂). One of the simplest amides is acetamide (CH₃CONH₂), which has a strong mousy odour.

Amiens /ˈæmiæn/ ancient city of NE France at the confluence of the rivers Somme and Avre; capital of Somme *département* and centre of a market-gardening region irrigated by canals; population (1982) 154,500. It has a magnificent Gothic cathedral with a spire 113 m/370 ft high and gave its name to the battles of Aug 1918, when British field marshal Douglas Haig launched his victorious offensive in World War I.

Amies /ˈeɪmiz/ (Edwin) Hardy 1909– . English couturier, one of Queen Elizabeth II's dressmakers. Noted from 1934 for his tailored clothes for women, he also designed for men from 1959.

Amin (Dada) /æˈmiːn ˈdɑːdɑː/ Idi 1926– . Ugandan politician, president 1971–79. He led the coup that deposed Milton Obote 1971, expelled the Asian community 1972, and exercised a reign of terror over his people. He fled to Libya when insurgent Ugandan and Tanzanian troops invaded the country 1979.

amine any of a class of organic chemical compounds in which one or more of the hydrogen atoms of ammonia (NH₃) have been replaced by other groups of atoms. *Methyl amines* have unpleasant ammonia odours and occur in decomposing fish. They are all gases at ordinary temperature. *Aromatic amine compounds* include aniline, which is used in dyeing.

amino acid water-soluble organic ◊molecule, mainly composed of carbon, oxygen, hydrogen, and nitrogen, containing both a basic amine group (NH₂) and an acidic carboxyl (COOH) group. When two or more amino acids are joined together, they are known as ◊peptides; ◊proteins are made up of interacting polypeptides (peptide chains consisting of more than three amino acids) and are folded or twisted in characteristic shapes.

Many different proteins are found in the cells of living organisms, but they are all made up of the same 20 amino acids, joined together in varying combinations, (although other types of amino acid do occur infrequently in nature). Eight of these, the *essential amino acids*, cannot be synthesized by humans and must be obtained from the diet. Children need a further two amino acids that are not essential for adults. Other animals also need some preformed amino acids in their diet, but green plants can manufacture all the amino acids they need from simpler molecules, relying on energy from the Sun and minerals (including nitrates) from the soil.

Amis /ˈeɪmɪs/ Kingsley 1922– . English novelist and poet. His works include *Lucky Jim* 1954, a comic portrayal of life in a provincial university, and *Take a Girl Like You* 1960. He won the UK's Booker Prize 1986 for *The Old Devils*. He is the father of Martin Amis.

Amis /ˈeɪmɪs/ Martin 1949– . English novelist. His works are characterized by their savage wit and include *The Rachel Papers* 1974, *Money* 1984, *London Fields* 1989, and *Time's Arrow* 1991.

Amman /əˈmɑːn/ capital and chief industrial centre of Jordan; population (1986) 1,160,000. It is a major communications centre, linking historic trade routes across the Middle East.

Amman is built on the site of the Old Testament Rabbath-Ammon (Philadelphia), capital of the Ammonites.

Ammon /ˈæmən/ in Egyptian mythology, the king of the gods, the equivalent of ◊Zeus or

◊Jupiter. The name is also spelt Amen/ Amun, as in the name of the pharaoh Tutankh*amen*. In art, he is represented as a ram, as a man with a ram's head, or as a man crowned with feathers. He had temples at Siwa oasis, Libya, and Thebes, Egypt.

ammonia NH_3 colourless pungent-smelling gas, lighter than air and very soluble in water. It is made on an industrial scale by the ◊Haber process, and used mainly to produce nitrogenous fertilizers, some explosives, and nitric acid.

In aquatic organisms and some insects, nitrogenous waste (from breakdown of amino acids and so on) is excreted in the form of ammonia, rather than urea as in mammals.

Ammonite member of an ancient Semitic people, mentioned in the Old Testament or Jewish Bible, who lived NW of the Dead Sea. Their capital was Amman, in present-day Jordan. They worshipped the god Moloch, to whom they offered human sacrifices. They were frequently at war with the Israelites.

ammonite extinct marine ◊cephalopod mollusc of the order Ammonoidea, related to the modern nautilus. The shell was curled in a plane spiral and made up of numerous gas-filled chambers, the outermost containing the body of the animal. Many species flourished between 200 million and 65 million years ago, ranging in size from that of a small coin to 2 m/6 ft across.

ammonium chloride or *sal ammoniac* NH_4Cl a volatile salt that forms white crystals around volcanic craters. It is prepared synthetically for use in 'dry-cell' batteries, fertilizers, and dyes.

amnesia loss or impairment of memory. As a clinical condition it may be caused by disease or injury to the brain, or by shock; in some cases it may be a symptom of an emotional disorder.

amnesty release of political prisoners under a general pardon, or a person or group of people from criminal liability for a particular action; for example, the occasional amnesties in the UK for those who surrender firearms that they hold illegally.

Amnesty International human-rights organization established in the UK 1961 to campaign for the release of political prisoners worldwide; it is politically unaligned. Amnesty International has 700,000 members, and section offices in 43 countries. The organization was awarded the Nobel Peace Prize 1977.

amniocentesis sampling the amniotic fluid surrounding a fetus in the womb for diagnostic purposes. It is used to detect Down's syndrome and other abnormalities.

amnion innermost of three membranes that enclose the embryo within the egg (reptiles and birds) or within the uterus (mammals). It contains the amniotic fluid that helps to cushion the embryo.

amoeba (plural *amoebae*) one of the simplest living animals, consisting of a single cell and belonging to the ◊protozoa group. The body consists of colourless protoplasm. Its activities are controlled by its nucleus, and it feeds by flowing round and engulfing organic debris. It reproduces by ◊binary fission. Some species of amoeba are harmful parasites.

amoebiasis ongoing infection of the intestines, caused by the amoeba *Entamoeba histolytica*, resulting in chronic dysentery and consequent weakness and dehydration. Endemic in the Third World, it is now occurring in North America and Europe.

Amorites /ˈæmərait/ ancient people of Semitic or Indo-European origin who were among the inhabitants of ◊Canaan at the time of the Israelite invasion. They provided a number of Babylonian kings.

amortization in finance, the ending of a debt by paying it off gradually, over a period of time. The term is used to describe either the paying off of a cash debt or the accounting procedure by which the value of an asset is progressively reduced ('depreciated') over a number of years.

Amos /ˈeɪmɒs/ book of the Old Testament written *c.* 750 BC. One of the ◊prophets, Amos was a shepherd who foretold the destruction of Israel because of the people's abandonment of their faith.

Amoy /əˈmɔɪ/ ancient name for ◊Xiamen, a port in SE China.

amp in physics, abbreviation for ◊ampere, a unit of electrical current.

ampere SI unit (abbreviation amp, symbol A) of electrical current. Electrical current is measured in a similar way to water current, in terms of an amount per unit time; one ampere represents a flow of about 6.28×10^{18} ◊electrons per second, or a rate of flow of charge of one coulomb per second.

The ampere is defined as the current that produces a specific magnetic force between two long, straight, parallel conductors placed one metre (3.3 ft) apart in a vacuum. It is named after the French scientist André Ampère.

Ampère /ɒmˈpeə/ André Marie 1775–1836. French physicist and mathematician who made many discoveries in electromagnetism and electrodynamics. He followed up the work of Hans ◊Oersted on the interaction between magnets and electric currents, developing a rule for determining the direction of the magnetic field associated with an electric current. The ampere is named after him.

Ampère's rule rule developed by André Ampère connecting the direction of an electric current and its associated magnetic currents. It states that if a person were travelling along a current-carrying wire in the direction of conventional current flow (from the positive to the negative terminal), and carrying a magnetic compass, then the north pole of the compass needle would be deflected to the left-hand side.

amphetamine or *speed* powerful synthetic ◊stimulant. Benzedrine was the earliest amphetamine marketed, used as a pep pill in World War II to help soldiers overcome fatigue, and until the 1970s amphetamines were prescribed by doctors as an appetite suppressant for weight loss; as an antidepressant, to induce euphoria; and as a stimulant, to increase alertness. Indications for its use today are very restricted because of severe side effects, including addiction and distorted behaviour. It is a sulphate or phosphate form of $C_9H_{13}N$.

Amphiaraus in Greek mythology, a visionary from Argos who foresaw his own death in the expedition of the ◊Seven against Thebes. An oracle bearing his name existed in antiquity at Oropos, near Thebes.

amphibian (Greek 'double life') member of the vertebrate class Amphibia (Greek 'double life'), which generally spend their larval (tadpole) stage in fresh water, transferring to land at maturity and generally returning to water to breed. Like fish and reptiles, they continue to grow throughout life, and cannot maintain a temperature greatly differing from that of their environment. The class includes caecilians, wormlike in appearance; salamanders; frogs; and toads.

amphibole any one of a large group of rock-forming silicate minerals with an internal structure based on double chains of silicon and oxygen, and with a general formula $X_2Y_5Si_8O_{22}(OH)_2$; closely related to ◊pyroxene. Amphiboles form orthorhombic, monoclinic, and triclinic ◊crystals.

Amphiboles occur in a wide range of igneous and metamorphic rocks. Common examples are ◊hornblende (X=Ca, Y=Mg, Fe, Al) and tremolite (X=Ca, Y=Mg).

amphioxus (or *lancelet*) filter-feeding animal about 6 cm/2.5 in long with a fishlike shape and a notochord, a flexible rod that forms the supporting structure of its body. It lacks organs such as heart or eyes, and lives half-buried on the sea bottom. It is a primitive relative of the vertebrates.

amphitheatre large oval or circular building used by the Romans for gladiatorial contests, fights of wild animals, and other similar events; it is a structure with an open space surrounded by rising rows of seats; the arena of an amphitheatre is completely surrounded by the seats of the spectators, hence the name (Greek *amphi*, 'around'). The ◊Colosseum in Rome, completed AD 80, held 50,000 spectators.

Amphitrite in Greek mythology, one of the daughters of Nereus and wife of the god ◊Poseidon.

Amphitryon in Greek mythology, the husband of ◊Alcmene, mother of ◊Heracles.

amphoteric term used to describe the ability of some chemical compounds to behave either as an ◊acid or a ◊base depending on their environment. For example, the metals aluminium and zinc, and their oxides and hydroxides, act as bases in acidic solutions and as acids in alkaline solutions.

Amino acids and proteins are also amphoteric, as they contain both a basic (amino, $-NH_2$) and an acidic (carboxyl, $-COOH$) group.

amplifier electronic device that magnifies the strength of a signal, such as a radio signal. The ratio of the amplitude of the output signal to that of the input signal is called the *gain* of the amplifier. As well as achieving high gain, an amplifier should be free from distortion and able to operate over a range of frequencies. Practical amplifiers are usually complex circuits, although simple amplifiers can be built from single transistors or valves.

amplitude maximum displacement of an oscillation from the equilibrium position. For a wave motion, it is the height of a crest (or the depth of a trough). With a sound wave, for example, amplitude corresponds to the intensity (loudness) of the sound. In AM (amplitude modulation) radio broadcasting, the required audio-frequency signal is made to modulate (vary slightly) the amplitude of a continuously transmitted radio carrier wave.

amplitude modulation (AM) method by which radio waves are altered for the transmission of broadcasting signals. AM is constant in frequency, and varies the amplitude of the transmitting wave in accordance with the signal being broadcast.

ampulla small vessel with a round body and narrow neck, used by the ancient Greeks and Romans for holding oil, perfumes, and so on; ampullae are used in the Christian church for holding water and wine at the Eucharist.

ampulla in biology, a slight swelling at the end of each semicircular canal in the inner ear. The sense of balance largely depends on sensitive hairs within the ampulla responding to movements of fluid within the canal.

Amritsar /æmˈrɪtsə/ industrial city in the Punjab, India; population (1981) 595,000. It is the holy city of ◊Sikhism, with the Guru Nanak University (named after the first Sikh guru) and the Golden Temple from which armed demonstrators were evicted by the Indian army under General Dayal 1984, 325 being killed. Subsequently, Indian prime minister Indira Gandhi was assassinated in reprisal. In 1919 it was the scene of the Amritsar Massacre.

Amritsar Massacre also called *Jallianwallah Bagh massacre* the killing of 379 Indians (and wounding of 1,200) in Amritsar, at the site of a Sikh religious shrine in the Punjab 1919. British troops under General Edward Dyer (1864–1927) opened fire without warning on a crowd of some 10,000, assembled to protest against the arrest of two Indian National Congress leaders (see ◊Congress Party).

Dyer was subsequently censured and resigned his commission, but gained popular support in the UK for his action, both by mention in the House of Lords and by private subscriptions totalling £926,000. The favourable treatment Dyer received spurred Mahatma ◊Gandhi to a policy of active noncooperation with the British.

Amsterdam /ˈæmstədæm/ capital of the Netherlands; population (1989) 1,038,382. Canals cut through the city link it with the North Sea and the Rhine, and as a Dutch port it is second only to Rotterdam. There is shipbuilding, printing, food processing, banking, and insurance.

Art galleries include the Rijksmuseum, Stedelijk, Vincent van Gogh Museum, and the Rembrandt house. Notable also are the Royal Palace 1655 and the Anne Frank house.

Amu Darya /æˈmuː dɑːriˈɑː/ (formerly *Oxus*) river in Soviet central Asia, flowing 2,530 km/1,578 mi from the ◊Pamirs to the ◊Aral Sea.

Amundsen /ˈæməndsən/ Roald 1872–1928. Norwegian explorer who in 1903–06 was the first person to navigate the ◊Northwest Passage. Beaten to the North Pole by US explorer Robert Peary 1910, he reached the South Pole ahead of Captain Scott 1911.

In 1918, Amundsen made an unsuccessful attempt to drift across the North Pole in the airship *Maud* and in 1925 tried unsuccessfully to fly from Spitsbergen, in the Arctic Ocean north of Norway, to the Pole by aeroplane. The following year he joined the Italian explorer Umberto Nobile (1885–1978) in the airship *Norge*, which circled the North Pole twice and landed in Alaska. Amundsen was killed in a plane crash over the Arctic Ocean while searching for Nobile and his airship *Italia*.

Amur /əˈmʊə/ river in E Asia. Formed by the Argun and Shilka rivers, the Amur enters the Sea of Okhotsk. At its mouth at Nikolaevsk it is 16 km/10 mi wide. For much of its course of over 4,400 km/2,730 mi it forms, together with its tributary, the Ussuri, the boundary between the USSR and China.

amyl alcohol former name for ◊pentanol.

amylase one of a group of ◊enzymes that breaks down starches into their component molecules (sugars) for use in the body. It occurs widely in both plants and animals. In humans, it is found in saliva and in pancreatic juices.

Anabaptist (Greek 'baptize again') member of any of various 16th-century radical Protestant sects. They believed in adult rather than child baptism, and sought to establish utopian communities. Anabaptist groups spread rapidly in N Europe, particularly in Germany, and were widely persecuted.

Notable Anabaptists included those in Moravia (the Hutterites) and Thomas Müntzer (1489–1525), a peasant leader who was executed for fomenting an uprising in Mühlhausen (now Mulhouse in E France). In Münster, Germany, Anabaptists controlled the city 1534–35. A number of Anabaptist groups, such as the Mennonites, Amish, and Hutterites, emigrated to North America, where they became known for their simple way of life and pacifism.

anabolic steroid any ◊hormone of the ◊steroid group that stimulates tissue growth. Its use in medicine is limited to the treatment of some anaemias and breast cancers; it may help to break up blood clots. Side effects include aggressive behaviour, masculinization in women, and, in children, reduced height.

It is used in sports, such as weightlifting and athletics, to increase muscle bulk for greater strength and stamina, but it is widely condemned because of the side effects. In 1988 the Canadian sprinter Ben Johnson was stripped of an Olympic gold medal for taking anabolic steroids.

anabranch (Greek *ana* 'again') stream that branches from a main river, then reunites with it. For example, the Great Anabranch in New South Wales, Australia, leaves the Darling near Menindee, and joins the Murray below the Darling–Murray confluence.

anaconda South American snake *Eunectes murinus* a member of the python and boa family, the Boidae. One of the largest snakes, growing to 6 m/20 ft or more, it is found in and near water, where it lies in wait for the birds and animals on which it feeds. The anaconda is not venomous, but kills its prey by coiling round it and squeezing until the creature suffocates.

anaemia condition caused by a shortage of haemoglobin, the oxygen-carrying component of red blood cells. The main symptoms are fatigue, pallor, breathlessness, palpitations, and poor resistance to infection. Treatment depends on the cause.

Anaemia arises either from abnormal loss or defective production of haemoglobin. Excessive loss occurs, for instance, with chronic slow bleeding or with accelerated destruction (◊haemolysis) of red blood cells. Defective production may be due to iron deficiency, vitamin B_{12} deficiency (pernicious anaemia), certain blood diseases (sickle-cell

disease and thalassemia), chronic infection, kidney disease, or certain kinds of poisoning. Untreated anaemia taxes the heart and may prove fatal.

anaerobic in biology, a description of those living organisms that do not require oxygen for the release of energy from food molecules such as glucose. Anaerobic organisms include many bacteria, yeasts, and internal parasites.

Obligate anaerobes such as certain primitive bacteria cannot function in the presence of oxygen; but *facultative anaerobes*, like the fermenting yeasts and most bacteria, can function with or without oxygen. Anaerobic organisms release 19 times less of the available energy from their food than do ◊aerobic organisms.

In plants, yeasts, and bacteria, anaerobic respiration results in the production of alcohol and carbon dioxide, a process that is exploited by both the brewing and the baking industries (see ◊fermentation). Normally aerobic animal cells can respire anaerobically for short periods of time when oxygen levels are low, but are ultimately fatigued by the build-up of the lactic acid produced in the process. This is seen particularly in muscle cells during intense activity, when the demand for oxygen can outstrip supply (see ◊oxygen debt).

anaesthetic drug that produces loss of sensation or consciousness; the resulting state is *anaesthesia*, in which the patient is insensitive to stimuli. Anaesthesia may also happen as a result of nerve disorder.

Ever since the first successful operation in 1846 on a patient rendered unconscious by ether, advances have been aimed at increasing safety and control. Sedatives may be given before the anaesthetic to make the process easier. The level and duration of unconsciousness are managed precisely. Where general anaesthesia may be inappropriate (for example, in childbirth, for a small procedure, or in the elderly), many other techniques are available. A topical substance may be applied to the skin or tissue surface; a local agent may be injected into the tissues under the skin in the area to be treated; or a regional block of sensation may be achieved by injection into a nerve. Spinal anaesthetic, such as epidural, is injected into the tissues surrounding the spinal cord, producing loss of feeling in the lower part of the body.

Less than one in 5,000 patients aged 20–40 may become sensitized to anaesthetics as a result of previously having undergone operations. Provided this is noticed promptly by the anaesthetist, no ill effects should ensue.

Analects /ˈænəlekts/ the most important of the four books that contain the teachings and ideas of ◊Confucianism.

analgesic agent for relieving ◊pain. ◊Opiates alter the perception or appreciation of pain and are effective in controlling 'deep' visceral (internal) pain. Non-opiates, such as ◊aspirin, ◊paracetamol, and ◊NSAIDs (nonsteroidal anti-inflammatory drugs), relieve musculoskeletal pain and reduce inflammation in soft tissues.

Pain is felt when electrical stimuli travel along a nerve pathway, from peripheral nerve fibres to the brain via the spinal cord. An anaesthetic agent acts either by preventing stimuli from being sent (local), or by removing awareness of them (general). Analgesic drugs act on both.

Temporary or permanent analgesia may be achieved by injection of an anaesthetic agent into, or the severing of, a nerve. Implanted devices enable patients to deliver controlled electrical stimulation to block pain impulses. Production of the body's natural opiates, ◊endorphins, can be manipulated by techniques such as relaxation and biofeedback. However, for the severe pain of, for example, terminal cancer, opiate analgesics are required.

analogous in biology, term describing a structure that has a similar function to a structure in another organism, but not a similar evolutionary path. For example, the wings of bees and of birds have the same purpose—to give powered flight—but have different origins. Compare ◊homologous.

analogue computer computing device that performs calculations through the interaction of continuously varying physical quantities, such as voltages (as distinct from the more common ◊digital computer, which works with discrete quantities). An analogue computer is said to operate in real time (corresponding to time in the real world), and can therefore be used to monitor and control other events as they happen.

Although common in engineering since the 1920s, analogue computers are not general-purpose computers, but specialize in solving ◊differential calculus and similar mathematical problems. The earliest analogue computing device is thought to be the flat, or planispheric, astrolabe, which originated in about the 8th century.

analysis branch of mathematics concerned with limiting processes on axiomatic number systems; ◊calculus of variations and infinitesimal calculus is now called analysis.

analysis in chemistry, the determination of the composition of substances; see ◊analytical chemistry.

analytic in philosophy, a term derived from ◊Kant: the converse of ◊synthetic. In an analytic judgement, the judgement provides no new knowledge; for example: 'All bachelors are unmarried.'

analytical chemistry branch of chemistry that deals with the determination of the chemical composition of substances. *Qualitative analysis* determines the identities of the substances in a given sample; *quantitative analysis* determines how much of a particular substance is present.

Simple qualitative techniques exploit the specific, easily observable properties of elements or compounds—for example, the flame test makes use of the different flame-colours produced by metal cations when their compounds are held in a hot flame. More sophisticated methods, such as those of ◊spectroscopy, are required where substances are present in very low concentrations or where several substances have similar properties.

Most quantitative analyses involve initial stages in which the substance to be measured is extracted from the test sample, and purified. The final analytical stages (or 'finishes') may involve measurement of the substance's mass (gravimetry) or volume (volumetry, titrimetry), or a number of techniques initially developed for qualitative analysis, such as fluorescence and absorption spectroscopy, chromatography, electrophoresis, and polarography. Many modern methods enable quantification by means of a detecting device that is integrated into the extraction procedure (as in gas–liquid chromatography).

analytical engine programmable computing device designed by Charles ◊Babbage in 1833. It was based on the ◊difference engine but was intended to automate the whole process of calculation. It introduced many of the concepts of the digital computer but, because of limitations in manufacturing processes, was never built.

Among the concepts introduced were input and output, an arithmetic unit, memory, sequential operation, and the ability to make decisions based on data. It would have required at least 50,000 moving parts. The design was largely forgotten until some of Babbage's writings were rediscovered in 1937.

analytical geometry another name for ◊coordinate geometry.

Ananda /əˈnændə/ 5th century BC. Favourite disciple of the Buddha. At his plea, a separate order was established for women. He played a major part in collecting the teachings of the Buddha after his death.

anarchism (Greek *anarkhos* 'without ruler') political belief that society should have no government, laws, police, or other authority, but should be a free association of all its members. It does not mean 'without order'; most theories of anarchism imply an order of a very strict and symmetrical kind, but they maintain that such order can be achieved by cooperation. Anarchism must not be confused with nihilism (a purely negative and destructive activity directed against society); anarchism is essentially a pacifist movement.

Religious anarchism, claimed by many anarchists to be exemplified in the early organization of the Christian church, has found expression in the social philosophy of the Russian writer Tolstoy and the Indian nationalist Gandhi. The growth of political anarchism may be traced through the British Romantic writers William Godwin and Shelley to the 1848 revolutionaries P J ◊Proudhon in France and the Russian ◊Bakunin, who had a strong following in Europe.

The theory of anarchism is expressed in the works of the Russian revolutionary ◊Kropotkin.

From the 1960s there were outbreaks of politically motivated violence popularly identified with anarchism; in the UK, the bombings and shootings carried out by the Angry Brigade 1968–71, and in the 1980s actions directed towards peace and animal-rights issues, and to demonstrate against large financial and business corporations.

anastomosis in medicine, a connection between two vessels (usually blood vessels) in the body. Surgical anastomosis involves the deliberate joining of two vessels or hollow parts of an organ; for example, when part of the intestine has been removed and the remaining free ends are brought together and stitched.

Anatolia /ˌænəˈtəʊliə/ (Turkish *Anadolu*) alternative name for Turkey-in-Asia.

anatomy the study of the structure of the body and its component parts, especially the ◊human body, as distinguished from physiology, which is the study of bodily functions.

Herophilus of Chalcedon (*c.* 330–*c.* 260 BC) is regarded as the founder of anatomy. In the 2nd century AD, the Graeco-Roman physician Galen produced an account of anatomy that was the only source of anatomical knowledge until *On the Working of the Human Body* 1543 by Andreas Vesalius. In 1628, William Harvey published his demonstration of the circulation of the blood. Following the invention of the microscope, the Italian Malpighi and the Dutch Leeuwenhoek were able to found the study of ◊histology. In 1747, Albinus (1697–1770), with the help of the artist Wandelaar (1691–1759), produced the most exact account of the bones and muscles, and in 1757–65 Albrecht von Haller gave the most complete and exact description of the organs that had yet appeared. Among the anatomical writers of the early 19th century are the surgeon Charles Bell (1774–1842), Jonas Quain (1796–1865), and Henry Gray (1825–1861). Later in the century came stain techniques for microscopic examination, and the method of mechanically cutting very thin sections of stained tissues (using X-rays; see ◊radiography). Radiographic anatomy has been one of the triumphs of the 20th century, which has also been marked by immense activity in embryological investigation.

Anaximander /æˌnæksɪˈmændə/ *c.* 610–*c.* 546 BC. Greek astronomer and philosopher. He claimed that the Earth was a cylinder three times wider than it is deep, motionless at the centre of the universe, and he is credited with drawing the first geographical map. He said that the celestial bodies were fire seen through holes in the hollow rims of wheels encircling the Earth. According to Anaximander, the first animals came into being from moisture and the first humans grew inside fish, emerging once fully developed.

ANC abbreviation for ◊*African National Congress*; South African nationalist organization.

ancestor worship religious rituals and beliefs oriented towards deceased members of a family or group, as a symbolic expression of values or in the belief that the souls of the dead remain involved in this world and are capable of influencing current events.

Zulus used to invoke the spirits of their great warriors before engaging in battle; the Greeks deified their early heroes; and the ancient Romans held in reverential honour the ◊Manes, or departed spirits of their forebears. Ancestor worship is a part of ◊Confucianism, and recent ancestors are venerated in the Shinto religion of Japan.

Anchises in classical mythology, a member of the Trojan royal family, loved by the goddess ◊Aphrodite. Their son ◊Aeneas rescued his father øn the fall of ◊Troy and carried him from the burning city on his shoulders. The story forms an episode in ◊Virgil's *Aeneid*.

Anchorage /ˈæŋkərɪdʒ/ port and largest town of Alaska, USA, at the head of Cook Inlet; population (1984) 244,030. Established 1918, Anchorage is a major centre of administration, communication, and commerce. Industries include salmon canning, and coal and gold are mined.

anchovy small fish *Engraulis encrasicholus* of the ◊herring family. It is fished extensively, being abundant in the Mediterranean, and is also found on the Atlantic coast of Europe and in the Black Sea. It grows to 20 cm/8 in. Pungently flavoured, it is processed into fish pastes and essences, and used as a garnish, rather than eaten fresh.

ancien régime the old order; the feudal, absolute monarchy in France before the French Revolution 1789.

ancient art art of prehistoric cultures and the ancient civilizations around the Mediterranean that predate the classical world of Greece and Rome: for example, Sumerian and Aegean art.

Artefacts range from simple relics of the Palaeolithic period, such as pebbles carved with symbolic figures, to the sophisticated art forms of ancient Egypt and Assyria: for example, mural paintings, sculpture, and jewellery.

Palaeolithic art The earliest surviving artefacts that qualify as art are mainly from Europe, dating from approximately 30,000 to 10,000 BC. This was a period of hunter-gatherer cultures. Items that survive are small sculptures, such as the *Willendorf Venus* (Kunsthistorisches Museum, Vienna) carved from a small stone and simply painted, and symbolic sculptures carved in ivory. The later cave paintings of Lascaux in France and Altamira in Spain depict animals— bison, bulls, horses, and deer—and a few

human figures. The animals are highly coloured and painted in profile, sometimes with lively and sinuous outlines.

Neolithic art In Europe the period 4000– 2400 BC produced great megaliths, such as Carnac in France and Stonehenge in Britain, and decorated ceramics, including pots and figurines—the pots sometimes covered in geometric ornament, heralding the later ornamental art of the Celts.

Egyptian art The history of ancient Egypt falls into three periods, the Old, the Middle, and the New Kingdoms, covering about 3,000 years between them. Within this period there is stylistic development, but also a remarkable continuity. Sculpture and painting are extremely stylized, using strict conventions and symbols based on religious beliefs. There is a strong emphasis on smooth and supple linear outlines throughout the period. Most extant Egyptian art is concerned with religion and funeral rites. During Egypt's slow decline in power, the style of art remained conservative, still subservient to the religion, but the level of technical expertise continued to be high, with an almost constant and prolific production of artefacts.

Egyptian Old Kingdom The monumental sculpture of the Sphinx dates from about 2530 BC. The rich treasure of grave goods that survives includes the clothes, ornaments, jewellery, and weapons of the dead, as well as statues in stone and precious metals and vivid wall paintings showing a variety of scenes from the life of the time.

Egyptian New Kingdom The style of painting became softer and more refined. The 18th dynasty, 1554–1305 BC, was a golden age, when the temples of Karnak and Luxor were built and the maze of tombs in the Valley of the Kings. During this period the pharaohs Ikhnaton and Tutankhamen created the most extravagant Egyptian style, exemplified by the carved images of these godlike creatures, the statues of Ikhnaton, and the golden coffins of Tutankhamen's mummified body, about 1361–1352 BC (Egyptian Museum, Cairo), and the head of Ikhnaton's queen, Nefertiti, about 1360 BC (Museo Archaeologico, Florence). The monumental statues of Ramses II in Abu Simbel date from the 13th century BC.

Sumerian art Sculpture was highly developed, for example, the remains of an inlaid harp (University Museum, Philadelphia) from the grave treasures of the royal tombs at Ur, about 2600 BC.

Assyrian art As in ancient Egypt, this is a stylized art with figures shown in profile and unconventional solutions to problems of perspective. This can be seen in the friezes of the palace of Nineveh, 7th century BC (examples in the British Museum, London).

Persian art Darius I's palace in Persepolis was magnificently decorated 518–516 BC with low- relief friezes cut in stone. This period also saw a marked development in metalwork techniques.

Aegean art Several cultures developed on the islands and mainland surrounding the Aegean Sea. In the Cyclades islands, simple sculpted figures were produced; in Crete, more sophisticated art forms were developed by the Minoans about 1800–1400 BC, exemplified by the stylized wall paintings at the palace in Knossos (fragments in the Archaeological Museum, Heraklion), brilliantly inventive ceramics, and naturalistic bull's heads in bronze and stone.

On the Greek mainland, Mycenean culture reached its peak around 1400 to 1200 BC. Surviving examples of this culture include the ruins of the palace at Mycenae, stylized gold masks, and other decorated metalwork. After the decline of Mycenae, there was little artistic activity for several centuries before the emergence of a distinctive Greek art.

Ancient Mariner, The Rime of the poem by Samuel Taylor Coleridge, published 1798, describing the curse that falls upon a mariner and his ship when he shoots an albatross.

Ancona /ænˈkəʊnə/ Italian town and naval base on the Adriatic Sea, capital of Marche region; population (1988) 104,000. It has a Romanesque cathedral and a former palace of the popes.

Andalusia /ˌændəˈluːsiə/ (Spanish *Andalucía*) fertile autonomous region of S Spain, including the provinces of Almería, Cádiz, Córdoba, Granada, Huelva, Jaén, Málaga, and Seville; area 87,300 sq km/33,698 sq mi; population (1986) 6,876,000. Málaga, Cádiz, and Algeciras are the chief ports and industrial centres. The Costa del Sol on the S coast has many tourist resorts, including Marbella and Torremolinos.

Andalusia has Moorish architecture, having been under Muslim rule 8th–15th centuries.

andalusite aluminium silicate, Al_2SiO_5, a white to pinkish mineral crystallizing as square-or rhomb-based prisms. It is common in metamorphic rocks formed from clay sediments under low pressure conditions. Andalusite, kyanite, and sillimanite are all polymorphs of Al_2SiO_5.

Andaman and Nicobar Islands /ˈændəmən, ˈnɪkəbɑː/ two groups of islands in the Bay of Bengal, between India and Myanmar, forming a Union Territory of the Republic of India; area 8,300 sq km/3,204 sq mi; population (1981) 188,000. The economy is based on fishing, timber, rubber, fruit, and rice.

Andean Group /ænˈdiːən/ (Spanish *Grupo Andino*) South American organization aimed at economic and social cooperation between member states. It was established under the Treaty of Cartagena 1969, by Bolivia, Chile, Colombia, Ecuador, and Peru; Venezuela joined 1973, but Chile withdrew 1976. The organization is based in Lima, Peru.

Andean Indian any indigenous inhabitant of the Andes range in South America, stretching from Ecuador to Peru to Chile, and including both the coast and the highlands. Many Andean civilizations developed in this region from local fishing-hunting-farming societies, all of which predated the ¢Inca, who consolidated the entire region and ruled from about 1200 to the 1530s, when the Spanish arrived and conquered. The earliest pan-Andean civilization was the Chavin, about 1200–800 BC, which was followed by large and important coastal city-states, such as the Mochica, the Chimú, the Nazca, and the Paracas. The region was dominated by the Tiahuanaco when the Inca started to expand, took them and outlying peoples into their empire, and imposed the Quechua language on all. It is now spoken by over 10 million people and is a member of the Andean-Equatorial family.

Andersen /ˈændəsən/ Hans Christian 1805–1875. Danish writer of fairy tales, such as 'The Ugly Duckling', 'The Snow Queen', 'The Little Mermaid', and 'The Emperor's New Clothes'. A gothic inventiveness, strong sense of wonder, and a redemptive evocation of material and spiritual poverty have given these stories perennial and universal appeal; they have been translated into many languages. He also wrote adult novels and travel books.

Anderson /ˈændəsən/ Carl David 1905–1991. US physicist who discovered the positron (positive electron) 1932; he shared a Nobel prize 1936.

Andersen The tales of the Danish writer Hans Christian Andersen earned him international acclaim.

Anderson /ˈændəsən/ Elizabeth Garrett 1836–1917. The first English woman to qualify in medicine. Refused entry into medical school, Anderson studied privately and was licensed by the Society of Apothecaries in London 1865. She was physician to the Marylebone Dispensary for Women and Children (later renamed the Elizabeth Garrett Anderson Hospital), a London hospital now staffed by women and serving women patients.

She helped found the London School of Medicine. She was the first woman member of the British Medical Association and the first woman mayor in Britain.

Anderson /ˈændəsən/ Marian 1902–1993. US contralto whose voice was remarkable for its range and richness. She toured Europe 1930, but in 1939 she was barred from singing at Constitution Hall, Washington DC, because she was black. In 1955 she sang at the Metropolitan Opera, the first black singer to appear there. In 1958 she was appointed an alternate (deputizing) delegate to the United Nations.

Anderson /ˈændəsən/ Maxwell 1888–1959. US playwright, whose *What Price Glory?* 1924, written with Laurence Stallings, is a realistic portrayal of the US soldier in action during World War I.

Anderson /ˈændəsən/ Sherwood 1876–1941. US writer of sensitive, experimental, and poetic stories of small-town Midwestern life as portrayed in *Winesburg, Ohio* 1919.

Andes /ˈændiːz/ the great mountain system or *cordillera* that forms the western fringe of South America, extending through some 67° of latitude and the republics of Colombia, Venezuela, Ecuador, Peru, Bolivia, Chile, and Argentina. The mountains exceed 3,600 m/12,000 ft for half their length of 6,500 km/4,000 mi.

Geologically speaking, the Andes are new mountains, having attained their present height by vertical upheaval of the entire strip of the Earth's crust as recently as the latter part of the Tertiary era and the Quaternary. But they have been greatly affected by weathering. Rivers have cut profound gorges, and glaciers have produced characteristic valleys. The majority of the individual mountains are volcanic; some are still active. The whole system may be divided into two almost parallel ranges. The southernmost extremity is Cape Horn, but the range extends into the sea and forms islands. Among the highest peaks are Cotopaxi and Chimborazo in Ecuador, Cerro de Pasco and Misti in Peru, Illampu and Illimani in Bolivia, Aconcagua (the highest mountain in the New World) in Argentina, and Ojos del Salado in Chile. Andean mineral resources include gold, silver, tin, tungsten, bismuth, vanadium, copper, and lead. Difficult communications make mining expensive. Transport for a long time was chiefly by pack animals, but air transport has greatly reduced difficulties of communications. Three railways cross the Andes from Valparaiso to Buenos Aires, Antofagasta to Salta, and Antofagasta via Uyuni to Asunción. New roads are being built, including the ◊Pan-American Highway. The majority of the sparse population is dependent on agriculture, the nature and products of which vary with the natural environment. Newcomers to the Andean plateau, which includes Lake ◊Titicaca, suffer from *puna*, mountain sickness, but indigenous peoples have hearts and lungs adapted to altitude.

andesite volcanic igneous rock, intermediate in silica content between rhyolite and basalt. It is characterized by a large quantity of the feldspar ◊minerals, giving it a light colour. Andesite erupts from volcanoes at destructive plate margins (where one plate of the Earth's surface moves beneath another; see ◊plate tectonics), including the Andes, from which it gets its name.

Andhra Pradesh /ˈændrə prɑːˈdeʃ/ state in E central India
area 276,700 sq km/106,845 sq mi
capital Hyderabad
towns Secunderabad
products rice, sugar cane, tobacco, ground-nuts, cotton
population (1981) 53,404,000
language Telugu, Urdu, Tamil
history formed 1953 from the Telegu-speaking areas of Madras, and enlarged 1956 from the former Hyderabad state.

Andorra /ænˈdɔːrə/ landlocked country in the E Pyrenees, bounded N by France and S by Spain.

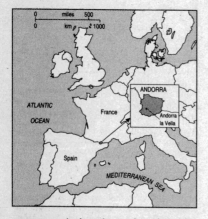

government Andorra has no formal constitution and the government is based on the country's feudal origins. Although administratively independent, it has no individual international status, its joint heads of state being the bishop of Urgel in Spain and the president of France. They are represented by permanent delegates, the vicar general of the Urgel diocese, and the prefect of the French *département* of Pyrénées-Orientales. There is a General Council of the villages, consisting of four people from each of the seven parishes, elected by Andorran citizens for a four-year term. The Council submits motions and proposals to the permanent delegates for approval.

Until 1982 the General Council elected an official called the First Syndic to act as its chief executive, but in that year an executive council was appointed, headed by a prime minister. This introduced a separation between legislative and executive powers and was an important step towards a more constitutional form of government. For the time being, reforms are dependent on the two co-princes, through their representatives.

history Co-princes have ruled Andorra since 1278. Until 1970 only third-generation Andorran males had the vote, now the franchise extends to all first-generation Andorrans of foreign parentage aged 28 or over. The electorate is small in relation to the total population, up to 70% of which consists of foreign residents who are demanding political and nationality rights. Immigration, controlled by a quota system, is restricted to French and Spanish nationals intending to work in Andorra. Since 1980 there have been signs of a fragile, but growing, democracy. There are loose political groupings but no direct party representation on the General Council. A technically illegal political organization, the Democratic Party of Andorra, may provide the basis for a future democratic system. In March 1993 the state's first constitution was approved in a referendum.

Andrássy /ænˈdræsi/ Gyula, Count Andrássy 1823–1890. Hungarian revolutionary and statesman who supported the Dual Monarchy of Austro-Hungary 1867 and was Hungary's first constitutional prime minister 1867–71. He became foreign minister of the Austro-Hungarian Empire 1871–79 and tried to halt Russian expansion into the Balkans.

André /ˈɑːndreɪ/ Carl 1935– . US sculptor, a Minimalist, who uses industrial materials to affirm basic formal and aesthetic principles. His *Equivalent VIII* 1976, an arrangement of bricks in Palladian proportion (Tate Gallery, London) was much criticized.

André /ˈændreɪ/ John 1751–1780. British army major in the American Revolution, with whom Benedict ◊Arnold plotted the surrender of ◊West Point. André was caught by Washington's army, tried, and hanged as a spy.

Andrea del Sarto /ˈændreɪə del ˈsɑːtəʊ/ (Andrea d'Agnola di Francesco) 1486–1531. Italian Renaissance painter active in Florence, one of the finest portraitists and religious painters of his time. His style is serene and noble, characteristic of High Renaissance art.

He trained under Piero de Cosimo and others but was chiefly influenced by ◊Masaccio and ◊Michelangelo. In 1518 he went to work for Francis I in France and returned to

Italy in 1519 with funds to enlarge the royal French art collection; he spent it on a house for himself and never went back. His pupils included Pontormo and Vasari. Del Sarto was the foremost painter in Florence after about 1510, along with Fra Bartolommeo, although he was gradually superseded by the emerging Mannerists during the 1520s. Apart from portraits, such as *A Young Man* (National Gallery, London), he painted many religious works, including the *Madonna of the Harpies* (Uffizi, Florence), an example of Classical beauty reminiscent of Raphael. He painted frescoes at Sta Annunziata and the Chiostro dello Scalzo, both in Florence.

Andreas Capellanus /ˈændriəs ˌkæpəˈleɪnəs/ Latin name for André le Chapelain.

André le Chapelain /ˈɒndreɪ lə ʃæˈplæn/ 12th century. French priest and author. He wrote *De Arte Honest Amandi/The Art of Virtuous Love*, a seminal work in ◊courtly love literature, at the request of ◊Marie de France, while he was chaplain at her court in Troyes, E France.

Andreotti /ˌændriˈɒti/ Giulio 1919– . Italian politician. From 1989 to 1992 he was prime minister for the sixth time having headed previous governments 1972–73, and four successive governments 1976–79. In addition he was defence minister eight times, and foreign minister five times. He is a fervent European.

Andrew /ˈændruː/ (full name Andrew Albert Christian Edward) 1960– . Prince of the UK, Duke of York, second son of Queen Elizabeth II. He married Sarah Ferguson 1986; their daughter, Princess Beatrice, was born in 1988, and their second daughter, Princess Eugenie was born in 1990. The couple separated 1992. Prince Andrew is a naval helicopter pilot.

Andrewes /ˈændruːz/ Lancelot 1555–1626. Church of England bishop. He helped prepare the text of the Authorized Version of the Bible, and was known for the intellectual and literary quality of his sermons. He was bishop of Chichester (1605), Ely (1609), and Winchester (1618).

Andrews /ˈændruːz/ John 1813–1885. Irish chemist who conducted a series of experiments on the behaviour of carbon dioxide under varying temperature and pressure. In 1869 he introduced the idea of a critical temperature: 30.9˚C in the case of carbon dioxide, beyond which no amount of pressure would liquefy the gas.

Andrews /ˈændruːz/ Julie. Stage name of Julia Elizabeth Wells 1935– . British-born US singer and actress. A child performer with her mother and stepfather in British music halls, she first appeared in the USA in the Broadway production *The Boy Friend* 1954. She was the original Eliza Doolittle in *My Fair Lady* 1956. In 1960 she appeared in Lerner and Loewe's *Camelot* on Broadway. Her films include *Mary Poppins* 1964, *The Americanization of Emily* 1963, *The Sound of Music* 1965, *'10'* 1980, and *Victor/Victoria* 1982.

Andrew, St /ˈændruː/ New Testament apostle, martyred on an X-shaped cross (*St Andrew's cross*). He is the patron saint of Scotland. Feast day 30 Nov.

A native of Bethsaida, he was Simon Peter's brother. With Peter, James, and John, who worked with him as fishermen at Capernaum, he formed the inner circle of Jesus' 12 disciples. According to tradition, he went with John to Ephesus, preached in Scythia, and was crucified at Patras.

Andrić /ˈændrɪtʃ/ Ivo 1892–1974. Yugoslavian novelist and nationalist. He became a diplomat, and was ambassador to Berlin 1940. *Na Drini Ćuprija/The Bridge on the Drina* 1945 is an epic history of a small Bosnian town. Nobel prize 1961.

Androcles /ˈændrəkliːz/ traditionally, a Roman slave who fled from a cruel master into the African desert, where he encountered and withdrew a thorn from the paw of a crippled lion. Recaptured and sentenced to combat a lion in the arena, he found his adversary was his old friend. The emperor Tiberius was said to have freed them both.

androecium male part of a flower, comprising a number of ◊stamens.

androgen general name for any male sex hormone, of which ◊testosterone is the most important. They are all ◊steroids and are principally involved in the production of male ◊secondary sexual characters (such as facial hair in humans).

Andromache /ænˈdrɒməki/ in Greek mythology, the faithful wife of Hector and mother of Astyanax. After the fall of Troy she was awarded to Neoptolemus, Achilles' son; she later married a Trojan seer called Helenus. Andromache is the heroine of Homer's ◊*Iliad* and the subject of a play by Euripides.

Andromeda /æn'drɒmɪdə/ in Greek mythology, an Ethiopian princess chained to a rock as a sacrifice to a sea monster. She was rescued by ◊Perseus, who married her.

Andromeda /æn'drɒmɪdə/ major constellation of the northern hemisphere, visible in autumn. Its main feature is the Andromeda galaxy. The star Alpha Andromedae forms one corner of the Square of Pegasus. It is named after the princess of Greek mythology.

Andromeda galaxy galaxy 2.2 million light years away from Earth in the constellation Andromeda, and the most distant object visible to the naked eye. It is the largest member of the ◊Local Group of galaxies. Like the Milky Way, it is a spiral orbited by several companion galaxies but contains about twice as many stars. It is about 200,000 light years across.

Andropov /æn'drɒpɒf/ Yuri 1914–1984. Soviet communist politician, president of the USSR 1983–84. As chief of the KGB 1967–82, he established a reputation for efficiently suppressing dissent.

Andropov was politically active from the 1930s. His part in quelling the Hungarian national uprising 1956, when he was Soviet ambassador, brought him into the Communist Party secretariat 1962 as a specialist on East European affairs. He became a member of the Politburo 1973 and succeeded Brezhnev as party general secretary 1982.

anechoic chamber room designed to be of high sound absorbency. All surfaces inside the chamber are covered by sound-absorbent materials such as rubber. The walls are often covered with inward-facing pyramids of rubber, to minimize reflections. It is used for experiments in ◊acoustics and for testing audio equipment.

anemone any plant of the genus *Anemone* of the buttercup family Ranunculaceae. The function of petals is performed by its sepals. The garden anemone *A. coronaria* is white, blue, red, or purple.

The Eurasian white wood anemone *A. nemorosa*, or windflower, grows in shady woods, flowering in spring. *Hepatica nobilis*, once included within *Anemone*, is common in the Alps. The ◊pasque flower is now placed in a separate genus.

anemophily type of ◊pollination in which the pollen is carried on the wind. Anemophilous flowers are usually unscented, have either very reduced petals and sepals or lack them altogether, and do not produce nectar.

In some species they are borne in ◊catkins. Male and female reproductive structures are commonly found in separate flowers. The male flowers have numerous exposed stamens, often on long filaments; the female flowers have long, often branched, feathery stigmas.

Many wind-pollinated plants, such as hazel *Corylus avellana*, bear their flowers before the leaves to facilitate the free transport of pollen. Since air movements are random, vast amounts of pollen are needed: a single birch catkin, for example, may produce over 5 million pollen grains.

anemometer device for measuring wind speed and liquid flow. A *cup-type anemometer* consists of cups at the ends of arms, which rotate when the wind blows. The speed of rotation indicates the wind speed. *Vane-type anemometers* have vanes, like a small windmill or propeller, that rotate when the wind blows. *Pressure-tube anemometers* use the pressure generated by the wind to indicate speed. The wind blowing into or across a tube develops a pressure, proportional to the wind speed, that is measured by a manometer or pressure gauge. *Hot-wire anemometers* work on the principle that the rate at which heat is transferred from a hot wire to the surrounding air is a measure of the air speed. Wind speed is determined by measuring either the electric current required to maintain a hot wire at a constant temperature, or the variation of resistance while a constant current is maintained.

Aneto, Pico /æˌnetəʊ'piːkəʊ/ highest peak of the Pyrenees mountains, rising to 3,400 m/11,052 ft in the Spanish province of Huesca.

Angad /'æŋgæd/ 1504–1552. Indian religious leader, second guru (teacher) of Sikhism 1539–52, succeeding Nanak. He popularized the alphabet known as *Gurmukhi*, in which the Sikh scriptures are written.

angel (Greek *angelos* 'messenger') in Jewish, Christian, and Muslim belief, a supernatural being intermediate between God and humans. The Christian hierarchy has nine orders: *Seraphim*, *Cherubim*, *Thrones* (who contemplate God and reflect his glory), *Dominations*, *Virtues*, *Powers* (who regulate the stars and the universe), *Principalities*, *Archangels*, and *Angels* (who minister to humanity). In traditional Catholic belief every human being has a guardian angel. The existence of angels was reasserted by the Pope in 1986.

angel dust popular name for the anaesthetic ◊*phencyclidine*.

Angel Falls /ˈeɪndʒəl/ highest waterfalls in the New World, on the river Caroní in the ropical rainforest of Bolívar Region, Venezuela; total height 978 m/3,210 ft. Named after the aviator and prospector James Angel who flew over the falls and crash-landed nearby 1935.

angelfish name for a number of unrelated fishes. The freshwater *angelfish*, genus *Pterophyllum*, of South America, is a tall, side-to-side flattened fish with a striped body, up to 26 cm/10 in long, but usually smaller in captivity. The *angelfish* or *monkfish*, of the genus *Squatina* is a bottom-living shark up to 1.8 m/6 ft long with a body flattened from top to bottom. The *marine angelfishes*, *Pomacanthus* and others, are long narrow-bodied fish with spiny fins, often brilliantly coloured, up to 60 cm/2 ft long, living around coral reefs in the tropics.

angelica any plant of the genus *Angelica* of the carrot family Umbelliferae. Mostly Eurasian in distribution, they are tall, perennial herbs with divided leaves and clusters of white or greenish flowers. The roots and fruits have long been used in cooking and for medicinal purposes.

A. archangelica is a culinary herb, the stems of which are preserved in sugar and used for cake decoration. *A. sylvestris*, the species found in Britain, has wedge-shaped leaves and clusters of white, pale violet, or pinkish flowers. The oil is used in perfume and liqueurs.

Angelico /ænˈdʒelɪkəʊ/ Fra (Guido di Pietro) *c.* 1400–1455. Italian painter of religious scenes, active in Florence. He was a monk and painted a series of frescoes at the monastery of San Marco, Florence, begun after 1436. He also produced several altarpieces in a simple style.

Fra Angelico joined the Dominican order about 1420. After his novitiate, he resumed a career as a painter of religious images and altarpieces, many of which have small predella scenes beneath them, depicting events in the life of a saint. The central images of the paintings are highly decorated with pastel colours and gold-leaf designs, while the predella scenes are often lively and relatively unsophisticated. There is a similar simplicity to his frescoes in the cells at San Marco, which are principally devotional works.

Angell /ˈeɪndʒəl/ Norman 1874–1967. British writer on politics and economics. In 1910 he acquired an international reputation with his book *The Great Illusion*, which maintained that any war must prove ruinous to the victors as well as to the vanquished. Nobel Peace Prize 1933.

Angelou /ˈændʒəluː/ Maya (born Marguerite Johnson) 1928– . US novelist, poet, playwright, and short-story writer. Her powerful autobiographical works, *I Know Why the Caged Bird Sings* 1970 and its three sequels, tell of the struggles towards physical and spiritual liberation of a black woman growing up in the South.

Angelou A telling commentator on American culture, US writer Maya Angelou achieved critical and popular success with her multi-volume autobiography.

Anger /ˈæŋgə/ Kenneth 1929– . US avant-garde filmmaker, brought up in Hollywood. His films, which dispense with conventional narrative, often use homosexual iconography and a personal form of mysticism. They include *Fireworks* 1947, *Scorpio Rising* 1964, and *Lucifer Rising* 1973.

He wrote the exposé *Hollywood Babylon*, the original version of which was published in France in 1959.

Angers /ɒnˈʒeɪ/ ancient French town, capital of Maine-et-Loire *département*, on the river Maine; population (1982) 196,000. Products include electrical machinery and Cointreau liqueur. It has a 12th–13th century cathedral and castle and was formerly the capital of the duchy and province of Anjou.

Angevin /ˈændʒɪvɪn/ relating to the reigns of the English kings Henry II, and Richard I (also known, with the later English kings up to Richard III, as the *Plantagenets*). Angevin derives from Anjou, the region in France controlled by English kings at this time. The *Angevin Empire* comprised the territories (including England) that belonged to the Anjou dynasty.

angina or *angina pectoris* severe pain in the chest due to impaired blood supply to the heart muscle because a coronary artery is narrowed.

angiosperm flowering plant in which the seeds are enclosed within an ovary, which ripens to a fruit. Angiosperms are divided into ◊monocotyledons (single seed leaf in the embryo) and ◊dicotyledons (two seed leaves in the embryo). They include the majority of flowers, herbs, grasses, and trees except conifers.

Angkor /ˈæŋkɔː/ site of the ancient capital of the Khmer Empire in NW Cambodia. N of Tonle Sap. The remains date mainly from the 10th–12th century AD, and comprise temples originally dedicated to the Hindu gods, shrines associated with Theravāda Buddhism, and royal palaces. Many are grouped within the enclosure called *Angkor Thom*, but the great temple of *Angkor Wat* (early 12th century) lies outside. Angkor was abandoned in the 15th century, and the ruins were overgrown by jungle and not adequately described until 1863. Buildings on the site suffered damage during the civil war 1970–75.

angle in geometry, an amount of rotation. By definition, an angle is a pair of rays (half-lines) that share a common endpoint but do not lie on the same line. Angles are measured in ◊degrees (°) or ◊radians, and are classified generally by their degree measures. *Acute angles* are less than 90°; *right angles* are exactly 90°; *obtuse angles* are greater than 90° but less than 180°; *reflex angles* are greater than 180° but less than 360°.

angler fish any of an order of fishes Lophiiformes, with flattened body and broad head and jaws. Many species have small, plant-like tufts on their skin. These act as camouflage for the fish as it waits, either floating among seaweed or lying on the sea bottom, twitching the enlarged tip of the thread-like first ray of its dorsal fin to entice prey.

There are over 200 species of angler fish, living in both deep and shallow water in temperate and tropical seas. The males of some species have become so small that they live as parasites on the females.

Anglesey /ˈæŋɡəlsɪ/ (Welsh *Ynys Môn*) island off the NW coast of Wales; area 720 sq km/278 sq mi; population (1981) 67,000. It is separated from the mainland by the Menai Straits, which are crossed by the Britannia tubular railway bridge and Telford's suspension bridge, built 1819–26 but since rebuilt. It is a holiday resort with rich fauna (notably bird life) and flora, and many buildings and relics of historic interest. The ancient granary of Wales, Anglesey now has industries such as toy-making, electrical goods, and bromine extraction from the sea. Holyhead is the principal town and port; Beaumaris was the county town until the county of Anglesey was merged into Gwynedd 1974.

Anglican Communion family of Christian churches including the Church of England, the US Episcopal Church, and those holding the same essential doctrines, that is the Lambeth Quadrilateral 1888 Holy Scripture as the basis of all doctrine, the Nicene and Apostles' Creeds, Holy Baptism and Holy Communion, and the historic episcopate.

In England the two archbishops head the provinces of Canterbury and York, which are subdivided into bishoprics. The Church Assembly 1919 was replaced 1970 by a General Synod with three houses (bishops, other clergy, and laity) to regulate church matters, subject to Parliament. A decennial Lambeth Conference (so called because the first was held there 1867), attended by bishops from all parts of the Anglican Communion, is presided over by the archbishop of Canterbury; it is not legislative but its decisions are often put into practice. In 1988 it passed a resolution seen as paving the way for the consecration of women bishops (the first was elected in the USA Sept 1988).

angling fishing with rod and line. It is the biggest participant sport in the UK.
Freshwater fishing embraces game fishing, in which members of the salmon family, such as salmon and trout, are taken by spinners (revolving lures) and flies (imitations of adult or larval insects); and coarse fishing, in which members of the carp family, pike, perch, and eels are taken by baits or lures, and (in the UK) are returned to the water virtually unharmed. In *seafishing* the catch includes flatfish, bass, and mackerel; big-

game fishes include shark, tuna or tunny, marlin, and swordfish. Competition angling exists and world championships take place for most branches of the sport. The oldest is the World Freshwater Championship, inaugurated 1957.

Anglo- combining language form with several related meanings. In *Anglo-Saxon* it refers to the Angles, a Germanic people who invaded Britain in the 5th to 7th centuries. In *Anglo-Welsh* it refers to England or the English. In *Anglo-American* it may refer either to England and the English or, commonly but less accurately, to Britain and the British (as in '*Anglo-American* relations'); it may also refer to the English language (as in '*Anglo-American* speech'); or to the Anglo-Saxon heritage in US society (as in WASP, white *Anglo-Saxon* Protestant).

Anglo-Irish Agreement or *Hillsborough Agreement* concord reached 1985 between the UK and Irish premiers, Margaret Thatcher and Garret FitzGerald. One sign of the improved relations between the two countries was increased cooperation between police and security forces across the border with Northern Ireland. The pact also gave the Irish Republic a greater voice in the conduct of Northern Ireland's affairs. However, the agreement was rejected by Northern Ireland Unionists as a step towards renunciation of British sovereignty.

Anglo-Saxon one of the several Germanic invaders (Angles, Saxons, and Jutes) who conquered much of Britain between the 5th and 7th centuries. After the conquest a number of kingdoms were set up, commonly referred to as the *Heptarchy*; these were united in the early 9th century under the overlordship of Wessex. The Norman invasion 1066 brought Anglo-Saxon rule to an end.

The Jutes probably came from the Rhineland and not, as was formerly believed, from Jutland. The Angles and Saxons came from Schleswig-Holstein, and may have united before invading. The Angles settled largely in East Anglia, Mercia, and Northumbria; the Saxons in Essex, Sussex, and Wessex; and the Jutes in Kent and S Hampshire.

There was probably considerable intermarriage with the Romanized Celts of ancient Britain, although the latter's language and civilization almost disappeared. The English-speaking peoples of Britain, the Commonwealth, and the USA are often referred to today as Anglo-Saxons, but the term is inaccurate, as the Welsh, Scots, and Irish are mainly of Celtic or Norse descent, and by the 1980s fewer than 15% of Americans were of British descent.

Anglo-Saxon art painting and sculpture of England from the 7th century to 1066. Sculpted crosses and ivories, manuscript painting, and gold and enamel jewellery survive. The relics of the Sutton Hoo ship burial, 7th century, and the *Lindisfarne Gospels*, about 690 (both British Museum, London), have typical Celtic ornamental patterns, but in manuscripts of southern England a different style emerged in the 9th century, with delicate, lively pen-and-ink figures and heavily decorative foliage borders.

Anglo-Saxon Chronicle history of England from the Roman invasion to the 11th century, in the form of a series of chronicles written in Old English by monks, begun in the 9th century (during the reign of King Alfred), and continuing to the 12th century.

The Chronicle, comprising seven different manuscripts, forms a unique record of early English history and of the development of Old English prose up to its final stages in the year 1154, by which date it had been superseded by Middle English.

Anglo-Saxon language group of dialects spoken by the Anglo-Saxon peoples who, in the 5th to 7th centuries, invaded and settled in Britain (in what became England and Lowland Scotland). Anglo-Saxon is traditionally known as Old English. See ◊English language.

Angola /æŋgəʊlə/ country in SW Africa, bounded W by the Atlantic ocean, N and

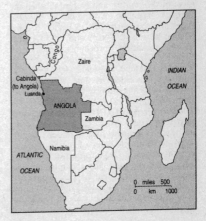

NE by Zaire, E by Zambia, and S by Namibia. The Cabinda enclave, a district of Angola, is bounded W by the Atlantic Ocean, N by the river Congo, and E and S by Zaire.

government The 1975 constitution, amended 1976, 1980, 1990 and 1992, created a one-party 'People's Republic', with political power held by the People's Movement for the Liberation of Angola–Workers' Party (MPLA–PT). The president, elected by the congress of MPLA–PT, chooses and chairs the council of ministers and is commander in chief of the armed forces. There is a 223-member people's assembly, 20 of whom are nominated by MPLA–PT and the rest elected by electoral colleges of 'loyal' citizens.

history Angola became a Portuguese colony 1491 and an Overseas Territory of Portugal 1951. A movement for complete independence, the MPLA, was established 1956, based originally in the Congo. This was followed by the formation of two other nationalist movements, the National Front for the Liberation of Angola (FNLA) and the National Union for the Total Independence of Angola (UNITA). War for independence from Portugal broke out 1961, with MPLA supported by socialist and communist states, UNITA helped by the Western powers and FNLA backed by the 'nonleft' power groups of southern Africa.

republic Three months of civil war followed the granting of full independence 1975, with MPLA and UNITA the main contestants, and foreign mercenaries and South African forces helping FNLA. By 1975 MPLA, with the help of mainly Cuban forces, controlled most of the country and had established the People's Republic of Angola in Luanda. Agostinho Neto, the MPLA leader, became its first president. FNLA and UNITA had, in the meantime, proclaimed their own People's Democratic Republic of Angola, based in Huambo. President Neto died 1979 and was succeeded by José Eduardo dos Santos, who maintained Neto's links with the Soviet bloc.

Lusaka Agreement UNITA guerrillas, supported by South Africa, continued to operate and combined forces raided Angola 1980–81 to attack bases of the South-West Africa People's Organization (◊SWAPO), who were fighting for Namibia's independence. South Africa proposed a complete withdrawal of its forces 1983 if Angola could guarantee that the areas vacated would not be filled by Cuban or SWAPO units. Angola accepted South Africa's proposals 1984, and a settlement was made (the Lusaka Agreement), whereby a Joint Monitoring Commission was set up to oversee South Africa's withdrawal, which was completed 1985. Relations between the two countries deteriorated 1986 when further South African raids into Angola occurred. UNITA also continued to receive South African support. Despite the securing of a peace treaty with South Africa and Cuba 1988, guerrilla activity by the UNITA rebels began again 1989.

cease-fire and peace A cease-fire negotiated June 1989 between the Luanda government and UNITA's Jonas ◊Savimbi collapsed two months later. However, a peace treaty was finally signed May 1991. President dos Santos promised a return to multiparty politics. A general election held in Sept 1992 was won by the MPLA, but the result was disputed by UNITA, which recommenced the civil war in Oct. By early Nov 1992 UNITA controlled more than half the country. In a reconciliatory gesture, UNITA was offered seats in the new government. Despite UNITA's eventual acceptance of the offer, fighting between government and rebel forces resumed. In 1993 fighting escalated, with famine reported in UNITA-besieged towns. The Dos Santos government was formally recognized by the USA. In Sept emergency airlifts began and the UN imposed sanctions against UNITA. In Aug 1994 the government and UNITA reached agreement on fair presidential elections.

Angora /ˈæŋɡɔːrə/ earlier form of ◊Ankara, Turkey, which gave its name to the Angora goat (see ◊mohair), and hence to other species of long-haired animal, such as the Angora rabbit (a native of the island of Madeira) and the Angora cat. Angora 'wool' from these animals has long, smooth fibres, and the demand for the fibre has led to wool farming in Europe, Japan, and the USA.

Angostura /ˌæŋɡəˈstjʊərə/ former name of ◊Ciudad Bolívar; port in Venezuela.

angostura flavouring prepared from oil distilled from the bitter, aromatic bark of either of two South American trees *Galipea officinalis* or *Cusparia trifoliata* of the rue family.

It is blended with herbs and other flavourings to give *angostura bitters*, which was first used as a stomach remedy and is now used to season food and fruit, to make a 'pink gin', and to prepare other alcoholic drinks.

Angry Young Men group of British writers who emerged about 1950 after the creative hiatus that followed World War II. They included Kingsley Amis, John Wain, John Osborne, and Colin Wilson. Also linked to the group were Iris Murdoch and Kenneth Tynan.

angst (German 'anxiety') an emotional state of anxiety without a specific cause. In ◊Existentialism, the term refers to general human anxiety at having free will, that is, of being responsible for one's actions.

angstrom unit (symbol Å) of length equal to 10–10 metre or one-hundred-millionth of a centimetre, used for atomic measurements and the wavelengths of electromagnetic radiation. It is named after the Swedish scientist A J Ångström.

Anguilla /æŋˈgwɪlə/ island in the E Caribbean
area 160 sq km/62 sq mi
capital The Valley
features white coral-sand beaches; has lost 80% of its coral reef through tourism (pollution and souvenir sales)
exports lobster, salt
currency Eastern Caribbean dollar
population (1988) 7,000
language English, Creole
government from 1982, governor, executive council, and legislative house of assembly (chief minister Emile Gumbs from 1984)
history a British colony from 1650, Anguilla was long associated with St Christopher-Nevis but revolted against alleged domination by the larger island and in 1969 declared itself a republic. A small British force restored order, and Anguilla retained a special position at its own request, since 1980 a separate dependency of the UK.

angular momentum see ◊momentum.

Angus /ˈæŋgəs/ former county and modern district on the E coast of Scotland, merged in 1975 in Tayside Region.

Anhui /ˌænˈhweɪ/ or *Anhwei* province of E China, watered by the Chang Jiang (Yangtze river)
area 139,900 sq km/54,000 sq mi
capital Hefei
products cereals in the N; cotton, rice, tea in the S
population (1986) 52,170,000.

Anhwei /ˌænˈhweɪ/ alternative spelling name of ◊Anhui.

anhydride chemical compound obtained by the removal of water from another compound; usually a dehydrated acid. For example, sulphur(VI) oxide (sulphur trioxide, SO_3) is the anhydride of sulphuric acid (H_2SO_4).

anhydrite naturally occurring anhydrous calcium sulphate ($CaSO_4$). It is used commercially for the manufacture of plaster of Paris and builders' plaster.

anhydrous of a chemical compound, containing no water. If the water of crystallization is removed from blue crystals of copper(II) sulphate, a white powder (anhydrous copper sulphate) results. Liquids from which all traces of water have been removed are also described as being anhydrous.

aniline (Portuguese *anil* 'indigo') $C_6H_5NH_2$ or *phenylamine* one of the simplest aromatic chemicals. When pure, it is a colourless oily liquid; it has a characteristic odour, and turns brown on contact with air. It occurs in coal tar, and is used in the rubber industry and to make drugs and dyes. It is highly poisonous.

Aniline was discovered in 1826, and was originally prepared by the dry distillation of ◊indigo, hence its name.

animal or *metazoan* member of the kingdom Animalia, one of the major categories of living things, the science of which is *zoology*. Animals are all ◊heterotrophs (they obtain their energy from organic substances produced by other organisms); they have ◊eukaryotic cells (the genetic material is contained within a distinct nucleus) bounded by a thin cell membrane rather than the thick cell wall of plants. In the past, it was common to include the single-celled ◊protozoa with the animals, but these are now classified as protists, together with single-celled plants. Thus all animals are multicellular. Most are capable of moving around for at least part of their life cycle.

The oldest land animals known date back 440 million years. Their remains were found in 1990 in a sandstone deposit near Ludlow, Shropshire, UK and included fragments of two centipedes a few centimetres long and a primitive spider measuring about 1 mm.

animal, domestic in general, a tame animal. In agriculture, it is an animal brought under human control for exploitation of its labour; use of its feathers, hide, or skin; or consumption of its eggs, milk, or meat. Common domestic animals include poultry, cattle (including buffalo), sheep, goats, and pigs. Staring about 10,000 years ago, the domestication of animals has only since World War II led to intensive ◊factory farming.

Increasing numbers of formerly wild species have been domesticated, with stress on scientific breeding for desired characteristics. At least 60% of the world's livestock is in developing countries, but the Third World consumes only 20% of all meat and milk produced. Most domestic animals graze plants that are not edible to humans, and 40% of the world's cereal production becomes animal feed; in the USA it is 90%.

animal liberation loose international movement against the infliction of suffering on animals, whether for scientific, military, or commercial research, or in raising them for food. The movement was sparked by the book *Animal Liberation* 1975 by Peter Singer and encompasses many different organizations.

animism in psychology and physiology, the view of human personality that attributes human life and behaviour to a force distinct from matter.

In religious theory, the conception of a spiritual reality behind the material one: for example, beliefs in the soul as a shadowy duplicate of the body capable of independent activity, both in life and death. In anthropology, the concept of spirits residing in all natural phenomena and objects.

Linked with this is the worship of natural objects such as stones and trees, thought to harbour spirits (naturism); fetishism; and ancestor worship.

anion ion carrying a negative charge. An electrolyte, such as the salt zinc chloride ($ZnCl_2$), is dissociated in aqueous solution or in the molten state into doubly-charged Zn^{2+} zinc ◊cations and singly-charged Cl^- anions. During electrolysis, the zinc cations flow to the cathode (to become discharged and liberate zinc metal) and the chloride anions flow to the anode.

anise plant *Pimpinella anisum*, of the carrot family Umbelliferae, whose fragrant seeds are used to flavour foods. Aniseed oil is used in cough medicines.

Anjou /ɑːnˈʒuː/ old countship and former province in N France; capital Angers. In 1154 the count of Anjou became king of England as Henry II, but the territory was lost by King John 1204. In 1480 the countship was annexed to the French crown. The *départements* of Maine-et-Loire and part of Indre-et-Loire, Mayenne, and Sarthe cover the area. The people are called Angevins—a name also applied by the English to the ◊Plantagenet kings.

Ankara /ˈæŋkərə/ (formerly *Angora*) capital of Turkey; population (1985) 2,252,000. Industries include cement, textiles, and leather products. It replaced Istanbul (then in Allied occupation) as capital 1923.

It has the presidential palace and Grand National Assembly buildings; three universities, including a technical university to serve the whole Middle East; the Atatürk mausoleum on a nearby hilltop; and the largest mosque in Turkey at Kocatepe.

ankh ancient Egyptian symbol (derived from the simplest form of sandal), meaning 'eternal life', as in Tut*ankh*amen. It consists of a T-shape surmounted by an oval.

Annaba /ˈænəbə/ (formerly *Bône*) seaport in Algeria; population (1983) 348,000. The name means 'city of jujube trees'. There are metallurgical industries, and iron ore and phosphates are exported.

Anna Comnena /ˈænə kɒmˈniːnə/ 1083–after 1148. Byzantine historian, daughter of the emperor ◊Alexius I, who was the historian of her father's reign. After a number of abortive attempts to alter the imperial succession in favour of her husband, Nicephorus Bryennius (*c.* 1062–1137), she retired to a convent to write her major work, the *Alexiad*. It describes the Byzantine view of public office, as well as the religious and intellectual life of the period.

Anna Karenina /kəˈrenɪnə/ a novel by Leo Tolstoy, published 1873–77. It describes a married woman's love affair with Vronski, a young officer, which ends with her suicide.

Annam /ˈænæm/ former country of SE Asia, incorporated in ◊Vietnam 1946 as Central Vietnam. A Bronze Age civilization was flourishing in the area when China conquered it about 214 BC. The Chinese named their conquest An-Nam, 'peaceful south'. Independent from 1428, Annam signed a treaty with France 1787 and became a French protectorate, part of Indochina 1884. During World War II, Annam was occupied by Japan.

Annamese member of the majority ethnic group in Vietnam, comprising 90% of the population. The Annamese language is distinct from Vietnamese, though it has been influenced by Chinese and has loan words from Khmer. Their religion combines elements of Buddhism, Confucianism, and Taoism, as well as ancestor worship.

Annapurna /ˌænəˈpɜːnə/ mountain 8,075 m/ 26,502 ft in the Himalayas, Nepal. The N face was first climbed by a French expedition (Maurice Herzog) 1950 and the S by a British team 1970.

Anne /æn/ 1665–1714. Queen of Great Britain and Ireland 1702–14. Second daughter of James, Duke of York, who became James II, and Anne Hyde. She succeeded William III in 1702. Events of her reign include the War of the Spanish Succession, Marlborough's victories at Blenheim, Ramillies, Oudenarde, and Malplaquet, and the union of the English and Scottish parliaments 1707. She was succeeded by George I.

She received a Protestant upbringing, and in 1683 married Prince George of Denmark (1653–1708). Of their many children only one survived infancy, William, Duke of Gloucester (1689–1700). For the greater part of her life Anne was a close friend of Sarah Churchill (1650–1744), wife of John Churchill (1650–1722), afterwards Duke of Marlborough; the Churchills' influence helped lead her to desert her father for her brother-in-law, William of Orange, during the Revolution of 1688, and later to engage in Jacobite intrigues. Her replacement of the Tories by a Whig government 1703–04 was her own act, not due to Churchillian influence. Anne finally broke with the Marlboroughs 1710, when Mrs Masham succeeded the duchess as her favourite, and supported the Tory government of the same year.

Anne /æn/ (full name Anne Elizabeth Alice Louise) 1950– . Princess of the UK, second child of Queen Elizabeth II, declared Princess Royal 1987. She is an excellent horsewoman, winning a gold medal at the 1976 Olympics, and is actively involved in global charity work, especially for children. In 1973 she married Captain Mark Phillips (1949–), of the Queen's Dragoon Guards; they separated in 1989. Their son Peter (1977–) was the first direct descendant of the Queen not to bear a title. They also have a daughter, Zara (1981–). In Dec 1992 she married Commander Tim Lawrence.

annealing process of heating a material (usually glass or metal) for a given time at a given temperature, followed by slow cooling, to increase ductility and strength. It is a common form of ◊heat treatment.

Ductile metals hardened by cold working may be softened by annealing. Thus thick wire may be annealed before being drawn into fine wire. Owing to internal stresses, glass objects made at high temperature can break spontaneously as they cool unless they are annealed. Annealing releases the stresses in a controlled way and, for glass for optical purposes, also improves the optical properties of the glass.

annelid any segmented worm of the phylum Annelida. Annelids include earthworms, leeches, and marine worms such as lugworms.

They have a distinct head and soft body, which is divided into a number of similar segments shut off from one another internally by membranous partitions.

Anne of Austria /æn/ 1601–1666. Queen of France from 1615 and regent 1643–61. Daughter of Philip III of Spain, she married Louis XIII of France (whose chief minister, Cardinal Richelieu, worked against her). On her husband's death she became regent for their son, Louis XIV, until his majority.

She was much under the influence of Cardinal Mazarin, her chief minister, to whom she was supposed to be secretly married.

Anne of Cleves /æn/ 1515–1557. Fourth wife of ◊Henry VIII of England 1540. She was the daughter of the Duke of Cleves, and was recommended to Henry as a wife by Thomas ◊Cromwell, who wanted an alliance with German Protestantism against the Holy Roman Empire. Henry did not like her looks, had the marriage declared void after six months, pensioned her, and had Cromwell beheaded.

annihilation in nuclear physics, a process in which a particle and its 'mirror image' particle or ◊antiparticle collide and disappear, with the creation of a burst of energy. The energy created is equivalent to the mass of the colliding particles in accordance with the ◊mass-energy equation. For example, an electron and a positron annihilate to produce a burst of high-energy X-rays.

anno Domini (Latin 'in the year of our Lord') in the Christian chronological system, refers to dates since the birth of Jesus, denoted by the letters AD. There is no year 0, so AD 1 follows immediately after the year 1 BC (before Christ). The system became the standard reckoning in the Western world after being adopted by the English historian Bede in the 8th century. The abbreviations CE (Common Era) and BCE (before

Common Era) are often used instead by scholars and writers as objective, rather than religious, terms.

The system is based on the calculations made 525 by Dionysius Exiguus, a Scythian monk, but the birth of Jesus should more correctly be placed about 4 BC.

annual general meeting (AGM) yearly meeting of the shareholders of a company or the members of an organization, at which business including consideration of the annual report and accounts, the election of officers, and the appointment of auditors is normally carried out.

UK company law requires an AGM to be called by the board of directors.

annual percentage rate (APR) the charge (including ◊interest) for granting consumer credit, expressed as an equivalent once-a-year percentage figure of the amount of the credit granted. It is usually approximately double the flat rate of interest, or simple interest. In the UK, lenders are legally required to state the APR when advertising loans.

annual plant plant that completes its life cycle within one year, during which time it germinates, grows to maturity, bears flowers, produces seed and then dies. Examples include the common poppy *Papaver rhoeas* and groundsel *Senecio vulgaris*. Among garden plants, some that are described as 'annuals' are actually perennials, although usually cultivated as annuals because they cannot survive winter frosts. See also ◊ephemeral plant, ◊biennial plant, ◊perennial plant.

annual rings or *growth rings* concentric rings visible on the wood of a cut tree trunk or other woody stem. Each ring represents a period of growth when new ◊xylem is laid down to replace tissue being converted into wood (secondary xylem). The wood formed from xylem produced in the spring and early summer has larger and more numerous vessels than the wood formed from xylem produced in autumn when growth is slowing down. The result is a clear boundary between the pale spring wood and the denser, darker autumn wood. Annual rings may be used to estimate the age of the plant (see ◊dendrochronology), although occasionally more than one growth ring is produced in a given year.

Annunciation in the New Testament, the announcement to Mary by the angel Gabriel that she was to be the mother of Christ; the feast of the Annunciation is 25 March (also known as Lady Day).

anode in chemistry, the positive electrode of an electrolytic ◊cell, towards which negative particles (anions), usually in solution, are attracted. See ◊electrolysis.

An anode is given its positive charge by the application of an external electrical potential, unlike the positive electrode of an an electrical (battery) cell, which acquires its charge in the course of a spontaneous chemical reaction taking place within the cell.

anodizing process that increases the resistance to ◊corrosion of a metal, such as aluminium, by building up a protective oxide layer on the surface. The natural corrosion resistance of aluminium is provided by a thin film of aluminium oxide; anodizing increases the thickness of this film and thus the corrosion protection.

It is so called because the metal becomes the ◊anode in an electrolytic bath containing a solution of, for example, sulphuric or chromic acid as the ◊electrolyte. During ◊electrolysis oxygen is produced at the anode, where it combines with the metal to form an oxide film.

anomie in the social sciences, a state of 'normlessness' created by the breakdown of commonly agreed standards of behaviour and morality; the term often refers to situations where the social order appears to have collapsed. The concept was developed by the French sociologist Emile Durkheim.

Durkheim used 'anomie' to describe societies in transition during industrialization. The term was adapted by the US sociologist Robert Merton to explain deviance and crime in the USA as a result of the disparity between high goals and limited opportunities.

anorexia lack of desire to eat, especially the pathological condition of *anorexia nervosa*, usually found in adolescent girls and young women, who may be obsessed with the desire to lose weight. Compulsive eating, or ◊bulimia, often accompanies anorexia.

Anouilh /ænuːiː/ Jean 1910–1987. French dramatist. His plays, influenced by the Neo-Classical tradition, include *Antigone* 1942, *L'Invitation au château/Ring Round the Moon* 1947, *Colombe* 1950, and *Becket* 1959, about St Thomas à Becket and Henry II.

anoxaemia shortage of oxygen in the blood; insufficient supply of oxygen to the tissues. Anoxaemia may result from breathing air that is deficient in oxygen (for instance, at high altitude or where there are noxious fumes), a disease of the lungs, or other disorder where the oxygen-carrying capacity of the blood is impaired.

Anquetil /ˌɒŋkəˈtiːl/ Jacques 1934–1988. French cyclist, the first person to win the Tour de France five times (between 1957 and 1964), a record later equalled by Eddie ◊Merckx and Bernard ◊Hinault.

Anschluss /ˈænʃlʊs/ (German 'union') the annexation of Austria with Germany, accomplished by the German chancellor Adolf Hitler 12 March 1938.

Anselm, St /ˈænselm/ c. 1033–1109. Medieval priest and philosopher. Born in Piedmont, he was educated at the abbey of Bec in Normandy, which as an abbot (from 1078) he made a centre of scholarship in Europe. He was appointed archbishop of Canterbury by William II of England 1093, but was later forced into exile. He holds an important place in the development of ◊Scholasticism.

Anshan /ˌænˈʃæn/ Chinese city in Liaoning province, 89 km/55 mi SE of Shenyang (Mukden); population (1986) 1,280,000. The iron and steel centre started here 1918 was expanded by the Japanese, dismantled by the Russians, and restored by the Communist government of China. It produces 6 million tonnes of steel annually.

ANSI (abbreviation for *American National Standards Institution*) US national standards body. It sets official procedures in (among other areas) computing and electronics.

Anson /ˈænsən/ George, 1st Baron Anson 1697–1762. English admiral who sailed around the world 1740–44. In 1740 he commanded the squadron attacking the Spanish colonies and shipping in South America; he returned home by circumnavigating the world, with £500,000 of Spanish treasure. He carried out reforms at the Admiralty, which increased the efficiency of the British fleet and contributed to its success in the Seven Years' War (1756–63) against France.

ant insect belonging to the family Formicidae, and to the same order (Hymenoptera) as bees and wasps. Ants are characterized by a conspicuous 'waist' and elbowed antennae. About 10,000 different species are known; all are social in habit, and all construct nests of various kinds. Ants are found in all parts

Anson An engraving (1744) of the English admiral George Anson, who circumnavigated the world and looted £500,000 of Spanish treasure.

of the world, except the polar regions. It is estimated that there are about 10 million billion ants.

Ant behaviour is complex, but it serves the colony rather than the individual. Ants find their way by light patterns, gravity (special sense organs are located in the joints of their legs), and chemical trails between food areas and the nest.

Communities include *workers*, sterile wingless females, often all alike, although in some species large-headed 'soldiers' are differentiated; *fertile females*, fewer in number and usually winged; and *males*, also winged and smaller than their consorts, with whom they leave the nest on a nuptial flight at certain times of the year. After aerial mating, the males die, and the fertilized queens lose their wings when they settle, laying eggs to found their own new colonies. The eggs hatch into wormlike larvae, which then pupate in silk cocoons before emerging as adults. *Remarkable species* include army (South American) and driver (African) ants, which march nomadically in huge columns, devouring even tethered animals in their path; leaf-cutter ants, genus *Atta*, which use pieces of leaf to grow edible fungus in underground 'gardens'; weaver ants, genus *Oecophylla*, which use their silk-producing larvae as living shuttles to bind the edges of leaves together to

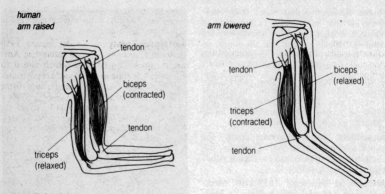

human
arm raised

tendon

biceps
(contracted)

tendon

triceps
(relaxed)

arm lowered

tendon

biceps
(relaxed)

triceps
(contracted)

tendon

antagonistic muscles

form the nest; Eurasian robber ants, *Formica sanguinea*, which raid the nests of another ant species *Formica fusca*, for pupae, then use the adults as 'slaves' when they hatch; and honey ants, in which some workers serve as distended honey stores. In some species, 'warfare' is conducted. Others are pastoralists, tending herds of ◊aphids and collecting a sweet secretion ('honeydew') from them.

Antabuse /ˈæntəbjuːz/ proprietary name for disulfiram, a synthetic chemical used in the treatment of alcoholism. It produces unpleasant side effects if combined with alcohol, such as nausea, headaches, palpitations, and collapse. The 'Antabuse effect' is produced coincidentally by certain antibiotics.

antacid any substance that neutralizes stomach acid, such as sodium bicarbonate or magnesium hydroxide ('milk of magnesia'). Antacids are weak ◊bases, swallowed as solids or emulsions. They may be taken between meals to relieve symptoms of hyperacidity, such as pain, bloating, nausea, and 'heartburn'. Excessive or prolonged need for antacids should be investigated medically.

antagonistic muscles in the body, a pair of muscles allowing coordinated movement of the skeletal joints. The extension of the arm, for example, requires one set of muscles to relax, while another set contracts. The individual components of antagonistic pairs can be classified into extensors (muscles that straighten a limb) and flexors (muscles that bend a limb).

Antakya /ænˈtɑːkjə/ or *Hatay* city in SE Turkey, site of the ancient ◊Antioch; population (1985) 109,200.

Antalya /ænˈtɑːljə/ Mediterranean port on the W coast of Turkey and capital of a province of the same name; population (1985) 258,000. The port trades in agricultural and forest produce.

Antananarivo /ˌæntənænəˈriːvəʊ/ (formerly *Tananarive*) capital of Madagascar, on the interior plateau, with a rail link to Tamatave; population (1986) 703,000.

Antarctica /ænˈtɑːktɪkə/ ice-covered continent surrounding the South Pole, arbitrarily defined as the region lying S of the Antarctic Circle. Occupying 10% of the world's surface, Antarctica contains 90% of the world's ice and 70% of its fresh water
area 13,900,000 sq km/5,400,000 sq mi (the size of Europe and the USA combined)
physical formed of two blocs of rock with an area of about 8 million sq km/3 million sq mi, Antarctica is covered by a cap of ice that flows slowly toward its 22,400 km/14,000 mi coastline, reaching the sea in high ice cliffs. The most southerly shores are near the 78th parallel in the Ross and Weddell Seas. E Antarctica is a massive bloc of ancient rocks that surface in the Transantarctic Mountains of Victoria Land. Separated by a deep channel, W Antarctica is characterized by the mountainous regions of Graham Land, the Antarctic Peninsula, Palmer Land, and Ellsworth Land; the highest peak is Vinson Massif (5,139 m/16,866 ft). Little more than 1% of the land is ice-free. With an estimated volume of 24 million cu m/5.9 million cu mi, the ice-cap has a mean thickness of 1,880 m/6,170 ft and in places reaches depths of 5,000 m/16,000 ft or more. Each annual layer

of snow preserves a record of global conditions, and where no melting at the surface of the bedrock has occurred the ice can be a million years old

climate winds are strong and temperatures are cold, particularly in the interior where temperatures can drop to $-70°C/-100°F$ and below. Precipitation is largely in the form of snow or hoar-frost rather than rain which rarely exceeds 50 mm/2 in per year (less than the Sahara Desert)

flora and fauna relatively few species of higher plants and animals, and a short food chain from iny marine plants to whales, seals, penguins, and other sea birds. Only two species of vascular plant are known, but there are about 60 species of moss, 100 species of lichen, and 400 species of algae

features Mount Erebus on Ross Island is the world's southernmost active volcano; the Ross Ice Shelf is formed by several glaciers coalescing in the Ross Sea

products cod, Antarctic icefish, and krill are fished in Antarctic waters. Whaling, which began in the early 20th century, ceased during the 1960s as a result of overfishing. Petroleum, coal, and minerals, such as palladium and platinum exist, but their exploitation is prevented by a 50-year ban on commercial mining agreed by 39 nations 1991

population no permanent residents; settlement limited to scientific research stations with maximum population of 2,000 to 3,000 during the summer months. Sectors of Antarctica are claimed by Argentina, Australia, Chile, France, the UK, Norway, and New Zealand.

Antarctic Circle imaginary line that encircles the South Pole at latitude 66° 32′ S. The line encompasses the continent of Antarctica and the Antarctic Ocean.

The region south of this line experiences at least one night during the southern summer during which the sun never sets, and at least one day during the southern winter during which the sun never rises.

Antarctic Ocean /ænt'ɑːktɪk/ popular name for the reaches of the Atlantic, Indian, and Pacific oceans extending S of the Antarctic Circle (66° 32′ S). The term is not used by the International Hydrographic Bureau.

Antarctic Peninsula /ænt'ɑːktɪk/ mountainous peninsula of W Antarctica extending 1,930 km/1,200 mi N towards South America; originally named *Palmer Land* after a US navigator, Captain Nathaniel Palmer, who was the first to explore the region 1820. It was claimed by Britain 1832, Chile 1942, and Argentina 1940. Its name was changed to the Antarctic Peninsula 1964.

Antarctic Treaty agreement signed 1959 between 12 nations with an interest in Antarctica (including Britain), which aimed to promote scientific research and keep Antarctica free from conflict. It came into force 1961 for a 30-year period, and by 1990 a total of 35 countries were party to it. Its provisions (covering the area south of latitude 60° S) neither accepted nor rejected any nation's territorial claims, but barred any new ones; imposed a ban on military operations and large-scale mineral extraction; and allowed for free exchange of scientific data from bases. Since 1980 the treaty has been extended to conserve marine resources within the larger area bordered by the Antarctic Convergence, and in 1991 a 50-year ban on mining activity was secured.

anteater mammal of the family Myrmecophagidae, order Edentata, native to Mexico, Central America, and tropical South America. An anteater lives almost entirely on ants and termites. It has toothless jaws, an extensile tongue, and claws for breaking into the nests of its prey.

Species include the giant anteater *Myrmecophaga tridactyla*, about 1.8 m/6 ft long including the tail, the tamandua or collared anteater *Tamandua tetradactyla*, about 90 cm/3.5 ft long, and the silky anteater *Cyclopes didactyla*, about 35 cm/14 in long. The name is also incorrectly applied to the aardvark, the echidna, and the pangolin.

antelope any of numerous kinds of even-toed, hoofed mammals belonging to the cow family, Bovidae. Most antelopes are lightly built and good runners. They are grazers or browsers, and chew the cud. They range in size from the dik-diks and duikers, only 30 cm/1 ft high, to the eland, which can be 1.8 m/6 ft at the shoulder.

The majority of antelopes are African, including the eland, gnu, kudu, springbok, and waterbuck, although other species live in Asia, including the deserts of Arabia and the Middle East. The pronghorn antelope *Antilocapra americana* of North America belongs to a different family, the Antilocapridae.

antenna in zoology, an appendage ('feeler') on the head. Insects, centipedes, and millipedes each have one pair of antennae but there are two pairs in crustaceans, such as shrimps. In insects, the antennae are usually involved with the senses of smell and touch;

they are frequently complex structures with large surface areas that increase the ability to detect scents.

antenna in radio and television, another name for ◊aerial.

anterior in biology, the front of an organism, usually the part that goes forward first when the animal is moving. The anterior end of the nervous system, over the course of evolution, has developed into a brain with associated receptor organs able to detect stimuli including light and chemicals.

anthelion (Greek 'antisun') solar halo caused by a reflection from the atmosphere, snow, or ice, sometimes appearing at the same altitude as the Sun but opposite to it.

anther in a flower, the terminal part of a stamen in which the ◊pollen grains are produced. It is usually borne on a slender stalk or filament, and has two lobes, each containing two chambers, or pollen sacs, within which the pollen is formed.

Anthony /ˈænθəni/ Susan B(rownell) 1820–1906. US pioneering campaigner for women's rights who also worked for the antislavery and temperance movements. Her causes included equality of pay for women teachers, married women's property rights, and women's suffrage. In 1869, with Elizabeth Cady ◊Stanton, she founded the National Woman Suffrage Association.

Anthony of Padua, St /ˈæntəni/ 1195–1231. Portuguese Franciscan preacher who opposed the relaxations introduced into the order. Born in Lisbon, the son of a nobleman, he became an Augustinian monk, but in 1220 joined the Franciscans. Like St Francis, he is said to have preached to animals. He died in Padua, Italy and was canonized 1232.

Anthony, St /ˈæntəni/ c. 251–356. Also known as Anthony of Thebes. Born in Egypt, he was the founder of Christian monasticism. At the age of 20, he renounced all his possessions and began a hermetic life of study and prayer, later seeking further solitude in a cave in the desert.

In 305 Anthony founded the first cenobitic order, a community of Christians following a rule of life under a superior. Late in his life he went to Alexandria and preached against ◊Arianism. He lived to over 100, and a good deal is known about his life since a biography (by St Athanasius) has survived. Anthony's temptations in the desert were a popular subject in art; he is also often depicted with a pig and a bell.

anthracene white, glistening, crystalline, tricyclic, aromatic hydrocarbon with a faint blue fluorescence when pure. Its melting point is about 216°C/421°F and its boiling point 351°C/664°F. It occurs in the high-boiling-point fractions of coal tar, where it was discovered 1832 by the French chemists Auguste Laurent (1808–1853) and Jean Dumas (1800–1884).

anthracite (from Greek *anthrax*, 'coal') hard, dense, glossy variety of ◊coal, containing over 90% of fixed carbon and a low percentage of ash and volatile matter, which causes it to burn without flame, smoke, or smell.

Anthracite gives intense heat, but is slow-burning and slow to light; it is therefore unsuitable for use in open fires. Its characteristic composition is thought to be due to the action of bacteria in disintegrating the coal-forming material when it was laid down during the ◊Carboniferous period.

Among the chief sources of anthracite coal are Pennsylvania in the USA; S Wales, UK; the Donbas, Ukraine and Russia; and Shanxi province, China.

anthrax cattle and sheep disease occasionally transmitted to humans, usually via infected hides and fleeces. It may develop as black skin pustules or severe pneumonia. Treatment is with antibiotics.

In the 17th century, some 60,000 cattle died in a European pandemic known as the Black Bane, thought to have been anthrax. The disease is described by the Roman poet Virgil and may have been the cause of the biblical fifth plague of Egypt.

A British biological-warfare experiment with anthrax during World War II rendered the island of Gruinard (off the west coast of Scotland) uninhabitable for more than 40 years.

In 1989 an outbreak of anthrax at Singret farm, in Wales, near Wrexham, killed 30 pigs, and the entire herd of 4,700 was subsequently destroyed.

anthropic principle in science, the idea that 'the universe is the way it is because if it were different we would not be here to observe it'. The principle arises from the observation that if the laws of science were even slightly different, it would have been impossible for intelligent life to evolve. For example, if the electric charge on the electron were only slightly different, stars would have been unable to burn hydrogen and produce the chemical elements that make up our bodies. Scientists are undecided whether the principle is an insight into the nature of the universe or a piece of circular reasoning.

anthropoid any primate belonging to the suborder Anthropoidea, including monkeys, apes, and humans.

anthropology (Greek *anthropos* 'man' and *logos* 'discourse') the study of humankind, which developed following 19th-century evolutionary theory to investigate the human species, past and present, physically, socially, and culturally.

anthropomorphism the attribution of human characteristics to animals, inanimate objects, or deities. It appears in the mythologies of many cultures and as a literary device in fables and allegories.

anthroposophy system of mystical philosophy developed by Rudolf ◊Steiner, who claimed to possess a power of intuition giving him access to knowledge not attainable by scientific means.

Antibes /onˈtiːb/ resort, which includes Juan les Pins, on the French Riviera, in the *département* of Alpes Maritimes; population (1982) 63,248. There is a Picasso collection in the 17th-century castle museum.

antibiotic drug that kills or inhibits the growth of bacteria and fungi. It is derived from living organisms such as fungi or bacteria, which distinguishes it from synthetic antimicrobials.

The earliest antibiotics, the ◊penicillins, came into use from 1941 and were quickly joined by ◊chloramphenicol, the ◊cephalosporins, erythromycins, tetracyclines, and aminoglycosides. A range of broad-spectrum antibiotics, the 4-quinolones, was developed 1989, of which ciprofloxacin was the first. Each class and individual antibiotic acts in a different way and may be effective against either a broad spectrum or a specific type of disease-causing agent. Use of antibiotics has become more selective as side effects, such as toxicity, allergy, and resistance, have become better understood. Bacteria have the ability to develop immunity following repeated or subclinical (insufficient) doses, so more advanced antibiotics are continually required to overcome them.

antibody protein molecule produced in the blood by ◊lymphocytes in response to the presence of invading substances, or ◊antigens, including the proteins carried on the surface of microorganisms. Antibody production is only one aspect of ◊immunity in vertebrates.

Each antibody is specific for its particular antigen and combines with it to form a 'complex'. This action may neutralize antigens such as toxins, or it may destroy microorganisms by setting off chemical changes that cause them to self-destruct. In other cases, the formation of a complex will cause antigens to form clumps that can then be detected and disposed of by immune cells, such as ◊macrophages and ◊phagocytes, which respond to the presence of the antibodies. Many diseases can only be contracted once because antibodies remain in the blood after the infection has passed, preventing any further invasion. Vaccination boosts a person's resistance by causing the production of antibodies specific to particular infections.

Large quantities of specific antibodies can now be obtained by the monoclonal technique (see ◊monoclonal antibodies). In 1989 a Cambridge University team developed genetically engineered bacteria to make a small part of an antibody (single domain antibodies) which bind to invaders such as toxins, bacteria, and viruses. Since they are smaller, they penetrate tissues more easily, and are potentially more effective in clearing organs of toxins. They can be produced more quickly, using fewer laboratory mice, and unlike conventional antibodies, they also disable viruses. In addition, single domain antibodies can be used to highlight other molecules, such as hormones in pregnancy testing.

anticholinergic any drug that blocks the passage of certain nerve impulses in the ◊central nervous system by inhibiting the production of acetylcholine, a neurotransmitter.

Its wide range of effects makes it an effective component of ◊premedication: it may be put in the eyes before examination or treatment to dilate the pupil and paralyse the muscles of accommodation, or inhaled to relieve constriction of the airways in bronchitis. Tremor and rigidity can be reduced in mild ◊Parkinson's disease. Bladder muscle tone may also be improved in the treatment of urinary frequency. Its usefulness as an ◊antispasmodic is limited by side effects, such as dry mouth, visual disturbances, and urinary retention.

Antichrist in Christian theology, the opponent of Christ. The appearance of the Antichrist was believed to signal the Second Coming, at which Christ would conquer his opponent. The concept may stem from the idea of conflict between Light and Darkness, which is present in Persian, Babylonian, and Jewish literature and which influenced early Christian thought. The Antichrist may be a false messiah, or be connected with false teaching, or be identified with an individual, for example Nero at the time of the persecution of Christians, and the pope and Napoleon in later Christian history.

anticline in geology, a fold in the rocks of the Earth's crust in which the layers or beds bulge upwards to form an arch (seldom preserved intact).

The fold of an anticline may be undulating or steeply curved. A steplike bend in otherwise gently dipping or horizontal beds is a *monocline*. The opposite of an anticline is a *syncline*.

anticoagulant substance that suppresses the formation of ◊blood clots. Common anticoagulants are heparin, produced by the liver and lungs, and derivatives of coumarin. Anticoagulants are used medically in treating heart attacks, for example. They are also produced by blood-feeding animals, such as mosquitoes, leeches, and vampire bats, to keep the victim's blood flowing.

Most anticoagulants prevent the production of thrombin, an enzyme that induces the formation from blood plasma of fibrinogen, to which blood platelets adhere and form clots.

Anti-Comintern Pact (Anti-Communist Pact) agreement signed between Germany and Japan 25 Nov 1936, opposing communism as a menace to peace and order. The pact was signed by Italy 1937 and by Hungary, Spain, and the Japanese puppet state of Manchukuo in 1939. While directed against the USSR, the agreement also had the effect of giving international recognition to Japanese rule in Manchuria.

anticonvulsant any drug used to prevent epileptic seizures (convulsions or fits); see ◊epilepsy.

In many cases, epilepsy can be controlled completely by careful therapy with one agent. Patients should stop or change treatment only under medical supervision.

Anti-Corn Law League in UK history, an extra-parliamentary pressure group formed 1838, led by the Liberals ◊Cobden and ◊Bright, which argued for free trade and campaigned successfully against duties on the import of foreign corn to Britain imposed by the ◊Corn Laws, which were repealed 1846.

Formed Sept 1838 by Manchester industrialists and campaigning on a single issue, the league initiated strategies for popular mobilization and agitation including mass meetings, lecture tours, pamphleteering, opinion polls, and parliamentary lobbying. Reaction by the conservative landed interests was organized with the establishment of the Central Agricultural Protection Society, nicknamed the Anti-League. In June 1846 political pressure, the state of the economy, and the Irish situation prompted Prime Minister ◊Peel to repeal the Corn Laws.

anticyclone area of high atmospheric pressure caused by descending air, which becomes warm and dry. Winds radiate from a calm centre, taking a clockwise direction in the northern hemisphere and an anticlockwise direction in the southern hemisphere. Anticyclones are characterized by clear weather and the absence of rain and violent winds. In summer they bring hot, sunny days and in winter they bring fine, frosty spells, although fog and low cloud are not uncommon. *Blocking anticyclones*, which prevent the normal air circulation of an area, can cause summer droughts and severe winters.

For example, the summer drought in Britain 1976, and the severe winters of 1947 and 1963 were caused by blocking anticyclones.

antidepressant any drug used to relieve symptoms in depressive illness. The two main groups are the tricyclic antidepressants (TCADs) and the monoamine oxidase inhibitors (MAOIs), which act by altering chemicals available to the central nervous system. Both may produce serious side effects and are restricted.

Antietam, Battle of /ænˈtiːtəm/ bloody but indecisive battle of the American Civil War 17 Sept 1862 at Antietam Creek, off the Potomac River. General McClellan of the Union blocked the advance of the Confederates under Robert E Lee on Maryland and Washington DC. This battle persuaded the British not to recognize the Confederacy.

antifreeze substance added to a water-cooling system (for example, that of a car) to prevent it freezing in cold weather. The most common types of antifreeze contain the chemical ethylene ◊glycol, an organic alcohol with a freezing point of about –15°C/5°F.

The addition of this chemical depresses the freezing point of water significantly. A solution containing 33.5% by volume of ethylene glycol will not freeze until about –20°C/–4°F. A 50% solution will not freeze until –35°C/–31°F.

antifungal any drug that acts against fungal infection, such as ringworm and athlete's foot.

antigen any substance that causes the production of ◊antibodies. Common antigens include the proteins carried on the surface of bacteria, viruses, and pollen grains. The proteins of incompatible blood groups or tissues also act as antigens, which has to be taken into account in medical procedures such as blood transfusions and organ transplants.

Antigone tragedy by Sophocles, written about 411 BC. Antigone buries her brother Polynices, in defiance of the Theban king Creon, but in accordance with the wishes of the gods. Creon imprisons Antigone in a cave, but after a warning that he has defied the gods, he goes to the cave and finds that Antigone has hanged herself.

Antigonus /æn'tɪgənəs/ 382–301 BC. A general of Alexander the Great, after whose death 323 he made himself master of Asia Minor. He was defeated and slain by ◊Seleucus I at the battle of Ipsus.

Antigua and Barbuda /æn'tiːgə, bɑːˈbjuːdə/ country comprising three islands in the E Caribbean (Antigua, Barbuda, and uninhabited Redonda).

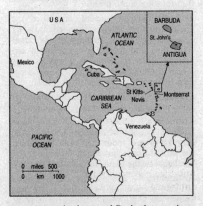

government Antigua and Barbuda constitute an independent sovereign nation within the ◊Commonwealth, with the British monarch as head of state. The constitution came into effect with independence 1981. The governor general, representing the British monarch, is appointed on the advice of the Antiguan prime minister, who is chosen by the governor general as the person most likely to have the support of the legislature. The parliament is similar to Britain's, with a prime minister and cabinet answerable to it. It consists of a senate and a house of representatives, each having 17 members. Senators are appointed for a five-year term by the governor general, 11 of them on the advice of the prime minister, four on the advice of the leader of the opposition, one at the governor general's own discretion, and one on the advice of the Barbuda Council, the main instrument for local government. Members of the house of representatives are elected by universal suffrage for a similar term. here are several political parties, the most significant being the Antigua Labour Party (ALP).

history The original inhabitants of Antigua and Barbuda were Carib Indians. The first Europeans to visit Antigua were with Christopher ◊Columbus 1493, although they did not go ashore. He named the island after the church of Santa María de la Antigua at Seville. Antigua was first colonized by Britain 1632. Charles II leased Barbuda 1685 to the Codrington family, who ran a sugar plantation on Antigua. Barbuda was a source of stock and provisions for the plantation and was inhabited almost entirely by black slaves, who used the relatively barren land cooperatively. The Codringtons finally surrendered the lease 1870. Barbuda reverted to the crown in the later 19th century. The Antiguan slaves were freed 1834 but remained poor, totally dependent on the sugar crop market. Between 1860 and 1959 the islands were administered by Britain within a federal system known as the ◊Leeward Islands. Antigua and Barbuda was made an Associated State of the UK and given full internal independence 1967, with Britain retaining responsibility for defence and foreign affairs. Barbuda, with a population of about 1,200 people, started a separatist movement 1969, fearing that Antigua would sell Barbudan land to foreign developers. Projects approved by the central government against the wishes of Barbudans include sand mining and a plan for a toxic-waste disposal site.

independence from Britain In the 1971 general election, the Progressive Labour Movement (PLM) won a decisive victory, and its leader, George Walter, replaced Vere Bird, leader of the ALP, as prime minister. The PLM fought the 1976 election on a call for early independence while the ALP urged caution until a firm economic foundation had been laid. The ALP won and declared 1978 that the country was ready for independence. Opposition from the inhabitants of Barbuda delayed the start of constitutional talks, and the territory eventually became independent as Antigua and Barbuda 1981. Despite its policy of ◊nonalignment, the ALP government actively assisted the US invasion of ◊Grenada 1983 and went on to win 16 of the 17 seats in the 1984 general election. In the 1989 general election Bird and the ALP won a sweeping victory.

antihistamine any substance that counteracts the effects of ◊histamine. Antihistamines may be naturally produced (such as vitamin C and epinephrin) or synthesized (pseudepinephrin).

H_1 antihistamines are used to relieve allergies, alleviating symptoms such as runny nose, itching, swelling, or asthma. H_2 antihistamines suppress acid production by the stomach, providing treatment for peptic ulcers that often makes surgery unnecessary.

antiknock substance added to petrol to reduce knocking in car engines. It is a mixture of dibromoethane and tetraethyl lead.

Its use in leaded petrol has resulted in atmospheric pollution by lead compounds. Children exposed to this form of pollution over long periods of time can suffer impaired learning ability. Unleaded petrol has been used in the USA for some years, and is increasingly popular in the UK. Leaded petrol cannot be used in cars fitted with ◊catalytic converters.

Anti-Lebanon /ˌænti'lebənən/ or *Antilibanus* mountain range on the Lebanese-Syrian border, including Mount Hermon, 2,800 m/9,200 ft. It is separated from the Lebanon mountains by the Bekaa valley.

Antilles /æn'tɪliːz/ the whole group of West Indian islands, divided N–S into the *Greater Antilles* (Cuba, Jamaica, Haiti–Dominican Republic, Puerto Rico) and *Lesser Antilles*, subdivided into the Leeward Islands (Virgin Islands, St Kitts–Nevis, Antigua and Barbuda, Anguilla, Montserrat, and Guadeloupe) and the Windward Islands (Dominica, Martinique, St Lucia, St Vincent and the Grenadines, Barbados, and Grenada).

antilogarithm or *antilog* the inverse of ◊logarithm, or the number whose logarithm to a given base is a given number. If $y = \log ax$, then $x = $ antilog ay.

antimacassar piece of cloth protecting a seat head-rest from staining by hair-oil. The term is derived from Rowland's Macassar Oil, first manufactured about 1793.

antimatter in physics, a form of matter in which most of the attributes (such as electrical charge, magnetic moment, and spin) of ◊elementary particles are reversed. Such particles (antiparticles) can be created in particle accelerators, such as those at ◊CERN in Geneva and at Fermilab in the USA.

antimony silver-white, brittle, semimetallic element (a metalloid), symbol Sb (from Latin *stibium*), atomic number 51, relative atomic mass 121.75. It occurs chiefly as the ore stibnite, and is used to make alloys harder; it is also used in photosensitive substances in colour photography, optical electronics, fireproofing, pigment, and medicine. It was employed by the ancient Egyptians in a mixture to protect the eyes from flies.

antinode in physics, the position in a ◊standing wave pattern at which the amplitude of vibration is greatest (compare ◊node). The standing wave of a stretched string vibrating in the fundamental mode has one antinode at its midpoint. A vibrating air column in a pipe has an antinode at the pipe's open end and at the place where the vibration is produced.

Antioch /ˈæntɪɒk/ ancient capital of the Greek kingdom of Syria, founded 300 BC by Seleucus Nicator in memory of his father Antiochus, and famed for its splendour and luxury. Under the Romans it was an early centre of Christianity. The site is now occupied by the Turkish town of ◊Antakya.

Antiochus /æn'taɪəkəs/ thirteen kings of Syria of the Seleucid dynasty, including:

Antiochus I *c.* 324–*c.* 261 BC. King of Syria from 281 BC, son of Seleucus I, one of the generals of Alexander the Great. He earned the title of Antiochus Soter, or Saviour, by his defeat of the Gauls in Galatia 278.

Antiochus II *c.* 286–*c.* 246 BC. King of Syria 261–246 BC, son of Antiochus I. He was known as Antiochus Theos, the Divine. During his reign the eastern provinces broke away from the Graeco-Macedonian rule and set up native princes. He made peace with Egypt by marrying the daughter of Ptolemy Philadelphus, but was a tyrant among his own people.

Antiochus III the Great *c.* 241–187 BC. King of Syria from 223 BC, nephew of Antiochus II. He secured a loose suzerainty over Armenia and Parthia 209, overcame Bactria, received the homage of the Indian king of the Kabul valley, and returned by way of the Persian Gulf 204. He took possession of Palestine, entering Jerusalem 198. He crossed into NW Greece, but was decisively defeated by the Romans at Thermopylae 191 and at Magnesia 190. He had to abandon his domains in Anatolia, and was killed by the people of Elymais.

Antiochus IV *c.* 215–164 BC. King of Syria from 175 BC, known as Antiochus Epiphanes, the Illustrious; second son of Antiochus III. He occupied Jerusalem in about 170, seizing much of the Temple treasure, and instituted worship of the Greek type in the Temple in an attempt to eradicate Judaism. This produced the revolt of the Hebrews under the Maccabees; Antiochus died before he could suppress it.

Antiochus VII Sidetes King of Syria from 138 BC. The last strong ruler of the Seleucid dynasty, he took Jerusalem 134, reducing the Maccabees to subjection, and fought successfully against the Parthians.

Antiope mother of the twins ◊Amphion and Zethus, whose father was Zeus.

She was imprisoned by the tyrant Lycus and his wife Dirce, and freed by her sons, who punished Dirce by tying her to a bull. The scene is represented in a classical marble group, the Farnese Bull, rediscovered in the Renaissance.

antioxidant any substance that prevents deterioration by oxidation in fats, oils, paints, plastics, and rubbers. When used as ◊food additives, antioxidants prevent fats and oils from becoming rancid when exposed to air, and thus extend their shelf life.

Vegetable oils contain natural antioxidants, such as vitamin E, which prevent spoilage, but antioxidants are nevertheless added to most oils. They are not always listed on food labels because if a food manufacturer buys an oil to make a food product, and the oil has antioxidant already added, it does not have to be listed on the label of the product. Some studies have shown that the antioxidants BHT and BHA cause behaviour disorders in animals.

antiparticle in nuclear physics, a particle corresponding in mass and properties to a given ◊elementary particle but with the opposite electrical charge, magnetic properties, or coupling to other fundamental forces. For example, an electron carries a negative charge whereas its antiparticle, the positron, carries a positive one. When a particle and its antiparticle collide, they destroy each other, in the process called 'annihilation', their total energy being converted to lighter particles and/or photons. A substance consisting entirely of antiparticles is known as ◊antimatter.

antiphony in music, a form of composition using widely spaced choirs or groups of instruments to create perspectives in sound. It was developed in 17th-century Venice by Giovanni ◊Gabrieli and his pupil Heinrich ◊Schütz.

antipodes (Greek 'opposite feet') places at opposite points on the globe.

In the UK, Australia and New Zealand are called the Antipodes.

antipope rival claimant to the elected pope for the leadership of the Roman Catholic church, for instance in the Great Schism 1378–1417 when there were rival popes in Rome and Avignon.

antiracism and antisexism active opposition to ◊racism and ◊sexism; positive action or a set of policies, such as 'equal opportunity' can be designed to counteract racism and sexism, often on the part of an official body or an institution, such as a school, a business, or a government agency.

The growth of antiracist and antisexist policies in the UK in the 1980s, for example in education, reflected the belief that to ensure equality of opportunity, conscious efforts should be made to counteract the effects of unconscious racism and sexism as well as the effects of previous systematic ◊discrimination against members of minority ethnic groups and women.

antirrhinum or *snapdragon* any of several plants, genus *Antirrhinum*, in the figwort family Scrophulariaceae. Antirrhinums are native to the Mediterranean region and W North America.

anti-Semitism literally, prejudice against Semitic people (see ◊Semite), but in practice it has meant prejudice or discrimination against, and persecution of, the Jews as an ethnic group. Anti-Semitism was a tenet of Hitler's Germany, and in the Holocaust 1933–45 about 6 million Jews died in concentration camps and in local extermination ◊pogroms, such as the siege of the Warsaw ghetto. In the USSR and the Eastern bloc, as well as in Islamic nations, anti-Semitism exists and is promulgated by neofascist groups. It is a form of ◊racism.

The destruction of Jerusalem AD 70 led many Jews to settle in Europe and throughout the Roman Empire. In the 4th century Christianity was adopted as the official religion of the Empire, which reinforced existing prejudice (dating back to pre-Christian times and referred to in the works of Seneca and Tacitus) against Jews who refused to convert. Anti-Semitism increased in the Middle Ages because of the Crusades, and legislation forbade Jews to own land or be members of a craft guild; to earn a living they had to become moneylenders and traders (and were then resented when they prospered). Britain expelled many Jews 1290, but they were formally readmitted 1655 by Cromwell. From the 16th century Jews were forced by law in many countries to live in a separate area, or *ghetto*, of a city.

Late 18th- and early 19th-century liberal thought improved the position of Jews in European society. In the Austro-Hungarian Empire, for example, they were allowed to own land, and after the French Revolution the 'rights of man' were extended to French Jews 1790. The rise of 19th-century nationalism and unscientific theories of race instigated new resentments. Anti-Semitism became strong in Austria, France (see ◊Dreyfus), and Germany, and from 1881 pogroms in Poland and Russia caused refugees to flee to the USA (where freedom of religion was enshrined in the constitution), to the UK, and to other European countries as well as Palestine (see ◊Zionism).

In the 20th century, fascism and the Nazi Party's application of racial theories led to organized persecution and genocide. After World War II, the creation of Israel 1948 provoked Palestinian anti-Zionism, backed by the Arab world. Anti-Semitism is still fostered by extreme right-wing groups, such as the National Front in the UK and France and the Neo-Nazis in the USA and Germany.

antiseptic any substance that kills or inhibits the growth of microorganisms. The use of antiseptics was pioneered by Joseph ◊Lister. He used carbolic acid (◊phenol), which is a weak antiseptic; substances such as TCP are derived from this.

antispasmodic any drug that reduces motility, the spontaneous action of the muscle walls. ◊Anti-cholinergics are a type of antispasmodic that act indirectly by way of the autonomic nervous system, which controls involuntary movement. Other drugs act directly on the smooth muscle to relieve spasm (contraction).

anti-submarine warfare all methods used to deter, attack, and destroy enemy submarines: missiles, torpedoes, depth charges, bombs, and direct-fire weapons from ships, other submarines, or aircraft. Frigates are the ships most commonly used to engage submarines in general. Submarines carrying nuclear missiles are tracked and attacked with 'hunter-killer', or attack, submarines, usually nuclear-powered.

antitrust laws in US economics, regulations preventing or restraining trusts, monopolies, or any business practice considered to be unfair or uncompetitive. Antitrust laws prevent mergers and acquisitions that might create a monopoly situation or ones in which restrictive practices might be stimulated.

antler 'horn' of a deer, often branched, and made of bone rather than horn. Antlers, unlike true horns, are shed and regrown each year. Reindeer of both sexes grow them, but in all other types of deer, only the males have antlers.

ant lion larva of one of the insects of the family Myrmeleontidae, order Neuroptera, which traps ants by waiting at the bottom of a pit dug in loose, sandy soil. Ant lions are mainly tropical, but also occur in parts of Europe and in the USA (where they are called doodlebugs).

Antofagasta /ˌæntəfəˈgæstə/ port of N Chile, capital of the region of Antofagasta; population (1987) 204,500. The area of the region is 125,300 sq km/48,366 sq mi; its population (1982) 341,000. Nitrates from the Atacama desert are exported.

Antonello da Messina /ˌæntəˈneləʊ/ *c.* 1430–1479. Italian painter, born in Messina, Sicily, a pioneer of the technique of oil painting, which he is said to have introduced to Italy from N Europe. Flemish influence is reflected in his technique, his use of light, and sometimes in his imagery. Surviving works include bust-length portraits and sombre religious paintings.

Antonescu /ˌæntəˈnesku/ Ion 1882–1946. Romanian general and politician who headed a pro-German government during World War II and was executed for war crimes 1946.

Antonine Wall /ˈæntənaɪn/ Roman line of fortification built AD 142–200. It was the Roman Empire's NW frontier, between the Clyde and Forth rivers, Scotland.

Antoninus Pius /ˌæntəˈninəs/ AD 86–161. Roman emperor who had been adopted 138 as Hadrian's heir, and succeeded him later that year. He enjoyed a prosperous reign, during which he built the Antonine Wall. His daughter married ◊Marcus Aurelius Antoninus.

Antonioni /ænˌtəʊniˈəʊni/ Michelangelo 1912– . Italian film director, famous for his subtle presentations of neuroses and personal relationships among the leisured classes. His work includes *L'Avventura* 1960, *Blow Up* 1966, and *The Passenger* 1975.

Antony and Cleopatra tragedy by William Shakespeare, written and first performed 1607–08. Mark Antony falls in love with the Egyptian queen Cleopatra in Alexandria, but returns to Rome when his wife, Fulvia, dies. He then marries Octavia to heal the rift between her brother Augustus Caesar and himself. Antony returns to Egypt and Cleopatra, but is finally defeated by Augustus. Believing Cleopatra dead, Antony kills himself, and Cleopatra takes her own life rather than surrender to Augustus.

antonymy near or precise oppositeness between or among words. *Good* and *evil* are antonyms. Antonyms may vary with context and situation: in discussing a colour, *dull* and *bright* are antonymous, but when talking about knives and blades, the opposite of *dull* is *sharp*.

Antrim /ˈæntrɪm/ county of Northern Ireland
area 2,830 sq km/1,092 sq mi
towns Belfast (county town), Larne (port)
features Giant's Causeway of natural hexagonal basalt columns, which, in legend, was built to enable the giants to cross between Ireland and Scotland; Antrim borders Lough Neagh, and is separated from Scotland by the 32 km/20 mi wide North Channel
products potatoes, oats, linen, synthetic textiles
population (1981) 642,000.

Antwerp /ˈæntwɜːp/ (Flemish *Antwerpen*, French *Anvers*) port in Belgium on the river Scheldt, capital of the province of Antwerp; population (1988) 476,000. One of the world's busiest ports, it has shipbuilding, oil-refining, petrochemical, textile, and diamond-cutting industries. The home of the artist Rubens is preserved, and many of his works are in the Gothic cathedral. The province of Antwerp has an area of 2,900 sq km/1,119 sq mi; population (1987) 1,588,000.

It was not until the 15th century that Antwerp rose to prosperity; from 1500 to 1560 it was the richest port in N Europe. After this Antwerp was beset by religious troubles and the Netherlands revolt against Spain. In 1648 the Treaty of Westphalia gave both shores of the Scheldt estuary to the United Provinces, which closed it to Antwerp trade. The Treaty of Paris 1814 opened the estuary to all nations on payment of a small toll to the Dutch, abandoned 1863. During World War I Antwerp was occupied by Germany Oct 1914–Nov 1918; during World War II, May 1940–Sept 1944.

Anu Mesopotamian sky god, commonly joined in a trinity with Enlil and Ea.

Anubis /əˈnjuː bɪs/ in Egyptian mythology, the jackal-headed god of the dead.

Anuradhapura /əˈnʊərədəpʊərə/ ancient holy city in Sri Lanka; population (1981) 36,000. It was the capital of the Sinhalese kings of Sri Lanka 5th century BC–8th century AD; rediscovered in the mid-19th century. Sacred in Buddhism it claims a Bo tree descended from the one under which the Buddha became enlightened.

anus opening at the end of the alimentary canal that allows undigested food and associated materials to pass out of an animal. It is found in all types of multicellular animal except the coelenterates (sponges) and the platyhelminthes (flat worms), which have a mouth only.

Anvers /ɒ̃ˈveə/ French form of ◊Antwerp, a province in N Belgium.

anxiety emotional state of fear or apprehension. Anxiety is a normal response to potentially dangerous situations. Abnormal anxiety can either be free-floating, experienced in a wide range of situations, or it may be phobic, when the sufferer is excessively afraid of an object or situation.

Anyang /ˈænˈjæŋ/ city in Henan province, E China; population (1980) 430,000. It was the capital of the Shang dynasty (13th–12th centuries BC). Rich archaeological remains have been uncovered since the 1930s.

ANZAC acronym from the initials of the *Australian and New Zealand Army Corps*, applied in general to all troops of both countries serving in World War I and to some extent those in World War II.

The date of their World War I landing in Gallipoli, Turkey, 25 April 1915, is marked by a public holiday, *Anzac Day*, in both Australia and New Zealand.

Anzio, Battle of /ˈænziəʊ/ in World War II, the beachhead invasion of Italy 22 Jan–23 May 1944 by Allied troops; failure to use information gained by deciphering German codes (see ◊Ultra) led to Allied troops being stranded temporarily after German attacks.

ANZUS acronym for *A*ustralia, *N*ew Zealand, and the *U*nited *S*tates (Pacific Security Treaty), a military alliance established 1951. It was replaced 1954 by the ◊Southeast Asia Treaty Organization, (SEATO).

Aomori /aʊˈmɔri/ port at the head of Mutsu Bay, on the N coast of Honshu Island, Japan; 40 km/ 25 mi NE of Hirosaki; population (1980) 288,000. It handles a large local trade in fish, rice, and timber.

aorta the chief ◊artery, the dorsal blood vessel carrying oxygenated blood from the left ventricle of the heart in birds and mammals. It branches to form smaller arteries, which in turn supply all body organs except the lungs. Loss of elasticity in the aorta provides evidence of ◊atherosclerosis, which may lead to heart disease.

Aouita /ɑːˈwiːtə/ Said 1960– . Moroccan runner. Outstanding at middle and long distances, he won the 1984 Olympic and 1987 World Championship 5,000-metres title, and has set many world records.

In 1985 he held world records at both 1,500 and 5,000 metres, the first person for 30 years to hold both. He has since broken the 2 miles, 3,000 metres, and 2,000 metres world records.

Aoun /ɑːˈuːn/ Michel 1935– . Lebanese soldier and Maronite Christian politician, president 1988–90. As commander of the Lebanese army, he was made president without Muslim support, his appointment precipitating a civil war between Christians and Muslims. His unwillingness to accept a 1989 Arab-League–sponsored peace agreement increased his isolation until the following year he surrendered to military pressure.

Born in Beirut, he joined the Lebanese army and rose to become, in 1984, its youngest commander. When, in 1988, the Chris-tian and Muslim communities failed to agree on a Maronite successor to the outgoing president Amin Gemayel (as required by the constitution), unilaterally appointed Aoun. This precipitated the creation of a rival Muslim government, and, eventually, a civil war. Aoun became isolated in the presidential palace and staunchly opposed the 1989 peace plan worked out by parliamentarians under the auspices of the Arab League. After defying the government led by Prime Minister Selim al-Hoss in the face of strong military opposition, in Oct 1990 Aoun sought political asylum in the French embassy. He obtained a pardon from the Lebanese government in 1991.

Aouzu Strip /ɑːˈuːzuː/ disputed territory 100 km/60 mi wide on the Chad–Libya frontier, occupied by Libya 1973. Lying to the N of the Tibesti massif, the area is rich in uranium and other minerals.

Apache /əˈpætʃi/ member of a group of North ◊American Indian peoples who lived as hunters in the Southwest. They are related to the Navajo, and now number about 10,000, living in reservations in Arizona, SW Oklahoma, and New Mexico. They were known as fierce raiders and horse warriors in the 18th and 19th centuries. Apache also refers to any of several southern Athabaskan languages and dialects spoken by these people.

apartheid (Afrikaans 'apartness') the racial-segregation policy of the government of South Africa, which was legislated 1948, when the Afrikaner National Party gained power. Nonwhites (Bantu, coloured or mixed, or Indian) do not share full rights of citizenship with the 4.5 million whites (for example, the 23 million black people cannot vote in parliamentary elections), and many public facilities and institutions were until 1990 and, in some cases, remain restricted to the use of one race only; the establishment of ◊Black National States is another manifestation of apartheid. In 1991 President de Klerk repealed the key elements of apartheid legislation.

The term has also been applied to similar movements and other forms of racial separation, for example social or educational, in other parts of the world.

The term 'apartheid' was coined in the late 1930s by the South African Bureau for Racial Affairs (SABRA), which called for a policy of 'separate development' of the races.

Internally, organizations opposed to apartheid were banned, for example the African National Congress and the United Democratic Front, and leading campaigners for its abolition have been, like Steve Biko, killed, or, like Archbishop Tutu, harassed. Anger at the policy has sparked off many uprisings, from ◊Sharpeville 1960 and ◊Soweto 1976 to the Crossroads squatter camps 1986.

Abroad, there are anti-apartheid movements in many countries. In 1961 South Africa was forced to withdraw from the Commonwealth because of apartheid; during the 1960s and 1970s there were calls for international ◊sanctions, especially boycotts of sporting and cultural links; and in the 1980s advocates of sanctions extended them into trade and finance.

The South African government's reaction to internal and international pressure was twofold: it abolished some of the more hated apartheid laws (the ban on interracial marriages was lifted 1985 and the pass laws, which restricted the movement of nonwhites, were repealed 1986); and it sought to replace the term 'apartheid' with 'plural democracy'. Under states of emergency 1985 and 1986 it used force to quell internal opposition, and from 1986 there was an official ban on the reporting of it in the media. In Oct 1989 President F W de Klerk permitted anti-apartheid demonstrations; the Separate Amenities Act was abolished 1990 and a new constitution promised. In 1990 Nelson Mandela, a leading figure in the African National Congress, was finally released. In 1991 the remaining major discriminating laws embodied in apartheid were repealed, including the Population Registration Act, which made it obligatory for every citizen to be classified into one of nine racial groups.

apatite common calcium phosphate mineral, $Ca_5(PO_4CO_3)_3(F,OH,Cl)$. Apatite has a hexagonal structure and occurs widely in igneous rocks, such as pegmatite, and in contact metamorphic rocks, such as marbles. It is used in the manufacture of fertilizer and as a source of phosphorus. Apatite is the chief constituent of tooth enamel while hydroxyapatite, $Ca_{10}(PO_4)_6(OH)_2$, is the chief inorganic constituent of bone marrow. Apatite ranks 5 on the ◊Mohs' scale of hardness.

apatosaurus /ˌæpətəʊˈsɔːrəs/ large plant-eating dinosaur, formerly called *brontosaurus*, which flourished about 145 million years ago. Up to 21 m/69 ft long and 30 tonnes in weight, it stood on four elephantlike legs and had a long tail, long neck, and small head. It probably snipped off low-growing vegetation with peglike front teeth, and swallowed it whole to be ground by pebbles in the stomach.

ape ◊primate of the family Pongidae, closely related to humans, including gibbon, orang-utan, chimpanzee, and gorilla.

Apeldoorn /ˈɑːpəldɔːn/ commercial city in Gelderland province, E central Netherlands; population (1982) 142,400. Het Loo, which is situated nearby, has been the summer residence of the Dutch royal family since the time of William of Orange.

Apelles 4th century BC. Greek painter, said to have been the greatest in antiquity. He was court painter to Philip of Macedonia and his son Alexander the Great. None of his work survives, only descriptions of his portraits and nude Venuses.

Apennines /ˈæpənaɪn/ chain of mountains stretching the length of the Italian peninsula. A continuation of the Maritime Alps, from Genoa it swings across the peninsula to Ancona on the E coast, and then back to the W coast and into the 'toe' of Italy. The system is continued over the Strait of Messina along the N Sicilian coast, then across the Mediterranean sea in a series of islands to the Atlas mountains of N Africa. The highest peak is Gran Sasso d'Italia at 2,914 m/9,560 ft.

aperture in photography, an opening in the camera that allows light to pass through the lens to strike the film. Controlled by shutter speed and the iris diaphragm, it can be set mechanically or electronically at various diameters.

aphelion the point at which an object, travelling in an elliptical orbit around the Sun, is at its furthest from the Sun.

aphid any of the family of small insects, Aphididae, in the order Homoptera, that live by sucking sap from plants. There are many species, often adapted to particular plants.

In some stages of their life cycle, wingless females rapidly produce large numbers of live young by ◊parthenogenesis, leading to enormous infestations, and numbers can approach 2 billion per hectare/1 billion per acre. They can also cause damage by transmitting viral diseases. An aphid that damages cypress and cedar trees appeared in

Malawi in 1985 and by 1991 was attacking millions of trees in central and E Africa. Some research suggests, however, that aphids may help promote fertility in the soil through the waste they secrete, termed 'honeydew'. Aphids are also known as plant lice, greenflies, or blackflies.

aphrodisiac (from Aphrodite, the Greek goddess of love) any substance that arouses or increases sexual desire.

Sexual activity can be stimulated in humans and animals by drugs affecting the pituitary gland. Preparations commonly sold for the purpose can be dangerous (cantharidin) or useless (rhinoceros horn), and alcohol and cannabis, popularly thought to be effective because they lessen inhibition, may have the opposite effect.

Aphrodite /ˌæfrəˈdaɪti/ in Greek mythology, the goddess of love (Roman Venus, Phoenician Astarte, Babylonian Ishtar); said to be either a daughter of Zeus (in Homer) or sprung from the foam of the sea (in Hesiod). She was the unfaithful wife of Hephaestus, the god of fire, and the mother of Eros.

Apia /ˈɑːpiə/ capital and port of Western ◊Samoa, on the N coast of Upolu island, in the W Pacific; population (1981) 33,000. It was the final home of the writer Robert Louis Stevenson.

Apis /ˈɑːpɪs/ ancient Egyptian god with a human body and a bull's head, linked with Osiris (and later merged with him into the Ptolemaic god Serapis); his cult centres were Memphis and Heliopolis, where sacred bulls were mummified.

Apocrypha appendix to the Old Testament of the Bible, not included in the final Hebrew canon but recognized by Roman Catholics. There are also disputed New Testament texts known as Apocrypha.

apogee the point at which an object, travelling in an elliptical orbit around the Earth, is at its furthest from the Earth.

Apollinaire /ˌəpɒlɪˈneə/ Guillaume. Pen name of Guillaume Apollinaire de Kostrowitsky 1880–1918. French poet of aristocratic Polish descent. He was a leader of the avant-garde in Parisian literary and artistic circles. His novel *Le Poète assassiné/The Poet Assassinated* 1916, followed by the experimental poems *Alcools/Alcohols* 1913 and *Calligrammes/Word Pictures* 1918, show him as a representative of the Cubist and Futurist movements.

Apollinarius of Laodicea /ˌæpɒlɪˈneəriəs/ Bishop of Laodicea, whose views on the nature of Christ were condemned by the Council of Constantine 381, but who nonetheless laid the foundations for the later ◊Nestorian controversy. Rather than seeing the nature of Jesus as a human and divine soul somehow joined in the person of Christ, he saw Christ as having a divine mind only, and not a human one.

Apollo /əˈpɒləʊ/ in Greek and Roman mythology, the god of sun, music, poetry, prophecy, agriculture, and pastoral life, and leader of the Muses. He was the twin child (with Artemis) of Zeus and Leto. Ancient statues show Apollo as the embodiment of the Greek ideal of male beauty.

His chief cult centres were his supposed birthplace on the island of Delos, in the Cyclades, and Delphi.

Apollo asteroid member of a group of ◊asteroids whose orbits cross that of the Earth. They are named after the first of their kind, Apollo, discovered 1932 and then lost until 1973. Apollo asteroids are so small and faint that they are difficult to see except when close to Earth (Apollo is about 2 km/1.2 mi across).

Apollonius of Perga /ˌæpəˈləʊniəs/ c. 260–c. 190 BC. Greek mathematician, called 'the Great Geometer'. In his work *Conic Sections* he showed that a plane intersecting a cone will generate an ellipse, a parabola, or a hyperbola, depending on the angle of intersection. In astronomy, he used a system of circles called epicycles and deferents to explain the motion of the planets; this system, as refined by Ptolemy, was used until the Renaissance.

Apollonius of Rhodes /ˌæpəˈləʊniəs/ c. 220–180 BC. Greek poet, author of the epic *Argonautica*, which tells the story of Jason and the Argonauts and their quest for the Golden Fleece.

Apollo of Rhodes the Greek statue of Apollo generally known as the ◊Colossus of Rhodes.

Apollo project US space project to land a person on the Moon, achieved 20 July 1969, when Neil Armstrong was the first to set foot there. He was accompanied on the Moon surface by Col Edwin E Aldrin Jr; Michael Collins remained in the orbiting command module.

The programme was announced 1961 by President Kennedy. The world's most powerful rocket, *Saturn V*, was built to launch the Apollo spacecraft, which carried three astronauts. When the spacecraft was in orbit around the Moon, two astronauts would descend to the surface in a lunar module to take samples of rock and set up experiments that would send data back to Earth. The first Apollo mission carrying a crew, *Apollo 7*, Oct 1968, was a test flight in orbit around the Earth. After three other preparatory flights, *Apollo 11* made the first lunar landing. Five more crewed landings followed, the last 1972. The total cost of the programme was over $24 billion.

Apollo–Soyuz test project joint US-Soviet space mission in which an Apollo and a Soyuz craft docked while in orbit around the Earth on 17 July 1975. The craft remained attached for two days and crew members were able to move from one craft to the other through an airlock attached to the nose of the Apollo. The mission was designed to test rescue procedures as well as having political significance.

apologetics philosophical writings that attempt to refute attacks on the Christian faith. Apologists include Justin Martyr, Origen, St Augustine, Thomas Aquinas, Blaise Pascal, and Joseph Butler. The questions raised by scientific, historical, and archaeological discoveries have widened the field of apologetics.

Apo, Mount /ˈɑːpəʊ/ active volcano and highest peak in the Philippines, rising to 2,954 m/9,692 ft on the island of Mindanao.

aposematic coloration in biology, the technical name for ◊warning coloration markings that make a dangerous, poisonous, or foul-tasting animal particularly conspicuous and recognizable to a predator. Examples include the yellow and black stripes of bees and wasps, and the bright red or yellow colours of many poisonous frogs. See also ◊mimicry.

a posteriori (Latin 'from the latter') in logic, an argument that deduces causes from their effects; inductive reasoning; the converse of ◊a priori.

apostle (Greek 'messenger') in the New Testament, any of the chosen 12 ◊disciples sent out by Jesus after his resurrection to preach the Gospel. In the earliest days of Christianity the term was extended to include some who had never known Jesus in the flesh, notably St Paul.

Apostles discussion group founded 1820 at Cambridge University, England; members have included the poet Tennyson, the philosophers G E Moore and Bertrand Russell, the writers Lytton Strachey and Leonard Woolf, the economist Keynes, and the spies Guy Burgess and Anthony Blunt.

Apostles' Creed one of the three ancient ◊creeds of the Christian church.

Apostolic Age early period in the Christian church dominated by those personally known to Jesus or his disciples.

apostolic succession doctrine in the Christian church that certain spiritual powers were received by the first apostles directly from Jesus, and have been handed down in the ceremony of 'laying on of hands' from generation to generation of bishops.

apostrophe mark (') used in written English and some other languages. In English it serves primarily to indicate either a missing letter (*mustn't* for *must not*) or number ('*47* for *1947*), or grammatical possession ('*John's* camera', '*women's* dresses'). It is often omitted in proper names (Publishers Association, Actors Studio, *Collins Dictionary*). Many people otherwise competent in writing have great difficulty with the apostrophe, which has never been stable at any point in its history.

An apostrophe may precede the plural *s* used with numbers and abbreviations (*the 1970's, a group of POW's*) but is equally often omitted (*the 1970s, a group of POWs*). For possessives of certain words ending with *s*, usage is split, as between *James's book* and *James' book*. Names and dates used adjectivally are not usually followed by an apostrophe ('a *1950s* car', 'a *Beatles* record'). The use of an apostrophe to help indicate a plural (as in a shopkeeper's *Apple's* and *Tomato's*, followed by their prices) is regarded by many as semiliterate.

apothecaries' weights obsolete units of mass, formerly used in pharmacy: 20 grains made one scruple; three scruples made one drachm; eight drachms made an apothecary's ounce (oz apoth.), and 12 such ounces made an apothecary's pound (lb apoth.). There are 7,000 grains in one pound avoirdupois (0.454 kg).

Appalachians /ˌæpəˈleɪtʃənz/ mountain system of E North America, stretching about 2,400 km/1,500 mi from Alabama to Québec, composed of very ancient eroded rocks.

The chain includes the Allegheny, Catskill, and Blue Ridge mountains, the latter having the highest peak, Mount Mitchell, 2,045 m/6,712 ft. The eastern edge has a fall line to the coastal plain where Philadelphia, Baltimore, and Washington stand.

appeal in law, an application for a rehearing of all or part of an issue that has already been dealt with by a lower court or tribunal. The outcome can be a new decision on all or part of the points raised, or the previous decision may be upheld. In criminal cases, an appeal may be against conviction and either the prosecution or the defence may appeal against sentence.

In the UK, summary trials (involving minor offences) are heard in the ◊magistrates' court and appeals against conviction or sentence are heard in the ◊crown court. The appeal in the crown court takes the form of a full retrial but no jury is present. Appeal against conviction or sentence in the crown court is heard by the criminal division of the Court of Appeal. The House of Lords is the highest appellate court within the UK. Further appeal may lie to either the ◊European Court of Justice or the ◊European Court of Human Rights.

In 1989, 31% of the appeals before the criminal division of the Court of Appeal were successful.

appeasement historically, the conciliatory policy adopted by the British government, in particular under Neville Chamberlain, towards the Nazi and Fascist dictators in Europe in the 1930s in an effort to maintain peace. It was strongly opposed by Winston Churchill, but the ◊Munich Agreement 1938 was almost universally hailed as its justification. Appeasement ended when Germany occupied Bohemia–Moravia March 1939.

appendicitis inflammation of the appendix, a small, blind extension of the bowel in the lower right abdomen. In an acute attack, the pus-filled appendix may burst, causing a potentially lethal spread of infection (see ◊peritonitis). Treatment is by removal (appendectomy).

appendix area of the mammalian gut, associated with the digestion of cellulose. In herbivores it may be large, containing millions of bacteria that secrete enzymes to digest grass. No vertebrate can produce the type of digestive enzyme that will digest cellulose, the main constituent of plant cell walls. Those herbivores that rely on cellulose for their energy have all evolved specialist mechanisms to make use of the correct type of bacteria.

Appert /ˈæpeə/ Nicolas 1750–1841. French pioneer of food preservation by ◊canning. He devised a system of sealing food in glass bottles and subjecting it to heat. His book *L'Art de conserver les substances animales et végétales* appeared in 1810. Shortly after, others applied the same principles to iron or sheet steel containers plated with tin.

apple fruit of *Malus pumila*, a tree of the family Rosaceae. There are several hundred varieties of cultivated apples, grown all over the world, which may be divided into eating, cooking, and cider apples. All are derived from the wild crab apple.

Apple trees grow best in temperate countries with a cool climate and plenty of rain during the winter. The apple has been an important food plant in Eurasia for thousands of years.

Appleton /ˈæpəltən/ Edward Victor 1892–1965. British physicist who worked at Cambridge under Ernest ◊Rutherford from 1920. He proved the existence of the Kennelly–Heaviside layer (now called the E layer) in the atmosphere, and the Appleton layer beyond it, and was involved in the initial work on the atom bomb. Nobel prize 1947.

applied kinesiology an extension of ◊chiropractic developed in the USA in the 1960s and '70s, principally by US practitioner Dr George Goodheart. Relating to the science of kinesiology, or muscle testing, the Chinese principle that there exist energy pathways in the body and that disease results from local energy blockages or imbalances, Goodheart developed both diagnostic and therapeutic techniques, working on the body's musculature, which have proved particularly effective with stress-related ailments.

appliqué embroidery used to create pictures or patterns by 'applying' pieces of material onto a background fabric. The pieces are cut into the appropriate shapes and sewn on, providing decoration for wall hangings, furnishing textiles, and clothes.

Appomattox /ˌæpəˈmætəks/ village in Virginia, USA, scene of the surrender 9 April 1865 of the Confederate army under Robert E Lee to the Union army under Ulysses S Grant, which ended the American Civil War.

apricot fruit of *Prunus armeniaca*, a tree of the rose family Rosaceae, closely related to the almond, peach, plum, and cherry. It has yellow-fleshed fruit. Although native to the Far East, it has long been cultivated in Armenia, from where it was introduced into Europe and the USA.

April Fools' Day the first day of April, when it is customary in W Europe and the USA to expose people to ridicule by a practical joke, causing them to believe some falsehood or to go on a fruitless errand.

The victim is known in England as an April Fool; in Scotland as a gowk (cuckoo or fool); and in France as a *poisson d'avril* (April fish). There is a similar Indian custom on the last day of the Holi festival in late March.

a priori (Latin 'from what comes before') in logic, an argument that is known to be true, or false, without reference to experience; the converse of ◊a posteriori.

Apuleius /æpjuːˈliːəs/ Lucius lived c. AD 160. Roman lawyer, philosopher, and author of *Metamorphoses*, or The ◊Golden Ass.

Apulia /puːˈljə/ English form of ◊Puglia, region of Italy.

Aqaba, Gulf of /ˈækəbə/ gulf extending for 160 km/100 mi between the Negev and the Red Sea; its coastline is uninhabited except at its head, where the frontiers of Israel, Egypt, Jordan, and Saudi Arabia converge. The two ports Eilat (Israeli 'Elath') and Aqaba, Jordan's only port are here.

aquaculture or *fish farming* raising fish (including molluscs and crustaceans) under controlled conditions in tanks and ponds, sometimes in offshore pens. It has been practised for centuries in the Far East, where Japan alone produces some 100,000 tonnes of fish a year. In the 1980s one-tenth of the world's consumption of fish was farmed, notably carp, catfish, trout, salmon, turbot, eel, mussels, clams, oysters, and shrimp.

The 300 trout farms in Britain produce over 9,000 tonnes per year, and account for 90% of home consumption.

aqualung or *scuba* acronym for *self-contained underwater breathing apparatus* worn by divers, developed in the early 1940s by the French diver Jacques Cousteau. Compressed-air cylinders strapped to the diver's back are regulated by a valve system and by a mouth tube provide air to the diver at the same pressure as that of the surrounding water (which increases with the depth).

The vital component of an aqualung is the demand-regulator, a two-stage valve in the diver's mouthpiece. When the diver breathes in, air first passes from the compressed-air cylinders through a valve to the inner chamber of the mouthpiece. There, water that has entered the outer chamber pressurizes the air to the surrounding pressure before the diver takes in the air.

aquamarine blue variety of the mineral ◊beryl.

aquaplaning phenomenon in which the tyres of a road vehicle cease to make direct contact with the road surface, due to the presence of a thin film of water. As a result, the vehicle can go out of control (particularly if the steered wheels are involved).

aquarium tank or similar container used for the study and display of living aquatic plants and animals. The same name is used for institutions that exhibit aquatic life. These have been common since Roman times, but the first modern public aquarium was opened in Regent's Park, London in 1853. A recent development is the oceanarium or seaquarium, a large display of marine life forms.

Aquarius /əˈkweərɪəs/ zodiacal constellation a little south of the celestial equator near Pegasus. Aquarius is represented as a man pouring water from a jar. The Sun passes through Aquarius from late Feb to early March. In astrology, the dates for Aquarius are between about 20 Jan and 18 Feb (see ◊precession).

aquatic living in water. All life on Earth originated in the early oceans, because the aquatic environment has several advantages for organisms. Dehydration is almost impossible, temperatures usually remain stable, and the heaviness of water provides physical support.

aquatint printmaking technique, usually combined with ◊etching to produce areas of subtle tone as well as more precisely etched lines. Aquatint became common in the late 18th century.

The etching plate is dusted with a fine layer of resin that is fixed to the plate by heating. The plate is then immersed in acid, which bites through the resin, causing tiny pits on the surface of the plate. When printed, this results in a fine, grainy tone. Areas of tone can be controlled by varnishing the plate with acid-resisting material. Denser tones are acquired by longer exposure to the acid.

Gainsborough experimented with aquatint but the first artist to become proficient in the technique was J B Le Prince (1733–1781). Others attracted to it include Goya, Degas, Pissarro, Picasso, and Rouault.

aqueduct any artificial channel or conduit for water, often an elevated structure of stone, wood, or iron built for conducting water across a valley.

The Greeks built a tunnel 1,280 m/4,200 ft long near Athens, 2,500 years ago. Many Roman aqueducts are still standing, for example the one at Nîmes in S France, built about AD 18 (which is 48 m/160 ft high). The largest Roman aqueduct is that at Carthage in Tunisia, which is 141 km/87 mi long and was built during the reign of Publius Aelius Hadrianus between AD 117 and 138. A recent aqueduct is the California State Water Project taking water from Lake Oroville in the north, through two power plants and across the Tehachapi mountains, more than 177 km/110 mi to S California.

The longest aqueduct in Britain is the Pont Cysylltau in Clwyd, Wales, opened 1805. It is 307 m/1,007 ft long, with 19 arches up to 36 m/121 ft high.

aqueous humour watery fluid found in the space between the cornea and lens of the vertebrate eye. Similar to blood serum in composition, it is renewed every four hours.

aqueous solution solution in which the solvent is water.

aquifer any rock formation containing water that can be extracted by a well.

The rock of an aquifer must be porous and permeable (full of interconnected holes) so that it can absorb water.

An aquifer may be underlain, overlain, or sandwiched between impermeable layers, called *aquicludes*, which impede water movement. Sand- stones and porous limestones make the best aquifers. They are actively sought in arid areas as sources of drinking and irrigation water.

Aquinas /əˈkwaɪnəs/ St Thomas *c.* 1226–1274. Neapolitan philosopher and theologian, the greatest figure of the school of ◊scholasticism. He was a Dominican monk, known as the 'Angelic Doctor'. In 1879 his works were recognized as the basis of Catholic theology. His *Summa contra Gentiles/ Against the Errors of the Infidels* 1259–64 argues that reason and faith are compatible. He assimilated the philosophy of Aristotle into Christian doctrine.

His unfinished *Summa Theologica*, begun 1265, deals with the nature of God, mor-

ality, and the work of Jesus. His works embodied the world view taught in universities until the mid-17th century, and include scientific ideas derived from Aristotle.

Aquino /əˈkiːnəʊ/ (Maria) Corazon (born Cojuangco) 1933– . President of the Philippines 1986–92. She was instrumental in the nonviolent overthrow of President Ferdinand Marcos 1986. She sought to rule in a conciliatory manner, but encountered opposition from left (communist guerrillas) and right (army coup attempts), and her land reforms were seen as inadequate.

The daughter of a sugar baron, she studied in the USA and in 1956 married the politician Benigno Aquino (1933–1983). The chief political opponent of the right-wing president Marcos, he was assassinated by a military guard at Manila airport on his return from exile. Corazon Aquino was drafted by the opposition to contest the Feb 1986 presidential election and claimed victory over Marcos, accusing the government of ballot-rigging. She led a nonviolent 'people's power' campaign, which overthrew Marcos 25 Feb. A devout Roman Catholic, Aquino enjoyed strong church backing in her 1986 campaign. Initially wary, the USA provided strong support and was instrumental in turning back a 1989 coup attempt. In 1991 she announced she would not enter the 1992 presidential elections.

Aquitaine /ˌækwɪˈteɪn/ region of SW France; capital Bordeaux; area 41,300 sq km/ 15,942 sq mi; population (1986) 2,718,000. It comprises the *départements* of Dordogne, Gironde, Landes, Lot-et-Garonne, and Pyrénées-Atlantiques. Red wines (Margaux, St Julien) are produced in the Médoc district, bordering the Gironde. Aquitaine was an English possession 1152–1452.

history early human remains have been found in the Dordogne region. Aquitaine coincides roughly with the Roman province of Aquitania and the ancient French province of Aquitaine. Eleanor of Aquitaine married the future Henry II of England 1152 and brought it to him as her dowry; it remained in English hands until 1452.

Arab any of a Semitic (see ◊Semite) people native to the Arabian peninsula, but now settled throughout North Africa and the nations of the Middle East.

The homeland of the Arabs comprises Saudi Arabia, Qatar, Kuwait, Bahrain, United Arab Emirates, Oman, and Yemen. Predominantly Arab nations also include

Iraq, Syria, Lebanon, and Jordan, and the N African Arab nations comprise Morocco, Algeria, Tunisia, Libya, Egypt, and Sudan, though the last-named has substantial non-Arab minorities. Although Mauritania and Somalia are not predominantly Arab, they support the ◊Arab League.

The term Arab was first recorded 853 BC but was not widely used until the end of the 6th century AD. The 7th century saw the rise of Islam and by the 8th century non-Arab converts were being assimilated by the Arabs. Arabic became the principal language of the Arab Empire. In 1258 the empire was broken up by the Mongols and it was not until the decline of the Ottoman Empire at the end of World War I that the Arab nations emerged again as separate, if not independent, states.

Arab Common Market organization providing for the abolition of customs duties on agricultural products, and reductions on other items, between the member states: Egypt, Iraq, Jordan, and Syria. It was founded 1965.

arabesque in ballet, a pose in which the dancer stands on one leg, straight or bent, with the other leg raised behind, fully extended. The arms are held in a harmonious position to give the longest possible line from fingertips to toes.

Arabia /əˈreɪbiə/ the peninsula between the Persian Gulf and the Red Sea, in SW Asia; area 2,590,000 sq km/1,000,000 sq mi. The peninsula contains the world's richest oil and gas reserves. It comprises the states of Bahrain, Kuwait, Oman, Qatar, Saudi Arabia, the United Arab Emirates, and Yemen.

physical A sandy coastal plain of varying width borders the Red Sea, behind which a mountain chain rises to about 2,000–2,500 m/6,600–8,200 ft. Behind this range is the plateau of the Nejd, averaging 1,000 m/3,300 ft. The interior comprises a vast desert area: part of the Hamad (Syrian) desert in the far N; Nafud in northern Saudi Arabia, and Rub'al Khali in S Saudi Arabia.

history The Arabian civilization was revived by Muhammad during the 7th century, but in the new empire created by militant Islam, Arabia became a subordinate state, and its cities were eclipsed by Damascus, Baghdad, and Cairo. Colonialism only touched the fringe of Arabia in the 19th century, and until the 20th century the interior was unknown to Europeans. Nationalism began

actively to emerge at the period of World War I (1914–18), and the oil discoveries from 1953 gave the peninsula significant economic power.

Arabian Gulf another name for the ◊Persian Gulf.

Arabian Nights /əˈreɪbiən/ tales in oral circulation among Arab storytellers from the 10th century, probably having their roots in India. They are also known as *The Thousand and One Nights* and include 'Ali Baba', 'Aladdin', 'Sinbad the Sailor', and 'The Old Man of the Sea'.

They were supposed to have been told to the sultan by his bride Scheherazade to avoid the fate of her predecessors, who were all executed following the wedding night to prevent their infidelity. She began a new tale each evening, which she would only agree to finish on the following night. Eventually the 'sentence' was rescinded.

The first European translation was by the French writer Antoine Galland (1646–1715) 1704, although the stories were known earlier. The first English translations were by E W Lane 1838–40 and Richard Burton 1885–88.

Arabian Sea NW branch of the ◊Indian Ocean.

Arabic language the major Semitic language of the Hamito-Semitic family of W Asia and North Africa, originating among the Arabs of the Arabian peninsula. It is spoken today by about 120 million people in the Middle East and N Africa. Arabic script is written from right to left.

The language has spread by way of conquest and trade as far west as Morocco and as far east as Malaysia, Indonesia, and the Philippines, and is also spoken in Arab communities scattered across the western hemisphere.

Forms of colloquial Arabic vary in the countries where it is the dominant language: Algeria, Bahrain, Egypt, Iraq, Jordan, Kuwait, Lebanon, Libya, Mali, Mauritania, Morocco, Oman, Saudi Arabia, Sudan, Syria, Tunisia, the United Arab Emirates, and Yemen. Arabic is also a language of religious and cultural significance in such other countries as Bangladesh, India, Iran, Israel, Pakistan, and Somalia. Arabic-speaking communities are growing in the USA and the West Indies.

A feature of the language is its consonantal roots. For example, *s–l–m* is the root for *salaam*, a greeting that implies peace; *Islam,* the creed of submission to God and calm acceptance of his will; and *Muslim*, one who submits to that will (a believer in Islam). The *Koran*, the sacred book of Islam, is 'for reading' by a *qari* ('reader') who is engaged in *qaraat* ('reading'). The 7th-century style of the Koran is the basis of Classical Arabic.

Arabic numerals the symbols 0, 1, 2, 3, 4, 5, 6, 7, 8, 9, early forms of which were in use among the Arabs before being adopted by the peoples of Europe during the Middle Ages in place of Roman numerals. They appear to have originated in India and probably reached Europe by way of Spain.

Arab–Israeli Wars series of wars between Israel and various Arab states in the Middle East since the founding of the state of Israel 1948.

background Arab opposition to an Israeli state began after the Balfour Declaration 1917, which supported the idea of a Jewish national homeland. In the 1920s there were anti-Zionist riots in Palestine, then governed by the UK under a League of Nations mandate. In 1936 an Arab revolt led to a British royal commission that recommended partition (approved by the United Nations 1947, but rejected by the Arabs).

Tension in the Middle East remained high, and the conflict was sharpened and given East–West overtones by Soviet adoption of the Arab cause and US support for Israel. Several wars only increased the confusion over who had a claim to what territory. articularly in view of the area's strategic sensitivity as an oil producer, pressure grew for a settlement, and in 1978 the ◊Camp David Agreements brought peace between Egypt and Israel, but this was denounced by other Arab countries. Israel withdrew from Sinai 1979–82, but no final agreement on Jerusalem and the establishment of a Palestinian state on the West Bank was reached. The continuing Israeli occupation of the Gaza Strip and the West Bank in the face of a determined uprising (◊Intifada) by the residents of these areas has seemingly hardened attitudes on both sides.

First Arab–Israeli War 14 Oct 1948–13 Jan/24 March 1949. As soon as the independent state of Israel had been proclaimed by the Jews in Palestine, it was invaded by combined Arab forces. The Israelis defeated them and went on to annex territory until they controlled 75% of what had been Palestine under British mandate.

Second Arab–Israeli War or *Suez War* 29 Oct–4 Nov 1956. After Egypt had taken control of the Suez Canal and, with British and French support, blockaded the Straits of Tiran, Israel, it invaded and captured Sinai and the Gaza Strip, from which it withdrew under heavy US pressure after the entry of a UN force.

Third Arab–Israeli War 5–10 June 1967, the *Six Day War*. It resulted in the Israeli capture of the Golan Heights from Syria, the eastern half of Jerusalem and the West Bank from Jordan, and, in the south, the Gaza Strip and Sinai Peninsula as far as the Suez Canal.

Fourth Arab–Israeli War 2–22/24 Oct 1973, the *Yom Kippur War*, so called because the Israeli forces were taken by surprise on the Day of ◊Atonement. It started with the re-crossing of the Suez Canal by Egyptian forces who made initial gains, as did the Syrians in the Golan Heights area. However, the Israelis stabilized the position in both cases.

Fifth Arab–Israeli War From 1978 the presence of Palestinian guerrillas in Lebanon led to Arab raids on Israel and Israeli retaliatory incursions, but on 6 June 1982 Israel launched a full-scale invasion. By 14 June Beirut was encircled, and ◊Palestine Liberation Organization (PLO) and Syrian forces were evacuated (mainly to Syria) 21–31 Aug, but in Feb 1985 there was a unilateral Israeli withdrawal from the country without any gain for losses incurred. Israel maintains a 'security zone' in S Lebanon and supports the South Lebanese Army militia as a buffer against Palestinian guerrilla incursions.

Arabistan /ˈærəbɪˈstɑːn/ former name of the Iranian province of Khuzestan, revived in the 1980s by the 2 million Sunni Arab inhabitants who demand autonomy. Unrest and sabotage 1979–80 led to a pledge of a degree of autonomy by Ayatollah Khomeini.

Arab League organization of Arab states established in Cairo 1945 to promote Arab unity, primarily in opposition to Israel. The original members were Egypt, Syria, Iraq, Lebanon, Transjordan (Jordan 1949), Saudi Arabia, and Yemen. In 1979 Egypt was suspended and the league's headquarters transferred to Tunis in protest against the Egypt-Israeli peace, but Egypt was re-admitted as a full member May 1989, and in March 1990 its headquarters returned to Cairo.

Arab Monetary Fund (AMF) money reserve established 1976 by 20 Arab states plus the Palestine Liberation Organization to provide a mechanism for promoting greater stability in exchange rates and to coordinate Arab economic and monetary policies. It operates mainly by regulating petrodollars within the Arab community to make member countries less dependent on the West for the handling of their surplus money. The fund's headquarters are in Abu Dhabi in the United Arab Emirates.

Arachne /əˈrækni/ (Greek 'spider') in Greek mythology, a Lydian woman who was so skilful a weaver that she challenged the goddess Athena to a contest. Athena tore Arachne's beautiful tapestries to pieces and Arachne hanged herself. She was transformed into a spider, and her weaving became a cobweb.

arachnid or *arachnoid* type of arthropod, including spiders, scorpions, and mites. They differ from insects in possessing only two main body regions, the cephalothorax and the abdomen.

Arafat /ˈærəfæt/ Yassir 1929– . Palestinian nationalist politician, cofounder of al-◊Fatah 1956 and president of the ◊Palestine Liberation Organization (PLO) from 1969. In the 1970s his activities in pursuit of an independent homeland for Palestinians made him a prominent figure in world politics, but in the 1980s the growth of factions within the PLO effectively reduced his power. His support for Saddam Hussein after Iraq's invasion of Kuwait 1990 weakened his international standing, but he was subsequently influential in the Middle East peace talks and Sept 1993 reached a historic peace accord with Israel. In 1994 he was awarded the Nobel Prize for Peace jointly with Yitzhak Rabin and Shimon Peres.

Arafura Sea /ærəˈfuərə/ area of the Pacific Ocean between N Australia and Indonesia, bounded by the Timor Sea in the W and the Coral Sea in the E. It is 1,290 km/800 mi long and 560 km/350 mi wide.

Arago /ˌærəˈgəʊ/ Dominique 1786–1853. French physicist and astronomer who made major contributions to the early study of electromagnetism. In 1820 he found out that iron enclosed in a wire coil could be magnetized by the passage of an electric current. Later, in 1824, he was the first to observe the ability of a floating copper disc to deflect a magnetic needle, the phenomenon of magnetic rotation.

Aragon /ˈærəgən/ autonomous region of NE Spain including the provinces of Huesca, Teruel, and Zaragoza; area 47,700 sq km/18,412 sq mi; population (1986) 1,215,000. Its capital is Zaragoza, and products include almonds, figs, grapes, and olives. Aragon was an independent kingdom 1035–1479.
history A Roman province until taken in the 5th century by the Visigoths, who lost it to the Moors in the 8th century, it became a kingdom 1035. It was united with Castile 1479 under Ferdinand and Isabella.

Aragon /ˌærəgɒn/ Louis 1897–1982. French poet and novelist. Beginning as a Dadaist, he became one of the leaders of Surrealism, published volumes of verse, and in 1930 joined the Communist party. Taken prisoner in World War II, he escaped to join the Resistance; his experiences are reflected in the poetry of *Le Crève-coeur* 1942 and *Les Yeux d'Elsa* 1944.

Arakan /ærəˈkɑːn/ state of Myanmar (formerly Burma) on the Bay of Bengal coast, some 645 km/400 mi long and strewn with islands; population (1983) 2,046,000. The chief town is Sittwe. It is bounded along its eastern side by the Arakan Yoma, a mountain range rising to 3,000 m/10,000 ft. The ancient kingdom of Arakan was conquered by Burma 1785.

Aral Sea /ˈɑːrəl/ inland sea; the world's fourth largest lake; divided between Kazakhstan and Uzbekistan; former area 62,000 sq km/24,000 sq mi, but decreasing. Water from its tributaries, the Amu Darya and Syr Darya, has been diverted for irrigation and city use, and the sea is disappearing, with long-term consequences for the climate.

Aramaic language Semitic language of the Hamito-Semitic family of W Asia, the everyday language of Palestine 2,000 years ago, during the Roman occupation and the time of Jesus.

In the 13th century BC Aramaean nomads set up states in Mesopotamia, and during the next 200 years spread into N Syria, where Damascus, Aleppo, and Carchemish were among their chief centres. Aramaic spread throughout Syria and Mesopotamia, becoming one of the official languages of the Persian empire under the Achaemenids and serving as a ◊lingua franca of the day.

Aramaic dialects survive among small Christian communities in various parts of W Asia, although Arabic spread widely with the acceptance of Islam.

Aran Islands /ˈærən/ three rocky islands (Inishmore, Inishmaan, Inisheer) in the mouth of Galway Bay, Republic of Ireland; population approximately 4,600. The capital is Kilronan. J M ◊Synge used the language of the islands in his plays.

Ararat /ˈærəræt/ double-peaked mountain on the Turkish-Iranian border; the higher, Great Ararat, 5,137 m/16,854 ft, was the reputed resting place of Noah's Ark after the Flood.

Araucanian Indian /ˌærɔːˈkeɪniən/ (Araucanian *Mapuche*) member of a group of South American Indian peoples native to central Chile and the Argentine pampas. They were agriculturalists and hunters, as well as renowned warriors, defeating the Incas and resisting the Spanish for 200 years. Originally, they lived in small villages; some 200,000 still survive in reserves. Scholars are divided over whether the Araucanian language belongs to the Penutian or the Andean-Equatorial family.

araucaria coniferous tree of genus *Araucaria*, allied to the firs, with flat, scalelike needles. Once widespread, it is now native only to the southern hemisphere. Some grow to gigantic size. Araucarias include the monkey-puzzle tree *A. araucana*, the Australian bunya bunya pine *A. bidwillii*, and the Norfolk Island pine *A. heterophylla*.

Arawak /ˈærəwæk/ member of an indigenous American people of the Caribbean and NE Amazon Basin. Arawaks lived mainly by shifting cultivation in tropical forests. They were driven out of many West Indian islands by another American Indian people, the Caribs, shortly before the arrival of the Spanish in the 16th century. Subsequently, their numbers on ◊Hispaniola declined from some 4 million in 1492 to a few thousand after their exploitation by the Spanish in their search for gold; the remaining few were eradicated by disease (smallpox was introduced 1518). Arawakan languages belong to the Andean-Equatorial group.

Arbenz Guzmán /ɑːˈbens ɡusˈmæn/ Jácobo 1913–1971. Guatemalan social democratic politician and president from 1951 until his overthrow 1954 by rebels operating with the help of the US Central Intelligence Agency.

Arbil /ˈɑːbɪl/ Kurdish town in a province of the same name in N Iraq. Occupied since Assyrian times, it was the site of a battle 331 BC at which Alexander the Great defeated the Persians under Darius III. In 1974 Arbil became the capital of a Kurdish autonomous region set up by the Iraqi government. Population (1985) 334,000.

arbitrageur in international finance, a person who buys securities (such as currency or commodities) in one country or market for immediate resale in another market, to take advantage of different prices. Arbitrage became widespread during the 1970s and 1980s with the increasing ◊deregulation of financial markets.

arbitration submission of a dispute to a third, unbiased party for settlement. Disputes suitable for arbitration include personal litigation, industrial disputes, or international grievances (as in the case of the warship ◊*Alabama*).

The first permanent international court was established in The Hague in the Netherlands 1900, and the League of Nations set up an additional Permanent Court of International Justice 1921 to deal with frontier disputes and the like. The latter was replaced 1945 with the International Court of Justice under the United Nations. Another arbiter is the European Court of Justice, which rules on disputes arising out of the Rome treaties regulating the European Community.

Arbuckle /ˈɑːbʌkəl/ Fatty (Roscoe Conkling) 1887–1933. US silent-film comedian, also a writer and director. His successful career in such films as *The Butcher Boy* 1917 and *The Hayseed* 1919 ended in 1921 after a sex-party scandal in which a starlet died. Although acquitted, he was spurned by the public and his films were banned.

Arbuthnot /ɑːˈbʌθnət/ John 1667–1735. Scottish writer and physician, attendant on Queen Anne 1705–14. He was a friend of Alexander Pope, Thomas Gray, and Jonathan Swift and was the chief author of the satiric *Memoirs of Martinus Scriblerus*. He created the English national character of John Bull, a prosperous farmer, in his *History of John Bull* 1712, pamphlets advocating peace with France.

arc in geometry, a section of a curved line. The arcs of a circle are classified thus: a *semicircle*, which is exactly half of the circle; *minor arcs*, which are less than the semicircle; and *major arcs*, which are greater than the semicircle.

A circle's arcs are measured in degrees. A semicircle is 180°, a minor arc is equal to the measure of its central angle (the angle formed by joining its two ends and the centre of the circle), and a major arc is 360° minus the degree measure of its corresponding minor arc.

Arcadia /ɑːˈkeɪdiə/ (Greek *Arkadhia*) central plateau of S Greece; area 4,419 sq km/1,706 sq mi; population (1981) 108,000. Tripolis is the capital town.

The English poet Philip ◊Sidney idealized the life of shepherds here in antiquity.

Arc de Triomphe /ˈɑːk də ˈtriːɒmf/ arch at the head of the Champs Elysées in the Place de l'Etoile, Paris, France, begun by Napoleon 1806 and completed 1836. It was intended to commemorate Napoleon's victories of 1805–06 and commissioned from Jean Chalgrin (1739–1811). Beneath it rests France's 'Unknown Soldier'.

Arc de Triomphe, Prix de l' French horse race run over 2,400 m/1.5 mi at Longchamp, near Paris. It is the leading 'open age' race in Europe, and one of the richest. It was first run 1920.

Arch /ɑːtʃ/ Joseph 1826–1919. English Radical member of Parliament and trade unionist, founder of the National Agricultural Union (the first of its kind) 1872. He was born in Warwickshire, the son of an agricultural labourer. Entirely self-taught, he became a Methodist preacher, and was Liberal-Labour MP for NW Norfolk.

arch curved structure of masonry that supports the weight of material over an open space, as in a bridge or doorway. It originally consisted of several wedge-shaped stones supported by their mutual pressure. The term is also applied to any curved structure that is an arch in form only.

Archaean /ɑːˈkiːən/ or *Archaeozoic* the earliest period of geological time; the first part of the Precambrian era, from the formation of Earth up to about 2,500 million years ago. It is a time when no life existed, and with every new discovery of ancient life its upper boundary is being pushed further back.

archaebacteria three groups of bacteria whose DNA differs significantly from that of other bacteria (called the 'eubacteria'). All are strict anaerobes, that is, they are killed by oxygen. This is thought to be a primitive condition and to indicate that the archaebacteria are related to the earliest life forms, which appeared about 4 billion years ago, when there was little oxygen in the Earth's atmosphere.

archaeology study of history (primarily but not exclusively the prehistoric and ancient periods), based on the examination of physical remains.

history Interest in the physical remains of the past began in the Renaissance among dealers in and collectors of ancient art. It was further stimulated by discoveries made in Africa, the Americas, and Asia by Europeans during the period of imperialist colonization in the 16th–19th centuries, such as the antiquities discovered during Napoleon's Egyptian campaign in the 1790s. Towards he end of the 19th century archaeology became an academic study, making increasing use of scientific techniques and systematic methodologies.

methods Principal activities include preliminary field (or site) surveys, excavation (where necessary), and the classification, dating, and interpretation of finds. Related disciplines that have been useful in archaeological reconstruction include stratigraphy (the study of geological strata), dendrochronology (the establishment of chronological sequences hrough the study of tree rings), palaeobotany (the study of ancient pollens, seeds, and grains), epigraphy (the study of inscriptions), and numismatics (the study of coins). Since 1958 radiocarbon dating has been used and refined to establish the age of archaeological strata and associated materials.

archaeopteryx extinct primitive bird, known from fossilized remains, about 160 million years old, found in limestone deposits in Bavaria, Germany. It is popularly known as 'the first bird', although some earlier bird ancestors are now known. It was about the size of a crow and had feathers and wings, but in many respects its skeleton is reptilian (teeth and a long, bony tail) and very like some small meat-eating dinosaurs of the time.

Archangel /ˈɑːkeɪndʒəl/ (Russian *Arkhangel'sk*) port in northern Russia; population (1987) 416,000. It was made an open port by Boris ◊Godunov and was of prime importance until Peter the Great built St Petersburg. It was used 1918–20 by the Allied interventionist armies in collaboration with the White Army in their effort to overthrow the newly established Soviet state. In World War II it was the receiving station for Anglo-American supplies. An open city in a closed area, it can be visited by foreigners only by air and is a centre for ICBMs (intercontinental ballistic missiles). Although the port is blocked by ice during half the year, it is the chief timber-exporting port of Russia. Plesetsk, to the south, is a launch site for crewed space flight.

archbishop in the Christian church, a bishop of superior rank who has authority over other bishops in his jurisdiction and often over an ecclesiastical province. The office exists in the Roman Catholic, Eastern Orthodox, and Anglican churches.

In the Church of England there are two archbishops—the archbishop of Canterbury ('Primate of All England') and the archbishop of York ('Primate of England').

archdeacon originally an ordained dignitary of the Christian church charged with the supervision of the deacons attached to a cathedral. Today in the Roman Catholic church the office is purely titular; in the Church of England an archdeacon still has many business duties, such as the periodic inspection of churches. It is not found in other Protestant churches.

archegonium female sex organ found in bryophytes (mosses and liverworts), pteridophytes (ferns, club mosses, and horsetails), and some gymnosperms. It is a multicellular, flask-shaped structure consisting of two parts: the swollen base or venter containing the egg cell, and the long, narrow neck. When the egg cell is mature, the cells of the neck dissolve, allowing the passage of the male gametes, or ◊antherozoids.

Archer /ɑːtʃə/ Frederick 1857–1886. English jockey. He rode 2,748 winners in 8,084 races 1870–86, including 21 classic winners.

He won the Derby five times, Oaks four times, St Leger six times, the Two Thousand Guineas four times, and the One Thousand Guineas twice. He rode 246 winners in the 1885 season, a record that stood until 1933 (see Gordon ◊Richards). Archer shot himself in a fit of depression.

Archer /ɑːtʃə/ Jeffrey 1940– . English writer and politician. A Conservative member of Parliament 1969–74, he lost a fortune in a disastrous investment, but recouped it as a best-selling novelist and dramatist. His books include *Not a Penny More, Not a Penny Less* 1975 and *First Among Equals*

1984. In 1985 he became deputy chair of the Conservative Party but resigned Nov 1986 after a scandal involving an alleged payment to a prostitute.

archerfish surface-living fish of the family Toxotidae, such as the genus *Toxotes*, native to SE Asia and Australia. The archerfish grows to about 25 cm/10 in and is able to shoot down insects up to 1.5 m/5 ft above the water by spitting a jet of water from its mouth.

archery use of the bow and arrow, originally in war and hunting, now as a competitive sport.

Flint arrowheads have been found in very ancient archaeological deposits, and bowmen are depicted in the sculptures of Assyria and Egypt, and indeed all nations of antiquity. The Japanese bow is larger and more sophisticated than the Western; its use is described in the medieval classic *Zen in the Art of Archery*. Until the introduction of gunpowder in the 14th century, bands of archers were to be found in every European army.

The English archers distinguished themselves in the French wars of the later Middle Ages; to this day the Queen's bodyguard in Scotland is known as the Royal Company of Archers. Up to the time of Charles II the practice of archery was fostered and encouraged by English rulers. Henry VIII in particular loved the sport and rewarded the scholar Roger ◊Ascham for his archery treatise *Toxophilus*. By the mid-17th century archery was no longer a significant skill in warfare and interest waned until the 1780s, although in the north of England shooting for the Scorton Arrow has been carried on, with few breaks, from 1673.

Organizations include the world governing body Fédération Internationale de Tir à l'Arc (FITA) 1931; the British Grand National Archery Society 1861; and in the USA the National Archery Association 1879 and, for actual hunting with the bow, the National Field Archery Association 1940. Competitions are usually based on double FITA rounds—that is, 72 arrows are fired at each of four targets from distances of 90, 70, 50, and 30 m for men, and from 70, 60, 50, and 30 m for women. The highest possible score is 2,880.

Archigram London-based group of English architects in the 1960s whose work was experimental and polemical; architecture was to be technological and flexible.

Archimedes /ˌɑːkɪˈmiːdiːz/ *c.* 287–212 BC. Greek mathematician who made major discoveries in geometry, hydrostatics, and mechanics. He formulated a law of fluid displacement (Archimedes' principle), and is credited with the invention of the Archimedes screw, a cylindrical device for raising water.

He was born at Syracuse in Sicily. It is alleged that Archimedes' principle was discovered when he stepped into the public bath and saw the water overflow. He was so delighted that he rushed home naked, crying 'Eureka! Eureka!' ('I have found it! I have found it!') He used his discovery to prove that the goldsmith of the king of Syracuse had adulterated a gold crown with silver. Archimedes designed engines of war for the defence of Syracuse, and was killed when the Romans besieged the town.

Archimedes' principle in physics, law stating that an object wholly or partly submerged in a fluid displaces a volume of fluid that weighs the same as the apparent loss in weight of the object (which, in turn, equals the upwards force, or upthrust, experienced by that object).

If the weight of the object is less than the upthrust exerted by the fluid, it will float partly or completely above the surface; if its weight is equal to the upthrust, the object will come to equilibrium below the surface; if its weight is greater than the upthrust, it will sink.

Archimedes screw one of the earliest kinds of pump, thought to have been invented by Archimedes. It consists of a spiral screw revolving inside a close-fitting cylinder. It is used, for example, to raise water for irrigation.

archipelago group of islands, or an area of sea containing a group of islands. The islands of an archipelago are usually volcanic in origin, and they sometimes represent the tops of peaks in areas around continental margins flooded by the sea.

Volcanic islands are formed either when a hot spot within the Earth's mantle produces a chain of volcanoes on the surface, such as the Hawaiian Archipelago, or at a destructive plate margin (see ◊plate tectonics) where the subduction of one plate beneath another produces an arc-shaped island group, such as the Aleutian Archipelago. Novaya Zemlya in the Arctic Ocean, the northern extension of the Ural Mountains, resulted from continental flooding.

Archipenko /ˌɑːkɪˈpeŋkəʊ/ Alexander 1887–1964. Russian-born abstract sculptor who lived in France from 1908 and in the USA from 1923. He pioneered Cubist works composed of angular forms and spaces and later experimented with clear plastic and sculptures incorporating lights.

architecture art of designing structures. The term covers the design of the visual appearance of structures; their internal arrangements of space; selection of external and internal building materials; design or selection of natural and artificial lighting systems, as well as mechanical, electrical, and plumbing systems; and design or selection of decorations and furnishings. Architectural style may emerge from evolution of techniques and styles particular to a culture in a given time period with or without identifiable individuals as architects, or may be attributed to specific individuals or groups of architects working together on a project.

early architecture Little remains of the earliest forms of architecture, but archaeologists have examined remains of prehistoric sites and documented ◊Stone Age villages of wooden post buildings with above-ground construction of organic materials such as mud or wattle and daub from the Upper Paleolithic, Mesolithic, and Neolithic periods in Asia, the Middle East, Europe, and the Americas. More extensive remains of stone-built structures have given clues to later Neolithic farming communities as well as habitations, storehouses, and religious and civic structures of early civilizations. The best documented are those of ancient Egypt, where exhaustive work in the 19th and 20th centuries revealed much about ordinary buildings, the monumental structures such as the pyramid tombs near modern Cairo, and the temple and tomb complexes concentrated at Luxor and Thebes.

Classical The basic forms of Classical architecture evolved in Greece between the 16th and 2nd centuries BC. Its hallmark is its post-and-lintel construction of temples and public structures, classified into the Doric, Ionic, and Corinthian orders, defined by simple, scrolled, and acanthus-leaf capitals for support columns, respectively. The Romans copied and expanded on Greek Classical forms, notably introducing bricks and concrete and inventing the vault, arch, and dome for public buildings and aqueducts.

Byzantine This form of architecture developed primarily in the E Roman Empire

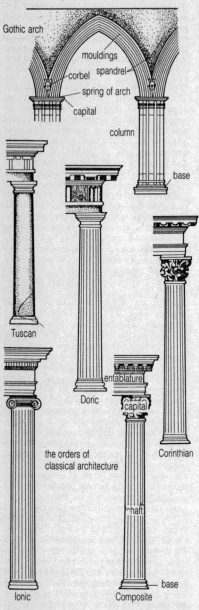

Gothic arch

mouldings

corbel spandrel

spring of arch

capital

column

base

Tuscan

entablature

Doric

capital

the orders of classical architecture

Corinthian

shaft

Ionic

Composite

base

Architecture

from the 4th century, with its centre at Byzantium (later named Constantinople, currently known as Istanbul). Its most notable features were construction of churches, some very large, based on the Greek cross plan (Hagia Sophia, Istanbul; St Mark's, Venice), with formalized painted and mosaic decoration.

Islamic This developed from the 8th century, when the Islamic religion spread from its centre in the Middle East west to Spain and E to China and parts of the Philippine Islands. Notable features are the development of the tower with dome and the pointed arch. Islamic architecture, chiefly through Spanish examples such as the *Great Mosque* at Córdoba and the *Alhambra* in Granada, profoundly influenced Christian church architecture—for example, by adoption of the pointed arch into the Gothic arch.

Romanesque This form of architecture is associated with Western European Christianity from the 8th to the 12th centuries. It is marked by churches with massive walls for structural integrity, rounded arches, small windows, and resulting dark volumes of interior space. In England this style is generally referred to as Norman architecture (Durham Cathedral). The style enjoyed a renewal of interest in Europe and the USA in the late 19th and early 20th centuries.

Gothic Gothic architecture emerged out of Romanesque, since the pointed arch and flying buttress made it possible to change from thick supporting walls to lighter curtain walls with extensive expansion of window areas (and stained-glass artwork) and resulting increases in interior light. Gothic architecture was developed mainly in France from the 12th to 16th centuries. The style is divided into Early Gothic (Sens Cathedral), High Gothic (Chartres Cathedral), and Late or Flamboyant Gothic. In England the corresponding divisions are Early English (Salisbury Cathedral), Decorated (Wells Cathedral), and Perpendicular (Kings College Chapel, Cambridge). Gothic was also developed extensively in Germany and neighbouring countries and in Italy.

Renaissance The 15th and 16th centuries in Europe saw the rebirth of Classical form and motifs in the Italian Neo-Classical movement. A major source of inspiration for the major Renaissance architects—Palladio, Alberti, Brunelleschi, Bramante, and Michelangelo—was the work of the 1st-century BC Roman engineer Vitruvius. The Palladian style was later used extensively in England by the likes of Inigo Jones; the Classical idiom was adopted by Christopher Wren. Classical or Neo-Classical style and its elements have been popular in the USA from the 18th century, as evidenced in much of the civic and commercial architecture since the time of the early republic (the US Capitol and Supreme Court buildings in Washington; many state capitols).

Baroque European architecture of the 17th and 18th centuries elaborated on Classical models with exuberant and extravagant decoration. In large-scale public buildings, the style is best seen in the innovative work of Giovanni Bernini and Francesco Borromini in Italy and later by John Vanbrugh, Nicholas Hawksmoor, and Christopher Wren in England. There were numerous practitioners in France and the German-speaking countries; Vienna is particularly Baroque.

Rococo This architecture extends the Baroque style with an even greater extravagance of design motifs, using a new lightness of detail and naturalistic elements, such as shells, flowers, and trees.

Neo-Classical European architecture of the 18th and 19th centuries again focused on the more severe Classical idiom (inspired by archaeological finds), producing, for example, the large-scale rebuilding of London by Robert Adam and John Nash and later of Paris by Georges Haussman.

Neo-Gothic The late 19th century saw a fussy Gothic revival in Europe and the USA, which was evident in churches and public buildings (such as the Houses of Parliament in London, designed by Charles Barry).

Art Nouveau This architecture arising at the end of the 19th century countered Neo-Gothic with sinuous, flowing shapes for buildings, room plans, and interior design. The style is characterized by the work of Charles Rennie Mackintosh in Scotland (Glasgow Art School) and Antonio Gaudí in Spain (Church of the Holy Family, Barcelona).

Modernist This architecture is also known as Functionalism or the International Style. It began in the 1900s with the Vienna school and the German Bauhaus but was also seen in the USA, Scandinavia, and France. It used spare line and form, an emphasis on rationalism, and the elimination of ornament. It makes great use of technological advances in materials such as glass, steel, and concrete and of construction techniques that allow flexibility of design. Notable practitioners include Frank Lloyd Wright, Mies van der Rohe, and Le Corbusier. Modern

architecture also furthered the notion of the planning of extensive multibuilding projects and of whole towns or communities.

Post-Modernist This style, which emerged in the 1980s in the USA, the UK, and Japan, rejected the functionalism of the Modern movement in favour of an eclectic mixture of styles and motifs, often classical. Its use of irony, parody, and illusion is in sharp distinction to the Modernist ideals of truth to materials and form following function.

High Tech This building style also developed in the 1980s. It took the ideals of the Modern movement and expressed them through highly developed structures and technical innovations (Norman Foster's Hong Kong and Shanghai Bank, Hong Kong; Richard Rogers's Lloyds Building in the City of London).

Deconstruction An architectural debate as much as a style, Deconstruction fragments forms and space by taking the usual building elements of floors, walls, and ceilings and sliding them apart to create a sense of disorientation and movement.

archive collection of historically valuable records, ranging from papers and documents to photographs, films, videotapes, and sound recordings.

The *National Register of Archives*, founded 1945, is in London; the *Public Record Office* (London and Kew) has documents of law and government departments from the Norman Conquest, including the ◊Domesday Book and ◊Magna Carta. Some government documents remain closed, normally for 30 years, but some for up to 100 years. The *National Portrait Gallery* has photographs, paintings, and sculptures; the *British Broadcasting Corporation Archives* have sound recordings, 500,000 cans of films, and 1.5 million videotapes (1990), and a contemporary Archive Unit to make films about the background to current events. In 1989 the British Film Institute launched a campaign for a national television archive to be funded from ITV advertising revenues.

archon (Greek 'ruler') in ancient Greece, title of the chief magistrate in many cities.

arc lamp or *arc light* electric light that uses the illumination of an electric arc maintained between two electrodes. The British scientist Humphry Davy developed an arc lamp 1808, and its major use in recent years has been in cinema projectors. The lamp consists of two carbon electrodes, between which a very high voltage is maintained.

Electric current arcs (jumps) between the two, creating a brilliant light.

The lamp incorporates a mechanism for automatically advancing the electrodes as they gradually burn away. Modern arc lamps (for example, searchlights) have the electrodes enclosed in an inert gas such as xenon.

arc minute, arc second units for measuring small angles, used in geometry, surveying, map-making, and astronomy. An arc minute is one- sixtieth of a degree, and an arc second one-sixtieth of an arc minute. Small distances in the sky, as between two close stars or the apparent width of a planet's disc, are expressed in minutes and seconds of arc.

Arctic, the /ˈɑːktɪk/ hat part of the northern hemisphere surrounding the North Pole; arbitrarily defined as the region lying N of the Arctic Circle (66° 32'N) or N of the tree line. There is no Arctic continent, the greater part of the region comprises the Arctic Ocean, which is the world's smallest ocean. Arctic climate, fauna, and flora extend over the islands and northern edges of continental land masses that surround the Arctic Ocean (Svalbard, Iceland, Greenland, Siberia, Scandinavia, Alaska, and Canada)

area 36,000,000 sq km/14,000,000 sq mi

physical pack-ice floating on the Arctic Ocean occupies almost the entire region between the North Pole and the coasts of North America and Eurasia, covering an area that ranges in diameter from 3,000 km/1,900 mi to 4,000 km/2,500 mi. The pack-ice reaches a maximum extent in February when its outer limit (influenced by the cold Labrador Current and the warm Gulf Stream), varies from 50°N along the coast of Labrador to 75°N in the Barents Sea N of Scandinavia. In spring the pack-ice begins to break up into ice floes which are carried by the S-flowing Greenland Current to the Atlantic Ocean. Arctic ice is at its minimum area in August. The greatest concentration of icebergs in Arctic regions is found in Baffin Bay. They are derived from the glaciers of W Greenland, then carried along Baffin Bay and down into the N Atlantic where they melt off Labrador and Newfoundland. The Bering Straits are icebound for more than six months each year, but the Barents Sea between Scandinavia and Svalbard is free of ice and is navigable throughout the year. Arctic coastlines, which have emerged from the sea since the last Ice Age, are characterized by deposits of gravel and disintegrated rock. Area covered by Arctic icecap shrank 2% 1978–1987

climate permanent ice sheets and year-round snow cover are found in regions where average monthly temperatures remain below 0°C/32°F, but on land areas where one or more summer months have average temperatures between freezing point and 10°C/50°F, a stunted, treeless tundra vegetation is found. Mean annual temperatures range from –23°C at the North Pole to –12°C on the coast of Alaska. In winter the Sun disappears below the horizon for a ime, but the cold is less severe than in parts of inland Siberia or Antartica. During the short summer season there is a maximum of 24 hours of daylight at the summer solstice on the Arctic Circle and six months constant light at the North Pole. Countries with Arctic coastlines established the International Arctic Sciences Committee in 1987 to study ozone depletion and climatic change

flora and fauna the plants of the relatively infertile Arctic tundra (lichens, mosses, grasses, cushion plants, and low shrubs) spring to life during the short summer season and remain dormant for the remaining en months of the year. There are no annual plants, only perennials. Animal species include reindeer, caribou, musk ox, fox, hare, lemming, wolf, polar bear, seal, and walrus. There are few birds except in summer when insects, such as mosquitoes, are plentiful

natural resources the Arctic is rich in coal (Svalbard, Russia), oil and natural gas (Alaska, Canadian Arctic, Russia), and mineral resources including gold, silver, copper, uranium, lead, zinc, nickel, and bauxite. Because of climatic conditions, the Arctic is not well-suited to navigation and the exploitation of these resources. Murmansk naval base on the Kola Peninsula is the largest in the world

population there are about one million aboriginal people including the Aleuts of Alaska, North American Indians, the Lapps of Scandinavia and Russia, the Yakuts, Samoyeds, Komi, Chukchi, Tungus and Dolgany of Russia, and the Inuit of Siberia, the Canadian Arctic and Greenland.

Arctic Circle /ˈɑːktɪk/ imaginary line that encircles the North Pole at latitude 66° 32 N. Within this line there is at least one day in the summer during which the Sun never sets, and at least one day in the winter during which the Sun never rises.

Arctic Ocean ocean surrounding the North Pole; area 14,000,000 sq km/5,400,000 sq mi. Because of the Siberian and North American rivers flowing into it, it has comparatively low salinity and freezes readily.

It comprises:

Beaufort Sea off Canada/Alaska coast, named after British admiral Francis ◊Beaufort; oil drilling allowed only in winter because the sea is the breeding and migration route of the bowhead whales, staple diet of the local Inuit;

Greenland Sea between Greenland and Svalbard;

Norwegian Sea between Greenland and Norway. From west to east along the N coast of Russia:

Barents Sea named after Willem ◊Barents, which has oil and gas reserves and is strategically significant as the meeting point of the NATO and Warsaw Pact forces. The ◊White Sea is its southernmost gulf;

Kara Sea renowned for bad weather and known as the 'great ice cellar';

Laptev Sea between Taimyr Peninsula and New Siberian Island;

East Siberian Sea and *Chukchi Sea* between Russia and the USA; the seminomadic Chukchi people of NE Siberia finally accepted Soviet rule in the 1930s.

The Arctic Ocean has the world's greatest concentration of nuclear submarines (40 of the 78 Soviet strategic nuclear submarines are here, plus their US counterparts), but at the same time there is much scientific cooperation on exploration, especially since Russia needs Western aid to develop oil and gas in its areas.

Ardebil /ɑːdəˈbiːl/ town in NW Iran, near the Azerbaijan frontier; population (1986) 281,973. Ardebil exports dried fruits, carpets, and rugs.

Ardèche /ɑːˈdeʃ/ river in SE France, a tributary of the Rhône. Near Vallon it flows under the Pont d'Arc, a natural bridge. It gives its name to a *département* (administrative region).

Arden /ˈɑːdn/ John 1930– . English playwright. His early plays *Serjeant Musgrave's Dance* 1959 and *The Workhouse Donkey* 1963 show the influence of Brecht. Subsequent works, often written in collaboration with his wife, Margaretta D'Arcy, show increasing concern with the political situation in Northern Ireland and a dissatisfaction with the professional and subsidized theatre world.

Arden, Forest of /ˈɑːdn/ former forest region of N Warwickshire, England, the setting for William Shakespeare's play *As You Like It*.

Ardennes /ɑːˈden/ wooded plateau in NE France, SE Belgium, and N Luxembourg, cut through by the river Meuse; also a *département* of ◊Champagne-Ardenne. There was heavy fighting here in World Wars I and II (see ◊Bulge, Battle of the).

are metric unit of area, equal to 100 square metres (119.6 sq yd); 100 ares make one ◊hectare.

area measure of surface. The SI unit of area is the metre squared.

Arecibo /ˌærerˈsiːbəʊ/ site in Puerto Rico of the world's largest single-dish ◊radio telescope, 305 m/1,000 ft in diameter. It is built in a natural hollow, and uses the rotation of the Earth to scan the sky. It has been used both for radar work on the planets and for conventional radio astronomy, and is operated by Cornell University, USA.

Arequipa /ˌærerˈkiːpə/ city in Peru at the base of the volcano El Misti; population (1990 est) 965,000. Founded by Pizarro 1540, it is the cultural focus of S Peru and a busy commercial (soap, textiles) centre.

Ares /ˈeəriː z/ in Greek mythology, the god of war (Roman ◊Mars). The son of Zeus and Hera, he was worshipped chiefly in Thrace.

arête (German *grat*; North American *combe-ridge*) sharp narrow ridge separating two ◊glacier valleys. The typical U-shaped cross sections of glacier valleys give arêtes very steep sides. Arêtes are common in glaciated mountain regions such as the Rockies, the Himalayas, and the Alps.

Arethusa /ˌærɪˈθjuːzə/ in Greek mythology, a nymph of the fountain and spring of Arethusa in the island of Ortygia near Syracuse, on the south coast of Sicily.

Aretino /ˌærəˈtiːnəʊ/ Pietro 1492–1556. Italian writer. He earned his living, both in Rome and Venice, by publishing satirical pamphlets while under the protection of a highly placed family. His *Letters* 1537–57 are a unique record of the cultural and political events of his time, and illustrate his vivacious, exuberant character. He also wrote poems and comedies.

Arevalo Bermejo /əˈrevələʊ bəˈmeɪx/ Juan José 1904–1990. Guatemalan president 1945–51, elected to head a civilian government after a popular revolt ended a 14-year period of military rule. However, many of his liberal reforms were later undone by subsequent military rulers.

Arezzo /ə'retsəʊ/ town in the Tuscan region of Italy; 80 km/50 mi SE of Florence; population (1981) 92,100. The writers Petrarch and Aretino were born here. It is a mining town and also trades in textiles, olive oil, and antiques.

argali wild sheep *Ovis ammon* of Central Asia. The male can grow to 1.2 m/4 ft at the shoulder, and has massive spiral horns.

Argand diagram /'ɑːgænd/ in mathematics, a method for representing complex numbers by Cartesian coordinates (x, y). Along the x-axis (horizontal axis) are plotted the real numbers, and along the y-axis (vertical axis) the nonreal, or ◊imaginary, numbers.

Argentina /ˌɑːdʒən'tiːnə/ country in South America, bounded W and S by Chile, N by Bolivia, and E by Paraguay, Brazil, Uruguay, and the Atlantic Ocean.

government The return of civilian rule 1983 brought a return of the 1853 constitution, with some changes in the electoral system. The constitution created a federal system with a president elected by popular vote through an electoral college, serving a six-year term. The president is head of both state and government and chooses the cabinet.

Argentina is a federal union of 22 provinces, one national territory, and the Federal District. The two-chamber Congress consists of a 46-member senate chosen by provincial legislatures for a nine-year term, and a directly elected chamber of 254 deputies serving a four-year term. Each province has its own elected governor and legislature that deal with matters not assigned to the federal government. The two most significant parties are the Radical Civic Union Party (UCR), and the Justicialist Party.

history Originally inhabited by South American Indian peoples, Argentina was first visited by Europeans in the early 16th century. Buenos Aires was founded first 1536 and again 1580 after being abandoned because of Indian attacks. Argentina was made a Spanish viceroyalty 1776, and the population rose against Spanish rule 1810. Full independence was achieved 1816. After a period of civil wars a stable government was established 1853 and the country developed as a democracy with active political parties.

rise of Perón Since 1930 Argentina has been subject to alternate civilian and military rule. The UCR held power from 1916 until the first military coup 1930. Civilian government returned 1932, and a second military coup 1943 paved the way for the rise of Lt-Gen Juan Domingo ◊Perón. Strengthened by the popularity of his wife, María Eva Duarte de ◊Perón (the legendary 'Evita'), Perón created the Peronista party, based on extreme nationalism and social improvement. Evita Perón died 1952, and her husband was overthrown and civilian rule restored 1955. Perón continued to direct the Peronista movement from exile in Spain. A coup 1966 restored military rule, and the success of a later Peronist party, Frente Justicialista de Liberación, brought Héctor Cámpora to the presidency 1973. After three months he resigned to make way for Perón, with his third wife, María Estela Martínez de Perón ('Isabel'), as vice president. Perón died 1974 and was succeeded by his widow.

Videla and the 'dirty war' Two years later, because of concern about the economy, a military coup ousted Isabel and a three-man junta, led by Lt-Gen Jorge Videla, was installed. The constitution was amended, and political and trade-union activity banned. The years 1976–83 witnessed a ferocious campaign by the junta against left-wing elements, the 'dirty war', during which it is believed that between 6,000 and 15,000 people 'disappeared'. Although confirmed in office until 1981, Videla retired 1978, to be succeeded by General Roberto Viola, who promised a return to democracy. Viola died

1981 and was replaced by General Leopoldo ◊Galtieri.

Falklands conflict Galtieri, seeking popular support and wishing to distract attention from the deteriorating economy, ordered 1982 the invasion of the *Islas Malvinas*, the ◊Falkland Islands, over which the UK's claim to sovereignty had long been disputed. After a short war, during which 750 Argentinians were killed, the islands were reoccupied by the UK. With the failure of the Falklands invasion, Galtieri was replaced in a bloodless coup by General Reynaldo Bignone. A military inquiry reported 1983 that Galtieri's junta was to blame for the defeat. Several officers were tried, and some, including Galtieri, given prison sentences. It was announced that the 1853 constitution would be revived, and an amnesty was granted to all those convicted of political crimes during the previous ten years. The ban on political and trade-union activity was lifted and general elections were held Oct 1983. The main parties were the UCR, led by Raúl ◊Alfonsín, and the Peronist Justicialist Party, led by Italo Lúder.

Alfonsín's reforms and investigations Having won the election, Alfonsín announced radical reforms in the armed forces (leading to the retirement of more than half the senior officers) and the trial of the first three military juntas that had ruled Argentina since 1976. He set up the National Commission on the Disappearance of Persons (CONADEP) to investigate the 'dirty war'. A report by CONADEP 1984 listed over 8,000 people who had disappeared and 1,300 army officers who had been involved in the campaign of repression. Alfonsín's government was soon faced with enormous economic problems, resulting in recourse to help from the ◊International Monetary Fund and an austerity programme.

Menem tackles high inflation The presidential election of May 1989 was won by the Justicialist candidate, Carlos ◊Menem. Alfonsín handed over power July 1989, five months before his term of office formally ended, to allow Menem to come to grips with the high inflation that threatened to bring about increasing social unrest. The new government soon established a rapport with the UK authorities and full diplomatic relations were restored Feb 1990 (the issue of sovereignty over the Falklands was skirted). President Menem was elected leader of the Justicialist Party Aug 1990 and in Dec a rebellion by junior army officers was put down. In Jan 1992 the government introduced a new currency, the peso, to replace the austral, which had been rendered almost worthless by inflation.

argon (Greek *argos* 'idle') colourless, odourless, nonmetallic, gaseous element, symbol Ar, atomic number 18, relative atomic mass 39.948. It is grouped with the ◊inert gases, since it was long believed not to react with other substances, but observations now indicate that it can be made to combine with boron fluoride to form compounds. It constitutes almost 1% of the Earth's atmosphere, and was discovered by British chemists John Rayleigh and William Ramsay after all oxygen and nitrogen had been removed chemically from a sample of air. It is used in electric discharge tubes and argon lasers.

argonaut or *paper nautilus* octopus living in the open sea, genus *Argonauta*. The female of the common paper nautilus, *A. argo*, is 20 cm/8 in across, and secretes a spiralled papery shell for her eggs from the web of the first pair of arms. The male is a shell-less dwarf, 1 cm/0.4 in across.

Argonauts /ˈɑːgənɔːts/ in Greek legend, the band of heroes who accompanied ◊Jason when he set sail in the *Argo* to find the ◊Golden Fleece.

Argos /ˈɑːgɒs/ city in ancient Greece, at the head of the Gulf of Nauplia, which was once a cult centre of the goddess Hera. In the Homeric age the name 'Argives' was sometimes used instead of 'Greeks'.

argument from design line of reasoning, argued by the English bishop William Paley 1794, that the universe is so complex that it can only have been designed by a superhuman power, and that we can learn something of it (God) by examining the world. The argument from design became popular with Protestant theologians in the 18th century as a means of accommodating Newtonian science. It was attacked by David ◊Hume, among others.

Argus /ˈɑː gəs/ in Greek mythology, a giant with 100 eyes. When he was killed by Hermes, Hera transplanted his eyes into the tail of her favourite bird, the peacock.

Argyll /ɑːgaɪl/ Archibald Campbell, 5th Earl of Argyll 1530–1573. Adherent of the Scottish presbyterian John ◊Knox. A supporter of Mary Queen of Scots from 1561, he commanded her forces after her escape from Lochleven Castle 1568. He revised his position and became Lord High Chancellor of Scotland 1572.

Argyllshire /ɑːˈɡaɪlʃə/ former county on the W coast of Scotland, including many of the Western Isles, which was for the most part merged in Strathclyde Region 1975, although a small area to the NW including Ballachulish, Ardgour, and Kingairloch went to Highland Region.

Århus /ˈɔːhuːs/ alternative form of ◊Aarhus, a port in Denmark.

aria (Italian 'air') solo vocal piece in an opera or oratorio, often in three sections, the third repeating the first after a contrasting central section.

Ariadne /ærɪˈædni/ in Greek mythology, the daughter of Minos, king of Crete. When Theseus came from Athens as one of the sacrificial victims offered to the Minotaur, she fell in love with him and gave him a ball of thread, which enabled him to find his way out of the labyrinth.

Ariane /ærɪˈæn/ launch vehicle built in a series by the European Space Agency (first flight 1979). The launch site is at Kourou in French Guiana. Ariane is a three-stage rocket using liquid fuels. Small solid-fuel and liquid-fuel boosters can be attached to its first stage to increase carrying power.

Since 1984 it has been operated commercially by Arianespace, a private company financed by European banks and aerospace industries. A future version, *Ariane 5*, is intended to carry astronauts aboard the Hermes spaceplane.

Arianism system of Christian theology that denied the complete divinity of Jesus. It was founded about 310 by ◊Arius, and condemned as heretical at the Council of Nicaea 325.

Some 17th- and 18th-century theologians held Arian views akin to those of ◊Unitarianism (that God is a single being, and that there is no such thing as the Trinity). In 1979 the heresy again caused concern to the Vatican in the writings of such theologians as Edouard Schillebeeckx of the Netherlands.

Arias Sanchez /ˈɑːrɪəs ˈsæntʃes/ Oscar 1940– . Costa Rican politician, president 1986–90, secretary general of the left-wing National Liberation Party (PLN) from 1979. He advocated a neutralist policy and in 1987 was the leading promoter of the Central American Peace Plan (see ◊Nicaragua). He lost the presidency to Rafael Angel Caldéron 1990.

Arica /əˈriːkə/ port in Chile; population (1987) 170,000. Much of Bolivia's trade passes through it, and there is contention over the use of Arica by Bolivia to allow access to the Pacific Ocean. It is Chile's northernmost city.

arid zone infertile area with a small, infrequent rainfall that rapidly evaporates because of high temperatures. The aridity of a region is defined by its *aridity index*—a function of the rainfall and also of the temperature, and hence the rate of evaporation. There are arid zones in Morocco, Pakistan, Australia, the USA, and elsewhere.

Scarcity of water is a problem for the inhabitants of arid zones, and constant research goes into discovering cheap methods of distilling sea water and artificially recharging natural groundwater reservoirs. Another problem is the eradication of salt in irrigation supplies from underground sources or where a surface deposit forms in poorly drained areas.

Ariel series of six UK satellites launched by the USA 1962–79, the most significant of which was *Ariel 5*, 1974, which made a pioneering survey of the sky at X-ray wavelengths.

Aries zodiacal constellation in the northern hemisphere between Pisces and Taurus, near Auriga, represented as the legendary ram whose golden fleece was sought by Jason and the Argonauts. Its most distinctive feature is a curve of three stars of decreasing brightness. The brightest of these is Hamal or Alpha Arietis, 65 light years from Earth. The Sun passes through Aries from late April to mid-May. In astrology, the dates for Aries are between about 21 March and 19 April (see ◊precession).

The spring ◊equinox once lay in Aries, but has now moved into Pisces through the effect of the Earth's precession (wobble).

aril accessory seed cover other than a ◊fruit; it may be fleshy and sometimes brightly coloured, woody, or hairy. In flowering plants, ◊angiosperms, it is often derived from the stalk that originally attached the ovule to the ovary wall. Examples of arils include the bright-red, fleshy layer surrounding the yew seed (yews are ◊gymnosperms so they lack true fruits), and the network of hard filaments that partially covers the nutmeg seed and yields the spice known as mace.

Ariosto /ˌærɪˈɒstəʊ/ Ludovico 1474–1533. Italian poet, born in Reggio. He wrote Latin poems and comedies on Classical lines, including the poem ◊*Orlando Furioso* 1516, published 1532, an epic treatment of the *Roland* story, and considered to be the perfect poetic expression of the Italian Renaissance.

Ariosto joined the household of Cardinal Ippolito d'Este 1503, and was frequently engaged in ambassadorial missions and diplomacy for the Duke of Ferrara. In 1521 he became governor of a province in the Apennines, and after three years retired to Ferrara, where he died.

Aristarchus of Samos /ˌærɪˈstɑːkəs/ *c.* 280–264 BC. Greek astronomer. The first to argue that the Earth moves around the Sun, he was ridiculed for his beliefs.

Aristide /ærɪˈstiːd/ Jean-Bertrand 1953– . President of Haiti Dec 1990–Oct 1991. A left-wing Catholic priest opposed to the right-wing regime of the Duvalier family, he campaigned for the National Front for Change and Democracy, representing a loose coalition of peasants, trade unionists, and clerics, and won 70% of the vote. He was deposed by the military Oct 1991.

Aristides /ˌærɪˈstaɪdiːz/ *c.* 530–468 BC. Athenian politician. He was one of the ten Athenian generals at the battle of ◊Marathon 490 BC and was elected chief archon, or magistrate. Later he came into conflict with the democratic leader Themistocles, and was exiled about 483 BC. He returned to fight against the Persians at Salamis 480 BC and in the following year commanded the Athenians at Plataea.

Aristippus /ˌærɪˈstɪpəs/ *c.* 435–356 BC. Greek philosopher, founder of the ◊Cyrenaic or hedonist school. A pupil of Socrates, he developed the doctrine that pleasure is the highest good in life. He lived at the court of ◊Dionysius of Syracuse and then with Laïs, a courtesan, in Corinth.

Aristophanes /ˌærɪˈstɒfəniːz/ *c.* 448–380 BC. Greek comedic dramatist. Of his 11 extant plays (of a total of over 40), the early comedies are remarkable for the violent satire with which he ridiculed the democratic war leaders. He also satirized contemporary issues such as the new learning of Socrates in *The Clouds* 423 BC and the power of women in ◊*Lysistrata* 411 BC. The chorus plays a prominent role, frequently giving the play its title, as in *The Wasps* 422 BC, *The Birds* 414 BC, and *The Frogs* 405 BC.

Aristotle /ˈærɪstɒtl/ 384–322 BC. Greek philosopher who advocated reason and moderation. He maintained that sense experience is our only source of knowledge, and that by reasoning we can discover the essences of things, that is, their distinguishing qualities. In his works on ethics and politics, he suggested that human happiness consists in living in conformity with nature. He derived his political theory from the recognition that mutual aid is natural to humankind, and refused to set up any one constitution as universally ideal. Of Aristotle's works some 22 treatises survive, dealing with logic, metaphysics, physics, astronomy, meteorology, biology, psychology, ethics, politics, and literary criticism.

Born in Stagira in Thrace, he studied in Athens, became tutor to ◊Alexander the Great, and in 335 BC opened a school in the Lyceum (grove sacred to Apollo) in Athens. It became known as the 'peripatetic school' because he walked up and down as he talked, and his works are a collection of his lecture notes. When Alexander died, Aristotle was forced to flee to Chalcis, where he died. Among his many contributions to political thought were the first systematic attempts to distinguish between different forms of government, ideas about the role of law in the state, and the conception of a science of politics.

In the Middle Ages, Aristotle's philosophy first became the foundation of Islamic philosophy, and was then incorporated into Christian theology; medieval scholars tended to accept his vast output without question. Aristotle held that all matter consisted of a single 'prime matter', which was always determined by some form. The simplest kinds of matter were the four elements—earth, water, air, and fire—which in varying proportions constituted all things. Aristotle saw nature as always striving to perfect itself, and first classified organisms into species and genera.

The principle of life he termed a soul, which he regarded as the form of the living creature, not as a substance separable from it. The intellect, he believed, can discover in sense impressions the universal, and since the soul thus transcends matter, it must be immortal. Art embodies nature, but in a more perfect fashion, its end being the purifying and ennobling of the affections. The essence of beauty is order and symmetry.

arithmetic branch of mathematics involving the study of numbers. The fundamental operations of arithmetic are addition, subtraction, multiplication, division, and, dependent on these four, raising to ◊powers and extraction of roots. Percentages, fractions, and ratios are developed from these operations. Fractions arise in the process of measurement.

Forms of simple arithmetic existed in prehistoric times. In China, Egypt, Babylon, and early civilizations generally, arithmetic was used for commercial purposes, records of taxation, and astronomy. During the Dark Ages in Europe, knowledge of arithmetic was preserved in India and later among the Arabs. European mathematics revived with the development of trade and overseas exploration. Hindu-Arabic numerals replaced Roman numerals, allowing calculations to be made on paper, instead of by the ◊abacus.

The essential feature of this number system was the introduction of zero, which allows us to have a *place–value* system. The decimal numeral system employs ten numerals (0,1,2,3,4,5,6, 7,8,9) and is said to operate in 'base ten'. In a base-ten number, each position has a value ten times that of the position to its immediate right; for example, in the number 23 the numeral 3 represents three units (ones), and the number 2 represents two tens. The Babylonians, however, used a complex base-sixty system, residues of which are found today in the number of minutes in each hour and in angular measurement (6×60 degrees). The Mayas used a base-twenty system.

There have been many inventions and developments to make the manipulation of the arithmetic processes easier, such as the invention of ◊logarithms by ◊Napier 1614 and of the slide rule in the period 1620–30. Since then, many forms of ready reckoners, mechanical and electronic calculators, and computers have been invented.

Modern computers fundamentally operate in base two, using only two numerals (0,1), known as a binary system. In binary, each position has a value twice as great as the position to its immediate right, so that for example binary 111 (111_2) is equal to 7 in the decimal system, and 1111 (1111_2) is equal to 15. Because the main operations of subtraction, multiplication, and division can be reduced mathematically to addition, digital computers carry out calculations by adding, usually in binary numbers in which the numerals 0 and 1 can be represented by off and on pulses of electric current.

Modulo arithmetic, sometimes known as residue arithmetic, can take only a specific number of digits, whatever the value. For example, in modulo 4 (mod 4) the only values any number can take are 0, 1, 2, or 3. In this system, 7 is written as 3 mod 4, and 35 is also 3 mod 4. Notice 3 is the residue, or remainder, when 7 or 35 is divided by 4. This form of arithmetic is often illustrated on a circle. It deals with events recurring in regular cycles, and is used in describing the functioning of petrol engines, electrical generators, and so on. For example, in the mod 12, the answer to a question as to what time it will be in five hours if it is now ten o'clock can be expressed $10 + 5 = 3$.

arithmetic and logic unit a computer component, see ◊ALU.

arithmetic sequence or *arithmetic progression* or *arithmetic series* sequence of numbers or terms that have a common difference between any one term and the next in the sequence. For example, 2, 7, 12, 17, 22, 27, ... is an arithmetic sequence with a common difference of 5. The general formula for the nth term is $a + (n-1)d$, where a is the first term and d is the common difference. An *arithmetic series* is the sum of the terms in an arithmetic sequence. The sum S of n terms is given by $S = (n/2)[2a + (n-1)d]$.

Arius /ˈeəriəs/ *c.* 256–336. Egyptian priest whose ideas gave rise to ◊Arianism, a Christian belief which denied the complete divinity of Jesus.

He was born in Libya, and became a priest in Alexandria 311. In 318 he was excommunicated and fled to Palestine, but his theology spread to such an extent that the emperor Constantine called a council at Nicaea 325 to resolve the question. Arius and his adherents were condemned and banished.

Arizona /ærɪˈzəʊnə/ state in SW US; nickname Grand Canyon State
area 294,100 sq km/113,523 sq mi
capital Phoenix
towns Tucson, Scottsdale, Tempe, Mesa, Glendale, Flagstaff
physical Colorado Plateau in the N and E, desert basins and mountains in the S and W, Colorado River, Grand Canyon
features Grand Canyon National Park (the multicoloured-rock gorge through which the Colorado River flows, 4–18 mi/6–29 km wide, up to 1.1 mi/1.7 km deep and 217

mi/350 km long); Organ Pipe Cactus National Monument Park; deserts: Painted (including the Petrified Forest of fossil rees), Gila, Sonoran; dams: Roosevelt, Hoover; old London Bridge (transported 1971 to the tourist resort of Lake Havasu City)

products cotton under irrigation, livestock, copper, molybdenum, silver, electronics, aircraft

population (1987) 3,469,000; including 4.5% American Indians (Navajo, Hopi, Apache), who by treaty own a quarter of the state

famous people Cochise, Wyatt Earp, Geronimo, Barry Goldwater, Zane Grey, Percival Lowell, Frank Lloyd Wright

history part of New Spain 1715; part of Mexico 1824; passed to the USA after Mexican War 1848; erritory 1863; statehood 1912.

Arizona is believed to derive its name from the Spanish *arida-zona* ('dry belt'). The first Spaniard to visit Arizona was the Franciscan Marcos de Niza 1539. After 1863 it developed rapidly as a result of the gold rush in neighbouring California. Irrigation has been carried out on a colossal scale since the 1920s. The Roosevelt dam on Salt River, and Hoover Dam on the Colorado River between Arizona and Nevada, provide the state with both hydroelectric power and irrigation water. At the end of the 19th century, rich copper deposits were found in Arizona and subsequently deposits of many other minerals. Aided by the use of air conditioning, the post-World War II era has seen a great increase in tourism.

Arjan /ˈɜːdʒən/ Indian religious leader, fifth guru (teacher) of Sikhism from 1581. He built the Golden Temple in ◊Amritsar and compiled the *Adi Granth*, the first volume of Sikh scriptures. He died in Muslim custody.

Arjuna /ˈɑːdʒʊnə/ Indian prince, one of the two main characters in the Hindu epic ◊*Mahābhārata*.

Arkansas /ˈɑːkənsɔː/ state in S central US; nickname Wonder State/Land of Opportunity

area 137,800 sq km/53,191 sq mi

capital Little Rock

towns Fort Smith, Pine Bluff, Fayetteville

physical Ozark mountains and plateau in the W, lowlands in he E; Arkansas River; many lakes

features Hot Springs National Park

products cotton, soybeans, rice, oil, natural gas, bauxite, timber, processed foods

population (1986) 2,372,000

famous people Johnny Cash, J William Fulbright, Douglas MacArthur, Winthrop Rockefeller *history* explored by de Soto 1541; European settlers 1648, who traded with local Indians; part of Louisiana Purchase 1803; statehood 1836.

Ark of the Covenant in the Old Testament, the chest that contained the Tablets of the Law as given to Moses. It is now the cupboard in a synagogue in which the ◊Torah scrolls are kept.

Arkwright /ˈɑːkraɪt/ Richard 1732–1792. English inventor and manufacturing pioneer who developed a machine for spinning cotton (he called it a 'spinning frame') 1768. He set up a water-powered spinning factory 1771 and installed steam power in another factory 1790.

Arkwright was born in Preston and experimented in machine designing with a watchmaker, John Kay of Warrington, until, with Kay and John Smalley, he set up the 'spinning frame'. Soon afterwards he moved to Nottingham to escape the fury of the spinners, who feared that their handicraft skills would become redundant. In 1771 he went into partnership with Jebediah Strutt, a Derby man who had improved the stocking frame, and Samuel Need, and built a water-powered factory at Cromford in Derbyshire. Steam power was used in his Nottingham works from 1790. This was part of the first phase of the ◊Industrial Revolution.

Arlington /ˈɑːlɪŋtən/ county in Virginia, USA, and suburb of Washington DC; population 152,599. It is the site of the National Cemetery for the dead of the US wars. The grounds were first used as a military cemetery 1864 during the American Civil War. By 1975, 165,142 military, naval, and civilian persons had been buried there and numbered, including the ◊Unknown Soldier of both world wars, President John F Kennedy, and his brother Robert Kennedy.

Armada fleet sent by Philip II of Spain against England 1588. See ◊Spanish Armada.

armadillo mammal of the family Dasypodidae, with an armour of bony plates on its back. Some 20 species live between Texas and Patagonia and range in size from the fairy armadillo at 13 cm/5 in to the giant armadillo, 1.5 m/4.5 ft long. Armadillos feed on insects, snakes, fruit, and carrion. Some can roll into an armoured ball if attacked; others rely on burrowing for protection.

They belong to the order Edentata ('without teeth') which also includes sloths and anteaters. However, only the latter are toothless. Some species of armadillos can have up to 90 peglike teeth.

Armageddon in the New Testament (Revelation 16), the site of the final battle between the nations that will end the world; it has been identified with ◊Megiddo in Israel.

Armagh /ɑːˈmɑː/ county of Northern Ireland
area 1,250 sq km/483 sq mi
towns Armagh (county town), Lurgan, Portadown, Keady
physical flat in the N, with many bogs; low hills in the S; Lough Neagh
features smallest county of Northern Ireland. There are crops in the better drained parts, especially flax. The chief rivers are the Bann and Blackwater, flowing into Lough Neagh, and the Callan tributary of the Blackwater
products chiefly agricultural: apples, potatoes, flax
population (1981) 119,000.

Armagnac /ˈɑːmənjæk/ deep-coloured brandy named after the district of Armagnac in Gascony, SW France, where it is produced.

Armani /ɑːˈmɑːni/ Giorgio 1935– . Italian fashion designer. He launched his first menswear collection 1974 and the following year started designing women's clothing. His work is known for fine tailoring and good fabrics. He designs for young men and women under the Emporio label.

armature in a motor or generator, the wire-wound coil that carries the current and rotates in a magnetic field. (In alternating-current machines, the armature is sometimes stationary.) The pole piece of a permanent magnet or electromagnet and the moving, iron part of a ◊solenoid, especially if the latter acts as a switch, may also be referred to as armatures.

armed forces state military organizations; see ◊services, armed.

Armenia /ɑːˈmiːniə/ country in W Asia, bounded E by Azerbaijan, N by Georgia, W by Turkey, and S by Iran.
government There is a 220-member legislature, the supreme soviet, to which deputies are elected by a majority system, and a second ballot 'run-off' race in contests in which there is no clear first-round majority. From the majority grouping within the supreme soviet, a prime minister (chair of the

cabinet of ministers) is drawn. The state president is directly elected.
history Armenia was in ancient times a kingdom occupying what is now the Van region of Turkey, part of NW Iran, and what is now Armenia. Under King Tigranes II (95–55 BC) the kingdom reached the height of its power, controlling an empire that stretched from the Mediterranean to the Caucasus. Thereafter, it fell under the sway of the ◊Byzantine Empire, then the Muslim Turks from the late 11th century, the Mongols in the 13th century, and the Ottomans from the 16th century. This domination by foreign powers bred an intense national consciousness and encouraged northward migration of the community.
under Soviet control With the advance of Russia into the Caucasus during the early 19th century, there was a struggle for independence which provoked an Ottoman backlash and growing international concern at Armenian maltreatment. In 1915 an estimated 1,750,000 Armenians were massacred or deported by the Turks. Conquered by Russia 1916, Armenia was briefly independent 1918 until occupied by the Red Army 1920. Along with Azerbaijan and Georgia, it formed part of the Transcaucasian Soviet Socialist Republic, but became a constituent republic of the USSR 1936.
growth of nationalism As a result of ◊glasnost, Armenian national identity was reawakened and in 1988 demands for reunion with ◊Nagorno-Karabakh led to a civil war 1989–91, resulting in the intervention of Soviet troops. The Armenian National Movement, which was formed Nov 1989 by Levon Ter-Petrossian and Vazguen Manukyan, and the militant Karabakh Committee were

at the fore of this growing nationalist campaign. The campaign included attempts to secure full control over the Azeri enclave of ◊Nakhichevan, leading to the flight of almost 200,000 Azeris from the republic. In the 1990 elections to the republic's supreme soviet (parliament) nationalists polled strongly and Ter-Petrossian and Manukyan were chosen as president and prime minister respectively.

struggle for independence On 23 Aug 1990 a declaration of independence was made but ignored by Moscow. The republic boycotted the March 1991 USSR referendum on the preservation of the Soviet Union and in April 1991 the property belonging to the Communist Party of Armenia (CPA) was nationalized. Four months later the CPA dissolved itself. In a referendum held Sept 1991, shortly after the failed anti-Gorbachev coup in Moscow, 94% voted for secession from the USSR. Two days later independence was formally proclaimed by President Ter-Petrossian, but this failed to secure Western recognition. A cease-fire agreement, brokered by the presidents of the Russian Federation and Kazakhstan, was signed by Armenia and Azerbaijan on 24 Sept 1991. It provided the basis for a negotiated settlement to the Nagorno-Karabakh dispute, including the disarming of local militias, the return of refugees, and the holding of free elections in the enclave. However, the agreement collapsed Nov 1991 when the Azeri parliament, dominated by communists-turned-nationalists, voted to annul Nagorno-Karabakh's autonomous status. Soviet troops were gradually withdrawn from the enclave, leaving it vulnerable to Azeri attacks. In response, after a referendum and elections Dec 1991, Nagorno-Karabakh's parliament declared its 'independence', precipitating an intensification of the conflict.

independence achieved On 16 Oct 1991, Ter-Petrossian was overwhelmingly re-elected president, capturing 83% of the vote, in the republic's first direct election. In Dec 1991 Armenia agreed to join the new confederal ◊Commonwealth of Independent States (CIS), which was formed to supersede the Soviet Union. Also in Dec Armenia was accorded diplomatic recognition by the USA and in Jan 1992 was admitted into the ◊Conference on Security and Cooperation in Europe (CSCE); in March 1992 it became a member of the United Nations (UN).

During early 1992 Armenia suffered a trade and energy embargo imposed by Azer-baijan in the escalating conflict over Nagorno-Karabakh. Despite capturing the Azeri strategic strongholds of Shusha and Lachin in May, Armenia had by Aug lost much of its newly gained territory in a surprise counteroffensive sprung by Azeri troops; however, it recovered its losses during 1993.

Armenian member of the largest ethnic group inhabiting the Republic of Armenia. There are Armenian minorities in the Republic of Azerbaijan, as well as in Turkey and Iran. Christianity was introduced to the ancient Armenian kingdom in the 3rd century. There are 4–5 million speakers of Armenian, which belongs to the Indo-European family of languages.

Armenian church /ɑːˈmiːnɪən/ form of Christianity adopted in Armenia in the 3rd century. The Catholicos, or exarch, is the supreme head, and Echmiadzin (near Yerevan) is his traditional seat.

About 295, Gregory the Illuminator (*c.* 257–332) was made exarch of the Armenian church, which has developed along national lines. The Seven Sacraments (or Mysteries) are administered, and baptism is immediately followed by confirmation. Believers number about 2 million.

Armenian language one of the main divisions of the Indo-European language family. Old Armenian, the classic literary language, is still used in the liturgy of the Armenian Church. Contemporary Armenian is used in the USSR, Iran, Turkey, Lebanon, and wherever Armenian emigrants have settled in significant numbers.

Armenian was not written down until the 5th century AD, when an alphabet of 36 (now 38) letters was evolved. Literature flourished in the 4th to 14th centuries, revived in the 18th, and continued throughout the 20th.

Armenian massacres series of massacres of Armenians by Turkish soldiers between 1895 and 1915. Reforms promised to Armenian Christians by Turkish rulers never materialized; unrest broke out and there were massacres by Turkish troops 1895. Again in 1909 and 1915, the Turks massacred altogether more than a million Armenians and deported others into the N Syrian desert, where they died of starvation; those who could flee to Russia or Persia. Only some 100,000 were left.

Armidale /ˈɑːmɪdeɪl/ town in New South Wales, Australia; population (1985) 21,500. The University of New England is here, and mansions of the ◊squatters (early settlers) survive.

Arminius /ɑːˈmɪnɪəs/ 17 BC–AD 21. German chieftain. An ex-soldier of the Roman army, he annihilated a Roman force led by Varus in the Teutoburger Forest area AD 9, and saved Germany from becoming a Roman province. He thus ensured that the empire's frontier did not extend beyond the Rhine.

Arminius /ɑːˈmɪnɪəs/ Jacobus. Latinized name of Jakob Harmensen 1560–1609. Dutch Protestant priest who founded Arminianism, a school of Christian theology opposed to Calvin's doctrine of predestination. His views were developed by Simon Episcopius (1583–1643). Arminianism is the basis of Wesleyan ◊Methodism.

armistice a cessation from hostilities while awaiting a peace settlement. 'The Armistice' refers specifically to the end of World War I between Germany and the Allies on 11 Nov 1918. On 22 June 1940 French representatives signed an armistice with Germany in the same railway carriage at Compiègne as in 1918. No armistice was signed with either Germany or Japan 1945; both nations surrendered and there was no provision for the suspension of fighting. The Korean armistice, signed at Panmunjom on 27 July 1953, terminated the Korean War 1950–53.

Armistice Day anniversary of the armistice signed 11 Nov 1918, ending World War I.

In the UK it is commemorated on the same day as ◊Remembrance Sunday.

Armory Show exhibition of Modern European art held Feb 1913 in New York. It marked the arrival of abstract art in the USA, and influenced US artists. A rioting crowd threatened to destroy Marcel Duchamp's *Nude Descending a Staircase* (now in the Museum of Art, Philadelphia).

armour body protection worn in battle. Body armour is depicted in Greek and Roman art. Chain mail was developed in the Middle Ages but the craft of the armourer in Europe reached its height in design in the 15th century, when knights were completely encased in plate armour that still allowed freedom of movement. Medieval Japanese armour was articulated, made of iron, gilded metal, leather, and silk. Contemporary bulletproof vests and riot gear are forms of armour. The term is used in a modern context to refer to a mechanized armoured vehicle, such as a tank.

Since World War II armour for tanks and ships has been developed beyond an increasing thickness of steel plate, with more emphasis on layered or 'sandwich' armour consisting of steel plates alternating with composite materials. More controversial is 'reactive' armour, consisting of 'shoeboxes' made of armour containing small, quick-acting explosive charges, which are attached at the most vulnerable points of a tank, in order to break up the force of entry of an enemy warhead. This type is used by Israel and the USSR, but the incorporation of explo-sive material in a tank has potential drawbacks.

The invention of gunpowder led, by degrees, to the virtual abandonment of armour until World War I, when the helmet reappeared as a defence against shrapnel. Suits of armour in the Tower of London were studied by US designers of astronaut wear. Modern armour, used by the army, police, security guards, and people at risk from assassination, uses nylon and fibreglass and is often worn beneath their clothing.

armoured personnel carrier (APC) wheeled or tracked military vehicle designed to transport up to ten people. Armoured to withstand small-arms fire and shell splinters, it is used on battlefields.

arms control attempts to limit the arms race between the superpowers by reaching agreements to restrict the production of certain weapons; see ◊disarmament.

arms trade the sale of arms from a manufacturing country to another nation. Nearly 50% of the world's arms exports end up in the Middle East, and most of the rest in Third World countries. Iraq, for instance, was armed in the years leading up to the 1991 Gulf War mainly by the USSR but also by France, Brazil, and South Africa.

Worldwide spending on arms was nearly $35 billion in 1987 (compared with $1 billion in 1960). The proportion of global arms spending accounted for by Third World countries was 24% in the late 1980s (up from 6% in 1965). During the 1980s, NATO countries supplied 31% of Third World Arms, with France supplying 11% and the Warsaw Pact countries supplying 58%. Arms exports are known in the trade as 'arms transfers'.

The Defence Export Services, a department of the Ministry of Defence, is responsible for British arms exports. Its annual budget is about 10 million.

Armstrong /ˈɑːmstrɒŋ/ Henry. Born Henry Jackson, nicknamed 'Homicide Hank' 1912–1988. US boxer. He was the only man to hold world titles at three different weights simultaneously. Between May and Nov 1938 he held the feather, welter-, and lightweight titles. He retired in 1945 and became a Baptist minister.

Armstrong /ˈɑːmstrɒŋ/ Louis ('Satchmo') 1901–1971. US jazz cornet and trumpet player and singer, born in New Orleans. His Chicago recordings in the 1920s with the Hot Five and Hot Seven brought him recognition for his warm and pure trumpet tone, his skill at improvisation, and his quirky, gravelly voice. From the 1930s he also appeared in films.

In 1923 Armstrong joined the Creole Jazz Band led by the cornet player Joe 'King' Oliver (1885–1938) in Chicago, but soon broke away and fronted various bands of his own. In 1947 he formed the Louis Armstrong All-Stars. He firmly established the pre-eminence of the virtuoso jazz soloist. He is also credited with the invention of scat singing (vocalizing meaningless syllables chosen for their sound).

Armstrong /ˈɑːmstrɒŋ/ Neil Alden 1930– . US astronaut. In 1969, he became the first person to set foot on the Moon, and said, 'That's one small step for a man, one giant leap for mankind.' The Moon landing was part of the ◊Apollo project.

Born in Ohio, he gained his pilot's licence at 16, and served as a naval pilot in Korea 1949–52 before joining NASA as a test pilot. He was selected to be an astronaut 1962 and landed on the Moon 20 July 1969.

Armstrong /ˈɑːmstrɒŋ/ Robert, Baron Armstrong of Ilminster 1927– . British civil servant, cabinet secretary in Margaret Thatcher's government. He achieved notoriety as a key witness in the *Spycatcher* trial in Australia 1987. After Oxford University he joined the civil service and rose rapidly to deputy-secretary rank. In 1970 he became Prime Minister Edward Heath's principal private secretary; Thatcher later made him cabinet secretary and head of the home civil service. He achieved considerable attention as a British Government witness in the 'Spycatcher' trial in Australia when, defending the Government's attempts to prevent Peter Wright's book alleging 'dirty tricks' from being published, to having been sometimes 'economical with the truth'. He retired in 1988 and was made a life peer.

Armstrong /ˈɑːmstrɒŋ/ William George 1810–1900. English engineer who developed a revolutionary method of making gun barrels 1855, by building a breech-loading artillery piece with a steel and wrought-iron barrel (previous guns were muzzle-loaded and had cast-bronze barrels). By 1880 the 150 mm/16 in Armstrong gun was the standard for all British ordnance.

army organized military force for fighting on land. A national army is used to further a political policy by force either within the state or on the territory of another state. Most countries have a national army, maintained at the expense of the state, raised either by conscription (compulsory military service) or voluntarily (paid professionals). Private armies may be employed by individuals and groups.

ancient armies (to 1066) Armies were common to all ancient civilizations. The Spartans trained from childhood for compulsory military service from age 21 to 26 in a full-time regular force as a heavily armed infantryman, or *hoplite*. Roman armies subjected all citizens to military service in *legions* of 6,000 men divided into *cohorts* of 600 men. Cohorts were similarly divided into six *centuries* of 100 men. The concept of duty to military service continued following the collapse of the Roman Empire. For example, the Anglo-Saxon *Fyrd* obliged all able-bodied men to serve in defence of Britain against Danish and then Norman invasion.
armies of knights and mercenaries (1066–1648) Medieval monarchs relied upon mounted men-at-arms, or *chevaliers*, who in turn called on serfs from the land. Feudal armies were thus inherently limited in size and could only fight for limited periods. Free *yeomen* armed with longbows were required by law to practise at the *butts* and provided an early form of indirect fire as *artillery*. In Europe paid troops, or *soldi*, and mounted troops, or *serviertes* (sergeants), made themselves available as *freelances*. By the end of the 15th century, *battles* or *battalions* or pikemen provided defence against the mounted knight. The hard gun, or *arquebus*, heralded the coming of infantrymen as known today. Those who wished to avoid military service could do so by paying *scutage*. For the majority the *conpane*, or *company*, was their home; they were placed under royal command by *ordonnances* and led by crown office holders, or *officiers*. Increased costs led to the formation of

the first mercenary armies. For example, the **Great Company** of 10,000 men acted as an international force, employing contractors, or **condottieri**, to serve the highest bidder. By the 16th century the long musket, pikemen, and the use of fortifications combined against the knight. **Sappers** became increasingly important in the creation and breaking of obstacles such as at Metz, a forerunner of the Maginot Line.

professional armies (1648–1792) The emergence of the nation-state saw the growth of more professional standing armies which trained in drills, used formations to maximize firepower, and introduced service discipline. The invention of the ring bayonet and the flintlock saw the demise of pikemen and the increased capability to fire from three ranks (today still the standard drill formation in the British Army). Artillery was now mobile and fully integrated into the army structure. The defects of raw levies, noble amateurs, and mercenaries led Oliver Cromwell to create the New Model Army for the larger campaigns of the English Civil War. After the Restoration, Charles II established a small standing army, which was expanded under James II and William III. In France, a model regiment was set up under de Martinet which set standards of uniformity for all to follow. State taxation provided for a formal system of army administration (uniforms, pay, ammunition). Nevertheless, recruits remained mainly society's misfits and delinquents. Collectively termed **other ranks**, they were divided from commissioned officers by a rigid hierarchical structure. The sheer cost of such armies forced wars to be fought by manoeuvre rather than by pitched battle, aiming to starve one's opponent into defeat while protecting one's own logistic chain.

armies of the revolution (1792–1819) Napoleon's organization of his army into autonomous **corps** of two to three **divisions**, in turn comprising two **brigades** of two **regiments** of two **battalions**, was a major step forward in allowing a rapid and flexible deployment of forces. Small-scale skirmishing by **light infantry**, coupled with the increasing devastation created by artillery or densely packed formations, saw the beginnings of the **dispersed battlefield**. Victory in war was now synonymous with the complete destruction of the enemy in battle. Reservists were conscripted to allow the mass army to fight wars through to the bitter end. (Only Britain, by virtue of the English Channel and the Royal Navy, was able to avoid the need to provide such large land forces.) Officers were now required to be professionally trained; the Royal Military College was set up in Britain 1802, St Cyr in France 1808, the Kriegsakademie in Berlin 1810, and the Russian Imperial Military Academy 1832. **Semaphore telegraph** and **observation balloons** were first steps to increasing the commander's ability to observe enemy movements. The British army, under Wellington, was very strong, but afterwards decreased in numbers.

19th-century armies The defeat of Revolutionary France saw a return to the traditions of the 18th century and a reduction in conscription. Meanwhile the railway revolutionized the deployment of forces, permitting quick mobilization, continuous resupply to the front, and rapid evacuation of casualties to the rear. The US Civil War has been called the Railway War. By 1870, the limitation of supply inherent to the Napoleonic army had been overcome and once again armies of over 1 million could be deployed. By 1914, continental armies numbered as many as 3 million and were based on conscription. A general staff was now required to manage these. **Breech-loading rifles** and **machine guns** ensured a higher casualty rate.

technological armies (1918–45) The advent of the internal combustion engine allowed new advances in mobility to overcome the supremacy of the defensive over the offensive. The **tank** and the **radio** were vital to the evolution of armoured warfare or **Blitzkrieg**. Armies were able to reorganize into highly mobile formations, such as the German **Panzer Divisions**, which utilized speed, firepower, and surprise to overwhelm static defences and thereby dislocate the army's rear.

The armies of World War II were very mobile, and were closely coordinated with the navy and air force. The requirement to fuel and maintain such huge fleets of vehicles again increased the need to maintain supplies. The complexity of the mechanized army demanded a wide range of skills not easily found through conscription.

armies of the nuclear age (1945–) The advent of tactical nuclear weapons severely compounded the problems of mass concentration and thus protected mobility assumed greater importance to allow rapid concentration and dispersal of forces in what could be a high chemical threat zone. From the 1960s there were sophisticated developments in tanks and antitank weapons, mortar-locating radar, and heat-seeking missiles. All armies of NATO and the Warsaw Pact are professional, except those of Canada, the UK, and the USA.

Arnauld /ɑːˈnəʊ/ French family closely associated with ◊Jansenism, a Christian church movement in the 17th century. *Antoine Arnauld* (1560–1619) was a Parisian advocate, strongly critical of the Jesuits; along with the philosopher Pascal and others, he produced not only Jansenist pamphlets, but works on logic, grammar, and geometry. Many of his 20 children were associated with the abbey of Port Royal, a convent of Cistercian nuns near Versailles which became the centre of Jansenism. His youngest child, *Antoine* (1612–1694), the 'great Arnauld', was religious director there.

Arne /ɑːn/ Thomas Augustus 1710–1778. English composer, whose musical drama *Alfred* 1740 includes the song 'Rule Britannia!'.

Arnhem, Battle of /ˈɑːnəm/ in World War II, airborne operation by the Allies, 17–26 Sept 1944, to secure a bridgehead over the Rhine, thereby opening the way for a thrust towards the Ruhr and a possible early end to the war. It was only partially successful, with 7,600 casualties. Arnhem is a city in the Netherlands, on the Rhine SE of Utrecht; population (1988) 297,000. It produces salt, chemicals, and pharmaceuticals.

Arnhem Land /ˈɑːnəm/ plateau of the central peninsula in Northern Territory, Australia. It is named after a Dutch ship which dropped anchor there in 1618. The chief town is Nhulunbuy. It is the largest of the Aboriginal reserves, and a traditional way of life is maintained, now threatened by mineral exploitation.

Arno /ˈɑːnəʊ/ Italian river 240 km/150 mi long, rising in the Apennines, and flowing westwards to the Mediterranean Sea. Florence and Pisa stand on its banks. A flood in 1966 damaged virtually every Renaissance landmark in Florence.

Arnold /ˈɑːnld/ Benedict 1741–1801. US soldier and military strategist who, during the American Revolution, won the turning point battle at Saratoga 1777 for the Americans. He is chiefly remembered as a traitor to the American side. A merchant in New Haven, Connecticut, he joined the colonial forces but in 1780 plotted to betray the strategic post at West Point to the British.

Arnold was bitter at having been passed over for promotion, and he contacted Henry Clinton to propose defection. Major André was sent by the British to discuss terms with him, but was caught and hanged as a spy. Arnold escaped to the British, who gave him an army command.

Arnold /ˈɑːnld/ Malcolm (Henry) 1921– . English composer. His work is tonal and includes a large amount of orchestral, chamber, ballet, and vocal music. His operas include *The Dancing Master* 1951, and he has written music for more than 80 films, including *The Bridge on the River Kwai* 1957, for which he won an Academy Award.

Arnold /ˈɑːnld/ Matthew 1822–1888. English poet and critic, son of Thomas Arnold. His poems, characterized by their elegiac mood and pastoral themes, include *The Forsaken Merman* 1849, *Thyrsis* 1867 (commemorating his friend Arthur Hugh Clough), *Dover Beach* 1867, and *The Scholar Gypsy* 1853. Arnold's critical works include *Essays in Criticism* 1865 and 1888, and *Culture and Anarchy* 1869, which attacks 19th-century philistinism.

Arnold /ˈɑːnld/ Thomas 1795–1842. English schoolmaster, father of the poet and critic Matthew Arnold. He was headmaster of Rugby School 1828–42. His regime has been graphically described in Thomas Hughes's *Tom Brown's Schooldays* 1857. He emphasized training of character, and had a profound influence on public school education.

aromatherapy use of aromatic essential oils to relieve tension or to induce a feeling of well-being, usually in combination with massage. It is also used to relieve minor skin complaints. Common in the Middle East for centuries, the practice was reintroduced to the West in France during the 1960s.

aromatic compound organic chemical compound in which some of the bonding electrons are delocalized (shared amongst several atoms within the molecule and not localized in the vicinity of the atoms involved in bonding). The commonest aromatic compounds have ring structures, the atoms comprising the ring being either all carbon or containing one or more different atoms (usually nitrogen, sulphur, or oxygen). Typical examples are benzene (C_6H_6) and pyridine (C_6H_5N).

Arp /ɑːp/ Hans or Jean 1887–1966. French abstract painter and sculptor. He was one of the founders of the ◊Dada movement about

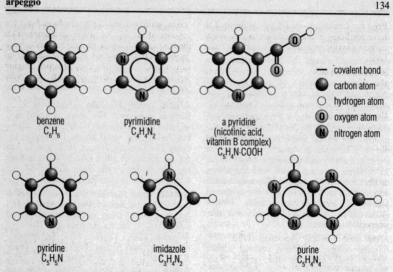

benzene
C_6H_6

pyrimidine
$C_4H_4N_2$

a pyridine
(nicotinic acid,
vitamin B complex)
$C_5H_4N \cdot COOH$

— covalent bond
● carbon atom
○ hydrogen atom
Ⓞ oxygen atom
Ⓝ nitrogen atom

pyridine
C_5H_5N

imidazole
$C_3H_4N_2$

purine
$C_5H_4N_4$

Aromatic compound Compounds whose molecules contain the benzene ring, or variations of it, are called aromatic.

1917, and later was associated with the Surrealists. His innovative wood sculptures use organic shapes in bright colours.

In his early experimental works, such as collages, he collaborated with his wife *Sophie Taeuber-Arp* (1889–1943).

arpeggio (Italian 'like a harp') in music, a chord played as a cascade of notes played in succession.

Arran /ˈærən/ large mountainous island in the Firth of Clyde, Scotland, in Strathclyde; area 427 sq km/165 sq mi; population (1981) 4,726. It is popular as a holiday resort. The chief town is Brodick.

Arras /ˈærəs/ French town on the Scarpe River NE of Paris; population (1982) 80,500 (conurbation). It is the capital of Pas-de-Calais *département*, and was formerly known for tapestry. It was the birthplace of the French revolutionary leader Robespierre.

Arras, Battle of /ˈærəs/ battle of World War I, April–May 1917. It was an effective but costly British attack on German forces in support of a French offensive, which was only partially successful, on the ◊Siegfried Line. British casualties totalled 84,000 as compared to 75,000 German casualties.

Arras, Congress and Treaty of meeting in N France 1435 between representatives of Henry VI of England, Charles VII of France, and Philip the Good of Burgundy to settle the Hundred Years' War. The outcome was a diplomatic victory for France. Although England refused to compromise on Henry VI's claim to the French crown, France signed a peace treaty with Burgundy, England's former ally.

arrest the apprehension and detention of a person suspected of a crime.

In Britain, an arrest may be made on a magistrate's warrant, but a police constable is empowered to arrest without warrant in all cases where he or she has reasonable ground for thinking a serious offence has been committed. A private citizen may arrest anyone committing a serious offence or breach of the peace in their presence. A person who makes a citizen's arrest must take the arrested person to the police or a magistrate as soon as is practicable or they may be guilty of false imprisonment. In the USA police officers and private persons have similar rights and duties.

Arrhenius /əˈreɪnɪəs/ Svante August 1859–1927. Swedish scientist, the founder of physical chemistry. Born near Uppsala, he became a professor at Stockholm in 1895, and made a special study of electrolysis. He wrote *Worlds in the Making* and *Destinies of the Stars*, and in 1903 received the Nobel

Prize for Chemistry. In 1905 he is reputed to have predicted global warming as a result of carbon dioxide emission from burning fossil fuels.

arrowroot starchy substance derived from the roots and tubers of various tropical plants with thick, clumpy roots. The true arrowroot *Maranta arundinacea* was used by the Indians of South America as an antidote against the effects of poisoned arrows.

The West Indian island of St Vincent is the main source of supply today. The edible starch is easily digested and is good for invalids.

arsenic brittle, greyish-white, semimetallic element (a metalloid), symbol As, atomic number 33, relative atomic mass 74.92. It occurs in many ores and occasionally in its elemental state, and is widely distributed, being present in minute quantities in the soil, the sea, and the human body. In larger quantities, it is poisonous. The chief source of arsenic compounds is as a by-product from metallurgical processes. It is used in making semiconductors, alloys, and solders.

art in the broadest sense, all the processes and products of human skill, imagination, and invention; the opposite of nature. In contemporary usage, definitions of art usually reflect aesthetic criteria, and the term may encompass literature, music, drama, painting, and sculpture. Popularly, the term is most commonly used to refer to the visual arts. In Western culture, aesthetic criteria introduced by the ancient Greeks still influence our perceptions and judgements of art.

Two currents of thought run through our ideas about art. In one, derived from Aristotle, art is concerned with *mimesis* ('imitation'), the representation of appearances, and gives pleasure through the accuracy and skill with which it depicts the real world. The other view, derived from Plato, holds that the artist is inspired by the Muses (or by God, or by the inner impulses, or by the collective unconscious) to express that which is beyond appearances—inner feelings, eternal truths, or the essence of the age. In the Middle Ages the term 'art' was used, chiefly in the plural, to signify a branch of learning which was regarded as an instrument of knowledge. The seven *liberal arts* consisted of the *trivium*, that is grammar, logic, and rhetoric, and the *quadrivium*, that is arithmetic, music, geometry, and astronomy. In the visual arts of Western civiliza-

tions, painting and sculpture have been the dominant forms for many centuries. This has not always been the case in other cultures. Islamic art, for example, is one of ornament, for under the Muslim religion artists were forbidden to usurp the divine right of creation by portraying living creatures. In some cultures masks, tattoos, pottery, and metalwork have been the main forms of visual art. Recent technology has made new art forms possible, such as photography and cinema, and today electronic media have led to entirely new ways of creating and presenting visual images. See also ◊ancient art, ◊medieval art, and the arts of individual countries, such as ◊French art, and individual movements, such as ◊Romanticism, ◊Cubism, and ◊Impressionism.

Artaud /ɑːˈtəʊ/ Antonin 1896–1948. French theatre director. Although his play, *Les Cenci/The Cenci* 1935, was a failure, his concept of the *Theatre of* ◊Cruelty, intended to release feelings usually repressed in the unconscious, has been an important influence on modern dramatists such as Albert Camus and Jean Genet and on directors and producers. Declared insane 1936, Artaud was confined in an asylum.

Art Deco /ɑːt ˈdekəʊ/ style in art and architecture that emerged in Europe in the 1920s and continued through the 1930s, using rather heavy, geometric simplification of form: for example, Radio City Music Hall, New York. It was a self-consciously modern style, with sharp lines, and dominated the decorative arts. The graphic artist Erté (1893–1989) was a fashionable exponent.

Artemis /ˈɑːtəmɪs/ in Greek mythology, the goddess (Roman Diana) of chastity, the Moon, and the hunt. She is the twin sister of ◊Apollo. Her cult centre was at Ephesus.

arteriography method of examining the interior of an artery by injecting into it a radio-opaque solution, which is visible on an X-ray photograph. It is used for the arteries of the heart (coronary arteriogram), for example.

artery vessel that carries blood from the heart to the rest of the body. It is built to withstand considerable pressure, having thick walls that are impregnated with muscle and elastic fibres. During contraction of the heart muscles, arteries expand in diameter to allow for the sudden increase in pressure that occurs; the resulting ◊pulse or pressure wave can be felt at the wrist. Not all arteries carry oxygenated (oxygen-rich) blood; the pulmonary arteries convey deoxygenated (oxygen-poor) blood from the heart to the lungs.

Arteries are flexible, elastic tubes, consisting of three layers, the middle of which is muscular; its rhythmic contraction aids the pumping of blood around the body. In middle and old age, the walls degenerate and are vulnerable to damage by the build-up of fatty deposits. These lower elasticity, hardening the arteries and decreasing the internal bore. This condition, known as ◊atherosclerosis, can lead to high blood pressure, loss of circulation, heart disease, and death. Research indicates that a typical Western diet, high in saturated fat, increases the chances of arterial disease developing.

artesian well well in which water rises from its ◊aquifer under natural pressure. Such a well may be drilled into an aquifer that is confined by impermeable beds both above and below. If the water table (the top of the region of water saturation) in that aquifer is above the level of the well head, hydrostatic pressure will force the water to the surface.

arthritis inflammation of the joints, with pain, swelling, and restricted motion. Many conditions may cause arthritis, including gout and trauma to the joint.

More common in women, *rheumatoid arthritis* usually begins in middle age in the small joints of the hands and feet, causing a greater or lesser degree of deformity and painfully restricted movement. It is alleviated by drugs, and surgery may be performed to correct deformity.

Osteoarthritis, a degenerative condition, tends to affect larger, load-bearing joints, such as the knee and hip. It appears in later life, especially in those whose joints may have been subject to earlier stress or damage; one or more joints stiffen and may give considerable pain. Joint replacement surgery is nearly always successful.

arthropod member of the phylum Arthropoda; an invertebrate animal with jointed legs and a segmented body with a horny or chitinous casing (exoskeleton), which is shed periodically and replaced as the animal grows. Included are arachnids such as spiders and mites, as well as crustaceans, millipedes, centipedes, and insects.

Arthur /ˈɑːθə/ 6th century AD. Legendary British king and hero in stories of ◊Camelot and the quest for the ◊Holy Grail. Arthur is said to have been born in Tintagel, Cornwall, and buried in Glastonbury, England. He may have been a Romano-Celtic leader against pagan Saxon invaders.

The legends of Arthur and the knights of the Round Table were developed in the 12th century by Geoffrey of Monmouth, Chrétien de Troyes, and the Norman writer Wace.

Arthur /ˈɑːθə/ Chester Alan 1830–1886. The 21st president of the USA. He was born in Vermont, the son of a Baptist minister, and became a lawyer and Republican political appointee in New York. In 1880, Arthur was chosen as ◊Garfield's vice president, and was his successor when Garfield was assassinated the following year. Arthur held office until 1885.

Arthur's Pass /ˈɑːθəz ˈpɑːs/ road-rail link across the Southern Alps, New Zealand, at 926 m/3,038 ft, linking Christchurch with Greymouth.

Arthur's Seat /ˈɑːθəz ˈsiːt/ hill of volcanic origin, Edinburgh, Scotland; height 251 m/823 ft; only fancifully linked with King Arthur.

artichoke two plants of the composite or sunflower family Compositae. The common or globe artichoke *Cynara scolymus* is tall, with purplish blue flowers; the bracts of the unopened flower are eaten. The Jerusalem artichoke *Helianthus tuberosus* has edible tubers.

The Jerusalem artichoke is a native of North America; its common name is a corruption of the Italian for sunflower, *girasole*.

article grammatical ◊part of speech. There are two articles in English: the *definite article* the, which serves to specify or identify a noun (as in 'This is *the* book I need'), and the *indefinite article* a or (before vowels) an, which indicates a single unidentified noun ('They gave me *a* piece of paper and *an* envelope').

Some people use the form 'an' before h ('an historic building'); this practice dates from the 17th century, when an initial h was often not pronounced (as in '*honour*'), and is nowadays widely considered rather grandiose.

articles of association in the UK, the rules governing the relationship between a registered company, its members (shareholders), and its directors. The articles of association are deposited with the registrar of companies. In the USA they are called *by-laws*.

artificial insemination (AI) mating achieved by mechanically injecting previously collected semen into the uterus without genital contact. It is commonly used with cattle since it allows farmers to select the type and quality of bull required for a herd, and to control the timing and organization of a breeding programme. The practice of artificially inseminating pigs has also become widespread in recent years.

In the UK in 1990 a Human Fertilisation and Embryology Bill proposed future identification of the donors. The Statutory Licensing Authority would hold central records of all children born in this way, and information on inherited conditions (and genealogical information, to avoid incest by marrying a sibling) would routinely be released.

artificial intelligence (AI) branch of cognitive science concerned with creating computer programs that can perform actions comparable with those of an intelligent human. Current AI research covers areas such as planning (for robot behaviour), language understanding, pattern recognition, and knowledge representation.

Early AI programs, developed in the 1960s, attempted simulations of human intelligence or were aimed at general problem-solving techniques. It is now thought that intelligent behaviour depends as much on the knowledge a system po sesses as on its reasoning power. Present emphasis is on ◊knowledge-based systems, such as ◊expert systems. Britain's largest AI laboratory is at the Turing Institute, University of Strathclyde, Glasgow. In May 1990 the first International Robot Olympics was held there, including table-tennis matches between robots of the UK and the USA.

artificial radioactivity natural and spontaneous radioactivity arising from radioactive isotopes or elements that are formed when elements are bombarded with subatomic particles–protons, neutrons, or electrons–or small nuclei.

artificial respiration maintenance of breathing when the natural process is suspended. If breathing is permanently suspended, as in paralysis, an ◊iron lung is used; in cases of electric shock or apparent drowning, for example, the first choice is the expired-air method, the *kiss of life* by mouth-to-mouth breathing until natural breathing is resumed.

artificial selection in biology, selective breeding of individuals that exhibit the particular characteristics that a plant or animal breeder wishes to develop. In plants, desirable features might include resistance to disease, high yield (in crop plants), or attractive appearance. In animal breeding, selection has led to the development of particular breeds of cattle for improved meat production (such as the Aberdeen Angus) or milk production (such as Jerseys).

artillery collective term for military ◊firearms too heavy to be carried. Artillery can be mounted on ships or aeroplanes and includes cannons and missile launchers.

14th century Cannons came into general use, and were most effective in siege warfare. The term had previously been applied to catapults used for hurling heavy objects.

16th century The howitzer, halfway between a gun and a mortar (muzzle-loading cannon), was first used in sieges.

early 19th century In the Napoleonic period, field artillery became smaller and more mobile.

1914–18 In World War I, howitzers were used to demolish trench systems. Giant cannons were used in the entrenched conditions of the Western Front and at sea against he lumbering, heavily armoured battleships, but their accuracy against small or moving targets was poor.

1939–45 In World War II artillery became more mobile, particularly in the form of self-propelled guns.

1980s The introduction of so-called smart munitions meant that artillery rounds could be guided to their target by means of a laser designator.

Art Nouveau /ɑː nuːˈvəʊ/ art style of about 1890–1910 in Europe, marked by sinuous lines and stylized flowers and foliage. It is also called *Jugendstil* (Germany) and *Stile Liberty* (Italy, after the fashionable London department store). Exponents included the illustrator Aubrey Beardsley, the architect and furniture designer Charles Rennie Mackintosh, and the glass and jewellery designer René Lalique.

Art Nouveau was primarily a decorative, two-dimensional style and pervaded the visual arts. The theatrical posters of Czech painter and designer Alphonse Mucha (1860–1939) exemplify the popular version.

Arts and Crafts movement English social movement, largely antimachine in spirit, based in design and architecture and founded by William Morris in the latter half of the 19th century. It was supported by the architect A W Pugin and by John ◊Ruskin and stressed the importance of handcrafting. The Art Nouveau style succeeded it.

Arts Council of Great Britain UK organization, incorporated 1946, which aids music, drama, and visual arts with government funds. It began 1940 as the Council for the Encouragement of Music and the Arts (CEMA) with a grant from the Pilgrim Trust.

Aruba /əˈruːbə/ island in the Caribbean, the westernmost of the Lesser Antilles; an overseas part of the Netherlands
area 193 sq km/75 sq mi
population (1985) 61,000
history Aruba obtained separate status from the other Netherlands Antilles 1986 and has full internal autonomy.

arum any plant of the genus *Arum*, family Araceae, especially the Old World genus *Arum*. The arum called trumpet lily *Zantedeschia aethio-pica*, an ornamental plant, is a native of South Africa.

The species *Arum maculatum*, known as cuckoopint or lords-and-ladies, is a common British hedgerow plant.

Arunachal Pradesh /ˌɑːrəˈnɑːtʃəl prɑːˈdeʃ/ state of India, in the Himalayas on the borders of Tibet and Myanmar
area 83,600 sq km/32,270 sq mi
capital Itanagar
products rubber, coffee, spices, fruit, timber
population (1981) 628,000
language 50 different dialects
history formerly nominally part of Assam, known as the renamed Arunachal Pradesh ('Hills of the Rising Sun'). It became a state 1986.

Arundel /ˈærəndl/ Thomas Howard, 2nd Earl of Arundel 1586–1646. English politician and patron of the arts. The Arundel Marbles, part of his collection of Italian sculptures, were given to Oxford University in 1667 by his grandson.

Arval Brethren (Latin *Fratres Arvales* 'brothers of the field') body of priests in ancient Rome who offered annual sacrifices to the *lares* or divinities of the fields to ensure a good harvest. They formed a college of 12 priests, and their chief festival fell in May.

Arvand River /ɑːˈvɑːnd/ Iranian name for the ◊Shatt al-Arab waterway.

Aryan the Indo-European family of languages; also the hypothetical parent language of an ancient people who are believed to have lived between Central Asia and E Europe and to have reached Persia and India in one direction and Europe in another, sometime in the 2nd century BC, diversifying into the various Indo-European language speakers of later times. In ◊Nazi Germany Hitler and other theorists erroneously propagated the idea of the Aryans as a white-skinned, blue-eyed, fair-haired master race.

Aryana /ˌeəriˈɑːnə/ ancient name of Afghanistan.

Arya Samaj /ˈɑːriə səˈmɑːdʒ/ Hindu religious sect founded by Dayanand Saraswati (1825–1888) about 1875. He renounced idol worship and urged a return to the purer principles of the Vedas (Hindu scriptures). For its time the movement was quite revolutionary in its social teachings, which included forbidding ◊caste practices, prohibiting child-marriage, and allowing widows to remarry.

ASA abbreviation for *Advertising Standards Authority*; *Association of South East Asia* (1961–67), replaced by ASEAN, ◊*Association of Southeast Asian Nations*.

ASA in photography, a numbering system for rating the speed of films, devised by the American Standards Association. It has now been superseded by ◊*ISO*, the International Standards Organization.

ASAT acronym for *anti*satellite weapon.

asbestos any of several related minerals of fibrous structure that offer great heat resistance because of their nonflammability and poor conductivity. Commercial asbestos is generally made from chrysolite, a ◊serpentine mineral, tremolite (a white ◊amphibole) and riebeckite (a blue amphibole, also known as crocidolite when in its fibrous form). Asbestos usage is now strictly controlled because exposure to its dust can cause cancer.

Asbestos has been used for brake linings, suits for fire fighters and astronauts, insulation of electric wires in furnaces, and fireproof materials for the building industry. Exposure to asbestos is a recognized cause of industrial cancer (mesothelioma), especially in the 'blue' form (from South Africa), rather than the more common 'white'. *Asbestosis* is a chronic lung inflammation caused by asbestos dust.

Ascension /əˈsenʃən/ British island of volcanic origin in the S Atlantic, a dependency of ◊St Helena since 1922; population (1982) 1,625. The chief settlement is Georgetown.

A Portuguese navigator landed there on Ascension Day 1501, but it remained uninhabited until occupied by Britain in 1815. There are sea turtles and sooty terns and for its role as a staging post to the Falkland Islands.

Ascension Day or *Holy Thursday* in the Christian calendar, the feast day commemorating Jesus' ascension into heaven. It is the 40th day after Easter.

ASCII /'æski/ (acronym for *A*merican *s*tandard *c*ode for *i*nformation *i*nterchange) in computing, a coding system in which numbers (between 0 and 127) are assigned to letters, digits, and punctuation symbols. For example, 45 represents a hyphen and 65 a capital A. The first 32 codes are used for control functions, such as carriage return and backspace. Strictly speaking, ASCII is a seven-bit code, but an eighth bit (binary digit) is often used to provide ◊parity or to allow for extra characters. The system is widely used for the storage of text and for the transmission of data between computers. Although computers work in binary code, ASCII numbers are usually quoted as decimal or ◊hexadecimal numbers.

ascorbic acid $C_6H_8O_6$ or *vitamin C* relatively simple organic acid found in fresh fruits and vegetables.

It is soluble in water and destroyed by prolonged boiling, so soaking or overcooking of vegetables reduces their vitamin C content. Lack of ascorbic acid results in scurvy.

In the human body, ascorbic acid is necessary for the correct synthesis of collagen. Lack of it causes skin sores or ulcers, tooth and gum problems, and burst capillaries (scurvy symptoms) owing to an abnormal type of collagen replacing the normal type in these tissues.

Ascot /'æskət/ village in Berkshire, England 9.5 km/6 mi SW of Windsor. Queen Anne established the racecourse on Ascot Heath 1711, and the Royal Ascot meeting is a social, as well as a sporting event. Horse races include the Gold Cup, Ascot Stakes, Coventry Stakes, and King George VI and Queen Elizabeth Stakes.

ASEAN acronym for ◊*A*ssociation of *S*outh *E*ast *A*sian *N*ations.

asepsis the practice of ensuring that bacteria are excluded from open sites during surgery, wound dressing, blood sampling, and other medical procedures. Aseptic technique is a first line of defence against infection.

asexual reproduction in biology, reproduction that does not involve the manufacture and fusion of sex cells, nor the necessity for two parents. The process carries a clear advantage in that there is no need to search for a mate nor to develop complex pollinating mechanisms; every asexual organism can reproduce on its own. Asexual reproduction can therefore lead to a rapid population build-up.

In evolutionary terms, the disadvantage of asexual reproduction arises from the fact that only identical individuals, or clones, are produced—there is no variation. In the field of horticulture, where standardized production is needed, this is useful, but in the wild, an asexual population that cannot adapt to a changing environment or evolve defences against a new disease is at risk of extinction. Many asexually reproducing organisms are therefore capable of reproducing sexually as well.

Asexual processes include ◊binary fission, in which the parent organism splits into two or more 'daughter' organisms, and ◊budding, in which a new organism is formed initially as an outgrowth of the parent organism. The asexual reproduction of spores, as in ferns and mosses, is also common and many plants reproduce asexually by means of runners, rhizomes, bulbs, and corms; see also ◊vegetative reproduction.

Asgard /'æzgɑːd/ in Scandinavian mythology, the place where the gods lived. It was reached by a bridge called Bifrost, the rainbow.

ash any tree of the worldwide genus *Fraxinus*, belonging to the olive family Oleaceae, with winged fruits. *F. excelsior* is the European species; its timber is of importance. The ◊*mountain ash* or *rowan* belongs to the family Rosaceae.

Ashanti /ə'ʃænti/ or *Asante* region of Ghana, W Africa; area 25,100 sq km/9,700 sq mi; population (1984) 2,089,683. Kumasi is the capital. Most Ashanti are cultivators and the main crop is cocoa, but the region is also noted for its metalwork and textiles. The Ashanti speak Akan (or Twi) which belongs to the Niger–Congo family of languages. For more than 200 years Ashanti was an independent kingdom. During the 19th century the Ashanti and the British fought for control of trade in West Africa. The British sent four expeditions against the Ashanti and formally annexed their country 1901.

Otomfuo Sir Osei Agyeman, nephew of the deposed king, Prempeh I, was made head of the re-established Ashanti confederation 1935 as Prempeh II. The Golden Stool (actually a chair), symbol of the Ashanti peoples since the 17th century, was returned to Kumasi in 1935 (the rest of the Ashanti treasure is in the British Museum). The Asantahene (King of the Ashanti) still holds ceremonies in which this stool is ceremonially paraded.

Ashbee /ˈæʃbi/ Charles Robert 1863–1942. British designer, architect, and writer, one of the major figures of the ◊Arts and Crafts movement. He founded a Guild and School of Handicraft in the East End of London in 1888, but later modified his views, accepting the importance of machinery and design for industry.

Ashbery /ˈæʃbəri/ John 1927– . US poet and art critic. His collections of poetry—including *Self-Portrait in a Convex Mirror* 1975, which won a Pulitzer prize—are distinguished by their strong visual element and narrative power. Other volumes include *Some Trees* 1956, *As We Know* 1979, and *Shadow Train* 1981.

Ashcan school group of US painters active about 1908–14, also known as the *Eight*. Members included Robert Henri (1865–1929), George Luks (1867–1933), William Glackens (1870–1938), Everett Shinn (1876–1953), and John Sloan (1871–1951). Their style is realist; their subjects centered on city life, the poor, and the outcast. They organized the ◊Armoury Show of 1913, which introduced modern European art to the USA.

Ashcroft /ˈæʃkrɒft/ Peggy 1907–1991. English actress. Her Shakespearean roles included Desdemona in *Othello* (with Paul Robeson), Juliet in *Romeo and Juliet* 1935 (with Laurence Olivier and John Gielgud), and she appeared in the British TV play *Caught on a Train* 1980 (BAFTA award), the series *The Jewel in the Crown* 1984, and the film *A Passage to India* 1985.

Ashdown /ˈæʃdaʊn/ Paddy (Jeremy John Durham) 1941– . English politician. Originally a Liberal MP, he became leader of the merged Social and Liberal Democrats 1988. He served in the Royal Marines as a commando, leading a Special Boat Section in

Borneo, and was a member of the Diplomatic Service 1971–76.

Ashe /æʃ/ Arthur Robert, Jr 1943–1993. US tennis player and coach. He won the US national men's singles title at Forest Hills and the first US Open 1968. Known for his exceptionally strong serve, Ashe turned professional 1969. He won the Australian men's title 1970 and Wimbledon 1975. Cardiac problems ended his playing career 1979, but he continued his involvement with the sport, serving as captain of the US Davis Cup team.

Ashes, the cricket trophy theoretically held by the winning team in the England–Australia test series.

The trophy is permanently held at ◊Lord's cricket ground no matter who wins the series. It is an urn containing the ashes of stumps and bails used in a match when England toured Australia 1882–83. The urn was given to the England captain Ivo Bligh by a group of Melbourne women. The action followed the appearance of an obituary notice in the *Sporting Times* the previous summer announcing the 'death' of English cricket after defeat by the Australians in the Oval test match.

Ashford /ˈæʃfəd/ town in Kent, England, on the river Stour, SW of Canterbury; population (1985) 47,000. It expanded in the 1980s as a new commercial and industrial centre for SE England.

Ashikaga in Japanese history, the family who held the office of shogun 1338–1573, a period of civil wars. Nō drama evolved under the patronage of Ashikaga shoguns. Relations with China improved intermittently and there was trade with Korea. The last (15th) Ashikaga shogun was ousted by Oda Nobunaga at the start of the Momoyama period. The Ashikaga belonged to the ◊Minamoto clan.

Ashkenazi /ˌæʃkəˈnɑːzɪ/ (plural *Ashkenazim*) a Jew of German or E European descent, as opposed to a Sephardi, of Spanish, Portuguese, or N African descent.

Ashkhabad /ˌæʃkəˈbæd/ capital of the Republic of Turkmenistan, population (1987) 382,000. 'Bukhara' carpets are made here.

It was established 1881 as a military fort on the Persian frontier, occupying an oasis on the edge of the Kara-Kum desert. It is the hottest place in the former USSR.

Ashmole /ˈæʃməʊl/ Elias 1617–1692. English antiquary, whose collection forms the basis of the Ashmolean Museum, Oxford, England.

He wrote books on alchemy and on antiquarian subjects, and amassed a fine library and a collection of curiosities, both of which he presented to Oxford University 1682. His collection was housed in the 'Old Ashmolean' (built 1679–83); the present Ashmolean Museum was erected 1897.

Ashmore and Cartier Islands /ˈæʃmɔː, ˈkɑːtieɪ/ group of uninhabited Australian islands comprising Middle, East, and West Islands (the Ashmores), and Cartier Island, in the Indian Ocean, about 190 km/120 mi off the NW coast of Australia; area 5 sq km/2 sq mi. They were transferred to the authority of Australia by Britain 1931. Formerly administered as part of the Northern Territory, they became a separate territory 1978. They are uninhabited, and West Ashmore has an automated weather station. Ashmore reef was declared a national nature reserve 1983.

ashram Indian community whose members lead a simple life of discipline and self-denial and devote themselves to social service. Noted ashrams are those founded by Mahatma Gandhi at Wardha and the poet Rabindranath Tagore at Santiniketan.

Ashton /ˈæʃtən/ Frederick 1904–1988. British choreographer, director of the Royal Ballet, London, 1963–70. He studied with Marie Rambert before joining the Vic-Wells (now Royal) Ballet 1935 as chief choreographer. His long association with Ninette de Valois and Margot Fonteyn, for whom he created many roles, gave the Royal Ballet a worldwide reputation.

His major works include *Façade* 1931 and *Les Rendezvous* 1933 for Rambert; *Cinderella* 1948, *Ondine* 1958, *La Fille mal gardée* 1960, *Marguerite and Armand*—for Margot Fonteyn and Rudolf Nureyev—1963, and *A Month in the Country* 1976. He contributed much to the popularity of ballet in the mid-20th century.

Ash Wednesday first day of Lent, the period in the Christian calendar leading up to Easter; in the Roman Catholic church the foreheads of the congregation are marked with a cross in ash, as a sign of penitence.

Asia /ˈeɪʃə/ largest of the continents, occupying one-third of the total land surface of the world
area 44,000,000 sq km/17,000,000 sq mi

largest cities (population over 5 million) Tokyo, Shanghai, Osaka, Beijing, Seoul, Calcutta, Bombay, Jakarta, Bangkok, Tehran, Hong Kong, Delhi, Tianjin, Karachi
physical lying in the eastern hemisphere, Asia extends from the Arctic Circle to just over 10° S of the Equator. The Asian mainland, which forms the greater part of the Eurasian continent, lies entirely in the northern hemisphere and stretches from Cape Chelyubinsk at its N extremity to Cape Piai at the S tip of the Malay Peninsula. From Dezhneva Cape in the E, the mainland extends W over more than 165° longitude to Cape Baba in Turkey. Containing the world's highest mountains and largest inland seas, Asia can be divided into five physical units:

1) at the heart of the continent, a central triangle of plateaux at varying altitudes (Tibetan Plateau, Tarim Basin, Gobi Desert), surrounded by huge mountain chains which spread in all directions (Himalayas, Karakoram, Hindu Kush, Pamirs, Kunlun, Tien Shan, Altai);

2) the W plateaux and ranges (Elburz, Zagros, Taurus, Great Caucasus mountains) of Afghanistan, Iran, N Iraq, Armenia, and Turkey;

3) the lowlands of Turkestan and Siberia which stretch N of the central mountains to the Arctic Ocean and include large areas in which the subsoil is permanently frozen;

4) the fertile and densely populated E lowlands and river plains of Korea, China, and Indochina, and the islands of the East Indies and Japan;

5) the southern plateaux of Arabia, and the Deccan, with the fertile alluvial plains of the Euphrates, Tigris, Indus, Ganges, Brahmaputra, and Irrawaddy rivers.

In Asiatic Russia are the largest areas of coniferous forest (taiga) in the world. The climate shows great extremes and contrasts, the heart of the continent becoming bitterly cold in winter and extremely hot in summer. When the heated air over land rises, moisture-laden air from the surrounding seas flows in, bringing heavy monsoon, rain to all SE Asia, China, and Japan between May and Oct.

features Mount Everest at 8,872 m/29,118 ft, is the world's highest mountain; Dead Sea –394 m/–1,293 ft is the world's lowest point below sea level; rivers (over 3,200 km/2,000 mi) include Chiang Jiang (Yangtze), Huang He (Yellow River), Ob-Irtysh, Amur, Lena, Mekong, Yeni sei; lakes (over 18,000 sq km/7,000 sq mi) include Caspian Sea (the largest inland body of water in the world), Aral Sea, Baikal (largest freshwater lake in Eurasia), Balkhash; deserts include the Gobi, Takla Makan, Syrian Desert, Arabian Desert, Negev

products 62% of the population are employed in agriculture; Asia produces 46% of the world's cereal crops (91% of the world's rice); other crops include mangoes (India), groundnuts (India, China), 84% of the world's copra (Philippines, Indonesia), 93% of the world's rubber (Indonesia, Malaysia, Thailand), tobacco (China), flax (China, Russia), 95% of the world's jute (India, Bangladesh, China), cotton (China, India, Pakistan), silk (China, India), fish (Japan, China, Korea, Thailand); China produces 55% of the world's tungsten; 45% of the world's tin is produced by Malaysia, China, and Indonesia; Saudi Arabia is the world's largest producer of coal

population (1988) 2,996,000; the world's largest, though not the fastest growing population, amounting to more than half the total number of people in the world; between 1950 and 1990 the death rate and infant mortality were reduced by more than 60%; annual growth rate 1.7%; projected to increase to 3,550,000 by the year 2000

language predominantly tonal languages (Chinese, Japanese) in the E, Indo-Iranian languages (Hindi, Urdu, Persian) in S Asia, Altaic languages (Mongolian, Turkish) in W and Central Asia, Semitic languages (Arabic, Hebrew) in the SW

religion the major religions of the world had their origins in Asia—Judaism and Christianity in the Middle East, Islam in Arabia, Buddhism, Hinduism, and Sikhism in India, Confucianism in China, and Shintoism in Japan.

Asia Minor /ˈeɪʃə ˈmaɪnə/ historical name for *Anatolia*, the Asian part of Turkey.

Asian and Pacific Council (ASPAC) organization established 1966 to encourage cultural and economic cooperation in Oceania and Asia. Its members include Australia, Japan, South Korea, Malaysia, New Zealand, the Philippines, Taiwan, and Thailand.

Asian Development Bank (ADB) bank founded 1966 to stimulate growth in Asia and the Far East by administering direct loans and technical assistance. Members include 30 countries within the region and 14 countries of W Europe and North America. The headquarters are in Manila, Philippines.

Japan played a leading role in the setting-up of the ADB, which was established under the aegis of the United Nations Economic and Social Council for Asia and the Pacific (ESCAP).

Asia-Pacific Economic Cooperation Conference (APEC) trade group comprising 12 Pacific Asian countries, formed Nov 1898 to promote multilateral trade and economic cooperation between member states. Its members are the USA, Canada, Japan, Australia, New Zealand, South Korea, Brunei, Indonesia, Malaysia, the Philippines, Singapore, and Thailand.

Asia, Soviet Central see ◊Soviet Central Asia.

Asimov /ˈæzɪmɒf/ Isaac 1920–1992. Russian-born US author and editor of science fiction and nonfiction.

He published more than 400 books including his science fiction *I, Robot* 1950 and the *Foundation* trilogy 1951–53, continued in *Foundation's Edge* 1983.

AS level General Certificate of Education *A*dvanced *S*upplementary examinations introduced in the UK 1988 as the equivalent to 'half an ◊A level' as a means of broadening the sixth form (age 16–18) curriculum, and including more students in the examination system.

Asmara /æsˈmɑːrə/ or *Asmera* capital of Eritrea; 64 km/40 mi SW of Massawa on the Red Sea; population (1984) 275,385. Products include beer, clothes, and textiles. In 1974, unrest here precipitated the end of the Ethiopian Empire. It has a naval school.

Asoka /əˈsəʊkə/ *c.* 273–238 BC. Indian emperor, and Buddhist convert from Hinduism. He issued edicts, carved on pillars and rock faces throughout his dominions, promoting wise government and the cultivation of moral virtues according to Buddhist teachings. Many still survive, and are amongst the oldest deciphered texts in India. In Patna there are the remains of a hall built by him.

asp any of several venomous snakes, including *Vipera aspis* of S Europe, allied to the adder, and the Egyptian cobra *Naja haje*, reputed to have been used by the Egyptian queen Cleopatra for her suicide.

ASPAC abbreviation of ◊*Asian and Pacific Council*.

asparagus any plant of the genus *Asparagus*, family Liliaceae, with small scalelike leaves and many needlelike branches. *A. officinalis* is cultivated, and the young shoots are eaten as a vegetable.

aspartame non-carbohydrate sweetener used in foods under the tradename Nutrasweet. It is about 200 times as sweet as sugar and, unlike saccharine, has no aftertaste.

aspen any of several species of ◊poplar tree, genus *Populus*. The quaking aspen *P. tremula* has flattened leafstalks that cause the leaves to flutter with every breeze.

asphalt semisolid brown or black ◊bitumen, used in the construction industry.

Considerable natural deposits of asphalt occur around the Dead Sea and in the Philippines, Cuba, Venezuela, and Trinidad. Bituminous limestone occurs at Neufchâtel, France. Asphalt is mixed with rock chips to form paving material, and the purer varieties are used for insulating material and for waterproofing masonry. Asphalt can be produced artificially by the distillation of ◊petroleum.

asphodel either of two related Old World genera (*Asphodeline* and *Asphodelus*) of plants of the lily family Liliaceae. *Asphodelus albus*, the white asphodel or king's spear, is found in Italy and Greece, sometimes covering large areas, and providing grazing for sheep. *Asphodeline lutea* is the yellow asphodel.

asphyxia suffocation; a lack of oxygen that produces a build-up of carbon dioxide waste in the tissues.

Asphyxia may arise from any one of a number of causes, including inhalation of smoke or poisonous gases, obstruction of the windpipe (by water, food, vomit, or foreign object), strangulation, or smothering. If it is not quickly relieved, brain damage or death ensues.

aspidistra Asiatic plant of the genus *Aspidistra* of the lily family Liliaceae. The Chinese *A. elatior* has broad, lanceolate leaves and, like all members of the genus, grows well in warm indoor conditions.

aspirin acetylsalicylic acid, a popular pain-relieving drug (◊analgesic) developed in the early 20th century for headaches and arthritis. It inhibits ◊prostaglandins, and is derived from the white willow tree *Salix alba*.

In the long term, even moderate use may cause stomach bleeding, kidney damage, and hearing defects, and aspirin is no longer considered suitable for children under 12, because of a suspected link with a rare disease, Reye's syndrome. However, recent medical research suggests that an aspirin a day may be of value in preventing heart attack and thrombosis.

Asquith /ˈæskwɪθ/ Herbert Henry, 1st Earl of Oxford and Asquith 1852–1928. British Liberal politician, prime minister 1908–16. As chancellor of the Exchequer he introduced old-age pensions 1908. He limited the powers of the House of Lords and attempted to give Ireland Home Rule.

Asquith was born in Yorkshire. Elected a member of Parliament 1886, he was home secretary in Gladstone's 1892–95 government. He was chancellor of the Exchequer 1905–08 and succeeded Campbell-Bannerman as prime minister. Forcing through the radical budget of his chancellor ◊Lloyd George led him into two elections 1910, which resulted in the Parliament Act 1911, limiting the right of the Lords to veto legislation. His endeavours to pass the Home Rule for Ireland Bill led to the ◊Curragh 'Mutiny' and incipient civil war. Unity was re-established by the outbreak of World War I 1914, and a coalition government was formed May 1915. However, his attitude of 'wait and see' was not adapted to all-out war, and in Dec 1916 he was replaced by Lloyd George. In 1918 the Liberal election defeat led to the eclipse of the party.

ass any of several horselike, odd-toed, hoofed mammals of the genus *Equus*, family Equidae. Species include the African wild ass *E. asinus*, and the Asian wild ass *E. hemionus*. They differ from horses in their smaller size, larger ears, tufted tail, and characteristic bray. Donkeys and burros are domesticated asses.

Assad /ˈæsæd/ Hafez al 1930– . Syrian Ba'athist politician, president from 1971. He became prime minister after a bloodless military coup 1970, and the following year was the first president to be elected by popular vote. Having suppressed dissent, he was re-elected 1978 and 1985. He is a Shia (Alawite) Muslim.

He has ruthlessly suppressed domestic opposition, and was Iran's only major Arab ally in its war against Iraq. He steadfastly pursued military parity with Israel, and has made himself a key player in any settlement of the Lebanese civil war or Middle East conflict generally. His support for UN action against Iraq following its invasion of

Kuwait 1990 raised his international standing.

Assam /æ'sæm/ state of NE India
area 78,400 sq km/30,262 sq mi
capital Dispur
towns Shilling
products half India's tea is grown and half its oil produced here; rice, jute, sugar, cotton, coal
population (1981) 19,903,000, including 12 million Assamese (Hindus), 5 million Bengalis (chiefly Muslim immigrants from Bangladesh), Nepalis, and 2,000,000 native people (Christian and traditional religions)
language Assamese
history a thriving region from 1000 BC; Assam migrants came from China and Myanmar (Burma). After Burmese invasion 1826, Britain took control; and made it a separate province 1874; included in the Dominion of India, except for most of the Muslim district of Silhet, which went to Pakistan 1947. Ethnic unrest started in the 1960s when Assamese was declared the official language. After protests, the Gara, Khasi, and Jainitia tribal hill districts became the state of Meghalaya 1971; the Mizo hill district became the Union Territory of Mizoram 1972. There were massacres of Muslim Bengalis by Hindus 1983. In 1987 members of Bodo ethnic group began fighting for a separate homeland. Direct rule was imposed by the Indian government Nov 1990 following separatist violence from the Marxist-militant United Liberation Front of Assam (ULFA), which had exhorted payments from tea-exporting companies. In March 1991 it was reported that the ULFA, operating from the jungles of Myanmar, had been involved in 97 killings, mainly of Congress I politicians, since 27 November 1990.

assassination murder, usually of a political, royal, or public person. The term derives from a sect of Muslim fanatics in the 11th and 12th centuries known as *hashshashin* ('takers of hashish'). They were reputed either to smoke cannabis before they went out to murder, or to receive hashish as payment.

assault intentional act or threat of physical violence against a person. In English law it is both a crime and a ◊tort (a civil wrong). The kinds of criminal assault are common (ordinary); aggravated (more serious, such as causing actual bodily harm); or indecent (of a sexual nature).

In the USA, 25% of violent crimes committed against women during the period 1973–1987 were carried out by people known to the victim, compared with 4% of crimes against men.

assault ship naval vessel designed to land and support troops and vehicles under hostile conditions.

assaying in chemistry, the determination of the quantity of a given substance present in a sample. Usually it refers to determining the purity of precious metals.

assembly code computer-programming language closely related to a computer's internal codes. It consists chiefly of a set of short mnemonics, which are translated, by a program called an assembler, into ◊machine code for the computer's ◊central processing unit (CPU) to follow directly. In assembly language, for example, 'JMP' means 'jump' and 'LDA' means 'load accumulator'. Assembly code is used by programmers who need to write very fast or efficient programs.

assembly line method of mass production in which a product is built up step by step by successive workers adding one part at a time.

US inventor Eli Whitney pioneered the concept of industrial assembly in the 1790s, when he employed unskilled labour to assemble muskets from sets of identical precision-made parts. In 1901 Ransome Olds in the USA began mass-producing motor cars on an assembly-line principle, a method further refined by the introduction of the moving conveyor belt by Henry ◊Ford 1913 and the time-and-motion studies of F W ◊Taylor. On the assembly line human workers now stand side by side with ◊robots.

asset in business accounting, a term that covers the land or property of a company or individual, payments due from bills, investments, and anything else owned that can be turned into cash. On a company's balance sheet, total assets must be equal to liabilities (money and services owed).

asset stripping sale or exploitation by other means of the assets of a business, often one that has been taken over for that very purpose. The parts of the business may be potentially more valuable separately than together. Asset stripping is a major force for the more efficient use of assets.

assimilation in animals, the process by which absorbed food molecules, circulating in the blood, pass into the cells and are used for growth, tissue repair, and other metabolic activities. The actual destiny of each food molecule depends not only on its type, but also on the body requirements at that time.

Assisi /əˈsiːzi/ town in Umbria, Italy, 19 km/ 12 mi SE of Perugia; population (1981) 25,000. St Francis was born here and is buried in the Franciscan monastery, completed 1253. The churches of St Francis are adorned with frescoes by Giotto, Cimabue, and others.

Assisted Places Scheme in UK education, a scheme established 1980 by which the government assists parents with the cost of fees at ◊independent schools on a means-tested basis.

Assiut /æˈsjuːt/ alternative transliteration of ◊Asyut, town in Egypt.

assize in medieval Europe, the passing of laws, either by the king with the consent of nobles, as in the Constitutions of ◊Clarendon 1164 by Henry II of England, or as a complete system, such as the *Assizes of Jerusalem*, a compilation of the law of the feudal kingdom of Jerusalem in the 13th century.

The term remained in use in the UK for the courts held by judges of the High Court in each county; they were abolished under the Courts Act 1971.

Associated State of the UK status of certain Commonwealth countries that have full power of internal government, but where Britain is responsible for external relations and defence.

Association of South East Asian Nations (ASEAN) regional alliance formed in Bangkok 1967; it took over the nonmilitary role of the Southeast Asia Treaty Organization 1975. Its members are Indonesia, Malaysia, the Philippines, Singapore, Thailand, and (from 1984) Brunei; its headquarters are in Jakarta, Indonesia.

associative operation in mathematics, an operation that is independent of the grouping of the numbers or symbols concerned. For example, multiplication is associative, as $4 \times (3 \times 2) = (4 \times 3) \times 2 = 24$; however, division is not, as $12 \div (4 \div 2) = 6$, but $(12 \div 4) \div 2 = 1.5$. Compare ◊commutative operation and ◊distributive operation.

ASSR abbreviation for *Autonomous Soviet Socialist Republic*.

Assuan /æˈswɑːn/ alternative transliteration of ◊Aswan.

Assyria /əˈsɪriə/ empire in the Middle East *c.* 2500–612 BC, in N Mesopotamia (now Iraq); early capital Ashur, later Nineveh. It was initially subject to Sumer and intermittently to Babylon. The Assyrians adopted in the main the Sumerian religion and structure of society. At its greatest extent the empire included Egypt and stretched from the E Mediterranean coast to the head of the Persian Gulf.

The land of Assyria originally consisted of a narrow strip of alluvial soil on each side of the river Tigris. The area was settled about 3500 BC and was dominated by Sumer until about 2350 BC. For nearly 200 years Assyria was subject first to the Babylonian dynasty of Akkad and then to the Gutians, barbarians from the north. The first Assyrian kings are mentioned during the wars following the decline of the 3rd dynasty of Ur (in Sumer), but Assyria continued under Babylonian and subsequently Egyptian suzerainty until about 1450 BC. Under King Ashur-uballit (reigned about 1380–1340 BC) Assyria became a military power. His work was continued by Adad-nirari I, Shalmaneser I, and Tukulti-enurta I, who conquered Babylonia and assumed the title of king of Sumer and Akkad.

During the reign of Nebuchadnezzar I (1150–1110 BC), Assyria was again subject to Babylonia, but was liberated by Tiglath-pileser I. In the Aramaean invasions, most of the ground gained was lost. From the accession of Adad-nirari II 911 BC Assyria pursued a course of expansion and conquest, culminating in the mastery over Elam, Mesopotamia, Syria, Palestine, the Arabian marches, and Egypt. Of this period the Old Testament records, and many 'documents' —such as the Black Obelisk celebrating the conquest of Shalmaneser III in the 9th century BC—survive.

The reign of Ashur-nazir-pal II (885–860 BC) was spent in unceasing warfare. Shalmaneser III warred against the Syrian states. At the battle of Qarqar 854 BC the Assyrian advance received a setback, and there followed a period of decline. The final period of Assyrian ascendancy began with the accession of Tiglath-pileser III (746–728 BC) and continued during the reigns of Sargon II, Sennacherib, Esarhaddon, and Ashurbanipal, culminating in the conquest of Egypt by Esarhaddon 671 BC. From this time the empire seems to have fallen into decay. Nabopolassar of Babylonia and Cyaxares of Media (see ◊Mede) united against it;

Nineveh was destroyed 612 BC; and Assyria became a Median province and subsequently a principality of the Persian Empire.

Much of Assyrian religion, law, social structure, and artistic achievement was derived from neighbouring sources. The Assyrians adopted the cuneiform script (invented by the Sumerians in 3500 BC) and took over the Sumerian pantheon, although the Assyrian god, Ashur (Assur), assumed the chief place in the cult. The library of Ashurbanipal excavated at Nineveh is evidence of the thoroughness with which Babylonian culture had been assimilated.

Astaire /əˈsteə/ Fred. Adopted name of Frederick Austerlitz 1899–1987. US dancer, actor, singer, and choreographer who starred in numerous films, including *Top Hat* 1935, *Easter Parade* 1948, and *Funny Face* 1957, many containing inventive sequences he designed and choreographed himself. He made ten classic films with the most popular of his dancing partners, Ginger Rogers. He later played straight dramatic roles in such films as *On the Beach* 1959.

Astaire US dancer, singer, and film star Fred Astaire with his dancing partner Ginger Rogers.

Astarte /əˈstɑːti/ alternative name for the Babylonian and Assyrian goddess ◊Ishtar.

astatine (Greek *astatos* 'unstable') nonmetallic, radioactive element, symbol At, atomic number 85, relative atomic mass 210. It is a member of the ◊halogen group, and is very rare in nature. Asta-tine is highly unstable, with many isotopes; the longest lived has a half-life of about eight hours.

aster any plant of the large genus *Aster*, family Compositae, belonging to the same subfamily as the daisy. All asters have starlike flowers with yellow centres and outer rays (not petals) varying from blue and purple to white and the genus comprises a great variety of size. Many are cultivated as garden flowers, including the Michaelmas daisy *A. nova-belgii*.

The sea aster *A. tripolium* grows wild on sea cliffs in the south of England.

Astérix the Gaul Belgian comic-strip character who first appeared 1959. Written originally by René Goscinny (1926–1977) with artwork by Albert Uderzo (1925–), it appears in 40 languages worldwide; 200 million Astérix comics were sold in 1990. The adventures are set in Roman times; Astérix and his friends are active in the resistance to the Roman occupation of ancient Gaul (modern France).

asteroid or ***minor planet*** any of many thousands of small bodies, composed of rock and iron, hat orbit the Sun. Most lie in a belt between the orbits of Mars and Jupiter, and are thought to be fragments left over from the formation of the ◊Solar System. About 100,000 may exist, but their total mass is only a few hundredths the mass of the Moon.

They include ◊Ceres (the largest asteroid, 9400 km/584 mi in diameter), Vesta (which has a light-coloured surface, and is the brightest as seen from Earth), ◊Eros, and ◊Icarus. Some asteroids are on orbits that bring them close to Earth, and some, such as the ◊Apollo asteroids, even cross Earth's orbit; at least some of these may be former comets that have lost their gas. One group, the Trojans, moves along the same orbit as Jupiter, 60° ahead and behind the planet. One unusual asteroid, ◊Chiron, orbits beyond Saturn. The first asteroid was discovered by the Italian astronomer Guiseppe Piazzi at the Palermo Observatory, Sicily, 1 Jan 1801.

asthenosphere division of the Earth's structure lying beneath the ◊lithosphere, at a depth of approximately 70 km/45 mi to 260 km/160 mi. It is thought to be the soft, partially molten layer of the ◊mantle on which the rigid plates of the Earth's surface move to produce the motions of ◊plate tectonics.

asthma difficulty in breathing due to spasm of the bronchi (air passages) in the lungs. Attacks may be provoked by allergy, infection, stress, or emotional upset. It may also be increasing as a result of air pollution and occupational hazards. Treatment is with ◊bronchodilators to relax the bronchial muscles and thereby ease the breathing, and with inhaled ◊steroids that reduce inflammation of the bronchi.

Although the symptoms are similar to those of bronchial asthma, *cardiac asthma* is an unrelated condition and is a symptom of heart deterioration.

Asthma sufferers may monitor their own status by use of a peak-flow meter, a device that measures how rapidly air is breathed out. Peak-flow meters are available on prescription in the UK.

Asti /ˈæsti/ town in Piedmont, SE of Turin, Italy; population (1983) 76,439. Asti province is famed for its sparkling wine. Other products include chemicals, textiles, and glass.

astigmatism aberration occurring in lenses, including that in the eye. It results when the curvature of the lens differs in two perpendicular planes, so that rays in one plane may be in focus while rays in the other are not. With astigmatic eyesight, the vertical and horizontal cannot be in focus at the same time; correction is by the use of a cylindrical lens that reduces the overall focal length of one plane so that both planes are seen in sharp focus.

Aston /ˈæstən/ Francis William 1877–1945. English physicist who developed the mass spectrometer, which separates ◊isotopes by projecting their ions (charged atoms) through a magnetic field. He received the Nobel Prize for Chemistry 1922.

Astor /ˈæstə/ prominent US and British family. *John Jacob Astor* (1763–1848) was a US millionaire. *Waldorf Astor*, 2nd Viscount Astor (1879–1952), was Conservative member of Parliament for Plymouth 1910–19, when he succeeded to the peerage. He was chief proprietor of the British *Observer* newspaper. His wife Nancy Witcher Langhorne (1879–1964), *Lady Astor*, was the first woman member of Parliament to take a seat in the House of Commons 1919, when

she succeeded her husband for the constituency of Plymouth. She was also a vehement temperance supporter and political hostess. Government policy was said to be decided at Cliveden, their country home.

Astrakhan /ˌæstrəˈkɑːn/ city in Russia, on the delta of the Volga, capital of Astrakhan region; population (1989) 509,000. In ancient times a Tatar capital, it became Russian 1556. It is the chief port for the Caspian fisheries.

astrolabe ancient navigational instrument, forerunner of the sextant. Astrolabes usually consisted of a flat disc with a sighting rod that could be pivoted to point at the Sun or bright stars. From the altitude of the Sun or star above the horizon, the local time could be estimated.

astrology (Greek *astron* 'star', *legein* 'speak') study of the relative position of the planets and stars in the belief that they influence events on Earth. The astrologer casts a ◊horoscope based on the time and place of the subject's birth. Astrology has no proven scientific basis, but has been widespread since ancient times. Western astrology is based on the 12 signs of the zodiac; Chinese astrology is based on a 60-year cycle and lunar calendar.

history A strongly held belief in ancient Babylon, astrology spread to the Mediterranean world, and was widely used by the Greeks and Romans. In Europe during the Middle Ages it had a powerful influence, since kings and other public figures had their own astrologers; astrological beliefs are reflected in Elizabethan and Jacobean literature. *popular prediction* In the UK, the first edition of *Old Moore's Almanac*, which gives a forecast of the year ahead, appeared 1700, and there have been annual editions since. Astrological forecasts in newspapers and magazines are usually very simplistic.

astrometry measurement of the precise positions of stars, planets, and other bodies in space. Such information is needed for practical purposes including accurate time-keeping, surveying and navigation, and calculating orbits and measuring distances in space. Astrometry is not concerned with the surface features or the physical nature of the body under study.

Before telescopes, astronomical observations were simple astrometry. Precise astrometry has shown that stars are not fixed in position, but have a ◊proper motion caused as they and the Sun orbit the Milky Way galaxy. The nearest stars also show ◊parallax (apparent change in position), from which their distances can be calculated. Above the distorting effects of the atmosphere, satellites such as ◊*Hipparcos* can make even more precise measurements than ground telescopes, so refining the distance scale of space.

astronaut Western term for a person making flights into space; the Soviet term is *cosmonaut*.

astronautics science of space travel. See ◊rocket; ◊satellite; ◊space probe.

Astronomer Royal honorary post in British astronomy. Originally it was held by the director of the Royal Greenwich Observatory; since 1972 the title of Astronomer Royal has been awarded separately. The Astronomer Royal from 1991 is Arnold Wolfendale (1927–). A separate post of Astronomer Royal for Scotland is attached to the directorship of the Royal Observatory, Edinburgh.

astronomical unit unit (symbol AU) equal to the mean distance of the Earth from the Sun: 149,597,870 km/92,955,800 mi. It is used to describe planetary distances. Light travels this distance in approximately 8.3 minutes.

astronomy science of the celestial bodies: the Sun, the Moon, and the planets; he stars and galaxies; and all other objects in the universe. It is concerned with their positions, motions, distances, and physical conditions; and with their origins and evolution. Astronomy thus divides into fields such as astrophysics, celestial mechanics, and cosmology. See also ◊gamma-ray astronomy, ◊infrared astronomy, ◊radio astronomy, ◊ultraviolet astronomy, and ◊X-ray astronomy.

Astronomy is perhaps the oldest science; there are observational records from Babylonia and from ancient China, Egypt, and Mexico. The first true astronomers, however, were the Greeks, who deduced that the Earth was a sphere, and attempted to measure its size. ◊Hipparchus drew star catalogues, and estimated the sizes and distances from the Earth of the Sun and Moon. Greek astronomy was summarized by ◊Ptolemy in his *Almagest*, which included the idea of an Earth-centred universe. This was still the prevailing view in 1543, when ◊Copernicus proposed that the Earth and the other planets revolve around the Sun. The next century saw the laws of planetary

motion expounded by Johann ◊Kepler, who used the accurate observations made by Tycho ◊Brahe, and ◊Galileo's discoveries 1609–10 with the **refractor** telescope (invented by Hans ◊Lippershey 1608): the moons of Jupiter, the phases of Venus, and the myriad of stars in the Milky Way. Isaac ◊Newton's *Principia* 1687 founded celestial mechanics, and firmly established the Copernican theory. About 1670 Newton built the first **reflector**, which used a mirror in place of the main lens. A hundred years later, William ◊Herschel began the construction of large telescopes, with which the discovered a planet, Uranus, and investigated double stars and nebulae, opening a new era in observational astronomy. In 1838 Friedrich ◊Bessel made the first reasonably accurate measurement of a star's distance from the Earth, and Neptune was discovered 1846 following mathematical prediction of its orbit. Photography, introduced at this time, was to have a great impact on astronomical research. Observations of the Sun's spectrum led to the introduction of spectroscopy and the development of astrophysics. Big telescopes built in the 20th century have revealed the distance and nature of the galaxies observed by Herschel. Pluto was discovered 1930. Edwin ◊Hubble found that all galaxies seem to be receding, the first evidence of an expanding, evolving universe, which forms the basis of the currently favoured ◊Big Bang theory. Advances in technology, especially electronics, have made it possible to study radiation from astronomical objects at all wavelengths, not just visible light, from radio wavelengths to X-rays and gamma rays. Discoveries since 1960 include ◊quasars and ◊pulsars, and a good understanding of how stars evolve. Artificial satellites, space probes, orbiting observatories, and giant optical telescopes are continually increasing our knowledge of the universe.

astrophotography use of photography in astronomical research. The first successful photograph of a celestial object was the daguerreotype plate of the Moon taken by John W Draper (1811–1882) of the USA in March 1840. The first photograph of a star, Vega, was taken by US astronomer William C Bond (1789–1859) in 1850.

Modern-day electronic innovations, notably ◊charge-coupled devices (CCDs), provide a more efficient light-gathering capability than photographic film as well as enabling information to be transferred to a computer for analysis. However, CCD images are expensive and very small in size compared to photographic plates. Photographic plates are better suited to wide-field images, whereas CCDs are used for individual objects, which may be very faint, within a narrow field of sky.

astrophysics study of the physical nature of stars, galaxies, and the universe. It began with the development of spectroscopy in the 19th century, which allowed astronomers to analyse the composition of stars from their light. Astrophysicists view the universe as a vast natural laboratory in which they can study matter under conditions of temperature, pressure, and density that are unattainable on Earth.

Asturias /æˈstʊəriəs/ autonomous region of N Spain; area 10,600 sq km/4,092 sq mi; population (1986) 1,114,000. Half of Spain's coal is produced from the mines of Asturias. Agricultural produce includes maize, fruit, and livestock. Oviedo and Gijón are the main industrial towns.

It was once a separate kingdom, and the eldest son of a king of Spain is still called prince of Asturias.

Astyanax in Greek mythology, the son of ◊Hector and ◊Andromache. After the death of all the sons of ◊Priam in battle at the siege of Troy, the child Astyanax was thrown from the city walls by the victorious Greeks.

Asunción /æˌsuːnsiˈɒn/ capital and port of Paraguay, on the Paraguay river; population (1984) 729,000. It produces textiles, footwear, and food products. Founded 1537, it was the first Spanish settlement in the La Plata region.

Aswan /ˌæsˈwɑːn/ winter resort town in Upper Egypt; population (1985) 183,000. It is near the High Dam built, 1960–70, which keeps the level of the Nile constant throughout the year without flooding. It produces steel and textiles.

asylum, political in international law, refuge granted in another country to a person who cannot return to their own country without putting themselves in danger. A person seeking asylum is a type of ◊refugee.

Under British immigration rules, asylum is granted in cases where the only country to which a person could be removed is one to which he or she is unwilling to go owing to a well-founded fear of being persecuted for reasons of race, religion, nationality, membership of a particular social group, or political opinion. A House of Lords ruling 1988 held that an applicant for asylum must be able to justify objectively his or her fears of persecution.

asymptote in ◊coordinate geometry, a straight line towards which a curve approaches more and more closely but never reaches. If a point on a curve approaches a straight line such that its distance from the straight line is d, then the line is an asymptote to the curve if limit d tends to zero as the point moves towards infinity. Among ◊conic sections (curves obtained by the intersection of a plane and a double cone), a ◊hyperbola has two asymptotes, which in the case of a rectangular hyperbola are at right angles to each other.

Atacama /ˌætəˈkɑːmə/ desert in N Chile; area about 80,000 sq km/31,000 sq mi. There are mountains inland, and the coastal area is rainless and barren. Atacama has silver and copper mines, and extensive nitrate deposits.

Atahualpa /ˌætəˈwɑːlpə/ c. 1502–1533. Last emperor of the Incas of Peru. He was taken prisoner 1532 when the Spaniards arrived, and agreed to pay a substantial ransom, but was accused of plotting against the conquistador Pizarro and sentenced to be burned. On his consenting to Christian baptism, the sentence was commuted to strangulation.

Atalanta /ˌætəˈlæntə/ in Greek mythology, a woman hunter who challenged all her suitors to a foot race; if they lost they were killed. Aphrodite gave Milanion three golden apples to drop so that when Atalanta stopped to pick them up, she lost the race.

AT&T (abbreviation of *American Telephone and Telegraph*) US telecommunications company that owns four out of five telephones in the USA. It was founded 1877 by the inventor of the telephone, Alexander Graham Bell as the Bell Telephone Company; it took its present name 1899.

Atatürk /ˈætətɜːk/ Kemal. Name assumed 1934 by Mustafa Kemal Pasha 1881–1938. ('Father of the Turks'). Turkish politician and general, first president of Turkey from 1923. After World War I he established a provisional rebel government and in 1921–22 the Turkish armies under his leadership expelled the Greeks who were occupying Turkey. He was the founder of the modern republic, which he ruled as virtual dictator, with a policy of consistent and radical westernization.

Kemal, born in Thessaloniki, was banished 1904 for joining a revolutionary society. Later he was pardoned and promoted in the army, and was largely responsible for the successful defence of the Dardanelles against the British 1915. In 1918, after Turkey had been defeated, he was sent into Anatolia to implement the demobilization of the Turkish forces in accordance with the armistice terms, but instead he established a provisional government opposed to that of Constantinople (under Allied control), and in 1921 led the Turkish armies against the Greeks, who had occupied a large part of Anatolia. He checked them at the Battle of the Sakaria, 23 Aug–13 Sept 1921, for which he was granted the title of Ghazi (the Victorious), and within a year had expelled the Greeks from Turkish soil. War with the British was averted by his diplomacy, and Turkey in Europe passed under Kemal's control. On 29 Oct 1923, Turkey was proclaimed a republic with Kemal as first president.

atavism (Latin *atavus* 'ancestor') in ◊genetics, the reappearance of a characteristic not apparent in the immediately preceding generations; in psychology, the manifestation of primitive forms of behaviour.

Athanasian creed one of the three ancient ◊creeds of the Christian church. Mainly a definition of the Trinity and Incarnation, it was written many years after the death of Athanasius, but was attributed to him as the chief upholder of Trinitarian doctrine.

Athanasius, St /ˌæθəˈneɪʃəs/ 298–373. Bishop of Alexandria, supporter of the doctrines of the Trinity and Incarnation. He was a disciple of St Anthony the hermit, and an opponent of ◊Arianism in the great Arian controversy. Following the official condemnation of Arianism at the Council of Nicaea 325, Athanasius was appointed bishop of Alexandria 328. The Athanasian creed was not actually written by him, although it reflects his views.

atheism nonbelief in, or the positive denial of, the existence of a God or gods.

Dogmatic atheism asserts that there is no God. *Sceptical atheism* maintains that the finite human mind is so constituted as to be incapable of discovering that there is or is not a God. *Critical atheism* holds that the evidence for atheism is inadequate. This is akin to *philosophical atheism*, which fails to find evidence of a God manifest in the universe. *Speculative atheism* comprises the

beliefs of those who, like the German philosopher Kant, find it impossible to demonstrate the existence of God. A related concept is ◊agnosticism.

Buddhism has been called an atheistic religion since it does not postulate any supreme being. The Jains are similarly atheistic, and so are those who adopt the Sankhya system of philosophy in Hinduism. Following the revolution of 1917 the USSR and later communist states, such as Albania, adopted an atheist position.

The first openly atheistic book published in Britain was *Answer to Dr Priestley's Letters to a Philosophical Unbeliever* 1782 by Matthew Turner, a Liverpool doctor.

Athelney, Isle of /ˈæθəlni/ area of firm ground in marshland near Taunton in Somerset, England, in 878 the headquarters of king ◊Alfred the Great when he was in hiding from the Danes. The legend of his burning the cakes is set here.

Athelstan /ˈæθəlstən/ *c.* 895–939. King of the Mercians and West Saxons. Son of Edward the Elder and grandson of Alfred the Great, he was crowned king 925 at Kingston upon Thames. He subdued parts of Cornwall and Wales, and defeated the Welsh, Scots, and Danes at Brunanburh 937.

Athena /əˈθiːnə/ in Greek mythology, the goddess (Roman Minerva) of war, wisdom, and the arts and crafts, who was supposed to have sprung fully grown from the head of Zeus. Her chief cult centre was Athens, where the ◊Parthenon was dedicated to her.

Athens /ˈæθɪnz/ (Greek *Athinai*) capital city of Greece and of ancient Attica; population (1981) 885,000, metropolitan area 3,027,000. Situated 8 km/5 mi NE of its port of Piraeus on the Gulf of Aegina, it is built around the rocky hills of the Acropolis 169 m/555 ft and the Areopagus 112 m/368 ft, and is overlooked from the northeast by the hill of Lycabettus, 277 m/909 ft high. It lies in the south of the central plain of Attica, watered by the mountain streams of Cephissus and Ilissus. It has less green space than any other European capital—4%—and severe air and noise pollution.

features The Acropolis dominates the city. Remains of ancient Greece include the Parthenon, the Erechtheum, and the temple of Athena Nike. Near the site of the ancient Agora (marketplace) stands the Theseum, and south of the Acropolis is the theatre of Dionysus. To the southeast stand the gate of Hadrian and the columns of the temple of

Olympian Zeus. Nearby is the marble stadium built about 330 BC and restored 1896.

history The site was first inhabited about 3000 BC, and Athens became the capital of a united Attica before 700 BC. Captured and sacked by the Persians 480 BC, subsequently under Pericles it was the first city of Greece in power and culture. After the death of Alexander the Great the city fell into comparative decline, but it flourished as an intellectual centre until AD 529, when the philosophical schools were closed by Justinian. In 1458 it was captured by the Turks who held it until 1833; it was chosen as the capital of Greece 1834. Among present day buildings are the royal palace and several museums.

atheroma furring-up of the interior of an artery by deposits, mainly of cholesterol, within its walls.

Associated with atherosclerosis, atheroma has the effect of narrowing the lumen (channel) of the artery, thus restricting blood flow. This predisposes to a number of conditions, including thrombosis, angina, and stroke.

atherosclerosis thickening and hardening of the walls of the arteries, associated with atheroma.

athletics competitive track and field events consisting of running, throwing, and jumping disciplines. *Running events* range from sprint races (100 metres) and hurdles to the marathon (26 miles 385 yards).

Jumping events are the high jump, long jump, triple jump, and pole vault (men only). *Throwing events* are javelin, discus, shot put, and hammer throw (men only).

history Among the Greeks, vase paintings show that competitive athletics were established at least by 1600 BC. Greek and Roman athletes were well paid and sponsored. The philosopher Aristotle paid the expenses of a boxer contestant at Olympia, and chariot races were sponsored by the Greek city-states. Today athletes are supposed to be unpaid amateurs. The concept of the unpaid amateur was popularised following the founding of the modern Olympic Games in 1896. However, athletes in the USA and Eastern bloc nations have become full-time, their incomes coming from commercial or state sponsorship, so that the status of athletics as an amateur sport is today rapidly disappearing at the senior level.

In aiming for the world record, nations may benefit from computer-aided training programmes and the specialization of equipment for maximum performance (for example, fibreglass vaulting poles, foam landing pads, aerodynamically designed javelins, and composition running tracks). In the course of the last twenty years there has been increasing controversy over the unlawful use of drugs, such as ◊anabolic steroids and growth hormones.

Athos /ˈeɪθɒs/ mountainous peninsula on the Macedonian coast of Greece. Its peak is 2,033 m/6,672 ft high. The promontory is occupied by a community of 20 Basilian monasteries inhabited by some 3,000 monks and lay brothers.

Atkins, Tommy popular name for the British soldier; see ◊Tommy Atkins.

Atlanta /ətˈlæntə/ capital and largest city of Georgia, USA; population (1988 est) 420,000, metropolitan area 2,010,000. There are Ford and Lockheed assembly plants, and it is the headquarters of Coca-Cola.

Originally named *Terminus* 1837, it was renamed 1845, was burned 1864 by General Sherman during the American Civil War. Nearby Stone Mountain Memorial shows the Confederate heroes Jefferson Davis, Robert E Lee, and Stonewall Jackson on horseback.

Atlantic, Battle of the /ətˈlæntɪk/ German campaign during World War I to prevent merchant shipping from delivering food supplies from the USA to the Allies, chiefly the UK. By 1917, some 875,000 tons of shipping had been lost. The odds were only turned by the belated use of naval *convoys* and *depth charges* to deter submarine attack.

Notable action included the British defeat at *Coronel* off Chile on 1 Nov 1914, the subsequent British success at the *Falkland Islands* on 8 Dec 1914, and the battle in the North Sea at *Jutland* on 31 May 1916, which effectively neutralized the German surface fleet for the rest of the war.

Atlantic, Battle of the continuous battle fought in the Atlantic Ocean throughout World War II (1939–45) by the sea and air forces of the Allies and Germany, to control the supply routes to the UK. The number of U-boats destroyed by the Allies during the war was nearly 800. At least 2,200 convoys of 75,000 merchant ships crossed the Atlantic, protected by US naval forces. Before the US entry into the war 1941, destroyers were suplied to the British under the Lend-Lease Act 1941.

The battle opened on the first night of the war, when on 4 Sept 1939 the ocean liner *Athenia*, sailing from Glasgow to New York, was torpedoed by a German submarine off the Irish coast. Germany tried U-boats, surface-raiders, indiscriminate mine-laying, and aircraft, but every method was successfully countered. The U-boats were the greatest menace, especially after the destruction of the German battleship *Bismarck* by British forces on 27 May 1941.

Atlantic Charter declaration issued during World War II by the British prime minister Churchill and the US president Roosevelt after meetings Aug 1941. It stressed their countries' broad strategy and war aims and was largely a propaganda exercise to demonstrate public solidarity between the Allies.

Atlantic City /ətˈlæntɪk ˈsɪti/ seaside resort in New Jersey, USA; population (1990) 38,000. It is known for its 'boardwalk' (a wooden pavement along the beach). Formerly a family resort, it has become a centre for casino gambling, which was legalized in New Jersey 1978.

Atlantic Ocean /ətˈlæntɪk/ ocean lying between Europe and Africa to the E and the Americas to the W, probably named after the legendary island ◊Atlantis; area of basin 81,500,000 sq km/31,500,000 sq mi; including Arctic Ocean, and Antarctic seas, 106,200,000 sq km/41,000,000 sq mi. The average depth is 3 km/2 mi; greatest depth the Milwaukee Depth in the Puerto Rico Trench 8,648 m/28,374 ft. The Mid-Atlantic Ridge, of which the Azores, Ascension, St Helena, and Tristan da Cunha form part, divides it from N to S. Lava welling up from this central area annually increases the distance between South America and Africa. The N Atlantic is the saltiest of the main oceans, and it has the largest tidal range. In the 1960s–80s average wave heights increased by 25%, the largest from 12 m/39 ft to 18 m/59 ft.

Atlantis legendary island continent, said to have sunk *c.* 9600 BC, following underwater convulsions. Although the Atlantic Ocean is probably named after it, the structure of the sea bottom rules out its ever having existed there.

One story told by the Greek philosopher Plato (derived from an account by Egyptian priests) may refer to the volcanic eruption that devastated Santorini in the ◊Cyclades, north of Crete, *c.* 1500 BC. The ensuing earthquakes and tidal waves brought about the collapse of the empire of Minoan Crete.

atlas book of maps. The atlas was introduced in the 16th century by ◊Mercator, who began work on it 1585; it was completed by his son 1594. Early atlases had a frontispiece showing Atlas supporting the globe.

Atlas /ˈætləs/ in Greek mythology, one of the ◊Titans who revolted against the gods; as a punishment, Atlas was compelled to support the heavens on his head and shoulders. Growing weary, he asked ◊Perseus to turn him into stone, and he was transformed into Mount Atlas.

Atlas Mountains /ˈætləs/ mountain system of NW Africa, stretching 2,400 km/1,500 mi from the Atlantic coast of Morocco to the Gulf of Gabes, Tunisia, and lying between the Mediterranean on the N and the Sahara on the S. The highest peak is Mount Toubkal 4,167 m/ 13,670 ft.

Atlas rocket US rocket, originally designed and built as an intercontinental missile, but subsequently adapted for space use. Atlas rockets launched astronauts in the Mercury series into orbit, as well as numerous other satellites and space probes.

atman in Hinduism, the individual soul or the eternal essential self.

atmosphere mixture of gases that surrounds the Earth, prevented from escaping by the pull of the Earth's gravity. Atmospheric pressure decreases with height in the atmosphere. In its lowest layer, the atmosphere consists of nitrogen (78%) and oxygen (21%), both in molecular form (two atoms bounded together). The other 1% is largely argon, with very small quantities of other gases, including water vapour and carbon dioxide. The atmosphere plays a major part in the various cycles of nature (the ◊water cycle, ◊carbon cycle, and ◊nitrogen cycle). It is the principal industrial source of nitrogen, oxygen, and argon, which are obtained by fractional distillation of liquid air.

The lowest level of the atmosphere, the ◊troposphere, is heated by the Earth, which is warmed by infrared and visible radiation from the Sun. Warm air cools as it rises in the troposphere, causing rain and most other weather phenomena. Infrared and visible radiations form only a part of the Sun's output of electromagnetic radiation. Almost all the shorter-wavelength ultraviolet radiation is filtered out by the upper layers of the atmosphere. The filtering process is an active one: at heights above about 50 km/31 mi ultraviolet photons collide with atoms, knocking out electrons to create a ◊plasma of electrons and positively charged ions. The resulting *ionosphere* acts as a reflector of radio waves, enabling radio transmissions to 'hop' between widely separated points on the Earth's surface. Waves of different wavelengths are reflected best at different heights. The collisions between ultraviolet photons and atoms lead to a heating of the upper atmosphere, although the emperature drops from top to bottom within the zone called the *thermosphere* as high-energy photons are progressively absorbed in collisions. Between the thermosphere and the tropopause (at which the warming effect of the Earth starts to be felt) there is a 'warm bulge' in the graph of temperature against height, at a level called the *stratopause.* This is due to longer-wavelength ultraviolet photons that have survived their journey through the upper layers; now they encounter molecules and split them apart into atoms. These atoms eventually bond together again, but often in different combinations. In particular, many ◊ozone molecules (oxygen-atom triplets) are formed. Ozone is a better absorber of ultraviolet than ordinary (two-atom) oxygen, and it is the *ozone layer* that prevents lethal amounts of ultraviolet from reaching he Earth's surface. Far above the atmosphere, as so far described, lie the *Van Allen radiation belts*. These are regions in which high-energy charged particles travelling outwards from the Sun (as the so-called solar wind) have been captured by the Earth's magnetic field. The outer belt (at about 1,600 km/1,000 mi) contains mainly protons, the inner belt (at about 2,000 km/1,250 mi) contains mainly electrons. Sometimes electrons spiral down towards the Earth, noticeably at polar latitudes, where the magnetic field is strongest. When such particles collide with atoms and ions in the thermosphere, light is emitted. This is the origin of the glows visible in the sky as the *aurora borealis* (northern lights) and the *aurora australis* (southern lights). A fainter, more widespread, *airglow* is caused by a similar mechanism.

atmosphere or *standard atmosphere* in physics, a unit (symbol atm) of pressure equal to 760 torr, 1013.25 millibars, or 1.01325×10^5 newtons per square metre. The actual pressure exerted by the atmosphere fluctuates around this value, which is assumed to be standard at sea level and 0°C, and is used when dealing with very high pressures.

atmospheric pressure pressure at a point in the atmosphere that is due to the weight of air above and so decreases with height. At sea level the pressure is about 101 kilopascals, 1013 millibars, 760 mmHg, or 14.7 lb per sq in. The exact value varies according to temperature and weather. Changes in atmospheric pressure, measured with a barometer, are used in weather forecasting.

atoll continuous or broken circle of ◊coral reef and low coral islands surrounding a lagoon.

atom the smallest unit of matter that can take part in a chemical reaction, and which cannot be broken down chemically into anything simpler. An atom is made up of protons and neutrons in a central nucleus surrounded by electrons (see ◊atomic structure). The atoms of the various elements differ in atomic number, relative atomic mass, and chemical behaviour. There are 109 different types of atom, corresponding with the 109 known elements as listed in the ◊periodic table of the elements.

Atoms are much too small to be seen even by the microscope (the largest, caesium, has a diameter of 0.0000005 mm/0.00000002 in), and they are in constant motion. Belief in the existence of atoms dates back to the ancient Greek natural philosophers. The first scientist to gather evidence for the existence of atoms was John Dalton, in the 19th century, who believed that every atom was a complete unbreakable entity. Ernest Rutherford showed by experiment that an atom in fact consists of a nucleus surrounded by negatively charged particles called electrons.

atom bomb bomb deriving its explosive force from nuclear fission (see ◊nuclear energy) as a result of a neutron chain reaction, developed in the 1940s in the USA into a usable weapon.

Research began in the UK 1940 and was transferred to the USA after its entry into World War II the following year. Known as the *Manhattan Project*, the work was carried out under the direction of the US physicist Oppenheimer at Los Alamos, New Mexico.

After one test explosion, two atom bombs were dropped on the Japanese cities of Hiroshima (6 Aug 1945) and Nagasaki (9 Aug 1945), each nominally equal to 200,000 tonnes of TNT. The USSR first detonated an atom bomb 1949 and the UK 1952.

The test site used by the UK was in the Monte Bello Islands off Australia. The development of the hydrogen bomb in the 1950s rendered the early atom bomb obsolete. See ◊nuclear warfare.

atomic clock timekeeping device regulated by various periodic processes occurring in atoms and molecules, such as atomic vibration or the frequency of absorbed or emitted radiation.

The first atomic clock was the *ammonia clock*, invented at the US National Bureau of Standards 1948. It was regulated by measuring the speed at which the nitrogen atom in an ammonia molecule vibrated back and forth. The rate of molecular vibration is not affected by temperature, pressure, or other external influences, and can be used to regulate an electronic clock.

A more accurate atomic clock is the *caesium clock*. Because of its internal structure, a caesium atom produces or absorbs radiation of a very precise frequency (9,192,631,770 Hz) that varies by less than one part in 10 billion. This frequency has been used to define the second, and is the basis of atomic clocks used in international time-keeping.

Hydrogen maser clocks, based on the radiation from hydrogen atoms, are the most accurate. The hydrogen maser clock at the US Naval Research Laboratory, Washington DC, is estimated to lose one second in 1,700,000 years. Cooled hydrogen maser clocks could theoretically be accurate to within one second in 300 million years.

atomic energy another name for ◊nuclear energy.

atomic force microscope (AFM) microscope developed in the late 1980s that produces a magnified image using a diamond probe, with a tip so fine that it may consist of a single atom, dragged over the surface of a specimen to 'feel' the contours of the surface. In effect, the tip acts like the stylus of a phonograph or record player, reading the surface. The tiny up-and-down movements of the probe are converted to an image of the surface by computer, and displayed on a screen. The AFM is useful for examination of biological specimens since, unlike the ◊scanning tunnelling microscope, the specimen does not have to be electrically conducting.

atomicity number of atoms of an ◊element that combine together to form a molecule. A molecule of oxygen (O_2) has atomicity 2; sulphur (S_8) has atomicity 8.

atomic mass unit or *dalton* unit (symbol amu or u) of mass that is used to measure the relative mass of atoms and molecules. It is equal to one-twelfth of the mass of a carbon-12 atom, which is equivalent to the mass of a proton or 1.66×10^{-27} kg. The ◊relative atomic mass of an atom has no units; thus oxygen-16 has an atomic mass of 16 daltons, but a relative atomic mass of 16.

atomic number or *proton number* the number (symbol Z) of protons in the nucleus of an atom. It is equal to the positive charge on the nucleus. In a neutral atom, it is also equal to the number of electrons surrounding the nucleus. The 109 elements are arranged in the ◊periodic table of the elements according to their atomic number. See also ◊nuclear notation.

atomic physics study of the properties of the ◊atom.

atomic radiation energy given out by disintegrating atoms during ◊radioactive decay. The energy may be in the form of fast-moving particles, known as ◊alpha particles and ◊beta particles, or in the form of high-energy electromagnetic waves known as ◊gamma radiation. Overlong exposure to atomic radiation can lead to ◊radiation sickness. Radiation biology studies the effect of radiation on living organisms.

atomic size or *atomic radius* size of an atom expressed as the radius in ◊angstroms or other units of length. The sodium atom has an atomic radius of 1.57 angstroms (1.57 $\times 10^{-8}$ cm). For metals, the size of the atom is always greater than the size of its ion. For non-metals the reverse is true.

atomic structure internal structure of an ◊atom. The core of the atom is the *nucleus*, a dense body only one-ten-thousandth the diameter of the atom itself. The simplest nucleus, that of hydrogen, comprises a single stable positively charged particle, the *proton*. Nuclei of other elements contain more protons and additional particles, called *neutrons*, of about the same mass as the proton but with no electrical charge. Each element has its own characteristic nucleus with a unique number of protons, the atomic number. The number of neutrons may vary. Where atoms of a single element have different numbers of neutrons, they are called

◊isotopes. Although some isotopes tend to be unstable and exhibit ◊radioactivity, they all have identical chemical properties.

The nucleus is surrounded by a number of moving *electrons*, each of which has a negative charge equal to the positive charge on a proton, but which weighs only 1/1,839 times as much. In a neutral atom, the nucleus is surrounded by the same number of electrons as it contains protons. According to ◊quantum theory, the position of an electron is uncertain; it may be found at any point. However, it is more likely to be found in some places than others. The region of space in which an electron is most likely to be found is called an orbital (see ◊orbital, atomic). The chemical properties of an element are determined by the ease with which its atoms can gain or lose electrons from its outer orbitals.

High-energy physics research has discovered the existence of subatomic particles (see ◊particle physics) other than the proton, neutron, and electron. More than 300 kinds of particle are now known, and these are classified into several classes according to their mass, electric charge, spin, magnetic moment, and interaction. The *elementary particles*, which include the electron, are indivisible and may be regarded as the fundamental units of matter; the *hadrons*, such as the proton and neutron, are composite particles made up of either two or three elementary particles called quarks.

Atoms are held together by the electrical forces of attraction between each negative electron and the positive protons within the nucleus. The latter repel one another with enormous forces; a nucleus holds together only because an even stronger force, called the strong nuclear force, attracts the protons and neutrons to one another. The strong force acts over a very short range—the protons and neutrons must be in virtual contact with one another. If, therefore, a fragment of a complex nucleus, containing some protons, becomes only slightly loosened from the main group of neutrons and protons, the natural repulsion between the protons will cause this fragment to fly apart from the rest of the nucleus at high speed. It is by such fragmentation of atomic nuclei (nuclear ◊fission) that nuclear energy is released.

atomic time time as given by ◊atomic clocks, which are regulated by natural resonance frequencies of particular atoms, and display a continuous count of seconds.

In 1967 a new definition of the second was adopted in the SI system of units: the duration of 9,192,631,770 periods of the radiation corresponding to the transition between two hyperfine levels of the ground state of the caesium-133 atom. The International Atomic Time Scale is based on clock data from a number of countries; it is a continuous scale in days, hours, minutes, and seconds from the origin on 1 Jan 1958, when the Atomic Time Scale was made 0 hr 0 min 0 sec when Greenwich Mean Time was at 0 hr 0 min 0 sec.

atomic weight another name for ◊relative atomic mass.

atomizer device that produces a spray of fine droplets of liquid. A vertical tube connected with a horizontal tube dips into a bottle of liquid, and at one end of the horizontal tube is a nozzle, at the other a rubber bulb. When the bulb is squeezed, air rushes over the top of the vertical tube and out through the nozzle. Following ◊Bernoulli's principle, the pressure at the top of the vertical tube is reduced, allowing the liquid to rise. The air stream picks up the liquid, breaks it up into tiny drops, and carries it out of the nozzle as a spray.

Aton /ˈɑːtɒn/ in ancient Egypt, the Sun's disc as an emblem of the single deity whose worship was promoted by ◊Ikhnaton in an attempt to replace the many gods traditionally worshipped.

atonality music in which there is an apparent absence of ◊key; often associated with an expressionist style.

Atonality is used by film and television composers for situations of mystery or horror; it exploits *dissonance* for its power to disturb. For ◊Schoenberg, pioneer of atonal music from 1909, the intention was to liberate tonal expression and not primarily to disturb, and he rejected the term as misleading.

atonement in Christian theology, the doctrine that Jesus suffered on the cross to bring about reconciliation and forgiveness between God and humanity.

Atonement, Day of Jewish holy day (*Yom Kippur*) held on the tenth day of Tishri (Sept–Oct), the first month of the Jewish year. It is a day of fasting, penitence, and cleansing from sin, ending the Ten Days of

Penitence that follow **Rosh Hashanah**, the Jewish New Year.

ATP abbreviation for **adenosine triphosphate**, a nucleotide molecule found in all cells. It can yield large amounts of energy, and is used to drive the thousands of biological processes needed to sustain life, growth, movement, and reproduction. Green plants use light energy to manufacture ATP as part of the process of ◊photosynthesis. In animals, ATP is formed by the breakdown of glucose molecules, usually obtained from the carbohydrate component of a diet, in a series of reactions termed ◊respiration. It is the driving force behind muscle contraction and the synthesis of complex molecules needed by individual cells.

atrium in architecture, an open inner courtyard. Originally the central court or main room of an ancient Roman house, open to the sky, often with a shallow pool to catch water.

atrium one of the upper chambers of the heart, receiving blood under low pressure as it returns from the body. Atrium walls are thin and stretch easily to allow blood into the heart. On contraction, the atria force blood into the thick-walled ventricles, which then give a second, more powerful beat.

atrophy in medicine, a diminution in size and function, or output, of a body tissue or organ. It is usually due to nutritional impairment, disease, or disuse (muscle).

atropine alkaloid derived from belladonna. It acts as an ◊anticholinergic, inhibiting the passage of certain nerve impulses. As atropine sulphate, it is administered as a mild antispasmodic drug.

attainder, bill of legislative device that allowed the English Parliament to declare guilt and impose a punishment on an individual without bringing the matter before the courts. Such bills were used intermittently from the Wars of the Roses until 1798. Some acts of attainder were also passed by US colonial legislators during the American Revolution to deal with 'loyalists' who continued to support the English crown.

attar of roses perfume derived from the essential oil of roses (usually damask roses), obtained by crushing and distilling the petals of the flowers.

attempt in law, a partial or unsuccessful commission of a crime. An attempt must be more than preparation for a crime; it must involve actual efforts to commit a crime.

In the UK, attempt is covered under the Criminal Attempts Act 1981, which repealed the 'suspected person offence', commonly known as the 'sus' law.

Attenborough /ˈætnbərə/ Richard 1923– . English actor, director and producer. He began his acting career in war films and comedies. His later films include *Brighton Rock* 1947 and *10 Rillington Place* 1970 (as actor), and *Oh! What a Lovely War* 1969, *Gandhi* (which won eight Academy Awards) 1982, and *Cry Freedom* 1987 (as director).

Attica /ˈætɪkə/ (Greek *Attiki*) region of Greece comprising Athens and the district around it; area 3,381 sq km/1,305 sq mi. It is renowned for its language, art, and philosophical thought in Classical times. It is a prefecture of modern Greece with Athens as its capital.

Attila /əˈtɪlə/ c. 406–453. King of the Huns in an area from the Alps to the Caspian Sea from 434, known to later Christian history as the 'Scourge of God'.

Attila first ruled jointly with his brother Bleda, whom he murdered in 444, and twice attacked the Eastern Roman Empire to increase the quantity of tribute paid to him, in 441–443 and 447–449. In 450 Honoria, the sister of the western Emperor Valentinian III, appealed to him to rescue her from an arranged marriage, and Attila used her appeal to attack the West. He was forced back from Orléans by Aetius and Theodoric, king of the Visigoths, and defeated by them on the ◊Catalaunian Fields in 451. In 452 he led the Huns into Italy, and was induced to withdraw by Pope ◊Leo I.

He died on the night of his marriage to the German Ildico, either by poison, or, as Chaucer represents it in his *Pardoner's Tale*, from a nasal haemorrhage induced by drunkenness.

Attila Line line dividing Greek and Turkish Cyprus, so called because of a fanciful identification of the Turks with the Huns.

Attis /ˈætɪs/ in Classical mythology, a Phrygian god whose death and resurrection symbolized the end of winter and the arrival of spring. Beloved by the goddess ◊Cybele, who drove him mad as a punishment for his infidelity, he castrated himself and bled to death.

Attlee /ˈætli/ Clement (Richard), 1st Earl 1883–1967. British Labour politician. In the coalition government during World War II he was Lord Privy Seal 1940–42, dominions secretary 1942–43, and Lord President of the Council 1943–45, as well as deputy prime minister from 1942. As prime minister 1945–51 he introduced a sweeping programme of nationalization and a whole new system of social services.

Attlee was educated at Oxford and practised at the Bar 1906–09. Social work in London's East End and cooperation in poor-law reform led him to become a socialist; he joined the Fabian Society and the Independent Labour Party 1908. He became lecturer in social science at the London School of Economics 1913. After service in World War I he was mayor of Stepney, E London, 1919–20; Labour member of Parliament for Limehouse 1922–50 and for W Walthamstow 1950–55. In the first and second Labour governments he was undersecretary for war 1924 and chancellor of the Duchy of Lancaster and postmaster general 1929–31. In 1935 he became leader of the opposition. In July 1945 he became prime minister after a Labour landslide in the general election. The government was returned to power with a much reduced majority 1950 and was defeated 1951.

Attorney General in the UK, principal law officer of the crown and head of the English Bar; the post is one of great political importance. In the USA, it is the chief law officer of the government and head of the Department of Justice.

In England, Wales, and Northern Ireland, the consent of the Attorney General is required for bringing certain criminal proceedings where offences against the state or public order are at issue (for example, the ◊*Spycatcher* litigation). Under the Criminal Justice Act 1988, cases can be referred to the Court of Appeal by the Attorney General if it appears to him or her that the sentencing of a person convicted of a serious offence has been unduly lenient.

Atwood /ˈætwʊd/ Margaret (Eleanor) 1939– . Canadian novelist, short-story writer, and poet. Her novels, which often treat feminist themes with wit and irony, include *The Edible Woman* 1969, *Life Before Man* 1979, *Bodily Harm* 1981, *The Handmaid's Tale* 1986, and *Cat's Eye* 1989.

Aube /əʊb/ river of NE France, a tributary of the Seine, length 248 km/155 mi; it gives its name to a *département* (administrative region).

aubergine or *eggplant* plant *Solanum melongena*, a member of the nightshade family Solanaceae. The aubergine is native to tropical Asia. Its purple-skinned, sometimes white, fruits are eaten as a vegetable.

Aubrey /ˈɔːbri/ John 1626–1697. English biographer and antiquary. His *Lives*, begun in 1667, contains gossip, anecdotes, and valuable insights into the celebrities of his time. Unpublished during his lifetime, a standard edition of the work appeared as *Brief Lives* 1898 in two volumes (edited by A Clark). Aubrey was the first to claim Stonehenge as a Druid temple.

aubrieta any spring-flowering dwarf perennial plant of the genus *Aubrieta* of the cress family Cruciferae. All are trailing plants with showy, purple flowers. Native to the Middle East, they are cultivated widely in rock gardens.

Auchinleck /ˈɔːkɪnlek/ Sir Claude John Eyre 1884–1981. British commander in World War II. He won the First Battle of El ◊Alamein 1942 in N Egypt. In 1943 he became commander in chief in India and founded the modern Indian and Pakistani armies. In 1946 he was promoted to field marshal; he retired in 1947.

Auchinleck, nicknamed 'the Auk', succeeded Wavell as commander in chief Middle East July 1941, and in the summer of 1942 was forced back to the Egyptian frontier by the German field marshal Rommel, but his victory at the First Battle of El Alamein is regarded by some as more important to the outcome of World War II than the Second Battle.

Auckland /ˈɔːklənd/ largest city in New Zealand, situated in N North Island; population (1987) 889,000. It fills the isthmus that separates its two harbours (Waitemata and Manukau), and its suburbs spread N across the Harbour Bridge. It is the country's chief port and leading industrial centre, having iron and steel plants, engineering, car assembly, textiles, food processing, sugar refining, and brewing.

There was a small whaling settlement on the site in the 1830s, and Auckland was officially founded as New Zealand's capital 1840, remaining so until 1865. The university was founded 1882.

Auckland /ˈɔːklənd/ George Eden, 1st Earl of Auckland 1784–1849. British Tory politician after whom Auckland, New Zealand, is named. He became a member of Parliament 1810, and 1835–41 was governor general of India.

auction the sale of goods or property in public to the highest bidder. There are usually conditions of sale by which all bidders are bound. Leading world auctioneers are Christie's and Sotheby's.

A bid may be withdrawn at any time before the auctioneer brings down the hammer, and the seller is likewise entitled to withdraw any lot before the hammer falls. In recent years, auction houses have been increasingly examined for illegal practices. It is illegal for the seller or anyone on their behalf to make a bid for their own goods unless their right to do so has been reserved and notified before the sale. 'Rings' of dealers agreeing to keep prices down are illegal. A reserve price is kept secret, but an upset price (the minimum price fixed for the property offered) is made public before the sale. An auction where property is first offered at a high price and gradually reduced until a bid is received is known as a *'Dutch auction'*.

In 1988, art auctioneers (handling not only pictures, but other items of value such as furniture) were required by a British judge's ruling to recognize the possibility of the item being of great value, and to carry out 'proper research' on their provenance.

auction bridge card game played by two pairs of players using all 52 cards in a standard deck. The chief characteristic is the selection of trumps by a preliminary bid or auction. It has been succeeded in popularity by ◊contract bridge.

Aude /əʊd/ river in SE France, 210 km/130 mi long, that gives its name to a *département*. Carcassonne is the main town through which it passes.

Auden /ˈɔːdn/ W(ystan) H(ugh) 1907–1973. English-born US poet. He wrote some of his most original poetry, such as *Look, Stranger!* 1936, in the 1930s when he led the influential left-wing literary group that included Louis MacNeice, Stephen Spender, and Cecil Day Lewis. He moved to the USA 1939, became a US citizen 1946, and adopted a more conservative and Christian viewpoint, for example in *The Age of Anxiety* 1947.

Born in York, Auden was associate professor of English literature at the University of Michigan from 1939, and professor of poetry at Oxford 1956–61. He also wrote verse dramas with Christopher ◊Isherwood, such as *The Dog Beneath the Skin* and *The Ascent of F6* 1951, and opera librettos, notably for Stravinsky's *The Rake's Progress* 1951.

Audenarde /əʊdˈnɑːd/ French form of ◊Oudenaarde, town in Belgium.

Audit Commission independent body in the UK established by the Local Government Finance Act 1982. It administers the District Audit Service (established 1844) and appoints auditors for the accounts of all UK local authorities. The Audit Commission consists of 15 members: its aims include finding ways of saving costs, and controlling illegal local-authority spending.

auditory canal tube leading from the outer ◊ear opening to the eardrum. It is found only in animals whose eardrums are located inside the skull, principally mammals and birds.

Audubon /ˈɔːdəbɒn/ John James 1785–1851. US naturalist and artist. In 1827, after extensive travels and observations of birds, he published the first part of his *Birds of North America*, with a remarkable series of colour plates. Later he produced a similar work on North American quadrupeds.

He was born in Santo Domingo (now Haiti) and educated in Paris. The National Audubon Society (founded 1886) has branches throughout the USA and Canada for the study and protection of birds.

Augean stables in Greek mythology, the stables of Augeas, king of Elis in Greece. One of the labours of ◊Heracles was to clean out the stables, which contained 3,000 cattle and had never been cleaned before. He was given only one day to do the labour and so diverted the river Alpheus through their yard.

auger tool used to collect sediment and soil samples below ground without hand excavation, or to determine the depth and type of archaeological deposits. The auger may be hand-or machine-powered.

Augsburg /ˈaʊksbɜːg/ industrial city in Bavaria, Germany, at the confluence of the Wertach and Lech rivers, 52 km/32 mi NW of Munich; population (1988) 246,000. It is named after the Roman emperor Augustus who founded it 15 BC.

Augsburg, Confession of /ˈaʊgzbʊəg/ statement of the Protestant faith as held by the German Reformers, composed by Philip ◊Melanchthon. Presented to the holy Roman emperor Charles V, at the conference known as the Diet of Augsburg

1530, it is the creed of the modern Lutheran church.

Augsburg, Peace of religious settlement following the Diet of Augsburg 1555, which established the right of princes in the Holy Roman Empire (rather than the emperor himself, Ferdinand I) to impose a religion on their subjects—later summarized by the maxim ◊*cuius regio, eius religio*. It initially applied only to Lutherans and Catholics.

augur member of a college of Roman priests who interpreted the will of the gods from signs or 'auspices' such as the flight of birds, the condition of entrails of sacrificed animals, and the direction of thunder and lightning. Their advice was sought before battle and on other important occasions. Consuls and other high officials had the right to consult the auspices themselves, and a campaign was said to be conducted 'under the auspices' of the general who had consulted the gods.

Augustan Age /ɔːˈgʌst(ə)n/ golden age of the Roman emperor ◊Augustus, during which art and literature flourished. The name is also given to later periods which used Classical ideals, such as that of Queen Anne in England.

Augustine of Hippo, St /ɔːˈgʌstɪn/ 354–430. One of the early Christian leaders and writers known as the Fathers of the Church. He was converted to Christianity by Ambrose in Milan and became bishop of Hippo (modern Annaba, Algeria) 396. Among Augustine's many writings are his *Confessions*, a spiritual autobiography, and *De Civitate Dei/The City of God*, vindicating the Christian church and divine providence in 22 books.

Born in Thagaste, Numidia (now Algeria), of Roman descent, he studied rhetoric in Carthage, where he became the father of an illegitimate son, Adeodatus. He lectured in Tagaste and Carthage and for ten years was attached to the Manichaeist belief. In 383 he went to Rome, and on moving to Milan came under the influence of Ambrose. After prolonged study of neo-Platonism he was baptized by Ambrose together with his son. Resigning his chair in rhetoric, he returned to Africa—his mother, St Monica, dying in Ostia on the journey—and settled in Thagaste. In 391, while visiting Hippo, Augustine was ordained priest, and in 396 he was appointed bishop of Hippo. He died there in 430, as the city was under siege by the Vandals.

Augustine, St /ɔːˈgʌstɪn/ first archbishop of Canterbury, England. He was sent from Rome to convert England to Christianity by Pope Gregory I. He landed at Ebbsfleet in Kent 597, and soon after baptized Ethelbert, King of Kent, along with many of his subjects. He was consecrated bishop of the English at Arles in the same year, and appointed archbishop 601, establishing his see at Canterbury. Feast day 26 May.

Augustinian /ɔːgəˈstɪnɪən/ member of a religious community that follows the Rule of St ◊Augustine of Hippo. It includes the Canons of St Augustine, Augustinian Friars and Hermits, Premonstratensians, Gilbertines, and Trinitarians.

Augustus /ɔːˈgʌstəs/ BC 63–AD 14. Title of Octavian (Gaius Julius Caesar Octavianus), first of the Roman emperors. He joined forces with Mark Antony and Lepidus the Second Triumvirate. Following Mark Antony's liaison with the Egyptian queen Cleopatra, Augustus defeated her troops at Actium 31 BC. As emperor (from 27 BC) he reformed the government of the empire, the army, and Rome's public services, and was a patron of the arts. The period of his rule is known as the ◊Augustan age.

He was the son of a senator who married a niece of Julius Caesar, and he became his great-uncle's adopted son and principal heir. Following Caesar's murder, Octavian formed with Mark Antony and Lepidus the Triumvirate that divided the Roman world between them and proceeded to eliminate the opposition. Antony's victory 42 BC over Brutus and Cassius had brought the republic to an end. Antony then became enamoured of Cleopatra and spent most of his time at Alexandria, while Octavian consolidated his hold on the western part of the Roman dominion. War was declared against Cleopatra, and the naval victory at Actium left Octavian in unchallenged supremacy, since Lepidus had been forced to retire. After his return to Rome 29 BC, Octavian was created *princeps senatus*, and in 27 BC he was given the title of Augustus ('venerable'). He then resigned his extraordinary powers and received from the Senate, in return, the proconsular command, which gave him control of the army, and the tribunician power, whereby he could initiate or veto legislation. In his programme of reforms Augustus received the support of three loyal and capable helpers, Agrippa, Maecenas, and his wife, Livia, while Virgil and Horace acted as the poets laureate of the new regime. A firm frontier for the empire was established: to the north, the friendly Batavians held the Rhine delta, and then the line followed the course of the Rhine and Danube; to the east, the Parthians were friendly, and the Euphrates gave the next line; to the south, the African colonies were protected by the desert; to the west were Spain and Gaul. The provinces were governed either by imperial legates responsible to the *princeps* or by proconsuls appointed by the Senate. The army was made a profession, with fixed pay and length of service, and a permanent fleet was established. Finally, Rome itself received an adequate water supply, a fire brigade, a police force, and a large number of public buildings. The years after 12 BC were marked by private and public calamities: the marriage of Augustus' daughter Julia to his stepson Tiberius proved disastrous; a serious revolt occurred in Pannonia AD 6; and in Germany three legions under Varus were annihilated in the Teutoburg Forest AD 9. Augustus died a broken man, but his work remained secure.

auk any member of the family Alcidae, consisting of marine diving birds including razorbills, puffins, murres, and guillemots. Confined to the northern hemisphere, they feed on fish and use their wings to 'fly' underwater in pursuit.

The smallest, at 20 cm/8 in is the *little auk Alle alle*, an arctic bird that winters as far south as Britain. The largest was the *great auk Pinguinis impennis*, 75 cm/2.5 ft and flightless, the last recorded individual being killed in 1844.

'Auld Lang Syne' song written by the Scottish poet Robert Burns about 1789, which is often sung at New Year's Eve gatherings; the title means 'old long since' or 'long ago'.

Aulis anchorage on the eastern coast of Greece, opposite ◊Euboea in Greek mythology, the point of departure for the Greek expedition against ◊Troy.

Aung San /aʊŋ 'sæn/ 1916–1947. Burmese politician. He was a founder and leader of the Anti-Fascist People's Freedom League, which led Burma's fight for independence from Great Britain. During World War II he collaborated first with Japan and then with the UK. In 1947 he became head of Burma's provisional government but was assassinated the same year by political opponents;

Burma (now Myanmar) became independent in 1948.

aura diagnosis ascertaining a person's state of health from the colour and luminosity of the aura, the 'energy envelope' of the physical body commonly claimed to be seen by psychics. A study carried out by the Charing Cross Hospital Medical School (London) confirmed that the aura can be viewed by high frequency electrophotography techniques and is broadly indicative of states of health, but concluded that aura diagnosis cannot identify specific abnormalities.

Aurangzeb /ˈɔːrənzeb/ or *Aurungzebe* 1618–1707. Mogul emperor of N India from 1658. Third son of Shah Jahan, he made himself master of the court by a palace revolution. His reign was the most brilliant period of the Mogul dynasty, but his despotic tendencies and Muslim fanaticism aroused much opposition. His latter years were spent in war with the princes of Rajputana and Maratha.

Aurelian /ɔːˈriːliən/ (Lucius Domitius Aurelianus) *c*. 214–AD 275. Roman emperor from 270. A successful soldier, he was chosen emperor by his troops on the death of Claudius II. He defeated the Goths and Vandals, defeated and captured ◊Zenobia of Palmyra, and was planning a campaign against Parthia when he was murdered. The *Aurelian Wall*, a fortification surrounding Rome, was built by Aurelian 271. It was made of concrete, and substantial ruins exist. The *Aurelian Way* ran from Rome through Pisa and Genoa to Antipolis (Antibes) in Gaul.

Aurelius Antoninus /ɔːˈriːliəs/ Marcus Roman emperor; see ◊Marcus Aurelius Antoninus.

auricula species of primrose *Primula auricula*, a plant whose leaves are said to resemble bear's ears. It is native to the Alps but popular in cool-climate areas and often cultivated in gardens.

Aurignacian /ɔːrɪgˈneɪʃ(ə)n/ in archaeology, an Old Stone Age culture that came between the Mousterian and the Solutrian in the Upper Palaeolithic. The name is derived from a cave at Aurignac in the Pyrenees of France. The earliest cave paintings are attributed to the Aurignacian peoples of W Europe about 16,000 BC.

Auriol /ˈɔːriˈəʊl/ Vincent 1884–1966. French Socialist politician. He was president of the two Constituent Assemblies of 1946 and first president of the Fourth Republic 1947–54.

aurochs (plural *aurochs*) extinct species of long-horned wild cattle *Bos primigenius* that formerly roamed Europe, SW Asia, and N Africa. It survived in Poland until 1627. Black to reddish or grey, it was up to 1.8 m/6 ft at the shoulder. It is depicted in many cave paintings, and is considered the ancestor of domestic cattle.

aurora /ɔːˈrɔːrə/ coloured light in the night sky near the Earth's magnetic poles, called *aurora borealis*, 'northern lights', in the northern hemisphere and *aurora australis* in the southern hemisphere. An aurora is usually in the form of a luminous arch followed by folded bands and rays, usually green but often showing shades of blue and red, and sometimes yellow or white. Auroras are caused at heights of over 100 km/60 mi by a fast stream of charged particles from solar flares and low-density 'holes' in the Sun's corona. These are guided by the Earth's magnetic field towards the north and south magnetic poles, where they enter the upper atmosphere and bombard the gases in the atmosphere, causing them to emit visible light.

Aurora /ɔːˈrɔːrə/ Roman goddess of the dawn. The Greek equivalent is *Eos*.

Auschwitz /ˈaʊʃvɪts/ (Polish *Oswiecim*) town near Kraków in Poland, the site of a notorious ◊concentration camp used by the Nazis in World War II to exterminate Jews and other political and social minorities, as part of the 'final solution'. Each of the four gas chambers could hold 6,000 people.

Ausgleich /ˈaʊsɡlaɪx/ compromise between Austria and Hungary 8 Feb 1867 that established the Austro–Hungarian Dual Monarchy under Habsburg rule. It endured until the collapse of Austria-Hungary 1918.

Austen /ˈɒstɪn/ Jane 1775–1817. English novelist who described her raw material as 'three or four families in a Country Village'. *Sense and Sensibility* was published 1811, *Pride and Prejudice* 1813, *Mansfield Park* 1814, *Emma* 1816, *Northanger Abbey* and *Persuasion* 1818, all anonymously. She observed speech and manners with wit and precision, revealing her characters' absurdities in relation to high standards of integrity and appropriateness.

She was born at Steventon, Hampshire, where her father was rector, and began writing early; the burlesque *Love and Freindship* (sic), published 1922, was written 1790. In 1801 the family moved to Bath and after the death of her father in 1805, to Southampton, finally settling in Chawton, Hampshire, with her brother Edward. She died in Winchester, and is buried in the cathedral.

Austerlitz, Battle of /ˈaʊstəlɪts/ battle on 2 Dec 1805 in which the French forces of Emperor Napoleon defeated those of Alexander I of Russia and Francis II of Austria at a small town in the Czech Republic (formerly in Austria), 19 km/12 mi E of Brno.

Austin /ˈɒstɪn/ capital of Texas, on the Colorado River; population (1980) 345,500. It is a centre for electronic and scientific research.

Austin /ˈɒstɪn/ Herbert, 1st Baron 1866–1941. English industrialist who began manufacturing cars 1905 in Northfield, Birmingham, notably the Austin Seven 1921.

Austin /ˈstɪn/ J(ohn) L(angshaw) 1911–1960. British philosopher. Influential in his later work on the philosophy of language, Austin was a pioneer in the investigation of the way words are used in everyday speech. His lectures *Sense and Sensibilia* and *How to do Things with Words* were published posthumously in 1962.

Australasia /ˌɒstrəˈleɪziə/ loosely applied geographical term, usually meaning Australia, New Zealand, and neighbouring islands.

Australia /ɒsˈtreɪliə/ country occupying all of the Earth's smallest continent, situated S of Indonesia, between the Pacific and Indian oceans.

government Australia is an independent sovereign nation within the Commonwealth, retaining the British monarch as head of state and represented by a governor general. The constitution came into effect 1 Jan 1901. As in the British system, the executive, comprising the prime minister and cabinet, is drawn from the federal parliament and is answerable to it. The parliament consists of two chambers: an elected senate of 76 (12 for each of the six states, two for the Australian Capital Territory, and two for the Northern Territory); and a house of Representatives of 148, elected by universal adult suffrage. Senators serve for six years, and members of the house for three years. Voting is compulsory; the senate is elected by proportional representation, but the house of representatives is elected as single-member constituencies with preferential voting. Each state has its own constitution, governor (the monarch's representative), executive (drawn from the parliament), and legislative and judicial system. Each territory has its own legislative assembly. The main political parties are the Liberal Party, the National Party (normally in coalition), the Australian Labor Party, and the Australian Democrats. The last relics of UK legislative control over Australia were removed 1986.

history Australia's native inhabitants, the Aborigines, arrived in Australia at least 40,000 years ago, according to present evidence. The first recorded sighting of Australia by Europeans was 1606, when the Dutch ship *Duyfken*, under the command of Willem ◊Jansz, sighted the W coast of Cape York and the Spanish ship of Luis Vaez de Torres sailed N of Cape York and through Torres Strait, thus proving that New Guinea was separate from any southern continent. Later voyagers include Dirk Hartog 1616, who left an inscribed pewter plate (Australia's most famous early European relic, now in Amsterdam) in W Australia, Abel ◊Tasman, and William ◊Dampier. A second wave of immigration began 1788, after Capt James ◊Cook had claimed New South Wales as a British colony 1770.

colonies established The gold rushes of the 1850s and 1880s contributed to the exploration as well as to the economic and constitutional growth of Australia, as did the pioneer work of the ◊overlanders. The creation of other separate colonies followed he first settlement in New South Wales at Sydney 1788: Tasmania 1825, Western Australia 1829, South Australia 1836, Victoria 1851, and Queensland 1859. The system of transportation of convicts from Britain was never introduced in South Australia and Victoria, and ended in New South Wales 1840, Queensland 1849, Tasmania 1852, and Western Australia 1868. The convicts' con-

tribution to the economic foundation of the country was considerable.

inland exploration by Europeans Exploration of the interior began with the crossing of the barrier of the ◊Blue Mountains 1813. Explorers include Hamilton Hume (1797–1873) and William Hovell (1786–1875) who reached Port Phillip Bay 1824 and were the first Europeans to see the Murray River; Charles ◊Sturt; Thomas Mitchell (1792–1855), surveyor general for New South Wales 1828–55, who opened up the fertile western area of Victoria; Edward ◊Eyre, Ludwig ◊Leichhardt, Robert O'Hara ◊Burke and William Wills (1834–1861), and John ◊Stuart. In the 1870s the last gaps were filled in by the crossings of W Australia by John ◊Forrest, (William) Ernest Giles (1835–1897) 1875–76, and Peter Warburton (1813–1889) 1873.

economic depression and growth In the 1890s there was a halt in the rapid expansion that Australia had enjoyed, and the resulting depression led to the formation of the Australian Labor Party and an increase in trade-union activity, which has characterized Australian politics ever since. State powers waned following the creation of the Commonwealth of Australia 1901. Australia played an important role in both world wars, and after World War II it embarked on a fresh period of expansion, with new mineral finds playing a large part in economic growth.

growth of nationalism Since 1945 Australia has strengthened its ties with India and other SE Asian countries; since Britain's entry into the EC 1973, and under the Whitlam Labor government, which came to power 1972, there was a growth of nationalism. After heading a Liberal–Country Party coalition government for 17 years, Robert Menzies resigned 1966 and was succeeded by Harold Holt, who died in a swimming accident 1967. John Gorton became prime minister 1968 but lost a vote of confidence in the House and was succeeded by a Liberal–Country Party coalition under William McMahon 1971. At the end of 1972 the Australian Labor Party took office, led by Gough Whitlam. The 1974 general election gave the Labor Party a fresh mandate to govern despite having a reduced majority in the house of representatives.

1975 constitutional crisis The senate blocked the government's financial legislation 1975 and, with Whitlam unwilling to resign, the governor general took the unprecedented

Australian prime ministers

date of taking office	name	party
1901	Sir Edmund Barton	Protectionist
1903	Alfred Deakin	Protectionist
1904	John Watson	Labor
1904	Sir G Reid	Free Trade
1905	Alfred Deakin	Protectionist
1908	Andrew Fisher	Labor
1909	Alfred Deakin	Protectionist Free Trade alliance
1910	Andrew Fisher	Labor
1913	Sir J Cook	Liberal
1914	Andrew Fisher	Labor
1915	W M Hughes	Labor
1917	W M Hughes	National Labor
1923	S M Bruce	Nationalist
1929	J H Scullin	Labor
1932	J A Lyons	United Australia Party
1939	Sir Earle Page	Country Party
1939	R G Menzies	United Australia Party
1941	A W Fadden	Country Party
1941	John Curtin	Labor
1945	F M Forde	Labor
1945	J B Chifley	Labor
1949	R G Menzies	Liberal–Country Party
1966	Harold Holt	Liberal–Country Party
1967	John McEwen	Liberal–Country Party
1968	J G Gorton	Liberal–Country Party
1971	William McMahon	Liberal–Country Party
1972	Gough Whitlam	Labor
1975	Malcolm Fraser	Liberal–Country Party
1983	Robert Hawke	Labor
1991	Paul Keating	Labor

Australia, Commonwealth of

state	capital	area in sq km
New South Wales	Sydney	801,600
Queensland	Brisbane	1,727,200
South Australia	Adelaide	984,000
Tasmania	Hobart	67,800
Victoria	Melbourne	227,600
Western Australia	Perth	2,525,500
territories		
Northern Territory	Darwin	1,346,200
Capital Territory	Canberra	2,400
		7,682,300
external territories		
Ashmore and Cartier Islands		5
Australian Antarctic Territory		6,044,000
Christmas Island		135
Cocos (Keeling) Islands	14	
Coral Sea Islands		1,000,000
Heard Island and McDonald Islands		410
Norfolk Island		40

SE Asia and imposed trading sanctions against South Africa as a means of influencing the dismantling of apartheid. In the 1987 general election, Labor marginally increased its majority in the House but did not have an overall majority in the Senate, where the balance was held by the Australian Democrats. The 1990 election was won by Labor, led by Bob Hawke, with a reduced majority in the house of representatives for a record fourth term in office.

Keating as prime minister In Dec 1991 Hawke's leadership of the Labor Party was successfully challenged by Paul Keating, who became the new party leader and prime minister. In Dec 1992 the Citizenship Act was amended to remove the oath of allegiance to the British Crown. In March 1993 the Labor Party won a surprising general election victory, entering an unprecedented fifth term of office.

Australia Day Australian national day and public holiday in Australia, the anniversary of Captain Phillip's arrival on 26 Jan 1788 at Sydney Cove in Port Jackson and the founding of the colony of New South Wales.

Australian Aboriginal religions beliefs associated with the creation legends recorded in the ◊Dreamtime stories. These are related to specific sacred sites. Each Aborigine has a Dreamtime ancestor associated

step of dismissing him and his cabinet and inviting Malcolm ◊Fraser to form a Liberal–Country Party coalition caretaker administration. The wisdom of this action was widely questioned, and eventually governor general John Kerr resigned 1977. In the 1977 general election the coalition was returned with a reduced majority that was further reduced 1980.

Hawke era In the 1983 general election the coalition was eventually defeated and the Australian Labor Party under Bob ◊Hawke again took office. Hawke called together employers and unions to a National Economic Summit to agree to a wage and price policy and to deal with unemployment. In 1984 he called a general election 15 months early and was returned with a reduced majority. Hawke has placed even greater emphasis than his predecessors on links with

with a particular animal that the person must not kill or injure.

Australian Aborigine any of the 500 groups of indigenous inhabitant of the continent of Australia, who migrated to this region from S Asia about 40,000 years ago. They were hunters and gatherers, living throughout the continent in small kin-based groups before European settlement. Several hundred different languages developed, the most important being Aranda (Arunta), spoken in central Australia, and Murngin, spoken in Arnhem Land. In recent years there has been a movement for the recognition of Aborigine rights and campaigning against racial discrimination in housing, education, wages, and medical facilities. Aboriginal culture has been protected by federal law since the passing of the Aboriginal and Torres Islander Heritage Protection Act in 1984.

There are about 227,645 Aborigines in Australia, making up about 1.5% of Australia's population of 16 million. 12% of Australia is owned by Aborigines and many live in reserves as well as among the general population (65% of Aborigines live in cities or towns). They have an infant mortality rate four times the national average and an adult life expectancy 20 years below the average 76 years of Australians generally.

Australian Antarctic Territory islands and territories S of 60° S, between 160° E and 45° E longitude, excluding Adélie Land; area 6,044,000 sq km/2,332,984 sq mi of land and 75,800 sq km/29,259 sq mi of ice shelf. The population on the Antarctic continent is limited to research personnel.

There are scientific bases at Mawson (1954) in MacRobertson Land, named after the explorer; at Davis (1957) on the coast of Princess Elizabeth Land, named in honour of Mawson's second-in-command; at Casey (1969) in Wilkes Land, named after Lord Casey; and at Macquarie Island (1948). The Australian Antarctic Territory came into being 1933, when established by a British Order in Council.

Australian architecture Aboriginal settlements tended to be based around caves, or a construction of bark huts, arranged in a circular group; there was some variation in different areas.

Architecture of the early settlers includes Vaucluse House and the Sydney home of William Charles Wentworth. Queensland has old-style homes built on stilts for cool-

ness beneath their floors. Outstanding examples of modern architecture are the layout of the town of Canberra, by Walter Burley Griffin (1876–1937); Victoria Arts Centre, Melbourne, by Roy Grounds (1905–   ), who also designed the Academy of Science, Canberra; and the Sydney Opera House 1956–73, by Joern Utzon.

Australian art art in Australia dates back to early Aboriginal works some 15,000 years ago. These are closely linked with religion and mythology and include rock and bark paintings. True Aboriginal art is now rare. European-style art developed in the 17th century, with landscape painting predominating.

precolonial art Pictures and decorated objects were produced in nearly all settled areas. Subjects included humans, animals, and geometric ornament. The 'X-ray style', showing the inner organs in an animal portrait, is unique to Australian Aboriginal art.

17th–18th centuries The first European paintings were topographical scenes of and around Sydney.

late 19th–early 20th century The landscape painters of the Heidelberg School, notably Tom Roberts and later Arthur Streeton (1867–1943), became known outside Australia.

20th century The figurative painters William Dobell, Russell Drysdale, Sidney Nolan, and Albert Namatjira are among Australia's modern artists.

Australian Capital Territory territory ceded to Australia by New South Wales 1911 to provide the site of ◊Canberra, with its port at Jervis Bay, ceded 1915; area 2,400 sq km/926 sq mi; population (1987) 261,000.

Australian literature Australian literature begins with the letters, journals, and memoirs of early settlers and explorers. The first poet of note was Charles Harpur (1813–1868); idioms and rhythms typical of the country were developed by, among others, Henry Kendall (1841–1882) and Andrew Barton (Banjo) Paterson (1864–1941). More recent poets include Christopher Brennan and Judith Wright, Kenneth Slessor (1901–1971), R D (Robert David) Fitzgerald (1902–   ), A D (Alec Derwent) Hope (1907–   ), and James McAuley (1917–1976). Among early Australian novelists are Marcus Clarke, Rolfe Boldrewood, and Henry Handel Richardson (1870–1946). Striking a harsh vein in contemporary themes are the dramatist Ray Lawler and novelist Patrick

◊White; the latter received the Nobel Prize for Literature in 1973. Thomas Keneally won the Booker Prize in 1982 for *Schindler's Ark*.

Australia Prize annual award for achievement internationally in science and technology, established 1990 and worth £115,000.

The first winners were Allan Kerr of Adelaide University, Australia; Eugene Nester of Washington University, USA; and Jeff Schell of the Max Planck Institute in Cologne, Germany. Their studies of the genetic systems of the crown-gall bacterium *Agrobacterium tumefaciens* led to the creation of genetically engineered plants resistant to herbicides, pests, and viruses.

Australia Telescope array of radio telescopes at three locations in Australia, operated by the Commonwealth Scientific and Industrial Research Organization (CSIRO). Six 22-m/72-ft dishes in a line 6 km/10 mi long at Culgoora, New South Wales, form the so-called Compact Array which can be used in combination with another 22 m dish at Siding Spring, NSW, and the 64-m/ 210-ft radio telescope at Parkes, NSW.

Austral Islands /ˈɒstrəl/ alternative name for ◊Tubuai Islands, part of ◊French Polynesia.

Austria /ˈɒstrɪə/ landlocked country in central Europe, bounded E by Hungary, S by Slovenia and Italy, W by Switzerland and Liechtenstein, NW by Germany, and N by the Czech Republic, and NE by the Slovak Republic.

government Austria is a federal republic consisting of nine provinces (*Länder*), each with its own provincial assembly (Landtag), provincial governor, and councillors. The 1920 constitution was amended 1929, suspended during ◊Hitler's regime, and reinstated 1945. The two-chamber federal assembly consists of a national council (Nationalrat) and a federal council (Bundesrat). The Nationalrat has 183 members, elected by universal suffrage through proportional representation, for a four-year term. The Bundesrat has 63 members elected by the provincial assemblies for varying terms. Each province provides a chair for the Bundesrat for a six-month term. The federal president, elected by popular vote for a six-year term, is formal head of state and chooses the federal chancellor on the basis of support in the Nationalrat. The federal chancellor is head of government and chooses the cabinet. Most significant of several political parties are the Socialist Party of Austria (SPÖ), the Austrian People's Party (ÖVP), and the Freedom Party of Austria (FPÖ).

history Austria was inhabited in prehistoric times by Celtic tribes; the country south of the Danube was conquered by the Romans 14 BC and became part of the Roman Empire. Following the fall of the empire in the 5th century AD, the region was occupied by Vandals, Goths, Huns, Lombards, and Avars. Having conquered the Avars 791, ◊Charlemagne established the East Mark, nucleus of the Austrian empire. Otto II granted the Mark to the House of Babenburg 973, which ruled until 1246. Rudolf of Habsburg, who became king of the Romans and Holy Roman emperor 1273, seized Austria and invested his son as duke 1282. Until the empire ceased to exist 1806, most of he dukes (from 1453, archdukes) of Austria were elected Holy Roman emperor.

Turks kept at bay Austria, which acquired control of ◊Bohemia 1526, was throughout the 16th century a bulwark of resistance against the Turks, who besieged Vienna 1529 without success. The ◊Thirty Years' War (1618–48) did not touch Austria, but it weakened its rulers. A second Turkish siege of Vienna 1683 failed, and by 1697 Hungary was liberated from the ◊Ottoman empire and incorporated in the Austrian dominion. As a result of their struggle with Louis XIV, the Habsburgs secured the Spanish Netherlands and Milan 1713. When Charles VI, last male Habsburg in the direct line, died 1740, his daughter Maria Theresa became archduchess of Austria and queen of Hungary, but the elector of Bavaria was elected emperor as Charles VII. Frederick II of Prussia seized Silesia, and the War of the ◊Austrian Succession (1740–48) followed. Charles VII died 1745, and Maria Theresa secured the election of her husband as Francis I, but she did not recover Silesia from Frederick. The archduke Francis who succeeded 1792 was also elected emperor as Francis II; sometimes opposing, sometimes allied with Napoleon, he proclaimed himself emperor of Austria 1804 as Francis I, and the name Holy Roman Empire fell out of use 1806. Under the Treaty of Vienna 1815, Francis failed to recover the Austrian Netherlands (annexed by France 1797) but received Lombardy and Venetia.

Austria–Hungary During the ◊revolutions of 1848 the grievances of mixed nationalities within the Austrian empire flared into a rebellion; revolutionaries in Vienna called for the resignation of ◊Metternich, who fled to the UK. By 1851 Austria had crushed all the revolts. As a result of he ◊Seven Weeks' War 1866 with Prussia, Austria lost Venetia to Italy. In the following year Emperor ◊Franz Joseph established the dual monarchy of Austria–Hungary. The treaty of Berlin 1878 gave Austria the administration of Bosnia and Herzegovina in the Balkans, though they remained nominally Turkish until Austria annexed hem 1908. World War I was precipitated 1914 by an Austrian attack on Serbia, following the assassination of Archduke Franz Ferdinand (Franz Joseph's nephew) and his wife by a Serbian nationalist. Austria–Hungary was defeated 1918, the last Habsburg emperor overthrown, and Austria became a republic, comprising only Vienna and its immediately surrounding provinces. The Treaty of St Germain, signed 1919 by Austria and the Allies, established Austria's present boundaries. Austria was invaded by Hitler's troops 1938 and incorporated into the German Reich (the *Anschluss*).

partition and independence With the conclusion of World War II Austria returned to its 1920 constitution, with a provisional government led by Dr Karl Renner. The Allies divided both the country and Vienna into four zones, occupied by the USSR, the USA, Britain, and France. The first postwar elections resulted in an SPÖ–ÖVP coalition government. The country was occupied until independence was formally recognized 1955. The first postwar noncoalition government was formed 1966 when the ÖVP came to power with Josef Klaus as chancellor. The SPÖ formed a minority government under Dr Bruno Kreisky 1970 and increased its majority in the 1971 and 1975 general elections. The government was nearly defeated 1978 over proposals to install the first nuclear power plant. The plan was abandoned, but nuclear energy remained a controversial issue. The SPÖ lost its majority 1983. Kreisky resigned, refusing to join a coalition. The SPÖ decline was partly attributed to the emergence of two environmentalist groups, the United Green Party (VGÖ) and the Austrian Alternative List (ALÖ). Dr Fred Sinowatz, the new SPÖ chairman, formed an SPÖ–FPÖ coalition government.

Waldheim controversy A controversy arose 1985 with the announcement that Dr Kurt Waldheim, former UN secretary general, was to be a presidential candidate. Despite allegations of his having been a Nazi officer in Yugoslavia, Waldheim eventually became president 1986, leading to diplomatic isolation by many countries. Later that year Sinowatz resigned as chancellor and was succeeded by Franz Vranitzky. The SPÖ–FPÖ coalition broke up when an extreme right-winger, Jorg Haider, became FPÖ leader. In the Nov elections the SPÖ's Nationalrat seats fell from 90 to 80, the ÖVP's from 81 to 77, while the FPÖ's increased from 12 to 18. For the first time the VGÖ was represented, winning eight seats. Vranitzky offered his resignation but was persuaded by the president to try to form a 'grand coalition' of the SPÖ and the ÖVP. Agreement was reached, and Vranitzky remained as chancellor with the ÖVP leader, Dr Alois Mock, as vice chancellor. Austria announced March 1989 that it intended to seek membership of the European Community (EC). In the Oct 1990 general election the Socialists won a clear lead over other parties and Vranitzky began another term as prime minister. The EC endorsed Aug 1991 Austria's earlier application for membership. Thomas Klestil of the People's Party replaced Waldheim as president May 1992.

Austrian Succession, War of the 1740–48 war between Austria (supported by England and Holland) and Prussia (supported by France and Spain)

1740 The Holy Roman emperor Charles VI died and the succession of his daughter Maria Theresa was disputed by a number of European powers. Frederick the Great of Prussia seized *Silesia* from Austria.

1743 At ◊*Dettingen* an army of British, Austrians, and Hanoverians under the command of George II was victorious over the French.
1745 An Austro–English army was defeated at ◊*Fontenoy* but British naval superiority was confirmed, and so there were gains in the Americas and India.
1748 The war was ended by the Treaty of Aix-la-Chapelle.

Austro–Hungarian Empire /ˌɒstrɔhʌŋˈgeəriən/ the Dual Monarchy established with the ◊Ausgleich by the Habsburg Franz Joseph 1867 between his empire of Austria and his kingdom of Hungary (including territory that became Czechoslovakia as well as parts of Poland, the Ukraine, Romania, Yugoslavia and Italy). In 1910 it had an area of 261,239 sq km/100,838 sq mi with a population of 51 million. It collapsed autumn 1918 with the end of World War I. Only two king-emperors ruled: Franz Joseph 1867–1916 and Charles 1916–18.

Austronesian languages (also known as *Malayo-Polynesian*) family of languages spoken in Malaysia, the Indonesian archipelago, parts of the region that was formerly Indochina, Taiwan, Madagascar, Melanesia, and Polynesia (excluding Australia and most of New Guinea). The group contains some 500 distinct languages, including Malay in Malaysia, Bahasa in Indonesia, Fijian, Hawaiian, and Maori.

authoritarianism rule of a country by a dominant elite who repress opponents and the press to maintain their own wealth and power. They are frequently indifferent to activities not affecting their security, and rival power centres, such as trade unions and political parties, are often allowed to exist, although under tight control. An extreme form is ◊totalitarianism.

autism, infantile rare syndrome, generally present from birth, characterized by a withdrawn state and a failure to develop normally in language or social behaviour, although the autistic child may, rarely, show signs of high intelligence in other areas, such as music. Many have impaired intellect, however. The cause is unknown, but is thought to involve a number of interacting factors, possibly including an inherent abnormality of the child's brain.

autobiography a person's own biography, or written account of his or her life, distinguished from the journal or diary by being a connected narrative, and from memoirs by dealing less with contemporary events and personalities. *The Boke of Margery Kempe* about 1432–36 is the oldest extant autobiography in English.

autochrome in photography, a single-plate additive colour process devised by the ◊Lumière brothers 1903. It was the first commercially available process, in use 1907–35.

autoclave pressurized vessel that uses superheated steam to sterilize materials and equipment such as surgical instruments. It is similar in principle to a pressure cooker.

autocracy form of government in which one person holds absolute power. The autocrat has uncontrolled and undisputed authority. Russian government under the tsars was an autocracy extending from the mid-16th century to the early 20th century. The title *Autocratix* (a female autocrat) was assumed by Catherine II of Russia in the 18th century.

auto-da-fé (Portuguese 'act of faith') religious ceremony, including a procession, solemn mass, and sermon, which accompanied the sentencing of heretics by the Spanish ◊Inquisition before they were handed over to the secular authorities for punishment, usually burning.

autogenics a system developed in the 1900s by German physician Johannes Schultz, designed to facilitate mental control of biological and physiological functions generally considered to be involuntary. Effective in inducing relaxation, assisting healing processes and relieving psychosomatic disorders, autogenics is regarded as a precursor of biofeedback.

autogiro or *autogyro* heavier-than-air craft that supports itself in the air with a rotary wing, or rotor. The Spanish aviator Juan de la ◊Cierva designed the first successful autogiro 1923. The autogiro's rotor provides only lift and not propulsion; it has been superseded by the helicopter, in which the rotor provides both. The autogiro is propelled by an orthodox propeller.

autoimmunity in medicine, condition where the body's immune responses are mobilized not against 'foreign' matter, such as invading germs, but against the body itself. Diseases considered to be of autoimmune origin include ◊myasthenia gravis, rheumatoid ◊arthritis, and ◊lupus erythematosus.

In autoimmune diseases T-lymphocytes reproduce to excess to home in on a target (properly a foreign disease-causing molecule);

however, molecules of the body's own tissue that resemble the target may also be attacked, for example insulin-producing cells, resulting in insulin-dependent diabetes; if certain joint membrane cells are attached, then rheumatoid arthritis may result; and if myelin, the basic protein of the nervous system, then multiple sclerosis. In 1990 in Israel a T-cell vaccine was produced that arrests the excessive reproduction of T-lymphocytes attacking healthy target tissues.

Autolycus /ɔːˈtɒlɪkəs/ in Greek mythology, an accomplished thief and trickster, son of the god ◊Hermes, who gave him the power of invisibility.

autolysis in biology, the destruction of a ◊cell after its death by the action of its own ◊enzymes, which break down its structural molecules.

automat snack bar where food is dispensed through coin-operated machines.

Automats were popular in the USA in the 1930s. The first was opened in Philadelphia, Pennsylvania 1902; the last closed in New York 1991.

automatic pilot control device that keeps an aeroplane flying automatically on a given course at a given height and speed. Devised by US businessman Lawrence Sperry 1912, the automatic pilot contains a set of ◊gyroscopes that provide references for the plane's course. Sensors detect when the plane deviates from this course and send signals to the control surfaces—the ailerons, elevators, and rudder—to take the appropriate action. Autopilot is also used in missiles.

automation widespread use of self-regulating machines in industry. Automation involves the addition of control devices, using electronic sensing and computing techniques, which often follow the pattern of human nervous and brain functions, to already mechanized physical processes of production and distribution; for example, steel processing, mining, chemical production, and road, rail, and air control.

The term was coined by US business consultant John Diebold. Automation builds on the process of ◊mechanization to improve manufacturing efficiency.

automatism performance of actions without awareness or conscious intent. It is seen in sleepwalking and in some (relatively rare) psychotic states.

automaton mechanical figure imitating human or animal performance. Automatons

are usually designed for aesthetic appeal as opposed to purely functional robots. The earliest recorded automaton is an Egyptian wooden pigeon of 400 BC.

Automobile Association *(AA)* motoring organization founded in Britain in 1905. Originally designed to protect motorists from the police, it gradually broadened its services to include signposting, technical and legal services, as well as roadside help for members. In 1914 membership stood at 83,000 and now exceeds 6 million.

autonomic nervous system in mammals, the part of the nervous system that controls the involuntary activities of the smooth muscles (of the digestive tract, blood vessels), the heart, and the glands. The *sympathetic* system responds to stress, when it speeds the heart rate, increases blood pressure and generally prepares the body for action. The *parasympathetic* system is more important when the body is at rest, since it slows the heart rate, decreases blood pressure, and stimulates the digestive system.

Autonomisti /aʊˌtɒnəˈmisti/ semiclandestine amalgam of Marxist student organizations in W Europe, linked with guerrilla groups and such acts as the kidnapping and murder of Italian former premier Aldo Moro by the Red Brigades 1978.

autosome any ◊chromosome in the cell other than a sex chromosome. Autosomes are of the same number and kind in both males and females of a given species.

autosuggestion conscious or unconscious acceptance of an idea as true, without demanding rational proof, but with potential subsequent effect for good or ill. Pioneered by the French psychotherapist Emile Coué (1857–1926) in healing, it is used in modern psychotherapy to conquer nervous habits and dependence on tobacco, alcohol, and so on.

autotroph any living organism that synthesizes organic substances from inorganic molecules by using light or chemical energy. Autotrophs are the *primary producers* in all food chains since the materials they synthesize and store are the energy sources of all other organisms. All green plants and many planktonic organisms are autotrophs, using sunlight to convert carbon dioxide and water into sugars by ◊photosynthesis.

The total ◊biomass of autotrophs is far greater than that of animals, reflecting the dependence of animals on plants, and the ultimate dependence of all life on energy from the sun—green plants convert light energy into a form of chemical energy (food) that animals can exploit. Some bacteria use the chemical energy of sulphur compounds to synthesize organic substances. See also ◊heterotroph.

autumnal equinox see ◊equinox.

autumn crocus or *meadow saffron* plant *Colchicum autumnale* of the family Liliaceae. It yields *colchicine*, which is used in treating gout and in plant breeding (it causes plants to double the numbers of their chromosomes, forming ◊polyploids).

Auvergne /əʊ'veən/ ancient province of central France and a modern region comprising the *départements* Allier, Cantal, Haute-Loire, and Puy-de-Dôme
area 26,000 sq km/10,036 sq mi
population (1986) 1,334,000
capital Clermont-Ferrand
physical mountainous, composed chiefly of volcanic rocks in several masses
products cattle, wheat, wine, and cheese
history named after the ancient Gallic Avenni tribe whose leader, Vercingetorix, led a revolt against the Romans 52 BC. In the 14th century the Auvergne was divided into a duchy, dauphiny, and countship. The duchy and dauphiny were united by the dukes of Bourbon before being confiscated by Francis I 1527. The countship united with France 1615.

auxin plant ◊hormone that promotes stem and root growth in plants. Auxins influence many aspects of plant growth and development, including cell enlargement, inhibition of development of axillary buds, ◊tropisms, and the initiation of roots. *Synthetic auxins* are used in rooting powders for cuttings, and in some weedkillers, where high auxin concentrations cause such rapid growth that the plants die. They are also used to prevent premature fruitdrop in orchards. The most common naturally occurring auxin is known as indoleacetic acid, or IAA. It is produced in the shoot apex and transported to other parts of the plant.

Ava /'ɑːvə/ former capital of Burma (now Myanmar), on the river Irrawaddy, founded by Thadomin Payä 1364. Thirty kings reigned there until 1782, when a new capital, Amarapura, was founded by Bodaw Payä. In 1823 the site of the capital was transferred back to Ava by King Baggidaw.

avalanche (from French *avaler* 'to swallow') fall of a mass of snow and ice down a steep slope. Avalanches occur because of the unstable nature of snow masses in mountain areas.

Changes of temperature, sudden sound, or earth-borne vibrations can cause a snowfield to start moving, particularly on slopes of more than 35°. The snow compacts into ice as it moves, and rocks may be carried along, adding to the damage caused.

Avalokiteśvara /ˌævələʊˌkɪteɪʃ'vɑːrə/ in Mahāyāna Buddhism, one of the most important ◊bodhisattvas, seen as embodying compassion. Known as *Guanyin* in China and *Kwannon* in Japan, he is one of the attendants of Amida Buddha.

Avalon in the romance and legend of ◊Arthur, the island ruled over by ◊Morgan le Fay to which King Arthur is conveyed after his final battle with ◊Mordred. It has been identified since the Middle Ages with Glastonbury in Somerset.

avant-garde (French 'advanced guard') in the arts, those artists or works that are in the forefront of new developments in their media. The term was introduced (as was 'reactionary') after the French Revolution, when it was used to describe any socialist political movement.

avant-garde dance experimental dance form that rejects the conventions of modern dance. It is often performed in informal spaces—museums, rooftops, even scaling walls.

In the USA, avant-garde dance stemmed mainly from the collaboration between Merce ◊Cunningham in New York and musician Robert Dunn which resulted in the Judson Dance Theater. While retaining technique and rhythm, Cunningham deleted the role of choreographer, thus giving dancers a new freedom. The Judson collective went further, denying even the necessity for technique and concentrating on the use of everyday movement—walking, spinning, jumping.

In the UK, leading exponents of avant-garde dance techniques include Michael ◊Clark from the mid-1980s and Rosemary Butcher. In Germany, Pina ◊Bausch with her Wuppertal Tanztheater (dance theatre), established 1974, has been considered the most compelling influence in European dance since ◊Diaghilev.

Avar member of a Central Asian nomadic people who in the 6th century invaded the area of Russia north of the Black Sea previously held by the Huns. They extended their dominion over the Bulgarians and Slavs in the 7th century and were finally defeated by Charlemagne 796.

Avatar in Hindu mythology, the descent of a deity to Earth in a visible form, for example the ten Avatars of ◊Vishnu.

Avebury /ˈeɪvbəri/ Europe's largest stone circle (diameter 412 m/1,352 ft), Wiltshire, England. It was probably constructed in the Neolithic period 3,500 years ago, and is linked with nearby ◊Silbury Hill. The village of Avebury was built within the circle, and many of the stones were used for building material.

Avebury /ˈeɪvbəri/ John Lubbock, 1st Baron Avebury 1834–1913. British banker. A Liberal (from 1886 Liberal Unionist) member of Parliament 1870–1900, he was responsible for the Bank Holidays Act 1871 introducing statutory public holidays.

Avedon /ˈeɪvdən/ Richard 1923– . US photographer. A fashion photographer with *Harper's Bazaar* magazine in New York from the mid-1940s, he moved to *Vogue* 1965. He later became the highest-paid fashion and advertising photographer in the world. Using large-format cameras, his work consists of intensely realistic images, chiefly portraits.

Ave Maria (Latin 'Hail, Mary') Christian prayer to the Virgin Mary, which takes its name from the archangel Gabriel's salutation to the Virgin Mary when announcing that she would be the mother of the Messiah (Luke 11:28).

avens any of several low-growing plants of the genus *Geum*, family Rosaceae. Species are distributed throughout Eurasia and N Africa.

Mountain avens *Dryas octopetala* belongs to a different genus and grows in mountain and arctic areas of Eurasia and North America. A creeping perennial, it has white flowers with yellow stamens.

Wood avens or herb bennet *Geum urbanum* grows in woods and shady places on damp soils, and has yellow five-petalled flowers and pinnate leaves. Water avens *G. rivale* has nodding pink flowers and is found in marshes and other damp places.

average number or value that represents the typical member of a group or set of numbers. The simplest averages include the arithmetic and geometric means (see ◊mean);

the ◊median and the ◊root-mean-square are more complex.

Averroës /əˈverəʊiːz/ (Arabic **Ibn Rushd**) 1126–1198. Arabian philosopher who argued for the eternity of matter and against the immortality of the individual soul. His philosophical writings, including commentaries on Aristotle and on Plato's *Republic*, became known to the West through Latin translations. He influenced Christian and Jewish writers into the Renaissance, and reconciled Islamic and Greek thought in that philosophic truth comes through reason. St Thomas Aquinas opposed this position.

Averroës was born in Córdoba, Spain, trained in medicine, and became physician to the caliph as well as judge of Seville and Córdoba. He was accused of heresy by the Islamic authorities and banished 1195. Later he was recalled, and died in Marrakesh. 'Averroism' was taught at Paris and elsewhere in the 13th century by the 'Averroists', who defended a distinction between philosophical truth and revealed religion.

Avery /ˈeɪvəri/ Milton 1893–1965. US painter, whose early work was inspired by Henri ◊Matisse, with subjects portrayed in thin, flat, richly coloured strokes. His later work, although it remained figurative, shows the influence of Mark ◊Rothko and other experimental US artists.

Avery /ˈeɪvəri/ Tex (Frederick Bean) 1907– 1980. US cartoon-film director who used violent, sometimes surreal humour. At Warner Bros he helped develop Bugs Bunny and Daffy Duck, before moving to MGM 1942 where he created, among others, Droopy the dog and Screwball Squirrel.

Avicenna /ˌævɪˈsenə/ (Arabic **Ibn Sina**) 979– 1037. Arabian philosopher and physician. His *Canon Medicinae* was a standard work for many centuries. His philosophical writings were influenced by al-Farabi, Aristotle, and the neo-Platonists, and in turn influenced the scholastics of the 13th century.

Aviemore /ˌævɪˈmɔː/ winter sports centre, in the Highlands, Scotland, SE of Inverness among the Cairngorm mountains.

Avignon /ˈævɪːnjɒn/ city in Provence, France, capital of Vaucluse *département*, on the river Rhône NW of Marseilles; population (1982) 174,000. An important Gallic and Roman city, it has a 12th-century bridge (only half still standing), a 13th-century cathedral, 14th-century walls, and two palaces built during the residence here of the popes,

Le Palais Vieux (1334–42) and Le Palais Nouveau (1342–52). Avignon was papal property 1348–1791.

Avila /ˈævɪlə/ town in Spain, 90 km/56 mi NW of Madrid; population (1986) 45,000. It is capital of the province of the same name. It has the remains of a Moorish castle, a Gothic cathedral, and the convent and church of St Teresa, who was born here. The medieval town walls are among the best preserved in Europe.

avocado tree *Persea americana* of the laurel family, native to Central America. Its dark-green, thick-skinned, pear-shaped fruit has buttery- textured flesh and is used in salads.

avocet wading bird, genus *Recurvirostra*, family Recurvirostridae, with characteristic long, narrow, upturned bill used in sifting water as it feeds in the shallows. It is about 45 cm/18 in long, and has long legs, partly-webbed feet, and black and white plumage. There are four species. Stilts belong to the same family.

Avogadro /ˌævəˈɡɑːdrəʊ/ Amedeo Conte di Quaregna 1776–1856. Italian physicist who proposed Avogadro's hypothesis on gases 1811. His work enabled scientists to calculate Avogadro's number, and still has relevance for today's atomic studies.

Avogadro's hypothesis /ˌævəˈɡɑːdrəʊ/ in chemistry, the law stating that equal volumes of all gases, when at the same temperature and pressure, have the same numbers of molecules. It was first propounded by Amadeo Avogadro.

Avogadro's number or *Avogadro's constant* the number of carbon atoms in 12 g of the carbon-12 isotope (6.022045×10^{23}). The relative atomic mass of any element, expressed in grams, contains this number of atoms.

avoirdupois system of units of mass based on the pound (0.45 kg), which consists of 16 ounces (each of 16 drams) or 7,000 grains (each equal to 65 mg).

Avon /ˈeɪvən/ county in SW England
area 1,340 sq km/517 sq mi
towns Bristol (administrative headquarters), Bath, Weston-super-Mare
features river Avon
products aircraft and other engineering, tobacco, chemicals, printing, dairy products
population (1987) 951,000
famous people John Cabot, Thomas Chatterton, W G Grace

history formed 1974 from the city and county of Bristol, part of S Gloucestershire, and part of N Somerset.

Avon /ˈeɪvən/ any of several rivers in England and Scotland. The Avon in Warwickshire is associated with Shakespeare.

The Upper or Warwickshire Avon, 154 km/96 mi, rises in the Northampton uplands near Naseby and joins the Severn at Tewkesbury. The Lower, or Bristol, Avon, 121 km/75 mi, rises in the Cotswolds and flows into the Bristol Channel at Avonmouth. The East, or Salisbury, Avon, 104 km/65 mi, rises S of the Marlborough Downs and flows into the English Channel at Christchurch.

AWACS /ˈeɪwæks/ (acronym for *Airborne Warning and Control System*) surveillance system that incorporates a long-range surveillance and detection radar mounted on a Boeing E-3 sentry aircraft. It was used with great success in the 1991 Gulf War.

Awash /ˈɑːwɑːʃ/ river that rises to the S of Addis Ababa in Ethiopia and flows NE to Lake Abba on the frontier with Djibouti. Although deep inside present-day Ethiopia, the Awash River was considered by Somalis to mark the eastern limit of Ethiopian sovereignty prior to the colonial division of Somaliland in the 19th century.

Awe /ɔː/ longest (37 km/23 mi) of the Scottish freshwater lochs, in Strathclyde, SE of Oban. It is drained by the river Awe into Loch Etive.

Axelrod /ˈæksəlrɒd/ Julius 1912– . US neuropharmacologist who shared the 1970 Nobel Prize for Medicine with the biophysicists Bernard Katz and Ulf von Euler (1905–1983) for his work on neurotransmitters (the chemical messengers of the brain).

axil upper angle between a leaf (or bract) and the stem from which it grows. Organs developing in the axil, such as shoots and buds, are termed axillary, or lateral.

axiom in mathematics, a statement that is assumed to be true and upon which theorems are proved by using logical deduction. The Greek mathematician ◊Euclid used a series of axioms that he considered could not be demonstrated in terms of simpler concepts to prove his geometrical theorems.

Axis the alliance of Nazi Germany and Fascist Italy before and during World War II. The *Rome–Berlin Axis* was formed 1936, when Italy was being threatened with sanctions because of its invasion of Ethiopia (Abyssinia). It became a full military and political alliance May 1939. A ten-year alliance between Germany, Italy, and Japan (*Rome–Berlin–Tokyo Axis*) was signed Sept 1940 and was subsequently joined by Hungary, Bulgaria, Romania, and the puppet states of Slovakia and Croatia. The Axis collapsed with the fall of Mussolini and the surrender of Italy 1943 and Germany and Japan 1945.

axis in mathematics, a line from which measurements may be taken, as in a *coordinate axis*; or a line alongside which an object may be symmetrical, as in an *axis of symmetry*; or a line about which an object or plane figure may revolve.

axolotl (Aztec 'water monster') aquatic larval form ('tadpole') of any of several North American species of salamander, belonging to the family Ambystomatidae. Axolotls are remarkable because they can breed without changing to the adult form and will only metamorphose into adult salamanders in response to the drying up of their ponds. The adults then migrate to another pond.

Axolotls may be up to 30 cm/12 in long. Species include the Mexican salamander *Ambystomum mexicanum* which lives in mountain lakes near Mexico City, and the tiger salamander *A. tigrinum*, found in North America, from Canada to Mexico. See also ◊neoteny.

axon long threadlike extension of a ◊nerve cell that conducts electrochemical impulses away from the cell body towards other nerve cells, or towards an effector organ such as a muscle. Axons terminate in ◊synapses with other nerve cells, muscles, or glands.

Axum /ˈɑːksʊm/ alternative transliteration of ◊Aksum, an ancient kingdom in Ethiopia.

Ayacucho /ˌaɪəˈkuːtʃaʊ/ capital of a province of the same name in the Andean mountains of central Peru; population (1988) 94,200. The last great battle in the war of independence against Spain was fought near here Dec 1824.

ayatollah (Arabic 'sign of God') honorific title awarded to Shi'ite Muslims in Iran by popular consent, as, for example, to Ayatollah Ruhollah ◊Khomeini.

Ayckbourn /ˈeɪkbɔːn/ Alan 1939– . English playwright. His prolific output, characterized by comic dialogue and experiments in dramatic structure, includes the trilogy *The Norman Conquests* 1974, *A Woman in Mind* 1986, *Henceforward* 1987, and *Man of the Moment* 1988.

aye-aye nocturnal tree-climbing prosimian *Daubentonia madagascariensis* of Madagascar, related to the lemurs. It is just over 1 m/3 ft long, including a tail 50 cm/20 in long.

It has an exceptionally long middle finger with which it probes for insects and their larvae under the bark of trees, and gnawing, rodentlike front teeth, with which it tears off the bark to get at its prey. The aye-aye has become rare through loss of its forest habitat, and is now classified as an endangered species.

aye-aye The aye-aye is a nocturnal animal that lives in the dense forests of Madagascar.

Ayer /eə/ A(lfred) J(ules) 1910–1989. English philosopher. He wrote *Language, Truth and Logic* 1936, an exposition of the theory of 'logical positivism', presenting a criterion by which meaningful statements (essentially truths of logic, as well as statements derived from experience) could be distinguished from meaningless metaphysical utterances (for example, claims that there is a God or that the world external to our own minds is illusory).

He was Wykeham professor of logic at Oxford 1959–78. Later works included *Probability and Evidence* 1972 and *Philosophy in the Twentieth Century* 1982.

Ayers Rock /eəz/ vast ovate mass of pinkish rock in Northern Territory, Australia; 335 m/1,110 ft high and 9 km/6 mi around. It is named after Henry Ayers, a premier of South Australia.

For the Aboriginals, whose paintings decorate its caves, it has magical significance. They call it Uluru.

Aymara member of an American Indian people of Bolivia and Peru, builders of a great culture, who were conquered first by the Incas and then by the Spaniards. Today 1.4 million Aymara farm and herd llamas and alpacas in the highlands; their language, belonging to the Andean-Equatorial language family, survives and their Roman Catholicism incorporates elements of their old beliefs.

Ayr /eə/ town in Strathclyde, Scotland, at the mouth of the river Ayr; population (1981) 49,500. Auld Bridge was built in the 5th century, the New Bridge 1788 (rebuilt 1879). Ayr has associations with Robert Burns.

Ayrshire /ˈeəʃə/ former county of SW Scotland, with a 113 km/70 mi coastline on the Firth of Clyde. In 1975 the major part was merged in the region of Strathclyde.

Ayrton /ˈeətn/ Michael 1921–1975. British painter, sculptor, illustrator, and writer. From 1961, he concentrated on the ◊Daedalus myth, producing bronzes of Icarus and a fictional autobiography of Daedalus, *The Maze Maker*, 1967.

Aytoun /ˈeɪtn/ W(illiam) E(dmonstoune) 1813–1865. Scottish poet, born in Edinburgh, chiefly remembered for his *Lays of the Scottish Cavaliers* 1848 and *Bon Gaultier Ballads* 1855, which he wrote in collaboration with the Scottish nationalist Theodore Martin (1816–1909).

Ayub Khan /ɑːˈjuːb/ Muhammad 1907–1974. Pakistani soldier and president from 1958 to 1969. He served in the Burma Campaign 1942–45, and was commander in chief of the Pakistan army 1951. In 1958 martial law was proclaimed in Pakistan and Ayub Khan assumed power after a bloodless army coup. He won the presidential elections 1960 and 1965, and established a stable economy and achieved limited land reforms. His militaristic form of government was unpopular, particularly with the Bengalis, and in 1968 student riots resulted in imprisonment of the opposition. He resigned 1969 after widespread opposition and civil disorder, notably in Kashmir.

Ayuraveda basically naturopathic system of medicine widely practised in India and based on principles derived from the ancient Hindu scriptures, the ◊Vedas. Hospital treatments and remedial prescriptions tend to be non-specific and to coordinate holistic therapies for body, mind, and spirit.

azalea any of various deciduous flowering shrubs, genus *Rhododendron*, of the heath family Ericaceae. There are several species native to Asia and North America, and from these many cultivated varieties have been derived. Azaleas are closely related to the evergreen ◊rhododendrons of the same genus.

Azaña /əˈθænjə/ Manuel 1880–1940. Spanish politician and first prime minister 1931–33 of the second Spanish republic. He was last president of the republic during the Civil War 1936–39, before the establishment of a dictatorship under Franco.

Azerbaijan /ˌæzəbɑɪˈdʒɑːn/ country in W Asia, bounded S by Iran, E by the Caspian Sea, W by Armenia and Georgia, and N by Russia.

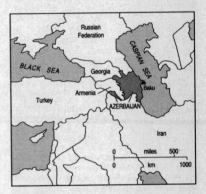

government There is a 360-seat legislature, the supreme soviet, and a 50-seat national assembly, the Milli Majlis, to which deputies are elected by a majority system, and a second-ballot runoff race in contests in which there is no clear first-round majority. From the majority grouping within the supreme soviet, a prime minister (chair of the cabinet of ministers) is drawn. The state president is directly elected.

history Azerbaijan shares a common language and culture with Turkey; however, before its conquest by tsarist Russia in the early 19th century, it was a province of Persia, and today 20 million Shi'ite Azeris live across the border in Iran. In the late 19th century, Baku became the centre of a growing oil industry. A member of the Transcaucasian Federation in 1917, Azerbaijan became an independent republic 1918, but was occupied by the Red Army two years later. The republic was secularized under Soviet rule.

growth of nationalism There was a growth in Azeri nationalism from the later 1980s, spearheaded by the Azeri Popular Front, founded in 1989, and fanned by the dispute with neighbouring Armenia over ◊Nagorno-Karabakh and ◊Nakhichevan. This dispute, which reawakened centuries-old enmities, flared up into full civil war from Dec 1989, prompting Azeri calls for secession from the USSR. In Jan 1990 Soviet troops were sent to Baku to restore order, and a state of emergency was imposed. The Azerbaijan Communist Party (ACP), led by Ayaz Mutalibov, allied itself with the nationalist cause and rejected compromise in the Nagorno-Karabakh dispute.

backlash In the Sept 1990 supreme soviet elections the Popular Front, having been on the verge of power before the Jan 1990 crackdown, was convincingly defeated by the ACP. A new state flag was adopted in Dec 1990 and the words 'Soviet Socialist' were dropped from the republic's name. In the March 1991 USSR constitutional referendum, the Azerbaijan population voted overwhelmingly in favour of preserving the Union and the Aug 1991 anti-Gorbachev coup in Moscow was warmly welcomed by President Mutalibov, who ordered the military suppression of demonstrations organized by the Popular Front.

independence declared After the failure of the Moscow coup, Mutalibov resigned from the ACP, which was soon disbanded, and on 30 Aug 1991 independence was declared. The state of emergency, still in force in Baku, was lifted. On 8 Sept 1991 Mutalibov was directly elected state president as the sole candidate in a contest boycotted by the opposition. In Dec 1991 Azerbaijan joined the new ◊Commonwealth of Independent States, which superseded the Soviet Union. In Jan 1992 Azerbaijan was admitted into the ◊Conference on Security and Cooperation in Europe (CSCE) and in March into the United Nations (UN). Azeri diplomatic and commercial links with Turkey improved and in Feb 1992 the republic joined the Economic Cooperation Organization (ECO), founded by Iran, Pakistan, and Turkey 1975, which aimed to reduce customs tariffs and eventually form a customs union. After independence, the state began to form its own armed forces. In Feb 1992 Azerbaijan switched from the Cyrillic alphabet, imposed by Moscow in 1937, to the Latin alphabet.

unstable leadership The Mutalibov administration and the supreme soviet remained under the domination of former members of the ACP, which was superseded by a new Republican Democratic Party, and much of the old system remained in place. Following Azeri defeats in Nagorno-Karabakh in March 1992, Mutalibov was forced to resign and various factions competed for power. In June 1992 Albufaz Elchibey, leader of the Popular Front, was elected president, pledging withdrawal from the CIS and a renewed campaign against Armenia over Nagorno-Karabakh. By Aug 1992 Azerbaijan had reclaimed much of its lost territory in the disputed enclave. Prime Minister Rakhim Guseinov resigned Jan 1993 because of differences with Elchibey. In June 1993 Elchibey fled following a military revolt, and was replaced by Communist Party leader, Geidar Aliyev, who was later elected president. The rebel military leader, Surat Huseynov, was appointed prime minister. In July Nagorno-Karabakh was overtaken by Armenian forces. Aliyev was dismissed 1994, accused of plotting a coup.

Azerbaijani or *Azeri* native of the Azerbaijan region of Iran (population 5,500,000) or the Azerbaijan republic (population 6,000,000). Azerbaijani is a Turkic language belonging to the Altaic family. Of the total population of Azerbaijanis, 70% are Shi'ite Muslims, 30% Sunni Muslims.

Azerbaijan, Iranian /ˌæzəbaɪˈdʒɑːn/ two provinces of NW Iran, *Eastern Azerbaijan* (capital Tabriz), population (1986) 4,114,000, and *Western Azerbaijan* (capital Orúmiyeh), population 1,972,000. Azerbaijanis in Iran, as in the Republic of Azerbaijan, are Shi'ite Muslim ethnic Turks, descendants of followers of the Khans from the Mongol Empire.

There are about 5 million Azerbaijanis, and 3 million distributed in the rest of the country, where they form a strong middle class. In 1946, with Soviet backing, they briefly established their own republic. Denied autonomy under the Shah, they rose 1979–80 against the supremacy of Ayatollah Khomeini and were forcibly repressed, although a degree of autonomy was promised.

Azhar, El /əˈzɑː/ Muslim university and mosque in Cairo, Egypt. Founded 970 by Jawhar, commander in chief of the army of the Fatimid caliph, it is claimed to be the oldest university in the world. It became the centre of Islamic learning, with several subsidiary foundations, and is now primarily a school of Koranic teaching.

azimuth in astronomy, the angular distance of an object from due north, measured eastwards (clockwise) along the horizon to a point directly beneath the object.

azo dye synthetic dye containing the azo group of two nitrogen atoms (N=N) connecting aromatic ring compounds. Azo dyes are usually red, brown, or yellow, and make up about half the dyes produced. They are manufactured from aromatic ◊amines.

Azores /ə'zɔːz/ group of nine islands in the N Atlantic, belonging to Portugal; area 2,247 sq km/867 sq mi; population (1987) 254,000. They are outlying peaks of the mid-Atlantic Ridge and are volcanic in origin. The capital is Ponta Delgada on the main island, San Miguel.

Portuguese from 1430, Azores were granted partial autonomy 1976, but remain a Portuguese overseas territory. The islands have a separatist movement. The Azores command the Western shipping lanes.

Azov /'eɪzɒv/ (Russian *Azovskoye More*) inland sea of Europe forming a gulf in the NE of the Black Sea between the Ukraine and Russia; area 37,555 sq km/14,500 sq mi. Principal ports include Rostov-on-Don, Kerch, and Taganrog. Azov is a good source of freshwater fish.

AZT drug used in the treatment of AIDS; see ◊zidovudine.

Aztec member of an ancient Mexican civilization that migrated south into the valley of Mexico in the 12th century, and in 1325 began reclaiming lake marshland to build their capital, Tenochtitlán, on the site of present-day Mexico City. Under Montezuma I (reigned from 1440), the Aztecs created a tribute empire in central Mexico. After the conquistador Cortès landed 1519, Montezuma II (reigned from 1502) was killed and Tenochitlán subsequently destroyed. Nahuatl is the Aztec language, it belongs to the Uto-Aztecan family of languages.

The Aztecs are known for their architecture, jewellery (gold, jade, and turquoise), sculpture, and textiles. Their form of writing combined hieroglyphs and pictographs, and they used a complex calendar that combined a sacred period of 260 days with the solar year of 365 days. Propitiatory rites were performed at the intersection of the two, called the 'dangerous' period, every 52 years, when temples were rebuilt. Their main god in a pantheon of gods was Huitzilopochtli (Hummingbird Wizard), but they also worshipped the feathered serpent ◊Quetzalcoatl, inherited from earlier Mexican civilizations. Religious ritual included human sacrifice on a large scale, the priests tearing the heart from the living victim or flaying people alive. War captives were obtained for this purpose, but their own people were also used. The Aztec state was a theocracy with farmers, artisans, and merchants taxed to support the priestly aristocracy. Tribute was collected from a federation of conquered nearby states.

Baabda /ˈbɑːbdə/ capital of the province of Jebel Lubnan in central Lebanon and site of the country's presidential palace. Situated to the SE of Beirut, it is the headquarters of the Christian military leader, General Michel Aoun.

Baade /ˈbɑːdə/ Walter 1893–1960. German-born US astronomer who made observations that doubled the distance scale and the age of the universe. Baade worked at Mount Wilson Observatory, USA, and discovered that stars are in two distinct populations according to their age, known as Population I (the younger) and Population II (the older). Later, he found that ◊Cepheid variable stars of Population I are brighter than had been supposed, and that distances calculated from them were wrong. Baade's figures showed that the universe was twice as large as previously thought, and twice as old.

Baader-Meinhof gang /ˈbɑːdə ˈmaɪnhɒf/ popular name for the West German guerrilla group the *Rote Armee Fraktion/Red Army Faction*, active from 1968 against what it perceived as US imperialism. The three main founding members were Andreas Baader, Gudrun Ensslin, and Ulrike Meinhof.

The group claimed responsibility in 1990 for the murder of Detlev Rohwedder, the government agent responsible for selling off state-owned companies of the former East German regime.

Baal /beɪl/ (Semitic 'lord' or 'owner') divine title given to their chief male gods by the Phoenicians, or Canaanites. Their worship as fertility gods, often orgiastic and of a phallic character, was strongly denounced by the Hebrew prophets.

Baalbek /ˈbɑːlbek/ city of ancient Syria, now in Lebanon, 60 km/36 mi NE of Beirut, 1,150 m/3,000 ft above sea level. It was originally a centre of Baal worship. The Greeks identified Baal with Helios, the sun, and renamed Baalbek *Heliopolis*. Its ruins, including Roman temples, survive; the Temple of Bacchus, built in the 2nd century AD, is still almost intact.

Ba'ath Party the ruling political party in Iraq and Syria. Despite public support of pan-Arab unity and its foundations 1943 as a party of Arab nationalism, its ideology has been so vague that it has fostered widely differing (and often opposing) parties in Syria and Iraq.

The Ba'ath party was founded in Damascus, Syria 1943 by three French-educated Syrian intellectuals, in opposition to both French rule and the older generation of Syrian Arab nationalists. Its constitution is an uncertain blend of neo-Marxist socialism and nationalism. The movement split into several factions after 1958 and again in 1966.

In Iraq, the Ba'ath party took control briefly in 1963 and gain from 1968 although its support here has always been limited. The rise of Saddam Hussein was not so much due to the popularity of the Ba'ath party itself as the exploitation and manipulation of an existing ideology by Hussein for his own purposes.

Babangida /bɑːˈbæŋgɪdɑː/ Ibrahim 1941– . Nigerian politician and soldier, president from 1985. He became head of the Nigerian army in 1983 and in 1985 led a coup against President Buhari, assuming the presidency himself.

Babangida was born in Minna, Niger state; he trained at military schools in Nigeria and the UK. He became an instructor in the Nigerian Defence Academy and by 1983 had reached the rank of major general. In 1983, after taking part in the overthrow of President Shehu Shagari, he was made army commander-in-chief. Responding to public pressure 1989, he allowed the formation of competing political parties and promised a return to a democratic civilian government in 1992. In an attempt to end corruption, he banned all persons ever having held elective office from being candidates in the new civilian government. Similarly, applications for recognition from former political parties were also rejected.

Babbage /ˈbæbɪdʒ/ Charles 1792–1871. English mathematician, who devised a precursor of the computer. He designed an ◊analytical engine, a general-purpose mechanical computing device for performing different calculations according to a program input on punched cards (an idea borrowed from the Jacquard loom). This device was never built, but it embodied many of the principles on which present digital computers are based.

His most important book was *On the Economy of Machinery and Manufactures* 1832, an analysis of industrial production systems and their economics. Altogether he wrote about 100 books.

In 1991, the British Science Museum completed Babbage's second difference engine (to demonstrate that it would have been possible to complete it with the materials then available), which evaluates polynomials up to the seventh power, with 30-figure accuracy.

Babbit metal soft, white metal, an ◊alloy of tin, lead, copper, and antimony, used to reduce friction in bearings, developed by the US inventor Isaac Babbit 1839.

Babbitt /ˈbæbɪt/ Milton 1916– . US composer. After studying with Roger ◊Sessions he developed a personal style of ◊serialism influenced by jazz.

babbler bird of the thrush family Muscicapidae with a loud babbling cry. Babblers, subfamily Timaliinae, are found in the Old World, and there are some 250 species in the group.

Babel /ˈbeɪbl/ Hebrew name for the city of ◊Babylon, chiefly associated with the *Tower of Babel* which, in the Genesis story in the Old Testament, was erected in the plain of Shinar by the descendants of Noah. It was a ziggurat, or staged temple, seven storeys high (100 m/300 ft) with a shrine of Marduk on the summit. It was built by Nabopolassar, father of Nebuchadnezzar, and was destroyed when Sennacherib sacked the city 689 BC.

Babel /ˈbɑːbl/ Isaak Emmanuilovich 1894–1939/40. Russian writer. Born in Odessa, he was an ardent supporter of the Revolution and fought under Budyenny's cavalry in the Polish campaign of 1921–22, an experience which inspired *Konarmiya/Red Cavalry* 1926. His other works include *Odesskie rasskazy/Stories from Odessa* 1924, which portrays the life of the Odessa Jews.

Bab-el-Mandeb /ˈbæb el ˈmændeb/ strait that joins the Red Sea and the Gulf of Aden, and separates Arabia and Africa. The name, meaning 'gate of tears', refers to its currents.

Babeuf /bɑːˈbɜːf/ François-Noël 1760–1797. French revolutionary journalist, a pioneer of practical socialism. In 1794 he founded a newspaper in Paris, later known as the *Tribune of the People*, in which he demanded the equality of all people. He was guillotined for conspiring against the ruling Directory during the French Revolution.

Babi faith /ˈbɑːbi/ alternative name for ◊Baha'i faith.

Babington /ˈbæbɪŋtən/ Anthony 1561–1586. English traitor who hatched a plot to assassinate Elizabeth I and replace her with ◊Mary Queen of Scots; its discovery led to Mary's execution and his own.

babirusa wild pig *Babirousa babyrussa*, becoming increasingly rare, found in the moist forests and by the water of Sulawesi, Buru, and nearby Indonesian islands. The male has large upper tusks which grow upwards through the skin of the snout and curve back towards the forehead. The babirusa is up to 80 cm/2.5 ft at the shoulder. It is nocturnal, and swims well.

Babism /ˈbɑːbɪzəm/ religious movement founded 1840's by Mirza Ali Mohammad ('the ◊Bab').

An offshoot of Islam, its main difference lies in the belief that Muhammad was not the last of the prophets. The movement split into two groups after the death of the Bab; Baha'ullah, the leader of one of these groups, founded the ◊Baha'i faith.

Babi Yar /ˈbɑːbi ˈjɑː/ ravine near Kiev, Ukraine, where more than 100,000 people were killed by the Nazis during World War II. The Soviet poet Yevtushenko wrote a poem called 'Babi Yar' 1961 in protest at plans for a sports centre on the site. It is also the name of a symphony (no. 13) by Soviet composer Dmitry Shostakovich.

baboon a large monkey, genus *Papio*, with a long doglike muzzle and large canine teeth, spending much of its time on the ground in open country. Males, with head and body up to 1.1 m/3.5 ft long, are larger than females and dominant males rule the 'troops' in which baboons live. They inhabit Africa and SW Arabia.

Species include the *olive baboon Papio anubis* from W Africa to Kenya, the *chacma Papio ursinus* from S Africa, and the *sacred baboon Papio hamadryas* from NE Africa and SW Arabia. The male sacred baboon has a 'cape' of long hair.

Bab, the /bɑːb/ name assumed by Mirza Ali Mohammad 1819–1850. Persian religious leader, born in Shiraz, founder of ◊Babism, an offshoot of Islam. In 1844 he proclaimed that he was a gateway to the Hidden Imam, a new messenger of Allah who was to come. He gained a large following whose activities caused the Persian authorities to fear a rebellion, and who were therefore persecuted. The Bab was executed for heresy.

Babylon /ˈbæbɪlən/ capital of ancient Babylonia, on the bank of the lower Euphrates River. The site is now in Iraq, 88 km/55 mi S of Baghdad and 8 km/5 mi N of Hilla, which is built chiefly of bricks from the ruins of Babylon. In 1986–89 President Saddam Hussein constructed a replica of the Southern Palace and citadel of Nebuchadnezzar II, on the plans of the German archaeologist Robert Koldeway. The *Hanging Gardens of Babylon*, one of the ◊Seven Wonders of the World, were probably erected on a vaulted stone base, the only stone construction in the mud-brick city. They formed a series of terraces, irrigated by a hydraulic system.

Babylonian captivity the exile of Jewish deportees to Babylon after Nebuchadnezzar II's capture of Jerusalem in 586 BC; according to tradition, the captivity lasted 70 years, but Cyrus of Persia, who conquered Babylon, actually allowed them to go home in 536 BC. By analogy, the name has also been applied to the papal exile to Avignon, France, 1309–77.

Bacall /bəˈkɔːl/ Lauren. Stage name of Betty Joan Perske 1924– . US actress who became an overnight star when cast by Howard Hawks opposite Humphrey Bogart in *To Have and Have Not* 1944. She and Bogart married in 1945, and starred together in *The Big Sleep* 1946. Her other films include *The Cobweb* 1955, *Harper* 1966, and *The Shootist* 1976.

Bacău /ˈbɑːkəʊ/ industrial city in Romania, 250 km/155 mi NNE of Bucharest, on the Bistrita; population (1985) 175,300. It is the capital of Bacău county, a leading oil-producing region.

Baccalauréat /ˌbækəlɔːreɪˈɑː/ French examination providing the school-leaving certificate and qualification for university entrance, also available on an international basis as an alternative to English ◊A levels.

Bacchus /ˈbækəs/ in Greek and Roman mythology, the god of fertility (see ◊Dionysus) and of wine; his rites (the *Bacchanalia*) were orgiastic.

Bach /bɑːx/ Carl Philip Emmanuel 1714–1788. German composer, third son of J S Bach. He introduced a new 'homophonic' style, light and easy to follow, which influenced Mozart, Haydn, and Beethoven.

Bach /bɑːx/ Johann Christian 1735–1782. German composer, the 11th son of J S Bach, who became celebrated in Italy as a composer of operas. In 1762 he was invited to London, where he became music master to the royal family. He remained in England until his death, enjoying great popularity both as composer and performer.

Bach /bɑːx/ Johann Sebastian 1685–1750. German composer. His appointments included positions at the courts of Weimar and Anhalt-Köthen, and from 1723 until his death he was musical director at St Thomas's choir school in Leipzig. Bach was a master of ◊counterpoint, and his music epitomizes the Baroque polyphonic style. His orchestral music includes the six *Brandenburg Concertos*, other concertos for keyboard instrument and violin, and four orchestral suites. Bach's keyboard music, for ◊clavier and organ, his fugues, and his choral music are of equal importance. He also wrote chamber music and songs.

Born at Eisenach, Bach came from a distinguished musical family. At 15 he became a chorister at Lüneburg, and at 19 he was organist at Arnstadt. He married twice and had over 20 children (although several died in infancy). His second wife, Anna Magdalena Wülkens, was a soprano; she also worked for him when his sight failed in later years.

Bach's sacred music includes 200 church cantatas, the Easter and Christmas oratorios, the two great Passions, of St Matthew and St John, and the Mass in B minor. His keyboard music includes a collection of 48 preludes and fugues known as the *Well-Tempered Clavier*, the *Goldberg Variations*, and the *Italian Concerto*. Of his organ music the finest examples are the chorale preludes. Two works written in his later years illustrate the principles and potential of his polyphonic art—the *Musical Offering* and *The Art of Fugue*.

Bach /bɑːx/ Wilhelm Friedemann 1710–1784. German composer, who was also an organist, improviser, and master of ◊counterpoint. He was the eldest son of J S Bach.

Bachelard /bæʃˈlɑː/ Gaston 1884–1962. French philosopher and scientist who argued for a creative interplay between reason and experience. He attacked both Cartesian and positivist positions, insisting that science was derived neither from first principles nor directly from experience.

Bach flower healing an essentially homoeopathic system of therapy developed in the 1920s by English physician Edward Bach. Based on the healing properties of wild flowers, it seeks to alleviate mental and emotional causes of disease rather than their physical symptoms.

bacillus member of a group of rodlike ◊bacteria that occur everywhere in the soil and air. Some are responsible for diseases such as anthrax or for causing food spoilage.

backgammon board game for two players, often used in gambling. It was known in Mesopotamia, Greece and Rome and in medieval England.

The board is marked out in 24 triangular points of alternating colours, 12 to each side. Throwing two dice, the players move their 15 pieces round the board to the six points that form their own 'inner table'; the first player to move all his or her pieces off the board is the winner.

back pain aches in the region of the spine. Low back pain can be caused by a very wide range of medical conditions. About half of all episodes of back pain will resolve within a week, but severe back pain can be chronic and disabling. The causes include muscle sprain, a prolapsed intervertebral disc, and vertebral collapse due to ◊osteoporosis or cancer. Treatment methods include rest, analgesics, physiotherapy, and exercises. Back pain is responsible for the loss of approximately 11.5 million working days each year in Britain.

Bacon /ˈbeɪkən/ Francis 1561–1626. English politician, philosopher, and essayist. He became Lord Chancellor 1618, and the same year confessed to bribe-taking, was fined £40,000 (which was paid by the king), and spent four days in the Tower of London. His works include *Essays* 1597, characterized by pith and brevity; *The Advancement of Learning* 1605, a seminal work discussing scientific method; the *Novum Organum* 1620, in which he redefined the task of natural science, seeing it as a means of empirical discovery and a method of increasing human power over nature; and *The New Atlantis* 1626,

Bacon English philosopher, politician, and author, Sir Francis Bacon.

describing a utopian state in which scientific knowledge is systematically sought and exploited.

Bacon was born in London, studied law at Cambridge from 1573, was part of the embassy in France until 1579, and became a member of Parliament 1584. He was the nephew of Queen Elizabeth's adviser Lord ◊Burghley, but turned against him when he failed to provide Bacon with patronage. He helped secure the execution of the earl of Essex as a traitor 1601, after formerly being his follower. Bacon was accused of ingratitude, but he defended himself in *Apology* 1604. The satirist Pope called Bacon 'the wisest, brightest, and meanest of mankind'. Knighted on the accession of James I 1603, he became Baron Verulam 1618 and Viscount St Albans 1621.

Bacon /ˈbeɪkən/ Francis 1909–1992. British painter, born in Dublin. He moved to London in 1925 and taught himself to paint. He practised abstract art, then developed a distorted Expressionist style with tortured figures presented in loosely defined space. From 1945 he focused on studies of figures, as in his series of screaming popes based on the portrait of Innocent X by Velázquez.

Bacon began to paint about 1930 and held his first show in London in 1949. He destroyed much of his early work. *Three Studies for Figures at the Base of a Crucifixion* 1944 (Tate Gallery, London) is an early example of his mature style.

Bacon /ˈbeɪkən/ Roger 1214–1292. English philosopher, scientist, and a teacher at Oxford University. In 1266, at the invitation of his friend Pope Clement IV, he began his *Opus Majus/Great Work*, a compendium of all branches of knowledge. In 1268 he sent this with his *Opus Minus/Lesser Work* and other writings to the pope. In 1277 Bacon was condemned and imprisoned by the church for 'certain novelties' (heresy) and not released until 1292. He was interested in alchemy, the biological and physical sciences and magic. Many discoveries have been credited to him, including the magnifying lens. He foresaw the extensive use of gunpowder and mechanical cars, boats, and planes.

Bacon was born in Somerset and educated at Oxford and Paris. He became a Franciscan monk and was in Paris until about 1251 lecturing on Aristotle. He wrote in Latin and is works include *On Mirrors, Metaphysical Questions,* and *On the Multiplication of Species.* He followed the maximum 'Cease to be ruled by dogmas and authorities; look at the world!'.

bacteria (singular *bacterium*) microscopic unicellular organisms with prokaryotic cells (see ◊prokaryote). They usually reproduce by ◊binary fission, and since this may occur approximately every 20 minutes, a single bacterium is potentially capable of producing 16 million copies of itself in a day.

Bacteria have a large loop of ◊DNA, sometimes called a bacterial chromosome. In addition there are often small, circular pieces of DNA known as ◊plasmids that carry spare genetic information. These plasmids can readily move from one bacterium to another, even though the bacteria are of different species. In a sense they are parasites within the bacterial cell, but they survive by coding their characteristics which promote the survival of their hosts. For example, some plasmids confer antibiotic resistance on the bacteria they inhabit. The rapid and problematic spread of antibiotic resistance among bacteria is due to plasmids, but they are also useful to humans in ◊genetic engineering. Although generally considered harmful, certain types of bacteria are vital in many food and industrial processes, while others play an essential role in

the ◊nitrogen cycle. Certain bacteria can influence the growth of others; for example, lactic acid bacteria will make conditions unfavourable for salmonella. Other strains produce nisin, which inhibits growth of listeria and botulism organisms. Plans in the food industry are underway to produce super strains of lactic acid bacteria to avoid food poisoning. In 1990, a British team of food scientists announced a new, rapid (five-minute) test for contamination of food by listeria or salmonella bacteria. Fluorescent dyes, added to a liquidized sample of food, reveal the presence of bacteria under laser light.

bacteriology the study of ◊bacteria.

bacteriophage virus that attacks ◊bacteria. Such viruses are now of use in genetic engineering.

Bactria /ˈbæktrɪə/ former region of central Asia (now Afghanistan, Pakistan, and Tajikistan) which was partly conquered by ◊Alexander the Great. During the 3rd–6th centuries BC it was a centre of East-West trade and cultural exchange.

Bactrian /ˈbæktrɪən/ one of the two species of ◊camel, found in Asia.

Species of camel *Camelus bactrianus* found in the Gobi Desert in Central Asia. Body fat is stored in two humps on the back. It has very long winter fur which is shed in ragged lumps. The head and body length is about 3 m/10 ft, and the camel is up to 2.1 m/6.8 ft tall at the shoulder. Most Bactrian camels are domesticated and are used as beasts of burden in W Asia.

Badajoz /ˌbædəˈxəʊθ/ city in Extremadura, Spain, on the Portuguese frontier; population (1986) 126,000. It has a 13th-century cathedral and ruins of a Moorish castle. Badajoz has often been besieged and was stormed by the Duke of Wellington 1812 with the loss of 59,000 British troops.

Baden /ˈbɑːdn/ former state of SW Germany, which had Karlsruhe as its capital. Baden was captured from the Romans in 282 by the Alemanni; later it became a margravate and in 1806, a grand duchy. A state of the German empire 1871–1918, then a republic, and under Hitler a *Gau* (province), it was divided between the *Länder* of Württemberg-Baden and Baden in 1945 and in 1952 made part of ◊Baden-Württemberg.

Baden /ˈbɑːdn/ town in Aargau canton, Switzerland, near Zurich; at an altitude of 366 m/ 1,273 ft; population (1990) 14,780. Its sulphur springs and mineral waters have been visited since Roman times.

Baden-Baden /ˈbɑːdn ˈbɑːdn/ Black Forest spa in Baden-Württemberg, Germany; population (1984) 49,000. Fashionable in the 19th century, it is now a conference centre.

Baden-Powell /ˈbeɪdn ˈpəʊəl/ Agnes 1854–1945. Sister of Robert Baden-Powell, she helped him found the ◊Girl Guides.

Baden-Powell /ˈbeɪdn ˈpəʊəl/ Lady Olave 1889–1977. wife of Robert Baden-Powell from 1912, she was the first and only World Chief Guide 1918–1977.

Baden-Powell /ˈbeɪdn ˈpəʊəl/ Robert Stephenson Smyth, 1st Baron Baden-Powell 1857–1941. British general, founder of the Scout Association. He fought in defence of Mafeking (now Mafikeng) during the Second South African War. After 1907 he devoted his time to developing the Scout movement, which rapidly spread throughout the world. He was created a peer in 1929.

Baden-Württemberg /ˈbɑːdn ˈvʊətəmbɜːg/ administrative region (German *Land*) of Germany
area 35,800 sq km/13,819 sq mi
capital Stuttgart
towns Mannheim, Karlsruhe, Freiburg, Heidelberg, Heilbronn, Pforzheim, Ulm
physical Black Forest; Rhine boundary S and W; source of the Danube; see also ◊Swabia
products wine, jewellery, watches, clocks, musical instruments, textiles, chemicals, iron, steel, electrical equipment, surgical instruments
population (1988) 9,390,000
history formed 1952 (following a plebiscite) by the merger of the *Länder* Baden, Württemberg-Baden, and Württemberg-Hohenzollern.

Bader /ˈbɑːdə/ Douglas 1910–1982. British fighter pilot. He lost both legs in a flying accident 1931, but had a distinguished flying career in World War II. He was knighted 1976 for his work with disabled people.

badger large mammal of the weasel family with molar teeth of a crushing type adapted to a partly vegetable diet, and short strong legs with long claws suitable for digging. The Eurasian *common badger Meles meles* is about 1 m/3 ft long, with long, coarse, greyish hair on the back, and a white face with a broad black stripe along each side. Mainly a woodland animal, it is harmless and nocturnal, and spends the day in a

Badger The American badger is slightly smaller than its Eurasian cousin.

system of burrows called a 'sett'. It feeds on roots, a variety of fruits and nuts, insects, worms, mice, and young rabbits.

The *American badger Taxidea taxus* is slightly smaller and lives in open country in North America. Various species of hog badger, ferret badger, and stink badger occur in S and E Asia, the last having the anal scent glands characteristic of the weasel family well developed.

Bad Godesburg /ˈbedˈgəʊdəsbɜːg/ SE suburb of ◊Bonn, Germany, formerly a spa, and the meeting place of Chamberlain and Hitler before the Munich Agreement 1938.

badlands barren landscape cut by erosion into a maze of ravines, pinnacles, gullies and sharp-edged ridges. South Dakota and Nebraska, USA, are examples.

Badlands, which can be created by overgrazing, are so called because of their total lack of value for agriculture and their inaccessibility.

badminton indoor racket game similar to lawn tennis but played on a smaller court and with a shuttlecock (a half sphere of cork or plastic with a feather or nylon skirt) instead of a ball. The object of the game is to prevent the opponent from being able to return the shuttlecock.

Badminton is played by two or four players. The court measures 6.1 m/20 ft by 13.4 m/44 ft. A net, 0.8 m/2.5 ft deep, is stretched across the middle of the court and at a height of 1.52 m/5 ft above the ground to the top of the net. The shuttlecock must be volleyed.

Only the server can win points. The sport is named after Badminton House, the seat of the duke of Beaufort, where the game was played in the 19th century. The major tournaments include the *Thomas Cup*, an international team championship for men, first held in 1949, and the *Uber Cup* a women's international team competition, first held in 1957. World championships have existed since 1977 in singles, doubles, and mixed doubles and are now held every two years.

Badoglio /baːˈdəʊljəʊ/ Pietro 1871–1956. Italian soldier and Fascist politician. A veteran of campaigns against the peoples of Tripoli and Cyrenaica, in 1935 he became commander in chief in Ethiopia, adopting ruthless measures to break patriot resistance. He was created viceroy of Ethiopia and duke of Addis Ababa in 1936. He resigned during the disastrous campaign into Greece 1940 and succeeded Mussolini as prime minister of Italy from July 1943 to June 1944, negotiating the armistice with the Allies.

Baedeker /ˈbeɪdɪkə/ Karl 1801–1859. German editor and publisher of foreign travel guides; the first was for Coblenz 1829. These are now published from Hamburg (before World War II from Leipzig).

Baekeland /ˈbeɪklənd/ Leo Hendrik 1863–1944. Belgian-born US chemist who invented ◊Bakelite, the first commercial plastic, made from formaldehyde and phenol. He later made a photographic paper, Velox, which could be developed in artificial light.

Baer /beə/ Karl Ernst von 1792–1876. German zoologist who was the founder of comparative ◊embryology.

Baez /baɪˈez/ Joan 1941– . US folk singer who emerged in the early 1960s with versions of traditional English and American folk songs such as 'Silver Dagger' and 'We Shall Overcome', the latter becoming the anthem of anti-Vietnam War protesters.

Baffin /ˈbæfɪn/ William 1584–1622. English explorer and navigator. In 1616, he and Robert Bylot explored Baffin Bay, NE Canada, and reached latitude 77° 45′ N, which for 236 years remained the 'furthest north'. In 1612, Baffin was chief pilot of an expedition in search of the Northwest Passage, and in 1613–14 commanded a whaling fleet near Spitsbergen, Norway. He piloted the *Discovery* on an expedition to Hudson Bay lead by Bylot in 1615. After 1617, Baffin worked for the ◊East India Company and made surveys of the Red Sea and Persian

Gulf. In 1622 he was killed in an Anglo-Persian attack on Hormuz.

Baffin Island /ˈbæfɪn/ island in the Northwest Territories, Canada
area 507,450 sq km/195,875 sq mi
features largest island in the Canadian Arctic; mountains rise above 2,000 m/6,000 ft, and there are several large lakes. The northernmost part of the strait separating Baffin Island from Greenland forms Baffin Bay, the southern end is Davis Strait.

It is named after William Baffin, who carried out research here 1614 during his search for the ◊Northwest Passage.

BAFTA /ˈbæftə/ acronym for *B*ritish *A*cademy of *F*ilm and *T*elevision *A*rts.

bagatelle /ˌbægəˈtel/ (French 'trifle') in music, a short character piece, often for piano.

bagatelle game resembling billiards but played on a board with numbered cups instead of pockets. The aim is to get the nine balls into the cups.

In *ordinary bagatelle* each player delivers all the balls in turn; in *French bagatelle* two or four players take part alternately.

Bagehot /ˈbædʒət/ Walter 1826–1877. British writer and economist, author of *The English Constitution* 1867, a classic analysis of the British political system. He was editor of *The Economist* magazine 1860–77.

Baggara /ˈbægərə/ member of a Bedouin people of the Nile Basin, principally in Kordofan, Sudan, west of the White Nile. They are Muslims, traditionally occupied in cattle breeding and big-game hunting. Their language is probably Afro-Asiatic.

Baghdad /ˈbægdæd/ historic city and capital of Iraq, on the Tigris river; population (1985) 4,649,000. Industries include oil refining, distilling, tanning, tobacco processing, and the manufacture of textiles and cement. Founded 762, it became Iraq's capital 1921.

To the SE, on the river Tigris, are the ruins of *Ctesiphon*, capital of Parthia about 250 BC–AD 226 and of the ◊Sassanian Empire about 226–641; the remains of the Great Palace include the world's largest single-span brick arch 26 m/85 ft wide and 29 m/95 ft high.

A route centre from the earliest times, it was developed by the 8th-century caliph Harun al-Rashid, although little of the *Arabian Nights* city remains. It was overrun 1258 by the Mongols, who destroyed the irrigation system. In 1639 it was taken by the

Turks. During World War I, Baghdad was captured by General Maude 1917.

Baghdad Pact military treaty of 1955 concluded by the UK, Iran, Iraq, Pakistan, and Turkey, with the USA cooperating; it was replaced by the ◊Central Treaty Organization (CENTO) when Iraq withdrew in 1958.

bagpipe ancient wind instrument used outdoors and incorporating a number of reed pipes powered from a single inflated bag. Known in Roman times, it is found in various forms throughout Europe.

The bag has the advantage of being more powerful than the unaided lungs and of being able to sustain notes indefinitely. The melody pipe, bent downwards, is called a *chanter* and the accompanying harmony pipes supported on the shoulder are *drones*, which emit invariable notes to supply a ground bass.

Bahadur Shah II /bə'hɑːdə 'ʃɑː/ 1775–1862. Last of the Mogul emperors of India. He reigned, though in name only, as king of Delhi 1837–57, when he was hailed by the mutineers of the ◊Indian Mutiny as an independent emperor at Delhi. After the rebellion he was exiled to Burma (now Myanmar) with his family.

Baha'i religion founded in the 19th century from a Muslim splinter group, ◊Babism, by the Persian ◊Baha'ullah. His message in essence was that all great religious leaders are manifestations of the unknowable God and all scriptures are sacred. There is no priesthood: all Baha'is are expected to teach, and to work towards world unification. There are about 4.5 million Baha'is worldwide.

Bahamas /bə'hɑːməz/ country comprising a group of about 700 islands and about 2,400 uninhabited islets and cays in the Caribbean, 80 km/50 mi from the SE coast of Florida. They extend for about 1,223 km/760 mi from NW to SE, but only 22 of the islands are inhabited.

government The Bahamas are an independent sovereign nation within the ◊Commonwealth, with the British monarch as head of state and represented by an appointed, resident governor general. The constitution, effective since independence 1973, provides for a two-chamber parliament with a senate and house of assembly. The governor general appoints a prime minister and cabinet drawn from and responsible to the legislature. The governor general appoints 16 senate members, nine on the advice of the

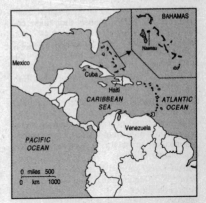

prime minister, four on the advice of the leader of the opposition, and three after consultation with the prime minister. The house of assembly has 49 members, elected by universal suffrage. Parliament has a maximum life of five years and may be dissolved within that period. The major political parties are the Progressive Liberal Party (PLP), and the Free National Movement (FNM).

history The Bahamas were reached by Christopher Columbus 1492, who first landed at San Salvador. The islands were a pirate area in the early 18th century and became a crown colony 1717 (although they were disputed by the Carolina colony until 1787). The Bahamas achieved internal self-government in 1964, and the first elections for the national assembly on a full voting register were held 1967. The PLP, drawing its support mainly from voters of African origin, won the same number of seats as the European-dominated United Bahamian Party (UBP). Lynden ◊Pindling became prime minister with support from outside his party. In the 1968 elections the PLP scored a resounding victory, repeated 1972, enabling Pindling to lead his country to full independence within the Commonwealth 1973 and increase his majority 1977.

The main contestants in the 1982 elections were the FNM (consisting of a number of factions that had split and reunited) and the PLP. Despite allegations of government complicity in drug trafficking, the PLP was again successful, and Pindling was unanimously endorsed as leader at a party convention in 1984. The 1987 general election was won by the PLP, led by Pindling. In Aug

1992 the FNM won 33 of the assembly's 49 seats and its leader Hubert Ingraham became prime minister.

Baha'ullah /ˌbɑːhɑːˈʊlə/ title of Mirza Hosein Ali 1817–1892. Persian founder of the ◊Baha'i religion. Baha'ullah, 'God's Glory', proclaimed himself as the prophet the ◊Bab had foretold.

Bahawalpur /bəˌhɑːwəlˈpʊə/ city in the Punjab, Pakistan; population (1981) 178,000. Once the capital of a former state of Bahawalpur, it is now an industrial town producing textiles and soap. It has a university, established 1975.

Bahia /bəˈiːə/ state of E Brazil
area 561,026 sq km/216,556 sq mi
capital Salvador
industry oil, chemicals, agriculture
population (1986) 10,949,000.

Bahía Blanca /bəˈiːə ˈblæŋkə/ port in S Argentina, on the river Naposta, 5 km/3 mi from its mouth; population (1980) 233,126. It is a major distribution centre for wool and food processing. The naval base of Puerto Belgrano is here.

Bahrain /bɑːˈreɪn/ country comprising a group of islands in the Persian Gulf, between Saudi Arabia and Iran.

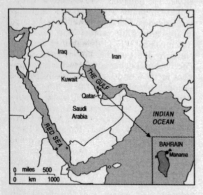

government The 1973 constitution provided for an elected national assembly of 30 members, but was dissolved 1975 after the prime minister refused to work with it. The Emir now governs Bahrain by decree, through a cabinet chosen by him. There are no recognizable political parties.
history Traditionally an Arab monarchy, Bahrain was under Portuguese rule during the 16th century and from 1602 was dominated by Persia (now Iran). Bahrain became a sheikdom 1783 under the control of the Khalifa dynasty. British assistance was sought to preserve the country's independence against claims of sovereignty made by Persia and the Ottoman Empire. It became a British protectorate 1861, with government shared between the ruling sheik and a British adviser. Persia claimed sovereignty 1928 but accepted a UN report 1970 showing that the inhabitants of Bahrain preferred independence.
independence achieved Britain announced the withdrawal of its forces 1968, and Bahrain joined two other territories under British protection, Qatar and the Trucial States (now the ◊United Arab Emirates), to form the Federation of Arab Emirates. Qatar and the Trucial States left the Federation 1971, and Bahrain became an independent state.

A new constitution 1973 provided for an elected national assembly, but two years later the prime minister, Sheik Khalifa (1933–), complained of obstruction by the assembly, which was then dissolved. Since then the Emir and his family have ruled with virtually absolute power.

Since the Iranian revolution of 1979, relations between the two countries have been uncertain, with fears of Iranian attempts to disturb Bahrain's stability. A causeway linking Bahrain with mainland Saudi Arabia was constructed 1986 (at 25 km/15.5 mi it is the longest in the world). During the 1991 Gulf War, Bahrain opposed Iraq's invasion of Kuwait.

Baikal /baɪˈkæl/ Russian *Baykal Ozero* largest freshwater lake in Asia, (area 31,500 sq km/12,150 sq mi) and deepest in the world (up to 1,740 m/5,710 ft), in S Siberia, Russia. Fed by more than 300 rivers, it is drained only by the Lower Angara. It has sturgeon fisheries and rich fauna.

Baikonur /ˌbaɪkəˈnʊə/ main Soviet launch site for spacecraft, located at Tyuratam, near the Aral Sea.

bail setting at liberty of a person in legal custody on an undertaking, (usually backed by some security, given either by that person or by someone else), to attend a legal proceeding at a stated time and place. If the person does not attend, the bail may be forfeited.

The Bail Act of 1976 presumes that a suspect will be granted bail, unless the police can give good reasons why not, for example, by showing that a further offence may take place.

Baile Atha Cliath /blɑː ˈklɪə/ official Gaelic name of ◊Dublin, capital of the Republic of Ireland, from 1922.

bailey an open space or court of a stone-built castle.

Bailey /ˈbeɪlɪ/ David 1938– . British fashion photographer, chiefly associated with *Vogue* magazine from the 1960s. He has published several books of his work, exhibited widely, and also made films.

Bailey /ˈbeɪlɪ/ Donald Coleman 1901–1985. English engineer, inventor in World War II of the portable *Bailey bridge*, made of interlocking, interchangeable, adjustable, and easily transportable units.

bailiff an officer of the court whose job, usually in the county courts, is to serve notices and enforce the court's orders involving seizure of the goods of a debtor.

Bailly /bɑːˈjiː/ Jean Sylvain 1736–1793. French astronomer who, early in the French Revolution, was president of the National Assembly and mayor of Paris, but resigned in 1791; he was guillotined during the Reign of Terror. He wrote about the satellites of Jupiter and the history of astronomy.

Baily's beads bright spots of sunlight seen around the edge of the Moon for a few seconds immediately before and after a total ◊eclipse of the Sun, caused by sunlight shining between mountains at the Moon's edge. Sometimes one bead is much brighter than the others, producing the so-called *diamond ring* effect. The effect was described 1836 by the English astronomer Francis Baily (1774–1844), a wealthy stockbroker who retired in 1825 to devote himself to astronomy.

Bainbridge /ˈbeɪnbrɪdʒ/ Beryl 1934– . English novelist, originally an actress, whose works have the drama and economy of a stage play. They include *The Dressmaker* 1973, *The Bottle Factory Outing* 1974, *Injury Time* 1977, *Young Adolf* 1978, *The Winter Garden* 1980, the collected short stories in *Mum and Mr Armitage* 1985, and *The Birthday Boys* 1991.

Bainbridge /ˈbeɪnbrɪdʒ/ Kenneth Tompkins 1904– . US physicist who was director of the first atomic bomb test at Alamogordo, New Mexico, in 1945.

Baird /beəd/ John Logie 1888–1946. Scottish electrical engineer who pioneered television. In 1925 he gave the first public demonstration of television and in 1926 pioneered fibre optics, radar (in advance of Robert ◊Watson-Watt), and 'noctovision', a system for seeing at night by using infrared rays.

Born at Helensburgh, Scotland, Baird studied electrical engineering in Glasgow at what is now the University of Strathclyde, at the same time serving several practical apprenticeships. He was working on television possibly as early as 1912, and he took out his first provisional patent 1923. He also developed video recording on both wax records and magnetic steel discs (1926–27), colour TV (1925–28), 3-D colour TV (1925–46), and transatlantic TV (1928). In 1936 his mechanically scanned 240-line system competed with EMI-Marconi's 405-line, but the latter was preferred for the BBC service from 1937, partly because it used electronic scanning and partly because it handled live indoor scenes with smaller, more manoeuvrable cameras. In 1944 he developed facsimile television, the forerunner of ◊Ceefax, and demonstrated the world's first all-electronic colour and 3-D colour receiver (500 lines).

Baja California /ˈbɑːhɑː/ mountainous peninsula that forms the twin NW states of Lower (Spanish *baja*) California, Mexico; area 143,396 sq km/55,351 sq mi; population (1980) 1,440,600. The northern state, Baja California Norte, includes the busy towns of Mexicali and Tijuana, but the southern state, Baja California Sur, is sparsely populated.

Bakelite first synthetic ◊plastic, created by Leo ◊Baekeland in 1909. Bakelite is hard, tough, and heatproof, and is used as an electrical insulator. It is made by the reaction of phenol with formaldehyde, producing a powdery resin that sets solid when heated. Objects are made by subjecting the resin to compression moulding (simultaneous heat and pressure in a mould).

Baker /ˈbeɪkə/ Benjamin 1840–1907. English engineer, who designed (with English engineer John Fowler (1817–1898)) London's first underground railway (the Metropolitan and District) in 1869, the Forth Bridge, Scotland, 1890, and the original Aswan Dam on the river Nile, Egypt.

Baker /ˈbeɪkə/ Chet (Chesney) 1929–1988. US jazz trumpeter of the cool school, whose good looks, occasional vocal performances, and romantic interpretations of ballads helped make him a cult figure. He became known with the Gerry Mulligan Quartet in 1952 and formed his own quartet 1953. Recordings include 'My Funny Valentine' and 'The Thrill Is Gone'.

Baker /'beɪkə/ James (Addison), III 1930– . US Republican politician. Under President Reagan, he was White House chief of staff 1981–85 and Treasury secretary 1985–88. After managing Bush's successful presidential campaign 1988, Baker was appointed secretary of state 1989 and played a prominent role in the 1990–91 Gulf crisis, and the subsequent search for a lasting Middle East peace settlement.

A lawyer from Houston, Texas, Baker entered politics 1970 as one of the managers of his friend George Bush's unsuccessful campaign for the Senate. He served as undersecretary of commerce 1975–76 in the Ford administration and was deputy manager of the 1976 and 1980 Ford and Bush presidential campaigns. Baker joined the Reagan administration 1981.

Baker /'beɪkə/ Janet 1933– . English mezzo-soprano who excels in lied, oratorio, and opera. Her performances include Dido in both *Dido and Aeneas* and *The Trojans*, and Marguerite in *Faust*. She retired from the stage in 1981 but continues to perform recitals, oratorio, and concerts.

Baker /'beɪkə/ Kenneth (Wilfrid) 1934– . British Conservative politician, home secretary 1990–92. He was environment secretary 1985–86, education secretary 1986–89, and chair of the Conservative Party 1989–90, retaining his cabinet seat, before becoming home secretary in John Major's government.

Baker /'beɪkə/ Samuel White 1821–1893. English explorer, in 1864 the first European to sight Lake Albert Nyanza (now Lake Mobutu Sese Seko) in central Africa, and discover that the river Nile flowed through it.

He founded an agricultural colony in Ceylon (now Sri Lanka), built a railway across the Dobruja, and in 1861 set out to discover the source of the Nile. His wife, Florence von Sass, accompanied him. From 1869 to 1873 he was governor general of the Nile equatorial regions.

Bakewell /'beɪkwel/ Robert 1725–1795. Pioneer improver of farm livestock. From his home in Leicestershire, England, he developed the Dishley or New Leicester breed of sheep and worked on raising the beef-producing qualities of Longhorn cattle.

Bakhtaran /ˌbæktəˈrɑːn/ (formerly (until 1980) *Kermanshah*) capital of Bakhtaran province, NW Iran; population (1986) 561,000. The province (area 23,700 sq km/9,148 sq mi; population 1,463,000) is on the Iraqi border and is mainly inhabited by Kurds. Industries include oil refining, carpets, and textiles.

Bakhuyzen /'bækhaʊzən/ Ludolf 1631–1708. Dutch painter of seascapes. *Stormy Sea* 1697 (Rijksmuseum, Amsterdam) is typically dramatic.

baking powder mixture of bicarbonate of soda (◊sodium hydrogencarbonate), an acidic compound, and a nonreactive filler (usually starch or calcium sulphate), used in baking as a raising agent. It gives a light open texture to cakes and scones, and is used as a substitute for yeast in making soda bread.

Several different acidic compounds (for example, tartaric acid, cream of tartar, sodium or calcium acid phosphates, and glucono-delta-lactone) may be used, any of which will react with the sodium hydrogencarbonate, in the presence of water and heat, to release the carbon dioxide that causes the cakemix or dough to rise.

Bakke /'bækə/ Allan 1940– . US student who, in 1978, gave his name to a test case claiming 'reverse discrimination' when appealing against his exclusion from medical school, since less well-qualified blacks were to be admitted as part of a special programme for ethnic minorities. He won his case against quotas before the Supreme Court, although other affirmative action for minority groups was still endorsed.

Bakst /bækst/ Leon. Assumed name of Leon Rosenberg 1886–1924. Russian painter and theatrical designer. He used intense colours and fantastic images from Oriental and folk art, with an Art Nouveau tendency to graceful surface pattern. His designs for Diaghilev's touring *Ballets Russes* made a deep impression in Paris 1909–14.

Baku /bɑːˈkuː/ capital city of the Republic of Azerbaijan, and industrial port (oil refining) on the Caspian Sea; population (1987) 1,741,000. Baku is a centre of the oil industry and is linked by pipelines with Batumi on the Black Sea. In Jan 1990 there were violent clashes between the Azeri majority and the Armenian minority, and Soviet troops were sent to the region. Over 13,000 Armenians subsequently fled from the city.

Bakunin /bəˈkuːnɪn/ Mikhail 1814–1876. Russian anarchist, active in Europe. In 1848 he was expelled from France as a revolutionary agitator. In Switzerland in the 1860s he became recognized as the leader of the anarchist movement. In 1869 he joined the First International (a coordinating socialist body) but, after stormy conflicts with Karl Marx, was expelled 1872.

Born of a noble family, Bakunin served in the Imperial Guard but, disgusted with tsarist methods in Poland, resigned his commission and travelled abroad. For his share in a brief revolt at Dresden 1849 he was sentenced to death. The sentence was commuted to imprisonment, and he was handed over to the tsar's government and sent to Siberia 1855. In 1861 he managed to escape to Switzerland. He had a large following, mainly in the Latin American countries. He wrote books and pamphlets, including *God and the State*.

Bala /ˈbælə/ (Welsh *Llyn Tegid*) lake in Gwynedd, N Wales, about 6.4 km/4 mi long and 1.6 km/1 mi wide. Lake Bala has a unique primitive fish, the gwyniad, protected from 1988.

Balaclava, Battle of /ˌbæləˈklɑːvə/ in the Crimean War, an engagement on 25 Oct 1854 near a town in Ukraine, 10 km/6 mi SE of Sevastopol. It was the scene of the ill-timed *Charge of the Light Brigade* of British cavalry against the Russian entrenched artillery. Of the 673 soldiers who took part, there were 272 casualties. *Balaclava helmets* were knitted hoods worn here by soldiers in the bitter weather.

Balakirev /bəˈlɑːkɪref/ Mily Alexeyevich 1837–1910. Russian composer. He wrote orchestral works including the fantasy *Islamey* 1869/1902, piano music, songs, and a symphonic poem *Tamara*, all imbued with the Russian national character and spirit. He was leader of the group known as the Five and taught its members, Mussorgsky, Cui, Rimsky-Korsakov, and Borodin.

balalaika Russian musical instrument, resembling a guitar. It has a triangular sound box, frets, and two, three, or four strings played by strumming with the fingers.

balance apparatus for weighing or measuring mass. The various types include the *beam balance* consisting of a centrally pivoted lever with pans hanging from each end, and the *spring balance*, in which the object to be weighed stretches (or compresses) a vertical coil spring fitted with a pointer that indicates the weight on a scale. Kitchen and bathroom scales are balances.

balance of nature in ecology, the idea that there is an inherent equilibrium in most ◊ecosystems, with plants and animals interacting so as to produce a stable, continuing system of life on earth. Organisms in the ecosystem are adapted to each other—for example, waste products produced by one species are used by another and resources used by some are replenished by others; the oxygen needed by animals is produced by plants while the waste product of animal respiration, carbon dioxide, is used by plants as a raw material in photosynthesis. The nitrogen cycle, the water cycle, and the control of animal populations by natural predators are other examples. The activities of human beings can, and frequently do, disrupt the balance of nature.

balance of payments in economics, a tabular account of a country's debit and credit transactions with other countries. Items are divided into the *current account*, which includes both visible trade (imports and exports) and invisible trade (such as transport, tourism, interest, and dividends), and the *capital account*, which includes investment in and out of the country, international grants, and loans. Deficits or surpluses on these accounts are brought into balance by buying and selling reserves of foreign currencies.

A *balance of payments crisis* arises when a country's current account deteriorates because the cost of imports exceeds income from exports. In developing countries persistent trade deficits often result in heavy government borrowing overseas, which in turn leads to a ◊debt crisis.

balance of power in politics, the theory that the best way of ensuring international order is to have power so distributed among states that no single state is able to achieve a dominant position. The term, which may also refer more simply to the actual distribution of power, is one of the most enduring concepts in international relations. Since the development of nuclear weapons, it has been asserted that the balance of power has been replaced by a *balance of terror*.

balance of trade the balance of trade transactions of a country recorded in its current account; it forms one component of the country's ◊balance of payments.

In Oct–Dec 1989 the invisible earnings component of the UK balance of trade was in deficit for the first time since records began, by over £713 million.

balance sheet a statement of the financial position of a company or individual on a specific date, showing both ◊assets and ◊liabilities.

Balanchine /ˌbælənˈtʃiːn/ George 1904–1983. Russian-born US choreographer. After leaving the USSR in 1924, he worked with ◊Diaghilev in France. Moving to the USA in 1933, he became a major influence on dance, starting the New York City Ballet in 1948. He was the most influential 20th-century choreographer of ballet in the USA. He developed an 'American Neo-Classic' dance style and made the New York City Ballet one of the world's great companies. He also pioneered choreography in Hollywood films.

Balboa /bælˈbəʊə/ Vasco Núñez de 1475–1519. Spanish ◊conquistador, the first European to see the eastern side of the Pacific Ocean, on 25 Sept 1513, from the isthmus of Darien (now Panama). He was made admiral of the Pacific and governor of Panama but was removed by Spanish court intrigue, imprisoned and executed.

Balchin /ˈbɔːltʃɪn/ Nigel Marlin 1908–1970. British author. During World War II he was engaged on scientific work for the army and wrote *The Small Back Room* 1943, a novel dealing with the psychology of the 'back room boys' of wartime research.

Balcon /ˈbɔːlkən/ Michael 1896–1977. British film producer, responsible for the influential 'Ealing comedies' of the 1940s and early 1950s, such as *Kind Hearts and Coronets* 1949, *Whisky Galore!* 1949, and *The Lavender Hill Mob* 1951.

Balder /ˈbɔːldə/ in Norse mythology, the son of ◊Odin and ◊Freya and husband of Nanna, and the best, wisest, and most loved of all the gods. He was killed, at ◊Loki's instigation, by a twig of mistletoe shot by the blind god Hodur.

baldness loss of hair from the upper scalp, common in older men. Its onset and extent are influenced by genetic make-up and the level of male sex ◊hormones. There is no cure, and expedients such as hair implants may have no lasting effect. Hair loss in both sexes may also occur as a result of ill health or following radiation treatment, such as for cancer. *Alopecia*, a condition in which the hair falls out, is different from the 'male pattern baldness' described above.

Baldung Grien /ˌbældʊŋˈgriːn/ Hans 1484/85–1545. German Renaissance painter, engraver, and designer, based in Strasbourg. He painted the theme *Death and the Maiden* in several versions.

Baldwin /ˈbɔːldwɪn/ James 1924–1987. US writer, born in New York City, who portrayed the condition of black Americans in contemporary society. His works include the novels *Go Tell It on the Mountain* 1953, *Another Country* 1962, and *Just Above My Head* 1979; the play *The Amen Corner* 1955; and the autobiographical essays *Notes of a Native Son* 1955 and *The Fire Next Time* 1963. He was active in the civil rights movement.

Baldwin /ˈbɔːldwɪn/ Stanley, 1st Earl Baldwin of Bewdley 1867–1947. British Conservative politician, prime minister 1923–24, 1924–29, and 1935–37; he weathered the general strike 1926, secured complete adult suffrage 1928, and handled the ◊abdication crisis of Edward VIII 1936, but failed to prepare Britain for World War II.

Born in Bewdley, Worcestershire, the son of an iron and steel magnate, in 1908 he was elected Unionist member of Parliament for Bewdley, and in 1916 he became parliamentary private secretary to Bonar Law. He was financial secretary to the Treasury 1917–21, and then appointed to the presidency of the Board of Trade. In 1919 he gave the Treasury £150,000 of War Loan for cancellation, representing about 20% of his fortune. He was a leader in the disruption of the Lloyd George coalition 1922, and, as chancellor under Bonar Law, achieved a settlement of war debts with the USA.

As prime minister 1923–24 and again 1924–29, Baldwin passed the Trades Disputes Act of 1927 after the general strike, granted widows' and orphans' pensions, and complete adult suffrage 1928. He joined the national government of Ramsay MacDonald 1931 as Lord President of the Council. He handled the abdication crisis during his third premiership 1935–37, but was later much criticized for his failures to resist popular desire for an accommodation with the dictators Hitler and Mussolini, and to rearm more effectively. Created 1st Earl Baldwin of Bewdley 1937.

Baldwin five kings of the Latin kingdom of Jerusalem, including:

Baldwin I /'bɔːldwɪn/ 1058–1118. King of Jerusalem from 1100. A French nobleman, he joined his brother ◊Godfrey de Bouillon on the First Crusade in 1096 and established the kingdom of Jerusalem in 1100. It was destroyed by Islamic conquest in 1187.

Balearic Islands /,bæliˈærɪk/ (Spanish **Baleares**) Mediterranean group of islands forming an autonomous region of Spain; including ◊Majorca, ◊Minorca, ◊Ibiza, Cabrera, and Formentera
area 5,000 sq km/1,930 sq mi
capital Palma de Mallorca
products figs, olives, oranges, wine, brandy, coal, iron, slate; tourism is crucial
population (1986) 755,000
history a Roman colony from 123 BC, the Balearic Islands were an independent Moorish kingdom 1009–1232; they were conquered by Aragón 1343.

Balewa /bəˈleɪwə/ alternative title of Nigerian politician ◊Tafawa Balewa.

Balfour /'bælfə/ Arthur James, 1st Earl of Balfour 1848–1930. British Conservative politician, prime minister 1902–05 and foreign secretary 1916–19, when he issued the Balfour Declaration 1917 and was involved in peace negotiations after World War I, signing the Treaty of Versailles.

Balfour Arthur Balfour, British statesman, formulator of the Balfour Declaration.

Son of a Scottish landowner, Balfour was elected a Conservative member of Parliament in 1874. In Lord Salisbury's ministry he was secretary for Ireland 1887, and for his ruthless vigour was called 'Bloody Balfour' by Irish nationalists. In 1891 and again in 1895 he became First Lord of the Treasury and leader of the Commons, and in 1902 he succeeded Salisbury as prime minister. His cabinet was divided over Joseph Chamberlain's tariff-reform proposals, and in the 1905 elections suffered a crushing defeat.

Balfour retired from the party leadership in 1911. In 1915 he joined the Asquith coalition as First Lord of the Admiralty. As foreign secretary 1916–19 he issued the Balfour Declaration in favour of a national home in Palestine for the Jews. He was Lord President of the Council 1919–22 and 1925–29. Created 1st Earl of Balfour 1922. He also wrote books on philosophy.

Balfour Eve 1898–1990. English agriculturalist and pioneer of modern organic farming. She established the Haughley Experiment, a farm research project at New Bells Farm near Haughley, Suffolk, to demonstrate that a more sustainable agricultural alternative existed. The experiment ran for almost 30 years, comparing organic and chemical farming systems. The wide-ranging support it attracted led to the formation of the ◊Soil Association 1946.

Balfour Declaration letter, dated 2 Nov 1917, from the British foreign secretary A J Balfour to Lord Rothschild (chair, British Zionist Federation) stating: 'HM government view with favour the establishment in Palestine of a national home for the Jewish people'. It led to the foundation of Israel 1948.

Bali /'bɑːli/ island of Indonesia, E of Java, one of the Sunda Islands
area 5,800 sq km/2,240 sq mi
capital Denpasar
physical volcanic mountains
features Balinese dancing, music, drama; one million tourists a year (1990)
products gold and silver work, woodcarving, weaving, copra, salt, coffee
population (1980) 2,470,000
history Bali's Hindu culture goes back to the 7th century; the Dutch gained control of the island by 1908.

Balikesir /,bɑːlɪkeˈsɪə/ city in NW Turkey, capital of Aydin province; population (1985) 152,000. There are silver mines nearby.

Balikpapan /ˌbɑːlɪkˈpɑːpən/ port in Indonesia, on the E coast of S Kalimantan, Borneo; population (1980) 280,900. It is an oil-refining centre.

Baliol /ˈbeɪliəl/ John de c. 1250–1314. King of Scotland 1292–96. As an heir to the Scottish throne on the death of Margaret, the Maid of Norway, his cause was supported by the English king, Edward I, against 12 other claimants. Having paid homage to Edward, Baliol was proclaimed king but soon rebelled and gave up the kingdom when English forces attacked Scotland.

Bali Strait /ˈbɑːli/ narrow strait between the two islands of Bali and Java, Indonesia. On 19–20 Feb 1942 it was the scene of a naval action between Japanese and Dutch forces that served to delay slightly the Japanese invasion of Java.

Balkans /ˈbɔːlkənz/ (Turkish 'mountains') peninsula of SE Europe, stretching into the Mediterranean Sea between the Adriatic and Aegean seas, comprising Albania, Bosnia-Herzegovina, Bulgaria, Croatia, Greece, Romania, Slovenia, Turkey-in-Europe and Yugoslavia. It is joined to the rest of Europe by an isthmus 1,200 km/750 mi wide between Rijeka on the west and the mouth of the Danube on the Black Sea to the east.

The great ethnic diversity resulting from successive waves of invasion has made the Balkans a byword for political dissension. The Balkans' economy developed comparatively slowly until after World War II, largely because of the predominantly mountainous terrain, apart from the plains of the Save-Danube basin in the north. Political differences have remained strong—for example, the confrontation of Greece and Turkey over Cyprus, and the differing types of communism prevailing in the rest—but in the later years of the 20th century a tendency to regional union emerged. To '*Balkanize*' is to divide into small warring states.

Balkan Wars two wars 1912–13 and 1913 (preceding World War I) which resulted in the expulsion by the Balkan states of Ottoman Turkey from Europe, except for a small area around Istanbul.

The *First Balkan War*, 1912, of Bulgaria, ◊Serbia, Greece, and Montenegro against Turkey, forced the Turks to ask for an armistice, but the London-held peace negotiations broke down when the Turks, while agreeing to surrender all Turkey-in-Europe W of the city of Edirne (formerly Adrianople), refused to give up the city itself. In Feb 1913 hostilities were resumed. Edirne fell on 26 March and on 30 May, by the Treaty of London, Turkey retained in Europe only a small piece of E Thrace and the Gallipoli peninsula.

The *Second Balkan War*, June–July 1913, took place when Bulgaria attacked Greece and Serbia, which were joined by Romania. Bulgaria was defeated, and Turkey secured from that country the cession of Edirne.

Balkhash /bælˈxɑːʃ/ salt lake in the Republic of Kazakhstan; area 17,300 sq km/6,678 sq mi. It is 600 km/375 mi long and receives several rivers, but has no outlet. Very shallow, it is frozen throughout the winter.

Ball /bɔːl/ John died 1381. English priest, one of the leaders of the ◊Peasants' Revolt 1381, known as 'the mad priest of Kent'. A follower of John Wycliffe and a believer in social equality, he was imprisoned for disagreeing with the archbishop of Canterbury. During the revolt he was released from prison, and when in Blackheath, London, preached from the text 'When Adam delved and Eve span, who was then the gentleman?' When the revolt collapsed he escaped but was captured near Coventry and executed.

Ball /bɔːl/ Lucille 1911–1989. US comedy actress. From 1951 to 1957 she starred with her husband, Cuban bandleader Desi Arnaz, in *I Love Lucy*, the first US television show filmed before an audience. It was followed by *The Lucy Show* 1962–68 and *Here's Lucy* 1968–74.

ballad (Latin *ballare* 'to dance') type of popular poem that tells a story. Of simple metrical form and dealing with some strongly emotional event, the ballad is halfway between the lyric and the epic. Most English ballads date from the 15th century. Poets of the Romantic movement both in England and in Germany were greatly influenced by the ballad revival, as seen in, for example, the *Lyrical Ballads* 1798 of Wordsworth and Coleridge. Other later forms are the 'broadsheets' with a satirical or political motive, and the testamentary 'hanging' ballads of the condemned criminal.

In 19th-century music the refined drawing-room ballad had a vogue, but a more robust tradition survived in the music hall; folk song played its part in the development of pop music, and slow songs are often called 'ballads' regardless of content.

ballade in music, an instrumental piece based on a story; a form used in piano works by ◊Chopin and ◊Liszt. In literature, a poetic form developed in France in the later Middle Ages from the ballad, generally consisting of one or more groups of three stanzas of seven or eight lines each, followed by a shorter stanza or envoy, the last line being repeated as a chorus.

Balladur Edouard 1929– . French Conservative politician, prime minister from 1993. During his first year of 'co-habitation' with socialist president, François Mitterrand, he demonstrated the sureness of his political touch, retaining popular support despite active opposition to some of his more right-wing policies. He is a strong supporter of the European Union and of maintaining close relations between France and Germany.

Ballance /'bæləns/ John 1839–1893. New Zealand Liberal politician, born in Northern Ireland; prime minister 1891–93. He emigrated to New Zealand, founded and edited the *Wanganui Herald*, and held many cabinet posts. He passed social legislation and opposed federation with Australia.

ball-and-socket-joint a joint allowing considerable movement in three dimensions, for instance the joint between the pelvis and the femur. To facilitate movement, such joints are lubricated by cartilage and synovial fluid. The bones are kept in place by ligaments and moved by muscles.

Ballantyne /'bæləntaɪn/ R(obert) M(ichael) 1825–1894. Scottish writer of children's books. Childhood visits to Canada and six years as a trapper for the Hudson's Bay Company provided material for his adventure stories, which include *The Young Fur Traders* 1856, *Coral Island* 1857, and *Martin Rattler* 1858.

Ballard /'bælɑːd/ J(ames) G(raham) 1930– . English novelist whose works include science fiction on the theme of disaster, such as *The Drowned World* 1962 and *High-Rise* 1975; the partly autobiographical *Empire of the Sun* 1984, dealing with his internment in China during World War II; and the autobiographical novel *The Kindness of Women* 1991.

Ballesteros /ˌbælɪˈstɪərɒs/ Seve(riano) 1957– . Spanish golfer who came to prominence 1976 and has won several leading tournaments in the USA, including the Masters Tournament. He has also won the British Open three times: in 1979, 1984, and 1988.

ballet (Italian *balletto* 'a little dance') theatrical representation in dance form in which music also plays a major part in telling a story or conveying a mood. Some such form of entertainment existed in ancient Greece, but Western ballet as we know it today first appeared in Italy. From there it was brought by Catherine de' Medici to France in the form of a spectacle combining singing, dancing, and declamation. In the 20th century Russian ballet has had a vital influence on the Classical tradition in the West, and ballet developed further in the USA through the work of George Balanchine and American Ballet Theater, and in the UK through the influence of Marie Rambert. ◊Modern dance is a separate development.

history The first important dramatic ballet, the *Ballet comique de la reine*, was produced 1581 by the Italian Balthasar de Beaujoyeux at the French court and was performed by male courtiers, with ladies of the court forming the *corps de ballet*. In 1661 Louis XIV founded *L'Académie royale de danse*, to which all subsequent ballet activities throughout the world can be traced. Long, flowing court dress was worn by the dancers until the 1720s when Marie-Anne Camargo, the first great ballerina, shortened her skirt to reveal her ankles, thus allowing greater movement *à terre* and the development of dancing *en l'air*. It was not until the early 19th century that a Paris costumier, Maillot, invented tights, thus allowing complete muscular freedom. The first of the great ballet masters was Jean-Georges ◊Noverre, and great contemporary dancers were Teresa Vestris (1726–1808), Anna Friedrike Heinel (1753–1808), Jean Dauberval (1742–1806), and Maximilien Gardel (1741–1787). Carlo Blasis is regarded as the founder of Classical ballet, since he defined the standard conventional steps and accompanying gestures.

Romantic ballet The great Romantic era of ◊Taglioni, Elssler, Grisi, Grahn, and Cerrito began about 1830 but survives today only in the ballets *Giselle* 1841 and *La Sylphide* 1832. Characteristics of this era were the new calf-length Romantic tutu and the introduction of dancing on the toes, *sur les pointes*. The technique of the female dancer was developed, but the role of the male dancer was reduced to that of her partner.

Russian ballet was introduced to the West by Sergei ◊Diaghilev, who set out for Paris 1909, at about the same time that Isadora ◊Duncan, a fervent opponent of classical ballet, was touring Europe. Associated with Diaghilev were Mikhail Fokine, Vaslav Nijinsky, Anna Pavlova, Léonide Massine, George Balanchine, and Serge Lifar. Ballets presented by his company, before its break-up after his death 1929, included *Les Sylphides*, *Schéhérazade*, *Petrouchka*, and *Blue Train*. Diaghilev and Fokine pioneered a new and exciting combination of the perfect technique of imperial Russian dancers and the appealing naturalism favoured by Isadora Duncan. In the USSR ballet continues to flourish, the two chief companies being the Kirov and the Bolshoi. Best-known ballerinas are Galina Ulanova and Maya Plisetskaya, and male dancers include Rudolf Nureyev, Mikhail Baryshnikov, and Alexander Godunov, now dancing in the West, as are the husband-and-wife team Vyacheslav Gordeyev and Nadezhda Pavlova.

American ballet was firmly established by the founding of Balanchine's School of American Ballet 1934, and by de Basil's Ballets Russes de Monte Carlo and Massine's Ballet Russe de Monte Carlo, which also carried on the Diaghilev tradition. In 1939 Lucia Chase and Richard Pleasant founded American Ballet Theater. From 1948 the New York City Ballet, under the guiding influence of Balanchine, developed a genuine American Neo-Classic style.

British ballet Marie Rambert initiated 1926 the company that developed into the Ballet Rambert, and launched the careers of choreographers such as Frederick Ashton and Anthony Tudor. The national company, the Royal Ballet (so named 1956), grew from foundations laid by Ninette de Valois and Frederick Ashton 1928. British dancers include Margot Fonteyn, Alicia Markova, Anton Dolin, Antoinette Sibley, Anthony Dowell, David Wall, Merle Park, and Lesley Collier; choreographers include Kenneth MacMillan.

ballistics study of the motion and impact of projectiles such as bullets, bombs, and missiles. For projectiles from a gun, relevant exterior factors include temperature, barometric pressure, and wind strength; and for nuclear missiles these extend to such factors as the speed at which the Earth turns.

balloon impermeable fabric bag that rises when filled with gas lighter than the surrounding air. In 1783, the first successful human ascent was in Paris, in a hot-air balloon designed by the ◊Montgolfier brothers. During the French Revolution balloons were used for observation; in World War II they were used to defend London against low-flying aircraft. They are now used for recreation and as a means of meteorological, infrared, gamma-ray, and ultraviolet observation. The first transatlantic crossing by balloon was made 11–17 Aug 1978 by a US team.

ballot the process of voting in an election. In political elections in democracies ballots are usually secret: voters indicate their choice of candidate on a voting slip which is placed in a sealed ballot box. *Ballot rigging* is a term used to describe elections that are fraudulent because of interference with the voting process or the counting of ◊votes.

ballroom dancing collective term for social dances such as the ◊foxtrot, quickstep, ◊tango, and ◊waltz.

ball valve valve used in lavatory cisterns to cut off the water supply when it reaches the correct level. It consists of a flat rubber washer at one end of a pivoting arm and a hollow ball at the other. The ball floats on the water surface, rising as the cistern fills, and at the correct level the rubber washer is pushed against the water-inlet pipe, cutting off the flow.

Balmer /ˈbælmə/ Johann Jakob 1825–1898. Swiss physicist and mathematician who developed a formula in 1884 that gave the wavelengths of the light emitted by the hydrogen atom (the hydrogen spectrum). This simple formula played a central role in the development of spectral and atomic theory.

Balmoral Castle /bælˈmɒrəl/ residence of the British royal family in Scotland on the river Dee, 10.5 km/6.5 mi NE of Braemar, Grampian region. The castle, built of granite in the Scottish baronial style, is dominated by a square tower and circular turret rising 30 m/100 ft. It was rebuilt 1853–55 by Prince Albert, who bought the estate in 1852.

balsam any of various garden plants of the genus *Impatiens* of the balsam family. They are usually annuals with spurred red or white flowers and pods that burst and scatter their seeds when ripe. In medicine and perfumery, balsam refers to various oily or gummy aromatic plant resins, such as balsam of Peru from the Central American tree *Myroxylon pereirae*.

Baltic, Battle of the naval battle fought off Copenhagen on 2 April 1801, in which a British fleet under Sir Hyde Parker, with ◊Nelson as second-in-command, annihilated the Danish navy.

Baltic Sea /ˈbɔːltɪk/ large shallow arm of the North Sea, extending NE from the narrow

Skagerrak and Kattegat, between Sweden and Denmark, to the Gulf of Bothnia between Sweden and Finland. Its coastline is 8,000 km/5,000 mi long, and its area, including the gulfs of Riga, Finland, and Bothnia, is 422,300 sq km/163,000 sq mi. Its shoreline is shared by Denmark, Germany, Poland, the Baltic States, Russia, Finland, and Sweden.

Many large rivers flow into it, including the Oder, Vistula, Niemen, W Dvina, Narva, and Neva. Tides are hardly perceptible, salt content is low; weather is often stormy and navigation dangerous. Most ports are closed by ice from Dec until May. The Kiel canal links the Baltic and North seas; the Göta canal connects the two seas by way of the S Swedish lakes. Since 1975 the Baltic Sea has been linked by the St Petersburg–Belomorsk seaway with the White Sea.

Baltic States /ˈbɔːltɪk/ collective name for the states of ◊Estonia, ◊Latvia, and ◊Lithuania, former constituent republics of the USSR (from 1940). They regained independence Sept 1991.

Baltimore /ˈbɔːltɪmɔː/ industrial port and largest city in Maryland, USA, on the W shore of Chesapeake Bay, NE of Washington DC; population (1980) 750,000; metropolitan area (1980) 2,300,000. Industries include shipbuilding, oil refining, food processing, and the manufacture of steel, chemicals, and aerospace equipment.

Named after the founder of Maryland, Lord Baltimore (1606–75), the city dates from 1729 and was incorporated 1797.

Baltistan /ˌbæltɪˈstɑːn/ region in the Karakoram range of NE Kashmir, held by Pakistan since 1949. It is the home of Balti Muslims of Tibetan origin. The chief town is Skardu, but Ghyari is of greater significance to Muslims as the site of a mosque built by Sayyid Ali Hamadani, a Persian who brought the Shia Muslim religion to Baltistan in the 14th century.

Baluch or **Baluchi** native to or an inhabitant of Baluchistan, a region in SW Pakistan and SE Iran on the Arabian Sea. The common religion of the Baluch is Islam, and they speak Baluchi, a member of the Iranian branch of the Indo-European language family.

Baluchistan /bəˌluːtʃɪˈstɑːn/ mountainous desert area, comprising a province of Pakistan, part of the Iranian province of Sistán and Balúchestan, and a small area of Afghanis-

tan. The Pakistani province has an area of 347,200 sq km/134,019 sq mi and a population (1985) of 4,908,000; its capital is Quetta. Sistán and Balúchestan has an area of 181,600 sq km/70,098 sq mi and a population (1986) of 1,197,000; its capital is Zahedan. The port of Gwadar in Pakistan is strategically important, on the Indian Ocean and the Strait of Hormuz.

history Originally a loose tribal confederation, Baluchistan was later divided into four principalities that were sometimes under Persian, sometimes under Afghan suzerainty. In the 19th century British troops tried to subdue the inhabitants until a treaty 1876 gave them autonomy in exchange for British army outposts along the Afghan border and strategic roads. On the partition of India 1947 the khan of Khalat declared Baluchistan independent; the insurrection was crushed by the new Pakistani army after eight months. Three rebellions followed, the last being from 1973 to 1977, when 3,300 Pakistani soldiers and some 6,000 Baluch were killed.

Balzac /ˈbælzæk/ Honoré de 1799–1850. French novelist. His first success was *Les Chouans/The Chouans* and *La Physiologie du mariage/The Physiology of Marriage* 1829, inspired by Walter Scott. This was the beginning of the long series of novels *La Comédie humaine/The Human Comedy*. He also wrote the Rabelaisian *Contes drolatiques/Ribald Tales* 1833.

Born in Tours, Balzac studied law and worked as a notary's clerk in Paris before turning to literature. His first attempts included tragedies such as *Cromwell* and novels published pseudonymously with no great success. A venture in printing and publishing 1825–28 involved him in a lifelong web of debt. His patroness, Madame de Berny, figures in *Le Lys dans la vallée/The Lily in the Valley* 1836. Balzac intended his major work *La Comédie humaine/The Human Comedy* to comprise 143 volumes, depicting every aspect of society in 19th-century France, of which he completed 80. The series includes *Eugénie Grandet* 1833, *Le Père Goriot* 1834, and *Cousine Bette* 1846. Balzac corresponded constantly with the Polish countess Evelinà Hanska after meeting her 1833, and they married four months before his death in Paris. He was buried in Père Lachaise cemetery.

Bamako /ˌbæməˈkəʊ/ capital and port of Mali on the river Niger; population (1976)

400,000. It produces pharmaceuticals, chemicals, textiles, tobacco, and metal products.

bamboo any of numerous plants of the subgroup Bambuseae within the grass family Gramineae, mainly found in tropical and subtropical countries. Some species grow as tall as 36 m/120 ft. The stems are hollow and jointed and can be used in furniture, house, and boat construction. The young shoots are edible; paper is made from the stem.

Bamboo flowers and seeds only once before the plant dies, sometimes after growing for as long as 120 years.

Banaba /ˈbɑːnəbə/ (formerly *Ocean Island*) island in the Republic of ◊Kiribati.

banana any of several treelike tropical plant of the genus *Musa*, family Musaceae, which grow up to 8 m/25 ft high. The edible banana is the fruit of a sterile hybrid form.

The curved yellow fruits of the commercial banana, arranged in rows of 'hands', form cylindrical masses of a hundred or more, and are exported green and ripened aboard refrigerated ships. The plant is destroyed after cropping. The *plantain*, a larger, coarser hybrid variety that is used green as a cooked vegetable, is a dietary staple in many countries. In the wild, bananas depend on bats for pollination.

Bananarama /bənɑːnəˈrɑːmə/ British pop group formed 1981, a vocal trio comprising, from 1988, founder members Sarah Dallin (1962–) and Keren Woodward (1963–), with Jackie O'Sullivan (1966–). Initially produced by the hitmaking factory of Stock, Aitken and Waterman, they were the top-selling female group of the 1980s.

Banaras /bəˈnɑːrəs/ alternative transliteration of ◊Varanasi, holy Hindu city in Uttar Pradesh, India.

Bancroft /ˈbænkrɒft/ George 1800–1891. US diplomat and historian. A Democrat, he was secretary of the navy 1845 when he established the US Naval Academy at Annapolis, Maryland, and as acting secretary of war (May 1846) was instrumental in bringing about the occupation of California and the ◊Mexican war. He wrote a *History of the United States* 1834–76.

band music group, usually falling into a special category: for example, *military*, comprising woodwind, brass, and percussion; *brass*, solely of brass and percussion; *marching*, a variant of brass; *dance* and *swing*, often like a small orchestra; *jazz*, with no fixed instrumentation; *rock and pop*,

generally electric guitar, bass, and drums, variously augmented; and *steel*, from the West Indies, in which percussion instruments made from oildrums sound like marimbas.

Banda /ˈbændə/ Hastings Kamuzu 1902– . Malawi politican, president from 1966. He led his country's independence movement and was prime minister of Nyasaland (the former name of Malawi) from 1963. He became Malawi's first president 1966 and 1971 was named president for life; his rule has been authoritarian.

Banda studied in the USA, and was a doctor in Britain until 1953.

Bandar Abbas /ˈbændər ˈæbəs/ port and winter resort in Iran on the Ormuz strait, Persian Gulf; population (1983) 175,000. Formerly called Gombroon, it was renamed and made prosperous by Shah Abbas I (1571–1629). It is a naval base.

Bandaranaike /ˌbændərəˈnaɪkə/ Sirimavo (born Ratwatte) 1916– . Sri Lankan politician, who succeeded her husband Solomon Bandaranaike to become the world's first female prime minister 1960–65 and 1970–77, but was expelled from parliament 1980 for abuse of her powers while in office. She was largely responsible for the new constitution 1972.

Bandaranaike /ˌbændərəˈnaɪkə/ Solomon West Ridgeway Dias 1899–1959. Sri Lankan nationalist politician. In 1951 he founded the Sri Lanka Freedom party and in 1956 became prime minister, pledged to a socialist programme and a neutral foreign policy. He failed to satisfy extremists and was assassinated by a Buddhist monk.

Bandar Seri Begawan /ˈbændə ˈseri bəˈgɑːwən/ formerly *Brunei Town* capital of Brunei; population (1983) 57,558.

bandicoot small marsupial mammal inhabiting Australia and New Guinea. There are about 11 species, family Peramelidae, rat- or rabbit-sized and living in burrows. They have long snouts, eat insects, and are nocturnal. A related group, the rabbit bandicoots or bilbys, is reduced to a single species that is now endangered and protected by law.

banding in UK education, the division of school pupils into broad streams by ability. Banding is used by some local authorities to ensure that comprehensive schools receive an intake of children spread right across the ability range. It is used internally by some schools as a means of avoiding groups of widely mixed ability.

Bandung /'bændʊŋ/ commercial city and capital of Jawa Barat province on the island of Java, Indonesia; population (1980) 1,463,000. Bandung is the third largest city in Indonesia and was the administrative centre when the country was the Netherlands East Indies.

Bandung Conference first conference 1955 of the Afro-Asian nations, proclaiming anticolonialism and neutrality between East and West.

bandy-bandy venomous Australian snake *Vermicella annulata* of the cobra family, which grows to about 75 cm/2.5 ft. It is banded in black and white. It is not aggressive toward humans.

Bangalore /ˌbæŋɡə'lɔː/ capital of Karnataka state, S India; population (1981) 2,600,000. Industries include electronics, aircraft and machine tools construction, and coffee.

Bangkok /ˌbæŋ'kɒk/ capital and port of Thailand, on the river Chao Phraya; population (1987) 5,609,000. Products include paper, ceramics, cement, textiles, and aircraft. It is the headquarters of the Southeast Asia Treaty Organization (SEATO).

Bangkok was established as the capital by Phra Chao Tak 1769, after the Burmese had burned down the former capital, Avuthia, about 65 km/40 mi to the N. Features include the temple of the Emerald Buddha and the vast palace complex.

Bangladesh /ˌbæŋglə'deʃ/ country in southern Asia, bounded N, W, and E by India, SE by Myanmar, and S by the Bay of Bengal.

government The 1972 constitution (suspended 1982–86) provides parliamentary democracy. Constitutional amendments were passed June 1989 restricting the president to two elected five-year terms and creating the post of elected vice president.

At the head of the present system is an executive president, popularly elected for a five-year term by universal suffrage, who serves as head of state and head of the armed forces, appointing cabinet ministers and judicial officers; the head of government is the prime minister. There is also a single-chamber legislative parliament Jatiya Sangsad, composed of 300 members directly elected for five-year terms from single-member constituencies and 30 women elected by the legislature itself.

history For history before 1947 see ◊India; for history 1947–1971 see ◊Pakistan. Present-day Bangladesh formerly comprised E Bengal province and Sylhet district of Assam in British India. Predominantly Muslim, it was formed into the eastern province of Pakistan when India was partitioned 1947. Substantially different in culture, language, and geography from the western provinces of Pakistan 1,000 miles away, and with a larger population, it resented the political and military dominance exerted by W Pakistan during the 1950s and 1960s. A movement for political autonomy grew after 1954, under the Awami League headed by Sheik Mujibur ◊Rahman. This gained strength as a result of W Pakistan's indifference 1970, when flooding killed 500,000 in E Pakistan.

republic proclaimed In Pakistan's first general elections 1970 the Awami League

Bandicoot

gained an overwhelming victory in E Pakistan and an overall majority in the all-Pakistan National Assembly. Talks on redrawing the constitution broke down, leading to E Pakistan's secession and the establishment of a Bangladesh ('Bengal Nation') government in exile in Calcutta, India, 1971. Civil war resulted in the flight of 10 million E Pakistani refugees to India, administrative breakdown, famine, and cholera. The W Pakistani forces in E Pakistan surrendered 1971 after India intervened on the secessionists' side. A republic of Bangladesh was proclaimed and rapidly gained international recognition 1972.

Sheik Mujibur assassinated Sheik Mujibur Rahman became prime minister 1972 under a secular, parliamentary constitution. He introduced a socialist economic programme of nationalization but became intolerant of opposition, establishing a one-party presidential system Jan 1975. Rahman, his wife and close relatives were assassinated in a military coup Aug 1975. The Awami League held power for three months under Khandakar Mushtaq Ahmed before a further military coup Nov 1975 established as president and chief martial-law administrator the nonpolitical chief justice Abu Sadat Mohammed Sayem.

martial law under Zia Maj-Gen Zia ur-Rahman (1936–1981) became chief martial law administrator 1976. President from 1977, he adopted an Islamic constitution, approved by a national referendum in May. In June he won a 4:1 majority in a direct presidential election. Zia's newly formed Bangladesh Nationalist Party (BNP) won a parliamentary majority. A civilian government was installed, and martial law and the state of emergency were lifted 1979. The administration was undermined, however, by charges of corruption and by a guerrilla movement in Chittagong 1980. On 30 May 1981 Zia was assassinated in an attempted coup, and interim power was assumed by Vice President Justice Abdus Sattar.

coup led by Ershad With disorder increasing, the civilian administration was overthrown March 1982 by a coup led by Lt-Gen Mohammad Hussain Ershad. Martial law was reimposed and political activity banned. Ershad governed first as chief martial-law administrator and then, from 1983, as president with an appointed council of ministers. The economy improved and a broad opposition coalition, the Movement for the Restoration of Democracy, was formed

1983. A move back to civilian rule began 1983–85 with local elections; Ershad promised presidential and parliamentary elections 1984, but both were cancelled after an opposition threat of a boycott and campaign of civil disobedience if martial law was not first lifted.

The ban on political activity was removed Jan 1986, and parliamentary elections were held in May. The Awami League agreed to participate in these elections, but the BNP and many other opposition parties boycotted them. With a campaign marked by violence, widespread abstentions, and claims of ballot-rigging, Ershad and his Jatiya Dal party gained the two-thirds majority required to pass a law granting retrospective immunity. Ershad was re-elected president in a direct election Oct 1986, and martial law was lifted Nov 1986.

opposition to government During 1987 the Awami League, led by Sheika Hasina Wazed (the daughter of Sheik Mujibur Rahman), and the BNP, led by Begum Khaleda Zia (the widow of Maj-Gen Zia ur-Rahman), stepped up their campaign against the Ershad government, demanding the president's resignation and free elections. In the wake of a wave of violent strikes and demonstrations, Ershad proclaimed a state of emergency Nov 1987, with urban curfews imposed, the two opposition leaders placed under house arrest, and antigovernment protests banned. A month later, parliament was dissolved and fresh elections called March 1988. As a result of both ballot-rigging and an opposition boycott, the ruling Jatiya Dal gained a sweeping victory. The state of emergency was lifted April 1988, and a bill was passed by parliament June 1988 making Islam the state religion.

Bangladesh received Sept 1988 the heaviest monsoon rains in 70 years; in the resulting floods several thousand people died and 30 million became homeless.

Ershad resigns On 4 Dec 1990, after a protracted campaign for the government's removal, Ershad resigned as president and the former prime minister, Kazi Zafar Ahmad, went into hiding. The state of emergency was lifted, parliament dissolved, and Ershad replaced by Shahabuddin Ahmad, the country's chief justice, who agreed to serve as an interim executive president pending the holding of free multiparty elections within three months. The new president immediately annulled the Special Powers Act (which had allowed the government to detain persons without trial and summarily close down newspapers), and also set about removing Ershad-installed personnel from key positions in the military and bureaucracy. Police raids on Ershad's residence revealed evidence of corruption. He was charged with illegal possession of firearms and embezzlement of public funds. He was accused of misappropriating funds in 1990 amounting to £3–4 million/$5–7 million. When the elections were held Feb 1991, the BNP emerged as the dominant force, capturing 140 of the 300 seats. It was helped by a big turnout from women and young people in the towns. Begum Khaleda Zia, leader of the BNP, formed a coalition government with minor parties in preparation for standing for president, and in March she was sworn in as the first woman prime minister of Bangladesh.

cyclone disaster Around 139,000 people were killed and thousands more threatened by epidemics after the devastating cyclone of 29–30 April 1991, which severely affected the area around Chittagong. Between 4 and 10 million people were made homeless and 1,300,000 sq km/500,000 sq mi inundated. Overall economic losses were put at US $3 billion by the government. By May 1991 emergency aid amounting to US $250 million had been provided by the international community, but there were criticisms of the government's management of the relief operation.

parliamentary government restored A nationwide referendum Sept 1991 restored a parliamentary system of government, and in the same month by-elections secured an absolute majority in parliament for the BNP. In Oct 1991 Abdur Rahman Biswas succeeded Shahabuddin Ahmad as state president. In Jan 1992 Bangladesh became a refuge for around 60,000 Muslims fleeing military crackdowns in Myanmar, stretching the country's already scanty resources.

living standards Bangladesh is the world's most densely populated country, with more than 2,255 people per sq mi. Only 15% of the people live in urban areas; 46.6% of the population is under 15, and 75% of women have their first child by the age of 17. There is an estimated one doctor for every 9,000 people and one nurse for every 20,000.

Bangor /'bæŋgə/ cathedral city in Gwynedd, N Wales; population (1981) 46,585. University College of the University of Wales is

here. The cathedral was begun 1495. Industries include chemicals and electrical goods.

Bangui /bɒŋɡiː/ capital and port of the Central African Republic, on the River Ubangi; population (1988) 597,000. Industries include beer, cigarettes, office machinery, and timber and metal products.

Banjermasin /ˌbɑːnjəˈmɑːsɪn/ river port in Indonesia, on Borneo; population (1980) 381,300. It is the capital of Kalimantan Selatan province. It exports rubber, timber, and precious stones.

banjo resonant stringed musical instrument, with a long fretted neck and circular drum-type sound box covered on the topside only by stretched skin (now usually plastic). It is played with a plectrum.

The banjo originated in the American South among black slaves (based on a similar instrument of African origin).

Banjul /bæn'dʒuːl/ capital and chief port of Gambia, on an island at the mouth of the river Gambia; population (1983) 44,536. Established as a settlement for freed slaves 1816, it was known as Bathurst until 1973.

bank financial institution that uses funds deposited with it to lend money to companies or individuals, and also provides financial services to its customers.

A *central bank* (in the UK, the Bank of England) issues currency for the government, in order to provide cash for circulation and exchange. In terms of assets, seven of the world's top ten banks were Japanese 1988.

Banka /'bæŋkə/ or *Bang Ka* island in Indonesia off the E coast of Sumatra
area 12,000 sq km/4,600 sq mi
capital Pangkalpinang
towns Mintok (port)
products tin (one of the world's largest producers)
population (1970) 300,000.

Bank for International Settlements (BIS) a bank established 1930 to handle German reparations settlements from World War I. The BIS (based in Basel, Switzerland) is today a centre for economic and monetary research and assists cooperation of central banks. Its financial activities are essentially short term. It has been superseded in some of its major functions by the ◊International Monetary Fund.

Bank of Commerce and Credit International (BCCI) international bank, founded 1972. By 1990 BCCI had offices in 69 countries, $15 billion in deposits, and $20 billion in assets. In July 1991 evidence of widespread systematic fraud at BCCI led regulators in seven countries to seize its assets, and BCCI operations in most of the remaining 62 countries were then also shut down. A subsequent investigation resulted in a New York criminal indictment of the institution and four of its units, and the arrest of some 20 BCCI officials in Abu Dhabi for alleged fraud.

BCCI was founded 1972 by Pakistani banker, Agha Hasan Abedi (1922–), who remained its chairman until 1989. From March 1990, it was under the control of Sheik Sultan Zayed bin al-Nahayan, the ruler of Abu Dhabi. In July 1990 five former officials of BCCI were convicted in Tampa, Florida, for laundering $32 million in cocaine profits for Colombia's Medellín drug cartel. Despite these convictions and later evidence of BCCI's fraudulent conduct, regulatory control was hampered by the fact that the bank had no central office under the jurisdiction of an individual government.

Bank of England UK central bank founded by act of Parliament 1694. It was entrusted with the note issue 1844 and nationalized 1946. It is banker to the clearing banks and the UK government. As the government's bank, it manages and arranges the financing of the ◊public-sector borrowing requirement and the national debt, implements monetary policy and exchange-rate policy through intervention in foreign-exchange markets, and supervises the UK banking system.

bank rate interest rate fixed by the Bank of England as a guide to mortgage, hire purchase rates, and so on, which was replaced 1972 by the *minimum lending rate* (lowest rate at which the Bank acts as lender of last resort to the money market), which from 1978 was again a 'bank rate' set by the Bank.

bankruptcy process by which the property of a person (in legal terms, an individual or corporation) unable to pay debts is taken away under a court order and divided fairly among the person's creditors, after preferential payments such as taxes and wages. Proceedings may be instituted either by the debtor (voluntary bankruptcy) or by any creditor for a substantial sum (involuntary bankruptcy). Until 'discharged', a bankrupt is severely restricted in financial activities.

When 'discharged' the person becomes free of most debts dating from the time of bankruptcy. The largest financial services bankruptcy, with liabilities of $3 billion, was filed by US securities firm Drexel Burnham Lambert in Feb 1990.

Banks /bæŋks/ Joseph 1744–1820. British naturalist and explorer. He accompanied Capt James ◊Cook on his voyage round the world 1768–71 and brought back 3,600 plants, 1,400 of them never before classified. The *Banksia* genus of shrubs is named after him.

banksia /ˈbæŋksɪə/ any shrub or tree of the genus *Banksia*, family Proteaceae, native to Australia and including the honeysuckle tree. The genus is named after Joseph Banks.

Banksias have spiny evergreen leaves and large flower spikes, made up of about 1,000 individual flowers formed around a central axis. The colours of the flower spikes can be gold, red, brown, purple, greenish-yellow, and grey.

Bannister /ˈbænɪstə/ Roger Gilbert 1929– . English track and field athlete, the first person to run a mile in under four minutes. He achieved this feat at Oxford, England, on 6 May 1954 in a time of 3 min 59.4 sec.

Bannockburn, Battle of battle on 24 June 1314 in which ◊Robert I of Scotland (known as Robert the Bruce) defeated the English under Edward II, who had come to relieve the besieged Stirling Castle. Named after the town of Bannockburn, S of Stirling.

bantam small variety of domestic chicken. Bantams can either be a small version of one of the large breeds, or a separate type. Some are prolific layers. Bantam cocks have a reputation as spirited fighters.

banteng wild species of cattle *Bos banteng*, now scarce, but formerly ranging from Myanmar (Burma) through SE Asia to Malaysia and Java, inhabiting hilly forests. Its colour varies from pale brown to blue-black, usually with white stockings and rump patch, and it is up to 1.5 m/5 ft at the shoulder.

Banting /ˈbæntɪŋ/ Frederick Grant 1891–1941. Canadian physician who discovered a technique for isolating the hormone insulin 1921 when, experimentally, he and his colleague Charles ◊Best tied off the ducts of the ◊pancreas to determine the function of the cells known as the islets of Langerhans. This allowed for the treatment of diabetes. Banting and John J R Macleod (1876–1935), his mentor, shared the 1923 Nobel Prize for Medicine, and Banting divided his prize with Best.

Bantu languages group of related languages spoken widely over the greater part of Africa south of the Sahara, including Swahili, Xhosa, and Zulu. Meaning 'people' in Zulu, the word Bantu itself illustrates a characteristic use of prefixes: *mu-ntu* 'man', *ba-ntu* 'people'.

Bantustan or *homeland* name until 1978 for a ◊Black National State in the Republic of South Africa.

banyan tropical Asian fig tree *Ficus benghalensis*, family Moraceae. It produces aerial roots that grow down from its spreading branches, forming supporting pillars that have the appearance of separate trunks.

baobab tree of the genus *Adansonia*, family Bombacaceae. It has rootlike branches, hence its nickname 'upside-down tree', and a disproportionately thick girth, up to 9 m/30 ft in diameter. The pulp of its fruit is edible and is known as monkey bread.

Baobabs may live for 1,000 years and are found in Africa (*A. digitata*) and Australia (*A. gregorii*), a relic of the time when both were part of ◊Gondwanaland.

baptism (Greek 'to dip') immersion in or sprinkling with water as a religious rite of initiation. It was practised long before the beginning of Christianity. In the Christian baptism ceremony, sponsors or godparents make vows on behalf of the child, which are renewed by the child at confirmation. It is one of the seven sacraments. The *amrit* ceremony in Sikhism is sometimes referred to as baptism.

Baptist /'bæptɪst/ member of any of several Protestant and evangelical Christian sects that practise baptism by immersion only upon profession of faith. Baptists seek their authority in the Bible. They originated among English Dissenters who took refuge in the Netherlands in the early 17th century, and spread by emigration and, later, missionary activity. Of the world total of approximately 31 million, some 26.5 million are in the USA and 265,000 in the UK.

bar c.g.s. unit of pressure equal to 10^5 pascals or 10^6 dynes/cm², approximately 750 mmHg or 0.987 atm. Its diminutive, the *millibar* (one-thousandth of a bar), is commonly used by meteorologists.

Bar, the in law, the profession of ◊barristers collectively. To be *called to the Bar* is to become a barrister.

Prospective barristers in the UK must not only complete a course of study in law but also be admitted to one of the four Inns of Court before they can be 'called'. The General Council of the Bar and of the Inns of Court (known as the Bar Council) is the professional governing body of the Bar.

bar in music, a modular unit of rhythm, shown in notation by vertical 'barring' of the musical continuum into sections of usually constant duration and rhythmic content. The alternative term is 'measure'.

Bara /'bɑːrə/ Theda. Stage name of Theodosia Goodman 1890–1955. US silent-film actress who became the movies' first sex symbol after appearing in *A Fool There Was* 1915, based on a poem by Rudyard Kipling, 'The Vampire'. The Vamp, as she became known, later played Carmen, Salome, and Cleopatra.

Barabbas /bə'ræbəs/ in the New Testament, a condemned robber released by Pilate at Passover instead of Jesus to appease a mob.

barb general name for fish of the genus *Barbus* and some related genera of the family Cyprinidae. As well as the ◊barbel, barbs include many small tropical Old World species, some of which are familiar aquarium species. They are active egg-laying species, usually of 'typical' fish shape and with barbels at the corner of the mouth.

Barbados /bɑː'beɪdɒs/ island country in the Caribbean, one of the Lesser Antilles. It is about 483 km/300 mi N of Venezuela.

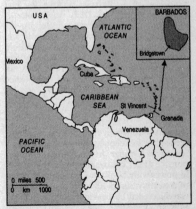

government The bicameral legislature dates from 1627, when the British settled. The constitution dates from 1966 and provides for a system of parliamentary government on the British model, with a prime minister and cabinet drawn from and responsible to the legislature, which consists of a senate and a house of assembly. The senate has 21 members appointed by the governor general, 12 on the advice of the prime minister, two on the advice of the leader of the opposition, and the rest on the basis of wider consultations. The house of assembly has 27 members elected by universal suffrage. The legislature has a maximum life of five years and may be dissolved within this period. The governor general appoints both the prime minister (on the basis of support in the house of assembly) and the leader of the opposition. The two main political parties are the Barbados Labour Party (BLP) and the Democratic Labour Party (DLP).

history Originally inhabited by Arawak Indians, who were wiped out soon after the arrival of the first Europeans, Barbados became a British colony 1627 and remained so until independence 1966. Universal adult suffrage was introduced 1951, and the BLP won the first general election. Ministerial government was established 1954, and the BLP leader Grantley Adams became the first prime minister. A group broke away from the BLP 1955 and formed the DLP. Six years later full internal self-government was achieved, and in the 1961 general election the DLP was victorious under its leader Errol Barrow.

When Barbados attained full independence 1966, Barrow became its first prime minister. The DLP was re-elected 1971, but in the 1976 general election the BLP—led now by Grantley Adams's son Tom—ended Barrow's 15-year rule. Both parties were committed to maintaining free enterprise and alignment with the USA, although the DLP government established diplomatic relations with Cuba 1972 and the BLP administration supported the US invasion of Grenada 1983.

The BLP was re-elected 1981. After Adams's sudden death 1985 he was succeeded by his deputy, Bernard St John, a former BLP leader. In the 1986 general election the DLP, led by Barrow, was returned to power with 24 of the 27 seats in the house of assembly. Errol Barrow died 1987 and was succeeded by Erskine Lloyd Sandiford. Foreign minister James Tudor resigned March 1989 in the face of charges that diplomatic staff had been involved in drug smuggling. The DLP obtained 18 seats with 49% of the vote in Jan 1991 elections, and the BLP only 10 seats with 44% of the vote.

In Sept 1994 the BLP was re-elected and Owen Arthur became prime minister.

Barbarossa /ˌbɑːbəˈrɒsə/ nickname 'red beard' given to the Holy Roman emperor ◊Frederick I, and also to two brothers, Horuk and Khair-ed-Din, who were Barbary pirates. Horuk was killed by the Spaniards 1518; Khair-ed-Din took Tunis 1534 and died in Constantinople 1546.

Barbary ape tailless, yellowish-brown macaque monkey *Macaca sylvanus*, found in the mountains and wilds of Algeria and Morocco. It was introduced to Gibraltar, where legend has it that the British will leave if the colony dies out.

Barbary Coast North African coast of the Mediterranean Sea (named after the ◊Berbers) from which pirates operated against US and European shipping from the 16th up to the 19th century. The pirates took hostages for ransom.

barbastelle insect-eating bat *Barbastella barbastellus* with 'frosted' black fur and a wingspan of about 25 cm/10 in, occasionally found in the UK but more common in Europe.

barbed wire cheap fencing material made of strands of galvanized wire (see ◊galvanizing), twisted together with sharp barbs at close intervals. In 1873 an American, Joseph Glidden, devised a machine to mass-produce barbed wire. Its use on the open grasslands of 19th-century America led to range warfare between farmers and cattle ranchers; the latter used to drive their herds cross-country.

barbel freshwater fish *Barbus barbus* found in fast-flowing rivers with sand or gravel bottoms in Britain and Europe. Long-bodied, and up to 1 m/3 ft long, the barbel has four *barbels* ('little beards'—sensory fleshy filaments) near the mouth.

Barber /ˈbɑːbə/ Samuel 1910–1981. US composer of a Neo-Classical, later somewhat dissonant style, whose works include *Adagio for Strings* 1936 and the opera *Vanessa* 1958, which won him one of his two Pulitzer prizes. Another Barber opera, *Antony and Cleopatra* 1966, was commissioned for the opening of the new Metropolitan Opera House at Lincoln Center, New York City. Barber's music is lyrical and fastidiously worked. His later works include *The Lovers* 1971.

barbershop in music, a style of unaccompanied close-harmony singing of sentimental ballads, revived in the USA during the 19th century. Traditionally sung by four male voices, since the 1970s it has developed as a style of ◊a cappella choral singing for both male and female voices.

Barbershop originated in 17th-century European barbers' shops, which offered dental and medical services. Waiting customers were provided with a cittern (almond-shaped, flat-backed stringed instrument, popular, cheap, and easy to play) or guitar by managements aware of the benefits of music to those undergoing pain.

barbet small, tropical bird, often brightly coloured. There are some 78 species of barbet in the family Capitonidae, about half living in Africa. Barbets eat insects and fruits and, being distant relations of woodpeckers, drill nest holes with their beaks. The name comes from the 'little beard' of bristles at the base of the beak.

Barbie /ˈbɑːbi/ Klaus 1913–1991. German Nazi, a member of the ◊SS from 1936. During World War II he was involved in the deportation of Jews from the occupied Netherlands 1940–42 and in tracking down Jews and Resistance workers in France 1942–45. Having escaped capture 1945, Barbie was employed by the US intelligence services in Germany before moving to Bolivia 1951 where he made a living as a businessman accompanied by his family. Expelled from there 1983, he was arrested and convicted of crimes against humanity in France 1987.

His work as SS commander, based in Lyon, included the rounding-up of Jewish children from an orphanage at Izieu and the torture of the Resistance leader Jean Moulin. His ruthlessness during this time earned him the epithet 'Butcher of Lyon'.

Barbirolli /ˌbɑːbɪˈrɒli/ John 1899–1970. English conductor. He made his name as a cellist, and in 1937 succeeded Toscanini as conductor of the New York Philharmonic Orchestra. He returned to England 1943, where he remained conductor of the Hallé Orchestra, Manchester, until his death.

barbiturate hypnosedative drug, commonly known as a 'sleeping pill', consisting of any salt or ester of barbituric acid $C_4H_4O_3N_2$. They work by depressing brain activity. Most barbiturates, being highly addictive, are no longer prescribed and are listed as controlled substances.

Tolerance develops quickly in the user so that increasingly large doses are required to induce sleep. A barbiturate's action persists for hours or days, causing confused, aggressive behaviour or disorientation.

Barbizon school /ˈbɑːbɪzɒn/ French school of landscape painters of the mid-19th century, based at Barbizon in the forest of Fontainebleau. Members included Jean-François Millet, Diaz de la Peña (1807–1876), and Théodore Rousseau (1812–1867). Their aim was to paint fresh, realistic scenes, sketching and painting their subjects in the open air.

Barbuda /bɑːˈbjuːdə/ one of the islands that form the state of ◊Antigua and Barbuda.

Barcelona /ˌbɑːsəˈləʊnə/ capital, industrial city (textiles, engineering, chemicals), and port of Catalonia, NE Spain; population (1986) 1,694,000. As the chief centre of anarchism and Catalonian nationalism, it was prominent in the overthrow of the monarchy 1931 and was the last city of the republic to surrender to Franco 1939.

features The Ramblas, tree-lined promenades leading from the Plaza de Cataluña, the largest square in Spain; ◊Gaudí's unfinished church of the Holy Family 1883; the Pueblo Español 1929, with specimens of Spanish architecture; a replica of Columbus's flagship the *Santa Maria*, in the Maritime Museum; a large collection of art by Picasso

history Founded in the 3rd century BC, Barcelona's importance grew until, in the 14th century, it had become one of the leading trade cities of the Mediterranean.

bar code pattern of bars and spaces that can be read by a computer. They are widely used in retailing, industrial distribution, and public libraries. The code is read by a scanning device; the computer determines the code from the widths of the bars and spaces.

The technique was patented 1949 but only became popular 1973, when the food industry in North America adopted the Universal Product Code system.

Bardeen /bɑːˈdiːn/ John 1908–1991. US physicist who won a Nobel prize 1956, with Walter Brattain and William Shockley, for the development of the transistor 1948. In 1972 he became the first double winner of a Nobel prize in the same subject (with Leon Cooper and John Schrieffer) for his work on superconductivity.

Bardot /bɑːˈdəʊ/ Brigitte 1934– . French film actress, whose sensual appeal did much to popularize French cinema internationally. Her films include *Et Dieu créa la femme/And*

God Created Woman 1950, *Viva Maria* 1965, and *Shalako* 1968.

Barebones Parliament /'beəbəʊnz/ English assembly called by Oliver ◊Cromwell to replace the 'Rump Parliament' July 1653. It consisted of 140 members nominated by the army and derived its name from one of its members, Praise-God Barbon. Although they attempted to pass sensible legislation (civil marriage; registration of births, deaths, and marriages; custody of lunatics), its members' attempts to abolish tithes, patronage, and the court of chancery, and to codify the law, led to the resignation of the moderates and its dissolution Dec 1653.

Bareilly /bə'reɪli/ industrial city in Uttar Pradesh, India; population (1981) 438,000. It was a Mogul capital 1657 and at the centre of the Indian Mutiny 1857.

Barenboim /'bærənbɔɪm/ Daniel 1942– . Israeli pianist and conductor, born in Argentina. Pianist/conductor with the English Chamber Orchestra from 1964, he became conductor of the New York Philharmonic Orchestra 1970 and musical director of the Orchestre de Paris 1975. Appointed artistic and musical director of the Opéra de la Bastille, Paris, July 1987, he was dismissed from his post July 1989, a few months before its opening, for reasons which he claimed were more political than artistic. He is a celebrated interpreter of Mozart and Beethoven.

Barents /'bærənts/ Willem *c.* 1550–1597. Dutch explorer and navigator. He made three expeditions to seek the ◊Northeast Passage; he died on the last voyage. The Barents Sea, part of the Arctic Ocean N of Norway, is named after him.

Bari /'bɑːri/ capital of Puglia region, S Italy, and industrial port on the Adriatic; population (1988) 359,000. It is the site of Italy's first nuclear power station; the part of the town known as Tecnopolis is the Italian equivalent of ◊Silicon Valley.

Barikot /ˌbɑːrɪ'kɒt/ garrison town in Konar province, E Afghanistan, near the Pakistan frontier. Besieged by Mujaheddin rebels 1985, the relief of Barikot by Soviet and Afghan troops was one of the largest military engagements of the Afghan war during Soviet occupation.

Barisal /ˌbʌrɪ'sɑːl/ river port and capital city of Barisal region, S Bangladesh; population (1981) 142,000. It trades in jute, rice, fish, and oilseed.

baritone lower-range male voice between bass and tenor.

barium (Greek *barytes* 'heavy') soft, silver-white, metallic element, symbol Ba, atomic number 56, relative atomic mass 137.33. It is one of the alkaline-earth metals, found in nature as barium carbonate and barium sulphate. As the sulphate it is used in medicine: taken as a suspension (a 'barium meal'), its progress is followed by using X-rays to reveal abnormalities of the alimentary canal. Barium is also used in alloys, pigments, and safety matches and, with strontium, forms the emissive surface in cathode-ray tubes. It was first discovered in barytes or heavy spar.

bark protective outer layer on the stems and roots of woody plants, composed mainly of dead cells. To allow for expansion of the stem, the bark is continually added to from within, and the outer surface often becomes fissured or is shed as scales. The bark from the cork oak *Quercus suber* is economically important and harvested commercially. The spice ◊cinnamon and the drugs cascara (used as a laxative and stimulant) and ◊quinine all come from bark.

Bark technically includes all the tissues external to the vascular ◊cambium (the ◊phloem, cortex, and periderm). Its thickness may vary from 2.5 mm/0.1 in to 30 cm/12 in or more, as in the giant redwood *Sequoia* where it forms a thick, spongy layer.

Barker /'bɑːkə/ Clive 1952– . British writer whose *Books of Blood* 1984–85 are in the sensationalist tradition of ◊horror fiction.

Barker /'bɑːkə/ George 1913– . British poet, known for his vivid imagery, as in *Calamiterror* 1937, *The True Confessions of George Barker* 1950, and *Collected Poems 1930–50*.

Barker /'bɑːkə/ Herbert 1869–1950. British mani-pulative surgeon, whose work established the popular standing of orthopaedics (the study and treatment of disorders of the spine and joints), but who was never recognized by the world of orthodox medicine.

Barker Howard 1946– . English playwright whose plays, renowned for their uncompromising and poetically dense language, confront the issues of private ambition and the exploitation of power. Among his works are *Victory* 1982; *The Castle* 1985; *The Last Supper*, *The Possibilities*, and *The Bite of the Night*, all in 1988; and *Seven Lears* 1989.

In 1988 he formed The Wrestling School, a theatre company dedicated to the performance of his own work.

Barking and Dagenham /ˈbɑːkɪŋ, ˈdægənəm/ borough of E Greater London
products Ford motor industry at Dagenham
population (1988) 147,600.

bark painting technique of painting on the inner side of a strip of tree bark, practised by Australian Aborigines. In red, yellow, white, brown, and black pigments, the works were often painted with the fingers as the artist lay inside a low bark-roofed shelter.

Barlach /ˈbɑːlæx/ Ernst 1870–1938. German Expressionist sculptor, painter, and poet. His simple, evocative figures carved in wood (for example, those in St Catherine's, Lübeck, 1930–32) often express melancholy.

barley cereal belonging to the grass family (Gramineae). Cultivated barley *Hordeum vulgare* comprises three main varieties—six-rowed, four-rowed, and two-rowed. Barley was one of the earliest cereals to be cultivated, about 5000 BC in Egypt, and no other cereal can thrive in so wide a range of climatic conditions; polar barley is sown and reaped well within the Arctic circle in Europe. Barley is no longer much used in bread-making, but it is used in soups and stews and as a starch. Its high-protein form finds a wide use for animal feeding, and its low-protein form is used in brewing and distilling alcoholic beverages.

bar mitzvah (Hebrew 'son of the commandment') in Judaism, initiation of a boy, which takes place at the age of 13, into the adult Jewish community; less common is the *bat* or *bas mitzvah* for girls aged 12. The child reads a passage from the Torah in the synagogue on the Sabbath, and is subsequently regarded as a full member of the congregation.

barn farm building traditionally used for the storage and processing of cereal crops and hay. On older farmsteads, the barn is usually the largest building. It is often characterized by ventilation openings rather than windows and has at least one set of big double doors for access. Before mechanization, wheat was threshed by hand on a specially prepared floor inside these doors.

Tithe barns were used in feudal England to store the produce paid as a tax to the parish priest by the local occupants of the land. In the Middle Ages, monasteries often controlled the collection of tithes over a wide area and, as a result, constructed some enormous tithe barns.

The best surviving example is the monastic barn at Great Coxwell in Oxfordshire, which was built in the middle of the 13th century and is 46.3 m/152 ft long by 13.4 m/44 ft wide by 14.6 m/48 ft high.

barnacle marine crustacean of the subclass Cirripedia. The larval form is free-swimming, but when mature, it fixes itself by the head to rock or floating wood. The animal then remains attached, enclosed in a shell through which the cirri (modified legs) protrude to sweep food into the mouth. Barnacles include the stalked *goose barnacle Lepas anatifera* found on ships' bottoms, and the *acorn barnacles*, such as *Balanus balanoides*, common on rocks.

Barnard /ˈbɑːnɑːd/ Christiaan (Neethling) 1922– . South African surgeon who performed the first human heart transplant 1967 in Cape Town. The patient, 54-year-old Louis Washkansky, lived for 18 days.

Barnardo /bəˈnɑːdəʊ/ Thomas John 1845–1905. British philanthropist, who was known as Dr Barnardo, although not medically qualified. He opened the first of a series of homes for destitute children 1867 in Stepney, E London.

Barnard's star /ˈbɑːnɑːd/ second closest star to the Sun, six light years away in the

Barley Barley was first cultivated in Egypt about 5000 BC.

constellation Ophiuchus. It is a faint red dwarf of 10th magnitude, visible only through a telescope. It is named after the US astronomer Edward E Barnard (1857–1923), who discovered 1916 that it has the fastest proper motion of any star, crossing 1 degree of sky every 350 years.

Barnes /bɑːnz/ Thomas 1785–1841. British journalist, forthright and influential editor of *The Times* from 1817, during whose editorship it became known as 'the Thunderer'.

Barnet /'bɑːnɪt/ borough of NW Greater London *features* site of the Battle of Barnet 1471 in one of the Wars of the ◊Roses; Hadley Woods; Hampstead Garden Suburb; department for newspapers and periodicals of the British Library at Colindale; residential district of *Hendon*, which includes Metropolitan Police Detective Training and Motor Driving schools and the Royal Air Force Battle of Britain and Bomber Command museums *population* (1981) 301,400.

Barnet, Battle of in the English Wars of the ◊Roses, the defeat of Lancaster by York on 14 April 1471 in Barnet (now in NW London).

Barnsley /'bɑːnzli/ town in S Yorkshire, England; population (1981) 128,200. It is an industrial town (iron and steel, glass, paper, carpet, clothing) on one of Britain's richest coalfields.

Barnum /'bɑːnəm/ Phineas T(aylor) 1810–1891. US showman. In 1871, after an adventurous career, he established the 'Greatest Show on Earth', which included the midget 'Tom Thumb', a circus, a menagerie, and an exhibition of 'freaks', conveyed in 100 rail cars. He coined the phrase 'there's a sucker born every minute'.

Barocci /bəˈrɒtʃi/ Federico c. 1535–1612. Italian artist, born and based in Urbino. He painted religious themes in a highly coloured, sensitive style that falls between Renaissance and Baroque. His *Madonna del Graffo* (National Gallery, London) shows the influence of Raphael (also from Urbino) and Correggio on his art.

barograph device for recording variations in atmospheric pressure. A pen, governed by the movements of an aneroid ◊barometer, makes a continuous line on a paper strip on a cylinder that rotates over a day or week to create a *barogram*, or permanent record of variations in atmospheric pressure.

barometer instrument that measures atmospheric pressure as an indication of weather. Most often used are the *mercury barometer* and the *aneroid barometer*.

In a mercury barometer a column of mercury in a glass tube, roughly 0.75 m/2.5 ft high (closed at one end, curved upwards at the other), is balanced by the pressure of the atmosphere on the open end; any change in the height of the column reflects a change in pressure. In an aneroid barometer, a shallow cylindrical metal box containing a vacuum expands or contracts in response to changes in pressure.

baron rank in the ◊peerage of the UK, above a baronet and below a viscount.

The first English barony by patent was created 1387, but barons by 'writ' existed earlier. Life peers, created under the Act of 1958, are always of this rank. The wife of a baron, or a woman holding a title in her own right, is a *baroness*.

baronet British order of chivalry below the rank of baron, but above that of knight, created 1611 by James I to finance the settlement of Ulster. It is a hereditary honour, although women cannot succeed to a baronetcy. A baronet does not have a seat in the House of Lords, but is entitled to the style *Sir* before his name. The sale of baronetcies was made illegal 1937.

Barons' Wars civil wars in England:
1215–17 between King ◊John and his barons, over his failure to honour ◊Magna Carta
1264–67 between ◊Henry III (and the future ◊Edward I) and his barons (led by Simon de ◊Montfort)
1264 14 May *Battle of Lewes* at which Henry III was defeated and captured
1265 4 Aug Simon de Montfort was defeated by the future Edward I at Evesham and killed.

Baroque style of art and architecture characterized by extravagance in ornament, asymmetry of design, and great expressiveness. It dominated European *art* for most of the 17th century, with artists such as the painter Rubens and the sculptor Bernini. In *architecture*, it often involved large-scale designs, such as Bernini's piazza in Rome and the palace of Versailles in France. In *music* the Baroque period lasted from about 1600 to 1750, and its major composers included Monteverdi, Vivaldi, J S Bach, and Handel.

In *painting*, Caravaggio, with his bold use of light and forceful compositions, was an early exponent, but the Carracci family was more typical of the early Baroque style, producing grandiose visions in ceiling paintings that deployed illusionistic displays of florid architectural decoration. In *sculpture*, the master of Baroque was Bernini, whose *Ecstasy of St Theresa* 1645–52 (Sta Maria della Vittoria, Rome) is a fine example of overt emotionalism. Most masterpieces of the new style emerged in churches and palaces in Rome, but the Baroque influence soon spread through Europe. The Swiss art historian Burckhardt was the first to use the term 'baroque'.

Barquisimeto /bɑːkiːsɪˈmeɪtəʊ/ capital of Lara state, NW Venezuela; population (1981) 523,000.

Barra /ˈbærə/ southernmost of the larger Outer Hebrides, Scotland; area 90 sq km/35 sq mi; population (1981) 1,340. It is separated from South Uist by the Sound of Barra. The main town is Castlebay.

barracuda large predatory fish *Sphyraena barracuda* found in the warmer seas of the world. It can grow over 2 m/6 ft long, and has a superficial resemblance to a pike. Young fish shoal but the older ones are solitary. The barracuda has very sharp shearing teeth, and may attack people.

Barrancabermeja /bəræŋkəbəmeɪxə/ port and oil-refining centre on the Magdalena River in the department of Santander, NE Colombia; population (1980 est) 70,000. It is a major outlet for oil from the De Mares fields, which are linked by pipeline to Cartagena on the Caribbean coast.

Barranquilla /ˌbærənˈkiːljə/ seaport in N Colombia, on the river Magdalena; population (1985) 1,120,900. Products include chemicals, tobacco, textiles, furniture, and footwear. It is Colombia's chief port on the Caribbean.

Barras /ˈbæˈrɑːs/ Paul François Jean Nicolas, Count 1755–1829. French revolutionary. He was elected to the National Convention 1792 and helped to overthrow Robespierre 1794. In 1795 he became a member of the ruling Directory (see ◊French Revolution). In 1796 he brought about the marriage of his former mistress, Joséphine de Beauharnais, with Napoleon and assumed dictatorial powers. After Napoleon's coup d'état 19 Nov 1799, Barras fell into disgrace.

Barrault /ˈbæˈrəʊ/ Jean-Louis 1910–1994. French actor and director. His films include

La Symphonie fantastique 1942, *Les Enfants du paradis* 1945, and *La Ronde* 1950.

He was producer and director to the ◊Comédie Française 1940–46, and director of the Théâtre de France (formerly Odéon) from 1959 until his dismissal 1968 because of statements made during the occupation of the theatre by student rebels.

Barre /bɑː/ Raymond 1924– . French politician, member of the centre-right Union pour la Démocratie Française; prime minister 1976–81, when he also held the Finance Ministry portfolio and gained a reputation as a tough and determined budget-cutter.

Barre, born on the French dependency of Réunion, was a liberal economist at the Sorbonne and vice president of the European Commission 1967–72. He served as minister of foreign trade to President Giscard d'Estaing and became prime minister on the resignation of Chirac 1976. He built up a strong political base in the Lyon region during the early 1980s. Once considered a candidate for the presidency, in 1988 he effectively ruled himself out of contention.

barrel unit of liquid capacity, the value of which depends on the liquid being measured. It is used for petroleum, a barrel of which contains 159 litres/35 imperial gallons; a barrel of alcohol contains 189 litres/41.5 imperial gallons.

barrel cylindrical container, tapering at each end, made of thick strips of wood bound together by metal hoops. Barrels are used for the bulk storage of fine wines and spirits.

barrel organ portable pipe organ, played by turning a handle. The handle works a pump and drives a replaceable cylinder upon which a pattern of ridges controls the passage of air to certain pipes, producing a variety of tunes.

It is often confused with the barrel or street piano used by buskers, which employed a barrel-and-pin mechanism to control a piano hammer action.

Barrett Browning /ˈbraʊnɪŋ/ Elizabeth 1806–1861. English poet. In 1844 she published *Poems* (including 'The Cry of the Children'), which led to her friendship with and secret marriage to Robert Browning 1846. The *Sonnets from the Portuguese* 1847 were written during their courtship. Later works include *Casa Guidi Windows* 1851 and the poetic novel *Aurora Leigh* 1857.

Barrie /'bæri/ J(ames) M(atthew) 1860–1937. Scottish playwright and novelist, author of *The Admirable Crichton* 1902 and the children's fantasy *Peter Pan* 1904.

He became known by his studies of Scottish rural life in plays such as *A Window in Thrums* 1889, which began the vogue of the Kailyard school. His reputation as a playwright was established with *The Professor's Love Story* 1894 and *The Little Minister* 1897. His later plays include *Quality Street* 1901 and *What Every Woman Knows* 1908.

barrier island long island of sand, lying offshore and parallel to the coast. Some of these islands are over 100 km/60 mi in length. Often several islands lie in a continuous row offshore. Coney Island and Jones Beach near New York City are well-known examples, as is Padre Island, Texas. The Frisian Islands are barrier islands along the coast of the Netherlands.

Most barrier islands are derived from marine sands piled up by shallow longshore currents that sweep sand parallel to the seashore. Others are derived from former spits, connected to land and built up by drifted sand, that were later severed from the mainland.

barrier reef ◊coral reef that lies offshore, separated from the mainland by a shallow lagoon.

barrister in the UK, a lawyer qualified by study at the ◊Inns of Court to plead for a client in court. In Scotland such lawyers are called ◊advocates. Barristers also undertake the writing of opinions on the prospects of a case before trial. They act for clients through the intermediary of ◊solicitors. In the highest courts, only barristers can represent litigants but this distinction between barristers and solicitors seems likely to change in the 1990s. When pupil barristers complete their training they are 'called to the Bar': this being the name of the ceremony in which they are admitted as members of the profession. A ◊Queen's Counsel (silk) is a senior barrister appointed on the recommendation of the Lord Chancellor.

Barrois de Chamorro Violeta President of Nicaragua from 1990; see ◊Chamorro.

barrow burial mound, usually composed of earth but sometimes of stones, examples of which are found in many parts of the world. The two main types are *long*, dating from the New Stone Age, or Neolithic, and *round*, dating from the later Mesolithic peoples of the early Bronze Age.

Long barrows may be mere mounds, but usually they contain a chamber of wood or stone slabs in which were placed the bodies of the deceased. They are common in southern England from Sussex to Dorset. The earthen (or unchambered) long barrows belong to the early and middle Neolithic, while others were constructed over Megalithic tombs.

Round barrows belong mainly to the Bronze Age, although in historic times some of the Saxon and most of the Danish invaders were barrow-builders. The commonest type is the bell barrow, consisting of a circular mound enclosed by a ditch and an outside bank of earth. Other types include the bowl barrow, pond barrow, and saucer barrow, all of which are associated with the Wessex culture (the Early Bronze Age culture of southern England dating to approximately 2000–1500 BC). Many barrows dot the Wiltshire downs in England.

Barrow /'bærəʊ/ most northerly town in the USA, at Point Barrow, Alaska; the world's largest Inuit settlement. There is oil at nearby Prudhoe Bay.

Barrow /'bærəʊ/ Clyde 1900–1934. US criminal; see ◊Bonnie and Clyde.

Barrow /'bærəʊ/ Isaac 1630–1677. British mathematician, theologian, and classicist. His *Lectiones geometricae* 1670 contains the essence of the theory of ◊calculus, which was later expanded by Isaac Newton and Gottfried Leibniz.

Barry /'bæri/ Charles 1795–1860. English architect of the Neo-Gothic Houses of Parliament at Westminster, London, 1840–60, in collaboration with ◊Pugin.

Barry /'bæri/ Comtesse du, see ◊Du Barry, mistress of Louis XV of France.

Barrymore /'bærɪmɔː/ US family of actors, the children of British-born Maurice Barrymore and Georgie Drew, both stage personalities.

Lionel Barrymore (1878–1954) first appeared on the stage with his grandmother, Mrs John Drew, 1893. He played numerous film roles from 1909, including *A Free Soul* 1931 and *Grand Hotel* 1932, but was perhaps best known for his annual radio portrayal of Scrooge in Dickens's *A Christmas Carol*.

Ethel Barrymore (1879–1959) played with the British actor Henry Irving in London 1898 and 1928 opened the Ethel Barrymore

Theatre in New York; she also appeared in many films from 1914, including *None but the Lonely Heart* 1944.

John Barrymore (1882–1942), a flamboyant actor who often appeared on stage and screen with his brother and sister. In his early years he was a Shakespearean actor. From 1923 he acted almost entirely in films, including *Dinner at Eight* 1933, and became a screen idol, nicknamed 'the Profile'.

Barstow /ˈbɑːstəʊ/ Stan 1928– . English novelist born in W Yorkshire. His novels describe northern working-class life and include *A Kind of Loving* 1960.

Barth /bɑːt/ Heinrich 1821–1865. German geographer and explorer who in explorations of N Africa between 1844 and 1855 established the exact course of the river Niger.

Barth /bɑːt/ John 1930– . US novelist and short-story writer who was influential in the 'academic' experimental movement of the 1960s. His works are usually interwoven fictions based on language games, since he is concerned with the relationship of language and reality. They include the novels *The Sot-Weed Factor* 1960, *Giles Goat-Boy* 1966, *Letters* 1979, *Sabbatical: A Romance* 1982, and *The Tidewater Tales* 1987. He also wrote the novella *Chimera* 1972 and *Lost in the Funhouse* 1968, a collection of short stories.

Barth /bɑːt/ Karl 1886–1968. Swiss Protestant theologian. A socialist in his political views, he attacked the Nazis. His *Church Dogmatics* 1932–62 makes the resurrection of Jesus the focal point of Christianity.

Barthes /bɑːt/ Roland 1915–1980. French critic and theorist of ◊semiology, the science of signs and symbols. One of the French 'new critics' and an exponent of ◊structuralism, he attacked traditional literary criticism in his early works, including *Le Degré zéro de l'ecriture/Writing Degree Zero* 1953 and *Sur Racine/On Racine* 1963. His structuralist approach involved exposing and analyzing the system of signs, patterns, and laws that may be conveyed by a novel or play. He also wrote an autobiographical novel *Roland Barthes sur Roland Barthes* 1975.

Bartholdi /bɑːˈtɒldi/ Frédéric Auguste 1834–1904. French sculptor. He designed the Statue of Liberty overlooking New York harbour, 1884.

Bartholomew, Massacre of St /bɑːˈθɒləmjuː/ see ◊St Bartholomew, Massacre of.

Bartholomew, St /bɑːˈθɒləmjuː/ in the New Testament, one of the apostles. Some legends relate that after the Crucifixion he took Christianity to India; others that he was a missionary in Anatolia and Armenia, where he suffered martyrdom by being flayed alive. Feast day 24 Aug.

Bartók /ˈbɑːtɒk/ Béla 1881–1945. Hungarian composer. A child prodigy, he studied music at the Budapest Conservatory, later working with ◊Kodály in recording and and transcribing local folk music for a government project. This led him to develop a personal musical language, combining folk elements with mathematical concepts of tone and rhythmic proportion. His large output includes six string quartets, a ballet *The Miraculous Mandarin* 1919, which was banned because of its subject matter (it was set in a brothel), concertos, an opera, and graded teaching pieces for piano. He died in the USA having fled from Hungary 1940.

Bartolommeo /bɑːtɒləˈmeɪəʊ/ Fra, also called *Baccio della Porta* c. 1472–c. 1517. Italian religious painter of the High Renaissance, active in Florence. His painting of *The Last Judgement* 1499 (Museo di San Marco, Florence) influenced Raphael.

Barton /ˈbɑːtn/ Edmund 1849–1920. Australian politician. He was leader of the federation movement from 1896 and first prime minister of Australia 1901–03.

baryon in nuclear physics, a heavy subatomic particle made up of three indivisible elementary particles called quarks. The baryons form a subclass of the ◊hadrons, and comprise the nucleons (protons and neutrons) and hyperons.

Baryshnikov /bəˈrɪʃnɪkɒf/ Mikhail 1948– . Soviet dancer, now in the USA. He joined the Kirov Ballet 1967 and became one of their most brilliant soloists. Defecting while on tour in Canada 1974, he joined American Ballet Theater (ABT) as principal dancer, partnering Gelsey Kirkland. He left to join the New York City Ballet 1978–80, but rejoined ABT as director 1980–90. From 1990 he has danced for various companies.

baryte barium sulphate, $BaSO_4$, the most common mineral of barium. It is white or light-coloured, and has a comparatively high density (specific gravity 4.6); the latter property makes it useful in the production of high-density drilling muds. Baryte occurs mainly in ore veins, where it is often found with calcite and with lead and zinc minerals.

It crystallizes in the orthorhombic system and can form tabular crystals or radiating fibrous masses.

baryton bowed stringed instrument producing an intense singing tone. It is based on an 18th-century viol and modified by the addition of sympathetic (freely vibrating) strings.

basal metabolic rate (BMR) amount of energy needed by an animal just to stay alive. It is measured when the animal is awake but resting, and includes the energy required to keep the heart beating, sustain breathing, repair tissues, and keep the brain and nerves functioning. Measuring the animal's consumption of oxygen gives an accurate value for BMR, because oxygen is needed to release energy from food.

basalt commonest volcanic ◊igneous rock, and the principal rock type on the ocean floor; it is basic, that is, it contains relatively little silica: under 50%. It is usually dark grey, but can also be green, brown, or black.

The groundmass may be glassy or finely crystalline, sometimes with large ◊crystals embedded. Basaltic lava tends to be runny and flows for great distances before solidifying. Successive eruptions of basalt have formed the great plateaux of Colorado and the Indian Deccan. In some places, such as Fingal's Cave in the Inner Hebrides of Scotland and the Giant's Causeway in Antrim, Northern Ireland, shrinkage during the solidification of the molten lava caused the formation of hexagonal columns.

bascule bridge type of drawbridge in which one or two counterweighted deck members pivot upwards to allow shipping to pass underneath. One example is the double bascule Tower Bridge, London.

base in mathematics, the number of different single-digit symbols used in a particular number system. In our usual (decimal) counting system of numbers (with symbols 0, 1, 2, 3, 4, 5, 6, 7, 8, 9) the base is 10. In the ◊binary number system, which has only the symbols 1 and 0, the base is two. A base is also a number that, when raised to a particular power (that is, when multiplied by itself a particular number of times as in $10^2 = 10 \times 10 = 100$), has a ◊logarithm equal to the power. For example, the logarithm of 100 to the base ten is 2.

For bases beyond 10, the denary numbers 10, 11, 12, and so on must be replaced by a single digit. Thus in base 16, all numbers up to 16 must be represented by single-digit

'numbers', since 10 in hexadecimal would mean 16 in decimal. Hence decimal 10, 11, 12, 13, 14, 15 are represented in hexadecimal by letters A, B, C, D, E, F.

base in chemistry, a substance that accepts protons, such as the hydroxide ion (OH^-) and ammonia (NH_3). Bases react with acids to give a salt. Those that dissolve in water are called ◊alkalis.

baseball national summer game of the USA, derived in the 19th century from the English game of ◊rounders. Baseball is a bat-and-ball game played between two teams, each of nine players, on a pitch ('field') marked out in the form of a diamond, with a base at each corner. The ball is struck with a cylindrical bat, and the players try to score ('make a run') by circuiting the bases. A 'home run' is a circuit on one hit.

The game is divided into nine innings, each with two halves, with each team taking turns to bat while the other team takes the field, pitching, catching, and fielding.

The pitcher throws the ball, and the batter tries to make a 'hit'. Having hit the ball, the batter tries to make a run, either in stages from home base to first, second, and third base, and back to home base, or in a 'home run'.

The batter is declared out if (1) he (or she, but the professional leagues have not yet admitted women) fails to hit the ball after 3 'strikes', (2) he hits the ball into the air and it is caught by a fielder, (3) he is touched by the ball in the hand of one of his opponents while he is between bases, and (4) a fielder standing on one of the bases catches the ball before the batter reaches the base.

The first batter is followed by the other members of his team in rotation until three members of the batting side are put out: the opposing team then take their turn to bat. After nine innings, the team scoring the most runs wins the game. The game is controlled by umpires.

The *World Series* was first held as an end-of-season game between the winners of the two professional leagues, the National League and the American League 1903, and was established as a series of seven games 1905. In the USA, the average salary in 1990 of a Major League baseball player in the USA was $890,844.

Basel /ˈbɑːzəl/ or *Basle* (French *Bâle*) financial, commercial, and industrial (dyes, vitamins, agrochemicals, dietary products, genetic products) city in Switzerland; population (1987) 363,000. Basel was a strong military station under the Romans. In 1501 it joined the Swiss confederation and later developed as a centre for the Reformation.

base pair in biochemistry, the linkage of two base (purine or pyrimidine) molecules in ◊DNA. They are found in nucleotides, and form the basis of the genetic code.

One base lies on one strand of the DNA double helix, and one on the other, so that the base pairs link the two strands like the rungs of a ladder. In DNA, there are four bases: adenine and guanine (purines) and cytosine and thymine (pyrimidines).

base rate in economics, the rate of interest to which most bank lending is linked, the actual rate depending on the status of the borrower. A prestigious company might command a rate only 1% above base rate, while an individual would be charged several points above.

An alternative method of interest rates is ◊LIBOR.

Bashkir /bæʃkɪə/ autonomous republic of Russia, with the Ural Mountains on the east
area 143,600 sq km/55,430 sq mi
capital Ufa
products minerals, oil
population (1982) 3,876,000
language Russian, Bashkir (c. 25%)
history annexed by Russia 1557; became the first Soviet autonomous republic 1919.

Bashkir member of the majority ethnic group of the Bashkir Autonomous Soviet Socialist Republic. The Bashkirs have been Muslims since the 13th century. The Bashkir language belongs to the Turkic branch of the Altaic family, and has about 1 million speakers.

Bashô /bɑːʃəʊ/ Pen name of Matsuo Munefusa 1644–1694. Japanese poet who was a master of the *haiku*, a 17-syllable poetic form with lines of 5, 7, and 5 syllables, which he infused with subtle allusiveness and made the accepted form of poetic expression in Japan. His *Oku-no-hosomichi/The Narrow Road to the Deep North* 1694, an account of a visit to northern Japan, consists of haikus interspersed with prose passages.

BASIC (acronym from *b*eginner's *a*ll-purpose *s*ymbolic *i*nstruction *c*ode) computer-programming language, developed 1964, originally designed to take advantage of ◊time-sharing computers (which can be used by many people at the same time). Most versions use an ◊interpreter program, which allows programs to be entered and run with no intermediate translation, although recent versions have been implemented as a ◊compiler. The language is relatively easy to learn and popular among microcomputer users.

Basic English simplified form of English devised and promoted by C K ◊Ogden in the 1920s and 1930s as an international auxiliary language; as a route into Standard English for foreign learners; and as a reminder to the English-speaking world of the virtues of plain language. Its name derives from the initial letters of *B*ritish, *A*merican, *s*cientific, *i*nternational, and *c*ommercial.

Basic has a vocabulary of 850 words (plus names, technical terms, and so on), only 18 of which are verbs or 'operators'. *Get* therefore replaces 'receive', 'obtain', and 'become', while *buy* is replaced by the phrase 'give money for'.

basicity number of replaceable hydrogen atoms in an acid. Nitric acid (HNO_3) is monobasic, sulphuric acid (H_2SO_4) is dibasic, and phosphoric acid (H_3PO_4) is tribasic.

basic-oxygen process most widely used method of steelmaking, involving the blasting of oxygen at supersonic speed into molten pig iron.

Pig iron from a blast furnace, together with steel scrap, is poured into a converter, and a jet of oxygen is then projected into the mixture. The excess carbon in the mix and other impurities quickly burn out or form a slag, and the converter is emptied by tilting. It takes only about 45 minutes to refine 350 tonnes/400 tons of steel. The basic-oxygen process was developed 1948 at a steelworks near the Austrian towns of Linz and Donawitz. It is a version of the ◊Bessemer process.

basidiocarp spore-bearing body, or 'fruiting body', of all basidiomycete fungi (see ◊fungus), except the rusts and smuts. A well-known example is the edible mushroom. Other types include globular basidiocarps (puffballs) or flat ones that project from tree trunks (brackets). They are made up of a mass of tightly packed, intermeshed ◊hyphae.

The tips of these hyphae develop into the reproductive cells, or *basidia*, that form a fertile layer known as the hymenium, or *gills*, of the basidiocarp. Four spores are budded off from the surface of each basidium.

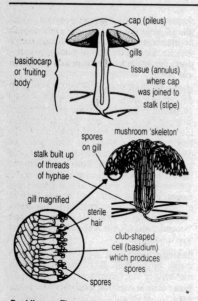

cap (pileus)

basidiocarp or 'fruiting body'

gills

tissue (annulus) where cap was joined to stalk (stipe)

spores on gill

mushroom 'skeleton'

stalk built up of threads of hyphae

gill magnified

sterile hair

club-shaped cell (basidium) which produces spores

spores

Basidiocarp The structure of the mushroom, an example of a basidiocarp.

Basie /ˈbeɪsi/ Count (William) 1904–1984. US jazz band leader, pianist, and organist who developed the big-band sound and a simplified, swinging style of music. He led impressive groups of musicians in a career spanning more than 50 years. Basie's compositions include 'One O'Clock Jump' and 'Jumpin at the Woodside'.

basil or *sweet basil* plant *Ocimum basilicum* of the mint family Labiatae. A native of the tropics, it is cultivated in Europe as a culinary herb.

Basil II /ˈbæzl/ *c.* 958–1025. Byzantine emperor from 976. His achievement as emperor was to contain, and later decisively defeat, the Bulgarians, earning for himself the title 'Bulgar-Slayer' after a victory 1014. After the battle he blinded almost all 15,000 of the defeated, leaving only a few men with one eye to lead their fellows home. The Byzantine empire had reached its largest extent at the time of his death.

Basildon /ˈbæzldən/ industrial ◊new town in Essex, England; population (1981) 152,500. It was designated as a new town 1949 from several townships. Industries include chemicals, clothing, printing, and engineering.

basilica Roman public building; a large roofed hall flanked by columns, generally with an aisle on each side, used for judicial or other public business. The earliest known basilica, at Pompeii, dates from the 2nd century BC. This architectural form was adopted by the early Christians for their churches.

Basilicata /bəˌzɪlɪrkɑːtə/ mountainous region of S Italy, comprising the provinces of Potenza and Matera; area 10,000 sq km/3,860 sq mi; population (1988) 622,000. Its capital is Potenza. It was the Roman province of Lucania.

basilisk South American lizard, genus *Basiliscus*. It is able to run on its hind legs when travelling fast (about 11 kph/7 mph) and may dash a short distance across the surface of water. The male has a well-developed crest on the head, body, and tail.

Basil, St /ˈbæzl/ *c.* 330–379. Cappadocian monk, known as 'the Great', founder of the Basilian monks. Elected bishop of Caesarea 370, Basil opposed the heresy of ◊Arianism. He wrote many theological works and composed the 'Liturgy of St Basil', in use in the Eastern Orthodox Church. Feast day 2 Jan.

Basingstoke /ˈbeɪzɪŋstəʊk/ industrial town in Hampshire, England, 72 km/45 mi WSW of London; population (1981) 67,500. It is the headquarters of the UK Civil Service Commission.

Baskerville /ˈbæskəvɪl/ John 1706–1775. English printer and typographer, who experimented in casting types from 1750 onwards.

He manufactured fine printing paper and inks, and in 1756 published a quarto edition of the Classical poet Virgil, which was followed by 54 highly crafted books. The Baskerville typeface is named after him.

basketball ball game between two teams of five players on an indoor enclosed court. The object is, via a series of passing moves, to throw the large inflated ball through a circular hoop and net positioned at each end of the court, 3.05 m/10 ft above the ground. Basketball was invented by YMCA instructor Dr James Naismith at Springfield, Massachusetts, 1891. The ◊Harlem Globetrotters helped to popularize the game worldwide. The first world championship for men was held in 1950, and in 1953 for women. They are now held every four years.

basketry ancient craft used to make a wide range of objects (from baskets to furniture) by interweaving or plaiting willows, rushes, cane, or other equally strong, natural fibres. ◊Wickerwork is a more rigid type of basketry.

Basketry flourished from the early Middle Ages until the late 19th century (a Basket Maker's Company was formed in London 1569), but cheap imports and alternative packaging led to a decline. In the UK, willow rods (osiers) were specially grown for basketry, and commercial osier beds still survive in Somerset.

Basle /bɑːl/ alternative form of ◊Basel, city in Switzerland.

Basov /ˈbɑːsɒf/ Nikolai Gennadievich 1912– . Soviet physicist who in 1953, with his compatriot Aleksandr Prokhorov, developed the microwave amplifier called a ◊maser. They were both awarded the Nobel Prize for Physics 1964, which they shared with Charles Townes of the USA.

Basque /bæsk/ member of a people who occupy the ◊Basque Country of central N Spain and the extreme SW of France. The Basques are a pre-Indo-European people who largely maintained their independence until the 19th century. During the Spanish Civil War 1936–39, they were on the republican side defeated by Franco. Their language (*Euskara*) is unrelated to any other language. The Basque separatist movement ETA (*Euskadi ta Askatasuna*, 'Basque Nation and Liberty') and the French organization *Iparretarrak* ('ETA fighters from the North Side') have engaged in guerrilla activity from 1968 in an unsuccessful attempt to secure a united Basque state.

Basque Country /bæsk/ (Basque *Euskal Herria*) homeland of the Basque people in the W Pyrenees, divided by the Franco-Spanish border. The Spanish Basque Country (Spanish *País Vasco* is an autonomous region (created 1979) of central N Spain, comprising the provinces of Vizcaya, Alava, and Guipúzcoa (Basque *Bizkaia, Araba*, and *Gipuzkoa*); area 7,300 sq km/ 2,818 sq mi; population (1988) 2,176,790. The French Basque Country (French *Pays Basque*) comprises the arrondissements of Labourd, Basse-Navarre, and Soule (Basque *Lapurdi, Nafarroa Beherea*, and *Zuberoa*). To Basque nationalists *Euskal Herria* also includes the autonomous Spanish province of Navarre.

Basque language language of W Europe known to its speakers, the Basques, as *Eu-skara*, and apparently unrelated to any other language on Earth. It is spoken by some half a million people in central N Spain and SW France, around the Bay of Biscay, as well as by emigrants in both Europe and the Americas.

Although previously forbidden in all public places for most of Franco's rule, Basque is now accepted as a regional language in both France and Spain, and is of central importance to the Basque nationalist movement.

Basra /ˈbæzrə/ (Arabic *al-Basrah*) principal port in Iraq, in the Shatt-al-Arab delta, 97 km/60 mi from the Persian Gulf, founded in the 7th century; population (1977) 1.5 million (1991) 850,000. Exports include wool, oil, cereal, and dates. Aerial bombing during the Gulf War destroyed bridges, factories, power stations, water treatment plants, sewage treatment plants, and the port. A Shi'ite rebellion March 1991 was crushed by the Iraqi army causing further death and destruction.

bass long-bodied scaly sea fish *Morone labrax* found in the N Atlantic and Mediterranean. They grow to 1 m/3 ft, and are often seen in shoals.

Other fish of the same family (Serranidae) are also called bass, as are North American freshwater fishes of the family Centrarchidae, such as black bass and small-mouthed bass.

Bass /bæs/ George 1763–*c.* 1808. English naval surgeon who with Matthew ◊Flinders explored the coast of New South Wales and the strait that bears his name between Tasmania and Australia 1795–98.

Bassein /bɑːˈseɪn/ port in Myanmar (Burma), in the Irrawaddy delta, 125 km/78 mi from the sea; population (1983) 355,588. Bassein was founded in the 13th century.

Basse-Normandie /bæs ˌnɔːmɒnˈdiː/ or *Lower Normandy* coastal region of NW France lying between Haute-Normandie and Brittany (Bretagne). It includes the *départements* of Calvados, Manche, and Orne; area 17,600 sq km/6,794 sq mi; population (1986) 1,373,000. Its capital is Caen. Apart from stock farming, dairy farming, and the production of textiles, the area produces Calvados (apple brandy).

basset type of dog with a long low body, wrinkled forehead, and long pendulous ears, originally bred in France for hunting hares.

Basseterre /bæs'teə/ capital and port of St Kitts–Nevis, in the Leeward Islands; population (1980) 14,000. Industries include data processing, rum, clothes, and electrical components.

Basse-Terre /bæs'teə/ port on the Leeward Island Basse-Terre; population (1982) 13,600. It is the capital of the French overseas *département* of Guadeloupe.

Basse-Terre /bæs'teə/ main island of the French West Indian island group of Guadeloupe; area 848 sq km/327 sq mi; population (1982) 141,300. It has an active volcano, Grande Soufrière, rising to 1,484 m/4,870 ft.

basset horn musical ◊woodwind instrument resembling a clarinet, pitched in F and ending in a brass bell.

bassoon double-reed ◊woodwind instrument, the bass of the oboe family. It doubles back on itself in a tube about 2.5 m/7.5 ft long. Its tone is rich and deep.

Bass Rock /bæs/ islet in the Firth of Forth, Scotland, about 107 m/350 ft high, with a lighthouse.

Bass Strait /bæs/ channel between Australia and Tasmania, named after British explorer George Bass; oil was discovered there in the 1960s.

bastard feudalism late medieval development of ◊feudalism in which grants of land were replaced by money as rewards for service.

Conditions of service were specified in a contract, or indenture, between lord and retainer. The system allowed large numbers of men to be raised quickly for wars or private feuds.

Bastille /bæs'tiːl/ castle of St Antoine, built about 1370 as part of the fortifications of Paris and used for centuries as a state prison; it was singled out for the initial attack by the mob that set the French Revolution in motion 14 July 1789. Only seven prisoners were found in the castle when it was stormed; the governor and most of the garrison were killed, and the Bastille was razed.

Basutoland /bə'suːtəʊlænd/ former name for ◊Lesotho, a kingdom in southern Africa.

bat flying mammal in which the forelimbs are developed as wings capable of rapid and sustained flight. There are two main groups of bats: *megabats*, or *flying foxes*, which eat fruit, and *microbats*, which mainly eat insects. Although by no means blind, many microbats rely largely on echolocation for navigation and finding prey, sending out pulses of high-pitched sound and listening for the echo. Bats are nocturnal, and those native to temperate countries hibernate in winter. There are about 1,000 species of bats forming the order Chiroptera, making this the second-largest mammalian order; bats make up nearly one-quarter of the world's mammals. Although bats are widely distributed, bat populations have declined alarmingly and many species are now endangered.

megabats The Megachiroptera live in the tropical regions of the Old World, Australia, and the Pacific, and feed on fruit, nectar, and pollen. The hind feet have five toes with sharp hooked claws which suspend the animal head downwards when resting. Relatively large, up to 900 g/2 lb with a 1.5 m/5 ft wingspan, they have large eyes and a long face earning them the name 'flying fox'. Many rainforest trees depend on bats for pollination and seed dispersal, and some 300 bat-dependent plant species yield more than 450 economically valuable products. Some bats are keystone species on whose survival whole ecosystems may depend.

microbats Most bats are Microchiroptera, mainly small and insect-eating, though some species feed on blood (◊vampire bats), frogs, or fish. They roost in caves, crevices, and hollow trees. A single bat may eat 3,000 insects in one night.

A bat's wings consist of thin hairless skin stretched between the four fingers of the hand, and from the last finger down to the hindlimb. The thumb is free and has a sharp claw to help in climbing. Some bats live to be over 30 years old. An adult female bat usually rears only one pup a year. The bumble bee bat, inhabiting SE Asian rainforests, is the smallest mammal in the world. In China bats are associated with good luck.

Bataan /bə'tɑːn/ peninsula in Luzon, the Philippines, which was defended against the Japanese in World War II by US and Filipino troops under Gen MacArthur 1 Jan–9 April 1942. MacArthur was evacuated, but some 67,000 Allied prisoners died on the *Bataan Death March* to camps in the interior.

Despite Bataan being in an earthquake zone, the ◊Marcos government built a nuclear power station there, near a dormant volcano. It has never generated any electricity, but in 1989 cost the country $350,000 a week in interest payments.

Batak /bɑːtæk/ member of the several distinct but related peoples of N Sumatra in Indonesia. Numbering approximately 2.5 million, the Batak speak languages belonging to the Austronesian family.

The most numerous and most centrally located are the Toba Batak who live S and W of Lake Toba. Although the Batak possess distinctive traditional beliefs, they were influenced by Hinduism between the 2nd and 15th centuries. The syllabic script of the Batak, which was inscribed on bamboo, horn, bone, and tree bark, is based on Indian scripts. Although the island of Sumatra has many Muslim peoples, most Batak did not adopt Islam. Since 1861 German and other missionaries have been active in N Sumatra and today over 80% of the Batak profess Christianity. Many Batak are rice farmers and produce handicrafts such as dyed textiles.

Batavia /bəˈteɪvɪə/ former name until 1949 for ◊Jakarta, capital of Indonesia on Java.

Batavian Republic /bəˈteɪvɪən/ name given to the Netherlands by the French 1795; it lasted until the establishment of the kingdom of the Netherlands 1814 at the end of the Napoleonic Wars.

batch system in computing, a system for processing data with little or no operator intervention. Batches of data are prepared in advance to be processed during regular 'runs' (for example, each night). This allows efficient use of the computer and is well suited to applications of a repetitive nature, such as a company payroll.

Bateman /ˈbeɪtmən/ H(enry) M(ayo) 1887–1970. Australian cartoonist who lived in England. His cartoons were based on themes of social embarrassment and confusion, in such series as *The Man who . . .* (as in *The Guardsman who Dropped his Rifle*).

Bates /beɪts/ Alan 1934– . English actor, a versatile male lead in over 60 plays and films. His films include *Zorba the Greek* 1965, *Far from the Madding Crowd* 1967, *Women in Love* 1970, *The Go-Between* 1971, and *The Shout* 1978.

Bates /beɪts/ H(enry) W(alter) 1825–1892. English naturalist and explorer, who spent 11 years collecting animals and plants in South America and identified 8,000 new species of insects. He made a special study of ◊camouflage in animals, and his observation of insect imitation of species that are un-

pleasant to predators is known as 'Batesian mimicry'.

Bates /beɪts/ H(erbert) E(rnest) 1906–1974. English author. Of his many novels and short stories, *The Jacaranda Tree* 1949 and *The Darling Buds of May* 1958 demonstrate the fineness of his natural observation and compassionate portrayal of character. *Fair Stood the Wind for France* 1944 was based on his experience as a Squadron Leader in World War II.

Bath /bɑːθ/ historic city in Avon, England; population (1981) 75,000.

features hot springs; the ruins of the baths for which it is named, as well as a great temple, are the finest Roman remains in Britain. Excavations 1979 revealed thousands of coins and 'curses', offered at a place which was thought to be the link between the upper and lower worlds. The Gothic Bath Abbey has an unusually decorated west front and fan vaulting. There is much 18th-century architecture, notably the Royal Crescent by John Wood. The Assembly Rooms 1771 were destroyed in an air raid 1942 but reconstructed 1963. The University of Technology was established 1966.

history the Roman city of Aquae Sulis ('waters of Sul'–the British goddess of wisdom) was built in the first 20 years after the Roman invasion. In medieval times the hot springs were crown property, administered by the church, but the city was transformed in the 18th century to a fashionable spa, presided over by 'Beau' ◊Nash. At his home here the astronomer Herschel discovered Uranus 1781. Visitors included the novelists Smollett, Fielding, and Jane Austen.

Bath, Order of the British order of knighthood, believed to have been founded in the reign of Henry IV (1399–1413). Formally instituted 1815, it included civilians from 1847 and women from 1970. There are three grades: Knights of the Grand Cross (GCB), Knights Commanders (KCB), and Knights Companions (CB).

Báthory /ˈbɑːtəri/ Stephen 1533–1586. King of Poland, elected by a diet convened 1575 and crowned 1576. Báthory succeeded in driving the Russian troops of Ivan the Terrible out of his country. His military successes brought potential conflicts with Sweden, but he died before these developed.

Bathurst /ˈbæθɜːst/ former name (until 1973) of ◊Banjul, capital of the Gambia.

bathyal zone upper part of the ocean, which lies on the continental shelf at a depth of between 200 and 2,000 metres.

bathyscaph or *bathyscaphe* or *bathyscape* deep-sea diving apparatus used for exploration at great depths in the ocean. In 1960, Jacques Piccard and Don Walsh took the bathyscaph *Trieste* to a depth of 10,917 m/ 35,820 ft in the Challenger Deep in the ◊Mariana Trench off the island of Guam in the Pacific Ocean.

batik Javanese technique of hand-applied colour design for fabric; areas to be left undyed in a colour are sealed with wax. Practised throughout Indonesia, the craft was introduced to the West by Dutch traders.

Batista /bə'tiːstə/ Fulgencio 1901–1973. Cuban dictator 1933–44 and 1952–59, whose authoritarian methods enabled him to jail his opponents and amass a large personal fortune. He was overthrown by rebel forces led by Fidel ◊Castro 1959.

Batman comic-strip character created 1939 by US cartoonist Bob Kane and his collaborator Bill Finger. A crime-busting superhero, disguised by a black batlike mask and cape, Batman is, with his sidekick Robin, a staple of the DC Comics group.

Batman's secret identity is that of millionaire playboy Bruce Wayne. His youthful aide, former circus performer Dick Grayson, is known as Robin the boy wonder. Together they zoom around in their 'batmobile' and combat the criminal activities of (among others) the Joker, the Penguin, the Riddler, and the Catwoman. Batman films appeared 1943, 1949, and 1989, and there was a Pop-art-inspired *Batman* television series in the 1960s.

In 1986 US comics writer and artist Frank Miller re-examined the legend in his graphic novel *Batman: The Dark Knight Returns*; his treatment of the ageing superhero as psychopathic vigilante proved highly influential.

Baton Rouge /'bætn 'ruːʒ/ port on the Mississippi River, USA, the capital of Louisiana; population (1987 est) 242,000. Industries include oil refining, petrochemicals, and iron. The bronze marble state capitol was built by Governor Huey ◊Long.

battalion or *unit* basic personnel unit in the military system, usually consisting of four or five companies. A battalion is commanded by a lieutenant colonel. Several battalions form a ◊brigade.

Batten /'bætn/ Jean 1909–1982. New Zealand aviator who made the first return solo flight by a woman Australia–Britain 1935, and established speed records.

Battersea /'bætəsi/ district of the Inner London borough of Wandsworth on the south bank of the Thames. It has a park (including a funfair 1951–74), a classically styled power station, now disused, and Battersea Dogs' Home (opened 1860) for strays.

battery any energy-storage device allowing release of electricity on demand. It is made up of one or more electrical ◊cells.

Primary-cell batteries are disposable; secondary-cell batteries are rechargeable. The common *dry cell* is a primary-cell battery based on the ◊Leclanché cell, and consists of a central carbon electrode immersed in a paste of manganese dioxide and ammonium chloride as the electrolyte. The zinc casing forms the other electrode. It is dangerous to try to recharge a primary-cell battery.

The lead–acid *car battery* is a secondary-cell battery, or accumulator. The car's generator continually recharges the battery. It consists of sets of lead (positive) and lead peroxide (negative) plates in an electrolyte of sulphuric acid (◊battery acid).

The introduction of rechargeable nickel-cadmium batteries has revolutionized portable electronic newsgathering (sound recording, video) and information processing (computing). These batteries offer a stable, short-term source of power free of noise and other hazards associated with mains electricity.

battery acid ◊sulphuric acid of approximately 70% concentration used in lead–acid cells (as found in car batteries).

The chemical reaction within the battery that is responsible for generating electricity also causes a change in the acid's composition. This can be detected as a change in its specific gravity: in a fully charged battery the acid's specific gravity is 1.270–1.290; in a half-charged battery it is 1.190–1.210; in a flat battery it is 1.110–1.130.

Batumi /bə'tuːmi/ port and capital in the Republic of Adzhar, Georgia; population (1984) 111,000. Main industries include oil refining, food canning, and engineering.

baud in engineering, a unit of electrical signalling speed equal to one pulse per second, measuring the rate at which signals are sent between electronic devices such as telegraphs and computers; 300 baud is about 300 words a minute.

Baudelaire /ˌbəʊdəˈleə/ Charles Pierre 1821–1867. French poet whose work combined rhythmical and musical perfection with a morbid romanticism and eroticism, finding beauty in decadence and evil. His first book of verse was *Les Fleurs du mal/Flowers of Evil* 1857.

Baudouin /ˌbəʊduˈæn/ 1930–1993. King of the Belgians from 1951. In 1950 his father, ◊Leopold III, abdicated and Baudouin was known until his succession July 1951 as *Le Prince Royal*. In 1960 he married Fabiola de Mora y Aragón (1928–), member of a Spanish noble family.

Bauhaus /ˈbaʊhaʊs/ German school of architecture and design founded 1919 by the architect Walter ◊Gropius at Weimar in Germany in an attempt to fuse all arts, design, architecture, and crafts into a unified whole. Moved to Dessau under political pressure 1925, it was closed by the Nazis 1933 because of 'decadence'. Associated with the Bauhaus were the artists Klee and Kandinsky and the architect Mies van der Rohe. Gropius and Marcel Breuer worked together in the USA 1937–40.

Bául /ˈbɑːʊl/ member of a Bengali mystical sect that emphasizes freedom from compulsion, from doctrine, and from social caste; they avoid all outward forms of religious worship. Not ascetic, they aim for harmony between physical and spiritual needs.

An oral tradition is passed down by gurus (teachers). The Báuls make extensive use of music and poetry.

Baum /bɔːm/ L(yman) Frank 1856–1919. US writer, author of the children's fantasy *The Wonderful Wizard of Oz* 1900 and its 13 sequels. The series was continued by another author after his death. The film *The Wizard of Oz* 1939 was one of the most popular of all time.

Bausch /baʊʃ/ Pina 1940– . German avant-garde dance choreographer and director from 1974 of the Wuppertal Tanztheater. Her works incorporate dialogue, elements of psychoanalysis, comedy, and drama, and have been performed on floors covered with churned earth, rose petals, or water.

bauxite principal ore of ◊aluminium, consisting of a mixture of hydrated aluminium oxides and hydroxides, generally contaminated with compounds of iron, which give it a red colour. Chief producers of bauxite are Australia, Guinea, Jamaica, Russia, Suriname, and Brazil.

Bavaria /bəˈveəriə/ (German *Bayern*) administrative region (German *Land*) of Germany
area 70,600 sq km/27,252 sq mi
capital Munich
towns Nuremberg, Augsburg, Würzburg, Regensburg
features largest of the German *Länder*; forms the Danube basin; festivals at Bayreuth and Oberammergau
products beer, electronics, electrical engineering, optics, cars, aerospace, chemicals, plastics, oil refining, textiles, glass, toys
population (1988) 11,000,000
famous people Lucas Cranach, Adolf Hitler, Franz Josef Strauss, Richard Strauss
religion 70% Roman Catholic, 26% Protestant
history the last king, Ludwig III, abdicated 1918, and Bavaria declared itself a republic.

The original Bavarians were Teutonic invaders from Bohemia who occupied the country at the end of the 5th century. They were later ruled by dukes who recognized the supremacy of the Holy Roman emperor. The house of Wittelsbach ruled parts or all of Bavaria 1181–1918; Napoleon made the ruler a king 1806. In 1871 Bavaria became a state of the German Empire.

Bawa /ˈbaʊə/ Geoffrey 1919– . Sri Lankan architect, formerly a barrister. His buildings are a contemporary interpretation of vernacular traditions, and include houses, hotels, and gardens. More recently he has designed public buildings such as the New Parliamentary Complex, Colombo 1982, and Ruhuru University, Matara 1984.

Baxter /ˈbækstə/ George 1804–1867. English engraver and printmaker; inventor 1834 of a special process for printing in oil colours, which he applied successfully in book illustrations.

bay various species of ◊laurel, genus *Laurus*. The aromatic evergreen leaves are used for flavouring in cookery. There is also a golden-leaved variety.

Bayard /ˈbeɪɑːd/ Pierre du Terrail, Chevalier de 1473–1524. French soldier. He served under Charles VIII, Louis XII, and Francis I and was killed in action at the crossing of the Sesia in Italy. His heroic exploits in battle and in tournaments, and his chivalry and magnanimity, won him the accolade of 'knight without fear and without reproach'.

Bayer (Farbenfabriken Bayer AG) German chemical and pharmaceutical company, the largest chemical multinational in Europe, founded 1863. Its 1990 profits were about $1 billion and it manufactures about 10,000 products for industry. Its headquarters are in Leverkusen, Germany.

The company was founded by industrialist Friedrich Bayer (1825–1880), initially to manufacture dyestuffs, and was reconstituted after World War II. It was a chemist employed by Bayer, C Witthauer, who developed and patented ◊aspirin 1899.

Bayes /beɪz/ Thomas 1702–1761. English mathematician whose investigations into probability led to what is now known as Bayes' theorem.

Bayesian statistics form of statistics that uses the knowledge of prior probability together with the probability of actual data to determine posterior probabilities, using Bayes' theorem.

Bayes' theorem in statistics, a theorem relating the ◊probability of particular events taking place to the probability that events conditional upon them have occurred.

For example, the probability of picking an ace at random out of a pack of cards is 4/52. If two cards are picked out, the probability of the second card being an ace is conditional on the first card: if the first card was an ace the probability will be 3/51; if not it will be 4/51. Bayes' theorem gives the probability that given that the second card is an ace, the first card is also.

Bayeux /baɪˈɜː/ town in N France; population (1982) 15,200. Its museum houses the Bayeux Tapestry. There is a 13th-century Gothic cathedral. Bayeux was the first town in W Europe to be liberated by the Allies in World War II, 8 June 1944.

Bayeux Tapestry linen hanging made about 1067–70, which gives a vivid pictorial record of the invasion of England by William I (the Conqueror) 1066. It is an embroidery rather than a true tapestry, sewn with woollen threads in blue, green, red, and yellow, 70 m/31 ft long and 50 cm/20 in wide and containing 72 separate scenes with descriptive wording in Latin. It is exhibited at the museum of Bayeaux in Normandy, France.

Bayle /beɪl/ Pierre 1647–1706. French critic and philosopher. He was suspended from the chair of philosophy at Rotterdam under suspicion of religious scepticism 1693. Three years later his *Dictionnaire historique et critique* appeared, which influenced among others the French *Encyclopédistes*.

Bayliss /ˈbeɪlɪs/ William Maddock 1860–1924. English physiologist who discovered the digestive hormone secretin with Ernest ◊Starling 1902. During World War I, Bayliss introduced the use of saline (salt water) injections to help the injured recover from ◊shock.

Bay of Pigs inlet on the S coast of Cuba about 145 km/90 mi SW of Havana. It was the site of an unsuccessful invasion attempt by 1,500 US-sponsored Cuban exiles 17–20 April 1961; 1,173 were taken prisoner.

The creation of this antirevolutionary force by the CIA had been authorized by the Eisenhower administration, and the project was executed under that of J F Kennedy. In 1962 most of the Cuban prisoners were ransomed for $53 million in food and medicine. The incident served to strengthen Cuba's links with the USSR.

bayonet short sword attached to the muzzle of a firearm. The bayonet was placed inside the barrel of the muzzle-loading muskets of the late 17th century. The *sock* or ring bayonet, invented 1700, allowed a weapon to be fired without interruption, leading to the demise of the pike.

Since the 1700s, bayonets have evolved into a variety of types. During World War I, the French used a long needle bayonet, while the Germans attached a bayonet, known as the butcher's knife, to their Mauser 98s. As armies have become more mechanized, bayonets have tended to decrease in length.

The new British Army rifle, the SA-80, is fitted with a bayonet; its predecessor, the SLR, was similarly equipped and used, with its bayonet, during the 1982 Falklands conflict.

Bayonne /baɪˈɒn/ river port in SW France; population (1983) 127,000. It trades in timber, steel, fertiliser, and brandy. It is a centre of ◊Basque life. The bayonet was invented here.

bayou (corruption of French *boyau* 'gut') in the Gulf States, USA, an ◊oxbow lake or marshy offshoot of a river.

Bayous may be formed, as in the lower Mississippi, by a river flowing in wide curves or meanders in flat country, and then cutting a straight course across them in times of flood, leaving loops of isolated water behind.

Bayreuth /baɪˈrɔɪt/ town in Bavaria, S Germany, where opera festivals are held every summer; population (1983) 71,000. It was the home of composer Richard ◊Wagner, and the Wagner theatre was established 1876.

Bazalgette /ˈbæzldʒet/ Joseph 1819–1890. British civil engineer who, as chief engineer to the London Board of Works, designed London's sewer system, a total of 155 km/83 mi of sewers, covering an area of 256 sq km/100 sq mi. It was completed 1865. He also designed the Victoria Embankment 1864–70, which was built over the river Thames and combined a main sewer, a water frontage, an underground railway, and a road.

BBC abbreviation for ◊*British Broadcasting Corporation*.

BBC English see ◊English language.

BCE abbreviation for *before the Common Era*; used with dates (instead of BC) by archaeologists in the Near East who are not Christian.

B cell or *B* ◊*lymphocyte* immune cell that produces ◊antibodies. Each B cell produces just one type of antibody, specific to a single ◊antigen.

BCG (abbreviation for *bacillus of Calmette and Guérin*) bacillus used as a vaccine to confer active immunity to ◊tuberculosis (TB).

BCG was developed by Albert Calmette and Camille Guérin in France 1921 from live bovine TB bacilli. These bacteria were bred in the laboratory over many generations until they became attenuated (weakened). Each inoculation contains just enough live, attenuated bacilli to provoke an immune response: the formation of specific ◊antibodies. The recipient then has lifelong protection against TB.

beach strip of land bordering the sea, normally consisting of boulders and pebbles on exposed coasts or sand on sheltered coasts. It is usually defined by the high- and low-water marks.

The material of the beach consists of a rocky debris eroded from exposed rocks and headlands. The material is transported to the beach, and along the beach, by waves that hit the coastline at an angle, resulting in a net movement of the material in one particular direction. This movement is known as *longshore drift*. Attempts are often made to halt longshore drift by erecting barriers, or jetties, at right angles to the movement. Pebbles are worn into round shapes by being battered against one another by wave action and the result is called *shingle*. The finer material, the *sand*, may be subsequently moved about by the wind and form sand dunes. Apart from the natural process of longshore drift, a beach may be threatened by the commercial use of sand and aggregate, by the mineral industry—since particles of metal ore are often concentrated into workable deposits by the wave action— and by pollution.

Concern for the conditions of bathing beaches led in the 1980s to a directive from the European Economic Community on water quality. In the UK, beaches free of industrial pollution, litter, and sewage, and with water of the highest quality, have the right (since 1988) to fly a blue flag.

Beach Boys, the US pop group formed 1961. They began as exponents of vocal-harmony surf music with Chuck Berry guitar riffs (their hits include 'Surfin' USA' 1963 and 'Help Me, Rhonda' 1965) but the compositions, arrangements, and production by Brian Wilson (1942–) became highly complex under the influence of psychedelic rock, peaking with 'Good Vibrations' 1966. Wilson spent most of the next 20 years in retirement but returned with a solo album 1988.

Beachy Head /ˈbiːtʃi/ (French *Bévéziers*) loftiest headland (162 m/532 ft high) on the south coast of England, between Seaford and Eastbourne in Sussex, the eastern termination of the South Downs. The lighthouse off the shore is 38 m/125 ft high.

Beadle /ˈbiːdl/ George Wells 1903–1989. US biologist. Born in Wahoo, Nebraska, he was professor of biology at the California Institute of Technology 1946–61. In 1958 he shared a Nobel prize with Edward L Tatum for his work in biochemical genetics, forming the 'one-gene–one-enzyme' hypothesis (a single gene codes for a single kind of enzyme).

beagle short-haired hound with pendant ears, sickle tail, and a bell-like voice for hunting hares on foot ('beagling').

Beagle Channel /ˈbiːgl/ channel to the south of Tierra del Fuego, South America, named after the ship of Charles ◊Darwin's voyage. Three islands at its eastern end, with krill and oil reserves within their 322 km/200 mi territorial waters, and the dependent sector of the Antarctic with its resources, were disputed between Argentina and Chile and awarded to Chile 1985.

beak horn-covered projecting jaws of a bird, or other horny jaws such as those of the tortoise or octopus. The beaks of birds are adapted by shape and size to specific diets.

Beaker people people thought to be of Iberian origin who spread out over Europe from the 3rd millennium BC. They were skilled in metalworking, and are identified by their use of distinctive earthenware beakers with stamped designs, of which the bell-beaker type was widely distributed throughout Europe. They favoured inhumation (burial of the intact body), in a trench or under a round ◊barrow, or secondary burials in some form of chamber tomb. A beaker accompanied each burial, to hold a drink for the deceased on their final journey.

In Britain, the Beaker people have been asso- ciated with later stages of the construction of ◊Stonehenge.

Beale /biːl/ Dorothea 1831–1906. British pioneer in women's education whose work helped to raise the standard of women's education and the status of women teachers. She was headmistress of the Ladies' College at Cheltenham from 1858, and founder of St Hilda's Hall, Oxford, 1892.

beam balance instrument for measuring mass (or weight). A simple form consists of a beam pivoted at its midpoint with a pan hanging at each end. The mass to be measured, in one pan, is compared with a variety of standard masses placed in the other. When the beam is balanced, the masses' turning effects or moments under gravity, and hence the masses themselves, are equal.

beam weapon weapon capable of destroying a target by means of a high-energy beam. Beam weapons similar to the 'death ray' of science fiction have been explored, most notably during Ronald Reagan's presidential term in the 1980s in the USA.

The *high-energy laser* (HEL) produces a beam of high accuracy that burns through the surface of its target. The USSR is thought to have an HEL able to put orbiting spacecraft out of action. The *charged particle beam* uses either electrons or protons, which have been accelerated almost to the speed of light, to slice through its target.

bean any seed of numerous leguminous plants. Beans are rich in nitrogenous or protein matter and are grown both for human consumption and as food for cattle and horses. Varieties of bean are grown throughout Europe, the USA, South America, China, Japan, SE Asia, and Australia.

The broad bean *Vicia faba* has been cultivated in Europe since prehistoric times. The French bean, kidney bean, or haricot *Phaseolus vulgaris* is probably of South American origin; the runner bean *Phaseolus coccineus* is closely allied to it, but differs in its climbing habit. Among beans of warmer countries are the lima or butter bean *Phaseolus lunatus* of South America, the soya bean *Glycine max*, extensively used in China and Japan, and the winged bean *Psophocarpus tetragonolobus* of SE Asia. The tuberous root of the winged bean has potential as a main crop in tropical areas where protein deficiency is common. The Asian mung bean *Phaseolus mungo* yields the bean sprouts used in Chinese cookery. Canned baked beans are usually a variety of *Phaseolus vulgaris*, which grows well in the USA.

bear large mammal with a heavily built body, short powerful limbs, and a very short tail. Bears breed once a year, producing one to four cubs. In northern regions they hibernate, and the young are born in the winter den. They are found mainly in North America and N Asia. The skin of the polar bear is black to conserve 80–90% of the solar energy trapped and channelled down the hollow hairs of its fur.

Bears walk on the soles of the feet and have long, nonretractable claws. There are seven species of bear, including the *brown bear Ursus arctos*, formerly ranging across most of Europe, N Asia, and North America, but now reduced in number. It varies in

Bear The polar bear ranges over the coasts and ice floes of the Arctic Ocean, to the southern limit of the ice.

size from under 2 m/7 ft long in parts of the Old World to 2.8 m/9 ft long and 780 kg/ 1,700 lb in Alaska. The *grizzly bear* is a North American variety of this species and another subspecies, the *Kodiak bear* of Alaska, is the largest living land carnivore. The white *polar bear Thalarctos maritimus* is up to 2.5 m/8 ft long, has furry undersides to the feet, and feeds mainly on seals. It is found in the north polar region. The North American *black bear Euarctos americanus* and the *Asian black bear Selenarctos thibetanus* are smaller, only about 1.6 m/5 ft long. The latter has a white V-mark on its chest. The *spectacled bear Tremarctos ornatus* of the Andes is similarly sized, as is the *sloth bear Melursus ursinus* of India and Sri Lanka, which has a shaggy coat and uses its claws and protrusile lips to obtain termites, one of its preferred foods. The smallest bear is the Malaysian *sun bear Helarctos malayanus*, rarely more than 1.2 m/4 ft long, a good climber, whose favourite food is honey. The bear family, Ursidae, is related to carnivores such as dogs and weasels, and all are capable of killing prey. The panda is probably related to both bears and raccoons.

bear in business, a speculator who sells stocks or shares on the stock exchange expecting a fall in the price in order to buy them back at a profit, the opposite of a ◊bull. In a bear market, prices fall, and bears prosper.

bearberry any of several species of evergreen trailing shrub, genus *Arctostaphylos*, of the heath family, found on uplands and rocky places. Most bearberries are North American but *A. uva-ursi* is also found in Asia and Europe in northern mountainous regions. It bears small pink flowers in spring, followed by red berries that are edible but dry.

Beardsley /ˈbɪədzli/ Aubrey (Vincent) 1872–1898. British illustrator. His meticulously executed black-and-white work displays the sinuous line and decorative mannerisms of Art Nouveau and was often charged with being grotesque and decadent.

bearing device used in a machine to allow free movement between two parts, typically the rotation of a shaft in a housing. *Ball bearings* consist of two rings, one fixed to a housing, one to the rotating shaft. Between them is a set, or race, of steel balls. They are widely used to support shafts, as in the spindle in the hub of a bicycle wheel.

The *sleeve*, or *journal, bearing* is the simplest bearing. It is a hollow cylinder, split into two halves. It is used for the big-end and main bearings on a car ◊crankshaft.

In some machinery the balls of ball bearings are replaced by cylindrical rollers or thinner, *needle bearings*. In precision equipment such as watches and aircraft instruments, bearings may be made from material such as ruby and are known as *jewel bearings*. For some applications bearings made from nylon and other plastics are used. They need no lubrication because their surfaces are naturally waxy.

bearing angle that a fixed, distant point makes with true or magnetic north at the point of observation, or the angle of the path of a moving object with respect to the north lines. Bearings are measured in degrees and given as three-digit numbers increasing clockwise. For instance, NE would be denoted as 045M or 045T, depending whether the reference line were magnetic (M) or true (T) north.

beat regular variation in the loudness of the sound when two notes of nearly equal pitch or ◊frequency are heard together. Beats result from the ◊interference between the sound waves of the notes. The frequency of the beats equals the difference in frequency of the notes.

Beat Generation or *Beat Movement* beatniks of the 1950s and 1960s, usually in their teens and early twenties, who rejected conventional lifestyles and opted for life on the road, drug experimentation, and antimaterialist values; and the associated literary movement whose members included William S Burroughs, Lawrence Ferlinghetti, Allen ◊Ginsberg, and Jack ◊Kerouac (who is credited with coining the term).

Beatitudes in the New Testament, the sayings of Jesus reported in Matthew 6: 1–12 and Luke 6: 20–38, depicting the spiritual qualities that characterize members of the Kingdom of God.

Beatles, the /ˈbiːtlz/ English pop group 1960–70. The members, all born in Liverpool, were John Lennon (1940–80, rhythm guitar, vocals), Paul McCartney (1942– , bass, vocals), George Harrison (1943– , lead guitar, vocals), and Ringo Starr (formerly Richard Starkey, 1940– , drums). Using songs written largely by Lennon and McCartney, the Beatles dominated rock music and pop culture in the 1960s.

Beatles The back cover of the album *A Hard Day's Night*

The Beatles gained early experience in Liverpool and Hamburg, West Germany. They had a top-30 hit with their first record, 'Love Me Do' 1962, and every subsequent single and album released until 1967 reached number one in the UK charts. At the peak of Beatlemania they starred in two films, *A Hard Day's Night* 1964 and *Help!* 1965, and provided the voices for the animated film *Yellow Submarine* 1968. Their song 'Yesterday' 1965 was covered by 1,186 different performers in the first ten years. The album *Sgt Pepper's Lonely Hearts Club Band* 1967, recorded on two four-track machines, anticipated subsequent technological developments.

beat music pop music that evolved in the UK in the early 1960s, known in its purest form as ◊Mersey beat, and as British Invasion in the USA. The beat groups characteristically had a simple, guitar-dominated line-up, vocal harmonies, and catchy tunes. They included the Beatles (1960–70), the Hollies (1962–), and the Zombies (1962–67).

Beaton /ˈbiːtn/ Cecil 1904–1980. English portrait and fashion photographer, designer, illustrator, diarist, and conversationalist. He produced portrait studies and also designed scenery and costumes for ballets, and sets for plays and films.

Beaton /ˈbiːtn/ David 1494–1546. Scottish nationalist cardinal and politician, adviser to James V. Under Mary Queen of Scots, he was opposed to the alliance with England and persecuted reformers such as George Wishart, who was condemned to the stake; he was killed by Wishart's friends.

Beatrix /ˈbɪətrɪks/ 1938– . Queen of the Netherlands. The eldest daughter of Queen ◊Juliana, she succeeded to the throne on her mother's abdication 1980. In 1966 she married West German diplomat Claus von Amsberg (1926–), who was created Prince of the Netherlands. Her heir is Prince Willem Alexander (1967–).

Beattie /ˈbiːti/ John Hugh Marshall 1915–1990. British anthropologist whose work on cross-cultural analysis influenced researchers in other fields, particularly philosophy. His book *Other Cultures: Aims, Methods and Achievements in Social Anthropology* 1964 has been translated into many languages. Beattie was appointed University Lecturer in Social Anthropology at Oxford 1953 and took up the Chair in Cultural Anthropology and Sociology of Africa in Leiden 1971.

Beatty /ˈbiːti/ David, 1st Earl 1871–1936. British admiral in World War I. He commanded the cruiser squadron 1912–16 and bore the brunt of the Battle of Jutland.

In 1916 he became commander of the fleet, and in 1918 received the surrender of the German fleet.

Beaufort /ˈbəʊfət/ Francis 1774–1857. British admiral, hydrographer to the Royal Navy from 1829; the Beaufort scale and the Beaufort Sea in the Arctic Ocean are named after him.

Beaufort /ˈbəʊfət/ Henry 1375–1447. English priest, bishop of Lincoln from 1398, of Winchester from 1405. As chancellor of England, he supported his half-brother Henry IV, and made enormous personal loans to Henry V to finance war against France. As a guardian of Henry VI from 1421, he was in effective control of the country until 1426. In the same year he was created a cardinal. In 1431 he crowned Henry VI as king of France in Paris.

Beaufort scale system of recording wind velocity, devised by Francis Beaufort 1806. It is a numerical scale ranging from 0 to 17, calm being indicated by 0 and a hurricane by 12; 13–17 indicate degrees of hurricane force.

In 1874, the scale received international recognition; it was modified 1926. Measurements are made at 10 m/33 ft above ground level.

Beaufort Sea /ˈbəʊfət/ section of the Arctic Ocean off Alaska and Canada, named after Francis Beaufort. Oil drilling is allowed only in the winter months because the sea is the breeding and migration route of bowhead whales, the staple diet of the local Inuit people.

Beauharnais /ˌbəʊɑːˈneɪ/ Alexandre, Vicomte de 1760–1794. French liberal aristocrat and general who served in the American Revolution and became a member of the National Convention in the early days of the French Revolution. He was the first husband of Josephine (consort of Napoleon I). Their daughter Hortense (1783–1837) married Louis, a younger brother of Napoleon, and their son became ◊Napoleon III. Beauharnais was guillotined during the Terror for his alleged lack of zeal for the revolutionary cause and his lack of success as Commander of the Republican Army of the North.

Beaujolais /ˈbəʊʒəleɪ/ light, fruity red wine produced in the area S of Burgundy in E France. Beaujolais is best drunk while young; the broaching date is the third Thursday in Nov, when the new vintage is rushed to the USA, the UK, Japan and other countries, so that the Beaujolais *nouveau* (new Beaujolais) may be marketed.

Beaulieu /ˈbjuːli/ village in Hampshire, England; 9 km/6 mi SW of Southampton; population (1985) 1,200. The former abbey is the home of Lord Montagu of Beaulieu and has the Montagu Museum of vintage cars.

Beauly Firth /ˈbjuːli/ arm of the North Sea cutting into Scotland N of Inverness, spanned by Kessock Bridge 1982.

Beaumarchais /ˌbəʊmɑːˈʃeɪ/ Pierre Augustin Caron de 1732–1799. French dramatist. His great comedies *Le Barbier de Seville/The Barber of Seville* 1775 and *Le Mariage de Figaro/The Marriage of Figaro* (1778, but prohibited until 1784) form the basis of operas by ◊Rossini and ◊Mozart.

Louis XVI entrusted Beaumarchais with secret missions, notably for the profitable shipment of arms to the American colonies during the War of Independence. Accused of treason 1792, he fled to Holland and England, but in 1799 he returned to Paris.

Beaumont /ˈbəʊmɒnt/ Francis 1584–1616. English dramatist and poet. From about 1608 he collaborated with John ◊Fletcher. Their joint plays include *Philaster* 1610, *The Maid's Tragedy* about 1611, and *A King and No King* about 1611. *The Woman Hater* about 1606 and *The Knight of the Burning Pestle* about 1607 are ascribed to Beaumont alone.

Beaumont /ˈbəʊmɒnt/ William 1785–1853. US surgeon who conducted pioneering experiments on the digestive system. In 1882 he saved the life of a Canadian trapper wounded in the side by a gun blast; the wound only partially healed and, through an opening in the stomach wall, Beaumont was able to observe the workings of the stomach. His *Experiments and Observations on the Gastric Juice and the Physiology of Digestion* was published 1833.

Beaufort scale

number and description	features	air speed mi per hr	m per sec
0 calm	smoke rises vertically; water smooth	less than 1	less than 0.3
1 light air	smoke shows wind direction; water ruffled	1–3	0.3–1.5
2 slight breeze	leaves rustle; wind felt on face	4–7	1.6–3.3
3 gentle breeze	loose paper blows around	8–12	3.4–5.4
4 moderate breeze	branches sway	13–18	5.5–7.9
5 fresh breeze	small trees sway, leaves blown off	19–24	8.0–10.7
6 strong breeze	whistling in telephone wires; sea spray from waves	25–31	10.8–13.8
7 moderate gale	large trees sway	32–38	13.9–17.1
8 fresh gale	twigs break from trees	39–46	17.2–20.7
9 strong gale	branches break from trees	47–54	20.8–24.4
10 whole gale	trees uprooted, weak buildings collapse	55–63	24.5–28.4
11 storm	widespread damage	64–72	28.5–32.6
12 hurricane	widespread structural damage	73–82	above 32.7

Beaune /bəʊn/ town SW of Dijon, France; population (1982) 21,100. It is the centre of the Burgundian wine trade, and has a wine museum. Other products include agricultural equipment and mustard.

Beauregard /ˌbəʊrəˈgɑː/ Pierre 1818–1893. US Confederate general whose opening fire on ◊Fort Sumter, South Carolina, started the American Civil War 1861.

'Beauty and the Beast' European folk tale about a traveller who receives mysterious overnight hospitality in a woodland palace, only meeting the benevolent owner, a hideous creature, the following morning. The Beast, furious at the theft of a rose by the traveller, agrees to forgive him on condition that his beautiful daughter comes willingly to live with him in the palace. Beauty consents and grows to love the Beast for his gentle character, finally breaking the spell of his hideous appearance by agreeing to marry him. The story first appeared in English 1757 in a translation from the French version of Madame de Beaumont.

Beauvais /bəʊˈveɪ/ town 76 km/47 mi NW of Paris, France; population (1982) 54,150. It is a market town trading in fruit, dairy produce, and agricultural machinery. Beauvais has a Gothic cathedral, the tallest in France: (68 m/223 ft), and is renowned for tapestries (which are now made at the ◊Gobelins factory, Paris).

Planned to be the greatest church ever built, the cathedral choir, built from 1250, was at 158 ft/48 m the tallest of any Gothic cathedral, but it collapsed 1284, and the tower over the crossing followed it 1573.

Beauvoir /bəʊˈvwɑː/ Simone de 1908–1986. French socialist, feminist, and writer who taught philosophy at the Sorbonne university in Paris 1931–43. Her book *Le Deuxième sexe/The Second Sex* 1949 became a seminal work for many feminists. Her novel of postwar Paris, *Les Mandarins/The Mandarins* 1954, has characters resembling the writers Albert Camus, Arthur Koestler, and Jean-Paul ◊Sartre. She also published autobiographical volumes.

beaver aquatic rodent *Castor fiber* with webbed hind feet, a broad flat scaly tail, and thick waterproof fur. It has very large incisor teeth and fells trees to feed on the bark and to use the logs to construct the 'lodge', in which the young are reared, food is stored, and where much of the winter is spent.

Beavers can construct dams on streams, and thus modify the environment considerably. They once ranged across Europe, N Asia, and North America, but in Europe now only survive where they are protected, and are reduced elsewhere, partly through trapping for their fur.

Beaverbrook /ˈbiːvəbrʊk/ (William) Max(well) Aitken, 1st Baron Beaverbrook 1879–1964. British financier, newspaper proprietor, and politician, born in Canada. He bought a majority interest in the *Daily Express* 1919, founded the *Sunday Express* 1921, and bought the London *Evening Standard* 1929. He served in Lloyd George's World War I cabinet and Churchill's World War II cabinet.

Between the wars he used his newspapers, in particular the *Daily Express*, to campaign for empire and free trade and against Prime Minister Baldwin.

Bebel /ˈbeɪbəl/ August 1840–1913. German socialist and founding member of the Verband deutsche Arbeitervereine (League of German Workers' Clubs), together with Wilhelm Liebknecht 1869. Also known as the Eisenach Party, he became its leading speaker in the Reichstag; it was based in Saxony and SW Germany before being incorporated into the SPD (Sozialdemokratische Partei Deutschlands/German Social Democratic Party) 1875.

Bebington /ˈbebɪŋtən/ town on Merseyside, England; population (1981) 64,150. Industries include oil and chemicals. There is a model housing estate originally built 1888 for Unilever workers, Port Sunlight.

bebop or *bop* hot jazz style, rhythmically complex, virtuosic, and highly improvisational, developed in New York 1945–55 by Charlie Parker, Dizzy Gillespie, Thelonius Monk, and other black musicians disaffected with dance bands and racism, and determined to create music that would be too difficult for white people to play.

Beccaria /bekəˈriːə/ Cesare, Marese di Beccaria 1738–1794. Italian philanthropist, born in Milan. He opposed capital punishment and torture; advocated education as a crime preventative; influenced English philosopher Jeremy ◊Bentham; and coined the phrase 'the greatest happiness of the greatest number', the tenet of ◊utilitarianism.

Bechet /ˈbeʃeɪ/ Sidney (Joseph) 1897–1959. US jazz musician, born in New Orleans. He played clarinet and was the first to forge an individual style on soprano saxophone. Bechet was based in Paris in the late 1920s and the 1950s, where he was recognized by classical musicians as a serious artist.

Bechuanaland /ˌbetʃuˈɑːnəlænd/ former name until 1966 of ◊Botswana.

Becker /bekə/ Boris 1967– . German lawn-tennis player. In 1985 he became the youngest winner of a singles title at Wimbledon at the age of 17. He has won the title three times and helped West Germany to win the Davis Cup 1988 and 1989. He also won the US Open 1989.

Becker /bekə/ Lydia 1827–1890. English botanist and campaigner for women's rights. She established the Manchester Ladies Literary Society 1865 as a forum for women to study scientific subjects. In 1867 she co-founded and became secretary of the National Society for Women's Suffrage. In 1870 she founded a monthly newsletter, *The Women's Suffrage Journal*.

Becket /bekɪt/ St Thomas à 1118–1170. English priest and politician. He was chancellor to ◊Henry II 1155–62, when he was appointed archbishop of Canterbury. The interests of the church soon conflicted with those of the crown and Becket was assassinated; he was canonized 1172.

In 1164 he opposed Henry's attempt to regulate the relations between church and state, and had to flee the country; he returned 1170, but the reconciliation soon broke down. Encouraged by a hasty outburst from the king, four knights murdered Becket before the altar of Canterbury cathedral. He was declared a saint, and his shrine became the busiest centre of pilgrimage in England until the Reformation.

Beckett /bekɪt/ Samuel 1906–1989. Irish novelist and dramatist who wrote in French and English. His *En attendant Godot/Waiting for Godot* 1952 is possibly the most universally known example of Theatre of the ◊Absurd, in which life is taken to be meaningless. This genre is taken to further extremes in *Fin de Partie/Endgame* 1957 and *Happy Days* 1961. Nobel Prize for Literature 1969.

Beckmann /bekmən/ Max 1884–1950. German Expressionist painter who fled the Nazi regime for the USA 1933. After World War I his art was devoted to themes of cruelty in human society, portraying sadists and their victims with a harsh style of realism.

becquerel SI unit (symbol Bq) of ◊radioactivity, equal to one radioactive disintegration (change in the nucleus of an atom when a particle or ray is given off) per second.

The becquerel is much smaller than the previous standard unit, the ◊curie, and so can be used for measuring smaller quantities of radioactivity. It is named after Antoine Becquerel.

Becquerel /ˌbekəˈrel/ Antoine Henri 1852–1908. French physicist who discovered penetrating radiation coming from uranium salts, the first indication of ◊radioactivity, and shared a Nobel prize with Marie and Pierre ◊Curie 1903.

bed in geology, a single ◊sedimentary rock unit with a distinct set of physical characteristics or contained fossils, readily distinguishable from those of beds above and below. Well-defined partings called *bedding planes* separate successive beds or strata.

The depth of a bed can vary from a fraction of a centimetre to several metres or feet, and can extend over any area. The term is also used to indicate the floor beneath a body of water (lake bed) and a layer formed by a fall of particles (lava bed).

bedbug flattened wingless red-brown insect *Cimex lectularius* with piercing mouthparts. It hides by day in crevices or bedclothes, and emerges at night to suck human blood.

Bede /biːd/ *c.* 673–735. English theologian and historian, known as *the Venerable Bede*, active in Durham and Northumbria. He wrote many scientific, theological, and historical works. His *Historia Ecclesiastica Gentis Anglorum/Ecclesiastical History of the English People* 731 is a seminal source for early English history.

Born at Monkwearmouth, Durham, he entered the local monastery at the age of seven, later transferring to Jarrow, where he became a priest in about 703.

Bedford /bedfəd/ administrative headquarters of Bedfordshire, England; population (1983) 89,200. Industries include agricultural machinery and airships. John Bunyan wrote *The Pilgrim's Progress* (1678) while imprisoned here.

Bedford /bedfəd/ John Robert Russell, 13th Duke of Bedford 1917– . English peer. Succeeding to the title 1953, he restored the family seat Woburn Abbey, Bedfordshire, now a tourist attraction.

bedford level peat portion of the ◊Fens.

Bedfordshire /ˈbedfədʃə/ county in S central England
area 1,240 sq km/479 sq mi
towns Bedford (administrative headquarters), Luton, Dunstable
features Whipsnade Zoo 1931, near Dunstable, a zoological park (200 hectares/500 acres) belonging to the London Zoological Society; Woburn Abbey, seat of the duke of Bedford
products cereals, vegetables, agricultural machinery, electrical goods
population (1987) 526,000
famous people John Bunyan, John Howard, Joseph Paxton.

Bedlam /ˈbedləm/ (abbreviation of *Bethlehem*) the earliest mental hospital in Europe. The hospital was opened in the 14th century in London and is now sited in Surrey. It is now used as a slang word meaning chaos.

Bedlington breed of ◊terrier with a short body, long legs, and curly hair, usually grey, named after a district of Northumberland, England.

Bedouin (Arabic 'desert-dweller') Arab of any of the nomadic peoples occupying the desert regions of Arabia and N Africa, now becoming increasingly settled. Their traditional trade was the rearing of horses and camels.

Beds abbreviation for ◊*Bedfordshire.*

bee four-winged insect of the superfamily Apoidea in the order Hymenoptera, usually with a sting. There are over 12,000 species, of which less than 1 in 20 are social in habit.

Most familiar is the *bumblebee*, genus *Bombus*, which is larger and stronger than the hive bee and so is adapted to fertilize plants in which the pollen and nectar lie deep, as in red clover; they can work in colder weather than the hive bee. The *hive* or *honey bee Apis mellifera* establishes perennial colonies of about 80,000, the majority being infertile females (workers), with a few larger fertile males (drones), and a single very large fertile female (the queen).

Solitary bees include species useful in pollinating orchards in spring, and may make their nests in tunnels under the ground or in hollow plant stems; 'cuckoo' bees lay their eggs in the nests of bumblebees, which they closely resemble.

Social bees, apart from the bumblebee and the hive bee, include the stingless South American *vulture bee Trigona hypogea*, discovered 1982, which is solely carnivorous.

Bees transmit information to each other about food sources by a 'dance', each movement giving rise to sound impulses which are picked up by tiny hairs on the back of the bee's head, the orientation of the dance also having significance. They use the Sun in navigation (see also under ◊migration). Besides their use in crop pollination and production of honey and wax, bees (by a measure of contaminants brought back to their hives) can provide an inexpensive and effective monitor of industrial and other pollution of the atmosphere and soil.

Most bees are pacific unless disturbed, but some South American species are aggressive. Bee stings may be fatal to people who are allergic to them, but this is comparatively rare. A vaccine treatment against bee stings, which uses concentrated venom, has been developed; see ◊melitin.

Beebe /ˈbiːb/ Charles 1877–1962. US naturalist, explorer, and writer. He was curator of birds for the New York Zoological Society 1899–1952. He wrote the comprehensive *Monograph of the Pheasants* 1918–22. His interest in deep-sea exploration led to a collaboration with the engineer Otis Barton and the development of a spherical diving vessel, the bathysphere. On 24 August 1934 the two men made a record-breaking dive to 923 m/3028 ft. Beebe's expeditions are described in a series of memoirs.

beech any tree of the genera *Fagus* and *Nothofagus*, family Fagaceae. The common beech *F. sylvaticus*, found in European forests, has a smooth grey trunk and edible nuts, or 'mast', which are used as animal feed or processed for oil. The timber is used in furniture.

Beecham /ˈbiːtʃəm/ Thomas 1879–1961. British conductor and impresario. He established the Royal Philharmonic Orchestra 1946 and fostered the works of composers such as Delius, Sibelius, and Richard Strauss.

Beeching /ˈbiːtʃɪŋ/ Richard, Baron Beeching 1913–1985. British scientist and administrator. He was chair of the British Railways Board 1963–65, producing the controversial *Beeching Report* 1963, which advocated concentrating resources on intercity passenger traffic and freight, at the cost of closing many rural and branch lines.

bee-eater bird *Merops apiaster* found in Africa, S Europe, and Asia. It feeds on a variety of insects, including bees, which it catches in its long narrow bill. Chestnut, yellow, and blue-green, it is gregarious, and generally nests in river banks and sandpits.

Beelzebub /biˈelzɪbʌb/ (Hebrew 'lord of the flies') in the New Testament, the leader of the devils, sometimes identified with Satan and sometimes with his chief assistant (see ◊devil). In the Old Testament Beelzebub was a fertility god worshipped by the Philistines and other Semitic groups (Baal).

beer alcoholic drink made from water and malt (fermented barley or other grain), flavoured with hops. Beer contains between 1% and 6% alcohol. One of the oldest alcoholic drinks, it was brewed in ancient China, Egypt and Babylon.

The medieval distinction between beer (containing hops) and *ale* (without hops) has now fallen into disuse and beer has come to be used strictly as a generic term including ale, stout, and lager. *Stout* is top fermented, but is sweet and strongly flavoured with roasted grain; *lager* is a light beer, bottom fermented and matured over a longer period (German *Lager*, 'store').

Beerbohm /ˈbɪəbəʊm/ Max 1872–1956. British caricaturist and author, the half-brother of actor and manager Herbert Beerbohm Tree. A perfectionist in style, he contributed to *The Yellow Book* 1894; wrote a novel of Oxford undergraduate life *Zuleika Dobson* 1911; and published volumes of caricature, including *Rossetti and His Circle* 1922. He succeeded George Bernard Shaw as critic to the *Saturday Review* 1898.

Beersheba /bɪəˈʃiːbə/ industrial town in Israel; population (1987) 115,000. It is the chief centre of the Negev desert and has been a settlement from the Stone Age.

beet plant of the genus *Beta* of the goosefoot family Chenapodiaceae. The common beet *B. vulgaris* is used in one variety to produce sugar, and another, the mangelwurzel, is grown as cattle fodder. The beetroot, or red beet, *B. rubra* is a salad plant.

Beethoven /ˈbeɪthəʊvən/ Ludwig van 1770–1827. German composer and pianist whose mastery of musical expression in every genre made him the dominant influence on 19th-century music. Beethoven's repertoire includes concert overtures; the opera *Fidelio*; five piano concertos and two for violin (one unfinished); 32 piano sonatas, including the *Moonlight* and *Appassionata*; 17 string quartets; the Mass in D *Missa solemnis*; and nine symphonies, as well many youthful works. He usually played his own piano pieces and conducted his orchestral works until he was hampered by deafness 1801; nevertheless he continued to compose.

Born in Bonn, the son and grandson of musicians, Beethoven became deputy organist at the court of the Elector of Cologne at Bonn before he was 12; later he studied under ◊Haydn and possibly ◊Mozart, whose influence dominated his early work. From 1809, he received a small allowance from aristocratic patrons.

beetle common name of insects in the order Coleoptera (Greek 'sheath-winged') with leathery forewings folding down in a protective sheath over the membranous hindwings, which are those used for flight. They pass through a complete metamorphosis. They include some of the largest and smallest of all insects: the largest is the *Hercules beetle Dynastes hercules* of the South American rainforest, 15 cm/6 in long; the smallest is only 0.05 cm/0.02 in long. Comprising more than 50% of the animal kingdom, beetles number some 370,000 named species, with many not yet described.

Beetles are found in almost every land and freshwater habitat, and feed on almost anything edible. Examples include: *click beetle* or *skipjack* species of the family Elateridae, so called because if they fall on their backs they pitch themselves with a jump and a loud click; the larvae, known as *wireworms*, feed on the roots of crops. In some tropical species of Elateridae the beetles have luminous organs between the head and abdomen and are known as *fireflies*. The potato pest *Colorado beetle Leptinotarsa decemlineata* is striped in black and yellow. The *blister beetle Lytta vesicatoria*, a shiny green species from S Europe, was once sold pulverized as an aphrodisiac and contains the toxin cantharidin. The larvae of the *furniture beetle Anobium punctatum* and the deathwatch beetle *Xestobium rufovillosum* and their relatives are serious pests of structural timbers and furniture (see ◊woodworm).

Beeton, Mrs /ˈbiːtn/ (Isabella Mary Mayson) 1836–1865. British writer on cookery and domestic management. She produced *Beeton's Household Management* 1859, the first comprehensive work on domestic science.

begging soliciting, usually for money and food. It is prohibited in many Western countries, including the UK, and stringent measures were taken against begging in the USSR. In the Middle East and Asia, almsgiving is often considered a religious obligation.

Legislation against begging is recorded in England from the 14th century and it is an offence to solicit alms on the public highway, to expose any sore or malformation to attract alms, to cause a child to beg, or to send begging letters containing false statements. In the 1980s begging reappeared in major UK cities and the 1824 ◊Vagrancy Act was much used against young homeless people. By 1990 there were at least 60 convictions a week under the act and there were calls for its repeal.

Begin /ˈbeɪɡɪn/ Menachem 1913–1992. Israeli politician. He was leader of the extremist Irgun Zvai Leumi organization in Palestine from 1942, and prime minister of Israel 1977–83, as head of the right-wing Likud party. In 1978 Begin shared a Nobel Peace Prize with President Sadat of Egypt for work on the ◊Camp David Agreements for a Middle East peace settlement.

Begin was born in Brest-Litovsk, Poland, studied law in Warsaw, and fled to the USSR 1939. As leader of the Irgun terrorist group, he was responsible in 1946 for a bomb attack at the King David Hotel, Jerusalem, which killed over 100 people.

begonia any plant of the genus *Begonia* of the tropical and subtropical family Begoniaceae. Begonias have fleshy and succulent leaves, and some have large, brilliant flowers. There are numerous species native to the tropics, in particular South America and India.

Behan /ˈbiːən/ Brendan 1923–1964. Irish dramatist. His early experience of prison and knowledge of the workings of the ◊IRA (recounted in his autobiography *Borstal Boy* 1958) provided him with two recurrent themes in his plays. *The Quare Fellow* 1954 was followed by the tragicomedy *The Hostage* 1958, first written in Gaelic.

behaviourism school of psychology originating in the USA, of which the leading exponent was John B ◊Watson. Behaviourists maintain that all human activity can ultimately be explained in terms of conditioned reactions or reflexes and habits formed in consequence. Leading behaviourists include Ivan ◊Pavlov and B F ◊Skinner.

behaviour therapy in psychology, the application of behavioural principles, derived from learning theories, to the treatment of clinical conditions such as ◊phobias, ◊obsessions, sexual and interpersonal problems. For example, in treating a phobia the person

is taken into the feared situation in gradual steps. Over time, the fear typically reduces, and the problem becomes less acute.

Behn /ben/ Aphra 1640–1689. English novelist and playwright, the first woman in England to earn her living as a writer. Her writings were criticized for their explicitness; they frequently present events from a woman's point of view. Her novel *Oronooko* 1688 is an attack on slavery.

Between 1670 and 1687 fifteen of her plays were produced, including *The Rover*, which attacked forced and mercenary marriages. She had the patronage of James I and was employed as a government spy in Holland 1666.

Behrens /ˈbeərənz/ Peter 1868–1940. German architect. He pioneered the adaptation of architecture to industry, and designed the AEG turbine factory in Berlin 1909, a landmark in industrial design. He taught ◊Le Corbusier and Walter ◊Gropius.

Behring /ˈbeərɪŋ/ Emil von 1854–1917. German physician who discovered that the body produces antitoxins, substances able to counteract poisons released by bacteria. Using this knowledge, he developed new treatments for diseases such as ◊diphtheria.

He won the first Nobel Prize for Medicine, in 1901.

Beiderbecke /ˈbaɪdəbek/ Bix (Leon Bismarck) 1903–1931. US jazz cornetist, composer, and pianist. A soloist with King Oliver, Louis Armstrong, and Paul Whiteman's orchestra, Beiderbecke was the first acknowledged white jazz innovator. He was inspired by the classical composers Debussy, Ravel, and Stravinsky.

Beijing /beɪˈdʒɪŋ/ or *Peking* capital of China; part of its NE border is formed by the Great Wall of China; population (1989) 6,800,000. The municipality of Beijing has an area of 17,800 sq km/6,871 sq mi and a population (1987) of 9,750,000. Industries include textiles, petrochemicals, steel, and engineering.

features Tiananmen Gate (Gate of Heavenly Peace) and Tiananmen Square, where, in 1989, Chinese troops massacred over 1,000 students and civilians demonstrating for greater freedom and democracy; the Forbidden City, built between 1406 and 1420 as Gu Gong (Imperial Palace) of the Ming Emperors, where there were 9,000 ladies-in-waiting and 10,000 eunuchs in service (it is now the seat of the government); the Great Hall of the People 1959 (used for official banquets); museums of Chinese history and of the Chinese revolution; Chairman Mao Memorial Hall 1977 (shared from 1983 with Zhou Enlai, Zhu De, and Liu Shaoqi); the Summer Palace built by the dowager empress Zi Xi (damaged by European powers 1900, but restored 1903); Temple of Heaven (Tiantan); and Ming tombs 50 km/30 mi to the NW.

history Beijing, founded 2,000 years ago, was the 13th-century capital of the Mongol emperor Kublai Khan. Later replaced by Nanking, it was again capital from 1421, except from 1928 to 1949, when it was renamed Peiping. Beijing was held by Japan 1937–45.

Beira /ˈbaɪrə/ port at the mouth of the river Pungwe, Mozambique; population (1986) 270,000. It exports minerals, cotton, and food products. A railway through the *Beira Corridor* links the port with Zimbabwe.

Beirut /ˌbeɪˈruːt/ or *Beyrouth* capital and port of ◊Lebanon, devastated by civil war in the 1970s and 1980s, when it was occupied by armies of neighbouring countries; population (1988 est) 1,500,000. The city is divided into a Christian eastern and a Muslim western sector by the Green Line.

history Beirut dates back to at least 1400 BC. Until the civil war 1975–76, Beirut was an international financial and educational centre, with four universities (Lebanese, Arab, French, and US); it was also a centre of espionage. It was besieged and virtually destroyed by the Israeli army July–Sept 1982 to enforce the withdrawal of the forces of the Palestinian Liberation Organization. After the cease-fire, 500 Palestinians were massacred in the Sabra–Chatila camps 16–18 Sept, 1982, by dissident ◊Phalangist and ◊Maronite troops, with alleged Israeli complicity. Civil disturbances continued, characterized by sporadic street fighting and hostage taking. In 1987 Syrian troops entered the city and remained as part of an Arab peacekeeping force. Intensive fighting broke out between Christian and Syrian troops in Beirut, and by 1990 the strength of Syrian military force in greater Beirut and E Lebanon was estimated at 42,000. In Oct 1990 President Elias Hwari formally invited Syrian troops to remove the Maronite Christian leader General Michel ◊Aoun from his E Beirut strong-hold; the troops then went on to dismantle the 'Green Line' separating Muslim W and Christian E Beirut, making the Beirut-Damascus highway fully passable

for the first time since 1985. The Syrian-backed 'Greater Beirut Security Plan' was subsequently implemented by the Lebanese government, enforcing the withdrawal of all militias from greater Beirut.

Bekka, the /ˈbekɑ/ or *El Beqa'a* governorate of E Lebanon separated from Syria by the Anti- Lebanon mountains. The Bekka Valley has been of strategic importance in the Syrian struggle for control of N Lebanon. In the early 1980s the valley was penetrated by Shia Muslims who established an extremist Hezbollah stronghold with the support of Iranian Revolutionary Guards. Zahlé and the ancient city of Baalbek are the chief towns.

Belarus or *Byelorussia* or *Belorussia* country in E central Europe, bounded S by Ukraine, E by Russia, W by Poland, and N by Latvia and Lithuania.

government There is a 260-seat legislature, the supreme soviet, to which deputies are elected by a majority system, and a second ballot runoff race in contests in which there is no clear first-round majority. The state president, who is also commander-in-chief of the armed forces, is directly elected and can serve a maximum of two five-year terms.

history A Byelorussian state developed in the Middle Ages around the city of Polotsk on the river Dvina. From the 13th century it became incorporated within the Slavonic Grand Duchy of Lithuania and from 1569 there was union with Poland.

brief independence Byelorussia was brought into the Russian Empire in the late 18th century and from the later 19th century there was an upsurge in national consciousness. Amid the chaos of the Bolshevik Revolution in Russia, an independent Byelorussian National Republic was declared in 1918, but failed to receive international recognition. Instead, a Byelorussian Soviet Republic was established in 1919, with some loss of territory to Poland.

nationalist revival National culture and language were encouraged until the Soviet dictator Stalin launched a Russification drive, with more than 100,000 people, predominantly writers and intellectuals, being executed between 1937 and 1941. Under the terms of the 1939 Nazi–Soviet pact, Byelorussia was reunified, but then suffered severely under German invasion and occupation 1941–44. Russification resumed in the 1960s and continued into the mid-1980s, when ◊glasnost brought a revival of national culture. A Popular Front, demanding greater autonomy, was established in Feb 1989. In the wake of the April 1986 ◊Chernobyl nuclear disaster, which forced the resettlement of several hundred thousand people, the Byelorussian Ecological Union (BEU) had been formed. Both the Popular Front and BEU contested the March–April 1990 Byelorussian supreme soviet elections under the Democratic Bloc banner, capturing more than a quarter of the seats. In response, Byelorussian was re-established as the republic's official state language from Sept 1990.

independence achieved Byelorussia's communist president, Nikolai Dementei, expressed support for the Aug 1991 coup attempt against President Gorbachev in Moscow. When it failed, Dementei resigned and the republic's supreme soviet declared Byelorussia's independence on 25 Aug 1991, suspending the activities of the Communist Party. In Sept 1991 the supreme soviet voted to adopt the name of Republic of Belarus and elected Stanislav Shushkevich, an advocate of democratic reform, as its chair, which also made him state president. Shushkevich played an important role in the creation in Dec 1991 of a new ◊Commonwealth of Independent States (CIS), the confederal successor to the USSR, with Mensk (Minsk) chosen as the CIS's early centre. In the same month, Belarus was formally acknowledged as independent by the USA and granted diplomatic recognition. In Jan 1992 it was admitted into the ◊Conference on Security and Cooperation in Europe (CSCE). It has been a member of the United Nations since its foundation in 1945.

economy and armed forces Belarus was cautious in its implementation of market-centred economic reform, with privatization and price liberalization introduced very gradually. It remained heavily dependent upon Russia for industrial raw materials. Belarus inherited substantial nuclear arms from the USSR. The Shushkevich administration pledged to gradually remove these to become nuclear-free, but Belarus also planned to establish its own independent armed forces. In May 1992, Belarus and Russia (as a single signatory), along with Ukraine and Kazakhstan, signed protocols with the USA agreeing to comply with START. It was also agreed to return all tactical nuclear weapons to Russia for destruction. In Feb 1993 parliament formally ratified START I and voted to adhere to the Nuclear Nonproliferation Treaty. The Communist Party re-established itself within the republic and a merger of Russian and Belarusian economies was agreed Jan 1994. President Shushkevich was dismissed and Alexandr Lukashenko elected president.

Belaúnde Terry /ˌbelɑːˈundeɪˈteri/ Fernando 1913– . President of Peru from 1963 to 1968 and from 1980 to 1985. He championed land reform and the construction of roads to open up the Amazon valley. He fled to the USA 1968 after being deposed by a military junta. After his return, his second term in office was marked by rampant inflation, enormous foreign debts, terrorism, mass killings, and human-rights violations by the armed forces.

Belau, Republic of /bəˈlaʊ/ (formerly *Palau*) self-governing island group in Micronesia; area 500 sq km/193 sq mi; population (1988) 14,000. It is part of the US Trust Territory of the Pacific Islands, and became internally self-governing 1980.

There are 26 larger islands (eight inhabited) and about 300 islets.

Spain held the islands from about 1600, and sold them to Germany 1899. Japan seized them in World War I, administered them by League of Nations mandate, and used them as a naval base during World War II. They were captured by the USA 1944, and became part of its Trust Territory 1947.

bel canto /ˈbel ˈkæntəʊ/ (Italian 'beautiful song') in music, an 18th-century Italian style of singing with emphasis on perfect technique and beautiful tone. The style reached its peak in the operas of Rossini, Donizetti, and Bellini.

Belém /bə'lem/ port and naval base in N Brazil; population (1980) 758,000. The chief trade centre of the Amazon Basin, it is also known as Pará, the name of the state of which it is capital.

Belfast /ˌbel'fɑːst/ industrial port (shipbuilding, engineering, electronics, textiles, tobacco) and capital of Northern Ireland since 1920; population (1985) 300,000. Since 1968 it has been heavily damaged by civil disturbances.

history Belfast grew up around a castle built 1177 by John de Courcy. With the settlement of English and Scots, Belfast became a centre of Irish Protestantism in the 17th century. An influx of Huguenots after 1685 extended the linen industry, and the 1800 Act of Union with England resulted in the promotion of Belfast as an industrial centre. It was created a city 1888, with a lord mayor from 1892. The former parliament buildings are to the south at Stormont.

Belgae people who lived in Gaul in Roman times, north of the Seine and Marne rivers. They were defeated by Caesar 57 BC. Many of the Belgae settled in SE England during the 2nd century BC.

Belgic remains in Britain include coins, minted in Gaul, pottery made on a wheel, and much of the finest Iron Age Celtic art.

Belgian Congo former name (1908–60) of ◊Zaire.

Belgium /'beldʒəm/ country in W Europe, bounded N by the Netherlands, NW by the North Sea, S and W by France, E by Luxembourg and Germany

government A parliamentary democracy under a constitutional monarch, with nine provinces, Belgium's constitution dates from 1831 and was most recently revised 1993. The prime minister and cabinet are drawn from and answerable to the legislature, which exercises considerable control over the executive. The legislature consists of a senate and a chamber of representatives. The senate has 182 members: 106 nationally elected, 50 representing the provinces, 25 co-opted and, by right, the heir to the throne. Senators are elected for four years. The chamber of representatives has 212 members elected by universal suffrage, through a system of proportional representation, for a four-year term. On the basis of parliamentary support, the monarch appoints the prime minister, who chooses the cabinet. The multiplicity of political parties reflects Belgium's linguistic and social divisions.

history The first recorded inhabitants were the Belgae, an ancient Celtic people. Conquered by the Romans, the area was known from 15 BC as the Roman province of Belgica; from the 3rd century AD onwards it was overrun by the Franks. Under ◊Charlemagne, Belgium became the centre of the Carolingian dynasty, and the peace and order during this period fostered the growth of such towns as Ghent, Bruges, and Brussels. Following the division of Charlemagne's empire 843 the area became part of Lotharingia. By the 11th century seven feudal states had emerged: the counties of Flanders, Hainaut, and Namur, the duchies of Brabant, Limburg, and Luxembourg, and the bishopric of Liège, all nominally subject to the French kings or the German emperor, but in practice independent. From the 12th century the economy flourished; Bruges, Ghent, and Ypres became centres of the textile industry, while the artisans of Dinant and Liège exploited the copper and tin of the Meuse valley. During the 15th century the states came one by one under the rule of the dukes of Burgundy, and, by the marriage of Mary (heir of Charles the Bold, duke of Burgundy) to Maximilian (archduke of Austria), passed into the ◊Habsburg dominions 1477.

under Spanish rule Other dynastic marriages brought all the Low Countries under Spain, and in the 16th century the religious and secular tyranny of Philip II led to revolt in the Netherlands. The independence of the Netherlands as the Dutch Republic was recognized 1648; the south, reconquered by Spain, remained Spanish until the Treaty of ◊Utrecht 1713 transferred it to Austria. The Austrian Netherlands were annexed 1719 by revolutionary France. The ◊Congress of Vienna 1815 reunited the North and South Netherlands as one kingdom under William, King of Orange-Nassau; but historical differences, and the fact that the language of the wealthy and powerful in the south was (as it remains) French, made the union uneasy.

recognition as an independent kingdom An uprising 1830 of the largely French-speaking people in the south, and continuing disturbances, led to the Great Powers' recognition 1839 of the South Netherlands as the independent and permanently neutral kingdom of Belgium, with Leopold of Saxe-Coburg (widower of Charlotte, daughter of George IV of England) as king, and a parliamentary constitution.

Although Prussia had been a party to the treaty 1839 recognizing Belgium's permanent neutrality, Germany invaded Belgium 1914 and occupied a large part of it until 1918. In 1940 Belgium was again overrun by Germany, to whom Leopold III surrendered. His government escaped to London, and Belgium had a strong resistance movement. After Belgium's liberation by the Allies 1944–45 the king's surrender caused acute controversy, ended only by his abdication 1951 in favour of his son Baudouin. Since 1945 Belgium has been a major force for international cooperation in Europe, being a founding member of the ◊Benelux Economic Union, the Council of Europe, and the European Economic Community.

language divisions Belgium's main problems stem from the division between French- and Flemish-speaking members of the population, aggravated by the polarization between the predominantly conservative Flanders in the north, and the mainly socialist French-speaking Wallonia in the south. About 55% of the population speak Flemish, 44% French, and the remainder German. During 1971–73 attempts to close the linguistic and social divisions included the transfer of greater power to the regions, the inclusion of German-speaking members in the cabinet, and linguistic parity in the government. Separate regional councils and ministerial committees were established 1974.

A coalition government, headed by Leo Tindemans (CVP) proposed 1977 the creation of a federal Belgium, based on Flanders, Wallonia, and Brussels, but the proposals were not adopted, and Tindemans resigned 1978. He was succeeded by Wilfried ◊Martens, heading another coalition.

administration decentralized The language conflict developed into open violence 1980, and it was eventually agreed that Flanders and Wallonia should be administered by separate regional assemblies, with powers to spend up to 10% of the national budget on cultural facilities, health, roads, and urban projects. Brussels was to be governed by a three-member executive. Such was the political instability that by 1980 Martens had formed no less than four coalition governments. A new coalition 1981, led by Mark Eyskens (CVP), lasted less than a year, and Martens again returned to power.

Economic difficulties 1981–82 resulted in a series of public sector strikes, and linguistic divisions again threatened the government 1983. Between 1983 and 1985 there was much debate about the siting of US cruise missiles in Belgium before a majority vote in parliament allowed their installation. Martens headed a series of coalition governments until Jan 1992 when the government was on the point of collapse. In March 1992 Jean-Luc Dehaene (CVP) formed a new coalition comprising the main centre-left parties. In 1993 King Baudouin died, and was succeeded by his brother, Prince Albert of Liege.

Belgrade /bel'greɪd/ (Serbo-Croat *Beograd*) capital of Yugoslavia and Serbia, and Danube river port linked with the port of Bar on the Adriatic; population (1981) 1,470,000. Industries include light engineering, food processing, textiles, pharmaceuticals, and electrical goods.

Belitung /brli:tʊŋ/ alternative name for the Indonesian island of ◊Billiton.

Belize /bəˈliːz/ country in Central America, bounded N by Mexico, W and S by Guatemala, and E by the Caribbean Sea.

government The 1981 constitution provides for a parliamentary government on the British model, with a prime minister and cabinet drawn from the legislature and accountable to it. The national assembly consists of a senate and a house of representatives. The senate has eight members appointed by the governor general for a five-year term, five on the advice of the prime minister, two on the advice of the leader of the opposition, and one after wider consultations. The house of representatives has 28 members elected by

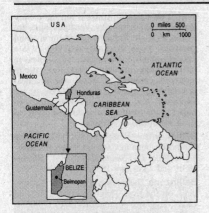

universal suffrage. The governor general appoints both the prime minister and the leader of the opposition.

history Once part of the ◊Maya civilization, and colonized in the 17th century, British Honduras (as it was called until 1973) became a recognized British colony 1862. A 1954 constitution provided for internal self-government, with the UK responsible for defence, external affairs, and internal security.

The first general election under the the new constitution, and all subsequent elections until 1984, were won by the People's United Party (PUP), led by George Price. Full internal self-government was granted 1964, and Price became prime minister. The capital was moved 1970 from Belize City to the new town of Belmopan. British troops were sent 1975 to defend the long-disputed frontier with Guatemala. Negotiations begun 1977 were inconclusive.

full independence achieved The UN called 1980 for full independence for Belize. A constitutional conference broke up 1981 over Guatemala's demand for territory rather than just access to the Caribbean. Full independence was achieved 1981 with George Price as the first prime minister. The UK agreed to protect the frontier and to assist in the training of Belizean forces. The PUP's uninterrupted 30-year rule ended 1984 when the United Democratic Party (UDP) leader, Manuel Esquivel, became prime minister. The UK reaffirmed its undertaking to protect Belize's disputed frontier. Still led by George Price, the PUP unexpectedly won the Sept 1989 general election. In Sept 1991 Guatemala recognized Belize's independence and withdrew threats of invasion. The July 1993 election was won by the UDP and Esquivel returned as prime minister.

Belize City /br'li:z/ chief port of Belize, and capital until 1970; population (1980) 40,000. After the city was destroyed by a hurricane 1961 it was decided to move the capital inland, to Belmopan.

bell musical instrument, made in many sizes, comprising a suspended hollow metal container with a beater attached, which rings when shaken. Church bells are massive instruments, cast in bronze, and mounted in towers from where their sound can be heard over a wide area. Their shape is a flared bowl with a thickened rim engineered to produce a clangorous mixture of tones. Orchestral *tubular bells*, made of brass or steel, offer a chromatic scale of pitches of reduced power, and are played by striking with a wooden mallet.

The world's largest bell is the 'Tsar Kolokol' or 'King of Bells', 220 tonnes, cast 1734, which stands on the ground of the Kremlin, Moscow, where it fell when being hung. The 'Peace Bell' at the United Nations headquarters, New York, was cast 1952 from coins presented by 64 countries.

Bell /bel/ Alexander Graham 1847–1922. Scottish scientist, inventor of the telephone. He patented his invention 1876, and later experimented with a type of phonograph and, in aeronautics, invented the tricycle undercarriage.

Bell /bel/ John 1928–1990. Irish physicist who in 1964 devised a test to verify a point in ◊quantum theory: whether two particles that were once connected are always afterwards interconnected even if they become widely separated. As well as investigating fundamental problems in theoretical physics, Bell contributed to the design of particle accelerators.

One of the most profound thinkers in modern physics, Bell worked for 30 years at CERN, the European research laboratory near Geneva, Switzerland. He demonstrated how to measure the continued interconnection of particles that had once been closely connected, and put forward mathematical criteria that had to be obeyed if such a connection existed, as required by quantum theory.

belladonna or *deadly nightshade* poisonous plant *Atropa belladonna*, found in Europe and Asia. The dried powdered leaves contain ◊alkaloids. Belladonna extract acts medicinally as an ◊anticholinergic (blocking the passage of certain nerve impulses), and is highly toxic in large doses.

Belladonna is of the nightshade family, *Solanaceae*. It grows to 5 ft/1.5 m, with dull green leaves to 8 in/20 cm and solitary greenish flowers that produce deadly black berries. The alkaloids contained are hyoscyamine, atropine, hyoscine, and belladonnine.

Bellay /beˈleɪ/ Joaquim du *c.* 1522–1560. French poet and prose writer who published the great manifesto of the new school of French poetry, the Pléiade: *Défense et illustration de la langue française* 1549.

Bellerophon in Greek mythology, a victim of slander who was sent against the monstrous ◊chimera, which he killed with the help of his winged horse Pegasus. After further trials, he ended his life as a beggar. His story was dramatized by ◊Euripides.

belles lettres (French 'fine letters') literature that is appreciated more for its aesthetic qualities than for its content.

bellflower general name for many plants of the family Campanulaceae, notably those of the genus *Campanula*. The Canterbury bell *C. medium* is the garden variety, originally from S Europe. The ◊harebell is also a *Campanula*.

The clustered bellflower *C. glomerata* is characteristic of chalk grassland, and found in Europe and N Asia. Erect and downy, it has tight clusters of violet bell-shaped flowers in late summer.

Bellingshausen /ˈbelɪnzhaʊzən/ Fabian Gottlieb von 1779–1852. Russian Antarctic explorer, the first to sight and circumnavigate the Antarctic continent 1819–21, although he did not realize what it was.

Bellini /beˈliːni/ family of Italian Renaissance painters, founders of the Venetian school.

Gentile (*c.* 1429–1507) assisted in the decoration of the Doge's Palace 1474 and worked in the court of Muhammad II at Constantinople (a portrait of the sultan is in the National Gallery, London). His also painted processional groups (Accademia, Venice).

Giovanni (*c.* 1430–1516), Gentile's younger brother, studied under his father, and painted portraits and various religious subjects. Giovanni Bellini's early works show the influence of his brother-in-law, Manteg-

na. His style developed from the static manner of mid-15th century Venetian work towards a High Renaissance harmony and grandeur, as in the altarpiece 1505 in Sta Zaccaria, Venice. He introduced softness in tone, harmony in composition, and a use of luminous colour that influenced the next generation of painters (including his pupils Giorgione and Titian). He worked in oil rather than tempera, a technique adopted from Antonello da Messina.

Bellini /beˈliːni/ Vincenzo 1801–1835. Italian composer, born in Catania, Sicily. His operas include *La Sonnambula* 1831, *Norma* 1831, and *I Puritani* 1835.

Bellinzona /ˌbelɪntˈsəʊnə/ town in Switzerland, on the river Ticino; 16 km/10 mi from Lake Maggiore; population (1980) 17,000. It is the capital of Ticino canton and a traffic centre for the St Gotthard Pass. It is also a tourist centre.

Belloc /ˈbelɒk/ (Joseph) Hilaire Pierre 1870–1953. English author, remembered primarily for his nonsense verse for children *The Bad Child's Book of Beasts* 1896 and *Cautionary Tales* 1907. Belloc also wrote travel and religious books (he was a devout Catholic).

Bellot /beˈləʊ/ Joseph René 1826–1853. French Arctic explorer who reached the strait now named after him 1852, and lost his life while searching for English explorer John ◊Franklin.

Bellow /ˈbeləʊ/ Saul 1915– . Canadian-born US novelist. Novels such as *Herzog* 1964, *Humboldt's Gift* 1975, and *The Dean's December* 1982 show his method of inhabiting the consciousness of a central character, frequently a Jewish-American intellectual whose suffering and reflectiveness deeply engage the reader. His sensitivity to mythic dimensions is evident in such novels as *Henderson the Rain King* 1959. Nobel Prize for Literature 1976.

bell ringing or *campanology* art of ringing church bells by hand, by means of a rope fastened to a wheel rotating the entire bell mechanism. *Change ringing* is an English art of ringing all the possible sequences of a number of bells in strict order, using one player to each bell. Fixed permutations of 5–12 bells are rung.

In Europe and the USA, the *carillon* performs arrangements of well-known music for up to 70 static bells. It is played by a single operator using a keyboard system of levers and pulleys acting on the striking mechanisms only. *Handbell* ringing is played solo or by a team of ringers selecting from a range of lightweight bells of pure tone resting on a table.

bells nautical term applied to half-hours of watch. A day is divided into seven watches, five of four hours each and two, called dogwatches, of two hours. Each half-hour of each watch is indicated by the striking of a bell, eight bells signalling the end of the watch.

Belmondo /bel'mɒndəʊ/ Jean-Paul 1933– . French film star who played the doomed gangster in Jean-Luc Godard's *A bout de souffle/Breathless* 1959. His other films include *Cartouche* 1962, *The Brain* 1968, and *Hold-up* 1985.

Belmopan /ˌbelməˈpæn/ capital of Belize from 1970; population (1980) 3,000. It replaced Belize City as administrative centre of the country.

Belo Horizonte /beləʊ ˌhɒrɪˈzɒnteɪ/ industrial city (steel, engineering, textiles) in SE Brazil, capital of the fast-developing state of Minas Gerais; population (1985) 3,060,000. Built in the 1890s, it was Brazil's first planned modern city.

Belorussia or *Byelorussia* former name 1919–91 of ◊Belarus.

Belshazzar /bel'ʃæzə/ in the Old Testament, the last king of Babylon, son of Nebuchadnezzar. During a feast (known as *Belshazzar's Feast*) he saw a message, interpreted by ◊Daniel as prophesying the fall of Babylon and death of Belshazzar.

Bemba /'bembə/ member of a people native to NE Zambia and neighbouring areas of Zaïre and Zimbabwe, although many reside in urban areas such as Lusaka and Copperbelt. They number about three million. The Bemba language belongs to the Bantu branch of the Niger–Congo family.

Ben Ali /ben 'æli/ Zine el Abidine 1936– . Tunisian politician, president from 1987. After training in France and the USA, he returned to Tunisia and became director-general of national security. He was made minister of the interior and then prime minister under the ageing president for life, Habib ◊Bourguiba, whom he deposed 1987 by a bloodless coup with the aid of ministerial colleagues. He ended the personality cult established by Bourguiba and moved toward a pluralist political system.

Benares /bɪ'nɑːrɪz/ transliteration of ◊Varanasi, holy city in India.

Ben Barka /ben 'bɑːkə/ Mehdi 1920–1965. Moroccan politician. He became president of the National Consultative Assembly 1956 on the country's independence from France. He was assassinated by Moroccan agents with the aid of the French secret service.

Ben Barka had been tutor to King Hassan. As a major opposition leader after independence he was increasingly leftist in his views, and was twice sentenced to death in his absence during 1963 following allegations of his involvement in an attempt on the king's life and for backing Algeria in border disputes.

Ben Bella /ben 'belə/ Ahmed 1916– . Algerian politician. He was leader of the National Liberation Front (FLN) from 1952, the first prime minister of independent Algeria 1962–63, and its first president 1963–65. In 1965 Ben Bella was overthrown by Col Houari ◊Boumédienne and detained until 1979. He founded a new party, Mouvement pour la Démocratie en Algérie 1985, and returned to Algerian 1990 after nine years in exile.

Benchley /'bentʃli/ Robert 1889–1945. US humorist, actor, and drama critic whose books include *Of All Things* 1921 and *Benchley Beside Himself* 1943. His film skit *How to Sleep* illustrates his ability to extract humour from everyday life.

benchmark in computing, a measure of the performance of a piece of equipment or software, usually consisting of a standard program or suite of programs. Benchmarks can indicate whether a computer is powerful enough to perform a particular task, and so enable machines to be compared. However, they provide only a very rough guide to practical performance, and may lead manufacturers to design systems that get high scores with the artificial benchmark programs but do not necessarily perform well with day-to-day programs or data.

Benchmark measures include *Whetstones*, *Dhrystones*, *SPECmarks*, and *TPC*. SPECmarks are based on ten programs adopted by the Systems Performance Evaluation Cooperative for benchmarking workstations; the Transaction Processing Performance Council's TPC-B benchmark is used to test databases and on-line systems in banking (debit/credit) environments.

bends popular name for a paralytic afflic-
tion of deep-sea divers, arising from too
rapid a release of nitrogen from solution in
their blood. If a diver surfaces too quickly,
nitrogen that had dissolved in the blood
under increasing water pressure is suddenly
released, forming bubbles in the bloodstream and causing paralysis. Immediate
treatment is compression and slow decompression in a special chamber.

Benedict /'benɪdɪkt/ 15 popes, including:

Benedict XV 1854–1922. Pope from 1914.
During World War I he endeavoured to
bring about a peace settlement, and it was
during his papacy that British, French, and
Dutch official relations were renewed with
the Vatican.

Benedictine order religious order of
monks and nuns in the Roman Catholic
church, founded by St ◊Benedict at Subiaco,
Italy, in the 6th century. It had a strong
influence on medieval learning and reached
the height of its prosperity early in the 14th
century.

St Augustine brought the order to England. A number of Oxford and Cambridge
colleges have a Benedictine origin. At the
Reformation there were nearly 300 Benedictine monasteries and nunneries in England,
all of which were suppressed. The English
novice house survived in France, and in the
19th century monks expelled from France
moved to England and built abbeys at
Downside, Ampleforth, and Woolhampton.
The monks from Pierre-qui-vive, who went
to England 1882, rebuilt Buckfast Abbey in
Devon on the ruins of a Cistercian monastery.

Benedict, St /'benɪdɪkt/ c. 480–c. 547.
Founder of Christian monasticism in the
West and of the ◊Benedictine order. He
founded the monastery of Monte Cassino,
Italy. Here he wrote out his rule for monastic life, and was visited shortly before his
death by the Ostrogothic king Totila, whom
he converted to the Christian faith. Feast
day 11 July.

benefice in the early Middle Ages, a dona-
tion of land or money to the Christian
church as an act of devotion; from the 12th
century, the term came to mean the income
enjoyed by clergy.

Benelux /'benɪlʌks/ (acronym from *Be*lgium,
the *Ne*therlands, and *Lux*embourg) customs
union agreed by Belgium, the Netherlands,
and Luxembourg 1944, fully effective 1960.

It was the precursor of the European Community.

Beneš /'beneʃ/ Eduard 1884–1948. Czechoslovak politician. He worked with Thomas
◊Masaryk towards Czechoslovak nationalism from 1918 and was foreign minister and
representative at the League of Nations. He
was president of the republic from 1935 until
forced to resign by the Germans; he headed
a government in exile in London during
World War II. He returned home as president 1945 but resigned again after the Communist coup 1948.

Bengal /,ben'gɔːl/ former province of British
India, divided 1947 into ◊West Bengal, a
state of India, and East Bengal, from 1972
◊Bangladesh. A famine in 1943, caused by a
slump in demand for jute and a bad harvest,
resulted in over three million deaths.

Bengali person of Bengali culture from
Bangladesh and India (W Bengal, Tripura).
There are 80–150 million speakers of Bengali, an Indo-Iranian language belonging to
the Indo-European family. It is the official
language of Bangladesh and of the state of
Bengal, and is also used by emigrant Ban-
gladeshi and Bengali communities in such
countries as the UK and the USA. Bengalis
in Bangladesh are predominantly Muslim,
whereas those in India are mainly Hindu.

Between the 8th and 12th centuries the
Bengalis were ruled by the Buddhist Pála
dynasty. From the 13th century they were
governed by semi-independent Muslim princes until their incorporation into the Mogul
Empire. In the 18th century Bengal was
annexed by the British and on independence
the region was partitioned by the successor
states of India and E Pakistan (now Bangladesh).

Benghazi /ben'gɑːzi/ or *Banghazi* historic
city and industrial port in N Libya on the
Gulf of Sirte; population (1982) 650,000. It
was controlled by Turkey between the 16th
century and 1911, and by Italy 1911–1942;
a major naval supply base during World
War II.

Colonized by the Greeks in the 7th century BC (*Euhesperides*), Benghazi was taken
by Rome in the 1st century BC (*Berenice*) and
by the Vandals in the 5th century AD. It
became Arab in the 7th century. With Tripoli, it was co-capital of Libya 1951–72.

Benguela current cold ocean current in
the S Atlantic Ocean, moving northwards
along the west coast of Southern Africa and

merging with the south equatorial current at a latitude of 15° S. Its rich plankton supports large, commercially exploited fish populations.

Ben-Gurion /ben 'guəriən/ David. Adopted name of David Gruen 1886–1973. Israeli statesman and socialist politician, one of the founders of the state of Israel, the country's first prime minister 1948–53, and again 1955–63.

He was born in Poland, and went to Palestine 1906 to farm. He was a leader of the Zionist movement, and as defence minister he presided over the development of Israel's armed forces into one of the strongest armies in the Middle East.

Benin /be'ni:n/ country in W Africa, bounded E by Nigeria, N by Niger and Burkina Faso, W by Togo, and S by the Gulf of Guinea.

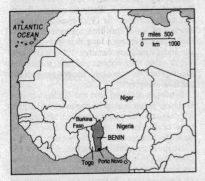

government The constitution is based on the Fundamental Law (*Loi fondamentale*) of 1977, which established a national revolutionary assembly with 196 members (representing socioprofessional classes rather than geographical constituencies) elected for a five-year term by universal suffrage. The assembly elects the president (head of state) also to serve a five-year term. From 1975 to 1989 Benin was a one-party state, committed to 'scientific socialism' under the Party of the People's Revolution of Benin (PRPB), chaired by the president.
history In the 12th–13th centuries the country was settled by the Aja, whose kingdom reached its peak in the 16th century. In the 17th–19th centuries the succeeding Dahomey kingdom (which gave the country its name until 1975) captured and sold its neighbours as slaves to Europeans.

Under French influence from the 1850s, Dahomey formed part of French West Africa from 1899, and became a self-governing dominion within the French Community 1958. It became fully independent 1960.

Dahomey went through a period of political instability 1960–72, with swings from civilian to military rule and disputes between regions. The deputy chief of the army, Mathieu Kerekou, established 1972 a military regime pledged to give fair representation to each region. His initial instrument of government was the National Council of the Revolution (CNR). Kerekou announced 1974 that as the People's Republic of Benin the country would follow 'scientific socialism', based on Marxist-Leninist principles.

CNR was dissolved 1977 and a 'national revolutionary assembly' established, which elected Kerekou 1980 as president and head of state. After initial economic and social difficulties, his government grew more stable; relations with France (Benin's biggest trading partner) improved considerably. President Mitterrand became the first French head of state to visit Benin 1983.

President Kerekou was re-elected Aug 1989 by the assembly for another five-year term. It was announced Dec 1989 that Marxist-Leninism was no longer the official ideology of Benin and that further constitutional reforms—allowing for more private enterprise—would be agreed upon. A preliminary referendum Dec 1990 showed overwhelming support for a multiparty political system, and multiparty elections were held Feb 1991. Kerekou was defeated and Nicéphore Soglo became president.

Benin /be'ni:n/ former African kingdom 1200–1897, now part of Nigeria. It reached the height of its power in the 14th–17th centuries when it ruled the area between the Niger Delta and Lagos. Benin traded in spices, ivory, palm oil, and slaves until its decline and eventual incorporation into Nigeria. The Oba (ruler) of Benin continues to rule his people as a divine monarch. The present Oba is considered an enlightened leader and one who is helping his people to become part of modern Nigeria.

Benn /ben/ Tony (Anthony Wedgwood) 1925–   . British Labour politician, formerly the leading figure on the party's left wing. He was minister of technology 1966–70 and of industry 1974–75, but his campaign against entry to the European Community led to his transfer to the Department of Energy 1975–79. He unsuccessfully contested Neil Kinnock for the party leadership 1988.

Son of Lord Stansgate, a Labour peer, Benn was elected MP for Bristol SE 1950–60, succeeded his father 1960, but never used his title and in 1963 was the first person to disclaim a title under the Peerage Act. He was again MP for Bristol SE 1963–83. In 1981 he challenged Denis Healey for the deputy leadership of the party and was so narrowly defeated that he established himself as the acknowledged leader of the left. His diaries cover in enormous detail the events of the period. In 1984 he became MP for Chesterfield.

Bennett /ˈbenɪt/ Alan 1934– . English playwright. His works (set in his native north of England) treat subjects such as class, senility, illness, and death with macabre comedy. They include TV films, for example *An Englishman Abroad* 1982; the cinema film *A Private Function* 1984; and plays such as *Forty Years On* 1968, *Getting On* 1971, *Kafka's Dick* 1986, and *The Madness of George III* 1991.

Bennett /ˈbenɪt/ (Enoch) Arnold 1867–1931. English novelist. He became a London journalist 1893 and editor of *Woman* 1896. His many novels include *Anna of the Five Towns* 1904, *The Old Wives' Tale* 1908, and the trilogy *Clayhanger*, *Hilda Lessways*, and *These Twain* 1910–16. Bennett came from one of the 'five towns' of the Potteries in Staffordshire, the setting for his major works.

Bennett /ˈbenɪt/ Richard Rodney 1936– . English composer of jazz, film music, symphonies, and operas. His film scores for *Far from the Madding Crowd* 1967, *Nicholas and Alexandra* 1971, and *Murder on the Orient Express* 1974 all received Oscar nominations. His operas include *The Mines of Sulphur* 1963 and *Victory* 1970.

Ben Nevis /ben ˈnevɪs/ highest mountain in the British Isles (1,342 m/4,406 ft), in the Grampians, Scotland.

Benny /ˈbeni/ Jack. Stage name of Benjamin Kubelsky 1894–1974. US comedian notable for his perfect timing and lugubrious manner. His radio programme, from 1932, made him a national institution. His film appearances, mostly in the 1930s and 1940s, included a starring role in *To Be or Not to Be* 1942.

Benoni /bɪˈnəʊni/ city in the Transvaal, South Africa, 27 km/17 mi E of Johannesburg; population (1980) 207,000. It was founded 1903 as a gold-mining centre.

Benson /ˈbensən/ Edward White 1829–1896. English cleric, first headmaster of Wellington College 1859–68, and, as archbishop of Canterbury from 1883, responsible for the 'Lincoln Judgment' on questions of ritual 1887.

bent or *bent grass* any grasses of the genus *Agrostris*. Creeping bent grass *A. stolonifera*, also known as fiorin, is common in N North America and Eurasia, including lowland Britain. It spreads by ◊stolons and bears large attractive panicles of yellow or purple flowers on thin stalks. It is often used on lawns and golf courses.

Bentham /ˈbenθəm/ Jeremy 1748–1832. English philosopher, legal and social reformer, and founder of ◊utilitarianism. The essence of his moral philosophy is found in the pronouncement of his *Principles of Morals and Legislation* (written 1780, published 1789): that 'the object of all legislation should be 'the greatest happiness for the greatest number'.

Bentham declared that the 'utility' of any law is to be measured by the extent to which it promotes the pleasure, good, and happiness of the people concerned. In 1776 he published *Fragments on Government*.

He made suggestions for the reform of the poor law 1798, which formed the basis of the reforms enacted 1834, and in his *Catechism of Parliamentary Reform* 1817 he proposed annual elections, the secret ballot, and universal male suffrage. He was also a pioneer of prison reform. In economics he was an apostle of *laissez-faire*, and in his *Defence of Usury* 1787 and *Manual of Political Economy* 1798 he contended that his principle of 'utility' was best served by allowing every man (sic) to pursue his own interests unhindered by restrictive legislation.

Bentinck /ˈbentɪŋk/ Lord William Cavendish 1774–1839. British colonial administrator, first governor general of India 1828–35. He acted against the ancient Indian rituals of thuggee and suttee, and established English as the medium of instruction.

Bentley /ˈbentli/ Edmund Clerihew 1875–1956. English author. He invented the four-line humorous verse form known as the ◊clerihew, used in *Biography for Beginners* 1905 and in *Baseless Biography* 1939. He was

also the author of the classic detective story
Trent's Last Case 1912.

Bentley /'bentli/ John Francis 1839–1902.
English architect, a convert to Catholicism,
who designed Westminster Cathedral, London (1895–1903). It is outwardly Byzantine
but inwardly shaped by shadowy vaults of
bare brickwork. The campanile is the tallest
church tower in London.

bentonite type of clay, consisting mainly of
montmorillonite and resembling ◊fuller's
earth, which swells when wet. It is used in
papermaking, moulding sands, drilling muds
for oil wells, and as a decolorant in food
processing.

bentwood type of furniture, originally
made by steam-heating and then bending
rods of wood to form panels. Initially a
country style, it was patented in the early
19th century in the USA. 20th-century designers such as Marcel ◊Breuer and Alvar
◊Aalto have developed a different form by
bending sheets of plywood.

Benue /'benueɪ/ river in Nigeria, largest
tributary of the Niger; it is navigable for
most of its length of 1,400 km/870 mi.

Benz /bents/ Karl Friedrich 1844–1929. German automobile engineer who produced the
world's first petrol-driven motor vehicle. He
built his first model engine 1878 and the
petrol-driven car 1885.

benzaldehyde C_6H_5CHO colourless liquid
with the characteristic odour of almonds. It
is used as a solvent and in the making of
perfumes and dyes. It occurs in certain
leaves, such as the cherry, laurel, and peach,
and in a combined form in certain nuts and
kernels. It can be extracted from such natural sources, but is usually made from ◊to-
luene.

Benzedrine /'benzədriːn/ trade name for
◊amphetamine, a stimulant drug.

benzene C_6H_6 clear liquid hydrocarbon of
characteristic odour, occurring in coal tar. It
is used as a solvent and in the synthesis of
many chemicals.

The benzene molecule consists of a ring of
six carbon atoms, all of which are in a single
plane, and it is one of the simplest ◊cyclic
compounds. Benzene is the simplest of a
class of compounds collectively known as
aromatic compounds. Some are considered
carcinogenic (cancer-inducing).

benzodiazepine any of a group of mood-
altering drugs (tranquillizers), for example

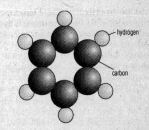

Benzene The molecule of benzene consists of
six carbon atoms arranged in a ring, with six
hydrogen atoms attached.

Librium and Valium. They are addictive and
interfere with the process by which information is transmitted between brain cells, and
various side-effects arise from continued use.

benzoic acid C_6H_5COOH white crystalline
solid, sparingly soluble in water, that is used
as a preservative for certain foods and as an
antiseptic. It is obtained chemically by the
direct oxidation of benzaldehyde and occurs
in certain natural resins, some essential oils,
and as hippuric acid.

benzoin resin obtained by making incisions
in the bark of *Styrax benzoin*, a tree native
to the East Indies. Benzoin is used in the
preparation of cosmetics, perfumes, and in-
cense.

Ben Zvi /ben 'zviː/ Izhak 1884–1963. Israeli
politician, president 1952–63. He was born
in Atpoltava, Russia, and became active in
the Zionist movement in Ukraine. In 1907 he
went to Palestine but was deported 1915
with ◊Ben-Gurion. They served in the Jewish
Legion under Field Marshal Allenby, who
commanded the British forces in the Middle
East.

Beowulf /'beɪəʊwʊlf/ Anglo-Saxon poem
(composed *c.* 700), the only complete surviving example of Germanic folk-epic. It exists
in a single manuscript copied about 1000 in
the Cottonian collection of the British Museum.

The hero Beowulf delivers the Danish king
Hrothgar from the water-demon Grendel
and its monstrous mother, and, returning
home, succeeds his cousin Heardred as king
of the Geats. After 50 years of prosperity, he
is killed in slaying a dragon.

Berber /'bɜːbə/ member of a people of North
Africa who since prehistoric times inhabited
Barbary, the Mediterranean coastlands from

Egypt to the Atlantic. Their language, Berber (a member of the Afro-Asiatic language family), is spoken by about one-third of Algerians and nearly two-thirds of Moroccans, ten million people.

Berbera /ˈbɜːbərə/ seaport in Somalia, with the only sheltered harbour on the S side of the Gulf of Aden; population (1982) 55,000. It is in a strategic position on the oil route and has a deep-sea port completed 1969. It was under British control 1884–1960.

Berchtold /ˈbeəxtəʊlt/ Count Leopold von 1863–1942. Prime minister and foreign minister of Austria–Hungary 1912–15 and, because his indecisive stance caused tension with Serbia, a crucial figure in the events that led to World War I.

Berdyaev /bɪəˈdjaɪef/ Nikolai Alexandrovich 1874–1948. Russian philosopher who often challenged official Soviet viewpoints after the Revolution of 1917. Although appointed professor of philosophy in 1919 at Moscow University, he was exiled 1922 for defending Orthodox Christian religion. His books include *The Meaning of History* 1923 and *The Destiny of Man* 1935.

Berdyansk /bɪəˈdjænsk/ city and port on the Berdyansk Gulf of the Sea of Azov, in SE Ukraine; population (1985) 130,000.

Bérégovoy Pierre 1925– . French socialist politician, prime minister 1992–3. A close ally of François ◊Mitterrand, he was named Chief of Staff 1981 after managing the successful presidential campaign. He was social affairs minister 1982–84 and finance minister 1984–86 and 1988–92.

The son of a Ukrainian immigrant, he was largely self-educated and his working-class background contrasted sharply with that of the other Socialist Party leaders. As finance minister, he was widely respected by France's financial community. He replaced the unpopular Edith ◊Cresson as prime minister in April 1992. He pledged to reduce unemployment and cut taxes to stimulate economic growth. He was replaced March 1993 by Edouard Balladur.

Berengaria of Navarre /ˌberənˈgeərɪə/ 1165–1230. Queen of England, the only English queen never to set foot in England. Daughter of King Sancho VI of Navarre, she married Richard I of England in Cyprus 1191, and accompanied him on his crusade to the Holy Land.

Berezniki /bɪˌrezˈnriːkiː/ city in Russia, on the Kama river N of Perm; population (1987) 200,000. It was formed 1932 by the amalgamation of several older towns. Industry includes chemicals and paper.

Berg /beəg/ Alban 1885–1935. Austrian composer. He studied under Arnold ◊Schoenberg and was associated with him as one of the leaders of the serial, or 12-tone, school of composition. His output includes orchestral, chamber, and vocal music as well as two operas, *Wozzeck* 1925, a grim story of working-class life, and the unfinished *Lulu* 1929–35.

Berg /bɜːg/ Paul 1926– . US molecular biologist. In 1972, using gene-splicing techniques developed by others, Berg spliced and combined into a single hybrid ◊DNA from an animal tumour virus (SV40) and DNA from a bacterial virus. Berg's work aroused fears in other workers and excited continuing controversy. He shared the 1980 Nobel Prize for Chemistry with Walter Gilbert and Frederick Sanger.

Bergama /ˈbeəgəmə/ modern form of ◊*Pergamum*, ancient city in W Turkey.

bergamot small, evergreen tree *Citrus bergamia* of the rue family Rutaceae. From the rind of its fruit a fragrant orange-scented essence used as a perfume is obtained. The sole source of supply is S Calabria, Italy, but the name comes from the town of Bergamo, in Lombardy.

Bergen /ˈbeəgən/ industrial port (shipbuilding, engineering, fishing) in SW Norway; population (1990) 211,800. Founded 1070, Bergen was a member of the ◊Hanseatic League.

Bergius /ˈbeəgɪəs/ Friedrich Karl Rudolph 1884–1949. German research chemist who invented processes for converting coal into oil and wood into sugar. He shared a Nobel prize 1931 with Carl Bosch for his part in inventing and developing high-pressure industrial methods.

Bergman /ˈbeəgmən/ Ingmar 1918– . Swedish stage producer (from the 1930s) and film director (from the 1950s). His work deals with complex moral, psychological, and metaphysical problems and is tinged with pessimism. His films include *Wild Strawberries* 1957, *The Seventh Seal* 1957, *Persona* 1966, and *Fanny and Alexander* 1982.

Bergman /ˈbeəgmən/ Ingrid 1917–1982. Swedish actress whose films include *Intermezzo* 1939, *Casablanca*, *For Whom the Bell Tolls* both 1943, and *Gaslight* 1944, for which she won an Academy Award. By leaving her husband to have a child with director Roberto Rossellini, she broke an unofficial moral code of Hollywood 'star' behaviour and was ostracized for many years. During her 'exile', she made films in Europe such as *Stromboli* 1949 (directed by Rossellini).

Bergson /beək'sɒn/ Henri 1859–1941. French philosopher who believed that time, change, and development were the essence of reality. He thought that time was not a succession of distinct and separate instants but a continuous process in which one period merged imperceptibly into the next. Nobel Prize for Literature 1928.

Beria /'beəriə/ Lavrenti 1899–1953. Soviet politician who became head of the Soviet police force and minister of the interior 1938. On Stalin's death 1953, he attempted to seize power but was foiled and shot after a secret trial.

beriberi endemic polyneuritis, an inflammation of the nerve endings, mostly occurring in the tropics and resulting from a deficiency of vitamin B_1 (thiamine).

Bering /'beərɪŋ/ Vitus 1681–1741. Danish explorer, the first European to sight Alaska. He died on Bering Island in the Bering Sea, both named after him, as is the Bering Strait, which separates Asia (Russia) from North America (Alaska).

Beringia /bə'rɪndʒiə/ former land bridge 1,600 km/1,000 mi wide between Asia and North America; it existed during the ice ages that occurred before 35000 BC and during the period 2400–9000 BC. It is now covered by the Bering Strait and Chukchi Sea.

Bering Sea /'beərɪŋ/ section of the N Pacific between Alaska and Siberia, from the Aleutian Islands north to the Bering Strait.

Bering Strait /'beərɪŋ/ strait between Alaska and Siberia, linking the N Pacific and Arctic oceans.

Berio /'beəriəʊ/ Luciano 1925– . Italian composer. His style has been described as graceful ♭serialism, and he has frequently experimented with electronic music and taped sound. His works include nine *Sequenzas/Sequences* 1957–75 for various solo instruments or voice, *Sinfonia* 1969 for voices and orchestra, *Points on the curve to find ...* 1974, and a number of dramatic works, including the opera *Un re in ascolto/A King Listens* 1984, loosely based on Shakespeare's *The Tempest*.

Beriosova /ˌberi'ɒsəvə/ Svetlana 1932– . British ballerina. Born in Lithuania and brought up partly in the USA, she danced with the Royal Ballet from 1952. Her style had a lyrical dignity and she excelled in *The Lady and the Fool*, *Ondine*, and *Giselle*.

Berkeley /'bɜːkli/ town on San Francisco Bay in California, USA; population (1988 est) 103,700. The Lawrence Radiation Laboratory at Berkeley was the scene of early experiments in atomic fission and a key centre in US development of the atomic bomb during World War II; the laboratory continues to provide facilities for research in high- energy physics and nuclear chemistry. During the 1960s, the University of California campus came to national attention as the site of major political demonstrations, largely directed against US military involvement in Vietnam.

Berkeley /'bɜːkli/ Busby. Stage name of William Berkeley Enos 1895–1976. US choreographer and film director who used ingenious and extravagant sets and teams of female dancers to create large-scale kaleidoscopic patterns through movement and costume when filmed from above, as in *Gold Diggers of 1933*.

Berkeley /'bɑːkli/ George 1685–1753. Irish philosopher and cleric who believed that nothing exists apart from perception, and that the all-seeing mind of God makes possible the continued apparent existence of things. For Berkeley, everyday objects are collections of ideas or sensations, hence the dictum *esse est percipi* ('to exist is to be perceived'). He became bishop of Cloyne 1734.

Berkeley /'bɑːkli/ Lennox (Randal Francis) 1903–1989. English composer. His works for the voice include *The Hill of the Graces* 1975, verses from Spenser's *Fairie Queene* set for eight-part unaccompanied chorus; and his operas *Nelson* 1953 and *Ruth* 1956.

berkelium synthesized, radioactive, metallic element of the actinide series, symbol Bk, atomic number 97, relative atomic mass 247. It was first produced 1949 by Glenn Seaborg and his team, at the University of California at Berkeley, USA, after which it is named.

Berks abbreviation for *Berkshire*.

Berkshire or *Royal Berkshire* county in S central England
area 1,260 sq km/486 sq mi

towns Reading (administrative headquarters), Eton, Slough, Maidenhead, Ascot, Bracknell, Newbury, Windsor

features rivers Thames and Kennet; Inkpen Beacon, 297 m/975 ft; Bagshot Heath; Windsor Forest and Windsor Castle; Eton College; Royal Military Academy at Sandhurst; atomic-weapons research establishment at Aldermaston; the former main UK base for US cruise missiles at Greenham Common, Newbury

products general agricultural and horticultural goods, electronics, plastics, pharmaceuticals

population (1987) 741,000

famous people Jethro Tull, William Laud, Stanley Spencer.

Berlage /ˈbeəlɑːgə/ Hendrikus 1856–1934. Dutch architect of the Amsterdam Stock Exchange 1897–1903. His individualist style marked a move away from 19th-century historicism and towards Dutch Expressionism.

Berlin /bɜːˈlɪn/ industrial city (machine tools, electrical goods, paper, printing) and capital of the Federal Republic of Germany; population (1990) 3,102,500. The Berlin Wall divided the city from 1961 to 1989, but in Oct 1990 Berlin became the capital of a unified Germany once more with East and West Berlin reunited as the 16th Land (state) of the Federal Republic.

First mentioned about 1230, the city grew out of a fishing village, joined the Hanseatic League in the 15th century, became the permanent seat of the Hohenzollerns, and was capital of the Brandenburg electorate 1486–1701, of the kingdom of Prussia 1701–1871, and of united Germany 1871–1945. From the middle of the 18th century it developed into a commercial and cultural centre. In World War II air raids and conquest by the Soviet army 23 Apr–2 May 1945, destroyed much of the city. After the war, Berlin was divided into four sectors—British, US, French, and Soviet—and until 1948 was under quadripartite government by the Allies. Following the ◊Berlin blockade the city was divided, with the USSR creating a separate municipal government in its sector. The other three sectors (West Berlin) were made a *Land* of the Federal Republic May 1949, and in Oct 1949 East Berlin was proclaimed capital of East Germany.

Berlin /bɜːˈlɪn/ Irving. Adopted name of Israel Baline 1888–1989. Russian-born US composer who wrote over 1,500 songs including such hits as 'Alexander's Ragtime

Band' 1911, 'Always' 1925, 'God Bless America' 1939, and 'White Christmas' 1942, and the musicals *Top Hat* 1935, *Annie Get Your Gun* 1950, and *Call Me Madam* 1953. He also wrote film scores such as *Blue Skies* and *Easter Parade*.

Berlin blockade in June 1948, the closing of entry to Berlin from the west by Soviet forces. It was an attempt to prevent the other Allies (the USA, France, and the UK) unifying the western part of Germany. The British and US forces responded by sending supplies to the city by air for over a year (the *Berlin airlift*). In May 1949 the blockade was lifted; the airlift continued until Sept. The blockade marked the formal division of the city into Eastern and Western sectors.

Berlin, Conference of conference 1884–85 of the major European powers (France, Germany, the UK, Belgium and Portugal) called by Chancellor Otto von Bismarck to decide on the colonial partition of Africa.

Berlin, Congress of congress of the European powers (Russia, Turkey, Austria–Hungary, the UK, France, Italy, and Germany) held in Berlin 1878 to determine the boundaries of the Balkan states after the Russo-Turkish war.

Berlinguer /ˌbeəlɪŋˈgweə/ Enrico 1922–1984. Italian Communist who freed the party from Soviet influence. Secretary general of the Italian Communist Party, by 1976 he was near to the premiership, but the murder of Aldo Moro, the prime minister, by Red Brigade guerrillas, prompted a move toward support for the socialists.

A leading spokesman for 'national communism', he sought to adapt Marxism to local requirements and to steer away from slavish obedience to Moscow. The rift between the Italian Communist Party and the Soviet Union widened during the late 1970s and early 1980s, when Berlinguer heavily criticized the Soviet Union's policies of intervention in Afghanistan and Poland.

Berlin Wall dividing barrier between East and West Berlin 1961–89, erected by East Germany to prevent East Germans from leaving for West Germany. Escapers were shot on sight.

From 13 Aug 1961, the East German security forces sealed off all but 12 of the 80 crossing points to West Berlin with a barbed wire barrier. It was reinforced with concrete by the Russians to prevent the escape of unwilling inhabitants of East Berlin to the rival political and economic system of West Berlin. The interconnecting link between East and West Berlin was *Checkpoint Charlie*, where both sides exchanged captured spies. On 9 Nov 1989 the East German government opened its borders to try to halt the mass exodus of its citizens to the West via other Eastern bloc countries, and the wall was gradually dismantled, with portions of it sold off as souvenirs.

Berlioz /ˈbeəliəʊz/ (Louis) Hector 1803–1869. French romantic composer, the founder of modern orchestration. Much of his music was inspired by drama and literature and has a theatrical quality. He wrote symphonic works, such as *Symphonie fantastique* 1830–31 and *Roméo et Juliette* 1839; dramatic cantatas including *La Damnation de Faust* 1846 and *L'Enfance du Christ* 1854; sacred music; and three operas, *Benvenuto Cellini* 1838, *Les Troyens* 1856–58, and *Béatrice et Bénédict* 1862.

Berlioz studied music at the Paris Conservatoire. He won the Prix de Rome 1830, and spent two years in Italy.

Bermuda /bəˈmjuːdə/ British colony in the NW Atlantic
area 54 sq km/21 sq mi
capital and chief port Hamilton
features consists of about 150 small islands, of which 20 are inhabited, linked by bridges and causeways; Britain's oldest colony
products Easter lilies, pharmaceuticals; tourism and banking are important
currency Bermuda dollar
population (1988) 58,100
language English
religion Christian
government under the constitution of 1968, Bermuda is a fully self-governing British colony, with a governor, senate, and elected House of Assembly (premier from 1982 John Swan, United Bermuda Party)
history the islands were named after Juan de Bermudez, who visited them in 1515, and were settled by British colonists in 1609. Indian and African slaves were transported from 1616, and soon outnumbered the white settlers. Racial violence 1977 led to intervention, at the request of the government, by British troops.

Bermuda Triangle /bəˈmjuːdə/ sea area bounded by Bermuda, Florida, and Puerto Rico, which gained the nickname 'Deadly Bermuda Triangle' in 1964 when it was suggested hat unexplained disappearances of ships and aircraft were exceptionally frequent there; analysis of the data has not confirmed the idea.

Bern /beən/ (French *Berne*) capital of Switzerland and of Bern canton, in W Switzerland on the Aare River; population (1987) 300,000. It joined the Swiss confederation 1353 and became the capital 1848. Industries include textiles, chocolate, pharmaceuticals, light metal, and electrical goods.

It was founded 1191 and made a free imperial city by Frederick II 1218. Its name is derived from the bear in its coat of arms, and there has been a bear pit in the city since the 16th century.

Bernadette, St /ˌbɜːnəˈdet/ 1844–1879. French saint, born in Lourdes in the French Pyrenees. In Feb 1858 she had a vision of the Virgin Mary in a grotto, and it became a centre of pilgrimage. Many sick people who were dipped in the water of a spring there were said to have been cured. Feast day 16 Apr.

The grotto of Massabielle was opened to the public by command of Napoleon III, and a church built on the rock above became a shrine. At the age of 20 Bernadette became a nun at Nevers, and nursed the wounded of the Franco-Prussian War.

Bernadotte /ˌbɜːnəˈdɒt/ Count Folke 1895–1948. Swedish diplomat and president of the Swedish Red Cross. In 1945 he conveyed Nazi commander Himmler's offer of capitulation to the British and US governments, and in 1948 was United Nations mediator in Palestine, where he was assassinated by Israeli Stern Gang guerrillas.

Bernadotte /ˌbɜːnəˈdɒt/ Jean-Baptiste Jules 1764–1844. Marshal in Napoleon's army who in 1818 became ◊Charles XIV of Sweden. Hence, Bernadotte is the family name of the present royal house of Sweden.

Bernard /beəˈnɑː/ Claude 1813–1878. French physiologist and founder of experimental medicine. Bernard first demonstrated that digestion is not restricted to the stomach, but takes place throughout the small intestine. He discovered the digestive input of the pancreas, several functions of the liver, and the vasomotor nerves which dilate and contract the blood vessels and thus regulate body temperature. This led him to the concept of the *milieu intérieur* ('internal environment') whose stability is essential to good health. Bernard was a member of the Académie Française and served in the French Senate.

Bernard of Clairvaux, St /kleəˈvəʊ/ 1090–1153. Christian founder in 1115 of Clairvaux monastery in Champagne, France. He reinvigorated the ◊Cistercian order, preached in support of the Second Crusade in 1146, and had the scholastic philosopher Abelard condemned for heresy. He is often depicted with a beehive. Feast day 20 Aug.

Bernard of Menthon, St /mɒnˈtɒn/ or *Bernard of Montjoux* 923–1008. Christian priest, founder of the hospices for travellers on the Alpine passes that bear his name. The large, heavily built *St Bernard* dogs, formerly employed to find travellers lost in the snow, were also named after him. He is the patron saint of mountaineers. Feast day 28 May.

Bernese Oberland /ˈbɜːniːz ˈəʊbələnd/ or *Bernese Alps* mountainous area in the S of Berne canton. It includes the Jungfrau, Eiger, and Finsteraarhorn peaks. Interlaken is the chief town.

Bernhard /ˈbeənɑːt/ Prince of the Netherlands 1911– . Formerly Prince Bernhard of Lippe-Biesterfeld, he married Princess ◊Juliana in 1937. When Germany invaded the Netherlands in 1940, he escaped to England and became liaison officer for the Dutch and British forces, playing a part in the organization of the Dutch Resistance.

Bernhardt /ˈbɜːnhɑːt/ Sarah. Stage name of Rosine Bernard 1845–1923. French actress who dominated the stage of her day, frequently performing at the Comédie-Française in Paris. She excelled in tragic roles, including Cordelia in Shakespeare's *King Lear*, the title role in Racine's *Phèdre*, and the male roles of Hamlet and of Napoleon's son in Edmond ◊Rostand's *L'Aiglon*.

Bernini /beəˈniːni/ Giovanni Lorenzo 1598–1680. Italian sculptor, architect, and painter, a leading figure in the development of the Baroque style. His work in Rome includes the colonnaded piazza in front of St Peter's Basilica (1656), fountains (as in the Piazza Navona), and papal monuments. His sculpture includes *The Ecstasy of St Theresa* 1645–52 (Sta Maria della Vittoria, Rome) and numerous portrait busts.

Bernini's sculptural style is full of movement and drama, as captured in billowing drapery and facial expressions. His subjects are religious and mythological. A fine example is the marble *Apollo and Daphne* for the Cardinal Borghese, 1622–25 (Borghese Palace, Rome), with the figures shown in full flight. Inside St Peter's, he created several marble monuments and the elaborate canopy over the high altar. He also produced many fine portrait busts, such as one of Louis XIV of France.

Bernoulli /bɜːˈnuːli/ Swiss family that produced many mathematicians and scientists in the 17th, 18th, and 19th centuries, in particular the brothers *Jakob* (1654–1705) and *Johann* (1667–1748).

Jakob and Johann were pioneers of ◊Leibniz's calculus. Jakob used calculus to study the forms of many curves arising in practical situations, and studied mathematical probability (*Ars conjectandi* 1713); *Bernoulli numbers* are named after him. Johann developed exponential calculus and contributed to many areas of applied mathematics, including the problem of a particle moving in a gravitational field. His son, *Daniel* (1700–82) worked on calculus and probability, and in physics proposed *Bernoulli's principle*, which states that the pressure of a moving fluid decreases the faster it flows (which explains the origin of lift on the aerofoil of an aircraft's wing). This and other work on hydrodynamics was published in *Hydrodynamica* 1738.

Bernstein /ˈbɜːnstaɪn/ Leonard 1918–1990. US composer, conductor, and pianist, one of

Bernstein US composer, conductor, and pianist Leonard Bernstein.

the most energetic and versatile of US musicians in the 20th century. His works, which established a vogue for realistic, contemporary themes, include symphonies such as *The Age of Anxiety* 1949, ballets such as *Fancy Free* 1944, and scores for musicals, including *West Side Story* 1957.

From 1958 to 1970 he was musical director of the New York Philharmonic. Among his other works are the symphony *Jeremiah* 1944, the ballet *Facsimile* 1946, the musicals *Wonderful Town* 1953 and *Candide* 1956, the *Chichester Psalms* 1965, and *Mass* 1971 in memory of President J F Kennedy.

Berri /'beri/ Nabih 1939– . Lebanese politician and soldier, leader of Amal ('Hope'), the Syrian-backed Shi'ite nationalist movement. He became minister of justice in the government of President ◊Gemayel 1984. In 1988 Amal was disbanded after defeat by the Iranian-backed Hezbollah ('Children of God') during the Lebanese civil wars, and Berri joined the cabinet of Selim Hoss 1989. In Dec 1990 Berri was made minister of state in the newly formed Karami cabinet.

berry fleshy, many-seeded ◊fruit that does not split open to release the seeds. The outer layer of tissue, the exocarp, forms an outer skin that is often brightly coloured to attract birds to eat the fruit and thus disperse the seeds. Examples of berries are the tomato and the grape.

A *pepo* is a type of berry that has developed a hard exterior, such as the cucumber fruit. Another is the *hesperidium*, which has a thick, leathery outer layer, such as that found in citrus fruits, and fluid-containing vesicles within, which form the segments.

Berry /'beri/ Chuck (Charles Edward) 1926– . US rock-and-roll singer, prolific songwriter, and guitarist. His characteristic guitar riffs became staples of rock music, and his humorous storytelling lyrics were also emulated. He had a string of hits in the 1950s and 1960s beginning with 'Maybellene' 1955 and enjoyed a resurgence of popularity in the 1980s.

Berryman /'berimən/ John 1914–1972. US poet whose complex and personal works include *Homage to Mistress Bradstreet* 1956, *77 Dream Songs* 1964 (Pulitzer Prize), and *His Toy, His Dream, His Rest* 1968.

berserker legendary Scandinavian warrior whose frenzy in battle transformed him into a wolf or bear howling and foaming at the mouth (hence 'to go berserk'), and rendered him immune to sword and flame.

Bertholet /ˌbeətə'leɪ/ Claude Louis 1748–1822. French chemist who carried out research into dyes and bleaches (introducing the use of ◊chlorine as a bleach) and determined the composition of ◊ammonia. Modern chemical nomenclature is based on a system worked out by Bertholet and Antoine ◊Lavoisier.

Bertolucci /ˌbeətəʊ'luːtʃi/ Bernardo 1940– . Italian film director whose work combines political and historical perspectives with an elegant and lyrical visual appeal. His films include *The Spider's Stratagem* 1970, *Last Tango in Paris* 1972, *1900* 1976, *The Last Emperor* 1987, for which he received an Academy Award, and *The Sheltering Sky* 1990.

Berwickshire /'berɪkʃə/ former county of SE Scotland, a district of Borders region from 1975.

Berwick-upon-Tweed /'berɪk əpɒn 'twiːd/ town in NE England, at the mouth of the Tweed, Northumberland, 5 km/3 mi SE of the Scottish border; population (1981) 26,230. It is a fishing port. Other industries include iron foundries and shipbuilding.

features Three bridges cross the Tweed: the Old Bridge 1611–34 with 15 arches, the Royal Border railway bridge 1850 constructed by Robert Stephenson, and the Royal Tweed Bridge 1928.

history Held alternately by England and Scotland for centuries, Berwick was made a neutral town 1551; it was attached to Northumberland in 1885.

beryl mineral, beryllium aluminium silicate, $Be_3Al_2Si_6O_{18}$, which forms crystals chiefly in granite. It is the chief ore of beryllium. Two of its gem forms are aquamarine (light-blue crystals) and emerald (dark-green crystals).

beryllium hard, light-weight, silver-white, metallic element, symbol Be, atomic number 4, relative atomic mass 9.012. It is one of the ◊alkaline-earth metals, with chemical properties similar to those of magnesium; in nature it is found only in combination with other elements. It is used to make sturdy, light alloys and to control the speed of neutrons in nuclear reactors. Beryllium oxide was discovered in 1798 by French chemist Louis-Nicolas Vauquelin (1763–1829), but the element was not isolated until 1828, by Friedrich Wöhler and Antoine-Alexandre-Brutus Bussy independently.

Berzelius /bə'ziːliəs/ Jöns Jakob 1779–1848. Swedish chemist who accurately determined more than 2,000 relative atomic and molecular masses. He devised (1813–14) the system of chemical symbols and formulae now in use and proposed oxygen as a reference standard for atomic masses. His discoveries include the elements cerium (1804), selenium (1817), and thorium (1828); he was the first to prepare silicon in its amorphous form and to isolate zirconium. The words *isomerism*, *allotropy*, and *protein* were coined by him.

Bes in Egyptian mythology, the god of music and dance, usually shown as a grotesque dwarf.

Besançon /bə'zɒnsɒn/ town on the river Doubs, France; population (1983) 120,000. It is the capital of Franche-Comté. The first factory to produce artificial fibres was established here 1890. Industries include textiles and clock-making. It has fortifications by ◊Vauban, Roman remains, and a Gothic cathedral. The writer Victor Hugo and the Lumière brothers, inventors of cinematography, were born here.

Besant /'besənt/ Annie 1847–1933. British socialist and feminist activist. Separated from her clerical husband in 1873 because of her freethinking views, she was associated with the radical atheist Charles Bradlaugh and the socialist ◊Fabian Society. She and Bradlaugh published a treatise advocating birth control and were prosecuted; as a result she lost custody of her daughter. In 1889 she became a disciple of Madame ◊Blavatsky. She thereafter preached theosophy and went to India. As a supporter of Indian independence, she founded the Central Hindu College 1898 and the Indian Home Rule League 1916, and became president of the Indian National Congress in 1917. Her *Theosophy and the New Psychology* was published 1904. She was the sister-in-law of Walter ◊Besant.

Besant /'besənt/ Walter 1836–1901. English writer. He wrote novels in partnership with James Rice (1844–1882), and produced an attack on the social evils of the East End of London, *All Sorts and Conditions of Men* 1882, and an unfinished *Survey of London* 1902–12. He was the brother-in-law of Annie ◊Besant.

Bessarabia /ˌbesə'reɪbiə/ territory in SE Europe, annexed by Russia 1812, that broke away at the Russian Revolution to join Romania. The cession was confirmed by the Allies, but not by Russia, in a Paris treaty of 1920; Russia reoccupied it 1940 and divided it between the Moldavian and Ukrainian republics. Romania recognized the position in the 1947 peace treaty.

Bessel /'besl/ Friedrich Wilhelm 1784–1846. German astronomer and mathematician, the first person to find the approximate distance to a star by direct methods when he measured the ◊parallax (annual displacement) of the star 61 Cygni in 1838. In mathematics, he introduced the series of functions now known as *Bessel functions*.

Bessemer process the first cheap method of making ◊steel, invented by Henry Bessemer in England 1856. It has since been superseded by more efficient steelmaking processes, such as the ◊basic-oxygen process. In the Bessemer process compressed air is blown into the bottom of a converter, a furnace shaped like a cement mixer, containing molten pig iron. The excess carbon in the iron burns out, other impurities form a slag, and the furnace is emptied by tilting.

Best /best/ Charles Herbert 1899–1978. Canadian physiologist, one of the team of Canadian scientists including Frederick ◊Banting whose research resulted in 1922 in the discovery of insulin as a treatment for diabetes.

Best /best/ George 1946– . Irish footballer. He won two League championship medals and was a member of the Manchester United side that won the European Cup in 1968.

Born in Belfast, he joined Manchester United as a youth and made his debut at 17; seven months later he made his international debut for Northern Ireland. Trouble with managers, fellow players, and the media led to his early retirement.

bestiary in medieval times, a book with stories and illustrations which depicted real and mythical animals or plants to illustrate a (usually Christian) moral. The stories were initially derived from the Greek *Physiologus*, a collection of 48 such stories, written in Alexandria around the 2nd century AD.

bestseller book that achieves large sales. Listings are based upon sales figures from bookstores and other retail stores.

The Bible has sold more copies than any other book over time, but popular and commercial examples include Charles Monroe Seldon's *In His Steps* 1897, Margaret Mitchell's *Gone With the Wind* 1936, and Dale Carnegie's *How to Win Friends and Influence*

People 1937. Current bestseller lists appear in newspapers, magazines, and book trade publications.

beta-blocker any of a class of drugs that block impulses that stimulate certain nerve endings (beta receptors) serving the heart muscles. This reduces the heart rate and the force of contraction, which in turn reduces the amount of oxygen (and therefore the blood supply) required by the heart. Beta-blockers are banned from use in competitive sports. They may be useful in the treatment of angina, arrhythmia, and raised blood pressure, and following myocardial infarctions. They must be withdrawn from use gradually.

beta decay the disintegration of the nucleus of an atom to produce a beta particle, or high-speed electron, and an electron-antineutrino. During beta decay, a proton in the nucleus changes into a neutron, thereby increasing the atomic number by one while the mass number stays the same. The mass lost in the change is converted into kinetic (movement) energy of the beta particle. Beta decay is caused by the weak nuclear force, one of the fundamental ◊forces of nature operating inside the nucleus.

beta particle electron ejected with great velocity from a radioactive atom that is undergoing spontaneous disintegration. Beta particles do not exist in the nucleus but are created on disintegration, beta decay, when a neutron converts to a proton to emit an electron.

Beta particles are more penetrating than ◊alpha particles, but less so than ◊gamma radiation; they can travel several metres in air, but are stopped by 2–3 mm of aluminium. They are less strongly ionizing than alpha particles and, like cathode rays, are easily deflected by magnetic and electric fields.

Betelgeuse /ˈbiːtldʒɜːz/ or *Alpha Orionis* red supergiant star in the constellation of Orion and the tenth brightest star in the sky, although its brightness varies. It is over 300 times the diameter of the Sun, about the same size as the orbit of Mars, is over 10,000 times as luminous as the Sun, and lies 650 light years from Earth.

betel nut fruit of the areca palm (*Areca catechu*), used together with lime and betel pepper as a masticatory stimulant by peoples of the East and Papua New Guinea.

Chewing it results in blackened teeth and a mouth stained deep red.

Bethe /ˈbeɪtə/ Hans Albrecht 1906– . German-born US physicist who worked on the first atom bomb. He was awarded a Nobel prize 1967 for his discoveries concerning energy production in stars.

Bethe left Germany for England in 1933, and worked at Manchester and Bristol universities. In 1935 he moved to the USA where he became professor of theoretical physics at Cornell University; his research was interrupted by the war and by his appointment as head of the theoretical division of the Los Alamos atom bomb project. He has since become a leading peace campaigner, and opposed the US government's Strategic Defense Initiative (Star Wars) programme.

Bethlehem /ˈbeθlɪhem/ (Hebrew *Beit-Lahm*) town on the W bank of the river Jordan, S of Jerusalem. Occupied by Israel in 1967; population (1980) 14,000. In the Bible it is mentioned as the birthplace of King David and Jesus.

Bethmann Hollweg /ˈbeɪtmæn ˈhɒlveɡ/ Theobald von 1856–1921. German politician, imperial chancellor 1909–17, largely responsible for engineering popular support for World War I in Germany, but his power was overthrown by a military dictatorship under ◊Ludendorff and ◊Hindenburg.

Betjeman /ˈbetʃɪmən/ John 1906–1984. English poet and essayist, originator of a peculiarly English light verse, nostalgic, and delighting in Victorian and Edwardian architecture. His *Collected Poems* appeared in 1968 and a verse autobiography *Summoned by Bells* in 1960. He was knighted in 1969 and became poet laureate in 1972.

betony plant, *Stachys* (formerly *Betonica*) *officinalis*, of the mint family, formerly used in medicine and dyeing. It has a hairy stem and leaves, and reddish-purple flowers.

Betony is found growing as a hedgerow weed in Britain.

Bettelheim /ˈbetlhaɪm/ Bruno 1903–1990. Austrian-born US child psychologist. Imprisoned in the Dachau and Buchenwald concentration camps 1933–35, he emigrated to the USA in 1939. At the University of Chicago he founded a treatment centre for emotionally disturbed children based on the principle of a supportive home environment. His books include *Love is Not Enough* 1950, *The Uses of Enchantment: The Meaning and*

Importance of Fairy Tales 1976, and *A Good Enough Parent* 1987. He took his own life.

Betti /ˈbeti/ Ugo 1892–1953. Italian poet and dramatist. His plays include *Delitto all'isola delle capre/Crime on Goat Island* 1948 and *La Regina e gli insorte/The Queen and the Rebels* 1949.

betting wagering money on the outcome of a game, race, or other event, not necessarily a sporting event.

In the UK, on-course betting on *horses* and *dogs* may be through individual bookmakers at given odds, or on the tote (totalizator), when the total amount (with fixed deductions) staked is divided among those making the correct forecast. Off-course betting is mainly through betting 'shops' (legalized 1960) which, like bookmakers, must have a licence. *Football* betting is in the hands of 'pools' promoters who must be registered with a local authority to which annual accounts are submitted. The size of the money prizes is determined by the number of successful forecasts of the results of matches received; the maximum first dividend on football pools is fixed at £1 million.

In France, there are no individual bookmakers; all betting is through the *Pari-mutuel*, the equivalent of the British totalizator.

Betty Boop comic-strip character created in the USA 1915 by Grim Natwick for Max Fleischer's 'Talkartoons'. Sexy and independent, she has short curly black hair, a minidress, and wide-eyed appeal. Her image and 'boop-a-doop' song were supposedly borrowed from US singer Helen Kane (1904–1966). Betty Boop was popular throughout the 1920s and 1930s, and the cartoons in which she appeared usually made comments on social follies of the time. Her film debut was in *Dizzy Dishes* 1930.

Beuys /bɔɪs/ Joseph 1921–1986. German sculptor and performance artist, one of the leaders of avant-garde art in Europe during the 1970s and 1980s. His sculpture makes use of unusual materials such as felt and fat. He was strongly influenced by his wartime experiences.

Bevan /ˈbevən/ Aneurin 1897–1960. British Labour politician. Son of a Welsh miner, and himself a miner at 13, he became member of Parliament for Ebbw Vale 1929–60. As minister of health 1945–51, he inaugurated the National Health Service (NHS); he was minister of labour Jan–April 1951, when he resigned (with Harold Wilson) on the introduction of NHS charges and led a Bevanite faction against the government. In 1956 he became chief Labour spokesman on foreign affairs, and deputy leader of the Labour party 1959. He was noted as an orator.

beverage any liquid for drinking other than pure water. Beverages are made with plant products to impart pleasant flavours, nutrients, and stimulants to people's fluid intake. Examples include juices, tea, coffee, cocoa, cola drinks, and alcoholic beverages. See also ⟡alcoholic liquor.

Beveridge /ˈbevərɪdʒ/ William Henry, 1st Baron Beveridge 1879–1963. British economist. A civil servant, he acted as Lloyd George's lieutenant in the social legislation of the Liberal government before World War I. The *Beveridge Report* 1942 formed the basis of the welfare state in Britain.

Beveridge Report, the popular name of *Social Insurance and Allied Services*, a report written by William Beveridge 1942 that formed the basis for the social reform legislation of the Labour Government of 1945–50.

Also known as the *Report on Social Security* it identified five 'giants': illness, ignorance, disease, squalor and want. It proposed a scheme of social insurance from 'the cradle to the grave', and recommended a national health service, social insurance and assistance, family allowances, and full-employment policies.

Beverly Hills /ˈbevəli/ residential part of greater Los Angeles, California, USA, known as the home of Hollywood film stars. Population (1980) 32,400.

Bevin /ˈbevɪn/ Ernest 1881–1951. British Labour politician. Chief creator of the Transport and General Workers' Union, he was its general secretary from 1921 to 1940, when he entered the war cabinet as minister of labour and national service. He organized the 'Bevin boys', chosen by ballot to work in the coal mines as war service, and was foreign secretary in the Labour government 1945–51.

Bezier curve curved line that connects a series of points (or 'nodes') in the smoothest possible way. The shape of the curve is governed by a series of complex mathematical formulae. They are used in ⟡computer graphics and ⟡CAD.

Béziers /bezˈjeɪ/ city in Languedoc-Roussillon, S France; population (1983) 84,000. It is a centre of the wine trade. It was once a

Roman station and was the site of a massacre 1209 in the Albigensian Crusade.

bézique (French *bésigue*) card game believed to have originated in Spain. Brought to England 1861 it became very popular and in 1887 the Portland Club drew up a standardized set of rules for the popular variety *Rubicon bézique*. Each player has a pack of cards but all cards with a face value of 2–6 are taken out.

BFI abbreviation for the *British Film Institute*. Founded in 1933, the organization was created to promote the cinema as a 'means of entertainment and instruction'. It includes the National Film Archive (1935) and the National Film Theatre (1951).

Bhagalpur /ˈbɑːɡlpʊə/ town in N India, on the river Ganges; population (1981) 225,000. It manufactures silk and textiles. Several Jain temples are here.

Bhagavad-Gītā /ˌbʌɡəvəd ˈɡiːtə/ (Hindu 'the Song of the Blessed') religious and philosophical Sanskrit poem, dating from around 300 BC, forming an episode in the sixth book of the *Mahābhārata*, one of the two great Hindu epics. It is the supreme religious work of Hinduism.

bhakti (Sanskrit 'devotion') in Hinduism, a tradition of worship that emphasizes love and devotion rather than ritual, sacrifice, or study.

bhangra pop music evolved in the UK in the late 1970s from traditional Punjabi music, combining electronic instruments and ethnic drums.

Bharat /ˈbʌrət/ Hindi name for ◊India.

Bhatgaon /bɑːˈtɡɑːɒn/ *Bhadgaon* or *Bhaktapur* town in Nepal, 11 km/7 mi SE of Katmandu; population (1981) 48,500. It has been a religious centre since the 9th century; there is a palace.

Bhavnagar /baʊˈnʌɡə/ port in Gujarat, NW India, in the Kathiawar peninsula; population (1981) 308,000. It is a centre for textile industry. It was capital of the former Rajput princely state of Bhavnagar.

bhikku Buddhist monk who is totally dependent on alms and the monastic community (*sangha*) for support.

Bhil member of a semi-nomadic people of Dravidian origin, living in NW India and numbering about 4 million. They are hunter-gatherers and also practise shifting cultivation. The Bhili language belongs to the Indo-European family, as does Gujarati, which is also spoken by the Bhil. Their religion is Hinduism.

Bhindranwale /ˈbɪndrəwɒlə/ Sant Jarnail Singh 1947–1984. Indian Sikh fundamentalist leader who campaigned for the creation of a separate state of Khalistan during the early 1980s, precipitating a bloody Hindu-Sikh conflict in the Punjab. Having taken refuge in the Golden Temple complex in Amritsar and built up an arms cache for guerrilla activities, Bhindranwale, along with around 500 followers, died at the hands of Indian security forces who stormed the temple in 'Operation Blue Star' June 1984.

Bhopal /bəʊˈpɑːl/ industrial city (textiles, chemicals, electrical goods, jewellery); capital of Madhya Pradesh, central India; population (1981) 672,000.

Nearby Bhimbetka Caves, discovered 1973, have the world's largest collection of prehistoric paintings, which are about 10,000 years old. In 1984 some 2,600 people died from an escape of the poisonous gas methyl isocyanate from a factory owned by the US company Union Carbide; another 300,000 are expected to suffer long-term health problems.

The city was capital of the former princely state of Bhopal, founded 1723, which became allied to Britain in 1817. It was merged with Madhya Pradesh in 1956.

Bhubaneswar /ˌbʊvəˈneɪʃwə/ city in NE India; population (1981) 219,200. It is the capital of Orissa state. Utkal University was founded 1843. A place of pilgrimage and centre of Siva worship, it has temples of the 6th–12th centuries.

It was capital of the Kesaris (Lion) dynasty of Orissa 474–950.

Bhumibol Adulyadej 1927– . King of Thailand from 1946. Born in the USA and educated in Bangkok and Switzerland, he succeeded to the throne on the assassination of his brother. In 1973 he was active, with popular support, in overthrowing the military government of Marshal Thanom Kittikachorn and thus ended a sequence of army-dominated regimes in power from 1932.

Bhutan /buːˈtɑːn/ mountainous, landlocked country in the eastern Himalayas (SE Asia), bounded N and W by Tibet (China) and to the S and E by India.

government Bhutan is a hereditary monarchy and although since 1953 there has been an elected national assembly (Tshogdu) and

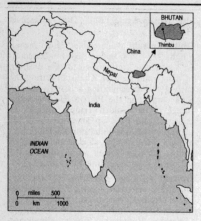

since 1965 a partially elected royal advisory council with whom the monarch shares power, in the absence of a written constitution or political parties it is in effect an absolute monarchy. There are, however, certain written rules governing the methods of electing members of the royal advisory council and Tshogdu. A gradual trend toward greater democracy is occurring.

history Bhutan was ruled by Tibet from the 16th century and by China from 1720. In 1774 the British East India Company concluded a treaty with the ruler of Bhutan, and British influence grew during the 19th century. A short border war in 1863 ended with a treaty in 1865, under which an annual subsidy was paid by Britain to Bhutan. In 1907 the first hereditary monarch was installed, and under the Anglo-Bhutanese Treaty signed three years later, Bhutan was granted internal autonomy while foreign relations were placed under the control of the British government in India.

Following India's independence 1947, an Indo-Bhutan Treaty of Friendship was signed 1949, under which Bhutan agreed to seek Indian advice on foreign relations but not necessarily to accept it. There is no formal defence treaty, but India would regard an attack on Bhutan as an act of aggression against itself. In 1952 King Jigme Dorji Wangchuk came to power, and in 1953 a national assembly was established.

In 1959, after the Chinese annexation of Tibet, Bhutan gave asylum to some 4,000 Tibetan refugees who in 1979 were given the choice of taking Bhutanese citizenship or returning to Tibet. Most became citizens,

and the rest went to India. In 1968, as part of a move towards greater democracy, the king appointed his first cabinet. He died 1972 and was succeeded by his Western-educated son Jigme Singye Wangchuk.

In 1983 Bhutan became a founding member of the South Asian Association for Regional Cooperation (SAARC), and in 1985 the first meeting of SAARC foreign ministers was held in Bhutan.

In 1988 the Buddhist Dzongkha ethnic minority, headed by the king, imposed its own language, religious practices, and national dress on the divided (mainly Hindu-Nepali) majority. Tension between the two communities increased; the Nepalese illegally formed a number of political parties to protest against Dzongkha policies. Several hundred people were reported to have been killed during prodemocracy demonstrations.

Bhutto /ˈbuːtəʊ/ Benazir 1953– . Pakistani politician, leader of the Pakistan People's Party (PPP) from 1984 (in exile until 1986), and prime minister of Pakistan 1988–90, when the opposition manoeuvred her from office and charged her with corruption and again from 1993. She was the first female leader of a Muslim state.

Benazir Bhutto was educated at Harvard and Oxford universities. She returned to Pakistan but was placed under house arrest after General ◊Zia ul-Haq seized power from her father, Prime Minister Zulfiqar Ali Bhutto. On her release she moved to the UK and became, with her mother Nusrat (1934–), the joint leader in exile of the opposition PPP. When martial law had been lifted, she returned to Pakistan April 1986 to launch a campaign for open elections. In her first year in office she struck an uneasy balance with the military establishment and improved Pakistan's relations with India.

She led her country back into the Commonwealth 1989, and became in 1990 the first head of government to bear a child while in office.

In Aug 1990, she was removed from office by presidential decree, and a caretaker government installed. Charges of corruption and abuse of power were levelled against her and her husband (who was also accused of mass murder, kidnapping and extortion), and her party was defeated in the subsequent general election. Bhutto and her husband claimed that the charges were fabrications, with the government's intention being to strike a deal whereby they would receive pardons on condition that they left the country and effectively abandoned politics. In May 1991 new charges (eight in all), alleging misuse of secret service funds, were brought against Benazir Bhutto. She denied all charges. Her husband, Asif Ali Zardari, who was acquitted on 5 May 1991 of fraudulently obtaining a bank loan, was charged on 13 May with criminal conspiracy leading to the death of political opponents.

Bhutto /ˈbuːtəʊ/ Zulfikar Ali 1928–1979. Pakistani politician, president 1971–73; prime minister from 1973 until the 1977 military coup led by Gen ◊Zia ul-Haq. In 1978 he was sentenced to death for conspiring to murder a political opponent and was hanged the following year.

Biafra, Bight of /biˈæfrə/ name until 1975 of the Bight of ◊Bonny, W Africa.

Biafra, Republic of /biˈæfrə/ African state proclaimed in 1967 when fears that Nigerian central government was increasingly in the hands of the rival Hausa tribe led the predominantly Ibo Eastern Region of Nigeria to secede under Lt Col Odumegwu Ojukwu. On the proclamation of Biafra, civil war ensued in the rest of the federation. In a bitterly fought campaign federal forces confined the Biafrans to a shrinking area of the interior by 1968, and by 1970 Biafra ceased to exist.

Białystok /bjæˈwɪstɒk/ city in E Poland; population (1985) 245,000. It is the capital city of Białystok region. Industries include textiles, chemicals, and tools. Founded 1310, the city belonged to Prussia 1795–1807 and to Russia 1807–1919.

Bible (Greek *ta biblia* 'the books') the sacred book of the Jewish and Christian religions. The Hebrew Bible, recognized by both Jews and Christians, is called the ◊*Old Testament* by Christians. The ◊*New Testament* comprises books recognized by the Christian church from the 4th century as canonical. The Roman Catholic Bible also includes the ◊*Apocrypha*. The first English translation of the entire Bible was by a priest, Miles Coverdale, 1535; the Authorized Version or *King James Bible* 1611, was long influential for the clarity and beauty of its language. A revision of the Authorized Version carried out 1959 by the British and Foreign Bible Society produced the widely used American translation, the

Revised Standard Version (New Testament 1946, Old Testament 1952, Apocrypha 1957). A conference of British churches 1946 recommended a completely new translation into English from the original Hebrew and Greek texts; work on this was carried out over the following two decades, resulting in the publication of the New English Bible (New Testament 1961, Old Testament and Apocrypha 1970). Another major new

The Bible

The Books of the Old Testament

name of book	chapters	date written
the Pentateuch or the Five Books of Moses		
Genesis	50	mid 8th-century BC
Exodus	40	950–586 BC
Leviticus	27	mid 7th-century BC
Numbers	36	850–650 BC
Deuteronomy	34	mid-7th century BC
Joshua	24	c. 550 BC
Judges	21	c. 550 BC
Ruth	4	end 3rd century BC
1 Samuel	31	c. 900 BC
2 Samuel	24	c. 900 BC
1 Kings	22	550–600 BC
2 Kings	25	550–600 BC
1 Chronicles	29	c. 300 BC
2 Chronicles	36	c. 300 BC
Ezra	10	c. 450 BC
Nehemiah	13	c. 450 BC
Esther	10	c. 200 BC
Job	42	600–400 BC
Psalms	150	6th–2nd century BC
Proverbs	31	350–150 BC
Ecclesiastes	12	c. 200 BC
Song of Solomon	8	3rd century BC
Isaiah	66	end 3rd century BC
Jeremiah	52	604 BC
Lamentations	5	586–536 BC
Ezekiel	48	6th century BC
Daniel	12	c. 166 BC
Hosea	14	c. 732 BC
Joel	3	c. 500 BC
Amos	9	775–750 BC
Obadiah	1	6th–3rd century BC
Jonah	4	600–200 BC
Micah	7	end 3rd century BC
Nahum	3	c. 626 BC
Habakkuk	3	c. 600 BC
Zephaniah	3	3rd century BC
Haggai	2	c. 520 BC
Zechariah	14	c. 520 BC
Malachi	4	c. 430 BC

The Bible (contd)

The Books of the New Testament

name of book	chapters	date written
the Gospels		
Matthew	28	before AD 70
Mark	16	before AD 70
Luke	24	AD 70–80
John	21	AD 90–100
The Acts	28	AD 70–80
Romans	16	AD 120
1 Corinthians	16	AD 57
2 Corinthians	13	AD 57
Galatians	6	AD 53
Ephesians	6	AD 140
Philippians	4	AD 63
Colossians	4	AD 140
1 Thessalonians	5	AD 50–54
2 Thessalonians	3	AD 50–54
1 Timothy	6	before AD 64
2 Timothy	4	before AD 64
Titus	3	before AD 64
Philemon	1	AD 60–62
Hebrews	13	AD 80–90
James	5	before AD 52
1 Peter	5	before AD 64
2 Peter	3	before AD 64
1 John	5	AD 90–100
2 John	1	AD 90–100
3 John	1	AD 90–100
Jude	1	AD 75–80
Revelation	22	AD 81–96

translation is the Jerusalem Bible, completed by Catholic scholars in 1966. Missionary activity led to the translation of the Bible into the languages of people they were trying to convert, and by 1975 parts of the Bible had been translated into over 1,500 different languages, with 261 complete translations.

Bible society society founded for the promotion of translation and distribution of the Scriptures. The four largest branches are the British and Foreign Bible Society, founded in 1804, the American Bible Society, the National Bible Society of Scotland, and the Netherlands Bible Society.

bicarbonate common name for ◊hydrogencarbonate

bicarbonate of soda former name for ◊sodium hydrogencarbonate (sodium bicarbonate).

Bichat /biːˈʃɑː/ Marie François Xavier 1771–1802. French physician and founder of ◊histology, the study of tissues. He studied the organs of the body, their structure, and the ways in which they are affected by disease. This led to his discovery and naming of 'tissue', a basic biological and medical concept; he identified 21 types.

bichir African fish, genus *Polypterus*, found in tropical swamps and rivers. Cylindrical in shape, some species grow to 70 cm/2.3 ft or more. They show many 'primitive' features, such as breathing air by using the swimbladder, having a spiral valve in the intestine, having heavy bony scales, and having larvae with external gills. These, and the fleshy fins, lead some scientists to think they are related to lungfish and coelacanths.

bicycle pedal-driven two-wheeled vehicle used in ◊cycling. It consists of a metal frame mounted on two large wire-spoked wheels, with handlebars in front and a seat between the front and back wheels. The bicycle is an energy-efficient, nonpolluting form of transport, and it is estimated that 800 million bicycles are in use throughout the world—twice the number of cars in existence. China, India, Denmark, and the Netherlands are countries with a high use of bicycles.

The first bicycle was seen in Paris 1791 and was a form of hobby-horse. The first treadle-propelled cycle was designed by Kirkpatrick Macmillan (Scotland) 1839. By the end of the 19th century wire wheels, metal frames (replacing wood), and pneumatic tyres (invented by J B Dunlop 1888) had been added. Among the bicycles of that time was the front-wheel driven 'Penny Farthing' with a large front wheel.

Bidault /biːˈdəʊ/ Georges 1899–1983. French politician. As a leader of the Mouvement Républicaine Populaire, he held office as prime minister and foreign minister in a number of unstable administrations 1944–54. In 1962 he became head of the ◊Organisation de l'Armée Secrète (OAS), formed 1961 by French settlers devoted to perpetuating their own rule in Algeria. He was charged with treason in 1963 and left the country, but was allowed to return in 1968.

Biedermeier /biːdəˌmaɪə/ mid-19th-century Germanic style of art and furniture design, derogatorily named after Gottlieb Biedermeier, a fictitious character embodying bourgeois taste.

biennial plant plant that completes its life cycle in two years. During the first year it grows vegetatively and the surplus food produced is stored in its ◊perennating organ, usually the root. In the following year these food reserves are used for the production of leaves, flowers, and seeds, after which the plant dies. Many root vegetables are biennials, including the carrot *Daucus carota* and parsnip *Pastinaca sativa*. Some garden plants that are grown as biennials are actually perennials, for example, the wallflower *Cheiranthus cheiri*.

Bierce /bɪəs/ Ambrose (Gwinett) 1842– c. 1914. US author. He established his reputation as a master of supernatural and psychological horror with *Tales of Soldiers and Civilians* 1891 and *Can Such Things Be?* 1893. He also wrote *The Devil's Dictionary* 1911 (first published as *The Cynic's Word Book* 1906), a collection of ironic definitions. He disappeared in Mexico 1913.

Bierstadt /ˈbɪəstæt/ Albert 1830–1902. German-born US landscape painter. His spectacular panoramas of the American wilderness fell out of favour after his death until interest in the Hudson River School rekindled late in the century. A classic work is *Thunderstorm in the Rocky Mountains* 1859 (Museum of Fine Arts, Boston).

Biffen /ˈbɪfɪn/ (William) John 1930– . British Conservative politician. In 1971 he was elected to Parliament for a Shropshire seat. Despite being to the left of Margaret Thatcher, he held key positions in government from 1979, including leader of the House of Commons from 1982, but was dropped after the general election of 1987.

big-band jazz ◊swing music created in the late 1930s and 1940s by bands of 13 or more players, such as those of Duke ◊Ellington and Benny ◊Goodman. Big-band jazz relied on fixed arrangements, where there is more than one instrument to some of the parts, rather than improvisation. Big bands were mainly dance bands, flourishing at a time when all dance music was live, and they ceased to be economically viable in the 1950s.

Big Bang in economics, popular term for the major changes instituted in late 1986 to the organization and practices of the City of London as Britain's financial centre, with the aim of ensuring that London retained its place as one of the leading world financial centres. Facilitated in part by computeriza-tion and on-line communications, the changes included the liberalization of the London ◊Stock Exchange. This involved merging the functions of jobber (dealer in stocks and shares) and broker (who mediates between the jobber and the public), introducing negotiated commission rates, and allowing foreign banks and financial companies to own British brokers/jobbers, or themselves to join the London Stock Exchange.

In the year before and after the Big Bang the City of London was marked by hyperactivity: there were many takeovers, mergers and acquisitions as companies sought to improve their competitiveness. Salaries reached unprecedented levels and there was a great deal of job mobility as British and foreign financial companies sought out the skills they needed. Share prices rose sharply and trading was helped by the introduction of highly sensitive computerized systems.

The level of activity could not be sustained, and in Oct 1987 the frenzied trading halted abruptly and share prices fell sharply around the world on what became known as ◊Black Monday.

Big Bang in astronomy, the hypothetical 'explosive' event that marked the origin of the universe as we know it. At the time of the Big Bang, the entire universe was squeezed into a hot, superdense state. The Big Bang explosion threw this compacted material outwards, producing the expanding universe (see ◊red shift). The cause of the Big Bang is unknown; observations of the current rate of expansion of the universe suggest that it took place about 15 billion years ago. See also ◊cosmology.

Big Ben popular name for the bell in the clock tower of the Houses of Parliament in London, cast at the Whitechapel Bell Foundry in 1858, and known as 'Big Ben' after Benjamin Hall, First Commissioner of Works at the time. It weighs 13.7 tonnes.

Biggin Hill /ˈbɪgɪn/ airport in the SE London borough of Bromley. It was the most famous of the Royal Air Force stations in the Battle of Britain in World War II.

bight coastal indentation, such as the Bight of ◊Bonny in W Africa and the Great Australian Bight.

Bihar /bɪˈhɑː/ or *Behar* state of NE India
area 173,900 sq km/67,125 sq mi
capital Patna

features river Ganges in the N, Rajmahal Hills in the S
products copper, iron, coal, rice, jute, sugar cane, grain, oilseed
population (1981) 69,823,000.
language Hindi, Bihari
famous people Chandragupta, Asoka
history the ancient kingdom of Magadha roughly corresponded to central and S Bihar. Many Bihari people were massacred as a result of their protest at the establishment of Bangladesh 1971.

Bihari member of a N Indian people, also living in Bangladesh, Nepal, and Pakistan, and numbering over 40 million. The Bihari are mainly Muslim. The Bihari language is related to Hindi and has several widely varying dialects. It belongs to the Indic branch of the Indo-European family. Many Bihari were massacred during the formation of Bangladesh, which they opposed.

Bijapur /ˌbɪdʒəˈpʊə/ ancient city in Karnataka, Republic of India. It was founded around AD 1489 Yusuf Adil Shah (died 1511), the son of Murad II, as the capital of the Muslim kingdom of Biafra. The city and kingdom was annexed by the Mogul emperor Aurangzeb in 1686.

Bikini /bɪˈkiːni/ atoll in the ◊Marshall Islands, W Pacific, where the USA carried out 23 atom-bomb tests 1946–63. In 1990 a US plan was announced to remove radioactive topsoil, allowing 800 islanders to return home. Its name was given to a two-piece swimsuit said to have an explosive effect.

Biko /ˈbiːkəʊ/ Steve (Stephen) 1946–1977. South African civil rights leader. An active opponent of ◊apartheid; he was arrested in Sept 1977; he died in detention six days later. Since his death in the custody of South African police he has been a symbol of the anti-apartheid movement.

He founded the South African Students Organization (SASO) in 1968 and was co-founder in 1972 of the Black People's Convention, also called the Black Consciousness movement, a radical association of South African students that aimed to develop black pride. His death while still in the hands of the police caused much controversy.

bilateralism in economics, a trade agreement between two countries or groups of countries in which they give each other preferential treatment. Usually the terms agreed result in balanced trade and are favoured by countries with limited foreign exchange reserves. Bilateralism is incompatible with free trade.

Bilbao /bɪlˈbaʊ/ industrial port (iron and steel, chemicals, cement, food) in N Spain, capital of Biscay province; population (1986) 378,000.

bilberry several species of shrubs of the genus *Vaccinium* of the heath family Ericaceae, closely related to North American blueberries.

bilby rabbit-eared bandicoot *Macrotis lagotis*, a lightly built marsupial with big ears and long nose. This burrowing animal is mainly carnivorous, and its pouch opens backwards.

Bildungsroman (German 'education novel') novel that deals with the psychological and emotional development of its protagonist, tracing his or her life from inexperienced youth to maturity. The first example of the type is generally considered to be ◊Wieland's *Agathon* 1765–66, but it was ◊Goethe's *Wilhelm Meisters Lehrjahr/Wilhelm Meister's Apprenticeship* 1795–96 that established the genre. Although taken up by writers in other languages, it remained chiefly a German form; later examples include Thomas ◊Mann's *Der Zauberberg/The Magic Mountain* 1924.

bile brownish fluid produced by the liver. In most vertebrates, it is stored in the gall bladder and emptied into the small intestine as food passes through. Bile consists of bile salts, bile pigments, cholesterol, and lecithin. *Bile salts* assist in the breakdown and absorption of fats; *bile pigments* are the breakdown products of old red blood cells that are passed into the gut to be eliminated with the faeces.

bilharzia or *schistosomiasis* disease that causes anaemia, inflammation, formation of scar tissue, dysentery, enlargement of the spleen and liver, cancer of the bladder, and cirrhosis of the liver. It is contracted by bathing in water contaminated with human sewage. Some 300 million people are thought to suffer from this disease in the tropics.

Freshwater snails that live in this water act as host to the first larval stage of flukes of the genus *Schistosoma*; when these larvae leave the snail in their second stage of development, they are able to pass through human skin, become sexually mature, and produce quantities of eggs, which pass to the intestine or bladder. The human host event-

ually dies of the infestation, but before then numerous eggs have passed from the body in urine or faeces to continue the cycle. Treatment is by means of drugs, usually containing antimony, to kill the parasites.

billiards indoor game played, normally by two players, with tapered poles (cues) and composition balls (one red, two white) on a rectangular table covered with a green baize cloth. The table has six pockets, one at each corner and in each of the long sides at the middle. Scoring strokes are made by potting the red ball, potting the opponent's ball, or potting another ball off one of these two. The cannon (when the cue ball hits the two other balls on the table) is another scoring stroke.

Billiards is played in many different forms. The most popular is the three-ball game played on a standard English billiards table, which is approximately 3.66 m/12 ft by 1.83 m/6 ft in size. *Carom*, played on a table without pockets, is popular in Europe. Another form is ◊pool, popular in the USA and Britain.

World Professional Championship was instituted in 1870 and organized on a challenge basis. It was restored as an annual tournament in 1980.

Billingsgate /'bılıŋzgeıt/ chief London wholesale fish market, formerly (from the 9th century) near London Bridge. It reopened in 1982 at the new Billingsgate market, West India Dock, Isle of Dogs.

billion the cardinal number represented by a 1 followed by nine zeros (1,000,000,000), equivalent to a thousand million.

Billiton /'bılıtɒn/ Indonesian island in the Java Sea, between Borneo and Sumatra, one of the Sunda Islands; area 4,830 sq km/1,860 sq mi. The chief port is Tanjungpandan. Tin mining is the chief industry.

Bill of Exchange form of commercial credit instrument, or IOU, used in international trade. In Britain, a Bill of Exchange is defined by the Bills of Exchange Act 1882 as an unconditional order in writing addressed by one person to another, signed by the person giving it, requiring the person to whom it is addressed to pay on demand or at a fixed or determinable future time a certain sum in money to or to the order of a specified person, or to the bearer. US practice is governed by the Uniform Negotiable Instruments Law, drafted on the same lines

as the British, and accepted by all states by 1927.

bill of lading document giving proof of particular goods having been loaded on a ship. The person to whom the goods are being sent normally needs to show the bill of lading in order to obtain the release of the goods. For air freight, there is an *air waybill*.

Bill of Rights in the USA, the first ten amendments to the US ◊Constitution:
1 guarantees freedom of worship, of speech, of the press, of assembly, and to petition the government;
2 grants the right to keep and bear arms (which has hindered recent attempts to control illicit use of arms);
3 prohibits billeting of soldiers in private homes in peacetime;
4 forbids unreasonable search and seizure;
5 guarantees none be 'deprived of life, liberty or property without due process of law' or be compelled in any criminal case to be a witness against oneself;
6 grants the right to speedy trial, to call witnesses, and to have defence counsel;
7 grants the right to trial by jury;
8 prevents the infliction of excessive bail or fines, or 'cruel and unusual punishment';
9 and *10* provide a safeguard to the states and people for all rights not specifically delegated to the central government.
Not originally part of the draft of the Constitution, the Bill of Rights was mooted during the period of ratification. Twelve amendments were proposed by Congress in 1789; the ten now called the Bill of Rights were ratified 1791.

In Britain, an act of Parliament 1689. It made provisions limiting ◊royal prerogative with respect to legislation, executive power, money levies, courts, and the army; required Parliament's consent to many government functions; and established rights of Parliament.

Billy the Kid, /'bılı/ nickname of William H Bonney 1859–1881. US outlaw, a leader in the Lincoln County cattle war in New Mexico, who allegedly killed his first victim at 12 and 22 people in all. He was sentenced to death for murdering a sheriff, but escaped (killing two guards), and was finally shot by Sheriff Pat Garrett while trying to avoid recapture.

bimetallic strip strip made from two metals each having a different coefficient of ◊thermal expansion; it therefore bends when subjected to a change in temperature. Such

Billy the Kid Although few details of his life are known, US outlaw Billy the Kid became the symbol of the discontented of his day. One of the American West's most notorious gunfighters, Billy had fallen into a career of thievery and lawlessness in his early teens, wandering throughout the southwest and northern Mexico, often with gangs.

strips are used widely for temperature measurement and control.

bimetallism monetary system in which two metals, traditionally gold and silver, both circulate at a ratio fixed by the state, are coined by the ◊mint on equal terms, and are legal tender to any amount. The system was in use in the 19th century.

Advocates of bimetallism have argued that the 'compensatory action of the double standard' makes for a currency more stable than one based only on gold, since the changes in the value of the two metals taken together may be expected to be less than the changes in one of them. One of the many arguments against the system is that the ratio of the prices of the metals is frozen regardless of the supply and demand.

binary fission in biology, a form of ◊asexual reproduction, whereby a single-celled organism, such as the amoeba, divides into two smaller 'daughter' cells. It can also occur in a few simple multicellular organisms, such as sea anemones, producing two smaller sea anemones of equal size.

binary number system or *binary number code* system of numbers to ◊base two, using combinations of the digits 1 and 0. Binary numbers play a key role in digital computers, in which they form the basis of the internal coding of information, the values of ◊bits (short for 'binary digits') being represented as on/off (1 and 0) states of switches and high/low voltages in circuits.

The value of any position in a binary number increases by powers of 2 (doubles) with each move from right to left (1, 2, 4, 8, 16, and so on). For example, 1011 in the binary number system means $(1 \times 8) + (0 \times 4) + (1 \times 2) + (1 \times 1)$, which adds up to 11 in the decimal system.

binary star pair of stars moving in orbit around their common centre of mass. Observations show that most stars are binary, or even multiple—for example, the nearest star system to the Sun, ◊Alpha Centauri.

A *spectroscopic binary* is a binary in which two stars are so close together that they cannot be seen separately, but their separate light spectra can be distinguished by a spectroscope. Another type is the ◊eclipsing binary.

binary weapon in chemical warfare, a weapon consisting of two substances that in isolation are harmless but when mixed together form a poisonous nerve gas. They are loaded into the delivery system separately and combine after launch.

With conventional chemical weapons, chemical stockpiles deteriorate, unstable compounds break down, and the handling and security of such deadly compounds present serious problems to any country possessing them. The development of binary chemical weapons in the USA served to minimize these risks, since the principle on which they are based is the combination of two individually harmless compounds into a deadly chemical agent only in the shell or bomb they are housed in, and then only when the projectile is armed or fired. This greatly reduces storage and handling problems.

binding energy in physics, the amount of energy needed to break the nucleus of an atom into the neutrons and protons of which it is made.

binding over UK court order that requires a recognizance, that is, a binding promise, that the defendant will be of good behaviour and keep the peace for a fixed period of time. If the defendant does not agree, or subsequently commits a breach of the peace, and is over 21, he or she may be imprisoned.

There is no power for the court to impose any conditions, but an order may be made in terms such as 'to keep the peace towards all Her Majesty's subjects, and especially towards X'.

bind over in law, to require a person to carry out some act, usually by an order given in a magistrates' court. A person may be bound over to appear in court at a particular time if bail has been granted or, most commonly, be bound over not to commit some offence; for example, causing a breach of the peace.

Binet /ˈbiːneɪ/ Alfred 1857–1911. French psychologist who introduced the first ◊intelligence tests 1905. They were standardized so that the last of a set of graded ests the child could successfully complete gave the level described as 'mental age'. If the test was passed by most children over 12, for instance, but failed by those younger, it was said to show a mental age of 12. Binet published these in collaboration with Theodore Simon.

binoculars optical instrument for viewing an object in magnification with both eyes; for example, field glasses and opera glasses. Binoculars consist of two telescopes containing lenses and prisms, which produce a stereoscopic effect as well as magnifying the image. Use of prisms has the effect of 'folding' the light path, allowing for a compact design.

The first binocular telescope was constructed by the Dutch inventor Hans Lippershey (c. 1570–c. 1619), in 1608. Later development was largely due to the German Ernst Abbé (1840–1905) of Jena, who at the end of the 19th century designed prism binoculars that foreshadowed the instruments of today, in which not only magnification but also stereoscopic effect is obtained.

binomial in algebra, an expression consisting of two terms, such as $a + b$ or $a - b$. The **binomial theorem**, discovered by Isaac ◊Newton and first published in 1676, is a formula whereby any power of a binomial quantity may be found without performing the progressive multiplications.

binomial system of nomenclature in biology, the system in which all organisms are identified by a two-part Latinized name. Devised by the biologist ◊Linnaeus, it is also known as the Linnaean system. The first name is capitalized and identifies the ◊genus; the second identifies the ◊species within that genus.

binturong shaggy-coated mammal *Arctitis binturong*, the largest member of the mongoose family, nearly 1 m/3 ft long excluding a long muscular tail with a prehensile tip. Mainly nocturnal and tree-dwelling, the binturong is found in the forests of SE Asia, feeding on fruit, eggs, and small animals.

Bío-Bío /ˈbiːəʊ ˈbiːəʊ/ longest river in Chile; length 370 km/230 mi from its source in the Andes to its mouth on the Pacific. The name is an Araucanian term meaning 'much water'.

biochemic tissue salts therapy the correction of imbalances or deficiencies in the body's resources of essential mineral salts. There are 12 tissue salts in the body and the healthy functioning of cells depends on their correct balance, but there is scant evidence that disease is due to their imbalance and can be cured by supplements, as claimed by German physician W H Schuessler in the 1870s, though many people profess to benefit from the 'Schuessler remedies'.

biochemistry science concerned with the chemistry of living organisms: the structure and reactions of proteins (such as enzymes), nucleic acids, carbohydrates, and lipids.

Its study has led to an increased understanding of life processes, such as those by which organisms synthesize essential chemicals from food materials, store and generate energy, and pass on their characteristics through their genetic material. A great deal of medical research is concerned with the ways in which these processes are disrupted. Biochemistry also has applications in agriculture and in the food industry (for instance, in the use of enzymes).

biodegradable capable of being broken down by living organisms, principally bacteria and fungi. Biodegradable substances, such as food and sewage, can therefore be rendered harmless by natural processes. The process of decay leads to compaction and ◊liquefaction, and to the release of nutrients that are then recycled by the ecosystem. Nonbiodegradable substances, such as glass, heavy metals, and most types of plastic, present major problems of disposal.

biodynamic farming agricultural practice based on the principle of ◊homeopathy: tiny quantities of a substance are applied to transmit vital qualities to the soil. It is a form of ◊organic farming, and was developed by the Austrian holistic mystic Rudolf ◊Steiner and Ehrenfried Pfiffer.

bioeconomics theory put forward in 1979 by Chicago economist Gary Becker that the concepts of sociobiology apply also in economics. The competitiveness and self-interest built into human genes are said to make capitalism an effective economic system, whereas the selflessness and collectivism proclaimed as the socialist ideal are held to be contrary to human genetic make-up and to produce an ineffective system.

biofeedback modification or control of a biological system by its results or effects. For example, a change in the position or ◊trophic level of one species affects all levels above it.

Many biological systems are controlled by negative feedback. When enough of the hormone thyroxine has been released into the blood, the hormone adjusts its own level by 'switching off' the gland that produces it. In ecology, as the numbers in a species rise, the food supply available to each individual is reduced. This acts to reduce the population to a sustainable level.

biofeedback in medicine, the use of electrophysiological monitoring devices to 'feed back' information about internal processes and thus facilitate conscious control. Developed in the USA in the 1960s, independently by neurophysiologist Barbara Brown and neuropsychiatrist Joseph Kamiya, the technique is effective in alleviating hypertension and preventing associated organic and physiological dysfunctions.

biofuel any solid, liquid, or gaseous fuel produced from organic (once living) matter, either directly from plants or indirectly from industrial, commercial, domestic, or agricultural wastes. There are three main avenues for the development of biofuels: the burning of dry organic wastes (such as household refuse, industrial and agricultural wastes, straw, wood, and peat); the fermentation of wet wastes (such as animal dung) in the absence of oxygen to produce biogas (containing up to 60% methane), or the fermentation of sugar cane or corn to produce alcohol; and energy forestry (producing fast-growing wood for fuel).

biogenesis biological term coined 1870 by T H Huxley to express the hypothesis that living matter always arises out of other similar forms of living matter. It superseded the opposite idea of ◊spontaneous generation or abiogenesis (that is, that living things may arise out of nonliving matter).

biogeography study of how and why plants and animals are distributed around the world, in the past as well as in the present; more specifically, a theory describing the geographical distribution of ◊species developed by Robert MacArthur and E O ◊Wilson. The theory argues that for many species, ecological specializations mean that suitable habitats are patchy in their occurrence. Thus for a dragonfly, ponds in which to breed are separated by large tracts of land, and for edelweiss adapted to alpine peaks the deep valleys between cannot be colonized.

biography account of a person's life. When it is written by that person, it is an ◊autobiography. Biography can be simply a factual narrative, but it was also established as a literary form in the 18th and 19th centuries. Among ancient biographers are Xenophon, Plutarch, Tacitus, Suetonius, and the authors of the Gospels of the New Testament. In the English language Lytton Strachey's *Eminent Victorians* opened the new era of frankness; 20th-century biographers include Richard Ellmann (James Joyce and Oscar Wilde), Michael Holroyd (1935–) (Lytton Strachey and George Bernard Shaw) and Elizabeth Longford (Queen Victoria and Wellington).

Medieval biography was mostly devoted to religious edification and produced chronicles of saints and martyrs; among the biographies of laymen are Einhard's *Charlemagne* and Asser's *Alfred*. In England true biography begins with the early Tudor period and such works as *Sir Thomas More* 1626, written by his son-in-law William Roper (1498–1578). By the 18th century it became a literary form in its own right through Johnson's *Lives of the Most Eminent English Poets* 1779–81 and Boswell's biography of Johnson 1791. 19th-century biographers include Robert Southey, Elizabeth Gaskell, G H Lewes, J Morley, and Thomas Carlyle. The general tendency was to provide irrelevant detail and suppress the more personal facts.

Bioko /biˈəʊkəʊ/ island in the Bight of Bonny, W Africa, part of Equatorial Guinea; area 2,017 sq km/786 sq mi; products include coffee, cacao, and copra; population (1983) 57,190. Formerly a Spanish possession, as *Fernando Po*, it was known 1973–79 as *Macías Nguema Bijogo*.

biological clock regular internal rhythm of activity, produced by unknown mechanisms, and not dependent on external time signals. Such clocks are known to exist in almost all animals, and also in many plants, fungi, and unicellular organisms. In higher organisms, there appears to be a series of clocks of graded importance. For example, although body temperature and activity cycles in human beings are normally 'set' to 24 hours, the two cycles may vary independently, showing that two clock mechanisms are involved.

biological control control of pests such as insects and fungi through biological means, rather than the use of chemicals. This can include breeding resistant crop strains; inducing sterility in the pest; infecting the pest species with disease organisms; or introducing the pest's natural predator. Biological control tends to be naturally self-regulating, but as ecosystems are so complex, it is difficult to predict all the consequences of introducing a biological controlling agent.

biological oxygen demand (BOD) the amount of dissolved oxygen taken up by microorganisms in a sample of water. Since these microorganisms live by decomposing organic matter, and the amount of oxygen used is proportional to their number and metabolic rate, BOD can be used as a measure of the extent to which the water is polluted with organic compounds.

biological shield shield around a nuclear reactor that is intended to protect personnel from the effects of ◊radiation. It usually consists of a thick wall of steel and concrete.

biological warfare use of living organisms, or of infectious material derived from them, to bring about death or disease in humans, animals, or plants. It was originally prohibited by the Geneva Protocol 1925, to which the United Nations has urged all states to adhere. Nevertheless research in this area continues; the Biological Weapons Convention 1972 permits research for defence purposes but does not define how this differs from offensive weapons development. In 1990 the US Department of Defense allocated $60 million to research, develop and test defence systems. Advances in genetic engineering make the development of new varieties of potentially offensive biological weapons more likely. At least ten countries have this capability. See also ◊chemical warfare.

biology science of life. Strictly speaking, biology includes all the life sciences—for example, anatomy and physiology, cytology, zoology and botany, ecology, genetics, biochemistry and biophysics, animal behaviour, embryology, and plant breeding. During the 1990s an important focus of biological research will be the international Human Genome Project, which will attempt to map the entire genetic code contained in the 23 pairs of human chromosomes.

bioluminescence production of light by living organisms. It is a feature of many deep-sea fishes, crustaceans, and other marine animals. On land, bioluminescence is seen in some nocturnal insects such as glow-worms and fireflies, and in certain bacteria and fungi. Light is usually produced by the oxidation of luciferin, a reaction catalysed by the ◊enzyme luciferase. This reaction is unique, being the only known biological oxidation that does not produce heat. Animal luminescence is involved in communication, camouflage, or the luring of prey, but its function in other organisms is unclear.

biomass the total mass of living organisms present in a given area. It may be specified for a particular species (such as earthworm biomass) or for a general category (such as herbivore biomass). Estimates also exist for the entire global plant biomass. Measurements of biomass can be used to study interactions between organisms, the stability of those interactions, and variations in population numbers.

biome broad natural assemblage of plants and animals shaped by common patterns of vegetation and climate. Examples include the tundra biome and the desert biome.

biomechanics study of natural structures to improve those produced by humans. For example, mother-of-pearl is structurally superior to glass fibre, and deer antlers have outstanding durability because they are composed of microscopic fibres. Such natural structures may form the basis of high-tech composites.

bionics (from 'biological electronics') design and development of electronic or mechanical artificial systems that imitate those of living things. The bionic arm, for example, is an artificial limb that uses electronics to amplify minute electrical signals generated in body muscles to work electric motors, which operate the joints of the fingers and wrist. *See* ◊prosthesis

biophysics application of physical laws to the properties of living organisms. Examples include using the principles of ◊mechanics to calculate the strength of bones and muscles, and ◊thermodynamics to study plant and animal energetics.

biopsy removal of a living tissue sample from the body for diagnostic examination.

biorhythm rhythmic change, mediated by ◊hormones, in the physical state and activity patterns of certain plants and animals that have seasonal activities. Examples include winter hibernation, spring flowering or breeding, and periodic migration. The hormonal changes themselves are often a response to changes in day length (◊photoperiodism); they signal the time of year to the animal or plant. Other biorhythms are innate and continue even if external stimuli such as day length are removed. These include a 24-hour or ◊circadian rhythm, a 28-day or circalunar rhythm (corresponding to the phases of the Moon), and even a year-long rhythm in some organisms.

Such innate biorhythms are linked to an internal or ◊biological clock, whose mechanism is still poorly understood. Often both types of rhythm operate; thus many birds have a circalunar rhythm that prepares them for the breeding season, and a photoperiodic response. There is also a theory that human activity is governed by three biorhythms: the *intellectual* (33 days), the *emotional* (28 days), and the *physical* (23 days). Certain days in each cycle are regarded as 'critical', even more so if one such day coincides with that of another cycle.

biosensor device based on microelectronic circuits that can directly measure medically significant variables for the purpose of diagnosis or monitoring treatment. One such device measures the blood sugar level of diabetics using a single drop of blood, and shows the result on a liquid crystal display within a few minutes.

biosphere or *ecosphere* the region of the Earth's surface (both land and water), together with the atmosphere above it, that can be occupied by living organisms.

BioSphere 2 (BS2) ecological test project, a 'planet in a bottle', in Arizona, USA. Under a glass dome, several different habitats are recreated, with representatives of nearly 4,000 species, including eight humans, sealed in the biosphere for two years from summer 1991 to see how effectively recycling of air, water, and waste can work in an enclosed environment and whether a stable ecosystem can be created; ultimately BS2 is a prototype space colony.

BS2 is in fact not the second in a series: Earth itself is regarded as BioSphere 1. Experiments with biospheres that hold only relatively simple life forms have been carried out for decades, and a 21-day trial period 1989 that included humans preceded the construction of BS2. The sealed area covers a total of 3.5 acres. Habitats represented in it are tropical rainforest, salt marsh, desert, coral reef, and savanna, as well as a section for intensive agriculture. The people within will be entirely self-sufficient, except for electricity: solar panels to provide energy for cooling, heating, pumping, and lighting would have been too expensive, so there is a 3.7-megawatt power station on the outside. The biospherians also have a computer link with the outside world.

The cost of setting up and maintaining the project has been estimated at $100 million, some of which will be covered by paying visitors, who can view the inhabitants through the geodesic glass dome. It is run by a private company, Space Biospheres Ventures, with funding from an ecology-minded oil millionaire, Edward P Bass (1945–), and other investors who expect to find commercial applications for the techniques that are developed in the course of the project.

biosynthesis synthesis of organic chemicals from simple inorganic ones by living cells—for example, the conversion of carbon dioxide and water to glucose by plants during ◊photosynthesis. Other biosynthetic reactions produce cell constituents including proteins and fats.

Biosynthesis requires energy; in the initial stages of photosynthesis this is obtained from sunlight, but more often it is supplied by the ◊ATP molecule. The term is also used in connection with biotechnology processes.

Biosynthesis requires energy; in the initial or light-dependent stages of photosynthesis this is obtained from sunlight, but in all other instances, it is supplied chemically by ◊ATP and NADPH. The term is also used in connection with the products achieved through biotechnology processes.

biotechnology industrial use of living organisms to manufacture food, drugs, or other products. The brewing and baking industries have long relied on the yeast microorganism for ◊fermentation purposes, while the dairy industry employs a range of bacteria and fungi to convert milk into cheeses and yoghurts. Recent advances include ◊genetic engineering, in which single-celled organisms with modified ◊DNA are used to produce insulin and other drugs. ◊Enzymes, whether extracted from cells or produced artificially, are central to most biotechnological applications.

biotin or *vitamin H* vitamin of the B complex, found in many different kinds of food; egg yolk, liver, and yeast contain large amounts.

biotite dark mica, $K(Mg, Fe)_3Al Si_3O_{10}(OH, F)_2$, a common silicate mineral It is colourless to silvery white with shiny surfaces, and like all micas, it splits into very thin flakes along its one perfect cleavage. Biotite is a mineral of igneous rocks such as granites, and metamorphic rocks such as schists and gneisses.

birch any tree of the genus *Betula*, including about 40 species found in cool temperate parts of the northern hemisphere. Birches grow rapidly, and their hard, beautiful wood is used for veneers and cabinet work.

The white or or silver birch *Betula pendula* is of great use to industry because its timber is quick-growing and durable. The bark is used for tanning and dyeing leather, and an oil is obtained from it.

bird backboned animal of the class Aves, the biggest group of land vertebrates, characterized by warm blood, feathers, wings, breathing through lungs, and egg-laying by the female.

Birds are bipedal, with the front limb modified to form a wing and retaining only three digits. The heart has four chambers, and the body is maintained at a high temperature (about 41°C/106°F). Most birds fly, but some groups (such as ostriches) are flightless, and others include flightless members. Many communicate by sounds, or by

visual displays, in connection with which many species are brightly coloured, usually the males. Birds have highly developed patterns of instinctive behaviour. Hearing and eyesight are well developed, but the sense of smell is usually poor. Typically the eggs are brooded in a nest and, on hatching, the young receive a period of parental care. There are nearly 8,500 species of birds.

Bird /bɜːd/ Isabella 1832–1904. British traveller and writer who wrote extensively of her journeys in the USA, Persia, Tibet, Kurdistan, China, Japan, and Korea.

Her published works include *The English-woman in America* 1856, *A Lady's Life in the Rocky Mountains* 1874, *Unbeaten Tracks in Japan* 1880, *Among the Tibetans* 1894, and *Pictures from China* 1900.

bird of paradise one of 40 species of crow-like birds, family Paradiseidae, native to New Guinea and neighbouring islands. Females are drably coloured, but the males have bright and elaborate plumage used in courtship display. Hunted almost to extinction for their plumage, they are now subject to conservation.

Birdseye /'bɜːdzaɪ/ Clarence 1886–1956. US inventor who pioneered food refrigeration processes. While working as a fur trader in Labrador 1912–16 he was struck by the ease with which food could be preserved in an Arctic climate. Back in the USA he found that the same effect could be obtained by rapidly freezing prepared food between two refrigerated metal plates. To market his products he founded the General Sea Foods Co. 1924, which he sold to General Foods 1929.

birdwatching observation and study of wild birds in their natural habitat. In the UK the Royal Society for the Protection of Birds, founded 1889, has a network of reserves in all types of habitat (73,000 ha/180,000 acres), and is the largest voluntary wildlife-conservation body in Europe, with a burgeoning membership of 827,000 (1990) due to a greater awareness of wildlife conservation. There are 116 bird reserves in the UK. In Europe, societies such as the Spanish Ornithological Society are fighting to preserve sanctuaries for birds such as the Coto Donana where bird watchers can be sure of seeing rare wildlife in their natural habitats.

Birkenhead /'bɜːkənhed/ seaport in Merseyside, England, on the Mersey estuary opposite Liverpool; population (1981) 123,884.

Chief industries include shipbuilding and engineering. The rail Mersey Tunnel 1886 and road Queensway Tunnel 1934 link Birkenhead with Liverpool.

Birkenhead /ˈbɜːkənhed/ Frederick Edwin Smith, 1st Earl of Birkenhead 1872–1930. British Conservative politician. A flamboyant character, known as 'FE', he joined with Edward Carson in organizing armed resistance in Ulster to Irish Home Rule. He was Lord Chancellor 1919–22 and a much criticized secretary for India 1924–28.

Birmingham /ˈbɜːmɪŋəm/ industrial city in the West Midlands, second largest city of the UK; population (1991 est) 934,900, metropolitan area 2,632,000. Industries include motor vehicles, machine tools, aerospace control systems, plastics, chemicals, and food.

features It is the site of the National Exhibition Centre and Sports Arena. Aston University is linked to a ◊science park; a school of music and symphony orchestra; the art gallery has a Pre-Raphaelite collection; the repertory theatre was founded 1913 by Sir Barry Jackson (1897–1961); since 1990 it has been the home of the ◊Royal Ballet; Symphony Hall (holding over 4,000) opened 1991.

history Lawn tennis was invented here. Sutton Park, in the residential suburb of Sutton Coldfield, has been a public country recreational area since the 16th century. As mayor, Joseph ◊Chamberlain carried out reforms in the 1870s.

Birmingham /ˈbɜːmɪŋhæm/ industrial city (iron, steel, chemicals, building materials, computers, cotton textiles) and commercial centre in Alabama, USA; population of the metropolitan area (1980) 847,500.

Birmingham Six Irish victims of a miscarriage of justice who spent nearly 17 years in British prisons convicted of an IRA terrorist bombing in Birmingham 1974. They were released 1991 when the Court of Appeal quashed their convictions. The methods of the police and prosecution were called into question.

Birobijan /bɪrəbɪˈdʒɑːn/ town in Kharabovsk Territory, E Russia, near the Chinese border; population (1989) 82,000. Industries include sawmills and clothing. It was capital of the Jewish Autonomous Region 1928–51 (sometimes also called Birobijan).

birth act of producing live young from within the body of female animals. Both viviparous and ovoviviparous animals give birth to young. In viviparous animals, embryos obtain nourishment from the mother via a ◊placenta or other means. In ovoviviparous animals, fertilized eggs develop and hatch in the oviduct of the mother and gain little or no nourishment from maternal tissues. See also ◊pregnancy.

birth control another name for ◊family planning; see also ◊contraceptive.

birth rate is measured as births per year per thousand of the population.

In the 20th century, the UK's birth rate has fallen from 28 to less than 10 due to increased use of contraception, better living standards and falling infant mortality. The average household now contains 1.8 children. The population growth rate remains high in developing countries. While it is now below replacement level in the UK, in Bangladesh it stands at 28, in Nigeria at 34, and in Brazil at 23 per thousand people per year.

Birtwistle /ˈbɜːtwɪsl/ Harrison 1934– . English avant-garde composer. He has specialized in chamber music, for example, his chamber opera *Punch and Judy* 1967 and *Down by the Greenwood Side* 1969.

Birtwistle's early music was influenced by ◊Stravinsky and by the medieval and Renaissance masters, and for many years he worked alongside Maxwell ◊Davies. Orchestral works include *The Triumph of Time* 1972 and *Silbury Air* 1977; he has also written operas including *The Mask of Orpheus* 1986 (with electronic music by Barry Anderson) and *Gawain* 1991 a reworking of the medieval English poem 'Sir Gawain and the Green Knight'. His *Chronometer* 1972 (assisted by Peter Zinovieff) is based on clock sounds.

Biscay, Bay of /ˈbɪskeɪ/ bay of the Atlantic Ocean between N Spain and W France, known for rough seas and exceptionally high tides.

biscuit small, flat, brittle cake of baked dough. The basic components of biscuit dough are weak flour and fat; other ingredients, such as eggs, sugar, chocolate, and spices, may be added to vary the flavour and texture. In the USA, 'biscuit' means something between a bread roll and a Yorkshire pudding, and 'cookie' means biscuit.

Originally made from slices of unleavened bread baked until hard and dry, biscuits could be stored for several years, and were a useful, though dull, source of carbohydrate on long sea voyages and military campaigns.

The first biscuit factory opened in Carlisle, N England, 1815 and the UK is now Europe's largest producer and consumer of factory-made biscuits.

bishop (Greek 'overseer') priest next in rank to an archbishop in the Roman Catholic, Eastern Orthodox, Anglican or episcopal churches. A bishop has charge of a district called a *diocese*.

Originally bishops were chosen by the congregation, but in the Roman Catholic church they are appointed by the pope, although in some countries, such as Spain, the political authority nominates appointees. In the Eastern Orthodox church bishops are always monks. In the Church of England the prime minister selects bishops on the advice of the archbishop of Canterbury; when a diocese is very large, assistant (suffragan) bishops are appointed. Bishops are responsible for meeting to settle matters of belief or discipline; they ordain priests and administer confirmation (as well as baptism in the Orthodox church). In the Methodist and Lutheran churches the bishop's role is mostly that of a supervisory official. In 1989 Barbara Harris of the US Episcopalian church was elected the first woman bishop in the ◊Anglican Communion.

Biskra /'bɪskrɑː/ oasis town in Algeria on the edge of the Sahara; population (1982) 123,100.

Bismarck /'bɪzmɑːk/ Otto Eduard Leopold, Prince von 1815–1898. German politician, prime minister of Prussia 1862–90 and chancellor of the German Empire 1871–90. He pursued an aggressively expansionist policy, waging wars against Denmark 1863–64, Austria 1866, and France 1870–71, which brought about the unification of Germany.

Bismarck was ambitious to establish Prussia's leadership within Germany and eliminate the influence of Austria. He secured Austria's support for his successful war against Denmark then, in 1866, went to war against Austria and its allies (the ◊Seven Weeks' War), his victory forcing Austria out of the German Bund and unifying the N German states into the North German Confederation under his own chancellorship 1867. He then defeated France, under Napoleon III, in the Franco-Prussian War 1870–71, proclaimed the German Empire 1871, and annexed Alsace-Lorraine. He tried to secure his work by the ◊Triple Alliance 1881 with Austria and Italy but ran into difficulties at home with the Roman Catholic church

and the socialist movement and was forced to resign by Wilhelm II 18 Mar 1890.

Bismarck in World War II, a small German battleship sunk 1942 in the Atlantic by the British Royal Navy.

Bismarck Archipelago /'bɪzmɑːk/ group of over 200 islands in SW Pacific Ocean, part of ◊Papua New Guinea; area 49,660 sq km/ 19,200 sq mi. The largest island is New Britain.

bismuth hard, brittle, pinkish-white, metallic element, symbol Bi, atomic number 83, relative atomic mass 208.98. It has the highest atomic number of all the stable elements (the elements from atomic number 84 up are radioactive). Bismuth occurs in ores and occasionally as a free metal (◊native metal). It is a poor conductor of heat and electricity, and is used in alloys of low melting point and in medical compounds to soothe gastric ulcers.

bison large, hoofed mammal of the bovine family. There are two species, both brown. The *European bison* or *wisent*, *Bison bonasus*, of which only a few protected herds survive, is about 2 m/7 ft high and weighs a tonne. The *North American bison* (often known as 'buffalo') *Bison bison* is slightly smaller, with a heavier mane and more sloping hindquarters. Formerly roaming the prairies in vast numbers, it was almost exterminated in the 19th century, but survives in protected areas.

Bissau /bɪ'saʊ/ capital and chief port of Guinea-Bissau, on an island at the mouth of the Geba river; population (1988) 125,000. Originally a fortified slave-trading centre, Bissau became a free port 1869.

bit in computing, the smallest unit of information; a binary digit or place in a binary number. A ◊byte contains eight bits (four bits is sometimes called a nybble).

Microcomputers are often described according to how many bits of information they can handle at once—for instance, the Intel 8088 microprocessor used in the original IBM PC had an 8-bit data bus (it fetched one byte at a time from memory) and 16-bit internal registers (it could store and work on 2-byte numbers). The maximum number of bits that a computer normally processes is called a *word*.

The first microprocessor, the Intel 4004 launched 1971, was a 4-bit device. Business micros of the 1980s used 32-bit processors such as the Intel 80386 and Motorola 68030.

In the 1990s 64-bit microprocessors first went into production.

bit pad computer input device; see ◊graphics tablet.

bittern any of several small herons, in particular the common bittern *Botaurus stellaris* of Europe and Asia. It is shy, stoutly built, has a streaked camouflage pattern and a loud, booming call. An inhabitant of marshy country, it is now quite rare in Britain.

bittersweet alternative name for the woody ◊nightshade plant.

bitumen impure mixture of hydrocarbons, including such deposits as petroleum, asphalt, and natural gas, although sometimes the term is restricted to a soft kind of pitch resembling asphalt.

Solid bitumen may have arisen as a residue from the evaporation of petroleum. If evaporation took place from a pool or lake of petroleum, the residue might form a pitch or asphalt lake, such as Pitch Lake in Trinidad. Bitumen was used in ancient times as a mortar, and by the Egyptians for embalming.

bivalent in biology, a name given to the pair of homologous chromosomes during reduction division (◊meiosis). In chemistry, the term is sometimes used to describe an element or group with a ◊valency of two, although the term 'divalent' is more common.

bivalve marine or freshwater mollusc whose body is enclosed between two shells hinged together by a ligament on the dorsal side of the body.

The shell is closed by strong 'adductor' muscles. Ventrally, a retractile 'foot' can be put out to assist movement in mud or sand. Two large platelike gills are used for breathing and also, with the ◊cilia present on them, make a mechanism for collecting the small particles of food on which bivalves depend. The bivalves form one of the five classes of molluscs, the Lamellibranchiata, otherwise known as Bivalvia or Pelycypoda, containing about 8,000 species.

Bizet /ˈbiːzeɪ/ Georges (Alexandre César Léopold) 1838–1875. French composer of operas, among them *Les Pêcheurs de perles/The Pearl Fishers* 1863, and *La jolie Fille de Perth/The Fair Maid of Perth* 1866. He also wrote the concert overture *Patrie* and incidental music to Daudet's *L'Arlésienne*. His operatic masterpiece *Carmen* was produced a few months before his death 1875.

Bjelke-Petersen /ˈbjelkə ˈpɪtəsən/ Joh(annes) 1911– . Australian right-wing politician, leader of the Queensland National Party (QNP) and premier of Queensland 1968–87.

Bjelke-Petersen was born in New Zealand. His Queensland state chauvinism and extremely conservative policies, such as lack of support for Aboriginal land rights or for conservation issues and attacks on the trade-union movement, made him a controversial figure outside as well as within Queensland, and he was accused more than once of electoral gerrymandering. In 1987 he broke the coalition of the QNP with the Australian Liberal Party to run for prime minister, but his action, by splitting the opposition, merely strengthened the hand of the Labor prime minister Bob Hawke. Amid reports of corruption in his government, Bjelke-Petersen was forced to resign the premiership 1987.

Björnson /ˈbjɜːnsɒn/ Björnstjerne 1832–1910. Norwegian novelist, playwright, poet, and journalist. His plays include *The Newly Married Couple* 1865 and *Beyond Human Power* 1883, dealing with politics and sexual morality. Among his novels is *In God's Way* 1889. Nobel Prize for Literature 1903.

black English term first used 1625 to describe West Africans, now used to refer to Africans south of the Sahara and to people of African descent living outside Africa. In some countries such as the UK (but not in North America) the term is sometimes also used for people originally from the Indian subcontinent, for Australian Aborigines, and peoples of Melanesia.

The term 'black', at one time considered offensive by many people, was first adopted by militants in the USA in the mid-1960s to emphasize ethnic pride; they rejected the terms 'coloured' and 'Negro' as euphemistic. 'Black' has since become the preferred term in the USA and largely in the UK. Currently, some US blacks prefer the term 'Afro-American' or 'African American'.

history Black Africans were first taken to the West Indies in large numbers as slaves by the Spanish in the early 16th century and to the North American mainland in the early 17th century. They were taken to South America by both the Spanish and Portuguese from the 16th century. African blacks were also taken to Europe to work as slaves and servants. Some of the indigenous coastal societies in W Africa were heavily involved in the slave trade and became wealthy on its proceeds. Sometimes, black sailors settled in European ports on the Atlantic seaboard, such as Liverpool and Bristol, England. Although blacks fought beside whites in the American Revolution, the US Constitution (ratified 1788) did not redress the slave trade, and slaves were given no ◊civil rights. Slavery was gradually abolished in the northern US states during the early 19th century, but as the South's economy had been based upon slavery, it was one of the issues concerning states' rights that led to the secession of the South, which provoked the American Civil War 1861–65. During the Civil War about 200,000 blacks fought in the Union (Northern) army, but in segregated units led by white officers.

The Emancipation Proclamation 1863 of President Abraham Lincoln officially freed the slaves (about 4 million), but it could not be enforced until the Union victory 1865 and the period after the war known as the ◊Reconstruction. Freed slaves were often resented by poor whites as economic competitors, and vigilante groups in the South, such as the ◊Ku Klux Klan were formed to intimidate them. In addition, although freed slaves had full US citizenship under the 14th Amendment to the Constitution, and were thus entitled to vote, they were often disenfranchised in practice by state and local literacy tests and poll taxes.

A 'separate but equal' policy was established when the US Supreme Court ruled 1896 (*Plessy* v. *Ferguson*) that segregation was legal if equal facilities were provided for blacks and whites. The ruling was overturned 1954 (*Brown* v. *Board of Education*) with the Supreme Court decision outlawing segregation in state schools. This led to a historic confrontation in Little Rock, Arkansas, 1957 when Governor Orval Faubus attempted to prevent black students from entering Central High School, and President Eisenhower sent federal troops to enforce their right to attend.

Another landmark in the blacks' struggle for civil rights was the ◊Montgomery bus boycott in Alabama 1955, which first brought Martin Luther ◊King Jr to national attention. In the early 1960s the civil-rights movement had gained impetus, largely under the leadership of King, who in 1957 had founded the ◊Southern Christian Leadership Conference (SCLC), a coalition group advocating nonviolence. Moderate groups such as the National Association for the Advancement of Colored People (NAACP) had been active since early in the century; for the first time they were joined in large numbers by whites, in particular students, as in the historic march converging on Washington DC 1963 from all over the USA. At about this time, impatient with the lack of results gained through moderation, the militant ◊Black Power movements began to emerge, such as the Black Panther Party founded 1966, and black separatist groups such as the ◊Black Muslims gained support.

Increasing pressure led to the passage of federal legislation, the Civil Rights acts of 1964 and 1968, and the Voting Rights Act of 1965, under President Johnson; they guaranteed equal rights under the law and prohibited discrimination in public facilities, schools, employment and voting. However, in the 1980s, despite some advances, legislation, and affirmative action (positive discrimination), blacks, who comprise some 12% of the US population, continued to suffer discrimination and inequality of opportunities in practice in such areas as education, employment, and housing. Despite these obstacles, many blacks have made positive contributions in the arts, the sciences, and politics.

Blacks in Britain Unlike the USA, Britain did not have a recent history of slavery at home, though slaves were used in Roman Britain. The UK outlawed the slave trade 1807 and abolished slavery in the British Empire 1833. In the UK only a tiny proportion of the population was black until after World War II, when immigration from Commonwealth countries increased. Legislation such as the Race Relations Act 1976 specifically outlawed discrimination on grounds of race and emphasized the official policy of equality of opportunity in all areas, and the Commission for Racial Equality was established 1977 to work towards eliminating discrimination; nevertheless, there is still considerable evidence of ◊racism in British society as a whole. The Swann Report on education 1985 emphasized that Britain was a multicultural society, and suggested various ways in which teachers could ensure that black children were able to reach their full potential. Black people are now beginning to take their place in public life in the UK; the election of Diane Abbott (1953–) as Britain's first black woman member of Parliament 1987 was an example.

Black /blæk/ Conrad (Moffat) 1940– . Canadian newspaper publisher. Between 1985 and 1990 he gained control of the right-wing *Daily Telegraph*, *Sunday Telegraph*, and *Spectator* weekly magazine in the UK, and he owns a number of Canadian newspapers.

Black /blæk/ James 1924– . British physiologist, director of therapeutic research at Wellcome Laboratories (near London) from 1978. He was active in the development of ◊beta-blockers (which reduce the rate of heartbeat) and anti-ulcer drugs. He shared the Nobel Prize for Medicine 1988 with US scientists Gertrude Elion (1918–) and George Hitchings (1905–).

Black /blæk/ Joseph 1728–1799. Scottish physicist and chemist who in 1754 discovered carbon dioxide (which he called 'fixed air'). By his investigations in 1761 of latent heat and specific heat, he laid the foundation for the work of his pupil, James Watt.

Black and Tans nickname of a special auxiliary force of the Royal Irish Constabulary employed by the British 1920–21 to combat the Sinn Féiners (Irish nationalists) in Ireland; the name derives from the colours of the uniforms, khaki with black hats and belts.

black beetle another name for ◊cockroach, although cockroaches belong to an entirely different order of insects (Dictyoptera) from the beetles (Coleoptera).

blackberry prickly shrub *Rubus fruticosus*, of the rose family, closely allied to raspberries and dewberries, that is native to northern parts of Europe. It produces pink or white blossoms and edible, black, compound fruits.

There are over 400 types of bramble found in Britain. In the past some have been regarded as distinct species.

blackbird bird *Turdus merula* of the thrush family. The male is black with a yellow bill and eyelids, the female dark brown with a dark beak. About 25 cm/10 in long, it lays three to five blue-green eggs with brown spots. ts song is rich and flutelike.

Found across Europe and Asia, the blackbird adapts well to human presence and gardens, and is one of the most common British birds. North American 'blackbirds' belong to a different family of birds, the Icteridae.

blackbirding formerly, the kidnapping of South Pacific islanders (kanakas) to provide virtual slave labour in Australia, Fiji, and Samoa. From 1847 to 1904 this practice was carried on extensively to provide workers for the sugar-cane plantations of Queensland. The Pacific Islanders Protection Act passed by the British Parliament 1872 brought the labour trade under control to some extent.

black body in physics, a hypothetical object that completely absorbs all thermal (heat) radiation striking it. It is also a perfect emitter of thermal radiation.

Although a black body is hypothetical, a practical approximation can be made by using a small hole in the wall of a constant-temperature enclosure. The radiation emitted by a black body is of all wavelengths, but with maximum radiation at a particular wavelength that depends on the body's temperature. As the temperature increases, the wavelength of maximum intensity becomes shorter (see ◊Wien's law). The total energy emitted at all wavelengths is proportional to the fourth power of the temperature (see ◊Stefan–Boltzmann law). Attempts to explain these facts failed until the development of ◊quantum theory 1900.

black box popular name for the unit containing an aeroplane's flight and voice recorders. These monitor the plane's behaviour and the crew's conversation, thus providing valuable clues to the cause of a disaster. The box is nearly indestructible and usually painted orange for easy recovery. The name also refers to any compact electronic device that can be quickly connected or disconnected as a unit.

The maritime equivalent is the *voyage recorder*, installed in ships from 1989. It has 350 sensors to record the performance of engines, pumps, navigation lights, alarms, radar, and hull stress.

blackbuck antelope *Antilope cervicapra* found in central and NW India. It is related to the gazelle, from which it differs in having spirally-twisted horns. The male is black above and white beneath, whereas the female and young are fawn-coloured above. It is about 76 cm/2.5 ft in height.

blackcap ◊warbler *Sylvia atricapilla*. The male has a black cap, the female a reddish-brown one. About 14 cm/5.5 in long, the blackcap likes wooded areas, and is a summer visitor to N Europe.

blackcock large grouse *Lyrurus tetrix* found on moors and in open woods in N Europe and Asia. The male is mainly black with a lyre-shaped tail, and grows up to 54 cm/1.7 ft in height. The female is speckled brown and only 40 cm/1.3 ft tall.

Black Country central area of England, around and to the N of Birmingham. Heavily industrialized, it gained its name in the 19th century from its belching chimneys, but antipollution laws have changed its aspect.

Black Death great epidemic of bubonic ◊plague that ravaged Europe in the 14th century, killing between one-third and half of the population. The cause of the plague was the bacterium *Pasteurella pestis*, transmitted by fleas borne by migrating Asian black rats. The name Black Death was first used in England in the early 19th century.

black earth exceedingly fertile soil that covers a belt of land in NE North America, Europe, and Asia.

In Europe and Asia it extends from Bohemia through Hungary, Romania, S Russia, and Siberia, as far as Manchuria, having been deposited when the great inland ice sheets melted at the close of the last ◊ice age.

black economy unofficial economy of a country, which includes undeclared earnings from a second job ('moonlighting'), and enjoyment of undervalued goods and services (such as company 'perks'), designed for tax evasion purposes. In industrialized countries, it has been estimated to equal about 10% of ◊gross domestic product.

Blackett /ˈblækɪt/ Patrick Maynard Stuart, Baron Blackett 1897–1974. British physicist. He was awarded a Nobel prize 1948 for work in cosmic radiation and his perfection of the Wilson cloud chamber.

Blackfoot /ˈblækfʊt/ member of a Plains ◊American Indian people, some 10,000 in number and consisting of three subtribes: the Blackfoot proper, the Blood, and the Piegan, who live in Montana, USA, and Saskatchewan and Alberta, Canada. They were skilled, horse-riding buffalo hunters until their territories were settled by Europeans. Their name derives from their black moccasins. Their language belongs to the Algonquian family.

Black Forest /blæk/ (German *Schwarzwald*) mountainous region of coniferous forest in Baden-Württemberg, W Germany. Bounded W and S by the Rhine, which separates it from the Vosges, it has an area of 4,660 sq km/1,800 sq mi and rises to 1,493 m/4,905 ft in the Feldberg. Parts of the forest have recently been affected by ◊acid rain.

Blackfoot Curley Bear (Car-io-scuse), a Blackfoot Indian chief photographed 1903.

Black Friday day, 24 September 1869, on which Jay Gould (1836–1892) and James Fisk (1834–1872) stock manipulators, attempted to corner the gold market by trying to prevent the government from selling gold. President Grant refused to agree, but they spread the rumour that the president was opposed to the sales. George S Boutweel (1818–1905) with Grant's approval ordered the sale of $4 million in gold. The gold price plunged and many speculators were ruined. The two men made about $11 million.

black hole object in space whose gravity is so great that nothing can escape from it, not even light. Thought to form when massive stars shrink at the ends of their lives, a black hole sucks in more matter, including other stars, from the space around it. Matter that falls into a black hole is squeezed to infinite density at the centre of the hole. Black holes can be detected because gas falling towards them becomes so hot that it emits X-rays.

Satellites above the Earth's atmosphere have detected X-rays from a number of objects in our Galaxy that might be black holes. Massive black holes containing the mass of millions of stars are thought to lie at the centres of ◊quasars. Microscopic black holes may have been formed in the chaotic conditions of the ◊Big Bang. The English physicist Stephen ◊Hawking has shown that such tiny black holes could 'evaporate' and explode in a flash of energy.

Black Hole of Calcutta incident in Anglo-Indian history: according to tradition, the nawab (ruler) of Bengal confined 146 British prisoners on the night of 20 June 1756 in one small room, of whom only 23 allegedly survived. Later research reduced the death count to 43, assigning negligence rather than intention.

blacking in an industrial dispute, the refusal of workers to handle particular goods or equipment, or to work with particular people.

Blacking /'blækɪŋ/ John 1928–1990. British anthropologist and ethnomusicologist who researched the relationship between music and body movement, and the patterns of social and musical organization. Blacking was from 1970 chair of social anthropology at Queen's University, Belfast, where he established a centre for ethnomusicology. His most widely read book is *How Musical is Man?* 1973.

Black Monday worldwide stockmarket crash that began 19 Oct 1987, prompted by the announcement of worse-than-expected US trade figures and the response by US Secretary of the Treasury, James Baker, who indicated that the sliding dollar needed to decline further. This caused a world panic as fears of the likely impact of a US recession were voiced by the major industrialized countries. Between 19 and 23 Oct, the New York Stock Exchange fell by 33%, the London Stock Exchange Financial Times 100 Index by 25%, the European index by 17%, and Tokyo by 12%. The total paper loss on the London Stock Exchange and other City of London institutions was £94 billion. The expected world recession did not occur; by the end of 1988 it was clear that the main effect had been a steadying in stock market activity and only a slight slowdown in world economic growth.

Blackmore /'blækmɔː/ R(ichard) D(oddridge) 1825–1900. English novelist, author of *Lorna Doone* 1869, a romance set on Exmoor, SW England, in the late 17th century.

Black Mountain poets group of experimental US poets of the 1950s who were linked with Black Mountain College, a liberal arts college in North Carolina. They rejected the formalistic constraints of rhyme and metre. Leading members included Charles Olson (1910–1970) and Robert Creeley (1926–).

Black Muslim member of a religious group founded 1929 in the USA and led, from 1934, by Elijah Muhammad (then Elijah Poole) (1897–1975) after he had a vision of ◊Allah. Its growth from 1946 as a black separatist organization was due to Malcolm X (1926–1965), the son of a Baptist minister who, in 1964, broke away and founded his own Organization for Afro-American Unity, preaching 'active self-defence'. Under the leadership of Louis Farrakhan, the movement underwent a recent revival.

black nationalism movement towards black separatism in the USA during the 1960s; see ◊Black Power.

Black National State area in the Republic of South Africa set aside for development towards self-government by black Africans in accordance with ◊apartheid. Before 1980 these areas were known as *black homelands* or *bantustans*. They make up less than 14% of the country and tend to be in arid areas (though some have mineral wealth), and may be in scattered blocks. Those that have so far achieved nominal independence are Transkei 1976, Bophuthatswana 1977, Venda 1979, and Ciskei 1981. They are not recognized outside South Africa due to their racial basis, although the repeal of the Land Acts and Group Areas Acts 1991 promises progressively to change their status. Since the accession of President de Klerk, outbreaks of violence have resulted in the overthrow of the governments in Ciskei and Venda, and calls for reintegration within South Africa in all four states. 11 million blacks live permanently in the country's white-designated areas.

Blackpool /'blækpuːl/ seaside resort in Lancashire, England, 45 km/28 mi N of Liverpool; population (1981) 148,000. The largest holiday resort in N England, the amusement facilities include 11 km/7 mi of promenades, known for their 'illuminations' of coloured lights, funfairs, and a tower 152 m/500 ft high. Political party conferences are often held here.

Black Power movement towards black separatism in the USA during the 1960s, embodied in the *Black Panther Party* founded

1966 by Huey Newton and Bobby Seale. Its declared aim was the establishment of a separate black state in the USA established by a black plebiscite under the aegis of the United Nations. Following a National Black Political Convention 1972, a National Black Assembly was established to exercise pressure on the Democratic and Republican parties.

The Black Power concept arose when existing ◊civil rights organizations such as the National Association for Advancement of Colored People and the Southern Christian Leadership Conference were perceived to be ineffective in producing major change in the status of black people. Stokely Carmichael then advocated the exploitation of political and economic power and abandonment of nonviolence, with a move towards the type of separatism first developed by the ◊Black Muslims. Leaders such as Martin Luther King rejected this approach, but the Black Panther Party (so named because the panther, though not generally aggressive, will fight to the death under attack) adopted it fully and, for a time, achieved nationwide influence.

Black Prince nickname of ◊Edward, Prince of Wales, eldest son of Edward III of England.

Black Sea (Russian *Chernoye More*) inland sea in SE Europe, linked with the seas of Azov and Marmara, and via the Dardanelles with the Mediterranean. Uranium deposits beneath it are among the world's largest.

Black September guerrilla splinter group of the ◊Palestine Liberation Organization formed 1970. Operating from bases in Syria and Lebanon, it was responsible for the kidnappings at the Munich Olympics 1972 that led to the deaths of 11 Israelis, and more recent hijack and bomb attempts. The group is named after the month in which Palestinian guerrillas were expelled from Jordan by King Hussein.

Blackshirts term widely used to describe fascist paramilitary organizations. Originating with Mussolini's fascist Squadristi in the 1920s, it was also applied to the Nazi SS (*Schutzstaffel*) and to the followers of Oswald Mosley's British Union of Fascists.

blacksnake any of several species of snake. The blacksnake *Pseudechis porphyriacus* is a venomous snake of the cobra family found in damp forests and swamps in E Australia. The blacksnake *Coluber constrictor* from the eastern USA, is a relative of the European grass snake, growing up to 1.2 m/4 ft long, and without venom.

Black Stone in Islam, the sacred stone built into the east corner of the ◊Kaaba which is a focal point of the *hajj*, or pilgrimage, to Mecca. There are a number of stories concerning its origin, one of which states that it was sent to Earth at the time of the first man, Adam; Muhammad declared that it was given to Abraham by Gabriel. It has been suggested that it is of meteoric origin.

blackthorn densely branched spiny European bush *Prunus spinosa*, family Rosaceae. It produces white blossom on black and leafless branches in early spring. Its sour, plumlike, blue-black fruit, the sloe, is used to flavour gin.

Black Thursday day of the Wall Street stock market crash 29 Oct 1929, which precipitated the ◊Depression in the USA and throughout the world.

Blackwall Tunnel road tunnel under the river Thames, London, linking the Bugsby Marshes (south) with the top end of the Isle of Dogs (north). The northbound tunnel, 7,056 km/4,410 ft long with an internal diameter of 7.2 m/24 ft, was built 1891–97 to a design by Sir Alexander Binnie; the southbound tunnel, 4,592 km/2,870 ft long with an internal diameter of 8.25 m/27.5 ft, was built 1960–67 to a design by Mott, Hay, and Anderson.

Blackwell /blækwel/ Elizabeth 1821–1910. English-born US physician, the first woman to qualify in medicine in the USA 1849, and the first woman to be recognized as a qualified physician in the UK 1869.

black widow North American spider *Latrodectus mactans*. The male is small and harmless, but the female is 1.3 cm/0.5 in long with a red patch below the abdomen and a powerful venomous bite. The bite causes pain and fever in human victims, but they usually recover.

bladder hollow elastic-walled organ in the ◊urinary systems of some fishes, most amphibians, some reptiles, and all mammals. Urine enters the bladder through two ureters, one leading from each kidney, and leaves it through the urethra.

bladderwort any of a large genus *Utricularia* of carnivorous aquatic plants of the family Lentibulariaceae. They have leaves with bladders that entrap small aquatic animals.

Blair Tony (Anthony Charles Lynton) 1953– . British politician, leader of the Labour Party from 1994. A centrist in the manner of his predecessor John Smith, he became Labour's youngest leader by a large majority in the first fully democratic elections to the post July 1994.

Blair practised as a lawyer before entering the House of Commons 1983 as member for the Durham constituency of Sedgfield. He was elected to Labour's shadow cabinet 1988 and given the energy portfolio; he shadowed employment from 1991 and home affairs from 1992. Like John Smith, he did not ally himself with any particular faction and, in drawing a distinction between 'academic and ethical socialism', succeeded in winning over most sections of his party, apart from the extreme left.

Blake /bleɪk/ George 1922– . British double agent who worked for MI6 (see ◊intelligence) and also for the USSR. Blake was unmasked by a Polish defector 1960 and imprisoned, but escaped to the Eastern bloc 1966.

Blake /bleɪk/ Quentin 1932– . English book illustrator whose animated pen-and-ink drawings for children's books are instantly recognizable. His own picture books include *The Marzipan Pig* 1986; he has illustrated more than 200 books.

Blake /bleɪk/ Robert 1599–1657. British admiral of the Parliamentary forces during the English ◊Civil War. Appointed 'general-at-sea' 1649, he destroyed Prince Rupert's privateering fleet off Cartagena, Spain, in the following year. In 1652 he won several engagements against the Dutch navy. In 1654 he bombarded Tunis, the stronghold of the Barbary corsairs, and in 1657 captured the Spanish treasure fleet in Santa Cruz.

Blake /bleɪk/ William 1757–1827. English poet, artist, and visionary. His lyrics, as in *Songs of Innocence* 1789 and *Songs of Experience* 1794 express spiritual wisdom in radiant imagery and symbolism. Prophetic books like *The Marriage of Heaven and Hell* 1790, *America* 1793, and *Milton* 1804 yield their meaning to careful study. He created a new composite art form in engraving and hand-colouring his own works.

Blake was born in Soho, London, and apprenticed to an engraver 1771–78. He illustrated the Bible, works by Dante and Shakespeare, and his own poems. His figures are heavily muscled, with elongated proportions.

Blakey /bleɪki/ Art. Muslim name Abdullah Ibn Buhaina 1919–1990. US jazz drummer and band-leader whose dynamic, innovative style made him one of the jazz greats. He contributed to the development of bebop in the 1940s and subsequently to hard bop, and formed the Jazz Messengers in the mid-1950s, continuing to lead the band for most of his life and discovering many talented musicians.

Blamey /bleɪmi/ Thomas Albert 1884–1951. The only Australian field marshal. Born in New South Wales, he served at Gallipoli, Turkey, and on the Western Front in World War I. In World War II he was commander, under MacArthur, in chief of the Allied Land Forces in the SW Pacific 1942–45.

Blanc /blɒŋ/ Louis 1811–1882. French socialist and journalist. In 1839 he founded the *Revue du progrès*, in which he published his *Organisation du travail*, advocating the establishment of cooperative workshops and other socialist schemes. He was a member of the provisional government of 1848 (see ◊revolutions of 1848) and from its fall lived in the UK until 1871.

Blanchard /blɒnˈʃɑː/ Jean Pierre 1753–1809. French balloonist who made the first hot air balloon flight across the English Channel with John Jeffries 1785. He made the first balloon flight in the USA 1793.

Blanche of Castile /blɒnʃ kæˈstiːl/ 1188–1252. Queen of France, wife of ◊Louis VIII of France, and regent for her son Louis IX (St Louis of France) from the death of her husband 1226 until Louis IX's majority 1234, and again from 1247 while he was on a Crusade.

blank verse in literature, the unrhymed iambic pentameter or ten-syllable line of five stresses. First used by the Italian Gian Giorgio Trissino in his tragedy *Sofonisba* 1514–15, it was introduced to England about 1540 by the Earl of Surrey, and developed by Christopher Marlowe. More recent exponents of blank verse in English include Thomas Hardy, T S Eliot, and Robert Frost.

After its introduction from Italy, blank verse was used with increasing freedom by Shakespeare, John Fletcher, John Webster, and Thomas Middleton. It was remodelled by Milton, who was imitated in the 18th century by James Thomson, Edward Young, and William Cowper; and revived in the early 19th century by Wordsworth, Shelley, and Keats, and later by Tennyson, Robert

Browning, and Algernon Charles Swinburne.

Blanqui /blɒŋˈkiː/ Louis Auguste 1805–1881. French revolutionary politician. He formulated the theory of the 'dictatorship of the proletariat', used by Karl Marx, and spent a total of 33 years in prison for insurrection. Although in prison, he was elected president of the Commune of Paris 1871. His followers, the Blanquists, joined with the Marxists 1881.

Blantyre-Limbe /ˈblæntaɪə ˈlɪmbeɪ/ chief industrial and commercial centre of Malawi, in the Shire highlands; population (1987) 331,600. It produces tea, coffee, rubber, tobacco, and textiles.

Blashford-Snell /ˈblæʃfəd ˈsnel/ John 1936– . British explorer and soldier. His expeditions have included the first descent and exploration of the Blue Nile 1968; the journey N to S from Alaska to Cape Horn, crossing the Darien Gap between Panama and Colombia for the first time 1971–72; and the first complete navigation of the Zaïre River, Africa 1974–75.

From 1963 he organized adventure training at Sandhurst military academy. He was director of Operation Drake 1977–81 and Operation Raleigh 1978–82. His books include *A Taste for Adventure* 1978.

blasphemy (Greek 'evil-speaking') written or spoken insult directed against religious belief or sacred things with deliberate intent to outrage believers.

Blasphemy was originally defined as 'publishing any matter which contradicts the teaching of the Church of England'; since 1883 it has been redefined as a 'vilification' or attack on Christianity, likely to 'outrage the feelings of believers'. Blasphemy is still an offence in English common law, despite several recommendations (for example by the Law Commission 1985) that the law of blasphemy should be abolished or widened to apply to all religious faiths. In 1977 the magazine *Gay News* and its editor were successfully prosecuted for publishing a poem that suggested Jesus was a homosexual. In 1989 Salman Rushdie was accused by orthodox Muslims of blasphemy against the Islamic faith in his book *The Satanic Verses*, but the Court of Appeal held it was not blasphemous under English law. Demands have since been made to extend blasphemy laws to cover Islam, or abolish blasphemy laws entirely.

blast freezing industrial method of freezing substances such as foods by blowing very cold air over them. See ◊deep freezing.

blast furnace smelting furnace in which temperature is raised by the injection of an air blast. It is employed in the extraction of metals from their ores, chiefly pig iron from iron ore.

The principle has been known for thousands of years, but the present blast furnace is a heavy engineering development combining a number of special techniques.

blastocyst in mammals, a stage in the development of the ◊embryo that is roughly equivalent to the ◊blastula of other animal groups.

blastomere in biology, a cell formed in the first stages of embryonic development, after the splitting of the fertilized ovum, but before the formation of the ◊blastula or blastocyst.

blastula early stage in the development of a fertilized egg, when the egg changes from a solid mass of cells (the morula) to a hollow ball of cells (the blastula), containing a fluid-filled cavity (the blastocoel). See also ◊embryology.

Blaue Reiter, der /ˈblaʊə ˈraɪtə/ (German 'the Blue Rider') group of German Expressionist painters based in Munich, some of whom had left *die* ◊*Brücke*. They were interested in the value of colours, in folk art, and in the necessity of painting 'the inner, spiritual side of nature', but styles were highly varied. Wassily Kandinsky and Franz Marc published a book of their views 1912, and there were two exhibitions 1911, 1912.

Blavatsky /bləˈvætski/ Helena Petrovna (born Hahn) 1831–1891. Russian spiritualist and mystic, cofounder of the Theosophical Society (see ◊theosophy) 1875, which has its headquarters near Madras, India. In Tibet she underwent spiritual training and later became a Buddhist. Her books include *Isis Unveiled* 1877 and *The Secret Doctrine* 1888. She was declared a fraud by the London Society for Psychical Research 1885.

bleaching decolorization of coloured materials. The two main types of bleaching agent are the *oxidizing bleaches*, which bring about the ◊oxidation of pigments, and include the ultraviolet rays in sunshine, hydrogen peroxide, and chlorine in household bleaches; and the *reducing bleaches*, which bring about ◊reduction, and include sulphur dioxide.

bleak freshwater fish *Alburnus alburnus* of the carp family. It is up to to 20cm/8 in long, and lives in still or slow-running clear water in Britain and Europe.

In E Europe its scales are used in the preparation of artificial pearls.

Blenheim, Battle of battle on 13 Aug 1704 in which English troops under ◊Marlborough defeated the French and Bavarian armies near the Bavarian village of Blenheim (now in Germany) on the left bank of the Danube.

blenny any fish of the family Blenniidae, mostly small fishes found near rocky shores, with elongated slimy bodies tapering from head to tail, no scales, and long pelvic fins set far forward.

The most common British species is the *shanny Blennius pholis*.

Blériot /'bleriəʊ/ Louis 1872–1936. French aviator who, in a 24-horsepower monoplane of his own construction, made the first flight across the English Channel on 25 July 1909.

blesbok African antelope *Damaliscus albifrons*, about 1 m/3 ft high, with curved horns, brownish body, and a white blaze on the face. It was seriously depleted in the wild at the end of the 19th century. A few protected herds survive in South Africa. It is farmed for meat.

Bligh /blaɪ/ William 1754–1817. British admiral who accompanied Captain James ◊Cook on his second voyage around the world 1772–74, and in 1787 commanded HMS *Bounty* on an expedition to the Pacific. On the return voyage the crew mutinied 1789, and Bligh was cast adrift in a boat with 18 men. He was appointed governor of New South Wales 1805, where his discipline again provoked a mutiny 1808 (the Rum Rebellion). He returned to Britain, and was made an admiral 1811.

blight any of a number of plant diseases caused mainly by parasitic species of ◊fungus, which produce a whitish appearance on leaf and stem surfaces—for instance *potato blight Phytophthora infestans*. General damage caused by aphids or pollution is sometimes known as blight.

blight notice in UK law, a statutory notice by which an owner–occupier can require a public authority to purchase land that is potentially liable to compulsory purchase for development.

Blighty popular name for England among British troops in World War I.

blimp airship: any self-propelled, lighter-than-air craft that can be steered. A blimp with a soft frame is also called a *dirigible*; a *zeppelin* is rigid-framed.

British lighter-than-air aircraft were divided in World War I into A-rigid and B-limp (that is, without rigid internal framework), a barrage balloon therefore becoming known as a blimp.

blindness complete absence or impairment of sight. It may be caused by heredity, accident, disease, or deterioration with age.

Education of the blind was begun by Valentin Haüy, who published a book with raised lettering 1784, and founded a school. Aids to the blind include the use of the ◊Braille and ◊Moon alphabets in reading and writing, and of electronic devices now under development that convert print to recognizable mechanical speech; guide dogs; and sonic torches.

blind spot area where the optic nerve and blood vessels pass through the retina of the ◊eye. No visual image can be formed as there are no light-sensitive cells in this part of the retina.

Bliss /blɪs/ Arthur (Drummond) 1891–1975. English composer and conductor who became Master of the Queen's Musick 1953. Among his works are *A Colour Symphony* 1922, music for ballets *Checkmate* 1937, *Miracle in the Gorbals* 1944, and *Adam Zero* 1946; an opera *The Olympians* 1949; and dramatic film music, including *Things to Come* 1935. He conducted the first performance of Stravinsky's *Ragtime* for eleven instruments 1918.

Blitzkrieg (German 'lightning war') swift military campaign, as used by Germany at the beginning of World War II 1939–41. The abbreviated *Blitz* was applied to the attempted saturation bombing of London by the German air force between Sept 1940 and May 1941.

Blixen /'blɪksən/ Karen, born Karen Dinesen 1885–1962. Danish writer. Her autobiography *Out of Africa* 1937 is based on her experience of running a coffee plantation in Kenya. She wrote fiction, mainly in English, under the pen name Isak Dinesen.

BL Lacertae object starlike object that forms the centre of a distant galaxy, with a prodigious energy output. BL Lac objects, as they are called, seem to be related to ◊quasars and are thought to be the brilliant nuclei of elliptical galaxies. They are so named because the first to be discovered lies in the constellation Lacerta.

Bloch /blɒk/ Ernest 1880–1959. Swiss-born US composer. Among his works are the lyrical drama *Macbeth* 1910, *Schelomo* for cello and orchestra 1916, five string quartets, and *Suite Hébraique*, for viola and orchestra 1953. He often used themes based on Jewish liturgical music and folk song.

Bloch /blɒk/ Felix 1905–1983. Swiss-US physicist who invented the analytical technique of nuclear magnetic resonance (NMR) ◊spectroscopy 1946. For this work he shared the Nobel Prize for Physics 1952 with US physicist Edward Purcell (1912–).

Bloch /blɒk/ Konrad 1912– . German-born US chemist. Making use of the ◊radio-isotope carbon-14 (the radioactive form of carbon), Bloch was able to follow the complex steps by which the body chemically transforms acetic acid into cholesterol. For his work in this field Bloch shared the 1964 Nobel Prize for Medicine with Feodor Lynen (1911–1979).

blockade cutting-off of a place by hostile forces by land, sea, or air so as to prevent any movement to or fro, in order to compel a surrender without attack or to achieve some other political aim (for example, the ◊Berlin blockade 1948.

During World War I Germany attempted to blockade Britain with intensive submarine warfare, and Britain attempted to blockade Germany. In 1990 a blockade by United Nations member countries was agreed in an attempt to force Iraq to withdraw from the invaded territory of Kuwait, but was superseded by open war.

No nation has the right to declare a blockade unless it has the power to enforce it, according to international law. The Declaration of London 1909 laid down that a blockade must not be extended beyond the coasts and ports belonging to or occupied by an enemy.

Bloemfontein /ˈbluːmfənteɪn/ capital of the Orange Free State and judicial capital of the Republic of South Africa; population (1985) 204,000. Founded 1846, the city produces canned fruit, glassware, furniture, and plastics.

Blok /blɒk/ Alexander Alexandrovich 1880–1921. Russian poet who, as a follower of the French Symbolist movement, used words for their symbolic rather than actual meaning. He backed the 1917 Revolution, as in his poems *The Twelve* 1918, and *The Scythians* 1918, the latter appealing to the West to join in the revolution.

Blomberg /ˈblɒmbeək/ Werner von 1878–1946. German soldier and Nazi politician, minister of defence 1933–35, minister of war, and head of the *Wehrmacht* (army) 1935–38 under Hitler's chancellorship. He was discredited by his marriage to a prostitute and dismissed in Jan 1938, enabling Hitler to exercise more direct control over the armed forces. In spite of his removal from office, Blomberg was put on trial for war crimes 1946 at Nuremberg.

Blondin /ˈblɒndɪn/ Charles. Assumed name of Jean François Gravelet 1824–1897. French tightrope walker who walked across a rope suspended above Niagara Falls, USA. He first crossed the falls 1859 at a height of 49 m/160 ft, and later repeated the feat blindfold and then pushing a wheelbarrow.

blood liquid circulating in the arteries, veins, and capillaries of vertebrate animals; the term also refers to the corresponding fluid in those invertebrates that possess a closed ◊circulatory system. Blood carries nutrients and oxygen to individual cells and removes waste products, such as carbon dioxide. It is also important in the immune response and, in many animals, in the distribution of heat throughout the body.

In humans it makes up 5% of the body weight, occupying a volume of 5.5 l/10 pt in the average adult. It consists of a colourless, transparent liquid called *plasma*, containing microscopic cells of three main varieties. *Red cells* (erythrocytes) form nearly half the volume of the blood, with 5 billion cells per litre. Their red colour is caused by ◊haemoglobin. *White cells* (leucocytes) are of various kinds. Some (phagocytes) ingest invading bacteria and so protect the body from disease; these also help to repair injured tissues. Others (lymphocytes) produce antibodies, which help provide immunity. Blood *platelets* (thrombocytes) assist in the clotting of blood.

Blood cells constantly wear out and die, and are replaced from the bone marrow. Dissolved in the plasma are salts, proteins, sugars, fats, hormones, and fibrinogen, which are transported around the body, the last having a role in clotting.

Blood /blʌd/ Thomas 1618–1680. Irish adventurer, known as Colonel Blood, who attempted to steal the crown jewels from the Tower of London, England, 1671.

blood–brain barrier theoretical term for the defence mechanism that prevents many substances circulating in the bloodstream (including some germs) from invading the brain.

The blood–brain barrier is not a single entity, but a defensive complex comprising various physical features and chemical reactions to do with the permeability of cells. It ensures that 'foreign' proteins, carried in the blood vessels supplying the brain, do not breach the vessel walls and enter the brain tissue. Many drugs are unable to cross the blood–brain barrier.

blood clotting complex series of events that prevents excessive bleeding after injury. The result is the formation of a meshwork of protein fibres (fibrin) and trapped blood cells over the cut blood vessels.

blood group any of the blood groups into which blood is classified according to antigenic activity. Red blood cells of one individual may carry molecules on their surface that act as ◊antigens in another individual whose red blood cells lack these molecules. The two main antigens are designated A and B. These give rise to four blood groups: having A only (A), having B only (B), having both (AB), and having neither (O). Each of these groups may or may not contain the ◊rhesus factor. Correct typing of blood groups is vital in transfusion, since incompatible types of donor and recipient blood will result in blood clotting, with possible death of the recipient.

These ABO blood groups were first described by Karl ◊Landsteiner 1902. Subsequent research revealed at least 14 main types of blood groupings, 11 of which are involved with induced ◊antibody production. Blood typing is also of importance in forensic medicine, cases of disputed paternity, and in anthropological studies.

bloodhound ancient breed of dog. Black and tan in colour, it has long, pendulous ears and distinctive wrinkled head and face. It grows to a height of about 65 cm/26 in at the shoulder. The breed originated as a hunting dog in Belgium in the Middle Ages, and its excellent powers of scent have been employed in tracking and criminal detection from very early times.

blood pressure pressure, or tension, of the blood against the inner walls of blood vessels, especially the arteries, due to the muscular pumping activity of the heart. Abnormally high blood pressure (see ◊hypertension) may be associated with various conditions or arise with no obvious cause; abnormally low blood pressure (hypotension) occurs in ◊shock and after excessive fluid or blood loss from any cause.

In mammals, the left ventricle of the ◊heart pumps blood into the arterial system. This pumping is assisted by waves of muscular contraction by the arteries themselves, but resisted by the elasticity of the inner and outer walls of the same arteries. Pressure is greatest when the heart ventricle contracts (*systolic pressure*) and least when the ventricle is filling up with blood and pressure is solely maintained by the elasticity of the arteries (*diastolic pressure*). Blood pressure is measured in millimetres of mercury (the height of a column on the measuring instrument, a sphygmomanometer). Normal human blood pressure is around 120/80 mm Hg; the first number represents the systolic pressure and the second the diastolic. Large deviations from this figure usually indicate ill health.

blood test laboratory evaluation of a blood sample. There are numerous blood tests, from simple typing to establish the ◊blood group to sophisticated biochemical assays of substances, such as hormones, present in the blood only in minute quantities.

The majority of tests fall into one of three categories: *haematology* (testing the state of the blood itself), *microbiology* (identifying infection), and *blood chemistry* (reflecting chemical events elsewhere in the body). Before operations, a common test is haemoglobin estimation to determine how well a patient might tolerate blood loss during surgery.

blood vessel specialist tube that carries blood around the body of multicellular animals. Blood vessels are highly evolved in vertebrates where the three main types, the arteries, veins, and capillaries, are all adapted for their particular role within the body.

bloom whitish powdery or waxlike coating over the surface of certain fruits that easily rubs off when handled. It often contains ◊yeasts that live on the sugars in the fruit. The term bloom is also used to describe a rapid increase in number of certain species of algae found in lakes, ponds, and oceans.

Such blooms may be natural but are often the result of nitrate pollution, in which artificial fertilizers, applied to surrounding fields, leach out into the waterways. This type of bloom can lead to the death of almost every other organism in the water; because light cannot penetrate the algal growth, the plants beneath can no longer photosynthesize and therefore do not release oxygen into the water. Only those organisms that are adapted to very low levels of oxygen survive.

Bloomer /'blu:mə/ Amelia Jenks 1818–1894. US campaigner for women's rights. In 1849, when unwieldy crinolines were the fashion, she introduced a knee-length skirt combined with loose trousers gathered at the ankles, which became known as *bloomers* (also called 'rational dress').

Bloomsbury Group group of writers and artists based in Bloomsbury, London. The group included the artists Duncan ◊Grant and Vanessa Bell, and the writers Lytton ◊Strachey, and Leonard (1880–1969) and Virginia ◊Woolf.

Blow /bləʊ/ John 1648–1708. British composer. He taught ◊Purcell, and wrote church music, for example the anthem 'I Was Glad when They Said unto Me' 1697. His masque *Venus and Adonis* 1685 is sometimes called the first English opera.

blowfly any fly of the genus *Calliphora*, also known as bluebottle, or of the related genus *Lucilia*, when it is greenbottle. It lays its eggs in dead flesh, on which the maggots feed.

blubber thick layer of ◊fat under the skin of marine mammals, which provides an energy store and an effective insulating layer, preventing the loss of body heat to the surrounding water. Blubber has been used (when boiled down) in engineering, food processing, cosmetics, and printing, but all of these products can now be produced synthetically, thus saving the lives of animals.

Blücher /'blu:kə/ Gebhard Leberecht von 1742–1819. Prussian general and field marshal, popular as 'Marshal Forward'. He took an active part in the patriotic movement, and in the War of German Liberation defeated the French as commander in chief at Leipzig 1813, crossed the Rhine to Paris 1814, and was made prince of Wahlstadt (Silesia).

In 1815 he was defeated by Napoleon at Ligny but played a crucial role in the British commander Wellington's victory at Waterloo, near Brussels.

blue sporting term used in the UK to describe a student of Oxford or Cambridge who represents their university at any game or sporting activity. The actual award is a ribbon, either light-blue (Cambridge) or dark-blue (Oxford), depending on which university is represented. The first blues are believed to have been awarded after the 1836 ◊Boat Race.

Blue Arrow UK company whose attempted purchase of the US company Manpower Inc 1987 prompted an investigation by the Serious Fraud Squad.

County NatWest, the investment banking company of the National Westminster Bank, failed to disclose that only 38% of a rights issue (sale of shares) by Blue Arrow, intended to finance the purchase, had been taken up, and concealed the ownership of some of the shares. Two National Westminster investment bankers, one securities company, and 11 individuals were charged with fraud and conspiracy Nov 1989.

Bluebeard /'blu:biəd/ folktale character, popularized by the writer Charles Perrault in France about 1697, and historically identified with Gilles de ◊Rais. Bluebeard murdered six wives for disobeying his command not to enter a locked room, but was himself killed before he could murder the seventh.

bluebell name given in Scotland to the harebell *Campanula rotundifolia*, and in England to the wild hyacinth *Endymion nonscriptus*, belonging to the family Liliaceae.

Bluebell The bluebell is a bulbous plant abundant in woods, hedgerows, and meadows adjoining woods.

bluebird three species of a North American bird, genus *Sialia*, belonging to the thrush subfamily, Turdinae. The eastern bluebird *Sialia sialis* is regarded as the herald of spring. About 18 cm/7 in long, it has a reddish breast, the upper plumage being sky-blue, and a distinctive song.

bluebuck any of several species of antelope, including the blue ◊duiker *Cephalophus* *monticola* of South Africa, about 33 cm/13 in high. The male of the Indian ◊nilgai antelope is also known as the bluebuck.

The bluebuck or blaubok, *Hippotragus leucophaeus*, was a large blue-grey South African antelope. Once abundant, it was hunted to extinction, the last being shot 1800.

blue chip in business and finance, a stock that is considered strong and reliable in terms of the dividend yield and capital value. Blue chip companies are favoured by stock market investors more interested in security than risk taking.

Bluefields /'bluːfiːldz/ one of three major port facilities on the E coast of Nicaragua, situated on an inlet of the Caribbean Sea.

bluegrass dense, spreading grass of the genus *Poa*, which is bluetinted and grows in clumps. Various species are known from the northern hemisphere. Kentucky bluegrass *P. pratensis*, introduced to the USA from Europe, provides pasture for horses.

blue-green algae or cyanobacteria single-celled, primitive organisms that resemble bacteria in their internal cell organization, sometimes joined together in colonies or filaments. Blue-green algae are among the oldest known living organisms and, with bacteria, belong to the kingdom Monera; remains have been found in rocks up to 3.5 billion years old. They are widely distributed in aquatic habitats, on the damp surfaces of rocks and trees, and in the soil.

Blue-green algae and bacteria are prokaryotic organisms. Some can fix nitrogen and thus are necessary to the nitrogen cycle, while others follow a symbiotic existence—for example, living in association with fungi to form lichens. Fresh water can become polluted by nitrates and phosphates from fertilizers and detergents. This eutrophication, or overenrichment, of the water causes multiplication of the algae in the form of algae blooms. The algae multiply and cover the water's surface, remaining harmless until they give of toxins as they decay. These toxins kill fish and other wildlife and can be harmful to domestic animals, cattle, and people.

blue gum either of two Australian trees: Tasmanian blue gum *Eucalyptus globulus* of the myrtle family, with bluish bark, a chief source of eucalyptus oil; and Sydney blue gum *E. saligna*, a tall, straight tree. The former is cultivated extensively in California

and has also been planted in South America, India, parts of Africa, and S Europe.

Blue Mountains part of the ◊Great Dividing Range, New South Wales, Australia, ranging 600–1,100 m/2,000–3,600 ft and blocking Sydney from the interior until the crossing 1813 by surveyor William Lawson, Gregory Blaxland, and William Wentworth.

Blue Nile (Arabic *Bahr el Azraq*) river rising in the mountains of Ethiopia. Flowing W then N for 2,000 km/1,250 mi, it eventually meets the White Nile at Khartoum. The river is dammed at Roseires where a hydroelectric scheme produces 70% of Sudan's electricity.

blueprint photographic process used for copying engineering drawings and architectural plans, so called because it produces a white copy of the original against a blue background.

The plan to be copied is made on transparent tracing paper, which is placed in contact with paper sensitized with a mixture of iron ammonium citrate and potassium hexacyanoferrate. The paper is exposed to ◊ultraviolet radiation and then washed in water. Where the light reaches the paper, it turns blue (Prussian blue). The paper underneath the lines of the drawing is unaffected, so remains white.

blue riband or *blue ribbon* the highest distinction in any sphere; for example, the blue riband of horse racing in the UK is held by the winner of the Derby.

The term derives from the blue riband of the Order of the Garter (see under ◊knighthood). The term *cordon bleu* in French has the same meaning.

Blue Ridge Mountains range extending from West Virginia to Georgia, USA, and including Mount Mitchell 2,045 m/6,712 ft; part of the ◊Appalachians.

blues African-American music that originated in the rural American South in the late 19th century, characterized by a 12-bar construction and frequently melancholy lyrics. Blues guitar and vocal styles have played a vital part in the development of jazz and pop music in general.

1920s–1930s The *rural* or *delta blues* was usually performed solo with guitar or harmonica, by such artists as Robert Johnson (1911–1938) and Bukka White (1906–1977), but the earliest recorded style, *classic blues*, by such musicians as W C Handy (1873–

1958) and Bessie Smith (1894–1937), was sung with a small band.

1940s–1950s The urban blues, using electric amplification, emerged in the northern cities, chiefly Chicago. As exemplified by Howlin' Wolf (adopted name of Chester Burnett, 1910–1976), Muddy Waters (adopted name of McKinley Morganfield, 1915–1983), and John Lee Hooker (1917–), urban blues became *rhythm and blues*.

1960s The jazz-influenced guitar style of B B King (1925–) inspired many musicians of the *British blues boom*, including Eric Clapton (1945–).

1980s The 'blues *noir*' of Robert Cray (1953–) found a wide audience.

blue shift in astronomy, a manifestation of the ◊Doppler effect in which an object appears bluer when it is moving towards the observer or the observer is moving towards it (blue light is of a higher frequency than other colours in the spectrum). The blue shift is the opposite of the ◊red shift.

bluestocking learned woman; the term is often used disparagingly. It originated 1750 in England with the literary gatherings of Elizabeth Vesey (1715–1791), the wife of an Irish MP, in Bath, and Elizabeth Montagu, a writer and patron, in London. According to the novelist Fanny Burney, the term arose when the poet Benjamin Stillingfleet protested that he had nothing formal to wear. She told him to come in his 'blue stockings'– that is, ordinary clothes. The regulars at these gatherings became known as the Blue Stocking Circle.

Blum /bluːm/ Léon 1872–1950. French politician. He was converted to socialism by the ◊Dreyfus affair 1899 and in 1936 became the first socialist prime minister of France. He was again premier for a few weeks 1938. Imprisoned under the ◊Vichy government 1942 as a danger to French security, he was released by the Allies 1945. He again became premier for a few weeks 1946.

Blunden /ˈblʌndən/ Edmund 1896–1974. English poet. He served in World War I and published the prose work *Undertones of War* 1928. His poetry is mainly about rural life. Among his scholarly contributions was the discovery and publication of some poems by the 19th-century poet John ◊Clare.

Blunt /blʌnt/ Anthony 1907–1983. British art historian and double agent. As a Cambridge lecturer, he recruited for the Soviet secret service and, as a member of the British Secret Service 1940–45, passed information to the USSR. In 1951 he assisted the defection to the USSR of the British agents Guy ◊Burgess and Donald Maclean (1913–1983). He was the author of many respected works on French and Italian art. Unmasked 1964, he was given immunity after his confession.

He was director of the Courtauld Institute of Art 1947–74 and Surveyor of the Queen's Pictures 1945–1972. He was stripped of his knighthood 1979 when the affair became public.

Blunt /blʌnt/ Wilfrid Scawen 1840–1922. British poet. He married Lady Anne Noel, Byron's grand-daughter, and travelled with her in the Middle East, becoming a supporter of Arab nationalism. He also supported Irish Home Rule (he was imprisoned 1887–88), and wrote anti-imperialist books, poetry, and diaries.

Blyth /blaɪð/ 'Chay' (Charles) 1940– . British sailing adventurer who rowed across the Atlantic with Capt John Ridgeway 1966 and sailed solo around the world in a westerly direction during 1970–71. He sailed around the world with a crew in the opposite direction 1973–74, and in 1977 he made a record-breaking transatlantic crossing from Cape Verde to Antigua.

BMA abbreviation for *British Medical Association*.

BMR abbreviation for ◊basal metabolic rate.

BNF abbreviation for *British Nuclear Fuels*.

boa any of various nonvenomous snakes of the family Boidae, found mainly in tropical and subtropical parts of the New World. Boas feed mainly on small mammals and birds. They catch these in their teeth or kill them by constriction (crushing the creature within their coils until it suffocates). The boa constrictor *Constrictor constrictor*, can grow up to 5.5 m/18.5 ft long, but rarely reaches more than 4 m/12 ft. Other boas include the anaconda and the emerald tree boa *Boa canina*, about 2 m/6 ft long and bright green.

Some small burrowing boas live in N Africa and W Asia, while other species live on Madagascar and some Pacific islands, but the majority of boas live in South and Central America. The name boa is sometimes used loosely to include the pythons of the Old World, which also belong to the Boidae family, and which share with boas vestiges of hind limbs and constricting habits.

Boadicea /ˌbəʊədɪˈsiːə/ alternative spelling of British queen ◊Boudicca.

boar wild member of the pig family, such as the Eurasian wild boar *Sus scrofa*, from which domestic pig breeds derive. The wild boar is sturdily built, being 1.5 m/4.5 ft long and 1 m/3 ft high, and possesses formidable tusks. Of gregarious nature and mainly woodland-dwelling, it feeds on roots, nuts, insects, and some carrion.

The dark coat of the adult boar is made up of coarse bristles with varying amounts of underfur, but the young are striped. The male domestic pig is also known as a boar, the female as a sow.

boarding school school offering board and lodging as well as tuition to its students.

Most boarding education in the UK is provided in the private, fee-paying sector, but there are a number of state schools with boarding facilities.

board of visitors in the UK penal system, a body of people independent of the government who supervise the state of prison premises, the administration of prisons, and the treatment of the prisoners. Boards of visitors also serve as disciplinary tribunals. Research has indicated that about 40% of members are magistrates.

Members of the various boards, who normally total between 9 and 16, meet once a month at the prison for which they are responsible and have access to all prisoners, all parts of the prison, and to prison records. The board must hear complaints and requests from prisoners and inspect the food. Members of the boards of visitors are appointed by the home secretary and normally serve for three-year terms.

boardsailing another name for ◊windsurfing, a watersport combining elements of surfing and sailing, also called sailboarding.

Boas /ˈbəʊæz/ Franz 1858–1942. German-born US anthropologist. One of America's first academic anthropologists, he stressed the need to study 'four fields'—ethnology, linguistics, physical anthropology, and archaeology—before generalizations might be made about any one culture or comparisons about any number of cultures.

Boateng /ˈbwɑːteŋ/ Paul 1951– . British Labour politician and broadcaster. Elected member of Parliament for Brent South 1987, he was appointed to Labour's Treasury team in 1989, the first black appointee to a frontbench post. He has served on numerous committees on crime and race relations.

boat people illegal emigrants arriving by sea, especially those Vietnamese who left their country after the takeover of South Vietnam 1975 by North Vietnam. Some 160,000 Vietnamese fled to Hong Kong, many being attacked at sea by Thai pirates, and in 1989 50,000 remained there in cramped, squalid refugee camps. The UK government began forced repatriation 1990.

Some 500,000 SE Asians became refugees in this way 1975–82 with an estimated 10%–15% mortality rate. Only 10% of those who have arrived in Hong Kong since the policy of 'screening' (questioning about reasons for leaving Vietnam) begun 1988 have been given refugee status; the others are classified as 'economic migrants'. In 1990 the total number of boat people in SE Asia was about 90,000, an increase of 30,000 from 1988.

Boat Race annual UK rowing race between the crews of Oxford and Cambridge universities. It is held during the Easter vacation over a 6.8 km/4.25 mi course on the river Thames between Putney and Mortlake, SW London.

The Boat Race was first held 1829 from Hambledon Lock to Henley Bridge. Up to and including the 1991 race it had been staged 137 times; Cambridge had 69 wins, Oxford 67 and there had been one dead heat 1877. The reserve crews also have their own races. The Cambridge reserve crew is called Goldie, Oxford's is called Isis.

bobcat cat *Felis rufa* living in a variety of habitats from S Canada through to S Mexico. It is similar to the lynx, but only 75 cm/2.5 ft long, with reddish fur and less well-developed ear-tufts.

bobolink North American songbird *Dolichonyx oryzivorus*, which takes its common name from the distinctive call of the male. Breeding males are mostly black, with a white rump. Breeding females are buff-coloured with dark streaks. Bobolinks are about 18 cm/7 in long, and build their nests on the ground in hayfields and weedy meadows.

bobsleighing or *bobsledding* port of racing steel-bodied, steerable toboggans, crewed by two or four people, down mountain ice chutes at speeds of up to 130 kph/80 mph. It was introduced as an Olympic event 1924 and world championships have been held every year since 1931. Included among the major bobsleighing events are the Olympic Championships (the four-crew event was introduced at the 1924 Winter Olympics and the two-crew 1932) and the World Championships, the four-crew championship introduced in 1924 and the two-crew in 1931. In Olympic years winners automatically become world champions.

Boccaccio /bɒˈkɑːtʃiəʊ/ Giovanni 1313–1375. Italian poet, chiefly known for the collection of tales called the ◊*Decameron* 1348–53.

Son of a Florentine merchant, he lived in Naples 1328–41, where he fell in love with the unfaithful 'Fiammetta' who inspired his early poetry. Before returning to Florence 1341 he had written *Filostrato* and *Teseide* (used by Chaucer in his *Troilus and Criseyde* and *Knight's Tale*). He was much influenced by ◊Petrarch, whom he met 1350.

Boccioni /ˌbɒtʃiˈəʊni/ Umberto 1882–1916. Italian painter and sculptor. One of the founders of the ◊Futurist movement, he was a pioneer of abstract art.

Böcklin /ˈbɜːklɪn/ Arnold 1827–1901. Swiss Romantic painter. His mainly imaginary landscapes have a dreamlike atmosphere: for example, *Island of the Dead* 1880 (Metropolitan Museum of Art, New York).

He was strongly attracted to Italy and lived for years in Rome. Many of his paintings are peopled with mythical beings, such as nymphs and naiads.

Bode /ˈbəʊdə/ Johann Elert 1747–1826. German astronomer, director of the Berlin observatory. He published the first atlas of all stars visible to the naked eye, *Uranographia* 1801, and devised Bode's Law.

Bode's law is a numerical sequence that gives the approximate distances, in astronomical units (distance between Earth and Sun = one astronomical unit), of the planets from the Sun by adding 4 to each term of the series 0, 3, 6, 12, 24, ... and then dividing by 10. Bode's law predicted the existence of a planet between ◊Mars and ◊Jupiter, which led to the discovery of the asteroids. The 'law' breaks down for ◊Neptune and ◊Pluto. The relationship was first noted 1772 by the German mathematician Johann Titius (1729–1796) 1772 (it is also known as the Titius-Bode law).

Bodhidharma /ˌbəʊdɪˈdɑːmə/ 6th century AD. Indian Buddhist and teacher. He entered China from S India about 520, and was the founder of the Ch'an school (◊Zen is the Japanese derivation). Ch'an focuses on contemplation leading to intuitive meditation, a direct pointing to and stilling of the human mind. In the 20th century, the Japanese variation, Zen, has attracted many followers in the west.

bodhisattva in Mahāyāna Buddhism, someone who seeks ◊enlightenment in order to help other living beings. A bodhisattva is free to enter ◊nirvana but voluntarily chooses to be reborn until all other beings have attained that state.

Bodichon /ˈbəʊdɪʃɒn/ Barbara (born Leigh-Smith) 1827–1891. English feminist and campaigner for women's education and suffrage. She wrote *Women and Work* 1857, and was a founder of the magazine *The Englishwoman's Journal* 1858.

Born into a radical family that believed in female equality, she attended Bedford College, London. She was a founder of the college for women that became Girton College, Cambridge.

Bodin /bɒˈdæn/ Jean 1530–1596. French political philosopher whose six-volume *De la République* 1576 is considered the first work on political economy.

An attorney in Paris, he published 1574 a tract explaining that prevalent high prices were due to the influx of precious metals from the New World. His theory of an ideal government emphasized obedience to a sovereign ruler.

Bodley /ˈbɒdli/ Thomas 1545–1613. English scholar and diplomat, after whom the Bodleian Library in Oxford is named. After retiring from Queen Elizabeth I's service 1597, he restored the university's library, which was opened as the Bodleian Library 1602.

The library had originally been founded in the 15th century by Humphrey, Duke of Gloucester (1391–1447).

Bodmin /ˈbɒdmɪn/ market town in Cornwall, England, 48 km/30 m from Plymouth; population (1984) 15,000. *Bodmin Moor* to the NE is a granite upland, culminating in Brown Willy 419 m/1,375 ft.

Bodoni /bəˈdəʊni/ Giambattista 1740–1813. Italian printer who managed the printing press of the duke of Parma and produced high-quality editions of the classics. He designed several typefaces, including one bearing his name, which is in use today.

Boehme /ˈbɜːmə/ Jakob 1575–1624. German mystic, who had many followers in Germany, Holland, and England. He claimed divine revelation of the unity of everything and nothing, and found in God's eternal nature a principle to reconcile good and evil. He was the author of the treatise *Aurora* 1612.

Boeing US military and commercial aircraft manufacturer, founded 1916 near Seattle, Oregon, by William E Boeing (1881–1956) as the Pacific Aero Products Company. Renamed the following year, the company built its first seaplane and in 1919 set up an airmail service between Seattle and Victoria, British Columbia.

Boeotia /bɪˈəʊʃə/ ancient district of central Greece, of which ◊Thebes was the chief city. The *Boeotian League* (formed by 10 city states in the 6th century BC) superseded ◊Sparta in the leadership of Greece in the 4th century BC.

Boer Dutch settler or descendant of Dutch and Huguenot settlers in South Africa; see also ◊Afrikaner.

Boer War the second of the ◊South African Wars 1899–1902, waged between the Dutch settlers in South Africa and the British.

Boethius /bəʊˈiːθɪəs/ Anicius Manilus Severinus AD 480–524. Roman philosopher. While imprisoned on suspicion of treason by the emperor ◊Theodoric the Great, he wrote treatises on music and mathematics and *De Consolatione Philosophiae/The Consolation of Philosophy*, a dialogue in prose.

bog type of wetland where decomposition is slowed down and dead plant matter accumulates as ◊peat. Bogs develop under conditions of low temperature, high acidity, low nutrient supply, stagnant water, and oxygen deficiency. The typical bog plant is sphagnum moss; rushes, cranberry, and cotton grass also grow under these conditions; insectivorous plants such as sundews and bladderworts are common in bogs (insect prey make up for the lack of nutrients).

Bogarde /ˈbəʊɡɑːd/ Dirk. Stage name of Derek van den Bogaerde 1921– . English actor who appeared in comedies and adventure films such as *Doctor in the House* 1954 and *Campbell's Kingdom* 1957, before acquiring international recognition for complex roles in Joseph Losey's *The Servant* 1963 and *Accident* 1967, and Luchino Visconti's *Death in Venice* 1971. He has also written autobiographical books and novels: *A Postillion Struck by Lightning* 1977, *Snakes and Ladders* 1978, *Orderly Man* 1983, and *Backcloth* 1986.

Bogarde English actor Dirk Bogarde.

Bogart /ˈbəʊɡɑːt/ Humphrey 1899–1957. US film actor who achieved fame as the gangster in *The Petrified Forest* 1936. He became an international cult figure as the tough, romantic loner in such films as *The Maltese Falcon* 1941 and *Casablanca* 1943, a status resurrected in the 1960s and still celebrated today. He won an Academy Award for his role in *The African Queen* 1952.

He co-starred in *To Have and Have Not* 1944 and *The Big Sleep* 1946 with Lauren Bacall, who became his fourth wife.

Boğazköy /bɔːˈɑːzkɔɪ/ village in Turkey 145 km/90 mi E of Ankara. It is on the site of *Hattusas*, the ancient ◊Hittite capital established about 1640 BC. Thousands of tablets excavated here over a number of years by the German Oriental Society revealed, when their cuneiform writing was deciphered by Bedrich Hrozny (1879–1952), a great deal about the customs, religion, and history of the Hittite people.

bogbean or *buckbean* aquatic or bog plant *Menyanthes trifoliata* of the gentian family, with a creeping rhizome and leaves and pink flower spikes held above water. It is found over much of the northern hemisphere.

Bognor Regis /ˈbɒɡnə ˈriːdʒɪs/ seaside resort in West Sussex, England, 105 km/66 mi SW of London; population (1981) 53,200. It owes the Regis part of its name to the convalescent visit by King George V 1929.

Bogomils /ˈbɒɡəmɪl/ Christian heretics who originated in 10th-century Bulgaria and spread throughout the Byzantine empire. Their name derives from Bogomilus, or Theophilus, who taught in Bulgaria 927–950. Despite persecution, they were expunged by the Ottomans only after the fall of Constantinople 1453.

Bogotá /ˌbɒɡəˈtɑː/ capital of Colombia, South America; 2,640 m/8,660 ft above sea level on the edge of the plateau of the E Cordillera; population (1985) 4,185,000. It was founded 1538.

Bohemia /bəʊˈhiːmiə/ area of the Czech Republic, a kingdom of central Europe from the 9th century. It was under Habsburg rule 1526–1918, when it was included in Czechoslovakia. The name Bohemia derives from the Celtic Boii, its earliest known inhabitants.

It became part of the Holy Roman Empire as the result of Charlemagne's establishment of a protectorate over the Celtic, Germanic, and Slav tribes settled in this area. Christianity was introduced in the 9th century, the See of Prague being established 975, and feudalism was introduced by King Ottaker I of Bohemia (1197–1230). From the 12th century onwards, mining attracted large numbers of German settlers, leading to a strong Germanic influence in culture and society. In 1310, John of Luxemburg (died 1346) founded a German-Czech royal dynasty that lasted until 1437. His son, Charles IV, became Holy Roman Emperor 1355, and during his reign the See of Prague was elevated to an archbishopric and a university was founded there. During the 15th century, divisions within the nobility and religious conflicts culminating in the Hussite Wars (1420–36) led to decline.

Bohr /bɔː/ Aage 1922– . Danish physicist who produced a new model of the nucleus 1952, known as the collective model. For this work, he shared the 1975 Nobel Prize for Physics. He was the son of Niels Bohr.

Bohr /bɔː/ Niels Henrik David 1885–1962. Danish physicist. His theoretic work produced a new model of atomic structure, now called the Bohr model, and helped establish the validity of ◊quantum theory.

After work with Ernest ◊Rutherford at Manchester, he became professor at Copenhagen 1916, and founded there the Institute of Theoretical Physics of which he became

director 1920. He was awarded the Nobel Prize for Physics 1922. Bohr fled from the Nazis in World War II and took part in work on the atomic bomb in the USA. In 1952, he helped to set up ◊CERN, the European nuclear research organization in Geneva.

Boiardo /bɔɪˈɑːdəʊ/ Matteo Maria, Count 1434–1494. Italian poet, famed for his *Orlando innamorato/Roland in Love* 1486, a chivalrous epic glorifying military honour, patriotism, and religion. ◊Ariosto's *Orlando Furioso* 1516 was conceived as a sequel to this work.

boil small abscess originating around a hair follicle or in a sweat gland, most likely to form if resistance is low or diet inadequate.

Boileau /bwæˈləʊ/ Nicolas 1636–1711. French poet and critic. After a series of contemporary satires, his *Epîtres/Epistles* 1669–77 led to his joint appointment with Racine as royal historiographer 1677. Later works include *L'Art poétique/The Art of Poetry* 1674 and the mock-heroic *Le Lutrin/The Lectern* 1674–83.

boiler any vessel that converts water into steam. Boilers are used in conventional power stations to generate steam to feed steam ◊turbines, which drive the electricity generators. They are also used in steamships, which are propelled by steam turbines, and in steam locomotives. Every boiler has a furnace in which fuel (coal, oil, or gas) is burned to produce hot gases, and a system of tubes in which heat is transferred from the gases to the water.

The common kind of boiler used in ships and power stations is the *water-tube* type, in which the water circulates in tubes surrounded by the hot furnace gases. The water-tube boilers at power stations produce steam at a pressure of up to 300 atmospheres and at a temperature of up to 600°C/1,100°F to feed to the steam turbines. It is more efficient than the *fire-tube* type that is used in steam locomotives. In this boiler the hot furnace gases are drawn through tubes surrounded by water.

boiling process of changing a liquid into its vapour, by heating it at the maximum possible temperature for that liquid (see ◊boiling point) at atmospheric pressure.

boiling point for any given liquid, the temperature at which the application of heat raises the temperature of the liquid no further, but converts it into vapour.

The boiling point of water under normal pressure is 100°C/212°F. The lower the pressure, the lower the boiling point and vice versa. See also ◊elevation of boiling point.

Bokassa /bɒˈkæsə/ Jean-Bédel 1921– . President of the Central African Republic 1966–79 (self-proclaimed emperor 1977–79). Commander in chief from 1963, in Dec 1965 he led the military coup that gave him the presidency. On 4 Dec 1976 he proclaimed the Central African Empire and one year later crowned himself as emperor for life. His regime was characterized by arbitrary state violence and cruelty. Overthrown in 1979, Bokassa was in exile until 1986. Upon his return he was sentenced to death, but this was commuted to life imprisonment 1988.

Boldrewood /ˈbəʊldəwʊd/ Rolf. Pen name of Thomas Alexander Browne 1826–1915. Australian writer. Born in London, he was taken to Australia as a child in 1830. He became a pioneer squatter, and a police magistrate in the goldfields. His books include *Robbery Under Arms* 1888.

bolero /bɒˈleərəʊ/ Spanish dance in triple time for a solo dancer or a couple, usually with castanet accompaniment. It was used as the title of a one-act ballet score by Ravel, choreographed by Nijinsky for Ida Rubinstein 1928.

boletus genus of fleshy fungi belonging to the class Basidiomycetes, with thick stems and caps of various colours. The European *Boletus edulis* is edible, but some species are poisonous.

Boleyn /bəˈlɪn/ Anne 1507–1536. Queen of England, the woman for whom Henry VIII broke with the pope and founded the Church of England (see ◊Reformation). Second wife of Henry, she was married to him 1533 and gave birth to the future Queen Elizabeth I in the same year. Accused of adultery and incest with her half-brother (a charge invented by Thomas ◊Cromwell), she was beheaded.

Bolger /ˈbɒldʒə/ Jim (James) Brendan 1935– . New Zealand politician and prime minister from 1990. A successful sheep and cattle farmer, Bolger was elected as a member of Parliament 1972. He held a variety of cabinet posts under Robert Muldoon's leadership 1977–84, and was an effective, if uncharismatic leader of he opposition from March 1986, taking the National Party to electoral victory Oct 1990.

Bolingbroke /ˈbɒlɪŋbrʊk/ title of Henry of Bolingbroke, ◊Henry IV of England.

Bolingbroke /ˈbɒlɪŋbrʊk/ Henry John, Viscount Bolingbroke 1678–1751. British Tory politician and political philosopher. He was foreign secretary 1710–14 and a Jacobite conspirator.

Secretary of war 1704–08, he became foreign secretary in Robert ◊Harley's ministry 1710, and in 1713 negotiated the Treaty of Utrecht. His plans to restore the 'Old Pretender' James Francis Edward Stuart were ruined by Queen Anne's death only five days after he had secured the dismissal of Harley 1714. He fled abroad, returning 1723, when he worked to overthrow Robert Walpole. His books, such as *Idea of a Patriot King* 1738 and *The Dissertation upon Parties* 1735, laid the foundations for 19th-century Toryism.

Bolívar /bɒˈliːvɑ/ Simón 1783–1830. South American nationalist, leader of revolutionary armies, known as *the Liberator*. He fought the Spanish colonial forces in several uprisings and eventually liberated his native Venezuela 1821, Colombia and Ecuador 1822, Peru 1824, and Bolivia (a new state named after him, formerly Upper Peru) 1825.

Born in Venezuela, Bolívar joined the nationalists working for Venezuelan independence, and was sent to Britain 1810 as the representative of their government. Forced to flee to Colombia 1812, he joined the revolutionaries there, and invaded Venezuela 1811. A bloody civil war followed and in 1814 Bolívar had to withdraw to Colombia, and eventually to the West Indies, from where he raided the Spanish-American coasts. In 1817 he returned to Venezuela to set up a provisional government, crossed into Colombia 1819, where he defeated the Spaniards, and returning to Angostura proclaimed the republic of Colombia, consisting of Venezuela, New Granada (present-day Colombia), and Quito (Ecuador), with himself as president. The independence of Venezuela was finally secured 1821, and in 1822 Bolívar (along with Antonio ◊Sucre) liberated Ecuador. He was invited to lead the Peruvian struggle 1823; and, final victory having been won by Sucre at Ayacucho 1824, he turned his attention to framing a constitution.

Bolivia /bəˈlɪvɪə/ landlocked country in central Andes mountains in South America, bounded N and E by Brazil, SE by Para-

guay, S by Argentina, and W by Chile and Peru.

government Achieving independence 1825 after nearly 300 years of Spanish rule, Bolivia adopted its first constitution 1826, and since then a number of variations have been produced. The present one provides for a congress consisting of a 27-member senate and a 130-member chamber of deputies, both elected for four years by universal suffrage. The president, directly elected for a four-year term, is head of both state and government and chooses the cabinet. For administrative purposes, the country is divided into nine departments, each governed by a prefect appointed by the president. Most significant among the many political parties are the National Revolutionary Movement (MNR), and the Nationalist Democratic Action Party (ADN).

history Once part of the ◊Inca civilization, Bolivia was conquered by Spain 1538 and remained under Spanish rule until liberated by Simón Bolívar 1825 (after whom the country took its name). Bolivia formed a Peruvian–Bolivian Confederation 1836–39 under Bolivian president Andrés Santa Cruz, a former president of Peru. Chile declared war on the confederation, Santa Cruz was defeated, and the confederation dissolved. Bolivia was again at war with Chile 1879–84, when it lost its coastal territory and land containing valuable mineral deposits, and with Paraguay (the Chaco War) 1932–35, again losing valuable territory.

In the 1951 election, Dr Víctor Paz Estenssoro, the MNR candidate exiled in Argentina since 1946, failed to win an absolute majority, and an army junta took over. A popular uprising, supported by MNR and a section of the army, demanded the return of Paz, who became president and began a programme of social reform. He lost the 1956 election but returned to power 1960. In 1964 a coup, led by Vice President General René Barrientos, overthrew Paz and installed a military junta. Two years later Barrientos won the presidency. He was opposed by left-wing groups and in 1967 a guerrilla uprising led by Dr Ernesto 'Che' ◊Guevara was only put down with US help.

frequent coups In 1969 President Barrientos died in an air crash and was replaced by the vice president. He was later replaced by General Alfredo Ovando, who was ousted by Gen Juan Torres, who in turn was ousted by Col Hugo Banzer Suárez 1971. Banzer announced a return to constitutional government, but another attempted coup 1974 prompted him to postpone elections, ban all trade union and political activity, and proclaim that military government would last until at least 1980. Banzer agreed to elections 1978, but they were declared invalid after allegations of fraud, and, in that year, two more military coups.

In the 1979 elections Dr Siles and Dr Paz received virtually equal votes, and an interim administration was installed. An election 1980 proved equally inconclusive and was followed by the 189th military coup in Bolivia's 154 years of independence. General Luis García became president but resigned the following year after allegations of drug trafficking. He was replaced by General Celso Torrelio, who promised to fight corruption and return the country to democracy within three years. In 1982 a mainly civilian cabinet was appointed, but rumours of an impending coup resulted in Torrelio's resignation. A military junta led by the hardline General Guido Vildoso was installed.

economy deteriorates With the economy deteriorating, the junta asked congress to elect a president, and Dr Siles Zuazo was chosen to head a coalition cabinet. Economic aid from Europe and the USA, cut off in 1980, was resumed, but the economy continued to deteriorate. The government's austerity measures proved unpopular, and in June the president was temporarily abducted by a group of right-wing army officers. In an attempt to secure national unity, President Siles embarked on a five-day hunger strike.

Siles resigned 1985 and an election was held. No candidate won an absolute majority and Dr Víctor Paz Estenssoro, aged 77, was chosen by congress. Austerity measures imposed by Estenssoro's administration reduced inflation from 24,000% in 1985 to 3% in the first half of 1989.

In the 1989 congressional elections the MNR won marginally more votes in the chamber of deputies than the ADN, but did not obtain a clear majority. After an indecisive presidential contest Jaime Paz Zamora of the Movement of the Revolutionary Left (MIR) was elected president by the congress after he negotiated a power-sharing arrangement with former military dictator Hugo Banzer Suárez. Zamora pledged to maintain fiscal and monetary discipline and preserve free-market policies.

The MNR won the 1993 congressional elections and Gonzalo Sanchez de Lozada was elected president.

Bolkiah /ˈbolkiːə/ Hassanal 1946– . Sultan of Brunei from 1967, following the abdication of his father, Omar Ali Saifuddin (1916–1986). As absolute ruler, Bolkiah also assumed the posts of prime minister and defence minister on independence 1984.

As head of an oil- and gas-rich microstate, the sultan is reputedly the world's richest individual, with an estimated total wealth of $22 billion, which includes the Dorchester and Beverly Hills hotels in London and Los Angeles, and, at a cost of $40 million, the world's largest palace. He was educated at a British military academy.

Böll /bɜːl/ Heinrich 1917–1985. German novelist. A radical Catholic and anti-Nazi, he attacked Germany's political past and the materialism of its contemporary society. His many publications include poems, short stories, and novels which satirize West German society, for example *Billard um Halbzehn/Billiards at Half-Past Nine* 1959 and *Gruppenbild mit Dame/Group Portrait with Lady* 1971. Nobel Prize for Literature 1972.

Bollandist member of a group of Belgian Jesuits who edit and publish the *Acta Sanctorum*, the standard collection of saints' lives and other scholarly publications. They are named after John Bolland (1596–1665), who published the first two volumes 1643.

boll-weevil small American beetle *Anthonomus grandis* of the weevil group. The female lays her eggs in the unripe pods or

'bolls' of the cotton plant, and on these the larvae feed, causing great destruction.

Bologna /bəˈlɒnjə/ industrial city and capital of Emilia-Romagna, Italy, 80 km/50 mi north of Florence; population (1988) 427,000. It was the site of an Etruscan town, later of a Roman colony, and became a republic in the 12th century. It came under papal rule 1506 and was united with Italy 1860.

bolometer sensitive ◊thermometer that measures the energy of radiation by registering the change in electrical resistance of a fine wire when it is exposed to heat or light. The US astronomer Samuel Langley devised it 1880 for measuring radiation from stars.

Bolshevik (from Russian *bolshinstvo*, 'a majority') member of the majority of the Russian Social Democratic Party who split from the ◊Mensheviks 1903. The Bolsheviks, under ◊Lenin, advocated the destruction of capitalist political and economic institutions, and the setting-up of a socialist state with power in the hands of the workers. The Bolsheviks set the ◊Russian Revolution 1917 in motion. They changed their name to the Russian Communist Party 1918.

Bolt /bəʊlt/ Robert (Oxton) 1924– . British dramatist, known for his historical plays, such as *A Man for All Seasons* 1960 (filmed 1967) about Thomas More, and for his screenplays, including *Lawrence of Arabia* 1962 and *Dr Zhivago* 1965.

Bolton /ˈbəʊltən/ city in Greater Manchester, England, 18 km/11 mi NW of Manchester; population (1985) 261,000. Industries include chemicals and textiles.

Boltzmann /ˈbɒltsmæn/ Ludwig 1844–1906. Austrian physicist who studied the kinetic theory of gases, which explains the properties of gases by reference to the motion of their constituent atoms and molecules.

He derived a formula, the *Boltzmann distribution*, which gives the number of atoms or molecules with a given energy at a specific temperature. The constant in the formula is called the *Boltzmann constant*.

Boltzmann constant in physics, the constant (symbol k) that relates the kinetic energy (energy of motion) of a gas atom or molecule to temperature. Its value is 1.380662×10^{-23} joules per Kelvin. It is equal to the gas constant R, divided by ◊Avogadro's number.

Boma /ˈbəʊmə/ port in Zaire, on the estuary of the river Zaïre 88 km/55 mi from the Atlantic; population (1976) 93,965. The oldest European settlement in Zaire, it was a centre of the slave trade, and capital of the Belgian Congo until 1927.

bomb container filled with explosive or chemical material and generally used in warfare. There are also ◊incendiary bombs and nuclear bombs and missiles (see ◊nuclear warfare). Any object designed to cause damage by explosion can be called a bomb (car bombs, letter bombs). Initially dropped from aeroplanes (from World War I), bombs were in World War II also launched by rocket (◊V1, V2). The 1960s saw the development of missiles that could be launched from aircraft, land sites, or submarines. In the 1970s laser guidance systems were developed to hit small targets with accuracy.

Aerial bombing started in World War I (1914–18) when the German air force carried out 103 raids on Britain, dropping 269 tonnes of bombs. In World War II (1939–45) nearly twice this tonnage was dropped on London in a single night, and at the peak of the Allied air offensive against Germany, more than ten times this tonnage was regularly dropped in successive nights on one target. Raids in which nearly 1,000 heavy bombers participated were frequent. They were delivered either in 'precision' or 'area' attacks and advances were made in *blind bombing*, in which the target is located solely by instruments and is not visible through a bombsight. In 1939 bombs were commonly about 115 kg/250 lb and 230 kg/500 lb, but by the end of the war the ten-tonner was being produced.

The fission or ◊*atom bomb* was developed in the 1940s and the USA exploded three during World War II: first a test explosion on 16 Jul 1945, at Alamogordo, New Mexico, USA, then on 6 Aug the first to be used in actual warfare was dropped over ◊Hiroshima and three days later another over Nagasaki, Japan.

The fusion or ◊hydrogen bomb was developed in the 1950s, and by the 1960s intercontinental 100-megatonne nuclear warheads could be produced (5,000 times more powerful than those of World War II). The USA and the former USSR between them possess stockpiles sufficient to destroy each other's countries and populations several times over (see also ◊nuclear winter). More recent bombs produce less fallout, a 'dirty' bomb being one that produces large quantities of radioactive debris from a U-238 (uranium isotope) casing.

The danger of nuclear weapons increases with the number of nations possessing them (USA 1945, USSR 1949, UK 1952, France 1960, China 1964), and nuclear-arms verification has been complicated by the ban on above-ground testing. Testing grounds include Lop Nor (China); Mururoa Atoll in the S Pacific (France); Nevada Desert, Amchitka Islands in the Aleutians (USA); Semipalatinsk in central Asia, Novaya Zemlya Islands in the Arctic (Russia).

Under the Outer Space Treaty 1966 nuclear warheads may not be sent into orbit, but this measure has been circumvented by more sophisticated weapons. The Fractional Orbital Bombardment System (FOBS) sends a warhead into a low partial orbit, followed by a rapid descent to Earth. This renders it both less vulnerable to ballistic missile defence systems and cuts the warning time to three minutes.

The rapid development of *laser guidance systems* in the 1970s meant that precise destruction of small but vital targets could be more effectively achieved with standard 450 kg/1,000 lb high-explosive bombs. The laser beam may be directed at the target by the army from the ground, but additional flexibility is gained by coupling ground-directed beams with those of guidance carried in high-performance aircraft accompanying the bombers, for example, the Laser Ranging Marker Target System (LRMTS). These systems' effectiveness was demonstrated during the ◊Gulf War of 1991.

Bombay /ˌbɒmˈbeɪ/ former province of British India; the capital was the city of Bombay. The major part became 1960 the two new states of ◊Gujarat and ◊Maharashtra.

Bombay /ˌbɒmˈbeɪ/ industrial port (textiles, engineering, pharmaceuticals, diamonds), commercial centre, and capital of Maharashtra, W India; population (1981) 8,227,000. It is the centre of the Hindi film industry.
features World Trade Centre 1975, National Centre for the Performing Arts 1969
history Bombay was founded in the 13th century, came under Mogul rule, was occupied by Portugal 1530, and passed to Britain 1662 as part of Catherine of Braganza's dowry. It was the headquarters of the East India Company 1685–1708. The city expanded rapidly with the development of the cotton trade and the railway in the 1860s.

bombay duck small fish *Harpodon nehereus*, also called the bummalow, found in the Indian Ocean. It has a thin body, up to

40 cm/16 in long, and sharp, pointed teeth. It feeds on shellfish and other small fish. It is valuable as a food fish, and is eaten, salted and dried, with dishes such as curry.

Bomberg /ˈbɒmbɜːg/ David 1890–1957. British painter who applied forms inspired by Cubism and Vorticism to traditional subjects in such early works as *The Mud Bath* 1914. Moving away from abstraction in the mid-1920s, his work became more representational and Expressionist.

Bonampak /ˌbɒnəmˈpæk/ site of a classic ◊Mayan city, on the river Usumacinta near the Mexico and Guatemala border, with extensive remains of wall paintings depicting battles, torture, and sacrifices. Rediscovered 1948, the paintings shed new light on Mayan society, which to that date had been considered peaceful.

Bonaparte /ˈbəʊnəpɑːt/ Corsican family of Italian origin that gave rise to the Napoleonic dynasty: see ◊Napoleon I, ◊Napoleon II, and ◊Napoleon III. Others were the brothers and sister of Napoleon I:
Joseph (1768–1844) whom Napoleon made king of Naples 1806 and Spain 1808;
Lucien (1775–1840) whose handling of the Council of Five Hundred on 10 Nov 1799 ensured Napoleon's future;
Louis (1778–1846) the father of Napoleon III, who was made king of Holland 1806–10;
Caroline (1782—1839) who married Joachim ◊Murat 1800;
Jerome (1784–1860) made king of Westphalia 1807.

Bonar Law British Conservative politician; see ◊Law, Andrew Bonar.

bona vacantia (Latin 'empty goods') in law, the property of a person who dies without making a will and without relatives or dependants who would be entitled or might reasonably expect to inherit. In the UK, in such a case the property goes to either the Crown or the duchies of Lancaster and Cornwall.

Bonaventura, St /ˌbɒnəvenˈtʊərə/ (John of Fidanza) 1221–1274. Italian Roman Catholic theologian. He entered the Franciscan order 1243, became professor of theology in Paris, and in 1256 general of his order. In 1273 he was created cardinal and bishop of Albano. Feast day 15 July.

bond in chemistry, the result of the forces of attraction that hold together atoms of an element or elements to form a molecule. The principal types of bonding are ◊ionic, ◊co-valent, ◊metallic, and ◊intermolecular (such as hydrogen bonding).

The type of bond formed depends on the elements concerned and their electronic structure. In an ionic or electrovalent bond, common in inorganic compounds, the combining atoms gain or lose electrons to become ions; for example, sodium (Na) loses an electron to form a sodium ion (Na$^+$) while chlorine (Cl) gains an electron to form a chloride ion (Cl$^-$) in the ionic bond of sodium chloride (NaCl).

In a covalent bond, the atomic orbitals of two atoms overlap to form a molecular orbital containing two electrons, which are thus effectively shared between the two atoms. Covalent bonds are common in organic compounds, such as the four carbon-hydrogen bonds in methane (CH$_4$). In a dative covalent or coordinate bond, one of the combining atoms supplies both of the valence electrons in the bond.

A metallic bond joins metals in a crystal lattice; the atoms occupy lattice positions as positive ions, and valence electrons are shared between all the ions in an 'electron gas'.

In a hydrogen bond, a hydrogen atom joined to an electronegative atom, such as nitrogen or oxygen, becomes partially positively charged, and is weakly attracted to another electronegative atom on a neighbouring molecule.

bond in commerce, a security issued by a government, local authority, company, bank, or other institution on fixed interest. Usually a long-term security, a bond may be irredeemable (with no date of redemption), secured (giving the investor a claim on the company's property or on a part of its assets), or unsecured (not protected by a lien). Property bonds are nonfixed securities with the yield fixed to property investment. See also ◊Eurobond.

Bond /bɒnd/ Alan 1938– . English-born Australian entrepreneur. He was chairman of the Bond Corporation 1969–90 during the years when its aggressive takeover strategy gave the company interests in brewing, the media, mining, and retailing. In 1983 Bond led a syndicate that sponsored the winning yacht in the America's Cup race. The collapse of the Bond empire 1990 left thousands of investors impoverished and shook both Australian and international business confidence.

Bond /bɒnd/ Edward 1935– . English dramatist. His early work aroused controversy because of the savagery of some of his imagery, for example, the brutal stoning of a baby by bored youths in *Saved* 1965. Other works include *Early Morning* 1968, the last play to be banned in the UK by the Lord Chamberlain; *Lear* 1972, a reworking of Shakespeare's play; *Bingo* 1973, an account of Shakespeare's last days; and *The War Plays* 1985.

Bondfield /'bɒndfiːld/ Margaret Grace 1873–1953. British socialist who became a trade-union organizer to improve working conditions for women. She was a Labour member of Parliament 1923–24 and 1926–31, and was the first woman to enter the cabinet–as minister of labour 1929–31.

Bondi /'bɒndi/ Hermann 1919– . Viennese-born British cosmologist. In 1948 he joined with Fred ◊Hoyle and Thomas Gold (1920–) in developing the steady-state theory of cosmology, which suggested that matter is continuously created in the universe.

bondservant another term for a slave or serf used in the Caribbean in the 18th and 19th centuries; a person who was offered a few acres of land in return for some years of compulsory service. The system was a means of obtaining labour from Europe.

bone hard connective tissue comprising the ◊skeleton of most vertebrate animals. It consists of a network of collagen fibres impregnated with inorganic salts, especially calcium phospate. Enclosed within this solid matrix are bone cells, blood vessels, and nerves. In strength, the toughest bone is comparable with reinforced concrete. There are two types of bone: those that develop by replacing ◊cartilage and those that form directly from connective tissue. The latter are usually platelike in shape, and form in the skin of the developing embryo. Humans have about 206 distinct bones in the skeleton. The interior of long bones consists of a spongy matrix filled with a soft marrow that produces blood cells.

Bône /bəʊn/ (or *Bohn*) former name of ◊Annaba, Algerian port.

bone china or *softpaste* semiporcelain made of 5% bone ash added to 95% kaolin; first made in the West in imitation of Chinese porcelain.

bone marrow substance found inside the cavity of bones. In early life it produces red blood cells but later on lipids (fat) accumul-

ate and its colour changes from red to yellow.

Bone marrow may be transplanted using immunosuppressive drugs in the recipient to prevent rejection.

bongo Central African antelope *Boocercus eurycerus*, living in dense humid forests. Up to 1.4 m/4.5 ft at the shoulder, it has spiral-shaped horns which may be 80 cm/2.6 ft or more in length. The body is rich chestnut, with narrow white stripes running vertically down the sides, and a black belly.

Bonham-Carter /'bɒnəm 'kɑːtə/ Violet, Lady Asquith of Yarnbury 1887–1969. British peeress, president of the Liberal party 1945–47.

Bonheur /bɒ'nɜː/ Rosa (Marie Rosalie) 1822–1899. French animal painter. Her realistic animal portraits include *Horse Fair* 1853 (Metropolitan Museum of Art, New York).

She exhibited at the Paris Salon every year from 1841, and received international awards. In 1894 she became the first woman Officer of the Légion d'Honneur.

Bonhoeffer /'bɒnhɜːfə/ Dietrich 1906–1945. German Lutheran theologian and opponent of Nazism. Involved in an anti-Hitler plot, he was executed by the Nazis in Flossenburg concentration camp. His *Letters and Papers from Prison* 1953 became the textbook of modern radical theology, advocating the idea of a 'religionless' Christianity.

Boniface /'bɒnɪfeɪs/ name of nine popes, including:

Boniface VIII Benedict Caetani *c.* 1228–1303. Pope from 1294. He clashed unsuccessfully with Philip IV of France over his taxation of the clergy, and also with Henry III of England.

Boniface, St /'bɒnɪfeɪs/ 680–754. English Benedictine monk, known as the 'Apostle of Germany'; originally named Wynfrith. After a missionary journey to Frisia 716, he was given the task of bringing Christianity to Germany 718 by Pope Gregory II, and was appointed archbishop of Mainz 746. He returned to Frisia 754 and was martyred near Dockum. Feast day 5 June.

Bonin and Volcano islands /'bəʊnɪn/ Japanese islands in the Pacific, N of the Marianas and 1,300 km/800 mi E of the Ryukyu islands. They were under US control 1945–68. The *Bonin Islands* (Japanese *Ogasawara Gunto*) number 27 (in 3 groups), the largest being Chichijima: area 104 sq km/40 sq mi, population (1991) 2,430. The

Volcano Islands (Japanese *Kazan Retto*) number 3, including ◊Iwo Jima, scene of some of the fiercest fighting of World War II; total area 28 sq km/11 sq mi. They have no civilian population, but a 200-strong maritime self-defence force and 100-strong air self-defence force are stationed there.

Bonington /'bɒnɪŋtən/ Chris(tian) 1934– . British mountaineer. He took part in the first ascent of Annapurna II 1960, Nuptse 1961, and the first British ascent of the north face of the Eiger 1962, climbed the central Tower of Paine in Patagonia 1963, and was the leader of an Everest expedition 1975 and again 1985, reaching the summit.

bonito any of various species of medium-sized tuna, predatory fish of the genus *Sarda*, in the mackerel family. The ocean bonito *Katsuwonus pelamis* grows to 1 m/3 ft and is common in tropical seas. The Atlantic bonito *Sarda sarda* is found in the Mediterranean and tropical Atlantic and grows to the same length but has a narrower body.

bon marché (French) cheap.

bon mot (French 'good word') witty remark.

Bonn /bɒn/ industrial city (chemicals, textiles, plastics, aluminium), and seat of government of the Federal Republic of Germany, 18 km/15 mi SSE of Cologne, on the left bank of the Rhine; population (1988) 292,000.

Once a Roman outpost, Bonn was captured by the French 1794, annexed 1801, and was allotted to Prussia 1815. Beethoven was born here. It was capital of West Germany 1949–90.

Bonnard /bɒ'nɑː/ Pierre 1867–1947. French Post-Impressionist painter. With other members of *les* ◊Nabis, he explored the decorative arts (posters, stained glass, furniture). He painted domestic interiors and nudes.

Bonner /'bɒnə/ Yelena 1923– . Soviet human-rights campaigner. Disillusioned by the Soviet invasion of Czechoslovakia 1968, she resigned from the Communist Party after marrying her second husband, Andrei ◊Sakharov 1971, and became active in the dissident movement.

Bonneville Salt Flats /'bɒnəvɪl/ bed of a prehistoric lake in Utah, USA, of which the Great Salt Lake is the surviving remnant. A number of world land speed records have been set here.

Bonnie and Clyde /'bɒni, klaɪd/ Bonnie Parker (1911–1934) and Clyde Barrow (1900–1934). Infamous US criminals who carried out a series of small-scale robberies in Texas, Oklahoma, New Mexico, and Missouri between Aug 1932 and May 1934. They were eventually betrayed and then killed in a police ambush.

Bonnie Prince Charlie Scottish name for ◊Charles Edward Stuart, pretender to the throne.

bonsai (Japanese 'bowl cultivation') art of producing miniature trees by selective pruning. It originated in China many centuries ago and later spread to Japan. Some specimens in the imperial Japanese collection are more than 300 years old.

Bonus Army or *Bonus Expeditionary Force* in US history, a march on Washington DC by unemployed ex-servicemen during the great ◊Depression to lobby Congress for immediate cash payment of a promised war veterans' bonus.

booby tropical seabird of the genus *Sula*, in the same family, Sulidae, as the northern ◊gannet. There are six species, including the circumtropical brown booby *Sula leucogaster*. They inhabit coastal waters, and dive to catch fish. The name was given by sailors who saw the bird's tameness as stupidity.

Booby Abbott's booby. It is thought that boobies were given their common name because of their unfortunate habit of allowing sailors to approach and kill them for food.

One species, *Abbott's booby*, breeds only on Christmas Island, in the western Indian Ocean. Unlike most boobies and gannets it nests high up in trees. Large parts of its breeding ground have been destroyed by phosphate mining, but conservation measures now protect the site.

boogie-woogie jazz played on the piano, using a repeated motif for the left hand. It was common in the USA from around 1900 to the 1950s. Boogie-woogie players included Pinetop Smith (1904–1929), Meade 'Lux' Lewis (1905–1964), and Jimmy Yancey (1898–1951). Rock-and-roll pianists like Jerry Lee Lewis adapted the style.

book portable written record. Substances used to make early books included leaves, bark, linen, silk, clay, leather, and papyrus. In about AD 100–150, the codex or paged book, as opposed to the roll or scroll, began to be adopted. Vellum was generally used for book pages by the beginning of the 4th century, and its use lasted until the 15th, when it was superseded by paper. Books only became widely available after the invention of the ◊printing press in the 15th century. Printed text is also reproduced and stored in ◊microform.

bookbinding securing of the pages of a book between protective covers by sewing and/or gluing. Cloth binding was first introduced 1822, but from the mid-20th century synthetic bindings were increasingly employed, and most hardback books are bound by machine.

Booker Prize /ˈbʊkə/ British literary prize of £20,000 awarded annually (from 1969) by the Booker company (formerly Booker McConnell) to a novel published in the UK during the previous year.

book-keeping process of recording commercial transactions in a systematic and established procedure. These records provide the basis for the preparation of accounts.

Booker Prize for fiction

1985	Keri Hulme *The Bone People*
1986	Kingsley Amis *The Old Devils*
1987	Penelope Lively *Moon Tiger*
1988	Peter Carey *Oscar and Lucinda*
1989	Kazuo Ishiguro *The Remains of the Day*
1990	A S Byatt *Possession*
1991	Ben Okri *The Femished Road*
1992	Barry Unsworth *Sacred Hunger* and Michael Ondaatje *The English Patient*
1993	Roddy Doyle *Paddy Clarke Ha Ha Ha*
1994	James Kelman *How Late It Was, How Late*

The earliest-known work on double-entry book-keeping, a system in which each item of a business transaction is entered twice—as debit and as credit—was by Luca Pacioli, published in Venice 1494. The method he advocated had, however, been practised by Italian merchants for several hundred years before that date. The first English work on the subject, by the schoolmaster Hugh Oldcastle, appeared 1543.

booklouse any of numerous species of tiny wingless insects of the order Psocoptera, especially *Atropus pulsatoria* that lives in books and papers, feeding on starches and moulds.

Most of the other species live in bark, leaves, and lichens. They thrive in dark, damp conditions.

Book of Hours see ◊Hours, Book of.

Book of the Dead ancient Egyptian book, known as the *Book of Coming Forth by Day*, buried with the dead as a guide to reaching the kingdom of Osiris, the god of the underworld. Similar practices were observed by Orphic communities (6th to 1st century BC) in S Italy and Crete, who deposited gold laminae, inscribed with directions about the next world, in the graves of their dead. In medieval times, Christians could obtain advice about dying from a book entitled *Ars Morendi/The Art of Dying*.

Boole /buːl/ George 1815–1864. English mathematician, whose work *The Mathematical Analysis of Logic* 1847 established the basis of modern mathematical logic, and whose ***Boolean algebra*** can be used in designing computers.

boomerang hand-thrown, flat wooden hunting missile shaped in a curved angle, formerly used throughout the world but developed by the Australian Aborigines to a great degree of diversity and elaboration. It is used to kill game and as a weapon or, in the case of the returning boomerang, as recreation.

boomslang rear-fanged venomous African snake *Dispholidus typus*, often green but sometimes brown or blackish, and growing to a length of 2 m/6 ft. It lives in trees, and feeds on tree-dwelling lizards such as chameleons. Its venom can be fatal to humans; however, boomslangs rarely attack people.

Boone /buːn/ Daniel 1734–1820. US pioneer who explored the Wilderness Road (East Virginia–Kentucky) 1775 and paved the way for the first westward migration of settlers.

Boorman /'bɔːmən/ John 1933– . English director who, after working in television, directed successful films both in Hollywood (*Point Blank* 1967, *Deliverance* 1972) and in Britain (*Excalibur* 1981, *Hope and Glory* 1987). He is the author of a telling book on film finance, *Money into Light* 1985.

booster first-stage rocket of a space-launching vehicle, or an additional rocket strapped to the main rocket to assist takeoff.

The US Delta rocket, for example, has a cluster of nine strap-on boosters that fire on lift off. Europe's Ariane 3 rocket uses twin strap-on boosters, as does the US space shuttle.

Boot /buːt/ Jesse 1850–1931. British entrepreneur and founder of the Boots pharmacy chain. In 1863 Boot took over his father's small Nottingham shop trading in medicinal herbs. Recognizing that the future lay with patent medicines, he concentrated on selling cheaply, advertising widely, and offering a wide range of medicines. In 1892, Boot also began to manufacture drugs. He had 126 shops by 1900 and more than 1,000 by his death.

boot or **bootstrap** in computing, the process of starting up the computer. Most computers have a small, built-in program whose only job is to load a slightly larger program, usually from a disc, which in turn loads the main ◊operating system.

Booth /buːð/ Charles 1840–1916. British sociologist, author of the study *Life and Labour of the People in London* 1891–1903, and pioneer of an ◊old-age pension scheme.

Booth /buːθ/ John Wilkes 1839–1865. US actor and fanatical Confederate sympathizer who assassinated President Abraham ◊Lincoln 14 April 1865; he escaped with a broken leg and was later shot in a barn in Virginia when he refused to surrender.

Booth /buːð/ William 1829–1912. British founder of the ◊Salvation Army 1878, and its first 'general'.

Born in Nottingham, the son of a builder, he experienced religious conversion at the age of 15. In 1865 he founded the Christian Mission in Whitechapel, E London, which became the Salvation Army 1878. *In Darkest England, and the Way Out* 1890 contained proposals for the physical and spiritual redemption of the many down-and-outs. His wife Catherine (1829–1890, born Mumford), whom he married 1855, became a public preacher about 1860, initiating the ministry of women. Their eldest son, *William Bramwell Booth* (1856–1929), became chief of staff of the Salvation Army 880 and was general from 1912 until his deposition 1929. *Evangeline Booth* (1865–1950), 7th child of General William Booth, was a prominent Salvation Army officer, and 1934–39 was general. She became a US citizen. *Catherine Bramwell Booth* (1884–1987), a granddaughter of William Booth, was a commissioner in the Salvation Army.

Boothby /'buːðbi/ Robert John Graham, Baron Boothby 1900–1986. Scottish politician. He became a Unionist member of Parliament 1924 and was parliamentary private secretary to Churchill 1926–29. He advocated Britain's entry into the European Community, and was a powerful speaker.

bootlegging illegal manufacture, distribution, or sale of a product. The term originated in the USA, when the sale of alcohol to American Indians was illegal and bottles were hidden for sale in the legs of the jackboots of unscrupulous traders. The term was later used for all illegal liquor sales during the period of ◊Prohibition in the USA 1920–33, and is often applied to unauthorized commercial tape recordings and the copying of computer software.

Bophuthatswana /bəʊˌpuːˈtætˈswɑːnə/ Republic of; self-governing black 'homeland' within South Africa
area 40,330 sq km/15,571 sq mi
capital Mmbatho or Sun City, a casino resort frequented by many white South Africans
features divided into six 'blocks'
exports platinum, chromium, vanadium, asbestos, manganese
currency South African rand
population (1985) 1,627,000
language Setswana, English
religion Christian
government executive president elected by the Assembly: Chief Lucas Mangope
recent history first 'independent' Black National State from 1977, but not recognized by any country other than South Africa.

Bora-Bora /ˌbɔːrəˈbɔːrə/ one of the 14 Society Islands of French Polynesia; situated 225 km/140 mi NW of Tahiti; area 39 sq km/15 sq mi. Exports include mother-of-pearl, fruit, and tobacco.

borage salad plant *Borago officinalis* native to S Europe and used in salads and medicinally. It has small blue flowers and hairy

Borage Borage is an annual plant, growing between 90 cm/3 ft and 120 cm/4 ft high.

leaves. It is cultivated in Britain and occasionally naturalized.

Borah /bɛːə/ William Edgar 1865–1940. US Republican politician. Born in Illinois, he was a senator for Idaho from 1906. An arch isolationist, he was chiefly responsible for the USA's repudiation of the League of Nations following World War I. .

borax hydrous sodium borate, $Na_2B_4O_7.10H_2O$, found as soft, whitish crystals or encrustations on the shores of hot springs and in the dry beds of salt lakes in arid regions, where it occurs with other borates, halite, and ◊gypsum. It is used in bleaches and washing powders.

A large industrial source is Borax Lake, California. Borax is also used in glazing pottery, in soldering, as a mild antiseptic, and as a metallurgical flux.

Bordeaux /bɔːˈdəʊ/ port on the Garonne, capital of Aquitaine, SW France, a centre for the wine trade, oil refining, and aeronautics and space industries; population (1982) 640,000. Bordeaux was under the English crown for three centuries until 1453. In 1870, 1914, and 1940 the French government was moved here because of German invasion.

Border /ˈbɔːdə/ Allan 1955– . Australian cricketer, captain of the Australian team from 1985. He has played for Australia (New South Wales and Queensland) since 1978, and in England for Gloucestershire and Essex. He now holds the world record for appearances in test matches (125) and one-day internationals (223).

Borders /ˈbɔːdəz/ region of Scotland
area 4,700 sq km/1,815 sq mi
towns Newtown St Boswells (administrative headquarters), Hawick, Jedburgh
features river Tweed; Lammermuir, Moorfoot, and Pentland hills; home of the novelist Walter Scott at Abbotsford; Dryburgh Abbey, burial place of Field Marshal Haig and Scott; ruins of 12th-century Melrose Abbey
products knitted goods, tweed, electronics, timber
population (1987) 102,000
famous people Duns Scotus, James Murray, Mungo Park.

Bordet /bɔːˈdeɪ/ Jules 1870–1961. Belgian bacteriologist and immunologist who researched the role of blood serum in the human immune response. He was the first to isolate 1906 the whooping cough bacillus.

bore surge of tidal water up an estuary or a river, caused by the funnelling of the rising tide by a narrowing river mouth. A very high tide, possibly fanned by wind, may build up when it is held back by a river current in the river mouth. The result is a broken wave, a metre or a few feet high, that rushes upstream.

Famous bores are found in the rivers Severn (England), Seine (France), Hooghly (India), and Chiang Jiang (China), where bores of over 4 m/13 ft have been reported.

Boreas in Greek mythology, the north wind which carried off Oreithyia, daughter of a legendary king of Athens. Their children were Calais and Zetes, two of the ◊Argonauts, who freed Phineus (a blind soothsayer, destined to be the future king of Salmydessus in Thrace) from the ◊Harpies.

Borelli /bəˈreli/ Giovanni Alfonso 1608–1679. Italian scientist who explored the links between physics and medicine and showed how mechanical principles could be applied to animal ◊physiology. This approach, known as iatrophysics, has proved basic to understanding how the mammalian body works.

Borg /bɔːg/ Bjorn 1956– . Swedish lawn-tennis player who won the men's singles title at Wimbledon five times 1976–80, a record since the abolition of the challenge system 1922. He also won six French Open singles titles 1974–75 and 1978–81 inclusive. In 1990

Borg announced tentative plans to return to professional tennis.

Borges /'bɔːxes/ Jorge Luis 1899–1986. Argentine poet and short-story writer, an exponent of ◊magic realism. In 1961 he became director of the National Library, Buenos Aires, and was professor of English literature at the university there. He is known for his fantastic and paradoxical work *Ficciones/Fictions* 1944.

Borges explored metaphysical themes in early works such as *Ficciones* and *El Aleph/The Aleph, and other Stories* 1949. In a later collection of tales *El informe de Brodie/Dr Brodie's Report* 1972, he adopted a more realistic style, reminiscent of the work of the young Rudyard ◊Kipling, of whom he was a great admirer. *El libro de arena/The Book of Sand* 1975 marked a return to more fantastic themes.

Borgia /'bɔːdʒə/ Cesare 1476–1507. Italian general, illegitimate son of Pope ◊Alexander VI. Made a cardinal at 17 by his father, he resigned to become captain-general of the papacy, campaigning successfully against the city republics of Italy. Ruthless and treacherous in war, he was an able ruler (the model for Machiavelli's *The Prince*), but his power crumbled on the death of his father. He was a patron of artists, including Leonardo da Vinci.

Borgia /'bɔːdʒə/ Lucrezia 1480–1519. Duchess of Ferrara from 1501. She was the illegitimate daughter of Pope ◊Alexander VI and sister of Cesare Borgia. She was married at 12 and again at 13 to further her father's ambitions, both marriages being annulled by him. At 18 she was married again, but her husband was murdered 1500 on the order of her brother, with whom (as well as with her father) she was said to have committed incest. Her final marriage was to the duke of Este, the son and heir of the duke of Ferrara. She made the court a centre of culture and was a patron of authors and artists such as Ariosto and Titian.

Borglum /'bɔːgləm/ Gutzon 1871–1941. US sculptor. He created a six-ton marble head of Lincoln in Washington, DC, and the series of giant heads of presidents Washington, Jefferson, Lincoln, and Theodore Roosevelt carved on Mount Rushmore, South Dakota (begun 1930).

boric acid or *boracic acid* H_3BO_3, acid formed by the combination of hydrogen and oxygen with nonmetallic boron. It is a weak

antiseptic and is used in the manufacture of glass and enamels. It is also an efficient insecticide against ants and cockroaches.

Boris III /'bɒrɪs/ 1894–1943. Tsar of Bulgaria from 1918, when he succeeded his father, Ferdinand I. From 1934 he was virtual dictator until his sudden and mysterious death following a visit to Hitler. His son Simeon II was tsar until deposed 1946.

Borlaug /'bɔːlɔːg/ Norman Ernest 1914– . US microbiologist and agronomist. He developed high-yielding varieties of wheat and other grain crops to be grown in Third World countries, and was the first to use the term 'Green Revolution'. Nobel Prize for Peace 1970.

Bormann /'bɔːmæn/ Martin 1900–1945. German Nazi leader. He took part in the abortive Munich ◊putsch (uprising) 1923 and rose to high positions in the Nazi (National Socialist) Party, becoming party chancellor May 1941. He was believed to have escaped the fall of Berlin May 1945 and was tried in his absence and sentenced to death at the ◊Nuremberg trials 1945–46, but a skeleton uncovered by a mechanical excavator in Berlin 1972 was officially recognized as his by forensic experts 1973.

Born /bɔːn/ Max 1882–1970. German physicist who received a Nobel prize 1954 for fundamental work on the ◊quantum theory. He left Germany for the UK during the Nazi era.

Borneo /'bɔːniəʊ/ third largest island in the world, one of the Sunda Islands in the W Pacific; area 754,000 sq km/290,000 sq mi. It comprises the Malaysian territories of ◊*Sabah* and ◊*Sarawak*; ◊*Brunei*; and, occupying by far the largest part, the Indonesian territory of ◊*Kalimantan*. It is mountainous and densely forested. In coastal areas the people of Borneo are mainly of Malaysian origin, with a few Chinese, and the interior is inhabited by the indigenous Dyaks. It was formerly under both Dutch and British colonial influence until Sarawak was formed 1841.

Bornholm /'bɔːnˈhəʊm/ Danish island in the Baltic Sea, 35 km/22 mi SE of the nearest point of the Swedish coast. It constitutes a county of the same name.
area 587 sq km/227 sq mi
capital Rönne
population (1985) 47,164.

Bornu /'bɔːnuː/ kingdom of the 9th–19th centuries to the W and S of Lake Chad, W central Africa. Converted to Islam in the 11th century, it reached its greatest strength in the 15th–18th centuries. From 1901 it was absorbed in the British, French, and German colonies in this area, which became the states of Niger, Cameroon, and Nigeria. The largest section of ancient Bornu is now the *state of Bornu* in Nigeria.

Borodin /ˈbɒrədɪn/ Alexander Porfir'yevich 1833–1887. Russian composer. Born in St Petersburg, the illegitimate son of a Russian prince, he became by profession an expert in medical chemistry, but in his spare time devoted himself to music. His principal work is the opera *Prince Igor*, left unfinished; it was completed by Rimsky-Korsakov and Glazunov and includes the Polovtsian Dances.

Borodino /ˌbɒrəˈdiːnəʊ/ battle 7 Sept 1812 where French troops under Napoleon defeated the Russians under Kutusov. Named after the village of Borodino, 110 km/70 mi NW of Moscow.

boron nonmetallic element, symbol B, atomic number 5, relative atomic mass 10.811. In nature it is found only in compounds, as with sodium and oxygen in borax. It exists in two allotropic forms (see ◊allotropy): brown amorphous powder and very hard, brilliant crystals. Its compounds are used in the preparation of boric acid, water softeners, soaps, enamels, glass, and pottery glazes. In alloys it is used to harden steel. Because it absorbs slow neutrons, it is used to make boron carbide control rods for nuclear reactors. It is a necessary trace element in the human diet. The element was named by Humphry Davy, who isolated it 1808.

borough unit of local government in the UK from the 8th century until 1974, when it continued as an honorary status granted by royal charter to a district council, entitling its leader to the title of mayor.

Borromeo, St /ˌbɒrəʊˈmeɪəʊ/ Carlo 1538–1584. Italian Roman Catholic saint and cardinal. He was instrumental in bringing the Council of Trent (1562–3) to a successful conclusion, and in drawing up the catechism that contained its findings. Feast day 4 Nov.

Borromini /ˌbɒrəʊˈmiːni/ Francesco 1599–1667. Italian Baroque architect, one of the two most important (with ◊Bernini) in 17th-century Rome. Whereas Bernini designed in a florid, expansive style, his pupil Borromini developed a highly idiosyncratic and austere use of the classical language of architecture. The churches of San Carlo alle Quattro Fontane and San Ivo in Rome demonstrate his revolutionary disregard for convention.

borstal in the UK, formerly a place of detention for offenders aged 15–21. The name was taken from Borstal prison near Rochester, Kent, where the system was first introduced 1908. From 1983 borstal institutions were officially known as youth custody centres, and have now been replaced by *young offender institutions*.

borzoi (Russian 'swift') large breed of dog originating in Russia, 75 cm/2.5 ft or more at the shoulder. It is of the greyhound type, white with darker markings, with a thick, silky coat.

Bosch /bɒʃ/ Carl 1874–1940. German metallurgist and chemist. He developed Fritz Haber's small-scale technique for the production of ammonia into an industrial high-pressure process that made use of water gas as a source of hydrogen; see ◊Haber process. He shared the Nobel Prize for Chemistry 1931 with Friedrich Bergius.

Bosch /bɒʃ/ Hieronymus (Jerome) 1460–1516. Early Netherlandish painter. His fantastic visions of weird and hellish creatures, as shown in *The Garden of Earthly Delights* about 1505–10 (Prado, Madrid), show astonishing imagination and a complex imagery. His religious subjects focused not on the holy figures but on the mass of ordinary witnesses, placing the religious event in a contemporary Netherlandish context and creating cruel caricatures of human sinfulness.

His work foreshadowed Surrealism and was probably inspired by a local religious brotherhood. However, he was an orthodox Catholic and a prosperous painter, not a heretic, as was once believed.

Bosch /bɒʃ/ Juan 1909– . President of the Dominican Republic 1963. His left-wing Partido Revolucionario Dominicano won a landslide victory in the 1962 elections. In office, he attempted agrarian reform and labour legislation. He was opposed by the USA, and overthrown by the army. His achievement was to establish a democratic political party after three decades of dictatorship.

Bose /bəʊs/ Jagadis Chunder 1858–1937. Indian physicist and plant physiologist. Born near Dakha, he was professor of physical science at Calcutta 1885–1915, and studied the growth and minute movements of plants, and their reaction to electrical stimuli. He founded the Bose Research Institute, Calcutta.

Bose /bəʊs/ Satyendra Nath 1894–1974. Indian physicist who formulated the Bose–Einstein law of quantum mechanics with ◊Einstein. He was professor of physics at the University of Calcutta 1945–58.

Bosnia-Herzegovina /ˈbɒzniə ˌhɜːtsɪɡəˈviːnə/ (Serbo-Croat *Bosna-Hercegovina*) country in central Europe, bounded N and W by Croatia, E by the Yugoslavian republic of Serbia, and E and S by the Yugoslavian republic of Montenegro.

government There is a 240-seat bicameral assembly and a directly elected seven-member state presidency. Election contests are by a majority system, there being a second-round runoff race if no candidate secures a majority of the vote in the first round.

history Once the Roman province of ◊Illyria, the area enjoyed brief periods of independence in medieval times, then was ruled by the Ottoman Empire 1463–1878 and Austria 1878–1918, when it was incorporated in the future Yugoslavia. It came under Nazi German rule 1941, and Marshal ◊Tito established his provisional government at liberated Jajce in Nov 1943. Bosnia-Herzegovina, kept undivided because of its ethnic and religious compound of Serbs (Orthodox Christians), Croats (Catholic Christians) and Serbo-Croatian-speaking Slavs (Muslims), became a republic within the Yugoslav Socialist Federal Republic in Nov 1945, after the expulsion of remaining German forces.

communist rule The republic's communist leadership became notorious for its corruption, racketeering, and authoritarianism, and from 1980 there was an upsurge in Islamic nationalism. Ethnic violence between Muslims and Serbs worsened 1989–90. In the Nov–Dec 1990 elections nationalist parties routed the ruling communists; subsequent divisions within the Bosnian ruling coalition, formed by the three leading Serb, Muslim, and Croatian parties, complicated the republic's dealings with Serbia.

civil unrest From the spring of 1991 the conflict between Serbia and Croatia and civil war in the latter spread disorder into Bosnia-Herzegovina, with Croats setting up barricades in an attempt to stop the predominantly Serb Yugoslav National Army (JNA) moving through into Croatia. In Aug 1991, the republic's president, Alija Izetbegović, a devout Muslim, expressed concern that Serbia intended to divide up Bosnia-Herzegovina between Serbia and Croatia, with a reduced Muslim buffer state in between, and appealed for support from Turkey and the European Community (EC). From Sept 1991 border areas began to fall into Serbian hands and Serbs began to form autonomous enclaves within the republic.

independence achieved In Oct 1991 the republic's 'sovereignty' was declared by its parliament, but was rejected by Serbs, who established an alternative assembly and held a referendum Nov 1991 on remaining in the rump Yugoslav federation. Muslims and Croats, in alliance in the republic's parliament, voted Jan 1992 to seek recognition of independence by the EC. A subsequent referendum Feb 1992, requested by the EC, voted overwhelmingly in favour of independence. The referendum was boycotted by Bosnian Serbs who fiercely opposed independence. Violent ethnic clashes ensued, with bombings in several Bosnian cities. Despite the worsening situation, the EC and the USA gave their official recognition of the country's independence in April. In May 1992 Bosnia-Herzegovina became a full member of the United Nations, and the UN called for the withdrawal of the JNA. Both UN and EC mediators vainly sought a solution to the conflict.

continued fighting Serb militia units, allegedly backed by Serbia, took control of border towns in E Bosnia and also launched attacks on the capital, Sarajevo. As Croats and Muslims also struggled to gain disputed territory, a state of emergency was declared. A number of cease-fires were quickly broken. By the end of May hundreds had been killed and hundreds of thousands were homeless. Bosnian Serbs established control over an area stretching from NW to the SE, comprising almost two-thirds of the country, and declared it independent. Croats dominated large portions of the western part of the country, and subsequently declared an independent Croatian state.

UN relief efforts placed in jeopardy From June 1992 Canadian/French UN forces were drafted into Sarajevo in an attempt to relieve a three-month Serbian siege of the capital.

In July Canadian forces handed over to a force of French, Egyptians, and Ukrainians. Continued Serbian offensives put the relief effort at risk, causing it to be temporarily abandoned Sept after relief workers were killed and a UN plane shot down. In Aug 1992 UN/EC-sponsored peace talks between all parties took place in London. Despite the reaching of an accord, the conflict continued to escalate.

war crimes reported From mid-1992 there was increased evidence of atrocities being perpetrated, particularly by Serbs, to enforce what was described as 'ethnic cleansing', and reports of 'death camps' and group slaughter of internees. In Sept 1992 the UN accepted French, Canadian, and UK offers of troops and in Oct the UN Security Council voted to create a war crimes commission and imposed a ban on all military flights over Bosnia-Herzegovina. In the same month, the first British troops were deployed in Bosnia-Herzegovina.

peace plan In January 1993 the UN–EC negotiated Vance–Owen peace plan, proposing a federal ethnic-based Bosnia-Herzegovina divided into 10 substantially autonomous, ethnically controlled provinces, was accepted in principle by Croats and Serbs, but Muslim politicians expressed strong reservations. Fighting continued, with Sarajevo subject to regular bombardment by Serbian forces. In March 1993 the USA commenced airdrops of food and medical supplies to war-ravaged eastern Bosnia and at the end of March a cease-fire was planned to take effect. By this date an estimated 1.8 million Bosnians, 40% of the population, had been made refugees. Since May 1992 at least 130,000 had been killed in the interethnic conflict.

A UN–EC peace plan wa rejected Jan 1993. The USA began airdrops of food and medical supplies; six UN 'safe areas' were created, intended as havens for Muslim civilians; a Bosnian Croat-Serb partition plan was rejected by the Muslims.

In Feb 1994 the Bosnian Serb siege of Sarajevo was lifted after a UN–NATO ultimatum, and Russian intervention accelerated Serb withdrawal. A Bosnian Croat–Muslim federation was formed after a cease-fire in the north. In April NATO bombed Bosnian Serb control positions around Gorazde in defence of a UN-declared 'safe area'. Bosnian Serbs later withdrew in response to a UN ultimatum. In August Serbia imposed a blockade against Bosnian Serbs. Hostilities renewed around Sarajevo and the 'safe area' of Bihac. In Nov the USA unilaterally lifted the arms embargo against Bosnian Muslims.

Bosnian Crisis period of international tension 1908 when Austria attempted to capitalize on Turkish weakness after the ◊Young Turk revolt by annexing the provinces of Bosnia and Herzegovina. Austria obtained Russian approval in exchange for conceding Russian access to the Bosporus straits (see ◊straits question).

The speed of Austrian action took Russia by surprise, and domestic opposition led to the resignation of Russian foreign minister Izvolsky. Russia also failed to obtain necessary French and British agreements on the straits.

boson in physics, an elementary particle whose spin can only take values that are whole numbers or zero. Bosons may be classified as ◊gauge bosons (carriers of the four fundamental forces) or ◊mesons. All elementary particles are either bosons or ◊fermions.

Bosporus /ˈbɒspərəs/ (Turkish *Karadeniz Boğaazi*) strait 27 km/17 mi long joining the Black Sea with the Sea of Marmara and forming part of the water division between Europe and Asia; its name may be derived from the Greek legend of ◊Io. Istanbul stands on its W side. The *Bosporus Bridge* 1973, 1,621 m/5,320 ft, links Istanbul and Turkey-in-Asia. In 1988 a second bridge across the straits was opened, linking Asia and Europe.

Bossuet /ˌbɒsjuˈeɪ/ Jacques Bénigne 1627–1704. French Roman Catholic priest and theologian. Appointed to the Chapel Royal,

Paris 1662, he became known for his funeral orations.

Boston /ˈbɒstən/ seaport in Lincolnshire, England, on the river Witham; population (1981) 26,500. St Botolph's is England's largest parish church, and its tower 'Boston stump' is a landmark for sailors.

Boston /ˈbɒstən/ industrial and commercial centre, capital of Massachusetts, USA; population (1980) 563,000; metropolitan area 2,800,000. It is a publishing centre, and the site of Harvard University. A centre of opposition to British trade restrictions, it was the scene of the Boston Tea Party.

Boston Tea Party protest 1773 against the British tea tax imposed by colonists in Massachusetts, America, before the ◊American Revolution.

When a valuable consignment of tea (belonging to the East India Company and intended for sale in the American colonies) arrived in Boston Harbour aboard three ships from England, it was thrown overboard by a group of Bostonians disguised as Indians during the night of 16 Dec 1773. The British government, angered by this and other colonial protests against British policy, took retaliatory measures 1774, including the closing of the port of Boston.

Boswell /ˈbɒzwəl/ James 1740–1795. Scottish biographer and diarist. He was a member of Samuel ◊Johnson's London Literary Club and the two men travelled to Scotland together 1773, as recorded in Boswell's *Journal of the Tour to the Hebrides* 1785. His classic English biography, *Life of Samuel Johnson*, was published 1791. His long-lost personal papers were acquired for publication by Yale University 1949, and the *Journals* are of exceptional interest.

Establishing a place in his intimate circle, he became a member of the Literary Club 1773, and in the same year accompanied Johnson on the journey later recorded in the *Journal of the Tour to the Hebrides* 1785. On his succession to his father's estate 1782, he made further attempts to enter Parliament, was called to the English Bar 1786, and was recorder of Carlisle 1788–90. In 1789 he settled in London, and in 1791 produced the classic English biography, the *Life of Samuel Johnson*.

Bosworth, Battle of /ˈbɒzwəθ/ last battle of the Wars of the ◊Roses, fought on 22 Aug 1485. Richard III, the Yorkist king, was defeated and slain by Henry of Richmond, who became Henry VII. The battlefield is near the village of Market Bosworth, 19 km/12 mi W of Leicester, England.

BOT abbreviation for ◊Board of Trade.

botanic garden place where a wide range of plants is grown, providing the opportunity to see a botanical diversity not likely to be encountered naturally. Among the earliest forms of botanic garden was the *physic garden*, devoted to the study and growth of medicinal plants; an example is the Chelsea Physic Garden in London, established 1673 and still in existence. Following increased botanical exploration, botanic gardens were used to test the commercial potential of new plants being sent back from all parts of the world.

Today a botanic garden serves many purposes: education, science, and conservation. Many are associated with universities and also maintain large collections of preserved specimens (see ◊herbarium), libraries, research laboratories, and gene banks.

botany the study of plants. It is subdivided into a number of specialized studies, such as the identification and classification of plants (taxonomy), their external formation (plant morphology), their internal arrangement (plant anatomy), their microscopic examination (plant histology), their functioning and life history (plant physiology), and their distribution over the Earth's surface in relation to their surroundings (plant ecology). Palaeobotany concerns the study of fossil plants, while economic botany deals with the utility of plants. Horticulture, agriculture, and forestry are branches of botany.

history The most ancient botanical record is carved on the walls of the temple at Karnak, Egypt, about 1500 BC. The Greeks in the 5th and 4th centuries BC used many plants for medicinal purposes, the first Greek *Herbal* being drawn up about 350 BC by Diocles of Carystus. Botanical information was collected into the works of Theophrastus of Eresus (380–287 BC), a pupil of Aristotle, who founded technical plant nomenclature. Cesalpino in the 16th century sketched out a system of classification based on flowers, fruits, and seeds, while Jung (1587–1658) used flowers only as his criterion. John Ray (1627–1705) arranged plants systematically, based on his findings on fruit, leaf, and flower, and described about 18,600 plants.

The Swedish botanist Carl von Linné, or ◊Linnaeus, who founded systematics in the 18th century, included in his classification all known plants and animals, giving each a ◊binomial descriptive label. His work greatly aided the future study of plants, as botanists found that all plants could be fitted into a systematic classification based on Linnaeus' work. Linnaeus was also the first to recognize the sexual nature of flowers. This was followed up by Charles ◊Darwin and others.

Later work revealed the detailed cellular structure of plant tissues and the exact nature of ◊photosynthesis. Julius von Sachs (1832–1897) defined the function of ◊chlorophyll and the significance of plant ◊stomata. In the second half of the 20th century, much has been learned about cell function, repair, and growth by the hybridization of plant cells (the combination of the nucleus of one cell with the cytoplasm of another).

Botany Bay /ˈbɒtənɪ/ inlet on the E coast of Australia, 8 km/5 mi S of Sydney, New South Wales. Chosen 1787 as the site for a penal colony, it proved unsuitable. Sydney now stands on the site of the former settlement. The name Botany Bay continued to be popularly used for any convict settlement in Australia.

botfly any fly of the family Oestridae. The larvae are parasites that feed on the skin (warblefly on cattle) or in the nasal cavity (nostrilflies on sheep and deer). The horse botfly belongs to another family, the Gasterophilidae. It has a parasitic larva that feeds in the horse's stomach.

Botha /ˈbəʊtə/ Louis 1862–1919. South African soldier and politician, a commander in the Second South African War. In 1907 Botha became premier of the Transvaal and in 1910 of the first Union South African government. On the outbreak of World War I 1914 he rallied South Africa to the Commonwealth, suppressed a Boer revolt, and conquered German South West Africa.

Botha was born in Natal. Elected a member of the Volksraad 1897, he supported the more moderate Joubert against Kruger. On the outbreak of the Second South African War he commanded the Boers besieging Ladysmith, and in 1900 succeeded Joubert in command of the Transvaal forces. When the Union of South Africa was formed 1910, Botha became prime minister, and at the Versailles peace conference 1919 he represented South Africa.

Botha /ˈbəʊtə/ P(ieter) W(illem) 1916– . South African politician, prime minister from 1978. Botha initiated a modification of ◊apartheid, which later slowed in the face of

Afrikaner (Boer) opposition. In 1984 he became the first executive state president. In 1989 he unwillingly resigned both party leadership and presidency after suffering a stroke, and was succeeded by F W de Klerk.

Botham /ˈbəʊθəm/ Ian (Terrence) 1955– . English cricketer whose test record places him among the world's greatest all-rounders. He has played county cricket for Somerset and Worcestershire as well as playing in Australia. He played for England 1977–89 and returned to the England side 1991.

Botham made his Somerset debut 1974 and first played for England against Australia at Trent Bridge 1977; he took five wickets for 74 runs in Australia's first innings. In 1987 he moved from Somerset to Worcestershire and helped them to win the Refuge Assurance League in his first season.

Botham also played Football League soccer for Scunthorpe United 1979–84. He raised money for leukaemia research with much-publicized walks from John o'Groats to Land's End in the UK, and Hannibal-style across the Alps.

Bothe /ˈbəʊtə/ Walther 1891–1957. German physicist who showed 1929 that the cosmic rays bombarding the Earth are composed not of photons but of more massive particles. Nobel Prize for Physics 1954.

Bothwell /ˈbɒθwəl/ James Hepburn, 4th Earl of Bothwell c. 1536–1578. Scottish nobleman, third husband of ◊Mary Queen of Scots, 1567–70, alleged to have arranged the explosion that killed Darnley, her previous husband, 1567.

Tried and acquitted a few weeks after the assassination, he abducted Mary, and (having divorced his wife) married her 15 May. A revolt ensued, and Bothwell was forced to flee to Norway and on to Sweden. In 1570 Mary obtained a divorce on the ground that she had been ravished by Bothwell before marriage. Later, Bothwell was confined in a castle in Zeeland, the Netherlands, where he died insane.

Botswana /bɒtˈswɑːnə/ landlocked country in central southern Africa, bounded S and SE by South Africa, W and N by Namibia, and NE by Zimbabwe.

government The 1966 constitution blends the British system of parliamentary accountability with representation for each of Botswana's major ethnic groups. It provides for a national assembly of 40 members—34 elected by universal suffrage, four by the assembly itself, plus the speaker and the

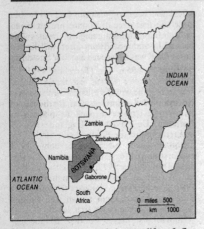

In 1963 High Commission rule ended, and in the legislative assembly elections the newly formed Bechuanaland Democratic Party (BDP) won a majority. Its leader, Seretse ◊Khama, had been deposed as chief of the Bamangwato tribe 1950 and had since lived in exile.

achieved independence In 1966 the country, renamed Botswana, became an independent state within the ◊Commonwealth with Sir Seretse Khama, as he had now become, as president. He continued to be re-elected until his death 1980 when he was succeeded by the vice president, Dr Quett Masire, who was re-elected 1984. In the Oct 1989 elections the BDP won 31 of the 34 national assembly seats and Quett Masire was again re-elected.

Since independence Botswana has earned a reputation for stability. It is a member of the ◊nonaligned movement. South Africa accused it of providing bases for the African National Congress (ANC) and Botswana was the target of several cross-border raids by South African forces. The presence of ANC bases was always denied by both Botswana and the ANC. Tension in this respect was dissipated by the legalization of the ANC by South Africa 1990. Normal relations with South Africa were restored 1994.

Botticelli /ˌbɒtˈtʃeli/ Sandro 1445–1510. Florentine painter of religious and mythological subjects. He was patronized by the ruling ◊Medici family, for whom he painted *Primavera* 1478 and *The Birth of Venus* about 1482–84 (both in the Uffizi, Florence). From the 1490s he was influenced by the religious fanatic ◊Savonarola and developed a harshly expressive and emotional style.

His real name was Filipepi, but his elder brother's nickname Botticelli 'little barrel' was passed on to him. His work for the Medicis was designed to cater to the educated classical tastes of the day. As well as his sentimental, beautiful young Madonnas, he produced a series of inventive compositions, including *tondi*, circular paintings. He broke with the Medicis after their execution of Savonarola.

Bottomley Virginia 1948– . British Conservative politician, health secretary from April 1992. Before entering Parliament she was a magistrate and psychiatric social worker. As an MP she became parliamentary private secretary to Chris Patten, then to Geoffrey Howe, and was made a junior environment minister 1988. Her husband,

attorney general—and has a life of five years. The president is elected by the assembly for its duration and is an ex-officio member of that body and answerable to it. There is also a 15-member house of chiefs, consisting of the chiefs of Botswana's eight principal ethnic groups, plus four members elected by the chiefs themselves and three elected by the house in general. The president may delay a bill for up to six months and then either sign it or dissolve the assembly and call a general election. The house of chiefs is consulted by the president and the assembly in matters affecting it. The president appoints a cabinet that is answerable to the assembly. Most significant of the seven political groupings are the Botswana Democratic Party (BDP), and the Botswana National Front (BNF).

history The first inhabitants were the ◊Kung, the hunter-gatherer groups living chiefly in the Kalahari Desert; from the 17th century the Tswana people became the principal inhabitants of the area, followed by the arrival of Bantu peoples in the early 19th century. Fearing an invasion by Boer farmers, the local rulers appealed to Britain and Bechuanaland (as it was originally called) became a British protectorate 1885.

On passing the Union of South Africa Act 1910, making South Africa independent, the British Parliament provided for the possibility of Bechuanaland becoming part of South Africa, but stipulated that this would not happen without popular consent. Successive South African governments requested the transfer, but Botswana preferred full independence.

Bottomley British Conservative politician and health secretary Virginia Bottomley, one of two women MPs included in John Major's April 1992 cabinet.

Peter Bottomley (1944–) is Conservative MP for Eltham.

botulism rare, often fatal type of ◊food poisoning. Symptoms include muscular paralysis and disturbed breathing and vision. It is· caused by a toxin produced by the bacterium *Clostridium botulinum*, sometimes found in improperly canned food. Thorough cooking destroys the toxin, which otherwise suppresses the cardiac and respiratory centres of the brain.

Boucher de Crèvecoeur de Perthes
/buːˈʃeɪ də krevˈkɜː də ˈpeət/ Jacques 1788–1868. French geologist whose discovery of Palaeolithic hand-axes 1837 challenged the acccepted view of human history dating only from 4004 BC, as proclaimed by the calculations of Bishop James ◊Usher.

Boudicca /buːˈdɪkə/ Queen of the Iceni (native Britons), often referred to by the Latin form *Boadicea*. Her husband, King Prasutagus, had been a tributary of the Romans, but on his death AD 60 the territory of the Iceni was violently annexed. Boudicca was scourged and her daughters raped. Boudicca raised the whole of SE England in revolt, and before the main Roman armies could return from campaigning in Wales she burned London, St Albans, and Colchester. Later the Romans under governor Suetonius Paulinus defeated the British between London and Chester; they were virtually annihilated and Boudicca poisoned herself.

Bougainville /ˈbuːɡənvɪl/ island province of Papua New Guinea; largest of the Solomon Islands archipelago
area 10,620 sq km/4,100 sq mi
capital Kieta
products copper, gold and silver
population (1989) 128,000
history named after the French navigator ◊Bougainville who arrived 768. In 1976 Bougainville became a province (with substantial autonomy) of Papua New Guinea. A state of emergency was declared 1989 after secessionist violence.

Bougainville /ˈbuːɡənvɪl/ Louis Antoine de 1729–1811. French navigator. After service with the French in Canada during the Seven Years' War, he made the first French circumnavigation of the world 1766–69 and the first systematic observations of longitude. Several Pacific islands are named after him, as is the climbing plant *bougainvillea*.

bougainvillea any plant of the genus of South American tropical vines *Bougainvillea*, family Nyctaginaceae, now cultivated in warm countries throughout the world for the red and purple bracts that cover the flowers.

Bougie /buːˈʒiː/ name until 1962 of ◊Bejaia, port in Algeria.

Bouguer anomaly in geophysics, an increase in the Earth's gravity observed near a mountain or dense rock mass. This is due to the gravitational force exerted by the rock mass of the rocks. It is named after its discoverer, the French mathematician Pierre Bouguer (1698–1758), who first observed it 1735.

Bou Kraa /buːˈkrɑː/ principal phosphate-mining centre of Western Sahara, linked by conveyor belt to the Atlantic coast near La'youn.

Boulanger /ˌbuːlɒnˈʒeɪ/ Lili (Juliette Marie Olga) 1893–1918. French composer, the younger sister of Nadia Boulanger. At the age of 19, she won the Prix de Rome with the cantata *Faust et Hélène* for voices and orchestra.

Boulanger /ˌbuːlɒnˈʒeɪ/ Nadia (Juliette) 1887–1979. French music teacher and conductor. A pupil of Fauré, and admirer of Stravinsky, she included among her composition pupils at the American Conservatory in Fontainebleau (from 1921) Aaron Copland, Roy Harris, Walter Piston, and Philip Glass.

boulder clay another name for ◊till, a type of glacial deposit.

boules (French 'balls') French game (also called *boccie* and *pétanque*) between two players or teams; it is similar to bowls.

Boules is derived from the ancient French game *jeu provençal*. The object is to deliver a boule (or boules) from a standing position to land as near the jack (target) as possible. The boule is approximately 8 cm/3 in in diameter and weighs 620–800 g/22–28 oz. The standard length of the court, normally with a sand base, is 27.5 m/90 ft.

Boulestin /ˌbuːleˈstæn/ Marcel 1878—1943. French cookery writer and restaurateur. He spread the principles of simple but high-quality French cooking in Britain in the first half of the 20th century, with a succession of popular books such as *What Shall We Have Today?* 1931.

Boulez /buːˈlez/ Pierre 1925– . French composer and conductor. He studied with ◊Messiaen and promoted contemporary music with a series of innovative *Domaine Musical* concerts and recordings in the 1950s, as conductor of the BBC Symphony and New York Philharmonic orchestras during the 1970s, and as founder and director of IRCAM, a music research studio in Paris opened 1977.

boulle or *buhl* ◊marquetry in brass and tortoiseshell. Originally Italian, it has acquired the name of its most skilful exponent, the French artisan André-Charles Boulle (1642–1732).

Boullée /buːˈleɪ/ Etienne-Louis 1729–1799. French Neo-Classical architect who, with Claude ◊Ledoux, influenced late 20th-century Rationalists such as the Italian Aldo Rossi. Boullée's abstract, geometric style is exemplified in his design for a spherical monument to the scientist Isaac Newton, 150 m/500 ft high. He built very little.

Boulogne-sur-Mer /buːˈlɔɪn sjuːə ˈmeə/ town on the English Channel, Pas-de-Calais *département*, France; population (1983) 99,000. Industries include oil refining, food processing, and fishing. It is also a ferry port (connecting with Dover and Folkestone) and seaside resort. Boulogne was a medieval countship, but became part of France 1477.

In World War II it was evacuated by the British 23 May 1940 and recaptured by the Canadians 22 Sept 1944.

Boult /bəʊlt/ Adrian (Cedric) 1889–1983. British conductor of the BBC Symphony Orchestra 1930–50 and the London Philharmonic 1950–57. He promoted the work of Holst and Vaughan Williams, and was a celebrated interpreter of Elgar. He was knighted in 1937.

Boulting /ˈbəʊltɪŋ/ John 1913–1985 and Roy 1913– . British director–producer team that was successful in the years following World War II. Their films include *Brighton Rock* 1947, *Lucky Jim* 1957, and *I'm All Right Jack* 1959. They were twins.

Boulton /ˈbəʊltən/ Matthew 1728–1809. British factory owner who helped to finance James ◊Watt's development of the steam engine.

Boumédienne /ˌbuːmeɪdˈjen/ Houari. Adopted name of Mohammed Boukharouba 1925–1978. Algerian politician who brought the nationalist leader Ben Bella to power by a revolt 1962, and superseded him as president in 1965 by a further coup.

Boundary Peak highest mountain in Nevada, USA, rising to 4,006 m/13,143 ft on the Nevada-California frontier.

***Bounty*, Mutiny on the** naval mutiny in the Pacific 1789 against British captain William ◊Bligh.

Bourbon /buːəbən/ name 1649–1815 of the French island of ◊Réunion, in the Indian Ocean.

Bourbon /buːəbən/ Charles, Duke of 1490–1527. Constable of France, honoured for his courage at the Battle of Marignano 1515. Later he served the Holy Roman Emperor Charles V, and helped to drive the French from Italy. In 1526 he was made duke of Milan, and in 1527 allowed his troops to sack Rome. He was killed by a shot the artist Cellini claimed to have fired.

Bourbon, duchy of originally a seigneury (feudal domain) created in the 10th century in the county of Bourges, central France, held by the Bourbon family. It became a duchy 1327.

The lands passed to the Capetian dynasty (see ◊Capet) as a result of the marriage of the Bourbon heiress Beatrix to Robert of

Clermont, son of Louis IX. Their son Pierre became the first duke of Bourbon 1327. The direct line ended with the death of Charles, Duke of Bourbon, in 1527.

Bourbon /ˈbuəbən/ French royal house (succeeding that of ◊Valois) beginning with Henry IV, and ending with Louis XVI, with a brief revival under Louis XVIII, Charles X, and Louis Phillippe. The Bourbons also ruled Spain almost uninterruptedly from Philip V to Alfonso XIII and were restored in 1975 (◊Juan Carlos); at one point they also ruled Naples and several Italian duchies. The Grand Duke of Luxembourg is also a Bourbon by male descent.

Bourdon gauge instrument for measuring pressure, invented by Eugène Bourdon 1849. The gauge contains a C-shaped tube, closed at one end. When the pressure inside the tube increases, the tube uncurls slightly causing a small movement at its closed end. A system of levers and gears magnifies this movement and turns a pointer, which indicates the pressure on a circular scale. Bourdon gauges are often fitted to cylinders of compressed gas used in industry and hospitals.

Bourgeois /ˈbuəˈʒwɑː/ Léon Victor Auguste 1851–1925. French politician. Entering politics as a Radical, he was prime minister in 1895, and later served in many cabinets. He was one of the pioneer advocates of the League of Nations. He was awarded the Nobel Peace Prize 1920.

bourgeoisie (French) the middle classes. The French word originally meant 'the freemen of a borough'. It came to mean the whole class above the workers and peasants, and below the nobility. Bourgeoisie (and *bourgeois*) has also acquired a contemptuous sense, implying commonplace, philistine respectability. By socialists it is applied to the whole propertied class, as distinct from the proletariat.

Bourgogne /buəˈɡɔɪn/ region of France, that includes the *départements* of Côte-d'Or, Nièvre, Sâone-et-Loire, and Yonne; area 31,600 sq km/12,198 sq mi; population (1986) 1,607,000. Its capital is Dijon. It is renowned for its wines, such as Chablis and Nuits-Saint-Georges, and for its cattle (the Charolais herd-book is maintained at Nevers). A former independent kingdom and duchy (English name ◊Burgundy), it was incorporated into France 1477.

Bourguiba /buəˈɡiːbə/ Habib ben Ali 1903– . Tunisian politician, first president of Tunisia 1957–87. He became prime minister 1956, president (for life from 1974) and prime minister of the Tunisian republic 1957; he was overthrown in a coup 1987.

Boutros-Ghali Boutros 1922– . Egyptian diplomat and politician, deputy prime minister 1991–92. He worked towards peace in the Middle East in the foreign ministry posts he held 1977–91. He became secretary general of the United Nations Jan 1992, and during his first year of office had to deal with the war in Bosnia-Herzegovina and famine in Somalia.

A professor at Cairo University 1949–77, Boutros-Ghali has expert knowledge of African affairs. In 1977 he accompanied President Sadat to Jerusalem on the diplomatic mission that led to the ◊Camp David Agreements and was appointed minister of state for foreign affairs that year.

Bouts /bauts/ Dierick *c.* 1420–1475. Early Netherlandish painter. Born in Haarlem, he settled in Louvain, painting portraits and religious scenes influenced by Rogier van der Weyden. *The Last Supper* 1464–68 (St Pierre, Louvain) is one of his finest works.

Bouvet Island /ˈbuːveɪ/ uninhabited island in the S Atlantic Ocean, a dependency of Norway since 1930; area 48 sq km/19 sq mi. Discovered by the French captain Jacques Bouvet in 1738, it was made the subject of a claim by Britain in 1825, but this was waived in Norway's favour in 1928.

Bouvines, Battle of /buːˈviːn/ victory for Philip II (Philip Augustus) of France in 1214, near the village of Bouvines in Flanders, over the Holy Roman emperor Otto IV and his allies. The battle, one of the most decisive in medieval Europe, ensured the succession of Frederick II as emperor and confirmed Philip as ruler of the whole of N France and Flanders; it led to the renunciation of all English claims to the region.

Bovet /bɔːˈveɪ/ Daniel 1907– . Swiss physiologist. He pioneered research into antihistamine drugs used in the treatment of nettle rash and hay fever, and was awarded a Nobel Prize for Medicine 1957 for his production of a synthetic form of curare, used as a muscle relaxant in anaesthesia.

bovine somatotropin (BST) hormone that increases an injected cow's milk yield by 10–40%. It is a protein naturally occurring in milk and breaks down within the human digestive tract into harmless amino acids. However, doubts have arisen recently as to whether such a degree of protein addition could in the long term be guaranteed harmless either to cattle or to humans.

Although no evidence of adverse side-effects had been found by 1990 there were calls for the drug to be banned because of potential consumer resistance to this method of increasing output of milk, which currently has a production surplus.

bovine spongiform encephalopathy (BSE) disease of cattle, allied to ◊scrapie, that renders the brain spongy and may drive an animal mad. It has been identified only in the UK, where more than 26,000 cases had been confirmed between the first diagnosis Nov 1986 and April 1991. The organism causing it is unknown; it is not a conventional virus because it is more resistant to chemicals and heat, cannot be seen even under an electron microscope, cannot be grown in tissue culture, and does not appear to provoke an immune response in the body. BSE is very similar to, and may be related to, Creutzfeld-Jakob disease and kuru, which affect humans.

The source of the disease has been traced to manufactured protein feed incorporating the rendered brains of scrapie-infected sheep. Following the animal-protein food ban in 1988, there was a single new case of BSE, indicating that the disease could be transmitted from cows to their calves.

BSE poses a threat to the valuable export trade in livestock, and has also killed pet cats and two wildlife-park animals.

Bow Bells the bells of St Mary-le-Bow church, Cheapside, London; a person born within the sound of Bow Bells is traditionally considered a true Cockney. The bells also feature in the legend of Dick ◊Whittington.

The church was nearly destroyed by bombs in 1941. The bells, recast from the old metal, were restored in 1961.

Bowdler /ˈbaʊdlə/ Thomas 1754–1825. British editor whose prudishly expurgated versions of Shakespeare and other authors gave rise to the verb *bowdlerize*.

Bowen /ˈbəʊɪn/ Elizabeth 1899–1973. Irish novelist. She published her first volume of short stories, *Encounters* in 1923. Her novels include *The Death of the Heart* 1938, *The Heat of the Day* 1949, and *The Little Girls* 1964.

bower bird New Guinean and N Australian bird of the family Ptilonorhynchidae, related to the ◊birds of paradise. The males are dull-coloured, and build elaborate bowers of sticks and grass, decorated with shells, feathers, or flowers, and even painted with the juice of berries, to attract the females. There are 17 species.

bowfin North American fish *Amia calva* with a swim bladder highly developed as an air sac, enabling it to breathe air. It is the only surviving member of a primitive group of bony fishes.

bowhead Arctic whale *Balaena mysticetus* with strongly curving upper jawbones supporting the plates of baleen with which it sifts planktonic crustaceans from the water. Averaging 15 m/50 ft long and 90 tonnes in weight, these slow-moving, placid whales were once extremely common, but by the 17th century were already becoming scarce through hunting. Only an estimated 3,000 remain, and continued hunting by the Inuit may result in extinction.

Bowie David. Stage name of David Jones 1947– . British pop singer, songwriter, and actor, He became a glam-rock star with the release of the album *The Rise and Fall of Ziggy Stardust and the Spiders from Mars* 1972, and collaborated in the mid-1970s with the electronic virtuoso Brian Eno (1948–) and Iggy Pop. He has also acted in plays and films, including Nicolas Roeg's *The Man Who Fell to Earth* 1976.

Bowles /bəʊlz/ Paul 1910– . US novelist and composer. Born in New York City, he studied with Aaron Copland and Virgil Thomson, writing scores for ballets, films, and an opera, *The Wind Remains* 1943, as well as incidental music for plays. He settled in Morocco, the setting of his novels *The Sheltering Sky* 1949 and *Let It Come Down* 1952. His autobiography, *Without Stopping*, was published in 1972.

bowls outdoor and indoor game popular in Commonwealth countries. It has been played in Britain since the 13th century at least and was popularized by Francis Drake, who is reputed to have played bowls on Plymouth Hoe as the Spanish Armada approached 1588.

The outdoor game is played on a finely cut grassed area called a rink, with biased bowls 13 cm/5 in in diameter. It is played as either singles, pairs, triples, or fours. The object is to get one's bowl (or bowls) as near as possible to the jack (target).

There are two popular forms: *lawn bowls*, played on a flat surface, and *crown green bowls*, played on a rink with undulations and a crown at the centre of the green. This latter version is more popular in the Midlands and N England. The major events include the World Championship first held in 1966 for men and in 1969 for women and the Waterloo Handicap, Crown Green bowling's principal tournament which was first held in 1907 at the Waterloo Hotel, Blackpool, England.

Bowman's capsule /ˈbəʊmən/ in the vertebrate kidney, a microscopic filtering device used in the initial stages of waste-removal and urine formation.

There are approximately a million of these capsules in a human kidney, each made up of a tight knot of capillaries and each leading into a kidney tubule or nephron. Blood at high pressure passes into the capillaries where water, dissolved nutrients, and urea move through the capillary wall into the tubule.

box any of several small evergreen trees and shrubs, genus *Buxus*, of the family Buxaceae, with small, leathery leaves. Some species are used as hedge plants and for shaping into garden ornaments. The common box *B. sempervirens* is slow-growing and ideal for hedging.

boxer breed of dog, about 60 cm/2 ft tall, with a smooth coat and a set-back nose. The tail is usually docked. Boxers are usually brown but may be brindled or white.

Boxer member of the *I ho ch'üan* ('Righteous Harmonious Fists'), a society of Chinese nationalists dedicated to fighting European influence. The *Boxer Rebellion* or *Uprising* 1900 was instigated by the Dowager Empress Tzu Hsi (1834–1908). European and US legations in Beijing were besieged and thousands of Chinese Christian converts and missionaries murdered. An international punitive force was dispatched, Beijing was captured 14 Aug 1900, and China agreed to pay a large indemnity.

boxfish or (*trunkfish* any fish of the family Ostraciodontidae, with scales that are hexagonal bony plates fused to form a box covering the body, only the mouth and fins being free of the armour. Boxfishes, also known as trunkfishes swim slowly. The cowfish, genus *Lactophrys*, with two 'horns' above the eyes, is a member of this group.

boxing fighting with the fists, almost entirely a male sport. The sport dates from the 18th century, when fights were fought with bare knuckles and untimed rounds. Each round ended with a knockdown. Fighting with gloves became the accepted form in the latter part of the 19th century after the formulation of the Queensberry Rules 1867. The last bare-knuckle championship fight was between John L Sullivan and Jake Kilrain 1899.

Jack Broughton (1704–1789) was one of the early champions and in 1743 drew up the first set of boxing rules. Today all boxing follows the original Queensberry Rules, but with modifications. Contests take place in a roped ring 4.3–6.1 m/14–20 ft square. All rounds last three minutes. Amateur bouts last three rounds and professional championship bouts for as many as twelve or fifteen rounds. Boxers are classified according to weight and may not fight in a division lighter than their own. The weight divisions in professional boxing range from *strawweight* (also known as paperweight and mini-flyweight), under 49 kg/108 lb, to *heavyweight*, over 88 kg/195 lb.

boyar landowner in the Russian aristocracy. During the 16th century boyars formed a powerful interest group threatening the tsar's power, until their influence was decisively broken in 1565 when Ivan the Terrible confiscated much of their land.

Boycott /ˈbɔɪkɒt/ Geoffrey 1940– . English cricketer born in Yorkshire, England's most prolific run-maker with 8,114 runs in test cricket. He was banned as a test player in 1982 for taking part in matches against South Africa.

He played in 108 test matches and in 1981 overtook Gary Sobers' world record total of test runs. Twice, in 1971 and 1979, his average was over 100 runs in an English season. He was released by Yorkshire after a dispute in 1986.

Boyd-Orr /ˈbɔɪd ˈɔː/ John 1880–1971. British nutritionist and health campaigner. He was awarded the Nobel Prize for Peace in 1949 in recognition of his work towards alleviating world hunger.

Boyle /bɔɪl/ Charles, 4th Earl of Orrery 1676–1731. Irish soldier and diplomat. The *orrery*, a mechanical model of the solar system in which the planets move at the correct relative velocities, is named after him.

Boyle /bɔɪl/ Robert 1627–1691. Irish physicist and chemist who published the seminal *The Sceptical Chymist* 1661. He was the first chemist to collect a sample of gas, formulated *Boyle's law* on the compressibility of a gas in 1662, was one of the founders of the Royal Society, and endowed the Boyle Lectures for the defence of Christianity.

Boyle's law law stating that the volume of a given mass of gas at a constant temperature is inversely proportional to its pressure. For example, if the pressure of a gas doubles, its volume will be reduced by a half, and vice versa. The law was discovered in 1662 by Robert Boyle. See also ◊gas laws.

Boyne /bɔɪn/ river in the Irish Republic. Rising in the Bog of Allen in County Kildare, it flows 110 km/69 mi NE to the Irish Sea near Drogheda. The Battle of the Boyne was fought at Oldbridge near the mouth of the river in 1690.

Boyne, Battle of the /bɔɪn/ battle fought 1 Jul 1690 in E Ireland, in which James II was defeated by William III and fled to France. It was the decisive battle of the War of English Succession, confirming a Protestant monarch. It took its name from the river Boyne in the Republic of Ireland 113 km/70 mi long, flowing past Drogheda into the Irish Sea.

Boyoma Falls /bɔɪˈəʊmə/ series of seven cataracts in under 100 km/60 mi in the Lualaba (upper Zaïre River) above Kisangani, central Africa. They have a total drop of over 60 m/200 ft.

Bo Zhu Yi /ˈbəʊ ˌdʒuː ˈjiː/ or **Po Chu-i** 772–846. Chinese poet. President from 841 of the imperial war department, he criticized government policy. He is said to have checked his work with an old peasant woman for clarity of expression.

Brabant /brəˈbænt/ (Flemish **Braband**) former duchy of W Europe, comprising the Dutch province of ◊North Brabant and the Belgian provinces of Brabant and Antwerp. They were divided when Belgium became independent 1830. The present-day Belgian province of Brabant has an area of 3,400 sq km/1,312 sq mi and a population (1987) of 2,222,000.

During the Middle Ages Brabant was an independent duchy, and after passing to Burgundy, and thence to the Spanish crown, was divided during the Dutch War of Independence. The southern portion was Spanish until 1713, then Austrian until 1815, when the whole area was included in the Netherlands. In 1830 the French-speaking part of the population in the S Netherlands rebelled, and when Belgium was recognized 1839, S Brabant was included in it.

Brabham /ˈbræbəm/ Grand Prix racing team started 1962 by the top Australian driver Jack Brabham (1926–). Their first car, designed by Ron Tauranac, had its first win 1964, and in 1966 Brabham won the world title in his own Repco engine-powered car.

Denny Hulme (1936–) won the title for the company the following year. Brabham retired in 1970 and the company lost some of its impetus. It returned to Grand Prix racing in 1989.

Brachiopoda any member of the phylum Brachiopoda, marine invertebrates with two shells, resembling but totally unrelated to bivalves. There are about 300 living species; they were much more numerous in past geological ages. They are suspension feeders, ingesting minute food particles from water. A single internal organ, the iophophore, handles feeding, aspiration, and excretion.

bracken large fern, especially *Pteridium aquilinum*, abundant in the northern hemisphere. A perennial rootstock throws up coarse fronds.

bracket fungus any ◊fungus of the class Basidiomycetes, with fruiting bodies that grow like shelves from trees.

Bracknell /ˈbræknəl/ ◊new town in Berkshire, England, founded 1949; population (1981) 49,000. The headquarters of the Meteorological Office is here, and (with Washington DC) is one of the two global area forecasting centres (of upper-level winds and temperatures) for the world's airlines.

bract leaflike structure in whose ◊axil a flower or inflorescence develops. Bracts are generally green and smaller than the true leaves. However, in some plants they may be brightly coloured and conspicuous, taking over the role of attracting pollinating insects to the flowers, whose own petals are small; examples include poinsettia *Euphorbia pulcherrima* and bougainvillea.

A whorl of bracts surrounding an ◊inflorescence is termed an **involucre**. A **bracteole** is a leaf-like organ that arises on an individual flower stalk, between the true bract and the ◊calyx.

Bradbury /'brædbəri/ Malcolm 1932– . British novelist and critic, whose writings include comic and satiric portrayals of academic life. Professor of American Studies at the University of East Anglia from 1970, his major work is *The History Man* 1975, set in a provincial English university. Other works include *Rates of Exchange* 1983.

Bradbury /'brædbəri/ Ray 1920– . US science-fiction writer, responsible for making the genre 'respectable' to a wider readership. His work shows nostalgia for small-town Midwestern life, and includes *The Martian Chronicles* 1950, *Fahrenheit 451*, 1953, *R is for Rocket* 1962, and *Something Wicked This Way Comes* 1962.

Bradford /'brædfəd/ industrial city (engineering, machine tools, electronics, printing) in West Yorkshire, England, 14 km/9 mi W of Leeds; population (1981) 281,000.
features a 15th-century cathedral; Cartwright Hall art gallery; the National Museum of Photography, Film, and Television 1983 (with Britain's largest cinema screen 14 × 20 m); and the Alhambra, built as a music hall and restored for ballet, plays, and pantomime.
history from the 13th century, Bradford developed as a great wool- and later, cloth-manufacturing centre, but the industry declined from the 1970s with Third World and Common Market competition. The city has received a succession of immigrants, Irish in the 1840s, German merchants in the mid-19th century, then Poles and Ukrainians, and more recently West Indians and Asians.

Bradlaugh /'brædlɔː/ Charles 1833–1891. British freethinker and radical politician. In 1880 he was elected Liberal member of Parliament for Northampton, but was not allowed to take his seat until 1886 because, as an atheist, he (unsuccessfully) claimed the right to affirm instead of taking the oath. He was associated with the feminist Annie Besant.

Bradley /'brædli/ Francis Herbert 1846–1924. British philosopher. In *Ethical Studies* 1876 and *Principles of Logic* 1883 he attacked the utilitarianism of J S Mill, and in *Appearance and Reality* 1893 and *Truth and Reality* 1914 he outlined his neo-Hegelian doctrine of the universe as a single ultimate reality.

Bradley /'brædli/ James 1693–1762. English astronomer who in 1728 discovered the ◊aberration of starlight. From the amount of aberration in star positions, he was able to calculate the speed of light. In 1748, he announced the discovery of ◊nutation (variation in the Earth's axial tilt).

Bradman /'brædmən/ Donald George 1908– . Australian test cricketer with the highest average in test history. From 52 test matches he averaged 99.94 runs per innings. He only needed four runs from his final test innings to average 100 but was dismissed at second ball.
Bradman was born in Bowral, New South Wales, came to prominence at an early age, and made his test debut in 1928. He played for Australia for 20 years and was captain 1936–48. He twice scored triple centuries against England and in 1930 scored 452 not out for New South Wales against Queensland, the highest first-class innings until 1959. In 1989 a Bradman Museum was opened in his home town.

Bradshaw /'brædʃɔː/ George 1801–1853. British publisher who brought out the first railway timetable in 1839. Thereafter *Bradshaw's Railway Companion* appeared at regular intervals.
He was apprenticed to an engraver on leaving school, and set up his own printing and engraving business in the 1820s, beginning in 1827 with an engraved map of Lancashire.

Brady /'breɪdi/ Mathew B *c.* 1823–1896. US photographer. Famed for his skill in photographic portraiture, he published *The Gallery of Illustrious Americans* 1850. With the outbreak of the US Civil War 1861, Brady and his staff became the foremost photographers of battle scenes and military life. Although his war photos were widely reproduced, Brady later suffered a series of financial reverses and died in poverty. Born in Warren County, New York, Brady served as an apprentice to a portrait painter. Learning the rudiments of photography from Samuel ◊Morse, Brady established his own ◊daguerreotype studio in New York 1844.

Braemar village in Grampian, Scotland, where the most celebrated of the ◊Highland Games, the *Braemar Gathering*, takes place every August.

Braga /'brɑːgə/ city in N Portugal 48 km/30 mi NNE of Oporto; population (1981) 63,800. Industries include textiles, electrical goods, and vehicle manufacture. It has a 12th-century cathedral, and the archbishop is primate of the Iberian peninsula. As Bracara Augusta it was capital of the Roman province Lusitania.

Bragança /brəˈgænsə/ capital of a province of the same name in NE Portugal, 176 km/110 mi NE of Oporto. Population (1981) 13,900. It was the original family seat of the House of Braganza.

Braganza /brəˈgænsə/ name of the royal house of Portugal whose members reigned 1640–1910; another branch were emperors of Brazil 1822–89.

Bragg /bræg/ William Henry 1862–1942. British physicist. In 1915 he shared with his son *(William) Lawrence Bragg* (1890–1971) the Nobel Prize for Physics for their research work on X-rays and crystals.

Brahe /ˈbrɑːhə/ Tycho 1546–1601. Danish astronomer who made accurate observations of the planets from which the German astronomer and mathematician Johann ◊Kepler proved that planets orbit the Sun in ellipses. His discovery and report of the 1572 supernova brought him recognition, and his observations of the comet of 1577 proved that it moved on an orbit among the planets, thus disproving the Greek view that comets were in the Earth's atmosphere.

Brahma /ˈbrɑːmə/ in Hinduism, the creator of the cosmos, who forms with Vishnu and Siva the Trimurti, or three aspects of the absolute spirit.

In the Hindu creation myth, Brahma, the demiurge, is born from the unfolding lotus flower that grows out of Vishnu's navel; after Brahma creates the world, Vishnu wakes and governs it for the duration of the cosmic cycle *kalpa*, the 'day of Brahma', which lasts for 4,200 million earthly years.

Brahman in Hinduism, the supreme being, an abstract, impersonal world-soul into whom the *atman*, or individual soul, will eventually be absorbed when its cycle of rebirth is ended.

Brahmanism /ˈbrɑːmənɪzəm/ earliest stage in the development of ◊Hinduism. Its sacred scriptures are the ◊Vedas, with their accompanying literature of comment and explanation known as Brahmanas, Aranyakas, and Upanishads.

Brahmaputra /ˌbrɑːməˈpuːtrə/ river in Asia 2,900 km/1,800 mi long, a tributary of the Ganges.

It rises in the Himalayan glaciers as Zangbo and runs eastward through Tibet, to the mountain mass of Namcha Barwa. Turning south, as the Dihang, it enters India and flows into the Assam valley near Sadiya, where it is now known as the Brahmaputra. It flows generally westwards until, shortly after reaching Bangladesh, it turns south and divides into the Brahmaputra proper, without much water, and the main stream, the Jamuna, which joins the Padma arm of the Ganges. The river is navigable for 1,285 km/800 mi from the sea.

Brahma Samaj /ˈbrɑːmə səˈmɑːdʒ/ Indian monotheistic religious movement, founded in 1830 in Calcutta by Ram Mohun Roy who attempted to recover the simple worship of the Vedas and purify Hinduism. The movement had split into a number of sects by the end of the 19th century and is now almost defunct.

Brahms /brɑːmz/ Johannes 1833–1897. German composer, pianist, and conductor. Considered one of the greatest composers of symphonic music and of songs, his works include four symphonies; ◊Lieder (songs); concertos for piano and for violin; chamber music; sonatas; and the choral *A German Requiem* 1868. He performed and conducted his own works.

Although his music belongs to a reflective strain of Romanticism, similar to Wordsworth in poetry, Brahms saw himself as continuing the Classical tradition from the point to which Beethoven had brought it. To his contemporaries, he was a strict formalist, in opposition to the romantic sensuality of Wagner.

Brǎila /brəˈiːlə/ port in Romania on the river Danube; 170 km/106 mi from its mouth; population (1983) 226,000. It is a naval base. Industries include the manufacture of artificial fibres, iron and steel, machinery, and paper. It was controlled by the Ottoman Empire 1544–1828.

Braille /breɪl/ system of writing for the blind. Letters are represented by a combination of raised dots on paper or other materials, which are then read by touch. It was invented in 1829 by *Louis Braille* (1809–1852), who became blind at the age of three.

brain in higher animals, a mass of interconnected ◊nerve cells, forming the anterior part of the ◊central nervous system, whose activities it coordinates and controls. In ◊vertebrates, the brain is contained by the skull. An enlarged portion of the upper spinal cord, the *medulla oblongata*, contains centres for the control of respiration, heartbeat rate and strength, and blood pressure. Overlying this is the *cerebellum*, which is concerned with coordinating complex muscular processes such as maintaining posture and moving limbs. The cerebral hemispheres (*cerebrum*) are paired outgrowths of the front end of the forebrain, in early vertebrates mainly concerned with the senses, but in higher vertebrates greatly developed and involved in the integration of all sensory input and motor output, and in intelligent behaviour.

In vertebrates, many of the nerve fibres from the two sides of the body cross over as they enter the brain, so that the left cerebral hemisphere is associated with the right side of the body and vice versa. In humans, a certain asymmetry develops in the two halves of the cerebrum. In right-handed people, the left hemisphere seems to play a greater role in controlling verbal and some mathematical skills, whereas the right hemisphere is more involved in spatial perception. In general, however, skills and abilities are not closely localized. In the brain, nerve impulses are passed across ◊synapses by neurotransmitters, in the same way as in other parts of the nervous system.

In mammals the cerebrum is the largest part of the brain, carrying the *cerebral cortex*. This consists of a thick surface layer of cell bodies (grey matter), below which fibre tracts (white matter) connect various parts of the cortex to each other and to other points in the central nervous system. As cerebral complexity grows, the surface of the brain becomes convoluted into deep folds. In higher mammals, there are large unassigned areas of the brain that seem to be connected with intelligence, personality, and higher mental faculties. Language is controlled in two special regions usually in the left side of the brain: *Broca's area* governs the ability to talk, and *Wernicke's area* is responsible for the comprehension of spoken and written words. In 1990, scientists at Johns Hopkins University, Baltimore, succeeded in culturing human brain cells.

Braine /breɪn/ John 1922–1986. English novelist. His novel *Room at the Top* 1957 created the character of Joe Lampton, one of the first of the northern working-class antiheroes.

brainstem central core of the brain, where the top of the spinal cord merges with the undersurface of the brain.

The oldest part of the brain in evolutionary terms, the brainstem is the body's life-support centre, containing regulatory mechanisms for vital functions such as breathing, heart rate, and blood pressure. It is also involved in controlling the level of consciousness by acting as a relay station for nerve connections to and from the higher centres of the brain.

In many countries, death of the brainstem is now formally recognized as death of the person as a whole. Such cases are the principal donors of organs for transplantation. So-called 'beating-heart donors' can be maintained for a limited period by life-support equipment.

Braithwaite /ˈbreɪθweɪt/ Eustace Adolph 1912– . Guyanese author. His experiences as a teacher in London prompted *To Sir With Love* 1959. His *Reluctant Neighbours* 1972 deals with black/white relations.

brake device used to slow down or stop the movement of a moving body or vehicle. The mechanically applied caliper brake used on bicycles uses a scissor action to press hard rubber blocks against the wheel rim. The main braking system of a car works hydraulically: when the driver depresses the brake pedal, liquid pressure forces pistons to apply brakes on each wheel.

Two types of car brakes are used. *Disc brakes* are used on the front wheels of some cars and on all wheels of sports and performance cars, since they are the more efficient and less prone to fading (losing their braking power) when they get hot. Braking pressure forces brake pads against both sides of a steel disc that rotates with the wheel. *Drum brakes* are fitted on the rear wheels of some cars and on all wheels of some passenger cars. Braking pressure forces brake shoes to expand outwards into contact with a drum rotating with the wheels. The brake pads and shoes have a tough ◊friction lining that grips well and withstands wear.

Many trucks and trains have *air brakes*, which work by compressed air. On landing, jet planes reverse the thrust of their engines to reduce their speed quickly. Space vehicles use retrorockets for braking in space, and use the air resistance, or drag of the atmosphere, to slow down when they return to Earth.

Bramah /ˈbrɑːmə/ Ernest. Pen name of Ernest Bramah Smith 1868–1948. British short story writer, creator of Kai Lung, and of Max Carrados, a blind detective.

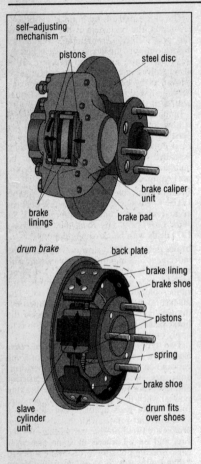

self–adjusting
mechanism

pistons

steel disc

brake caliper
unit

brake
linings

brake pad

drum brake

back plate

brake lining

brake shoe

pistons

spring

brake shoe

slave
cylinder
unit

drum fits
over shoes

Brake Two common braking systems: the disc brake (top) and the drum brake (bottom).

Bramah /brɑːmə/ Joseph 1748–1814. British inventor of a flushing water closet 1778, an 'unpickable' lock 1784, and the hydraulic press 1795. The press made use of ◊Pascal's principle (that pressure in fluid contained in a vessel is evenly distributed) and employed water as the hydraulic fluid; it enabled the 19th-century bridge-builders to lift massive girders.

Bramante /brəˈmænti/ Donato c. 1444–1514. Italian Renaissance architect and artist. Inspired by Classical designs, he was employed by Pope Julius II in rebuilding part of the Vatican and St Peter's in Rome.

bramble any prickly bush of a genus *Rubus* belonging to the rose family Rosaceae. Examples are ◊blackberry, raspberry, and dewberry.

brambling bird *Fringilla montifringilla* belonging to the finch family, about 15 cm/6 in long. It breeds in N Europe and Asia.

Branagh /brænə/ Kenneth 1960– . British actor and director. He cofounded, with David Parfitt, the Renaissance Theatre Company 1987, was a notable Hamlet and Touchstone in 1988, and in 1989 directed and starred in a film of Shakespeare's *Henry V*.

Branagh Hailed by some as a new Olivier, Northern Irish actor and director Kenneth Branagh has played a wide variety of Shakespearean and contemporary roles on stage, film, and television.

Brancusi /brænˈkuːzi/ Constantin 1876–1957. Romanian sculptor, active in Paris from 1904, a pioneer of abstract forms and conceptual art. He was one of the first sculptors in the 20th century to carve directly from his material, working with marble, granite, wood, and other materials. He developed increasingly simplified natural or organic forms, such as the sculpted head that gradually came to resemble an egg (*Sleeping Muse* 1910, Musée National d'Art Moderne, Paris). By the 1930s he had achieved monumental simplicity with structures of simple repeated forms (*Endless Col-*

umn and other works in Tirgu Jiu public park, Romania). Brancusi was revered by his contemporaries and remains a seminal figure in 20th-century sculpture.

Brandeis /'brændaɪs/ Louis Dembitz 1856–1941. US jurist. As a crusader for progressive causes, he helped draft social-welfare and labour legislation. In 1916, with his appointment o the US Supreme Court by President Wilson, he became the first Jewish justice and maintained his support of individual rights in his opposition to the 1917 Espionage Act and in his dissenting opinion in he first wiretap case, *Olmstead* v *US* 1928.

Brandenburg /'brændənbɜːg/ administrative *Land* (state) of the Federal Republic of Germany
area 25,000 sq km/10,000 sq mi
capital Potsdam
towns Cottbus, Brandenburg, Frankfurt-on-Oder
products iron and steel, paper, pulp, metal products, semiconductors
population (1990) 2,700,000
history the Hohenzollern rulers who took control of Brandenburg in 1415 later acquired the powerful duchy of Prussia and became emperors of Germany. At the end of World War II, Brandenburg lost over 12,950 sq km/5,000 sq mi of territory when Poland advanced its frontier to the line of the Oder and Neisse rivers. The remainder, which became a region of East Germany, was divided 1952 into the districts of Frankfurt-on-Oder, Potsdam, and Cottbus. When Germany was reunited 1990, Brandenburg reappeared as a state of the Federal Republic.

Brandenburg /'brændənbɜːg/ town in the Federal Republic of Germany, on the river Havel; 60 km/36 mi W of Berlin; population (1981) 94,700. Industries include textiles, cars, and aircraft. It has a 12th-century cathedral.

Brando /'brændəʊ/ Marlon 1924– . US actor whose casual style, mumbling speech, and use of ◊Method acting made him one of cinema's most distinctive stars. He won best-actor Academy Awards for *On the Waterfront* 1954 and *The Godfather* 1972.

He made his Broadway debut in *I Remember Mama* 1944, appeared in *Candida* 1946, and achieved fame in *A Streetcar Named Desire* 1947. His films include *The Men* 1950, *A Streetcar Named Desire* 1951, *Julius Caesar* 1953, *The Wild One* 1954, *Mutiny on the Bounty* 1962, *Last Tango in Paris* 1973,

Brando The film role as the biker Johnny in The Wild One 1954 helped create Marlon Brando's image as moody and difficult.

Apocalypse Now 1979, and *The Freshman* 1990.

Brandt /brænt/ Bill 1905–1983. British photographer who produced a large body of richly printed and romantic black-and-white studies of people, London life, and social behaviour.

Brandt /brænt/ Willy. Adopted name of Karl Herbert Frahm 1913–1992. West German socialist politician, federal chancellor 1969–74. He played a key role in the remoulding of the Social Democratic Party (SPD) as a moderate socialist force (leader 1964–87). As mayor of West Berlin 1957–66, Brandt became internationally known during the Berlin Wall crisis 1961. He received the Nobel Peace Prize 1971.

Brandt, born in Lübeck, changed his name when he fled to Norway 1933 and became active in the anti-Nazi resistance. He returned 1945 and entered the Bundestag (federal parliament) 1949. In the 'grand coalition' 1966–69 he served as foreign minister and introduced *Ostpolitik*, a policy of reconciliation between East and West Europe, which was continued when he became federal chancellor 1969, and culminated in the 1972 signing of the Basic Treaty with East Germany.

He resigned from the chancellorship 1974 following the discovery that a close aide, Günther Guillaume, had been an East German spy. Brandt continued to wield considerable influence in the SPD, in particular over the party's new radical left wing. He chaired the ◊Brandt Commission on Third World problems 1977–83 and was a member of the European Parliament 1979–83.

Brandt Commission officially the Independent Commission on International Development Issues, established in 1977 and chaired by the former West German chancellor Willy ◊Brandt. Consisting of 18 eminent persons acting independently of governments, the commission examined the problems of developing countries and sought to identify corrective measures that would command international support. It was disbanded in 1983.

Its main report, published in 1980 under the title *North–South: A Programme for Survival*, made detailed recommendations for accelerating the development of poorer countries (involving the transfer of resources to the latter from the rich countries).

brandy (Dutch *brandewijn* 'burnt wine') spirit distilled from fermented grape juice (wine). Best-known examples are produced in France, notably Armagnac and Cognac. Brandy can also be prepared from other fruits, for example, apples (Calvados) and cherries (Kirschwasser). Brandies contain up to 55% alcohol.

Branson /'brænsən/ Richard 1950– . British entrepreneur whose Virgin company developed quickly, diversifying from retailing records to the airline business.

Braque /brɑːk/ Georges 1882–1963. French painter who, with Picasso, founded the Cubist movement around 1907–10. They worked together at L'Estaque in the south of France and in Paris. Braque began to experiment in collages and invented a technique of gluing paper, wood, and other materials to canvas. His later work became more decorative.

Brasília /brə'zɪlɪə/ capital of Brazil from 1960, 1,000 m/3,000 ft above sea level; population (1980) 411,500. It was designed by Lucio Costa (1902–1963), with Oscar Niemeyer as chief architect, as a completely new city to bring life to the interior.

Brasov /brɑː'sɒv/ (Hungarian *Brassó*, German *Krondstadt*) industrial city (machine tools, industrial equipment, chemicals, cement, woollens) in central Romania at the foot of the Transylvanian Alps; population (1985) 347,000. It belonged to Hungary until 1920.

brass metal ◊alloy of copper and zinc, with not more than 5% or 6% of other metals. The zinc content ranges from 20% to 45%, and the colour of brass varies accordingly from coppery to whitish yellow. Brasses are characterized by the ease with which they may be shaped and machined; they are strong and ductile, resist many forms of corrosion, and are used for electrical fittings, ammunition cases, screws, household fittings, and ornaments.

Brasses are usually classed into those that can be worked cold (up to 25% zinc) and those that are better worked hot (about 40% zinc).

Brassaï /brɑː'sɑːiː/ adopted name of Gyula Halesz 1899–1986. French photographer of Hungarian origin. From the early 1930s on he documented, mainly by flash, the nightlife of Paris, before turning to more abstract work.

Brassica genus of plants of the family Cruciferae. The most familiar species is the common cabbage *Brassica oleracea*, with its varieties broccoli, cauliflower, kale, and brussels sprouts.

brass instrument in music, any instrument made of brass or other metal, which is directly blown through a 'cup' or 'funnel' mouthpiece.

In the symphony orchestra they comprise: the *French horn* a descendant of the natural hunting horn, valved, and curved into a circular loop, with a wide bell; the *trumpet* a cylindrical tube curved into an oblong, with a narrow bell and three valves (the state *fanfare trumpet* has no valves); the *trombone*, an instrument with a 'slide' to vary the effective length of the tube (the *sackbut*, common from the 14th century, was its forerunner); the *tuba*, normally the lowest toned instrument of the orchestra, which is valved and with a very wide bore to give sonority, and a bell that points upward.

In the brass band (in descending order of pitch) they comprise: the *cornet* three-valved instrument, looking like a shorter, broader trumpet, and with a wider bore; the *flugelhorn* valved instrument, rather similar in range to the cornet; the *tenor horn*; *B-flat baritone*; *euphonium*; *trombone*; and *bombardon* (bass tuba). A brass band normally also includes bass and side drums, triangle, and cymbals.

Bratby /'brætbi/ John 1928– . British artist, one of the leaders of the 'kitchen-sink' school of the 1950s because of a preoccupation in early work with working-class domestic interiors.

Bratislava /'brætɪslɑːvə/ (German *Pressburg*) industrial port (engineering, chemicals, oil refining) and capital of the Slovak Republic, on the river Danube; population (1986) 417,000. It was the capital of Hungary 1526–1784 and capital of Slovakia (within Czechoslovakia) until 1993.

Brattain /'brætn/ Walter Houser 1902–1987. US physicist. In 1956 he was awarded a Nobel prize jointly with William Shockley and John Bardeen for their work on the development of the transistor, which replaced the comparatively costly and clumsy vacuum tube in electronics.

Braun /braʊn/ Eva 1910–1945. German mistress of Adolf Hitler. Secretary to Hitler's photographer and personal friend, Heinrich Hoffmann, she became Hitler's mistress in the 1930s and married him in the air-raid shelter of the Chancellery in Berlin on 29 Apr 1945. The next day they committed suicide together.

Brautigan /'brɔtɪgən/ Richard 1935–1984. US novelist, author of playful fictions set in California, such as *Trout Fishing in America* 1967, and Gothic works like *The Hawkline Monster* 1974.

Brazil /brə'zɪl/ largest country in South America, (almost half the continent) bounded SW by Uruguay, Argentina, Paraguay and Bolivia; W by Peru and Colombia; N by Venezuela, Guyana, Surinam, and French Guiana; and NE and SE by the Atlantic Ocean.

government Brazil is a federal republic of 23 states, three territories, and a federal district (Brasília). The two-chamber national congress consists of a senate of 69 members (on the basis of one senator per state) elected for an eight-year term, and a chamber of deputies, whose numbers vary, elected for a four-year term. The number of deputies is determined by the population of each state, and each territory is represented by one deputy. Elections to both chambers are by universal suffrage. The cabinet is chosen by the president, who is elected by universal

adult suffrage for a five-year term and is not eligible for re-election. The states and the federal district each have an elected governor.

history Inhabited by various South American Indians, Brazil was colonized by the Portuguese from 1500. In 1808, after ◊Napoleon invaded Portugal, King John VI moved his capital from Lisbon to Rio de Janeiro. In 1821 he returned to Lisbon, leaving his son, Crown Prince Pedro, as regent. In 1822 Pedro declared Brazil an independent kingdom, and took the title Emperor Pedro I. His son, Pedro II, persuaded large numbers of Portuguese to emigrate, and the centre of Brazil developed quickly, largely on the basis of slavery. In 1888 slavery was abolished and in 1889 a republic was founded, followed by the adoption of a constitution for a federated nation 1891.

After social unrest in the 1920s, the world economic crisis of 1930 produced a revolt that brought Dr Getúlio Vargas to the presidency. He held office, as a benevolent dictator, until the army forced him to resign 1945 and General Eurico Dutra became president. In 1951 Vargas returned to power but committed suicide 1954 and was succeeded by Dr Juscelino Kubitschek.

In 1961 Dr Janio Quadros became president but resigned after seven months, to be succeeded by Vice President João Goulart. Suspecting him of left-wing leanings, the army forced a restriction of presidential powers and created the office of prime minister. A referendum brought back the presidential system 1963, with Goulart choosing his own cabinet.

free political parties banned In a bloodless coup 1964, General Castelo Branco assumed dictatorial powers and banned all political groupings except for two artificially created parties, the progovernment National Renewal Alliance (ARENA) and the opposition Brazilian Democratic Movement Party (PMBD). In 1967 Branco named Marshal da Costa e Silva as his successor, and a new constitution was adopted. In 1969 da Costa e Silva resigned because of ill health, and a military junta took over. In 1974 General Ernesto Geisel became president until succeeded by General Baptista de Figueiredo 1978. The ban on opposition parties was lifted 1979.

civilian presidency restored President Figueiredo held office until 1985, his last few years as president witnessing economic decline, strikes, and calls for the return of democracy. In 1985 Tancredo Neves became the first civilian president in 21 years, but died within months of taking office. He was succeeded by Vice President José ◊Sarney, who continued to work with Neves's cabinet and policies. The constitution was again amended to allow direct presidential elections.

In the Dec 1989 presidential election Fernando Collor of the National Reconstruction Party (PRN) narrowly defeated Luis Inácio da Silva of the Workers' Party (PT). He advocated free-market economic policies and a crackdown on government corruption. In Sept 1992, facing trial on corruption charges, Collor was stripped of his powers by the national congress and replaced by Vice President Itamar Franco. Collor resigned in Dec and was subsequently banned from public office for eight years. In April 1993 Collor was indicted for 'passive corruption'. In Oct 1994 Fernando Henrique Cardoso was elected president.

Brazil nut seed, rich in oil and highly nutritious, of the gigantic South American tree *Bertholletia excelsa*. The seeds are enclosed in a hard outer casing, each fruit containing 10–20 seeds arranged like the segments of an orange. The timber of the tree is also valuable.

brazing method of joining two metals by melting an ◊alloy into the joint. It is similar to soldering but takes place at a much higher temperature. Copper and silver alloys are widely used for brazing, at temperatures up to about 900°C/1,650°F.

Brazzaville /ˈbræzəvɪl/ capital of the Congo, industrial port (foundries, railway repairs, shipbuilding, shoes, soap, furniture, bricks) on the river Zaïre, opposite Kinshasa; population (1984) 595,000.

There is a cathedral 1892 and the Pasteur Institute 1908. It stands on Pool Malebo (Stanley Pool).

Brazzaville was founded by the Italian Count Pierre Savorgnan de Brazza (1852–1905), employed in African expeditions by the French government. It was the African headquarters of the Free (later Fighting) French during World War II.

bread food baked from a kneaded dough or batter made with ground cereals, usually wheat, and water; many other ingredients may be added. The dough may be unleavened or raised (usually with yeast).

Bread has been a staple of human diet in many civilizations as long as agriculture has been practised, and some hunter-gatherer peoples made it from crushed acorns or beech nuts. Potato, banana, and cassava bread are among some local varieties, but most breads are made from fermented cereals which form glutens when mixed with water. The earliest bread was unleavened and was made from a mixture of flour and water and dried in the sun on flat stones. The Egyptians first used ovens and made leavened bread. The yeast creates gas, making the dough rise. Traditionally bread has been made from whole grains: wheat, barley, rye and oats, ground into a meal which varied in quality. White bread was developed by the end of the 19th century by roller-milling, which removed the wheat germ to satisfy fashionable consumer demand. Today, some of the nutrients removed in the processing of bread are synthetically replaced.

breadfruit fruit of the tropical trees *Artocarpus communis* and *A. altilis* of the mulberry family Moraceae. It is highly nutritious and when baked is said to taste like bread. It is native to many South Pacific islands.

Breakspear /ˈbreɪkspɪə/ Nicholas. Original name of ◊Adrian IV, the only English pope.

bream deep-bodied, flattened fish *Abramis brama* of the carp family, growing to about 50 cm/1.6 ft, typically found in lowland rivers across Europe.

The sea-breams are also deep-bodied flattened fish, but belong to the family Sparidae, and are unrelated to the true breams. The red sea-bream *Pagellus bogaraveo* up to 45 cm/1.5 ft, is heavily exploited as a food fish in the Mediterranean.

Bream /briːm/ Julian (Alexander) 1933– . British virtuoso of the guitar and lute. He has revived much Elizabethan lute music and encouraged composition by contemporaries for both instruments. Britten and Henze have written for him.

breast one of a pair of organs on the upper front of the human female, also known as a ◊mammary gland. Each of the two breasts contains milk-producing cells, and a network of tubes or ducts that lead to an opening in the nipple.

Milk-producing cells in the breast do not become active until a woman has given birth to a baby. Breast milk is made from substances extracted from the mother's blood as it passes through the breasts. It contains all the nourishment a baby needs, including antibodies to help fight infection.

Breathalyzer /ˈbreθəlaɪzə/ trademark for an instrument for on-the-spot checking by police of the amount of alcohol consumed by a suspect driver. The driver breathes into a plastic bag connected to a tube containing a chemical (such as a diluted solution of potassium dichromate in 50% sulphuric acid) that changes colour in the presence of alcohol. Another method is to use a gas chromatograph, again from a breath sample.

Breath testing was introduced in the UK in 1967. The approved device is now the Lion Intoximeter 3000, which is used by police to indicate the proportion of alcohol in the blood.

breathing in terrestrial animals, the muscular movements whereby air is taken into the lungs and then expelled, a form of ◊gas exchange. Breathing is sometimes referred to as external respiration, for true respiration is a cellular (internal) process.

Lungs are specialized for gas exchange but are not themselves muscular, consisting of spongy material. In order for oxygen to be passed to the blood and carbon dioxide removed, air is forced in and out of the chest region by the ribs and accompanying intercostal muscles, the rate of breathing being controlled by the brain. High levels of activity lead to a greater demand for oxygen and a subsequent higher rate of breathing.

breathing rate the number of times a minute the lungs inhale and exhale. The rate increases during exercise because the muscles require an increased supply of oxygen and nutrients. At the same time very active muscles produce a greater volume of carbon dioxide, a waste gas that must be removed by the lungs via the blood.

The regulation of the breathing rate is under both voluntary and involuntary control, although a person can only forcibly stop breathing for a limited time. The regulatory system includes the use of chemoreceptors, which can detect levels of carbon dioxide in the blood. High concentrations of carbon dioxide, occurring for example during exercise, stimulate a fast breathing rate.

breccia a coarse clastic ◊sedimentary rock, made up of broken fragments (clasts) of pre-existing rocks. It is similar to ◊conglomerate but the fragments in breccia are large and jagged.

Brecht /brext/ Bertolt 1898–1956. German dramatist and poet, who aimed to destroy the 'suspension of disbelief' usual in the theatre and to express Marxist ideas. He adapted John Gay's *Beggar's Opera* as *Die Dreigroschenoper/The Threepenny Opera* 1928, set to music by Kurt Weill. Later plays include *Mutter Courage/Mother Courage* 1941, set during the Thirty Years' War, and *Der kaukasische Kreidekreis/The Caucasian Chalk Circle* 1949.

Breda, Treaty of /breɪdɑː/ 1667 treaty that ended the Second Anglo-Dutch War (1664–67). By the terms of the treaty, England gained New Amsterdam, which was renamed New York.

breeder reactor or *fast breeder* alternative names for ◊fast reactor, a type of nuclear reactor.

Breeders' Cup end-of-season horse race in the USA. Leading horses from the USA and Europe compete for $10 million in prize money, the top prize going to the winner of the Breeders' Cup Turf. It was first held 1984.

breeding in nuclear physics, a process in a reactor in which more fissionable material is produced than is consumed in running the reactor.

For example, plutonium-239 can be made from the relatively plentiful (but nonfissile) uranium-238, or uranium-233 can be produced from thorium. The Pu-239 or U-233 can then be used to fuel other reactors. The

French breeder reactor *Superphénix*, one of the most successful, generates 250 megawatts of electrical power.

Bremen /ˈbreɪmən/ industrial port (iron, steel, oil refining, chemicals, aircraft, shipbuilding, cars) in Germany, on the Weser 69 km/43 mi from the open sea; population (1988) 522,000.

Bremen was a member of the ◊Hanseatic League, and a free imperial city from 1646. It became a member of the North German Confederation 1867 and of the German Empire 1871.

Bremen /ˈbreɪmən/ administrative region (German *Land*) of Germany, consisting of the cities of Bremen and Bremerhaven; area 400 sq km/154 sq mi; population (1988) 652,000.

Brendel /ˈbrendl/ Alfred 1931– . Austrian pianist, known for his fastidious and searching interpretations of Beethoven, Schubert, and Liszt. He is the author of *Musical Thoughts and Afterthoughts* 1976 and *Music Sounded Out* 1990.

Brennan /ˈbrenən/ Christopher (John) 1870–1932. Australian Symbolist poet, influenced by Baudelaire and Mallarmé. Although one of Australia's greatest poets, he is virtually unknown outside his native country. His complex, idiosyncratic verse includes *Poems 1914* and *A Chant of Doom and Other Verses* 1918.

Brennan /ˈbrenən/ Walter 1894–1974. US actor, often seen in Westerns as the hero's sidekick. His work includes *The Westerner* 1940, *Bad Day at Black Rock* 1955, and *Rio Bravo* 1959.

Brennan /ˈbrenən/ William Joseph, Jr 1906– . US jurist and associate justice of the US Supreme Court 1956–90. He wrote many important Supreme Court majority decisions that assured the freedoms set forth in the First Amendment and established the rights of minority groups.

Brenner /ˈbrenə/ Sidney 1927– . South African scientist, one of the pioneers of genetic engineering. Brenner discovered messenger ◊RNA (a link between ◊DNA and the ◊ribosomes in which proteins are synthesized) 1960.

Brenner Pass /ˈbrenə/ lowest of the Alpine passes, 1,370 m/4,495 ft; it leads from Trentino–Alto Adige, Italy, to the Austrian Tirol, and is 19 km/12 mi long.

Brentano /brenˈtɑːnəʊ/ Klemens 1778–1842. German writer, leader of the Young ◊Romantics. He published a seminal collection of folk-tales and songs with Ludwig von ◊Arnim (*Des Knaben Wunderhorn*) 1805–08, and popularized the legend of the Lorelei (a rock in the river ◊Rhine). He also wrote mystic religious verse, as in *Romanzen vom Rosenkranz* 1852.

Brenton /ˈbrentən/ Howard 1942– . British dramatist, whose works include *The Romans in Britain* 1980, and a translation of Brecht's *The Life of Galileo*.

Brescia /ˈbreʃə/ (ancient *Brixia*) historic and industrial city (textiles, engineering, firearms, metal products) in N Italy, 84 km/52 mi E of Milan; population (1988) 199,000. It has medieval walls and two cathedrals (12th and 17th century).

Breslau /ˈbreslaʊ/ German name of ◊Wrocław, town in Poland.

Brest /brest/ naval base and industrial port (electronics, engineering, chemicals) on *Rade de Brest* (Brest Roads), a great bay at the western extremity of Bretagne, France; population (1983) 201,000. Occupied as a U-boat base by the Germans 1940–44, the town was destroyed by Allied bombing and rebuilt.

Brest /brest/ town in Belarus, on the river Bug and the Polish frontier; population (1987) 238,000. It was in Poland (*Brześć nad Bugiem*) until 1795 and again 1921–39. The *Treaty of* ◊Brest-Litovsk (an older Russian name of the town) was signed here.

Brest-Litovsk, Treaty of /ˈbrest lɪˈtɒfsk/ bilateral treaty signed 3 March 1918 between Russia and Germany, Austria–Hungary, and their allies. Under it, Russia agreed to recognize the independence of Georgia, Ukraine, Poland and the Baltic States, and pay heavy compensation. It was annulled under the Nov 1918 Armistice that ended World War I.

Bretagne /brɪˈtɑːni/ region of NW France, see ◊Brittany.

Brétigny, Treaty of /ˌbretɪnˈjiː/ treaty made between Edward III of England and John II of France in 1360 at the end of the first phase of the Hundred Years' War, under which Edward received Aquitaine and its dependencies in exchange for renunciation of his claim to the French throne.

Breton /ˈbretɒn/ André 1896–1966. French author, among the leaders of the ◊Dada art movement. *Les Champs magnétiques/Magnetic Fields* 1921, an experiment in automatic writing, was one of the products of the movement. He was also a founder of ◊Surrealism, publishing *Le Manifeste de surréalisme/Surrealist Manifesto* 1924. Other works include *Najda* 1928, the story of his love affair with a medium.

Breton language member of the Celtic branch of the Indo-European language family; the language of Brittany in France, related to Welsh and Cornish, and descended from the speech of Celts who left Britain as a consequence of the Anglo Saxon invasions of the 5th and 6th centuries. Officially neglected for centuries, Breton is now a recognized language of France.

Bretton Woods Conference the United Nations Monetary and Financial Conference held 1944 in Bretton Woods, New Hampshire, USA to discuss post-war international payments problems. The agreements reached on financial assistance and measures to stabilize exchange rates led to the creation of the International Bank for Reconstruction and Development in 1945 and the International Monetary Fund.

Breuer /ˈbrɔɪə/ Josef 1842–1925. Viennese physician, one of the pioneers of psychoanalysis. He applied it successfully to cases of hysteria, and collaborated with Freud in *Studien über Hysterie/Studies in Hysteria* 1895.

Breuer /ˈbrɔɪə/ Marcel 1902–1981. Hungarian-born architect and designer who studied and taught at the ◊Bauhaus school in Germany. His tubular steel chair 1925 was the first of its kind. He moved to England, then to the USA, where he was in partnership with Walter Gropius 1937–40. His buildings show an affinity with natural materials; the best known is the Bijenkorf, Rotterdam, the Netherlands (with Elzas) 1953.

Breuil /ˈbrɔɪ/ Henri 1877–1961. French prehistorian, professor of historic ethnography and director of research at the Institute of Human Palaeontology, Paris, from 1910. He established the genuine antiquity of Palaeolithic cave art and stressed the anthropological approach to human prehistory.

breviary (Latin, 'a summary or abridgement') in the Roman Catholic church, the book of instructions for reciting the daily services. It is usually in four volumes, one for each season.

brewing making of beer, ale, or other alcoholic beverages from ◊malt and ◊barley by steeping (mashing), boiling, and fermenting.

Mashing the barley releases its sugars. Yeast is then added, which contains the enzymes needed to convert the sugars into ethanol (alcohol) and carbon dioxide. Hops are added to give a bitter taste.

brewster unit (symbol B) for measuring the reaction of optical materials to stress, defined in terms of the slowing down of light passing through the material when it is stretched or compressed.

Brewster /ˈbruːstə/ David 1781–1868. Scottish physicist who made discoveries about the diffraction and polarization of light, and invented the kaleidoscope.

Brezhnev /ˈbreʒnef/ Leonid Ilyich 1906–1982. Soviet leader. A protégé of Stalin and Khrushchev, he came to power (after he and ◊Kosygin forced Khrushchev to resign) as general secretary of the Soviet Communist Party (CPSU) 1964–82 and was president 1977–82. Domestically he was conservative; abroad the USSR was established as a military and political superpower during the Brezhnev era, extending its influence in Africa and Asia.

Brezhnev, born in the Ukraine, joined the CPSU in the 1920s. In 1938 he was made head of propaganda by the new Ukrainian party chief Khrushchev and ascended in the local party hierarchy. After World War II he caught the attention of the CPSU leader Stalin, who inducted Brezhnev into the secretariat and Politburo 1952. Brezhnev was removed from these posts after Stalin's death 1953, but returned 1956 with Khrushchev's patronage. In 1960, as criticism of Khrushchev mounted, Brezhnev was moved to the ceremonial post of state president and began to criticize Khrushchev's policies.

Brezhnev stepped down as president 1963 and returned to the Politburo and secretariat. He was elected CPSU general secretary 1964, when Khrushchev was ousted, and gradually came to dominate the conservative and consensual coalition. In 1977 he regained the additional title of state president under the new constitution. He suffered an illness (thought to have been a stroke or heart attack) March–April 1976 that was believed to have affected his thought and speech so severely that he was not able to make decisions. These were made by his entourage, for example committing troops to Afghanistan to prop up the government.

Within the USSR, economic difficulties mounted; the Brezhnev era was a period of caution and stagnation, although outwardly imperialist.

Brezhnev Doctrine Soviet doctrine 1968 designed to justify the invasion of Czechoslovakia. It laid down for the USSR as a duty the direct maintenance of 'correct' socialism in countries within the Soviet sphere of influence. In 1979 it was extended, by the invasion of Afghanistan, to the direct establishment of 'correct' socialism in countries not already within its sphere. The doctrine was renounced by Mikhail ◊Gorbachev in 1989. Soviet troops were withdrawn from Afghanistan and the satellite states of E Europe were allowed to decide their own forms of government, with noncommunist and 'reform communist' governments being established from Sept 1989.

Brian /ˈbraɪən/ known as *Brian Boru* ('Brian of the Tribute') 926–1014. High king of Ireland from 976, who took Munster, Leinster, and Connacht to become ruler of all Ireland. He defeated the Norse at Clontarf, thus ending Norse control of Dublin, although he was himself killed. He was the last high king with jurisdiction over most of Scotland. His exploits were celebrated in several chronicles.

Briand /briˈɒn/ Aristide 1862–1932. French radical socialist politician. He was prime minister 1909-11, 1913, 1915–17, 1921–22, 1925–26 and 1929, and foreign minister 1925–32. In 1925 he concluded the ◊Locarno Pact (settling Germany's western frontier) and in 1928 the ◊Kellogg-Briand Pact renouncing war; in 1930 he outlined a scheme for a United States of Europe.

brick common building material, rectangular in shape, made of clay and fired in a kiln. Bricks are made by kneading a mixture of crushed clay and other materials into a stiff mud and extruding it into a ribbon. The ribbon is cut into individual bricks, which are fired at a temperature of up to about 1,000°C/1,800°F. Bricks may alternatively be pressed into shape in moulds.

Refractory bricks used to line furnaces are made from heat-resistant materials such as silica and dolomite. They must withstand operating temperatures of 1,500°C/2,700°F or more. Sun-dried bricks of mud reinforced with straw were first used in Mesopotamia some 8,000 years ago. Similar mud bricks, called adobe, are still used today in Mexico and other areas where the climate is warm and dry.

Established in England by the Romans, brickmaking was later reintroduced in the 13th century, becoming widespread in domestic building only in the 19th century. Brick sizes were first regulated 1729.

bridewealth or *brideprice* goods or property presented by a man's family to his prospective wife's as part of the marriage agreement. It was the usual practice among many societies in Africa, Asia, and the Pacific, and among many American Indian groups. In most European and S Asian countries the alternative custom was ◊dowry.

Bridewealth is regarded as compensation to the woman's family for giving her away in marriage, and it usually means that the children she bears will belong to her husband's family group rather than her own. It may require a large amount of valuables such as livestock, shell items, or cash.

bridewell jail or house of correction. The word comes from the royal palace of Bridewell, built 1522 by Henry VIII. In 1555 it was converted to a type of prison where the 'sturdy and idle' as well as certain petty criminals were made to labour. Various other towns set up their own institutions following the same regime.

bridge structure that provides a continuous path or road over water, valleys, ravines, or above other roads. Bridges can be designed according to four principles: *arch* for example, Sydney Harbour Bridge, Australia, a steel arch with a span of 503 m/1,650 ft; *beam or girder* for example, Rio-Niteroi, Guanabara Bay, Brazil, centre span 300 m/984 ft; length 13,900 m/8 mi 3,380 ft; ◊*cantilever* for example, Forth Rail Bridge, Scotland, 1,658 m/5,440 ft long with two main spans, two cantilevers each, one from each tower; *suspension* for example, Humber Bridge, England, with a centre span of 1,410 m/4,628 ft.

The types of bridge differ in the way they bear the weight of the structure and its load. Beam, or girder, bridges are supported at each end by the ground with the weight thrusting downwards. Cantilever bridges are a complex form of girder. Arch bridges thrust outwards but downwards at their ends; they are in compression. Suspension bridges use cables under tension to pull inwards against anchorages on either side of the span, so that the roadway hangs from the main cables by the network of vertical cables. Some bridges are too low to allow traffic to pass beneath easily, so they are designed with movable parts, like swing and draw bridges.

history In prehistory, people used logs or wove vines into ropes that were thrown across the obstacle. By 4000 BC arched structures of stone and/or brick were used in the Middle East, and the Romans built long arched spans, many of which are still standing. Wooden bridges proved vulnerable to fire and rot and many were replaced with cast and wrought iron, but these were disadvantaged by low tensile strength. The Bessemer process produced steel that made it possible to build long-lived framed structures that support great weight over long spans.

The world's longest bridge span is the main span of the Humber Estuary Bridge, England, at 1,410 m/4,626 ft. The single-span bridge under construction across the Messina Straits between Sicily and the mainland of Italy will be 3,320 m/10,892 ft long, the world's largest by far. Steel is pre-eminent in the construction of long-span bridges because of its high strength-to-weight ratio, but in other circumstances reinforced concrete has the advantage of lower maintenance costs. The Newport Transporter Bridge (built 1906 in Wales) is a high-level suspension bridge which carries a car suspended a few feet above the water. It was used in preference to a conventional bridge where expensive high approach roads would have to be built.

bridge card game derived from whist. First played among members of the Indian Civil Service about 1900, bridge was brought to England in 1903 and played at the Portland Club in 1908. It is played in two forms: ◊auction bridge and ◊contract bridge.

Bridges /ˈbrɪdʒɪz/ Robert (Seymour) 1844–1930. British poet, poet laureate from 1913, author of *The Testament of Beauty* 1929, a long philosophical poem. In 1918 he edited and published posthumously the poems of Gerard Manley ◊Hopkins.

Bridgetown /ˈbrɪdʒtaʊn/ port and capital of Barbados, founded 1628; population (1987) 8,000. Sugar is exported through the nearby deep-water port.

Bridget, St /ˈbrɪdʒɪt/ 453–523. A patron saint of Ireland, also known as *St Brigit* or *St Bride*. She founded a church and monastery at Kildare, and is said to have been the daughter of a prince of Ulster. Feast day 1 Feb.

Bridgewater /ˈbrɪdʒwɔːtə/ Francis Egerton, 3rd Duke of 1736–1803. Pioneer of British inland navigation. With James ◊Brindley as his engineer, he constructed 1762–72 the Bridgewater canal from Worsley to Manchester, and thence to the Mersey, a distance of 67.5 km/42 mi.

Bridgman /ˈbrɪdʒmən/ Percy Williams 1882–1961. US physicist. His research into machinery producing high pressure led in 1955 to the creation of synthetic diamonds by General Electric. He was awarded the Nobel Prize for Physics 1946.

Bridlington agreement /ˈbrɪdlɪŋtən/ in UK industrial relations, a set of principles agreed 1939 at a Trades Union Congress conference in Bridlington, Humberside, to prevent the poaching of members of one trade union by another, and to discourage breakaway unions.

brief in law, the written instructions sent by a solicitor to a barrister before a court hearing.

Traditionally, in the UK, briefs are tied with red tape and the barrister writes the outcome of the case on the 'backsheet' of the brief before returning it to the solicitor.

Brieux /briˈɜː/ Eugène 1858–1932. French dramatist, an exponent of the naturalistic problem play attacking social evils. His most powerful plays are *Les trois filles de M Dupont* 1897; *Les Avariés/ Damaged Goods* 1901, long banned for its outspoken treatment of syphilis; and *Maternité* 1903.

brigade military formation consisting of a minimum of two battalions, but more usually three or more, as well as supporting arms. There are typically about 5,000 soldiers in a brigade, which is commanded by a brigadier. Two or more brigades form a ◊division.

An infantry brigade is one that contains more infantry than armour; it is said to be 'infantry-heavy'. A typical armoured brigade ('armour-heavy') consists of two armoured battalions and one infantry battalion supported by an artillery battalion and a field-engineer battalion as well as other logistic support.

Briggs /ˈbrɪgz/ Barry 1934– . New Zealand motorcyclist who won four individual world speedway titles 1957–66 and took part in a record 87 world championship races.

Brighouse /ˈbrɪghaʊs/ Harold 1882–1958. English playwright. Born and bred in Lancashire, in his most famous play, *Hobson's Choice* 1916, he dealt with a Salford bootmaker's courtship, using the local idiom.

Bright /braɪt/ John 1811–1889. British Liberal politician, a campaigner for free trade, peace, and social reform. A Quaker millowner, he was among the founders of the Anti-Corn Law League in 1839, and was largely instrumental in securing the passage of the Reform Bill of 1867.

After entering Parliament in 1843 Bright led the struggle there for free trade, together with Richard ◊Cobden, which achieved success in 1846. His *laissez-faire* principles also made him a prominent opponent of factory reform. His influence was constantly exerted on behalf of peace, as when he opposed the Crimean War, Palmerston's aggressive policy in China, Disraeli's anti-Russian policy, and the bombardment of Alexandria. During the American Civil War he was outspoken in support of the North. He sat in Gladstone's cabinets as president of the Board of Trade 1868–70 and chancellor of the Duchy of Lancaster 1873–74 and 1880–82, but broke with him over the Irish Home Rule Bill. Bright owed much of his influence to his skill as a speaker.

Bright John Bright, British Victorian politician and humanitarian campaigner against the Corn Laws and the Crimean War.

Bright /braɪt/ Richard 1789–1858. British physician who described many conditions and linked oedema to kidney disease. *Bright's disease*, an inflammation of the kidneys, is named after him; see ◊nephritis.

Brighton /ˈbraɪtn/ resort on the E Sussex coast, England; population (1981) 146,000. It has Regency architecture and The Royal Pavilion 1782 in Oriental style. There are two piers and an aquarium. The University of Sussex was founded 1963.

history Originally a fishing village called Brighthelmstone, it became known as Brighton at the beginning of the 19th century, when it was already a fashionable health resort patronized by the Prince Regent, afterwards George IV. In 1990 the Royal Pavilion reopened after nine years of restoration.

brill flatfish *Scophthalmus laevis*, living in shallow water over sandy bottoms in the NE Atlantic and Mediterranean. It is a freckled sandy brown, and grows to 60 cm/2 ft.

Brindisi /ˈbrɪndɪzɪ/ (ancient *Brundisium*) port and naval base on the Adriatic, in Puglia, on the heel of Italy; population (1981) 90,000. Industries include food processing and petrochemicals. It is one of the oldest Mediterranean ports, at the end of the Appian Way from Rome. The poet Virgil died here 19 BC.

Brindley /ˈbrɪndlɪ/ James 1716–1772. British canal builder, the first to employ tunnels and aqueducts extensively, in order to reduce the number of locks on a direct-route canal. His 580 km/360 mi of canals included the Bridgewater (Manchester–Liverpool) and Grand Union (Manchester–Potteries) canals.

brine common name for a solution of sodium chloride ($NaCl$) in water. Brines are used extensively in the food-manufacturing industry for canning vegetables, pickling vegetables (sauerkraut manufacture), and curing meat. Industrially, brine is the source from which chlorine, caustic soda (sodium hydroxide), and sodium carbonate are made.

Brinell /brɪˈnel/ Johann Auguste 1849–1925. Swedish engineer who devised the Brinell hardness test, for measuring the hardness of substances, in 1900.

Brinell hardness test test of the hardness of a substance according to the area of indentation made by a 10 mm/0.4 in hardened steel or sintered tungsten carbide ball under standard loading conditions in a test machine. The resulting Brinell number is equal to the load (kg) divided by the surface area (mm²) and is named after its inventor Johann Brinell.

Brisbane /'brɪzbən/ industrial port (brewing, engineering, tanning, tobacco, shoes; oil pipeline from Moonie), capital of Queensland, E Australia, near the mouth of Brisbane river, dredged to carry ocean-going ships; population (1986) 1,171,300.

Brisbane /'brɪzbən/ Thomas Makdougall 1773–1860. Scottish soldier, colonial administrator, and astronomer. After serving in the Napoleonic Wars under Wellington, he was governor of New South Wales 1821–25. Brisbane in Queensland is named after him. He catalogued over 7,000 stars.

brisling processed form of sprat *Sprattus sprattus* a small herring, fished in Norwegian fjords, then seasoned and canned.

bristlecone pine The oldest living species of ◊pine.

bristletail primitive wingless insect of the order Thysanura. Up to 2 cm/0.8 in long, bristletails have a body tapering from front to back, two long antennae, and three 'tails' at the rear end. They include the *silverfish Lepisma saccharina* and the *firebrat Thermobia domestica*. Two-tailed bristletails constitute another insect order, the Diplura. They live under stones and fallen branches, feeding on decaying material.

Bristol /'brɪstəl/ industrial port (aircraft engines, engineering, microelectronics, tobacco, chemicals, paper, printing), administrative headquarters of Avon, SW England; population (1991 est) 370,300. The old docks have been redeveloped for housing, industry, yachting facilities, and the National Lifeboat Museum. Further developments include a new city centre, with Brunel's Temple Meads railway station at its focus, and a weir across the Avon nearby to improve the waterside environment.

features 12th-century cathedral; 14th-century St Mary Redcliffe; 16th-century Acton Court, built by Sir Nicholas Poynz, a courtier of Henry VIII; Georgian residential area of Clifton; the Clifton Suspension Bridge designed by Brunel, and his *SS Great Britain*, which is being restored in dry dock.

history John Cabot sailed from here 1497 to Newfoundland, and there was a great trade with the American colonies and the West Indies in the 17th–18th centuries, including slaves. The poet Chatterton was born here.

Bristow /'brɪstəʊ/ Eric 1957– . English darts player nicknamed 'the Crafty Cock-

ney'. He has won all the game's major titles, including the world professional title a record five times between 1980 and 1986.

Britain /'brɪtn/ or *Great Britain* island off the NW coast of Europe, one of the British Isles. It consists of ◊England, ◊Scotland, and ◊Wales, and is part of the ◊United Kingdom. The name is derived from the Roman name Britannia, which in turn is derived from ancient Celtic name of the inhabitants, *Bryttas*.

Britain, ancient /'brɪtn/ period in the history of the British Isles (excluding Ireland) from prehistory to the Roman occupation. After the last glacial retreat of the Ice Age about 15,000 BC, Britain was inhabited by hunters who became neolithic farming villagers. They built stone circles and buried their chiefs in ◊barrow mounds. Around 400 BC Britain was conquered by the ◊Celts and 54 BC by the Romans under Julius Caesar; ◊Boudicca led an uprising against their occupation.

The original inhabitants gradually changed from hunting and gathering to keeping livestock and growing corn; traces of human occupation in the *Old Stone Age* have been found at Cheddar Caves, Somerset. In the *New Stone Age* the farming villagers buried their chiefs in long barrows; remains of flint mining can be found at Grimes Graves, Norfolk. In the *Bronze Age* burials were made in round barrows. About 2300 BC, the ◊Beaker people invaded, and left traces of their occupation at Avebury and Stonehenge (stone circles). About 700 BC the *Iron Age* began, and shortly afterwards Britain was conquered by the Celts, who built hillforts and left burial sites containing chariots. The Celts were a tall, fair-haired people who migrated in two waves from Europe. First came the Goidelic Celts, of whom traces may still be seen in the Gaels of Ireland and the Scottish Highlands; there followed the Brythonic Celts or Bretons, who were closely allied in descent and culture to the Gauls of France. The early Britons were highly skilled in pottery and metalwork. Tin mines in Cornwall attracted merchant sailors from Carthage. In 55–54 BC Julius Caesar raided England. AD 43 marked the start of the Roman conquest; among the most visible surviving remains are those found in Bath, Fishbourne (near Chichester), Hadrian's Wall, Watling Street, London (Temple of Mithras), Dover, St Albans, and Dorchester. In 407 the Romans withdrew, but partly reoccupied the country about 417–27 and about 450. For later history, see ◊England, history; ◊Scotland, history; ◊Wales, history; and ◊United Kingdom.

Britain, Battle of /'brɪtn/ World War II air battle between German and British air forces over Britain lasting 10 Jul–31 Oct 1940.

At the outset the Germans had the advantage because they had seized airfields in the Netherlands, Belgium, and France, which were basically safe from attack and from which SE England was within easy range. On 1 Aug 1940 the Luftwaffe had about 4,500 aircraft of all kinds, compared to about 3,000 for the RAF. The Battle of Britain had been intended as a preliminary to the German invasion plan *Seelöwe* (Sea Lion), which Hitler indefinitely postponed 17 Sept and abandoned 10 Oct, choosing instead to invade the USSR.

Britannicus /brɪ'tænɪkəs/ Tiberius Claudius *c.* AD 41–55. Roman prince, son of the Emperor Claudius and Messalina; so-called from his father's expedition to Britain. He was poisoned by Nero.

British Antarctic Territory colony created in 1962 and comprising all British territories S of latitude 60° S: the South Orkney Islands, the South Shetland Islands, the Antarctic Peninsula and all adjacent lands, and Coats Land, extending to the South Pole; total land area 660,000 sq km/170,874 sq mi. Population (exclusively scientific personnel): about 300.

British Broadcasting Corporation (BBC) the UK state-owned broadcasting network. It operates television and national and local radio stations, and is financed solely by the sale of television viewing licences. It is not allowed to carry advertisements, but overseas radio broadcasts (World Service) have a government subsidy.

The BBC was converted from a private company (established 1922) to a public body under royal charter 1927. Under the Charter, news programmes were required to be politically impartial. The first director-general 1922–1938 was John Reith.

British Columbia /kə'lʌmbɪə/ province of Canada on the Pacific.
area 947,800 sq km/365,851 sq mi
capital Victoria
towns Vancouver, Prince George, Kamloops, Kelowna

physical Rocky Mountains and Coast Range; deeply indented coast; rivers include the Fraser and Columbia; over 80 lakes; more than half the land is forested
products fruit and vegetables; timber and wood products; fish; coal, copper, iron, lead; oil and natural gas; hydroelectricity
population (1986) 2,889,000
history Capt Cook explored the coast in 1778; a British colony was founded on Vancouver Island in 1849, and the gold rush of 1858 extended settlement to the mainland; it became a province in 1871. In 1885 the Canadian Pacific Railroad linking British Columbia to the E coast was completed.

British Commonwealth of Nations former official name of the ◊Commonwealth.

British Empire the various territories all over the world conquered or colonized by Britain from about 1600, most now independent or ruled by other powers; the British Empire was at its largest at the end of World War I, with over 25% of the world's population and area. The ◊Commonwealth is composed of former and remaining territories of the British Empire.

The first successful British colony was Jamestown, Virginia, founded 1607. British settlement spread up and down the east coast of North America and by 1664, when the British secured New Amsterdam (New York) from the Dutch, there was a continuous fringe of colonies from the present South Carolina in the south to what is now New Hampshire. These colonies, and others formed later, had their own democratic institutions. The attempt of George III and his minister Lord North to coerce the colonists into paying special taxes to Britain roused them to resistance, which came to a head in the ◊American Revolution 1775–81 and led to the creation of the United States of America from the 13 English colonies then lost. Colonies and trading posts were set up in many parts of the world by the British, who also captured them from other European empire builders.

Settlements were made in the Gambia and on the Gold Coast of Africa 1618; in Bermuda 1609 and other islands of the West Indies; Jamaica was taken from Spain 1655; in Canada, Acadia (Nova Scotia) was secured from France by the Treaty of Utrecht 1713, which recognized Newfoundland and Hudson Bay (as well as Gibraltar in Europe) as British. New France (Québec), Cape Breton Island, and Prince Edward Island became

British as a result of the Seven Years' War 1756–63.

In the Far East, the ◊East India Company, chartered 1600, set up a number of factories, as their trading posts were called, and steadily increased its possessions and the territories over which it held treaty rights up to the eve of the ◊Indian Mutiny 1857.

Although this revolt was put down, it resulted in the taking over of the government of British India by the crown 1858; Queen Victoria was proclaimed empress of India 1 Jan 1877. Ceylon (now Sri Lanka) had also been annexed to the East India Company 1796, and Burma (now Myanmar), after a series of Anglo-Burmese Wars from 1824, became a province of British India 1886. Burma and Ceylon became independent 1948 and the republic of Sri Lanka dates from 1972. British India, as the two dominions of India and Pakistan, was given independence in 1947. In 1950 India became a republic but remained a member of the Commonwealth.

Constitutional development in Canada started with an act of 1791 which set up Lower Canada (Québec), mainly French-speaking, and Upper Canada (Ontario), mainly English-speaking. In the War of 1812, the USA wrongly assumed that Canada would join the union. But there was sufficient discontent there to lead to rebellion 1837 in both Canadas. After the suppression of these risings, Lord Durham was sent out to advise on the affairs of British North America; his report, published 1839, became the basis for the future structure of the Empire. In accordance with its recommendations, the two Canadas were united 1840 and given a representative legislative council: the beginning of colonial self-government. With the British North America Act 1867, the self-governing dominion of Canada came into existence; to the original union of Ontario, Québec, New Brunswick, and Nova Scotia were later added further territories until the federal government of Canada controlled all the northern part of the continent except Alaska.

In the antipodes, colonization began with the desire to find a place for penal settlement after the loss of the original American colonies. The first shipload of British convicts landed in Australia 1788 on the site of the future city of Sydney. New South Wales was opened to free settlers 1819, and in 1853 transportation of convicts was abolished. Before the end of the century five Australian colonies—New South Wales, Western Australia, South Australia, Victoria, Queensland—and the island colony of Tasmania had each achieved self-government; an act of the Imperial Parliament at Westminster created the federal commonwealth of Australia, an independent dominion, 1901. New Zealand, annexed 1840, was at first a dependency of New South Wales. It became a separate colony 1853 and a dominion 1907.

The Cape of Good Hope in South Africa was occupied by two English captains 1620, but neither the home government nor the East India Company was interested. The Dutch occupied it 1650, and Cape Town remained a port of call for their East India Company until 1795 when, French revolutionary armies having occupied the Dutch Republic, the British seized it to keep it from the French. Under the Treaty of Paris 1814, the UK bought Cape Town from the new kingdom of the Netherlands for $6 million. British settlement began 1824 on the coast of Natal, proclaimed a British colony 1843. The need to find new farmland and establish independence from British rule led a body of Boers (Dutch 'farmers') from the Cape to make the Great Trek northeast 1836, to found Transvaal and Orange Free State. Conflict between the British government, which claimed sovereignty over those areas (since the settlers were legally British subjects), and the Boers culminated, after the discovery of gold in the Boer territories, in the South African War 1899–1902, which brought Transvaal and Orange Free State definitely under British sovereignty. Given self-government 1907, they were formed, with Cape Colony (self-governing 1872) and Natal (self-governing 1893), into the Union of South Africa 1910.

In the early years of the century, a series of Colonial Conferences (renamed Imperial Conferences 1907) were held by the representatives of Australia, New Zealand, Canada, and South Africa, together with the United Kingdom. These four self-governing countries came to be known as Dominions within the British Empire. Their meetings were the basis for the idea of the Commonwealth of Nations.

The British South Africa Company, chartered 1889, extended British influence over Southern Rhodesia (a colony 1923) and Northern Rhodesia (a protectorate 1924); with Nyasaland, taken under British protection 1891, the Rhodesias were formed into a federation 1953–63 with representative government. Uganda was made a British protectorate 1894. Kenya, formerly a protectorate, became a colony 1920, certain districts on the coast forming part of the sultan of Zanzibar's dominions remained a protectorate.

In W Africa, Sierra Leone colony was founded 1788 with the cession of a strip of land to provide a home for liberated slaves; a protectorate was established over the hinterland 1896. British influence in Nigeria began through he activities of the National Africa Company (the Royal Niger Company from 1886), which bought Lagos from an African chief 1861 and steadily extended its hold over the Niger Valley until it surrendered its charter 1899; in 1900 the two protectorates of North and South Nigeria were proclaimed. World War I ousted Germany from the African continent, and in 1921–22, under League of Nations mandate, Tanganyika was transferred to British administration, SW Africa to South Africa; Cameroons and Togoland, in West Africa, were divided between Britain and France. The establishment of the greater part of Ireland as the Irish Free State, with dominion status, occurred 1922. A new constitution adopted by the Free State 1937 dropped the name and declared Ireland (Eire) to be a 'sovereign independent state'; in 1949 Southern Ireland became a republic outside the Commonwealth, hough remaining in a special relationship with Britain.

British Empire, Order of the British order of chivalry, instituted by George V in 1917. There are military and civil divisions, and the ranks are GBE, Knight Grand Cross or Dame Grand Cross; KBE, Knight Commander; DBE, Dame Commander; CBE, Commander; OBE, Officer; MBE, Member.

British Honduras /hɒnˈdjuərəs/ former name of ◊Belize.

British Indian Ocean Territory British colony in the Indian Ocean directly administered by the Foreign and Commonwealth Office. It consists of the Chagos Archipelago some 1,900 km/1,200 mi NE of Mauritius.
area 60 sq km/23 sq mi
features lagoons; US naval and air base on Diego Garcia
products copra, salt fish, tortoiseshell
population (1982) 3,000
history purchased in 1965 for $3 million by Britain from Mauritius to provide a joint US/UK base. The island of Aldabra, Farquhar, and Desroches, some 485 km/300 mi

N of Madagascar, originally formed part of the British Indian Ocean Territory but were returned to the administration of the Seychelles in 1976.

British Isles group of islands off the NW coast of Europe, consisting of Great Britain (England, Wales, and Scotland), Ireland, the Channel Islands, the Orkney and Shetland islands, the Isle of Man, and many other islands that are included in various counties, such as the Isle of Wight, Scilly Isles, Lundy Island, and the Inner and Outer Hebrides. The islands are divided from Europe by the North Sea, Strait of Dover, and the English Channel, and face the Atlantic to the W.

British Legion organization to promote the welfare of British veterans of war service and their dependants. Established under the leadership of Douglas Haig in 1921 (royal charter 1925) it became the *Royal British Legion* 1971; it is nonpolitical.

British Library national library of the UK. Created 1973, it comprises the *reference division* (the former library departments of the British Museum, being rehoused in Euston Road, London); *lending division* at Boston Spa, Yorkshire, from which full text documents and graphics can be sent by satellite link to other countries; *bibliographic services division* (incorporating the British National Bibliography); and the *National Sound Archive* in South Kensington, London.

British Museum largest museum of the UK. Founded in 1753, it opened in London in 1759. In 1881 the Natural History Museum was transferred to South Kensington.

The museum began with the purchase of Hans Sloane's library and art collection, and the subsequent acquisition of the Cottonian, Harleian, and other libraries. It was first housed at Montagu House in Bloomsbury. Its present buildings (1823–47) were designed by Robert Smirke, with later extensions in the circular reading room 1857, and the north wing or Edward VII galleries 1914.

British Petroleum (BP) one of the world's largest oil concerns and Britain's largest company, with more than 128,000 employees in 70 countries. It was formed as the Anglo-Persian Oil Company 1909 and acquired the chemical interests of the Distillers Company 1967.

British Somaliland /səmɑlilænd/ a British protectorate comprising over 176,000 sq km/67,980 sq mi of territory on the Somali coast of E Africa from 1884 until the independence of Somalia in 1960. British authorities were harassed by Somali nationalists under the leadership of Muhammad bin Abdullah Hassan.

British Standards Institute (BSI) UK national standards body. Although government funded, the institute is independent. The BSI interprets international technical standards for the UK, and also sets its own.

For consumer goods, it sets standards which products should reach (the BS standard), as well as testing products to see that they conform to that standard (as a result of which the product may be given the BSI 'kite' mark).

British Technology Group (BTG) UK corporation exploiting inventions derived from public or private sources, usually jointly with industrial firms. It was set up 1967 under the Development of Inventions Acts 1948–65 and known as the National Research Development Council until 1981. BTG holds more than 8,000 patents and was responsible for marketing the hovercraft, magnetic resonance imaging (MRI), and cephalosporin antibiotics. In 1990 it returned royalties worth £13 million to British research bodies.

British Telecom (BT) British company that formed part of the Post Office until 1980, and was privatized in 1984. It is responsible for ◊telecommunications, including the telephone network, and radio and television broadcasting. Previously a monopoly, it now faces commercial competition for some of its services. It operates Britain's ◊viewdata network called ◊Prestel.

British thermal unit imperial unit (symbol Btu) of heat, now replaced in the SI system by the ◊joule (one British thermal unit is approximately 1,055 joules). Burning one cubic foot of natural gas releases about 1,000 Btu of heat.

One British thermal unit is defined as the amount of heat required to raise the temperature of 0.45 kg/1 lb of water by 1°F. The exact value depends on the original temperature of the water.

British Virgin Islands part of the ◊Virgin Islands group in the W est Indies.

British Volunteer Programme name embracing the various schemes under which volunteers from the UK are sent to work in overseas developing countries since 1966. Voluntary Service Overseas (VSO), (1958) is

the best known of these organizations, which inspired the US ◊Peace Corps.

Brittain /ˈbrɪtn/ Vera 1894–1970. English socialist writer, a nurse to the troops overseas 1915–19, as told in her *Testament of Youth* 1933; *Testament of Friendship* 1950 commemorated Winifred ◊Holtby.

Brittan /ˈbrɪtn/ Leon 1939– . British Conservative politician and lawyer. Chief secretary to the Treasury 1981–83, home secretary 1983–85, secretary for trade and industry 1985–86 (resigned over his part in the ◊Westland affair) and senior European Commissioner from 1988.

Brittany /ˈbrətænj/ (French *Bretagne*, Breton *Breiz*) region of NW France in the Breton peninsula between the Bay of Biscay and the English Channel; area 27,200 sq km/10,499 sq mi; population (1987) 2,767,000. Its capital is Rennes and includes the *départements* of Côtes-du-Nord, Finistère, Ille-et-Vilaine, and Morbihan. It is a farming region.
history Brittany was the Gallo-Roman province of Armorica after being conquered by Julius Caesar 56 BC. It was devastated by Norsemen after the Roman withdrawal. It was established under the name of Brittany in the 5th century AD by Celts fleeing the Anglo-Saxon invasion of Britain. It became a strong, expansionist state that maintained its cultural and political independence, despite pressure from the Carolingians, Normans, and Capetians. In 1171, the duchy of Brittany was inherited by Geoffrey, son of Henry II of England, and remained in the Angevin dynasty's possession until 1203, when Geoffrey's son Arthur was murdered by King ◊John, and the title passed to the Capetian Peter of Dreux. Under the Angevins, feudalism was introduced, and French influence increased under the Capetians. By 1547 it had been formally annexed by France, and the ◊Breton language was banned in education. A separatist movement developed after World War II, and there has been guerrilla activity.

Britten /ˈbrɪtn/ (Edward) Benjamin, 1913–1976. English composer. He often wrote for the individual voice; for example, the role in the opera *Peter Grimes* 1945, based on verses by Crabbe, was created for Peter ◊Pears. Among his many works are the *Young Person's Guide to the Orchestra* 1946; the chamber opera *The Rape of Lucretia* 1946; *Billy Budd* 1951; *A Midsummer Night's Dream* 1960; and *Death in Venice* 1973.

brittle-star any member of the echinoderm class Ophiuroidea. A brittle-star resembles a starfish, and has a small, central, rounded body and long, flexible, spiny arms used for walking. The small brittle-star *Amphipholis squamata* is greyish, about 4.5 cm/2 in across, and found on sea bottoms worldwide. It broods its young, and its arms can be luminous.

BRM abbreviation for *British Racing Motors* racing-car manufacturer founded 1949 by Raymond Mays (1899–1980). Their early days in Grand Prix racing were disastrous and it was not until 1956 that they started having moderate success. Their first Grand Prix win was 1959, and in the next 30 years they won 17 Grands Prix.

Brno /ˈbɜːnəʊ/ industrial city in the Czech Republic (chemicals, arms, textiles, machinery); population (1984) 380,800. Now the second largest city in the Czech Republic, Brno was formerly the capital of the Austrian crown land of Moravia.

Broad /brɔːd/ Charles Dunbar 1887–1971. British philosopher. His books include *Perception, Physics and Reality* 1914, and *Lectures on Psychic Research* 1962, discussing scientific evidence for survival after death.

broadbill primitive perching bird of the family Eurylaimidae, found in Africa and S Asia. Broadbills are forest birds and are often found near water. They are gregarious and noisy, have brilliant coloration and wide bills, and feed largely on insects.

broadcasting the transmission of sound and vision programmes by radio and television. Broadcasting may be organized under complete state control, as in the former USSR, or private enterprise, as in the USA, or may operate under a compromise system, as in Britain, where there is a television and radio service controlled by the state-regulated ◊British Broadcasting Corporation (BBC) and also the commercial ◊Independent Television Commission (known as the Independent Broadcasting Authority before 1991).

In the USA, broadcasting is only limited by the issue of licences from the Federal Communications Commission to competing commercial companies; in Britain, the BBC is a centralized body appointed by the state and responsible to Parliament, but with policy and programme content not controlled by the state; in Japan, which ranks next to the USA in the number of television sets owned, there is a semigovernmental radio and television broadcasting corporation (NHK) and numerous private television companies.

Television broadcasting entered a new era with the introduction of high-powered communications satellites in the 1980s. The signals broadcast by these satellites are sufficiently strong to be picked up by a small dish aerial located, for example, on the roof of a house. Direct broadcast by satellite thus became a feasible alternative to land-based television services. See also ◊cable television.

Broadcasting Standards Council UK body concerned with handling complaints on treatment of sex and violence. It was established 1988 and is responsible for drawing up a code on standards of taste and decency in TV and radio.

broad-leaved tree another name for a tree belonging to the ◊angiosperms, such as ash, beech, oak, maple, or birch. The leaves are generally broad and flat, in contrast to the needlelike leaves of most ◊conifers. See also ◊deciduous tree.

Broadmoor /ˈbrɔːdmɔː/ special hospital (established 1863) in Crowthorne, Berkshire, England, for those formerly described as 'criminally insane'. Patients are admitted if considered by a psychiatrist to be both mentally disordered and potentially dangerous. The average length of stay is eight years; in 1991 patients numbered 515.

Broads, Norfolk /brɔːdz/ area of navigable lakes and rivers in England, see ◊Norfolk Broads.

Broadway /ˈbrɔːdweɪ/ major avenue in New York running from the tip of Manhattan NW and crossing Times Square at 42nd Street, at the heart of the theatre district, where Broadway is known as 'the Great White Way'. New York theatres situated outside this area are described as *off-Broadway*; those even smaller and farther away are *off-off-Broadway*.

Broch /brɒx/ Hermann 1886–1951. Austrian novelist, who used experimental techniques in *Die Schlafwandler/The Sleepwalkers* 1932, *Der Tod des Vergil/The Death of Virgil* 1945, and *Die Schuldlosen/The Guiltless*, a novel in 11 stories. He moved to the US 1938 after being persecuted by the Nazis.

Brocken /ˈbrɒkən/ highest peak of the Harz Mountains (1,142 m/3,746 ft) in Germany. On 1 May (Walpurgis night), witches are said to gather here. The *Brocken Spectre* is a phenomenon of mountainous areas, so named because it was first scientifically observed at Brocken in 1780. The greatly enlarged shadow of the observer, accompanied by coloured rings, is cast by a low sun upon a cloud bank.

brocket name for a male European red deer in its second year, when it has short, straight, pointed antlers. Brocket deer, genus *Mazama*, include a number of species of small, shy, solitary deer found in Central and South America. They are up to 1.3 m/4 ft in body length and 65 cm/2 ft at the shoulder, and have similar small, straight antlers even when adult.

broderie anglaise (French 'English embroidery') embroidered fabric, usually white cotton, in which holes are cut in patterns and oversewn, often to decorate lingerie, shirts, and skirts.

Brodsky /'brɒdski/ Joseph 1940– . Russian poet, who emigrated to the USA in 1972. His work, often dealing with themes of exile,

Brodsky The protégé of the great Russian poet Anna Akhmatova during the 1950s, Joseph Brodsky was arrested by the Soviet authorities 1964 as a 'parasite'.

is admired for its wit and economy of language, particularly in its use of understatement. Many of his poems, written in Russian, have been translated into English (*A Part of Speech* 1980). More recently he has also written in English. He was awarded the Nobel Prize for Literature in 1987 and became US poet laureate 1991.

Broglie /də 'brəʊli/ Louis de, 7th Duc de Broglie 1892–1987. French theoretical physicist. He established that all subatomic particles can be described either by particle equations or by wave equations, thus laying the foundations of wave mechanics. He was awarded the 1929 Nobel Prize for Physics.

Broglie /də 'brəʊli/ Maurice de, 6th Duc de Broglie 1875–1960. French physicist. He worked on X-rays and gamma rays, and helped to establish the Einsteinian description of light in terms of photons. He was the brother of Louis de Broglie.

Broken Hill /'brəʊkən/ former name (until 1967) of ◊Kabwe, town in Zambia.

brolga or *native companion*, Australian crane *Grus rubicunda*, about 1.5 m/5 ft tall, mainly grey with a red patch on the head.

Bromberg /'brɒmbɜːg/ German name of ◊Bydgoszcz, port in Poland.

brome grass any annual grasses of the genus *Bromus* of the temperate zone; some are used for forage, but many are weeds.

Soft brome *Bromus interruptus*, discovered in England 1849 and widespread in 1970, was thought to have died out by 1972, until rediscovered 1979 in an Edinburgh botanical collection.

bromeliad any tropical or subtropical plant of the pineapple family Bromeliaceae, usually with stiff leathery leaves and bright flower spikes.

Bromeliads are native to tropical America, where there are some 1,400 species. Some are terrestrial, growing in habitats ranging from scrub desert to tropical forest floor. Many, however, are epiphytes and grow on trees. The epiphytes are supported by the tree but do not take nourishment from it, using rain and decayed plant and animal remains for independent sustenance.

In many bromeliads the stiff, leathery leaves are arranged in rosettes, and in some the leaf bases trap water to form little pools, in which organisms ranging from microorganisms to frogs may pass their whole life cycles. Many bromeliads have attractive flowers; often, too, the leaves are coloured and patterned. They are therefore popular greenhouse plants.

Bromfield /'brɒmfiːld/ Louis 1896–1956. US novelist. Among his books are *The Strange Case of Miss Annie Spragg* 1928, *The Rains Came* 1937, and *Mrs Parkington* 1943, dealing with the golden age of New York society.

bromide salt of the halide series containing the Br⁻ ion, which is formed when a bromine atom gains an electron.

The term 'bromide' is sometimes used to describe an organic compound containing a bromine atom, even though it is not ionic. Modern naming uses the term 'bromo-' in such cases. For example, the compound C_2H_5Br is now called bromoethane; its traditional name, still used sometimes, is ethyl bromide.

bromine (Greek *bromos* 'stench') dark, reddish-brown, nonmetallic element, a volatile liquid at room temperature, symbol Br, atomic number 35, relative atomic mass 79.904. It is a member of the ◊halogen group, has an unpleasant odour, and is very irritating to mucous membranes. Its salts are known as bromides.

Bromine was formerly extracted from salt beds but is now mostly obtained from sea water, where it occurs in small quantities. Its compounds are used in photography and in the chemical and pharmaceutical industries.

bromocriptine drug that mimics the actions of the naturally occurring biochemical substance dopamine, a neurotransmitter. Bromocriptine acts on the pituitary gland to inhibit the release of prolactin, the hormone that regulates lactation, and thus reduces or suppresses milk production. It is also used in the treatment of ◊Parkinson's disease.

Bromocriptine may also be given to control excessive prolactin secretion and to treat prolactinoma (a hormone-producing tumour). Recent research has established its effectiveness in reversing some cases of infertility.

bronchiole small-bore air tube found in the vertebrate lung responsible for delivering air to the main respiratory surfaces. Bronchioles lead off from the larger bronchus and branch extensively before terminating in the many thousand alveoli that form the bulk of lung tissue.

bronchitis inflammation of the bronchii (air passages) of the lungs, usually caused initially by a viral infection, such as a cold

or flu. It is aggravated by environmental pollutants, especially smoking, and results in a persistent cough, irritated mucus-secreting glands, and large amounts of sputum. The total number of deaths from bronchitis in England and Wales 1988 was 7,796.

bronchus one of a pair of large tubes (bronchii) splitting off from the windpipe and passing into the vertebrate lung. Apart from their size, bronchii differ from the bronchioles in possessing cartilaginous rings, which give rigidity and prevent collapse during breathing movements.

Numerous glands secrete a slimy mucus, which traps dust and other particles; the mucus is constantly being propelled upwards to the mouth by thousands of tiny hairs or cilia. The bronchus is adversely effected by several respiratory diseases and by smoking, which damages the cilia and therefore the lung-cleaning mechanism.

Brontë /'brɒnti/ three English novelists, daughters of a Yorkshire parson. *Charlotte* (1816–1855), notably with *Jane Eyre* 1847 and *Villette* 1853, reshaped autobiographical material into vivid narrative. *Emily* (1818–1848) in *Wuthering Heights* 1847 expressed the intensity and nature mysticism which also pervades her poetry (*Poems* 1846). The more modest talent of *Anne* (1820–49) produced *Agnes Grey* 1847 and *The Tenant of Wildfell Hall* 1848.

The Brontës were brought up by an aunt at Haworth rectory (now a museum) in Yorkshire. During 1848–49 Emily, Anne, and their brother Patrick Branwell all died of tuberculosis, aided in Branwell's case by alcohol and opium addiction; he is remembered for his portrait of the sisters.

brontosaurus former name of a type of large, plant-eating dinosaur, now better known as ◊apatosaurus.

Bronx, the /brɒŋks/ borough of New York City, USA, NE of Harlem River; area 109 sq km/ 42 sq mi; population (1980) 1,169,000. Largely residential, it is named after an early Dutch settler, James Bronck. The Bronx Zoo is here.

bronze alloy of copper and tin, yellow or brown in colour. It is harder than pure copper, more suitable for ◊casting, and also resists ◊corrosion. Bronze may contain as much as 25% tin, together with small amounts of other metals, mainly lead.

Bronze is one of the first metallic alloys known and used widely by early peoples during the period of history known as the ◊Bronze Age.

Bell metal, the bronze used for casting bells, contains 15% or more tin. **Phosphor bronze** is hardened by the addition of a small percentage of phosphorus. **Silicon bronze** (for telegraph wires) and **aluminium bronze** are similar alloys of copper with silicon or aluminium and small amounts of iron, nickel, or manganese, but usually no tin.

Bronze Age stage of prehistory and early history when bronze became the first metal worked extensively and used for tools and weapons. It developed out of the Stone Age, preceded the Iron Age and may be dated 5000–1200 BC in the Middle East and about 2000–500 BC in Europe. Recent discoveries in Thailand suggest that the Far East, rather than the Middle East, was the cradle of the Bronze Age.

Mining and metalworking were the first specialized industries, and the invention of the wheel during this time revolutionized transport. Agricultural productivity (which began during the New Stone Age, or Neolithic period, about 10,000 BC), and hence the size of the population that could be supported, was transformed by the ox-drawn plough.

Bronzino /brɒndˈziːnəʊ/ Agnolo 1503–1572. Italian painter active in Florence, court painter to Cosimo I, Duke of Tuscany. He painted in an elegant, Mannerist style and is best known for portraits and the allegory *Venus, Cupid, Folly and Time* about 1545 (National Gallery, London).

Brook /brʊk/ Peter 1925– . English director renowned for his experimental productions. His work with the Royal Shakespeare Company included a production of Shakespeare's *A Midsummer Night's Dream* 1970, set in a white gymnasium and combining elements of circus and commedia dell'arte. In the same year he established Le Centre International de Créations Théâtrales/The International Centre for Theatre Research in Paris. Brook's later productions transcend Western theatre conventions and include *The Conference of the Birds* 1973, based on a Persian story, and *The Mahabarata* 1985/8, a cycle of three plays based on the Hindu epic. His films include *Lord of the Flies* 1962 and *Meetings with Remarkable Men* 1979.

Brooke /brʊk/ James 1803–1868. British administrator who became rajah of Sarawak, on Borneo, 1841.

Born near Varanasi, he served in the army of the East India Company. In 1838 he headed a private expedition to Borneo, where he helped to suppress a revolt, and when the sultan gave him the title of rajah of Sarawak, Brooke became known as the 'white rajah'. He was succeeded as rajah by his nephew, Sir Charles Johnson (1829–1917), whose son Sir Charles Vyner (1874–1963) in 1946 arranged for the transfer of Sarawak to the British crown.

Brooke /brʊk/ Peter Leonard 1934– . British Conservative politician, a member of Parliament from 1977. He was appointed chair of the Conservative Party by Margaret Thatcher 1987, and was made Northern Ireland secretary 1989–92.

Brooke was educated at Oxford and worked as a management consultant in New York and Brussels. The son of a former home secretary, Lord Brooke of Cumnor, he became an MP in 1977 and entered Thatcher's government in 1979. Following a number of junior appointments, he succeeded Norman Tebbit as chair of the Conservative Party 1987. After an undistinguished two years in that office, he succeeded Tom King as Northern Ireland secretary 1989. He aroused criticism (and praise) for observing that at some future time negotiations with the IRA might take place. In 1991 his efforts to institute all-party, and all-Ireland, talks on reconciliation eventually proved abortive but he continued to be held in high regard on both sides of the border.

Brooke /brʊk/ Rupert Chawner 1887–1915. English poet, symbol of the World War I 'lost generation'. His five war sonnets, the best-known of which is 'The Patriot', were published posthumously. Other notable works include 'Grantchester' and 'The Great Lover'.

Brookeborough /ˈbrʊkbərə/ Basil Brooke, Viscount Brookeborough 1888–1973. Unionist politician of Northern Ireland. He entered Parliament in 1929, held ministerial posts 1933–45, and was prime minister of Northern Ireland 1943–63. He was a staunch advocate of strong links with Britain.

Brooklands /ˈbrʊklandz/ former UK motor racing track near Weybridge, Surrey. One of the world's first purpose-built circuits, it was opened 1907 as a testing ground for early motorcars. It was the venue for the first British Grand Prix (then known as the RAC

Grand Prix) 1926. It was sold to aircraft builders Vickers 1946.

Brooklyn /'brʊklɪn/ borough of New York City, USA, occupying the SW end of Long Island. It is linked to Manhattan Island by Brooklyn Bridge 1883 and others, and to Staten Island by the Verrazano-Narrows Bridge 1964. There are more than 60 parks of which Prospect is the largest. There is also a botanic garden, and a beach and amusement area at Coney Island.

Brookner /'brʊknə/ Anita 1928– . British novelist and art historian, whose novels include *Hotel du Lac* 1984, winner of the Booker prize, *A Misalliance* 1986, and *Latecomers* 1988.

Brooks /brʊks/ Louise 1906–1985. US actress, known for her roles in silent films such as *A Girl in Every Port* 1928, *Die Büchse der Pandora/Pandora's Box*, and *Das Tagebuch einer Verlorenen/Diary of a Lost Girl* both 1929, both directed by G W ◊Pabst. At 25 she had appeared in 17 films. She retired from the screen 1938.

Brooks /brʊks/ Mel. Stage name of Melvin Kaminsky 1926– . US film director and comedian, known for madcap and slapstick verbal humour. He became well known with his record album *The 2,000-Year-Old Man* 1960. His films include *The Producers* 1968, *Blazing Saddles* 1974, *Young Frankenstein* 1975, *History of the World Part I* 1981, and *To Be or Not to Be* 1983.

Brooks /brʊks/ Van Wyck 1886–1963. US literary critic and biographer. His five-volume *Makers and Finders: A History of the Writer in America, 1800–1915* 1936–52 was an influential series of critical works on US literature. The first volume *The Flowering of New England* 1936 won a Pulitzer prize.

broom any shrub of the family Leguminosae especially species of the *Cytisus* and *Spartium*, often cultivated for their bright yellow flowers.

In Britain the yellow-flowered Scots broom *Cytisus scoparius* predominates.

Broome /brʊm/ David 1940– . British show jumper. He won the 1970 world title on a horse named Beethoven. His sister Liz Edgar is also a top-class show jumper.

Brothers Karamazov, The /ˌkærəˈmɑːzɒv/ novel by Dostoievsky, published 1879–80. It describes the reactions and emotions of four brothers after their father's murder. One of them is falsely convicted of the crime, although his illegitimate brother is guilty.

Brougham /brʊm/ Henry Peter, 1st Baron Brougham and Vaux 1778–1868. British Whig politician and lawyer. From 1811 he was chief adviser to the Princess of Wales (afterwards Queen Caroline), and in 1820 he defeated the attempt of George IV to divorce her. He was Lord Chancellor 1830–34, supporting the Reform Bill.

Brown /braʊn/ (James) Gordon 1951– . British Labour politician. He entered Parliament in 1983, rising quickly to the opposition front bench, with a reputation as an outstanding debater.

Brown /braʊn/ Capability (Lancelot) 1715–1783. English landscape gardener. He acquired his nickname because of his continual enthusiasm for the 'capabilities' of natural landscapes.

He advised on gardens of stately homes, including Blenheim, Oxfordshire; Stowe, Buckinghamshire; and Petworth, W Sussex, sometimes also contributing to the architectural designs.

Brown /braʊn/ Charles Brockden 1771–1810. US novelist and magazine editor. He introduced the American Indian into fiction and is called the 'father of the American novel' for his *Wieland* 1798, *Ormond* 1799, *Edgar Huntly* 1799, and *Arthur Mervyn* 1800. His works also pioneered the Gothic and fantastic traditions in US fiction.

Brown /braʊn/ Earle 1926– . US composer who pioneered ◊graphic notation and mobile form during the 1950s, as in *Available Forms II* 1958 for ensemble and two conductors. He was an associate of John ◊Cage.

Brown /braʊn/ Ford Madox 1821–1893. British painter associated with the ◊Pre-Raphaelite Brotherhood. His pictures include *The Last of England* 1855 (Birmingham Art Gallery) and *Work* 1852–65 (City Art Gallery, Manchester), packed with realistic detail and symbolic incident.

Brown /braʊn/ George, Baron George-Brown 1914–1985. British Labour politician. He entered Parliament in 1945, was briefly minister of works 1951, and contested the leadership of the party on the death of Gaitskell, but was defeated by Harold Wilson. He was secretary for economic affairs 1964–66 and foreign secretary 1966–68. He was created a life peer 1970.

Brown /braʊn/ James 1928– . US rhythm-and-blues singer, a pioneer of funk and much sampled in hip-hop and techno dance music. Staccato horn arrangements and shouted vocals characterize his hits, which include 'Please, Please, Please' 1956, 'Papa's Got a Brand New Bag' 1965, and 'Say It Loud, I'm Black and I'm Proud' 1968.

Brown /braʊn/ John 1800–1859. US slavery abolitionist. With 18 men, on the night of 16 Oct 1859, he siezed the government arsenal at Harper's Ferry in W Virginia, apparently intending to distribute weapons to runaway slaves who would then defend the mountain stronghold, which Brown hoped would become a republic of former slaves. On 18 Oct the arsenal was stormed by US Marines under Col Robert E ◊Lee. Brown was tried and hanged on 2 Dec, becoming a martyr and the hero of the popular song 'John Brown's Body' *c.* 1860.

Born in Connecticut, he settled as a farmer in Kansas in 1855. In 1856 he was responsible for the 'Pottawatomie massacre' when five proslavery farmers were killed. In 1858 he formed the plan for a refuge for runaway slaves in the mountains of Virginia.

Brown /braʊn/ John 1825–1883. Scottish servant and confidant of Queen Victoria from 1858.

Brown /braʊn/ Robert 1773–1858. Scottish botanist, a pioneer of plant classification and the first to describe and name the cell nucleus.

On an expedition to Australia in 1801 he collected 4,000 species of plant and later classified them using the 'natural' system of Bernard de Jussieu (1699–1777) rather than relying upon the system of Carolus ◊Linnaeus. The agitated movement of small particles suspended in water, now explained by kinetic theory, was described by Brown in 1827 and later became known as *Brownian movement*.

brown dwarf hypothetical object less massive than a star, but heavier than a planet. Brown dwarfs would not have enough mass to ignite nuclear reactions at their centres, but would shine by heat released during their contraction from a gas cloud. Because of the difficulty of detection, no brown dwarfs have been spotted with certainty, but some astronomers believe that vast numbers of them may exist throughout the Galaxy.

Browne /braʊn/ Hablot Knight 1815–1882. British illustrator, pseudonym Phiz, known for his illustrations of Charles Dickens's works.

Browne /braʊn/ Robert 1550–1633. English Puritan leader, founder of the Brownists. He founded a community in Norwich, East Anglia, and in the Netherlands which developed into present-day ◊Congregationalism.

Browne /braʊn/ Thomas 1605–1682. English author and physician. Born in London, he travelled widely in Europe before settling in Norwich in 1637. His works display a richness of style as in *Religio Medici/The Religion of a Doctor* 1643, a justification of his profession; *Vulgar Errors* 1646, an examination of popular legend and superstition; *Urn Burial* and *The Garden of Cyrus* 1658; and *Christian Morals*, published posthumously in 1717.

Brownian movement the continuous random motion of particles in a fluid medium (gas or liquid) as they are subjected to impact from the molecules of the medium. The phenomenon was explained by Albert Einstein in 1905 but was observed as long ago as 1827 by the Scottish botanist Robert Brown.

Browning /braʊnɪŋ/ Robert 1812–1889. English poet, married to Elizabeth Barrett Browning. His work is characterized by the use of dramatic monologue and an interest in obscure literary and historical figures. It includes the play *Pippa Passes* 1841 and the poems 'The Pied Piper of Hamelin' 1842, 'My Last Duchess' 1842, 'Home Thoughts from Abroad' 1845, and 'Rabbi Ben Ezra' 1864.

Browning, born in Camberwell, London, wrote his first poem 'Pauline' 1833 under the influence of Shelley; it was followed by 'Paracelsus' 1835 and 'Sordello' 1840. From 1837 he achieved moderate success with his play *Strafford* and several other works. In the pamphlet series of *Bells and Pomegranates* 1841–46, which contained *Pippa Passes*, *Dramatic Lyrics* 1842 and *Dramatic Romances* 1845, he included the dramas *King Victor and King Charles*, *Return of the Druses*, and *Colombe's Birthday*.

In 1846 he met Elizabeth Barrett; they married the same year and went to Italy. There he wrote *Christmas Eve and Easter Day* 1850 and *Men and Women* 1855, the latter containing some of his finest love poems and dramatic monologues, which were followed by *Dramatis Personae* 1864 and *The Ring and the Book* 1868–69, based on an Italian murder story.

brown ring test in analytical chemistry, a test for the presence of ◊nitrates.

To an aqueous solution containing the test substance is added iron(II) sulphate. Concentrated sulphuric acid is then carefully poured down the inside wall of the test tube so that it forms a distinct layer at the bottom. The formation of a brown colour at the boundary between the two layers indicates the presence of nitrate.

Browns Ferry /ˌbraʊnz ˈferi/ site of a nuclear power station on the Alabama River, central Alabama, USA. A nuclear accident in 1975 resulted in the closure of the plant for 18 months. This incident marked the beginning of widespread disenchantment with nuclear power in the USA.

Brownshirts the SA (*Sturmabteilung*), or Storm Troops, the private army of the German Nazi party who derived their name from the colour of their uniform.

Brown v Board of Education (of Topeka, Kansas) US Supreme Court decision 1954 that consolidated several suits challenging segregation laws in four states and the District of Columbia. The petitioner, Brown, was the father of a schoolgirl who lived near a school but was forced to travel across town to attend class in an all-black school. In a landmark decision the Court did away with the long-standing 'separate but equal' doctrine of ◊*Plessy* v *Ferguson*, ruling that segregated educational facilities are intrinsically unequal and are therefore in violation of the 14th Amendment. Lower courts were directed to desegregate schools with all deliberate speed.

Brubeck /ˈbruːbek/ Dave (David Warren) 1920– . US jazz pianist, a student of the French composer Milhaud and Arnold Schoenberg, inventor of the 12-tone composition system. The Dave Brubeck Quartet (formed 1951) combined improvisation with classical discipline. Included in his large body of compositions is the internationally popular 'Take Five'.

Bruce /bruːs/ one of the chief Scottish noble houses. Robert I (Robert the Bruce) and his son, David II, were both kings of Scotland descended from Robert de Bruis (died 1094), a Norman knight who arrived in England with William the Conqueror 1066.

Bruce /bruːs/ James 1730–1794. Scottish explorer, the first European to reach the source of the Blue Nile 1770, and to follow the river downstream to Cairo 1773.

Bruce Robert. King of Scotland; see ◊Robert I.

Bruce /bruːs/ Stanley Melbourne, 1st Viscount Bruce of Melbourne 1883–1967. Australian National Party politician, prime minister 1923–29. He was elected to parliament in 1918. As prime minister he introduced a number of social welfare measures.

brucellosis disease of cattle, goats, and pigs, also known when transmitted to humans as ***undulant fever*** since it remains in the body and recurs. It was named after Australian doctor David Bruce (1855–1931), and is caused by bacteria (genus *Brucella*) present in the milk of infected cattle.

Bruch /brʊx/ Max 1838–1920. German composer, professor at the Berlin Academy 1891. He wrote three operas including *Hermoine* 1872. Among the most celebrated of his works are the *Kol Nidrei* for cello and orchestra, violin concertos, and many choral pieces.

Brücke, die /ˈbrʊkə/ (German 'the bridge') German Expressionist art movement 1905–13, formed in Dresden. Ernst Ludwig Kirchner was one of its founders, and Emil Nolde was a member 1906–07. Influenced by African art, they strove for spiritual significance, using raw colours to express different emotions. In 1911 the ◊*Blaue Reiter* took over as the leading group in German art.

Bruckner /ˈbrʊknə/ (Joseph) Anton 1824–1896. Austrian Romantic composer. He was cathedral organist at Linz 1856–68, and from 1868 he was professor at the Vienna Conservatoire. His works include many choral pieces and 11 symphonies, the last unfinished. His compositions were influenced by Richard ◊Wagner and Beethoven.

Brüderhof /ˈbruːdəhɒf/ (German 'Society of Brothers') Christian Protestant sect with beliefs similar to the Mennonites. They live in groups of families (single persons are assigned to a family), marry only within the sect (divorce is not allowed), and retain a 'modest' dress for women (cap or headscarf, and long skirts).

Brueghel /ˈbrɜːxəl/ family of Flemish painters. *Pieter Brueghel the Elder* (*c.* 1525–69) was one of the greatest artists of his time. He painted satirical and humorous pictures of peasant life, many of which include symbolic details illustrating folly and inhumanity, and a series of Months, (five survive), including *Hunters in the Snow* (Kunsthistorisches Museum, Vienna).

The elder Pieter was nicknamed 'Peasant' Brueghel. Two of his sons were painters.

Pieter Brueghel the Younger (1564–1638), called 'Hell' Brueghel, specialized in religious subjects, and another son, *Jan Brueghel* (1568–1625), called 'Velvet' Brueghel, painted flowers, landscapes, and seascapes.

Bruges /bruːʒ/ (Flemish *Brugge*) historic city in NW Belgium; capital of W Flanders province, 16 km/10 mi from the North Sea, with which it is connected by canal; population (1985) 117,700. Bruges was the capital of medieval ◊Flanders and was the chief European wool manufacturing town as well as its chief market.

features Among many fine buildings are the 14th-century cathedral, the church of Nôtre Dame with a Michelangelo statue of the Virgin and Child, the Gothic town hall and market hall; there are remarkable art collections. It was named for its many bridges. The College of Europe is the oldest centre of European studies. The contemporary port handles coal, iron ore, oil, and fish. Local manufactures include lace, textiles, paint, steel, beer, furniture, and motors.

Brugge Flemish form of ◊Bruges, town in Belgium.

Brummell /'brʌməl/ Beau (George Bryan) 1778–1840. British dandy and leader of fashion. He introduced long trousers as conventional day and evening wear for men. A friend of the Prince of Wales, the future George IV, he later quarrelled with him, and was driven by gambling losses to exile in France in 1816 and died in an asylum.

Brundtland /'brʊntlænd/ Gro Harlem 1939– . Norwegian Labour politician. Environment minister 1974–76, she briefly took over as prime minister 1981, and was elected prime minister in 1986 and again in 1990. She chaired the World Commission on Environment and Development which produced the *Brundtland Report* 1987.

Brundtland Report the findings of the World Commission on Environment and Development, published 1987 as *Our Common Future*. It stressed the necessity of environmental protection and popularized the phrase 'sustainable development'. The commission was chaired by the Norwegian prime minister Gro Harlem Brundtland.

Brunei /bruːˈnaɪ/ country comprising two enclaves on the NW coast of the island of Borneo, bounded to the landward side by Sarawak and to the NW by the South China Sea.

government The 1959 constitution gives supreme authority to the sultan, advised by various councils. Since the constitution was suspended after a revolution 1962, the sultan rules by decree. One political party is allowed, the Brunei National United Party (BNUP), a multiethnic splinter group formed by former members of the Brunei National Democratic Party (BNDP). While loyal to the sultan, it favours the establishment of an elected prime ministerial system. Other parties have been banned or have closed down.

history An independent Islamic sultanate from the 15th century, Brunei was a powerful state by the early 16th century, with dominion over all of Borneo, its neighbouring islands, and parts of the Philippines. With the growing presence of the Portuguese and Dutch in the region its influence declined in the late 16th century. In 1888 Brunei became a British protectorate, and under an agreement of 1906 accepted the appointment of a British Resident as adviser to the sultan. The discovery of large oilfields in the 1920s brought economic prosperity to Brunei. The country was occupied by the Japanese 1941 and liberated by the Australians 1945, when it was returned to Britain. In 1950 Sir Muda Omar Ali Saiffuddin Saadul Khairi Waddien (1916–1986), popularly known as Sir Omar, became sultan.

In 1959, a new constitution gave Brunei internal self-government but made Britain responsible for defence and external affairs; a proposal in 1962 that Brunei should join the Federation of Malaysia was opposed by a revolution that was put down with British help. As a result the sultan decided to rule by decree. In 1967, he abdicated in favour of his son, Hassanal Bolkiah, but continued to be his chief adviser. In 1971 Brunei gained full internal self-government.

independence achieved In 1984 full independence was achieved, the sultan becoming prime minister and minister of finance and home affairs, presiding over a cabinet of six, three of whom were close relatives. Britain agreed to maintain a small force to protect the gas and oilfields that make Brunei the wealthiest nation, per head, in Asia. In 1985, the sultan cautiously allowed the formation of the loyal and reliable Brunei National Democratic Party (BNDP), an organization dominated by businessmen. A year later, ethnic Chinese and government employees (who were debarred from joining the BNDP) formed, with breakaway members of the other party, the Brunei National United Party (BNUP), the country's only political party after the dissolution by the sultan of the BNDP 1988.

Since the death of Sir Omar 1986, the pace of political reform has quickened, with key cabinet portfolios being assigned to nonmembers of the royal family. A more nationalist socioeconomic policy has also begun, with preferential treatment given to native Malays in the commercial sphere rather than the traditional Chinese, and an Islamic state is being constructed. During the Iranian arms scandal 1987, it was revealed that the sultan of Brunei donated $10 million to the Nicaraguan Contras (antigovernment guerrillas).

Brunei Town /ˈbruːnaɪ/ former name (until 1970) of ◊Bandar Seri Begawan, Brunei.

Brunel /bruːˈnel/ Isambard Kingdom 1806–1859. British engineer and inventor. In 1833 he became engineer to the Great Western Railway, which adopted the 2.1 m/7 ft gauge on his advice. He built the Clifton Suspension Bridge over the river Avon at Bristol and the Saltash Bridge over the river Tamar near Plymouth. His shipbuilding designs include the *Great Western* 1838, the first steamship to cross the Atlantic regularly; the *Great Britain* 1843, the first large iron ship to have a screw propeller; and the *Great Eastern* 1857, which laid the first transatlantic telegraph cable.

Brunel /bruːˈnel/ Marc Isambard 1769–1849. British engineer and inventor, father of Isambard Kingdom Brunel. He constructed the Rotherhithe tunnel under the river Thames in London from Wapping to Rotherhithe 1825–43.

Brunelleschi /ˌbruːnəˈleski/ Filippo 1377–1446. Italian Renaissance architect. One of the earliest and greatest Renaissance architects, he pioneered the scientific use of perspective. He was responsible for the construction of the dome of Florence Cathedral (completed 1438), a feat deemed impossible by many of his contemporaries.

Bruning /ˈbruːnɪŋ/ Heinrich 1885–1970. German politician. Elected to the Reichstag (parliament) 1924, he led the Catholic Centre Party from 1929 and was federal chancellor 1930–32 when political and economic crisis forced his resignation.

Brünn German form of ◊Brno, town in the Czech Republic.

Bruno, St /ˈbruːnəʊ/ 1030–1101. German founder of the monastic Catholic ◊Carthusian order. He was born in Cologne, became a priest, and controlled the cathedral school of Rheims 1057–76. Withdrawing to the mountains near Grenoble after an ecclesiastical controversy, he founded the monastery at Chartreuse in 1084. Feast day 6 Oct.

Brunswick /ˈbrʌnzwɪk/ (German *Braunschweig*) former independent duchy, a republic from 1918, which is now part of ◊Lower Saxony, Germany.

Brunswick /ˈbrʌnzwɪk/ (German *Braunschweig*) industrial city (chemical engineering, precision engineering, food processing) in Lower Saxony, Germany; population (1988) 248,000. It was one of the chief cities of N Germany in the Middle Ages and a member of the ◊Hanseatic League. It was capital of the duchy of Brunswick from 1671.

Brusa alternative form of ◊Bursa, town in Turkey.

Brussels /ˈbrʌsəlz/ (Flemish *Brussel*; French *Bruxelles*) capital of Belgium, industrial city (lace, textiles, machinery, chemicals); population (1987) 974,000 (80% French-speaking, the suburbs Flemish-speaking). It is the headquarters of the European Economic Community and since 1967 of the international secretariat of ◊NATO. First settled in the 6th century, and a city from 1312, Brussels became the capital of the Spanish Netherlands 1530 and of Belgium 1830.

Brussels, Treaty of /ˈbrʌsəlz/ pact of economic, political, cultural, and military alliance established 17 March 1948, for 50 years, by the UK, France, and the Benelux countries, joined by West Germany and Italy 1955. It was the forerunner of the North Atlantic Treaty Organization and the European Community.

Brutalism architectural style of the 1950s and 1960s that evolved from the work of Le Corbusier and Mies van der Rohe. It stresses fuctionalism and honesty to materials; steel and concrete are favoured. In the UK the style was developed by Alison and Peter ◊Smithson.

Brutus /'bruːtəs/ Marcus Junius *c.* 78–42 BC. Roman soldier, a supporter of ◊Pompey (against Caesar) in the civil war. Pardoned by ◊Caesar and raised to high office by him, he nevertheless plotted Caesar's assassination to restore the purity of the Republic. Brutus committed suicide when he was defeated (with ◊Cassius) by ◊Mark Antony, Caesar's lieutenant, at Philippi 42 BC.

Bruxelles French form of ◊Brussels, capital of Belgium.

Bryansk /bri'ænsk/ city in Russia, SW of Moscow on the Desna; population (1987) 445,000. Industries include sawmills, textiles, and steel.

Bryant /'braɪənt/ Arthur 1899–1985. British historian who produced studies of Restoration figures such as Pepys and Charles II, and a series covering the Napoleonic Wars including *The Age of Elegance* 1950.

Bryant /'braɪənt/ David 1931– . English flat-green (lawn) bowls player. He has won every honour the game has offered, including four outdoor world titles (three singles and one triples) 1966–88 and three indoor titles 1979–81.

Bryce /braɪs/ James, 1st Viscount Bryce 1838–1922. British Liberal politician, professor of civil law at Oxford University 1870–93. He entered Parliament 1880, holding office under Gladstone and Rosebery. He was author of *The American Commonwealth* 1888, ambassador to Washington 1907–13, and improved US-Canadian relations.

Brynner /'brɪnə/ Yul 1915–1985. Actor, in the USA from 1940, who made a shaven head his trademark. He played the king in *The King and I* both on stage 1951 and on film 1956, and was the leader of *The Magnificent Seven* 1960.

bryony either of two hedgerow climbing plants found in Britain: *white bryony Bryonia dioca* belonging to the gourd family

Cucurbitaceae, and *black bryony Tamus communis* of the yam family Dioscoreaceae.

bryophyte member of the Bryophyta, a division of the plant kingdom containing three classes: the Hepaticae (◊liverwort), Musci (◊moss), and Anthocerotae (◊hornwort). Bryophytes are generally small, low-growing, terrestrial plants with no vascular (water-conducting) system as in higher plants. Their life cycle shows a marked ◊alternation of generations. Bryophytes chiefly occur in damp habitats and require water for the dispersal of the male gametes (◊antherozoids).

In bryophytes, the ◊sporophyte, consisting only of a spore-bearing capsule on a slender stalk, is wholly or partially dependent on the ◊gametophyte for water and nutrients. In some liverworts the plant body is a simple ◊thallus, but in the majority of bryophytes it is differentiated into stem, leaves, and ◊rhizoids.

Brześć nad Bugiem Polish name of ◊Brest, a town in Belarus.

Brzezinski /brə'ʒɪnski/ Zbigniew 1928– . US Democrat politician, born in Poland; he taught at Harvard University, USA, and became a US citizen 1949. He was national security adviser to President Carter 1977–81 and chief architect of Carter's human-rights policy.

BSc abbreviation for *Bachelor of Science* degree. The US abbreviation is *BS*.

BSE abbreviation for ◊bovine spongiform encephalopathy.

BSI abbreviation for ◊*British Standards Institution*.

BST abbreviation for *British Summer Time*; ◊*bovine somatotropin*.

BT abbreviation for *British Telecom*.

Btu symbol for ◊*British thermal unit*.

bubble chamber in physics, a device for observing the nature and movement of atomic particles, and their interaction with radiations. It is a vessel filled with a superheated liquid through which ionizing particles move and collide. The paths of these particles are shown by strings of bubbles, which can be photographed and studied. By using a pressurized liquid medium instead of a gas, it overcomes drawbacks inherent in the earlier ◊cloud chamber. It was invented by Donald ◊Glaser 1952.

bubble memory in computing, a memory device based on the creation of small 'bubbles' on a magnetic surface. Bubble memories typically store up to 4 megabits (4 million ◊bits) of information. They are not sensitive to shock and vibration, unlike other memory devices such as disc drives, yet, like magnetic discs, they do not lose their information when the computer is switched off.

Buber /'buːbə/ Martin 1878–1965. Austrian-born Israeli philosopher, a Zionist and advocate of the reappraisal of ancient Jewish thought in contemporary terms. His book *I and Thou* 1923 posited a direct dialogue between the individual and God; it had great impact on Christian and Jewish theology. When forced by the Nazis to abandon a professorship in comparative religion at Frankfurt, he went to Jerusalem and taught social philosophy at the Hebrew University 1937–51.

bubonic plague epidemic disease of the Middle Ages; see ◊plague and ◊Black Death.

Bucaramanga /buˌkɑːrəˈmæŋgə/ industrial (coffee, tobacco, cacao, cotton) and commercial city in N central Colombia; population (1985) 493,929. It was founded by the Spanish 1622.

buccaneer member of various groups of seafarers who plundered Spanish ships and colonies on the Spanish American coast in the 17th century. Unlike true pirates, they were acting on (sometimes spurious) commission.

Buchan /'bʌxən, 'bʌkən/ John, Baron Tweedsmuir 1875–1940. Scottish politician and author. Called to the Bar 1901, he was Conservative member of Parliament for the Scottish universities 1927–35, and governor general of Canada 1934–40. His adventure stories, today criticized for their anti-semitism, include *The Thirty-Nine Steps* 1915, *Greenmantle* 1916, and *The Three Hostages* 1924.

Bucharest /ˌbuːkəˈrest/ (Romanian *Bucuresti*) capital and largest city of Romania; population (1985) 1,976,000, the conurbation of Bucharest district having an area of 1,520 sq km/587 sq mi and a population of 2,273,000. It was originally a citadel built by Vlad the Impaler (see ◊Dracula) to stop the advance of the Ottoman invasion in the 14th century. Bucharest became the capital of the princes of Wallachia 1698 and of Romania 1861. Savage fighting took place in the city during Romania's 1989 revolution.

Buchenwald /'buːxənvælt/ site of a Nazi ◊concentration camp 1937–45 at a village NE of Weimar, E Germany.

Buchman /'bʊkmən/ Frank N D 1878–1961. US Christian evangelist. In 1938 he launched in London the anticommunist campaign, the Moral Re-Armament movement.

Buchner /'bʊxnə/ Eduard 1860–1917. German chemist who researched the process of fermentation. In 1897 he observed that fermentation could be produced mechanically, by cell-free extracts. Buchner argued that it was not the whole yeast cell that produced fermentation, but only the presence of the enzyme he named zymase. Nobel prize 1907.

Buck /bʌk/ Pearl S(ydenstricker) 1892–1973. US novelist. Daughter of missionaries to China, she spent much of her life there and wrote novels about Chinese life, such as *East Wind–West Wind* 1930 and *The Good Earth* 1931, for which she received a Pulitzer prize 1932. She received the Nobel Prize for Literature 1938.

Buckingham /'bʌkɪŋəm/ market town in Buckinghamshire, England, on the river Ouse. University College was established 1974, and was given a royal charter as the University of Buckingham 1983.

Buckingham /'bʌkɪŋəm/ George Villiers, 1st Duke of Buckingham 1592–1628. English courtier, adviser to James I and later Charles I. After Charles's accession, Buckingham attempted to form a Protestant coalition in Europe, which led to war with France, but he failed to relieve the Protestants (◊Huguenots) besieged in La Rochelle 1627. This added to his unpopularity with Parliament, and he was assassinated.

Buckingham /'bʌkɪŋəm/ George Villiers, 2nd Duke of Buckingham 1628–1687. English politician, a member of the ◊Cabal under Charles II. A dissolute son of the first duke, he was brought up with the royal children. His play *The Rehearsal* satirized the style of the poet Dryden, who portrayed him as Zimri in *Absalom and Achitophel*.

Buckingham Palace London home of the British sovereign, built 1703 for the duke of Buckingham, but bought by George III 1762 and reconstructed by ◊Nash 1821–36; a new front was added 1913.

Buckinghamshire /'bʌkɪŋəmʃə/ county in SE central England
area 1,880 sq km/726 sq mi

towns Aylesbury (administrative headquarters), Buckingham, High Wycombe, Beaconsfield, Olney, Milton Keynes
features ◊Chequers (country seat of the prime minister); Burnham Beeches and the church of the poet Gray's 'Elegy' at Stoke Poges; Cliveden, a country house designed by Charles Barry (now a hotel, it was used by the newspaper-owning Astors for house parties); Bletchley Park, home of World War II code-breaking activities, now used as a training post for GCHQ (Britain's electronic surveillance centre); Open University at Walton Hall; homes of the poets William Cowper at Olney and John Milton at Chalfont St Giles, and of the Tory prime minister Disraeli at Hughenden; Stowe gardens
products furniture, chiefly beech; agricultural goods
population (1989 est) 634,400
famous people William Herschel, George Gilbert Scott, Edmund Waller, John Hampden, Ben Nicholson.

Buckley /'bʌkli/ William F(rank) 1925– . US conservative political writer, novelist, and founder-editor of the *National Review* 1955. In such books as *Up from Liberalism* 1959, and in a weekly television debate *Firing Line*, he represented the 'intellectual' right-wing, antiliberal stance in US political thought.

buckthorn any of several thorny shrubs of the family Rhamnaceae. The buckthorn *Rhamnus catharticus* is native to Britain and has berries formerly used in medicine as a purgative.

buckwheat any of several plants of the genus *Fagopyrum*, family Polygonaceae. The name usually refers to *F. esculentum*, which grows to about 1 m/3 ft and can grow on poor soil in a short summer. The highly nutritious black, triangular seeds (groats) are consumed by both animals and humans. They can be eaten either cooked whole or or as a cracked meal (kasha) or ground into flour, often made into pancakes.

bud undeveloped shoot usually enclosed by protective scales; inside is a very short stem and numerous undeveloped leaves, or flower parts, or both. Terminal buds are found at the tips of shoots, while axillary buds develop in the ◊axils of the leaves, often remaining dormant unless the terminal bud is removed or damaged. Adventitious buds may be produced anywhere on the plant, their formation sometimes stimulated by an injury, such as that caused by pruning.

Budaeus /buːˈdiːəs/ Latin form of the name of Guillaume Budé 1467–1540. French scholar. He persuaded Francis I to found the Collège de France, and also the library that formed the nucleus of the French national library, the Bibliothèque Nationale.

Budapest /ˌbjuːdəˈpest/ capital of Hungary, industrial city (chemicals, textiles) on the river Danube; population (1989) 2,115,000. Buda, on the right bank of the Danube, became the Hungarian capital 1867 and was joined with Pest, on the left bank, 1872.

Buddha /'budə/ 'enlightened one', title of Prince *Gautama Siddhàrtha c.* 563–483 BC. religious leader, founder of Buddhism, born at Lumbini in Nepal. At the age of 29 he left his wife and son and a life of luxury, to escape from the material burdens of existence. After six years of austerity he realized that asceticism, like overindulgence, was futile, and chose the middle way of meditation. He became enlightened under a bo, or bodhi, tree near Buddh Gaya in Bihar, India. He began teaching at Varanasi, and founded the Sangha, or order of monks. He spent the rest of his life travelling around N India, and died at Kusinagara in Uttar Pradesh.

The Buddha's teaching consisted of the Four Noble Truths: the fact of frustration or suffering; that suffering has a cause; that it can be ended; and that it can be ended by following the Noble Eightfold Path—right views, right intention, right speech, right action, right livelihood, right effort, right mindfulness, and right concentration—eventually arriving at nirvana, the extinction of all craving for things of the senses and release from the cycle of rebirth.

Buddh Gaya /'bud gəˈjɑː/ village in Bihar, India, where Gautama became the Buddha while sitting beneath a bo (*bodhi* 'wisdom') tree; a descendant of the original tree is preserved.

Buddhism /'budiz(ə)m/ one of the great world religions, which originated in India about 500 BC. It derives from the teaching of the Buddha, who is regarded as one of a series of such enlightened beings; there are no gods. The chief doctrine is that of *karma*, good or evil deeds meeting an appropriate reward or punishment either in this life or (through reincarnation) a long succession of lives. The main divisions in Buddhism are *Theravàda* (or Hinayàna) in SE Asia and *Mahàyàna* in N Asia; *Lamaism* in Tibet and *Zen* in Japan are among the many

Mahāyāna sects. Its symbol is the lotus. There are over 247.5 million Buddhists worldwide.

scriptures The only complete canon of the Buddhist scriptures is that of the Sinhalese (Sri Lanka) Buddhists, in Pāli, but other schools have essentially the same canon in Sanskrit. The scriptures, known as *pitaka*s (baskets), date from the 2nd to 6th centuries AD. There are three divisions: *vinaya* (discipline), listing offences and rules of life; the *sūtras* (discourse), or *dharma* (doctrine), the exposition of Buddhism by the Buddha and his disciples; and *abhidharma* (further doctrine), later discussions on doctrine.

beliefs The self is not regarded as permanent, as it is subject to change and decay. It is attachment to the things that are essentially impermanent that causes delusion, suffering, greed, and aversion, the origin of karma, and they in turn create further karma and the sense of self is reinforced. Actions which incline towards selflessness are called 'skilful karma' and they are on the path leading to enlightenment. In the *Four Noble Truths* the Buddha acknowledged the existence and source of suffering, and showed the way of deliverance from it through the *Eightfold Path*. The aim of following the Eightfold Path is to break the chain of karma and achieve dissociation from the body by attaining *nirvana* ('blowing out')—the eradication of all desires, either in annihilation or by absorption of the self in the infinite.

Supreme reverence is accorded to the historical Buddha (Sākyamuni, or, when referred to by his clan name, Gautama), who is seen as one in a long and ongoing line of Buddhas, the next one (Maitreya) being due *c.* AD 3000.

Theravāda Buddhism, the School of the Elders, also known as *Hinayāna* or Lesser Vehicle, prevails in SE Asia (Sri Lanka, Thailand, and Myanmar), and emphasizes the mendicant, meditative life as the way to break the cycle of *samsāra*, or death and rebirth. Its three alternative goals are *arahat*: one who has gained insight into the true nature of things; *Paccekabuddha*, an enlightened one who lives alone and does not teach; and fully awakened *Buddha*. Its scriptures are written in Pāli, an Indo-Aryan language with its roots in N India. In India itself Buddhism had virtually died out by the 13th century, and was replaced by Hinduism. However, it has 5 million devotees in the 20th century and is still growing.

Mahāyāna Buddhism, or Greater Vehicle arose at the beginning of the Christian era. This tradition emphasized the eternal, formless principle of the Buddha as the essence of all things. It exhorts the individual not merely to attain personal nirvana, but to become a trainee Buddha, or *bodhisattva*, and so save others; this meant the faithful could be brought to enlightenment by a bodhisattva without following the austerities of Theravāda, and the cults of various Buddhas and bodhisattvas arose. Mahāyāna Buddhism also emphasizes *shunyata*, or the experiential understanding of the emptiness of all things, even Buddhist doctrine.

Mahāyāna Buddhism prevails in N Asia (China, Korea, Japan, and Tibet). In the 6th century AD Mahāyāna spread to China with the teachings of Bodhidharma and formed Ch'an, which became established in Japan from the 12th century as *Zen Buddhism*. Zen emphasizes silent meditation with sudden interruptions from a master to encourage awakening of the mind. Japan also has the lay organization *Sōka Gakkai* (Value Creation Society), founded 1930, which equates absolute faith with immediate material benefit; by the 1980s it was followed by more than 7 million households.

Esoteric, Tantric, or *Diamond Buddhism* became popular in Tibet and Japan, and holds that enlightenment is already within the disciple and with the proper guidance (that is privately passed on by a master) can be realised. Buddhist believers worldwide are estimated at 350 million.

budding type of ◊asexual reproduction in which an outgrowth develops from a cell to form a new individual. Most yeasts reproduce in this way.

In a suitable environment, yeasts grow rapidly, forming long chains of cells as the buds themselves produce further buds before being separated from the parent. Simple invertebrates, such as ◊hydra, can also reproduce by budding.

In horticulture, the term is used for a technique of plant propagation whereby a bud (or scion) and a sliver of bark from one plant are transferred to an incision made in the bark of another plant (the stock). This method of ◊grafting is often used for roses.

buddleia any shrub or tree of the tropical genus *Buddleia*, family Buddleiaceae. The purple or white flower heads of the butterfly bush *B. davidii* attract large numbers of butterflies.

Budge /bʌdʒ/ Donald 1915– . US tennis player. He was the first to perform the Grand Slam when he won the Wimbledon, French, US, and Australian championships all in 1938. He won 14 Grand Slam events, including Wimbledon singles twice. He turned professional 1938.

budgerigar small Australian parakeet *Melopsittacus undulatus* that feeds mainly on grass seeds. Normally it is bright green, but yellow, white, blue, and mauve varieties have been bred for the pet market. It breeds freely in captivity.

budget estimate of income and expenditure for some future period, used in financial planning. National budgets set out estimates of government income and expenditure and generally include projected changes in taxation and growth. Interim budgets are not uncommon, in particular, when dramatic changes in economic conditions occur. Governments will sometimes construct a budget deficit or surplus as part of macroeconomic policy.

Budějovice see ◊České Budějovice, town in the Czech Republic.

Budweis /ˈbʊdvaɪs/ German form of České Budějovice, a town in the Czech Republic.

Buenos Aires /ˈbweɪnɒs ˈaɪrɪz/ capital and industrial city of Argentina, on the S bank of the Río de la Plata; population (1980) 2,922,829, metropolitan area 9,969,826. It was founded 1536, and became the capital 1853.

buffalo either of two species of wild cattle. The Asiatic water buffalo *Bubalis bubalis* is found domesticated throughout S Asia and wild in parts of India and Nepal. It likes moist conditions. Usually grey or black, up to 1.8 m/6 ft high, both sexes carry large horns. The African buffalo *Syncerus caffer* is found in Africa, south of the Sahara, where there is grass, water, and cover in which to retreat. There are a number of subspecies, the biggest up to 1.6 m/5 ft high, and black, with massive horns set close together over the head. The name is also commonly applied to the American bison.

Buffalo /ˈbʌfələʊ/ industrial port in New York State, USA, at the E end of Lake Erie; population (1980) 1,200,000. It is linked with New York City by the New York State Barge Canal.

buffer in computing, part of the memory used to hold data while it is waiting to be used. For example, a program might store data in a printer buffer until the printer is ready to print it.

buffer mixture of chemical compounds chosen to maintain a steady ◊pH. The commonest buffers consist of a mixture of a weak organic acid and one of its salts or a mixture of acid salts of phosphoric acid. The addition of either an acid or a base causes a shift in the ◊chemical equilibrium, thus keeping the pH constant.

Buffon /buːˈfɒn/ George Louis Leclerc, Comte de 1707–1778. French naturalist and author of the 18th century's most significant work of natural history, the 44-volume *Histoire naturelle* (1749–67). In *The Epochs of Nature*, one of the volumes, he questioned biblical chronology for the first time, and raised the Earth's age from the traditional figure of 6,000 years to the seemingly colossal estimate of 75,000 years.

bug in computing, an error in a program. It can be an error in the logical structure of a program or a syntactic error, such as a spelling mistake. Some bugs cause a program to fail immediately; others remain dormant, causing problems only when a particular combination of events occurs. See also ◊debugging.

bug in entomology, an insect belonging to the order Hemiptera. All these have two pairs of wings with forewings partly thickened. They also have piercing mouthparts adapted for sucking the juices of plants or animals, the 'beak' being tucked under the body when not in use.

They include: the bedbug, which sucks human blood; the shieldbug, or stinkbug, which has a strong odour and feeds on plants; the water boatman and other water bugs.

Bug /buːg/ name of two rivers in E Europe: the *West Bug* rises in SW Ukraine and flows to the Vistula, and the *South Bug* rises in W Ukraine and flows to the Black Sea.

Buganda /buːˈgændə/ two provinces (North and South Buganda) of Uganda, home of the Baganda people and formerly a kingdom from the 17th century. The *kabaka* or king, Edward Mutesa II (1924–1969), was the first president of independent Uganda 1962–66, and his son Ronald Mutebi (1955–) is *sabataka* (head of the Baganda clans).

Bugatti /bjuːˈgæti/ racing and sports-car company, founded by the Italian Ettore Bugatti (1881–1947). The first car was produced

1908, but it was not until 1924 that one of the great Bugattis, Type 35, was produced. Bugatti cars are credited with more race wins than any other. The company was taken over by Hispano Suiza after Bugatti's death 1947.

buggery or *sodomy* anal intercourse by a man with another man or a woman, or sexual intercourse by a man or woman with an animal (bestiality). In English law, buggery may be committed by a man with his wife, or with another man in private if both parties consent and are over 21 years old. In all other circumstances it is an offence.

bugle in music, a valveless brass instrument with a shorter tube and less flared bell than the trumpet. Constructed of copper plated with brass, it has long been used as a military instrument for giving a range of signals based on the tones of a harmonic series. The bugle is conical whereas the trumpet is cylindrical.

bugle any of a genus *Ajuga* of low-growing plants of the mint family Labiatae, with spikes of white, pink, or blue flowers. They are often grown as ground cover.

The leaves may be smooth-edged or faintly toothed, the lower ones with a long stalk. Bugle is found across Europe and N Africa, usually in damp woods or pastures.

bugloss any of several genera of plants of the family Boraginaceae, distinguished by their rough, bristly leaves and small blue flowers.

Bugs Bunny cartoon-film character created by US cartoonist Bob Clampett for *Porky's Hare Hunt* 1938. The cynical, carrot-crunching rabbit with its goofy incisors and catchphrase 'Eh, what's up, Doc?' starred again in *A Wild Hare* 1940. By 1962 he had appeared in 159 films, and won an Academy Award for *Knighty Knight Bugs* 1958.

buhl alternative spelling for ◊boulle, a type of marquetry.

building society in the UK, a financial institution that attracts investment in order to lend money, repayable at interest, for the purchase or building of a house on security of a ◊mortgage. Since the 1970s building societies have considerably expanded their services and in many ways now compete with clearing banks.

Building societies originated 1781 from the ◊friendly societies in England. In Britain, the Building Societies Act 1986 enabled societies

to raise up to 20% of their funds on the international capital market. Among other changes, the act provided that building societies could grant unsecured loans of up to £5,000; they were also able to offer interest-bearing cheque accounts, a challenge to the clearing banks' traditional role in this area. From 1988 societies were able to operate in other EC countries. In the USA the equivalent institution is called a *savings and loan association*; the first was founded 1831.

Bujumbura /ˌbuːdʒʊmˈbuərə/ capital of Burundi; population (1986) 272,600. Formerly called *Usumbura* (until 1962), it was founded 1899 by German colonists. The university was established 1960.

Bukavu /buːˈkɑːvuː/ port in E Zaire, on Lake Kivu; population (1984) 171,100. Mining is the chief industry. Called *Costermansville* until 1966, it is the capital of Itivu region.

Bukhara /buˈxɑːrə/ city in Uzbekistan; population (1987) 220,000. It is the capital of Bukhara region, which has given its name to carpets (made in Ashkhabad). It is an Islamic centre, with a Muslim theological training centre. An ancient city in central Asia, it was formerly the capital of the independent emirate of Bukhara, annexed to Russia 1868.

It was included in Bukhara region 1924.

Bukharest alternative form of ◊Bucharest, capital of Romania.

Bukharin /buˈxɑːrɪn/ Nikolai Ivanovich 1888–1938. Soviet politician and theorist. A moderate, he was the chief Bolshevik thinker after Lenin. Executed on Stalin's orders for treason 1938, he was posthumously rehabilitated 1988.

He wrote the major defence of war communism in his *Economics of the Transition Period* 1920. He drafted the Soviet constitution of 1936 but in 1938 was imprisoned and tried for treason in one of Stalin's 'show trials'. He pleaded guilty to treason, but defended his moderate policies and denied criminal charges. Nevertheless, he was executed, as were all other former members of Lenin's Politburo except Trotsky, who was murdered, and Stalin himself.

Bukovina /ˌbukəˈviːnə/ region in SE Europe, divided between Ukraine and Romania. It covers 10,500 sq km/4,050 sq mi.

history Part of Moldavia during the Turkish regime, it was ceded by the Ottoman Empire to Austria 1777, becoming a duchy of the Dual Monarchy 1867–1918; then it was included in Romania. N Bukovina was ceded to the USSR 1940 and included in Ukraine as the region of Chernovtsy; the cession was confirmed by the peace treaty 1947, but the question of its return has been raised by Romania. The part of Bukovina remaining in Romania became the district of Suceava.

Bulawayo /ˌbʊləˈweɪəʊ/ industrial city and railway junction in Zimbabwe; population (1982) 415,000. It lies at an altitude of 1,355 m/4,450 ft on the river Matsheumlope, a tributary of the Zambezi, and was founded on the site of the kraal (enclosed village), burned down 1893, of the Matabele chief, Lobenguela. It produces agricultural and electrical equipment. The former capital of Matabeleland, Bulawayo developed with the exploitation of gold mines in the neighbourhood.

bulb underground bud with fleshy leaves containing a reserve food supply and with roots growing from its base. Bulbs function in vegetative reproduction and are characteristic of many monocotyledonous plants such as the daffodil, snowdrop, and onion. Bulbs are grown on a commercial scale in temperate countries, such as England and the Netherlands.

bulbil small bulb that develops above ground from a bud. Bulbils may be formed on the stem from axillary buds, as in members of the saxifrage family, or in the place of flowers, as seen in many species of onion *Allium*. They drop off the parent plant and develop into new individuals, providing a means of ◊vegetative reproduction and dispersal.

bulbul small fruit-eating passerine bird of the family Pycnonotidae. There are about 120 species, mainly in the forests of the Old World tropics.

Bulgakov /bʊlˈɡɑːkɒf/ Mikhail Afanasyevich 1891–1940. Russian novelist and playwright. His novel *The White Guard* 1924, dramatized as *The Days of the Turbins* 1926, deals with the Revolution and the civil war.

Bulganin /bʊlˈɡɑːnɪn/ Nikolai 1895–1975. Soviet military leader and politician. He helped to organize Moscow's defence in World War II, became a marshal of the USSR 1947, and was minister of defence 1947–49 and 1953–55. On the fall of Malenkov he became prime minister (chair of Council of Ministers) 1955–58 until ousted by Khrushchev.

Bulgaria /bʌlˈɡeərɪə/ country in SE Europe, bounded N by Romania, W by Yugoslavia and Macedonia, S by Greece, SE by Turkey, and E by the Black Sea.

government Under the 1991 constitution, Bulgaria is a parliamentary republic. There is a single-chamber legislature, the 240-member national assembly, directly elected every five years by a system of proportional representation. The prime minister is the leader of the party or group with a majority in the assembly. The state president, who is also commander in chief of the armed forces, is popularly elected for a five-year term. The controlling force has traditionally been the Bulgarian Communist Party (BCP), renamed the Bulgarian Socialist Party 1990.

history In the ancient world Bulgaria comprised ◊Thrace and Moesia and was the Roman province of Moesia Inferior. It was occupied in the 6th century AD by the Slavs (from whom the language derives), followed by Bulgars from Asia in the 7th century. In 865 Khan Boris adopted Eastern Orthodox Christianity, and under his son Simeon (893–927), who assumed the title of tsar, Bulgaria became a leading power. It was ruled by ◊Byzantium from the 11th century and, although a second Bulgarian empire was founded after the 14th century, Bulgaria formed part of the ◊Ottoman Empire for almost 500 years, becoming an independent kingdom 1908.

Bulgaria allied itself with Germany during World War I. From 1919 a government of the leftist Agrarian Party introduced land reforms, but was overthrown 1923 by a fascist coup. A monarchical-fascist dictatorship was established 1934 under King ◊Boris III. During World War II Bulgaria again allied itself with Germany, being occupied 1944 by the USSR.

republic In 1946 the monarchy was abolished, and a republic was proclaimed under a communist-leaning alliance, the Fatherland Front, led by Georgi ◊Dimitrov (1882–1949). Bulgaria reverted largely to its 1919 frontiers. The new republic adopted a Soviet-style constitution 1947, with nationalized industries and cooperative farming introduced. Vulko Chervenkov, Dimitrov's brother-in-law, became the dominant political figure 1950–54, introducing a Stalinist regime. He was succeeded by the more moderate Todor ◊Zhivkov, under whom Bulgaria became one of the Soviet Union's most loyal satellites.

haphazard reforms During the 1980s the country faced mounting economic problems, chiefly caused by the rising cost of energy imports. During 1985–89, under the promptings of the Soviet leader Mikhail Gorbachev, a haphazard series of administrative and economic reforms was instituted. This proved insufficient to placate reformists either inside or outside the BCP. In Nov 1989, influenced by the democratization movements sweeping other East European countries and backed by the army and the USSR, the foreign secretary Petar ◊Mladenov ousted Zhivkov. Mladenov became leader of the BCP and president of the state council, and quickly promoted genuine political pluralism. In Dec 1989 legislation was passed to end the BCP's 'leading role' in the state and allow the formation of free opposition parties and trade unions; political prisoners were freed; the secret police wing responsible for dissident surveillance was abolished; and free elections were promised for 1990. In Feb 1990 Alexander Lilov, a reformer, was elected party chief, and Andrei Lukanov became prime minister. A special commission was established to investigate allegations of nepotism and high-level embezzlement of state funds under Zhivkov. Zhivkov was placed under house arrest and later imprisoned, pending trial on charges of corruption and abuse of power.

relations with Turkey Bulgaria's relations with neighbouring Turkey deteriorated during 1989, following the flight of 310,000 ethnic Turks from Bulgaria to Turkey after the Bulgarian government's violent suppression of their protests at the programme of 'Bulgarianization' (forcing them to adopt Slavic names and resettle elsewhere). The new Mladenov government announced Dec 1989 that the forced assimilation programme would be abandoned; this provoked demonstrations by anti-Turk nationalists (abetted by BCP conservatives) but encouraged more than 100,000 refugees to return from Turkey.

market economy In Feb 1990 a government decree relegalized private farming and a phased lifting of price controls commenced April 1990 as part of a drive towards a market economy. Huge price rises and food shortages were the result. Also in April, the BCP renamed itself the Bulgarian Socialist Party (BSP). Petar Mladenov resigned as president July 1990 and in Aug the opposition leader Dr Zhelyu Zhelev was elected in his place. In Nov 1990, following mass demonstrations in Sofia, a general strike, and a boycott of parliament by opposition deputies, the government of Andrei Lukanov resigned. He was replaced in Dec 1990 by a nonparty politician, Dimitur Popov (1927–), heading a caretaker coalition government, and the strikes by workers and students were called off.

In national elections held Oct 1991 the right-of-centre Union of Democratic Forces (UDF) edged out the BSP, but fell short of an outright majority. In 1992, Lyuben Berov became prime minister, replacing Popov. Berov resigned Sept 1994 and Reneta Indjova was appointed interim prime minister.

Bulgarian member of an ethnic group living mainly in Bulgaria. There are 8–8.5 million speakers of Bulgarian, a Slavic language belonging to the Indo-European family. The Bulgarians use the Cyrillic alphabet and are known for their folk arts.

Bulge, Battle of the or *Ardennes offensive* in World War II, Hitler's plan, code-named 'Watch on the Rhine', for a breakthrough by his field marshal ◊Rundstedt aimed at the US line in the Ardennes 16 Dec 1944–28 Jan 1945. There were 77,000 Allied casualties and 130,000 German, including Hitler's last powerful reserve, his Panzer elite. Although US troops were encircled for some weeks at Bastogne, the German counteroffensive failed.

bulgur wheat cracked wholewheat, made by cooking the grains, then drying and cracking them. It is widely eaten in the Middle East.

bulimia (Greek 'ox hunger') condition of continuous, uncontrolled hunger. Considered a counteraction to stress or depression, this eating disorder is found chiefly in young women. When compensated for by forced vomiting or overdoses of laxatives, the condition is called *bulimia nervosa*. It is sometimes associated with ◊anorexia.

bull speculator who buys stocks or shares on the stock exchange expecting a rise in the price in order to sell them later at a profit, the opposite of a ◊bear. In a bull market, prices rise and bulls profit.

bull or *papal bull* document or edict issued by the pope; so called from the circular seals (medieval Latin *bulla*) attached to them. Some of the most celebrated bulls include Leo X's condemnation of Luther 1520 and Pius IX's proclamation of papal infallibility 1870.

Bull /bʊl/ John. Imaginary figure personifying England; see ◊John Bull.

bull-baiting the setting of dogs to attack a chained bull, one-time 'sport' popular in the UK and Europe. It became illegal in Britain 1835.

bulldog British dog of ancient but uncertain origin. The head is broad and square, with deeply wrinkled cheeks, small folded ears, and the nose laid back between the eyes. The bulldog grows to about 45 cm/18 in at the shoulder.

It was bred for bull-baiting, the peculiar set of the lower jaw making it difficult for the dog to release its grip.

bulldozer earth-moving machine widely used in construction work for clearing rocks and tree stumps and levelling a site. The bulldozer is a kind of ◊tractor with a powerful engine and a curved, shovel-like blade at the front, which can be lifted and forced down by hydraulic rams. It usually has ◊caterpillar tracks so that it can move easily over rough ground.

bullfighting the national 'sport' of Spain, (where there are more than 400 bullrings), which is also popular in Mexico, Portugal, and much of Latin America. It involves the ritualized taunting of a bull in a circular ring, until its eventual death at the hands of the matador. Originally popular in Greece and Rome, it was introduced into Spain by the Moors in the 11th century.

In some parts of France and in Portugal it is illegal to kill the bulls. Opponents of the sport are appalled by the cruelty involved and efforts have been made to outlaw it.

bullfinch Eurasian finch *Pyrrhula pyrrhula*, with a thick head and neck, and short heavy bill. It is small and blue-grey or black, the males being reddish and the females brown on the breast. Bullfinches are 15 cm/6 in long, and usually seen in pairs. They feed on tree buds as well as seeds and berries, and are usually seen in woodland. They also live in the Aleutians and on the Alaska mainland.

bullhead or *miller's thumb*. small fish *Cottus gobio* found in fresh water in the northern hemisphere, often under stones. It has a large head, a spine on the gill cover, and grows to 10 cm/4 in.

Related bullheads, such as the *father lasher Myxocephalus scorpius*, live in coastal waters. They are up to 30 cm/1 ft long. The male guards the eggs and fans them with his tail.

Bullock Report the report of a committee of inquiry headed by Lord Bullock, published 1975, on the teaching of English in the UK. The report, *A Language for Life*, recommended improvements in the teaching of reading, writing, and spoken English in both primary and secondary schools.

bullroarer musical instrument used by Australian Aborigines during religious rites consisting of a piece of wood or stone, fastened to a cord. It is twirled around the head to make a whirring noise and is a highly sacred object carved with mythical designs. It is also used in many other parts of the world, including Britain.

Bull Run, Battles of /bʊl rʌn/ in the American Civil War, two victories for the Confederate army under General Robert E Lee at *Manassas* Junction, NE Virginia: *1st Battle of Bull Run* 21 July 1861; *2nd Battle of Bull Run* 29–30 Aug 1862.

bull terrier heavily built, smooth-coated breed of dog, usually white, originating as a cross between a terrier and a bulldog. It grows to about 40 cm/16 in tall, and was formerly used in bull-baiting. Pit bull terriers are used in illegal dog fights.

Bülow /ˈbjuːləʊ/ Bernhard, Prince von 1849–1929. German diplomat and politician. He was chancellor of the German Empire 1900–09 under Kaiser Wilhelm II and, holding that self-interest was the only rule for any state, adopted attitudes to France and Russia that unintentionally reinforced the trend towards opposing European power groups: the ◊Triple Entente (Britain, France, Russia) and ◊Triple Alliance (Germany, Austria–Hungary, Italy).

Bülow /'bjuːləʊ/ Hans (Guido) Frieherr von 1830–1894. German conductor and pianist. He studied with Richard ◊Wagner and Franz ◊Liszt, and in 1857 married Cosima, daughter of Liszt. From 1864 he served Ludwig II of Bavaria, conducting first performances of Wagner's *Tristan und Isolde* and *Die Meistersinger*. His wife left him and married Wagner 1870.

bulrush either of two plants: the great reed mace or cat's tail *Typha latifolia* with chocolate-brown tight-packed flower spikes reaching up to 15 cm/ 6 in long; and a type of sedge *Scirpus lacustris* with tufts of reddish-brown flowers at the top of a rounded, rushlike stem.

Bulwer-Lytton /'bʊlwə 'lɪtn/ Edward George Earle Lytton, Ist Baron Lytton 1803–1873. See ◊Lytton.

bumblebee any large ◊bee, usually dark-coloured but banded with yellow, orange or white, belonging to the genus *Bombus*.

Most species live in small colonies, usually underground, often in an old mousehole. The queen lays her eggs in a hollow nest of moss or grass at the beginning of the season. The larvae are fed on pollen and honey, and develop into workers. All the bees die at the end of the season except fertilized females, which hibernate and produce fresh colonies in the spring. Bumblebees are found naturally all over the world, with the exception of Australia, where they have been introduced to facilitate the pollination of some cultivated varieties of clover.

Bunche /bʌntʃ/ Ralph 1904–1971. US diplomat. Grandson of a slave, he was principal director of the UN Department of Trusteeship 1947–54, and UN undersecretary acting as mediator in Palestine 1948–49 and as special representative in the Congo 1960. He taught at Harvard and Howard universities and was involved in the planning of the ◊United Nations. In 1950 he was awarded the Nobel Prize for Peace, the first awarded to a black man.

Bundelas /bʊnˈdeɪləz/ Rajput clan prominent in the 14th century, which gave its name to the Bundelkhand in N central India. The clan had replaced the ◊Chandelā in the 11th century and continued to resist

the attacks of other Indian rulers until coming under British control after 1812.

Bunin /'buːnɪn/ Ivan Alexeyevich 1870–1953. Russian writer, author of *Derevnya/The Village* 1910, which tells of the passing of peasant life; and *Gospodin iz San Frantsisko/The Gentleman from San Francisco* 1916 (about the death of a millionaire on Capri), for which he received a Nobel prize 1933. He was also a poet and translated Byron into Russian.

Bunker Hill, Battle of /'bʌŋkə/ the first considerable engagement in the ◊American Revolution, 17 June 1775, near a small hill in Charlestown (now part of Boston), Massachusetts, USA; although the colonists were defeated they were able to retreat to Boston and suffered fewer casualties than the British.

Bunsen /'bʊnzən/ Robert Wilhelm von 1811–1899. German chemist credited with the invention of the *Bunsen burner*. His name is also given to the carbon–zinc electric cell, which he invented 1841 for use in arc lamps. In 1859 he discovered two new elements, caesium and rubidium.

bunsen burner gas burner used in laboratories, consisting of a vertical metal tube through which a fine jet of fuel gas is directed. Air is drawn in through airholes near the base of the tube and the mixture is ignited and burns at the tube's upper opening.

The invention of the burner is attributed to Robert von Bunsen 1855 but Michael Faraday is known to have produced a similar device at an earlier date.

Bunshaft /'bʌnʃaft/ Gordon 1909–1990. US architect whose Modernist buildings include the first to be completely enclosed in curtain walling (walls which hang from a rigid steel frame), the Lever Building 1952 in New York. He also designed the Heinz Company's UK headquarters 1965 at Hayes Park, London.

bunting any of a number of sturdy, finch-like, passerine birds with short, thick bills, of the family Emberizidae, especially the genera *Passerim* and *Emberiza*. Most of these brightly coloured birds are native to the New World.

Some live in the Old World, such as the ◊ortolan, the ◊yellowhammer, and the *snow bunting* of the far north, which is largely white-plumaged, and migrates to temperate Europe in the winter.

Buñuel /ˈbuːnjuel/ Luis 1900–1983. Spanish Surrealist film director. He collaborated with Salvador Dali on *Un Chien andalou* 1928 and *L'Age d'or/The Golden Age* 1930, and established his solo career with *Los olvidados/The Young and the Damned* 1950. His works are often anticlerical, with black humour and erotic imagery. Later films include *Le Charme discret de la bourgeoisie/The Discreet Charm of the Bourgeoisie* 1972 (Academy Award winner) and *Cet Obscur Objet du désir/That Obscure Object of Desire* 1977.

Bunyan /ˈbʌnjən/ John 1628–1688. English author. A Baptist, he was imprisoned in Bedford 1660–72 for unlicensed preaching. During a second jail sentence 1675 he started to write *The Pilgrim's Progress*, the first part of which was published 1678. Other works include *Grace Abounding* 1666, *The Life and Death of Mr Badman* 1680, and *The Holy War* 1682.

At 16, during the Civil War, he was conscripted into the Parliamentary army. Released 1646, he passed through a period of religious doubt before joining the ◊Baptists 1653. In 1660 he was committed to Bedford county jail for preaching, where he remained for 12 years, refusing all offers of release conditional on his not preaching again. During his confinement he wrote *Grace Abounding* describing his early spiritual struggles. Set free 1672, he was elected pastor of the Bedford congregation, but in 1675 he was again arrested and imprisoned for six months in the jail on Bedford Bridge, where he began *The Pilgrim's Progress*.

buoy floating object used to mark channels for shipping or warn of hazards to navigation. Buoys come in different shapes, such as a pole (spar buoy), cylinder (car buoy), and cone (nun buoy). Light buoys carry a small tower surmounted by a flashing lantern, and bell buoys house a bell, which rings as the buoy moves up and down with the waves. Mooring buoys are heavy and have a ring on top to which a ship can be tied.

buoyancy lifting effect of a fluid on a body wholly or partly immersed in it. This was studied by ◊Archimedes in the 3rd century BC.

bur or *burr* in botany, a type of 'false fruit' or ◊pseudocarp, surrounded by numerous hooks; for instance, that of burdock *Arctium*. The term is also used to include any type of fruit or seed-bearing hooks, such as that of goosegrass *Galium aparine* and wood

avens *Geum urbanum*. Burs catch in the feathers or fur of passing animals, and thus may be dispersed over considerable distances.

Burbage /ˈbɜːbɪdʒ/ Richard *c.* 1567–1619. English actor, thought to have been ◊Shakespeare's original Hamlet, Othello, and Lear. He also appeared in first productions of works by Ben Jonson, Thomas Kyd, and John Webster. His father *James Burbage* (c. 1530–1597) built the first English playhouse, known as 'the Theatre'; his brother *Cuthbert Burbage* (*c.* 1566–1636) built the original ◊Globe Theatre 1599 in London.

burbot long, rounded fish *Lota lota* of the cod family, the only one living entirely in fresh water. Up to 1 m/3 ft long, it lives on the bottom of clear lakes and rivers, often in holes or under rocks, throughout Europe, Asia, and North America.

burden of proof in court proceedings, the duty of a party to produce sufficient evidence to prove that his case is true.

In English and US law a higher standard of proof is required in criminal cases (beyond all reasonable doubt), than in civil cases (on the balance of probabilities).

burdock any of the bushy herbs belonging to the genus *Arctium* of the family Compositae, characterized by hairy leaves and ripe fruit enclosed in ◊burs with strong hooks. It is a common roadside weed in Britain.

bureaucracy organization whose structure and operations are governed to a high degree by written rules and a hierarchy of offices; in its broadest sense, all forms of administration, and in its narrowest, rule by officials.

The early civilizations of Mesopotamia, Egypt, China, and India were organized hierarchically, thus forming the bureaucratic tradition of government. The German sociologist Max Weber saw the growth of bureaucracy in industrial societies as an inevitable reflection of the underlying shift from traditional authority to a rational and legal system of organization and control. In Weber's view, bureaucracy established a relation between legally enstated authorities and their subordinate officials. This relationship is characterized by defined rights and duties prescribed in written regulations.

Contemporary writers have highlighted the problems of bureaucracy, such as its inflexibility and rigid adherence to rules, so that today the term is often used as a criticism rather than its original neutral sense.

burette in chemistry, a piece of apparatus, used in ◊titration, for the controlled delivery of measured variable quantities of a liquid.

It consists of a long, narrow, calibrated glass tube, with a tap at the bottom, leading to a narrow-bore exit.

Burgenland /ˈbuəɡənlænd/ federal state of SE Austria, extending from the Danube S along the W border of the Hungarian plain; area 4,000 sq km/1,544 sq mi; population (1989) 267,200. It is a largely agricultural region adjoining the Neusiedler See, and produces timber, fruit, sugar, wine, lignite, antimony, and limestone. Its capital is Eisenstadt.

Burgess /ˈbɜːdʒɪs/ Anthony. Pen name of Anthony John Burgess Wilson 1917–1993. British novelist, critic, and composer. His prolific work includes *A Clockwork Orange* 1962, set in a future London terrorized by teenage gangs, and the panoramic *Earthly Powers* 1980. His vision has been described as bleak and pessimistic, but his work is also comic and satiric, as in his novels featuring the poet Enderby.

Burgess /ˈbɜːdʒɪs/ Guy (Francis de Moncy) 1910–1963. British spy, a diplomat recruited by the USSR as an agent. He was linked with Kim ◊Philby, Donald Maclean (1913–1983), and Anthony ◊Blunt.

Burgess Shale Site /ˈbɜːdʒɪs/ site of unique fossil-bearing rock formations created 530 million years ago by a mud slide, in Yoho National Park, British Colombia, Canada. The shales in this corner of the Rocky Mountains contain more than 120 species of marine invertebrate fossils. Although discovered 1909 by US geologist Charles Walcott, the Burgess Shales have only recently been used as evidence in the debate concerning the evolution of life. In *Wonderful Life* 1990 Stephen Jay Gould drew attention to a body of scientific opinion interpreting the fossil finds as evidence of parallel early evolutionary trends extinguished by chance rather than natural selection.

burgh former unit of Scottish local government, abolished 1975; the terms *burgh* and *royal burgh* once gave mercantile privilege but are now only an honorary distinction.

burgh (burh or borough) term originating in Germanic lands in the 9th–10th centuries referring to a fortified settlement, usually surrounding a monastery or castle. Later, it was used to mean new towns, or towns that enjoyed particular privileges relating to gov-

ernment and taxation and whose citizens were called *burghers*.

Burgh /də ˈbɜːɡ/ Hubert de died 1243. English ◊justiciar and regent of England. He began his career in the administration of Richard I, and was promoted to the justiciarship by King John; he remained in that position under Henry III from 1216 until his dismissal. He was a supporter of King John against the barons, and ended French intervention in England by his defeat of the French fleet in the Strait of Dover 1217. He reorganized royal administration and the Common Law.

burgher term used from the 11th century to describe citizens of ◊burghs who were freemen of a burgh, and had the right to participate in its government. They usually had to possess a house within the burgh.

Burghley /ˈbɜːli/ William Cecil, Baron Burghley 1520–1598. English politician, chief adviser to Elizabeth I as secretary of state from 1558 and Lord High Treasurer from 1572. He was largely responsible for the religious settlement of 1559, and took a leading role in the events preceding the execution of Mary Queen of Scots 1587.

One of Edward VI's secretaries, he lost office under Queen Mary, but on Queen Elizabeth's succession became one of her most trusted ministers. He carefully avoided a premature breach with Spain in the difficult period leading up to the attack by the Spanish Armada 1588, did a great deal towards abolishing monopolies and opening up trade, and was created Baron Burghley 1571.

burglary offence committed when a trespasser enters a building intending to steal, do damage to property, grievously harm any person, or rape a woman. Entry need only be effective so, for example, a person who puts their hand through a broken shop window to steal something may be guilty of burglary.

UK research 1991 suggested that the average age of burglars was 15 years. In England and Wales 1990, burglary formed 22% of all recorded crime, with 1,006,500 offences, an 11% increase from 1987 (these figures do not include theft from or of vehicles).

Burgos /ˈbuəɡɒs/ city in Castilla-León, Spain, 217 km/135 mi N of Madrid; population (1986) 164,000. It produces textiles, motor parts, and chemicals. It was capital of the old kingdom of Castile, and the national hero El Cid is buried in the Gothic cathedral, built 1221–1567.

Burgundy /ˈbɜːgəndi/ ancient kingdom and duchy in the valleys of the rivers Saône and Rhône, France. The Burgundi were a Teutonic tribe that overran the country about 400. From the 9th century to the death of Duke ◊Charles the Bold 1477, Burgundy was the nucleus of a powerful principality. On Charles's death the duchy was incorporated into France. The capital of Burgundy was Dijon. Today the region to which it corresponds is ◊Bourgogne.

Burke /bɜːk/ Edmund 1729–1797. British Whig politician and political theorist, born in Dublin, Ireland. In Parliament from 1765, he opposed the government's attempts to coerce the American colonists, for example in *Thoughts on the Present Discontents* 1770, and supported the emancipation of Ireland, but denounced the French Revolution, for example in *Reflections on the Revolution in France* 1790.

Burke wrote *A Philosophical Inquiry into the Origin of our Ideas on the Sublime and Beautiful* 1756, on aesthetics. He was paymaster of the forces in Rockingham's government 1782 and in the Fox–North coalition 1783, and after the collapse of the latter spent the rest of his career in opposition. He attacked Warren Hastings's misgovernment in India and promoted his impeachment. Burke defended his inconsistency in supporting the American but not the French Revolution in his *Appeal from the New to the Old Whigs* 1791 and *Letter to a Noble Lord* 1796, and attacked the suggestion of peace with France in *Letters on a Regicide Peace* 1795–97. He retired 1794. He was a skilled orator and is regarded by British Conservatives as the greatest of their political theorists.

Burke /bɜːk/ John 1787–1848. First publisher, in 1826, of ◊*Burke's Peerage*.

Burke /bɜːk/ Martha Jane *c.* 1852–1903. Real name of US heroine ◊Calamity Jane.

Burke /bɜːk/ Robert O'Hara 1820–1861. Australian explorer who made the first south-north crossing of Australia (from Victoria to the Gulf of Carpentaria), with William Wills (1834–1861). Both died on the return journey, and only one of their party survived. He was born in Galway, Ireland, and became a police inspector in the goldfields of Victoria.

Burke /bɜːk/ William 1792–1829. Irish murderer. He and his partner William Hare, living in Edinburgh, sold the body of an old man who had died from natural causes in their lodging house. After that, they increased their supplies by murdering at least 15 people. Burke was hanged on the evidence of Hare. Hare is said to have died a beggar in London in the 1860s.

Burke's Peerage popular name of the *Genealogical and Heraldic History of the Peerage, Baronetage, and Knightage of the United Kingdom*, first issued by John Burke 1826. The most recent edition was 1970.

Burkina Faso /bɜːˈkiːnə ˈfæsəʊ/ (formerly Upper Volta) landlocked country in W Africa, bounded E by Niger, NW and W by Mali, S by Ivory Coast, Ghana, Togo, and Benin.

government The 1991 constitution provides for a 107-member national assembly, Assemblée des Députés Populaires (ADP), elected by universal suffrage for a five-year term, and a president, similarly elected for a seven-year term renewable only once.

history The area known from 1984 as Burkina Faso was invaded in the 11th to 13th centuries by the Mossi people, whose powerful warrior kingdoms lasted for over 500 years. In the 1890s it became a province of French West Africa, known as Upper Volta.

In 1958 it became a self-governing republic and in 1960 achieved full independence with Maurice Yaméogo as president. A military coup 1966 removed Yaméogo and installed Col Sangoulé Lamizana as president and prime minister. He suspended the constitution, dissolved the national assembly, banned political activity, and set up a supreme council of the armed forces as the instrument of government.

In 1969 the ban on political activity was lifted, and in 1970 a referendum approved a new constitution, based on civilian rule, that was to come into effect after four years of combined military and civilian government. After disagreements between military and civilian members of the government, General Lamizana announced 1974 a return to army rule and dissolved the national assembly.

Lamizana overthrown In 1977 political activity was allowed again, and a referendum approved a constitution that would create a civilian government. In the 1978 elections the Volta Democratic Union (UDV) won a majority in the national assembly, and Lamizana became president. But a deteriorating economy led to strikes, and a bloodless coup led by Col Zerbo overthrew Lamizana 1980. Zerbo formed a government of national recovery, suspended the constitution, and dissolved the national assembly.

In 1982 Zerbo was ousted, and Maj Jean-Baptiste Ouédraogo emerged as leader of a military regime, with Capt Thomas Sankara as prime minister. In 1983 Sankara seized power in another coup, becoming president and ruling through a council of ministers. Opposition members were arrested, the national assembly was dissolved, and a National Revolutionary Council (CNR) set up. In 1984 Sankara announced that the country would be known as Burkina Faso ('land of upright men'), symbolizing a break with its colonial past; his government strengthened ties with Ghana and established links with Benin and Libya. Sankara was killed Oct 1987 in a military coup led by a former close colleague, Capt Blaise Compaoré (1951–). A new constitution, providing for a multi-party system, was approved 1991. Compaore was re-elected president Dec 1991. Prompted by widespread unrest, multiparty elections were held May 1992. The ruling FP–Popular Front won a clear majority, amid opposition claims of electoral fraud.

burlesque in the 17th and 18th centuries, a form of satirical comedy parodying a particular play or dramatic genre. For example, John ◊Gay's *The Beggar's Opera* 1728 is a burlesque of 18th-century opera, and Richard Brinsley ◊Sheridan's *The Critic* 1777 satirizes the sentimentality in contemporary drama. In the USA from the mid-19th century, burlesque referred to a sex and comedy show invented by Michael Bennett Leavitt 1866 with acts including acrobats, singers,

and comedians. During the 1920s striptease was introduced in order to counteract the growing popularity of the movies.

Burma /ˈbɜːmə/ former name (to 1989) of ◊Myanmar.

Burman member of the largest ethnic group in Myanmar (formerly Burma). The Burmans, speakers of a Sino-Tibetan language, migrated from the hills of Tibet, settling in the areas around Mandalay by the 11th century AD.

From the Mons, a neighbouring people, the Burmans acquired Hinayana Buddhism and a written script based on Indian syllables. The Burmans are mainly settled in the valleys where they cultivate rice in irrigated fields.

burn destruction of body tissue by extremes of temperature, corrosive chemicals, electricity, or radiation. *First-degree burns* may cause reddening; *second-degree burns* cause blistering and irritation but usually heal spontaneously; *third-degree burns* are disfiguring and may be life-threatening.

Burns cause plasma, the fluid component of the blood, to leak from the blood vessels, and it 'is this loss of circulating fluid that engenders ◊shock. Emergency treatment is needed for third-degree burns in order to replace the fluid volume, prevent infection (a dire threat to the severely burned), and reduce the pain.

Burne-Jones /ˈbɜːn ˈdʒəʊnz/ Edward Coley 1833–1898. English painter. In 1856 he was apprenticed to the Pre-Raphaelite painter Dante Gabriel ◊Rossetti, who remained a dominant influence. His paintings, inspired by legend and myth, were characterized by elongated forms as in *King Cophetua and the Beggar Maid* 1880–84 (Tate Gallery, London). He later moved towards Symbolism. He also designed tapestries and stained glass in association with William ◊Morris. The best collection of his work is in the Birmingham City Art Gallery.

Burnell /ˈbel bɜːˈnel/ (Susan) Jocelyn (Bell) 1943– . British astronomer. In 1967 she discovered the first ◊pulsar (rapidly flashing star) with Antony ◊Hewish and colleagues at Cambridge University, England.

burnet herb *Sanguisorba minor* of the rose family, also known as *salad burnet*. It smells of cucumber and can be used in salads. The term is also used for other members of the genus *Sanguisorba*.

Burnet /ˈbɜːnɪt/ Macfarlane 1899–1985. Australian physician, an authority on immunology and viral diseases. He was awarded the Order of Merit 1958 in recognition of his work on such diseases as influenza, poliomyelitis, and cholera, and shared the 1960 Nobel Prize for Medicine with Peter Medawar for his work on skin grafting.

Burnett /bəˈnet/ Frances (Eliza) Hodgson 1849–1924. English writer who emigrated with her family to the USA 1865. Her novels for children include the rags-to-riches tale *Little Lord Fauntleroy* 1886 and the sentimental *The Secret Garden* 1909.

Burney /ˈbɜːni/ Frances (Fanny) 1752–1840. English novelist and diarist, daughter of musician Dr Charles Burney (1726–1814). She achieved success with *Evelina*, published anonymously 1778, became a member of Dr ◊Johnson's circle, received a post at court from Queen Charlotte, and in 1793 married the French émigré General d'Arblay. She published three further novels, *Cecilia* 1782, *Camilla* 1796, and *The Wanderer* 1814; her diaries and letters appeared 1842.

Burnham /ˈbɜːnəm/ Forbes 1923–1985. Guyanese Marxist-Leninist politician. He was prime minister 1964–80, leading the country to independence 1966 and declaring it the world's first cooperative republic 1970. He was executive president 1980–85. Resistance to the US landing in Grenada 1983 was said to be due to his forewarning the Grenadans of the attack.

Burnham /ˈbɜːnəm/ James 1905–1987. US philosopher who argued in *The Managerial Revolution* 1941 that world control is passing from politicians and capitalists to the new class of business executives, the managers.

burning common name for ◊combustion.

Burns /bɜːnz/ John 1858–1943. British labour leader, sentenced to six weeks' imprisonment for his part in the Trafalgar Square demonstration on 'Bloody Sunday' 13 Nov 1887, and leader of the strike in 1889 securing the 'dockers' tanner' (wage of 6d per hour). An Independent Labour member of Parliament 1892–1918, he was the first working-class person to be a member of the cabinet, as president of the Local Government Board 1906–14.

Burns /bɜːnz/ Robert 1759–1796. Scottish poet who used the Scots dialect at a time when it was not considered suitably 'elevated' for literature. Burns's first volume, *Poems, Chiefly in the Scottish Dialect*, appeared 1786. In addition to his poetry, Burns wrote or adapted many songs, including 'Auld Lang Syne'.

Born at Alloway near Ayr, he became joint tenant with his brother of his late father's farm at Mossgiel in 1784, but it was unsuccessful. Following the publication of his first volume of poems in 1786 he farmed at Ellisland, near Dumfries. He became district excise officer on the failure of his farm in 1791.

Burns' fame rests equally on his poems (such as 'Holy Willie's Prayer', 'Tam o' Shanter', 'The Jolly Beggars', and 'To a Mouse') and his songs—sometimes wholly original, sometimes adaptations—of which he contributed some 300 to Johnson's *Scots Musical Museum* 1787–1803 and Thomson's *Scottish Airs with Poetry* 1793–1811.

Burns /bɜːnz/ Terence 1944– . British economist. A monetarist, he was director of the London Business School for Economic Forecasting 1976–79, and became chief economic adviser to the Thatcher government 1980.

Burr /bɜː/ Aaron 1756–1836. US politician, Republican vice president 1800–04, in which year he killed his political rival Alexander ◊Hamilton in a duel.

Burr was born in Newark, New Jersey of an eminent Puritan family. He was on George Washington's staff during the ◊American Revolution but was critical of the general and was distrusted in turn. He tied with Thomas Jefferson in the presidential election of 1800, but Alexander ◊Hamilton, Burr's longtime adversary, influenced the House of Representatives to vote Jefferson in; Burr becoming vice president. After killing Hamilton he fled to South Carolina, but returned briefly to Washington to complete his term of office.

In 1807 Burr was tried and acquitted of treason charges, which implicated him variously in a scheme to conquer Mexico, or part of Florida, or to rule over a seceded Louisiana. He spent some years in Europe, seeking British and French aid in overthrowing Jefferson, but re-entered the USA 1812 under an assumed name. He died in poverty at the age of 80.

Burra /ˈbʌrə/ Edward 1905–1976. English painter devoted to themes of city life, its hustle, humour, and grimy squalor. *The Snack Bar* 1930 (Tate Gallery, London) and his watercolour scenes of Harlem, New York, 1933–34, are characteristic. Postwar works include religious paintings and landscapes.

Burroughs /ˈbʌrəuz/ Edgar Rice 1875–1950. US novelist. He wrote *Tarzan of the Apes* 1914, the story of an aristocratic child lost in the jungle and reared by apes and followed it with over 20 more books about the Tarzan character. He also wrote about life on Mars.

Burroughs /ˈbʌrəuz/ William S 1914– . US novelist. He 'dropped out' and, as part of the ◊Beat Generation, wrote *Junkie* 1953, describing his addiction to heroin; *The Naked Lunch* 1959; *The Soft Machine* 1961; and *Dead Fingers Talk* 1963. His later novels include *Queer* and *Mind Wars*, both 1985.

Burroughs /ˈbʌrəuz/ William Steward 1857–1898. US industrialist who invented the first hand-operated adding machine to give printed results.

Bursa /ˈbɜːsə/ city in NW Turkey, with a port at Mudania; population (1985) 614,000. It was the capital of the Ottoman Empire 1326–1423.

Burt /bɜːt/ Cyril Lodowic 1883–1971. British psychologist. A specialist in child and mental development, he argued in *The Young Delinquent* 1925 the importance of social and environmental factors in delinquency. After his death it was claimed that he had falsified experimental results in an attempt to prove his theory that intelligence is largely inherited.

Burton /ˈbɜːtn/ Richard Francis 1821–1890. British explorer and translator (he knew 35 oriental languages). He travelled mainly in the Middle East and NE Africa, often disguised as a Muslim; made two attempts to find the source of the Nile, 1855 and 1857–58 (on the second, with ◊Speke, he reached Lake Tanganyika); and wrote many travel books. He translated oriental erotica and the *Arabian Nights* 1885–88.

After military service in India, Burton explored the Arabian peninsula and Somaliland. In 1853 he visited Mecca and Medina disguised as an Afghan pilgrim; he was then commissioned by the Foreign Office to explore the sources of the Nile. Later travels took him to North and South America. His translations include the *Kama Sutra of Vatsyayana* 1883 and *The Perfumed Garden* 1886. His wife, who had accompanied him on some journeys, burned his unpublished manuscripts and diaries after his death.

Burton /ˈbɜːtn/ Richard. Stage name of Richard Jenkins 1925–1984. Welsh actor of stage and screen. He was remarkable for his rich, dramatic voice, and for his marital and acting partnership with Elizabeth Taylor, with whom he appeared in several films, including *Cleopatra* 1962 and *Who's Afraid of Virginia Woolf?* 1966. Among his later films are *Equus* 1977 and *Nineteen Eighty-Four* 1984.

Burton /ˈbɜːtn/ Robert 1577–1640. English philosopher who wrote an analysis of depression, *Anatomy of Melancholy* 1621, a compendium of information on the medical and religious opinions of the time, much used by later authors.

Burundi /buˈrundi/ country in E central Africa, bounded N by Rwanda, W by Zaire, SW by Lake Tanganyika, and SE and E by Tanzania.

government The 1992 constitution provides for a multiparty system. The president, elected by universal suffrage for a maximum of two five-year terms, shares power with the prime minister, who appoints and heads a council of ministers. There is a single-chamber, 81-member national assembly, elected by universal suffrage for a five-year term.

history Originally inhabited by the Twa pygmies, Burundi was taken over by Bantu Hutus in the 13th century, and overrun in the 15th century by the Tutsi. In 1890, ruled by a Tutsi king and known as Urundi, it became part of German East Africa and during World War I was occupied by Belgium. Later, as part of Ruanda-Urundi, it was administered by Belgium as a League of Nations (and then United Nations) trust territory.

The 1961 elections, supervised by the UN, were won by UPRONA, a party formed by Louis, one of the sons of the reigning king,

Mwambutsa IV. Louis was assassinated after only two weeks as prime minister and was succeeded by his brother-in-law, André Muhirwa. In 1962 Urundi separated from Ruanda and, as Burundi, was given internal self-government and then full independence.

republic In 1966 King Mwambutsa IV, after a 50-year reign, was deposed by another son, Charles, with army help, and the constitution was suspended. Later that year Charles, now Ntare V, was deposed by his prime minister, Capt Michel Micombero, who declared Burundi a republic. Micombero was a Tutsi, whose main rivals were the numerically superior Hutu. In 1972 the deposed Ntare V was killed, allegedly by the Hutu, giving the Tutsi an excuse to massacre large numbers of Hutu.

In 1973 amendments to the constitution made Micombero president and prime minister and in the following year UPRONA was declared the only political party. In 1976 Micombero was deposed in an army coup led by Col Jean-Baptiste Bagaza, who became president, with a prime minister and a new council of ministers. In 1977 the prime minister announced a return to civilian rule and a five-year plan to eliminate corruption and secure social justice, including promoting some Hutu to government positions.

army massacre In 1978 the post of prime minister was abolished and a new constitution, providing for a national assembly, was adopted 1981 after a referendum. Bagaza was re-elected 1984 (he was the only presidential candidate) but was deposed in a military coup Sept 1987, his government being replaced by a 'Military Council for National Redemption' headed by Maj Pierre Buyoya, believed to be a Tutsi. In Aug 1988 the minority-Tutsi-controlled Burundian army massacred thousands of Hutus in the NE section of the country. Despite Buoya's pledges to end interethnic violence, this massacre was seen by many as a continuation of the strife that began following an abortive Hutu rebellion 1972. In March 1992 a new constitution, providing for multiparty politics, was resoundingly approved by referendum. In June 1993 Melchior Ndadaye, a Hutu, was elected president. He was killed in a military coup in Oct and intertribal massacres followed.

In Jan 1994 Cyprien Ntaryamira, a Hutu, was elected president, but died in a plane crash with Rwandan president Juvenal Habyarimana in April.

Bury /'beri/ town in Greater Manchester, England, on the river Irwell, 16 km/10 mi N of central Manchester; population (1986) 173,650. Industries include cotton, chemicals, and engineering.

Buryat /ˌbʊriˈɑːt/ autonomous republic of Russia, in East Siberia.
area 351,300 sq km/135,600 sq mi
capital Ulan-Udé
physical bounded on the S by Mongolia, on the W by Lake Baikal; mountainous and forested
products coal, timber, building materials, fish, sheep, cattle
population (1986) 1,014,000
history settled by Russians 17th century; annexed from China by treaties 1689 and 1727.

Bury St Edmunds /'beri/ market town in Suffolk, England, on the river Lark; population (1985) 29,500. It was named after St Edmund, and there are remains of a large Benedictine abbey founded 1020.

bus in computing, the electrical connection through which a computer processor communicates with some of its parts and/or peripherals. It may be thought of as a multi-lane (perhaps 100-lane) highway system. The bus may include a control bus, a data bus, a memory bus, or all of these. Standard buses include the Eurobus, Futurebus, and VME.

Early microcomputers and microprocessor-based systems were typically bus-based: they were made up of different ◊printed circuit boards (PCBs) whose functions (processor card, display controller, floppy disc controller, etc) communicated by means of a *central bus*. Nowadays most such functions are provided on the main circuit board (or motherboard) while the bus is used for expansion options such as network cards, hard disc cards, and modems. The bus may therefore be referred to as an *expansion bus*.

bus or *omnibus* vehicle that carries fare-paying passengers on a fixed route, with frequent stops where passengers can get on and off.

An omnibus appeared briefly on the streets of Paris in the 1660s, when the mathematician Blaise Pascal introduced the first horse-drawn vehicles for public use. But a successful service, again in Paris, was not established until 1827. Two years later George Shillibeer introduced a horse-drawn bus in London.

Many bus companies sprang up in the UK, the most successful being the London General Omnibus Company, which operated from 1856 until 1911, by which time petrol-driven buses had taken over. Following deregulation in the 1980s, private bus operators in Britain were allowed outside London to set up fare-paying routes.

Bush /buʃ/ George 1924– . 41st president of the USA 1989–93, a Republican. He was director of the Central Intelligence Agency (CIA) 1976–81 and US vice president 1981–89. As president, his response to the Soviet leader Gorbachev's diplomatic initiatives were initially criticized as inadequate, but his sending of US troops to depose his former ally, General ◊Noriega of Panama, proved a popular move at home. Success in the 1991 Gulf War against Iraq further raised his standing. Domestic economic problems 1991–92 were followed by his defeat in the 1992 presidential elections by Democrat Bill Clinton.

Bush The US president 1989–93, George Bush.

Bush, son of a Connecticut senator, moved to Texas 1948 to build up an oil-drilling company. A congressman 1967–70, he was appointed US ambassador to the United Nations (UN) (1971–73) and Republican national chair (1973–74) by President Nixon, and special envoy to China 1974–75 under President Ford.

During Bush's time as head of the CIA, General Noriega of Panama was on its payroll, and Panama was later used as a channel for the secret supply of arms to Iran and the Nicaraguan Contra guerrillas. Evidence came to light 1987 linking him with the ◊Irangate scandal. But Noriega became uncontrollable and, in Dec 1989, Bush sent an invasion force to Panama and set up a puppet government.

As president, Bush soon reneged on his election pledge of 'no new taxes', but not before he had introduced a cut in capital-gains tax which predominantly benefited the richest 3% of the population. In 1990, having proclaimed a 'new world order' as the Cold War was officially declared over and facing economic recession in the USA, he sent a large army to Saudi Arabia after Iraq's annexation of Kuwait, and ruled out negotiations. His response to Iraq's action contrasted sharply with his policy of support for Israel's refusal to honour various UN Security Council resolutions calling for its withdrawal from occupied territories, but the ousting of Iraqi forces from Kuwait was greeted as a great US victory. Despite this success, the signing of the long-awaited ◊Strategic Arms Reduction Treaty July 1991, and Bush's unprecedented unilateral reduction in US nuclear weapons two months later, his popularity at home waned as criticism of his handling of domestic affairs mounted.

bushbuck antelope *Tragelaphus scriptus* found over most of Africa S of the Sahara. Up to 1 m/3 ft high, the males have keeled horns twisted into spirals, and are brown to blackish. The females are generally hornless, lighter, and redder. All have white markings, including stripes or vertical rows of dots down the sides. Rarely far from water, bushbuck live in woods and thick brush.

bushel dry or liquid measure equal to eight gallons or four pecks (2,219.36 cu in/36.37 litres) in the UK; some US states have different standards according to the goods measured.

Bushman former name for the ◊Kung, ◊San, and other hunter-gatherer groups (for example, the Gikwe, Heikom, and Sekhoin) living in and around the Kalahari Desert in southern Africa. They number approximately 50,000 and speak San and other languages of the ◊Khoisan family.

bushmaster large snake *Lachesis muta*. It is a type of pit viper, and is related to the rattlesnakes. Up to 4 m/12 ft long, it is found in wooded areas of South and Central America, and is the largest venomous snake in the New World. It has a powerful venomous bite. When alarmed, it produces a noise by vibrating its tail amongst dry leaves.

bushranger Australian armed robber of the 19th century. The first bushrangers were escaped convicts. The last gang was led by Ned ◊Kelly and his brother Dan in 1878–80. They form the subject of many Australian ballads.

Business Expansion Scheme UK government scheme, launched 1981, offering tax relief to encourage private investment in high-risk ventures, later extended to forms of investment in property.

Busoni /buːˈsəʊni/ Ferruccio (Dante Benvenuto) 1866–1924. Italian pianist, composer, and music critic. Much of his music was for the piano, but he also composed several operas including *Doktor Faust*, completed by a pupil after his death. An apostle of Futurism, he encouraged the French composer ◊Varèse.

Buss /bʌs/ Frances Mary 1827–1894. British pioneer in education for women. She first taught in a school run by her mother, and at 18 she founded her own school for girls in London, which became the North London Collegiate School in 1850. She founded the Camden School for Girls in 1871.

Her work helped to raise the status of women teachers and the academic standard of women's education in the UK. She is often associated with Dorothea ◊Beale, a fellow pioneer.

Bustamante /ˌbʌstəˈmænti/ (William) Alexander (born Clarke) 1884–1977. Jamaican socialist politician. As leader of the Labour Party, he was the first prime minister of independent Jamaica 1962–67.

bustard bird of the family Otididae, related to cranes but with a rounder body, a thicker neck, and a relatively short beak. Bustards are found on the ground on open plains and fields.

The great bustard *Otis tarda* is one of the heaviest flying birds at 18 kg/40 lb, and the larger males may have a length of 1 m/3 ft and wingspan of 2.3 m/7.5 ft. It is found in Europe and N Asia.

It has been extinct in Britain for some time, although attempts are being made by the Great Bustard Trust (1970) to naturalize

it again on Salisbury Plain. The little bustard *Otis tetrax* is less than half the size of the great bustard, and is also found in continental Europe. The great Indian bustard is endangered because of hunting and loss of its habitat to agriculture; there are less than 1,000 individuals left.

butadiene or *buta-1, 3-diene* $CH_2{:}CHCH{:}CH_2$ inflammable gas derived from petroleum, used in making synthetic rubber and resins.

butane C_4H_{10} one of two gaseous alkanes (paraffin hydrocarbons) having the same formula but differing in structure. Normal butane is derived from natural gas; isobutane is a by-product of petroleum manufacture. Liquefied under pressure, it is used as a fuel for industrial and domestic purposes (for example, in portable cookers).

Bute /bjuːt/ island and resort in the Firth of Clyde, Scotland; area 120 sq km/46 sq mi. The chief town is Rothesay. It is separated from the mainland in the north by a winding channel, the *Kyles of Bute*. With Arran and the adjacent islands it comprised the former county of Bute, merged 1975 in the region of Strathclyde.

Bute /bjuːt/ John Stuart, 3rd Earl of Bute 1713–1792. British Tory politician, prime minister 1762–63. On the accession of George III in 1760, he became the chief instrument in the king's policy for breaking the power of the Whigs and establishing the personal rule of the monarch through Parliament.

Bute succeeded his father 1723, and in 1737 was elected a representative peer for Scotland. His position as the king's favourite and supplanter of the popular prime minister Pitt the Elder made him hated in the country. He resigned 1763 after the Seven Years' War.

Buthelezi /ˌbuːtəˈleɪzi/ Chief Gatsha 1928– . Zulu leader and politician, chief minister of KwaZulu, a black 'homeland' in the Republic of South Africa from 1970. He is the founder (1975) and president of ◊Inkatha, a paramilitary organization for attaining a nonracial democratic political system.

Buthelezi, great-grandson of King ◊Cetewayo, opposed KwaZulu becoming a ◊Black National State, arguing instead for a confederation of black areas, with eventual majority rule over all South Africa under a one-party socialist system.

Butler /ˈbʌtlə/ Joseph 1692–1752. English priest and theologian who became dean of St Paul's in 1740 and bishop of Durham in 1750; his *Analogy of Religion* 1736 argued that it is no more rational to accept ◊deism (arguing for God as the first cause) than revealed religion (not arrived at by reasoning).

Butler /ˈbʌtlə/ Josephine (born Gray) 1828–1906. English social reformer. She promoted women's education and the Married Women's Property Act, and campaigned against the Contagious Diseases Acts of 1862–70, which made women in garrison towns suspected of prostitution liable to compulsory examination for venereal disease. Refusal to undergo examination meant imprisonment. As a result of her campaigns the acts were repealed in 1883.

Butler /ˈbʌtlə/ Reg 1913–1981. English sculptor who taught architecture 1937–39 and then was a blacksmith for many years before becoming known for cast and forged iron works, abstract and figurative.

In 1953 he won the international competition for a monument to The Unknown Political Prisoner (a model is in the Tate Gallery, London).

Butler /ˈbʌtlə/ Richard Austen ('Rab'), Baron Butler 1902–1982. British Conservative politician. As minister of education 1941–45, he was responsible for the 1944 Education Act; he was chancellor of the Exchequer 1951–55, Lord Privy Seal 1955–59, and foreign minister 1963–64. As a candidate for the prime ministership, he was defeated by Harold Macmillan in 1957 (under whom he was home secretary 1957–62), and by Alec Douglas-Home in 1963.

Butler /ˈbʌtlə/ Samuel 1612–1680. English satirist. His poem *Hudibras*, published in three parts 1663, 1664, and 1678, became immediately popular for its biting satire against the Puritans.

Butler /ˈbʌtlə/ Samuel 1835–1902. English author who made his name 1872 with a satiric attack on contemporary utopianism, *Erewhon* (*nowhere* reversed), but is now remembered for his autobiographical *The Way of All Flesh* written 1872–85 and published 1903.

The Fair Haven 1873 examined the miraculous element in Christianity. *Life and Habit* 1877 and other works were devoted to a criticism of the theory of natural selection. In *The Authoress of the Odyssey* 1897 he maintained that Homer's *Odyssey* was the work of a woman.

Butlin /ˈbʌtlɪn/ Billy (William) 1899–1980. British holiday-camp entrepreneur. Born in South Africa, he went in early life to Canada, but later entered the fairground business in the UK. He originated a chain of camps (the first was at Skegness 1936) that provided accommodation, meals, and amusements at an inclusive price.

Butor /bjuːˈtɔː/ Michel 1926– . French writer, one of the *nouveau roman* novelists who made radical changes in the traditional form. His works include *Passage de Milan/Passage from Milan* 1954, *Dégrès/Degrees* 1960, and *L'Emploi du temps/Passing Time* 1963. *Mobile* 1962 is a volume of essays.

butte /bjuːt/ a steep-sided flat-topped hill, formed in horizontally layered sedimentary rocks, largely in arid areas. A large butte with a pronounced tablelike profile is a ◊mesa.

Buttes and mesas are characteristic of semi-arid areas where remnants of resistant rock layers protect softer rock underneath, as in the plateau regions of Colorado, Utah, and Arizona, USA.

Butte /bjuːt/ mining town in Montana, USA, in the Rocky Mountains; population (1980) 37,200. Butte was founded in 1864 during a rush for gold, soon exhausted; copper was found some 20 years later.

buttercup plant of the genus *Ranunculus* with divided leaves and yellow flowers. Species include the common buttercup *R. acris* and the creeping buttercup *R. repens*.

Butterfield /ˈbʌtəfiːld/ William 1814–1900. English Gothic Revival architect. His work is characterized by vigorous, aggressive forms and multicoloured striped and patterned brickwork, as in the church of All Saints, Margaret Street, London 1850–59, and Keble College, Oxford 1867–83.

His schools, parsonages, and cottages develop an appealing functional secular style that anticipates of Philip ◊Webb and other ◊Arts and Crafts architects. At Baldersby, Yorkshire, UK, he designed a whole village of church, rectory, almshouse, school, and cottages 1855–57.

butterfly insect belonging, like moths, to the order Lepidoptera, in which the wings are covered with tiny scales, often brightly coloured. There are some 15,000 species of butterfly, many of which are under threat throughout the world because of the destruction of habitat.

Butterflies have a tubular proboscis through which they suck up nectar, or, in some species, carrion, dung, or urine. ◊Metamorphosis is complete; the pupa, or chrysalis, is usually without the protection of a cocoon. Adult lifespan may be only a few weeks, but some species hibernate and lay eggs in the spring.

The largest family, Nymphalidae, has some 6,000 species; it includes the peacock, tortoiseshells, and fritillaries. The family Pieridae includes the *cabbage white*, one of the few butterflies injurious to crops. The Lycaenidae are chiefly small, often with metallic coloration, for example the blues, coppers, and hairstreaks. The *large blue Lycaena arion* (extinct in Britain from 1979, but re-established 1984) has a complex life history: it lays its eggs on wild thyme, and the caterpillars are then taken by Myrmica ants to their nests. The ants milk their honey glands, while the caterpillars feed on the ant larvae. In the spring, the caterpillars finally pupate and emerge as butterflies. The mainly tropical Papilionidae, or swallowtails, are large and very beautiful, especially the South American species. The world's largest butterfly is *Queen Alexandra's birdwing Ornithoptera alexandrae* of Papua New Guinea, with a body 7.5 cm/3 in long and a wingspan of 25 cm/10 in. The most spectacular migrant is the orange and black *monarch butterfly Danaus plexippus*, which may fly from N Canada to Mexico in the autumn.

Butterflies usually differ from moths in having the antennae club-shaped rather than plumed or feathery, no 'lock' between the fore and hindwing, and resting with the wings in the vertical position rather than flat or sloping.

butterfly fish any of several fishes, not all related. The freshwater butterfly fish *Pantodon buchholzi* of W Africa can leap from the water and glide for a short distance on its large wing-like pectoral fins. Up to 10 cm/4 in long, it lives in stagnant water. The tropical marine butterfly fishes, family Chaetodontidae, are brightly coloured with laterally flattened bodies, often with long snouts which they poke into crevices in rocks and coral when feeding.

butterwort insectivorous plant, genus *Pinguicula*, of the bladderwort family, with purplish flowers and a rosette of flat leaves covered with a sticky secretion that traps insects.

button (French *bouton* 'bud', 'knob') fastener for clothing, originating with Bronze Age fasteners. In medieval Europe buttons were replaced by pins but were reintroduced in the 13th century as a decorative trim and in the 16th century as a functional fastener.

In the 15th and 16th centuries, gold- and silver-plated handmade buttons were popular with the nobility. By the early 19th century, machine-made fabric buttons and ones made of glass and ceramics existed, but they were not strongly featured on garments. By the middle of the 19th century, shell, mother-of-pearl, moulded horn, stamped steel, and brass buttons were popular. In the 1880s there was a revival of the use of enamel buttons developed in the 18th century. The 1920s Art Deco movement increased the popularity of buttons and in the 1930s they were produced in wood, cork, Perspex, and various plastics.

buttress reinforcement in brick or masonry, built against a wall to give it strength. A *flying buttress* is an arc transmitting the force of the wall to be supported to an outer buttress, common in Gothic architecture.

Buxtehude /ˌbʊkstəˈhuːdə/ Diderik 1637–1707. Danish composer and organist at Lübeck, Germany, who influenced ◊Bach and ◊Handel. He is remembered for his organ works and cantatas, written for his evening concerts or *Abendmusiken*.

Buxton /ˈbʌkstən/ spa town in Derbyshire, England; population (1981) 21,000. Known from Roman times for its hot springs, it is today a source for bottled mineral water. It has a restored Edwardian opera house and an annual opera festival.

buzzard any of a number of species of medium-sized hawks with broad wings, often seen soaring. The *common buzzard Buteo buteo* of Europe and Asia is about 55 cm/1.8 ft long with a wingspan of over 1.2 m/4 ft. It preys on a variety of small animals up to the size of a rabbit.

The *rough-legged buzzard Buzzard lagopus* lives in the northern tundra and eats lemmings. The *honey buzzard Pernis apivora* feeds largely, as its name suggests, on honey and insect larvae. It summers in Europe and W Asia and winters in Africa.

Byatt /ˈbaɪət/ A(ntonia) S(usan) 1936– . English novelist and critic. Her fifth novel, *Possession*, won the 1990 Booker Prize. *The*

Virgin in the Garden 1978 is a confident, zestfully handled account of a varied group of characters putting on a school play during Coronation year, 1953. It has a sequel, *Still Life* 1985.

Byblos /ˈbɪblɒs/ ancient Phoenician city (modern Jebeil), 32 km/20 mi N of Beirut, Lebanon. Known to the Assyrians and Babylonians as *Gubla*, it had a thriving export of cedar and pinewood to Egypt as early as 1500 BC. In Roman times it boasted an amphitheatre, baths, and a temple dedicated to an unknown male god, and was known for its celebration of the resurrection of Adonis, worshipped as a god of vegetation.

Bydgoszcz /ˈbɪdɡɒʃtʃ/ industrial river port in N Poland, 105 km/65 mi NE of Poznań on the Warta; population (1985) 361,000. As *Bromberg* it was under Prussian control 1772–1919.

Byelorussia or *Belorussia* (Russian *Belaruskaya* or 'White Russia') former name 1919–91 of ◊Belarus.

Byelorussian or *Belorussian* 'White Russian' a native of the Republic of Belarus. Byelorussian, a Balto-Slavic language belonging to the Indo-European family, is spoken by about 10 million people, including some in Poland. It is written in the Cyrillic script. Byelorussian literature dates to the 11th century AD.

The Byelorussians are descended from E S' ic tribes who moved into the region between the 6th and 8th centuries AD. They were ruled by Kiev until 1240 when Byelorussian lands went to Lithuania. In the 18th century Catherine the Great acquired Byelorussia, but W Byelorussia was under Polish rule 1921–39.

Byng /bɪŋ/ George, Viscount Torrington 1663–1733. British admiral. He captured Gibraltar 1704, commanded the fleet that prevented an invasion of England by the 'Old Pretender' James Francis Edward Stuart 1708, and destroyed the Spanish fleet at Messina 1718. John ◊Byng was his fourth son.

Byng /bɪŋ/ John 1704–1757. British admiral. Byng failed in the attempt to relieve Fort St Philip when in 1756 the island of Minorca was invaded by France. He was court-martialled and shot. The French writer Voltaire ironically commented that it was done 'to encourage the others'.

Byng /bɪŋ/ Julian, 1st Viscount of Vimy 1862–1935. British general in World War I,

commanding troops in Turkey and France, where, after a victory at Vimy Ridge, he took command of the Third Army.

Byrd /bɜːd/ Richard Evelyn 1888–1957. US aviator and explorer. The first to fly over the North Pole (1926), he also flew over the South Pole (1929), and led five overland expeditions in Antarctica.

Byrd /bɜːd/ William 1543–1623. English composer. His church choral music (set to Latin words, as he was a firm Catholic), notably masses for three, four, and five voices, is among the greatest Renaissance music. He also composed secular vocal and instrumental music.

Probably born in Lincoln, he became organist at Lincoln cathedral in 1563. He shared with ◊Tallis the honorary post of organist in Queen Elizabeth's Chapel Royal, and in 1575 he and Tallis were granted a monopoly in the printing and selling of music.

Byrds, the /bɜːdz/ US pioneering folk-rock group 1964–73. Emulated for their 12-string guitar sound, as on the hits 'Mr Tambourine Man' (a 1965 version of Bob Dylan's song) and 'Eight Miles High' 1966, they moved towards country rock in the late 1960s.

Byron /ˈbaɪrən/ Augusta Ada 1815–1851. English mathematician, daughter of Lord ◊Byron. She has been credited by some as the world's first computer programmer for her work with ◊Babbage's mechanical invention. In 1983 a new, high-level computer language, ADA, was named after her.

Byron /ˈbaɪrən/ George Gordon, 6th Baron Byron 1788–1824. English poet who became the symbol of Romanticism and political liberalism throughout Europe in the 19th century. His reputation was established with the first two cantos of *Childe Harold* 1812. Later works include *The Prisoner of Chillon* 1816, *Beppo* 1818, *Mazeppa* 1819, and, most notably, the satirical *Don Juan* 1819–24. He left England in 1816, spending most of his later life in Italy.

Born in London and educated at Harrow and Cambridge, Byron published his first volume *Hours of Idleness* 1807 and attacked its harsh critics in *English Bards and Scotch Reviewers* 1809. Overnight fame came with the first two cantos of *Childe Harold*, romantically describing his tours in Portugal, Spain, and the Balkans (third canto 1816, fourth 1818). In 1815 he married mathematician Anne Milbanke (1792–1860), with whom he had a daughter, Augusta Ada Byron, separating from her a year later amid much scandal. He then went to Europe, where he became friendly with Percy and Mary ◊Shelley. He engaged in Italian revolutionary politics and sailed for Greece in 1823 to further the Greek struggle for independence, but died of fever at Missolonghi. He is remembered for his lyrics, his colloquially easy *Letters*, and as the 'patron saint' of Romantic liberalism.

byte in computing, a basic unit of storage of information. A byte contains 8 ◊bits and can specify 256 values, such as the numbers from 0 to 255, or 256 colours at one byte per pixel (picture element). Three bytes (24 bits) can specify 16,777,216 values. Twenty-four-bit colour graphics with 16.8 million colours can provide a photo-realistic colour display.

The term also refers to a single memory location; large computer memory size is measured in thousands of bytes (kilobytes or KB) or millions of bytes (megabytes or MB).

Byzantine art and architecture art that originated in the 4th–5th centuries in Byzantium (the capital of the Eastern Roman Empire), and spread to Italy, throughout the Balkans, and to Russia, where it survived for many centuries. It is characterized by heavy stylization, strong linear emphasis, the use of rigid artistic stereotypes and rich colours such as gold. Byzantine artists excelled in mosaic work and manuscript painting. In architecture, the dome supported on pendentives was in widespread use.

Classical examples of Byzantine architecture are the churches of Sta Sophia, Constantinople, and St Mark's, Venice. Medieval painting styles were influenced by Byzantine art; a more naturalistic style emerged from the 13th century onwards in the West. See also ◊medieval art.

Byzantine Empire /bɪˈzæntaɪn, baɪ-/ the *Eastern Roman Empire* 395–1453, with its capital at Constantinople (formerly Byzantium, modern Istanbul).

330 Emperor Constantine converted to Christianity and moved his capital to Constantinople.
395 The Roman Empire was divided into eastern and western halves.
476 The Western Empire was overrun by barbarian invaders.
527–565 Emperor Justinian I temporarily recovered Italy, N Africa, and parts of Spain.

7th–8th centuries Syria, Egypt, and N Africa were lost to the Muslims, who twice besieged Constantinople (673–77, 718), but the Christian Byzantines maintained their hold on Anatolia.
8th–11th centuries The ◊Iconoclastic controversy brought the emperors into conflict with the papacy, and in 1054 the Greek Orthodox Church broke with the Roman.
867–1056 Under the Macedonian dynasty the Byzantine Empire reached the height of its prosperity; the Bulgars proved a formidable danger, but after a long struggle were finally crushed in 1018 by ◊Basil II ('the Bulgar-Slayer'). After Basil's death the Byzantine Empire declined because of internal factions.
1071–73 The Seljuk Turks conquered most of Anatolia.
1204 The Fourth Crusade sacked Constantinople and set Baldwin of Flanders (1171–1205) on the throne of the new Latin (W European) Empire.
1261 The Greeks recaptured the Latin (W European) Empire and restored the Byzantine Empire, but it maintained a precarious existence.
1453 The Turks captured Constantinople and founded the ◊Ottoman Empire.

Byzantine literature written mainly in the Greek *koinē*, a form of Greek accepted as the literary language of the 1st century AD and increasingly separate from the spoken tongue of the people. Byzantine literature is chiefly concerned with theology, history, and commentaries on the Greek classics. Its chief authors are the theologians St Basil, Gregory of Nyssa, Gregory of Nazianzus, Chrysostom (4th century AD) and John of Damascus (8th century); the historians Zosimus (about 500), Procopius (6th century), Bryennius and his wife ◊Anna Comnena (about 1100), and Georgius Acropolita (1220–1282); and the encyclopedist Suidas (about 975). Drama was nonexistent, and poetry, save for the hymns of the 6th–8th centuries, scanty and stilted, but there were many popular works about the lives of the saints.

Byzantium /baɪˈzæntiəm/ (modern Istanbul) ancient Greek city on the Bosporus, founded as a colony of the Greek city of Megara, near Corinth, about 660BC. In AD 330 the capital of the Roman Empire was transferred there by Constantine the Great, who renamed it ◊Constantinople.

C general-purpose computer-programming language popular on minicomputers and microcomputers. Developed in the early 1970s from an earlier language called BCPL, C is closely associated with the operating system ◊Unix. It is useful for writing fast and efficient systems programs, such as operating systems (which control the operations of the computer).

c. abbreviation for *circa* (Latin 'about'); used with dates that are uncertain.

˚C symbol for degrees ◊Celsius, commonly called centigrade.

Cabal, the /kəˈbæl/ (from *kabbala*) group of politicians, the English king Charles II's counsellors 1667–73, whose initials made up the word by coincidence—Clifford (Thomas Clifford 1630–1673), Ashley (Anthony Ashley Cooper, 1st Earl of ◊Shaftesbury), ◊Buckingham (George Villiers, 2nd Duke of Buckingham), Arlington (Henry Bennett, 1st Earl of Arlington 1618–1685), and ◊Lauderdale (John Maitland, Duke of Lauderdale).

cabaletta in music, a short aria with repeats which the singer could freely embellish as a display of virtuosity. In the 19th century the term came to be used for the final section of an elaborate aria.

cabbage plant *Brassica oleracea* of the cress family Cruciferae, allied to the turnip and wild mustard, or charlock. It is a table vegetable, cultivated as early as 2000 BC, and the numerous commercial varieties include kale, Brussels sprouts, common cabbage, savoy, cauliflower, sprouting broccoli, and kohlrabi.

cabbala alternative spelling of ◊kabbala.

caber, tossing the (Gaelic *cabar* 'pole') Scottish athletic sport, a ◊Highland Games

event. The caber (a tapered tree-trunk about 6 m/20 ft long, weighing about 100 kg/220 lb) is held in the palms of the cupped hands and rests on the shoulder. The thrower runs forward and tosses the caber, rotating it through 180 degrees so that it lands on its opposite end and falls forward. The best competitors toss the caber about 12 m/40 ft.

Cabinda /kəˈbɪndə/ or *Kabinda* African coastal enclave, a province of ◊Angola; area 7,770 sq km/3,000 sq mi; population (1980) 81,300. The capital is Cabinda. There are oil reserves. Cabinda, which was attached to Angola in 1886, has made claims to independence.

cabinet (a small room, implying secrecy) in politics, the group of ministers holding a country's highest executive offices who decide government policy. In Britain the cabinet system originated under the Stuarts. Under William III it became customary for the king to select his ministers from the party with a parliamentary majority. The US cabinet, unlike the British, does not initiate legislation, and its members, appointed by the president, must not be members of Congress.

The first British 'cabinet councils' or sub-committees of the ◊Privy Council undertook special tasks. When George I ceased to attend cabinet meetings, the office of prime minister, not officially recognized until 1905, came into existence to provide a chair (Robert Walpole was the first). Cabinet members are chosen by the prime minister; policy is collective and the meetings are secret, minutes being taken by the secretary of the cabinet, a high civil servant; secrecy has been infringed in recent years by 'leaks', or unauthorized disclosures to the press.

cable unit of length, used on ships, originally the length of a ship's anchor cable or 120 fathoms (219 m/720 ft), but now taken as one-tenth of a ◊nautical mile (185.3 m/608 ft).

cable car method of transporting passengers up steep slopes by cable. In the *cable railway*, passenger cars are hauled along rails by a cable wound by a powerful winch. A pair of cars usually operates together on the funicular principle, one going up as the other goes down. The other main type is the *aerial cable car*, where the passenger car is suspended from a trolley that runs along an aerial cableway.

Cable News Network (CNN) international television news channel; the 24-hour service was founded 1980 by US entrepreneur Ted Turner and has its headquarters in Atlanta, Georgia. It established its global reputation 1991 with eyewitness accounts from Baghdad of the beginning of the Gulf War.

cable television distribution of broadcast signals through cable relay systems. Narrowband systems were originally used to deliver services to areas with poor regular reception; systems with wider bands using coaxial and fibreoptic cable are increasingly used for distribution and development of home-based interactive services.

Cabot /ˈkæbət/ Sebastian 1474–1557. Italian navigator and cartographer, the second son of Giovanni ◊Caboto. He explored the Brazilian coast and the Río de la Plata for the Holy Roman Emperor Charles V 1526–30.

Caboto /kæˈbəʊtəʊ/ Giovanni or *John Cabot* 1450–1498. Italian navigator. Commissioned, with his three sons, by Henry VII of England to discover unknown lands, he arrived at Cape Breton Island on 24 June 1497, thus becoming the first European to reach the North American mainland (he thought he was in NE Asia). In 1498 he sailed again, touching Greenland, and probably died on the voyage.

Cabral /kəˈbrɑːl/ Pedro Alvarez 1460–1526. Portuguese explorer. He set sail from Lisbon for the East Indies in March 1500, and accidentally reached Brazil by taking a course too far west. He claimed the country for Portugal 25 April, since Spain had not followed up Vicente Pinzón's (c. 1460–1523) landing there earlier in the year. Continuing around Africa, he lost seven of his fleet of thirteen ships (the explorer Bartolomeu ◊Diaz was one of those drowned), and landed in Mozambique. Proceeding to India, he negotiated the first Indo-Portuguese treaties for trade, and returned to Lisbon July 1501.

Cabrini /kəˈbriːni/ Frances or Francesca ('Mother Cabrini') 1850—1917. First Roman Catholic US citizen to become a saint. Born in Lombardy, Italy, she founded the Missionary Sisters of the Sacred Heart, and established many schools and hospitals in the care of her nuns. She was canonized 1946. Her feast day is 22 Dec.

cacao tropical American evergreen tree *Theobroma cacao* of the Sterculia family, now also cultivated in West Africa and Sri

UK cabinet

Prime Minister
Lord President and Leader of the House of Commons
Lord Chancellor
Secretary of State for Foreign and Commonwealth Affairs
Chancellor of the Exchequer
Home Secretary
Secretary of State for Trade and Industry
Secretary of State for Defence
Secretary of State for Scotland
Secretary of State for Wales
Secretary of State for Northern Ireland
Secretary of State for the Environment
Secretary of State for Employment
Secretary of State for Health
Secretary of State for Social Security
Secretary of State for Education and Science
Secretary of State for Transport
Secretary of State for Energy
Secretary of State for Agriculture, Fisheries, and Food
Chief Secretary to the Treasury
Chancellor of the Duchy of Lancaster and chair of the Conservative Party
Lord Privy Seal and Leader of the House of Lords

Lanka. Its seeds are cocoa beans, from which ◊cocoa and chocolate are prepared.

The trees mature at five to eight years and produce two crops a year. The fruit is 17 cm/6.5 in–25 cm/9.5 in long, hard and ridged, with the beans inside. The seeds are called cocoa nibs; when left to ferment, then roasted and separated from the husks, they contain about 50% fat, part of which is removed to make chocolate and cocoa. The Aztecs revered cacao and made a drink for the nobility only from cocoa beans and chillis, which they called chocolatl. In the 16th century Spanish traders brought cacao to Europe. It was used to make a drink, which came to rival coffee and tea in popularity.

cachalot alternative name for the sperm whale; see ◊whale.

CACM abbreviation for ◊*Central American Common Market*.

cactus (plural *cacti*) plant of the family Cactaceae, although the term is commonly applied to many different succulent and prickly plants. True cacti have a woody axis (central core) overlaid with an enlarged

Cactus The strawberry cactus *Echinocereus enneacanthus*, which bears bright pink flowers and edible fruit.

fleshy stem, which assumes various forms and is usually covered with spines (actually reduced leaves). They all have special adaptations to growing in dry areas.

Cactus flowers are often large and brightly coloured; the fruit is fleshy and often edible, as in the case of the prickly pear. The Cactaceae are a New World family and include the treelike saguaro and the night-blooming cerus with blossoms 30 cm/12 in across.

CAD (acronym for *c*omputer-*a*ided *d*esign) the use of computers for creating and editing design drawings. CAD also allows such things as automatic testing of designs and multiple or animated three-dimensional views of designs. CAD systems are widely used in architecture, electronics, and engineering, for example in the motor-vehicle industry, where cars designed with the assistance of computers are now commonplace. A related development is ◊CAM (computer-assisted manufacture).

caddis fly insect of the order Trichoptera. Adults are generally dull brown, mothlike, with wings covered in tiny hairs. Mouthparts are poorly developed, and many do not feed as adults. They are usually found near water.

The larvae are aquatic, and many live in cases, open at both ends, which they make out of sand or plant remains. Some species make silk nets among aquatic vegetation to help trap food.

Cade /keɪd/ Jack died 1450.. English rebel. He was a prosperous landowner, but led a revolt 1450 in Kent against the high taxes and court corruption of Henry VI and demanded the recall from Ireland of Richard, Duke of York. The rebels defeated the royal forces at Sevenoaks and occupied London. After being promised reforms and pardon they dispersed, but Cade was hunted down and killed.

cadenza /kəˈdenzə/ in music, an unaccompanied bravura passage (requiring elaborate, virtuoso execution) in the style of an improvisation for the soloist during a concerto.

Cadiz /kəˈdɪz/ Spanish city and naval base, capital and seaport of the province of Cadiz, standing on Cadiz Bay, an inlet of the Atlantic, 103 km/64 mi S of Seville; population (1986) 154,000. After the discovery of the Americas 1492, Cadiz became one of Europe's most vital trade ports. The English adventurer Francis Drake burned a Spanish fleet here 1587 to prevent the sailing of the ◊Armada.

cadmium soft, silver-white, ductile, and malleable metallic element, symbol Cd, atomic number 48, relative atomic mass 112.40. Cadmium occurs in nature as a sulphide or carbonate in zinc ores. It is a toxic metal that, because of industrial dumping, has become an environmental pollutant. It is used in batteries, electroplating, and as a constituent of alloys used for bearings with low coefficients of friction; it is also a constituent of an alloy with a very low melting point.

Cadmium is also used in the control rods of nuclear reactors, because of its high absorption of neutrons. It was named in 1817 by the German chemist Friedrich Strohmeyer (1776–1835) after Greek mythological character Cadmus.

Cadmus /ˈkædməs/ in Greek mythology, a Phoenician from ◊Tyre, brother of ◊Europa. He founded the city of Thebes in Greece. Obeying the oracle of Athena, Cadmus killed the sacred dragon that guarded the spring of Ares. He sowed the teeth of the dragon, from which sprang a multitude of fierce warriors who fought among themselves; the survivors were considered to be the ancestors of the Theban aristocracy.

caecilian tropical amphibian of rather wormlike appearance. There are about 170 species known, forming the amphibian order Apoda (also known as Caecilia or Gymnophiona). Caecilians have a grooved skin that gives a 'segmented' appearance, have no trace of limbs, and mostly live below ground. Some species bear live young, others lay eggs.

caecum in the ◊digestive system of animals, a blind-ending tube branching off from the first part of the large intestine, terminating in the appendix. It has no function in humans but is used for the digestion of cellulose by some grass-eating mammals. The rabbit caecum and appendix contains millions of bacteria that produce cellulase, the enzyme necessary for the breakdown of cellulose to glucose.

Caedmon /ˈkædmən/ 7th century. Earliest known English poet. According to the Northumbrian historian Bede, when Caedmon was a cowherd at the Christian monastery of Whitby, he was commanded to sing by a stranger in a dream, and on waking produced a hymn on the Creation. The poem is preserved in some manuscripts. Caedmon became a monk and may have composed other religious poems.

Caen /kɑːn/ capital of Calvados *département*, France, on the river Orne; population (1982) 183,526. It is a business centre, with ironworks and electric and electronic industries. Caen building stone has a fine reputation. The town is linked by canal with the nearby English Channel to the northeast. The church of St Etienne was founded by William the Conqueror, and the university by Henry VI of England in 1432. Caen was captured by British forces in World War II on 9 July 1944 after five weeks' fighting, during which the town was badly damaged.

Caerleon /kɑːˈliːən/ small town in Gwent, Wales, on the Usk, 5 km/3 mi NE of Newport; population (1981) 6,711. It stands on the site of the Roman fortress of Isca. There is a Legionary Museum and remains of an amphitheatre.

Caernarvon /kəˈnɑːvən/ or *Caernarfon* administrative headquarters of Gwynedd, N Wales, situated on the SW shore of the Menai Strait; population (1981) 10,000. Formerly a Roman station, it is now a market town and port. The first Prince of Wales (later ◊Edward II) was born in Caernarvon Castle; Edward VIII was invested here 1911 and Prince Charles 1969.

Caernarvonshire /kəˈnɑːvənʃə/ (Welsh *Sir Gaernarfon*) former county of N Wales, merged in ◊Gwynedd 1974.

Caerphilly /kəˈfɪli/ (Welsh *Caerffili*) market town in Mid Glamorgan, Wales, 11 km/7 mi N of Cardiff; population (1981) 42,736. The castle was built by Edward I. The town gives its name to the mild Caerphilly cheese.

Caesar /ˈsiːzə/ powerful family of ancient Rome, which included Gaius Julius ◊Caesar, whose grand-nephew and adopted son ◊Augustus assumed the name of Caesar and passed it on to his adopted son ◊Tiberius. Henceforth, it was used by the successive emperors, becoming a title of the Roman rulers. The titles 'tsar' in Russia and 'kaiser' in Germany were both derived from the name Caesar.

Caesar /ˈsiːzə/ Gaius Julius *c.* 100–44 BC. Roman statesman and general. He formed with Pompey and Crassus the First Triumvirate in 60 BC. He conquered Gaul 58–50 and invaded Britain 55 and 54. He fought against Pompey 49–48, defeating him at Pharsalus. After a period in Egypt Caesar returned to Rome as dictator from 46. He was assassinated by conspirators on the ◊Ides of March 44.

A patrician, Caesar allied himself with the popular party, and when elected to the office of aedile 65 nearly ruined himself with lavish amusements for the Roman populace. Although a free thinker, he was elected chief pontiff 63 and appointed governor of Spain 61. Returning to Rome 60, he formed with Pompey and Crassus the First Triumvirate. As governor of Gaul, he was engaged in its subjugation 58–50, defeating the Germans under Ariovistus and selling thousands of the Belgic tribes into slavery. In 55 he crossed into Britain, returning for a further campaigning visit 54. A revolt by the Gauls under Vercingetorix 52 was crushed 51. His governorship of Spain was to end 49, and, Crassus being dead, Pompey became his rival. Declaring 'the die is cast', Caesar crossed the Rubicon (the small river separating Gaul from Italy) to meet the army raised against him by Pompey. In the ensuing civil war, he followed Pompey to Epirus 48, defeated him at Pharsalus, and chased him to Egypt, where he was murdered. Caesar stayed some months in Egypt, where Cleopatra, queen of Egypt, gave birth to his son, Caesarion. He executed a lightning campaign 47 against King Pharnaces II (ruled 63–47 BC) in Asia Minor, which he summarized: *Veni vidi vici* 'I came, I saw, I conquered'. With his final victory over the sons of Pompey at Munda in Spain 45, he established his position, having been awarded a ten-year dictatorship 46. On 15 Mar 44 he was stabbed to death at the foot of Pompey's statue (see ◊Brutus, ◊Cassius) in the Senate house. His commentaries on the campaigns and the civil war survive.

Caesarea /ˌsiːzəˈriə/ ancient city in Palestine (now ◊Qisarya). It was built by Herod the Great 22–12 BC, who also constructed a port (*portus Augusti*). Caesarea was the administrative capital of the province of Judaea.

Caesarean section /sɪˈzeərɪən/ surgical operation to deliver a baby by cutting through the mother's abdominal and intra-uterine walls. It may be recommended for almost any obstetric complication implying a threat to mother or baby. In the USA in 1990, appoximately 25% of all births were by Caesarean section.

Caesarean section was named after the Roman emperor Julius Caesar, who was born this way. In medieval Europe, it was performed mostly in attempts to save the life of a child whose mother had died in labour. The Christian church forbade cutting open the mother before she was dead.

caesium (Latin *caesius* 'bluish-grey') soft, silvery-white, ductile, metallic element, symbol Cs, atomic number 55, relative atomic mass 132.905. It is one of the ◊alkali metals, and is the most electropositive of all the elements. In air it ignites spontaneously, and it reacts vigorously with water. It is used in the manufacture of photoelectric cells. The name comes from the blueness of its spectral line.

The rate of vibration of caesium atoms is used as the standard of measuring time. Its radioactive isotope Cs-137 (half-life 30.17 years) is a product of fission in nuclear explosions and in nuclear reactors; it is one of the most dangerous waste products of the nuclear industry, being a highly radioactive biological analogue for potassium.

caffeine ◊alkaloid organic substance found in tea, coffee, and kola nuts; it stimulates the heart and central nervous system. When isolated, it is a bitter crystalline compound, $C_8H_{10}N_4O_2$. Too much caffeine (more than six average cups of tea or coffee a day) can be detrimental to health.

Cage /keɪdʒ/ John 1912–1992. US composer. A pupil of ◊Schoenberg and ◊Cowell,

he joined others in reacting against the European music tradition in favour of a more realistic idiom open to non-Western attitudes. He invented the ◊prepared piano to tour as accompanist with the dancer Merce Cunningham, a lifelong collaborator. He also worked to reduce the control of the composer over the music, introducing randomness (◊aleatory music) and inexactitude and allowing sounds to 'be themselves'.

Cagliari /kælˈjɑːri/ capital and port of Sardinia, Italy, on the Gulf of Cagliari; population (1988) 222,000.

Cagnes-sur-Mer /kæn sjʊə ˈmeə/ capital of the *département* of Alpes-Maritimes; SW of Nice, France; population (1986) 35,214. The château (13th–17th century) contains mementoes of the impressionist painter Renoir, who lived here 1900–19.

Cagney /ˈkægni/ James 1899–1986. US actor who moved to films from Broadway. Usually associated with gangster roles (*The Public Enemy* 1931), he was an actor of great versatility, playing Bottom in *A Midsummer Night's Dream* 1935 and singing and dancing in *Yankee Doodle Dandy* 1942.

Cahora Bassa /kəˈhɒɪrə ˈbæsə/ largest hydroelectric scheme in Africa, created as a result of the damming of the Zambezi River to form a 230 km/144 mi-long reservoir in W Mozambique.

Cain /keɪn/ in the Old Testament, the firstborn son of Adam and Eve. Motivated by jealousy, he murdered his brother Abel because the latter's sacrifice was more acceptable to God than his own.

Caine /keɪn/ Michael. Stage name of Maurice Micklewhite 1933– . English actor, an accomplished performer with an enduring Cockney streak. His films include *Alfie* 1966, *The Man Who Would Be King* 1975, *Educating Rita* 1983, and *Hannah and Her Sisters* 1986.

'Ça Ira' /sɑː ɪəˈrɑː/ song of the French Revolution, written by a street singer, Ladré, and set to an existing tune by Bécourt, a drummer of the Paris Opéra.

cairn Scottish breed of ◊terrier. Shaggy, short-legged, and compact, it can be sandy, greyish brindle, or red. It was formerly used for flushing out foxes and badgers.

Cairngorms /ˈkeəŋɡɔːmz/ mountain group in Scotland, northern part of the ◊Grampians, the highest peak being Ben Macdhui 1,309 m/4,296 ft.

Aviemore (Britain's first complete holiday and sports centre) was opened in 1966, and 11 km/7 mi to the south is the Highland Wildlife Park at Kincraig.

Cairns /keənz/ seaport of Queensland, Australia; population (1984) 38,700. Its chief industry is sugar exporting.

Cairo /ˈkaɪrəʊ/ (Arabic *El Qahira*) capital of Egypt, on the E bank of the Nile 13 km/8 mi above the apex of the Delta and 160 km/100 mi from the Mediterranean; the largest city in Africa and in the Middle East; population (1985) 6,205,000, Greater Cairo (1987) 13,300,000. El Fustat (Old Cairo) was founded by Arabs about AD 642, Al Qahira about 1000 by the ◊Fatimid ruler Gowhar. It was also the capital of the Ayyubid dynasty who built the citadel in the late 1100s. Under the Mamelukes from 1250–1517 the city prospered, but declined in the 16th century after conquest by the Turks. It became the capital of the virtually autonomous kingdom of Egypt established by Mehmet Ali in 1805. During World War II it was the headquarters of the Allied forces in North Africa.

Cairo is the site of the mosque that houses the El Azhar university (972). The Mosque of Amr dates from 643; the Citadel, built by Sultan Saladin in the 12th century, contains the impressive 19th-century Muhammad Ali mosque. The city is 32 km/20 mi N of the site of the ancient Egyptian centre of ◊Memphis. The Great Pyramids and Sphinx are at nearby Gîza.

The government and business quarters reflect Cairo's position as a leading administrative and commercial centre, and the semi-official newspaper *al Ahram* is an influential voice in the Arab world. Cairo's industries include the manufacture of textiles, cement, vegetable oils, and beer. At Helwan, 24 km/15 mi to the S, an industrial centre is developing, with iron and steelworks powered by electricity from the Aswan High Dam. There are two secular universities: Cairo University (1908) and Ein Shams (1950).

caisson hollow cylindrical or boxlike structure, usually of reinforced ◊concrete, sunk into a riverbed to form the foundations of a bridge.

An *open caisson* is open at the top and at the bottom, where there is a wedge-shaped cutting edge. Material is excavated from inside, allowing the caisson to sink. A *pneumatic caisson* has a pressurized chamber at the bottom, in which workers carry out the excavation. The air pressure prevents the surrounding water entering; the workers enter and leave the chamber through an airlock, allowing for a suitable decompression period to prevent ◊decompression sickness (the so-called bends).

Cajun /ˈkeɪdʒən/ member of a French-speaking community of Louisiana, USA, descended from French-Canadians who, in the 18th century, were driven there from Nova Scotia (then known as Acadia, from which the name Cajun comes). *Cajun music* has a lively rhythm and features steel guitar, fiddle, and accordion.

cal symbol for ◊*calorie*.

CAL (acronym for *c*omputer-*a*ssisted *l*earning) the use of computers in education and training: the computer displays instructional material to a student and asks questions about the information given; the student's answers determine the sequence of the lessons.

Calabar /ˈkæləbɑː/ port and capital of Cross River State, SE Nigeria, on the Cross River, 64 km/40 mi from the Atlantic; population (1983) 126,000. Rubber, timber, and vegetable oils are exported. It was a centre of the slave trade in the 18th and 19th centuries.

calabash tropical South American evergreen tree *Crescentia cujete*, family Bignoniaceae, with gourds 50 cm/20 in across, which are used as water containers. The Old World tropical vine bottle gourd *Lagenaria siceraria* of the gourd family Cucurbitaceae is sometimes called calabash, and it produces equally large true gourds.

Calabria /kəˈlæbriə/ mountainous earthquake region occupying the 'toe' of Italy, comprising the provinces of Catanzaro, Cosenza, and Reggio; capital Catanzaro; area 15,100 sq km/ 5,829 sq mi; population (1988) 2,146,000. Reggio is the industrial centre.

Calais /ˈkæleɪ/ port in N France; population (1982) 101,000. Taken by England's Edward III in 1347, it was saved from destruction by the personal surrender of the Burghers of Calais commemorated in Rodin's sculpture; the French retook it 1558. Following German occupation May 1940–Oct 1944, it surrendered to the Canadians.

calamine $ZnCO_3$ zinc carbonate, an ore of zinc. The term also refers to a pink powder made of a mixture of zinc oxide and iron(II) oxide used in lotions and ointments as an astringent for treating, for example, sunburn, eczema, measles rash, and insect bites and stings.

Calamity Jane /dʒeɪn/ nickname of Martha Jane Burke *c.* 1852–1903. US heroine of Deadwood, South Dakota. She worked as a teamster, transporting supplies to the mining camps, adopted male dress and, as an excellent shot, promised 'calamity' to any aggressor. Many fictional accounts of the Wild West featured her exploits.

Calchas in Greek mythology, a visionary and interpreter of omens for the Greek expedition against ◊Troy, responsible for recommending the sacrifice of ◊Iphigenia by her father ◊Agamemnon, as an atonement for an offence against the goddess ◊Artemis.

calcite common, colourless, white, or light-coloured rock-forming mineral, calcium carbonate, CaCO₃. It is the main constituent of ◊limestone and marble, and forms many types of invertebrate shell.

Calcite often forms ◊stalactites and ◊stalagmites in caves and is also found deposited in veins through many rocks because of the ease with which it is dissolved and transported by groundwater; ◊oolite is its spheroidal form. It rates 3 on the ◊Mohs' scale of hardness. Large crystals up to 1 m/3 ft have been found in Oklahoma and Missouri, USA. ◊Iceland spar is a transparent form of calcite used in the optical industry; as limestone it is used in the building industry.

calcium (Latin *calcis* 'lime') soft, silvery-white, metallic element, symbol Ca, atomic number 20, relative atomic mass 40.08. It is one of the ◊alkaline-earth metals. It is the fifth most abundant element (the third most abundant metal) in the Earth's crust. It is found mainly as its carbonate CaCO₃, which occurs in a fairly pure condition as chalk and limestone (see ◊calcite). Calcium is an essential component of bones, teeth, shells, milk, and leaves, and it forms 1.5% of the human body by mass.

Calcium ions in animal cells are involved in regulating muscle contraction, hormone secretion, digestion, and glycogen metabolism in the liver.

The element was discovered and named by the English chemist Humphry Davy in 1808. Its compounds include slaked lime (calcium hydroxide, Ca(OH)₂); plaster of Paris (calcium sulphate, CaSO₄2H₂O); calcium phosphate (Ca₃(PO₄)₂, the main constituent of animal bones; calcium hypochlorite (CaOCl₂), a bleaching agent; calcium nitrate (Ca(NO₃)₂4H₂O), a nitrogenous fertilizer;

calcium carbide (CaC₂), which reacts with water to give ethyne (acetylene); calcium cyanamide (CaCN₂), the basis of many pharmaceuticals, fertilizers, and plastics, including melamine; calcium cyanide (Ca(CN)₂), used in the extraction of gold and silver and in electroplating; and others used in baking powders and fillers for paints.

calculator pocket-sized electronic computing device for performing numerical calculations. It can add, subtract, multiply, and divide; many calculators also compute squares and roots, and have advanced trigonometric and statistical functions. Input is by a small keyboard and results are shown on a one-line computer screen, typically a ◊liquid crystal display (LCD) or a light-emitting diode (LED). The first electronic calculator was manufactured by the Bell Punch Company in the USA in 1963.

calculus (Latin 'pebble') branch of mathematics that permits the manipulation of continuously varying quantities, used in practical problems involving such matters as changing speeds, problems of flight, varying stresses in the framework of a bridge, and alternating current theory. *Integral calculus* deals with the method of summation or adding together the effects of continuously varying quantities. *Differential calculus* deals in a similar way with rates of change. Many of its applications arose from the study of the gradients of the tangents to curves.

There are several other branches of calculus, including calculus of errors and calculus of variation. Differential and integral calculus, each of which deals with small quantities which during manipulation are made smaller and smaller, compose the *infinitesimal calculus*. Differential equations relate to the derivatives of a set of variables and may include the variables. Many give the mathematical models for physical phenomena such as ◊simple harmonic motion. Differential equations are solved generally through integrative means, depending on their degrees. If no known mathematical processes are available, integration can be performed graphically or by computers.

history Calculus originated with Archimedes in the 3rd century BC as a method for finding the areas of curved shapes and for drawing tangents to curves. These ideas were not developed until the 17th century, when the French philosopher Descartes introduced ◊coordinate geometry, showing how geometrical curves can be described and manipulated by means of algebraic expressions. Then the French mathematician Fermat used these algebraic forms in the early stages of the development of differentiation. Later the German philosopher Leibniz and the English scientist Newton advanced the study.

Calcutta /kælˈkʌtə/ largest city of India, on the river Hooghly, the westernmost mouth of the river Ganges, some 130 km/80 mi N of the Bay of Bengal. It is the capital of West Bengal; population (1981) 9,166,000. It is chiefly a commercial and industrial centre (engineering, shipbuilding, jute, and other textiles). Calcutta was the seat of government of British India 1773–1912. There is severe air pollution.

Buildings include a magnificent Jain temple, the palaces of former Indian princes; and the Law Courts and Government House, survivals of the British Raj. Across the river is ◊Howrah, and between Calcutta and the sea there is a new bulk cargo port, Haldia, which is the focus of oil refineries, petrochemical plants, and fertilizer factories.

There is a fine museum; educational institutions include the University of Calcutta (1857), oldest of several universities; the Visva Bharati at Santiniketan, founded by Rabindranath Tagore; and the Bose Research Institute.

history Calcutta was founded 1686–90 by Job Charnock of the East India Company as a trading post. Captured by Suraj-ud-Dowlah in 1756, during the Anglo-French wars in India, in 1757 it was retaken by Robert Clive.

Calder /ˈkɔːldə/ Alexander 1898–1976. US abstract sculptor, the inventor of *mobiles*, suspended shapes that move in the lightest current of air. In the 1920s he began making wire sculptures with movable parts; in the 1960s he created *stabiles*, large coloured sculptures of sheet metal.

caldera in geology, a very large basin-shaped ◊crater. Calderas are found at the tops of volcanoes, where the original peak has collapsed into an empty chamber beneath. The basin, many times larger than the original volcanic vent, may be flooded, producing a crater lake, or the flat floor may contain a number of small volcanic cones, produced by volcanic activity after the collapse.

Typical calderas are Kilauea, Hawaii; Crater Lake, Oregon, USA; and the summit of Olympus Mons, on Mars.

Calderón de la Barca /ˌkældəˈrɒn deɪ lɑːˈbɑːkə/ Pedro 1600–1681. Spanish dramatist and poet. After the death of Lope de Vega in 1635, he was considered to be the leading Spanish dramatist. Most celebrated of the 118 plays is the philosophical *La vida es sueño/Life is a Dream* 1635.

Caledonian Canal /ˌkælɪˈdəʊniən/ waterway in NW Scotland, 98 km/61 mi long, linking the Atlantic and the North Sea. Of its 98 km/61 mi length only a 37 km/23 mi stretch is artificial, the rest being composed of lochs Lochy, Oich, and Ness. The canal was built by Thomas ◊Telford 1803–23.

calendar the division of the ◊year into months, weeks, and days and the method of ordering the years. From year one, an assumed date of the birth of Jesus, dates are calculated backwards (BC 'before Christ' or BCE 'before common era') and forwards (AD, Latin *anno Domini* 'in the year of the Lord' or CE 'common era'). The *lunar month* (period between one new moon and the next) naturally averages 29.5 days, but the Western calendar uses for convenience a *calendar month* with a complete number of days, 30 or 31 (Feb has 28). For adjustments, since there are slightly fewer than six extra hours a year left over, they are added to Feb as a 29th day every fourth year (*leap year*), century years being excepted unless they are divisible by 400. For example, 1896 was a leap year; 1900 was not.

The *month names* in most European languages were probably derived as follows: January from Janus, Roman god; February from *Februar*, Roman festival of purification; March from Mars, Roman god; April from Latin *aperire*, 'to open'; May from Maia, Roman goddess; June from Juno, Roman goddess; July from Julius Caesar, Roman general; August from Augustus, Roman emperor; September, October, November, December (originally the seventh–tenth months) from the Latin words meaning seventh, eighth, ninth, and tenth, respectively.

The *days of the week* are Monday named after the Moon; Tuesday from Tiu or Tyr, Anglo-Saxon and Norse god; Wednesday from Woden or Odin, Norse god; Thursday from Thor, Norse god; Friday from Freya, Norse goddess; Saturday from Saturn, Roman god; and Sunday named after the Sun.

All early calendars except the ancient Egyptian were lunar. The word calendar comes from the Latin *Kalendae* or *calendae*, the first day of each month on which, in ancient Rome, solemn proclamation was made of the appearance of the new moon.

The *Western* or *Gregorian calendar* derives from the *Julian calendar* instituted by Julius Caesar 46 BC. It was adjusted by Pope Gregory XIII 1582, who eliminated the accumulated error caused by a faulty calculation of the length of a year and avoided its recurrence by restricting century leap years to those divisible by 400. Other states only gradually changed from ◊Old Style to New Style; Britain and its colonies adopted the Gregorian calendar 1752, when the error amounted to 11 days, and 3 Sept 1752 became 14 Sept (at the same time the beginning of the year was put back from 25 March to 1 Jan). Russia did not adopt it until the October Revolution of 1917, so that the event (then 25 Oct) is currently celebrated 7 Nov.

The *Jewish calendar* is a complex combination of lunar and solar cycles, varied by considerations of religious observance. A year may have 12 or 13 months, each of which normally alternates between 29 and 30 days; the New Year (Rosh Hashanah) falls between 5 Sept and 5 Oct. The calendar dates from the hypothetical creation of the world (taken as 7 Oct 3761 BC).

The *Chinese calendar* is lunar, with a cycle of 60 years. Both the traditional and, from 1911, the Western calendar are in use in China.

The *Muslim calendar*, also lunar, has 12 months of alternately 30 and 29 days, and a year of 354 days. This results in the calendar rotating around the seasons in a 30-year cycle. The era is counted as beginning on the day Muhammad fled from Mecca AD 622.

Calgary /ˈkælgəri/ city in Alberta, Canada, on the Bow River, in the foothills of the Rockies; at 1,048 m/3,440 ft it is one of the highest Canadian towns; population (1986) 671,000. It is the centre of a large agricultural region and is the oil and financial centre of Alberta and W Canada. Founded as Fort Calgary by the North West Mounted Police 1875, it was reached by the Canadian Pacific Railway 1885 and developed rapidly after the discovery of oil 1914. The 1988 Winter Olympic Games were held here.

Calhoun /kælˈhuːn/ John Caldwell 1782–1850. US politician, born in South Carolina. He was vice president 1825–29 under John Quincy Adams and 1829–33 under Andrew Jackson. Throughout he was a defender of the *states' rights* against the federal government, and of the institution of black slavery.

Cali /ˈkæliː/ city in SW Colombia, in the Cauca Valley 975 m/3,200 ft above sea level, founded in 1536. Cali has textile, sugar, and engineering industries. Population (1985) 1,398,276.

calibration the preparation of a usable scale on a measuring instrument. A mercury ◊thermometer, for example, can be calibrated with a Celsius scale by noting the heights of the mercury column at two standard temperatures—the freezing point (0°C) and boiling point (100°C) of water—and dividing the distance between them into 100 equal parts and continuing these divisions above and below.

calico cotton fabric: in the USA, it is a printed cotton; in the UK, a plain woven cotton material. The name derives from Calicut, India, an original source of calico.

California /ˌkælɪˈfɔːniə/ state of the Pacific USA; nicknamed the Golden State, originally because of its gold mines, but more recently because of its sunshine
area 411,100 sq km/158,685 sq mi
capital Sacramento
towns Los Angeles, San Diego, San Francisco, San José, Fresno
physical Sierra Nevada (including Yosemite and Sequoia National Parks, Lake Tahoe, and Mount Whitney, 4,418 m/14,500 ft, the highest mountain in the lower 48 states) and the Coast Range; Death Valley 86 m/282 ft below sea level; Colorado and Mojave deserts (Edwards Air Force base is in the latter); Monterey Peninsula; Salton Sea; offshore in the Pacific there are vast underwater volcanoes with tops 8 km/5 mi across
features California Institute of Technology (Caltech); Lawrence Livermore Laboratory (named after Ernest Lawrence), which shares nuclear weapons research with Los Alamos; Stanford University, which has the Hoover Institute and is the powerhouse of ◊Silicon Valley; Paul Getty art museum at Malibu, built in the style of a Roman villa
products leading agricultural state with fruit (peaches, citrus, grapes in the valley of the San Joaquin and Sacramento rivers), nuts, wheat, vegetables, cotton, rice, all mostly grown by irrigation, the water being carried by immense concrete-lined canals to the Central Valley and Imperial Valley; beef cattle, timber, fish, oil, natural gas, aerospace, electronics (Silicon Valley), food pro-

cessing, films, and television programmes. There are also great reserves of energy (geothermal) in the hot water which lies beneath much of the state
population (1987) 27,663,000, most populous state of the USA, 66% non-Hispanic white; 20% Hispanic; 7.5% black; 7% Asian (including many Vietnamese)
famous people Bret Harte, W R Hearst, Jack London, Marilyn Monroe, Richard Nixon, William Saroyan, John Steinbeck
history colonized by Spain 1769, it was ceded to the USA after the Mexican War 1848, and became a state 1850. Gold had been discovered in the Sierra Nevada Jan 1848, and was followed by the gold rush 1849–56.

California, Lower /ˌkælɪˈfɔːnɪə/ English name for ◊Baja California.

californium synthesized, radioactive, metallic element of the actinide series, symbol Cf, atomic number 98, relative atomic mass 251. It is produced in very small quantities and used in nuclear reactors as a neutron source. The longest-lived isotope, Cf-251, has a half-life of 800 years.

It is named after the state of California, where it was first synthesized in 1950 by Glenn Seaborg and his team at the University of California at Berkeley.

Caligula /kəˈlɪgjʊlə/ Gaius Caesar AD 12–41. Roman emperor, son of Germanicus and successor to Tiberius in AD 37. Caligula was a cruel tyrant and was assassinated by an officer of his guard. Believed to have been mentally unstable, he is remembered for giving a consulship to his horse Incitatus.

calima (Spanish 'haze') dust cloud in Europe, coming from the Sahara Desert, which sometimes causes heatwaves and eye irritation.

caliph title of civic and religious heads of the world of Islam. The first caliph was ◊Abu Bakr. Nominally elective, the office became hereditary, held by the Ummayyad dynasty 661–750 and then by the ◊Abbasid. During the 10th century the political and military power passed to the leader of the caliph's Turkish bodyguard; about the same time, an independent ◊Fatimid caliphate sprang up in Egypt. After the death of the last Abbasid (1258), the title was claimed by a number of Muslim chieftains in Egypt, Turkey, and India. The most powerful of these were the Turkish sultans of the Ottoman Empire.

The title was adopted by the prophet Muhammad's successors. The last of the Turkish caliphs was deposed by Kemal ◊Atatürk in 1924.

calla alternative name for ◊arum lily.

Callaghan /ˈkæləhæn/ (Leonard) James, Baron Callaghan 1912– . British Labour politician. As chancellor of the Exchequer 1964–67, he introduced corporation and capital-gains taxes, and resigned following devaluation. He was home secretary 1967–70 and prime minister 1976–79 in a period of increasing economic stress.

Callaghan British Labour politician James Callaghan, prime minister 1976—79.

As foreign secretary 1974, Callaghan renegotiated Britain's membership of the European Community. In 1976 he succeeded Harold Wilson as prime minister and in 1977 entered into a pact with the Liberals to maintain his government in office. Strikes in the so-called 'winter of discontent' 1978–79 led to the government's losing a vote of no confidence in the Commons, forcing him to call an election, and his party was defeated at the polls May 1979.

This made Callaghan the first prime minister since Ramsay MacDonald 1924 to be forced into an election by the will of the Commons. In 1980 he resigned the party leadership under left-wing pressure, and in

1985 announced that he would not stand for Parliament in the next election.

Callao /kaɪ̆aʊ/ chief commercial and fishing port of Peru, 12 km/7 mi SW of Lima; population (1988) 318,000. Founded 1537, it was destroyed by an earthquake 1746. It is Peru's main naval base, and produces fertilizers.

Callas /ˈkæləs/ Maria. Adopted name of Maria Kalogeropoulos 1923–1977. US lyric soprano, born in New York of Greek parents. With a voice of fine range and a gift for dramatic expression, she excelled in operas including *Norma*, *Madame Butterfly*, *Aïda*, *Lucia di Lammermoor*, and *Medea*.

calligraphy art of handwriting, regarded in China and Japan as the greatest of the visual arts, and playing a large part in Islamic art because the depiction of the human and animal form is forbidden.

The present letter forms have gradually evolved from originals shaped by the tools used to make them—the flat brush on paper, the chisel on stone, the stylus on wax and clay, and the reed and quill on papyrus and skin.

In Europe during the 4th and 5th centuries books were written in square capitals ('majuscules') derived from classical Roman inscriptions (Trajan's Column in Rome is the outstanding example). The *rustic* capitals of the same period were written more freely, the pen being held at a severe angle so that the scribe was less frequently inclined to change the angle for special flourishes. *Uncial* capitals, more rounded, were used from the 4th to the 8th centuries. During this period the *cursive* hand was also developing, and the interplay of this with the formal hands, coupled with the need for speedier writing, led to the small letter forms ('minuscules'). During the 7th century the *half-uncial* was developed with ascending and descending strokes and was adopted by all countries under Roman rule. The cursive forms developed differently in different countries. In Italy the italic script was evolved and became the model for italic typefaces. Printing and the typewriter reduced the need for calligraphy in the West. In the UK there was a 20th-century revival inspired by Edward Johnston (1872–1944) and Irene Wellington (1904–1984).

Calliope /kəˈlaɪəpi/ in Greek mythology, the ◊Muse of epic poetry and chief of the Muses.

callipers measuring instrument used, for example, to measure the internal and external diameter of pipes. Some callipers are made like a pair of compasses, having two legs, often curved, pivoting about a screw at one end. The ends of the legs are placed in contact with the object to be measured, and the gap between the ends is then measured against a rule. The slide calliper looks like an adjustable spanner, and carries a scale for direct measuring, usually with a ◊vernier scale for accuracy.

Callisto /kəˈlɪstəʊ/ in Greek mythology, ◊nymph beloved by Zeus (Roman Jupiter) who was changed into a bear by his jealous wife Hera.

Callisto /kəˈlɪstəʊ/ second largest moon of Jupiter, 4,800 km/3,000 mi in diameter, orbiting every 16.7 days at a distance of 1.9 million km/1.2 million mi from the planet. Its surface is covered with large craters.

callus in botany, a tissue that forms at a damaged plant surface. Composed of large, thin-walled ◊parenchyma cells, it grows over and around the wound, eventually covering the exposed area.

Calmette /kælˈmet/ Albert 1863–1933. French bacteriologist. A student of Pasteur, he developed (with Camille Guérin, 1872–1961) the ◊BCG vaccine against tuberculosis in 1921.

calomel Hg_2Cl_2 (technical name *mercury(I) chloride*) white, heavy powder formerly used as a laxative, now used as a pesticide and fungicide.

calorie c.g.s. unit of heat, now replaced by the ◊joule (one calorie is approximately 4.2 joules). It is the heat required to raise the temperature of one gram of water by 1°C. In dietetics, the calorie or kilocalorie is equal to 1,000 calories.

The kilocalorie measures the energy value of food in terms of its heat output: 28 g/1 oz of protein yields 120 kilocalories, of carbohydrate 110, of fat 270, and of alcohol 200.

calorimeter instrument used in physics to measure heat. A simple calorimeter consists of a heavy copper vessel that is polished (to reduce heat losses by radiation) and covered with insulating material (to reduce losses by convection and conduction).

In a typical experiment, such as to measure the heat capacity of a piece of metal, the calorimeter is filled with water, whose temperature rise is measured using a thermometer when a known mass of the heated metal is immersed in it. Chemists use a bomb calorimeter to measure the heat produced by burning a fuel completely in oxygen.

calotype paper-based photograph using a wax paper negative, the first example of the ◊negative/positive process invented by the English photographer Fox Talbot around 1834.

Calpe /ˈkælpi/ former name of ◊Gibraltar.

Calvados /ˌkælvaˈdɒs/ French brandy distilled from apple cider, named after the *département* in the Basse-Normandie region of NW France where it is produced.

Calvary /ˈkælvəri/ (Aramaic *Golgotha* 'skull') in the New Testament, the site of Jesus' crucifixion at Jerusalem. Two chief locations are suggested: the site where the Church of the Sepulchre now stands, and the hill beyond the Damascus gate.

Calvin /ˈkælvɪn/ John (also known as *Cauvin* or *Chauvin*) 1509–1564. French-born Swiss Protestant church reformer and theologian. He was a leader of the Reformation in Geneva and set up a strict religious community there. His theological system is known as Calvinism, and his church government as ◊Presbyterianism. Calvin wrote (in Latin) *Institutes of the Christian Religion* 1536 and commentaries on the New Testament and much of the Old Testament.

Calvin, born in Noyon, Picardie, studied theology and then law, and about 1533 became prominent in Paris as an evangelical preacher. In 1534 he was obliged to leave Paris and retired to Basel, where he studied Hebrew. In 1536 he accepted an invitation to go to Geneva, Switzerland, and assist in the Reformation, but was expelled 1538 because of public resentment against the numerous and too drastic changes he introduced. He returned to Geneva 1541 and, in the face of strong opposition, established a rigorous theocracy (government by priests). In 1553 he had the Spanish theologian Servetus burned for heresy. He supported the Huguenots in their struggle in France and the English Protestants persecuted by Queen Mary I.

Calvin /ˈkælvɪn/ Melvin 1911– . US chemist who, using radioactive carbon-14 as a tracer, determined the biochemical processes of ◊photosynthesis, in which green plants use ◊chlorophyll to convert carbon dioxide and water into sugar and oxygen. He was awarded a Nobel prize 1961.

Calvinism /ˈkælvɪnɪz(ə)m/ Christian doctrine as interpreted by John Calvin and

adopted in Scotland, parts of Switzerland, and the Netherlands; by the ◊Puritans in England and New England, USA; and by the subsequent Congregational and Presbyterian churches in the USA. Its central doctrine is predestination, under which certain souls (the elect) are predestined by God through the sacrifice of Jesus to salvation, and the rest to damnation. Although Calvinism is rarely accepted today in its strictest interpretation, the 20th century has seen a Neo-Calvinist revival through the work of Karl ◊Barth.

Calypso /kəˈlɪpsəʊ/ in Greek mythology, a sea ◊nymph who waylaid the homeward-bound Odysseus for seven years.

calypso /kəˈlɪpsəʊ/ West Indian satirical ballad with a syncopated beat. Calypso is a traditional song form of Trinidad, a feature of its annual carnival, with roots in W African praise singing. It was first popularized in the USA by Harry Belafonte (1927–) in 1956. Mighty Sparrow (1935–) is Trinidad's best-known calypso singer.

calyx collective term for the ◊sepals of a flower, forming the outermost whorl of the ◊perianth. It surrounds the other flower parts and protects them while in bud. In some flowers, for example, the campions *Silene*, the sepals are fused along their sides, forming a tubular calyx.

cam part of a machine that converts circular motion to linear motion or vice versa. The *edge cam* in a car engine is in the form of a rounded projection on a shaft, the camshaft. When the camshaft turns, the cams press against linkages (plungers or followers) that open the valves in the cylinders. A *face cam* is a disc with a groove in its face, in which the follower travels. A *cylindrical cam* carries angled parallel grooves, which impart a to and fro motion to the follower when it rotates.

CAM (acronym for *computer-aided manufacture*) use of computers to control production processes; in particular, the control of machine tools and ◊robots in factories. In some factories, the whole design and production system has been automated by linking ◊CAD (computer-aided design) to CAM.

Camagüey /ˌkæməˈgweɪ/ city in Cuba; population (1986) 260,800. It is the capital of Camagüey province in the centre of the island. Founded about 1514, it was the capital of the Spanish West Indies during the 19th century. It has a 17th-century cathedral.

Camargo /kæmɑːˈɡəʊ/ Marie-Anne de Cupis 1710–1770. French ballerina, born in Brussels. She became a ballet star in Paris in 1726 and was the first ballerina to attain the 'batterie' (movements involving beating the legs together) previously danced only by men. She shortened her skirt to expose the ankles and her brilliant footwork, gaining more liberty of movement.

Camargue /kæˈmɑːɡ/ marshy area of the ◊Rhône delta, south of Arles, France; about 780 sq km/300 sq mi. Bulls and horses are bred there, and the nature reserve, which is known for its bird life, forms the southern part.

cambium in botany, a layer of actively dividing cells (lateral ◊meristem), found within stems and roots, that gives rise to ◊secondary growth in perennial plants, causing an increase in girth. There are two main types of cambium: vascular cambium which gives rise to secondary ◊xylem and ◊phloem tissues, and cork cambium (or phellogen) which gives rise to secondary cortex and cork tissues (see ◊bark).

Cambodia /kæmˈbəʊdiə/ (formerly *Khmer Republic* 1970–76, *Democratic Kampuchea* 1976–79, and *People's Republic of Kampuchea* 1979–89) country in SE Asia, bounded N and NW by Thailand, N by Laos, E and SE by Vietnam, and SW by the Gulf of Thailand.

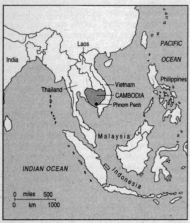

government Under the terms of the 1991 United Nations transitional arrangements, political power is shared between the all-party Supreme National Council (SNC) and the UN Transitional Authority in Cambodia (UNTAC).

history The area now known as Cambodia was once occupied by the Khmer empire, an ancient civilization that flourished during the 6th–15th centuries. After this, the region was subject to attacks by the neighbouring Vietnamese and Thai, and in 1863 became a French protectorate. A nationalist movement began in the 1930s, and anti-French feeling was fuelled 1940–41 when the French agreed to Japanese demands for bases in Cambodia, and allowed Thailand to annex Cambodian territory.

During World War II Cambodia was occupied by Japan. France regained control of the country 1946, but it achieved semi-autonomy within the French Union 1949 and full independence 1953. Prince Norodom ◊Sihanouk, who had been elected king 1941, abdicated in favour of his parents and became prime minister as leader of the Popular Socialist Community 1955. When his father died 1960, he became head of state.

Khmer Republic Sihanouk remained neutral during the Vietnam War and was overthrown by a right-wing revolt led by pro-USA Lt-Gen Lon Nol in 1970. Lon Nol first became prime minister (1971–72) and then president (1972–75) of what was termed the new Khmer Republic. His regime was opposed by the exiled Sihanouk and by the communist Khmer Rouge (backed by North Vietnam and China) who merged to form the National United Front of Cambodia. A civil war developed and, despite substantial military aid from the USA during its early stages, Lon Nol's government fell 1975. The country was renamed Kampuchea, with Prince Sihanouk as head of state.

Khmer Rouge Regime The Khmer Rouge proceeded ruthlessly to introduce an extreme communist programme, forcing urban groups into rural areas, which led to over 2.5 million deaths from famine, disease, and maltreatment. In 1976 a new constitution removed Prince Sihanouk from power, appointed Khieu Samphan (the former deputy prime minister) president and placed the Communist Party of Kampuchea, led by ◊Pol Pot, in control. The Khmer Rouge developed close links with China and fell out with its former sponsors, Vietnam and the USSR.

In a Vietnamese invasion of Kampuchea launched 1978, Pol Pot was overthrown and a pro-Vietnamese puppet government was set up under Heng Samrin. The defeated regime kept up guerrilla resistance under Pol Pot, causing over 300,000 Kampuchean refugees to flee to Thailand in 1979 alone.

resistance movement In 1982 the resistance movement broadened with the formation in Kuala Lumpur, Malaysia, of an anti-Vietnamese coalition and Democratic Kampuchea government-in-exile with Prince Sihanouk (then living in North Korea) as president, Khieu Samphan (political leader of the now less extreme Khmer Rouge) as vice president, and Son Sann (an ex-premier and contemporary leader of the noncommunist Khmer People's National Liberation Front (KPNLF)) as prime minister. The coalition received sympathetic support from ◊ASEAN countries and China. However, its 60,000 troops were outnumbered by the 170,000 Vietnamese who supported the Heng Samrin government. With the resistance coalition's base camps being overrun 1985, a military victory appeared unlikely. During 1982–91 the USA aided the KPNLF and the Sihanoukist National Army (ANS)—allies of the Khmer Rouge—with millions of dollars in 'humanitarian' aid and secret 'nonlethal' military aid.

political settlement Hopes of a political settlement were improved by the retirement of the reviled Pol Pot as Khmer Rouge military leader 1985 and by the appointment of the reformist Hun Sen as prime minister. A mixed-economy domestic approach was adopted and indigenous Khmers promoted to key government posts; at the same time, prompted by the new Soviet leader, Mikhail Gorbachev, the Vietnamese began a phased withdrawal. In spring 1989, after talks with the resistance coalition, the Phnom Penh government agreed to a package of constitutional reforms, including the adoption of Buddhism as the state religion and the readoption of the ideologically neutral name State of Cambodia. Withdrawal of the Vietnamese army was completed Sept 1989. However, the United Nations continued to refuse recognition of the Hun Sen government and the civil war intensified, with the Khmer Rouge making advances in the western provinces, capturing the border town of Pailin Oct 1989. The Phnom Penh government was left with an army of 40,000, backed by a 100,000-strong militia, against the resistance coalition's 45,000 guerrillas, half of whom belonged to the Khmer Rouge. In Nov 1990 the five permanent members of the UN Security Council, including the USA, USSR, and China, agreed on the final draft of a Cambodian peace settlement, which provided for an immediate cease-fire and the formation of an interim administration under UN auspices. The Phnom Penh government dismissed it, objecting to the establishment of a UN administration within the country.

accord reached Guerrilla fighting intensified Jan 1991 but, for the first time in 12 years, a cease-fire was implemented May 1991. The cease-fire broke down June 1991 after talks in Jakarta foundered once again. However, later in the month an accord was reached by the all-party Supreme National Council (SNC) at Pattaya, Thailand, between Prince Sihanouk, the guerrillas' nominal leader, and the Hun Sen government.

end of civil war On 23 Oct 1991, after nearly four years of intermittent negotiations, Cambodia's four warring factions and 18 interested countries signed a peace agreement in Paris, ending 13 years of civil war. The UN peacekeeping operation provided for a UN Trasitional Authority in Cambodia (UNTAC) to administer the country in conjuction with the Supreme National Council comprising representatives from Cambodia's four warring factions until the UN-administered general elections in 1993.

return of Sihanouk and Khmer Rouge The ruling Kampuchean People's Revolutionary Party, anxious to make itself more attractive to voters, formally abandoned its Marxist-Leninist ideology in Oct 1991 and changed its name to the Khmer/ Cambodian People's Party. Heng Samrin was replaced as party chair by the powerful Chea Sim and the party endorsed a multiparty democratic system, a free-market economy, and the protection of human rights. It upheld Buddhism as the state religion and declared support for Prince Sihanouk's future candidacy for the state presidency. Prince Sihanouk returned to Phnom Penh on 23 Nov 1991 after a 13-year absence. Khieu Samphan, leader of the Khmer Rouge, also returned but was forced to fly back to Thailand after being attacked by an angry mob. Despite promises Aug 1992 that the Khmer Rouge would cooperate in the peace process, they were still refusing to disarm in Oct.   In Jan 1992 political prisoners were released from Cambodia's jails and it was announced that freedom of speech and the formation of new political parties would be allowed. Free general elections 1993 resulted in a surprise win by the moderate FUNCINPEC party with Prince Norodom Ranariddh appointed prime minister.

Cambrai /kɒmˈbreɪ/ chief town of Nord *département*, France; on the river Escaut (Scheldt); population (1982) 36,600. Industries include light textiles (cambric is named after the town) and confectionery. The Peace of Cambrai or Ladies' Peace (1529) was concluded on behalf of Francis I of France by his mother Louise of Savoy and on behalf of Charles V by his aunt Margaret of Austria.

Cambrai, Battles of /kɒmˈbreɪ/ two battles in World War I at Cambrai in NE France: *First Battle* Nov–Dec 1917; the town was almost captured by the British when large numbers of tanks were used for the first time. *Second Battle* 26 Aug–5 Oct 1918, the town was taken during the final British offensive.

Cambrian /ˈkæmbrɪən/ period of geological time 590–505 million years ago; the first period of the Palaeozoic era. All invertebrate animal life appeared, and marine algae were widespread. The earliest fossils with hard shells, such as trilobites, date from this period.

Cambridge /ˈkeɪmbrɪdʒ/ city in England, on the river Cam (a river sometimes called by its earlier name, Granta), 80 km/50 mi N of London; population (1989) 101,000. It is the administrative headquarters of Cambridgeshire. The city is centred on Cambridge University (founded 12th century).
history As early as 100 BC, a Roman settlement grew up on a slight rise in the low-lying plain, commanding a ford over the river. Apart from those of Cambridge University, fine buildings include St Benet's church, the oldest building in Cambridge, the round church of the Holy Sepulchre, and the Guildhall 1939.
Industries include the manufacture of scientific instruments, radio, electronics, paper, flour milling, and fertilizers.

Cambridge /ˈkeɪmbrɪdʒ/ city in Massachusetts, USA; population (1980) 95,322. Industries include paper and publishing. Harvard University 1636 (the oldest educational institution in the USA, named after John Harvard 1607–38, who bequeathed his library to it along with half his estate), Massachusetts Institute of Technology 1861, and the John F Kennedy School of Government and

Memorial Library are here, as well as a park named after him.

Cambridgeshire /ˈkeɪmbrɪdʒʃə/ county in E England
area 3,410 sq km/1,316 sq mi
towns Cambridge (administrative headquarters), Ely, Huntingdon, Peterborough
features rivers: Ouse, Cam, Nene; Isle of Ely; Cambridge University; at RAF Molesworth, near Huntingdon, Britain's second ♭cruise missile base was deactivated Jan 1989
products mainly agricultural
population (1989) 642,000
famous people Oliver Cromwell, Octavia Hill, John Maynard Keynes.

Cambridge University English university, one of the earliest in Europe, probably founded in the 12th century, though the earliest of the existing colleges, Peterhouse, was not founded until about 1284. In 1990, there were 10,000 undergraduate and 3,000 postgraduate students.
The chancellor is the titular head, and the vice chancellor the active head. The Regent House is the legislative and executive body, with the Senate as the court of appeal. Each college has its own corporation, and is largely independent. The head of each college, assisted by a council of fellows, manages its affairs. Among the departments held in high repute is the Cavendish Laboratory for experimental physics, established 1873. The Cambridge Science Park was set up by Trinity College in 1973. The Royal Greenwich Observatory moved there in 1990.

Cambs abbreviation for ♭*Cambridgeshire*.

Cambyses /kæmˈbaɪsiːz/ 6th century BC. Emperor of Persia 529–522 BC. Succeeding his father Cyrus, he assassinated his brother Smerdis and conquered Egypt in 525 BC. There he outraged many of the local religious customs and was said to have become insane. He died in Syria on his journey home, probably by suicide.

Camden /ˈkæmdən/ inner borough of NW Greater London; population (1981) 171,563. It includes the districts of (1) *Bloomsbury*, site of London University, Royal Academy of Dramatic Art (RADA), and the British Museum; home between World Wars I and II of writers and artists including Leonard and Virginia Woolf and Lytton Strachey; (2) *Fitzrovia*, W of Tottenham Court Road, with the Telecom Tower and Fitzroy Square as its focus; (3) *Hampstead*, site of Primrose Hill, Hampstead Heath, and nearby Kenwood House; Keats's home, now a museum; the churchyard where the painter Constable is buried; and Hampstead Garden Suburb; (4) *Highgate*, with the burial site of George Eliot, Michael Faraday, and Karl Marx; (5) *Holborn*, with the Inns of Court (Lincoln's Inn and Gray's Inn); Hatton Garden (diamond dealers), the London Silver Vaults; and (6) *Somers Town*, between Euston and King's Cross railway stations.

Camden Town Group school of British painters 1911–13, based in Camden, London, inspired by W R ◊Sickert. The work of Spencer Gore (1878–1914) and Harold Gilman (1876–1919) is typical of the group, rendering everyday town scenes in Post-Impressionist style.

camel large cud-chewing mammal of the even-toed hoofed order Artiodactyla. Unlike typical ruminants, it has a three-chambered stomach. It has two toes which have broad soft soles for walking on sand, and hooves resembling nails. There are two species, the single-humped *Arabian camel Camelus dromedarius*, and the twin-humped *Bactrian camel*, *C. bactrianus* from Asia. They carry a food reserve of fatty tissue in the hump, can go without drinking for long periods, can feed on salty vegetation, and withstand extremes of heat and cold, thus being well adapted to desert conditions.

Smaller, flat-backed members of the camel family include the ◊alpaca, the ◊guanaco, the ◊llama, and the ◊vicuna.

camellia any oriental evergreen shrub with roselike flowers of the genus *Camellia*, tea family Theaceae. Numerous species, including *C. japonica* and *C. reticulata*, have been introduced into Europe, the USA, and Australia.

Camelot /ˈkæmələt/ legendary seat of King ◊Arthur.

cameo small relief carving of semiprecious stone, shell, or glass. A pale-coloured surface layer is carved to reveal a darker ground. Fine cameos were produced in ancient Greece and Rome, during the Renaissance, and in the Victorian era. They were used for decorating goblets and vases, and as jewellery.

camera apparatus used in ◊photography, consisting of a light-proof box with a lens at one end and sensitized film at the other. The lens collects rays of light reflected from the subject and brings them together as a sharp image on the film; it has marked numbers known as ◊apertures, or F stops, that reduce or increase the amount of light. Apertures also control depth of field. A shutter controls the amount of time light has to affect the film. There are small-, medium-, and large-format cameras; the format refers to the size of recorded image and the dimensions of the print obtained.

A simple camera has a fixed shutter speed and aperture, chosen so that on a sunny day the correct amount of light is admitted. More complex cameras allow the shutter speed and aperture to be adjusted; most have a built-in exposure meter to help choose the correct combination of shutter speed and aperture for the ambient conditions and subject matter. The most versatile camera is the single lens reflex (◊SLR) which allows the lens to be removed and special lenses attached. A pin-hole camera has a small (pin-sized) hole instead of a lens. It must be left on a firm support during exposures, which are up to ten seconds with slow film, two seconds with fast film and five minutes for paper negatives in daylight. The pin-hole camera gives sharp images from close-up to infinity.

camera obscura darkened box with a tiny hole for projecting the inverted image of the scene outside on to a screen inside. For its development as a device for producing photographs, see ◊photography.

Cameron /ˈkæmərən/ Charles 1746–1812. Scottish architect. He trained under Isaac Ware in the Palladian tradition before being summoned to Russia in 1779. He created the palace complex at Tsarskoe Selo (now Pushkin), planned the town of Sofia, and from 1803, as chief architect of the Admiralty, executed many buildings, including the Naval Hospital and barracks at Kronstadt 1805.

Cameron /ˈkæmərən/ Julia Margaret 1815–1879. British photographer. She made lively, revealing portraits of the Victorian intelligentsia using a large camera, five-minute exposures, and wet plates. Her subjects included Charles Darwin and Alfred Tennyson.

Cameroon /ˌkæməˈruːn/ country in W Africa, bounded NW by Nigeria, NE by Chad, E by the Central African Republic, S by Congo, Gabon, and Equatorial Guinea, and W by the Atlantic.

government Cameroon was a federal state until 1972 when a new constitution, revised 1975, made it unitary. The constitution provides for a president and a single-chamber

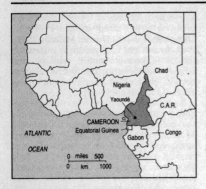

national assembly of 180, each elected for a five-year term. The president has the power to choose the cabinet, to lengthen or shorten the life of the assembly, and may stand for re-election. The only political party is the Democratic Assembly of the Cameroon People (RDPC), formed 1966 by a merger of the governing party of each state of the original federation and the four opposition parties. The state president is also president of the party.

history The area was first visited by Europeans 1472, when the Portuguese began slave trading in the area. In 1884 Cameroon became a German protectorate. After World War I, France governed about 80% of the area under a League of Nations mandate, with Britain administering the remainder. In 1946 both became UN trust territories.

In 1957 French Cameroon became a state within the French Community and three years later achieved full independence as the Republic of Cameroon. After a plebiscite 1961, the northern part of British Cameroons merged with Nigeria, and the southern part joined the Republic of Cameroon to form the Federal Republic of Cameroon. The French zone became East Cameroon and the British part West Cameroon.

Ahmadou Ahidjo, who had been the first president of the republic 1960, became president of the federal republic and was re-elected 1965. In 1966 Cameroon was made a one-party state when the two government parties and most of the opposition parties merged into the Cameroon National Union (UNC). Extreme left-wing opposition to the UNC was crushed 1971. In 1972 the federal system was abolished, and a new national assembly was elected 1973.

Biya's presidency In 1982 Ahidjo resigned, nominating Paul Biya as his successor. In 1983 Biya began to remove Ahidjo's supporters, and in protest Ahidjo resigned the presidency of UNC. Biya was re-elected 1984, while Ahidjo went into exile in France. Biya strengthened his position by abolishing the post of prime minister and reshuffling his cabinet. He also changed the nation's name from the United Republic of Cameroon to the Republic of Cameroon. Many of Ahidjo's supporters were executed after a failed attempt to overthrow Biya. In 1985 UNC changed its name to RDPC, and Biya tightened his control by more cabinet changes.

In 1988 Biya was re-elected president with 98.75% of the vote. In 1990 widespread public disorder resulted from the arrests of lawyers, lecturers, and students. Biya granted amnesty to political prisoners and promised multiparty elections. In March 1992 the first multiparty assembly elections in 28 years were held. The ruling RDPC secured a majority only with the support of a small pro-Biya opposition group. Biya also won the Oct 1992 presidential election, but his victory was questioned by the opposition.

Camoëns /ˈkæməʊenz/ or *Camões* Luís Vaz de 1524–1580. Portuguese poet and soldier. He went on various military expeditions, and was shipwrecked in 1558. His poem *Os Lusiades/The Lusiads* 1572 tells the story of the explorer Vasco da Gama and incorporates much Portuguese history; it has become the country's national epic. His posthumously published lyric poetry is also now valued.

Having wounded an equerry of the king in 1552, he was banished to India. He received a small pension, but died in poverty of plague.

Camorra /kəˈmɒrə/ Italian secret society formed about 1820 by criminals in the dungeons of Naples and continued once they were freed. It dominated politics from 1848, was suppressed in 1911, but many members eventually surfaced in the US ◊Mafia. The Camorra still operates in the Naples area.

camouflage colours or structures that allow an animal to blend with its surroundings to avoid detection by other animals. Camouflage can take the form of matching the background colour, of countershading (darker on top, lighter below, to counteract natural shadows), or of irregular patterns that break up the outline of the animal's body. More elaborate camouflage involves closely resembling a feature of the natural environment, as with the stick insect; this is closely akin to ◊mimicry.

Campagna Romana /kæm'pænjə rəʊ'mɑːnə/ lowland stretch of the Italian peninsula, including and surrounding the city of Rome. Lying between the Tyrrhenian Sea and the Sabine Hills to the NE, and the Alban Hills to the SE, it is drained by the lower course of the river Tiber and a number of small streams, most of which dry up in the summer. Prosperous in Roman times, it later became virtually derelict through overgrazing, lack of water, and the arrival in the area of the malaria-carrying *Anopheles* mosquito. Extensive land reclamation and drainage in the 19th and 20th centuries restored its usefulness.

Campaign for Nuclear Disarmament (CND) nonparty-political British organization advocating the abolition of nuclear weapons worldwide: CND seeks unilateral British initiatives to help start the multilateral process and end the arms race.

The movement was launched by the philosopher Bertrand Russell and Canon John Collins in 1958. It grew out of the demonstration held outside the government's Atomic Weapons Research Establishment at Aldermaston, Berkshire, at Easter 1956. It held annual marches from Aldermaston to London 1959–63, after the initial march in 1958 which was routed from London to Aldermaston. From 1970 CND has also opposed nuclear power. Its membership peaked in the early 1980s, during the campaign against the presence of US Pershing and cruise nuclear missiles on British soil.

Campania /kæm'pænjə/ agricultural region (wheat, citrus, wine, vegetables, tobacco) of S Italy, including the volcano ◊Vesuvius; capital Naples; industrial centres Benevento, Caserta, and Salerno; area 13,600 sq km/5,250 sq mi; population (1988) 5,732,000. There are ancient sites at Pompeii, Herculaneum, and Paestum.

campanile originally a bell tower erected near, or attached to, a church or town hall in Italy. The leaning tower of Pisa is an example; another is the great campanile of Florence, 90 m/275 ft high.

Campbell /'kæmbəl/ Colin, 1st Baron Clyde 1792–1863. British field marshal. He commanded the Highland Brigade at ◊Balaclava in the Crimean War and, as commander in

chief during the Indian Mutiny, raised the siege of Lucknow and captured Cawnpore.

Campbell /'kæmbəl/ Donald Malcolm 1921–1967. British car and speedboat enthusiast, son of Malcolm Campbell, who simultaneously held the land-speed and water-speed records. In 1964 he set the world water-speed record of 444.57 kph/276.3 mph on Lake Dumbleyung, Australia, with the turbojet hydroplane *Bluebird*, and achieved the land-speed record of 648.7 kph/403.1 mph at Lake Eyre salt flats, Australia. He was killed in an attempt to raise his water-speed record on Coniston Water, England.

He was invalided out of the RAF in World War II and took up the interests of his father, Malcolm ◊Campbell.

Campbell /'kæmbəl/ Malcolm 1885–1948. British racing driver who, at one time, held both land- and water-speed records. His car and boat were both called *Bluebird*.

He set the land-speed record nine times, pushing it up to 484.8 kph/301.1 mph at Bonneville Flats, Utah, USA, in 1935, and broke the water-speed record three times, the best being 228.2 kph/141.74 mph on Coniston Water, England, in 1939.

Campbell /'kæmbəl/ Mrs Patrick (born Beatrice Stella Tanner) 1865–1940. British actress whose roles included Paula in Pinero's *The Second Mrs Tanqueray* 1893 and Eliza in *Pygmalion*, written for her by G B Shaw, with whom she had an amusing correspondence.

Campbell /'kæmbəl/ Roy 1901–1957. South African poet, author of *The Flaming Terrapin* 1924. Born in Durban, he became a professional jouster and bullfighter in Spain and Provence, France. He fought for Franco in the Spanish Civil War and was with the Commonwealth forces in World War II.

Campbell /'kæmbəl/ Thomas 1777–1844. Scottish poet. After the successful publication of his *Pleasures of Hope* in 1799, he travelled in Europe, and there wrote his war poems 'Hohenlinden' and 'Ye Mariners of England'.

Campbell-Bannerman /'kæmbəl 'bænəmən/ Henry 1836–1908. British Liberal politician, prime minister 1905–08. It was during his term of office that the South African colonies achieved self-government, and the Trades Disputes Act 1906 was passed.

Camp David /'kæmp 'deɪvɪd/ official country home of US presidents, situated in the Appalachian mountains, Maryland; it was originally named Shangri-la by F D Roosevelt, but was renamed Camp David by Eisenhower (after his grandson).

Camp David Agreements two framework agreements signed at Camp David, Maryland, USA, in 1978 by the Israeli prime minister Begin and Egyptian president Sadat, under the guidance of US president Carter, covering an Egypt–Israel peace treaty and phased withdrawal of Israel from Sinai, which was completed in 1982, and an overall Middle East settlement including the election by the West Bank and Gaza Strip Palestinians of a 'self-governing authority'. The latter issue stalled over questions of who should represent the Palestinians and what form the self-governing body should take.

Campeche /kæm'petʃi/ port on the Bay of ♦Campeche, Mexico; population (1984) 120,000. It is the capital of Campeche state. Timber and fish are exported, and there is a university, established 1756.

Camperdown /'kæmpədaʊn/ (Dutch *Kamperduin*) village on the NW Netherlands coast, off which a British fleet defeated the Dutch 11 Oct 1797 in the Revolutionary Wars.

camphor $C_{10}H_{16}O$ volatile, aromatic ♦ketone substance obtained from the camphor tree *Cinnamomum camphora*. It is distilled from chips of the wood, and is used in insect repellents and medicinal inhalants and liniments, and in the manufacture of celluloid.

Camphylobacter genus of bacteria that cause serious outbreaks of gastroenteritis. They grow best at 43°C, and so are well suited to the digestive tract of birds. Poultry is therefore the most likely source of a *Camphylobacter* outbreak, although the bacteria can also be transmitted via beef or milk. *Camphylobacter* can survive in water for up to 15 days, so may be present in drinking water if supplies are contaminated by sewage or reservoirs are polluted by seagulls. In 1990 the incidence of *Camphylobacter* poisoning equalled salmonella incidence.

Campin /kɒm'piːn/ Robert, also known as the *Master of Flémalle* c. 1378–1444. Netherlandish painter of the early Renaissance, active in Tournai from 1406, one of the first northern masters to use oil. His outstanding work is the *Mérode altarpiece*, about 1425 (Metropolitan Museum of Art, New York), which shows a distinctly naturalistic style, with a new subtlety in modelling and a grasp of pictorial space.

Campinas /kæm'piːnəs/ city of São Paulo, Brazil, situated on the central plateau; population (1980) 566,700. It is a coffee-trading centre. There are also metallurgical and food industries.

campion /'kæmpiən/ any of several plants of the genera *Lychnis* and *Silene*, belonging to the pink family Caryophyllaceae, which include the garden campion *L. coronaria*, the wild white and red campions *S. alba* and *S. dioica*, and the bladder campion *S. vulgaris*.

Campion /'kæmpiən/ Edmund 1540–1581. English Jesuit and Roman Catholic martyr. He took orders as a deacon in the English church, but fled to Douai, France, where he recanted Protestantism 1571. In 1573 he became a Jesuit in Rome, and in 1580 was sent to England as a missionary. He was betrayed as a spy 1581, imprisoned in the Tower of London, and hanged, drawn, and quartered as a traitor.

Campion /'kæmpiən/ Thomas 1567–1620. English poet and musician. He was the author of the critical *Art of English Poesie* 1602, and four *Bookes of Ayres*, for which he composed both words and music.

Campobasso /ˌkæmpəʊ'bæsəʊ/ capital of Molise region, Italy, about 190 km/120 mi SE of Rome; population (1981) 48,300. It has a high reputation for its cutlery.

Campo-Formio, Treaty of /'kæmpəʊ 'fɔːmiəʊ/ peace settlement 1797 during the Revolutionary Wars between Napoleon and Austria, by which France gained the region that is now Belgium and Austria was compensated with Venice and part of that area which now reaches into Slovenia and Croatia.

Camus /kæ'mjuː/ Albert 1913–1960. Algerian-born French writer. A journalist in France, he was active in the Resistance during World War II. His novels, which owe much to ♦existentialism, include *L'Etranger/The Outsider* 1942, *La Peste/The Plague* 1948, and *L'Homme révolté/The Rebel* 1952. He was awarded the Nobel Prize for Literature 1957.

Canaan /'keɪnən/ ancient region between the Mediterranean and the Dead Sea, called in the Bible the 'Promised Land' of the Israelites. It was occupied as early as the 3rd millennium BC by the Canaanites, a Semitic-speaking people who were known to the Greeks of the 1st millennium BC as Phoenicians. The capital was Ebla (now Tell Mardikh, Syria).

The Canaanite Empire included Syria, Palestine, and part of Mesopotamia. It was conquered by the Israelites during the 13th to 10th centuries BC. Ebla was excavated 1976–77, revealing an archive of inscribed tablets dating from the 3rd millennium BC, which includes place names such as Gaza and Jerusalem (no excavations at the latter had suggested occupation at so early a date).

Canada /'kænədə/ country occupying the northern part of the North American continent, bounded S by the USA, N by the Arctic Ocean, NW by Alaska, E by the Atlantic Ocean, and W by the Pacific Ocean.

government The Canada Act of 1982 gave Canada power to amend its constitution and added a charter of rights and freedoms. This represented Canada's complete independence, though it remains a member of the British ◊Commonwealth.

Canada is a federation of ten provinces: Alberta, British Columbia, Manitoba, New Brunswick, Newfoundland, Nova Scotia, Ontario, Prince Edward Island, Québec, and Saskatchewan; and two territories: Northwest Territories and Yukon. Each province has a single-chamber assembly, popularly elected; the premier (the leader of the party with the most seats in the legislature) chooses the cabinet. The two-chamber federal parliament consists of the Senate, whose 104 members are appointed by the government for life or until the age of 75 and

Canada: prime ministers

1867	John A Macdonald	(Conservative)
1873	Alexander Mackenzie	(Liberal)
1878	John A Macdonald	(Conservative)
1891	John J Abbott	(Conservative)
1892	John S D Thompson	(Conservative)
1894	Mackenzie Bowell	(Conservative)
1896	Charles Tupper	(Conservative)
1896	Wilfred Laurier	(Liberal)
1911	Robert L Borden	(Conservative)
1920	Arthur Meighen	(Conservative)
1921	William Lyon Mackenzie King	(Liberal)
1926	Arthur Meighen	(Conservative)
1926	William Lyon Mackenzie King	(Liberal)
1930	Richard Bedford Bennett	(Conservative)
1935	William Lyon Mackenzie King	(Liberal)
1948	Louis Stephen St Laurent	(Liberal)
1957	John G Diefenbaker	(Conservative)
1963	Lester Bowles Pearson	(Liberal)
1968	Pierre Elliot Trudeau	(Liberal)
1979	Joseph Clark	(Progressive Conservative)
1980	Pierre Elliot Trudeau	(Liberal)
1984	John Turner	(Liberal)
1984	Brian Mulroney	(Progressive Conservative)
1993	Kim Campbell	(Conservative)
1993	Jean Chrétien	(Liberal)

Canada: provinces

province	capital	area in sq km
Alberta	Edmonton	661,200
British Columbia	Victoria	947,800
Manitoba	Winnipeg	650,000
New Brunswick	Fredericton	73,400
Newfoundland	St John's	405,700
Nova Scotia	Halifax	55,500
Ontario	Toronto	1,068,600
Prince Edward Island	Charlottetown	5,700
Québec	Québec	1,540,700
Saskatchewan	Regina	652,300

territory	capital	area in sq km
Northwest Territories	Yellowknife	3,426,300
Yukon Territory	Whitehorse	483,500

who must be resident in the provinces they represent; and the House of Commons, which has 295 members, elected by universal suffrage in single-member constituencies.

The federal prime minister is the leader of the best-supported party in the House of Commons and is accountable, with the cabinet, to it. Parliament has a maximum life of five years. Legislation must be passed by both chambers and then signed by the governor general.

history Inhabited by indigenous Indian and Eskimo groups, Canada was reached by an English expedition led by John Cabot 1497 and a French expedition under Jacques Cartier 1534. Both countries developed colonies from the 17th century, with hostility between them culminating in the French and Indian Wars (1689–1763), in which France was defeated. Antagonism continued, and in 1791 Canada was divided into English-speaking Upper Canada (much of modern Ontario) and French-speaking Lower Canada (much of modern Québec and all of modern mainland Newfoundland). The two were united as Canada Province 1841, when the self-governing Dominion of Canada was founded.

In 1870 the province of Manitoba was added to the confederation, British Columbia joined 1871, and Prince Edward Island 1873. The new provinces of Alberta and Saskatchewan were created from the Northwest Territories 1905. An improving economy led to vast areas of fertile prairie land being opened up for settlement; the discovery of gold and other metals, the exploitation of forests for lumber and paper, the development of fisheries and tourism, and investment from other countries gradually transformed Canada's economy into one of the most important manufacturing and trading nations in the world. World War II stimulated further rapid industrialization, and in the postwar period discovery and exploitation of mineral resources took place on a vast scale. Newfoundland joined the confederation 1949.

Trudeau's era The Progressive Conservatives returned to power 1957, after 22 years of Liberal Party rule. In 1963 the Liberals were reinstated in office under Lester Pearson, who was succeeded by Pierre Trudeau 1968. Trudeau maintained Canada's defensive alliance with the USA but sought to widen its influence internationally. Faced with the problem of Québec's separatist movement, he promised to create equal opportunities

for both English- and French-speaking Canadians throughout the country. He won both the 1972 and 1974 elections.

In 1979, with no party having an overall majority in the Commons, the Progressive Conservatives formed a government under Joe Clark. Later that year Trudeau announced his retirement from politics, but when, in Dec 1979, Clark was defeated on his budget proposals, Trudeau reconsidered his decision and won the 1980 general election with a large majority.

Trudeau's third administration was concerned with 'patriation', or the extent to which the British Parliament should determine Canada's constitution. The position was resolved with the passing of the Constitution Act 1982, the last piece of UK legislation to have force in Canada.

In 1983 Clark was replaced as leader of the Progressive Conservatives by Brian Mulroney, a corporate lawyer who had never run for public office, and in 1984 Trudeau retired to be replaced as Liberal Party leader and prime minister by John Turner, a former minister of finance. Within nine days of taking office, Turner called a general election, and the Progressive Conservatives, under Mulroney, won 211 seats, the largest majority in Canadian history, with the Liberal Party and the New Democratic Party (NDP) winning 40 and 30 seats respectively.

changing direction Soon after taking office, Mulroney began an international realignment, placing less emphasis on links established by Trudeau with Asia, Africa, and Latin America and more on cooperation with Europe and a closer relationship with the USA. The election of 1988 was fought on the issue of free trade with the USA, and the Conservatives won with a reduced majority. Despite the majority of voters opting for the Liberals or NDP, who both opposed free trade, an agreement was signed with the USA 1989. In 1990–91, Canada joined the coalition opposing Iraq's invasion of Kuwait. A national referendum Nov 1992 rejected the Charlottetown Accord, a constitutional reform package giving greater autonomy to Québec. In Feb 1993 Mulroney resigned the leadership of the Conservative Party, and was replaced as prime minister by Kim Campbell in June. The North American Free Trade Agreement (NAFTA) with the USA and Mexico was ratified the same month. The Conservatives were defeated in

Canada: history

c. 35,000 BC	People arrived in North America from Asia by way of Beringia.
c. 2000 BC	Eskimo begin settling Arctic coast from Siberia E to Greenland.
c. AD 1000	Vikings, including Leif Ericsson, landed in NE Canada, and started settlements that did not survive.
1497	John Cabot landed on Cape Breton Island.
1534	Jacques Cartier reached the Gulf of St Lawrence.
1603	Samuel Champlain began his exploration of Canada.
1608	Champlain founded Québec.
1759	James Wolfe captured Québec.
1763	France ceded Canada to Britain under the Treaty of Paris.
1775–83	American Revolution caused Loyalist influx to New Brunswick and Ontario.
1791	Canada divided into English-speaking Upper Canada (much of modern Ontario) and French-speaking Lower Canada (much of modern Québec and mainland Newfoundland).
1793	Alexander Mackenzie reached Pacific by land.
1812–14	War of 1812 between Britain and the USA. US invasions repelled by both provinces.
1837	Rebellions led by William Lyon Mackenzie in Upper Canada and Louis Joseph Papineau in Lower Canada.
1840	Upper and Lower Canada united to form the Province of Canada.
1867	British North America Act created the Dominion of Canada (Ontario, Québec, Nova Scotia, and New Brunswick).
1869	Rising, led by Louis Riel, against the Canadian government and the threat of a flood of white settlers into Rupert's Land.
1870	Manitoba created (from part of Rupert's Land) and joined confederation. North West (later Northwest) Territories created.
1871	British Columbia entered confederation.
1873	Prince Edward Island entered confederation.
1885	Northwest Rebellion crushed and leader Louis Riel hanged. Canadian Pacific Railway completed.
1905	Alberta and Saskatchewan formed from the Northwest Territories and entered confederation
1914–18	World War I—Canadian troops at 2nd Battle of Ypres, Vimy Ridge, Passchendaele, the Somme, and Cambrai.
1931	Canada became an independent nation. Norway renounced its claim to the Sverdrup Islands, confirming Canadian sovereignty in the entire Arctic Archipelago north of the Canadian mainland.
1939–45	World War II—Canadian participation in all theatres.
1949	Newfoundland joined the confederation.
1950–53	Korean War—Canada participated in United Nations force, and subsequently in almost all UN peacekeeping operations.
1968	Pierre Trudeau became prime minister.

the Oct general election, with Liberal leader Jean Chrétien becoming prime minister.

Canadian art painting and sculpture of Canada after colonization. Early painters of Canadian life include Cornelius Krieghoff (1815–1872), who recorded Indian and pioneer life, and Paul Kane (1810–1871), painter of the Plains Indians. In the late 19th century, a Canadian style developed with the landscapes of Tom Thomson (1877–1917) and the 'Group of Seven', formed 1913, that developed an expressive landscape style. Maurice Cullen (1866–1934), an Impressionist, and James Wilson Morrice (1865–

1924), a Fauve, introduced new European trends.

Before World War II Emily Carr (1871–1945) was one of the most original talents, developing eloquent studies of nature. Canadian artists have since joined the international arena. The Automatistes, led by the Surrealist Paul-Emile Borduas (1905–1960), rebelled against the Canadian establishment. Jean-Paul Riopelle (1923–) has made a significant contribution to Abstract Expressionism.

Canadian literature Canadian literature in English began early in the 19th century in

canals and waterways

name	country	opened	length km	mi
Amsterdam	Netherlands	1876	26.6	16.5
Baltic–Volga	USSR	1964	2,430	1,510
Baltic–White Sea	USSR	1933	235	146
Corinth	Greece	1893	6.4	4
Elbe and Trave	Germany	1900	66	41
Erie	USA	1825	580	360
Göta	Sweden	1832	185	115
Grand Canal	China	485 BC–AD 1972	1,050	650
Kiel	Germany	1895	98	61
Manchester	England	1894	57	35.5
Panama	Panama (US zone)	1914	81	50.5
Princess Juliana	Netherlands	1935	32	20
St Lawrence	Canada	1959	3,700	2,342
Sault Ste Marie	USA	1855	2.6	1.6
Sault Ste Marie	Canada	1895	1.8	1.1
Welland	Canada	1929	45	28
Suez	Egypt	1869	166	103

the Maritime Provinces with the humorous tales of T C Haliburton (1796–1865); Charles Heavysege (1816–1876), a poet of note, was from Kingston, Ontario. The late 19th century brought the lyrical output of Charles G D Roberts (1860–1943), Bliss Carman (1861–1929), Archibald Lampman (1861–1899), and Duncan Campbell Scott (1862–1944).

Realism in fiction developed with Frederick P Grove (1871–1948), Mazo de la Roche (1885–1961), creator of the 'Jalna' series, and Hugh MacLennan (1907–). Humour of worldwide appeal emerged in Stephen Leacock (1869–1944); Brian Moore (1921–), author of *The Luck of Ginger Coffey* 1960; and Mordecai Richler. Also widely read outside Canada was L M Montgomery (1874–1942), whose *Anne of Green Gables* 1908 became a children's classic. Saul Bellow and Marshall ◊McLuhan were both Canadian-born, as were contemporary novelists Robertson ◊Davies and Margaret ◊Atwood. See also ◊French Canadian literature.

canal artificial waterway constructed for drainage, irrigation, or navigation. *Irrigation canals* carry water for irrigation from rivers, reservoirs, or wells, and are carefully designed to maintain an even flow of water over the whole length. *Navigation and ship canals* are constructed at one level between ◊locks, and frequently link with other forms of waterway—rivers and sea links—to form a waterway system. The world's two major international ship canals are the Suez Canal 1869 and the Panama Canal 1914, which provide invaluable short cuts for shipping between Europe and the East and between the east and west coasts of the Americas.

Irrigation canals fed from the Nile have maintained life in Egypt since the earliest times; the division of the waters of the Upper Indus and its tributaries form the extensive system in Pakistan and Punjab, India, was, for more than ten years, major cause of dispute between India and Pakistan, settled by a treaty 1960; the Murray basin, Victoria, Australia, and the Imperial and Central Valley projects in California, USA, are examples of 19th- and 20th-century irrigation canal development.

Probably the oldest *ship canal* to be still in use, as well as the longest, is the Grand Canal in China, which links Tianjin and Hangzhou and connects the Huang He (Yellow River) and Chang Jiang. It was originally built in three stages 485 BC–AD 283, reaching a total length of 1,780 km/1,107 mi. Large sections silted up in later years, but the entire system was dredged, widened, and rebuilt 1958–72 in conjunction with work on flood protection, irrigation, and hydroelectric schemes.

The first major British canal was the Bridgewater Canal 1759–61, constructed for the 3rd Duke of Bridgewater to carry coal from his collieries to Manchester. The engineer, James ◊Brindley, overcame great difficulties in the route. Today, many of Britain's canals form part of an interconnecting system of waterways some 4,000 km/2,500 mi long. Many that have become disused commercially have been restored for recreation and the use of pleasure craft.

Where speed is not a prime factor, the cost-effectiveness of transporting goods by canal has encouraged a revival and Belgium, France, Germany, and the USSR are among countries that have extended and streamlined their canals.

Canaletto /ˌkænəˈletəʊ/ Antonio (Giovanni Antonio Canale) 1697–1768. Italian painter celebrated for his paintings of views (*vedute*) of Venice (his native city) and of the river Thames and London 1746–56. Much of his work is very detailed and precise, with a warm light and a sparkling of tiny highlights on the green waters of canals and rivers. His later style became clumsier and more static.

Canaries current cold ocean current in the North Atlantic Ocean flowing SW from Spain along the NW coast of Africa. It meets the northern equatorial current at a latitude of 20°N.

canary bird *Serinus canaria* of the finch family, found wild in the Canary Islands and Madeira. It is greenish with a yellow underside. Canaries have been bred as cage birds in Europe since the 15th century, and many domestic varieties are yellow or orange.

Canary Islands /kəˈneəri/ (Spanish *Canarias*) group of volcanic islands 100 km/60 mi off the NW coast of Africa, forming the Spanish provinces of Las Palmas and Santa Cruz de Tenerife; area 7,300 sq km/2,818 sq mi; population (1986) 1,615,000.

features The chief centres are Santa Cruz on Tenerife (which also has the highest peak in extra-continental Spain, Pico de Teide, 3,713 m/12,186 ft), and Las Palmas on Gran Canaria. The province of Santa Cruz comprises Tenerife, Palma, Gomera, and Hierro; the province of Las Palmas comprises Gran Canaria, Lanzarote, and Fuerteventura. There are also six uninhabited islets. The Northern Hemisphere Observatory (1981) is on the island of La Palma, the first in the world to be controlled remotely. Observation conditions are among the best in the world, since there is no moisture, no artificial light pollution, and little natural ◊airglow. The Organization of African Unity (OAU) supports an independent Guanch Republic (so called from the indigenous islanders, a branch of the N African Berbers) and revival of the Guanch language.

Canberra /ˈkænbərə/ capital of Australia (since 1908), situated in the Australian Capital Territory, enclosed within New South Wales, on a tributary of the Murrumbidgee River; area (Australian Capital Territory including the port at Jervis Bay) 2,432 sq km/939 sq mi; population (1988) 297,300.

It contains the Parliament House (first used by the Commonwealth Parliament 1927), the Australian National University 1946, the Canberra School of Music 1965, and the National War Memorial.

cancan /ˈkænkæn/ high-kicking stage dance for women (solo or line of dancers) originating in Paris about 1830. The music usually associated with the cancan is the *galop* from Offenbach's *Orpheus in the Underworld*.

cancer group of diseases characterized by abnormal proliferation of cells. Cancer (malignant) cells are usually degenerate, capable only of reproducing themselves (tumour formation). Malignant cells tend to spread from their site of origin by travelling through the bloodstream or lymphatic system.

There are more than 100 types of cancer. Some, like lung or bowel cancer, are common; others are rare. The likely cause remains unexplained. Triggering agents (◊carcinogens) include chemicals such as those found in cigarette smoke, other forms of smoke, asbestos dust, exhaust fumes, and many industrial chemicals. Some viruses can also trigger the cancerous growth of cells (see ◊oncogenes), as can X-rays and radioactivity. Dietary factors are important in some cancers; for example, lack of fibre in the diet may predispose people to bowel cancer and a diet high in animal fats and low in fresh vegetables and fruit increases the risk of breast cancer. Psychological ◊stress may increase the risk of cancer, more so if the person concerned is not able to control the source of the stress. In some families there is a genetic tendency towards a particular type of cancer.

Cancer is one of the leading causes of death in the industrialized world, yet it is by no means incurable, particularly in the case of certain tumours, including Hodgkin's disease, acute leukaemia, and testicular cancer. Cures are sometimes achieved with specialized treatments, such as surgery, chemotherapy with ◊cytotoxic drugs, and irradiation, or a combination of all three. ◊Monoclonal antibodies have been used therapeutically against some cancers, with limited success. There is also hope of combining a monoclonal antibody with a drug that will kill the cancer cell to produce a highly specific ◊magic bullet drug. In 1990 it was discovered that the presence in some patients of a particular protein, p-glycoprotein, actively protects the cancer cells from drugs intended to destroy them. If this action can be blocked, the cancer should become far easier to treat. However, at present public health programmes are more concerned with prevention and early detection.

Cancer /ˈkænsə(r)/ faintest of the zodiacal constellations (its brightest stars are fourth magnitude). It lies in the northern hemisphere, between Leo and Gemini, and is represented as a crab. Cancer's most distinctive feature is the star cluster Praesepe, popularly known as the Beehive. The Sun passes through the constellation during late July and early Aug. In astrology, the dates for Cancer are between about 22 June and 22 July (see ◊precession).

Cancún /kænˈkuːn/ Caribbean resort in Mexico where, in 1981, a North–South summit was held to discuss the widening gap between the industrialized countries and the Third World.

candela /kænˈdeɪlə/ SI unit (symbol cd) of luminous intensity, which replaced the old units of candle and standard candle. It measures the brightness of a light itself rather than the amount of light falling on an object, which is called *illuminance* and measured in ◊lux.

One candela is defined as the luminous intensity in a given direction of a source that emits monochromatic radiation of frequency 540×10^{-12} Hz and whose radiant energy in that direction is 1/683 watt per steradian.

Candela /kænˈdeɪlə/ Félix 1910– . Spanish-born Mexican architect, originator of the hypar (hyperbolic paraboloid) from 1951, in which doubly curved surfaces are built up on a framework of planks sprayed with cement.

Candia /ˈkændiə/ Italian name for the Greek island of ◊Crete. Also, formerly the name of Crete's largest city, ◊Iráklion, founded about AD 824.

Candida albicans /ˈʃændɪdə ˈælbɪkænz/ yeastlike fungus present in the human digestive tract and in the vagina, which causes no harm in most healthy people. However, it can cause problems if it multiplies excessively, as in vaginal candidiasis or ◊thrush, the main symptom of which is intense itching.

The most common form of thrush is oral, which often occurs in those taking steroids or prolonged courses of antibiotics.

Newborn babies may pick up the yeast during birth and suffer an infection of the mouth and throat. There is also some evidence that over-growth of *Candida* may occur in the intestines, causing diarrhoea, bloating, and other symptoms such as headache and fatigue, but this is not yet proven. Occasionally, *Candida* can infect immunocompromised patients, such as those with AIDS. Treatment for candidiasis is based on antifungal drugs.

Candide /ˌkɒnˈdiːd/ satire by ◊Voltaire, published 1759. The hero experiences extremes of fortune in the company of Dr Pangloss, a personification of the popular belief of the time (partly based on a misunderstanding of ◊Leibniz) that 'all is for the best in the best of all possible worlds'. Voltaire exuberantly demonstrates that this idea is absurd and inhumane.

candle vertical cylinder of wax (such as tallow or paraffin wax) with a central wick of string. A flame applied to the end of the wick melts the wax, thereby producing a luminous flame. The wick is treated with a substance such as alum so that it carbonizes but does not rapidly burn out.

The candle was also the name of a unit of luminous intensity, replaced 1940 by the candela (cd), equal to 1/60 of the luminance of 1 sq cm of a black body radiator at a temperature of 2,042K (the temperature of solidification of platinum).

Candlemas in the Christian church, the Feast of the Purification of the Blessed Virgin Mary and the Presentation of the Infant Christ in the Temple, celebrated on 2 Feb; church candles are blessed on this day.

cane reedlike stem of various plants such as the sugar cane, bamboo, and, in particular, the group of palms called rattans, consisting of the genus *Calamus* and its allies. Their slender stems are dried and used for making walking sticks, baskets, and furniture.

Canea /kɑːˈniə/ (Greek *Khaniá*) capital and administrative centre of Crete, on the NW coast; population (1981) 47,338. It was founded 1252 by the Venetians and is surrounded by a wall. Vegetable oils, soap, and leather are exported. Heavy fighting took place here during World War II, after the landing of German parachutists in May 1941.

Canetti /kə'neti/ Elias 1905– . Bulgarian-born writer. He was exiled from Austria as a Jew 1938 and settled in England 1939. His books, written in German, include three volumes of memoirs —*Die gerettete Zunge: Geschichte einer Jugend/The Tongue Set Free: Remembrance of a European childhood* 1977, *Die Fackel im Ohr: Lebensgeschichte 1921–31/The Torch in My Ear* 1980, and *Das Augenspeil/The Play of the Eyes* 1985 —and *Die Blendung/Auto da Fé* 1935. He was awarded a Nobel prize 1981.

canine in mammalian carnivores, long, often pointed teeth found at the front of the mouth between the incisors and premolars. They are used for catching prey, for killing, and for tearing flesh. Canines are absent in herbivores such as rabbits and sheep, and are much reduced in humans.

Canis Major /'keɪnɪs/ brilliant constellation of the southern hemisphere, identified with one of the two dogs following at the heel of Orion. Its main star, Sirius, is the brightest star in the sky.

Canis Minor small constellation along the celestial equator, identified with the second of the two dogs of Orion (the other dog is Canis Major). Its brightest star is Procyon.

cannabis dried leaves and female flowers (marijuana) and resin (hashish) of certain varieties of ◊hemp *Cannabis sativa*, which are smoked or eaten and have an intoxicating effect.

Cannabis is a soft drug in that any dependence is psychological rather than physical. It has medicinal use in countering depression and the side effects of cancer therapy (pain and nausea).

Cultivation of cannabis is illegal in the UK and USA except under licence.

Cannes /kæn/ resort in Alpes-Maritimes *département*, S France; population (1982) 73,000, conurbation 296,000. A prestigious film festival is held here annually. Formerly only a small seaport, in 1834 it attracted the patronage of Lord ◊Brougham and other distinguished visitors and soon became a fashionable holiday resort. A new town (La Bocca) grew up facing the Mediterranean.

Cannes Film Festival international film festival held every year in Cannes, France. A number of important prizes are awarded, including the Palme d'Or (Golden Palm) for the best film.

The first festival was held 1946. The main award is the Palme d'Or (known as The

Grand Prix prior to 1955); other awards are made for best direction, best actor, and best actress. Awards for supporting performances were introduced 1979.

cannibalism practice of eating human flesh, also called *anthropophagy*. The name is derived from the Caribs, a South American and West Indian people, alleged by the conquering Spaniards to eat their captives.

canning /'kænɪŋ/ food preservation in hermetically sealed containers by the application of heat. Originated by Nicolas Appert in France 1809 with glass containers, it was developed by Peter Durand in England 1810 with cans made of sheet steel thinly coated with tin to delay corrosion. Cans for beer and soft drinks are now generally made of aluminium.

Canneries were established in the USA before 1820, but the US canning industry began to grow considerably in the 1870s when the manufacture of cans was mechanized and factory methods of processing were used. The quality and taste of early canned food was frequently dubious but by the end of the 19th century, scientific research made greater understanding possible of the food-preserving process, and standards improved.

In Britain, imports of canned fruit, beef, vegetables, and condensed milk rose substantially after World War I. A British canning industry was slow to develop compared to the USA or Australia, but it began to grow during the 1920s, and by 1932, the Metal Box Company was producing over 100 million cans a year.

Canning /'kænɪŋ/ Charles John, 1st Earl 1812–1862. British administrator, first viceroy of India from 1858. As governor general of India from 1856, he suppressed the Indian Mutiny with a fair but firm hand which earned him the nickname 'Clemency Canning'. He was the son of George Canning.

Canning /'kænɪŋ/ George 1770–1827. British Tory politician, foreign secretary 1807–10 and 1822–27, and prime minister 1827 in coalition with the Whigs. He was largely responsible, during the Napoleonic Wars, for the seizure of the Danish fleet and British intervention in the Spanish peninsula.

Canning entered Parliament 1793. His verse, satires, and parodies for the *Anti-Jacobin* 1797–98 led to his advancement by Pitt the Younger. His disapproval of the ◊Walcheren expedition 1809 involved him in a duel with the war minister, ◊Castlereagh, and led to Canning's resignation as foreign secretary. He was president of the Board of Control 1816–20. On Castlereagh's death 1822, he again became foreign secretary, supported the national movements in Greece and South America, and was made prime minister 1827. When Wellington, Peel, and other Tories refused to serve under him, he formed a coalition with the Whigs. He died in office.

Cannizzaro /kæni'zɑːrəʊ/ Stanislao 1826–1910. Italian chemist who revived interest in the work of Avogadro that had, in 1811, revealed the difference between ◊atoms and ◊molecules, and so established atomic and molecular weights as the basis of chemical calculations.

Cannon /'kænən/ Annie Jump 1863–1941. US astronomer who, from 1896, worked at Harvard College Observatory and carried out revolutionary work on the classification of stars by examining their spectra. Her system, still used today, has spectra arranged according to temperature and runs from O through B, A, F, G, K, and M. O-type stars are the hottest, with surface temperatures of over 25,000K.

Cano /'kɑːnəʊ/ Alonso 1601–1667. Spanish sculptor, painter, and architect, an exponent of the Baroque style in Spain. He was active in Seville, Madrid, and Granada and designed the façade of Granada Cathedral 1667.

Cano /'kɑːnəʊ/ Juan Sebastian del c. 1476–1526. Spanish voyager. It is claimed that he was the first sea captain to sail around the world. He sailed with Magellan 1519 and, after the latter's death in the Philippines, brought the *Victoria* safely home to Spain.

canoeing sport of propelling a lightweight, shallow boat, pointed at both ends, by paddles or sails. Currently, canoes are made from fibreglass, but original boats were of wooden construction covered in bark or skin. Canoeing was popularized as a sport in the 19th century.

Two types of canoe are used: the *kayak*, and the *Canadian-style* canoe. The kayak, derived from the Eskimo model, has a keel and the canoeist sits. The Canadian-style canoe has no keel and the canoeist kneels. In addition to straightforward racing, there are slalom courses, with up to 30 'gates' to be negotiated through rapids and round artificial rock formations. Penalty seconds are added to course time for touching suspended

gate poles or missing a gate. One to four canoeists are carried. The sport was introduced into the Olympic Games 1936.

canon in the Roman Catholic and Anglican churches, a type of priest. Canons, headed by the dean, are attached to a cathedral and constitute the *chapter*.

Originally, in the Catholic church, a canon was a priest in a cathedral or collegiate church. Canons lived within its precinct, and their lives were ordered by ecclesiastical rules (termed ◊canon law). About the 11th century, a distinction was drawn between *regular* or *Augustinian canons* who observed the rules, and *secular canons* who lived outside the precinct and were, in effect, the administrative officers of a cathedral, but in holy orders. After the Reformation, all canons in England became secular canons.

canon in theology, the collection of writings that is accepted as authoritative in a given religion, such as the *Tripitaka* in Theravāda Buddhism. In the Christian church, it comprises the books of the ◊Bible.

The canon of the Old Testament was drawn up at the assembly of rabbis held at Jamnia in Palestine between AD 90 and 100; certain excluded books were included in the ◊Apocrypha. The earliest list of New Testament books is known as the Muratorian Canon (about 160–70). Bishop Athanasius promulgated a list (c. 365) which corresponds with that in modern Bibles.

canon in music, an echo form for two or more parts repeating and following a leading melody at regular time intervals to achieve a harmonious effect. It is often found in classical music, for example ◊Vivaldi and J S ◊Bach.

canonization in the Catholic church, the admission of one of its members to the Calendar of ◊Saints. The evidence of the candidate's exceptional piety is contested before the Congregation for the Causes of Saints by the Promotor Fidei, popularly known as the *devil's advocate*. Papal ratification of a favourable verdict results in ◊beatification, and full sainthood (conferred in St Peter's basilica, the Vatican) follows after further proof.

Under a system laid down mainly in the 17th century, the process of investigation was seldom completed in under 50 years, although in the case of a martyr it took less time. Since 1969 the gathering of the proof of the candidate's virtues has been left to the bishop of the birthplace, and, miracles being difficult to substantiate, stress is placed on extraordinary 'favours' or 'graces' that can be proved or attested by serious investigation.

Many recent saints have come from the Third World where the expansion of the Catholic church is most rapid, for example the American Mohawk Indian Kateri Tekakwitha (died 1680), beatified 1980.

canon law rules and regulations of the Christian church, especially the Greek Orthodox, Roman Catholic, and Anglican churches. Its origin is sought in the declarations of Jesus and the apostles. In 1983 Pope John Paul II issued a new canon law code reducing offences carrying automatic excommunication, extending the grounds for annulment of marriage, removing the ban on marriage with non-Catholics, and banning trade union and political activity by priests.

The earliest compilations were in the East, and the canon law of the Eastern Orthodox Church is comparatively small. Through the centuries, a great mass of canon law was accumulated in the Western church which, in 1918, was condensed in the *Corpus juris canonici* under Benedict XV. Even so, this is supplemented by many papal decrees.

The canon law of the Church of England remained almost unchanged from 1603 until it was completely revised 1969, and is kept under constant review by the Canon Law Commission of the General Synod.

Canopus /kəˈnəupəs/ or *Alpha Carinae* second brightest star in the sky (after Sirius), lying in the constellation Carina. It is a yellow-white supergiant about 120 light years from Earth, and thousands of times more luminous than the Sun.

Canova /kəˈnəuvə/ Antonio 1757–1822. Italian Neo-Classical sculptor, based in Rome from 1781. He received commissions from popes, kings, and emperors for his highly finished marble portrait busts and groups. He made several portraits of Napoleon.

Canova was born near Treviso. His reclining marble *Pauline Borghese* 1805–07 (Borghese Gallery, Rome) is a fine example of cool, polished Classicism. He executed the tombs of popes Clement XIII, Pius VII, and Clement XIV. His marble sculptures include *Cupid and Psyche* (Louvre, Paris) and *The Three Graces*; the latter has been held in the Victoria and Albert Museum, London, since 1990 while efforts were made to raise £7.6 million necessary to keep it in the UK.

Cánovas del Castillo /ˈkænəvæs del kæˈstɪljəu/ Antonio 1828–1897. Spanish pol-

itician and chief architect of the political system known as the *turno politico* through which his own Conservative party, and that of the Liberals under Práxedes Sagasta, alternated in power. Elections were rigged to ensure the appropriate majorities. Cánovas was assassinated 1897 by anarchists.

Cantab abbreviation for *Cantabrigiensis* (Latin 'of Cambridge').

Cantabria /kænˈtæbriə/ autonomous region of N Spain; area 5,300 sq km/2,046 sq mi; population (1986) 525,000; capital Santander.

Cantabrian Mountains /kænˌtæbriən/ (Spanish *Cordillera Cantabrica*) mountains running along the N coast of Spain, reaching 2,648 m/8,688 ft in the Picos de Europa massif. The mountains contain coal and iron deposits.

Cantal /kɒnˈtɑːl/ volcanic mountain range in central France, which gives its name to Cantal *département*. The highest point is the Plomb du Cantal, 1,858 m/6,096 ft.

cantata in music, an extended work for voices, from the Italian, meaning 'sung', as opposed to *sonata* ('sounded') for instruments. A cantata can be sacred or secular, sometimes uses solo voices, and usually has orchestral accompaniment. The first printed collection of sacred cantata texts dates from 1670.

Canterbury /ˈkæntəbəri/ city in Kent, England, on the river Stour, 100 km/62 mi SE of London; population (1984) 39,000.

The Roman *Durovernum*, Canterbury was the Saxon capital of Kent. The present name derives from *Cantwarabyrig* (Old English 'fortress of the men of Kent'). In 597 King Ethelbert welcomed ◊Augustine's mission to England here, and the city has since been the metropolis of the Anglican Communion and seat of the archbishop of Canterbury.

Canterbury, archbishop of /ˈkæntəbəri/ primate of all England, archbishop of the Church of England (Anglican), and first peer of the realm, ranking next to royalty. He crowns the sovereign, has a seat in the House of Lords, and is a member of the Privy Council. He is appointed by the prime minister.

Formerly selected by political consultation, since 1980 the new archbishops have been selected by a church group, the Crown Appointments Commission (formed 1977). The first holder of the office was St Augustine 601–04; his 20th-century successors have been Randal T Davidson 1903, C G Lang 1928, William Temple 1942, G F Fisher 1945, Michael Ramsey 1961, Donald Coggan 1974, Robert Runcie 1980, and George Carey 1991.

Canterbury Plains /ˈkæntəbəri/ area of rich grassland between the mountains and the sea on the E coast of South Island, New Zealand, source of Canterbury lamb; area 10,000 sq km/4,000 sq mi.

Canterbury Tales, The unfinished collection of stories in prose and verse (c. 1387) by Geoffrey ◊Chaucer, told in Middle English by a group of pilgrims on their way to Thomas á ◊Becket's tomb at Canterbury. The tales and preludes are remarkable for their vivid character portrayal and colloquial language.

cantilever beam or structure that is fixed at one end only, though it may be supported at some point along its length; for example, a diving board. The cantilever principle, widely used in construction engineering, eliminates the need for a second main support at the free end of the beam, allowing for more elegant structures and reducing the amount of materials required. Many large-span bridges have been built on the cantilever principle.

A typical cantilever bridge consists of two beams cantilevered out from either bank, each supported part way along, with their free ends meeting in the middle. The multiple-cantilever Forth Rail Bridge (completed 1890) across the Firth of Forth in Scotland has twin main spans of 521 m/1,710 ft.

canton /ˈkænˈtɒn/ in France, an administrative district, a subdivision of the *arrondissement*; in Switzerland, one of the 23 subdivisions forming the Confederation.

Canton /ˌkænˈtɒn/ alternative spelling of Kwangchow or ◊Guangzhou in China.

cantor (Latin *cantare* 'to sing') in Judaism, the prayer leader and choir master in a synagogue; the cantor is not a rabbi, and the position can be held by any lay person.

Cantor /ˈkæntɔː/ Georg 1845–1918. German mathematician who followed his work on number theory and trigonometry by considering the foundations of mathematics. He defined real numbers and produced a treatment of irrational numbers using a series of transfinite numbers. antor's set theory has been used in the development of topology and real function theory.

Canute /kəˈnjuːt/ *c.* 995–1035. King of England from 1016, Denmark from 1018, and Norway from 1028. Having invaded England 1013 with his father, Sweyn, king of Denmark, he was acclaimed king on his father's death 1014 by his ◊Viking army. Canute defeated ◊Edmund II Ironside at Assandun, Essex, 1016, and became king of all England on Edmund's death. He succeeded his brother Harold as king of Denmark 1018, compelled King Malcolm to pay homage by invading Scotland about 1027, and conquered Norway 1028. He was succeeded by his illegitimate son Harold I.

The legend of Canute disenchanting his flattering courtiers by showing that the sea would not retreat at his command was first told by Henry of Huntingdon 1130.

Canute VI /kəˈnjuːt/ (*Cnut VI*) 1163–1202. King of Denmark from 1182, son and successor of Waldemar Knudsson. With his brother and successor, Waldemar II, he resisted Frederick I's northward expansion, and established Denmark as the dominant power in the Baltic.

canyon (Spanish *cañon* 'tube') deep, narrow valley or gorge running through mountains. Canyons are formed by stream down-cutting, usually in areas of low rainfall, where the stream or river receives water from outside the area.

There are many canyons in the western USA and in Mexico, for example the Grand Canyon of the Colorado River in Arizona, the canyon in Yellowstone National Park, and the Black Canyon in Colorado.

Cao Chan /tsaʊ ˈtʃæn/ or *Ts'ao Chan* 1719–1763. Chinese novelist. His tragic love story *Hung Lou Meng/The Dream of the Red Chamber* published 1792, involves the downfall of a Manchu family and is semiautobiographical.

cap another name for a ◊diaphragm contraceptive.

CAP abbreviation for ◊*Common Agricultural Policy*.

capacitor or *condenser* device for storing electric charge, used in electronic circuits; it consists of two or more metal plates separated by an insulating layer called a dielectric.

Its *capacitance* is the ratio of the charge stored on either plate to the potential difference between the plates. The SI unit of capacitance is the farad, but most capacitors have much smaller capacitances, and the microfarad (a millionth of a farad) is the commonly used practical unit.

capacity in economics, the maximum amount that can be produced when all the resources in an economy, industry, or firm are employed as fully as possible. Capacity constraints can be caused by lack of investment and skills shortages, and spare capacity can be caused by lack of demand.

Cape Breton /'keɪp 'bretn/ island forming the northern part of the province of Nova Scotia, Canada; area 10,282 sq km/3,970 sq mi; population (1988) 170,000. Bisected by a waterway, it has road and rail links with the mainland across the Strait of Canso. It has coal resources and steelworks, and there has been substantial development in the strait area, with docks, oil refineries, and newsprint production from local timber. In the north, the surface rises to 550 m/1,800 ft at North Cape, and the coast has many fine harbours. here are cod fisheries. The climate is mild and very moist. The chief towns are Sydney and Glace Bay.
history The first British colony was established 1629 but was driven out by the French. In 1763 Cape Breton was ceded to Britain and attached to Nova Scotia 1763–84 and from 1820.

Cape Canaveral /'keɪp kə'nævərəl/ promontory on the Atlantic coast of Florida, USA, 367 km/228 mi N of Miami, used as a rocket launch site by ◊NASA. First mentioned 1513, it was known 1963–73 as Cape Kennedy. The ◊Kennedy Space Center is nearby.

Cape Coast /'keɪp 'kəust/ port of Ghana, W Africa, 130 km/80 mi W of Accra; population (1982) 73,000. It has been superseded as the main port since 1962 by Tema. The town, first established by the Portuguese in the 16th century, is built on a natural breakwater, adjoining the castle.

Cape Cod /'keɪp 'kɒd/ hook-shaped peninsula in SE Massachusetts, USA; 100 km/60 mi long and 1.6–32 km/1–20 mi wide; population (1980) 150,000. Its beaches and woods make it a popular tourist area. It is separated from the rest of the state by the Cape Cod Canal. The islands of Martha's Vineyard and Nantucket are just south of the cape. Basque and Norse fisherfolk are believed to have visited Cape Cod many years before the English Pilgrims landed at Provincetown 1620. It was named after the cod which were caught in the dangerous shoals

of the cape. The ◊Kennedy family home is at the resort of Hyannis Port.

Cape Coloured South African term for people of mixed African and European descent, mainly living in Cape Province.

Cape gooseberry plant *Physalis peruviana* of the potato family. Originating in South America, it is grown in South Africa, from where it takes its name. It is cultivated for its fruit, a yellow berry surrounded by a papery ◊calyx.

Cape Horn /'keɪp hɔn/ southernmost point of South America, in the Chilean part of the archipelago of ◊Tierra del Fuego; notorious for gales and heavy seas. It was named in 1616 by Dutch explorer Willem Schouten (1580–1625) after his birthplace (Hoorn).

Čapek /'tʃæpek/ Karel 1890–1938. Czech writer whose works often deal with social injustice in an imaginative, satirical way. *R.U.R.* 1921 is a play in which robots (a term he coined) rebel against their controllers; the novel *Válka s Mloky/War With the Newts* 1936 is a science-fiction classic.

Capella /kə'pelə/ or *Alpha Aurigae* brightest star in the constellation Auriga and the sixth brightest star in the sky. It consists of a pair of yellow giant stars 41 light years from Earth, orbiting each other every 104 days.

Cape of Good Hope /'keɪp əv gud 'həu/ South African headland forming a peninsula between Table Bay and False Bay, Cape Town. The first European to sail around it was Bartholomew Diaz 1488. Formerly named Cape of Storms, it was given its present name by King John II of Portugal.

Cape Province /'keɪp 'prɒvɪns/ (Afrikaans *Kaapprovinsie*) largest province of the Republic of South Africa, named after the Cape of Good Hope
area 641,379 sq km/247,638 sq mi, excluding Walvis Bay
capital Cape Town
towns Port Elizabeth, East London, Kimberley, Grahamstown, Stellenbosch
physical Orange River, Drakensberg, Table mountain (highest point Maclear's Beacon, 1,087 m/3,567 ft); Great Karoo Plateau, Walvis Bay
products fruit, vegetables, wine; meat, ostrich feathers; diamonds, copper, asbestos, manganese
population (1985) 5,041,000; officially including 44% coloured; 31% black; 25% white; 0.6% Asian

history the Dutch occupied the Cape 1652, but it was taken by the British 1795, after the French Revolutionary armies had occupied the Netherlands, and was sold to Britain for £6 million 1814. The Cape achieved self-government 1872. It was an original province of the Union 1910.

The Orange River was proclaimed the northern boundary 1825. Griqualand West (1880) and the southern part of Bechuanaland (1895) were later incorporated; Walvis Bay, although formerly administered with Namibia, is legally an integral part of Cape Province.

caper trailing shrub *Capparis spinosa*, native to the Mediterranean and belonging to the family Capparidaceae. Its flower buds are preserved in vinegar as a condiment.

capercaillie large bird *Tetrao urogallus* of the grouse type found in coniferous woodland in Europe and N Asia. At nearly 1 m/3 ft long, the male is the biggest gamebird in Europe, with a largely black plumage and rounded tail which is fanned out in courtship. The female is speckled brown and about 60 cm/2 ft long.

Capet /kæ'pet/ Hugh 938–996. King of France from 987, when he claimed the throne on the death of Louis V. He founded the Capetian dynasty, of which various branches continued to reign until the French Revolution, for example, ◊Valois and ◊Bourbon.

Cape Town /'keiptaʊn/ (Afrikaans *Kaapstad*) port and oldest town in South Africa, situated in the SW on Table Bay; population (1985) 776,617. Industries include horticulture and trade in wool, wine, fruit, grain, and oil. It is the legislative capital of the Republic of South Africa and capital of Cape Province; it was founded 1652.

It includes the Houses of Parliament, City Hall, Cape Town Castle 1666, and Groote Schuur ('great barn'), the estate of Cecil Rhodes (he designated the house as the home of the premier, and a university and the National Botanical Gardens occupy part of the grounds). The naval base of *Simonstown* is to the SE; in 1975 Britain's use of its facilities was ended by the Labour government in disapproval of South Africa's racial policies.

Cape Verde /keip 'vɜːd/ group of islands in the Atlantic, W of Senegal (W Africa).
government The 1980 constitution provides for a national people's assembly of 83,

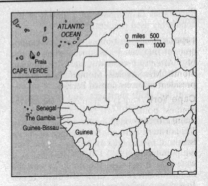

elected by universal suffrage for a five-year term, and a president, elected for a similar term by the assembly. From 1981 to 1990 the African Party for the Independence of Cape Verde (PAICV) was the only political party.
history The Cape Verde islands were first settled in the 15th century by Portugal, the first black inhabitants being slaves imported from W Africa. Over the next five centuries of Portuguese rule the islands were gradually peopled with Portuguese, African slaves, and people of mixed African-European descent who became the majority. The Cape Verdians kept some African culture but came to speak Portuguese or the Portuguese-derived Creole language, and became Catholics.

A liberation movement developed in the 1950s. The mainland territory to which Cape Verde is linked, Guinea-Bissau, achieved independence 1974, and a process began for their eventual union. A transitional government was set up, composed of Portuguese and members of the African Party for the Independence of Portuguese Guinea and Cape Verde (PAIGC).
after independence In 1975 a national people's assembly was elected, and Aristides Pereira, PAIGC secretary general, became president and head of government of Cape Verde. The 1980 constitution provided for the union of the two states but in 1981 this aspect was deleted because of insufficient support, and the PAIGC became the African Party for the Independence of Cape Verde (PAICV). Pereira was re-elected, and relations with Guinea-Bissau improved. Under President Pereira, Cape Verde adopted a nonaligned policy and achieved considerable respect within the region. An opposition party, the Independent Democratic Union

of Cape Verde (UCID), operated from Portugal.

In the first multiparty elections, held Jan 1991, a new party, Movement for Democracy (MPD), won a majority in the assembly. After a very low poll the following month, Mascarenhas Monteiro was elected president in succession to Pereira.

Cape York /'keɪp jɔːk/ peninsula, the northernmost point (10° 41′ S) of the Australian mainland, named by Capt James ◊Cook 1770. The peninsula is about 800 km/500 mi long and 640 km/400 mi wide at its junction with the mainland. Its barrenness deterred early Dutch explorers, although the south is being developed for cattle (Brahmin type). In the north there are large bauxite deposits.

capillarity spontaneous movement of liquids up or down narrow tubes, or capillaries. The movement is due to unbalanced molecular attraction at the boundary between the liquid and the tube. If liquid molecules near the boundary are more strongly attracted to molecules in the material of the tube than to other nearby liquid molecules, the liquid will rise in the tube. If liquid molecules are less attracted to the material of the tube than to other liquid molecules, the liquid will fall.

capillary narrowest blood vessel in vertebrates, between 8- and 20-thousandths of a millimetre in diameter, barely wider than a red blood cell. Capillaries are distributed as *beds*, complex networks connecting arteries and veins. Capillary walls are extremely thin, consisting of a single layer of cells, and so nutrients, dissolved gases, and waste products can easily pass through them. This makes the capillaries the main area of exchange between the fluid (◊lymph) bathing body tissues and the blood.

capillary in physics, a very narrow, thick-walled tube, usually made of glass, such as in a thermometer. Properties of fluids, such as surface tension and viscosity, can be studied using capillary tubes.

capital in architecture, a stone placed on the top of a column, pier, or pilaster, and usually wider on the upper surface than the diameter of the supporting shaft. A capital consists of three parts: the top member, called the *abacus*, a block that acts as the supporting surface to the superstructure; the middle portion, known as the bell or *echinus*; and the lower part, called the necking or *astragal*.

capital in economics, accumulated or inherited wealth held in the form of assets (such as stocks and shares, property, and bank deposits). In stricter terms, capital is defined as the stock of goods used in the production of other goods, and may be *fixed capital* (such as buildings, plant, and machinery) that is durable, or *circulating capital* (raw materials and components) that is used up quickly.

capital bond in economics, an investment bond that is purchased by a single payment, set up for a fixed period, and offered for sale by a life insurance company. The emphasis is on capital growth of the lump sum invested rather than on income.

capital gains tax income tax levied on the change of value of a person's assets, often property.

capitalism economic system in which the principal means of production, distribution, and exchange are in private (individual or corporate) hands and competitively operated for profit. A *mixed economy* combines the private enterprise of capitalism and a degree of state monopoly, as in nationalized industries.

capital punishment punishment by death. Capital punishment, abolished in the UK 1965 for all crimes except treason, is retained in 92 countries and territories (1990), including the USA (37 states), China, and the USSR. Methods of execution include electrocution, lethal gas, hanging, shooting, lethal injection, garrotting, and decapitation.

Countries that have abolished the death penalty fall into three categories: those that have abolished it for all crimes (44 countries); those that retain it only for exceptional crimes such as war crimes (17 countries); and those that retain the death penalty for ordinary crimes but have not executed anyone since 1980 (25 countries and territories). The first country in Europe to abolish the death penalty was Portugal 1867. In the USA, the Supreme Court declared capital punishment unconstitutional 1972 (as a cruel and unusual punishment) but decided 1976 that this was not so in all circumstances. It was therefore reintroduced in some states, and in 1990 there were over 2,000 prisoners on death row (awaiting execution) in the USA.

In Britain, the number of capital offences was reduced from over 200 at the end of the 18th century, until capital punishment was abolished 1866 for all crimes except murder, treason, piracy, and certain arson attacks. Its use was subject to the royal prerogative of mercy. The punishment was carried out by hanging (in public until 1866). Capital punishment for murder was abolished 1965 but still exists for treason. In 1990, Ireland abolished the death penalty for all offences.

Many countries use capital punishment for crimes other than murder, including corruption and theft (USSR) and drug offences (Malaysia and elsewhere). In South Africa, over 1,500 death sentences were passed 1978–1987. There were 1,500 executions in China 1983–89, and 64 in the USSR 1985–88, although the true figure may be higher in both cases. In 1989 the number of capital offences in the USSR was reduced to six. The International Covenant on Civil and Political Rights 1977 ruled out imposition of the death penalty on those under the age of 18. The covenant was signed by President Carter on behalf of the USA, but in 1989 the US Supreme Court decided that it could be imposed from the age of 16 for murder, and that the mentally retarded could also face the death penalty.

capitulum in botany, a flattened or rounded head (inflorescence) of numerous, small, stalkless flowers. The capitulum is surrounded by a circlet of petal-like bracts and has the appearance of a large, single flower. It is characteristic of plants belonging to the daisy family (Compositae) such as the daisy *Bellis perennis* and the garden marigold *Calendula officinalis*; but is also seen in parts of other families, such as scabious *Knautia* and teasels *Dipsacus*. The individual flowers are known as ◊florets.

Capodimonte /kæpəʊ di ˈmɒnteɪ/ porcelain produced in S Italy, usually white, painted with colourful folk figures, landscapes, or flowers. It was first produced under King Charles III of Naples about 1740, and is named after a village N of Naples.

Capone /kəˈpəʊn/ Al(phonse) 1898–1947. US gangster, born in Brooklyn, New York, the son of an Italian barber. His nickname was *Scarface*. During the ◊Prohibition period, Capone built a formidable criminal organization in Chicago. He was brutal in his pursuit of dominance, killing seven members of a rival gang in the St Valentine's Day massacre. He was imprisoned 1931–39 for income-tax evasion, the only charge that could be sustained against him.

Caporetto /kæpəˈretəʊ/ former name of ◊Kobarid, Yugoslavia.

Capote /kəˈpəʊti/ Truman. Pen name of Truman Streckfus Persons 1924–1984. US novelist, journalist and playwright. He wrote *Breakfast at Tiffany's* 1958; set a trend with the first 'nonfiction novel', *In Cold Blood* 1966, reconstructing a Kansas killing; and mingled recollection and fiction in *Music for Chameleons* 1980.

Cappadocia /kæpəˈdəʊʃə/ ancient region of Asia Minor, in E central Turkey. It was conquered by the Persians 584 BC but in the 3rd century BC became an independent kingdom. The region was annexed as a province of the Roman Empire AD 17.

Capra /ˈkæprə/ Frank 1897–1991. Italian-born US film director. His films, satirical social comedies that often have idealistic heroes, include *It Happened One Night* 1934, *Mr Deeds Goes to Town* 1936, and *You Can't Take It With You* 1938, for each of which he received an Academy Award.

Capri /kəˈpriː/ Italian island at the southern entrance of the Bay of Naples; 32 km/20 mi S of Naples; area 13 sq km/5 sq mi. It has two towns, Capri and Anacapri, a profusion of flowers, beautiful scenery, and an ideal climate.

Capricornus /ˌkæprɪˈkɔːnəs/ zodiacal constellation in the southern hemisphere next to Sagittarius. It is represented as a fish-tailed goat, and its brightest stars are third magnitude. The Sun passes through it late Jan to mid-Feb. In astrology, the dates for Capricornus are between about 22 Dec and 19 Jan (see ◊precession).

Caprivi /kəˈpriːvi/ Georg Leo, Graf von 1831–1899. German soldier and politician. While chief of the admiralty (1883–88) he reorganized the German navy. He became imperial chancellor 1890–94 succeeding Bismarck and renewed the Triple Alliance but wavered between European allies and Russia. Although he strengthened the army, he alienated the conservatives.

Caprivi Strip /kəˈpriːvi/ NE part of Namibia, a narrow strip between Angola and Botswana, giving the country access to the Zambezi River.

capsicum any pepper plant of the genus *Capsicum* of the nightshade family Solanaceae, native to Central and South America. The differing species produce green to red fruits that vary in size. The small ones are used whole to give the hot flavour of chilli, or ground to produce cayenne pepper; the large pointed or squarish pods, known as sweet peppers, are mild-flavoured and used as a vegetable.

capsule in botany, a dry, usually many-seeded fruit formed from an ovary composed of two or more fused ◊carpels, which splits open to release the seeds. The same term is used for the spore-containing structure of mosses and liverworts; this is borne at the top of a long stalk or seta.

Captain Marvel US comic-book character created 1940 by C(larence) C(harles) Beale (1910–1989). Captain Marvel is a 15-year-old schoolboy, Billy Batson, who transforms himself by saying 'Shazam' into a superhuman hero wearing a red-and-yellow caped athletic suit.

capuchin monkey of the genus *Cebus* found in Central and South America, so called because the hairs on the head resemble the cowl of a capuchin monk. Capuchins live in small groups, feed on fruit and insects, and have a tail that is semiprehensile and can give support when climbing through the trees.

Capuchin /kæpjʊtʃɪn/ member of the Franciscan order of monks in the Roman Catholic church, instituted by the Italian monk Matteo di Bassi (died 1552), who wished to return to the literal observance of the rule of St Francis. The Capuchin rule was drawn up 1529 and the order recognized by the pope 1619. The name was derived from the French term for the brown habit and pointed hood (*capuche*) that they wore. The order has been involved in missionary activity.

capybara world's largest rodent *Hydrochoerus hydrochaeris*, up to 1.3 m/4 ft long and 50 kg/110 lb in weight. It is found in South America, and belongs to the guinea pig family. The capybara inhabits marshes and dense vegetation around water. It has thin, yellowish hair, swims well, and can rest underwater with just eyes, ears, and nose above the surface.

car small, driver-guided, passenger-carrying motor vehicle; originally the automated version of the horse-drawn carriage, meant to convey people and their goods over streets and roads. Over 300 million motor vehicles are produced each year worldwide. Most are four-wheeled and have water-cooled, piston-type internal-combustion engines fuelled by petrol or diesel. Variations have existed for decades that use ingenious and often non-polluting power plants, but the motor industry long ago settled on this general formula

for the consumer market. Experimental and sports models are streamlined, energy-efficient, and hand-built.

Although it is recorded that in 1479 Gilles de Dom was paid 25 livres (the equivalent of 25 pounds of silver) by the treasurer of Antwerp in the Low Countries for supplying a self-propelled vehicle, the ancestor of the automobile is generally agreed to be the cumbersome steam carriage made by Nicolas-Joseph Cugnot 1769, still preserved in Paris. Steam was an attractive form of power to the English pioneers, and in 1808 Richard Trevithick built a working steam carriage. Later in the 19th century, practical steam coaches were used for public transport until stifled out of existence by punitive road tolls and legislation.

Although a Frenchman, Jean Etienne Lenoir, patented the first internal combustion engine (gas-driven) 1860, and an Austrian, Siegfried Marcus, built a vehicle which was shown at the Vienna Exhibition (1873), two Germans, Gottlieb Daimler and Karl Benz are generally regarded as the creators of the motorcar. In 1885 Daimler and Benz built and ran the first petrol-driven motorcar. The pattern for the modern motorcar was set by Panhard 1890 (front radiator, engine under bonnet, sliding-pinion gearbox, wooden ladder-chassis) and Mercedes 1901 (honeycomb radiator, in-line four-cylinder engine, gate-change gearbox, pressed-steel chassis) set the pattern for the modern car. Emerging with Haynes and Duryea in the early 1890s, US demand was so fervent that 300 makers existed by 1895; only 109 were left by 1900.

In England, cars were still considered to be light locomotives in the eyes of the law and, since the Red Flag Act 1865, had theoretically required someone to walk in front with a red flag (by night, a lantern). Despite these obstacles, which put UK development another ten years behind all others, in 1896 Frederick Lanchester produced an advanced and reliable vehicle, later much copied. The period 1905–06 inaugurated a world motor-car boom continuing to the present day.

Among the legendary cars of the early 20th century are: De Dion Bouton, with the first practical high-speed engines; Mors, notable first for racing and later as a silent tourer ; Napier, the 24-hour record-holder at Brooklands 1907, unbeaten for 17 years; the incomparable Silver Ghost Rolls-Royce; the enduring Model T ◊Ford; and the many types of Bugatti and Delage, from record-breakers to luxury tourers.

After World War I popular motoring began with the era of cheap, light (baby) cars made by Citroën, Peugeot, and Renault (France); Austin, Morris, Clyno, and Swift (England); Fiat (Italy); Volks-wagen (Germany); and the cheap though bigger Ford, Chevrolet, and Dodge in the USA. During the interwar years a great deal of racing took place, and the experience gained benefited the everyday motorist in improved efficiency, reliability, and safety. There was a divergence between the lighter, economical European car, with its good handling, and the heavier US car, cheap, rugged, and well adapted to long distances on straight roads at speed. By this time motoring had become a universal pursuit.

After World War II small European cars tended to fall into three categories, in about equal numbers: front engine and rear drive, the classic arrangement; front engine and front-wheel drive; rear engine and rear-wheel drive. Racing cars have the engine situated in the middle for balance. From the 1950s a creative resurgence produced in practical form automatic transmission for small cars, rubber suspension, transverse engine mounting, self-levelling ride, disc brakes, and safer wet-weather tyres. The drive against pollution from the 1960s and the fuel crisis from the 1970s led to experiments with steam cars (cumbersome), diesel engines (slow and heavy, though economical), solar-powered cars, and hybrid cars using both electricity (in town centres) and petrol (on the open road). The industry brought on the market the stratified-charge petrol engine, using a fuel injector to achieve 20% improvement in petrol consumption; weight reduction in the body by the use of aluminium and plastics; and 'slippery' body designs with low air resistance, or drag. Microprocessors were also developed to measure temperature, engine speed, pressure, and oxygen/CO_2 content of exhaust gases, and readjust the engine accordingly.

A typical present-day European medium-sized saloon car has a semi-monocoque construction in which the body panels, suitably reinforced, support the road loads through independent front and rear sprung suspension, with seats located within the wheelbase for comfort. It is usually powered by a ◊petrol engine using a carburettor to mix petrol and air for feeding to the engine cylinders (typically four or six), and the engine is usually water cooled. In the 1980s high-performance diesel engines were being developed for use in private cars, and it is anticipated that this trend will continue for reasons of economy. From the engine, power is transmitted through a clutch to a four- or five-speed gearbox and from there, in a front-engine rear-drive car, through a drive (propeller) shaft to a ◊differential gear, which drives the rear wheels. In a front-engine, front-wheel drive car, clutch, gearbox, and final drive are incorporated with the engine unit. An increasing number of high-performance cars are being offered with four-wheel drive. This gives superior roadholding in wet and icy conditions.

In the UK, the Ministry of Transport was established 1919, roads were improved, and various laws and safety precautions imposed to govern the use of cars. A driver must possess a licence, and a vehicle must be registered with the local licensing authority, displaying the number assigned to it. A road tax is imposed, and the law also insists on insurance for third-party risks. Motoring organizations include the Automobile Association (AA) and the Royal Automobile Club (RAC). From 1951 to 1988 the number of cars on British roads increased from 2 million to 18 million; the Ministry of Transport predicts that this figure will rise to 43 million by 2025.

caracal cat *Felis caracal* related to the ◊lynx. It has long black ear-tufts, a short tail, and short reddish-fawn fur. It lives in bush and desert country in Africa, Arabia, and India, hunting birds and small mammals at night. Head and body length is about 75 cm/2.5 ft.

Caracalla /ˌkærəˈkælə/ Marcus Aurelius Antoninus AD 186–217. Roman emperor. He succeeded his father Septimus Severus AD 211, ruled with cruelty and extravagance, and was assassinated. He was nicknamed after the Celtic cloak (*caracalla*) that he wore.

With the support of the army he murdered his brother Geta and thousands of his followers to secure sole possession of the throne. During his reign, Roman citizenship was given to all subjects of the empire.

Caracas /kəˈrækəs/ chief city and capital of Venezuela; situated on the Andean slopes, 13 km/8 mi S of its port La Guaira on the Caribbean coast; population of metropolitan area (1981) 1,817,000. Founded 1567, it is now a large industrial and commercial centre, notably for oil companies.

Caracalla A contemporary marble sculpture of Caracalla.

Caractacus /kəˈræktəkəs/ died *c.* AD 54. British chieftain who headed resistance to the Romans in SE England AD 43–51, but was defeated on the Welsh border. Shown in Claudius's triumphal procession, he was released in tribute to his courage and died in Rome.

carambola small evergreen tree *Averrhoa carambola* of SE Asia. The fruits, called *star fruit*, are yellowish, about 12 cm/4 in long, with a five-pointed star-shaped cross-section. They may be eaten raw, cooked, or pickled, and are juicily acidic. The juice is also used to remove stains from hands and clothes.

carat (Arabic *quirrat* 'seed') unit for measuring the mass of precious stones; it is equal to 0.2 g/0.00705 oz, and is part of the troy system of weights. It is also the unit of purity in gold (US karat). Pure gold is 24-carat; 22-carat (the purest used in jewellery) is 22 parts gold and two parts alloy (to give greater strength).

Caravaggio /ˌkærəˈvædʒiəʊ/ Michelangelo Merisi da 1573–1610. Italian early Baroque painter, active in Rome 1592–1606, then in Naples, and finally in Malta. His life was as dramatic as his art (he had to leave Rome after killing a man). He created a forceful style, using contrasts of light and shade and focusing closely on the subject figures, sometimes using dramatic foreshortening.

Caravaggio's compositions were unusual, strong designs in the two-dimensional plane with little extraneous material. He painted from models, making portraits of real Roman people as saints and madonnas, which caused outrage. An example is *The Conversion of St Paul* (Sta Maria del Popolo, Rome).

caravan vehicle fitted to provide living accommodation. Originally intended as permanent homes, caravans are widely used for holiday purposes.

Caravans for travelling show troupes were in use in England by 1840. Romany caravans became a familiar sight from the 1870s onwards, and a few luxury versions were made for wealthy people. The first car-towed caravan was made by Eccles Motor Transport 1919, the pioneer of today's compact and ingeniously fitted 'tourer'. Other developments have included the large 'mobile home' and the conversion of commercial vans to 'motor caravans'.

caraway herb *Carum carvi* of the carrot family Umbelliferae. It is grown for its spicy, aromatic seeds, which are used in cookery, medicine, and perfumery.

carbide compound of carbon and one other chemical element, usually a metal, silicon, or boron.

Calcium carbide (CaC_2) can be used as the starting material for many basic organic chemical syntheses, by the addition of water and generation of ethyne (acetylene). Some metallic carbides are used in engineering because of their extreme hardness and strength. Tungsten carbide is an essential ingredient of carbide tools and high-speed tools. The 'carbide process' was used during World War II to make organic chemicals from coal rather than from oil.

carbohydrate chemical compound composed of carbon, hydrogen, and oxygen, with the basic formula $Cm(H_2O)n$, and related compounds with the same basic structure but modified ◊functional groups.

The simplest carbohydrates are sugars (*monosaccharides*, such as glucose and fructose, and *disaccharides*, such as sucrose), which are soluble compounds, some with a sweet taste. When these basic sugar units are joined together in long chains or branching structures they form *polysaccharides*, such as starch and glycogen, which often serve as food stores in living organisms. As such they form a major energy-providing part of the human diet. Even more complex carbohydrates are known, including ◊chitin, which is found in the cell walls of fungi and the hard outer skeletons of insects, and ◊cellulose, which makes up the cell walls of plants. Carbohydrates form the chief foodstuffs of herbivorous animals.

carbolic acid common name for the aromatic compound ◊phenol.

carbon (Latin *carbo* (*carbonaris*) 'coal') nonmetallic element, symbol C, atomic number 6, relative atomic mass 12.011. It is one of the most widely distributed elements, both inorganically and organically, and occurs in combination with other elements in all plants and animals. The atoms of carbon can link with one another in rings or chains, giving rise to innumerable complex compounds. It occurs in nature (1) in the pure state in the crystalline forms of graphite and diamond; (2) as calcium carbonate ($CaCO_3$) in carbonaceous rocks such as chalk and limestone; (3) as carbon dioxide (CO_2) in the atmosphere; and (4) as hydrocarbons in the fossil fuels petroleum, coal, and natural gas. Noncrystalline forms of pure carbon include charcoal and coal. When added to steel, carbon forms a wide range of alloys. In its elemental form, it is widely used as a moderator in nuclear reactors; as colloidal graphite it is a good lubricant, which, when deposited on a surface in a vacuum, obviates photoelectric and secondary emission of electrons. The radioactive isotope C-14 (half-life 5,730 years) is widely used in archaeological dating and as a tracer in biological research.

Carbonari /kɑːbəˈnɑːri/ secret revolutionary society in S Italy in the first half of the 19th century that advocated constitutional government. The movement spread to N Italy but support dwindled after the formation of ◊Mazzini's nationalist Young Italy movement, although it helped prove the way for the unification of Italy (see ◊Risorgimento).

carbonate CO_3^{2-} ion formed when carbon dioxide dissolves in water; any salt formed by this ion and another chemical element, usually a metal.

Carbon dioxide (CO_2) dissolves sparingly in water (for example, when rain falls through the air) to form carbonic acid (H_2CO_3), which unites with various basic substances to form carbonates. Calcium carbonate ($CaCO_3$) (chalk, limestone, and marble) is one of the most abundant carbonates known, being a constituent of mollusc shells and the hard outer skeletons of crustaceans.

carbonated water water in which carbon dioxide is dissolved under pressure. It forms the basis of many fizzy soft drinks such as soda water and lemonade.

carbon cycle sequence by which ◊carbon circulates and is recycled through the natural world. The carbon element from carbon dioxide, released into the atmosphere by living things as a result of ◊respiration, is taken up by plants during ◊photosynthesis and converted into carbohydrates; the oxygen component is released back into the atmosphere. The simplest link in the carbon cycle, however, occurs when an animal eats a plant and carbon is transferred from, say, a leaf cell to the animal body. Today, the carbon cycle is in danger of being disrupted by the increased consumption and burning of fossil fuels, and the burning of large tracts of tropical forests, as a result of which levels of carbon dioxide are building up in the atmosphere and probably contributing to the ◊greenhouse effect.

carbon dating alternative name for ◊radiocarbon dating.

carbon dioxide CO_2 colourless gas, slightly soluble in water and denser than air. It is formed by the complete oxidation of carbon.

It is produced by living things during the processes of respiration and the decay of organic matter. Its increasing density contributes to the ◊greenhouse effect and ◊global warming.

carbon fibre fine, black, silky filament of pure carbon produced by heat treatment from a special grade of Courtelle acrylic fibre, used for reinforcing plastics. The resulting composite is very stiff and, weight for weight, has four times the strength of high-tensile steel. It is used in the aerospace industry, cars, and electrical and sports equipment.

Carboniferous /kɑːbəˈnɪfərəs/ period of geological time 360–286 million years ago, the fifth period of the Palaeozoic era. In the USA it is divided into two periods: the Mississippian (lower) and the Pennsylvanian (upper). Typical of the lower-Carboniferous rocks are shallow-water ◊limestone, while upper-Carboniferous rocks have ◊delta deposits with ◊coal (hence the name). Amphibians were abundant, and reptiles evolved during this period.

carbon monoxide CO colourless, odourless gas formed when carbon is oxidized in a limited supply of air. It is a poisonous constituent of car exhaust fumes, forming a stable compound with haemoglobin in the blood, thus preventing the haemoglobin from transporting oxygen to the body tissues.

In industry it is used as a reducing agent in metallurgical processes—for example, in the extraction of iron in ◊blast furnaces—and is a constituent of cheap fuels such as water gas.

carbon tetrachloride former name for ◊tetrachloromethane.

Carborundum /ˌkɑːbərʌndəm/ trademark for a very hard, black abrasive, consisting of silicon carbide (SiC), an artificial compound of carbon and silicon. It is harder than ◊corundum but not as hard as ◊diamond. It was first produced 1891 by US chemist Edward Acheson (1856–1931).

carboxyl group –COOH in organic chemistry, the acidic functional group that determines the properties of fatty acids (carboxylic acids) and amino acids.

carboxylic acid alternative name for ◊fatty acid.

carbuncle in medicine, a bacterial infection of the skin, similar to a ◊boil but deeper and more widespread. It is treated with drawing salves, lancing, or antibiotics.

carbuncle in gemology, a garnet cut to resemble a rounded knob.

carburation mixing of a gas, such as air, with a volatile hydrocarbon fuel, such as petrol, kerosene, or fuel oil, in order to form an explosive mixture. The process, which increases the amount of potential heat energy released during combustion, is used in internal-combustion engines. In most petrol engines the liquid fuel is atomized and mixed with air by means of a device called a **carburettor**.

Carcassonne /ˌkɑːkəˈsɒn/ city in SW France, capital of Aude *département*, on the river Aude, which divides it into the ancient and modern town; population (1982) 42,450. Its medieval fortifications (restored) are the finest in France.

Carchemish /ˈkɑːkəmɪʃ/ (now *Karkamis*, Turkey) centre of the ◊Hittite New Empire (*c*. 1400–1200 BC) on the river Euphrates, 80 km/50 mi NE of Aleppo, and taken by Sargon II of Assyria 717 BC. Nebuchadnezzar II of Babylon defeated the Egyptians here 605 BC.

carcinogen any agent that increases the chance of a cell becoming cancerous (see ◊cancer), including various chemical compounds, some viruses, X-rays, and other forms of ionizing radiation. The term is often used more narrowly to mean chemical carcinogens only.

carcinoma malignant ◊tumour arising from the skin, the glandular tissues, or the mucous membranes that line the gut and lungs.

Cardano /kɑːˈdɑːnəʊ/ Girolamo 1501–1576. Italian physician, mathematician, philosopher, astrologer, and gambler. He is remembered for his theory of chance, his use of algebra, and many medical publications, notably the first clinical description of typhus fever.

Cárdenas /ˈkɑːdɪnæs/ Lázaro 1895–1970. Mexican centre-left politician and general, president 1934–40. A civil servant in early life, Cárdenas took part in the revolutionary campaigns 1915–29 that followed the fall of President Díaz (1830–1915). As president of the republic, he attempted to achieve the goals of the revolution by building schools, distributing land to the peasants, and developing transport and industry. He was minister of defence 1943–45.

cardiac pertaining to the ◊heart.

Cardiff /ˈkɑːdɪf/ (Welsh *Caerdydd*) capital of Wales (from 1955) and administrative headquarters of South and Mid Glamorgan, at the mouth of the Taff, Rhymney, and Ely rivers; population (1983) 279,800. Besides steelworks, there are car-component, flour-milling, paper, cigar, and other industries.

The city dates from Roman times, the later town being built around a Norman castle. The castle was the residence of the earls and marquesses of Bute from the 18th century and was given to the city 1947 by the fifth marquess. Coal was exported until the 1920s. As coal declined, iron and steel exports continued to grow, and an import trade in timber, grain and flour, tobacco, meat, and citrus fruit developed.

The docks on the Bristol Channel were opened 1839 and greatly extended by the second marquess of Bute (1793–1848). The derelict docks have now been redeveloped for industry.

Llandaff, on the right bank of the river Taff, was included in Cardiff 1922; its cathedral, virtually rebuilt in the 19th century and restored 1948–57 after air-raid damage in World War II, has Jacob Epstein's sculpture

Christ in Majesty. At St Fagan's is the Welsh National Folk Museum, containing small, rebuilt historical buildings from rural Wales in wich crafts are demonstrated. The city is the headquaters of the Welsh National Opera.

Cardiff Arms Park (Welsh *Parc yr Arfau*) Welsh rugby ground officially known as the National Stadium, situated in Cardiff. The stadium became the permanent home of the Welsh national team 1964 and has a capacity of 64,000.

Cardiganshire /ˌkɑːdɪɡənʃə/ (Welsh *Ceredigion* or *Sir Aberteifi*) former county of Wales. In 1974 it was merged, together with Pembrokeshire and Carmarthenshire, into Dyfed.

Cardin /ˈkɑːdæn/ Pierre 1922– . French fashion designer, the first women's designer to show a collection for men, in 1960, and the first to sell his own ready-to-wear collections to department stores.

cardinal in the Roman Catholic church, the highest rank next to the pope. Cardinals act as an advisory body to the pope and elect him. Their red hat is the badge of office. The number of cardinals has varied; there were 151 in 1989.

Originally a cardinal was any priest in charge of a major parish, but in 1567 the term was confined to the members of the Sacred College, 120 of whom (below the age of 80) elect the pope and are themselves elected by him (since 1973). They advise on all matters of doctrine, canonizations, convocation of councils, liturgy, and temporal business.

cardinal number in mathematics, one of the series of numbers 0, 1, 2, 3, 4, ... Cardinal numbers relate to quantity, whereas ordinal numbers (first, second, third, fourth, . . .) relate to order.

cardioid heart-shaped curve traced out by a point on the circumference of a circle that rolls around the edge of another circle of the same diameter. The polar equation of the cardioid is of the form $r = a(1 + \cos \theta)$.

Carducci /kɑːˈduːtʃi/ Giosuè 1835–1907. Italian poet. Born in Tuscany, he was appointed professor of Italian literature at Bologna 1860, and won distinction through his lecturing, critical work, and poetry. His revolutionary *Inno a Satana/Hymn to Satan* 1865 was followed by several other volumes of verse, in which his nationalist sympathies are apparent. Nobel prize 1906.

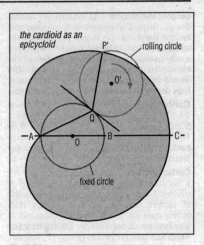

the cardioid as an epicycloid

Cardioid

Carême /kəˈreɪm/ Antonin 1784–1833. French chef who is regarded as the founder of classic French *haute cuisine*. At various times he was chief cook to the Prince Regent in England and Tsar Alexander I in Russia.

care order in Britain, a court order that places a child in the care of a local authority.

From Oct 1991 a person who is a parent or guardian of the child may exercise responsibility independently of the authority, provided that the person does not act in a manner incompatible with the care order, for example, by taking the child away from his or her placement without permission.

Carew /kəˈruː/ Thomas *c.* 1595–*c.* 1640. English poet. He was a gentleman of the privy chamber to Charles I in 1628, and a lyricist as well as member of the school of ◊Cavalier poets.

Carey George Leonard 1935– . 103rd archbishop of Canterbury from 1991. A product of a liberal evangelical background, he was appointed bishop of Bath and Wells 1987.

His support of the ◊ordination of women priests brought disagreement to his first meeting with Pope John Paul II in 1992.

Carey /ˈkeəri/ Peter 1943– . Australian novelist. His works include *Bliss* 1981, *Illywhacker* (Australian slang for 'con man') 1985, and *Oscar and Lucinda* 1988, which won the Booker Prize.

cargo cult Melanesian religious movement, dating from the 19th century. Adherents believe the arrival of cargo is through the agency of a messianic spirit figure, heralding a new paradise free of white dominance. The movement became active during and after World War II with the apparently miraculous dropping of supplies from aeroplanes.

Carib /ˈkærɪb/ member of a group of ◊American Indian people of the northern coast of South America and the islands of the S West Indies in the Caribbean. Those who moved north to take the islands from the Arawak Indians were alleged by the conquering Spaniards to be fierce cannibals. In 1796, the English in the West Indies deported most of them to Roatan Island, off Honduras. Carib languages belong to the Ge-Pano-Carib family.

Caribbean Community and Common Market (CARICOM) organization for economic and foreign policy coordination in the Caribbean region, established by the Treaty of Chaguaramas 1973 to replace the former Caribbean Free Trade Association. Its headquarters are in Georgetown, Guyana. The leading member is Trinidad and Tobago; other members are Antigua and Barbuda, Barbados, Belize, Dominica, Grenada, Guyana, Jamaica, Montserrat, St Kitts-Nevis, Anguilla, St Lucia, and St Vincent. From 1979, a left-wing Grenadan coup led to a progressive regional subgroup including St Lucia and Dominica.

Caribbean Sea /ˌkærɪˈbiːən/ part of the Atlantic Ocean between the north coasts of South and Central America and the West Indies, about 2,740 km/1,700 mi long and 650 km/400 mi 1,500 km/900 mi wide. It is here that the Gulf Stream turns towards Europe. It is heavily polluted by untreated sewage, which destroys mangrove forests and coral reefs.

caribou ◊reindeer of North America.

caricature exaggerated portrayal of individuals or types, aiming to ridicule or otherwise expose the subject. Classical and medieval examples survive. Artists of the 18th, 19th, and 20th centuries have often used caricature as a way of satirizing society and politics. Notable exponents include Daumier and Grosz.

Grotesque drawings have been discovered in Pompeii and Herculaneum, and Pliny refers to a grotesque portrait of the poet Hipponax. Humorous drawings were executed by the ◊Carracci family and their Bolognese followers (the Italian 'eclectic' school of the 16th century). In 1830, Charles Philipon (1800–1862) founded in Paris *La Caricature*, probably the first periodical to specialize in caricature.

CARICOM /ˈkænkɒm/ abbreviation for ◊Caribbean Community and Common Market.

caries decay and disintegration, usually of the substance of teeth (cavity) or bone. It is caused by acids produced when the bacteria that live in the mouth break down sugars in the food. Fluoride, a low sugar intake, and regular brushing are all protective. Caries forms mainly in the 45 minutes following an intake of sugary food, so the most dangerous diet for the teeth is one in which frequent sugary snacks and drinks are consumed.

Carina /kəˈriːnə/ constellation of the southern hemisphere, represented as a ship's keel. Its brightest star is Canopus; it also contains Eta Carinae, a massive and highly luminous star embedded in a gas cloud, perhaps 8,000 light years away. It has varied unpredictably in the past; some astronomers think it is likely to explode as a supernova within 10,000 years.

Carinthia /kəˈrɪnθiə/ (German *Kärnten*) federal province of alpine SE Austria, bordering Italy and Slovenia in the south; capital Klagenfurt; area 9,500 sq km/3,667 sq mi; population (1987) 542,000. It was an independent duchy from 976 and a possession of the Habsburg dynasty 1276–1918.

Carissimi /kəˈrɪsɪmi/ Giacomo 1605–1674. Italian composer of church music. Chief choirmaster at Sant' Apollinaire, Rome, 1630–74, he pioneered the use of expressive solo aria as a commentary on the Latin biblical text. He wrote five oratorios, including *Jephtha* 1650.

Carl XVI Gustaf /kɑːl/ 1946– . King of Sweden from 1973. He succeeded his grandfather Gustaf VI, his father having been killed in an air crash 1947. Under the new Swedish constitution, which became effective on his grandfather's death, the monarchy was stripped of all power at his accession.

Carlisle /kɑːˈlaɪl/ city in Cumbria, NW England, situated on the river Eden at the west end of Hadrian's Wall, administrative centre of the county; population (1981) 71,000. It is a leading railway centre; textiles, engineering, and biscuit making are the chief industries. There is a Norman cathedral and a castle. The bishopric dates from 1133.

Carlist /'kɑ:lɪst/ supporter of the claims of the Spanish pretender Don Carlos de Bourbon (1788–1855), and his descendants, to the Spanish crown. The Carlist revolt continued, primarily in the Basque provinces, until 1839. In 1977 the Carlist political party was legalized and Carlos Hugo de Bourbon Parma (1930–) renounced his claim as pretender and became reconciled with King Juan Carlos. See also ◊Bourbon.

Carlos /'kɑ:lɒs/ four kings of Spain; see ◊Charles.

Carlos I /'kɑ:lɒs/ 1863–1908. King of Portugal, of the Braganza-Coburg line, from 1889 until he was assassinated in Lisbon with his elder son Luis. He was succeeded by his younger son Manuel.

Carlos /'kɑ:lɒs/ Don 1545–1568. Spanish prince. Son of Philip II, he was recognized as heir to the thrones of Castile and Aragon but became mentally unstable and had to be placed under restraint following a plot to assassinate his father. His story was the subject of plays by Schiller, Vittorio Alfieri, Thomas Otway, and others.

Carlow /'kɑ:ləʊ/ county in the Republic of Ireland, in the province of Leinster; county town Carlow; area 900 sq km/347 sq mi; population (1986) 41,000. Mostly flat except for mountains in the south, the land is fertile, and well suited to dairy farming.

Carlsbad /'kɑ:lzbæd/ German name of ◊Karlovy Vary, a spa town in W Bohemia, Czech Republic.

Carlsson /'kɑ:lsən/ Ingvar (Gösta) 1934– . Swedish socialist politician, leader of the Social Democratic Party, deputy prime minister 1982–86 and prime minister 1986–91.

Carlucci /kɑ:'lu:tʃi/ Frank (Charles) 1930– . US politician, a pragmatic moderate. A former diplomat and deputy director of the CIA, he was national security adviser 1986–87 and defence secretary 1987–89 under Reagan, supporting Soviet-US arms reduction.

Carlyle /kɑ:'laɪl/ Thomas 1795–1881. Scottish essayist and social historian. His works include *Sartor Resartus* 1833–34, describing his loss of Christian belief, *French Revolution* 1837, *Chartism* 1839, and *Past and Present* 1843. His prose style was idiosyncratic, encompassing grand, thunderous rhetoric and deliberate obscurity. His suspicion of democracy together with a streak of anti-Semitism foreshadow 20th-century fascist ideology.

Carmarthenshire /kə'mɑ:ðənʃə/ (Welsh *Sir Gaerfyrddin*) former county of S Wales, now part of ◊Dyfed. The county town was Carmarthen.

Carmelite order /'kɑ:məlaɪt/ mendicant order of friars in the Roman Catholic church. The order was founded on Mount Carmel in Palestine by Berthold, a crusader from Calabria, about 1155, and spread to Europe in the 13th century. The Carmelites have devoted themselves largely to missionary work and mystical theology. They are known as *White Friars* because of the white overmantle they wear (over a brown habit).

Traditionally Carmelites originated in the days of Elijah, who according to the Old Testament is supposed to have lived on Mount Carmel. Following the rule which the patriarch of Jerusalem drew up for them about 1210, they lived as hermits in separate huts. About 1240, the Muslim conquests compelled them to move from Palestine and they spread to the west, mostly in France and England, where the order began to live communally. The most momentous reform movement was initiated by St ◊Teresa. In 1562 she founded a convent in Avila and, with the cooperation of St John of the Cross and others, she established a stricter order of barefoot friars and nuns (the *Discalced Carmelites*).

Carmichael /kɑ:'maɪkəl/ Hoagy (Hoagland Howard) 1899–1981. US jazz composer, pianist, singer, and actor. His songs include 'Stardust' 1927, 'Rockin'' Chair' 1930, 'Lazy River' 1931, and 'In the Cool, Cool, Cool of the Evening' 1951 (Academy Award).

Carmina Burana /'kɑ:mɪnə bʊ'rɑ:nə/ medieval lyric miscellany compiled from the work of wandering 13th-century scholars and including secular (love songs and drinking songs) as well as religious verse. Carl ◊Orff composed a cantata 1937 based on the material.

Carnac /'kɑ:næk/ Megalithic site in Brittany, France, where remains of tombs and stone alignments of the period 2000–1500 BC have been found. The largest of the latter has 1,000 stones up to 4 m/13 ft high arranged in 11 rows, with a circle at the western end. Named after the village of Carnac; population about 4,000.

Carnarvon Range /kə'nɑ:vən/ section of the Great Divide, Queensland, Australia, about 900 m/1,000 ft high. There are many Aboriginal paintings in the sandstone caves along its 160 km/100 mi length.

carnassial tooth powerful scissor-like pair of molars, found in all mammalian carnivores except seals. Carnassials are formed from an upper premolar and lower molar, and are shaped to produce a sharp cutting surface. Carnivores such as dogs transfer meat to the back of the mouth, where the carnassials slice up the food ready for swallowing.

Carnatic /kɑːˈnætɪk/ region of SE India, in Madras state. It is situated between the Eastern Ghats and the Coromandel Coast and was formerly a leading trading centre.

carnation any of numerous double-flowered cultivated varieties of a plant *Dianthus caryophyllus* of the pink family. The flowers smell like cloves; they are divided into flake, bizarre, and picotees, according to whether the petals exhibit one or more colours on their white ground, have the colour dispersed in strips, or have a coloured border to the petals.

Carné /kɑːˈneɪ/ Marcel 1909– . French director known for the romantic fatalism of such films as *Drôle de Drame* 1936, *Hôtel du Nord* 1938, *Le Quai des brumes/Port of Shadows* 1938, and *Le Jour se lève/Daybreak* 1939. His masterpiece, *Les Enfants du paradis/The Children of Paradise* 1943–45, was made with his longtime collaborator, the poet and screenwriter Jacques Prévert (1900–1977).

Carnegie /kɑːˈneɪgi/ Andrew 1835–1919. US industrialist and philanthropist, born in Scotland, who developed the Pittsburgh iron and steel industries, making the USA the world's leading producer. He endowed public libraries, education and various research trusts. On his death the Carnegie Trusts continued his benevolent activities. *Carnegie Hall* in New York, opened 1891 as the Music Hall, was renamed 1898 because of his large contribution to its construction.

Carnegie Medal (full name *Library Association Carnegie Medal*) annual award for an outstanding book for children written in English and published in the UK. The medal was first awarded 1937 to Arthur Ransome's *Pigeon Post* (in the ◊*Swallows and Amazons* series). Named after US industrialist and philanthropist Andrew Carnegie.

carnelian semiprecious gemstone variety of ◊chalcedony consisting of quartz (silica) with iron impurities, which give it a translu-

cent red colour. It is found mainly in Brazil, India, and Japan.

Carniola /kɑːniˈəʊlə/ former crownland and duchy of Austria, most of which was included in Slovenia, part of the kingdom of the Serbs, Croats, and Slovenes (later Yugoslavia) 1919. The western districts of Idrija and Postojna, then allocated to Italy, were transferred to Yugoslavia 1947.

carnivore animal that eats other animals. Although the term is sometimes confined to those that eat the flesh of ◊vertebrate prey, it is often used more broadly to include any animal that eats other animals, even microscopic ones. Carrion-eaters may or may not be included.

The mammalian order Carnivora includes cats, dogs, bears, badgers, and weasels.

Carnot /kɑːnəʊ/ (Nicolas Leonard) Sadi 1796–1832. French scientist and military engineer who founded the science of ◊thermodynamics. His pioneering work was *Réflexions sur la puissance motrice du feu/On the Motive Power of Fire*.

Carnot /kɑːnəʊ/ Lazare Nicolas Marguerite 1753–1823. French general and politician. A member of the National Convention in the French Revolution, he organized the armies of the republic. He was war minister 1800–01 and minister of the interior 1815 under Napoleon. His work on fortification, *De la défense de places fortes* 1810, became a military textbook. Minister of the interior during the ◊Hundred Days, he was proscribed at the restoration of the monarchy and retired to Germany.

Carnot /kɑːnəʊ/ Marie François Sadi 1837–1894. French president from 1887, grandson of Lazare Carnot. He successfully countered the Boulangist anti-German movement (see ◊Boulanger) and in 1892 the scandals arising out of French financial activities in Panama. He was assassinated by an Italian anarchist in Lyon.

carnotite potassium uranium vanadate, $K_2(UO_2)_2 (VO_4)_2 3H_2O$, a radioactive ore of vanadium and uranium with traces of radium. A yellow powdery mineral, it is mined chiefly in the Colorado Plateau, USA; Radium Hill, Australia; and Shaba, Zaire.

Caro /kɑːrəʊ/ Anthony 1924– . British sculptor who made bold, large abstracts using ready-made angular metal shapes, often without bases. His works include *Fathom* (outside the Economist Building, London).

carob small Mediterranean tree *Ceratonia siliqua* of the legume family Leguminosae. Its 20-cm/8-in pods are used as animal fodder; they are also the source of a chocolate substitute.

carol song that in medieval times was associated with a round dance; now those that are sung at annual festivals, such as Easter, and Christmas.

Christmas carols were common as early as the 15th century. The custom of singing carols from house to house, collecting gifts, was called wassailing. Many carols such as 'God Rest You Merry Gentlemen' and 'The First Noel', date from the 16th century or earlier.

Carol /'kærəl/ two kings of Romania:

Carol I 1839–1914. First king of Romania 1881–1914. A prince of the house of Hohenzollern-Sigmaringen, he was invited to become prince of Romania, then part of the Ottoman Empire, 1866. In 1877, in alliance with Russia, he declared war on Turkey, and the Congress of Berlin 1878 recognized Romanian independence.

He promoted economic development and industrial reforms but failed to address rural problems. This led to a peasant rebellion 1907 which he brutally crushed. At the beginning of World War I, King Carol declared Romania's neutrality but his successor (his nephew King Ferdinand I) declared for the Allies.

Carol II 1893–1953. King of Romania 1930–40. Son of King Ferdinand, he married Princess Helen of Greece and they had a son, Michael. In 1925 he renounced the succession and settled in Paris with his mistress, Mme Lupescu. Michael succeeded to the throne 1927, but in 1930 Carol returned to Romania and was proclaimed king. In 1938 he introduced a new constitution under which he practically became an absolute ruler. He was forced to abdicate by the pro-Nazi ◊Iron Guard Sept 1940, went to Mexico, and married his mistress 1947.

Carolina /ˌkærə'laɪnə/ two separate states of the USA; see ◊North Carolina and ◊South Carolina.

Caroline of Anspach /'kærəlaɪn, 'ænspæx/ 1683–1737. Queen of George II of Great Britain and Ireland. The daughter of the Margrave of Brandenburg-Anspach, she married George, Electoral Prince of Hanover, 1705, and followed him to England 1714 when his father became King George I.

She was the patron of many leading writers and politicians such as Alexander Pope, John Gay, and Chesterfield. She supported Sir Robert Walpole and kept him in power and acted as regent during her husband's four absences.

Caroline of Brunswick /'kærəlaɪn, 'brʌnzwɪk/ 1768–1821. Queen of George IV of Great Britain, who unsuccessfully attempted to divorce her on his accession to the throne 1820.

Second daughter of Karl Wilhelm, Duke of Brunswick, and Augusta, sister of George III, she married her first cousin, the Prince of Wales, 1795, but after the birth of Princess ◊Charlotte Augusta a separation was arranged. When her husband ascended the throne 1820 she was offered an annuity of £50,000 provided she agreed to renounce the title of queen and to continue to live abroad. She returned forthwith to London, where she assumed royal state. In July 1820 the government brought in a bill to dissolve the marriage, but Lord ◊Brougham's splendid defence led to the bill's abandonment. On 19 July 1821 Caroline was prevented by royal order from entering Westminster Abbey for the coronation. Her funeral was the occasion of popular riots.

Carolines /'kærəlaɪnz/ scattered archipelago in Micronesia, Pacific Ocean, consisting of over 500 coral islets; area 1,200 sq km/463 sq mi. The chief islands are Ponape, Kusai, and Truk in the eastern group, and Yap and Belau in the western group.

The Carolines are well watered and productive. Occupied by Germany 1899, and Japan 1914, and mandated by the League of Nations to Japan 1919, they were fortified, contrary to the terms of the mandate. Under Allied air attack in World War II they remained unconquered. In 1947 they became part of the US trust territory of the ◊Pacific Islands.

Carolingian dynasty /ˌkærə'lɪndʒɪən/ Frankish dynasty descending from ◊Pepin the Short (died 768) and named after his son Charlemagne; its last ruler was Louis V of France (reigned 966–87), who was followed by Hugh ◊Capet.

carotene naturally occurring pigment of the carotenoid group. Carotenes produce the orange, yellow, and red colours of carrots, tomatoes, oranges, and crustaceans.

carotenoids any of a group of yellow, orange, red, or brown pigments found in many living organisms, particularly in the ◊chloroplasts of plants. There are two main types, the *carotenes* and the *xanthophylls*. Both types are long-chain lipids (◊fats).

Some carotenoids act as accessory pigments in ◊photosynthesis, and in certain algae they are the principal light-absorbing pigments functioning more efficiently than ◊chlorophyll in low-intensity light. Carotenoids can also occur in organs such as petals, roots, and fruits, giving them their characteristic colour, as in the yellow and orange petals of wallflowers *Cheiranthus*. They are also responsible for the autumn colours of leaves, persisting longer than the green chlorophyll, which masks them during the summer.

Carothers /kəˈrʌðəz/ Wallace 1896–1937. US chemist who carried out research into polymerization. By 1930 he had discovered that some polymers were fibre-forming, and in 1937 he produced ◊nylon.

carotid artery one of a pair of major blood vessels, one on each side of the neck, supplying blood to the head.

carp fish *Cyprinus carpio* found all over the world. It commonly grows to 50 cm/1.8 ft and 3 kg/7 lb, but may be even larger. It lives in lakes, ponds, and slow rivers. The wild form is drab, but cultivated forms may be golden, or may have few large scales (mirror carp) or be scaleless (leather carp). *Koi* carp are highly prized and can grow up to 1 m/3 ft long with a distinctive pink, red, white, or black colouring.

Carpaccio /kɑːˈpætʃiəʊ/ Vittorio 1450/60–1525/ 26. Italian painter known for scenes of his native Venice. His series *The Legend of St Ursula* 1490–98 (Accademia, Venice) is full of detail of contemporary Venetian life. His other great series is the lives of saints George and Jerome 1502–07 (S Giorgio degli Schiavoni, Venice).

Carpathian Mountains /kɑːˈpeɪθiən/ Central European mountain system, forming a semicircle through Slovakia–Poland–Ukraine–Moldova–Romania, 1,450 km/900 mi long. The central *Tatra mountains* on the Slovak–Poland frontier include the highest peak, Gerlachovka, 2,663 m/8,737 ft.

Carpeaux /kɑːˈpəʊ/ Jean-Baptiste 1827–1875. French sculptor whose lively naturalistic subjects include *La Danse* 1865–69 for the Opéra, Paris.

Another example is the *Neapolitan Fisherboy* 1858 (Louvre, Paris). The Romantic charm of his work belies his admiration of Michelangelo. He studied in Italy 1856–62 and won the Prix de Rome scholarship 1854.

carpel female reproductive unit in flowering plants (◊angiosperms). It usually comprises an ◊ovary containing one or more ovules, the stalk or style, and a ◊stigma at its top which receives the pollen. A flower may have one or more carpels, and they may be separate or fused together. Collectively the carpels of a flower are known as the ◊gynoecium.

Carpentaria, Gulf of /ˌkɑːpənˈteəriə/ shallow gulf opening out of the Arafura Sea, N of Australia. It was discovered by Tasman 1606 and named 1623 in honour of Pieter Carpentier, governor general of the Dutch East Indies.

carpet thick textile fabric, generally made of wool, used for covering floors and stairs. There is a long tradition of fine handmade carpets in the Middle East, India, Pakistan, and China. Western carpets are machine-made. Carpets and rugs have also often been made in the home as a pastime, cross and tent stitch on canvas being widely used in the 18th and 19th centuries.

history The earliest known carpets date from *c.* 500 BC and were excavated at Passypych in SE Siberia, but it was not until the later Middle Ages that carpets reached W Europe from Turkey. Persian carpets (see ◊Islamic art), which reached a still unrivalled peak of artistry in the 15th and 16th centuries, were rare in Britain until the mid-19th century, reaching North America a little later. The subsequent demand led to a revival of organized carpet-making in Persia. Europe copied oriental technique, but developed Western designs: France produced beautiful work at the Savonnerie and Beauvais establishments under Louis XIV and Louis XV; and Exeter, Axminster, London, and Wilton became British carpetmaking centres in the 18th century, though Kidderminster is the biggest centre today. The first carpet factory in the USA was established in Philadelphia 1791; it is still a large carpet-producing centre.

carpetbagger in US history, derogatory name for the entrepreneurs and politicians from the North who moved to the Southern states during ◊Reconstruction 1861–65 after the Civil War.

With the votes of newly enfranchised blacks and some local white people (called scalawags), they won posts in newly created Republican state governments, but were resented by many white Southerners as outsiders and opportunists. The term thus came to mean a corrupt outsider who profits from an area's political instability, although some arrivals had good motives. They were so called because they were supposed to own no property except what they carried in their small satchels made of carpeting.

Carracci /kəˈrɑːtʃi/ Italian family of painters in Bologna, whose forte was murals and ceilings. The foremost of them, *Annibale Carracci* (1560–1609), decorated the Farnese Palace, Rome, with a series of mythological paintings united by simulated architectural ornamental surrounds (completed 1604).

Ludovico Carracci (1555–1619), with his cousin *Agostino Carracci* (1557–1602), founded Bologna's Academy of Art. Agostino collaborated with his brother Annibale on the Farnese Palace decorative scheme, which paved the way for a host of elaborate murals in Rome's palaces and churches, ever-more inventive illusions of pictorial depth and architectural ornament. Annibale also painted early landscapes such as *Flight into Egypt* 1603 (Doria Gallery, Rome).

Carradine /ˈkærədiːn/ John (Richmond Reed) 1906–1988. US film actor who often played sinister roles. He appeared in many major Hollywood films, such as *Stagecoach* 1939 and *The Grapes of Wrath* 1940, but was later seen mostly in horror B-movies, including *House of Frankenstein* 1944.

carragheen species of deep-reddish, branched seaweed *Chondrus crispus*. Named after Carragheen in Ireland, it is found on rocky shores on both sides of the Atlantic. It is exploited commercially in food and medicinal preparations and as cattle feed.

Carrara /kəˈrɑːrə/ town in Tuscany, Italy, 60 km/37 mi NW of Livorno; population (1981) 66,000. It is known for its quarries of fine white marble, which were worked by the Romans, abandoned in the 5th century, and came into use again with the revival of sculpture and architecture in the 12th century.

Carrel /kəˈrel/ Alexis 1873–1944. US surgeon born in France, whose experiments paved the way for organ transplantation. Working at the Rockefeller Institute, New York City, he devised a way of joining blood vessels end to end (anastomosing). This was a key move in the development of transplant surgery, as was his work on keeping organs viable outside the body, for which he was awarded the Nobel Prize for Medicine 1912.

Carreras /kəˈreərəs/ José 1947– . Spanish tenor whose roles include Handel's Samson, and whose recordings include *West Side Story* 1984. He made a dramatic recovery from leukaemia in 1988 and, together with Placido Domingo and Luciano Pavarotti, achieved world-wide fame in a recording of operatic hits released to coincide with the soccer World Cup series in Rome 1990.

Carreras Spanish lyric tenor José Carreras made his mark playing opposite Montserrat Caballé.

Carrhae, Battle of /ˈkæriː/ battle 53 BC in which the invading Roman general Crassus was defeated and killed by the Parthians. The ancient town of Carrhae is near Haran, Turkey.

carriage driving sport in which two- or four-wheeled carriages are pulled by two or four horses. Events include ◊dressage, obstacle driving, and the marathon. The Duke of Edinburgh is one of the sport's leading exponents.

carrier /ˈkæriə/ in medicine, anyone who harbours an infectious organism without ill effects but can pass the infection to others. The term is also applied to those who carry a recessive gene for a disease or defect without manifesting the condition.

carrier warfare naval warfare involving ◊aircraft carriers. Carrier warfare was conducted during World War II in the battle of the Coral Sea May 1942, which stopped the Japanese advance in the South Pacific, and in the battle of Midway Islands June 1942, which weakened the Japanese navy through the loss of four aircraft carriers. The US Navy deployed six aircraft carriers during the Gulf War 1991.

Carrington /ˈkærɪŋtən/ Peter Alexander Rupert, 6th Baron Carrington 1919– . British Conservative politician. He was defence secretary 1970–74, and led the opposition in the House of Lords 1964–70 and 1974–79. While foreign secretary 1979–82, he negotiated independence for Zimbabwe, but resigned after failing to anticipate the Falklands crisis. He was secretary general of NATO 1984–88. He chaired EC-sponsored peace talks on Yugoslavia 1991.

Carroll /ˈkærəl/ Lewis. Pen name of Charles Lutwidge Dodgson 1832–1898. English author of children's classics *Alice's Adventures in Wonderland* 1865 and *Alice Through the Looking Glass* 1872. An Oxford don and mathematician, he first told the stories to Alice Liddell and her sisters, daughters of the Dean of Christ Church. He also published mathematical works.

During his lifetime Dodgson refused to acknowledge any connection with any books not published under his own name. Among later works was the mock-heroic nonsense poem *The Hunting of the Snark* 1876. He was among the pioneers of portrait photography.

carrot hardy European biennial *Daucus carota* of the family Umbelliferae. Cultivated since the 16th century for its edible root, it has a high sugar content and also contains ◊carotene, which is converted by the human liver to vitamin A.

carrying capacity in ecology, the maximum number of animals of a given species that a particular area can support. When the carrying capacity is exceeded, there is insufficient food (or other resources) for the members of the population. The population may then be reduced by emigration, reproductive failure, or death through starvation.

Carry on **films** series of low-budget British comedies with an emphasis on the unsubtle double entendre; they were probably the most successful film run in postwar Britain. The first was *Carry on Sergeant* 1958 and the series continued for 20 years with such titles as *Carry on Nurse, Carry on Spying, Carry on Screaming*, and *Carry on Doctor*.

All were produced by Peter Rogers and directed by Gerald Thomas. Regular stars included Kenneth Williams, Charles Hawtrey, Sid James, and Joan Sims.

Carson /ˈkɑːsən/ Kit (Christopher) 1809–68. US frontier settler, guide, and Indian agent, who later fought for the Federal side in the Civil War. Carson City was named after him.

Carson /ˈkɑːsən/ Rachel 1907–1964. US naturalist. An aquatic biologist with the US Fish and Wildlife Service 1936–49, she then became its editor-in-chief until 1952. In 1951 she published *The Sea Around Us* and in 1963 *Silent Spring*, attacking the indiscriminate use of pesticides.

Carson /ˈkɑːsən/ Willie (William) 1942– . British jockey, born in Scotland, who has ridden three Epsom Derby winners as well as the winners of most major races worldwide.

The top flat-race jockey on five occasions, he has had over 3,000 wins in Britain. For many years he has ridden for the royal trainer, Major Dick Hern.

Carson City /ˈkɑːsən ˈsɪti/ capital of Nevada, USA; population (1980) 30,000. Smallest of the state capitals, it is named after Kit ◊Carson.

Cartagena /ˌkɑːtəˈdʒiːnə/ city in the province of Murcia, Spain, on the Mediterranean; population (1986) 169,000. It is a seaport and naval base. It was founded as *Carthago Nova* about 225 BC by the Carthaginian Hasdrubal, son-in-law of Hamilcar Barca. It continued to flourish under the Romans and the Moors and was conquered by the Spanish 1269. It has a 13th-century cathedral and Roman remains.

Cartagena /ˌkɑːtəˈdʒiːnə/ or *Cartagena de los Indes* port, industrial centre, and capital of the department of Bolívar, NW Colombia; population (1985) 531,000. Plastics and chemicals are produced here.

It was founded 1533 and taken by English buccaneer Francis Drake 1586. A pipeline brings petroleum to the city from the De Manes oilfields.

carte blanche (French 'white paper') no instructions, complete freedom to do as one wishes.

cartel (German *Kartell* 'a group') agreement among national or international firms to set mutually acceptable prices for their products. A cartel may restrict supply, or output, or raise prices to prevent entrants to the market and increase member profits. It therefore represents a form of ◊oligopoly. ◊OPEC, for example, is an oil cartel.

National laws concerning cartels differ widely, and international agreement is difficult to achieve. Both the Treaty of Rome and the Stockholm Convention governing the European Community (EC) and the European Free Trade Association (EFTA), respectively contain provisions for control. In Germany, cartels are the most common form of monopolistic organization.

Carter /'kɑːtə/ Angela 1940–1992. English writer of the ◊magic realist school. Her novels include *The Magic Toyshop* (filmed by David Wheatley 1987) and *Nights at the Circus* 1984. She co-wrote the script for the film *The Company of Wolves* 1984, based on one of her stories.

Carter /'kɑːtə/ Elliott (Cook) 1908– . US composer. His early music shows the influence of ◊Stravinsky, but after 1950 it became increasingly intricate and densely written in a manner resembling ◊Ives. He invented 'metrical modulation' which allows different instruments or groups to stay in touch while playing at different speeds. He has written four string quartets, the *Symphony for Three Orchestras* 1967, and the song cycle *A Mirror on Which to Dwell* 1975.

Carter /'kɑːtə/ Jimmy (James Earl) 1924– . 39th president of the USA 1977–81, a Democrat. In 1976 he narrowly wrested the presidency from Gerald Ford. Features of his presidency were the return of the Panama Canal Zone to Panama, the Camp David Agreements for peace in the Middle East, and the Iranian seizure of US embassy hostages. He was defeated by Ronald Reagan 1980.

Carter Doctrine assertion 1980 by President Carter of a vital US interest in the Persian Gulf region (prompted by the Soviet invasion of Afghanistan and instability in Iran): any outside attempt at control would be met by military force if necessary.

Cartesian coordinates /kɑː'tɪːzjən/ in ◊coordinate geometry, the components of a system used to denote the position of a point on a plane (two dimensions) or in space (three dimensions) with reference to a set of two or more axes. The Cartesian coordinate system can be extended to any finite number of dimensions (axes), and is used thus in theoretical mathematics. It is named after the French mathematician, Descartes.

For a plane defined by two axes at right angles (a horizontal x-axis and a vertical y-axis), the coordinates of a point are given by its perpendicular distances from the y-axis and x-axis, written in the form (x,y). For example, a point P that lies three units from the y-axis and four units from the x-axis has Cartesian coordinates (3,4). In three-dimensional coordinate geometry, points are located with reference to a third, z-axis. The system is useful in creating technical drawings of machines or buildings, and in computer-aided design (◊CAD).

Carthage /'kɑːθɪdʒ/ ancient Phoenician port in N Africa; it lay 16 km/10 mi N of Tunis, Tunisia. A leading trading centre, it was in conflict with Greece from the 6th century BC, and then with Rome, and was destroyed by Roman forces 146 BC at the end of the ◊*Punic Wars*. About 45 BC, Roman colonists settled in Carthage, and it became the wealthy capital of the province of Africa. After its capture by the Vandals AD 439 it was little more than a pirate stronghold. From 533 it formed part of the Byzantine Empire until its final destruction by Arabs 698, during their conquest in the name of Islam.

Carthage is said to have been founded 814 BC by Phoenician emigrants from Tyre, led by Princess Dido. It developed an extensive commerce throughout the Mediterranean and traded with the Tin Islands, whose location is believed to have been either Cornwall, England, or SW Spain. After the capture of Tyre by the Babylonians in the 6th century BC, it became the natural leader of the Phoenician colonies in N Africa and Spain, and there soon began a prolonged struggle with the Greeks, which centred mainly on Sicily, the east of which was dominated by Greek colonies, while the west was held by Carthaginian trading stations. About 540 BC the Carthaginians defeated a Greek attempt to land in Corsica, and 480 BC a Carthaginian attempt to conquer the whole of Sicily was defeated by the Greeks at Himera.

The population of Carthage before its destruction by the Romans is said to have numbered over 700,000. The constitution was an aristocratic republic with two chief magistrates elected annually and a senate of 300 life members. The religion was Phoenician, including the worship of the Moon goddess Tanit, the great Sun god Baal-Hammon, and the Tyrian Meklarth; human sacrifices were not unknown. The real strength of Carthage lay in its commerce and its powerful navy; its armies were for the most part mercenaries.

Carthusian order /kɑː'θjuːzɪən/ Roman Catholic order of monks and, later, nuns, founded by St Bruno 1084 at Chartreuse, near Grenoble, France. Living chiefly in unbroken silence, they ate one vegetarian meal a day and supported themselves by their own labours; the rule is still one of severe austerity.

The first rule was drawn up by Guigo, the fifth prior. The order was introduced into England about 1178, when the first Charterhouse was founded at Witham in Essex. They were suppressed at the Reformation, but there is a Charterhouse at Parkminster, Sussex, established 1833.

Cartier /ka:tĭeɪ/ Georges Étienne 1814–1873. French-Canadian politician. He fought against the British in the rebellion 1837, was elected to the Canadian parliament 1848, and was joint prime minister with John A Macdonald 1858–62. He brought Québec into the Canadian federation 1867.

Cartier /ˌka:tĭeɪ/ Jacques 1491–1557. French navigator who was the first European to sail up the St Lawrence River 1534. He named the site of Montréal.

Cartier-Bresson /ˌka:tĭeɪ brɛˈsɒn/ Henri 1908– . French photographer, considered one of the greatest photographic artists. His documentary work was shot in black and white, using a small-format camera. His work is remarkable for its tighly structured composition and his ability to capture the decisive moment.

cartilage flexible bluish-white connective ♦tissue made up of the protein collagen. In cartilaginous fish it forms the skeleton; in other vertebrates it forms the greater part of the the embryonic skeleton, and is replaced by ♦bone in the course of development, except in areas of wear such as bone endings, and the discs between the backbones. It also forms structural tissue in the larynx, nose, and external ear of mammals.

Cartland /ˈka:tlənd/ Barbara 1904– . English romantic novelist. She published her first book, *Jigsaw* 1921 and since then has produced a prolific stream of stories of chastely romantic love, usually in idealized or exotic settings, for a mainly female audience (such as *Love Climbs In* 1978 and *Moments of Love* 1981).

cartography art and practice of drawing ♦maps.

cartoon humorous or satirical drawing or ♦caricature; a strip cartoon or ♦comic strip; traditionally, the base design for a large fresco, mosaic, or tapestry, transferred to wall or canvas by tracing or picking out

(pouncing). Surviving examples include Leonardo da Vinci's *Virgin and St Anne* (National Gallery, London).

Cartwright /ˈka:traɪt/ Edmund 1743–1823. British inventor. He patented the power loom 1785, built a weaving mill 1787, and patented a wool-combing machine 1789.

Caruso /kəˈruːsəʊ/ Enrico 1873–1921. Italian operatic tenor. In 1902 he starred, with Nellie Melba, in Puccini's *La Bohème*. He was one of the first opera singers to profit from gramophone recordings.

Carver /ˈka:və/ George Washington 1864–1943. US agricultural chemist. Born a slave in Missouri, he was kidnapped and raised by his former owner, Moses Carver. He devoted his life to improving the economy of the US South and the condition of blacks. He advocated the diversification of crops, promoted peanut production, and was a pioneer in the field of plastics.

Carver /ˈka:və/ Raymond 1939–1988. US short-story writer and poet, author of vivid tales of contemporary US life, a collection of which were published in *Cathedral* 1983. *Fires* 1985 includes his essays and poems.

Cary /ˈkeəri/ (Arthur) Joyce (Lunel) 1888–1957. British novelist. He used his experiences gained in Nigeria in the Colonial Service (which he entered 1918) as a backdrop to such novels as *Mister Johnson* 1939. Other books include *The Horse's Mouth* 1944.

caryatid building support or pillar in the shape of a woman, the name deriving from the Karyatides, who were priestesses at the temple of Artemis at Karyai; the male equivalent is a *telamon* or *atlas*.

caryopsis dry, one-seeded ♦fruit in which the wall of the seed becomes fused to the carpel wall during its development. It is a type of ♦achene, and therefore develops from one ovary and does not split open to release the seed. Caryopses are typical of members of the grass family (Gramineae), including the cereals.

Casablanca /ˌkæsəˈblæŋkə/ (Arabic *Dar el-Beida*) port, commercial and industrial centre on the Atlantic coast of Morocco; population (1982) 2,139,000. It trades in fish, phosphates, and manganese. The Great Hassan II Mosque, completed 1989, is the world's largest; it is built on a platform (40,000 sq m/430,000 sq ft) jutting out over the Atlantic, with walls 60 m/200 ft high, topped by a hydraulic sliding roof, and a minaret 175 m/574 ft high.

Casablanca was occupied by the French from 1907 until Morocco became independent 1956.

Casablanca Conference World War II meeting of the US and UK leaders Roosevelt and Churchill, 14–24 Jan 1943, at which the Allied demand for the unconditional surrender of Germany, Italy, and Japan was issued.

Casals /kəˈsɑːlz/ Pablo 1876–1973. Catalan cellist, composer, and conductor. As a cellist, he was celebrated for his interpretations of J S Bach's unaccompanied suites. He left Spain 1939 to live in Prades, in the French Pyrenees, where he founded an annual music festival. In 1956 he moved to Puerto Rico, where he launched the Casals Festival 1957, and toured extensively in the USA. He wrote instrumental and choral works, including the Christmas oratorio *The Manger.*

Casanova de Seingalt /ˌkæsəˈnəʊvə də sæŋˈɡælt/ Giovanni Jacopo 1725–1798. Italian adventurer, spy, violinist, librarian, and, according to his *Memoirs,* one of the world's great lovers. From 1774 he was a spy in the Venetian police service. In 1782 a libel got him into trouble, and after more wanderings he was appointed 1785 librarian to Count Waldstein at his castle of Dûx in Bohemia. Here Casanova wrote his *Memoirs* (published 1826–38, although the complete text did not appear until 1960–61).

Cascade Range /kæˈskeɪd/ volcanic mountains in the western USA and Canada, extending 1,120 km/700 mi from N California through Oregon and Washington to the Fraser River. They include Mount St Helens and Mount Rainier (the highest peak, 4,392 m/14,408 ft), which is noteworthy for its glaciers. The mountains are the most active in the USA, excluding Alaska and Hawaii.

case grammar theory of language that proposes that the underlying structure should contain some sort of functional information about the roles of its components; thus in the sentence 'The girl opened the door', the phrase *the girl* would have the role of agent, not merely that of grammatical subject.

casein main protein of milk, from which it can be separated by the action of acid, the enzyme rennin, or bacteria (souring); it is also the main component of cheese. Casein is used commercially in cosmetics, glues, and as a sizing for coating paper.

Casement /ˈkeɪsmənt/ Roger David 1864–1916. Irish nationalist. While in the British consular service, he exposed the ruthless exploitation of the people of the Belgian Congo and Peru, for which he was knighted 1911 (degraded 1916). He was hanged for treason by the British for his involvement in the Irish nationalist cause.

In 1914 Casement went to Germany and attempted to induce Irish prisoners of war to form an Irish brigade to take part in a republican insurrection. He returned to Ireland in a submarine 1916 (actually to postpone, not start, the Easter Rising), was arrested, tried for treason, and hanged.

Caserta /kəˈzɜːtə/ town in S Italy 33 km/21 mi NE of Naples; population (1981) 66,318. It trades in chemicals, olive oil, wine, and grain. The base for Garibaldi's campaigns in the 19th century, it was the Allied headquarters in Italy 1943–45, and the German forces surrendered to Field Marshal Alexander here 1945.

Cash /kæʃ/ Johnny 1932– . US country singer, songwriter, and guitarist. His early hits, recorded for Sun Records in Memphis, Tennessee, include the million-selling 'I Walk the Line' 1956. Cash's gruff delivery and storytelling ability distinguish his work. He is widely respected outside the country-music field for his concern for the underprivileged, expressed in albums like *Bitter Tears* 1964 about American Indians and the live *At Folsom Prison* 1968.

cash crop crop grown solely for sale rather than for the farmer's own use, for example, coffee, cotton, or sugar beet. Many Third World countries grow cash crops to meet their debt repayments rather than grow food for their own people. The price for these crops depends on financial interests, such as those of the multinational companies and the International Monetary Fund.

cashew tropical American tree *Anacardium occidentale,* family Anacardiaceae. Extensively cultivated in India and Africa, it produces poisonous kidney-shaped nuts that become edible after being roasted.

cash flow input of cash required to cover all expenses of a business, whether revenue or capital. Alternatively, the actual or prospective balance between the various outgoing and incoming movements which are designated in total, positive or negative according to which is greater.

cashmere natural fibre originating from the wool of the goats of Kashmir, India, used for shawls, scarves, sweaters, and coats. It can also be made artificially.

Caspian Sea /'kæspiən/ world's largest inland sea, divided between Iran, Azerbaijan, Russia, Kazakhstan, and Turkmenistan; area about 400,000 sq km/155,000 sq mi, with a maximum depth of 1,000 m/3,250 ft. The chief ports are Astrakhan and Baku. It is now approximately 28 m/90 ft below sea level owing to drainage in the north, and the damming of the Volga and Ural rivers for hydroelectric power.

An underwater ridge divides it into two halves, of which the shallow northern half is almost salt-free. There are no tides. The damming has led to shrinkage over the last 50 years, and the growth of industry along its shores has caused pollution and damaged the Russian and Iranian caviar industries.

Cassandra /kə'sændrə/ in Greek mythology, the daughter of ◊Priam, king of Troy. Her prophecies (for example, of the fall of Troy) were never believed, because she had rejected the love of Apollo. She was murdered with Agamemnon by his wife Clytemnestra.

Cassatt /kə'sæt/ Mary 1845–1926. US Impressionist painter and printmaker. In 1868 she settled in Paris. Her popular, colourful pictures of mothers and children show the influence of Japanese prints, for example *The Bath* 1892 (Art Institute, Chicago).

cassava or *manioc* plant *Manihot utilissima*, belonging to the spurge family Euphorbiaceae. Native to South America, it is now widely grown throughout the tropics for its starch-containing roots, from which tapioca and bread are made.

Cassavetes /kæsə'veitiːz/ John 1929–1989. US director and actor whose experimental, apparently improvised films include *Shadows* 1960 and *The Killing of a Chinese Bookie* 1980. He acted in *The Dirty Dozen* 1967 and *Rosemary's Baby* 1968.

cassia bark of a SE Asian plant *Cinnamomum cassia* of the laurel family Lauraceae. It is aromatic and closely resembles true cinnamon, for which it is a widely used substitute. *Cassia* is also a genus of pod-bearing tropical plants of the family Caesalpiniaceae, many of which have strong purgative properties; *Cassia senna* is the source of the laxative drug senna.

Cassini /kæ'siːni/ Giovanni Domenico 1625–1712. Italian-French astronomer who discovered four moons of Saturn and the gap in the rings of Saturn now called the *Cassini division*.

Cassini joint space probe of the US agency NASA and the European Space Agency to the planet Saturn. *Cassini* is scheduled to be launched Nov 1995 and to go into orbit around Saturn Dec 2003, dropping off a sub-probe, *Huygens*, to land on Saturn's largest moon, Titan.

Cassino /kæ'siːnəʊ/ town in S Italy, 80 km/50 mi NW of Naples, at the foot of Monte Cassino; population (1981) 31,139. It was the scene of heavy fighting during World War II in 1944, when most of the town was destroyed. It was rebuilt 1.5 km/1 mi to the north. The abbey on the summit of Monte Cassino, founded by St Benedict 529, was rebuilt 1956.

Cassiopeia /kæsiə'peiə/ prominent constellation of the northern hemisphere, named after the mother of Andromeda. It has a distinctive W-shape, and contains one of the most powerful radio sources in the sky, Cassiopeia A, the remains of a ◊supernova (star explosion).

cassiterite or *tinstone* chief ore of tin, consisting of reddish-brown to black stannic oxide (SnO_2), usually found in granite rocks. When fresh it has a bright ('adamantine') lustre. It was formerly extensively mined in Cornwall, England; today Malaysia is the world's main supplier. Other sources of cassiterite are in Africa, Indonesia, and South America.

Cassius /'kæsiəs/ Gaius died 42 BC. Roman soldier, one of the conspirators who killed Julius ◊Caesar 44 BC. He fought at Carrhae 53, and with the republicans against Caesar at Pharsalus 48; was pardoned and appointed praetor, but became a leader in the conspiracy of 44, and after Caesar's death joined Brutus. He committed suicide after his defeat at ◊Philippi 42.

Casson /'kæsən/ Hugh 1910– . British architect, professor at the Royal College of Art 1953–75, and president of the Royal Academy 1976–84. His books include *Victorian Architecture* 1948. He was director of architecture for the Festival of Britain 1948–51.

cassowary large flightless bird, genus *Casuarius*, found in New Guinea and N Australia, usually in forests. Related to the emu, the cassowary has a bare head with a horny casque, or helmet, on top, and brightly

Cassowary The common cassowary of N Australia and New Guinea.

coloured skin on the neck. Its loose plumage is black and its wings tiny, but it can run and leap well and defends itself by kicking. Cassowaries stand up to 1.5 m/5 ft tall.

Castagno /kæˈstænjəʊ/ Andrea del *c.* 1421–1457. Italian Renaissance painter, active in Florence. In his frescoes in Sta Apollonia, Florence, he adapted the pictorial space to the architectural framework and followed ◊Masaccio's lead in perspective.

Castagno's work is sculptural and strongly expressive, anticipating the Florentine late 15th-century style, as in his *David*, about 1450–57 (National Gallery, Washington, DC).

castanets Spanish percussion instrument made of two hollowed wooden shells, clapped in the hand to produce a rhythmic accompaniment to dance.

caste (Portuguese *casta* 'race') stratifying of Hindu society dating from ancient times split into four main groups from which over 3,000 subsequent divisions derive: ***Brahmans*** (priests), ***Kshatriyas*** (nobles and warriors), ***Vaisyas*** (traders and farmers), and ***Sudras*** (servants); plus a fifth group, ***Harijan*** (untouchables). No upward or downward mobility exists, as in classed societies.

In Hindu tradition, the four main castes are said to have originated from the head, arms, thighs, and feet respectively of Brahma, the creator; the members of the fifth were probably the aboriginal inhabi-

tants of the country, known variously as Scheduled Castes, Depressed Classes, Untouchables, or Harijan (name coined by Gandhi, 'children of God'). This lowest caste handled animal products, garbage, and human wastes and so was considered to be polluting by touch, or even by sight, to others. Discrimination against them was made illegal 1947 when India became independent, but persists.

Castel Gandolfo /kæsˈtel gænˈdɒlfəʊ/ castle built by Pope Urban VIII in the 17th century and still used by the pope as a summer residence; it is situated in a village in Italy 24 km/15 mi SE of Rome.

Castello Branco /kəʃˈtelu ˈbræŋkuː/ Camillo Ferreira Botelho, Visconde de Corrêa Botelho 1825–1890. Portuguese novelist. His work fluctuates between mysticism and bohemianism, and includes *Amor de perdição/Love of Perdition* 1862, written during his imprisonment for adultery, and *Novelas do Minho* 1875, stories of the rural north.

Castellón de la Plana /ˌkæstelˈjɒn delɑː ˈplɑːnə/ port in Spain, facing the Mediterranean to the east; population (1981) 124,500. It is the capital of Castellón province and is the centre of an orange-growing district.

Castiglione /kæsˌtiːliˈəʊni/ Baldassare, Count Castiglione 1478–1529. Italian author and diplomat, who described the perfect Renaissance gentleman in *Il Cortegiano/The Courtier* 1528.

Castile /kæsˈtiːl/ kingdom founded in the 10th century, occupying the central plateau of Spain. Its union with ◊Aragon 1479, based on the marriage of ◊Ferdinand and Isabella, effected the foundation of the Spanish state, which at the time was occupied and ruled by the ◊Moors. Castile comprised the two great basins separated by the Sierra de Gredos and the Sierra de Guadarrama, known traditionally as Old and New Castile. The area now forms the regions of ◊Castilla-León and ◊Castilla-La Mancha.

The kingdom of Castile grew from a small area in the north. In the 11th century, Old Castile was united with León; the kingdom of Toledo was captured from the Moors 1085 and became New Castile, with Toledo the capital of the whole. Castile was united with Aragon 1479, and in 1492, after routing the Moors, Ferdinand and Isabella established the Catholic kingdom of Spain.

Castilian language /kæ'stɪlɪən/ member of the Romance branch of the Indo-European language family, originating in NW Spain, in the provinces of Old and New Castile. It is the basis of present-day standard Spanish (see ◊Spanish language) and is often seen as the same language, the terms *castellano* and *español* being used interchangeably in both Spain and the Spanish-speaking countries of the Americas.

Castilla–La Mancha /kæ'stiːljə lɑː 'mæntʃə/ autonomous region of central Spain; area 79,200 sq km/30,571 sq mi; population (1986) 1,665,000. It includes the provinces of Albacete, Ciudad Real, Cuenca, Guadalajara, and Toledo. Irrigated land produces grain and chickpeas, and merino sheep graze here.

Castilla–León /kæ'stiːljə ler'ɒn/ autonomous region of central Spain; area 94,100 sq km/36,323 sq mi; population (1986) 2,600,000. It includes the provinces of Ávila, Burgos, León, Palencia, Salamanca, Segovia, Soria, Valladolid, and Zamora. Irrigated land produces wheat and rye. Cattle, sheep, and fighting bulls are bred in the uplands.

casting process of producing solid objects by pouring molten material into a shaped mould and allowing it to cool. Casting is used to shape such materials as glass and plastics, as well as metals and alloys.

The casting of metals has been practised for more than 6,000 years, using first copper and bronze, then iron. The traditional method of casting metal is *sand casting*. Using a model of the object to be produced, a hollow mould is made in a damp sand and clay mix. Molten metal is then poured into the mould, taking its shape when it cools and solidifies. The sand mould is broken up to release the casting. Permanent metal moulds called *dies* are also used for casting, in particular, small items in mass-production processes where molten metal is injected under pressure into cooled dies. *Continuous casting* is a method of shaping bars and slabs that involves pouring molten metal into a hollow, water-cooled mould of the desired cross section.

cast iron cheap but invaluable constructional material, most commonly used for car engine blocks. Cast iron is partly refined pig (crude) ◊iron, which is very fluid when molten and highly suitable for shaping by ◊casting; it contains too many impurities (for example, carbon) to be readily shaped in any other way. Solid cast iron is heavy and can absorb great shock but is very brittle.

castle /'kɑːsəl/ private fortress of a king or noble. The earliest castles in Britain were built following the Norman Conquest, and the art of castle building reached a peak in the 13th century. By the 15th century, the need for castles for domestic defence had largely disappeared, and the advent of gunpowder made them largely useless against attack. See also ◊château.

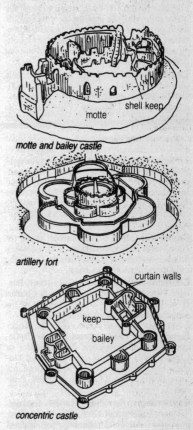

motte and bailey castle

artillery fort

concentric castle

Castle Three stages in the development of the castle. (Top) the motte and bailey, an earthwork with a palisade or wall; (centre) an artillery fort, typical of 16th-century coastal defences in England; (bottom) a 13th-century concentric castle.

structure The main parts of a typical castle are: the *keep*, a large central tower containing store rooms, soldiers' quarters, and a hall for the lord and his family; the *inner bailey* or walled courtyard surrounding the keep; the *outer bailey* or second courtyard, separated from the inner bailey by a wall; crenellated *embattlements* through which missiles were discharged against an attacking enemy; rectangular or round *towers* projecting from the walls; the *portcullis*, a heavy grating which could be let down to close the main gate; and the *drawbridge* crossing the ditch or moat surrounding the castle. Sometimes a tower called a *barbican* was constructed over a gateway as an additional defensive measure.

Castle /ˈkɑːsəl/ Barbara, Baroness Castle (born Betts) 1911– . British Labour politician, a cabinet minister in the Labour governments of the 1960s and 1970s. She led the Labour group in the European Parliament 1979–89.

She was minister of overseas development 1964–65, transport 1965–68, employment 1968–70 (when her White Paper 'In Place of Strife', on trade-union reform, was abandoned because it suggested state intervention in industrial relations), and social services 1974–76, when she was dropped from the cabinet by Prime Minister James Callaghan. She criticized him in her *Diaries* 1980.

Castle Hill rising Irish convict revolt in New South Wales, Australia, 4 Mar 1804; a number were killed while parleying with the military under a flag of truce.

Castlemaine /ˈkɑːsəlmeɪn/ Lady (born Barbara Villiers) 1641–1709. Mistress of Charles II of England 1660–70 and mother of his son, the Duke of Grafton (1663–1690).

She was the wife from 1659 of Roger Palmer (1634–1705), created Earl of Castlemaine 1661. She became chief mistress of Charles 1660–70, when she was created Duchess of Cleveland. Among her descendants through the Duke of Grafton is Diana, Princess of Wales.

Castlereagh /ˈkɑːsəlreɪ/ Robert Stewart, Viscount Castlereagh 1769–1822. British Tory politician. As chief secretary for Ireland 1797–1801, he suppressed the rebellion of 1798 and helped the younger Pitt secure the union of England, Scotland, and Ireland 1801. As foreign secretary 1812–22, he coordinated European opposition to Napoleon and represented Britain at the Congress of Vienna 1814–15.

Castlereagh sat in the Irish House of Commons from 1790. When his father, an Ulster landowner, was made an earl 1796, he took the courtesy title of Viscount Castlereagh. In Parliament he was secretary for war and the colonies 1805–06 and 1807–09, when he had to resign after a duel with foreign secretary George ◊Canning. Castlereagh was foreign secretary from 1812, when he devoted himself to the overthrow of Napoleon and subsequently to the Congress of Vienna and the congress system. Abroad his policy favoured the development of material liberalism, but at home he repressed the Reform movement, and popular opinion held him responsible for the Peterloo massacre of peaceful demonstrators 1819. In 1821 he succeeded his father as Marquess of Londonderry.

Castor /ˈkɑːstə(r)/ or *Alpha Geminorum* second brightest star in the constellation Gemini and the 23rd brightest star in the sky. Along with ◊Pollux, it forms a prominent pair at the eastern end of Gemini.

Castor is 45 light years from Earth, and is one of the finest ◊binary stars in the sky for small telescopes. The two main components orbit each other over a period of 467 years. A third, much fainter, star orbits the main pair over a period probably exceeding 10,000 years. Each of the three visible components is a spectroscopic binary, making Castor a sextuple star system.

Castor and Pollux/Polydeuces /ˈkɑːstə, ˌpɒlʌks, pɒlɪˈdjuːsiːz/ in Greek mythology, twin sons of Leda (by ◊Zeus), brothers of ◊Helen and ◊Clytemnestra. Protectors of mariners, they were transformed at death into the constellation Gemini.

castor-oil plant tall, tropical and subtropical shrub *Ricinus communis* of the spurge family Euphorbiaceae. The seeds, in North America called castor beans, yield the purgative castor oil and also ricin, one of the most powerful poisons known, which can be targeted to destroy cancer cells, while leaving normal cells untouched.

castration removal of the testicles. Male domestic animals may be castrated to prevent reproduction, to make them larger or more docile, or to remove a disease site.

Castration of humans was used in ancient and medieval times and occasionally later to preserve the treble voice of boy singers or, by Muslims, to provide trustworthy harem guards, called eunuchs. If done in childhood, it greatly modifies the secondary sexual characteristics: for instance, the voice may remain high, and growth of hair on the face and body may become weak or cease, owing to the removal of the hormones normally secreted by the testes.

Male domestic animals, mainly stallions and bulls, are castrated to prevent undesirable sires from reproducing, to moderate their aggressive and savage disposition and, for bulls, to improve their value as beef cattle (steers). Cockerels are castrated (capons) to improve their flavour and increase their size. The effects of castration can also be achieved by administration of hormones.

castrato in music, a high male voice of unusual brilliance and power achieved by castration before puberty. The practice was outlawed in the mid-19th century.

Castries /kæˈstriːz/ port and capital of St Lucia, on the NW coast of the island in the Caribbean; population (1988) 53,000. It produces textiles, chemicals, tobacco, and wood and rubber products.

Castro /ˈkæstrəʊ/ Cipriano 1858–1924. Venezuelan dictator 1899–1908, known as 'the Lion of the Andes'. When he refused to pay off foreign debts 1902, British, German, and Italian ships blockaded the country. He presided over a corrupt government. There were frequent rebellions during his rule, and opponents of his regime were exiled or murdered.

Castro (Ruz) /ˈkæstrəʊ ˈruːs/ Fidel 1927– . Cuban communist politician, prime minister 1959–76 and president from 1976. He led two unsuccessful coups against the right-wing Batista regime and led the revolution that overthrew the dictator 1959. From 1979 he was also president of the nonaligned movement, although promoting the line of the USSR, which subsidized his regime.

Of wealthy parentage, Castro was educated at Jesuit schools and, after studying law at the University of Havana, he gained a reputation through his work for poor clients. He opposed the Batista dictatorship, and took part in an unsuccessful attack on the army barracks at Santiago de Cuba 1953. After some time in exile in the USA and Mexico, Castro attempted a secret landing in Cuba 1956 in which all but 11 of his supporters were killed. He eventually gathered an army of over 5,000 which overthrew Batista 1959 and he became prime minister a few months later. His brother Raúl was appointed minister of armed forces.

The Castro regime introduced a centrally planned economy based on the production for export of sugar, tobacco, and nickel. Aid for development has been provided by the USSR while Cuba joined ◊Comecon 1972. By nationalizing US-owned businesses 1960 Castro gained the enmity of the USA, which came to a head in the ◊Cuban missile crisis 1962. His regime became socialist and he espoused Marxism-Leninism until, in 1974, he rejected Marx's formula 'from each according to his ability and to each according to his need' and decreed that each Cuban should 'receive according to his work'.

casuarina any tree or shrub of the genus *Casuarina*, family Casuarinaceae, with many species native to Australia and New Guinea but also found in Africa and Asia. Commonly known as she-oaks, casuarinas have taken their Latin name from the resemblance of their long, drooping branchlets to the feathers of the cassowary, whose genus is *Casuarius*.

cat small, domesticated, carnivorous mammal *Felis catus*, often kept as a pet or for catching small pests such as rodents. Found in many colour variants, it may have short, long, or no hair, but the general shape and size is constant. All cats walk on the pads of their toes, and have retractile claws. They have strong limbs, large eyes, and acute hearing. The canine teeth are long and well-developed, as are the shearing teeth in the side of the mouth.

Domestic cats have a common ancestor, the *African wild cat Felis libyca*, found across Africa and Arabia. This is similar to the *European wild cat Felis silvestris*. Domestic cats can interbreed with either of these wild relatives. Various other species of small wild cat live in all continents except Antarctica and Australia. Large cats such as the lion and tiger also belong to the cat family Felidae.

catacomb underground cemetery, such as the catacombs of the early Christians. Examples include those beneath the basilica of St Sebastian in Rome, where bodies were buried in niches in the walls of the tunnels.

Catalan language /ˈkætələn, -lən/ member of the Romance branch of the Indo-European language family, an Iberian language closely related to Provençal in France. It is spoken in Catalonia in NE Spain, the Balearic Islands, Andorra, and a corner of SW France.

Since the end of the Franco regime in Spain 1975, Catalan nationalists have vigorously promoted their regional language as being coequal in Catalonia with Castilian Spanish, and it is now accepted as an official language of the European Community. The official languages of the 1992 Olympics in Barcelona are English, French, Spanish, and Catalan.

Catalaunian Fields /ˌkætəˈlɔːniən/ plain near Troyes, France, scene of the defeat of Attila the Hun by the Romans and Goths under the Roman general Aëtius (died 454) 451.

catalepsy in medicine, an abnormal state in which the patient is apparently or actually unconscious and the muscles become rigid.

There is no response to stimuli, and the rate of heartbeat and breathing is slow. A similar condition can be drug-induced or produced by hypnosis, but catalepsy as ordinarily understood occurs spontaneously in epilepsy, schizophrenia, and other nervous disorders.

Çatal Hüyük /tʃæˈtɑːl huːˈjuːk/ Neolithic site (6000 BC) in Turkey-in-Asia, SE of Konya. It was a fortified city and had temples with wall paintings, and objects such as jewellery, obsidian, and mirrors. Finds at Jericho and Catal Hüyük together indicated much earlier development of urban life in the ancient world than was previously imagined.

Catalonia /ˌkætəˈləʊniə/ (Spanish *Cataluña*, Catalan *Catalunya*) autonomous region of NE Spain; area 31,900 sq km/12,313 sq mi; population (1986) 5,977,000. It includes Barcelona (the capital), Gerona, Lérida, and Tarragona. Industries include wool and cotton textiles; hydroelectric power is produced.

The north is mountainous, and the Ebro basin breaks through the Castellón mountains in the south. The soil is fertile, but the climate in the interior is arid. Catalonia leads Spain in industrial development. Tourist resorts have developed along the Costa Brava.

history The region has a long tradition of independence. It enjoyed autonomy 1932–39 but lost its privileges for supporting the republican cause in the ◊Spanish Civil War. Autonomy and official use of the ◊Catalan language were restored 1980.

catalpa any tree of the genus *Catalpa* belonging to the trumpet creeper Bignoniaceae family, found in North America, China, and the West Indies. The northern catalpa *C.*

speciosa of North America grows to 30 m/100 ft and has heart-shaped, deciduous leaves and tubular white flowers with purple borders.

Cataluña Spanish name for ◊Catalonia.

Catalunya Catalan name for ◊Catalonia.

catalyst substance that alters the speed of, or makes possible, a chemical or biochemical reaction but remains unchanged at the end of the reaction. ◊Enzymes are natural biochemical catalysts. In practice most catalysts are used to speed up reactions.

catalytic converter device for reducing toxic emissions from the ◊internal-combustion engine. It converts harmful exhaust products to relatively harmless ones by passing exhaust gases over a mixture of catalysts. *Oxidation catalysts* convert hydrocarbons into carbon dioxide and water; *three-way catalysts* convert oxides of nitrogen back into nitrogen.

Over the lifetime of a vehicle, a catalytic converter can reduce hydrocarbon emissions by 87%, carbon monoxide emissions by 85%, and nitrogen oxide emissions by 62%, but will cause a slight increase in the amount of carbon dioxide emitted. Catalytic converters are standard in the USA, where a 90% reduction in pollution from cars was achieved without loss of engine performance or fuel economy.

catamaran (Tamil 'tied log') twin-hulled sailing vessel, based on the aboriginal craft of South America and the Indies, made of logs lashed together, with an outrigger. A similar vessel with three hulls is known as a trimaran. Car ferries with a wave-piercing catamaran design are also in use in parts of Europe and North America. They have a pointed main hull and two outriggers and travel at a speed of 35 knots (84.5 kph/52.5 mph).

Cat and Mouse Act popular name for the *Prisoners, Temporary Discharge for Health, Act* 1913; an attempt by the UK Liberal government under Herbert Asquith to reduce embarrassment caused by the incarceration of ◊suffragettes accused of violent offences against property.

When the suffragettes embarked on hunger strikes, prison authorities introduced forced feeding, which proved humiliating and sometimes dangerous to the women. Following a public outcry, the hunger strikers were released on a licence that could be revoked without further trial. The government was accused of playing cat to suffragette mice by its adoption of powers of release and rearrest.

cataract eye disease in which the crystalline lens or its capsule becomes opaque, causing blindness. Fluid accumulates between the fibres of the lens and gives place to deposits of ◊albumin. These coalesce into rounded bodies, the lens fibres break down, and areas of the lens or the lens capsule become filled with opaque products of degeneration.

catastrophe theory mathematical theory developed by René Thom in 1972, in which he showed that the growth of an organism proceeds by a series of gradual changes that are triggered by, and in turn trigger, large-scale changes or 'catastrophic' jumps. It also has applications in engineering—for example, the gradual strain on the structure of a bridge that can eventually result in a sudden collapse—and has been extended to economic and psychological events.

catastrophism theory that the geological features of the Earth were formed by a series of sudden, violent 'catastrophes' beyond the ordinary workings of nature. The theory was largely the work of Georges ◊Cuvier. It was later replaced by the concepts of ◊uniformitarianism and ◊evolution.

Catch-22 black-humour novel by Joseph Heller, published 1961, about a US squadron that is ordered to fly an increased number of bombing missions in Italy in World War II; the crazed military justifications involved were described by the novel's phrase 'Catch-22', which has come to represent the dilemma of all false authoritarian logic.

catch crop crop that is inserted between two principal crops in a rotation in order to provide some quick livestock feed or soil improvement at a time when the land would otherwise be lying idle.

catchment area area from which water is collected by a river and its tributaries.

Cateau-Cambresis, Treaty of /kæˈtəʊ kæmˈbresɪs/ treaty that ended the dynastic wars between the Valois of France and the Habsburg Empire, 2–3 April 1559.

catechism teaching by question and answer on the Socratic method, but chiefly as a means of instructing children in the basics of the Christian creed. A person being instructed in this way in preparation for baptism or confirmation is called a *catechumen*.

A form of catechism was used for the catechumens in the early Christian church. Little books of catechism became numerous at the Reformation. Luther published simple catechisms for children and uneducated people, and a larger catechism for the use of teachers. The popular Roman Catholic catechism was that of Peter Canisius 1555; that with the widest circulation now is the 'Explanatory Catechism of Christian Doctrine'. Protestant catechisms include Calvin's Geneva Catechism 1537; that composed by Cranmer and Ridley with additions by Overall 1549–1661, incorporated in the Book of Common Prayer; the Presbyterian Catechism 1647–48; and the Evangelical Free Church Catechism 1898.

catecholamine chemical that functions as a ◊neurotransmitter or a ◊hormone. Dopamine, epinephrine (adrenaline), and norepinephrine (noradrenaline) are catecholamines.

categorical imperative technical term in ◊Kant's moral philosophy designating the supreme principle of morality for rational beings. The imperative orders us to act only in such a way that we can wish a maxim, or subjective principle, of our action to be a universal law.

category in philosophy, a fundamental concept applied to being that cannot be reduced to anything more elementary. Aristotle listed ten categories: substance, quantity, quality, relation, place, time, position, state, action, and passion.

caterpillar larval stage of a ◊butterfly or ◊moth. Wormlike in form, the body is segmented, may be hairy, and often has scent glands. The head has strong biting mandibles, silk glands, and a spinneret.

Many caterpillars resemble the plant on which they feed, dry twigs, or rolled leaves. Others are highly coloured and rely for their protection on their irritant hairs, disagreeable smell, or on their power to eject a corrosive fluid. Yet others take up a 'threat attitude' when attacked.

Caterpillars emerge from eggs that have been laid by the female insect on the food plant and feed greedily, increasing greatly in size and casting their skins several times, until the pupal stage is reached. The abdominal segments bear a varying number of 'pro-legs' as well as the six true legs on the thoracic segments.

caterpillar track endless flexible belt of metal plates on which certain vehicles such as tanks and bulldozers run, which takes the place of ordinary tyred wheels. A track-laying vehicle has a track on each side, and its engine drives small cogwheels that run along the top of the track in contact with the ground. The advantage of such tracks over wheels is that they distribute the vehicle's weight over a wider area and are thus ideal for use on soft and waterlogged as well as rough and rocky ground.

catfish fish belonging to the order Siluriformes, in which barbels (feelers) on the head are well- developed, so giving a resemblance to the whiskers of a cat. Catfishes are found worldwide, mainly but not exclusively in fresh water, and are plentiful in South America.

The E European **giant catfish** or **wels** *Silurus glanis* grows to 1.5 m/5 ft long or more. It has been introduced to several places in Britain.

Cathar /ˈkæθə/ (medieval Latin 'the pure') member of a sect in medieval Europe usually numbered among the Christian heretics. Influenced by ◊Manichaeism, they started about the 10th century in the Balkans where they were called 'Bogomils', spread to SW Europe where they were often identified with the ◊Albigenses, and by the middle of the 14th century had been destroyed or driven underground by the Inquisition.

The Cathars believed that this world is under the domination of Satan, and men and women are the terrestrial embodiment of spirits who were inspired by him to revolt and were driven out of heaven. At death, the soul will be reincarnated (whether in human or animal form) unless it has been united through the Cathar faith with Christ.

For someone who has become a Cathar, death brings release, the Beatific Vision, and immortality in Christ's presence. Baptism with the spirit—the *consolamentum*—was the central rite, believed to remedy the disaster of the Fall. The spirit received was the Paraclete, the Comforter, and it was imparted by imposition of hands. The Believers, or *Credentes*, could approach God only through the Perfect (the ordained priesthood), who were implicitly obeyed in everything, and lived lives of the strictest self-denial and chastity.

cathedral (Latin *cathedra*, 'seat' or 'throne') Christian church containing the throne of a bishop or archbishop, which is usually situated on the south side of the choir. A cathedral is governed by a dean and chapter.

Formerly, cathedrals were distinguished as either monastic or secular, the clergy of the latter not being members of a regular monastic order. Some British cathedrals, such as Lincoln and York, are referred to as 'minsters', the term originating in the name given to the bishop and cathedral clergy who were often referred to as a *monasterium*. After the dissolution of the monasteries by Henry VIII, most of the monastic churches were refounded and are called Cathedrals of the New Foundation. Cathedrals of dioceses founded since 1836 include St Albans, Southwark, Truro, Birmingham, and Liverpool. There are cathedrals in most of the chief cities of Europe; UK cathedrals include Canterbury Cathedral (spanning the Norman to Perpendicular periods), Exeter Cathedral (13th-century Gothic), and Coventry Cathedral (rebuilt after World War II, consecrated 1962).

Cather /ˈkæðə/ Willa (Sibert) 1876–1947. US novelist and short-story writer. Born in Virginia, she moved to Nebraska as a child. Her novels frequently explore life in the pioneer West, both in her own time and in past eras; for example, *O Pioneers!* 1913 and *My Antonia* 1918, and *A Lost Lady* 1923. *Death Comes for the Archbishop* 1927 is a celebration of the spiritual pioneering of the Catholic church in New Mexico. She also wrote poetry and essays on fiction.

Catherine I /ˈkæθrɪn/ 1684–1727. Empress of Russia from 1725. A Lithuanian peasant girl, born Martha Skavronsky, she married a Swedish dragoon and eventually became the mistress of Peter the Great. In 1703 she was rechristened as Katarina Alexeievna, and in 1711 the tsar divorced his wife and married Catherine 1712. She accompanied him on his campaigns, and showed tact and shrewdness. In 1724 she was proclaimed empress, and after Peter's death 1725 she ruled capably with the help of her ministers. She allied Russia with Austria and Spain in an anti-English bloc.

Catherine II *the Great* 1729–1796. Empress of Russia from 1762, and daughter of the German prince of Anhalt-Zerbst. In 1745, she married the Russian grand duke Peter. Catherine was able to dominate him; six months after he became Tsar Peter III 1762, he was murdered in a coup and Catherine ruled alone. During her reign Russia extended its boundaries to include territory from wars with the Turks 1768–72, 1787–92, and from the partitions of Poland 1772, 1793, and 1795.

Catherine's private life was notorious throughout Europe, but except for Grigory ◊Potemkin she did not permit her lovers to influence her policy.

Catherine de' Medici /deɪ ˈmedɪtʃi/ 1519–1589. French queen consort of Henry II, whom she married 1533; daughter of Lorenzo de' Medici, duke of Urbino; and mother of Francis II, Charles IX, and Henry III. At first outshone by Henry's mistress Diane de Poitiers (1490–1566), she became regent 1560–63 for Charles IX and remained in power until his death 1574.

During the religious wars of 1562–69, she first supported the Protestant ◊Huguenots against the Roman Catholic *Guises* to ensure her own position as ruler; she later opposed them, and has been traditionally implicated in the Massacre of ◊St Bartholomew 1572.

Catherine of Alexandria, St Christian martyr. According to legend she disputed with 50 scholars, refusing to give up her faith and marry Emperor Maxentius. Her emblem is a wheel, on which her persecutors tried to kill her (the wheel broke and she was beheaded). Feast day 25 Nov.

Catherine of Aragon /ˈærəgən/ 1485–1536. First queen of Henry VIII of England, 1509–33, and mother of Mary I; Henry divorced her without papal approval, thus beginning the English ◊Reformation.

Catherine had married Henry's elder brother Prince Arthur 1501 and on his death 1502 was betrothed to Henry, marrying him on his accession 1509. Of their six children, only Mary lived. Wanting a male heir, Henry sought an annulment 1526 when Catherine was too old to bear children. When the pope demanded that the case be referred to him, Henry married Anne Boleyn, afterwards receiving the desired decree of nullity from Cranmer, the archbishop of Canterbury, in 1533. The Reformation in England followed, and Catherine went into retirement until her death.

Catherine of Braganza /brəˈgænzə/ 1638–1705. Queen of Charles II of England 1662–85. The daughter of John IV of Portugal (1604–1656), she brought the Portuguese possessions of Bombay and Tangier as her dowry and introduced tea drinking and citrus fruits to England. Her childlessness and practice of her Catholic faith were unpopular, but Charles resisted pressure for divorce. She returned to Lisbon 1692, after his death.

Catherine of Siena /siˈenə/ 1347–1380. Italian mystic, born in Siena. She persuaded Pope Gregory XI to return to Rome from Avignon 1376. In 1375 she is said to have received on her body the stigmata, the impression of Jesus' wounds. Her *Dialogue* is a classic mystical work. Feast day 29 April.

Catherine of Valois /ˈvælˈwɑ/ 1401–1437. Queen of Henry V of England, whom she married 1420; the mother of Henry VI. After the death of Henry V, she secretly married Owen Tudor (c. 1400–1461) about 1425, and their son Edmund Tudor became the father of Henry VII.

Catherwood /ˈkæθəwʊd/ Frederick 1799–1854. British topographical artist and archaeological illustrator who accompanied John Lloyd ◊Stephens in his exploration of Central America 1839–40 and the Yucatán 1841–42. His engravings, published 1844, were the first accurate representation of Mayan civilization in the West.

catheter fine tube inserted into the body to introduce or remove fluids. The original catheter was the urinary one, passed by way of the urethra (the duct that leads urine away from the bladder). In today's practice, catheters can be inserted into blood vessels, either in the limbs or trunk, to provide blood samples and local pressure measurements, and to deliver drugs and/or nutrients directly into the bloodstream.

cathode in chemistry, the negative electrode of an electrolytic ◊cell, towards which positive particles (cations), usually in solution, are attracted. See ◊electrolysis.

A cathode is given its negative charge by connecting it to the negative side of an external electrical supply. This is in contrast to the negative electrode of an electrical (battery) cell, which acquires its charge in the course of a spontaneous chemical reaction taking place within the cell.

cathode in electronics, the part of an electronic device in which electrons are generated. In a thermionic valve, electrons are produced by the heating effect of an applied current; in a photoelectric cell, they are produced by the interaction of light and a semiconducting material. The cathode is kept at a negative potential relative to the device's other electrodes (anodes) in order to ensure that the liberated electrons stream away from the cathode and towards the anodes.

cathode-ray oscilloscope (CRO) instrument that measures and displays the waveform of voltages that vary over time; see ◊oscilloscope.

cathode-ray tube vacuum tube in which a beam of electrons is produced and focused onto a fluorescent screen. It is an essential component of television receivers, computer visual display units, and oscilloscopes.

Catholic church whole body of the Christian church, though usually referring to the Roman Catholic Church (see ◊Roman Catholicism).

Catholic Emancipation in British history, acts of Parliament passed 1780–1829 to relieve Roman Catholics of civil and political restrictions imposed from the time of Henry VIII and the Reformation.

Catiline /ˈkætɪlaɪn/ (Lucius Sergius Catilina) c. 108–62 BC. Roman politician. Twice failing to be elected to the consulship in 64/63 BC, he planned a military coup, but ◊Cicero exposed his conspiracy. He died at the head of the insurgents.

cation ◊ion carrying a positive charge. During electrolysis, cations in the electrolyte move to the cathode (negative electrode).

catkin in flowering plants (◊angiosperms), a pendulous inflorescence, bearing numerous small, usually unisexual flowers. The tiny flowers are stalkless and the petals and sepals are usually absent or much reduced in size. Many types of trees bear catkins, including willows, poplars, and birches. Most plants with catkins are wind-pollinated, so the male catkins produce large quantities of pollen. Some ◊gymnosperms also have catkin-like structures that produce pollen, for example, the swamp cypress *Taxodium*.

Catlin /ˈkætlɪn/ George 1796–1872. US painter and explorer. From the 1830s he made a series of visits to the Great Plains, painting landscapes and scenes of American Indian life.

He produced an exhibition of over 500 paintings with which he toured America and Europe. His style is factual, with close attention to detail. Many of his pictures are in the Smithsonian Institution, Washington DC.

Cato /ˈkeɪtəʊ/ Marcus Porcius 234–149 BC. Roman politician. Appointed censor (senior magistrate) in 184 BC, he excluded from the Senate those who did not meet his high standards. He was so impressed by the power of ◊Carthage, on a visit in 157, that he ended every speech by saying: 'Carthage must be destroyed.' His farming manual is the earliest surviving work in Latin prose.

Cato Street Conspiracy in British history, unsuccessful plot hatched in Cato Street, London, to murder the Tory foreign secretary Robert Castlereagh and all his ministers on 20 Feb 1820. The leader, the Radical Arthur Thistlewood (1770–1820), who intended to set up a provisional government, was hanged with four others.

CAT scan or *CT scan* (acronym for *c*omputerized *a*xial *t*omography) in medicine, a sophisticated method of X-ray imaging. Quick and noninvasive, CAT scanning is an aid to diagnosis, helping to pinpoint problem areas without the need for exploratory surgery.

The CAT scanner passes a narrow fan of X-rays through successive slices of the suspect body part. These slices are picked up by crystal detectors in a scintillator and converted electronically into cross-sectional images displayed on a viewing screen. Gradually, using views taken from various angles, a three-dimensional picture of the organ or tissue can be built up and suspect irregularities analysed.

cat's eyes reflective studs used to mark the limits of traffic lanes, invented by Percy Shaw (1890–1976) in England, as a road safety device in 1934.

A cat's eye stud has two pairs of reflective prisms (the eyes) set in a rubber pad, which reflect the light of a vehicle's headlamps back to the driver. When a vehicle goes over a stud, it moves down inside an outer rubber case; the surfaces of the prisms brush against the rubber and are thereby cleaned.

Catskills /ˈkætskɪlz/ US mountain range, mainly in SE New York State; the highest point is Slide Mountain, 1,281 m/4,204 ft.

cattle any large, ruminant, even-toed, hoofed mammal of the genus *Bos*, family Bovidae, including wild species such as yak, gaur, gayal, banteng, and kouprey, as well as domestic breeds. Asiatic water buffalos *Bubalus*, African buffalos *Syncerus*, and American bison *Bison* are not considered true cattle. Cattle were first domesticated in the Middle East during the Neolithic period, about 8000 BC. They were brought north into Europe by migrating Neolithic farmers.

Fermentation in the four-chambered stomach allows cattle to make good use of the grass that is normally the main part of the diet. There are two main types of domesticated cattle: the European breeds, variants of *Bos taurus* descended from the ◊aurochs, and the various breeds of *zebu Bos indicus*, the humped cattle of India, which are useful in the tropics for their ability to withstand the heat and diseases to which European breeds succumb. Cattle are bred to achieve maximum yields of meat (beef cattle) or milk (dairy cattle). The old established beef breeds are mostly British in origin. The Hereford, for example, is the premier English breed, ideally suited to rich lowland pastures but it will also thrive on poorer land such as that found in the US Midwest and the Argentine pampas. Of the Scottish beef breeds, the Aberdeen Angus, a black and hornless variety, produces high-quality meat through intensive feeding methods. Other breeds include the Devon, a hardy early-maturing type, and the Beef Shorthorn, now less important than formerly, but still valued for an ability to produce good calves when crossed with less promising cattle. In recent years, more interest has been shown in other European breeds, their tendency to have less fat being more suited to modern tastes. Examples include the Charolais and the Limousin from central France, and the Simmental, originally from Switzerland. In the USA, four varieties of zebus, called Brahmans, have been introduced. They interbreed with *B. taurus* varieties and produce valuable hybrids that resist heat, ticks, and insects. For dairying purposes, a breed raised in many countries is variously known as the Friesian, Holstein, or Black and White. It can give enormous milk yields, up to 13,000 l/3,450 gal in a single lactation, and will produce calves ideally suited for intensive beef production. Other dairying types include the Jersey and Guernsey, whose milk has a high butterfat content, and the Ayrshire, a smaller breed capable of staying outside all year.

Catullus /kəˈtʌləs/ Gaius Valerius *c.* 84–54 BC. Roman lyric poet, born in Verona of a well-to-do family. He moved in the literary and political society of Rome and wrote lyrics describing his unhappy love affair with Clodia, probably the wife of the consul Metellus, calling her Lesbia. His longer poems include two wedding songs. Many of his poems are short verses to his friends.

Caucasoid /ˈkɔːkəsɔɪd/ or *Caucasian* former racial classification used for any of the light-skinned peoples; so named because the German anthropologist J F Blumenbach (1752–1840) theorized that they originated in the Caucasus.

Caucasus /ˈkɔːkəsəs/ series of mountain ranges between the Caspian and Black Seas, in Russia, Georgia, Armenia, and Azerbaijan; 1,200 km/750 mi long. The highest is Elbruz, 5,633 m/18,480 ft.

Cauchy /ˈkəʊʃi/ Augustin Louis 1789–1857. French mathematician who employed rigorous methods of analysis. His prolific output included work on complex functions, determinants, and probability, and on the convergence of infinite series. In calculus, he refined the concepts of the limit and the definite integral.

caucus in the USA, a closed meeting of regular party members; for example, to choose a candidate for office. The term was originally used in the 18th century in Boston, Massachusetts.

In the UK, it was first applied to the organization introduced by the Liberal politician Joseph Chamberlain in 1878 and is generally used to mean a local party committee.

cauda tail, or taillike appendage; part of the *cauda equina*, a bundle of nerves at the bottom of the spinal cord in vertebrates.

cauliflower variety of ◊cabbage *Brassica oleracea*, distinguished by its large, flattened head of fleshy, aborted flowers. It is similar to broccoli but less hardy.

causality in philosophy, a consideration of the connection between cause and effect, usually referred to as the 'causal relationship'. If an event is assumed to have a cause, two important questions arise: what is the relationship between cause and effect, and must it follow that every event is caused? The Scottish philosopher David Hume considered these questions to be, in principle, unanswerable.

Causley /ˈkɔːzli/ Charles (Stanley) 1917– . English poet. He published his first volume *Hands to Dance* in 1951. Later volumes include *Johnny Alleluia* 1961, *Underneath the Water* 1968, and *Figgie Hobbin* 1970. His work is characterized by simple diction and rhythms, reflecting the ballad tradition, and religious imagery.

caustic soda former name for ◊sodium hydroxide (NaOH).

cauterization in medicine, the use of special instruments to burn or fuse small areas of body tissue to destroy dead cells, prevent the spread of infection, or seal tiny blood vessels to minimize blood loss during surgery.

Cauthen /ˈkɔːθən/ Steve 1960– . US jockey. He rode Affirmed to the US Triple Crown in 1978 at the age of 18 and won 487 races in 1977.

He has ridden in England since 1979 and has twice won the Derby, on Slip Anchor in 1985 and on Reference Point in 1987. He was UK champion jockey in 1984, 1985, and 1987.

caution legal term for a warning given by police questioning a suspect, which in the UK must be couched in the following terms: 'You do not have to say anything unless you wish to do so, but what you say may be given in evidence.' Persons not under arrest must also be told that they do not have to remain at the police station or with the police officer but that if they do, they may obtain legal advice if they wish. A suspect should be cautioned again after a break in questioning and upon arrest.

Cautions are given in pursuance of the general principle of English law that a person need not provide any information that might tend to incriminate them, and that no adverse inferences from this silence may be drawn at any criminal trial. However, refusal to provide a name and address when charged with an offence may result in detention.

Cauvery /ˈkɔːvəri/ or **Kaveri** river of S India, rising in the W Ghats and flowing 765 km/475 mi SE to meet the Bay of Bengal in a wide delta. It has been a major source of hydroelectric power since 1902 when India's first hydropower plant was built on the river.

Cavaco Silva /kəˈvækəʊ ˈsɪlvə/ Anibal 1939– . Portuguese politician, finance minister 1980–81, and prime minister and Social Democratic Party (PSD) leader from 1985. Under his leadership Portugal joined the European Community 1985 and the Western European Union 1988.

Cavaco Silva studied economics in Britain and the USA, and was a university teacher and research director in the Bank of Portugal. In 1978, with the return of constitutional government, he entered politics. His first government fell in 1987, but an election later that year gave him Portugal's first absolute majority since democracy was restored.

cavalier horseman of noble birth, but mainly used to describe a male supporter of Charles I in the English Civil War, typically with courtly dress and long hair (as distinct from a Roundhead); also a supporter of Charles II after the Restoration.

Cavalier poets poets of Charles I's court, including Thomas Carew, Robert Herrick, Richard Lovelace, and John Suckling. They wrote witty, light-hearted love lyrics.

Cavan /ˈkævən/ agricultural county of the Republic of Ireland, in the province of Ulster; area 1,890 sq km/730 sq mi; population (1986) 54,000.

The river Erne divides it into a narrow, mostly low-lying peninsula, 30 km/20 mi long, between Leitrim and Fermanagh, and an eastern section of wild and bare hill country. The soil is generally poor and the climate moist and cold. The chief towns are Cavan, the capital, population about 3,000; Kilmore, seat of Roman Catholic and Protestant bishoprics; and Virginia.

cave roofed-over cavity in the Earth's crust usually produced by the action of underground water or by waves on a seacoast. Caves of the former type commonly occur in areas underlain by limestone, such as Kentucky and many Balkan regions, where the rocks are soluble in water. A **pothole** is a vertical hole in rock caused by water descending a crack and is thus open to the sky.

Cave animals often show loss of pigmentation or sight, and under isolation, specialized species may develop. The scientific study of caves is called *speleology*.

Celebrated caves include the Mammoth Cave in Kentucky, 6.4 km/4 mi long and 38 m/125 ft high; the Caverns of Adelsberg (Postumia) near Trieste, Italy, which extend for many miles; Carlsbad Cave, New Mexico, the largest in the USA; the Cheddar caves, England; Fingal's Cave, Scotland, which has a range of basalt columns; and Peak Cavern, England.

Cave /keɪv/ Edward 1691–1754. British printer and founder, under the pseudonym Sylvanus Urban, of *The Gentleman's Magazine* 1731–1914, the first periodical to be called a magazine. Samuel ◊Johnson was a contributor 1738–44.

caveat emptor (Latin 'let the buyer beware') dictum that professes the buyer is responsible for checking the quality of non-warrantied goods purchased.

cavefish cave-dwelling fish, which may belong to one of several quite unrelated groups, independently adapted to life in underground waters. Cavefish have in common a tendency to blindness and atrophy of the eye, enhanced touch-sensitive organs in the skin, and loss of pigment.

The *Kentucky blindfish Amblyopsis spelaea*, which lives underground in limestone caves, has eyes which are vestigial and beneath the skin, and a colourless body. The Mexican *cave characin* is a blind, colourless form of *Astyanax fasciatus* found in surface rivers of Mexico.

Cavell /ˈkævəl/ Edith Louisa 1865–1915. British matron of a Red Cross hospital in Brussels, Belgium, in World War I, who helped Allied soldiers escape to the Dutch frontier. She was court-martialled by the Germans and condemned to death.

Cavendish /ˈkævəndɪʃ/ Frederick Charles, Lord Cavendish 1836–1882. British administrator, second son of the 7th Duke of Devonshire. He was appointed chief secretary to the lord lieutenant of Ireland in 1882.

On the evening of his arrival in Dublin he was murdered in Phoenix Park with Thomas Burke, the permanent Irish undersecretary, by members of the Irish Invincibles, a group of Irish Fenian extremists founded 1881.

Cavendish /ˈkævəndɪʃ/ Henry 1731–1810. English physicist. He discovered hydrogen (which he called 'inflammable air') 1766, and determined the compositions of water and of nitric acid. The ◊Cavendish experiment enabled him to discover the mass and density of the Earth.

Cavendish Spencer see ◊Hartington, Spencer Compton Cavendish, British politician.

Cavendish /ˈkævəndɪʃ/ Thomas 1555–1592. English navigator, and commander of the third circumnavigation of the world. He sailed in July 1586, touched Brazil, sailed down the coast to Patagonia, passed through the Straits of Magellan, and returned to Britain via the Philippines, the Cape of Good Hope, and St Helena, reaching Plymouth after two years and 50 days.

Cavendish experiment measurement of the gravitational attraction between lead and gold spheres, which enabled Henry ◊Cavendish to calculate a mean value for the mass and density of Earth, using Newton's law of universal gravitation.

caviar salted roe (eggs) of sturgeon, salmon and other fishes. Caviar is prepared by beating and straining the egg sacs until the eggs are free from fats and then adding salt. Russia and Iran are the main exporters of the most prized variety of caviar, derived from

Caspian Sea sturgeon. Iceland produces various high-quality, lower-priced caviars.

cavitation formation of partial vacuums in fluids at high velocities, produced by propellers or other machine parts in hydraulic engines, in accordance with ◊Bernoulli's principle. When these vacuums collapse, pitting, vibration, and noise can occur in the metal parts in contact with the fluids.

Cavite /kəˈviti/ town and port of the Philippine Republic; 13 km/8 mi S of Manila; population (1980) 88,000. It is the capital of Cavite province, Luzon. It was in Japanese hands Dec 1941–Feb 1945. After the Philippines achieved independence in 1946, the US Seventh Fleet continued to use the naval base.

Cavour /kəˈvuə/ Camillo Benso di, Count 1810–1861. Italian nationalist politician. Editor of *Il ◊Risorgimento* from 1847. As prime minister of Piedmont 1852–59 and 1860–61, he enlisted the support of Britain and France for the concept of a united Italy achieved in 1861; after expelling the Austrians 1859, he assisted Garibaldi in liberating southern Italy 1860.

As prime minister, Cavour sought to secure French and British sympathy for the cause of Italian unity by sending Piedmontese troops to fight in the Crimean War. In 1858 he had a secret meeting with Napoleon III at Plombières, where they planned the war of 1859 against Austria, which resulted in the union of Lombardy with Piedmont. Then the central Italian states joined the kingdom of Italy, although Savoy and Nice were to be ceded to France. With Cavour's approval Garibaldi overthrew the Neapolitan monarchy, but Cavour occupied part of the Papal States which, with Naples and Sicily, were annexed to Italy, to prevent Garibaldi from marching on Rome.

cavy short-tailed South American rodent, family Caviidae, of which the *guinea-pig Cavia porcellus* is an example. Wild cavies are greyish or brownish with rather coarse hair. They live in small groups in burrows, and have been kept for food since ancient times.

Cawnpore /kɔːnˈpɔː/ former spelling of ◊Kanpur, Indian city.

Caxton /ˈkækstən/ William *c.* 1422–1491. The first English printer. He learned the art of printing in Cologne, Germany, 1471 and set up a press in Belgium where he produced the first book printed in English, his own version of a French romance, *Recuyell of the Historyes of Troye* 1474. Returning to England in 1476, he established himself in London, where he produced the first book printed in England, *Dictes or Sayengis of the Philosophres* 1477.

The books from Caxton's press in Westminster included editions of the poets Chaucer, Gower, and John Lydgate (c. 1370–1449). He translated many texts from French and Latin and revised some English ones, such as Malory's *Morte d'Arthur*. Altogether he printed about 100 books.

Cayenne /keɪen/ capital and chief port of French Guiana, on Cayenne island at the mouth of the river Cayenne; population (1982) 38,135.

It was founded in 1634, and used as a penal settlement from 1854 to 1946.

cayenne pepper condiment derived from the dried fruits of various species of ◊capsicum (especially *Capsicum frutescens*), a tropical American genus of plants of the family Solanaceae. It is wholly distinct in its origin from black or white pepper, which is derived from an East Indian plant (*Piper nigrum*).

Cayley /keɪli/ Arthur 1821–1895. British mathematician who developed matrix algebra, used by ◊Heisenberg in his elucidation of quantum mechanics.

Cayley /keɪli/ George 1773–1857. British aviation pioneer, inventor of the first piloted glider in 1853, and the caterpillar tractor.

cayman or *caiman*, large reptile, resembling the ◊crocodile.

Cayman Islands /keɪmən/ British island group in the West Indies
area 260 sq km/100 sq mi
features comprises three low-lying islands: Grand Cayman, Cayman Brac, and Little Cayman
exports seawhip coral, a source of ◊prostaglandins; shrimps; honey; jewellery
currency CI dollar
population (1988) 22,000
language English
government governor, executive council, and legislative assembly
history settled by military deserters in the 17th century, the islands became a pirate lair in the 18th century. Administered with Jamaica until 1962, when the Caymans became a separate colony, they are now a tourist resort, international financial centre, and tax haven.

CBI abbreviation for ◊*Confederation of British Industry*.

cc symbol for *cubic centimetre*; abbreviation for *carbon copy/copies*.

CCASG abbreviation of ◊*Cooperative Council for the Arab States of the Gulf*.

CD-ROM in computing, a storage device, consisting of a metal disc with a plastic coating, on which information is etched in the form of microscopic pits. A CD-ROM typically holds about 550 ◊megabytes of data. CD-ROMs cannot have information written on to them by the computer, but must be manufactured from a master.

They are used for distributing large quantities of text, such as dictionaries, encyclopedias, and technical manuals. The technology is similar to that of the audio ◊compact disc.

CDU abbreviation for the centre-right *Christian Democratic Union* in the Federal Republic of Germany.

CE abbreviation for *Common Era* (see ◊calendar); *Church of England* (often *C of E*).

Ceauşescu /tʃaʊˈʃesku/ Nicolae 1918–1989. Romanian politician, leader of the Romanian Communist Party (RCP), in power 1965–89. He pursued a policy line independent of and critical of the USSR. He appointed family members, including his wife *Elena Ceauşescu*, to senior state and party posts, and governed in an increasingly repressive manner, zealously implementing schemes that impoverished the nation. The Ceauşescus were overthrown in a bloody revolutionary coup Dec 1989 and executed.

Ceauşescu joined the underground RCP in 1933 and was imprisoned for antifascist activities 1936–38 and 1940–44. After World War II he was elected to the Grand National Assembly and was soon given ministerial posts. He was inducted into the party secretariat and Politburo in 1954–55. In 1965 Ceauşescu became leader of the RCP and from 1967 chair of the state council. He was elected president in 1974. As revolutionary changes rocked E Europe 1989, protests in Romania escalated until the Ceauşescu regime was toppled. Following his execution, the full extent of his repressive rule and personal extravagance became public.

In June 1991, Ceauşescu's son, Nicu, was sentenced to 16 years' imprisonment, followed by eight years' loss of civil liberties, after being convicted of genocide. The charge arose from his ordering of troops to fire on demonstrators during the Dec 1989 riots which led to his father's overthrow.

Cebu /seɪˈbuː/ chief city and port of the island of Cebu in the Philippines; population (1980) 490,000; area of the island 5,086 sq km/1,964 sq mi; population (1980) 1,234,000. The oldest city of the Philippines, Cebu was founded as San Miguel in 1565 and became the capital of the Spanish Philippines.

Cecil /ˈsesəl/ Henry Richard Amherst 1943– . Scottish-born racehorse trainer with stables at Warren Place, Newmarket. He was the first trainer to win over £1 million in a season (1985). He trained Slip Anchor and Reference Point to win the Epsom Derby.

Cecil /ˈsɪsəl/ Robert, 1st Earl of Salisbury 1563–1612. Secretary of state to Elizabeth I of England, succeeding his father, Lord Burghley; he was afterwards chief minister to James I, who created him Earl of Salisbury 1605.

Cecilia, St /səˈsiːliə/ Christian patron saint of music, martyred in Rome in the 2nd or 3rd century, who is said to have sung hymns while undergoing torture. Feast day 22 Nov.

CEDA (acronym for Confederación Español de Derechas Autónomas) federation of right-wing parties under the leadership of José Maria Gil Robles, founded during the Second Spanish Republic 1933 to provide a right-wing coalition in the Spanish Cortes. Supporting the Catholic and monarchist causes, the federation was uncommitted as to the form of government.

Cedar The true cedars are evergreen conifers growing from the Mediterranean to the Himalayas.

cedar any of an Old World genus *Cedrus* of coniferous trees of the pine family Pinaceae. The *cedar of Lebanon C. libani* grows to great heights and age in the mountains of Syria and Asia Minor. Of the historic forests on Mount Lebanon itself, only a few stands of trees remain.

The Australian ◊red cedar *Toona australis* is a non-coniferous tree. Together with the *Himalayan cedar C. deodara* and the *Atlas cedar C. atlantica*, it has been introduced into England.

Cedar Rapids /ˈsiːdə ˈræpɪdʒ/ town in E Iowa, USA; population (1980) 110,243. Communications equipment is manufactured here.

Ceefax /ˈsiːfæks/ ('see facts') one of Britain's two ◊teletext systems (the other is Oracle), or 'magazines of the air', developed by the BBC and first broadcast in 1973.

CEGB abbreviation for the former (until 1990) UK *Central Electricity Generating Board*.

Cela /ˈθelə/ Camilo José 1916– . Spanish novelist. Among his novels, characterized by their violence and brutal realism, are *La familia de Pascual Duarte/The Family of Pascal Duarte* 1942, and *La colmena/The Hive* 1951. He was awarded the Nobel Prize for Literature 1989.

celandine either of two plants belonging to different families, and resembling each other only in their bright yellow flowers. The *greater celandine Chelidonium majus* belongs to the poppy family, and is common in hedgerows. The *lesser celandine Ranunculus ficaria* is a member of the buttercup family, and is a familiar wayside and meadow plant in Europe.

Celebes /səˈliːbɪz/ English name for ◊Sulawesi, island of Indonesia.

celeriac variety of garden celery *Apium graveolens* var. *rapaceum* of the carrot family Umbelliferae, with an edible, turniplike root and small, bitter stems.

celery Old World plant *Apium graveolens* of the carrot family Umbelliferae. It grows wild in ditches and salt marshes and has a coarse texture and acrid taste. Cultivated varieties of celery are grown under cover to make them less bitter.

celesta keyboard glockenspiel producing sounds of disembodied purity. It was invented by Auguste Mustel 1886 and first used to effect by Tchaikovsky in *Nutcracker* ballet music.

celestial mechanics the branch of astronomy that deals with the calculation of the orbits of celestial bodies, their gravitational attractions (such as those that produce the Earth's tides), and also the orbits of artificial satellites and space probes. It is based on the laws of motion and gravity laid down by ◊Newton.

Celestial Police group of astronomers in Germany 1800–15, who set out to discover a supposed missing planet thought to be orbiting the Sun between Mars and Jupiter, a region now known to be occupied by types of ◊asteroid. Although they did not discover the first asteroid (found 1801), they discovered the second, Pallas (1802), third, Juno (1804), and fourth, Vesta (1807).

celestial sphere imaginary sphere surrounding the Earth, on which the celestial bodies seem to lie. The positions of bodies such as stars, planets, and galaxies are specified by their coordinates on the celestial sphere. The equivalents of latitude and longitude on the celestial sphere are called ◊declination and ◊right ascension (which is measured in hours from 0 to 24). The *celestial poles* lie directly above the Earth's poles, and the *celestial equator* lies over the Earth's equator. The celestial sphere appears to rotate once around the Earth each day, actually a result of the rotation of the Earth on its axis.

celestine or *celestite* mineral consisting of strontium sulphate, $SrSO_4$, occurring as white or light blue crystals. It is the principal source of strontium. Celestine is found in small quantities in Germany, Italy, and the USA. In the UK it is found in Somerset.

celibacy way of life involving voluntary abstinence from sexual intercourse. In some religions, such as Christianity and Buddhism, celibacy is a requirement for certain religious roles, such as the priesthood or a monastic life. Other religions, including Judaism, strongly discourage celibacy.

Céline /se'li:n/ Louis Ferdinand. Pen name of Louis Destouches 1884–1961. French novelist whose writings (the first of which was *Voyage au bout de la nuit/Journey to the End of the Night* 1932) aroused controversy over their cynicism and misanthropy.

cell in biology, a discrete, membrane-bound portion of living matter, the smallest unit capable of an independent existence. All living organisms consist of one or more cells, with the exception of ◊viruses. Bacteria, protozoa, and many other microorganisms consist of single cells, whereas a human is made up of billions of cells. Essential features of a cell are the membrane, which encloses it and restricts the flow of substances in and out; the jellylike material within, often known as ◊protoplasm; the ◊ribosomes, which carry out protein synthesis; and the ◊DNA, which forms the hereditary material.

cell, electrical or *voltaic cell* or *galvanic cell* device in which chemical energy is converted into electrical energy; the popular name is 'battery', but this actually refers to a collection of cells in one unit.

Each cell contains two conducting ◊electrodes immersed in an ◊electrolyte, in a container. A spontaneous chemical reaction within the cell generates a negative charge (excess of electrons) on one electrode, and a positive charge (deficiency of electrons) on the other. The accumulation of these equal but opposite charges prevents the reaction from continuing unless an outer connection (external circuit) is made between the electrodes allowing the charges to dissipate. When this occurs, electrons escape from the cell's negative terminal and are replaced at the positive, causing a current to flow.

The reactive chemicals of a *primary cell* cannot be replenished, and so, after prolonged use, the cell will become flat (cease to supply current). *Secondary cells*, or accumulators, are rechargeable: their chemical reactions can be reversed and the original condition restored by applying an electric current. It is dangerous to attempt to recharge a primary cell.

The first cell was made by Alessandro Volta in 1800.

cell, electrolytic device to which electrical energy is applied in order to bring about a chemical reaction; see ◊electrolysis.

Cellini /tʃe'li:ni/ Benvenuto 1500–1571. Italian sculptor and goldsmith working in the Mannerist style; author of an arrogant autobiography (begun 1558). Among his works are a graceful bronze *Perseus* 1545–54 (Loggia dei Lanzi, Florence) and a gold salt cellar made for Francis I of France 1540–43 (Kunsthistorisches Museum, Vienna), topped by nude reclining figures.

cell membrane or *plasma membrane* thin layer of protein and fat surrounding cells that controls substances passing between the cytoplasm and the intercellular space. The membrane is semipermeable, allowing some substances to pass through and some not. Generally, small molecules such as water, glucose, and amino acids can penetrate the membrane, while large molecules such as starch cannot.

Membranes also play a part in ⟡active transport, hormonal response, and cell metabolism.

cello abbreviation for *violoncello*, a member of the violin family, and fourth member of a string quartet. The cello has been much in demand as a solo instrument because of its exeptional range and brilliance of tone, and its repertoire extends from Bach to Beethoven, Dvořák, and Elgar.

cellophane transparent wrapping film made from wood ⟡cellulose, widely used for packaging, first produced by Swiss chemist Jacques Edwin Brandenberger in 1908.

cellphone telephone based on a ⟡cellular radio network.

cell sap dilute fluid found in the large central vacuole of many plant cells. It is made up of water, amino acids, glucose, and salts. The sap has many functions, including storage of useful materials, and provides mechanical support for non-woody plants.

cellular radio or *cellphone* mobile radio telephone, one of a network connected to the telephone system by a computer-controlled communication system. Service areas are divided into small 'cells', about 5 km/3 mi across, each with a separate low-power transmitter.

The cellular system allows the use of the same set of frequencies with the minimum risk of interference. Nevertheless, in crowded city areas, cells can become overloaded. This has led to a move away from analogue transmissions to digital methods that allow more calls to be made within a limited frequency range.

cellulite /ˈseljulaɪt/ fatty compound alleged by some dietitians to be produced in the body by liver disorder and to cause lumpy deposits on the hips and thighs. Medical opinion generally denies its existence, attributing the lumpy appearance to a type of subcutaneous fat deposit.

celluloid transparent or translucent, highly inflammable, plastic material (a ⟡thermoplastic) made from cellulose nitrate and camphor. It was once used for toilet articles, novelties, and photographic film, but has now been replaced by the non-flammable substance ⟡cellulose acetate.

cellulose complex ⟡carbohydrate composed of long chains of glucose units. It is the principal constituent of the cell wall of higher plants, and a vital ingredient in the diet of many ⟡herbivores. Molecules of cellulose are organized into long, unbranched microfibrils that give support to the cell wall. No mammal produces the enzyme (cellulase) necessary for digesting cellulose; mammals such as rabbits and cows are only able to digest grass because the bacteria present in their gut manufacture the appropriate enzyme.

Cellulose is the most abundant substance found in the plant kingdom. It has numerous uses in industry: in rope-making; as a source of textiles (linen, cotton, viscose, and acetate) and plastics (cellophane and celluloid); in the manufacture of nondrip paint; and in such foods as whipped dessert toppings.

cellulose acetate or *cellulose ethanoate* chemical (an ⟡ester) made by the action of acetic acid (ethanoic acid) on cellulose. It is used in making transparent film, especially photographic film; unlike its predecessor, celluloid, it is not flammable.

cellulose nitrate or *nitrocellulose* series of esters of cellulose with up to three nitrate (NO_3) groups per monosaccharide unit. It is made by the action of concentrated nitric acid on cellulose (for example, cotton waste) in the presence of concentrated sulphuric acid. Fully nitrated cellulose (gun cotton) is explosive, but esters with fewer nitrate groups were once used in making lacquers, rayon, and plastics, such as coloured and photographic film, until replaced by the non-flammable cellulose acetate. ⟡Celluloid is a form of cellulose nitrate.

cell wall in plants, the tough outer surface of the cell. It is constructed from a mesh of ⟡cellulose and is very strong and relatively inelastic. Most living cells are turgid (swollen with water; see ⟡turgor) and develop an internal hydrostatic pressure (wall pressure) that acts against the cellulose wall. The result of this turgor pressure is to give the cell, and therefore the plant, rigidity. Plants that are not woody are particularly reliant on this form of support.

The cellulose in cell walls plays a vital role in global nutrition. No vertebrate is able to produce cellulase, the enzyme necessary for the breakdown of cellulose into sugar. Yet most mammalian herbivores rely on cellulose, using secretions from microorganisms living in the gut to break it down. Humans cannot digest the cellulose of the cell walls; they possess neither the correct gut microorganisms nor the necessary grinding teeth. However, cellulose still forms a necessary part of the human diet as ◊fibre (roughage).

Celsius /'selsiəs/ temperature scale in which one division or degree is taken as one hundredth part of the interval between the freezing point (0˚C) and the boiling point (100˚C) of water at standard atmospheric pressure.

The degree centigrade (˚C) was officially renamed Celsius in 1948 to avoid confusion with the angular measure known as the centigrade (one hundredth of a grade). The Celsius scale is named after the Swedish astronomer Anders Celsius (1701–1744), who devised it in 1742 but in reverse (freezing point was 100˚; boiling point 0˚).

Celt /kelt/ (Greek *Keltoi*) member of an Indo-European people of alpine Europe and Iberia whose first known territory was in central Europe about 1200 BC, in the basin of the upper Danube, the Alps, and parts of France and S Germany. In the 6th century they spread into Spain and Portugal. Over the next 300 years, they also spread into the British Isles (see ◊Britain, ancient), N Italy (sacking Rome 390 BC), Greece, the Balkans, and parts of Asia Minor, although they never established a united empire. In the 1st century BC they were defeated by the Roman Empire and by Germanic tribes and confined largely to Britain, Ireland, and N France.

Between the Bronze and Iron Ages, in the 9th–5th centuries BC, they developed a transitional culture (named the *Hallstatt* culture after its archaeological site SW of Salzburg). They farmed, raised cattle, and were pioneers of ironworking, reaching their peak in the period from the 5th century to the Roman conquest (the *La Tène* culture). Celtic languages survive in Ireland, Wales, Scotland, the Isle of Man, and Brittany, and have been revived in Cornwall.

Celtic art style of art that originated about 500 BC, probably on the Rhine, and spread westwards to Gaul and the British Isles and southwards to Italy and Turkey. Celtic manuscript illumination and sculpture from Ireland and Anglo-Saxon Britain of the 6th–8th centuries has intricate spiral and geometric ornament, as in *The Book of Kells*

(Trinity College, Dublin) and the *Lindisfarne Gospels* (British Museum, London).

Metalwork using curving incised lines and inlays of coloured enamel and coral survived at La Tène, a site at Lake Neuchâtel, Switzerland.

Celtic languages branch of the Indo-European family, divided into two groups: the *Brythonic* or *P-Celtic* (Welsh, Cornish, Breton, and Gaulish) and the *Goidelic* or *Q-Celtic* (Irish, Scottish, and Manx Gaelic). Celtic languages once stretched from the Black Sea to Britain, but have been in decline for centuries, limited to the so-called 'Celtic Fringe' of western Europe.

As their names suggest, a major distinction between the two groups is that where Brythonic has p (as in Old Welsh *map*, 'son') and Goidelic has a q sound (as in Gaelic *mac*, 'son'). Gaulish is the long-extinct language of ancient Gaul. Cornish died out as a natural language in the late 18th century and Manx in 1974. All surviving Celtic languages have experienced official neglect in recent centuries and have suffered from emigration; currently, however, governments are more inclined than in the past to encourage their use.

Celtic Sea /'keltɪk/ name commonly used by workers in the oil industry for the sea area bounded by Wales, Ireland, and SW England, to avoid nationalist significance. It is separated from the Irish Sea by St George's Channel.

cement any bonding agent used to unite particles in a single mass or to cause one surface to adhere to another. *Portland cement* is a powder obtained from burning together a mixture of lime (or chalk) and clay, and when mixed with water and sand or gravel, turns into mortar or concrete. In geology, a chemically precipitated material such as carbonate that occupies the interstices of clastic rocks is called cement.

cenotaph (Greek 'empty tomb') monument to commemorate a person or persons not actually buried at the site, as in the Whitehall Cenotaph, London, designed by Edwin Lutyens to commemorate the dead of both world wars.

Cenozoic /ˌsiːnəʊ'zəʊɪk/ or *Caenozoic* era of geological time that began 65 million years ago and is still in process. It is divided into the Tertiary and Quaternary periods.

The Cenozoic marks the emergence of mammals as a dominant group, including humans, and the formation of the mountain chains of the Himalayas and the Alps.

censor in ancient Rome, either of two senior magistrates, high officials elected every five years to hold office for 18 months. Their responsibilities included public morality, a census of the citizens, and a revision of the Senatorial list.

censorship the suppression by authority of material considered immoral, heretical, subversive, libellous, damaging to state security, or otherwise offensive. It is generally more stringent under totalitarian or strongly religious regimes and in wartime.

The British government uses the ◊D-notice and the ◊Official Secrets Act to protect itself. Laws relating to obscenity, libel, and blasphemy act as a form of censorship. The media exercise a degree of self-censorship; for example, in the British Board of Film Classification, run by the film industry. There is a similar body, popularly called the Hays Office (after its first president, 1922–45, Will H Hays), in the USA. During the Gulf War 1991, access to the theatre of war was controlled by the US military: only certain reporters were allowed in and their movements were restricted.

census official count of the population of a country, originally for military call-up and taxation, later for assessment of social trends as other information regarding age, sex, and occupation of each individual was included. They may become unnecessary as computerized databanks are developed.

The first US census was taken in 1790 and the first in Britain in 1801.

centaur in Greek mythology, a creature half-human and half-horse. Centaurs were supposed to live in Thessaly, and be wild and lawless; the mentor of Heracles, Chiron, was an exception.

The earliest representations of centaurs (c. 1800–1000 BC) were excavated near Famagusta, Cyprus, in 1962, and are two-headed. Some female representations also exist.

Centaurus /enˈtɔːrəs/ large bright constellation of the southern hemisphere, represented as a centaur. It contains the closest star to the Sun, Proxima Centauri. Omega Centauri, the largest and brightest globular cluster of stars in the sky, is 16,000 light years away. Centaurus A, a peculiar galaxy 15 million light years away, is a strong source of radio waves and X-rays.

centigrade common name for the ◊Celsius temperature scale.

centipede jointed-legged animal of the group Chilopoda, members of which have a distinct head and a single pair of long antennae. Their bodies are composed of segments (which may number nearly 200), each of similar form and bearing a single pair of legs. Most are small, but the tropical *Scolopendra gigantea* may reach 30 cm/1 ft in length. *Millipedes*, class Diplopoda, have fewer segments (up to 100), but have two pairs of legs on each.

Nocturnal, frequently blind, and all carnivorous, centipedes live in moist, dark places, and protect themselves by a poisonous secretion. They have a pair of poison claws, and strong jaws with poison fangs. The bite of some tropical species is dangerous to humans. Several species live in Britain, *Lithobius forficatus* being the most common.

Central African Republic /ˈsentrəl ˈæfrɪkən rɪˈpʌblɪk/ landlocked country in Central Africa, bordered NE and E by Sudan, S by Zaire and the Congo, W by Cameroon, and NW by Chad.

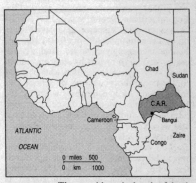

government The president is head of both state and government and presides over the 22-member council of ministers, composed of both military and civilian members. All political activity has been banned since the 1981 coup, but the main opposition groups, although passive, still exist. They are the Patriotic Front Ubangi Workers' Party (FPO-PT), the Central African Movement for National Liberation (MCLN), and the Movement for the Liberation of the Central African People (MPLC). A new constitution was approved by referendum 1986, providing for a 52-member national assembly elected for a five-year term at the summons of the president. Despite this manifesto, however, the country remains under military rule.

history A French colony from the late 19th century, the territory of Ubangi-Shari became self-governing within French Equatorial Africa in 1958 and two years later achieved full independence. Barthélémy Boganda, who had founded the Movement for the Social Evolution of Black Africa (MESAN), had been a leading figure in the campaign for independence and became the country's first prime minister. A year before full independence he was killed in an air crash and was succeeded by his nephew, David Dacko, who became president 1960 and 1962 established a one-party state, with MESAN as the only political organization.

Bokassa's rule Dacko was overthrown in a military coup Dec 1965, and the commander in chief of the army, Col Jean-Bédel ◊Bokassa, assumed power. Bokassa annulled the constitution and made himself president for life 1972 and marshal of the republic 1974. An authoritarian regime was established, and in 1976 ex-president Dacko was recalled to be the president's personal adviser. At the end of that year the republic was restyled the Central African Empire, and in 1977 Bokassa was crowned emperor at a lavish ceremony his country could ill afford. His rule became increasingly dictatorial and idiosyncratic, leading to revolts by students and, in April 1979, by schoolchildren who objected to the compulsory wearing of school uniforms made by a company owned by the Bokassa family. Many of the children were imprisoned, and it is estimated that at least 100 were killed, with the emperor allegedly personally involved.

Dacko's coup In Sept 1979, while Bokassa was in Libya, Dacko ousted him in a bloodless coup, backed by France. The country became a republic again, with Dacko as president. He initially retained a number of Bokassa's former ministers but, following student unrest, they were dropped, and in Feb 1981 a new constitution was adopted, with an elected national assembly. Dacko was elected president for a six-year term in March, but opposition to him grew and in Sept 1981 he was deposed in another bloodless coup, led by the armed forces' chief of staff, General André Kolingba.

military government The constitution and all political organizations were suspended, and a military government installed. Undercover opposition to the Kolingba regime continued, with some French support, but relations with France were improved by an unofficial visit by President Mitterrand in Oct 1982. By 1984 there was evidence of a gradual return to constitutional government. The leaders of the banned political parties were granted an amnesty, and at the end of the year the French president paid a state visit. In Jan 1985 proposals for a new constitution were announced and in Sept civilians were included in Kolingba's administration. In 1986 Bokassa returned from exile in France, expecting to be returned to power. Instead, he was tried for his part in the killing of the schoolchildren in 1979 and condemned to death; the sentence was commuted to life imprisonment 1988. In Oct 1990 there were widespread demonstrations calling for the restoration of multiparty politics. In Sept 1993 Ange Patasse was elected president, ending twelve years of military dictatorship. Jean-Luc Mandaba was appointed prime minister.

Central America /sentrəl əˈmerikə/ the part of the Americas that links Mexico with the isthmus of Panama, comprising Belize, Costa Rica, El Salvador, Guatemala, Honduras, Nicaragua, and Panama.

It is also an isthmus, crossed by mountains that form part of the Cordilleras. Much of Central America formed part of the Maya civilization. Spanish settlers married indigenous women, and the area remained out of the mainstream of Spanish Empire history. When the Spanish Empire collapsed in the early 1800s, the area formed the Central American Federation, with a constitution based on that of the USA. Demand for cash crops (bananas, coffee, cotton), especially from the USA, created a strong landowning class controlling a serflike peasantry by military means. There has been US military intervention in the area, for example in Nicaragua, where the dynasty of General Anastasio Somoza was founded. US president Carter reversed support for such regimes, but in the 1980s, the Reagan and Bush administrations again favoured military and financial aid to right-wing political groups, including the ◊Contras in Nicaragua.

Central American Common Market (CACM) (*Mercado Común Centroamericana: MCCA*) economic alliance established 1960 by El Salvador, Guatemala, Honduras (seceded 1970), and Nicaragua; Costa Rica joined 1962. Formed to encourage economic development and cooperation between the smaller Central American nations and to attract industrial capital, CACM failed to live up to early expectations: nationalist interests remained strong and by the mid-1980s political instability in the region and border conflicts between members were hindering its activities.

Central American States, Organization of (ODECA) (*Organización de Estados Centroamericanos*) international association promoting common economic, political, educational, and military aims in Central America. Its members are Costa Rica, El Salvador, Guatemala, Honduras, and Nicaragua, provision being made for Panama to join at a later date. The first organization, established 1951, was superseded 1962. ODECA comprises executive, legislative, and economic councils and the Central American Court of Justice; it was responsible for establishing the ◊Central American Common Market 1960. The permanent headquarters are in Guatemala City.

Central Command military strike force consisting of units from the US army, navy, and air force, which operates in the Middle East and North Africa. Its headquarters are in Fort McDill, Florida. It was established 1979, following the Iranian hostage crisis and the Soviet invasion of Afghanistan, and was known as the Rapid Deployment Force until 1983. It commanded coalition forces in the Gulf War 1991.

Central Criminal Court in the UK, crown court in the City of London, able to try all treasons and serious offences committed in the City or Greater London. First established 1834, it is popularly known as the *Old Bailey* after part of the medieval defences of London; the present building is on the site of Newgate Prison.

central dogma in genetics and evolution, the fundamental belief that ◊genes can affect the nature of the physical body, but that changes in the body (for example, through use or accident) cannot be translated into changes in the genes.

central heating system of heating from a central source, typically of a house, larger building, or group of buildings, as opposed to heating each room individually. Steam heat and hot-water heat are the most common systems in use. Water is heated in a furnace burning oil, gas or solid fuel, and, as steam or hot water, is then pumped through radiators in each room. The level of temperature can be selected by adjusting a ◊thermostat on the burner or in a room.

Central heating has its origins in the ◊hypocaust heating system introduced by the Romans nearly 2,000 years ago. Central heating systems are usually switched on and off by a time switch. Another kind of central heating system uses hot air, which is pumped through ducts (called risers) to grills in the rooms. Underfloor heating (called radiant heat) is used in some houses, the heat coming from electric elements buried in the floor.

Central Intelligence Agency (CIA) US intelligence organization established 1947. It has actively intervened overseas, generally to undermine left-wing regimes or to protect US financial interests; for example, in the Congo (now Zaire) and Nicaragua. From 1980 all covert activity by the CIA has by law to be reported to Congress, preferably beforehand, and must be authorized by the president. A fire in the US embassy in Moscow 1991 led to the loss of much sensitive material and, in May, William Webster stepped down as director, followed criticisms of the agency's intelligence gathering prior to the 1989 US invasion of Panama and the 1991 Gulf War and was replaced by Robert Gates 1991–93. Robert James Woolsey became CIA director 1993.

Developed from the wartime Office of Strategic Services and set up by Congress, as part of the National Security Act, on the lines of the British Secret Service, the CIA was intended solely for use overseas in the Cold War. It was involved in, for example, the restoration of the shah of Iran 1953, South Vietnam (during the Vietnam War), Chile (the coup against President Allende), and Cuba (the ◊Bay of Pigs). On the domestic front, it was illegally involved in the ◊Watergate political scandal and in the 1970s lost public confidence when US influence collapsed in Iran, Afghanistan, Nicaragua, Yemen, and elsewhere.

CIA headquarters is in Langley, Virginia. Past directors include William Casey, Richard ◊Helms, and George ◊Bush. Domestic intelligence functions are performed by the ◊Federal Bureau of Investigation.

Central Lowlands one of the three geographical divisions of Scotland, occupying the fertile and densely populated plain that lies between two geological fault lines, which run nearly parallel NE–SW across Scotland from Stonehaven to Dumbarton and from Dunbar to Girvan.

Central Mount Stuart /stju:ət/ flat-topped mountain 844 m/2,770 ft high, at approximately the central point of Australia. It was originally named in 1860 by explorer J McDouall Stuart after another explorer, Charles Sturt—Central Mount Sturt—but later became known by his own name.

central nervous system the part of the nervous system with a concentration of ◊nerve cells which coordinates various body functions. In ◊vertebrates, the central nervous system consists of a brain and a dorsal nerve cord (the spinal cord) within the spinal column. In worms, insects, and crustaceans, it consists of a paired ventral nerve cord with concentrations of nerve cells, known as ◊*ganglia* in each segment, and a small brain in the head.

Some simple invertebrates, such as sponges and jellyfishes, have no central nervous system but a simple network of nerve cells called a *nerve net*.

Central Powers originally the signatories of the ◊Triple Alliance 1882: Germany, Austria-Hungary, and Italy. During the World War I, Italy remained neutral before joining the ◊Allies.

central processing unit (CPU) the main component of a computer, the part that executes individual program instructions and controls the operation of other parts. It is sometimes called the central processor or, simply, the processor.

The CPU comprises three main components: the ◊ALU (arithmetic and logic unit), where all calculations and logical operations are carried out; a control unit, which decodes, synchronizes and executes program instruction, and the immediate access memory, which stores the data and programs on which the computer is currently working. All these components contain ◊registers, which are memory locations reserved for specific purposes.

Central Provinces and Berar /berrɑː/ former British province of India, now part of ◊Madhya Pradesh.

Central Scotland region of Scotland, formed 1975 from the counties of Stirling, S Perthshire, and West Lothian
area 2,600 sq km/1,004 sq mi
towns Stirling (administrative headquarters), Falkirk, Alloa, Grangemouth

features Stirling Castle; field of Bannockburn; Loch Lomond; the Trossachs
products agriculture; industries including brewing and distilling, engineering, electronics
population (1987) 272,000
famous people William Alexander (founder of Nova Scotia), Rob Roy Macgregor.

Central Treaty Organization (CENTO) military alliance that replaced the ◊Baghdad Pact 1959; it collapsed when the withdrawal of Iran, Pakistan, and Turkey 1979 left the UK as the only member.

Centre /sɒntr/ region of N central France; area 39,200 sq km/15,131 sq mi; population (1986) 2,324,000. It includes the *départements* of Cher, Eure-et-Loire, Indre, Indre-et-Loire, Loire-et-Cher, and Loiret. Its capital is Orléans.

Centre, the /ˈsentə/ region of central Australia, including the tourist area between the Musgrave and MacDonnell ranges which contains Ayers Rock and Lake Amadeus.

centre of gravity the point in an object about which its weight is evenly balanced. In a uniform gravitational field, this is the same as the centre of mass.

centre of mass or *centre of gravity* the point in or near an object from which its total weight appears to originate and can be assumed to act. A symmetrical homogeneous object such as a sphere or cube has its centre of mass at its physical centre; a hollow shape (such as a cup) may have its centre of mass in space inside the hollow.

Centre Party (German *Zentrumspartei*) German political party established 1871 to protect Catholic interests. Although alienated by Chancellor Bismarck's ◊*Kulturkampf* 1873–78, in the following years the *Zentrum* became an essential component in the government of imperial Germany. The party continued to play a part in the politics of Weimar Germany before being barred by Hitler in the summer of 1933.

centrifugal force useful concept in physics, based on an apparent (but not real) force. It may be regarded as a force that acts radially outwards from a spinning or orbiting object, thus balancing the ◊centripetal force (which is real). For an object of mass m moving with a velocity v in a circle of radius r, the centrifugal force F equals mv^2/r (outwards).

centrifuge apparatus that rotates at high speeds, causing substances inside it to be thrown outwards. One use is for separating mixtures of substances of different densities.

The mixtures are usually spun horizontally in balanced containers ('buckets'), and the rotation sets up centrifugal forces, causing their components to separate according to their densities. A common example is the separation of the lighter plasma from the heavier blood corpuscles in certain blood tests. The *ultracentrifuge* is a very high-speed centrifuge, used in biochemistry for separating ◊colloids and organic substances; it may operate at several million revolutions per minute.

centriole structure found in the ◊cells of animals that plays a role in the processes of ◊meiosis and ◊mitosis (cell division).

centripetal force force that acts radially inwards on an object moving in a curved path. For example, with a weight whirled in a circle at the end of a length of string, the centripetal force is the tension in the string. For an object of mass m moving with a velocity v in a circle of radius r, the centripetal force F equals mv^2/r (inwards). The reaction to this force is the ◊centrifugal force.

centromere part of the ◊chromosome where there are no ◊genes. Under the microscope, it usually appears as a constriction in the strand of the chromosome, and is the point at which the spindle fibres are attached during ◊meiosis and ◊mitosis (cell division).

Cephalonia /ˌsefəˈləʊniə/ English form of ◊Kefallinia, largest of the Ionian islands, off the W coast of Greece.

cephalopod any predatory marine mollusc of the class Cephalopoda, with the mouth and head surrounded by tentacles. Cephalopods are the most intelligent, the fastest-moving, and the largest of all animals without backbones, and there are remarkable luminescent forms which swim or drift at great depths. They have the most highly developed nervous and sensory systems of all invertebrates, the eye in some closely paralleling that found in vertebrates. Examples include octopus, squid, and cuttlefish. Shells are rudimentary or absent in most cephalopods.

Typically, they move by swimming with the mantle (fold of outer skin) aided by the arms, but can squirt water out of the siphon (funnel) to propel themselves backwards by jet propulsion. They grow very rapidly and may be mature in a year. The female common octopus lays 150,000 eggs after copulation, and stays to brood them for as long as six weeks. After they hatch the female dies, and, although reproductive habits of many cephalopods are not known, it is thought that dying after spawning may be typical.

cephalosporin any of a class of broad-spectrum antibiotics derived from a fungus (genus *Cephalosporium*). It is similar to penicillin and is used on penicillin-resistant infections.

Cepheid variable /ˈsiːfɪɪd/ yellow supergiant star that varies regularly in brightness every few days or weeks as a result of pulsations. The time that a Cepheid variable takes to pulsate is directly related to its average brightness; the longer the pulsation period, the brighter the star.

This relationship, the *period luminosity law* (discovered by Henrietta ◊Leavitt), allows astronomers to use Cepheid variables as 'standard candles' to measure distances in our Galaxy and to nearby galaxies. They are named after their prototype, Delta Cephei, whose light variations were observed 1784 by English astronomer John Goodricke (1764–1786).

Cepheus /ˈsiːfiəs/ constellation of the north polar region, named after King Cepheus of Greek mythology, husband of Cassiopeia and father of Andromeda. It contains the Garnet Star (Mu Cephei), a red supergiant of variable brightness that is one of the reddest-coloured stars known, and Delta Cephei, prototype of the ◊Cepheid variables.

Ceram /səˈræm/ or *Seram* Indonesian island, in the Moluccas; area 17,142 sq km/6,621 sq mi. The chief town is Ambon.

ceramic nonmetallic mineral (clay) used to form articles that are then fired at high temperatures. Ceramics are divided into heavy clay products (bricks, roof tiles, drainpipes, sanitary ware), refractories or high-temperature materials (linings for furnaces used to manufacture steel, fuel elements in nuclear reactors), and pottery, which uses china clay, ball clay, china stone, and flint. Superceramics, such as silicon carbide, are lighter, stronger, and more heat-resistant than steel for use in motor and aircraft engines and have to be cast to shape since they are too hard to machine.

Cerberus /ˈsɜːbərəs/ in Greek mythology, the three-headed dog guarding the entrance to ◊Hades, the underworld.

cereal grass grown for its edible, nutrient-rich, starchy seeds. The term refers primarily to wheat, oats, rye, and barley, but may also refer to corn, millet, and rice. Cereals contain about 75% complex carbohydrates and 10% protein, plus fats and fibre (roughage). They store easily. In 1984, world production exceeded 2 billion tonnes. If all the world's cereal crop were consumed as wholegrain products directly by humans, everyone could obtain adequate protein and carbohydrate; however, a large proportion of cereal production in affluent nations is used as animal feed to boost the production of meat, dairy products, and eggs.

cerebellum part of the brain of ◊vertebrate animals which controls muscular movements, balance, and coordination. It is relatively small in lower animals such as newts and lizards, but large in birds since flight demands precise coordination. The human cerebellum is also well developed, because of the need for balance when walking or running, and for coordinated hand movements.

cerebral pertaining to the brain, especially the part known as the cerebrum, concerned with higher brain functions.

cerebral haemorrhage or *apoplectic fit* in medicine, a ◊stroke in which a blood vessel bursts in the brain, caused by factors such as high blood pressure combined with hardening of the arteries, or chronic poisoning with lead or alcohol. It may cause death or damage parts of the brain, leading to paralysis or mental impairment. The effects are usually long-term and the condition may recur.

cerebral hemisphere one of the two halves of the ◊cerebrum.

cerebral palsy any nonprogressive abnormality of the brain caused by oxygen deprivation before birth, injury during birth, haemorrhage, meningitis, viral infection, or faulty development. It is characterized by muscle spasm, weakness, lack of coordination, and impaired movement. Intelligence is not always affected.

cerebrum part of the vertebrate ◊brain, formed from the two paired cerebral hemispheres. In birds and mammals it is the largest part of the brain. It is covered with an infolded layer of grey matter, the cerebral cortex, which integrates brain functions. The cerebrum coordinates the senses, and is responsible for learning and other higher mental faculties.

Ceres /ˈsɪəriːz/ in Roman mythology, the goddess of agriculture; see ◊Demeter.

Ceres /ˈsɪəriːz/ the largest asteroid, 940 km/ 584 mi in diameter, and the first to be discovered (by Giuseppe Piazzi 1801). Ceres orbits the Sun every 4.6 years at an average distance of 414 million km/257 million mi. Its mass is about one-seventieth of that of the Moon.

cerium malleable and ductile, grey, metallic element, symbol Ce, atomic number 58, relative atomic mass 140.12. It is the most abundant member of the lanthanide series, and is used in alloys, electronic components, nuclear fuels, and lighter flints. It was discovered 1804 by the Swedish chemists Jöns Berzelius and Wilhelm Hisinger (1766–1852), and, independently, by Martin Klaproth. The element was named after the then recently discovered asteroid Ceres.

cermet bonded material containing ceramics and metal, widely used in jet engines and nuclear reactors. Cermets behave much like metals but have the great heat resistance of ceramics. Tungsten carbide, molybdenum boride, and aluminium oxide are among the ceramics used; iron, cobalt, nickel, and chromium are among the metals.

CERN nuclear research organization founded 1954 as a cooperative enterprise among European governments. It has laboratories at Meyrin, near Geneva, Switzerland. It was originally known as the *Conseil Européen pour la Recherche Nucléaire* but subsequently renamed *Organisation Européenne pour la Recherche Nucléaire*, although still familiarly known as CERN. It houses the world's largest particle ◊accelerator, the ◊Large Electron–Positron Collider (LEP), with which notable advances have been made in ◊particle physics.

Cernăuţi /ˌtʃɛənəˈuts/ Romanian form of ◊Chernovtsy, city in Ukraine.

Cerro Tololo Inter-American Observatory observatory on Cerro Tololo mountain in the Chilean Andes operated by AURA (the Association of Universities for Research into Astronomy). Its main instrument is a 4-m/158-in reflector, opened 1974, a twin of that at Kitt Peak.

certiorari in UK ◊administrative law, a remedy available by ◊judicial review whereby a superior court may quash an order or decision made by an inferior body. It has become less important in recent years following the extension of alternative remedies by judicial review. It originally took the form of a prerogative ◊writ.

Cervantes /sɜːˈvæntiːz/ Saavedra, Miguel de 1547–1616. Spanish novelist, playwright, and poet whose masterpiece, ◊*Don Quixote* (in full *El ingenioso hidalgo Don Quixote de la Mancha*), was published 1605. In 1613, his *Novelas ejemplares/Exemplary Novels* appeared, followed by *Viaje del Parnaso/The Voyage to Parnassus* 1614. A spurious second part of *Don Quixote* prompted Cervantes to bring out his own second part in 1615, often considered superior to the first in construction and characterization.

cervical cancer ◊cancer of the cervix (the neck of the womb).

cervical smear removal of a small sample of tissue from the cervix (neck of the womb) to screen for changes implying a likelihood of cancer. The procedure is also known as the *Pap test* after its originator, George Papanicolau.

cervix (Latin 'neck') abbreviation for *cervix uteri*, the neck of the womb.

César /seˈzɑː/ adopted name of César Baldaccini 1921– . French sculptor who uses iron and scrap metal and, in the 1960s, crushed car bodies. His subjects are imaginary insects and animals.

České Budějovice /ˈtʃeskeɪ ˈbuːdʒɪəʊˌviːtseɪ/ (German *Budweis*) town in the Czech Republic, on the river Vltava; population (1989) 97,000. It is a commercial and industrial centre for S Bohemia, producing beer, timber, and metal products.

Cetewayo /ketʃˈwaɪəʊ/ (Cetshwayo) *c.* 1826–1884. King of Zululand, South Africa, 1873–83, whose rule was threatened by British annexation of the Transvaal 1877. Although he defeated the British at Isandhlwana 1879, he was later that year defeated by them at Ulundi. Restored to his throne 1883, he was then expelled by his subjects.

Cetinje /ˈtsetiːnjeɪ/ town in Montenegro, Yugoslavia, 19 km/12 mi SE of Kotor; population (1981) 20,213. Founded 1484 by Ivan the Black, it was capital of Montenegro until 1918. It has a palace built by Nicholas, the last king of Montenegro.

Cetus /ˈsiːtəs/ (Latin 'whale') constellation straddling the celestial equator (see ◊celestial sphere), represented as a sea monster. Cetus contains the long-period variable star ◊Mira, and ◊Tau Ceti, one of the nearest stars visible with the naked eye.

Cévennes /seˈven/ series of mountain ranges on the southern, southeastern, and east-ern borders of the Central Plateau of France. The highest peak is Mount Mézenc, 1,754 m/5,755 ft.

Ceylon /sɪˈlɒn/ former name (until 1972) of ◊Sri Lanka.

Cézanne /seɪˈzæn/ Paul 1839–1906. French Post-Impressionist painter, a leading figure in the development of modern art. He broke away from the Impressionists' spontaneous vision to develop a style that captured not only light and life, but the structure of natural forms in landscapes, still lifes, portraits, and his series of bathers.

His series of Mont Sainte-Victoire in Provence from the 1880's in the 1900's show an increasing fragmentation of the painting's surface and a movement towards abstraction, with layers of colour and square brushstrokes achieving monumental solidity. He was greatly revered by early abstract painters, notably Picasso and Braque.

CFC abbreviation for ◊*chlorofluorocarbon*.

CFE abbreviation for *conventional forces in Europe*. Talks between government representatives began in Vienna, Austria, in March 1989 designed to reduce the 'conventional'—that is, non-nuclear—forces (US, Soviet, French, British, and German) in Europe. A treaty was signed by NATO and Warsaw Pact representatives in Nov 1990, reducing the number of tanks, missiles, aircraft, and other forms of military hardware held by member states, but doubts remain about its verification. The 1990 Paris Conference on Security and Cooperation in Europe (CSCE) and the dissolution of the Warsaw Pact as a military alliance dramatically changed the arms-control climate.

c.g.s. system or *C.G.s. system* system of units based on the centimetre, gram, and second, as units of length, mass, and time, respectively. It has been replaced for scientific work by the ◊SI units to avoid inconsistencies in definition of the thermal calorie and electrical quantities.

Chabrol /ʃæˈbrɒl/ Claude 1930– . French film director. Originally a critic, he was one of the French New Wave directors. His works of murder and suspense, which owe much to Hitchcock, include *Les Cousins/The Cousins* 1959, *Les Biches/The Girlfriends* 1968, *Le Boucher/The Butcher* 1970, and *Cop au Vin* 1984.

chacma species of ◊baboon.

Chaco /ˈtʃɑːkəʊ/ province of Argentina; area 99,633 sq km/38,458 sq mi; population (1989 est) 824,400. Its capital is Resistencia, in the southeast. The chief crop is cotton, and there is forestry.

It includes many lakes, swamps, and forests, producing timber and quebracho (a type of wood used in tanning). Until 1951 it was a territory, part of Gran Chaco, a great zone, mostly level, stretching into Paraguay and Bolivia. The north of Gran Chaco was the scene of the Chaco War.

Chaco War /'tʃɑːkəʊ/ war between Bolivia and Paraguay 1932–35 over boundaries in the N Gran Chaco, settled by arbitration 1938.

Chad /tʃæd/ landlocked country in central N Africa, bounded N by Libya, E by Sudan, S by the Central African Republic, and W by Cameroon, Nigeria, and Niger.

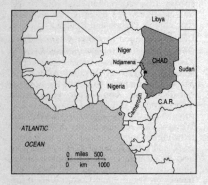

government The 1982 provisional constitution provides for a president who appoints and leads a council of ministers that exercises executive and legislative power. In 1984 a new regrouping, the National Union for Independence and Revolution (UNIR), was undertaken in an attempt to consolidate the president's position, but a number of opposition groups exist.

history Called Kanem when settled by Arabs in the 7th–13th centuries, the area later became known as Bornu and in the 19th century was conquered by Sudan. From 1913 a province of French Equatorial Africa, Chad became an autonomous state within the French Community 1958, with François Tombalbaye as prime minister.

Full independence was achieved 1960, and Tombalbaye became president. He soon faced disagreements between the Arabs of the north, who saw Libya as an ally, and the black African Christians of the south, who

felt more sympathy for Nigeria. In the north the Chadian National Liberation Front (Frolinat) revolted against the government. In 1975 Tombalbaye was killed in a coup led by former army Chief of Staff Félix Malloum, who became president of a supreme military council and appealed for national unity. Frolinat continued its opposition, however, supported by Libya, which held a strip of land in the north, believed to contain uranium.

Frolinat expansion By 1978 Frolinat, led by General Goukouni Oueddi, had expanded its territory but was halted with French aid. Malloum tried to reach a settlement by making former Frolinat leader, Hissène Habré, prime minister, but disagreements developed between them.

In 1979 fighting broke out again between government and Frolinat forces, and Malloum fled the country. Talks resulted in the formation of a provisional government (GUNT), with Goukouni holding the presidency with Libyan support. A proposed merger with Libya was rejected, and Libya withdrew most of its forces.

civil war The Organization for African Unity (OAU) set up a peacekeeping force but civil war broke out and by 1981 Hissène Habré's Armed Forces of the North (FAN) controlled half the country. Goukouni fled and set up a 'government in exile'. In 1983 a majority of OAU members agreed to recognize Habré's regime, but Goukouni, with Libyan support, fought on.

cease-fire After Libyan bombing, Habré appealed to France for help. Three thousand troops were sent as instructors, with orders to retaliate if attacked. Following a Franco-African summit 1984, a cease-fire was agreed, with latitude 16°N dividing the opposing forces. Libyan president Col Khaddhafi's proposal of a simultaneous withdrawal of French and Libyan troops was accepted. By Dec all French troops had left, but Libya's withdrawal was doubtful.

Habré dissolved the military arm of Frolinat 1984 and formed a new party, the National Union for Independence and Revolution (UNIR), but opposition to his regime grew. In 1987 Goukouni was reported to be under house arrest in Tripoli. Meanwhile Libya intensified its military operations in northern Chad, Habré's government retaliated, and France renewed (if reluctantly) its support.

OAU cease-fire It was announced March 1989 that France, Chad, and Libya had agreed to observe a cease-fire proposed by the OAU. A meeting July 1989 between Habré and Khaddhafi reflected the improvement in relations between Chad and Libya. Habré was endorsed as president Dec 1989 for another seven-year term, under a revised constitution. The new constitution was introduced July 1990, providing for a new national assembly of 123 elective seats to replace the appointed National Consultative Council. In Dec 1990 the government fell to rebel opposition forces, Hissène Habré was reported killed, and the rebel leader Idriss Deby became president. In March 1992 the new government moved nearer to multiparty politics when two opposition groups were approved.

Chad, Lake /tʃæd/ lake on the NE boundary of Nigeria. It once varied in extent between rainy and dry seasons from 50,000 sq km/20,000 sq mi to 20,000 sq km/7,000 sq mi, but a series of droughts 1979–89 reduced its area by 80%. Almost £1billion has been spent on the S Chad irrigation project to use the lake waters to irrigate the surrounding desert; the 4,000 km/2,500 mi of canals dug for the project are now permanently dry because of the shrinking size of the lake. The Lake Chad basin is being jointly developed for oil and natron by Cameroon, Chad, Niger, and Nigeria.

Chadli /ʃædˈliː/ Benjedid 1929– . Algerian socialist politician, president 1979–92. An army colonel, he supported Boumédienne in the overthrow of Ben Bella 1965, and succeeded Boumédienne 1979, pursuing more moderate policies.

chador (Hindi 'square of cloth') all-enveloping black garment for women worn by some Muslims and Hindus.

The origin of the chador dates to the 6th century BC under Cyrus the Great and the Achaemenian empire in Persia. Together with the ◊purdah (Persian 'veil') and the idea of female seclusion, it persisted under Alexander the Great and the Byzantine Empire, and was adopted by the Arab conquerors of the Byzantines. Its use was revived in Iran in the 1970s by Ayatollah Khomeini in response to the Koranic request for 'modesty' in dress.

Chadwick /tʃædwɪk/ Edwin 1800–1890. English social reformer, author of the Poor Law Report 1834. He played a prominent part in the campaign which resulted in the ◊Public Health Act 1848. He was commissioner of the first Board of Health 1848–54.

A self-educated protégé of Jeremy ◊Bentham and advocate of ◊utilitarianism, he used his influence to implement measures to eradicate cholera, improve sanitation in urban areas, and clear slums in British cities.

Chadwick /tʃædwɪk/ James 1891–1974. British physicist. In 1932 he discovered the particle in the nucleus of an atom that became known as the neutron because it has no electric charge. Nobel prize 1935.

chafer beetle of the family Scarabeidae. The adults eat foliage or flowers, and the underground larvae feed on roots, chiefly those of grasses and cereals, and can be very destructive. Examples are the ◊cockchafer and the **rose chafer** *Cetonia aurata*, about 2 cm/0.8 in long and bright green.

chaffinch bird *Fringilla coelebs* of the finch family, common throughout much of Europe and W Asia. About 15 cm/6 in long, the male is olive-brown above, with a bright chestnut breast, a bluish-grey cap, and two white bands on the upper part of the wing; the female is duller.

Chagall /ʃæˈgæl/ Marc 1887–1985. Russian-born French painter and designer; much of his highly coloured, fantastic imagery was inspired by the village life of his boyhood. He also designed stained glass, mosaics (for Israel's Knesset in the 1960s), tapestries, and stage sets.

Chagall is an original figure, often seen as a precursor of Surrealism, as in *The Dream* (Metropolitan Museum of Art, New York). His stained glass can be found in, notably, a chapel in Vence, the south of France, 1950s, and a synagogue near Jerusalem. He also produced illustrated books.

Chagas's disease /ˈʃɑːgəs/ disease common in Central and South America, caused by a trypanosome parasite transmitted by insects; it results in incurable damage to the heart, intestines, and brain. It is named after Brazilian doctor Carlos Chagas (1879–1934).

Chagos Archipelago /tʃɑːgəs ˌɑːkɪˈpeləgəʊ/ island group in the Indian Ocean; area 60 sq km/23 sq mi. Formerly a dependency of Mauritius, it now forms the ◊British Indian Ocean Territory. The chief island is Diego Garcia, now a US-British strategic base.

Chain /tʃeɪn/ Ernst Boris 1906–1979. German-born British biochemist who worked on the development of ◊penicillin. Chain fled to Britain from the Nazis 1933. After the discovery of penicillin by Alexander Fleming, Chain worked to isolate and purify it. For this work, he shared the 1945 Nobel Prize for Medicine with Fleming and Howard Florey. Chain also discovered penicillinase, an enzyme that destroys penicillin.

chain reaction in nuclear physics, a fission reaction that is maintained because neutrons released by the splitting of some atomic nuclei themselves go on to split others, releasing even more neutrons. Such a reaction can be controlled (as in a nuclear reactor) by using moderators to absorb excess neutrons. Uncontrolled, a chain reaction produces a nuclear explosion (as in an atom bomb).

Chaka /ˈʃɑːgə/ alternative spelling of ◊Shaka, Zulu chief.

Chalatenango /tʃəˌlætɪˈnæŋgəʊ/ department on the N frontier of El Salvador; area 2,507 sq km/968 sq mi; population (1981) 235,700; capital Chalatenango. It is largely controlled by FMLN guerrilla insurgents.

chalaza glutinous mass of transparent albumen supporting the yolk inside birds' eggs. The chalaza is formed as the egg slowly passes down the oviduct, when it also acquires its coiled structure.

Chalcedon, Council of /kælˈsiːd(ə)n/ ecumenical council of the early Christian church, convoked 451 by the Roman emperor Marcian, and held at Chalcedon (now Kadiköy, Turkey). The council, attended by over 500 bishops, resulted in the *Definition of Chalcedon*, an agreed doctrine for both the eastern and western churches.

The council was assembled to repudiate the ideas of ◊Eutyches on Jesus' divine nature subsuming the human; it also rejected the ◊Monophysite doctrine that Jesus had only one nature, and repudiated ◊Nestorianism. It reached a compromise definition of Jesus' nature which it was hoped would satisfy all factions: Jesus was one person in two natures, united 'unconfusedly, unchangeably, indivisibly, inseparably'.

chalcedony form of quartz, SiO_2, in which the crystals are so fine-grained that they are impos-sible to distinguish with a microscope (cryptocrystalline). Agate, onyx, tiger's eye, and carnelian are ◊gem varieties of chalcedony.

chalcopyrite copper iron sulphide, Cu, FeS_2, the most common ore of copper. It is brassy yellow in colour and may have an iridescent surface tarnish. It occurs in many different types of mineral vein, in rocks ranging from basalt to limestone.

Chaldaea /kælˈdiːə/ ancient region of Babylonia.

Chaliapin /ʃælɪˈæpɪn/ Fyodor Ivanovich 1873–1938. Russian bass singer, born in Kazan. His greatest role was that of Boris Godunov in Mussorgsky's opera of the same name.

chalice cup, usually of precious metal, used in celebrating the ◊Eucharist in the Christian church.

chalk soft, fine-grained, whitish rock composed of calcium carbonate, $CaCO_3$, extensively quarried for use in cement, lime, and mortar, and in the manufacture of cosmetics and toothpaste. *Blackboard chalk* in fact consists of ◊gypsum (calcium sulphate, $CaSO_4$).

Chalk was once thought to derive from the remains of microscopic animals or foraminifera. In 1953, however, it was seen under the electron microscope to be composed chiefly of ◊coccolithophores, unicellular lime-secreting algae, and hence primarily of plant origin. It is formed from deposits of deep-sea sediments called oozes.

Chalk was laid down in the later ◊Cretaceous period and covers a wide area in Europe. In England it stretches in a belt from Wiltshire and Dorset continuously across Buckinghamshire and Cambridgeshire to Lincolnshire and Yorkshire, and also forms the North and South Downs, and the cliffs of S and SE England.

Chalmers /ˈtʃɑːməz/ Thomas 1780–1847. Scottish theologian. At the Disruption of the ◊Church of Scotland 1843, Chalmers withdrew from the church along with a large number of other priests, and became principal of the Free Church college, thus founding the ◊Free Church of Scotland.

Chamberlain /ˈtʃeɪmbəlɪn/ (Arthur) Neville 1869–1940. British Conservative politician, son of Joseph Chamberlain. He was prime minister 1937–40; his policy of appeasement towards the fascist dictators Mussolini and Hitler (with whom he concluded the ◊Munich Agreement 1938) failed to prevent the outbreak of World War II. He resigned 1940 following the defeat of the British forces in Norway.

Chamberlain was minister of health 1923 and 1924–29 and worked at slum clearance. In 1931 he was chancellor of the Exchequer in the national government, and in 1937 succeeded Baldwin as prime minister. Trying to close the old Anglo-Irish feud, he agreed to return to Eire those ports that had been occupied by the navy. He also attempted to appease the demands of the European dictators, particularly Mussolini. In 1938 he went to Munich and negotiated with Hitler the settlement of the Czechoslovak question. He was ecstatically received on his return, and claimed that the Munich Agreement brought 'peace in our time'. Within a year, however, Britain was at war with Germany.

Chamberlain /ˈtʃeɪmbəlɪn/ (Joseph) Austen 1863–1937. British Conservative politician, elder son of Joseph Chamberlain; as foreign secretary 1924–29 he negotiated the Pact of ◊Locarno, for which he won the Nobel Peace Prize 1925, and signed the ◊Kellogg–Briand pact to outlaw war 1928.

During World War I he was secretary of state for India 1915–17 and member of the war cabinet 1918. He was chancellor of the Exchequer 1919–21 and Lord Privy Seal 1921–22, but failed to secure the leadership of the party 1922, as many Conservatives resented the part he had taken in the Irish settlement of 1921. He was foreign secretary in the Baldwin government 1924–29, and negotiated and signed the Locarno Pact 1925 to fix the boundaries of Germany, and the Kellogg–Briand pact 1928 to ban war and provide for peaceful settlement of disputes.

Chamberlain /ˈtʃeɪmbəlɪn/ Joseph 1836–1914. British politician, reformist mayor of and member of Parliament for Birmingham; in 1886, he resigned from the cabinet over Gladstone's policy of home rule for Ireland, and led the revolt of the Liberal-Unionists.

By 1874 Chamberlain had made a sufficient fortune in the Birmingham screw-manufacturing business to devote himself entirely to politics. He adopted radical views, and took an active part in local affairs. Three times mayor of Birmingham, he carried through many schemes of municipal development. In 1876 he was elected to Parliament and joined the republican group led by Charles Dilke, the extreme left wing of the Liberal Party. In 1880 he entered Gladstone's cabinet as president of the Board of Trade. The climax of his radical period was reached with the unauthorized programme, advocating, among other things, free education, graduated taxation, and smallholdings of 'three acres and a cow'.

As colonial secretary in Salisbury's Conservative government, Chamberlain was responsible for relations with the Boer republics up to the outbreak of war 1899. In 1903 he resigned to campaign for imperial preference or tariff reform as a means of consolidating the empire. From 1906 he was incapacitated by a stroke. Chamberlain was one of the most colourful figures of British politics, and his monocle and orchid made him a favourite subject for political cartoonists.

Chamberlain /ˈtʃeɪmbəlɪn/ Owen 1920– . US physicist whose graduate studies were interrupted by wartime work on the Manhattan Project at Los Alamos. After World War II, working with Italian physicist Emilio Segrè, he discovered the existence of the antiproton. Both men were awarded the Nobel Prize for Physics 1959.

Chamberlain, Lord /ˈtʃeɪmbəlɪn/ in the UK, chief officer of the royal household who engages staff and appoints retail suppliers. Until 1968 the Lord Chamberlain licensed and censored plays before their public performance.

Chamberlain, Lord Great /ˈtʃeɪmbəlɪn/ in the UK, the only officer of state whose position survives from Norman times; responsibilities include the arrangements for the opening of Parliament, assisting with the regalia at coronations, and organizing the ceremony when bishops and peers are created.

chamber music music suitable for performance in a small room or chamber, rather than in the concert hall, and usually written for instrumental combinations, played with one instrument to a part, as in the string quartet.

It came into use as a reaction to earlier music for voices such as the madrigal, which allowed accompanying instruments little freedom for technical display. At first a purely instrumental style, it developed through Haydn and Beethoven into a private and often experimental medium making unusual demands on players and audiences alike. During the 20th century the limitations of recording and radio have encouraged many composers to scale down their orchestras to chamber proportions, as in Berg's *Chamber Concerto* and Stravinsky's *Agon*.

Chambers /ˈtʃeɪmbəz/ William 1726–1796. British architect and popularizer of Chinese influence (for example, the pagoda in Kew Gardens, London) and designer of Somerset House, London.

chameleon any of some 80 or so species of lizard of the family Chameleontidae. Some species have highly developed colour-changing abilities, which are caused by changes in the intensity of light, of temperature, and of emotion altering the dispersal of pigment granules in the layers of cells beneath the outer skin.

The tail is long and highly prehensile, assisting the animal when climbing. Most chameleons live in trees and move very slowly. The tongue is very long, protrusile, and covered with a viscous secretion; it can be shot out with great rapidity to 20 cm/8 in for the capture of insects. The eyes are on 'turrets', move independently, and can swivel forward to give stereoscopic vision for 'shooting'. Most live in Africa and Madagascar, but the **common chameleon** *Chameleo chameleon* is found in Mediterranean countries.

chamois goatlike mammal *Rupicapra rupicapra* found in mountain ranges of S Europe and Asia Minor. It is brown, with dark patches running through the eyes, and can be up to 80 cm/2.6 ft high. Chamois are very sure-footed, and live in herds of up to 30 members.

Both sexes have horns which may be 20 cm/8 in long. These are set close together and go up vertically, forming a hook at the top. Chamois skin is very soft, and excellent for cleaning glass, but the chamois is now comparatively rare and 'chamois leather' is often made from the skin of sheep and goats.

Chamorro /ʃəˈmɒrəʊ/ Violeta Barrios de *c.* 1939– . President of Nicaragua from 1990. With strong US support, she was elected as the candidate for the National Opposition Union (UNO) 1989, winning the presidency from David Ortega Saavedra Feb 1990 and thus ending the period of Sandinista rule.

Chamorro's political career began 1978 with the assassination by the right-wing dictatorship of her husband, Pedro Joaquín Chamorro. Violeta became candidate for UNO, a 14-party coalition, Sept 1989; In the 1990 elections, UNO won 51 of the 92 seats in the National Assembly. The Sandinista Liberation Front (FSLN) however remained the largest party, and together with reactionary elements within Chamorro's own coalition, obstructed the implementation of her policies. Her early presidency was marked by rising unemployment, strikes, and continuing skirmishes between ◊Contra rebels and Sandinista militants in the mountains (despite official disbanding of the Contras June 1990).

Champagne sparkling white wine invented by Dom Pérignon, a Benedictine monk, 1668. It is made from a blend of grapes (*pinot noir* and *pinot chardonnay*) grown in the Marne River region around Rheims and Epernay, in Champagne, NE France. After a first fermentation, sugar and yeast are added to the still wine, which, when bottled, undergoes a second fermentation to produce the sparkle. Sugar syrup may be added to make the wine sweet (*sec*) or dry (*brut*).

Champagne has become a symbol of luxurious living and is used worldwide to celebrate special occasions. Rising demand has given rise to the production of similar wines outside France, in the USA, for example, and Spain. Although these wines imitate Champagnes closely, they are referred to as *méthode champenoise*; only wines produced in the Champagne region of France can be termed 'Champagne'. The pop when a bottle is opened is due to the sudden release of pressure that allows the accumulated carbon dioxide to escape: a bottle may contain up to five times its volume in gas.

Production in 1844 was 7 million bottles; in 1987, it was about 217 million bottles (of which the UK was the world's largest consumer, importing about 15 million bottles).

Champagne-Ardenne /ʃæmˌpeɪn ɑːˈden/ region of NE France; area 25,600 sq km/9,882 sq mi; population (1986) 1,353,000. Its capital is Reims, and it comprises the *départements* of Ardennes, Aube, Marne, and Haute-Marne. It has sheep and dairy farming and vineyards.

Champaigne /ʃæmˈpeɪn/ Philippe de 1602–1674. French artist, the leading portrait painter of the court of Louis XIII. Of Flemish origin, he went to Paris 1621 and gained the patronage of Cardinal Richelieu. His style is elegant, cool, and restrained.

Champlain /ʃæmˈpleɪn/ lake situated in the northeastern USA, named after Samuel de Champlain, who saw it 1609. It is linked to the St Lawrence and Hudson rivers.

Champlain /ʃæmˈpleɪn/ Samuel de 1567–1635. French pioneer, soldier, and explorer in Canada. Having served in the army of Henry IV and on an expedition to the West Indies, he began his exploration of Canada 1603. In a third expedition 1608 he founded and named Québec, and was appointed lieutenant governor of French Canada 1612.

Champollion /ʃɒmpɒlˈjɒn/ Jean François, le Jeune 1790–1832. French Egyptologist who in 1822 deciphered Egyptian hieroglyphics with the aid of the ◊Rosetta Stone.

chance likelihood, or ◊probability, of an event taking place. As a science, it originated when the Chevalier de Méré consulted ◊Pascal about how to reduce his gambling losses. In correspondence with another mathematician, ◊Fermat, Pascal worked out the foundations of the theory of chance. This underlies the science of statistics.

chancel part of a Christian church where the choir and clergy sit, formerly kept separate from the nave.

The term originated in the early Middle Ages, when chancels were raised above the level of the nave, from which they were separated by a rood screen, a pierced partition bearing the image of the Crucifixion. The chancel has usually been considered the preserve and responsibility of the clergy, while the upkeep and repair of the nave was left to the parishioners.

Chancellor, Lord UK state official, originally the royal secretary, today a member of the cabinet, whose office ends with a change of government. The Lord Chancellor acts as Speaker of the House of Lords, may preside over the Court of Appeal, and is head of the judiciary.

Until the 14th century he was always an ecclesiastic, who also acted as royal chaplain and Keeper of the Great Seal. Under Edward III the Lord Chancellor became head of a permanent court to consider petitions to the king: the *Court of Chancery*. In order of precedence the Lord Chancellor comes after the archbishop of Canterbury.

chancellor of the Duchy of Lancaster in the UK, honorary post held by a cabinet minister who has other nondepartmental responsibilities. The chancellor of the Duchy of Lancaster was originally the monarch's representative controlling the royal lands and courts within the duchy.

chancellor of the Exchequer in the UK, senior cabinet minister responsible for the national economy. The office, established under Henry III, originally entailed keeping the Exchequer seal.

Chancery in the UK, a division of the High Court that deals with such matters as the administration of the estates of deceased persons, the execution of trusts, the enforcement of sales of land, and ◊foreclosure of mortgages. Before reorganization of the court system 1875, it administered the rules of ◊equity as distinct from ◊common law.

Chan Chan /ˈtʃæn ˈtʃæn/ capital of the pre-Inca ◊Chimu kingdom in Peru.

Chandelā /tʃʌnˈdeɪlɑː/ or **Candella** Rajput dynasty that ruled the Bundelkhand region of central India from the 9th to the 11th century. The Chandelās fought against Muslim invaders, until they were replaced by the Bundelās.

Chandernagore /ˌtʃʌndənəˈgɔː/ ('city of sandalwood') city on the river Hooghly, India, in the state of West Bengal; population (1981) 102,000. Formerly a French settlement, it was ceded to India by treaty 1952.

Chandigarh /ˌtʃʌndɪˈgɑː/ city of N India, in the foothills of the Himalayas; population (1981) 421,000. It is also a Union Territory; area 114 sq km/44 sq mi; population (1981) 450,000.

Planned by the architect Le Corbusier, it was inaugurated 1953 to replace Lahore (capital of British Punjab), which went to Pakistan under partition 1947. Since 1966, when it became a Union Territory, it has been the capital city of both Haryana and Punjab, until a new capital is built for the former.

Chandler /ˈtʃɑːndlə/ Raymond 1888–1959. US crime writer who created the hard-boiled private eye Philip Marlowe in books that include *The Big Sleep* 1939, *Farewell, My Lovely* 1940, and *The Long Goodbye* 1954.

Chandragupta Maurya /ˈtʃʌndrəɡuptə ˈmaʊriə/ ruler of N India *c.* 321–*c.* 297 BC, founder of the Maurya dynasty. He overthrew the Nanda dynasty 325 and then conquered the Punjab 322 after the death of ◊Alexander the Great, expanding his empire west to Persia. He is credited with having united most of India.

Chandrasekhar /ˌtʃændrəˈseɪkə/ Subrahmanyan 1910– . Indian-born US astrophysicist who made pioneering studies of the structure and evolution of stars. The *Chandrasekhar limit* of 1.4 Suns is the maximum mass of a ◊white dwarf before it turns into a ◊neutron star. Born in Lahore, he studied in Madras, India, and Cambridge, England, before emigrating to the USA. Nobel Prize for Physics 1983.

Chanel /ʃæˈnel/ Coco (Gabrielle) 1883–1971. French fashion designer, creator of the 'little black dress', informal cardigan suit, costume jewellery, and perfumes.

Chanel The French couturier Coco Chanel in 1937.

Chaney /'tʃeɪni/ Lon (Alonso) 1883–1930. US star of silent films, often in grotesque or monstrous roles such as *The Phantom of the Opera* 1925. A master of make-up, he was nicknamed 'the Man of a Thousand Faces'. He sometimes used extremely painful devices for added effect, as in the title role in *The Hunchback of Notre Dame* 1923, when he carried over 30 kg/70 lbs of costume in the form of a heavy hump and harness.

Chaney /'tʃeɪni/ Lon, Jr (Creighton) 1906–1973. US actor, son of Lon Chaney, who gave an acclaimed performance as Lennie in *Of Mice and Men* 1940. He went on to star in many 1940s horror films, including the title role in *The Wolf Man* 1941. His other work includes *My Favorite Brunette* 1947 and *The Haunted Palace* 1963.

Changchiakow /'tʃæŋ ˌtʃɪə 'kaʊ/ alternative transcription of ◊Zhangjiakou, trading centre in Hesei province, China.

Changchun /ˌtʃæŋ'tʃʊn/ industrial city and capital of Jilin province, China; population (1989) 2,020,000. Machinery and motor vehicles are manufactured. It is also the centre of an agricultural district.

As Hsingking ('new capital') it was the capital of Manchukuo 1932–45 during Japanese occupation.

change of state in science, a change in the physical state (solid, liquid, or gas) of a material. For instance, melting, boiling, evaporation, and their opposites, solidification and condensation, are changes of state.

The former set of changes are brought about by heating or decreased pressure; the latter by cooling or increased pressure.

These changes involve the absorption or release of heat energy, called ◊latent heat, even though the temperature of the material does not change during the transition between states.

In the unusual change of state called *sublimation*, a solid changes directly to a gas without passing through the liquid state. For example, solid carbon dioxide (dry ice) sublimes to carbon dioxide gas.

Chang Jiang /'tʃæŋ dʒi'æŋ/ or *Yangtze Kiang* longest river of China, flowing about 6,300 km/3,900 mi from Tibet to the Yellow Sea. It is a main commercial waterway.

It has 204 km/127 mi of gorges, below which is Gezhou Ba, the first dam to harness the river. The entire length of the river was first navigated 1986.

Changsha /ˌtʃæŋ'ʃɑː/ port on the river Chang Jiang, capital of Hunan province, China; population (1989) 1,260,000. It trades in rice, tea, timber, and non-ferrous metals; works antimony, lead, and silver; and produces chemicals, electronics, porcelain, and embroideries.

Channel, English stretch of water between England and France, leading in the west to the Atlantic Ocean, and in the east via the Strait of Dover to the North Sea; also known as *La Manche* (French 'the sleeve') from its shape.

The English Channel is 450 km/280 mi long W–E; 27 km/17 mi wide at its narrowest (Cap Gris Nez–Dover) and 117 km/110 mi wide at its widest (Ushant–Land's End).

Channel Country /'tʃænl/ area of SW Queensland, Australia, in which channels such as Cooper's Creek (where explorers Robert Burke and William Wills died 1861) are cut by intermittent rivers. Summer rains supply rich grass for cattle, and there are the 'beef roads', down which herds are taken in linked trucks for slaughter.

Channel Islands /'tʃænl/ group of islands in the English Channel, off the NW coast of France; they are a possession of the British crown; they comprise the islands of Jersey, Guernsey, Alderney, Great and Little Sark, with the lesser Herm, Brechou, Jethou, and Lihou
area 194 sq km/75 sq mi
features very mild climate, productive soil; financially the islands are a tax haven

exports flowers, early potatoes, tomatoes, butterflies
currency English pound, also local coinage
population (1981) 128,878
language official language French (◊Norman French) but English more widely used
religion chiefly Anglican
famous people Lillie Langtry
government the main islands have their own parliaments and laws. Unless specially signified, the Channel Islands are not bound by British acts of Parliament, though the British government is responsible for defence and external relations
history originally under the duchy of Normandy, they are the only part still held by Britain. The islands came under the same rule as England 1066, and are dependent territories of the British crown. Germany occupied the islands during World War II June 1940–May 1945.

Channel swimming popular test of endurance since Captain Matthew Webb (1848–1883) first swam across the English Channel from Dover to Calais 1875. His time was 21 hr 45 min for the 34 km/21 mi journey.

The current record is 7 hr 40 min by Penny Dean of the USA 1978. The first to swim nonstop in both directions was the Argentine Antonio Abertondo 1961. The Channel Swimming Association was formed 1927, and records exist for various feats; double crossing, most crossings, and youngest and oldest to complete a crossing.

Channel Tunnel tunnel built beneath the English Channel, linking Britain with mainland Europe. It comprises twin rail tunnels, 50 km/31 mi long and 7.3 m/24 ft in diameter, located 40 m/130 ft beneath the seabed. Specially designed shuttle trains carrying cars and lorries will run between terminals at Folkestone, Kent, and Sangatte, W of Calais, France. It was begun 1986 and was officially opened May 1994. The French and English sections were linked Dec 1990.

In the 1880s British financier and railway promoter Edward Watkin started boring a tunnel near Dover, abandoning it 1894 because of governmental opposition after driving some 1.6 km/1 mile out to sea. In 1973 Britain and France agreed to back a tunnel, but a year later Britain pulled out following a change of government. The estimated cost has continually been revised upwards and in 1989 was £6 billion.

chanson de geste epic poetry of the High Middle Ages in Europe. It probably developed from oral poetry recited in royal or princely courts, and takes as its subject the exploits of heroes, such as those associated with Charlemagne and the crusades.

Chanson de Roland /ʃɑːˈsɒn də rəʊˈlɒn/ early 12th-century epic poem which tells of the real and imaginary deeds of Roland and other knights of Charlemagne, and their last stand against the Basques at Roncesvalles. It is an example of the *chanson de geste*.

chanterelle edible fungus *Cantharellus cibarius* that is bright yellow and funnel-shaped. It grows in deciduous woodland.

Chantilly /ʃænˈtɪli/ town in Oise *département*, France, NE of Paris; population (1982) 10,208. It is the centre of French horseracing and was the headquarters of the French military chief Joseph Joffre 1914–17. It was formerly renowned for its lace and porcelain.

chantry in medieval Europe, a religious ceremony in which, in return for an endowment of land, the souls of the donor and the donor's family and friends would be prayed for. A chantry could be held at an existing altar, or in a specially constructed chantry chapel, in which the donor's body was usually buried.

Chantries became widespread in the later Middle Ages, reflecting the acceptance of the doctrine of ◊purgatory, together with the growth of individualistic piety (as in the ◊*devotio moderna*) and the decline in the popularity of monasteries, to which they were seen as an alternative. Their foundation required the consent of the local bishop and a licence from the king for the alienation of land in ◊mortmain. They were suppressed in Protestant countries during the Reformation, and abolished in England 1547.

Chao Phraya /ˈtʃaʊ prəˈjɑː/ chief river (formerly Menam) of Thailand, flowing 1,200 km/750 mi into the Bight of Bangkok, an inlet of the Gulf of Thailand.

chaos theory or *chaology* branch of mathematics used to deal with chaotic systems—for example, an engineered structure, such as an oil platform, that is subjected to irregular, unpredictable wave stress.

chaparral thick scrub country of the southwestern USA. Thorny bushes have replaced what was largely evergreen oak trees.

chapel place of worship used by some Christian denominations; also, a part of a building used for Christian worship. A large church or cathedral may have several chapels.

Chapel Royal in the UK, the royal retinue of priests, singers, and musicians (including Tallis, Byrd, and Purcell) of the English court from 1135.

Chaplin /ˈtʃæplɪn/ Charlie (Charles Spencer) 1889–1977. English film actor and director. He made his reputation as a tramp with a smudge moustache, bowler hat, and twirling cane in silent comedies from the mid-1910s, including *The Rink* 1916, *The Kid* 1920, and *The Gold Rush* 1925. His work often contrasts buffoonery with pathos, and his later films combine dialogue with mime and music, as in *The Great Dictator* 1940 and *Limelight* 1952. He was one of cinema's most popular and greatest stars.

Chaplin was born in south London and first appeared on the stage at the age of five. His other films include *City Lights* 1931, *Modern Times* 1936, and *Monsieur Verdoux* (in which he spoke for the first time) 1947. *Limelight* 1952 was awarded an Oscar for Chaplin's musical theme. When accused of communist sympathies during the McCarthy witchhunt, he left the USA 1952 and moved to Switzerland. He received special Oscars 1928 and 1972.

Chapman /ˈtʃæpmən/ Frederick Spencer 1907–1971. British explorer, mountaineer, and writer who explored Greenland, the Himalayas, and Malaysia. He accompanied Gino Watkins on the British Arctic Air Routes Expedition 1930–31, recalled in *Northern Lights* 1932, and in 1935 he joined a climbing expedition to the Himalayas. For two years he participated in a government mission to Tibet described in *Lhasa, the Holy City* 1938, before setting out to climb the 7,315 m/24,000 ft peak Chomollari.

Chapman /ˈtʃæpmən/ George 1559–1634. English poet and dramatist. His translations of the Greek epics of Homer (completed 1616) were celebrated; his plays include the comedy *Eastward Ho!* (with Jonson and Marston) 1605 and the tragedy *Bussy d'Amboise* 1607.

chapter in the Christian church, the collective assembly of canons (priests) who together administer a cathedral.

char or *charr* fish *Salvelinus alpinus* related to the trout, living in the Arctic coastal waters, and also in Europe and North America in some upland lakes. It is one of Britain's rarest fish, and is at risk from growing acidification.

characin freshwater fish belonging to the family Characidae. There are over 1,300 species, mostly in South and Central America, but also in Africa. Most are carnivores. In typical characins, unlike the somewhat similar carp family, the mouth is toothed, and there is a small dorsal adipose fin just in front of the tail. Characins include ◊tetras and ◊piranhas.

characteristic in mathematics, the integral part (whole number) of a ◊logarithm. For example, in base ten, $10^0 = 1$, $10^1 = 10$, $10^2 = 100$, and so on, the powers to which 10 is raised are the characteristics. To determine the power to which 10 must be raised to obtain a number between 10 and 100, say 20, the logarithm for 2 is found (0.3010), and the characteristic 1 added to make 1.3010. The fractional part (in this case 0.3010) is the ◊mantissa.

charcoal black, porous form of ◊carbon, produced by heating wood or other organic materials in the absence of air. It is used as a fuel in the smelting of metals such as copper and zinc, and by artists for making black line drawings. *Activated charcoal* has been powdered and dried so that it presents a much increased surface area for adsorption; it is used for filtering and purifying liquids and gases—for example, in drinking-water filters and gas masks.

Charcoal had many uses in earlier centuries. Because of the high temperature at which it burns (1,100°C), it was used in furnaces and blast furnaces before the development of ◊coke. It was also used in an industrial process for obtaining ethanoic acid (acetic acid), in producing wood tar and ◊wood pitch, and (when produced from alder or willow trees) as a component of gunpowder.

Charcot /ʃɑːˈkəʊ/ Jean-Martin 1825–1893. French neurologist who studied hysteria, sclerosis, locomotor ataxia, and senile diseases. Among his pupils was Sigmund ◊Freud.

Charcot worked at a hospital in Paris, where he studied the way certain mental illnesses cause physical changes in the brain. He exhibited hysterical women at weekly public lectures, which became highly fashionable events.

Chardin /ʃɑːˈdæn/ Jean-Baptiste-Siméon 1699–1779. French painter of naturalistic still lifes and quiet domestic scenes that recall the Dutch tradition. His work is a complete contrast to that of his contemporaries, the Rococo painters. He developed his own technique using successive layers of paint to achieve depth of tone and is generally considered one of the finest exponents of the genre.

Charente /ʃæˈrɒnt/ French river, rising in Haute-Vienne *département* and flowing past Angoulême and Cognac into the Bay of Biscay below Rochefort. It is 360 km/225 mi long. Its wide estuary is much silted up. It gives its name to two *départements*, Charente and Charente-Maritime (formerly Charente-Inférieure).

charge see ◊electric charge.

charge-coupled device (CCD) device for forming images electronically, using a layer of silicon that releases electrons when struck by incoming light. The electrons are stored in ◊pixels and read off into a computer at the end of the exposure. CCDs have now almost entirely replaced photographic film for applications such as astrophotography where extreme sensitivity to light is paramount.

charged particle beam high-energy beam of electrons or protons that does not burn through the surface of its target like a ◊laser, but cuts through it. Such beams are being developed as weapons.

Charge of the Light Brigade disastrous attack by the British Light Brigade of cavalry against the Russian entrenched artillery on 25 Oct 1854 during the Crimean War at the Battle of ◊Balaclava.

Charing Cross /ˈtʃeərɪŋ ˈkrɒs/ district in Westminster, London, around Charing Cross railway station. It derives its name from the site of the last of 12 stone crosses erected by Edward I 1290 at the resting-places of the coffin of his queen, Eleanor. The present cross was designed by A S Barry 1865.

chariot horse-drawn carriage with two wheels, used in ancient Egypt, Greece, and Rome, for fighting, processions, and races; it is thought to have originated in Asia. Typically, the fighting chariot contained a driver and a warrior, who would fight on foot, with the chariot providing rapid mobility.

Julius Caesar and Tacitus both write of chariots being used by the British against Roman armies in the 1st century AD. The most complete remains of a chariot found in Britain were at Llyn Cerrig Bach in Anglesey, Wales, but many parts of chariots, such as axle-caps and harness mounts, have been found.

charismatic movement late 20th-century movement within the Christian church that empha-sizes the role of the Holy Spirit in the life of the individual believer and in the life of the church. See ◊Pentecostal movement.

Charlemagne /ˈʃɑːləˌmeɪn/ · Charles I *the Great* 742–814. King of the Franks from 768 and Holy Roman emperor from 800. By inheritance (his father was ◊Pepin the Short) and extensive campaigns of conquest, he united most of W Europe by 804, when after 30 years of war the Saxons came under his control. He reformed the legal, judicial, and military systems; established schools; and promoted Christianity, commerce, agriculture, arts, and literature. In his capital, Aachen, scholars gathered from all over Europe.

Pepin had been mayor of the palace in Merovingian Neustria until he was crowned king by Pope Stephen II (died 757) in 754, and his sons Carl (Charlemagne) and Carloman were crowned as joint heirs. When Pepin died 768, Charlemagne inherited the N Frankish kingdom, and when Carloman died 771, he also took possession of his domains.

He was engaged in his first Saxon campaign when the Pope's call for help against the Lombards reached him; he crossed the Alps, captured Pavia, and took the title of king of the Lombards. The pacification and christianizing of the Saxon peoples occupied the greater part of Charlemagne's reign. From 792 N Saxony was subdued, and in 804 the whole region came under his rule.

In 777 the emir of Zaragoza asked for Charlemagne's help against the emir of Córdoba. Charlemagne crossed the Pyrenees 778 and reached the Ebro but had to turn back from Zaragoza. The rearguard action of Roncesvalles, in which ◊Roland, warden of the Breton March, and other Frankish nobles were ambushed and killed by Basques, was later glorified in the *Chanson de Roland*. In 801 the district between the Pyrenees and the Llobregat was organized as the Spanish March. The independent duchy of Bavaria was incorporated in the kingdom 788, and the ◊Avar people were subdued 791–96 and accepted Christianity. Charlemagne's last campaign was against a Danish attack on his northern frontier 810.

The supremacy of the Frankish king in Europe found outward expression in the bestowal of the imperial title: in Rome, during Mass on Christmas Day 800, Pope Leo III crowned Charlemagne emperor. He enjoyed diplomatic relations with Byzantium, Baghdad, Mercia, Northumbria, and other regions. Jury courts were introduced, the laws of the Franks revised, and other peoples' laws written down. A new coinage was introduced, weights and measures were reformed, and communications were improved. Charlemagne also took a lively interest in theology, organized the church in his dominions, and furthered missionary enterprises and monastic reform.

The *Carolingian Renaissance* of learning began when he persuaded the Northumbrian scholar Alcuin to enter his service 781. Charlemagne gathered a kind of academy around him. Although he never learned to read, he collected the old heroic sagas, began a Frankish grammar, and promoted religious instruction in the vernacular. He died 28 Jan 814 in Aachen, where he was buried. Soon a cycle of heroic legends and romances developed around him, including epics by Ariosto, Boiardo, and Tasso.

Charles /tʃɑːlz/ (Mary) Eugenia 1919– . Dominican politician, prime minister from 1980; cofounder and first leader of the centrist Dominica Freedom Party (DFP).

Charles qualified as a barrister in England and returned to practise in the Windward and Leeward Islands in the West Indies. Two years after Dominica's independence the DFP won the 1980 general election and she became the Caribbean's first female prime minister.

Charles /ʃɑːl/ Jacques Alexandre César 1746–1823. French physicist who studied gases and made the first ascent in a hydrogen-filled balloon 1783. His work on the expansion of gases led to the formulation of ◊Charles's law.

Charles /tʃɑːlz/ Ray 1930– . US singer, songwriter, and pianist whose first hits were 'I've Got A Woman' 1955, 'What'd I Say' 1959, and 'Georgia on My Mind' 1960. He has recorded gospel, blues, rock, soul, country, and rhythm and blues.

Charles /tʃɑːlz/ two kings of Britain:

Charles I 1600–1649. King of Great Britain and Ireland from 1625, son of James I of England (James VI of Scotland). He accepted the ◊petition of right 1628 but then dissolved Parliament and ruled without a parliament 1629–40. His advisers were ◊Strafford and ◊Laud, who persecuted the Puritans and provoked the Scots to revolt. The ◊Short Parliament, summoned 1640, refused funds, and the ◊Long Parliament later that year rebelled. Charles declared war on Parliament 1642 but surrendered 1646 and was beheaded 1649. He was the father of Charles II.

Charles was born at Dunfermline, and became heir to the throne on the death of his brother Henry 1612. He married Henrietta Maria, daughter of Henry IV of France. When he succeeded his father, friction with Parliament began at once. The parliaments of 1625 and 1626 were dissolved, and that of 1628 refused supplies until Charles had accepted the Petition of Right. In 1629 it attacked Charles's illegal taxation and support of the Arminians (see Jacobus ◊Arminius) in the church, whereupon he dissolved Parliament and imprisoned its leaders.

For 11 years he ruled without a parliament, the Eleven Years' Tyranny, raising money by expedients, such as ◊ship money, that alienated the nation, while the ◊Star Chamber suppressed opposition by persecuting the Puritans. When Charles attempted 1637 to force a prayer book on the English model on Presbyterian Scotland he found himself confronted with a nation in arms. The Short Parliament, which met April 1640, refused to grant money until grievances were redressed, and was speedily dissolved. The Scots then advanced into England and forced their own terms on Charles. The Long Parliament met 3 Nov 1640 and declared extraparliamentary taxation illegal, abolished the Star Chamber and other prerogative courts, and voted that Parliament could not be dissolved without its own consent. Laud and other ministers were imprisoned, and Strafford condemned to death. After the failure of his attempt to arrest the parliamentary leaders 4 Jan 1642, Charles, confident that he had substantial support among those who felt that Parliament was becoming too radical and zealous, withdrew from London, and on 22 Aug declared war on Parliament by raising his standard at Nottingham (see English ◊Civil War).

Charles's defeat at Naseby June 1645 ended all hopes of victory; in May 1646 he surrendered at Newark to the Scots, who handed him over to Parliament Jan 1647. In June the army seized him and carried him off to Hampton Court. While the army leaders strove to find a settlement, Charles secretly intrigued for a Scottish invasion. In Nov he escaped, but was recaptured and held at Carisbrooke Castle; a Scottish invasion followed 1648, and was shattered by ◊Cromwell at Preston. In Jan 1649 the House of Commons set up a high court of justice, which ried Charles and condemned him to death. He was beheaded 30 Jan before the Banqueting House in Whitehall.

Charles II 1630–1685. King of Great Britain and Ireland from 1660, when Parliament accepted he restoration of the monarchy; son of Charles I. His chief minister Clarendon, who arranged his marriage 1662 with Catherine of Braganza, was replaced 1667 with the ◊Cabal of advisers. His plans to restore Catholicism in Britain led to war with the Netherlands 1672–74 and a break with Parliament, which he dissolved 1681. He was succeeded by James II.

Charles was born in St James's Palace, London; during the Civil War he lived with his father at Oxford 1642–45, and after the victory of Cromwell's Parliamentary forces withdrew to France. Accepting the ◊Covenanters' offer to make him king, he landed in Scotland 1650, and was crowned at Scone 1 Jan 1651. An attempt to invade England was ended 3 Sept by Cromwell's victory at Worcester. Charles escaped, and for nine years he wandered through France, Germany, Flanders, Spain, and Holland until the opening of negotiations by George Monk (1608–1670) 1660. In April Charles issued the Declaration of ◊Breda, promising a general amnesty and freedom of conscience. Parliament accepted the Declaration and he was proclaimed king 8 May 1660, landed at Dover on 26 May, and entered London three days later.

Charles wanted to make himself absolute, and favoured Catholicism for his subjects as most consistent with absolute monarchy. The disasters of the Dutch war furnished an excuse for banishing Clarendon 1667, and he was replaced by the Cabal of Clifford and Arlington, both secret Catholics, and ◊Buckingham, Ashley (Lord ◊Shaftesbury), and ◊Lauderdale, who had links with the ◊Dissenters. In 1670 Charles signed the Secret Treaty of Dover, he full details of which were known only to Clifford and Arlington, whereby he promised Louis XIV of France

he would declare himself a Catholic, re-establish Catholicism in England, and support Louis's projected war against the Dutch; in return Louis was to finance Charles and in the event of resistance to supply him with troops. War with the Netherlands followed 1672, and at the same time Charles issued the Declaration of Indulgence, suspending all penal laws against Catholics and Dissenters.

In 1673, Parliament forced Charles to withdraw the Indulgence and accept a Test Act excluding all Catholics from office, and in 1674 to end the Dutch war. The Test Act broke up the Cabal, while Shaftesbury, who had learned the truth about the treaty, assumed the leadership of the opposition. ◊Danby, the new chief minister, built up a court party in the Commons by bribery, while subsidies from Louis relieved Charles from dependence on Parliament. In 1678 Titus ◊Oates's announcement of a 'popish plot' released a general panic, which Shaftesbury exploited to introduce his Exclusion Bill, excluding James, Duke of York, from the succession as a Catholic; instead he hoped to substitute Charles's illegitimate son ◊Monmouth.

In 1681 Parliament was summoned at Oxford, which had been the Royalist headquarters during the Civil War. The Whigs attended armed, but when Shaftesbury rejected a last compromise, Charles dissolved Parliament and the Whigs fled in terror. Charles now ruled without a parliament, financed by Louis XIV. When the Whigs plotted a revolt, their leaders were executed, while Shaftesbury and Monmouth fled to the Netherlands.

Charles was a patron of the arts and science. His mistresses included Lady ◊Castlemaine, Nell ◊Gwyn, Lady ◊Portsmouth, and Lucy ◊Walter.

Charles (full name Charles Philip Arthur George) 1948– . Prince of the UK, heir to the British throne, and Prince of Wales since 1958 (invested 1969). He is the first-born child of Queen Elizabeth II and the Duke of Edinburgh. He studied at Trinity College, Cambridge, 1967–70, before serving in the Royal Air Force and Royal Navy. He is the first royal heir since 1659 to have an English wife, Lady Diana Spencer, daughter of the 8th Earl Spencer. They have two sons and heirs, William (1982–) and Henry (1984–). Amid much publicity, Charles and Diana separated 1992. Prince Charles's concern for social and environmental issues has led to many self-help projects for the young and underprivileged, and he is a leading critic of contemporary architecture.

Charles /tʃɑːlz/ ten kings of France, including:

Charles I better known as the emperor ◊Charlemagne.

Charles II *the Bald*; see ◊Charles II, Holy Roman emperor.

Charles III /ʃɑːlz, ʃɑːl/ *the Simple* 879–929. King of France 893–922, son of Louis the Stammerer. He was crowned at Reims. In 911 he ceded what later became the duchy of Normandy to he Norman chief Rollo.

Charles IV *the Fair* 1294–1328. King of France from 1322, when he succeeded Philip V as the last of the direct Capetian line.

Charles V *the Wise* 1337–1380. King of France from 1364. He was regent during the captivity of his father, John II, in England 1356–60, and became king on John's death. He reconquered nearly all France from England 1369–80.

Charles VI *the Mad* or *the Well-Beloved* 1368–1422. King of France from 1380, succeeding his father Charles V; he was under the regency of his uncles until 1388. He became mentally unstable 1392, and civil war broke out between the dukes of Orléans and Burgundy. Henry V of England invaded France 1415, conquering Normandy, and in 1420 forced Charles to sign the Treaty of Troyes, recognizing Henry as his successor.

Charles VII 1403–1461. King of France from 1429. Son of Charles VI, he was excluded from the succession by the Treaty of Troyes, but recognized by the south of France. In 1429 Joan of Arc raised the siege of Orléans and had him crowned at Reims. He organized France's first standing army and by 1453 he had expelled the English from all of France except Calais.

Charles VIII 1470–1498. King of France from 1483, when he succeeded his father, Louis XI. In 1494 he unsuccessfully tried to claim the Neapolitan crown, and when he entered Naples 1495 was forced to withdraw by a coalition of Milan, Venice, Spain, and the Holy Roman Empire. He defeated them at Fornovo, but lost Naples. He died while preparing a second expedition.

Charles IX 1550–1574. King of France from 1560. Second son of Henry II and Catherine de' Medici, he succeeded his brother Francis II at the age of ten but remained under the domination of his mother's regency for ten years while France was torn by religious wars. In 1570 he fell under the influence of the ◊Huguenot leader Gaspard de Coligny; alarmed by this, Catherine instigated his order for the Massacre of ◊St Bartholomew, which led to a new religious war.

Charles X 1757–1836. King of France from 1824. Grandson of Louis XV and brother of Louis XVI and Louis XVIII, he was known as the comte d'Artois before his accession. He fled to England at the beginning of the French Revolution, and when he came to the throne on the death of Louis XVIII, he attempted to reverse the achievements of the Revolution. A revolt ensued 1830, and he again fled to England.

Charles /tʃɑːlz/ seven rulers of the Holy Roman Empire:

Charles I better known as ◊Charlemagne.

Charles II *the Bald* 823–877. Holy Roman emperor from 875 and (as Charles II) king of France from 843. Younger son of Louis I (the Pious), he warred against his eldest brother, Emperor Lothair I. The Treaty of Verdun 843 made him king of the West Frankish Kingdom (now France and the Spanish Marches).

Charles III *the Fat* 839–888. Holy Roman emperor 881–87; he became king of the West Franks 885, thus uniting for the last time the whole of Charlemagne's dominions, but was deposed.

Charles IV 1316–1378. Holy Roman emperor from 1355 and king of Bohemia from 1346. Son of John of Luxembourg, king of Bohemia, he was elected king of Germany 1346 and ruled all Germany from 1347. He was the founder of the first German university in Prague 1348.

Charles V 1500–1558. Holy Roman emperor 1519–56. Son of Philip of Burgundy and Joanna of Castile, he inherited vast possessions, which led to rivalry from Francis I of France, whose alliance with the Ottoman Empire brought Vienna under siege 1529 and 1532. Charles was also in conflict with the Protestants in Germany until the Treaty of Passau 1552, which allowed the Lutherans religious liberty.

Charles was born in Ghent and received the Netherlands from his father 1506; Spain, Naples, Sicily, Sardinia, and the Spanish dominions in N Africa and the Americas on the death of his maternal grandfather, Ferdinand V of Castile (1452–1516); and from his paternal grandfather, Maximilian I, the Habsburg dominions 1519, when he was elected emperor. He was crowned in Aachen 1520. From 1517 the empire was split by the rise of Lutheranism, Charles making unsuccessful attempts to reach a settlement at Augsburg 1530 (see Confession of ◊Augsburg), and being forced by the Treaty of Passau to yield most of the Protestant demands. Worn out, he abdicated in favour of his son Philip II in the Netherlands 1555 and Spain 1556. He yielded the imperial crown to his brother Ferdinand I, and retired to the monastery of Yuste, Spain.

Charles VI 1685–1740. Holy Roman emperor from 1711, father of ◊Maria Theresa, whose succession to his Austrian dominions he tried to ensure, and himself claimant to the Spanish throne 1700, thus causing the War of the ◊Spanish Succession.

Charles VII 1697–1745. Holy Roman emperor from 1742, opponent of ◊Maria Theresa's claim to the Austrian dominions of Charles VI.

Charles /tʃɑːlz/ (Karl Franz Josef) 1887–1922. Emperor of Austria and king of Hungary from 1916, the last of the Habsburg emperors. He succeeded his great-uncle Franz Josef 1916 but was forced to withdraw to Switzerland 1918, although he refused to abdicate. In 1921 he attempted unsuccessfully to regain the crown of Hungary and was deported to Madeira, where he died.

Charles /tʃɑːlz/ (Spanish *Carlos*) four kings of Spain:

Charles I 1500–1558. See ◊Charles V, Holy Roman emperor.

Charles II 1661–1700. King of Spain from 1665. The second son of Philip IV, he was the last of the Spanish Habsburg kings. Mentally handicapped from birth, he bequeathed his dominions to Philip of Anjou, grandson of Louis XIV, which led to the War of the ◊Spanish Succession.

Charles III 1716–1788. King of Spain from 1759. Son of Philip V, he became duke of Parma 1732 and conquered Naples and Sicily 1734. On the death of his half-brother Ferdinand VI (1713–1759), he became king of Spain, handing over Naples and Sicily to his son Ferdinand (1751–1825). During his reign, Spain was twice at war with Britain: during the Seven Years' War, when he sided with France and lost Florida; and when he

backed the colonists in the American Revolution and regained it. At home he carried out a programme of reforms and expelled the Jesuits.

Charles IV 1748–1819. King of Spain from 1788, when he succeeded his father, Charles III, but left the government in the hands of his wife and her lover, the minister Manuel de Godoy (1767–1851). In 1808 Charles was induced to abdicate by Napoleon's machinations in favour of his son Ferdinand VII (1784–1833), who was subsequently deposed by Napoleon's brother Joseph. Charles was awarded a pension by Napoleon and died in Rome.

Charles /tʃɑːlz/ (Swedish *Carl*) fifteen kings of Sweden (the first six were local chieftains):

Charles VII King of Sweden from about 1161. He helped to establish Christianity in Sweden.

Charles VIII 1408–1470. King of Sweden from 1448. He was elected regent of Sweden 1438, when Sweden broke away from Denmark and Norway. He stepped down 1441 when Christopher III of Bavaria (1418–1448) was elected king, but after his death became king. He was twice expelled by the Danes and twice restored.

Charles IX 1550–1611. King of Sweden from 1604, the youngest son of Gustavus Vasa. In 1568 he and his brother John led the rebellion against Eric XIV (1533–1577); John became king as John III and attempted to Catholicize Sweden, and Charles led the opposition. John's son Sigismund, king of Poland and a Catholic, succeeded to the Swedish throne 1592, and Charles led the Protestants. He was made regent 1595 and deposed Sigismund 1599. Charles was elected king of Sweden 1604 and was involved in unsuccessful wars with Russia, Poland, and Denmark. He was the father of Gustavus Adolphus.

Charles X 1622–1660. King of Sweden from 1654, when he succeeded his cousin Christina. He waged war with Poland and Denmark and in 1657 invaded Denmark by leading his army over the frozen sea.

Charles XI 1655–1697. King of Sweden from 1660, when he succeeded his father Charles X. His mother acted as regent until 1672 when Charles took over the government. He was a remarkable general and reformed the administration.

Charles XII 1682–1718. King of Sweden from 1697, when he succeeded his father,

Charles XI. From 1700 he was involved in wars with Denmark, Poland, and Russia. He won a succession of victories until, in 1709 while invading Russia, he was defeated at Poltava in the Ukraine, and forced to take refuge in Turkey until 1714. He was killed while besieging Fredrikshall.

Charles XIII 1748–1818. King of Sweden from 1809, when he was elected; he became the first king of Sweden and Norway 1814.

Charles XIV (Jean Baptiste Jules ◊Bernadotte) 1763–1844. King of Sweden and Norway from 1818. A former marshal in the French army, in 1810 he was elected crown prince of Sweden under the name of Charles John (Carl Johan). Loyal to his adopted country, he brought Sweden into the alliance against Napoleon 1813, as a reward for which Sweden received Norway. He was the founder of the present dynasty.

Charles XV 1826–1872. King of Sweden and Norway from 1859, when he succeeded his father Oscar I. A popular and liberal monarch, his main achievement was the reform of the constitution.

Charles Albert /tsɑːlz ˈælbət/ 1798–1849. King of Sardinia from 1831. He showed liberal sympathies in early life, and after his accession introduced some reforms. On the outbreak of the 1848 revolution he granted a constitution and declared war on Austria. His troops were defeated at Custozza and Novara. In 1849 he abdicated in favour of his son Victor Emmanuel and retired to a monastery, where he died.

Charles Edward Stuart /tʃɑːlz ˈedwəd ˈstjuːət/ 1720–1788. British prince, known as the Young Pretender or Bonnie Prince Charlie, grandson of James II. In the Jacobite rebellion 1745 Charles won the support of the Scottish Highlanders; his army invaded England but was beaten back by the Duke of ◊Cumberland and routed at ◊Culloden 1746. Charles went into exile.

He was born in Rome, the son of James, the Old Pretender, and created Prince of Wales at birth. In July 1745 he sailed for Scotland, and landed in Inverness-shire with seven companions. On 19 Aug he raised his father's standard, and within a week had rallied an army of 2,000 Highlanders. He entered Edinburgh almost without resistance, won an easy victory at Prestonpans, invaded England, and by 4 Dec had reached Derby, where his officers insisted on a retreat. The army returned to Scotland and

won a victory at Falkirk, but was forced to retire to the Highlands before Cumberland's advance. On 16 April at Culloden Charles's army was routed by Cumberland, and he fled. For five months he wandered through the Highlands with a price of £30,000 on his head before escaping to France. He visited England secretly in 1750, and may have made other visits. In later life he degenerated into a friendless drunkard. He settled in Italy 1766.

Charles Martel /tʃɑːlz mɑːˈtel/ c. 688–741. Frankish ruler (Mayor of the Palace) of the E Frankish kingdom from 717 and the whole kingdom from 731. His victory against the Moors at Moussais-la-Bataille near Tours in 732 earned him his nickname of Martel, 'the Hammer', because he halted the Islamic advance by the ◊Moors into Europe. An illegitimate son of Pepin of Heristal (Pepin II, Mayor of the Palace c. 640–714), he was a grandfather of Charlemagne.

Charles's law law stating that the volume of a given mass of gas at constant pressure is directly proportional to its absolute temperature (temperature in kelvin). It was discovered by Jacques Charles in 1787, and independently by Joseph Gay-Lussac in 1802.

Charles the Bold /tʃɑːlz/ Duke of Burgundy 1433–1477. Son of Philip the Good, he inherited Burgundy and the Low Countries from him 1465. He waged wars attempting to free the duchy from dependence on France and restore it as a kingdom. He was killed in battle.

Charles' ambition was to create a kingdom stretching from the mouth of the Rhine to the mouth of the Rhône. He formed the League of the Public Weal against Louis XI of France, invaded France 1471, and conquered the country as far as Rouen. The Holy Roman emperor, the Swiss, and Lorraine united against him; he captured Nancy, but was defeated at Granson and again at Morat 1476. Nancy was lost, and he was killed while attempting to recapture it. His possessions in the Netherlands passed to the Habsburgs by the marriage of his daughter Mary to Maximilian I of Austria.

Charleston /tʃɑːlstən/ main port and city of South Carolina, USA; population (1980) 486,000. Industries include textiles, clothing, and paper products. The city dates from 1670. Fort Sumter, in the sheltered harbour of Charleston, was bombarded by Confederate batteries 12–13 April 1861, thus beginning the Civil War. There are many historic houses and fine gardens.

Charleston /ˈtʃɑːlstən/ chief city of West Virginia, USA, on the Kanawha River; population (1980) 64,000. It is the centre of a district producing coal, natural gas, salt, clay, timber, and oil and was the home of the pioneer Daniel ◊Boone.

Charleston /ˈtʃɑːlstən/ back-kicking dance of the 1920s that originated in Charleston, South Carolina, and became an American craze.

Charlotte /ˈʃɑːlət/ city in North Carolina, USA, on the border with South Carolina; population (1980) 314,500. Industries include data processing, textiles, chemicals, machinery, and food products. It was the gold-mining centre of the country until 1849. The Mint Museum of Arts has paintings, sculpture, and ceramics. Charlotte is the birthplace of James K Polk, 11th president of the USA.

Charlotte Amalie /ˈʃɑːlət əˈmɑːljə/ capital and tourist resort of the US Virgin Islands; population (1980) 11,756.

Charlotte Augusta /ˈʃɑːlət ɔːˈɡʌstə/ Princess 1796–1817. Only child of George IV and Caroline of Brunswick, and heir to the British throne. In 1816 she married Prince Leopold of Saxe-Coburg (later Leopold I of the Belgians), but died in childbirth 18 months later.

Charlotte Sophia /ˈʃɑːlət səˈfaɪə/ 1744–1818. British queen consort. The daughter of the German duke of Mecklenburg-Strelitz, she married George III of Great Britain and Ireland 1761, and they had nine sons and six daughters.

Charlottetown /ˈʃɑːləttaʊn/ capital of Prince Edward Island, Canada; population (1986) 16,000. The city trades in textiles, fish, timber, vegetables, and dairy produce. It was founded by the French in the 1720s.

Charlton /ˈtʃɑːltən/ Bobby (Robert) 1937– . English footballer, younger brother of Jack Charlton, who scored a record 49 goals in 106 appearances. He spent most of his playing career with Manchester United.

He was an elegant midfield player who specialized in fierce long-range shots. On retiring he had an unsuccessful spell as manager of Preston North End. He later became a director of Manchester United.

Charlton /ˈtʃɑːltən/ Jack 1935– . English footballer, older brother of Robert (Bobby)

and nephew of Jackie Milburn. He spent all his playing career with Leeds United and played more than 750 games for them.

He and his brother both appeared in the England team that won the World Cup 1966. After retiring, Charlton managed Middlesborough to the 2nd division title. Appointed manager of the Republic of Ireland national squad in 1986, he took the team to the 1988 European Championship finals, after which he was made an 'honorary Irishman'. He led Ireland to the World Cup finals for the first time in 1990.

charm in physics, a property possessed by one type of ◊quark (very small particles found inside protons and neutrons), called the charm quark. The effects of charm are only seen in experiments with particle ◊accelerators. See ◊elementary particles.

Charon /ˈkeərən/ in Greek mythology, the boatman who ferried the dead over the river Styx to the underworld.

Charter 88 British political campaign begun 1988, calling for a written constitution to prevent what it termed the development of 'an elective dictatorship'. Those who signed the charter, including many figures from the arts, objected to what they saw as the autocratic premiership of Margaret Thatcher.

Charteris /ˈtʃɑːtərɪs/ Leslie 1907–1993. British novelist, a US citizen from 1946. His varied career in many exotic occupations gave authentic background to some 40 novels about Simon Templar, the 'Saint', a gentleman-adventurer on the wrong side of the law, which have been adapted for films, radio, and television. The first was *The Saint Meets the Tiger* 1928.

Chartism radical British democratic movement, mainly of the working classes, which flourished around 1838–50. It derived its name from the People's Charter, a six-point programme comprising: universal male suffrage, equal electoral districts, secret ballot, annual parliaments, abolition of the property qualification for, and payment of, members of Parliament. Greater prosperity, lack of organization, and rivalry in the leadership led to its demise.

Chartres /ˈʃɑːtrə/ capital of the *département* of Eure-et-Loir, NW France, 96 km/59 mi SW of Paris, on the river Eure; population (1982) 39,243. The city is an agricultural centre for the fertile Plaine de la Beauce. Its cathedral of Nôtre Dame, completed about

1240, is a masterpiece of Gothic architecture.

Chartreuse /ʃɑːˈtrɜːz/ trademark for a green or yellow liqueur distilled since 1607 by the Carthusian monks at La Grande Chartreuse monastery, France, and also in Tarragona, Spain.

Chartreuse, La Grande /ʃɑːˈtrɜːz/ the original home of the Carthusian order of Roman Catholic monks, established by St Bruno around 1084 in a valley near Grenoble, France. The present buildings date from the 17th century.

Charybdis /kəˈrɪbdɪs/ in Greek mythology, a whirlpool formed by a monster of the same name on one side of the narrow straits of Messina, Sicily, opposite the monster Scylla.

chasing indentation of a design on metal by small chisels and hammers. This method of decoration was familiar in ancient Egypt, Assyria, and Greece; it is used today on fine silverware.

chasuble the outer garment worn by the priest in the celebration of the Christian Mass. The colour of the chasuble depends on which feast is being celebrated.

château term originally applied to a French medieval castle, but now used to describe a country house or important residence in France. The château was first used as a domestic building in the late 15th century; by the reign of Louis XIII (1610–43) fortifications such as moats and keeps were no longer used for defensive purposes, but merely as decorative features. The Loire valley contains some fine examples of châteaux.

Chateaubriand /ʃæˌtəʊbriˈɒn/ François René, vicomte de 1768–1848. French author. In exile from the French Revolution 1794–99, he wrote *Atala* 1801 (after his encounters with North American Indians) and the autobiographical *René*, which formed part of *Le Génie du Christianisme/The Genius of Christianity* 1802.

Châtelet /ʃɑːtəˈleɪ/ Emilie de Breteuil, Marquise du 1706–1749. French scientific writer and translator into French of Newton's *Principia*.

Her marriage to the Marquis du Châtelet in 1725 gave her the leisure to study physics and mathematics. She met Voltaire in 1733, and settled with him at her husband's estate at Cirey, in the Duchy of Lorraine. Her study of Newton, with whom she collaborated on various scientific works, influenced Voltaire's work. She independently produced the first (and only) French translation of Newton's *Principia Mathematica* (published posthumously in 1759).

Chatham /ˈtʃætəm/ town in Kent, England; population (1983) 146,000. The Royal Dockyard 1588–1984 was from 1985 converted to an industrial area, marina, and museum as a focus of revival for the whole Medway area.

Chatham Islands /ˈtʃætəm/ two Pacific islands (Chatham and Pitt), forming a county of South Island, New Zealand; area 960 sq km/371 sq mi; population (1981) 750. The chief settlement is Waitangi.

Chattanooga /ˌtʃætəˈnuːɡə/ city in Tennessee, USA, on the Tennessee River; population (1986) 426,000. It is the focus of the ◊Tennessee Valley Authority area. Developed as a salt-trading centre after 1835, it now produces chemicals, textiles, and metal products.

Chatterji /ˈtʃætədʒiː/ Bankim Chandra 1838–1894. Indian novelist. Born in Bengal, where he established his reputation with his first book, *Durges-Nandini* 1864, he became a favourite of the nationalists. His book *Ananda Math* 1882 contains the Indian national song 'Bande-Mataram'.

Chatterton /ˈtʃætətən/ Thomas 1752–1770. English poet whose medieval-style poems and brief life were to inspire English Romanticism. Born in Bristol, he studied ancient documents he found in the Church of St Mary Redcliffe and composed poems he ascribed to a 15th-century monk, 'Thomas Rowley', which were accepted as genuine. He committed suicide in London, after becoming destitute.

Chatwin /ˈtʃætwɪn/ Bruce 1940–1989. English writer. His works include *The Songlines* 1987, written after living with Aborigines, the novel *Utz* 1988, about a manic porcelain collector in Prague, and travel pieces and journalism collected in *What Am I Doing Here* 1989.

Chaucer /ˈtʃɔːsə/ Geoffrey c. 1340–1400. The first great English poet. *The Canterbury Tales*, a collection of stories told by a group of pilgrims on their way to Canterbury, reveals his knowledge of human nature and his stylistic variety, from urbane and ironic to simple and bawdy. His *Troilus and Criseyde* is a substantial narrative poem about the tragic betrayal of an idealized courtly love.

Chaucer was born in London. Taken prisoner in the French wars, he had to be ransomed by Edward III 1360. He married Philippa Roet 1366, becoming in later life the brother-in-law of ◊John of Gaunt. He achieved various appointments and was sent on missions to Italy (where he may have met ◊Boccaccio and ◊Petrarch), France, and Flanders. His early work showed formal French influence, as in his adaptation of the French allegorical poem on courtly love, *Romance of the Rose*; more mature works reflected the influence of Italian realism, as in his long narrative poem *Troilus and Criseyde*, adapted from Boccaccio. In *The Canterbury Tales* he showed his own genius for metre and characterization.

chauvinism warlike, often unthinking, patriotism, as exhibited by Nicholas Chauvin, one of Napoleon I's veterans and his fanatical admirer. In the mid-20th century the expression *male chauvinism* was coined to mean an assumed superiority of the male sex over the female.

Checheno-Ingush /tʃɪtʃenəʊ ɪŋˈguːʃ/ autonomous republic in S Russia on the northern slopes of the Caucasus Mountains; area 19,000 km/7,350 sq mi; population (1986) 1,230,000. It was conquered in the 1850s, and is a major oilfield. The capital is Grozny. The population includes Chechens (53%) and Ingushes (12%).

check digit in computing, a digit added to important codes for ◊error detection.

Checkpoint Charlie Western-controlled crossing point for non-Germans between West Berlin and East Berlin, opened 1961 as the only crossing point between the Allied and Soviet sectors. Its dismantling in June 1990 was seen as a symbol of the ending of the ◊Cold War.

Cheddar /tʃedə/ village in Somerset, England where Cheddar cheese was first produced. Nearby are a limestone gorge and caves with stalactites and stalagmites. In 1962 excavation revealed the site of a Saxon palace.

cheese food made from the *curds* (solids) of soured milk from cows, sheep, or goats, separated from the *whey* (liquid), then salted, put into moulds, and pressed into firm blocks. Cheese is ripened with bacteria or surface fungi, and kept for a time to mature before eating.

There are six main types of cheese. *Soft cheeses* may be ripe or unripe, and include cottage cheese and high-fat soft cheeses such as Bel Paese, Camembert, and Neufchatel. *Semi-hard cheeses* are ripened by bacteria (Munster) or by bacteria and surface fungi (Port Salut, Gouda, St Paulin); they may also have penicillin moulds injected into them (Roquefort, Gorgonzola, Blue Stilton, Wensleydale). *Hard cheeses* are ripened by bacteria, and include Cheddar, Cheshire, and Cucciocavallo; some have large cavities within them, such as Swiss Emmental and Gruyère. *Very hard cheeses*, such as Parmesan and Spalen, are made with skimmed milk. *Processed cheese* is made with dried skim-milk powder and additives, and *whey cheese* is made by heat coagulation of the proteins from whey; examples are Mysost and Primost. In France (from 1980) a cheese has the same *appellation controlée* status as wine if it is made only in a special defined area—for example, Cantal and Roquefort are *appellation controlée* cheeses, but not Camembert and Brie, which are made in more than one region.

cheesecloth fine muslin or cotton fabric of very loose weave, originally used to press curds during the cheesemaking process; it was popular for clothing in the 1970s.

cheetah large wild cat *Acinonyx jubatus* native to Africa, Arabia, and SW Asia, but now rare in some areas. Yellowish with black spots, it has a slim lithe build. It is up to 1 m/3 ft tall at the shoulder, and up to 1.5 m/5 ft long. It can reach 110 kph/70 mph, but tires after about 400 metres. Cheetahs live in open country where they hunt small antelopes, hares, and birds.

Cheever /tʃiːvə/ John 1912–1982. US writer. His short stories and novels include *The Wapshot Chronicle* 1937, *Bullet Park* 1969, *World of Apples* 1973, and *Falconer* 1977.

Chefoo /tʃiːˈfuː/ former name of part of ◊Yantai in China.

Cheka secret police operating in the USSR 1917–23. It originated from the tsarist Okhrana (the security police under the tsar 1881–1917), and became successively the OGPU (GPU) 1923–34, NKVD 1934–46, and MVD 1946–53, before its present form, the ◊KGB.

The name is formed from the initials *che* and *ka* of the two Russian words meaning 'extraordinary commission', formed for 'the repression of counter-revolutionary activities and of speculation', and extended to cover such matters as espionage and smuggling.

Chekhov /ˈtʃekɒf/ Anton (Pavlovich) 1860–1904. Russian dramatist and writer. He began to write short stories and comic sketches as a medical student. His plays concentrate on the creation of atmosphere and delineation of internal development, rather than external action. His first play *Ivanov* 1887 was a failure, as was *The Seagull* 1896 until revived by Stanislavsky 1898 at the Moscow Art Theatre, for which Chekhov went on to write his major plays: *Uncle Vanya* 1899, *The Three Sisters* 1901 and *The Cherry Orchard* 1904.

Born at Taganrog, he qualified as a doctor 1884, but devoted himself to writing short stories rather than practising medicine. The collection *Particoloured Stories* 1886 consolidated his reputation and gave him leisure to develop his style, as seen in *My Life* 1895, *The Lady with the Dog* 1898, and *In the Ravine* 1900.

Chekiang /ˌtʃekiˈæŋ/ alternative transcription of ◊Zhejiang, province of SE China.

chela in Hinduism, a follower or pupil of a guru (teacher).

chelate chemical compound whose molecules consist of one or more metal atoms or charged ions joined to chains of organic residues by coordinate (or dative covalent) chemical ◊bonds.

Chelates are used in analytical chemistry, in agriculture and horticulture as carriers of essential trace metals, in water softening, and in the treatment of thalassaemia by removing excess iron, which may build up to toxic levels in the body. Metalloproteins (natural chelates) may influence the performance of enzymes or provide a mechanism for the storage of iron in the spleen and plasma of the human body.

Chelmsford /ˈtʃelmzfəd/ town in Essex, England, 48 km/30 mi NE of London; population (1981) 58,000. It is the administrative headquarters of the county, and a market town with radio, electrical, engineering, and agricultural machinery industries.

Chelsea /ˈtʃelsi/ historic area of the Royal Borough of Kensington and Chelsea, London, immediately N of the Thames where it is crossed by the Albert and Chelsea bridges.

The Royal Hospital was founded in 1682 by Charles II for old and disabled soldiers, 'Chelsea Pensioners', and the National Army Museum, founded 1960, covers campaigns 1485–1914. The Physic Garden for botanical research was established in the 17th century; the home of the essayist Thomas Carlyle in Cheyne Row is a museum. The Chelsea Flower Show is held annually by the Royal Horticultural Society in the grounds of Royal Hospital. Ranelagh Gardens 1742–1804 and Cremorne Gardens 1845–77 were popular places of entertainment.

Chelsea porcelain factory porcelain factory thought to be the first in England. Based in SW London, it dated from the 1740s, when it was known as the Chelsea Porcelain Works. It produced softpaste porcelain in imitation of Chinese high-fired porcelain. Later items are distinguished by the anchor mark on the base. Chelsea porcelain includes plates and other items decorated with botanical, bird, and insect paintings.

The factory was taken over by William Duesbury of Derby 1769 (after which the so-called 'Chelsea-Derby' was produced), and pulled down 1784.

Cheltenham /ˈtʃeltənəm/ spa at the foot of the Cotswolds, Gloucestershire, England; population (1981) 73,000. There are annual literary and music festivals, a racecourse (the Cheltenham Gold Cup is held annually), and Cheltenham College (founded 1854).

Chelyabinsk /ˌtʃeliˈæbɪnsk/ industrial town and capital of Chelyabinsk region, W Siberia, Russia; population (1987) 1,119,000. It has iron and engineering works and makes chemicals, motor vehicles, and aircraft.

chemical change change that occurs when two or more substances (reactants) interact with each other, resulting in the production of different substances (products) with different chemical compositions. A simple example of chemical change is the burning of carbon in oxygen to produce carbon dioxide.

chemical equation method of indicating the reactants and products of a chemical reaction by using chemical symbols and formulae. A chemical equation gives two basic pieces of information: (1) the reactants (on the left-hand side) and products (right-hand side); and (2) the reacting proportions (stoichiometry)—that is, how many units of each reactant and product are involved. The equation must balance; that is, the total number of atoms of a particular element on the left-hand side must be the same as the number of atoms of that element on the right-hand side.

chemical equilibrium condition in which the products of a reversible chemical reaction are formed at the same rate at which they decompose back into the reactants, so that the concentration of each reactant and product remains constant.

The amounts of reactant and product present at equilibrium are defined by the *equilibrium constant* for that reaction and specific temperature.

chemical oxygen demand (COD) measure of water and effluent quality, expressed as the amount of oxygen (in parts per million) required to oxidize the reducing substances present.

Under controlled conditions of time and temperature, a chemical oxidizing agent (potassium permanganate or dichromate) is added to the sample of water or effluent under consideration, and the amount needed to oxidize the reducing materials present is measured. From this the chemically equivalent amount of oxygen can be calculated. Since the reducing substances typically include organic compounds, COD may be regarded as reflecting the extent to which the sample is polluted. Compare ◊biological oxygen demand.

chemical warfare use in war of gaseous, liquid, or solid substances intended to have a toxic effect on humans, animals, or plants. Together with ◊biological warfare, it was banned by the Geneva Protocol 1925 (which remains the only international legal mechanism for the control of chemical weapons) although this has not always been observed. In 1989 the 149-nation UN Conference on Disarmament unanimously voted to outlaw chemical weapons, and drew up a draft Convention on Chemical Weapons (CCW), intended as the basis for a new international agreement on chemical warfare. At the time of the conference, the total US stockpile was estimated at 30,000 tonnes and the Soviet stockpile at 50,000. The USA and USSR agreed bilaterally in June 1990 to reduce their stockpile to 5,000 tonnes each by 2002. The USA began replacing its stocks with new nerve-gas ◊binary weapons.

Some 20 nations currently hold chemical weapons, including Iraq, Iran, Israel, Syria, Libya, South Africa, China, Ethiopia, North Korea, Myanmar, Taiwan, and Vietnam. Iraq used chemical weapons during the 1980–88 Iran–Iraq war, inflicting massive casualties on largely unprotected Iranian Revolutionary Guards and on civilians; it threatened the use of chemical weapons during the 1991 Gulf War but did not use them.

There are several types of chemical weapons. *Irritant gases* may cause permanent injury or death. Examples include chlorine, phosgene (Cl_2CO), and mustard gas ($C_4H_8Cl_2S$), used in World War I (1914–18) and allegedly used by Soviet forces in Afghanistan, by Vietnamese forces in Laos, and by Iraq against Iran during their 1980–88 war. *Tear gases*, such as CS gas, used in riot control, affect the lungs and eyes, causing temporary blindness. *Nerve gases* are organophosphorus compounds similar to insecticides, which are taken into the body through the skin and lungs and break down the action of the nervous system. Developed by the Germans for World War II, they were not used.

Incapacitants are drugs designed to put an enemy temporarily out of action by, for example, impairing vision or inducing hallucinations. They have not so far been used. *Toxins* are poisons to be eaten, drunk, or injected; for example, ricin (derived from the castor-oil plant) and the botulism toxin. Ricin has been used in individual cases, and other toxins have allegedly been used by Soviet forces in Afghanistan and Vietnamese forces in Cambodia. *Herbicides* are defoliants used to destroy vegetation sheltering troops and the crops of hostile populations. They were used in Vietnam by the USA and in Malaya (now Malaysia) by the UK. ◊Agent Orange became notorious because it caused cancer and birth abnormalities among Vietnam War veterans and US factory staff. ◊*Binary weapons* are two chemical components that become toxic in combination, after the shell containing them is fired.

chemiluminescence the emission of light from a substance as a result of a chemical reaction (rather than raising its temperature). See ◊luminescence.

chemistry science concerned with the composition of matter and of the changes that take place in it under certain conditions.

All matter can exist in three states: gas, liquid, or solid. It is composed of minute particles termed *molecules*, which are constantly moving, and may be further divided into ◊*atoms*.

Molecules that contain atoms of one kind only are known as *elements*; those that

Nobel prize for Chemistry : recent winners

1985	Herbert A Hauptman (USA) and Jerome Karle (USA): methods of determining crystal structures
1986	Dudley Herschback (USA), Yuan Lee (USA), and John Polanyi (Canada): dynamics of chemical elementary processes
1987	Donald Cram (USA), Jean-Marie Lehn (France), and Charles Pedersen (USA): molecules with highly selective structure-specific interactions
1988	Johann Deisenhofer (Germany), Robert Huber (Germany), and Hartmut Michel (Germany): three-dimensional structure of the reaction centre of photosynthesis
1989	Sydney Altman (USA) and Thomas Cech (USA): discovery of catalytic function of RNA
1990	Elias James Corey (USA): new methods of synthesizing chemical compounds
1991	Richard R Ernst (Switzerland): improvements in the technology of nuclear magnetic resonance (NMR) imaging
1992	Rudolph A. Marcus (USA): theoretical discoveries relating to reduction and oxidation reactions.
1993	Kary Mullis (USA): invention of the polymerase chain reaction technique for amplifying DNA. Michael Smith (Canada) splicing foreign genetic segments into an organism's DNA in order to modify the proteins produced.
1994	George A Olah (USA): development of technique for examining hydrocarbon molecules

contain atoms of different kinds are called *compounds*.

Chemical compounds are produced by a chemical action that alters the arrangement of the atoms in the reacting molecules. Heat, light, vibration, catalytic action, radiation, or pressure, as well as moisture (for ionization), may be necessary to produce a chemical change. Examination and possible breakdown of compounds to determine their components is *analysis*, and the building up of compounds from their components is *synthesis*. When substances are brought together without changing their molecular structures they are said to be *mixtures*.

Organic chemistry is the branch of chemistry that deals with carbon compounds. *Inorganic chemistry* deals with the description, properties, reactions, and preparation of all the elements and their compounds, with the exception of carbon compounds. *Physical chemistry* is concerned with the quantitative explanation of chemical phenomena and reactions, and the measurement of data required for such explanations. This branch studies in particular the movement of molecules and the effects of temperature and pressure, often with regard to gases and liquids.

Symbols are used to denote the elements. The symbol is usually the first letter or letters of the English or Latin name of the element—for example, C for carbon; Ca for calcium; Fe for iron (*ferrum*). These symbols represent one atom of the element; molecules containing more than one atom of an element are denoted by a subscript figure—for

example, water is H_2O. In some substances a group of atoms acts as a single entity, and these are enclosed in parentheses in the symbol—for example $(NH_4)_2SO_4$ denotes ammonium sulphate. The symbolic representation of a molecule is known as a *formula*. A figure placed before a formula represents the number of molecules of a substance taking part in, or being produced by, a reaction—for example, $2H_2O$ indicates two molecules of water. Chemical reactions are expressed by means of *equations*, as in:

$$NaCl + H_2SO_4 \rightarrow NaHSO_4 + HCl.$$

This equation states the fact that sodium chloride (NaCl) on being treated with sulphuric acid (H_2SO_4) is converted into sodium bisulphate (sodium hydrogensulphate, $NaHSO_4$) and hydrogen chloride (HCl).

Elements are divided into *metals*, which have lustre and conduct heat and electricity, and *nonmetals*, which usually lack these properties. The *periodic system*, developed by John Newlands in 1863 and established by Dmitri Mendeleyev in 1869, classified elements according to their relative atomic masses. Those elements that resemble each other in general properties were found to bear a relation to one another by weight, and these were placed in groups or families. Certain anomalies in this system were later removed by classifying the elements according to their atomic numbers. The latter is equivalent to the positive charge on the nucleus of the atom.

history Ancient civilizations were familiar with certain chemical processes—for example, extracting metals from their ores, and making alloys. The alchemists endeavoured to turn base (nonprecious) metals into gold, and chemistry evolved towards the end of the 17th century from the techniques and insights developed during alchemical experiments. Robert Boyle defined elements as the simplest substances into which matter could be resolved. The alchemical doctrine of the four elements (earth, air, fire, and water) gradually lost its hold, and the theory that all combustible bodies contain a substance called phlogiston (a weightless 'fire element' generated during combustion) was discredited in the 18th century by the experimental work of Joseph Black, Antoine Lavoisier, and Joseph Priestley (who discovered the presence of oxygen in air). Henry Cavendish discovered the composition of water, and John Dalton put forward the atomic theory, which ascribed a precise relative weight to the 'simple atom' characteristic of each element. Much research then took place leading to the development of ◊biochemistry, ◊chemotherapy, and ◊plastics.

Chemnitz /ˈkemnɪts/ industrial city (engineering, textiles, chemicals) in the state of Saxony, Federal Republic of Germany, on the Chemnitz river, 65 km/40 mi SSE of Leipzig; population (1990) 310,000. As a former district capital of East Germany it was named **Karl-Marx-Stadt** 1953–90.

chemosynthesis method of making ◊protoplasm (contents of a cell) using the energy from chemical reactions, in contrast to the use of light energy employed for the same purpose in ◊photosynthesis. The process is used by certain bacteria, which can synthesize organic compounds from carbon dioxide and water using the energy from special methods of ◊respiration.

Nitrifying bacteria are a group of chemosynthetic organisms which change free nitrogen into a form that can be taken up by plants; nitrobacteria, for example, oxidize nitrites to nitrates. This is a vital part of the ◊nitrogen cycle. As chemosynthetic bacteria can survive without light energy, they can live in dark and inhospitable regions, including the hydrothermal vents of the Pacific ocean. Around these vents, where temperatures reach up to 350°C/662°F, the chemosythetic bacteria are the basis of a food web supporting fishes and other marine life.

chemotherapy any medical treatment with chemicals. It usually refers to treatment of cancer with cytotoxic and other drugs. The term was coined by the German bacteriologist Paul Ehrlich for the use of synthetic chemicals against infectious diseases.

chemotropism movement by part of a plant in response to a chemical stimulus. The response by the plant is termed 'positive' if the growth is towards the stimulus or 'negative' if the growth is away from the stimulus. Fertilization of flowers by pollen is achieved because the ovary releases chemicals that produce a positive chemotrophic response from the developing pollen tube.

Chemulpo /ˌtʃemulˈpəʊ/ former name for ◊Inchon, port and summer resort on the W coast of South Korea.

Chengchow /ˌtʃeŋˈtʃaʊ/ alternative transcription of ◊Zhengzhou, capital of Henan province of China.

Chengde /ˌtʃeŋˈdeɪ/ or **Chengteh** town in Hebei province, China, NE of Beijing; population (1984) 325,800. It is a market town for agricultural and forestry products. It was the summer residence of the Manchu rulers and has an 18th-century palace and temples.

Chengdu /ˌtʃeŋˈduː/ or **Chengtu** ancient city, capital of Sichuan province, China; population (1986) 2,580,000. It is a busy rail junction and has railway workshops, and textile, electronics, and engineering industries. It has well-preserved temples.

cheque (US **check**) order written by the drawer to a commercial or central bank to pay a specific sum on demand.

Usually the cheque should bear the date on which it is payable, a definite sum of money to be paid, written in words and figures, to a named person or body, or to the bearer, and be signed by the drawer. It is then payable on presentation at the bank on which it is drawn. If the cheque is 'crossed', as is usual British practice, it is not negotiable and can be paid only through a bank; in the USA a cheque is always negotiable.

cheque card card issued from 1968 by savings and clearings banks in Europe, which guarantees payment by the issuing bank when it is presented with a cheque for payment of goods or service.

It bears the customer's signature and account number, for comparison with those on the cheque; payment to the vendor by the issuing bank is immediate, no commission being charged. It is also known as a banker's card.

Chequers /ˈtʃekəz/ country home of the prime minister of the UK. It is an

Elizabethan mansion in the Chiltern hills near Princes Risborough, Buckinghamshire, and was given to the nation by Lord Lee of Fareham under the Chequers Estate Act 1917, which came into effect 1921.

Cher /ʃeə/ French river that rises in Creuse *département* and flows into the river Loire below Tours, length 355 km/220 mi. It gives its name to a *département*.

Cherbourg /ʃeəbuəg/ French port and naval station at the northern end of the Cotentin peninsula, in Manche *département*; population (1982) 85,500 (conurbation). There is an institute for studies in nuclear warfare, and Cherbourg has large shipbuilding yards. During World War II, Cherbourg was captured June 1944 by the Allies, who thus gained their first large port of entry into France. Cherbourg was severely damaged; restoration of the harbour was completed 1952. There is a nuclear processing plant at nearby Cap la Hague. There are ferry links to Southampton, Weymouth, and Rosslare.

Cherenkov /tʃɪˈrenkɒf/ Pavel 1904– . Soviet physicist. In 1934 he discovered *Cherenkov radiation*; this occurs as a bluish light when charged atomic particles pass through water or other media at a speed in excess of that of light. He shared a Nobel prize 1958 with his colleagues Ilya ◊Frank and Igor Tamm.

Chernenko /tʃɜːˈnenkəʊ/ Konstantin 1911–1985. Soviet politician, leader of the Soviet Communist Party (CPSU) and president 1984–85. He was a protégé of Brezhnev and from 1978 a member of the Politburo.

Chernenko, born in central Siberia, joined the Komsomol (Communist Youth League) 1929 and the CPSU 1931. The future CPSU leader Brezhnev brought him to Moscow to work in the central apparatus 1956 and later sought to establish Chernenko as his successor, but he was passed over in favour of the KGB chief Andropov. When Andropov died Feb 1984 Chernenko was selected as the CPSU's stopgap leader by cautious party colleagues and was also elected president. From July 1984 he gradually retired from public life because of failing health.

Chernobyl /tʃəˈnəʊbəl/ town in Ukraine; site of nuclear power station. In April 1986 a leak, caused by overheating, occurred in a non-pressurized boiling-water nuclear reactor. The resulting clouds of radioactive isotopes were traced as far away as Sweden;

over 250 people were killed, and thousands of square miles contaminated.

Chernovtsy /ˌtʃɜːnɒftˈsiː/ city in Ukraine; population (1987) 254,000. Industries include textiles, clothing, and machinery. Former names: Czernowitz (before 1918), Cernăuţi (1918–1940, when it was part of Romania), Chrenovitsy (1940–44).

Cherokee /tʃerəkiː/ member of a North ◊American Indian people, formerly living in the S Allegheny Mountains of what is now Alabama, the Carolinas, Georgia, and Tennessee. Their scholarly leader Sequoyah (c. 1770-1843) devised the syllabary used for writing their language. Their language belongs to the Macro-Siouan family.

cherry any of various trees of the genus *Prunus*, of the rose family, distinguished from plums and apricots by their fruits, which are spherical and smooth and not covered with a bloom.

Cultivated cherries are derived from two species, the sour cherry *P. cerasus* and the gean *P. avium*, which grow wild in Britain. The former is the ancestor of morello, duke, and Kentish cherries; the latter of the sweet cherries–hearts, mazzards, and bigarreaus. Besides those varieties that are grown for their fruit, others are planted as ornamental trees.

cherub (Hebrew *kerubh*) type of angel in Christian belief, usually depicted as a young child with wings. Cherubim form the second order of ◊angels.

Cherubini /ˌkeruˈbiːni/ Luigi (Carlo Zanobi Salvadore Maria) 1760–1842. Italian composer. His first opera *Quinto Fabio* 1779 was produced at Alessandria. In 1784 he went to London and became composer to King George III, but from 1788 he lived in Paris, where he produced a number of dramatic works including *Médée* 1797, *Les Deux Journées* 1800, and the ballet *Anacréon* 1803. After 1809 he devoted himself largely to church music.

chervil several plants of the carrot family Umbelliferae. The garden chervil *Anthriscus cerefolium* has leaves with a sweetish odour, resembling parsley. It is used as a garnish and in soups.

Cherwell /tʃɑːwəl/ Frederick Alexander Lindemann 1886–1957. British physicist. He was director of the Physical Laboratory of the RAF at Farnborough in World War I, and personal adviser to ◊Churchill on scientific and statistical matters during World

Chervil Chervil is a small annual with a delicate parsleylike appearance, growing to a height of 30–45 cm/12–18 in.

War II. Cherwell served as director of the Clarendon Laboratory, Oxford 1919–56, and, though his own scientific output was slight, oversaw its transformation into a major research institute.

Chesapeake Bay /ˈtʃesəpiːk/ largest of the inlets on the Atlantic coast of the USA, bordered by Maryland and Virginia. Its wildlife is threatened by urban and industrial development.

Cheshire /ˈtʃeʃə/ county in NW England
area 2,320 sq km/896 sq mi
towns Chester (administrative headquarters), Warrington, Crewe, Widnes, Macclesfield, Congleton
physical chiefly a fertile plain; rivers: Mersey, Dee, Weaver
features salt mines and geologically rich former copper workings at Alderley Edge (in use from Roman times until the 1920s); Little Moreton Hall; discovery of Lindow Man, the first 'bogman', dating from around 500 BC, to be found in mainland Britain; Quarry Bank Mill at Styal is a cotton-industry museum
products textiles, chemicals, dairy products
population (1987) 952,000
famous people Charles Dodgson (Lewis Carroll); the novelist Mrs Gaskell lived at Knutsford (the locale of *Cranford*)

Cheshire /ˈtʃeʃə/ (Geoffrey) Leonard 1917– . British pilot. Commissioned into the Royal Air Force on the outbreak of the World War II, he won the Victoria Cross, Distinguished Service Order (with 2 bars), and Distinguished Flying Cross. A devout Roman Catholic, he founded the first Cheshire Foundation Home for the Incurably Sick 1948. In 1959 he married Susan Ryder (1923–) who established a foundation for the sick and disabled of all ages and became a life peeress 1978.

chess board game originating as early as the 2nd century AD. Two players use 16 pieces each, on a board of 64 squares of alternating colour, to try to force the opponent into a position where the main piece (the king) is threatened and cannot move to another position without remaining threatened.

Chess originated in India, and spread to Russia, China, Japan, and Iran, and from there was introduced to the Mediterranean area by Arab invaders. It reached Britain in the 12th century via Spain and Italy. The first official world championships were recognized in 1886.

Chester /ˈtʃestə/ city in Cheshire, England, on the river Dee 26 km/16 mi S of Liverpool; population (1984) 117,000. It is the administrative headquarters of Cheshire. Industries include engineering and the manufacture of car components. Its name derives from the Roman *Castra Devana*, ('the camp on the Dee'), and there are many Roman and later remains. It is the only English city to retain its city walls (2 mi/3 km long) intact. The cathedral dates from the 11th century but was restored in 1876. The church of St John the Baptist is a well-known example of early Norman architecture. The 'Rows' are covered arcades dating from the Middle Ages.

From 1070 to the reign of Henry III, Chester was the seat of a ◊county palatine (a county whose lord exercised some of the roles usually reserved for the monarch).

Chesterfield /ˈtʃestəfiːld/ Philip Dormer Stanhope, 4th Earl of Chesterfield 1694–1773. English politician and writer, author of *Letters to his Son* 1774. A member of the literary circle of Swift, Pope, and Bolingbroke, he incurred the wrath of Dr Samuel ◊Johnson by failing to carry out an offer of patronage.

He was ambassador to Holland 1728–32 and 1744. In Ireland, he established schools, helped to reconcile Protestants and Catholics, and encouraged manufacturing. An opponent of Walpole, he was a Whig MP 1715–26, Lord-Lieutenant of Ireland 1745–46, and Secretary of State 1746–48.

Chesterton /ˈtʃestətən/ G(ilbert) K(eith) 1874–1936. English novelist, essayist, and satirical poet, author of a series of novels featuring the naive priest-detective Father Brown. Other novels include *The Napoleon of Notting Hill* 1904 and *The Man Who Knew Too Much* 1922.

chestnut tree of the genus *Castanea*, belonging to the beech family Fagaceae. The Spanish or sweet chestnut *C. sativa* produces edible nuts inside husks; its timber is also valuable. ◊Horse chestnuts are quite distinct, belonging to the genus *Aesculus*, family Hippocastanaceae.

Chestnut Chestnut trees come in two types: the sweet or Spanish chestnut (illustrated) and the horse chestnut.

Chetnik /ˈtʃetnɪk/ member of a Serbian nationalist group that operated underground during the German occupation of Yugoslavia during World War II. Led by Col Draza ◊Mihailovič, the Chetniks initially received aid from the Allies, but this was later transferred to the communist partisans led by Tito.

Chevalier /ʃəˈvælieɪ/ Maurice 1888–1972. French singer and actor. He began as dancing partner to the revue artiste Mistinguett at the ◊Folies-Bergère, and made numerous films including *Innocents of Paris* 1929, which revived his song 'Louise', *The Merry Widow* 1934, and *Gigi* 1958.

Cheviots /ˈtʃiːviəts/ range of hills 56 km/35 mi long, mainly in Northumberland, forming the border between England and Scotland for some 48 km/30 mi. The highest point is the Cheviot, 816 m/2,676 ft. For centuries the area was a battleground between the

English and the Scots. It gives its name to a breed of sheep.

Chevreul /ʃəˈvrɜːl/ Michel-Eugène 1786–1889. French chemist who studied the composition of fats and identified a number of fatty acids, including 'margaric acid', which became the basis of margarine.

chewing gum gummy confectionery to be chewed not swallowed. It is composed mainly of chicle (milky juice of the tropical sapodilla tree *Achras zapota* of Central America), usually flavoured with mint, sweetened, and pressed flat. The first patent was taken out in the USA in 1871. *Bubble gum* is a variety that allows chewers to blow bubbles.

Chiang Ching /dʒiˈæŋ ˈtʃɪŋ/ alternative transcription of the name of the Chinese actress ◊Jiang Qing, third wife of Mao Zedong.

Chiang Kai-shek /ˈtʃæŋ kaɪ ˈʃek/ Pinyin *Jiang Jie Shi* 1887–1975. Chinese Nationalist ◊Guomindang (Kuomintang) general and politician, president of China 1928–31 and 1943–49, and of Taiwan from 1949, where he set up a US-supported right-wing government on his expulsion from the mainland by the Communist forces. He was a commander in the civil war that lasted from the end of imperial rule 1911 to the Second ◊Sino-Japanese War and beyond, having split with the Communist leader Mao Zedong 1927.

Chiang took part in the revolution of 1911 that overthrew the Qing dynasty of the Manchus, and on the death of the Nationalist Guomindang leader Sun Yat-sen was made commander in chief of the Nationalist armies in S China 1925. Collaboration with the communists, broken 1927, was resumed after the ◊Xian incident 1936 when China needed to pool military strength, and Chiang nominally headed the struggle against the Japanese invaders of World War II, receiving the Japanese surrender 1945. The following year, civil war between the Nationalists and Communists erupted, and in Dec 1949 Chiang and hiss followers took refuge on the island of Taiwan, maintaining a large army in the hope of reclaiming the mainland. His authoritarian regime enjoyed US support until his death. His son, Chiang Ching-kuo (1910–1988), then became president.

Chibcha /ˈtʃɪbtʃɑːz/ member of a South American Indian people of Colombia, whose high chiefdom was conquered by the Spanish in 1538. Their practice of covering their chief with gold dust, during rituals, fostered the legend of the 'Lost City' of El Dorado (the Golden), which was responsible for many failed expeditions into the interior of the continent.

Chicago /ʃɪˈkɑːgəʊ/ financial and industrial (iron, steel, chemicals, textiles) city in Illinois, USA, on Lake Michigan; population (1980) 3,005,000, metropolitan area 7,581,000. The famous stockyards are now closed.

It contains the world's first skyscraper (built 1887–88) and some of the world's tallest buildings, including the Sears Tower, 443 m/1,454 ft. The Museum of Science and Industry, opened 1893, has 'hands on' exhibits including a coal-mine, a World War II U-boat, an Apollo spacecraft and lunar module, and exhibits by industrial firms. 50 km/30 mi to the west is the Fermilab, the US centre for particle physics. The Chicago River cuts the city into three 'sides'. Chicago is known as the Windy City, possibly from the breezes of Lake Michigan, and from its citizens' (and, allegedly, politicians') voluble talk. It has a renowned symphony orchestra, an art institute, the University of Chicago, and five professional sports teams.

history The site of Chicago was visited by Jesuit missionaries 1673, and Fort Dearborn, then a frontier fort, was built here 1803. The original layout of Chicago was a rectangular grid, but many outer boulevards have been constructed on less rigid lines. As late as 1831 Chicago was still an insignificant village, but railways connected it with the east coast by 1852, and by 1871, when it suffered a disastrous fire, it was a city of more than 300,000 inhabitants. Rapid development began again in the 1920s, and during the years of Prohibition 1919–33, the city became notorious for the activities of its gangsters. The opening of the St Lawrence Seaway 1959 brought Atlantic shipping to its docks.

Chicano /tʃɪˈkɑːnəʊ/ citizen or resident of the USA of Mexican descent. The term was originally used for those who became US citizens after the ◊Mexican War.

Chichen Itzá /tʃɪˈtʃen ɪtˈsɑː/ Toltec city situated among the Mayan city-states of Yucatán, Mexico. It flourished AD 900–1200 and displays Classic and Post-Classic architecture of the Toltec style. The site has temples with sculptures and colour reliefs, an observatory, and a sacred well into which sacrifices, including human beings, were cast.

Chichester /tʃɪtʃɪstə/ city and market town in Sussex; 111 km/69 mi SW of London, near Chichester Harbour; population (1981) 24,000. It is the administrative headquarters of West Sussex. It was a Roman township, and the remains of the Roman palace built around AD 80 at nearby Fishbourne are unique outside Italy. There is a cathedral consecrated 1108, later much rebuilt and restored, and the Chichester Festival Theatre (1962).

Chichester /tʃɪtʃɪstə/ Francis 1901–1972. English sailor and navigator. In 1931 he made the first east–west crossing of the Tasman Sea in *Gipsy Moth*, and in 1966–67 circumnavigated the world in his yacht *Gipsy Moth IV*.

chicken domestic fowl; see under ◊poultry.

chickenpox or *varicella* common acute disease, caused by a virus of the ◊herpes group and transmitted by airborne droplets. Chickenpox chiefly attacks children under ten. The incubation period is two to three weeks. One attack normally gives immunity for life.

The temperature rises and spots (later inflamed blisters) develop on the torso, then on the face and limbs. The sufferer recovers within a week, but remains infectious until the last scab disappears.

chickpea annual plant *Cicer arietinum*, family Leguminosae, which is grown for food in India and the Middle East. Its short, hairy pods contain edible pealike seeds.

chickweed any of several low-growing plants of the genera *Stellaria* and *Cerastium* of the pink family Caryophyllaceae, with small, white, starlike flowers.

chicle milky juice from the sapodilla tree *Achras zapota* of Central America; it forms the basis of chewing gum.

chicory plant *Cichorium intybus*, family Compositae. Native to Europe and W Asia, it has large, usually blue, flowers. Its long taproot is used dried and roasted as a coffee substitute. As a garden vegetable, grown under cover, its blanched leaves are used in salads. It is related to ◊endive.

Chiengmai /dʒiˈeŋ ˈmaɪ/ or *Chiang Mai* town in N Thailand; population (1982) 104,910. There is a trade in teak and lac (as shellac, a resin used in varnishes and polishes) and many handicraft industries. It is the former capital of the Lan Na Thai kingdom.

chiffchaff bird *Phylloscopus collybita* of the warbler family, found in woodlands and thickets in Europe and N Asia during the summer, migrating south for winter. About 11 cm/4.3 in long, olive above, greyish below, with an eyestripe and usually dark legs, it looks similar to a willow-warbler but has a distinctive song.

Chifley /tʃɪfli/ Ben (Joseph Benedict) 1885–1951. Australian Labor prime minister 1945–49. He united the party in fulfilling a welfare and nationalization programme 1945–49 (although he failed in an attempt to nationalize the banks 1947) and initiated an immigration programme and the Snowy Mountains hydroelectric project.

chigger or **harvest mite** scarlet or rusty brown ◊mite of the family Trombiculidae, common in summer and autumn. Their tiny red larvae cause intensely irritating bites.

Chihuahua /tʃɪrwɑːwə/ capital of Chihuahua state, Mexico, 1,285 km/800 mi NW of Mexico City; population (1984) 375,000. Founded in 1707, it is the centre of a mining district.

chihuahua smallest breed of dog, developed in the USA from Mexican origins. It may weigh only 1 kg/2.2 lb. The domed head and wide-set ears are characteristic, and the skull is large compared to the body. It can be almost any colour, and occurs in both smooth (or even hairless) and long-coated varieties.

child abuse the molesting of children by parents and other adults. It can give rise to various criminal charges and has become a growing concern since the early 1980s.

In the UK a local authority can take abused children away from their parents by obtaining a care order from a juvenile court under the Children's and Young Persons Act 1969 (replaced by the Children's Act 1989). Controversial methods of diagnosing sexual abuse led to a public inquiry in Cleveland, England 1988, which severely criticized the handling of such cases. The standard of proof required for criminal proceedings is greater than that required for a local authority to take children into care. This has led to highly publicized cases where children have been taken into care but prosecutions have eventually not been brought, as in Rochdale, Lancashire, and the Orkneys, Scotland in 1990.

Child, Convention on the Rights of the United Nations document designed to make the wellbeing of children an international obligation. It was adopted 1989 and covers children from birth up to 18.

It laid down international standards for: *provision* of a name, nationality, health care, education, rest, and play; *protection* from commercial or sexual exploitation, physical or mental abuse, and engagement in warfare; *participation* in decisions affecting a child's own future.

Childers /tʃɪldəz/ (Robert) Erskine 1870–1922. Irish Sinn Féin politician, author of the spy novel *The Riddle of the Sands* 1903. He was executed as a Republican terrorist.

Before turning to Irish politics, Childers was a clerk in the House of Commons in London. In 1921 he was elected to the Irish Parliament as a supporter of the Sinn Féin leader de Valera, and took up arms against the Irish Free State 1922. Shortly afterwards he was captured, court-martialled, and shot by the Irish Free State government of William T Cosgrave.

child prodigy a young person who has developed a remarkable talent for one or more subjects or pursuits. Unlike ◊idiots savants, child prodigies are usually taught by an adult. ◊Mozart was a child prodigy of musical genius.

Children's Crusade a ◊Crusade by some 10,000 children from France, the Low Countries, and Germany, in 1212, to recapture Jerusalem for Christianity. Motivated by religious piety, many of them were sold into slavery or died of disease.

children's literature works specifically written for children. The earliest known illustrated children's book in English is *Goody Two Shoes* 1765, possibly written by Oliver Goldsmith. *Fairy tales* were originally part of a vast range of oral literature, credited only to the writer who first recorded them, such as Charles Perrault. During the 19th century several writers, including Hans Christian Andersen, wrote original stories in the fairy tale genre; others, such as the Grimm brothers, collected (and sometimes adapted) existing stories.

Early children's stories were written with a moral purpose; this was particularly true in the 19th century, apart from the unique case of Lewis Carroll's *Alice* books. The late 19th century was the great era of children's literature in the UK, with Lewis Carroll, Beatrix Potter, Charles Kingsley, and J M Barrie. It was also the golden age of illustrated children's books, with such artists as

Kate Greenaway and Randolph Caldecott. In the USA, Louise May Alcott's *Little Women* 1868 and its sequels found a wide audience. Among the most popular 20th-century children's writers in English have been Kenneth Grahame (*The Wind in the Willows* 1908) and A A Milne (*Winnie the Pooh* 1926) in the UK; and, in the USA, Laura Ingalls Wilder (*Little House on the Prairie* 1935), E B White (*Stuart Little* 1945, *Charlotte's Web* 1952), and Dr Seuss (*Cat in the Hat* 1957).

Many recent children's writers have been influenced by J R R ◊Tolkien whose *The Hobbit* 1937, and its sequel, the three-volume *Lord of the Rings* 1954–55, are set in the comprehensively imagined world of 'Middle-earth'. His friend C S ◊Lewis produced the allegorical chronicles of Narnia, beginning with *The Lion the Witch and the Wardrobe* 1950. Rosemary Sutcliff's *The Eagle of the Ninth* 1954, Philippa Pearce's *Tom's Midnight Garden* 1958, and Penelope Lively's *The Wild Hunt of Hagworthy* 1971 are other outstanding books by children's authors who have exploited a perennial fascination with time travel.

Writers for younger children combining stories and illustrations of equally high quality include Maurice ◊Sendak, *Where the Wild Things Are* 1963, and Quentin Blake *Mister Magnolia* 1980. Roald ◊Dahl's *James and the Giant Peach* 1961 is the first of his popular children's books which summon up primitive emotions and have an imperious morality. More 'realistic' stories for teenagers are written by US authors such as Judy Blume and S E Hinton.

Child Support Bill UK Act of Parliament 1990 that proposed a new system of child maintenance with the establishment of a Child Support Agency which would carry out the assessment, review, collection, and enforcement of maintenance payments. In cases where the parent caring for the child is receiving income support or family credit (see ◊social security), the parent caring for the child would be required to make a claim for maintenance to the agency. If the parent does not do so, the parent's allowance, but not that of her children, may be reduced. The agency would be part of the Department of Social Security and cost an estimated £30 million over three years.

Chile /ˈtʃɪli/ South American country, bounded N by Peru and Bolivia, E by Argentina, and S and W by the Pacific Ocean.

government Since 1973 Chile has been ruled by a military junta. A new constitution announced 1981 took effect 1989. It provides for the election of a president for an eight-year, nonrenewable term and a legislature consisting of a senate with 26 elected and nine appointed members and a chamber of deputies with 120 elected members, all serving four-year terms. Strikes in the public services are not allowed, and the economy is based on 'free market principles'.

history The area now known as Chile was originally occupied by the Araucanian Indians and invaded by the ◊Incas in the 15th century. The first European to reach it was ◊Magellan, who in 1520 sailed through the strait now named after him. A Spanish expedition under Pedro de Valdivia founded Santiago 1541, and Chile was subsequently colonized by Spanish settlers who established an agricultural society, although the Indians continued to rebel until the late 19th century. Becoming independent from Spain 1818, Chile went to war with Peru and Bolivia 1879 and gained considerable territory from them.

Most of the 20th century has been characterized by left-versus right-wing struggles. The Christian Democrats under Eduardo Frei held power 1964–70, followed by a left-wing coalition led by Dr Salvador ◊Allende, the first democratically elected Marxist head of state. He promised social justice by constitutional means and began nationalizing industries, including US-owned copper mines.

'authoritarian democracy' The ◊CIA saw Allende as a pro-Cuban communist and encouraged opposition to him. In 1973 the army, led by General Augusto ◊Pinochet, overthrew the government. Allende was killed or, as the new regime claimed, committed suicide. Pinochet became president, and his opponents were tortured, imprisoned, or just 'disappeared'. In 1976 Pinochet proclaimed an 'authoritarian democracy' and in 1977 banned all political parties. His policies were 'endorsed' by a referendum 1978.

opposition to government In 1980 a 'transition to democracy' by 1989 was announced, but imprisonment and torture continued. By 1983 opposition to Pinochet had increased, with demands for a return to democratic government. He attempted to placate opposition by initiating public works. In 1984 an antigovernment bombing campaign began, aimed mainly at electricity installations, resulting in a 90-day state of emergency, followed by a 90-day state of siege. In 1985, as opposition grew in the Catholic church and the army as well as among the public, another state of emergency was declared, but the bombings and killings continued.

pluralist politics In Oct 1988 Pinochet's proposal to remain in office for another eight-year term was rejected in a plebiscite. Another plebiscite Aug 1989 approved constitutional changes leading to a return to pluralist politics and in Dec the moderate Christian Democratic Party (PDC) candidate, Patricio Aylwin, was elected president, his term of office beginning March 1990.

In Jan 1990, the junta approved the disbanding of the secret police of the National Information Centre (CNI), which had replaced the National Information Bureau (DINA) 1977. In Sept 1990 a government commission was set up to investigate some 2,000 political executions 1973–78, 500 political murders 1978–90, and 700 disappearances. In the same month the formerly discredited politician, Salvador Allende, was officially recognized by being buried in a marked grave, and President Aylwin censured General Pinochet for trying to return to active politics. In 1991 the official report for President Aylwin revealed 2,279 deaths during Pinochet's term, of which over 2,115 were executions carried out by the secret police. Eduardo Frei replaced Aylwin as president March 1994.

chilli (North American *chili*) pod, or powder made from the pod, of a variety of ◊capsicum, *Capsicum frutescens*, a hot, red pepper. It is widely used in cooking.

Chiltern Hundreds, stewardship of /ˈtsɪltən/ in the UK, a nominal office of profit under the crown. British members of Parliament must not resign; therefore, if they wish to leave office during a Parliament, they may apply for this office, a formality that disqualifies them from being an MP.

Chilterns /ˈtʃɪltənz/ range of chalk hills extending for some 72 km/45 mi in a curve from a point north of Reading to the Suffolk border. Coombe Hill, near Wendover, 260 m/852 ft high, is the highest point.

chimaera fish of the group Holocephali. Chimaeras have thick bodies that taper to a long thin tail, large fins, smooth skin, and a cartilaginous skeleton. They can grow to 1.5 m/4.5 ft. Most chimaeras are deep-water fish, and even *Chimaera monstrosa*, a relatively shallow-living form caught around European coasts, lives at a depth of 300–500 m/1,000–1,600 ft.

chimera in biology, an organism composed of tissues that are genetically different. Chimeras can develop naturally if a ◊mutation occurs in a cell of a developing embryo, but are more commonly produced artificially by implanting cells from one organism into the embryo of another.

chimera or *chimaera* in Greek mythology, a fire-breathing animal with a lion's head, a goat's body, and tail in the form of a snake; hence any apparent hybrid of two or more creatures. The chimera was killed by the hero Bellerophon on the winged horse Pegasus.

chimpanzee highly intelligent African ape *Pan troglodytes* that lives mainly in rainforests but sometimes in wooded savannah. Chimpanzees are covered in thin but long black body hair, except for the face, hands, and feet, which may have pink or black skin. They normally walk on all fours, supporting the front of the body on the knuckles of the fingers, but can stand or walk upright for a short distance. They can grow to 1.4 m/4.5 ft tall, and weigh up to 50 kg/110 lb. They are strong, and climb well, but spend time on the ground. They live in loose social groups. The bulk of the diet is fruit, with some leaves, insects, and occasional meat. Chimpanzees can use 'tools', fashioning twigs to extract termites from their nests.

Chimpanzees are found in an area from W Africa to W Uganda and Tanzania in the east. Studies of chromosomes suggest that chimpanzees are the closest apes to humans, perhaps sharing 99% of the same genes. Trained chimpanzees can communicate with humans with the aid of machines or sign language, but are probably precluded from human speech by the position of the voice-box.

Chimu /ˈtʃiːmuː/ South American civilization that flourished on the coast of Peru from about 1250 to about 1470, when it was conquered by the Incas. The Chimu people produced fine work in gold, realistic portrait pottery, savage fanged feline images in clay, and possibly a system of writing or recording by painting patterns on beans. They built aqueducts carrying water many miles, and the huge, mazelike city of Chan Chan, 36 sq km/ 14 sq mi, on the coast near Trujillo.

chimurenga (Shona 'struggle') Zimbabwean pop music developed in the 1970s, particularly by Thomas Mapfumo (1945–), transposing to electric guitar the sound of the *mbira*, or thumb piano, an instrument of the region. Mapfumo used traditional rhythms and melodies in new ways combined with a political message.

China /ˈtʃaɪnə/ the largest country in E Asia, bounded N by Mongolia; NW by Tajikistan, Kyrgyzstan, Kazakhstan, and Afghanistan; SW by India and Nepal; S by Bhutan, Myanmar (Burma), Laos, and Vietnam; SE by the South China Sea; and E by the East China Sea, North Korea, and the Yellow Sea; and NE by Russia.

government China is divided into 22 provinces, five autonomous regions, and three municipalities (Beijing, Shanghai, and Tianjin), each with an elected local people's government with policy-making power in defined areas. Ultimate authority resides in he single-chamber National People's Congress (NPC), composed of 2,970 deputies indirectly elected every five years through local people's congresses. Deputies to local people's congresses are directly elected through universal suffrage in constituency contests.

The NPC, the 'highest organ of state power', meets annually and elects a permanent, 133-member committee to assume its functions between sittings. The committee has an inner body comprising a chair and 19 vice chairs. The NPC also elects for a five-year term a State Central Military Commission (SCMC), leading members of the judiciary, the vice president, and the state president, who must be at least 45 years of age. The president is restricted to two terms in office and performs primarily ceremonial functions. Executive administration is effected by a prime minister and a cabinet (state council) that includes three vice premiers, 31 departmental ministers, eight commission chiefs, an auditor general, and a secretary general, and is appointed by the NPC.

China's controlling force is the Chinese Communist Party (CCP). It has a parallel hierarchy comprising elected congresses and committees functioning from village level upwards and taking orders from above. A national party congress every five years elects a 285-member central committee (175 of whom have full voting powers) that meets twice a year and elects an 18-member Politburo and 5-member secretariat to exercise day-to-day control over the party and to frame state and party policy goals. The Politburo meets weekly and is China's most significant political body.

history For early history see ◊China, history. Imperial rule ended 1911 with the formation of a republic 1912. After several years of civil war the nationalist ◊Guomindang, led by ◊Chiang Kai-shek, was firmly installed in power 1926, with communist aid. In 1927 Chiang Kai-shek began a purge of the communists, who began the 'Long March' (1934–36) to Shaanxi, which became their base.

In 1931 Japan began its penetration of Manchuria and in 1937 began the second

◊Sino-Japanese War, during which both communists and nationalists fought Japan. Civil war resumed after the Japanese surrender 1945, until in 1949, following their elimination of nationalist resistance on the mainland, the communists inaugurated the People's Republic of China, the nationalists having retired to ◊Taiwan.

China: history

500,000 BC	The oldest human remains found in China were those of 'Peking man' (*Sinanthropus pekinensis* later known as *Homo erectus*).
25,000 BC	Humans of the Upper Palaeolithic modern type (*Homo sapiens sapiens*) inhabited the region.
5000 BC	A simple Neolithic agricultural society was established.
c. 2800–c. 2200 BC	The **Sage kings**, a period of agricultural development, known only from legend.
c. 2200–c. 1500 BC	The **Xia dynasty**, a bronze-age early civilization, with further agricultural developments, including irrigation, and the first known use of writing in this area.
c. 1500–c. 1066 BC	The **Shang dynasty** is the first of which we have documentary evidence. Writing became well-developed; bronze vases survive in ceremonial burials. The first Chinese calendar was made.
c. 1066–221 BC	During the **Zhou dynasty** the feudal structure of society broke down in a period of political upheaval, though iron, money, and written laws were all in use, and philosophy flourished (see ◊Confucius). The dynasty ended in the 'Warring States' period (403–221 BC), with the country divided into small kingdoms.
221–206 BC	The **Qin dynasty** corresponds to the reign of Shih Huang Ti, who curbed the feudal nobility and introduced orderly bureaucratic government; he had roads and canals built and began the ◊Great Wall of China to keep out invaders from the north.
206 BC–AD 220	The **Han dynasty** was a long period of peace, during which territory was incorporated, the keeping of historical records was systematized, and an extensive civil service set up. Art and literature flourished, and ◊Buddhism was introduced. The first census was taken in AD 2, registering a population of 57 million. Chinese caravans traded with the Parthians.
220–581	The area was divided into **Three Kingdoms**: the Wei, Shu, and Wu. Confucianism was superseded by Buddhism and Taoism; glass was introduced from the West. Following prolonged fighting, the Wei became the most powerful kingdom, eventually founding the **Jin dynasty** (265–304), which expanded to take over from the barbarian invaders who ruled much of China at that time, but from 305 to 580 lost the territory they had gained to the Tatar invaders from the north.
581–618	Reunification came with the **Sui dynasty**: the government was reinstated, the barbarian invasions stopped, and the Great Wall refortified.
618–907	During the **Tang dynasty** the system of government became more highly developed and centralized, and the empire covered most of SE and much of central Asia. Sculpture, painting, and poetry flourished again, and trade relations were established with the Islamic world and the Byzantine Empire.
907–960	The period known as the **Five Dynasties and Ten Kingdoms** beheld war, economic depression, and loss of territory in N China, central Asia, and Korea, but printing was developed, including the first use of paper money, and porcelain was traded to Islamic lands.
960–1279	The **Song dynasty** was a period of calm and creativity. Central government was restored, and movable type was invented. At the end of the dynasty, the northern and western frontiers were neglected, and Mongol invasions took place. Marco Polo visited the court of the Great Khan in 1275.
1279–1368	The **Yuan dynasty** saw the beginning of Mongol rule in China, with Kublai Khan on the throne in Beijing 1293; there were widespread revolts. Marco Polo served the Kublai Khan.
1368–1644	The Mongols were expelled by the first of the native Chinese **Ming dynasty**, who expanded the empire. Chinese ships sailed to the Sunda Islands 1403, Ceylon 1408, and the Red Sea 1430. Mongolia was captured by the second Ming emperor.

China: history

1368–1644	Architecture developed and Beijing flourished as the new capital. Portuguese explorers reached Macao 1516 and Canton 1517; other Europeans followed. Chinese porcelain arrived in Europe 1580. The Jesuits reached Beijing 1600.
1644–1912	The last of the dynasties was the **Manchu** or **Ching**, who were non-Chinese nomads from Manchuria. Initially trade and culture flourished, but during the 19th century it seemed that China would be partitioned among the US and European imperialist nations, since all trade was conducted through treaty ports in their control. The ◊Boxer Rebellion 1900 against Western influence was suppressed by European troops.
1911–12	Revolution broke out, and the infant emperor Henry ◊P'u-i was deposed. For history 1911–present, see ◊Chinese Revolution and ◊China.

To begin with, the communist regime concentrated on economic reconstruction. A centralized Soviet-style constitution was adopted 1954, industries were nationalized, and central planning and moderate land reform introduced. The USSR provided economic aid, while China intervened in the ◊Korean War. Development during this period was based on material incentives and industrialization.

Great Leap Forward From 1958, under state president and CCP chair ◊Mao Zedong, China embarked on a major new policy, the ◊Great Leap Forward. This created large self-sufficient agricultural and industrial communes in an effort to achieve classless 'true communism'. The experiment proved unpopular and impossible to coordinate, and over 20 million people died in the floods and famines of 1959–62. The failure of the 'Great Leap' reduced Mao's influence 1962–65, and a successful 'recovery programme' was begun under President Liu Shaoqi. Private farming plots and markets were reintroduced, communes reduced in size, and income differentials and material incentives restored.

Cultural Revolution Mao struck back against what he saw as a return to capitalism by launching the Great Proletarian Cultural Revolution (1966–69), a 'rectification campaign' directed against 'rightists' in the CCP that sought to re-establish the supremacy of (Maoist) ideology over economics. During the anarchic campaign, Mao, supported by People's Liberation Army (PLA) chief ◊Lin Biao and the Shanghai-based ◊Gang of Four (comprising Mao's wife Jiang Qing, radical intellectuals Zhang Chunqiao and Yao Wenyuan, and former millworker Wang Hongwen), encouraged student (Red Guard) demonstrations against party and government leaders. The chief targets were Liu Shaoqi, ◊Deng Xiaoping (head of the CCP secretariat), and Peng Zhen (mayor of Beijing). All were forced out of office. Government institutions fell into abeyance during the Cultural Revolution, and new 'Three Part Revolutionary Committees', comprising Maoist party officials, trade unionists, and PLA commanders, took over administration. By 1970, Mao sided with pragmatic prime minister ◊Zhou Enlai and began restoring order and a more balanced system. In 1972–73 Deng Xiaoping, finance minister Li Xiannian, and others were rehabilitated, and a policy of détente towards the USA began. This reconstruction movement was climaxed by the summoning of the NPC in 1975 for the first time in 11 years to ratify a new constitution and approve an economic plan termed the 'Four Modernizations'—agriculture, industry, armed forces, and science and technology—that aimed at placing China on a par with the West by the year 2000.

after Mao The deaths of Zhou Enlai and Mao Zedong 1976 unleashed a violent succession struggle between the leftist Gang of Four, led by Jiang Qing, and moderate 'rightists', grouped around Vice Premier Deng Xiaoping. Deng was forced into hiding by the Gang; and Mao's moderate protégé ◊Hua Guofeng became CCP chair and head of government 1976. Hua arrested the Gang on charges of treason and held power 1976–78 as a stop-gap leader, continuing Zhou Enlai's modernization programme. His authority was progressively challenged, however, by Deng Xiaoping, who returned to office 1977 after campaigns in Beijing. By 1979, after further popular campaigns, Deng had gained effective charge of the government, controlling a majority in the Politburo. State and judicial bodies began to meet again, Liu Shaoqi was rehabilitated as a party hero, and economic reforms were introduced. These involved the dismantling of the commune system, the introduction of direct farm incentives under a new 'responsibility system', and the encouragement of foreign investment in 'Special Economic Zones' in coastal enclaves. By June 1981 Deng's supremacy was assured when his protégés ◊Hu Yaobang and ◊Zhao Ziyang had become party chair and prime minister and the Gang of Four were sentenced to life imprisonment. In 1982, Hua Guofeng and a number of senior colleagues were ousted from the Politburo, and the NPC adopted a definitive constitution, restoring the post of state president (abolished since 1975) and establishing a new civil rights code. The new administration was a collective leadership, with Hu Yaobang in control of party affairs, Zhao Ziyang overseeing state administration, and Deng Xiaoping (a party vice chair and SCMC chair) formulating long-term strategy and supervising the PLA. The triumvirate pursued a three-pronged policy aimed firstly at streamlining the party and state bureaucracies and promoting to power new, younger, and better-educated technocrats. Secondly, they sought to curb PLA influence by retiring senior commanders and reducing manpower numbers from 4.2 to 3 million. Thirdly, they gave priority to economic modernization by extending market incentives and local autonomy and by introducing a new 'open door' policy to encourage foreign trade and investment.

prodemocracy movement These economic reforms met with substantial success in the agricultural sector (output more than doubled 1978–85) but had adverse side effects, widening regional and social income differentials and fuelling a wave of 'mass consumerism' that created balance of payments problems. Contact with the West brought demands for full-scale democratization in China. These calls led in 1986 to widespread student demonstrations, and party chief Hu Yaobang was dismissed 1987 for failing to check the disturbances. Hu's departure imperilled the post-Dengist reform programme, as conservative forces, grouped around the veteran Politburo members Chen Yun and Peng Zhen, sought to halt the changes and re-establish central party control. Chen Yun, Peng Zhen, and Deng Xiaoping all retired from the Politburo Oct 1987, and soon after ◊Li Peng took over as prime minister, Zhao Ziyang having

become CCP chairman. With inflation spiralling, economic reform was halted in the autumn of 1988 and an austerity budget introduced 1989. This provoked urban unrest and a student-led prodemocracy movement was launched in Beijing and rapidly spread to provincial cities.

There were mass demonstrations during the Soviet leader Mikhail Gorbachev's visit to China in May 1989. Soon after Gorbachev's departure a brutal crackdown was launched against the demonstrators by Li Peng and President Yang Shangkun, with Deng Xiaoping's support. Martial law was proclaimed and in June 1989 more than 2,000 unarmed protesters were massacred by army troops in the capital's Tiananmen Square. Arrests, executions, martial law, and expulsion of foreign correspondents brought international condemnation and economic sanctions. Communist Party general secretary Zhao Ziyang was ousted and replaced by Jiang Zemin (the Shanghai party chief and new protégé of Deng Xiaoping), a move that consolidated the power of the hardline faction of President Yang Shangkun and Premier Li Peng. Deng officially retired from the last of his party and army posts but remained a dominant figure. A crackdown on dissidents was launched as the pendulum swung sharply away from reform towards conservatism. Several dozen prodemocracy activists arrested 1989 were tried early 1991 and received sentences of 2–13 years. In 1993 Jiang Zemin replaced Yang Shangkun as president.

foreign affairs In foreign affairs, China's 1960 rift with ◊Khrushchev's Soviet Union over policy differences became irrevocable 1962 when the USSR sided with India during a brief Sino-Indian border war. Relations with the Soviet Union deteriorated further 1969 after border clashes in the disputed Ussuri River region. China pursued a ◊nonaligned strategy, projecting itself as the voice of Third World nations, although it achieved nuclear capability by 1964. During the early 1970s, concern with Soviet expansionism brought rapprochement with the USA, bringing about China's entry to the UN 1971 (at ◊Taiwan's expense), and culminating in the establishment of full Sino-American diplomatic relations 1979. In the 1980s there was a partial rapprochement with the USSR, culminating in Gorbachev's visit May 1989. However, a new rift became evident 1990, with the Chinese government denouncing the Soviet leader's 'revisionism'.

Until the Tiananmen Square massacre June 1989, relations with the West were warm during the Deng administration, with economic contacts broadening. After the massacre, the USA imposed an embargo on sales of military equipment and announced the scaling-back of government contacts. But in Dec 1989 US president Bush sent a surprise mission to China, defending the contact as an effort to prevent dangerous isolation of the Chinese and as a way to engage them in constructive peace proposals for Cambodia. And during the Gulf crisis of 1990–91, China used its UN Security Council vote to back much of the policy of the US-led anti-Iraq alliance, although it abstained in the vote authorizing the war. By March 1991 Japan and the European Community had dropped most of the sanctions imposed in the wake of the Tiananmen massacre. In May 1991 Jiang Zemin visited the USSR for talks with Gorbachev. This was the first visit to the USSR of a Chinese Communist Party leader since Mao Zedong visited Moscow 1957. An agreement on the demarcation of the Sino-Soviet border was signed. By Aug 1991 more than 200 million had been 'affected' and several thousand killed by major floods.

Nevertheless, China's economy, after stalling 1989–90, was expanding rapidly once again. In Sept 1991 the British prime minister, John Major, became the first Western leader to pay an official visit to China since the 1989 Tiananmen Square massacre. This was despite the fact that more than 1,000 prisoners detained for their role in the 1989 protests were still held in Chinese jails. In the same month, Premier Li Peng stated that relations with Vietnam 'will gradually resume towards normalization', 12 years after the Sino-Vietnamese border war.

china clay clay mineral formed by the decomposition of ◊feldspars. The alteration of aluminium silicates results in the formation of *kaolinite*, $Al_2Si_2O_5(OH)_2$, from which *kaolin*, or white china clay, is derived.

China Sea /ˈtʃaɪnə/ area of the Pacific Ocean bordered by China, Vietnam, Borneo, the Philippines, and Japan. Various groups of small islands and shoals, including the Paracels, 500 km/300 mi E of Vietnam, have been disputed by China and other powers because they lie in oil-rich areas.

North of Taiwan it is known as the *East China Sea* and to the south as the *South China Sea*.

chinchilla South American rodent *Chinchilla laniger* found in high, rather barren areas of the Andes in Bolivia and Chile. About the size of a small rabbit, it has long ears and a long bushy tail, and shelters in rock crevices. These gregarious animals have thick soft silver-grey fur, and were hunted almost to extinction for it. They are now farmed and protected in the wild.

Chindits /ˈtʃɪndɪts/ Indian division of the British army in World War II that carried out guerrilla operations against the Japanese in Burma (now Myanmar) under the command of Brigadier General Orde Wingate (1903–44). The name derived from the mythical Chinthay—half lion, half eagle—placed at the entrance of Burmese pagodas to scare away evil spirits.

Chinese /ˈtʃɑːniː/ native to or an inhabitant of China and Taiwan, or a person of Chinese descent. The Chinese comprise more than 25% of the world's population, and the Chinese language (Mandarin) is the largest member of the Sino-Tibetan family.

Chinese traditions are ancient, many going back to at least 3000 BC. They include a range of philosophies and religions, including Confucianism, Taoism, and Buddhism. The veneration of ancestors was an enduring feature of Chinese culture, as were patrilineal-based villages. The extended family was the traditional unit, the five-generation family being the ideal. Recent attempts by the People's Republic of China have included the restriction of traditions and the limit of one child to a married couple.

The majority of Chinese are engaged in agriculture, cultivating irrigated rice fields in the south, and growing millet and wheat in the north. Many other Chinese work in commerce, industry, and government. Descendants of Chinese migrants are found throughout SE Asia, the Pacific, Australia, North and South America, and Europe. Within China many minorities speak non-Chinese languages belonging to the Sino-Tibetan family (such as Tibetan, Hmong, and Zhuang). Some peoples speak languages belonging to the Altaic (such as Uigur, Mongol, and Manchu) and Indo-European (such as Russian) families, while in the northeast there are Koreans. The Chinese were governed for long periods by the Mongol

(AD 1271–1368) and Manchu (AD 1644–1911) dynasties. See ◊China, history.

Chinese architecture style of building in China. Traditionally of timber construction, few existing buildings predated the Ming dynasty (1368–1644), but records such as the *Ying Tsao Fa Shih/Method of Architecture* 1103 show that Chinese architecture changed little throughout the ages, both for the peasants and for the well-to-do. Curved roofs are a characteristic feature; also typical is the pagoda with a number of curved tiled roofs, one above the other. The Chinese are renowned for their wall-building. The Great Wall of China was built about 228–210 BC as a northern frontier defence, and Beijing's fine city walls, of which only a small section remains, date from the Ming period.

Chinese buildings usually face south, a convention which can be traced back to the 'Hall of Brightness', a building from the Zhou dynasty (1050–221 BC), and is still retained in the functionally Western-style Chinese architecture of the present day. Although some sections of Beijing have been destroyed by modernization it still contains fine examples of buildings from the Ming dynasty, such as the Altar of Heaven, the ancestral temple of the Ming tombs, and the Five Pagoda Temple. The introduction of Buddhism from India exerted considerable influence on Chinese architecture.

Chinese art the painting and sculpture of China. From the Bronze Age to the Cultural Revolution, Chinese art shows a stylistic unity unparalleled in any other culture. From about the 1st century AD Buddhism inspired much sculpture and painting.

Neolithic art accomplished pottery dates back to about 2500 BC, already showing a distinctive Chinese approach to form.

Bronze Age art rich burial goods, with bronzes and jade carvings, survive from the second millennium BC, decorated with hieroglyphs and simple stylized animal forms. Astonishing life-size terracotta figures from the Qin period (about 221–206 BC) guard the tomb of Emperor Shi Huangdi in the old capital of Xian. Bronze horses, naturalistic but displaying the soft curving lines of the Chinese style, are a feature of the Han dynasty.

early Buddhist art once Buddhism was established in China it inspired a monumental art, with huge rock-cut Buddhas and graceful linear relief sculptures at the monasteries of Yungang, about 460–535, and Longmen. Bronze images show the same curving lines and rounded forms.

Tang dynasty (618–907) art shows increasing sophistication in idealized images and naturalistic portraits, such as the carved figures of Buddhist monks (Luohan). This period also produced brilliant metalwork and delicate ceramics. It is known that the aims and, broadly speaking, the style of Chinese painting were already well established, but few paintings survive, with the exception of some Tang scrolls and silk paintings.

Song dynasty the golden age of painting was the Song dynasty (960–1278). The imperial court created its own workshop, fostering a fine calligraphic art, mainly devoted to natural subjects—landscape, mountains, trees, flowers, birds, and horses—though genre scenes of court beauties were also popular. Scrolls, albums, and fans of silk or paper were painted with watercolours and ink, using soft brushes that produced many different textures. Painting was associated with literature, and painters added poems or quotations to their work to intensify the effect. Ma Yuan (*c.* 1190–1224) and Xia Gui (active *c.* 1180–1230) are among the painters; Muqi (1180–*c.* 1270), was a monk known for exquisite brushwork. The Song dynasty also produced the first true porcelain, achieving a classic simplicity and delicacy in colouring and form.

Ming dynasty (1368–1644) painters continued the landscape tradition, setting new standards in idealized visions. The painter Dong Qichang wrote a history and theory of Chinese painting. The Song style of porcelain gradually gave way to increasingly elaborate decorative work, and pale shades were superseded by rich colours, as in Ming blue-and-white patterned ware.

Qing dynasty (1644–1911) the so-called Individualist Spirits emerged, painters who developed bolder, personal styles of brushwork.

20th century the strong spirit that supported traditional art began to fade in the 19th and 20th centuries, but attempts to incorporate modernist ideas have been frowned on by the authorities. Not directly concerned with the representation of political events, Chinese art took some years before responding to the political upheavals of this century. Subsequently, response to offical directives produced a period of Soviet-style realism followed by a reversion to a peasant school of painting, which was the officially favoured direction for art during the Cultural Revolution.

influence Chinese art had a great impact on surrounding countries. The art of Korea was almost wholly inspired by Chinese example for many centuries. Along with Buddhism, Chinese styles of art were established in Japan in the 6th–7th centuries BC and continued to exert a profound influence, though Japanese culture soon developed an independent style.

Chinese language language or group of languages of the Sino-Tibetan family, spoken in China, Taiwan, Hong Kong, Singapore, and Chinese communities throughout the world. Varieties of spoken Chinese differ greatly, but all share a written form using thousands of ideographic symbols—characters—which have changed little in 2,000 years. Nowadays, *putonghua* ('common speech'), based on the educated Beijing dialect known as Mandarin Chinese, is promoted throughout China as the national spoken and written language.

Because the writing system has a symbolic form (like numbers and music notes) it can be read and interpreted regardless of the reader's own dialect. The Chinese dialects are tonal, that is, they depend upon the tone of a syllable to indicate its meaning: *ma* with one tone means 'mother', with another means 'horse'. The characters of Chinese script were traditionally written down the page from right to left. Today they are commonly written horizontally and read left to right, using 2,000 simplified characters. A variant of the Roman alphabet has been introduced and is used in schools to help with pronunciation. This, called *Pinyin*, is prescribed for international use by the People's Republic of China for personal and place names (as in *Beijing* rather than *Peking*). Pinyin spellings are generally used in this volume, but they are not accepted by the government of Taiwan.

Chinese literature *Poetry* Chinese poems, often only four lines long, and written in the ancient literary language understood throughout China, consist of rhymed lines of a fixed number of syllables, ornamented by parallel phrasing and tonal pattern. The oldest poems are contained in the *Book of Songs* (800–600 BC). Some of the most celebrated Chinese poets are the nature poet T'ao Ch'ien (372–427), the master of technique Li Po (701–62), the autobiographical

Po Chüi (772–846), and the wide-ranging Su Tung-p'o (1036–1101); and among the moderns using the colloquial language under European influence and experimenting in free verse are Hsu Chih-mo (1895–1931), and Pien Chih-lin (1910–   ).

Prose histories are not so much literary works as they are collections of edited documents with moral comment, while the essay has long been cultivated under strict rules of form and style. A famous example of the latter genre is *Upon the Original Way* by Han Yü (768–824), recalling the nation to Confucianism. Until the 16th century the short story was confined to the anecdote, startling by its strangeness and written in the literary language—for example, the stories of the poetic Tuan Ch'eng-shih (died 863); but after that time the more novelistic type of short story, written in the colloquial tongue, developed by its side. The Chinese novel evolved from the street storyteller's art and has consequently always used the popular language. The early romances *Three Kingdoms*, *All Men are Brothers*, and *Golden Lotus* are anonymous, the earliest known author of this genre being Wu Che'ng-en (*c.* 1505–1580); the most realistic of the great novelists is Ts'ao Chan (died 1763). Twentieth-century Chinese novels have largely adopted European form, and have been influenced by Russia, as have the realistic stories of Lu Hsün. In typical Chinese drama, the stage presentation far surpasses the text in importance (the dialogue was not even preserved in early plays), but the present century has seen experiments in the European manner.

Chinese Revolution a series of major political upheavals in China 1911–49 that eventually led to Communist party rule and the establishment of the People's Republic of China. In 1912, a Nationalist revolt overthrew the imperial Manchu (or Ching) dynasty. Led by Sun Yat-sen 1923–25, and by Chiang Kai-shek 1925–49, the Nationalists, or Guomindang, were increasing challenged by the growing Communist movement. The 10,000 km/6,000 mi *Long March* to the NW by the Communists 1934–35 to escape from attacks by the Nationalist forces resulted in Mao Zedong's emergence as Communist leader. During World War II 1939–45, the various Chinese political groups pooled military resources against the Japanese invaders. After World War II, the conflict reignited into open civil war 1946–49, until the

Nationalists were defeated at Nanking and forced to flee to Taiwan. Communist rule was established in the People's Republic of China under the leadership of Mao.

The Chinese revolution came about with the collapse of the Manchu (or Ching) dynasty, a result of increasing internal disorders, pressure from foreign governments, and the weakness of central government. A Nationalist revolt led to a provisional republican constitution being proclaimed and a government established in Beijing (Peking). Led by Sun Yat Sen and Chiang Kai-shek, the Nationalists were faced with the problems of restoring the authority of central government and meeting the challenges from militaristic factions and the growing Communist movement. After 1930, Chiang launched a series of attacks that encircled the communists in SE China and led to an attempt by communist army commander Chu Teh to break out. The resulting Long March to NW China from Oct 1934–Oct 1935 reduced the Communists' army from over 100,000 to little more than 8,000, mainly as a result of skirmishes with Chiang's forces and the severity of the conditions. During the march, a power struggle developed between Mao Zedong and Chang Kuo T'ao that eventually split the force. Mao's group finally based itself in Yen'an, where it remained throughout the war with the Japanese, forming an uneasy alliance with the Nationalists to expel the invaders. Mao's troops formed the basis of the Red Army that renewed the civil war against the nationalists 1946 and emerged victorious after defeating them at Nanking 1949. As a result, Communist rule was established in China under Mao's leadership.

Chinghai /ˌtʃɪŋˈhaɪ/ alternative transcription of ◊Qinghai, NW province of China.

chinook (American Indian 'snow-eater') a warm dry wind that blows downhill on the eastern side of the Rocky Mountains. It often occurs in winter and spring when it produces a rapid thaw, and so is important to the agriculture of the area.

chintz printed fabric, usually glazed, popular for furnishings. In England in the late 16th and 17th centuries the term was used for Indian painted and printed cotton fabrics (calicos) and later for European printed fabrics.

Such textiles were made in India from very early times. In England chintz became so popular by the early 18th century that in 1722 Parliament legislated against the importation and manufacture of chintz, to protect the British silk and wool industries. The legislation against manufacture was repealed 1744. In the mid-19th century chintz was superseded by a stronger fabric, ◊cretonne, but it has become popular again for soft furnishings.

chip complete electronic circuit on a slice of silicon (or other ◊semiconductor) crystal only a few millimetres square. It is also called ◊silicon chip and ◊integrated circuit.

chipmunk several species of small ground squirrel with characteristic stripes along its side. Chipmunks live in North America and E Asia, in a variety of habitats, usually wooded, and take shelter in burrows. They have pouches in their cheeks for carrying food. They climb well but spend most of their time on or near the ground.

Chippendale /ˈtʃɪpəndeɪl/ Thomas c. 1718–1779. English furniture designer. He set up his workshop in St Martin's Lane, London 1753. His book *The Gentleman and Cabinet Maker's Director* 1754, was a significant contribution to furniture design. He favoured Louis XVI, Chinese, Gothic, and Neo-Classical styles, and worked mainly in mahogany.

Chirac /ˈʃɪəræk/ Jacques 1932– . French conservative politician, prime minister 1974–76 and 1986–88. He established the neo-Gaullist Rassemblement pour la République (RPR) 1976, and became mayor of Paris 1977.

Chirac held ministerial posts during the Pompidou presidency and gained the nickname 'the Bulldozer'. In 1974 he became prime minister to President Giscard d'Estaing, but the relationship was uneasy. Chirac contested the 1981 presidential election and emerged as the National Assembly leader for the parties of the right during the socialist administration of 1981–86. Following the rightist coalition's victory 1986, Chirac was appointed prime minister by President Mitterrand in a 'cohabitation' experiment. The term was marked by economic decline, nationality reforms, and student unrest.

Student demonstrations in autumn 1986 forced him to scrap plans for educational reform. He stood in the May 1988 presidential elections and was defeated by Mitterrand, who replaced him with the moderate Socialist Michel Rocard.

Chirico /ˈkɪərɪkəʊ/ Giorgio de 1888–1978. Italian painter born in Greece, whose style presaged Surrealism in its use of enigmatic imagery and dreamlike settings, for example, *Nostalgia of the Infinite* 1911, Museum of Modern Art, New York.

In 1917, with Carlo Carrà (1881–1966), he founded Metaphysical painting, which aimed to convey a sense of mystery and hallucination. This was achieved by distorted perspective, dramatic lighting, and the use of dummies and statues in place of human figures.

Chiron /ˈkaɪrən/ in Greek mythology, the son of Kronos by a sea nymph. A ◊centaur, he was the wise tutor of ◊Jason and ◊Achilles, among others.

Chiron /ˈkaɪrən/ unusual Solar-System object orbiting between Saturn and Uranus, discovered 1977 by US astronomer Charles T Kowal (1940–). Initially classified as an asteroid, it is now believed to be a giant cometary nucleus about 200 km/120 mi across, composed of ice with a dark crust of carbon dust.

chiropractic technique of manipulation of the spine and other parts of the body, based on the principle that disorders are attributable to aberrations in the functioning of the nervous system, which manipulation can correct.

Developed in the 1890s by US practitioner Daniel David Palmer, chiropractic is widely practised today by accredited therapists, although orthodox medicine remains sceptical of its efficacy except for the treatment of back problems.

Chissano /ʃɪˈsɑːnəʊ/ Joaquim 1939– . Mozambique nationalist politician, president from 1986; foreign minister 1975–86. In 1992 Chissano signed a peace accord with the leader of the rebel Mozambique National Resistance (MNR) party, bringing to an end 16 years of civil war.

He was secretary to Samora ◊Machel, who led the National Front for the Liberation of Mozambique (Frelimo) during the campaign for independence in the early 1960s. When Mozambique achieved internal self-government 1974, Chissano was appointed prime minister. After independence he served under Machel as foreign minister and on his death succeeded him as president.

chitin complex long-chain compound, or ◊polymer; a nitrogenous derivative of glucose. Chitin is found principally in the ◊exo-

skeleton of insects and other arthropods. It combines with protein to form a covering that can be hard and tough, as in beetles, or soft and flexible, as in caterpillars and other insect larvae. In crustaceans such as crabs, it is impregnated with calcium carbonate for extra strength.

In 1991 scientists discovered that chitin can be converted into carbomethylchitosan, a water-soluble, biodegradable material which is also non-toxic. Its uses include coating apples (still fresh after 6 months), coating seeds, clearing water of heavy metals, and dressing wounds.

Chittagong /ˈtʃɪtəgɒŋ/ city and port in Bangladesh, 16 km/10 mi from the mouth of the Karnaphuli River, on the Bay of Bengal; population (1981) 1,388,476. Industries include steel, engineering, chemicals, and textiles.

chivalry code of gallantry and honour that medieval knights were pledged to observe. The word originally meant the knightly class of the feudal Middle Ages.

chive or *chives* bulbous perennial plant *Allium schoenoprasum* of the lily family Liliaceae. It has long, tubular leaves and dense, round flower heads in blue or lilac, and is used as a garnish for salads.

chlamydia single-celled bacterium that can only live parasitically in animal cells. Chlamydiae are thought to be descendants of bacteria that have lost certain metabolic processes. In humans, they cause ◊trachoma, a disease found mainly in the tropics (a leading cause of blindness), and psittacosis, a disease which may be contracted from birds by inhaling particles of dried droppings and which can cause inflammation of the lungs and pneumonia.

chloral or *trichloroethanal* CCl_3CHO oily, colourless liquid with a characteristic pungent smell, produced by the action of chlorine on ethanol. It is soluble in water and its compound chloral hydrate is a powerful sleep-inducing agent.

chloramphenicol first of the broad-spectrum antibiotics to be used commercially. It was discovered 1947 in a Venezuelan soil sample containing the bacillus *Streptomyces venezuelae*, which produces the antibiotic substance $C_{11}H_{12}Cl_2N_2O_5$, now synthesized. Because of its toxicity, its use is limited to treatment of life-threatening infections, such as meningitis and typhoid fever.

chloride Cl⁻ negative ion formed when hydrogen chloride dissolves in water, and any salt containing this ion, commonly formed by the action of hydrochloric acid (HCl) on various metals or by direct combination of a metal and chlorine. Sodium chloride (NaCl) is common table salt.

chlorinated solvents liquid organic compounds that contain chlorine atoms, often two or more. They are very effective solvents for fats and greases, but many have toxic properties. They include trichloromethane (chloroform, $CHCl_3$), tetrachloromethane (carbon tetrachloride, CCl_4), and trichloroethene ($CH_2ClCHCl_2$).

chlorine (Greek *chloros* 'green') greenish-yellow, gaseous, nonmetallic element with a pungent odour, symbol Cl, atomic number 17, relative atomic mass 35.453. It is a member of the ◊halogen group and is widely distributed, in combination with the ◊alkali metals, as chlorates or chlorides.

In nature it is always found in the combined form, as in hydrochloric acid, produced in the mammalian stomach for digestion. Chlorine is obtained commercially by the electrolysis of concentrated brine and is an important bleaching agent and germicide, used for both drinking and swimming-pool water. As an oxidizing agent it finds many applications in organic chemistry. The pure gas (Cl_2) is a poison and was used in gas warfare in World War I, where its release seared the membranes of the nose, throat, and lungs, producing pneumonia. Chlorine is a component of chlorofluorocarbons (CFCs) and is partially responsible for the depletion of the ◊ozone layer; it is released from the CFC molecule by the action of ultraviolet radiation in the upper atmosphere, making it available to react with and destroy the ozone.

Chlorine was discovered 1774 by the German chemist Karl Scheele, but Humphry Davy first proved it to be an element 1810 and named it after its colour.

chlorofluorocarbon (CFC) synthetic chemical, which is odourless, nontoxic, nonflammable, and chemically inert. CFCs are used as propellants in ◊aerosol cans, as refrigerants in refrigerators and air conditioners, and in the manufacture of foam boxes for take-away food cartons. They are partly responsible for the destruction of the ◊ozone layer. In June 1990 representatives of 93 nations, including the UK and the USA, agreed to phase out production of CFCs and

various other ozone-depleting chemicals by the end of the 20th century.

When CFCs are released into the atmosphere, they drift up slowly into the stratosphere, where, under the influence of ultraviolet radiation from the Sun, they break down into chlorine atoms which destroy the ozone layer and allow harmful radiation from the Sun to reach the Earth's surface. CFCs can remain in the atmosphere for more than 100 years.

chloroform (technical name *trichloromethane*) CCl_3 clear, colourless, toxic, carcinogenic liquid with a characteristic pungent, sickly sweet smell and taste, formerly used as an anaesthetic (now superseded by less harmful substances). It is used as a solvent and in the synthesis of organic chemical compounds.

chlorophyll green pigment present in most plants; it is responsible for the absorption of light energy during ◊photosynthesis. The pigment absorbs the red and blue-violet parts of sunlight but reflects the green, thus giving plants their characteristic colour.

Chlorophyll is found within chloroplasts, present in large numbers in leaves. Cyanobacteria (blue-green algae) and other photosynthetic bacteria also have chlorophyll, though of a slightly different type. Chlorophyll is similar in structure to ◊haemoglobin, but with magnesium instead of iron as the reactive part of the molecule.

chloroplast structure (◊organelle) within a plant cell containing the green pigment chlorophyll. Chloroplasts occur in most cells of the green plant that are exposed to light,

chloroplast

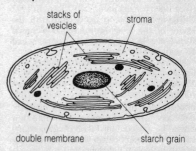

Chloroplast Green chlorophyll molecules on the membranes of the vesicle stacks capture light energy to produce food by photosynthesis.

often in large numbers. Typically, they are flattened and disc-like, with a double membrane enclosing the stroma, a gel-like matrix. Within the stroma are stacks of fluid-containing cavities, or vesicles, where ◊photosynthesis occurs.

It is thought that the chloroplasts were originally free-living cyanobacteria (blue-green algae) which invaded larger, non-photosynthetic cells and developed a symbiotic relationship with them. Like ◊mitochondria, they contain a small amount of DNA and divide by fission. Chloroplasts are a type of ◊plastid.

chlorosis abnormal condition of green plants in which the stems and leaves turn pale green or yellow. The yellowing is due to a reduction in the levels of the green chlorophyll pigments. It may be caused by a deficiency in essential elements (such as magnesium, iron, or manganese), a lack of light, genetic factors, or viral infection.

chocolate powder, syrup, confectionery, or beverage derived from cacao seeds. See ◊cocoa and chocolate.

choir body of singers, normally divided into two or more parts, and commonly four (soprano, alto, tenor, bass). The words *choir* and *chorus* are frequently interchangeable, although all church groups use the former, while larger groups, which may have several hundred members, invariably use the latter.

Choiseul /ʃwæˈzɜːl/ Étienne François, duc de Choiseul 1719–1785. French politician. Originally a protégé of Mme de Pompadour, the mistress of Louis XV, he became minister for foreign affairs 1758, and held this and other offices until 1770. He banished the Jesuits, and was a supporter of the Enlightenment philosophers Diderot and Voltaire.

cholecystectomy surgical removal of the ◊gall bladder. It is carried out when gallstones or infection lead to inflammation of the gallbladder, which may then be removed either via a ◊laparotomy or by ◊endoscopy; the latter method, which performs the operation without making a large wound, is increasing in popularity.

cholera any of several intestinal diseases, especially *Asiatic cholera*, an infection caused by a bacterium *Vibrio cholerae* transmitted in contaminated water and characterized by violent diarrhoea and vomiting. It is prevalent in many tropical areas. The formerly high death rate during epidemics has been much reduced by treatments to

prevent dehydration and loss of body salts. There is an effective vaccine that must be repeated at frequent intervals for people exposed to continuous risk of infection.

The worst epidemic in the Western hemisphere for 70 years occurred in Peru 1991, with 55,000 confirmed cases and 258 deaths. It was believed to have been spread by the consumption of seafood contaminated by untreated sewage.

cholesterol white, crystalline ◊sterol found throughout the body, especially in fats, blood, nerve tissue, and bile; it is also provided in the diet by foods such as eggs, meat, and butter. A high level of cholesterol in the blood is thought to contribute to atherosclerosis (hardening of the arteries).

Cholesterol is an integral part of all cell membranes and the starting point for steroid hormones, including the sex hormones. *Low-density lipoprotein cholesterol* (LDL-cholesterol), when present in excess, can enter the tissues and become deposited on the surface of the arteries, causing atherosclerosis. *High-density lipoprotein cholesterol* (HDL-cholesterol) acts as a scavenger, transporting fat and cholesterol from the tissues to the liver to be broken down. Blood cholesterol levels can be altered by reducing the amount of alcohol and fat in the diet and by substituting some of the saturated fat for polyunsaturated fat, which gives a reduction in LDL-cholesterol. HDL-cholesterol can be increased by exercise.

Chomsky /ˈtʃɒmski/ Noam 1928– . US professor of linguistics. He proposed a theory of transformational generative grammar, which attracted widespread interest because of the claims it made about the relationship between language and the mind and the universality of an underlying language structure. He has been a leading critic of the imperialist tendencies of the US government.

Chongjin /ˌtʃʊŋˈdʒɪn/ capital of North Hamgyong province on the NE coast of North Korea; population (1984) 754,000.

Chongqing /ˌtʃʊŋˈtʃɪŋ/ or *Chungking*, also known as *Pahsien* city in Sichuan province, China, that stands at the the ◊Chang Jiang and Jialing Jiang rivers; population (1984) 2,733,700. Industries include iron, steel, chemicals, synthetic rubber, and textiles.

For over 4,000 years it has been a major commercial centre in one of the most remote and economically deprived regions of China. It was opened to foreign trade 1891, and remains a focal point of road, river, and rail transport. When both Beijing and Nanjing were occupied by the Japanese, it was the capital of China 1938–46.

Choonhavan /ʃuːnˈhævən/ Chatichai 1922– . Thai conservative politician, prime minister of Thailand 1988–91. He promoted a peace settlement in neighbouring Cambodia as part of a vision of transforming Indochina into a thriving open-trade zone. Despite economic success, he was ousted in a bloodless military coup 1991.

Chopin /ˈʃɒpæn/ Frédéric (François) 1810–1849. Polish composer and pianist. He made his debut as a pianist at the age of eight. As a performer, Chopin revolutionized the technique of pianoforte-playing, turning the hands outwards and favouring a light, responsive touch. His compositions for piano, which include two concertos and other works with orchestra, are characterized by great volatility of mood, and rhythmic fluidity.

From 1831 he lived in Paris, where he became known in the fashionable salons, although he rarely performed in public. In 1836 Liszt introduced him to Mme Dudevant (George ◊Sand), with whom he had a close relationship 1838–46. During this time she nursed him in Majorca for tuberculosis, while he composed intensively and for a time regained his health. His music was made the basis of the ballet *Les Sylphides* by Fokine 1909 and orchestrated by Alexander Gretchaninov (1864–1956), a pupil of Rimsky-Korsakov.

chord in geometry, a straight line joining any two points on a curve. The chord that passes through the centre of a circle (its longest chord) is the diameter. The longest and shortest chords of an ellipse (a regular oval) are called the major and minor axes respectively.

chord in music, a group of three or more notes sounded together. The resulting combination of tones may be either harmonious or dissonant.

chordate animal belonging to the phylum Chordata, which includes vertebrates, sea squirts, amphioxi, and others. All these animals, at some stage of their lives, have a supporting rod of tissue (notochord or backbone) running down their bodies.

chorea disease of the nervous system marked by involuntary movements of the face muscles and limbs, formerly called St

Vitus's dance. ◊Huntington's chorea is also characterized by such movements.

chorion outermost of the three membranes enclosing the embryo of reptiles, birds, and mammals; the ◊amnion is the innermost membrane.

chorion villus sampling (CVS) ◊biopsy of a small sample of placental tissue, carried out in early pregnancy at 10–12 weeks' gestation. Since the placenta forms from embryonic cells, the tissue obtained can be tested to reveal genetic abnormality in the fetus. The advantage of CVS over ◊amniocentesis is that it provides an earlier diagnosis, so that if any abnormality is discovered, and the parents opt for an abortion, it can be carried out more safely.

choroid black layer found at the rear of the ◊eye beneath the retina. By absorbing light that has already passed through the retina, it stops back-reflection and so aids vision.

Chou En-lai /ˈtʃəʊ en ˈlaɪ/ alternative transcription of ◊Zhou Enlai.

chough bird *Pyrrhocorax pyrrhocorax* of the crow family, about 38 cm/15 in long, black- feathered, and with red bill and legs. It lives on sea-cliffs and mountains from Europe to E Asia, but is now rare.

The *alpine chough Pyrrhocorax graculus* is similar, but has a yellow bill and is found up to the snowline in mountains from the Pyrenees to Central Asia.

chow chow breed of dog originating in China in ancient times. About 45 cm/1.5 ft tall, it has a broad neck and head, round catlike feet, a soft woolly undercoat with a coarse outer coat, and a mane. Its coat should be of one colour, and it has an unusual blue-black tongue.

Chrétien de Troyes /ˌkretiˈæn də ˈtrwɑː/ medieval French poet, born in Champagne about the middle of the 12th century. His epics, which introduced the concept of the ◊Holy Grail, include *Lancelot, ou le chevalier de la charrette*; *Perceval, ou le conte du Graal*, written for Philip, Count of Flanders; *Erec*; *Yvain, ou le chevalier au Lion*; and other Arthurian romances.

Christ /kraɪs/ (Greek *khristos* 'anointed one') the ◊Messiah as prophesied in the Hebrew Bible, or Old Testament.

Christchurch /ˈkraɪstʃɜːtʃ/ city on South Island, New Zealand, 11 km/7 mi from the mouth of the Avon River; population (1986) 299,300. It is the principal city of the Canterbury plains and the seat of the University of Canterbury. Industries include fertilizers and chemicals, canning and meat processing, rail workshops, and shoes.

Christchurch uses as its port a bay in the sheltered Lyttelton Harbour on the northern shore of the Banks Peninsula, which forms a denuded volcanic mass. Land has been reclaimed for service facilities, and rail and road tunnels (1867 and 1964 respectively) link Christchurch with Lyttelton.

christening Christian ceremony of ◊baptism of infants, including giving a name.

Christian /ˈkrɪstjən/ follower of ◊Christianity, the religion derived from the teachings of Jesus. In the New Testament (Acts 11:26) it is stated that the first to be called Christians were the disciples in Antioch (now Antakya, Turkey).

Christian /ˈkrɪstjən/ ten kings of Denmark and Norway, including:

Christian I 1426–1481. King of Denmark from 1448, and founder of the Oldenburg dynasty. In 1450 he established the union of Denmark and Norway that lasted until 1814.

Christian IV 1577–1648. King of Denmark and Norway from 1588. He sided with the Protestants in the Thirty Years' War (1618–48), and founded Christiania (now Oslo, capital of Norway). He was succeeded by Frederick II 1648.

Christian VIII 1786–1848. King of Denmark 1839–48. He was unpopular because of his opposition to reform. His attempt to encourage the Danish language and culture in Schleswig and Holstein led to an insurrection there shortly after his death. He was succeeded by Frederick VII.

Christian IX 1818–1906. King of Denmark from 1863. His daughter Alexandra married Edward VII of the UK and another, Dagmar, married Tsar Alexander III of Russia; his second son, George, became king of Greece. In 1864 he lost the duchies of Schleswig and Holstein after a war with Austria and Prussia.

Christian X 1870–1947. King of Denmark and Iceland from 1912, when he succeeded his father Frederick VIII. He married Alexandrine, Duchess of Mecklenburg-Schwerin, and was popular for his democratic attitude. During World War II he was held prisoner by the Germans in Copenhagen. He was succeeded by Frederick IX.

Christiania /ˌkrɪstiˈɑːniə/ former name of the Norwegian capital of ◊Oslo (1624–1924), after King Christian IV who replanned it following a fire 1624.

Christianity world religion derived from the teaching of Jesus in the first third of the 1st century, with a present-day membership of about 1 billion. It is divided into different groups or denominations which differ in some areas of belief and practice. Its main divisions are the ◊Roman Catholic, ◊Eastern Orthodox, and ◊Protestant churches.

beliefs Christians believe in one God with three aspects: God the Father, God the Son (Jesus), and God the Holy Spirit, who is the power of God working in the world. God created everything that exists and showed his love for the world by coming to Earth as Jesus, and suffering and dying in order to be reconciled with humanity. Christians believe that three days after his death by crucifixion Jesus was raised to life by God's power, appearing many times in bodily form to his followers, and that he is now alive in the world hrough the Holy Spirit. Christians speak of the sufferings they may have to endure because of their faith, and the reward of everlasting life in God's presence which is promised to those who have faith in Jesus Christ and who live according to his teaching.

Christian Science sect, the Church of Christ, Scientist, established in the USA by Mary Baker Eddy 1879. Christian Scientists believe that since God is good and is a spirit, matter and evil are not ultimately real. Consequently they refuse all medical treatment. The church has its own daily newspaper, the *Christian Science Monitor*.

Christian Science is regarded by its adherents as the restatement of primitive Christianity with its full gospel of salvation from all evil, including sickness and disease as well as sin. According to its adherents, Christian Science healing is brought about by the operation of truth in human conscience. There is no ordained priesthood, but there are public practitioners of Christian Science healing who are officially authorized.

Christians of St Thomas sect of Indian Christians on the Malabar Coast, named after the apostle who is supposed to have carried his mission to India. In fact the Christians of St Thomas were established in the 5th century by Nestorians from Persia. They now form part of the Assyrian church (see under ◊Nestorianism) and have their own patriarch.

Christianity: chronology

1st century	The Christian church is traditionally said to have originated at Pentecost, and separated from the parent Jewish religion by the declaration of Saints Barnabas and Paul that the distinctive rites of Judaism were not necessary for entry into the Christian church.
3rd century	Christians were persecuted under the Roman emperors Severus, Decius, and Diocletian.
312	Emperor Constantine established Christianity as the religion of the Roman Empire.
4th century	A settled doctrine of Christian belief evolved, with deviating beliefs condemned as heresies. Questions of discipline threatened disruption within the Church; to settle these, Constantine called the Council of Arles 314, followed by the councils of Nicaea 325 and Constantinople 381.
5th century	Councils of Ephesus 431 and Chalcedon 451. Christianity was carried northwards by figures such as Saints Columba and Augustine.
800	Holy Roman Emperor Charlemagne crowned by the Pope. The Church assisted the growth of the feudal system of which it formed the apex.
1054	The Eastern Orthodox Church split from the Roman Catholic Church.
11th–12th centuries	Secular and ecclesiastical jurisdiction were often in conflict, for example, Emperor Henry IV and Pope Gregory VII, Henry II of England and his archbishop Becket.
1096–1291	The Church supported a series of wars in the Middle East, called the Crusades.
1233	The Inquisition was established to suppress heresy.
14th century	Increasing worldliness (against which the foundation of the Dominican and Franciscan monastic orders was a protest) and ecclesiastical abuses led to dissatisfaction and the appearance of the reformers Wycliffe and Huss.
early 16th century	The Renaissance brought a re-examination of Christianity in N Europe by the humanists Erasmus, More, and Colet.
1517	The German priest Martin Luther started the Reformation, an attempt to return to a pure form of Christianity, and became leader of the Protestant movement.
1519–64	In Switzerland the Reformation was carried out by Calvin and Zwingli.
1529	Henry VIII renounced papal supremacy and proclaimed himself head of the Church of England.
1545–63	The Counter-Reformation was initiated by the Catholic church at the Council of Trent.
1560	The Church of Scotland was established according to Calvin's Presbyterian system.
17th century	Jesuit missionaries established themselves in China and Japan. Puritans, Quakers, and other sects seeking religious freedom established themselves in North America.
18th century	During the Age of Reason, Christian dogmas were questioned, and intellectuals began to examine society in purely secular terms. In England and America, religious revivals occurred among the working classes in the form of Methodism and the Great Awakening. In England the Church of England suffered the loss of large numbers of Nonconformists.
19th century	The evolutionary theories of Darwin and the historical criticism of the Bible challenged the Book of Genesis. Missionaries converted natives of Africa and Asia, suppressing indigenous faiths and cultures.
1948	The World Council of Churches was founded as part of the ecumenical movement to reunite various Protestant sects and, to some extent, the Protestant churches and the Catholic church.
1950s–80s	Protestant evangelicism grew rapidly in the USA, spread by television.
1969	A liberation theology of freeing the poor from oppression emerged in South America, and attracted papal disapproval.
1972	The United Reformed Church was formed by the union of the Presbyterian Church in England and the Congregational Church. In the USA, the 1960s-70s saw the growth of cults, some of them nominally Christian, which were a source of social concern.

Christianity: chronology

1980s	The Roman Catholic Church played a major role in the liberalization of the Polish government; and in the USSR the Orthodox Church and other sects were tolerated and even encouraged under President Gorbachev.
1989	Barbara Harris, first female bishop, ordained in the USA.
1992	The Church of England General Synod voted in favour of the ordination of women priests.

Christie /krɪsti/ Agatha 1890–1976. English detective novelist who created the characters Hercule ◊Poirot and Miss Jane ◊Marple. She wrote more than 70 novels including *The Murder of Roger Ackroyd* 1926 and *Ten Little Indians* 1939. Her play *The Mousetrap*, which opened in London 25 Nov 1952, is the longest continuous running show in the world.

Her first crime novel, *The Mysterious Affair at Styles* 1920, introduced Hercule Poirot. She often broke 'purist' rules, as in *The Murder of Roger Ackroyd* in which the narrator is the murderer. She caused a nationwide sensation 1926 by disappearing for ten days when her husband fell in love with another woman.

Christie /krɪsti/ Linford 1960– . Jamaican-born English sprinter. In 1986, Christie won the European 100-metres championship and finished second to Ben Johnson in the Commonwealth Games. At the 1988 Seoul Olympics, he won two silver medals in the 100 metres and 4 × 100 metres relay. In 1990 he won gold medals in the Commonwealth Games for the 100 metres and 4 × 100 metres relay.

Christina /krɪsˈtiːnə/ 1626–1689. Queen of Sweden 1632–54. Succeeding her father Gustavus Adolphus at the age of six, she assumed power 1644, but disagreed with the former regent ◊Oxenstjerna. Refusing to marry, she eventually nominated her cousin Charles Gustavus (Charles X) as her successor. As a secret convert to Roman Catholicism, which was then illegal in Sweden, she had to abdicate 1654, and went to live in Rome, twice returning to Sweden unsuccessfully to claim the throne.

Christine de Pisan /krɪstiːn də 'piːzɒn/ 1364–1430. French poet and historian. Her works include love lyrics, philosophical poems, a poem in praise of Joan of Arc, a history of Charles V, and various defences of women, including *La Cité des dames/The City of Ladies* 1405.

Christmas /krɪsməs/ 25 Dec, a Christian religious holiday, observed throughout the Western world and traditionally marked by feasting and giving of gifts. In the Christian church, it is the day on which the birth of Jesus is celebrated, although the actual birth date is unknown. Many of its customs have a non-Christian origin and were adapted from celebrations of the winter ◊solstice.

Christmas Island /krɪsməs/ island in the Indian Ocean, 360 km/224 mi S of Java; area 140 sq km/54 sq mi; population (1986) 2,000. It has phosphate deposits. Found to be uninhabited when reached by Capt W Mynars on Christmas Day 1643, it was annexed by Britain 1888, occupied by Japan 1942–45, and transferred to Australia 1958. After a referendum 1984, it was included in Northern Territory.

Christmas rose see ◊hellebore.

Christo /krɪstəʊ/ adopted name of Christo Javacheff 1935– . US sculptor, born in Bulgaria, active in Paris in the 1950s and in New York from 1964. He is known for his wrapped works: structures, such as bridges and buildings and even areas of coastline, are temporarily wrapped in synthetic fabric tied down with rope. The *Running Fence* 1976 across California was another temporary work.

Christophe /kriːˈstɒf/ Henri 1767–1820. West Indian slave, one of the leaders of the revolt against the French 1791, who was proclaimed king of Haiti 1811. His government distributed plantations to military leaders. He shot himself when his troops deserted him because of his alleged cruelty.

Christopher, St /krɪstəfə/ patron saint of travellers. His feast day, 25 July, was dropped from the Roman Catholic liturgical calendar 1969.

Traditionally he was a martyr in Syria in the 3rd century, and legend describes his carrying the child Jesus over the stream; despite his great strength, he found the burden increasingly heavy, and was told that the child was Jesus Christ bearing the sins of all the world.

chromatic scale musical scale proceeding by semitones. All 12 notes in the octave are used rather than the 7 notes of the diatonic scale.

chromatography technique used for separating the components of a mixture. This is brought about by means of two immiscible substances, one of which (the *mobile phase*) transports the sample mixture through the other (the stationary phase). The mobile phase may be a gas or a liquid; the stationary phase may be a liquid or a solid, and may be in a column, on paper, or in a thin layer on a glass or plastic support. The components of the mixture are absorbed or impeded by the stationary phase to different extents and therefore become separated.

chromite Fe,Cr_2O_4, iron chromium oxide, the main chromium ore. It is one of the ◊spinel group of minerals, and crystallizes in dark-coloured octahedra of the cubic system. Chromite is usually found in association with ultrabasic and basic rocks; in Cyprus, for example, it occurs with ◊serpentine, and in South Africa it forms continuous layers in a layered ◊intrusion.

chromium (Greek *chromos* 'colour') hard, brittle, grey-white, metallic element, symbol Cr, atomic number 24, relative atomic mass 51.996. It takes a high polish, has a high melting point, and is very resistant to corrosion. It is used in chromium electroplating, in the manufacture of stainless steel and other alloys, and as a catalyst. Its compounds are used for tanning leather and for ◊alums. In human nutrition it is a vital trace element. In nature, it occurs chiefly as chrome iron ore or chromite (Fe,Cr_2O_4). The former USSR, Zimbabwe, and Brazil are sources.

The element was named 1797 by the French chemist Louis Vauquelin (1763–1829) after its brightly coloured compounds.

chromosome structure in a cell nucleus that carries the ◊genes. Each chromosome consists of one very long strand of DNA, coiled and folded to produce a compact body. The point on a chromosome where a particular gene occurs is known as its locus. Most higher organisms have two copies of each chromosome (they are ◊diploid) but some have only one (they are ◊haploid). See also ◊mitosis and ◊meiosis.

chromosphere (Greek 'colour' and 'sphere') layer of mostly hydrogen gas 10,000 km/6,000 mi deep above the visible surface of the Sun (the photosphere). It appears pinkish-red during ◊eclipses of the Sun.

chronic in medicine, term used to describe a condition that is of slow onset and then runs a prolonged course, such as rheumatoid arthritis or chronic bronchitis. In contrast, an *acute* condition develops quickly and may be of relatively short duration.

Chronicles two books of the Old Testament containing genealogy and history.

chronicles, medieval books modelled on the Old Testament Books of Chronicles. Until the later Middle Ages, they were usually written in Latin by clerics, who borrowed extensively from one another.

Two early examples were written by Gregory of Tours in the 6th century and by ◊Bede. In the later Middle Ages, vernacular chronicles appear, written by laymen, but by then the chronicle tradition was in decline, supplanted by Renaissance histories.

chronometer instrument for measuring time precisely, originally used at sea. It is designed to remain accurate through all conditions of temperature and pressure. The first accurate marine chronometer, capable of an accuracy of half a minute a year, was made 1761 by John Harrison in England.

chrysanthemum any plant of the genus *Chrysanthemum* of the family Compositae, with about 200 species. There are hundreds of cultivated varieties, whose exact wild ancestry is uncertain. In the Far East the common chrysanthemum has been cultivated for more than 2,000 years and is the national emblem of Japan. Chrysanthemums may be grown from seed, but are more usually propagated by cutting or division.

Chuang member of the largest minority group in China, numbering about 15 million. They live in S China, where they cultivate rice fields. Their religion includes elements of ancestor worship. The Chuang language belongs to the Tai family.

chub freshwater fish *Leuciscus cephalus* of the carp family. Rather thickset and cylindrical, it grows up to 60 cm/2 ft, is dark greenish or grey on the back, silvery yellow below, with metallic flashes on the flanks. It lives generally in clean rivers throughout Europe.